Thailand
Handbook

Andrew Spooner with
Matt Crook and Jenny Hedstrom

66 99

As the sun sets, the Bangkok Night comes
to life. The air cools, the traffic calms, and
Bangkok's faults disappear into a glossy and
seductive darkness, music drifting through
nighttime breezes scented with jasmine and
the smoke from ten thousand food stalls ...

Chris Coles (from the blog Bangkok Noir)

Footprint story

It was 1921

Ireland had just been partitioned, the British miners were striking for more pay and the federation of British industry had an idea. Exports were booming in South America – how about a handbook for businessmen trading in that far away continent? The Anglo-South American Handbook was born that year, written by W Koebel, the most prolific writer on Latin America of his day.

1924

Two editions later the book was 'privatized' and in 1924, in the hands of Royal Mail, the steamship company for South America, it became The South American Handbook, subtitled 'South America in a nutshell'. This annual publication became the 'bible' for generations of travellers to South America and remains so to this day. In the early days travel was by sea and the Handbook gave all the details needed for the long voyage from Europe. What to wear for dinner; how to arrange a cricket match with the Cable & Wireless staff on the Cape Verde Islands and a full account of the journey from Liverpool up the Amazon to Manaus: 5898 miles without changing cabin!

1939

As the continent opened up, The South American Handbook reported the new Pan Am flying boat services, and the fortnightly airship service from Rio to Europe on the Graf Zeppelin. For reasons still unclear but with extraordinary determination, the annual editions continued through the Second World War.

1970s

Many more people discovered South America and the backpacking trail started to develop. All the while the Handbook was gathering fans, including literary vagabonds such as Paul Theroux and Graham Greene (who once sent some updates addressed to "The publishers of the best travel guide in the world, Bath, England").

1990s

During the 1990s the company set about developing a new travel guide series using this legendary title as the flagship. By 1997 there were over a dozen guides in the series and the Footprint imprint was launched.

2000s

The series grew quickly and there were soon Footprint travel guides covering more than 150 countries. In 2004, Footprint launched its first thematic guide: Surfing Europe, packed with colour photographs, maps and charts. This was followed by further thematic guides such as Diving the World, Snowboarding the World, Body and Soul escapes, Travel with Kids and European City Breaks.

2009

Today we continue the traditions of the last 87 years that has served legions of travellers so well. We believe that these help to make Footprint guides different. Our policy is to use authors who are genuine experts who write for independent travellers; people possessing a spirit of adventure, looking to get off the beaten track.

Title page: Thailand's street food is some of the best on the planet. **Above**: Travellers heading to Koh Tao aren't the only early risers – fishermen near Chumphon.

The ancient kingdom of Thailand is a proud and independent place that burns fiercely with the white heat of modernity while revering the links to its historic past. Ancient Siam, authentic street food and gorgeous silks sit side by side with massive industry, a thick fug of traffic jams, fast food and seminal hi-tech. Get used to the idea that Thailand is rapidly becoming a highly advanced 21st-century society and you can then enjoy its other countless attractions with a hint of realism.

Why not start with the weird and wonderful? Grab a mouthful of cooked bugs off a street or watch *kooey* (transexual) kickboxing. If you prefer misty vistas shrouding antique temples, then make for Sukhothai and Isaan. Or head for its 2600-km coastline – the tourist fleshpots of Pattaya or Phuket, or the isolated, verdant islands such as Koh Tarutao and the dive mecca of Koh Similan.

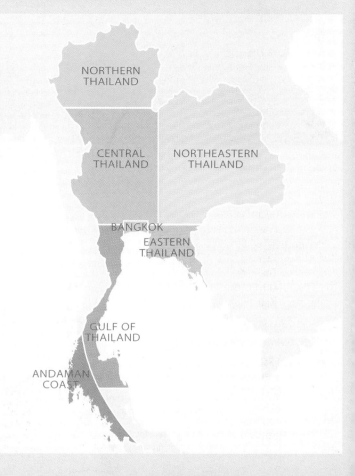

NORTHERN THAILAND

CENTRAL THAILAND

NORTHEASTERN THAILAND

BANGKOK

EASTERN THAILAND

GULF OF THAILAND

ANDAMAN COAST

Contents

Thai architecture, Grand Palace,
Bangkok.

ATIKARN/SHUTTERSTOCK

Where to go

Top of the list for many people visiting Thailand, especially if they come from a less than tropical country, is a beach. Most of Thailand's beaches are concentrated in the south and east. The southern coast stretches over 1000 km to the border with Malaysia while the eastern coastal fringe of the Gulf of Thailand runs 400 km to Cambodia. Pattaya, Phuket, Koh Samui, Koh Phi Phi, Koh Phangan, Koh Samet, Krabi, Koh Chang and Hua Hin are probably the best-known beach resorts, but there are scores of lesser-known (or up-and-coming) islands and stretches of sand, including Koh Turatao and Koh Lipe, Koh Phayam, Trang's Andaman Islands and the tiny islands a short hop from Phuket, Koh Lanta and Koh Chang. Whether you are looking for a luxury hotel in a resort with nightlife and restaurants, or a quiet out-of-the-way place with just a handful of A-frame huts metres from the sea, it is here to be found.

The hilltribes of the north are another Thailand and sometimes it can seem like another era too; an age when people lived distinctive, coherent lives untrammelled by the homogenizing forces of globalization. Taking the time to trek through the hills and forests of the north, rafting down its rivers and staying with the ethnic minorities are the highlights of many visitors' stay. Lives are moulded by the seasons and the demands of farming, and world views have as much to do with ancient beliefs and outlooks as they have with modernity. Combining a stretch by the sea with a trek in the hills of the north is a popular option. The unofficial capital of the north is Chiang Mai. The hill people of this region, with their distinctive material and non-material cultures, their characteristic livelihoods and lifestyles, provide a vivid counterpoint to the lowland Thais.

Above: The Full Moon Party, Koh Phangan.
Opposite left: Damnoen Saduak Floating Market, west of Bangkok.
Opposite right: Doi Suthep, a popular pilgrimage spot for Thais, near Chiang Mai.

The central plains are the heartland of the Thai nation. This is the site of the glorious former capitals of Sukhothai, Si Satchanalai and Ayutthaya. To the west of the central plains, en route to the border with Burma, is Kanchanaburi, site of the infamous bridge over the River Kwai. The northeast, the forgotten corner of Thailand, is the least visited region of the country. Poor and environmentally harsh, it was formerly part of the Khmer Empire that built Angkor Wat in neighbouring Cambodia. In the northeast the Khmer have left their mark in the ruins of Phimai, Phnom Rung, Muang Tam and many other temples and towers. The Mekong River, which skirts the northern and eastern edges of the region and forms the border with Laos, also attracts visitors.

Most visitors begin their stay in Thailand in Bangkok. The capital has a poor reputation for pollution and congestion but it's not just an urban nightmare. The city has impressive historical sights, the canals which gave it the label (along with several other cities in Asia) 'Venice of the East', great food, a throbbing nightlife and good shopping.

Itineraries

One or two weeks

Bangkok provides the perfect stopover for people travelling to other points in Asia or heading further south to Australia and New Zealand. A long weekend taking in the markets and temples of the Thai capital could easily combine with a few days on the beach at nearby Koh Samet. If beaches are not your thing, Khao Yai National Park is only a couple of hours north of Bangkok, while the stunning Khmer ruins at Phnom Rung, further east, make for a very worthwhile diversion. Alternatively, you could just head straight to the sands of Phuket (some international flights land here) or one of the Gulf islands – Koh Samui, Koh Phangan and Koh Tao – and have a satisfying week-long beach holiday. If you have a bit more time then you could also squeeze in a few days in the north in either Chiang Mai or Chiang Rai. The ancient ruins of Ayutthaya and Sukhothai could be visited en route, while the famous bridge over the River Kwai in the engaging riverside town of Kanchanaburi is only a couple of hours west of Bangkok.

Three or four weeks

A typical three-week travellers' itinerary would combine beach with city and possibly the northern hills. Bangkok is essential and a week-long stay will give you a chance to explore more than just the obvious sights. If you want to get a better sense of the Thai capital try one of the canal (*khlong*) ferries or base yourself in Chinatown and feast on the extra-ordinary food.

PAVOL KMETO/SHUTTERSTOCK

Above: Maya Bay, Ko Phi Phi. **Opposite page:** Wat Chang Rob, Sukhothai.

Head south from Bangkok and stop in the royal resort town of Hua Hin before taking in Prachuap Khiri Khan and the stunning beach at Ao Manao. Take a train to Surat Thani and a boat to Koh Samui, or keep going south to the beaches of Krabi, Phuket or Trang. There are plenty of tropical islands here, ranging from the famous charms of Koh Phi Phi to the laid-back vibe of Koh Yao Noi or Koh Lanta, now a firm fixture for foreign tourists.

Head in the opposite direction from Bangkok and there are a number of choices. North and east will take you to Isaan, Khmer heritage and the Mekong River. East reveals the gaudy, sinful resort of Pattaya and the more chilled island of Koh Chang. Directly north takes you to the flat, endless plains and ancient ruins of Central Thailand, the largest of which is Sukhothai. Just to the west of here is the Burmese border and Mae Sot, where the hills and forests spread out to the trekking centre of Umphang.

In the far north is Chiang Mai whose laid-back charms are well known for seducing travellers into staying longer than they'd planned. The capital of the north makes for a great trekking base or you can rent a motorbike and complete the legendary Mae Hong Son loop, stopping off in Pai on the way. Chiang Rai is also a good jumping-off point, and a week or so exploring the furthest-flung corners of the kingdom in and around the Golden Triangle are richly rewarding.

NICOLA GIBBS

A month or more

One of the great things about Thailand is that it is such an easy place to feel at home, and this fact can dramatically change a traveller's plans. Don't get too worried if a six-week trip exploring the country ends up with you completely relaxed on a hammock on some remote island. If you make the effort, escaping the hordes can be very rewarding.

Journey through Isaan to Ubon Ratch-atani and follow the mighty Mekong up the Thai border to Chiang Khan, taking in the elegant riverside towns of Nakhon Phanom and Nong Khai en route. From there the gorgeous hills that surround Loei are just a short hop, and you can pick up a bus to take you to one of Thailand's most famous temples: Wat Yai, in Phitsanulouk. The more intrepid visitor can then head to the remote and beautiful province of Nan before the road curls through endless mountains, and links back up with the Mekong near Chiang Khong. Trace the route of the Mekong a little further and you'll come to the Golden Triangle, before swinging south to reach the engaging hill and border towns of Mae Sai and Mae Salong. Don't forget to stop in at Chiang Rai and Chiang Mai while heading south, and a visit to the lesser-known antiquities of Kamphaeng Phet and Si Satchanalai is definitely worth considering.

From Bangkok the road south takes in Cha-am and Phetburi. The almost deserted beaches of Chumphon, where you'll find kitesurfing schools, are a perfect spot to unwind and spend a few days, and to the south and west of here is boisterous Ranong, the beaches at Khao Lak, and the lakes and forests of Khao Sok National Park.

Carry on past Krabi and Phuket and you'll arrive at the friendly southern town of Trang where a host of islands are easily reached. Further south still you'll find one of Thailand's best-kept secrets, the Tarutao National Park where dazzling beaches and crystalline seas await.

Thailand highlights & itineraries

See colour maps in centre of book

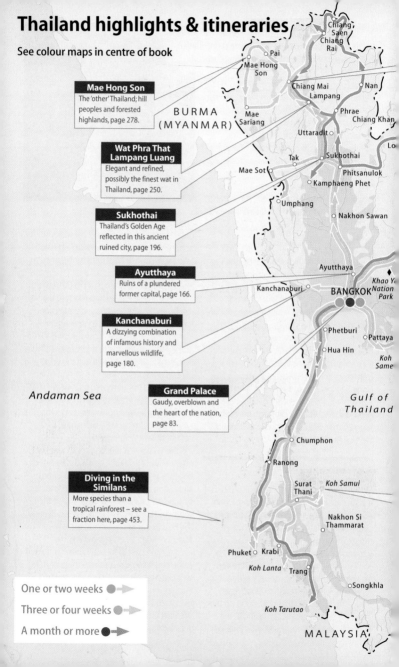

Mae Hong Son
The 'other' Thailand; hill peoples and forested highlands, page 278.

Wat Phra That Lampang Luang
Elegant and refined, possibly the finest wat in Thailand, page 250.

Sukhothai
Thailand's Golden Age reflected in this ancient ruined city, page 196.

Ayutthaya
Ruins of a plundered former capital, page 166.

Kanchanaburi
A dizzying combination of infamous history and marvellous wildlife, page 180.

Grand Palace
Gaudy, overblown and the heart of the nation, page 83.

Diving in the Similans
More species than a tropical rainforest – see a fraction here, page 453.

One or two weeks
Three or four weeks
A month or more

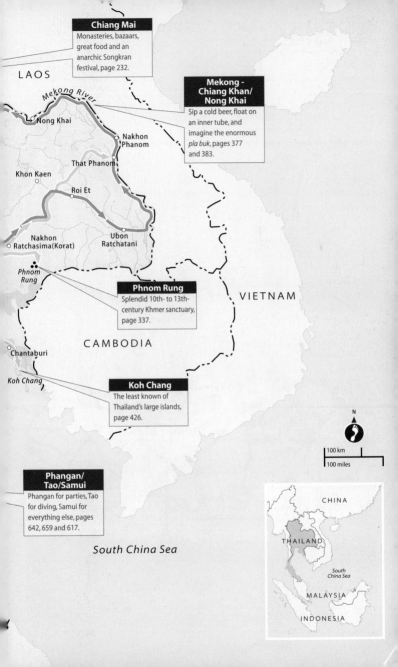

Chiang Mai
Monasteries, bazaars, great food and an anarchic Songkran festival, page 232.

Mekong – Chiang Khan/ Nong Khai
Sip a cold beer, float on an inner tube, and imagine the enormous *pla buk*, pages 377 and 383.

LAOS

Mekong River

Nong Khai

Nakhon Phanom

That Phanom

Khon Kaen

Roi Et

Nakhon Ratchasima(Korat)

Ubon Ratchatani

Phnom Rung

Phnom Rung
Splendid 10th- to 13th-century Khmer sanctuary, page 337.

VIETNAM

CAMBODIA

Chantaburi

Koh Chang

Koh Chang
The least known of Thailand's large islands, page 426.

N

100 km
100 miles

Phangan/ Tao/Samui
Phangan for parties, Tao for diving, Samui for everything else, pages 642, 659 and 617.

South China Sea

CHINA

THAILAND

South China Sea

MALAYSIA

INDONESIA

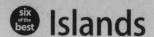

Islands

Koh Si Chang

Regularly overlooked by travellers, Koh Si Chang is the nearest island to Bangkok, just a short hop from the capital and the transit ferry point of Si Racha. It attracts a fair number of devotees, who don't come for the beaches – there is only one of any reasonable note. What you do get on Si Chang, though, is some of the best seafood in Thailand, great small places to stay and an authentic slice of Thai life long-lost on the islands on the usual tourist-trail. The island also has its own troop of monkeys, one of the most-visited Chinese temples in Thailand and an old, abandoned royal palace. For more information, see page 403.

Koh Tao

While the nearby larger islands of Koh Samui and Koh Phangan are now firmly on their way to being totally overrun, tiny Koh Tao still retains a lot of charm, with some pretty beaches and at least some semblance of serenity. While not lazing about learning yoga, many of Tao's visitors come here to learn to dive (see Six of the best dive regions, page 16). If you visit Koh Tao to learn to scuba then make sure you pick your training school carefully – a few have poor safety standards. For more information on Koh Tao, see page 659.

Koh Lanta

Despite the building of an airport at nearby Krabi and the establishment of several upmarket resorts, Koh Lanta still retains much of its original atmosphere. Even in the throes of high season you're pretty much guaranteed a slice of beach or a patch of tropical forest to yourself. The west coast of the island is where you'll find all the resorts and bungalow hang-outs. On the east side is the small authentic village of Ban Koh Lanta Yai, one of the nicest spots to stay. For more information, see page 543.

GINA SMITH/SHUTTERSTOCK

Opposite page: Find a deserted stretch of beach on Koh Lanta. **Above left:** Koh Lipe has some of the clearest waters in the Andaman Sea. **Above right:** Laze on the beach or learn to dive on Koh Tao.

Koh Lipe

Located in the far south of Thailand, Lipe is a part of an archipelago that forms the Tarutao National Park. A postcard vision of a tropical island getaway, Lipe has stunning beaches, gorgeous turquoise seas and a chilled friendly vibe making it popular with families and those looking for respite. Pricier than it once was, Lipe can be tricky to reach at certain times of the year, particularly during low season, but is always worth the effort. Plans are now afoot to run a year-long ferry. For more information, see page 575.

Koh Yao Noi

Tucked away in stunning Phangnga Bay, and easily accessible from both Krabi and Phuket, Koh Yao Noi is noted for its tranquillity. The friendly local community are almost entirely Muslim and have fought hard to protect Yao Noi from the worst ravages of tourism. There are some fantastic local projects and homestays here and, with a large fishing fleet, some awesome seafood. Resorts range from top end through to tiny and lowkey so there is something for every budget. The beaches are not fantastic but plenty of smaller unpopulated islands can be reached by hiring boats. For more information, see page 501.

Phuket

If you're after glamour, fine food and an upmarket experience, Phuket has some of the best resort hotels in Thailand. But there's plenty more to experience than just that, Phuket offers a massive diversity of distractions. There's a kicking club scene, some beautiful colonial architecture, fine beaches and fantastic scuba-diving operators. It is expensive – outside of Bangkok, it is easily the priciest place in Thailand – but if you have the cash there are few better places to spend it. For more information, see page 462

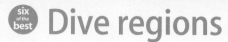

Dive regions

Koh Phi Phi

Phi Phi is dramatically beautiful and the rugged limestone cliffs that explode vertically from the sea are equally impressive below sea level. Long caves, fantastic overhangs and swim-throughs create some adventurous diving, but need to be approached with care. Hard coral gardens have suffered a little from inexperienced boat handlers and natural disasters, but soft corals are healthy and host many small fish and crustaceans.

Shark Point is less than an hour away and equally accessible from southern Phuket. Regarded as one of South Thailand's best dives, this tiny exposed pinnacle is no indication of the large and prolific reef beneath it. The area is characterized by a mass of pink and purple corals. Currents can be strong and visibility varies from 2-25 m.

Similan Islands

This chain of nine tiny islands is ringed by perfect beaches and amazing coral reefs. The park can be reached in a long day trip but a liveaboard is best. Visibility rarely drops below 20 m and can reach mythical proportions. Currents sometimes catch divers unawares, but from November to April conditions are usually excellent with February to April the calmest.

What makes the Similans so attractive are their two completely different sides. To the east the islands have pure white sand and hard coral gardens that slope gently to over 30 m. Colourful soft corals and sea fans are plentiful, the diving is easy and the pace calm. The west, however, is much more dramatic, with currents that swirl around huge granite boulders creating spectacular swim-throughs. It's a bit like diving between flooded skyscrapers that have been reclaimed by the sea. The variety of diving is extensive also, with more sites than you can name.

The region is not known for an abundance of wrecks but one is worth diving. The *Boon Song* wreck, a tin-mining boat, was sunk deliberately and now lies on her side at 18 m. Although not particularly big nor all that substantial a structure, the hull is covered in a mass of life. Leopard sharks patrol the sands

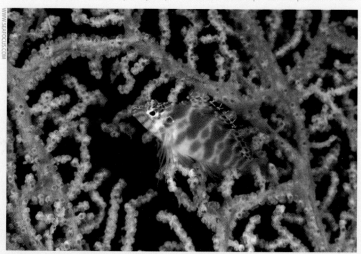

and a wide range of nudibranchs, morays and other fish inhabit the cracks and crevices.

Koh Bon, Koh Tachai

North of the Similans, Koh Bon and Koh Tachai are both enveloped by excellent reefs and prolific marine life. As they're exposed to deep ocean upwellings, currents and visibility vary considerably. Sometimes, what starts as a gentle drift may end up with a fierce upwelling, so care is needed. However, the rocky landscapes are very dramatic and even on a murky day there are frequent pelagic sightings. Leopard sharks seem to lurk permanently at Koh Tachai and in April and May manta rays are regular visitors to Koh Bon.

Richelieu Rock

The dive site that has it all is Richelieu Rock. Even compared with the rest of Thailand, this is the one 'do not miss' dive of your life. Completely submerged at high tide, currents and visibility around the rock can change quickly. On a single dive you can see mating pairs of harlequin shrimps, many ornate ghost pipefish and elegant sea horses. Down on the sand, giant grouper pose for photos while curious turtles watch over your shoulder. And that's not to mention the many different types of moray eels, nudibranchs and schooling fish. The rock is famous, though, as it is one the rare places you can dive with the enormous and endangered whaleshark, which might be seen from February through April.

The Burma Banks

Because of its political isolation, access to diving at Burma Banks has been mostly limited to Thai liveaboards that hold special permits. As such, the reefs are regarded as virgin, with areas of pristine coral and plenty of life. Conditions are similar to the Similan Islands.

The Banks are an area some 1500 km sq studded with plateaux that rise up from great depths to reasonable diving limits. This is a great shark-spotting destination. Western Rocky is a set of three pinnacles that are washed by some pretty good surges and

Opposite page: Threadfin hawkfish hiding on a fan coral. **Above:** Gold coral fan reflecting the sea.

you are likely to encounter schools of squid, seasnakes and tiny orangutan crabs.

Koh Tao

Koh Tao has become the epicentre of diving in the Gulf of Thailand and the reason is simple. This area has great diving just seconds from the beach. Ideal for beginners or those who like peaceful dive days. Even in peak season visibility can be as minimal as 3 m, but will clear to an incredible 40 m in an instant. Currents away from shore can be quite strong and care is required.

The best dive in the area is undoubtedly Chumphon Pinnacle. A massive rock pinnacle soars from 40 m to within 16 m of the surface and is surrounded by a group of smaller ones. There is a huge variety of life-like giant groupers and batfish amongst colourful black coral gardens. Not only are huge schools of jacks spotted regularly, occasionally sailfish, whalesharks and even whales are seen too.

Food experiences

Isaan food

The vast populous northeast region of Thailand produces some of the most popular food in the kingdom. Spicy *som tams* (green papaya salads) of numerous descriptions are central to a lot of Isaan food, as is *khao niaow* (sticky rice) and various grilled meats. A lot of the tastes are very closely related to Lao food with their *som tam* being far saltier and fishier and less zesty than Thai *som tam*, which normally comes filled with lime juice, dried shrimps and peanuts. *Larb*, a minced meat salad usually served with roasted broken rice, plenty of mint, lime and chilli is another Isaan staple. The more rustic and original version of *larb* is made with uncooked meat and often comes filled with blood. You should be able to find Isaan food anywhere in the country.

EHASELWANTER/SHUTTERSTOCK

Seafood

Aharn talay – Thai for seafood – is an essential part of eating in Thailand. From *tom yam kungs*, sour and spicy soups served with *kung* (fresh prawn), through to grilled *pla muek* (squid) served from a street stall, the range of produce is mouth-watering. If you want to avoid farmed prawn and crab head to Koh Yao Noi in Phangnga Bay, where the local Muslim fishermen have instigated an environmentally sustainable protection programme. While not strictly 'sea' food, *pla duk* (catfish) is available pretty much everywhere in Thailand and is often sold attached to a stick, kebab-style, making for healthy fast food.

Mango

One of the most anticipated times in the Thai epicurean calendar are the Thai summer months of March and April when the mango season is in full flourish. It's then that this wonderful fruit is piled high on street stalls and the delightful dessert, *khao niaow mamuang* (sticky rice, served with slices of mango and a sweet coconut sauce) is enjoyed by the whole nation. Of course *mamuang* (mango) is available all year round but it is certainly at its best, like other fruit, when it is in season. There are several main varieties on sale but the most famous is *num dok mai* (water flower), a pale yellowish fruit, often with small black spots. The mango should be soft and firm to the touch and the flesh, at its best, will be delectably sweet with a slightly tart aftertaste.

Rice

The Thai relationship with rice is highly symbolic and deeply entrenched in the psyche of the nation. At times, Thailand has been the biggest rice exporter on the planet, being rightly famous for its fragrant, high-quality jasmine rice. Even the Thai word for

Opposite page: Spicy soups for sale on the streets of Bangkok.
Above: Grasshoppers, beetles and grubs make for an unusual snack.

rice, *khao*, means eat. A question Thais often ask each other is *kin khao rue yung* (have you eaten)? But don't think Thai rice stops at white jasmine rice. Head into a Thai market and you are bound to find either a shop or stall selling dozens of colours, qualities, lengths and tastes. There's special rice for cooking sticky rice, brown rice, black rice and red rice. And if you plan to spend a long time in one place in Thailand make sure you buy that ubiquitous and indispensable Thai culinary gadget – the rice cooker.

Street food

If you don't eat on the street in Thailand you'll be missing out on one of the planet's best eating experiences. Supping on a bowl of *kway tiaow* (noodle soup) or dealing with some seriously *pet* (spicy) food while watching the world go by is quintessentially Thai. The best thing about Thai streetfood is that the seller will make it to your specifications – learn a few key phrases and you'll get your favourite dish with just the right amount of what you like. One of the best phrases to use

is *mai sai* which means don't add. So try *mai sai nam taan* (don't add sugar) or *mai sai pong choo rod* (no MSG). If you like it just a little bit hot, say *pet nit noi* and for a splash of fish sauce, say *sai nam plaa nit noi*. Look for the popular sellers and just jump in.

Weird food

Some of the things you might see on either a Thai menu or lined up on a street-side stall may strike you as a little weird. The locals have been quick to turn this to their advantage and *malang* (insect) sellers now proffer their overpriced grasshoppers and beetles to the tourists on Bangkok's Khao San and Sukhumvit roads. Another common local snack is the *duang*, a deep-fried yellowish grub rich in protein and high in cholesterol. *Teen ped* (duck beak) and *kob* (frog) are also popular, while buffalo embryos are sometimes glimpsed in rural markets. Much of this insect and grub eating has its roots in poverty, with the dry, vast plains of Isaan providing the focus of such culinary practices.

When to go

The hottest time of year is April and May. The wet season runs from May to October in most parts of the country (as you travel south from Bangkok the seasons change). The best time to visit – for most parts of the country – is between December and February. But don't imagine that the wet season means being stuck in your room or bogged down in a tropical storm. Travel to almost all corners of the country is possible at any time of year.

During the rainy season clear skies are interspersed with heavy showers, and it is perfectly sensible to visit Thailand during the monsoon. Flooding is most likely towards the end of the rainy season in September and October. Five to six hours of daily sunshine are normal, even during the rainy season. Visitors will also benefit from lower hotel room rates.

For the central (including Bangkok), northern and northeastern regions, the best time to visit is November to February when the rains have ended and temperatures are at their lowest. However, don't expect Bangkok to be cool. Note that in the south the seasons are less pronounced – and

Above: A couple of surfers riding waves, Phuket. **Opposite page:** Traditional Thai windmill at the floating market, Pattaya.

become more so the further you travel south. Generally the best times to visit the west side of the peninsula (Phuket, Krabi, Phi Phi, etc) are between November and April, while the east coast (Koh Samui, Koh Phangan, etc) is drier between May and October.

Thailand

Activity	J	F	M	A	M	J	J	A	S	O	N	D
Cycling	★	★									★	★
Diving in the Andaman Sea	★	★	★	★							★	★
Diving the eastern Gulf Coast	★	★	★								★	★
Diving the western Gulf Coast			★	★	★	★						
Motorbike touring in the north	★	★									★	★
Kitesurfing in the Gulf of Thailand	★	★	★	★	★						★	★
Trekking in the north	★	★									★	★
Rock climbing	★	★	★	★							★	★
Lazing in a hammock	★	★	★	★	★	★	★	★	★	★	★	★

Rainfall and climate charts

Bangkok

Month	Average temperature in °C max-min	Average rainfall in mm
Jan	32 - 23	07
Feb	33 - 24	13
Mar	34 - 26	32
Apr	35 - 27	58
May	34 - 27	170
Jun	33 - 26	112
Jul	33 - 26	118
Aug	33 - 26	160
Sep	33 - 25	256
Oct	32 - 25	207
Nov	32 - 24	32
Dec	32 - 22	03

Chiang Mai

Month	Average temperature in °C max-min	Average rainfall in mm
Jan	30 - 15	03
Feb	33 - 16	09
Mar	35 - 20	17
Apr	36 - 23	38
May	34 - 24	125
Jun	32 - 24	88
Jul	32 - 24	104
Aug	32 - 24	160
Sep	32 - 23	156
Oct	31 - 22	85
Nov	30 - 19	39
Dec	28 - 16	11

Nan

Month	Average temperature in °C max-min	Average rainfall in mm
Jan	31 - 14	03
Feb	33 - 16	07
Mar	36 - 19	30
Apr	37 - 22	34
May	35 - 24	138
Jun	33 - 24	103
Jul	32 - 24	153
Aug	32 - 24	202
Sep	32 - 23	151
Oct	32 - 22	46
Nov	31 - 18	14
Dec	30 - 14	06

Nakhon Ratchasima

Month	Average temperature in °C max-min	Average rainfall in mm
Jan	31 - 18	03
Feb	34 - 21	11
Mar	36 - 23	25
Apr	37 - 25	49
May	35 - 25	114
Jun	34 - 25	87
Jul	34 - 25	85
Aug	33 - 24	124
Sep	32 - 24	163
Oct	31 - 23	94
Nov	30 - 21	14
Dec	29 - 18	02

Ubon Ratchathani

Month	Average temperature in °C max-min	Average rainfall in mm
Jan	32 - 18	01
Feb	34 - 20	12
Mar	36 - 23	18
Apr	36 - 25	61
May	35 - 25	156
Jun	33 - 25	185
Jul	32 - 24	193
Aug	32 - 24	191
Sep	32 - 24	207
Oct	32 - 22	76
Nov	31 - 20	17
Dec	30 - 18	00

Chantaburi

Month	Average temperature in °C max-min	Average rainfall in mm
Jan	33 - 22	16
Feb	33 - 23	24
Mar	33 - 24	49
Apr	34 - 25	81
May	33 - 25	257
Jun	32 - 25	376
Jul	31 - 25	346
Aug	31 - 25	364
Sep	31 - 24	370
Oct	32 - 24	195
Nov	32 - 23	39
Dec	32 - 21	05

Phuket

Month	Average temperature in °C max-min	Average rainfall in mm
Jan	33 - 24	20
Feb	34 - 25	19
Mar	34 - 25	44
Apr	34 - 26	78
May	33 - 26	165
Jun	32 - 26	144
Jul	32 - 25	168
Aug	32 - 25	208
Sep	31 - 25	246
Oct	31 - 24	244
Nov	32 - 25	138
Dec	32 - 24	48

Hua Hin

Month	Average temperature in °C max-min	Average rainfall in mm
Jan	30 - 22	10
Feb	31 - 23	11
Mar	32 - 24	37
Apr	34 - 26	27
May	34 - 26	73
Jun	33 - 26	56
Jul	33 - 26	65
Aug	33 - 26	48
Sep	32 - 25	97
Oct	31 - 24	206
Nov	30 - 24	58
Dec	29 - 24	04

Nakhon Si Thammarat

Month	Average temperature in °C max-min	Average rainfall in mm
Jan	30 - 22	100
Feb	32 - 22	49
Mar	33 - 23	69
Apr	34 - 24	66
May	34 - 24	121
Jun	34 - 24	91
Jul	34 - 24	97
Aug	34 - 24	98
Sep	33 - 23	119
Oct	32 - 23	238
Nov	30 - 23	424
Dec	30 - 23	328

Sport and activities

Bungee jumping and canopying

Some people get their kicks bungee jumping, others choose to zip through the jungle on cables (canopying). You can try both if you're in Phuket, see pages 491-492. Canopying with **Phuket Cable Jungle Adventure**, 232/17 Bansuanneramit, Moo 8, Srisoonthorn, T076-527054, www.phuket-canopy.com, will cost you ฿1600 and they'll pick you up from pretty much anywhere on the island. There's also canopying in Koh Chang, see page 438.

Caving

The main cave systems are in the northern, western and southern regions of the country. In the most part, when open to the public, they are pretty sedate affairs and not exactly of interest to the specialist caver (but they can be enjoyable for the non-specialist). More adventurous cave expeditions are provided in Soppong (see page 277). On Koh Phangan, the Seaflower Guesthouse, Ao Chaophao, will arrange caving trips, see page 652.

Cycling

Thailand's main highways are certainly not for cycling; some would say, not even for driving. However, there is an extensive network of village roads and trails that provide excellent biking trails, particularly in the northeastern region. **Click and Travel Ltd**, T053-281553, www.clickandtravelonline.com, a young 'Soft Adventure Company' is based in Chiang Mai and specializes in bicycle tours in the north.

Diving

Of all Southeast Asia's countries, for divers Thailand is perhaps one of the most blessed. With some of the richest reefs in the region, it might be hard to choose where to dive

AGE FOTOSTOCK/SUPERSTOCK

Above: An elephant camp near Chiang Mai. **Opposite page**: Scuba diver, Thailand's Indian Ocean.

and when, until you learn that Thai diving is seasonal. At its simplest, half the year you dive on the west, the other half on the east. The western Andaman Sea is where the best and most varied diving is found. Corals are lush and marine life prolific. From November to late April, seas are mostly calm and visibility varies from good to outstanding and currents are acceptable to most divers. The east coast is a good choice for those months when the monsoon is blowing in across the Andaman Sea. The shallower waters of the Gulf of Thailand are calm from May to October. The water in Thailand is invariably warm, with temperatures between 25-28°C (23°C at the lowest). There are more than enough operators and in general, dive businesses are extremely professional. Many work closely with one of the international governing bodies (PADI, NAUI, CMAS, BSAC), however, some facilities in far-flung areas may be limited. For further information, see Six of the best dive regions, page 16.

Fishing

There is little sport river fishing, but travel agents in Kanchanaburi (see page 194) can help organize fishing trips on the Kwai River, Khao Laem and Srinakharin reservoirs. The main beach resorts – Pattaya, Phuket, Koh Phi Phi, Koh Samui and others – offer game fishing in both the Andaman Sea and Gulf of Thailand.

Elephant trekking

There are several elephant camps in the north of Thailand where visitors can go on a short saunter. In the northern region these include the Thai Elephant Conservation Centre outside Lampang, see page 251, where you can also train to be a mahoot; the Elephant Training Camp in the Mae Sa Valley outside Chiang Mai, see page 246; and the Chiang Dao Elephant Training Centre near Chiang Dao, also not far from Chiang Mai, see page 247. In the northeastern region there is the rather tacky Khao Yai Elephant Camp linked to the Khao Yai National Park (see page 333), and Ban Tha Klang, a village of traditional elephant tamers and trainers outside Surin, see page 347. Slightly more adventurous elephant treks are sometimes included in longer trekking programmes.

Golf

In the 1990s golf became one of Thailand's boom industries. Courses were constructed right across the country – many hoping to cash in on a wave of foreigners, particularly Japanese, enticed by the comparative cheapness of playing here. Environmental activists railed against the process, lamenting the use of chemicals to keep greens and fairways artificially lush and bright, the massive use of water in a country where water is a scarce and valuable resource, and the land disputes that sometimes arose as 'Big Money' leveraged land from poor farmers. Be that as it may, Thailand has an impressive network of courses, some of international standard and many attached to luxury hotels. There are courses for example in Bangkok (see page 150), Chiang Mai (page 269), and Phuket (see page 493).

Above: There is some excellent rock climbing in Thailand. **Opposite**: Thai massage lesson at the Wat Po temple, Bangkok.

Horse riding

Horse riding is not big business in Thailand. Most of the places that offer horse riding are pretty sedate affairs with gentle and controlled trots and canters around enclosed spaces. Chiang Mai has more opportunities than anywhere else (see page 270) but there is also riding on offer in Phuket (see page 494) and Pattaya (see page 412).

Motorbike and quad bike 'treks'

Many people hire trail bikes and make their own way into the hills of the northern region. Biking maps are available in book shops in Chiang Mai and Bangkok and there are some well-established routes. If you would rather go on a tour, many trekking outfits will arrange this. For more information on motorbiking in the north, see page 271.

Parasailing

Along with banana boating, parasailing is found at the more commercial beaches in Thailand like Pattaya Bay and Jomtien in Pattaya and Patong in Phuket. Perhaps one of the best places to enjoy this sport is Koh Lan, near Pattaya, where floating 'take-off and landing' platforms means that the flight occurs exclusively above the sea and you don't even have to get wet.

Rock climbing

Most of the country's mountains are modest with 'trekking' or 'hiking' being the operative words, rather than 'climbing'. Leave the crampons at home. However, there is some excellent rock climbing, for example at Ao Nang, just outside Krabi (see page 531) and on Koh Phi Phi (see page 541).

Thai massage

One of the most effective and stimulating massages around, Thai massage is based on the theory that we have 10 major life energy lines running through our bodies, known as *sen sib*. To balance energy and release blocks, the therapist uses her palms, fingers, elbows, forearms and feet to perform intense stretches and pressure-point massage along these 10 lines, pulling, pressing, lifting and loosening muscles and joints. Also called Thai yoga massage, it is sometimes referred to as a 'lazy person's yoga', but it is actually far from a lazy experience, and can hurt like hell, depending on how stiff you are. You lie on a wide mat, dressed in loose, comfortable clothing, and the more you relax and give yourself up to the pain, the more effective the massage will be.

Though the Thais are experts at the art, its origins can be traced back to India and an ayurvedic doctor called Shivago Komarpaj, who is said to have treated the Buddha himself. Thousands of years later, some of his notes still remain intact, and Thai King Rama III commissioned the carving of them onto the walls of Wat Po temple in Bangkok, which was founded in 1788 as Thailand's first university.

At the temple today you'll find life-sized figurines of devotees in pretzel-like yoga and massage shapes pulling pained faces; but it's not all agony at the Wat Po School of Thai Massage, www.watpomassage.com. Set in the grounds of the temple, it offers authentic and affordable massage in communal, fan-cooled rooms by practitioners who are trained on site. If you want to master the fine art yourself, you can also learn massage here – you'll be black and blue by the end of it from each other's mistakes but you'll become a pretty good masseuse. The Institute of Thai Massage in Chiang Mai, T+66 (0)5-321 8632, www.itm.infothai.com, offers 13 different courses, including a five-day foundation in Thai massage for US$150.

Above: Kayaking near limestone rocks, Krabi.

Sea kayaking

This has become popular over the last decade or so. Limestone areas of the south such as Phangnga Bay provide a pock-marked coast of cliffs, sea caverns and rocky islets. Specialist companies, see below, have now been joined by many other companies based in Phuket, Krabi, Ao Nang, Koh Tao and Phi Phi. Kayaks can be hired on many commercial beaches by the hour but for a comprehensive tour including a guide and organized itinerary, the following tour operators offer trips for all: **Discover Asia**, 19/9 Soi Suk Chai, Sukhumvit 42, Prakhanong, Klongtoey, Bangkok, T02-381 7742, www.asiantraveladventures.com, runs day trips from October-June and longer tours around south Thailand's marine parks and islands. **Paddle Asia**, 9/71 Moo 3, Thanon, Rasdanusorn, Ban Kuku, Phuket, T076-216 145, www.seakayaking-thailand.com, offers traditional kayak tours around the marine parks, specifically for bird- and nature-lovers. **Sea Canoe Thailand**, 367/4 Yaowarat Rd, Phuket, T076-212172, www.seacanoe.net,

is an established watersports company offering day trips and longer tours from Phuket (see page 495).

Trekking

Hundreds of thousands of tourists each year take a trek into the hills of the northern and western regions, partly to experience Thailand's (declining) natural wealth and partly to see and stay with one or more of the country's hilltribes. Treks are often combined with elephant rides and rafting and can stretch from single day outings to two-week expeditions. The main trekking centres are Chiang Mai, Chiang Rai, Mae Hong Son, Mae Sot, Mae Sariang, Pai, Soppong, Fang, Tha Ton, Chiang Saen, Sop Ruak, Mae Sai, Nan and Umphang.

    The best time to trek is during the cool, dry season between October and February. In March and April, although it is dry, temperatures can be high and the vegetation is parched. During the wet season, paths are muddy and walking can be difficult. For more information on trekking, see page 268.

Wakeboarding and kitesurfing

Offered as an option in a few watersports centres, wakeboarding has its own specialist school in Thailand, **Air Time**, 99/9 Tambon Mae Nam Khu, Amphur Pluak Daeng, Dok Krai, Rayong, T08-6838 7841, www.air-time. net. It runs wakeboard camps near Pattaya with dedicated English-, French-, German-, Dutch- and Thai-speaking coaches and the chance to try out monoboards, kneeboards, skyski and tubes. **Thailand Kitesurfing School**, Rawai, Muang, Phuket, T076-288258, www.kitethailand.com, also runs courses and there is a kitesurfing school in Hua Hin that offers one- to three-day courses and instructor training.

Whitewater rafting

There are two forms of rafting in Thailand: gentle drifting on bamboo rafts down languid rivers like the Kwai in the western region and the Kok in the north as well as the alternative high-adrenalin version.

Whitewater rafting is a year-round activity. Among the popular locations are Pai (on the Pai River, see page 287) and the Mae Taeng and Mae Cham close to Chiang Mai. There is whitewater rafting in Sangkhlaburi in the western region (see page 194) and there are also opportunities on the resort island of Phuket. June to November is a particularly good time due to higher rainfall. **K-Trekking**, 238/5, Chiangmai-hod Road, A Muang, Chiang Mai T053-431447, F053-431447, offers day tours from US$55; **New Frontier Adventure Co**, 53/54 Onnutch 17, Suan Luang, Bangkok, T02-391 1785, F02-717 9950, offers rafting and whitewater rafting plus options of elephant safaris and

trekking for one to three days; and **Sea Canoe Thailand**, Yaowarat Road, Phuket, T076-212172, www.seacanoe.net, organizes full- and half-day tours from Phuket from US$65 per day.

Wildlife watching

Thailand has an extensive network of national parks and protected areas. The more popular – such as Khao Yai and Phu Kradung in the northeast, Doi Inthanon in the north, and Khao Sok in the south – have trails, camping grounds, hides, accommodation, visitor centres and more. However, compared with other countries with a rich natural heritage, it is difficult not to feel that Thailand has not made the most of its potential. Trails are, generally, not well laid out and true nature lovers may find themselves disappointed rather than enthralled. But for those from temperate regions the sheer luxuriance and abundance of the tropical forest, and the unusual birds, insects and more, will probably make up for this. See also Land and environment, page 759.

Thai cookery courses

There has been an explosion of interest in Thai cuisine, and the number of Thai cookery classes has blossomed. Bangkok (see page 149) and Chiang Mai (see page 267) offer the largest choice, but many hotels and even some guesthouses (such as the Apple Guesthouse in Kanchanaburi) offer classes of varying length of time and intensity. You can find classes in Koh Samui (see page 637), Phuket (see page 492), Mae Sot (see page 227) and Koh Lanta (see page 556), to name but a few.

Family travel in Thailand

According to the Thai psyche, anything worth doing should involve an element of *sanuk* or fun – something that fraught parents might question when cajoling overheated kids around manic Bangkok. Overwhelmingly, though, Thailand is bursting with excuses for having fun. You could start with some jetlag-recovery time on the tropical island of Koh Samet or take a sleeper train to the hill country around Chiang Mai – ideal if *sanuk* equates to some cool relief from the hot and humid lowlands. Elsewhere, children will be all smiles riding elephants, paddling sea kayaks and snorkelling on coral reefs.

One day in Bangkok

Prepare to be dazzled by Bangkok's temple monasteries or wats. These architectural gems with their gleaming orange-and-green roof tiles, mosaic-clad stupas and gilded ornamentation are a must-see. Head first to Wat Phra Kaew where the diminutive 66-cm-tall Emerald Buddha resides in a lavishly decorated *bot* (chapel) guarded by statues of mythical giants (see page 83). Adjoining Wat Phra Kaew is the Grand Palace, another impressive monument (see page 83), but only worth a quick look with kids in tow. Before they get 'templed out' or frazzled by the heat, you need to stroll along to nearby Wat Pho to show them the reclining Buddha (see page 82). Measuring 46 m in length and 15 m in height, it is completely clad in gold leaf and mother-of-pearl. Next, hop on a long-tail boat for a refreshing zip around Bangkok's canals and river tributaries – a veritable 'Venice of the East', see page 93. If the kids are up for another temple, squeeze in a stop at Wat Arun with its impressive 82-m-tall central spire (see page 95). That's the essential sightseeing stuff over with. So, how do you keep children entertained for the rest of the day? Older children may want to mingle with trendy Thai teens in MBK, a shopping centre crammed with shops and stalls selling cheap 'designer' clothing and just about everything else (see pages 100 and 142). For somewhere green and clean, Lumpini Park (see page 105) has lawns to run about on, a lake to boat on and even a kite-flying season from February to April. There's a

SWISSMACKY/SHUTTERSTOCK

Bangkok

▸▸ Most of the famous sights in the royal district are within walking distance of each other, but get there early in the morning before temperatures soar.

▸▸ Jump in a tuk-tuk to get around or catch the cool river breezes on a Chao Phraya River Express boat.

▸▸ Warn children not to approach dogs as rabies is relatively common in Thailand.

LUCIANO MORTULA/SHUTTERSTOCK

Above: Don't forget the suncream when visiting Bangkok's Grand Palace. **Opposite Page:** Jump into a tuk-tuk to get around.

Children's Discovery Museum at Chatuchak Park, a collection of rare indigenous wildlife at Dusit Zoo and a nest of vipers at the Thai Red Cross Snake Farm, where lethal snakes are 'milked' in order to produce anti-venoms.

Out of town

A 69-ha wildlife park located 45 km east of Bangkok, Safari World (www.safari world.com) has rare white pandas and a drive-through safari experience, while Muang Boran (www.ancientcity.com),

Thailand for kids

▸▸ Explore the ancient tropical rainforest of Khao Sok National Park by elephant-back, then discover the jungle's strange nocturnal wildlife during a night safari. See page 449.

▸▸ Ride the sleeper train from Bangkok to Chiang Mai, scale the Dragon Staircase to Doi Suthep Temple and visit the elephant sanctuary at nearby Lampang (see page 251).

▸▸ Learn to scuba dive on Koh Tao, see psychedelic coral reefs and (fingers crossed) spot a whaleshark. See page 659.

▸▸ Taste delicious Thai food, like *kaeng phet kai naw mai* (chicken and bamboo shoot curry) and *kuaytiaw plaa* (rice noodles with fish balls) – but steer clear of the really spicy stuff like *yam phrik chii faa*.

▸▸ Trek in the hilltribe region, sleeping in local villages and finding out how people live in this remote corner of northern Thailand. See page 243.

▸▸ Paddle a kayak into the sea caves of Ao Phangnga Marine National Park. See page 500.

▸▸ Discover beach bliss, lazing under coconut palms and snorkelling over coral reefs at islands like Koh Samet, Koh Samui, Koh Phangan, Koh Phi Phi, and Koh Lanta. See pages 415, 617, 642, 533 and 543.

▸▸ Shop in markets for traditional souvenirs like hilltribe embroidery, Thai silk and shadow puppets.

33 km from the city, is an open-air museum with scaled replicas of Thailand's famous monuments. Further afield, you can catch a train or bus to Kanchanaburi and visit the famous bridge over the River Kwai and take a dip in the natural pools fed by the seven-tiered waterfalls of Erawan National Park. To the south, meanwhile, the beach-side resort of Hua Hin has calm waters, plenty of restaurants and pony rides on the beach.

How big is your footprint?

Travel to the furthest corners of the globe is now commonplace and the mass movement of people for leisure and business is a major source of foreign exchange and economic development in Thailand. In some regions it is the most significant economic activity.

The benefits of international travel are self-evident for both hosts and travellers: employment, increased understanding of different cultures, business and leisure opportunities. At the same time there is clearly a downside to the industry. Where visitor pressure is high and/or poorly regulated, adverse impacts to society and the natural environment may be apparent. Paradoxically, this is as true in undeveloped and pristine areas (where culture and the natural environment are less 'prepared' for even small numbers of visitors) as in major resort destinations.

The travel industry is growing rapidly and increasingly the impacts of this supposedly 'smokeless' industry are becoming apparent. These impacts can seem remote and unrelated to an individual trip or holiday (eg air travel is clearly implicated in global warming and damage to the ozone layer, resort location and construction can destroy natural habitats and restrict traditional rights and activities), but individual choice and awareness can make a difference in many instances and, collectively, travellers are having a significant effect in shaping a more responsible and sustainable industry.

Of course travel can have beneficial impacts and this is something to which every traveller can contribute. Many national parks are partly funded by receipts from visitors. Similarly, travellers can promote patronage and protection of important archaeological sites and heritage through their interest and contributions via entrance and performance fees. They can also support small-scale enterprises by staying in locally run hotels and hostels, eating in local restaurants and by purchasing local goods, supplies and arts and crafts.

Go Green: Europe to Thailand overland

If you've around three weeks to spare, you can travel from the UK to Thailand overland by Trans-Siberian Railway. It's safe, comfortable and relatively inexpensive, but good organizational skills are called for.

▸▸ London to Moscow takes 48 hours by Eurostar and high-speed train to Cologne then a direct Russian sleeping-car from Cologne to Moscow. Fares from around £175 one-way.
▸▸ Moscow to Beijing takes six nights on one of the two-weekly Trans-Siberian trains: train No 4 every Tuesday via Mongolia and the Gobi Desert, or train No 20 every Friday via Manchuria. Tickets cost around £300.
▸▸ Beijing to Hanoi (Vietnam) takes two nights on a twice-weekly train leaving every Sunday and Thursday, soft-sleeper fare £80.
▸▸ From Hanoi to Thailand, the direct route means a rough but scenic 24-hour bus ride to Vientiane then an overnight train from Nong Khai on the Thai border to Bangkok. The easier but more roundabout option is a train to Ho Chi Minh City (two nights, several daily), a daily bus to Phnom Penh and on to Aranyaprathet on the Thai frontier for a train to Bangkok. Details can be found at www.seat61.com/Thailand.htm.

Responsible travel

▸▸ Where possible choose a destination, tour operator or hotel with a proven ethical and environmental commitment – if in doubt, ask.

▸▸ Spend money on locally produced (rather than imported) goods and services, buy directly from the producer or from a 'fair trade' shop, and use common sense when bargaining – the few dollars you save may be a week's salary to others.

▸▸ Use water and electricity carefully – travellers may receive preferential supply while the needs of local communities are overlooked.

▸▸ Learn about local etiquette and culture – consider local norms and behaviour and dress appropriately for local cultures and situations.

▸▸ Protect wildlife and other natural resources – don't buy souvenirs or goods unless they are clearly sustainably produced and are not protected under CITES legislation.

▸▸ Always ask before taking photographs or videos of people.

▸▸ Consider staying in local accommodation rather than foreign-owned hotels – the economic benefits for host communities are far greater – and there are more opportunities to learn about local culture.

▸▸ Make a voluntary contribution to Climate Care, www.co2.org, to help counteract the pollution caused by tax-free fuel on your flight.

Wooden chalets, Rock View, Koh Tao.

Thailand on screen and page

Books to read

Kampoon Boontawee's *Luuk Isan* (A Child of the Northeast) won a national Thai literature prize in 1979 and tells of a year in the life of a village in the 1930s. *Letters from Thailand* (1991) by Botan takes the form of a series of letters from a young immigrant in 1950s and 1960s Bangkok to his mother back in China. Sanitsuda Ekachai's insightful *Behind the Smile: Voices of Thailand* (1990) is a series of vignettes of contemporary Thai life, written in English by a *Bangkok Post* reporter, whilst Khammaan Khonkhai's *The Teacher of Mad Dog Swamp* (1992) centres upon the experiences of a young teacher who, on graduation, is sent to an up-country primary school. The book was originally published in Thai as *Khru Ban Nok* (Rural Teacher) in 1978 and is semi-autobiographical.

Foreigners have also written extensively about Thailand and one of the most famous books is Alex Garland's *The Beach* (1997), a notorious account of travellers coming unstuck on an island in southern Thailand.

If you want a gaudy and detailed telling of all those arcane bits of Thai popular culture, Philip Cornwel-Smith's *Very Thai* (2007) is excellent.

Films to watch

At various points over the last few years Thailand has seemed on the cusp of developing a truly inspiring and inter-nationally acceptable film industry. Yet, with each wave of talent, this industry seems to retreat to the Thai staples of gory ghost stories, saccharine-sweet teen romances and dubious comedies poking fun at the 'simple' folk of Isaan.

There is still a hefty back-catalogue of decent films with the more notable productions of the last few years being the martial arts epic *Ong Bak* (2003), the tale of an assassin; *Bangkok Dangerous* (1999), the original, not the dire Nicholas Cage remake; and the surrealist cowboy film, *Tears of the Black Tiger* (2000).

A number of Western and regional films choose Thailand as a backdrop.

Kar Wai Wong's *In The Mood For Love* (2000) was filmed on the streets of Bangkok; Di Caprio's *The Beach* (2000) was set on Koh Phi Phi; and Werner Herzog pushed Christian Bale to the limit in the jungles of Thailand (doubling as Vietnam) in *Rescue Dawn* (2006).

Contents

Footprint features

Essentials

Getting there

Air

The majority of visitors arrive in Thailand through Bangkok's **Suvarnabhumi International Airport**, which opened in 2006 but has been plagued with problems. The city's old airport, Don Muang, has been re-opened to help cope with the overflow (for details, see Bangkok, page 76). Chiang Mai in the north and Phuket in the south also have international airports. More than 35 airlines and charter companies fly to Bangkok. THAI is the national carrier. Fares inflate by up to 50% during high season.

Flights from Europe

The approximate flight time from London to Bangkok (non-stop) is 12 hours. From London Heathrow, airlines offering non-stop flights include **Qantas, British Airways, THAI** and **Eva Air**. You can easily connect to Thailand from the UK via most other European capitals. **Finnair** flies daily from Helsinki, **KLM** via Amsterdam and **Lufthansa** via Frankfurt. **SAS** flies from Copenhagen and **Swiss Air** from Zurich. Further afield, **Etihad** flies via Abu Dhabi, **Gulf Air** via Bahrain and **Qatar** via Muscat and Doha. Non-direct flights can work out much cheaper, so if you want a bargain, shop around. **Finnair**, www.finnair.com, often offers some of the cheapest fares. It is also possible to fly direct to Chiang Mai from Dusseldorf, Frankfurt and Munich in Germany, and to Phuket from Dusseldorf and Munich.

Flight from the USA and Canada

The approximate flight time from Los Angeles to Bangkok is 21 hours. There are one-stop flights from Los Angeles on **THAI** and two-stops on **Delta**; one-stop flights from San Francisco on **Northwest** and **United** and two-stops on **Delta**; and one-stop flights from Vancouver on **Canadian**. THAI have now started a non-stop flight from New York to Bangkok, which takes 16 hours.

Flight from Australasia

There are flights from Sydney and Melbourne (approximately nine hours) daily with Qantas and THAI. There is also a choice of other flights with **British Airways, Alitalia, Lufthansa** and **Lauda Air**, which are less frequent. There are flights from Perth with THAI and Qantas. From Auckland, **Air New Zealand, THAI** and **British Airways** fly to Bangkok.

Flight from Asia

THAI, **Air India** and **Indian Airlines, Air Lanka,** THAI and **Cathay Pacific** fly from Colombo. From Dhaka, there are flights with **Biman Bangladesh Airlines** and THAI. PIA and THAI fly from Karachi. **Balkan** flies from Male. **Royal Nepal Airlines** and THAI fly from Kathmandu. It is also possible to fly to Chiang Mai from Kunming (China) and Singapore and to Phuket from Hong Kong, Kuala Lumpur, Penang, Singapore, Taipei and Tokyo. Numerous airlines fly from Hong Kong, Tokyo, Manila, Kuala Lumpur, Singapore and Jakarta to Bangkok. There are daily connections from Singapore and Kuala Lumpur to Hat Yai and from Singapore and Hong Kong to Koh Samui. It is also possible to fly to Phuket from Hong Kong, Kuala Lumpur, Penang, Singapore, Taipei and Tokyo.

There has been a massive proliferation of budget airlines in Southeast Asia with Bangkok becoming one of the primary hubs. There are cheap fares available to/from Laos,

Packing for Thailand

Travellers usually tend to take too much. Almost everything is available in Thailand's main towns and cities – and often at a lower price than in the West. Even apparently remote areas will have shops that stock most things that a traveller might require from toiletries and batteries to pharmaceuticals.

Suitcases are not appropriate if you are intending to travel overland by bus. A backpack, or a travelpack (where the straps can be zipped out of sight), is recommended. Travelpacks have the advantage of being hybrid backpacks-suitcases. For serious hikers, a backpack with an internal frame is still by far the better option for longer treks.

In terms of clothing, dress in Thailand is relatively casual – even at formal functions. Jackets and ties are not necessary except in a few of the most expensive hotel restaurants; the door policy of the more exclusive bars, clubs and restaurants in Bangkok increasingly discourages open-toe footwear of the beach variety (you may be prevented from entry if you arrive in flip-flops). Although formal attire may be the exception, dressing tidily is the norm. For further advice on what to wear and cultural sensitivities, see Clothing page 53.

There is a tendency, rather than to take inappropriate articles of clothing, to pack too many of the same article. Laundry services are cheap, and the turn-around rapid. The exception to the former statement is at more upmarket hotels, where laundry services can be pricey – if you are staying in an expensive hotel you should be able to find a laundry nearby that will do an equally good job.

Checklist Bumbag; first-aid kit; hiking boots (if intending to visit any of the national parks); insect repellent and/or electric mosquito mats, coils; International Driving Licence; money belt; passports (valid for at least six months); photocopies of essential documents; short-wave radio; spare passport photographs; sun hat; sun protection; sunglasses; Swiss Army knife; torch; umbrella; wet wipes; zip-lock bags. When travelling to out-of-the-way places, carry toilet paper, as locals don't always use it (readily available for purchase in Thailand). The Thais have a completely different concept of what constitutes loud noise and earplugs are essential. Those intending to stay in budget accommodation might also include: cotton sheet sleeping bag; padlock (for hotel room and pack); soap; student card; toilet paper; towel; travel wash.

Cambodia, Singapore, China, Macau, Maldives, Hong Kong and Malaysia. The situation is changing rapidly with carriers going in and out of business and routes/frequencies fluctuating – check www.asiaoz.com/thailand_airlines.html for a full, up-to-date list of budget air connections. The main players are **One Two Go** (www.fly12go.com), **Air Asia** (www.airasia.com) and **Bangkok Airways** (www.bangkokair.com). **Air Asia** currently do exceptionally cheap flights to Burma (Myanmar). Bangkok has a concentration of tour companies specializing in Indochina and Burma and is a good place to arrange a visa (although most of these countries now issue visas on arrival).

Flight from the Middle East
Etihad, flies from Abu Dhabi, **Gulf Air** flies from Bahrain, and **Egyptair** from Cairo.

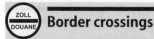

Border crossings

Travellers should always check the political and immigration situation before setting off.

Thailand–Burma (Myanmar)
Saam Ong–Payathonzu (Three Pagodas Pass), see page 187.
Mae Sot–Myawady, see page 223.
Mae Sai–Tachilek (Golden Triangle), see page 310.

Thailand–Cambodia
Aranya Prathet–Poipet, see page 425.
Ban Hat Lek–Koh Kong, see page 425.
Pong Nam Ron–Pailin, see page 425.

Thailand–China
Chiang Saen–Jin Hang, see page 306.

Thailand–Laos
Chiang Khong–Ban Houei Xai, see page 308.
Chongmek–Pakxe (near Ubon Ratchathani), see page 352.
Friendship Bridge, see page 386.

Thailand–Malaysia
Sungei Golok–Rantau Panjang, see page 560.
Satun–Kuala Perlis, see page 577.

Road

The main road access is from **Malaysia**. The principal land border crossings are near Betong in Yala Province, from Sungei Golok in Narathiwat Province and at Padang Besar, where the railway line crosses the border. In April 1994 the Friendship Bridge linking Nong Khai with **Laos** opened and became the first bridge across the Mekong River. In addition to the Nong Khai/Friendship Bridge crossing, it is also possible to enter Thailand from Laos at the following places: Pakse to Chongmek (near Ubon Ratchathani); Savannakhet to Mukdahan; Thakhek to Nakhon Phanom; and Ban Houei Xai to Chiang Khong. All four require travellers to cross the Mekong by boat; in the latter three cases the river forms the border while in the first case the river is entirely within the territory of Laos (see also box, page 361).

Border crossings with **Burma (Myanmar)** have been in a state of flux ever since the first – at Mae Sai in the north – opened in 1992. Officially you're only allowed to fly into Burma from Thailand. Depending on the state of relations between Burma and Thailand, and on security conditions in the borderland regions, restrictions on travel are lifted and re-imposed at a day's notice. This applies to the crossing at Mae Sai in the north, Saam Ong in the west and at Mae Sot in the northwest. Sometimes, only Thai passport holders are permitted to cross. If foreigners are permitted to enter Burma it is usually only for forays into the immediate vicinity and sometimes only for day trips.

Crossing the border into **Cambodia** has also become much easier; visas are available at nearly all entry points and there are both sea and land routes (see box, page 425, for details).

Boat

No regular, scheduled cruise liners sail to Thailand any longer but it is sometimes possible to enter the country on a **freighter**, arriving at Khlong Toey Port in Bangkok. The *Bangkok Post* publishes weekly shipping details on ships leaving the kingdom.

There are frequent **passenger ferries** from Pak Bara, near Satun, in southern Thailand to Perlis and Langkawi Island, both in **Malaysia**. The passenger and car ferries at Ta Ba, near the town of Tak Bai, south of Narathiwat, make for a fast border crossing to Pengkalan Kubor in Malaysia. An alternative is to hitch a lift on a yacht from Phuket (Thailand) or from Penang (Malaysia). Check at the respective yacht clubs for information.

Rail

Regular services link Singapore and Bangkok, via Kuala Lumpur, Butterworth and the major southern Thai towns. Express air-conditioned trains take two days from Singapore, 34 hours from Kuala Lumpur, 24 hours from Butterworth. The **Magic Arrow Express** leaves Singapore on Sunday, Tuesday and Thursday. An additional train from Butterworth departs at 1420, arriving Bangkok 1210 the next day. The train from Bangkok to Butterworth departs 1420, arriving Butterworth 1255. See www.ktmb.com.my for a timetable for trains between Thailand and Malaysia. All tickets should be booked in advance. **Orient-Express Hotels**, which operates the *Venice Simplon Orient-Express* also runs the luxury *Eastern & Oriental Express* between Bangkok, Kuala Lumpur and Singapore. The air-conditioned train runs once a week from Singapore to Bangkok and back. This locomotive extravaganza departs from Bangkok on Sunday and returns from Singapore every Thursday. The journey takes 45 hours (three nights, two days) to cover the 2000-km one-way trip. Passengers can disembark at Hua Hin, Butterworth (Penang) and Kuala Lumpur. Reservations can be made at **Orient-Express Hotels**, T020-7921400, www.orient-express.com. **Orient-Express Hotels** also has agents in Bangkok (T02-2168661), Singapore (32-01 Shaw Towers, Beach Road, T3923500, F3923600) and Kuala Lumpur to handle reservations, as well as sales offices in Australia, Japan, USA, France and Germany. See the website for details.

Getting around

Air

The budget airline boom has finally arrived in Thailand with carriers now offering cheap flights all over the country. **Air Asia**, **Bangkok Airways**, **Nok Air** and **One Two Go** are the present major players in this market offering dirt cheap flights – but only if you book online and in advance. **Thai Airways (THAI)** is the national flag carrier and is also by far the largest domestic airline. Although it has had a relatively turbulent few years and standards have declined since the halcyon days of the late 1980s, it is still okay.

THAI flies to several destinations in Thailand. It has a three-stop 'Amazing Thailand Air Pass'. The three coupons entitle you to fly economy to any of THAI's domestic airports for a period of three months. You can add a maximum of eight coupons. The pass must be bought prior to arrival in Thailand as part of an international trip to or via Thailand. THAI head office is found at 89 Vibhavadi Rangsit Road, Jompol, Jatujak, Bangkok 10900, T02-2451000, www.thaiair.com. It is better to book flights through a local office or travel agent displaying the THAI logo. THAI domestic routes leave from Suvarnabhumi Airport in Bangkok.

Bangkok Airways head office is at 99 Mu 14, Vibhavadirangsit Road, Chom Phon, Chatuchak, Bangkok 10900, T02-265 5678 (ext 1771 for reservations centre), www.bangkokair.com; the European Regional Office is at Bethmannstrasse 58, D-60311 Frankfurt/Main, Germany, T0049 69-13377565, T0049 69-13377566, info@bangkok airways.de). **Bangkok Airways** flies from Bangkok to Chiang Mai via Sukhothai, Koh Samui, Phuket, Krabi, Trat and from Koh Samui to Phuket and Pattaya (U-Tapao). From Phuket it flies to Pattaya. The airline has domestic offices at all the airports it flies to and from: Dong Muang Airport, Chiang Mai, Krabi, Pattaya, Phuket, Samui, and Sukhothai airports. **Bangkok Airways** also offers an airpass deal in conjunction with **Laos Airlines** and Siem Reap Airways (Cambodia). Coupons for each sector start at US$55 and a minimum of three or maximum of six must be bought. Local departure taxes are not included. See the website for full details.

One Two Go, head office: 18 Ratchadapisak Road, Klongtoey, Bangkok 10110, T1126, www.fly12go.com, flies from Bangkok to Chiang Rai via Chiang Mai, Hat Yai and Phuket. Malaysian-based **Air Asia**, T02-515 9999, www.airasia.com, offers routes from Bangkok to Chiang Mai, Chiang Rai, Udon Thani, Hat Yai, Phuket, Ubon Ratchathani and Narathiwat. **Nok Air**, T1318, www.nokair.com, has flights to Chiang Mai, Hat Yai, Phuket, Nakhon Si Thammarat, Udon Thani, Trang, Loei and Krabi.

Road

Bicycle
The advice below is collated from travellers who have bicycled through Thailand and is meant to provide a general guideline for those intending to tour the country by bicycle (which is becoming more and more common).

Bicycle type Touring, hybrid or mountain bikes are fine for most roads and tracks in Thailand. Spares are readily available and even small towns have bicycle repair shops where it is often possible to borrow larger tools such as vices. Mountain bikes have made an impact, so accessories for these are also widely available. Components made of more unusual materials – such as titanium and rarer composites – are harder to find.

Attitudes to cyclists It is still comparatively rare to see foreigners cycling in Thailand, so expect to be an object of interest. Be aware that bicyclists give way to everything and everyone! Cars and buses often travel along the hard shoulder; be very wary, especially on main roads. Avoid cycling at night.

Useful equipment Basic tool kit – although there always seems to be help near at hand, and local workshops seem to be able to improvise a solution to just about any problem – including a puncture repair kit, spare tubes, spare tyre and pump. Also take a good map of the area, bungee cords, first-aid kit and water filter. Cover up well, including a hat, and take sunscreen and mosquito repellent.

Buses in Thailand: sample routes and times

Ticket prices are now linked to fuel costs, so can fluctuate.

Route	Time (hours)
Bangkok north to:	
Ayutthaya	1½
Sukhothai	7
Mae Sot	9
Chiang Mai	9¾
Chiang Rai	12
Mae Hong Son	12½
Bangkok northeast to:	
Korat	4½
Udon Thani	9
Ubon Ratchathani	10
Nakhon Phanom	10
Bangkok south to:	
Hua Hin	3
Chumphon	7
Surat Thani	11
Nakhon Si Thammarat	12
Phuket	13
Krabi	12
Satun	13
Bangkok east to:	
Pattaya	3
Chantaburi	4½
Trat	5½
Phuket to:	
Surat Thani	5
Trang	5
Nakhon Si Thammarat	8
Hat Yai	6
Satun	7
Chiang Mai to:	
Nan	6
Mae Sot	6
Sukhothai	5
Khon Kaen	12
Chiang Rai	3
Mae Hong Son	7
Udon Thani	12

Bicycle hire Guesthouses and specialized outlets hire out touring and mountain bikes. Expect to pay ฿80-150 per day.

Transporting your bicycle Bikes can be taken on trains, but check the security in the guards' van. Buses are used to taking bicycles (but the more expensive air-conditioned tour buses may prove reluctant), and most carry them for free, although some drivers may ask for a surcharge. Many international airlines take bicycles free of charge, provided they are not boxed. Check your carrier's policy before checking in.

Bus

Private and state-run buses leave Bangkok for every town in Thailand; it is an extensive network and a cheap way to travel. The government bus company is called **Bor Kor Sor**, and every town in Thailand will have a BKS terminal. There are small stop-in-every-town local buses plus the faster long-distance buses (*rot duan* – express; or *rot air* – air-conditioned). **Air-conditioned buses** come in two grades: *chan nung* (first class, blue colour) and *chan song* (second class, orange colour). *Chan song* have more seats but less elbow and leg room, and will not offer hostess, food and drink services, or a toilet. *Chan nung* buses will have all of these as well as a maximum of 42 seats (adjustable to 70° recline). For longer/overnight journeys, air-conditioned de luxe (sometimes known as *rot tour*, officially Standard 1A buses, also blue like the *chan rung*) or VIP buses, stewardess service is provided with food and drink supplied en route and more leg room plus constant Thai music or videos. There should be no more than 24 seats (adjustable to 135° recline). Many fares include meals at roadside restaurants, so keep hold of your ticket. For sample routes, see box on page 39. If you're travelling on an overnight air-conditioned bus bring a light sweater and some earplugs – both the volume of the entertainment system and cooling system are likely to be turned up full blast.

The local buses are slower and cramped but worth it for those wishing to sample local life. The seats at the very back are reserved for monks, so be ready to move if necessary.

Private tour buses Many tour companies operate bus services in Thailand; travel agents in Bangkok will supply information. These buses are seldom more comfortable than the state buses but are usually more expensive. Overnight trips usually involve a meal stop (included in price of ticket) and stewardess service for drinks and snacks. They often leave from outside the company office, which may not be located at the central bus station.

Car
There are two schools of thought on car hire in Thailand: one, that under no circumstances should *farangs* (foreigners) drive themselves; and second, that hiring a car is one of the best ways of seeing the country and reaching the more inaccessible sights. Increasing numbers of visitors are hiring their own cars and internationally respected car hire firms are expanding their operations (such as **Hertz** and **Avis**). Roads and service stations are generally excellent. Driving is on the left-hand side of the road.

Car hire The average cost of hiring a car from a reputable firm is ฿1000-2000 per day, ฿6000-10,000 per week, or ฿20,000-30,000 per month. Some companies automatically include insurance; for others it must be specifically requested and a surcharge is added. An international driver's licence, or a UK, US, French, German, Australian, New Zealand, Singapore or Hong Kong licence is required. The lower age limit is 20 years (higher for some firms). Addresses of car hire firms are included in the sections on the main tourist destinations. If the mere thought of competing with Thai drivers is terrifying, an option is to hire a chauffeur along with the car. For this service an extra ฿300-500 per day is usually charged, more at weekends and if an overnight stay is included. Note that local car hire firms are cheaper although the cars are likely to be less well maintained and will have tens of thousands of kilometres on the clock.

Safety There are a few points that should be kept in mind: accidents in Thailand are often horrific. If involved in an accident, and they occur with great frequency, you – as a foreigner – are likely to be found the guilty party and expected to meet the costs. Ensure the cost of hire includes insurance cover. Many local residents recommend that if a foreigner is involved in an accident, they should not stop but drive on to the nearest police station – if possible, of course.

Hitchhiking
Thai people rarely hitchhike and tourists who try could find themselves waiting for a long time at the roadside. It is sometimes possible to wave down vehicles at the more popular beach resorts.

Motorbike
Hiring a motorbike has long been a popular way for visitors to explore the local area. Off the main roads and in quieter areas it can be an enjoyable and cheap way to see the country. Some travellers are now not just hiring motorbikes to explore a local area, but are touring the entire country by motorcycle. It is the cheapest way to be independent of public transport, but the risks rise accordingly (see below).

Motorbike hire Rental is mostly confined to holiday resorts and prices vary from place to place; ฿150-300 per day is usual for a 100-150cc machine. Often licences do not have to be shown and insurance will not be available. Riding in shorts and flip-flops is dangerous – a foot injury is easily acquired even at low speeds and broken toes are a nightmare to heal – always wear shoes. Borrow a helmet or, if you're planning to ride a motorbike on more than one occasion, consider buying one – decent helmets can be found for ฿1500 and are better than the 'salad bowls' usually offered by hire companies.

Safety In most areas of Thailand it is compulsory to wear a helmet and while this law is not always enforced there are now periodic checks everywhere – even on remote roads. Fines are usually ฿300; if you have an accident without a helmet the price could be much higher. Thousands of Thais are killed in motorcycle accidents each year and large numbers of tourists also suffer injuries (Koh Samui has been said to have the highest death rate anywhere in the world). Expect anything larger than you to ignore your presence on the road. Be extremely wary and drive defensively.

Motorbike taxi
These are becoming increasingly popular, and are the cheapest, quickest and most dangerous way to get from 'A' to 'B'. They are usually used for short rides down *sois* or to better local transport points. Riders wear coloured vests (sometimes numbered) and tend to congregate at key intersections or outside shopping centres for example. Agree a price before boarding – expect to pay ฿10 upwards for a short *soi* hop.

Songthaew ('two rows')
Songthaews are pick-up trucks fitted with two benches and can be found in many upcountry towns. They normally run fixed routes, with set fares, but can often be hired and used as a taxi service (agree a price before setting out). To let the driver know you want to stop, press the electric buzzers or tap the side of the vehicle with a coin.

Taxi
Standard air-conditioned taxis are found in very few Thai towns with the majority in the capital. In Bangkok all taxis have meters. Most Bangkok taxis will also take you on long-distance journeys either for an agreed fee or with the meter running. In the south of Thailand, shared long-distance taxis are common.

Tuk-tuks
These come in the form of pedal or motorized machines. Fares should be negotiated and agreed before setting off. It will not take long to discover what is a reasonable price, but don't expect to pay the same as a Thai. Drivers are a useful source of local information and will know most places of interest, plus hotels and restaurants (and sometimes their prices). In Bangkok, and most other towns, these vehicles are a motorized, gas-powered scooter. Pedal-powered *saamlors* (meaning 'three wheels') were outlawed in Bangkok a few years ago and they are now gradually being replaced by the noisier motorized version throughout the country.

Boat

The waterways of Thailand are extensive. However, most people limit their water travel to trips around Bangkok or to Ayutthaya. *Hang-yaaws* (long-tailed boats) are a common form of water travel and are motorized, fast and fun.

Cruise holidays

An alternative to the usual overland tour of Thailand is to book a berth on the *Andaman Princess*. This cruise ship sails to Koh Tao and back (three days and two nights). Passengers can snorkel at Koh Tao and the level of service and safety is high. Large numbers of young, middle-class Thais make the journey and there is lots of entertainment. It costs around ฿5000 for a single berth. Contact **Siam Cruise**, 33/10-11 Sukhumvit Soi Chaiyod (Soi 11), T02-2554563, www.siamcruise.com.

Sea travel

There are numerous boats to and from the Gulf Coast Islands of Koh Samui, Koh Phangan and Koh Tao. Principal services run from Chumphon to Koh Tao and from Surat Thani and the port of Don Sak to Koh Samui and then on to Koh Phangan. Fast ferries, slow boats and night boats run services daily. On the Andaman Coast there are services to and from Phuket, Koh Phi Phi, Krabi, Koh Lanta, the islands off Trang and from Ban Pak Bara and Koh Tarutao National Park. The islands off the eastern seaboard are also connected by regular services to the mainland. Note that services become irregular and are suspended during certain times of year because of the wet season and rough seas. Each section details information on the months that will affect regular boat services.

Rail

The **State Railway of Thailand**, www.railway.co.th/english, is efficient, clean and comfortable, with five main routes to the north, northeast, west, east and south. It is safer than bus travel but can take longer. The choice is **first-class air-conditioned compartments**, **second-class sleepers**, **second-class air-conditioned sit-ups** with reclining chairs and **third-class sit-ups**. Travelling third class is often cheaper than taking a bus; first and second class are more expensive than the bus but infinitely more comfortable. **Express trains** are known as *rot duan*, **special express trains** as *rot duan phiset* and **rapid trains** as *rot raew*. Express and rapid trains are faster as they make fewer stops; there is a surcharge for the service.

Reservations for sleepers should be made in advance (up to 60 days ahead) at Bangkok's **Hualamphong station** ① *T1690, T02-220 4444, the advance booking office is open daily 0700-0400.* Some travel agencies also book tickets. A queue-by-ticket arrangement works efficiently, and travellers do not have to wait long. If you change a reservation the charge is ฿10. It is advisable to book the bottom sleeper, as lights are bright on top (in second-class compartments) and the ride more uncomfortable. It still may be difficult to get a seat at certain times of year, such as during festivals (like **Songkran** in April). Personal luggage allowance is 50 kg in first class, 40 kg in second and 30 kg in third class. Children aged three to 12 years old and under 150 cm in height pay half fare; those under three years old and less than 100 cm in height travel free, but do not get a seat. It is possible to pick up timetables at Hualamphong station (from the information booth in the main concourse). There are two types: the 'condensed' timetable (by region) showing all rapid routes, and complete,

State railways of Thailand: sample routes

Route	Time	Distance (km)
Bangkok north to:		
Don Muang	45 mins	22
Ayutthaya	1½ hrs	71
Lopburi	2½ hrs	133
Nakhon Sawan	4 hrs	246
Phitsanulok	5-6 hrs	389
Uttaradit	8 hrs	485
Den Chai	8 hrs	534
Nakhon Lampang	11¾ hrs	642
Lamphun	8½ hrs	729
Chiang Mai	11-13 hrs	751
Bangkok northeast to:		
Nakhon Ratchasima	5 hrs	264
Surin	8 hrs	420
Si Saket	9½ hrs	515
Ubon Ratchathani	10 hrs	575
Bua Yai Jn	5 hrs	346
Ban Phai	8 hrs	408
Khon Kaen	8 hrs	450
Udon Thani	9½ hrs	569
Nong Khai	11 hrs	624
Bangkok east to:		
Chachoengsao	1½ hrs	61
Prachin Buri	3 hrs	122
Kabin Buri	3½ hrs	161
Aranya Prathet	4½ hrs	255
Chonburi	2¾ hrs	108
Pattaya	3¾ hrs	155
Bangkok south to:		
Nakhon Pathom	1½ hrs	64
Kanchanaburi	2½ hrs	133
Rachaburi	2 hrs	117
Phetburi	3 hrs	167
Hua Hin	4 hrs 10 mins	229
Prachuap Khiri Khan	5 hrs	318
Chumphon	7¾ hrs	485
Surat Thani	11 hrs	651
Trang	15 hrs	845
Nakhon Si Thammarat	15 hrs	832

To view full details visit www.railway.co.th/english

separate timetables for all classes. Timetables are available from stations and some tourist offices. If travelling north or south during the day, try to get a seat on the side of the carriage out of the sun.

You can buy a 20-day **rail pass** (blue pass) which is valid on all trains, second and third class (supplementary charges are NOT included). A more expensive red pass includes supplementary charges. For further details visit the Advance Booking Office at Hualamphong station in Bangkok, T02-223 3762, T02-224 7788.

Maps

Although maps of Thailand and Southeast Asia are available locally, it is sometimes useful to buy one prior to departure in order to plan routes and itineraries.

Regional maps Bartholomew *Southeast Asia* (1:5,800,000); ITM (International Travel Maps) *Southeast Asia* (1:6,000,000); Nelles *Southeast Asia* (1:4,000,000); Hildebrand *Thailand, Burma, Malaysia and Singapore* (1:2,800,000).

Country maps Bartholomew *Thailand* (1:1,500,000); ITM (International Travel Maps) *Thailand* (1:1,000,000); Nelles *Thailand* (1:1,500,000).

Road maps The best (and cheapest) road maps are available locally and can be easily picked up from a petrol station. They are especially handy because they often give place names in Thai and English and therefore can help when you are trying to get somewhere (but no one understands you!). Michelin also produces a good book or road maps for the country.

Other maps Tactical Pilotage Charts (TPC, US Airforce) (1:500,000); Operational Navigational Charts (ONC, US Airforce) (1:500,000). Both of these are good at showing relief features, which are good for planning treks but less useful for roads, towns and facilities.

Map shops in the UK The best selection is available from **Stanfords**, 12-14 Long Acre, Covent Garden, London, T020-78361321, www.stanfords.co.uk, or 29 Corn Street, Bristol, and 39 Spring Gardens, Manchester. Recommended. Also recommended is **McCarta**, 15 Highbury Place, London, T020-73541616. ➤➤ *For a map of Bangkok, see page 77.*

Sleeping

Thailand has a large selection of hotels, including some of the best in the world. Standards outside of the usual tourist areas have improved immensely over recent years and while such places might not be geared to Western tastes they offer some of the best-value accommodation in the country. Due to its popularity with backpackers, Thailand also has many small guesthouses, serving Western food and catering to the foibles of foreigners. These are concentrated in the main tourist areas.

Hotels and guesthouses

Hotels and guesthouses are listed under eight categories, according to the average price of a double/twin room for one night. It should be noted that many hotels will have a

Sleeping price codes

LL Over US$200, **L** US$151-200 and **AL** US$101-150 **International**: rooms will be air-conditioned, have a minibar, in-room safe, coffee- and tea-making facilities and cable TV. They will have the entire range of business services, sports facilities (gym, swimming pool), possibly a spa, Asian and Western restaurants and bars. It is likely they will offer tutorials on Thai cooking, flower arranging and massage, for example.

A US$66-100 **First class**: usually offer comprehensive business, sports and recreational facilities, with a range of restaurants and bars. Rooms are likely to have all or the majority of the facilities mentioned above.

B US$46-65 **Tourist class**: these will probably have a swimming pool and all rooms will have air conditioning and an attached bathroom. Other services include one or more restaurants. The majority will have cable TV.

C US$31-45 **Economy**: rooms may be air-conditioned and have attached bathrooms with hot water. A restaurant and room service will probably be available. Sports facilities are unlikely.

D US$21-30 **Budget**: rooms are likely to be fan-cooled and they should have an attached bathroom. Toilets may be either Western-style or of the squat variety, depending on whether the town is on the tourist route. Many in this price range, out of tourist areas, are 'Thai' hotels. Bed linen, towels and toilet paper are usually provided, and there may be a restaurant.

E US$12-20 **Guesthouse**: fan-cooled rooms, in some cases with shared bathroom facilities. Toilets are likely to be of the squat variety, with no toilet paper provided. Bed linen should be provided, although towels may not. Rooms are small, facilities few. Guesthouses popular with foreigners may be excellent sources of information and also sometimes offer cheap tours and services such as bicycle and motorcycle hire. Places in this category vary a great deal, and can change very rapidly. One year's best bargain becomes the following year's health hazard – or, it has been upgraded and is beyond the budget traveller's reach. Other travellers are the best source of up-to-the-minute reviews on whether standards have plummeted.

F US$7-11 and **G** US$6 and under **Guesthouse**: fan-cooled rooms, usually with shared bathroom facilities. Toilets are likely to be of the squat variety with no toilet paper provided. Some of these guesthouses can be filthy, vermin-infested places. Others are superb value. As in the category above, standards change very fast and other travellers are the best source of information.

range of rooms, some with air conditioning (a/c) and attached bathroom facilities, others with just a fan and shared facilities. Prices can therefore vary a great deal. If a hotel entry lists 'some a/c', then these rooms are likely to be in the upper part of the range, perhaps even in the next range. Few hotels in Thailand provide breakfast in the price of the room. A service charge of 10% and government tax of 7% will usually be added to the bill in the more expensive hotels (categories **L-C**). Ask whether the quoted price includes tax when checking in. Prices in Bangkok are inflated.

During the off-season, hotels and guesthouses in tourist destinations may halve their room rates so it is always worthwhile bargaining or asking whether there is a special price. Given the fierce competition among hotels, it is even worth trying during the peak season.

Over-building has meant that there is a glut of rooms in some towns and hotels are desperate for business.

Until 10 years ago, most guesthouses offered shared facilities with cold-water showers and squat toilets. Levels of cleanliness were also less than pristine. Nowadays, Western toilet imperialism is making inroads into Thai culture and many of the better-run guesthouses will have good, clean toilets with sit-down facilities and, sometimes, hot water. Some are even quite stylish in their bathroom facilities. Fans are the norm in most guesthouses although, again, to cash in on the buying power of backpackers with more disposable income more and more offer air-conditioned rooms as well. Check that mosquito nets are provided.

Security is a problem, particularly in beach resort areas where flimsy bungalows offer easy access to thieves. Keep valuables with the office for safekeeping (although there are regular cases of people losing valuables that have been left in 'safekeeping') or on your person when you go out. Guesthouses can be tremendous value for money. With limited overheads, family labour and using local foods they can cut their rates in a way that larger hotels with armies of staff, imported food and expensive facilities simply cannot.

Camping and national park accommodation

It is possible to camp in Thailand and **national parks** are becoming much better at providing campsites and associated facilities. Most parks will have public toilets with basic facilities. Some parks also offer bungalows; these fall into our **C** accommodation category but because they can often accommodate large groups their per person cost is less than this. The more popular parks will often also have privately run accommodation including sophisticated resorts, sometimes within the park boundaries. For reservations at any of the national parks contact: Reservation Office, National Parks Division, Royal Forestry Department, 61 Phanhonyothin Road, Ladyao, Jatujak, Bangkok, T02-56142923. The official website, www.dnp.go.th/parkreserve, is excellent for making online bookings. Alternatively, you can phone the park offices listed in the relevant sections of this guide. **Beaches** are considered public property – anybody can camp on them for free.

In terms of what to bring and wear, bear in mind that at night at high elevations, even in muggy Thailand, it can be cold. In the north and northeast it can fall to close to freezing during the cooler months. So make sure you have a thick coat and a warm sleeping bag. During the day, long trousers (to avoid scratches), sturdy shoes (if you are thinking of trekking any distance), and a hat are recommended. In the evening, long-sleeved shirts (to keep the mosquitoes at bay) are required. If you are camping, remember that while the more popular parks have tents for hire, the rest – and this means most – do not. Bring your own torch, camp stove, fuel and toilet paper.

Eating and drinking

Thai food, for long an exotic cuisine distant from the average northerner's mind and tongue, has become an international success story. The Thai government, recognizing the marketing potential of their food, has instituted a plan called 'Global Thai' to boost the profile of Thai food worldwide as a means of attracting more people to visit its country of origin. Thai food has become, in short, one of Thailand's most effective advertisements.

Thai food is an intermingling of Tai, Chinese and, to a lesser extent, Indian cuisines. This helps to explain why restaurants produce dishes that must be some of the (spicy) hottest in

Eating price codes

♥♥♥ **Expensive** over US$12   ♥♥ **Mid-range** US$6-12   ♥ **Cheap** under US$6

Prices refer to the cost of an average main dish. They do not include drinks.

the world, as well as others that are rather bland. *Larb* (traditionally raw – but now more frequently cooked – chopped beef mixed with rice, herbs and spices) is a traditional 'Tai' dish; *pla priaw waan* (whole fish with soy and ginger) is Chinese in origin; while *gaeng mussaman* (beef 'Muslim' curry) was brought to Thailand by Muslim immigrants. Even satay, paraded by most restaurants as a Thai dish, was introduced from Malaysia and Indonesia (which themselves adopted it from Arab traders during the Middle Ages).

Despite these various influences, Thai cooking is distinctive. Thais have managed to combine the best of each tradition, adapting elements to fit their own preferences. Remarkably, considering how ubiquitous it is in Thai cooking, the chilli pepper is a New World fruit and was not introduced into Thailand until the late 16th century (along with the pineapple and the papaya).

A Thai meal is based around rice, and many wealthy Bangkokians own farms upcountry where they cultivate their favourite variety. When a Thai asks another Thai whether he has eaten he will ask, literally, whether he has 'eaten rice' (*kin khaaw*). Similarly, the accompanying dishes are referred to as food 'with the rice'. There are two main types of rice – 'sticky' or glutinous (*khao niaw*) and non-glutinous (*khao jao*). Sticky rice is usually used to make sweets (desserts) although it is the staple in the northeastern region and parts of the north. *Khao jao* is standard white rice.

In addition to rice, a meal usually consists of a soup like *tom yam kung* (prawn soup), *kaeng* (a curry) and *krueng kieng* (a number of side dishes). Thai food is spicy, and aromatic herbs and grasses (like lemongrass, coriander, tamarind and ginger) are used to give a distinctive flavour. *Nam pla* (fish sauce made from fermented fish and used as a condiment) and *nam prik* (*nam pla*, chillies, garlic, sugar, shrimps and lime juice) are two condiments that are taken with almost all meals. *Nam pla* is made from steeping fish, usually anchovies, in brine for long periods and then bottling the peatish-coloured liquor produced. Chillies deserve a special mention because most Thais like their food HOT! Some chillies are fairly mild; others – like the tiny, red *prik khii nuu* ('mouse shit pepper') – are fiendishly hot.

Isaan food – from the northeast of Thailand – is also distinctive and very popular. Most of the labourers, prostitutes and service staff come from Isaan, particularly in Bangkok, and you won't have to go far to find a rickety street stall selling sticky rice, aromatic *kai yang* (grilled chicken) and fiery *som tam* (papaya salad).

Due to Thailand's large Chinese population (or at least Thais with Chinese roots), there are also many Chinese-style restaurants whose cuisine is variously 'Thai-ified'. Many of the snacks available on the streets show this mixture of Thai and Chinese, not to mention Arab and Malay. *Bah jang*, for example, are small pyramids of leaves stuffed with sticky rice, Chinese sausage, salted eggs, pork and dried shrimp. They were reputedly first created for the Chinese dragon boat festival but are now available 12 months a year – for around ฿20.

To sample Thai food it is best to go in a group to a restaurant and order a range of dishes. To eat alone is regarded as slightly strange. However, there are a number of 'one-dish' meals like fried rice and *phat thai* (fried noodles) and restaurants will also usually provide *raat khao* ('over rice'), which is a dish like a curry served on a bed of rice for a single person.

Strict non-fish-eating **vegetarians** and **vegans** are in for a tough time. Nearly every cooked meal you will eat in Thailand will be liberally doused in *nam pla* or cooked with shrimp paste. At more expensive and upmarket international restaurants you'll probably be able to find something suitable – in the rural areas, you'll be eating fruit, fried eggs and rice, though not all at once. There are a network of Taoist restaurants offering more strict veggie fare throughout the country – look out for yellow flags with red Chinese lettering. Also asking for 'mai sai nam pla' (no *nam pla* please)– when ordering what should be veggie food might keep the fish sauce out of harm's reach.

Eating out

It is possible to get a tasty and nutritious meal almost anywhere – and at any time – in Thailand. Thais eat out a great deal so that most towns have a range of places. Starting at the top, in pecuniary terms at any rate, the more sophisticated restaurants are usually air-conditioned, and sometimes attached to a hotel. In places like Bangkok and Chiang Mai they may be Western in style and atmosphere. In towns less frequented by foreigners they are likely to be rather more functional – although the food will be just as good. In addition to these more upmarket restaurants are a whole range of places from **noodle shops** to **curry houses** and **seafood restaurants**. Many small restaurants have no menus. But often the speciality of the house will be clear – roasted, honeyed ducks hanging in the window, crab and fish laid out on crushed ice outside. Away from the main tourist spots, 'Western' breakfasts are commonly unavailable, so be prepared to eat Thai-style (noodle or rice soup or fried rice).

Towards the bottom of the scale are **stalls and food carts**. These tend to congregate at particular places in town – often in the evening, from dusk – although they can be found just about anywhere: outside the local provincial offices, along a cul-de-sac, or under a conveniently placed shady tree. Stall holders will tend to specialize in either noodles, rice dishes, fruit drinks, sweets and so on. Hot meals are usually prepared to order. While stall food may be cheap – a meal costs only around ฿15-20 – they are frequented by people from all walks of life. A well-heeled businessman in a suit is just as likely to be seen bent over a bowl of noodles at a rickety table on a busy street corner as a construction worker.

A popular innovation over the last 10 years or so has been the *suan a-haan* or **garden restaurant**. These are often on the edge of towns, with tables set in gardens, sometimes with bamboo furniture and ponds. Another type of restaurant worth a mention is the **Thai-style coffee shop**. These are sometimes attached to hotels in provincial towns and feature hostesses dressed in Imelda-esque or skimpy spangly costumes. The hostesses, when they are not crooning to the house band, sit with customers, laugh at their jokes and assiduously make sure that their glasses are always full.

In the north, *khantoke* dining is de rigueur – or so one might imagine from the number of restaurants offering it. It is a northern Thai tradition, when people sit on the floor to eat at low tables, often to the accompaniment of traditional music and dance.

Tourist centres also provide good European, American and Japanese food at reasonable prices. Bangkok boasts some superb restaurants. Less expensive Western **fast-food** restaurants can also be found, including McDonald's and Kentucky Fried Chicken.

The etiquette of eating

The Thai philosophy on eating is 'often', and most Thais will snack their way through the day. Eating is a relaxed, communal affair and it is not necessary to get too worked up about etiquette. Dishes are placed in the middle of the table where diners can help themselves. In a restaurant rice is usually spooned out by a waiter or waitress – and it is considered good manners to start a meal with a spoon of rice. While food is eaten with a spoon and fork, the fork is only used to manoeuvre food onto the spoon. Because most food is prepared in bite-sized pieces it is not usually necessary to use a knife. At noodle stalls chopsticks and china soup spoons are used while in the northeast most people – at least at home – use their fingers. Sticky rice is compressed into a ball using the ends of the fingers and then dipped in the other dishes. Thais will not pile their plates with food but take several small portions from the dishes arranged on a table. It is also considered good manners when invited out to leave some food on your plate, as well as on the serving dishes on the table. This demonstrates the generosity of the host.

Drink

Water in smaller restaurants can be risky, so many people recommend that visitors drink bottled water or hot tea. Many hotels provide bottles of water gratis in their rooms.

Coffee is consumed throughout Thailand. In stalls and restaurants, coffee comes with a glass of Chinese tea. Soft drinks are widely available too. Many roadside stalls prepare fresh fruit juices in liquidizers while hotels produce all the usual cocktails.

Major brands of **spirits** are served in most hotels and bars, although not always off the tourist path. The most popular spirit among Thais is Mekhong – local cane whisky – which can be drunk straight or with mixers such as Coca-Cola. However, due to its hangover-inducing properties, more sophisticated Thais prefer Johnny Walker or an equivalent brand.

Beer drinking is spreading fast. The most popular local beer is Singha beer brewed by Boon Rawd. Singha, Chang and Heineken are the three most popular beers in Thailand. Leo and Cheers are agreeable budget options although they are seldom sold in restaurants. Beer is relatively expensive in Thai terms as it is heavily taxed by the government. It is a high status drink, so the burgeoning middle class, especially the young, are turning to beer in preference to traditional, local whiskies – which explains why brewers are so keen to set up shop in this traditionally non-beer drinking country. Some pubs and bars also sell beer on tap – which is known as *bier sot*, 'fresh' beer.

Thais are fast developing a penchant for **wine**. Imported wines are expensive by international standards but Thailand now has six wineries, mainly in the northeastern region around Nakhon Ratchasima. For tours around the wine regions (including to a vineyard where the workers use elephants) contact Laurence Civil (laurence@csloxinfo.com).

Entertainment

Bars and clubs

Thais are great clubbers and partygoers, although provincial nightclubs and coffee shops might not be to everyone's tastes. Karaoke is also very popular across the country. Unsurprisingly, the most sophisticated nightlife is to be found in the largest towns and in tourist centres. Jazz and blues, nightclubs, rock, discos, wine bars, gay and lesbian bars, cabaret, straight bars, beer gardens and more are all available. The ousted prime minister,

Thaksin, brought in laws to close down most bars and clubs by midnight though special licences are granted for later hours. Nightclubs tend to close between 0200 and 0300 while opening hours are more variable, anywhere from 1800 to 2200. Bars tend to open and close earlier than nightclubs; happy hours are usually between 1700 and 1900. For the latest offerings, including music, dance and theatre check out the many free newspapers and magazines available in the country's tourist centres.

If you want a taste of tradition, then visit one of the upcountry coffee shops. Some of these are innocuous places where men gather to drink strong coffee, accompanied by Chinese tea, and chat about the price of rice and the latest political scandal. Others are really nightclubs where men drink prodigious quantities of whisky while accompanied by girls dressed in a weird assortment of dresses from figure-hugging little black numbers to Marie Antoinette extravagances. They also take it in turns to croon popular Thai ballads and rock songs to bad backing bands. Upstairs is, commonly, a brothel.

Cinema

In Bangkok, a range of cinemas show films either with an English soundtrack or English subtitles (listed in the *Bangkok Post* and *The Nation*). Up-country cinemas will often have a separate glass enclosed section where it is possible to listen to the English soundtrack of dubbed films. Generally films are screened at 1200, 1400, 1700, 1900, 2100, and at 1000 on Saturday and Sunday. In Bangkok, cultural centres such as the Alliance Française and the Goethe Institute show European films. It is also possible to rent videos in some towns. In the main tourist centres, bars and restaurants will often screen videos or DVDs on large-screen televisions, the night's offerings advertised in advance.

Festivals and events

A booklet of holidays and festivals is available from most TAT offices. For movable festivals (where only the month is listed), check the TAT's website, www.tourismthailand.org. Regional and local festivals are noted in appropriate sections.

January
New Year's Day (1 Jan, public holiday).

February/March
Chinese New Year (late Jan/early Feb; movable) is celebrated by Thailand's large Chinese population. The festival extends over 15 days; spirits are appeased, and offerings are made to the ancestors and to the spirits. Good wishes and lucky money are exchanged, and Chinese-run shops and businesses shut.
Magha Puja (movable, full moon; public holiday) is a Buddhist holy day and celebrates the occasion when the Buddha's disciples miraculously gathered together to hear him preach. Culminates in a candle-lit procession

around the temple bot (or ordination hall). The faithful make offerings and gain merit.

April
Chakri Day (6 Apr; public holiday) commemorates the founding of the present Chakri Dynasty.
Songkran (movable; public holiday) marks the beginning of the Buddhist New Year. The festival is particularly big in the north, much less so in the south and (understandably) the Muslim far south. It is a 3- to 5-day celebration with parades, dancing and folk entertainment. Traditionally, the first day represents the last chance for a 'spring clean'. Rubbish is burnt, in the belief that old and dirty things will cause misfortune in the coming year. The wat is the

focal point of celebrations. Revered Buddha images are carried through the streets, accompanied by singers and dancers. The second day is the main water-throwing day. The water-throwing practice was originally an act of homage to ancestors and family elders. Young people pay respect by pouring scented water over the elders heads. The older generation sprinkle water over Buddha images. Gifts are given. This uninhibited water-throwing continues for all 3 days. On the third day birds, fish and turtles are all released, to gain merit and in remembrance of departed souls.

May/June
Labour Day (1 May; public holiday).
Coronation Day (5 May; public holiday) commemorates the present King Bhumibol's crowning in 1950.
Visakha Puja (full moon; public holiday) holiest of all Buddhist days, it marks the Buddha's birth, enlightenment and death. Candlelit processions are held at most temples.
Ploughing Ceremony (movable; public holiday) is performed by the king at Sanaam Luang near the Grand Palace in Bangkok. Brahmanic in origin, it traditionally marks the auspicious date when farmers could begin preparing their rice land. Bulls decorated with flowers pull a sacred gold plough.

July
Asalha Puja and **Khao Phansa** (movable, full moon; public holiday) commemorates the Buddha's first sermon to his disciples and marks the beginning of the Buddhist Lent. Monks reside in their monasteries for the 3-month Buddhist Rains Retreat to study and meditate, and young men temporarily become monks. Ordination ceremonies take place and villagers give monks white cotton robes to wear during the Lent ritual bathing.

August
Queen's Birthday (12 Aug; public holiday).

October
Chulalongkorn Day (23 Oct; public holiday) honours King Chulalongkorn (1868-1910), one of Thailand's most beloved and revered kings.
Ok Phansa (3 lunar months after Asalha Puja) marks the end of the Buddhist Lent and the beginning of Krathin, when gifts (usually a new set of cotton robes) are offered to the monks. Particularly venerated monks are sometimes given silk robes as a sign of respect and esteem.
Krathin itself is celebrated over 2 days. It marks the end of the monks' retreat and the re-entry of novices into secular society. Processions and fairs are held all over the country; villagers wear their best clothes, and food, money, pillows and bed linen are offered to the monks of the local wat.

November
Loi Krathong (full moon) comes at the end of the rainy season and honours the goddess of water. A *krathong* is a model boat made to contain a candle, incense and flowers. The little boats are pushed out onto canals, lakes and rivers. Sadly, few *krathongs* are now made of leaves: polystyrene has taken over and the morning after Loi Krathong lakes and river banks are littered with the wrecks of the previous night. The 'quaint' candles in pots sold in many shops at this time, are in fact large firecrackers.

December
King's Birthday (5 Dec; public holiday). Flags and portraits of the king are erected all over Bangkok, especially down Rachdamnern Av and around the Grand Palace.
Constitution Day (10 Dec; public holiday).
New Year's Eve (31 Dec; public holiday).

Shopping

→ For VAT refunds, see Customs and duty free, page 56.

Bangkok and Chiang Mai are the shopping 'centres' of Thailand. Many people now prefer Chiang Mai, as the shops are concentrated in a smaller area and there is a good range of quality products, especially handicrafts. Bangkok still offers the greatest variety and choice but it is difficult to find bargains any longer; the department stores and shopping malls contain high-price, high-quality merchandise (at a fixed price), much of which is imported.

Between shopkeepers competition is fierce. Do not be cajoled into buying something before having a chance to price it elsewhere – Thais can be very persuasive. Also, watch out for guarantees of authenticity – fake antiques abound, and even professionals find it difficult to know a 1990 Khmer sculpture from a 10th-century one.

Thailand has had a reputation as being a mecca for pirated goods: CDs and DVDs, Lacoste shirts, Gucci leather goods, Rolex watches, computer software and so on. These items are still available, but pressure from the US to protect intellectual copyright is leading to more enthusiastic crackdowns by the police. In Bangkok, genuine CDs can be bought at what are still bargain prices compared with the West; buying pirated DVDs often requires a retreat to some back room. Strangely though, most DVD sellers are quite honest and if your fake doesn't work they will replace it. When buying DVDs ask for 'master' copies – this way you should avoid purchasing a film shot from the back of a cinema.

The widest selection of **Thai silk** is available in Bangkok although cheaper silk, as well as good quality cotton, can be found in the northeast (the traditional centre of silk weaving). **Tailor-made clothing** is available although designs are sometimes outdated; it might be better for the tailor to copy an article of your own clothing (see page 144). However, times are changing and there are now some top designers in Bangkok. **Leather goods** include custom-made crocodile skin shoes and boots (for those who aren't squeamish).

Bangkok is also a good place to buy **jewellery** – gold, sapphires and rubies – as well as **antiques**, **bronzeware** and **celadon**. (See Tricksters, below, and Safety page 64.) **Handicrafts** are best purchased up-country.

Bargaining

Bargaining is common, except in the large department stores (although they may give a discount on expensive items of jewellery or furniture) and on items like soap, books and most necessities. Expect to pay anything from 25-75% less than the asking price, depending on the bargainer's skill and the shopkeeper's mood.

Tricksters

Tricksters, rip-off artists, fraudsters, less than honest salesmen – call them what you will – are likely to be far more of a problem than simple theft. People may well approach you in the street offering incredible one-off bargains, and giving what might seem to be very plausible reasons for your sudden good fortune. Be wary in all such cases and do not be pressed into making a hasty decision. Unfortunately, more often than not, the salesman is trying to pull a fast one. Favourite 'bargains' are precious stones, whose authenticity is 'demonstrated' before your very eyes (see page 147). Although many Thais genuinely do like to talk to *farangs* and practise their English, in tourist areas there are also those who offer their friendship for pecuniary rather than linguistic reasons. Sad as it is to say, it is probably a good idea to be suspicious. For up-to-date information, visit www.bangkokscams.com.

Local customs and laws

Thais are generally very understanding of the foibles and habits of *farangs* (foreigners) and will forgive and forget most indiscretions. However, there are a number of 'dos and don'ts' that are worth observing.

Clothing In towns and at religious sights, it is courteous to avoid wearing shorts and sleeveless tops. Visitors who are inappropriately dressed may not be allowed into wats (temples); make sure your shoulders and knees are covered up and avoid wearing flip-flops. The same is true of mosques (in the Muslim-dominated far south). In the most expensive restaurants in Bangkok diners may well be expected to wear a jacket and tie. This does not apply on beaches and islands where (almost) anything goes and sarongs, flip-flops, etc are de rigueur. However, topless sunbathing or nudity is still very much frowned upon by Thais, especially in Muslim areas in the south. Most Thais always look neat and clean; *mai rieb-roi* means 'not neat' and is considered a great insult. Dirty, unkempt Westerns are sometimes given the pejorative, and decidedly racist, name of *kee nok farang* – or 'bird shit Westerners'.

Cool and hot hearts Among Thais, the personal characteristic of *jai yen* is very highly regarded; literally, this means to have a 'cool heart'. It embodies calmness, having an even temper and not displaying emotion. Although foreigners generally receive special dispensation, and are not expected to conform to Thai customs (all *farang* are thought to have *jai rawn* or 'hot hearts'), it is important to keep calm in any disagreement – losing one's temper leads to loss of face and loss of respect. An associated personal trait which Thais try to develop is *kreng jai*; this embodies being understanding of other people's needs, desires and feelings – in short, not imposing oneself.

Greeting people Traditionally, Thais greet one another with a *wai* – the equivalent of a handshake. In a *wai*, hands are held together as if in prayer, and the higher the *wai*, the more respectful the greeting. By watching Thai's *wai* it is possible to ascertain their relative seniority where a combination of class, age, wealth, power and gender all play a part. Juniors or inferiors should initiate a *wai*, and hold it higher and for longer than the senior or superior. Foreigners are not expected to conform to this custom – a simple *wai* at chest to chin height is all that is required. You should not *wai* to children or to waiters, waitresses and other people offering a service. When *farangs* and Thais do business it is common to shake hands. The respectful term of address is *khun*, which applies to both men and women. This is usually paired with a Thai's first name so that, for example, Somchai Bamruang would be greeted as Khun Somchai. The closest equivalent to the English Mr and Mrs/Miss are *Nai* and *Nang*, which are also used as formal terms of address. Thais also have nicknames like *Kai* (chicken), *Ooy* (sugar) or *Kung* (shrimp) while people from certain professions will also have respectful titles – like *ajaan* for a teacher or lecturer.

Heads and feet Try to not openly point your feet at anyone – feet are viewed as spiritually the lowest part of the body. At the same time, never touch anyone's (even a child's) head, which is the holiest as well as the highest part. Resting your feet on a table would be regarded as highly disrespectful while stepping over someone sitting on the floor is also frowned upon. If sitting on the floor, try to tuck your feet under your body – although Westerners unused to this posture may find it uncomfortable after a short time.

The strange case of Harry Nicolaides

The reverence shown to their king is a Thai national trait – pictures of him hang in nearly every home and giant poster boards depicting the monarch are seemingly festooned on every street corner.

To protect the king, and other royals, from criticism and slander, Thailand has some of the toughest lese-majesty laws on the planet with lengthy jail sentences awaiting miscreants.

A completely unknown Australian author, Harry Nicolaides, was sentenced to three years in prison in January 2009 (he received a royal pardon in February 2009 and returned to Australia) after a single paragraph in a book he'd self-published in 2005 (only 50 copies were printed) was deemed lese-majesty by a Thai court. Only seven copies of Nicolaides' book had ever been sold and without the intervention of the Thai courts this tome would have disappeared into the obscurity it likely deserved. Instead, the obvious outcome has been the dissemination of the offending text across the internet.

The new Democrat Party government, installed in December 2008, have sought to extend prosecution of alleged lese-majesty offences, implementing a far-reaching crackdown. Thousands of Thai websites have been closed down; leading left-wing academic, Giles Ji Ungpakorn has been charged (he fled Thailand in February 2009); several other Thai political activists are in prison and the BBC's Bangkok correspondent Jonathan Head is under investigation.

Visitors to Thailand are warned to be very careful about voicing an opinion on Thai royalty, to treat coinage, stamps and anything depicting the Thai royal family with the utmost respect and to be ready to stand, or follow direction, should the national or royal anthem be played.

The monarchy Never criticize any member of the royal family or the institution itself. The monarchy is held in very high esteem and *lese-majesty* remains an offence carrying a sentence of up to 15 years in prison. You should treat coins and bank notes with respect as they bear the image of the king, as well as postage stamps which are moistened with a sponge rather than the tongue. In cinemas, the national anthem is played before the show and the audience is expected to stand. At other events, take your lead from the crowd as to how to behave. A dying custom, but one which is still adhered to in smaller towns as well as certain parts of Bangkok, like Hualamphong railway station, is that everybody stops in their tracks at 0800 and 1800, when the national anthem is relayed over loudspeakers.

Monastery (wat) and monk etiquette Remove shoes on entering any monastery building, do not climb over Buddha images or have your picture taken in front of one, and when sitting in a *bot* or *viharn* ensure that your feet are not pointing towards a Buddha image. Wear modest clothing – women should not expose their shoulders or wear dresses that are too short (see Clothing, above). Ideally, they should be calf length although knee-length dresses or skirts are usually acceptable. Women should never touch a monk, hand anything directly to a monk or venture into the monks' quarters. They should also avoid climbing *chedis* (stupas). As in any other place of worship, visitors should not disturb the peace of a wat.

Open shows of affection Visitors will notice that men and women rarely show open, public signs of affection. It is not uncommon, however, to see men holding hands – this is usually a sign of simple friendship, nothing more. That said, in Bangkok, traditional customs have broken down and in areas such as Siam Square it is common to see young lovers, hand-in-hand.

Sanuk A quality of *sanuk*, which can be roughly translated as 'fun' or *joie de vivre*, is important to Thais. Activities are undertaken because they are *sanuk*, others avoided because they are *mai sanuk* ('not fun'). Perhaps it is because of this apparent love of life that so many visitors returning from Thailand remark on how Thais always appear happy and smiling. However, it is worth bearing in mind that the interplay of *jai yen* and *kreng jai* means that everything may not be quite as it appears.

Smoking This is now illegal in all air-conditioned areas. Fines are heavy, although not always enforced. Bangkok police regularly fine people up to ฿3000 for discarding cigarette butts anywhere other than in official ashtrays.

Essentials A-Z

Accident and emergency

Emergency services Police: T191, T123. **Tourist police:** T1155. **Fire:** T199. **Ambulance:** T02-2551134-6. **Tourist Assistance Centre:** Rachdamnern Nok Av, Bangkok, T02-356 0655.

Calling one of the emergency numbers will not usually be very productive as few operators speak English. It is better to call the tourist police or have a hotel employee or other English-speaking Thai telephone for you. For more intractable problems contact your embassy or consulate.

Children

Many people are daunted by the prospect of taking a child to Southeast Asia and there are disadvantages: travelling is slower and more expensive and there are additional health risks for the child or baby. But it can be a most rewarding experience and, with sufficient care and planning, it can also be safe. Children are excellent passports into a local culture. Thais love kids so are more than willing to accommodate, look after, feed, tolerate and adore your children. You will also receive the best service and

help from officials and members of the public when in difficulty. A non-Asian child is still something of a novelty, especially in more remote areas, and parents may find their child frequently taken off their hands.

Disposable nappies can be bought in Thailand but remember that you're adding to the rubbish-disposal problem. Many Western baby products are available in Thailand: shampoo, talcum powder, soap and lotion. Baby wipes are expensive and not always easy to find. Other things worth packing are child paracetamol; first-aid kit; decongestant for colds; instant food for under one year olds; ORS (Oral Rehydration Salts) such as Dioralyte, widely available in Thailand, and the most effective way to alleviate diarrhoea (it is not a cure); sarong or backpack for carrying child (and/or lightweight collapsible buggy); sterilizing tablets (and container for sterilizing bottles, teats, utensils); cream for nappy rash and other skin complaints, such as Sudocrem; sunblock, factor 15 or higher; sun hat; thermometer; zip-lock bags for snacks, etc.

Eating
Be aware that even expensive hotels may have squalid cooking conditions;

the cheapest street stall is often more hygienic. Where possible, try to watch food being prepared. Stir-fried vegetables and rice or noodles are the best bet; meat and fish may be pre-cooked and then left out before being re-heated. Fruit can be bought cheaply – papaya, banana and avocado are all excellent sources of nutrition. Western-style baby foods and products are widely available in good supermarkets. Powdered milk is also available throughout the region, although most brands have added sugar. If taking a baby, breast-feeding is strongly recommended. Powdered food, bottled water and fizzy drinks are also sold widely.

Health

More preparation is probably necessary for babies and children than for an adult, and particularly when travelling to remote areas where health services are primitive. A travel insurance policy which has an air ambulance provision is strongly recommended. When planning a route, try to stay within 24 hrs' travel of a hospital with good care and facilities. For advice about common problems, see Health, page 58. **Note** Never allow your child to be exposed to the harsh tropical sun without protection. A child can burn in minutes. Loose cotton clothing with long sleeves and legs and a sunhat are best. High-factor sun-protection cream is essential.

Vaccinations

Children should already be properly protected against diphtheria, poliomyelitis and pertussis (whooping cough), measles and HIB, all of which can be more serious infections in Southeast Asia than at home. The measles, mumps and rubella vaccine is also given to children throughout the world, but those teenage girls who have not had rubella (German measles) should be tested and vaccinated. Hepatitis B vaccination for babies is now routine in some countries. See also Health, page 58.

Sleeping

At the hottest time of year, air conditioning may be essential for a baby or young child's comfort. This rules out many of the cheaper hotels, but air-conditioned accommodation is available in all but the most out-of-the-way spots. When the child is bathing, be aware that the water could carry parasites, so avoid letting him or her drink it.

Transport

Public transport may be a problem; trains are fine, but long bus journeys are restrictive and uncomfortable. Hiring a car is undoubtedly the most convenient way to see a country with a small child. It is possible to buy child-seats in larger cities.

Customs and duty free

Customs

Non-residents can bring in unlimited foreign and Thai currency although amounts exceeding US$10,000 must be declared. Maximum amount permitted to take out of Thailand is ฿50,000 per person.

Prohibited items

All narcotics; obscene literature, pornography; firearms (except with a permit from the Police Department or local registration office); and some species of plants and animals (for more information contact the **Royal Forestry Department**, Phahonyothin Rd, Bangkok, T02-561 0777).

Duty free

500 g of cigars/cigarettes (or 200 cigarettes) and one litre of wine or spirits.

Export restrictions

No Buddha or Bodhisattva images or fragments should be taken out of Thailand, except for worshipping by Buddhists, for cultural exchanges or for research. However, it is obvious that many people do – you only have to look in the antique shops to see the abundance for sale. A licence should be obtained from the **Department of Fine Arts**, Na Prathat Rd, Bangkok, T02-224 1370, from **Chiang Mai National Museum**, T02-221308, or from the **Songkhla National Museum**, Songkhla, T02-311728. 5-days' notice is needed; take 2 passport photos of the object and photocopies of your passport.

VAT refunds
Most of the major department stores have a VAT refund desk. Go to them on your day of purchase with receipts and ask them to complete VAT refund form, which you then present, with purchased goods, at appropriate desk in any international airport in Thailand. They'll give you another form that you exchange for cash in the departure lounge. You'll need to spend at least ฿4000 to qualify for a refund.

Disabled travellers

Disabled travellers will find Thailand a challenge. The difficulties that even the able bodied encounter in crossing roads when pedestrian crossings are either non-existent or ignored by most motorists are amplified for the disabled. Cracked pavements, high curbs and lack of ramps add to the problems for even the most wheelchair savvy. Buses and taxis are not designed for disabled access either and there are relatively few hotels and restaurants that are wheelchair-friendly. This is particularly true of cheaper and older establishments. This is not to suggest that travel in Thailand is impossible for the disabled. On the plus side, you will find Thais to be extremely helpful and because taxis and tuk-tuks are cheap it is usually not necessary to rely on buses. The **Global Access – Disabled Travel Network** website, www.globalaccess news.com, is useful. Another informative site, with lots of advice on how to travel with specific disabilities, plus listings and links, belongs to the **Society for Accessible Travel and Hospitality**, www.sath.org. Another site,

www.access-able.com has a specific section for travel in Thailand.

Electricity

Voltage is 220 volts (50 cycles). Most first- and tourist-class hotels have outlets for shavers and hairdryers. Adaptors are recommended, as almost all sockets are 2-pronged.

Embassies and consulates

Thai embassies worldwide
www.thaiembassy.org is a useful resource.
Australia 131 Macquarie St, Level 8, Sydney 2000, T02-9241 2542.
Austria Cottagegasse 48, 1180 Vienna, T01-478 3335.
Belgium 2 Sq du Val de la Cambre, 1050 Brussels, T02-640 6810.
Canada 180 Island Park Drive, Ottawa, Ontario, K1Y 0A2, T613-722 4444.
Germany Lepsiusstrasse 64-66, 12163 Berlin, T030-794810.
Israel 21 Shaul Hamelech Boulevard, Tel Aviv 64367, T03-695 8980.
Italy Via Nomentana132, 00162 Rome, T06-862 2051.
Japan 3-14-6, Kami-Osaki, Shinagawa-Ku, Tokyo 14-0021, T03-3447 2247.
Laos Rte Phonekheng, Vientiane, PO Box 128, T021-214581.
Malaysia 206 Jalan Ampang, 50450 Kuala Lumpur, T03-2148 8222.
Netherlands Laan Copes Van Cattenburch 123, 2585 EZ, The Hague, T3170-345 9703.
New Zealand 2 Cook St, Karori, PO Box 17226, Wellington, T04-476 8616.
Sweden Floragatan 3, 26220, Stockholm 100 40, T08-7917340.
Switzerland Kirchstrasse 56, 3097 Liebefeld-Bern, T031-9703030.
UK 29-30 Queens Gate, London, SW7 5JB, T020-7589 2944.
USA 1024 Wisconsin Av, NW, Suite 401, Washington, DC 20007, T202-944 3600.

Gay and lesbian travellers

On the surface, Thailand is incredibly tolerant of homosexuals and lesbians. In Bangkok and other major cities there's an openness that can make even San Francisco look tame. It is for this reason that Thailand's gay scene has flourished and, more particularly, has grown in line with international tourism. However, overt public displays of affection are still frowned upon (see Local customs and laws, page 55). Attitudes in the more traditional rural areas, particularly the Muslim regions, are far more conservative than in the cities. By exercising a degree of cultural sensitivity any visit should be hassle free.

Several of the free tourist magazines distributed through hotels and restaurants in Bangkok, Pattaya, Phuket and Koh Samui provide information on the gay and lesbian scene, including bars and meeting points. The essential website before you get there is www.utopia-asia.com which provides good material on where to go, current events, and background information on the Thai gay scene in Bangkok and beyond. **Utopia tours** at Tarntawan Palace Hotel, 119/5-10 Suriwong Rd, T02-634 0273, www.utopia-tours.com, provides tours for gay and lesbian visitors. There's also a map of gay Bangkok. Gay clubs are listed in *Bangkok Metro* magazine (www.bkkmetro. co.th) and include **DJ Station** (by far the most famous Bangkok gay club) and its sister club **Freeman Dance Arena**, 60/18-21 Silom Rd, www.dj-station.com. The main centres of activity in Bangkok are Silom Rd sois 2 and 4 and Sukhumvit Soi 23. There is also a thriving gay scene in Pattaya and, to a lesser extent, on Phuket, Koh Samui and in Chiang Mai. See also the Thai section of www.fridae.com, one of Asia's most comprehensive gay sites.

Health

Hospitals/medical services are listed in the Directory sections of each chapter.

Staying healthy in Thailand is straight-forward. With the following advice and precautions you should keep as healthy as you do at home. Most visitors return home having experienced no problems at all beyond an upset stomach. However, in Thailand the health risks, especially in the tropical areas, are different from those encountered in Europe or the USA. It also depends on how you travel and where. The country has a mainly tropical climate; nevertheless the acquisition of true tropical disease by the visitor is probably conditioned as much by the rural nature and standard of hygiene of the surroundings than by the climate. Malaria is common in certain areas, particularly in the jungle. There is an obvious difference in health risks between the business traveller who tends to stay in international class hotels in the large cities and the backpacker trekking through the rural areas. There are no hard and fast rules to follow; you will often have to make your own judgement on the healthiness or otherwise of your surroundings. Check with your doctor on the status of Avian flu before you go. At the time of writing, Thailand was clear of bird flu.

Before you go

Ideally, you should see your GP/practice nurse or travel clinic at least 6 weeks before your departure for general advice on travel risks, malaria and recommended vaccinations. Your local pharmacist can also be a good source of readily accessible advice. Make sure you have travel insurance, get a dental check (especially if you are going to be away for more than a month), know your own blood group and if you suffer a long-term condition such as diabetes or epilepsy make sure some-one knows or that you have a **Medic Alert** bracelet/necklace with this information on it.

Recommended vaccinations

No vaccinations are specifically required for Thailand unless coming from an infected area, but tuberculosis, rabies, Japanese B encephalitis and hepatitis B are commonly recommended. The final decision, however, should be based on a consultation with your GP or travel clinic. You should also confirm that your primary courses and boosters are up to date (diphtheria, tetanus, poliomyelitis, hepatitis A, typhoid).

A yellow fever certificate is required by visitors who have been in an infected area in the 10 days before arrival. Those without a vaccination certificate will be vaccinated and kept in quarantine for 6 days, or deported.

A-Z of health risks
Bites and stings

This is a very rare event indeed for travellers, but if you are unlucky (or careless) enough to be bitten by a venomous snake, spider, scorpion or sea creature, try to identify the culprit, without putting yourself in further danger (do not try to catch a live snake).

Snake bites in particular are very frightening, but in fact rarely poisonous – even venomous snakes bite without injecting venom. Victims should be taken to a hospital or a doctor without delay. It is not advised for travellers to carry snake bite anti-venom as it can do more harm than good in inexperienced hands. Reassure and comfort the victim frequently. Immobilize the limb with a bandage or a splint and get the patient to lie still with the affected area below the heart. Do not slash the bite area and try to suck out the poison. This also does more harm than good. You should only apply a tourniquet if you know how to do so; do not attempt this unless you are experienced.

Certain tropical fish inject venom into bathers' feet when trodden on, which can be exceptionally painful. Wear plastic shoes if such creatures are reported. The pain can be relieved by immersing the foot in hot water (as hot as you can bear) for as long as the pain persists.

Dengue fever

This is a viral disease spread by mosquitoes that tend to bite during the day. The symptoms are fever and often intense joint pains, also some people develop a rash. Symptoms last about a week but it can take a few weeks to recover fully. Dengue can be difficult to distinguish from malaria as both diseases tend to occur in the same places. There are no effective vaccines or antiviral drugs though, fortunately, travellers rarely develop the more severe form of the disease (which can prove fatal). Rest, plenty of fluids and paracetamol (not aspirin) is the recommended treatment. **Note** The number of cases in Thailand has risen in the last year, consult your GP for further advice.

Diarrhoea and intestinal upset

Diarrhoea can refer either to loose stools or an increased frequency of bowel movement, both of which can be a nuisance. Symptoms should be relatively short-lived but if they persist beyond 2 weeks specialist medical attention should be sought. Also seek medical help if there is blood in the stools and/or fever.

Adults can use an anti-diarrhoeal medication such as loperamide to control the symptoms but only for up to 24 hrs. In addition keep well hydrated by drinking plenty of fluids and eat bland foods. Oral rehydration sachets taken after each loose stool are a useful way to keep hydrated. These should always be used when treating children and the elderly.

Bacterial traveller's diarrhoea is the most common form. Ciproxin (Ciprofloxacin) is a useful antibiotic and can be obtained by private prescription in the UK. You need to take one 500 mg tablet when the diarrhoea starts. If there are so signs of improvement after 24 hrs the diarrhoea is likely to be viral and not bacterial. If it is due to other organisms such as those causing giardia or amoebic dysentery, different antibiotics will be required.

The standard advice to prevent problems is be careful with water and ice for drinking. Ask yourself where the water came from. If you have any doubts then boil it or filter and treat it. There are many filter/treatment devices now available on the market. Food can also transmit disease. Be wary of salads (what were they washed in, who handled them), re-heated foods or food that has been left out in the sun having been cooked earlier in the day. There is a simple adage: wash it, peel it, boil it or forget it. Also be wary of unpasteurized dairy products as these can transmit a range of diseases.

Hepatitis

Hepatitis means inflammation of the liver. Viral causes of the disease can be acquired anywhere in the world. The most obvious symptom is a yellowing of your skin or the whites of your eyes. However, prior to this all that you may notice is itching and tiredness. Pre-travel hepatitis A vaccine is the best bet. Hepatitis B (for which there is a vaccine) is spread through blood and unprotected sexual intercourse, both of which can be avoided.

Japanese encephalitis B

This is a viral disease of the brain spread by mosquitoes in parts of Asia. It is very rare in travellers but those visiting rural areas during the wet season may be advised to have the vaccine.

Malaria

Malaria can cause death within 24 hrs and can start as something just resembling an attack of flu. You may feel tired, lethargic, headachy, feverish; more seriously you may develop fits, followed by coma and then death. Have a low index of suspicion because it is very easy to write off vague symptoms, which may actually be malaria. If you have a temperature, visit a doctor as soon as you can and ask for a malaria test. On your return home, if you suffer any of these symptoms, have a test as soon as possible. Even if a previous test proved negative, this could save your life.

Treatment is with drugs and may be oral or into a vein depending on the seriousness of the infection. Remember ABCD: Awareness

(of whether the disease is present in the area you are travelling in); Bite avoidance, Chemoprohylaxis; Diagnosis.

To prevent mosquito bites wear clothes that cover arms and legs, use effective insect repellents in areas with known risks of insect-spread disease and use a mosquito net treated with an insecticide. Repellents containing 30-50% DEET (Di-ethyltoluamide) are recommended when visiting malaria-endemic areas; lemon eucalyptus (Mosiguard) is a reasonable alternative. The key advice is to guard against contracting malaria by taking the correct anti-malarials and finishing the recommended course. If you are a popular target for insect bites or develop lumps quite soon after being bitten use antihistamine tablets and apply a cream such as hydrocortisone.

Remember that it is risky to buy medicine, and in particular anti-malarials, in some developing countries. These may be sub-standard or part of a trade in counterfeit drugs.

Rabies

Rabies is prevalent in Thailand so be aware of the dangers of the bite from any animal. Rabies vaccination before travel can be considered but if bitten always seek urgent medical attention – whether or not you have been previously vaccinated – after first cleaning the wound and treating with an iodine-base disinfectant or alcohol.

Sun

Take good heed of advice regarding protecting yourself against the sun. Overexposure can lead to sunburn and, in the longer term, skin cancers and premature skin aging. The best advice is simply to avoid exposure to the sun by covering exposed skin, wearing a hat and staying out of the sun if possible, particularly between late morning and early afternoon. Apply a high-factor sunscreen (at least SPF15) and also make sure it screens against UVB. A further danger in tropical climates is heat exhaustion or more seriously heatstroke. This can be avoided by good hydration, which means drinking water past the point of simply quenching thirst. Also when first exposed to tropical heat take time to acclimatize by avoiding strenuous activity in the middle of the day. If you cannot avoid heavy exercise it is also a good idea to increase salt intake.

Underwater health

If you plan to dive make sure that you are fit do so. The British Sub-Aqua Club (BSAC), Telford's Quay, South Pier Rd, Ellesmere Port, Cheshire CH65 4FL, UK, T0151-350 6200, F0151-350 6215, www.bsac.com, can put you in touch with doctors who will carry out medical examinations. Check that any dive company you use are reputable and have appropriate certification from BSAC or Professional Association of Diving Instructors (PADI), Unit 7, St Philips Central, Albert Rd, St Philips, Bristol, BS2 0TD, T0117-300 7234, www.padi.com.

There are a few simple rules to avoid getting the bends: don't dive too deep; don't ascend too quickly; use – and obey – your computer; drink a lot to avoid dehydration. Should you, however, become victim to a suspected decompression attack, contact one of the following facilities immediately: Apakorn Kiatiwong Naval Hospital, Sattahip, Chonburi, T038-437171, 26 km east of Pattaya, urgent care available 24 hrs; Department of Underwater & Aviation Medicine, Phra Pinklao Naval Hospital, Taksin Rd, Thonburi, Bangkok, T02-4600000-19, ext 341, or T02-4601105; Hyperbaric Services Thailand, 233 Raj-U-thit 200 Pee Rd, Patong Beach, Phuket, T076-342518, T342519, after hrs emergency number T08-1797 5984, T08-1978 5976 (mob); Hyperbaric Services Thailand, 34/8 Moo 4, Bo Phut, T077-427427, after hours emergency number: T08-1081 0848.

Water

There are a number of ways of purifying water. Dirty water should first be strained through a filter bag and then boiled or treated.

Bring water to a rolling boil for several minutes. There are sterilizing methods that can be used and products generally contain chlorine (eg Puritabs) or iodine (eg Pota Aqua) compounds. There are a number of water sterilizers now on the market available in personal and expedition size. Make sure you take the spare parts or spare chemicals with you and do not believe everything the manufacturers say.

Other diseases and risks

There are a range of other insect-borne diseases that are quite rare in travellers, but worth finding out about if going to particular destinations. Examples are sleeping sickness, river blindness and leishmaniasis. Fresh water can also be a source of diseases such as bilharzia and leptospirosis and it is worth investigating if these are a danger before bathing in lakes and streams. Also remember that unprotected sex always carries a risk and extra care is required when visiting some parts of the world.

Useful websites

www.nathnac.org National Travel Health Network and Centre.
www.who.int World Health Organisation.
www.fitfortravel.scot.nhs.uk Fit for Travel. This site from Scotland provides a quick A-Z of vaccine and travel health advice requirements for each country.

Books

Dawood R, editor. *Travellers' health* (3rd edition, Oxford University Press, 2002). *Expedition Medicine* (The Royal Geographic Society) Editors David Warrell and Sarah Anderson ISBN 1 86197 040-4.

Internet

Apart from a few remote islands Thailand has an excellent internet network. Tourist areas tend to be well catered for with numerous internet shops offering a connection for between ฿30-90 per hr. Some guesthouses and hotels have free wireless while the more expensive ones charge extortionate rates of up ฿1000 per day. You might also be able to pick up wireless for free from office blocks, etc. The cheapest internet options tend to be the small games rooms run primarily for Thai kids who eagerly play online games, usually ฿10-20 per hr, or by using your web-enabled mobile phone with a local simcard – see Mobiles, page 66.

Insurance

Always take out travel insurance before you set off and read the small print carefully. Check that the policy covers any activities that you may end up doing. Also check exactly what your medical cover includes, ie ambulance, helicopter rescue or emergency flights back home. And check the payment protocol; you may have to cough up first (literally) before the insurance company reimburses you. It is always best to dig out all the receipts for expensive personal effects like jewellery or cameras. Take photos of these items and note down all serial numbers. You are advised to shop around. STA Travel and other reputable student travel organizations offer good-value policies. Young travellers from North America can try the International Student Insurance Service (ISIS), which is available through STA Travel, T1-800-7814040, www.sta-travel.com. Other recommended travel insurance companies in North America include: Travel Guard, T1-800-8261300, www.noelgroup.com; Access America, T1-800-2848300; Travel Insurance Services, T1-800-9371387; and Travel Assistance International, T1-800-821 2828. Older travellers should note that some companies will not cover people over 65 years old, or may charge higher premiums. The best policies for older travellers (UK) are offered by Age Concern, T0845-601 2234.

If diving in Thailand, it's worth noting that there are no air evacuation services,

and hyperbaric services can charge as much as US$800 per hr so good dive insurance is imperative. It is inexpensive and well worth it in case of a problem, real or perceived. Many general travel insurance policies will not cover diving. Contact DAN (the Divers' Alert Network) for more information, www.diversalertnetwork.org; DAN Europe, www.daneurope.org; or DAN South East Asia Pacific, www.danseap.org.

Language

English is reasonably widely spoken and is taught to all school children. Off the tourist trail, making yourself understood becomes more difficult. It is handy to buy a Thai/English road atlas of the country (most petrol stations sell them) – you can then point to destinations.

The Thai language is tonal and, strictly speaking, monosyllabic. There are 5 tones: high, low, rising, falling and mid-tone. These are used to distinguish between words which would otherwise be identical. For example: *mai* (low tone, new), *mai* (rising, silk), *mai* (mid-tone, burn), *mai* (high tone, question indicator), and *mai* (falling tone, negative indicator). Not surprisingly, many visitors find it hard to hear the different tones, and it is difficult to make much progress during a short visit. The tonal nature of the language also explains why so much of Thai humour is based around homonyms – and especially when *farangs* (foreigners) say what they do not mean. Although tones make Thai a challenge for foreign visitors, other aspects of the language are easier to grasp: there are no marked plurals in nouns, no marked tenses in verbs, no definite or indefinite articles, and no affixes or suffixes.

Visitors may well experience 2 oddities of the Thai language being reflected in the way that Thais speak English. An 'l' or 'r' at the end of a word in Thai becomes an 'n', while an 's' becomes a 't'. So some Thais refer to the 'Shell' Oil Company as 'Shen', a name like 'Les' becomes 'Let', while 'cheque bill' becomes 'cheque bin'. It is also impossible to have 2 consonants after one another in Thai. If it occurs, a Thai will automatically insert a vowel (even though it is not written). So the soft drink 'Sprite' becomes 'Sa-prite', and the English word 'start', 'sa-tart'. See also page 774.

Despite Thai being a difficult language to pick up, it is worth trying to learn a few words, even if your visit to Thailand is short. Thais generally feel honoured that a *farang* is bothering to learn their language, and will be patient and helpful. If they laugh at some of your pronunciations do not be put off – it is not meant to be critical.

Media

Newspapers and magazines

There are 2 major English-language dailies – the *Bangkok Post* (www.bangkokpost.net) and *The Nation* (www.nationmultimedia.com). They provide good international coverage. There are a number of Thai-language dailies and weeklies, as well as Chinese-language newspapers. The local papers are sometimes scandalously colourful, with gruesome pictures of traffic accidents and murder victims.

International newspapers are available in Bangkok, Chiang Mai, Pattaya and on Koh Samui.

Television and radio

CNN and BBC are available in most mid- or upper-range hotels. Local cable networks will sometimes provide English language films, while a full satellite package will give you English football and various movie and other channels. Programme listings are available in *The Nation* and *Bangkok Post*.

Short wave radio frequencies are BBC, London, Southeast Asian service 3915, 6195, 9570, 9740, 11750, 11955, 15360; Singapore service 88.9MHz; East Asian service 5995, 6195, 7180, 9740, 11715, 11750, 11945, 11955, 15140, 15280, 15360, 17830, 21715.

Voice of America (VoA, Washington), Southeast Asian service 1143, 1575, 7120, 9760, 9770, 15185, 15425; Indonesian service 6110, 11760, 15425. **Radio Beijing**, Southeast Asian service (English) 11600, 11660. **Radio Japan** (Tokyo), Southeast Asian service (English) 11815, 17810, 21610. For information on Asian radio and television broadcasts.

Internet

Recent events in Thailand have exposed the vested interests hiding in the background of papers such as *The Nation* and they are no longer reliable news sources. Into this gap has sprung up a number of excellent blogs: **angkokpundit.blogspot.com**, continually update, excellent news resource; **facthai.wordpress.com**, campaign against censorship, will publish hard to get articles; **rspas.anu.edu.au/rmap/newmandala/**, excellent analysis and coverage of current events; **news.inbangkok.org**, straight news resource; **www.prachatai.com/english**, Thai bloggers producing independent news and analysis; **www.khikwai.com**, cultural and social analysis of current affairs; www.notthe nation, irreverent and highly entertaining send-up of Thai politics and *The Nation* newspaper – Thailand's *Private Eye*.

Money

Currency

Exchange rates €1=฿46, £1=฿50, US$1=฿36 (Mar 2009). For up-to-the-minute exchange rates visit www.xe.com.

The unit of Thai currency is the **baht** (฿), which is divided into 100 **satang**. Notes in circulation include ฿20 (green), ฿50 (blue), ฿100 (red), ฿500 (purple) and ฿1000 (orange and grey). Coins include 25 satang and 50 satang, and ฿1, ฿2, ฿5, and ฿10. The 2 smaller coins are disappearing from circulation and the 25 satang coin, equivalent to the princely sum of US$0.003, is rarely found. The colloquial term for 25 satang is saleng.

Exchange

It is best to change money at banks or money changers which give better rates than hotels. The exchange booths at Bangkok airport have some of the best rates available. There is no black market. First-class hotels have 24-hr money changers. Indonesian rupiah, Nepalese rupees, Burmese kyat, Vietnamese dong, Lao kip and Cambodian riels cannot be exchanged for baht at Thai banks. (Money changers will sometimes exchange kyat, dong, kip and riel and it can be a good idea to buy the currencies in Bangkok before departure for these countries as the black-market rate often applies.) There is a charge of ฿23 per cheque when changing traveller's cheques (passport required) so it works out cheaper to travel with large denomination traveller's cheques (or avoid them altogether).

Credit and debit cards

Plastic is increasingly used in Thailand and just about every town of any size will have a bank with an ATM. Visa and MasterCard are the most widely taken credit cards, and cash cards with the Cirrus logo can also be used to withdraw cash at many banks. Generally speaking, AMEX can be used at branches of the **Bangkok Bank**; JCB at **Siam Commercial Bank**; MasterCard at **Siam Commercial** and **Bangkok Bank**; and Visa at **Thai Farmers' Bank** and **Bangkok Bank**. Most larger hotels and more expensive restaurants take credit cards as well. Because Thailand has embraced the ATM with such exuberance, many foreign visitors no longer bother with traveller's cheques or cash and rely entirely on plastic. Even so, a small stash of US dollars cash can come in handy in a sticky situation.

Notification of credit card loss: **American Express**, SP Building, 388 Phahonyothin Rd, Bangkok 10400, T02-2735544; **Diners Club**, Dusit Thani Building, Rama IV Rd, T02-233 5644, T02-238 3660; **JCB**, T02-256 1361, T02-2561351; **Visa** and **MasterCard**, Thai Farmers Bank Building, Phahonyothin Rd, T02-251 6333, T02-273 1199.

Cost of living

A day's work in the fields will earn a Thai around ฿100-150, depending on the type of work and the region. The minimum daily wage in Bangkok is around ฿165 (US$5) and in most provincial areas, ฿133 (US$4). The average salary of a civil servant is around US$250 a month. Of course, Thailand's middle classes – and especially those engaged in business in Bangkok – will earn far more than this. Thailand has appalling wealth distribution yet Thai society is remarkably cohesive. A simple but good meal out will cost ฿60; the rental of a modern house in a provincial city will cost perhaps ฿4000 a month.

Cost of travelling

Visitors staying in the best hotels and eating in hotel restaurants will probably spend at least ฿2000 per day, conceivably much much more. Tourists staying in cheaper a/c accommodation and eating in local restaurants will probably spend about ฿600-900 per day. Backpackers staying in fan-cooled guesthouses and eating cheaply, should be able to live on ฿300 per day. In Bangkok, expect to pay 20-30% more.

Opening hours

Hours of business Banks: Mon-Fri 0830-1530. **Exchange**: daily 0830-2200 in Bangkok, Pattaya, Phuket and Chiang Mai. In other towns opening hours are usually shorter. **Government offices**: Mon-Fri 0830-1200, 1300-1630. **Shops**: 0830-1700, larger shops: 1000-1900 or 2100. **Tourist offices**: 0830-1630.

Safety

In general, Thailand is a safe country to visit. The vast majority of visitors to Thailand will not experience any physical threat what so ever. However, there have been some widely publicized murders of foreign tourists in recent years and the country does have a very high murder rate. It is best to avoid any situation where violence can occur – what would be a simple punch-up or pushing bout in the West can quickly escalate in Thailand to extreme violence. This is mostly due to loss of face. Getting drunk with Thais can be a risky business – Westerners visiting the country for short periods won't be versed in the intricacies of Thai social interaction and may commit unwitting and terrible faux pas. A general rule of thumb if confronted with a situation is to appear conciliatory and offer a way for the other party to back out gracefully. It should be noted that even some police officers in Thailand represent a threat – at least 3 young Western travellers have been shot and murdered by drunken Thai policemen in the last few years. Confidence tricksters, touts, all operate, particularly in more popular tourist centres. Robbery is also a threat; it ranges from pick-pocketing to the drugging (and subsequent robbing) of bus and train passengers. Watchfulness and simple common sense should be employed. Women travelling alone should be careful (see also page 71). Always lock hotel rooms and place valuables in a safe deposit if available (if not, take them with you).

If you do get any problems contact the tourist police rather than the ordinary police – they will speak English and are used to helping resolve any disputes, issues, etc. The country's health infrastructure, especially in provincial capitals and tourist destinations, is good.

For background information on staying healthy, see page 58. The UK's Foreign and Commonwealth Office's 'Know Before You Go' campaign, www.fco.gov.uk/travel, offers some advice.

Foreign and Commonwealth Office (FCO), T0845-850 2829, www.fco.gov.uk/travel. The UK Foreign and Commonwealth Office's travel warning section.
US State Department, www.travel.state. gov/travel_warnings.html. The US State Department updates travel advisories on its 'Travel Warnings and Consular Information Sheets'. It also has a hotline for American travellers, T202-647-5225.

Bribery

The way to make your way in life, for some people in Thailand, is through the strategic offering of gifts. A Chulalongkorn University report recently estimated that it 'costs' ฿10 million to become Bangkok Police Chief. Apparently this can be recouped in just 2 years of hard graft. Although bribing officials is by no means recommended, resident *farangs* report that they often resort to such gifts to avoid the time and hassle involved in filling in the forms and making the requisite visit to a police station for a minor traffic offence. As a visitor, it's best to play it straight.

Drugs and prostitution

Many prostitutes and drug dealers are in league with the police and may find it more profitable to report you than to take your custom (or they may try to do both). They receive a reward from the police, and the police in turn receive a bonus for the detective work. Note that foreigners on buses may be searched for drugs. Sentences for possession of illegal drugs vary from a fine or one year in jail for marijuana up to life imprisonment or execution for possession or smuggling of heroin. The death penalty is usually commuted.

Insurgency and security in the south

The UK Foreign and Commonwealth office (www.fco.gov.uk/travel) advises against all but essential travel to the 4 provinces of Yala, Pattani, Narathiwat and Songkhla. The US State Department (www.travel.state.gov) does the same and includes Hat Yai town in its warning. These areas are the main home of Thailand's Muslim minority and have been the home of a major uprising that while long term escalated considerably in 2004. Thousands have died with appalling atrocities committed on both sides. Westerners have also become victims in what is essentially a localized civil war. There is little doubt that more could have been done to assuage concerns in the region by considering the political demands and cultural sensitivities of the people of the far south. The lack of sensitivity represents a considerable political failure – and a long-term one. See also page 670, page 672, page 674, and Background, page 711.

Prisons

Thai prisons are very grim. Most foreigners are held in 2 Bangkok prisons – Khlong Prem and Bangkwang. One resident who visits overseas prisoners in jail wrote to us saying: "You cannot over-estimate the horrors! Khlong Prem has 7000 prisoners, 5 to a cell, with not enough room to stretch out, no recreation, one meal a day (an egg on Sundays) … ". One hundred prisoners in a dormitory is not uncommon, and prisoners on Death Row have waist chains and ankle fetters permanently welded on.

Tourist police

In 1982 the government set up a special arm of the police to deal with the demands of the tourist industry – the tourist police. Now, there is no important tourist destination that doesn't have a tourist police office. The Thai police have come in for a great deal of scrutiny over recent years, although most policemen are honest and only too happy to help the luckless visitor. **Tourist Police**, Bangkok, T02-2815051 or T02-2216206. Daily 0800-2400.

Traffic

Perhaps the greatest danger is from the traffic – especially if you are attempting to drive yourself. More foreign visitors are killed or injured in traffic accidents than in any other way. Thai drivers have a 'devil may care' attitude towards the highway code, and there are many horrific accidents. Be very careful when crossing the road – just because there is a pedestrian crossing, do not expect drivers to stop. Be particularly wary when driving or riding a motorcycle (see page 40).

Student travellers

Anyone in full-time education is entitled to an **International Student Identity Card (ISIC)**. These are issued by student travel offices and travel agencies across the world and offer special rates on all forms of transport and other concessions and services. The ISIC head office is: **ISIC Association**, Box 9048, 1000 Copenhagen, Denmark, T45-3393 9303. Students are eligible for discounts at some museums but the use of student cards is not widespread so don't expect to save a fortune.

Tax

Airport tax is now included in the price of a ticket. For VAT refunds, see Shopping, page 52.

Telephone

→ *Country code +66.*

From Bangkok there is direct dialling to most countries. To call overseas, you first need to dial the international direct dial (IDD) access code, which is 001, followed by the country code. Outside Bangkok, it's best to go to a local telephone exchange if calling internationally.

Local area codes vary according to province. Individual area codes are listed through the book; the code can be found at the front of the telephone directory.

Calls from a telephone box cost ฿1. All telephone numbers marked in the text with a prefix 'B' are Bangkok numbers.

Directory enquiries

For domestic long-distance calls including Malaysia and Vientiane (Laos): T101 (free), Greater Bangkok BMA T183, international calls T02-2350030-5, although hotel operators will invariably help make the call if asked.

Mobiles

Mobiles are common and increasingly popular – reflecting the difficulties of getting a landline as well as a desire to be contactable at all times and places. Coverage is good except in some border areas. As of 2006, all mobile phone numbers had an extra digit added and now begin '08'. If you call an old number there is a message, first in Thai and then in English, telling you to insert the number 8.

A Thai sim card is very easy for visitors to acquire and highly recommended if you are staying for any period of time in Thailand. You will need an unlocked phone (cheap, unlocked second-hand phones are available throughout Thailand from about ฿700) and a valid ID when buying a sim card or top-up.

AIS and *Happy D Prompt* sim cards and top ups are available throughout the country and cost ฿200 with domestic call charges from ฿3 per min and international calls from ฿8 per min. This is a very good deal and much cheaper than either phone boxes or hotels.

Internet

GPRS data deals are also incredible cheap – the AIS network offers 100 hrs of mobile internet connection for ฿300 per month. Speeds are slow though the network is perfectly adequate for text emails, basic web-browsing and social sites such as Facebook.

Time

GMT plus 7 hrs.

Tipping

Tipping is generally unnecessary. However, a 10% service charge is now expected on room, food and drinks bills in the smarter hotels as well as for any personal service. Increasingly, the more expensive restaurants add a 10% service charge; others expect a small tip.

Tour operators

Australia and New Zealand

Flight Centres, 82 Elizabeth St, Sydney, T9235 3522; 205 Queen St, Auckland, T09-309 6171.

STA Travel, T1300-360960, www.statravel.com.au; 855 George St, Sydney, and 240 Flinders St, Melbourne. In NZ: www.statravel.co.nz, 187 Queen St, Auckland, T09-309 0458.

Travel.com.au, 80 Clarence St, Sydney, T02-1300 130 482, www.travel.com.au.

UK

Asean Explorer, PO Box 82, 37 High St, Alderney, GY9 3DG, T01481-823417, www.asean-explorer.com. Holidays for adventurers and golfers in Thailand.

Exodus Travels, 9 Weir Rd, London, T020-9500039, T020-8673 0859, www.exodus.co.uk. Small group travel for walking and trekking holidays, adventure tours and more.

Magic of the Orient, 14 Frederick Place, Bristol, BS8 1AS, T0117-3116050, www.magic oftheorient.com. Tailor-made holidays to the region. Established in 1989 the company's philosophy is to deliver first-class service from knowledgeable staff at good value.

Ornitholidays, 29 Straight Mile, Romsey, SO51 9BB, T01794-519445, www.ornit holidays.co.uk. Birdwatching holidays.

Pettitts, T01892-515966, www.pettitts.co.uk. Travel to unusual locations.

Ramblers Holidays, Lemsford Mill, Lemsford Village, Welwyn Garden City, Herts, AL8 7TR, T01707-331133, www.ramblersholidays.co.uk.

Silk Steps, Compass House, Rowdens Rd, Wells, Somerset, BA5 1TU, T01749-685162, www.silk steps.co.uk. Tailor-made and group travel.

STA Travel, 33 Bedford St, Covent Garden, London, WC2E 9ED, T0871-468 0612, www.statravel.co.uk. Specialists in low-cost student/youth flights and tours, also good for student IDs and insurance.

Steppes Travel, 51 Castle St, Cirencester, GL7 1QD, T01285-880980, www.steppestravel.co.uk.

Symbiosis Expedition Planning, Holly House, Whilton, Daventry, Northamptonshire, T0845-1232844, www.symbiosis-travel.com. Specialists in tailor-made and small group adventure holidays for those concerned about the impact of tourism on environments.
Trailfinders, 194 Kensington High St, London, W8 7RG, T020-7938 3939, www.trailfinders.co.uk.
Trans Indus, 75 St Mary's Rd and the Old Fire Station, Ealing, London, W5 5RW, T020-8566 2729, www.transindus.co.uk. Tours to Thailand and other Southeast Asian countries.
Travelmood, 214 Edgware Rd, London, W2 1DH; 230 High St, Guildford, GU1 3JD; 54 Park St, Bristol, BS1 5JN; 36 Mill Lane, Solihull, B91 3BA; 1 Brunswick Court, Bridge St, Leeds, LS2 7QU; Queen Buildings, 24 Queen Av, Liverpool, L2 4TZ; 16 Reform St, Dundee, DD1 1RG, T0800-298 9822, www.travelmood.com. 21 years' experience as a top travel specialist offering tailor-made trips to the Far East and adventure and activity travel in Asia.

North America
Air Brokers International, 323 Geary St, Suite 411, San Francisco, CA 94102, T01-800-883 3273, www.airbrokers.com. Consolidator and specialist on RTW and Circle Pacific tickets.
Discount Airfares Worldwide On-Line, www.etn.nl/discount.htm. A hub of consolidator and discount agent links.
Global Spectrum, 3907 Laro Court, Fairfax, VA 22031, USA, T1800-419 4446, www.globalspectrumtravel.com.
International Travel Network/Airlines of the Web, www.itn.net/airlines. Online air travel information and reservations.
Nine Dragons Travel & Tours, 1476 Orange Grove Rd, Charleston, SC 29407, USA, T1317-281 3895, www.nine-dragons.com. Guided and individually customized tours.
Princess Cruises, 24844 Av Rockefeller, Santa Clarita, CA 91355, www.princess.com.
STA Travel, 920 Westwood Blvd, Los Angeles, CA 90024, T1-310-824 1574, www.statravel.com.

Travel CUTS, T1-866-246 9762, www.travelcuts.com. Specialist in student discount fares, IDs and other travel services. Branches in other Canadian cities.
Travelocity, www.travelocity.com.

Tourist information

Tourist Authority of Thailand (TAT), 1600 New Phetburi Rd, Makkasan, Ratchathewi, T02-2505500, www.tourismthailand.org; also at 4 Rachdamnern Nok Av (intersection with Chakrapatdipong Rd), Mon-Fri 0830-1630; in addition there are 2 counters at Suvarnabhumi Airport, in the Arrivals halls of Domestic and International Terminals, T02-134 0040, T02-134 0041, 0800-2400. Local offices are found in most major tourist destinations in the country. Most offices open daily 0830-1630. TAT offices are a useful source of local information, often providing maps of the town, listings of hotels/guesthouses and information on local tourist attractions. The website is a useful first stop and is generally well regarded.

Tourism authorities abroad
Australia, Suite 2002, 2nd floor, 56 Pitt St, Sydney, NSW 2000, T9247-7549, F9251-2465, www. thailand.net.au.
France, 90 Ave des Champs Elysées, 75008 Paris, T5353-4700, F4563-7888, tatpar@wanadoo.fr.
Germany, Bethmannstr 58, D-60311, Frankfurt/Main 1, T69-1381390, F69-281468, tatfra@t-online.de.
Hong Kong, 401 Fairmont House, 8 Cotton Tree Drive, Central, T2868-0732, F2868-4585, tathkg@hk.super.net.
Italy, 4th floor, Via Barberini 68, 00187 Roma, T06-487 3479, F06-4873500.
Japan, Yurakucho Denki Building, South Tower 2F, Room 259, 1-7-1, Yurakucho, Chiyoda-ku, Tokyo 100-0006, T03-218 0337, F03-218 0655, tattky@criss cross.com.
Malaysia, c/o Royal Thai Embassy 206 Jalan Ampang, 50450 Kuala Lumpur, T26-23480, F26-23486, sawatdi@po.jaring.my.

Singapore, c/o Royal Thai Embassy, 370 Orchard Rd, Singapore 238870, T2357901, F7335653, tatsir@mbox5.signet.com.sg.
UK, 1st floor, 17-19 Cockspur St, Trafalgar Sq, London SW1Y 5BL, T0870-900 2007, www.tourismthailand.co.uk.
USA, 1st floor, 611 North Larchmont Blvd, Los Angeles, CA 90004, T461-9814, F461-9834, tatla@ix.netcom.com.

Useful websites

www.asiasociety.org Homepage of the Asia Society with papers, reports and speeches as well as nearly 1000 links to what they consider to be the best educational, political and cultural sites on the web.
www.asiatravelmart.com Includes deals on flights, hotels and more; especially good on cheap hotel deals in the Asian region.
www.bang-kok.com Search engine with links to websites on flights, travel and hotels.
www.bangkokpost.net Homepage for the *Bangkok Post* including back issues and main stories of the day.
www.bangkokrecorder.com Instant access to the hipper side of Thai life from current events, comment, chat and lifestyle features to the best of Bangkok clubbing.
www.chula.ac.th Managed by Thailand's premier university, Chulalongkorn, introduces people to Thailand's history, culture, society, politics and economics. Look for English language link in top right-hand corner.
www.geocities.com/~nesst Homepage of the Network for Environmentally and Socially Sustainable Tourism (Thailand), with information on tourism in Thailand, book reviews and a discussion page.
www.nationmultimedia.com Homepage for *The Nation*, one of Thailand's main English-language daily newspapers.
www.thaifolk.com Good site for Thai culture from folk songs and handicrafts through to festivals like Loi Kratong and Thai myths and legends. Information posted in both English and Thai – although the Thai version of the site is better.

Visas and immigration

For the latest information on visas and tourist visa exemptions see the consular information section of the **Thai Ministry of Foreign Affairs** website, www.mfa.go.th. The immigration office is at **Immigration Bureau**, Soi Suan Plu, Thanon Sathorn Tai, Bangkok 10120, T02-287 3101, www.immigration.go.th. Open Mon-Fri 0830-1630, closed Sat, Sun and official holidays (tourists only). The Thai government is currently considering making changes to tourist visas. Plans include an extension to the 30-day entry permit and a waiving of fees for the 2-month tourist visa. Nothing has been confirmed, but visitors may want to check with their local embassy before travel.

Thai immigration authorities will only issue 15-day visa-free entry permits if you enter Thailand by a land crossing from any neighbouring country. How long this will stay in force is unknown.

There are several types of visa, only a few of which concern visitors: transit visa, tourist visa and non-immigrant visa.
1 Transit visa (TS): for those who are in transit; visitors are permitted to stay 30 days.
2 Tourist visa (TR): for tourists; visitors are permitted to stay for 60 days.
3 Non-immigrant visa: for foreigners who wish to undertake official or private work, study, research or stay with family; duration 90 days.

Tourist visa requirements are detailed below; for other visa types contact your embassy or www.mfa.go.th; for independent advice see www.thaivisa.com.

Visas on arrival

For tourists from 20 countries (all Western countries, plus most Arabic and other Asian states; see www.mfa.go.th for a full list) it is possible to have a special 30-day entry permit issued on arrival. These permits are not strictly visas and differ from 'visa on arrival' service signposted at the airports. Applicants must also have an outbound (return) ticket and possess funds to meet living expenses of ฿20,000 per person or ฿40,000 per family.

Before 2006 it was possible to make unlimited border crossings in order to gain repeated entry for 30 days as a tourist. Now visitors are not allowed to stay more than 90 days every 6 months using this method. If you intend to stay in Thailand for a lengthy period over 30 days you'd be best advised to get a 2-month visa before travel.

Tourist visas

These are valid for 60 days from date of entry (single or multiple entry) and must be obtained from a Thai embassy before arrival. They can be extended for a further 30 days.

90-day non-immigrant visas

These can be obtained in the applicant's home country (about US$30 per entry). A letter from the applicant's company or organization guaranteeing their repatriation should be submitted at the same time.

Re-entry permit

For those who wish to leave and then re-enter Thailand before their visa expires, it is possible to apply for a re-entry permit (฿1900) from the Immigration office.

Visa extensions

These are obtainable from the immigration office in Bangkok (see above) for ฿1900. Applicants must bring 2 photocopies of their passport ID page and the page on which their tourist visa is stamped, together with 3 passport photographs. It is also advisable to dress neatly. Visas are issued by all Thai embassies and consulates. The length of time a visa is extended varies according to the office and the official.

Weather

For daily weather reports visit the website www.thaimet.tmd.go.th. For more details on climate, see When to go, page 20.

Weights and measures

Thailand uses the metric system, although there are some traditional measures still in use, in particular the *rai*, which equals 0.16 ha. There are 4 *ngaan* in a *rai*. Other local measures include the *krasorp* (sack) which equals 25 kg and the *tang* which is 10-11 kg. However, for most purchases (for example fruit) the kg is the norm. Both kg and km are often referred to as lo – as in ki-lo.

Women travellers

Compared with neighbouring East and South Asia, women in Southeast Asia enjoy relative equality of opportunity. While this is a contentious issue, scholars have pointed to the lack of pronouns in Southeast Asian languages, the role of women in trade and commerce, the important part that women play in reproductive decisions, the characteristically egalitarian patterns of inheritance and so on. This is not to suggest that there is complete equality between the sexes. Buddhism, for example – at least as it is practised in Thailand – accords women a lower position and it is notable how few women are in positions of political power.

The implications for women travellers, and especially solo women travellers, is that they may face some difficulties not encountered by men – for example the possibility of some low-key sexual harassment. Women should make sure that rooms are secure at night and if travelling in remote regions, should try to team up with other travellers.

Working in Thailand

Most visitors to Thailand who wish to work take up a post teaching English. Some guesthouses will provide free accommodation for guests who are willing to allot a portion of the day to English conversation classes. Those with a qualification, for example a TEFL certificate, can usually command a higher salary. There are also various NGOs/voluntary organizations that employ people. See www.thaivisa.com or www.goabroad.com. The former provides background information on getting a visa while the latter has information on language schools, volunteer work and more.

Volunteering

Projects range from conservation and teaching English to looking after elephants. They vary in length from 2 weeks and beyond and generally need to be organized before you arrive. The application process almost always involves submitting a statement of intent, although generally no formal qualifications or experience are required; usually volunteers need to be over 18 and will pay fees upfront. Consult individual organizations about visas and lodgings – most include basic shared accommodation in the price but not travel to and from Thailand. The following international organizations run projects in Thailand.

British Trust for Conservation Volunteers, Sedum House, Mallard Way, Potteric Carr, Doncaster, DN4 8DB, T01302-388888, www.btcv.org. Mangrove conservation and turtle monitoring from 2 weeks in duration.

Cross Cultural Solutions, 2 Clinton Place, New Rochelle, NY 10801, USA, T1800 3804777 (US only), T191 4632 0022, www.crossculturalsolutions.org. Community work and research into local development.

Earthwatch, 267 Banbury Rd, Oxford, OX2 7HT, T01865-318838, www.earthwatch.org.

Elephant Nature Park, 209/2 Sridorn Chai Rd, Chiang Mai 50100, Thailand, T053-272855, www.thaifocus.com/elephant/. Under 1 month, office work and working with elephants.

Global Services Corps, 300 Broadway, Suite 28, San Francisco, CA 94133-3312, USA, T415-788-3666, ext128, www.globalservice corps.org. Volunteers must be over 18 with an interest in international issues and sustainable development.

Involvement Volunteers, PO Box 218, Port Melbourne, Vic 3207, Australia, T613-9646 5504, www.volunteering.org.au. Australian network with international reach, organic farming, teaching and community work.

VSO, 317 Putney Bridge Rd, London, SW15 2PN, UK, T0208-780 7200, www.vso.org.uk. Worldwide voluntary organization.

Contents

Footprint features

Bangkok

At a glance

⊖ **Getting around** A motorcycle taxi will get you around quickly. Take a ferry along the *khlongs* or river to escape the smog, but for the best skylines catch the Skytrain.

◉ **Time required** Everything from a day to a lifetime.

☾ **Weather** Dec and Jan can sometimes be pleasantly cool.

✗ **When not to go** Avoid the heat of Mar and Apr. Peak monsoon months are Sep and Oct.

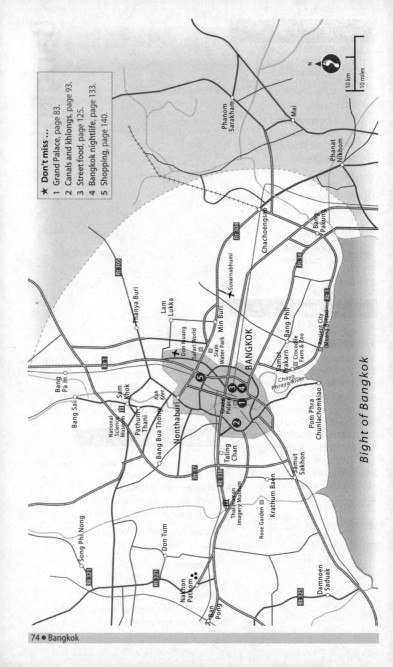

★ **Don't miss ...**
1 Grand Palace, page 83.
2 Canals and khlongs, page 93.
3 Street food, page 125.
4 Bangkok nightlife, page 133.
5 Shopping, page 140.

Bight of Bangkok

Dirty, dynamic, wild and sweaty, Bangkok is a heaving scrum of humanity blended with ancient beauty, booming youth culture and the rituals of a bygone age. The Thais call it the City of Angels but there's nothing angelic about Bangkok. Don't arrive expecting an exotic, languid, dreamy place trapped in some imagined, traditional past. What will hit you is the size, pace, endless olfactory cacophony, friendliness of the locals and interminable gridlocked traffic. The whole place resembles a giant, out-of-control car-boot sale whose pavements are humming with open-air kitchens, clothes stalls, hawkers and touts.

Some of the old *King and I* romanticism does persist. There are the *khlongs*, palaces and temples but ultimately, what marks Bangkok out from the imaginings of its visitors, is its thrusting modernity in open struggle with the ancient, rural traditions of Thai culture. Neon, steel and glass futuristic transport rubs shoulders with lumbering elephants, alms-collecting monks and crumbling teak villas. It's all here: poverty and wealth, smog-filled thoroughfares and backstreets smothered in alluring exotic aromas, cybercafés and barrows laden with fried bugs.

With your senses fully overloaded don't forget the sheer luxury that's on offer. Bangkok is home to some of the best, and most affordable, hotels in the world. Add the numerous spas, the futuristic super-hip nightlife and the incredibly diverse range of markets and shops selling everything from amulets and sarongs to Prada and hi-tech gadgets – your head will be spinning. And when the urban theatre of Bangkok finally overwhelms take a day trip to the ancient summer residence of the Thai kings at Bang Pa In or drift upriver to Nonthaburi for its provincial charm. Crocodile farms, wax works and other oddities will also provide Thai-style kitsch.

Getting there

Suvarnabhumi International Airport (pronounced su-wan-na-poom), is 25 km southeast of the city. Currently, the airport is only accessible by road but a 28-km overhead city rail link between downtown Bangkok and the airport is scheduled for completion by 2009. The new and old airports are relatively equidistant from Central Bangkok and although the travel links are considerably improved, it can still take well over an hour to get to the city centre by car. Taking the expressway cuts the travel time down significantly and outside of rush-hour the transit time to Central Bangkok should be 35-45 minutes.

Bangkok is Thailand's domestic transport hub with flights to around 25 towns and cities; trains head south to the Malaysian border (and onward to Kuala Lumpur and Singapore), north to Chiang Mai and northeast to Nong Khai and Ubon Ratchathani; and buses of every kind make their way to all corners of the country. It is often necessary to transit through Bangkok if working your way north to south by whatever means of transport. From April 2009 THAI will no longer fly domestic routes from **Don Muang**, the old airport, 25 km north of the city. At the time of publication the situation regarding Don Muang's remaining budget carriers was unknown, so if you have a connecting flight check which airport it is going to/from. ➤ *For Transport from the airports to the city, see page 155.*

Airport information

Suvarnabhumi airport opened in September 2006, much later than originally promised. Controversy clung to the project from the start with allegations of backhanders involving the contracts for construction and ground services, and the troubled airport is still in the headlines. Thai newspapers are forever uncovering scandals involving cracked runways sinking into the swamp and the creaking infrastructure. Many complain about the labyrinthine layout, paucity of toilets and inadequacy of the air-conditioning. Travellers should also be aware that crime has spiralled at the airport since it opened, the number of thefts has rocketed. The Thai police report that pickpockets journey across Asia to descend on distracted passengers. In 2007, due to a mixture of runway cracks and lack of working facilities at Suvarnabhumi, the old airport, Don Muang was forced to re-open. For information on the airport siege that took place in Bangkok in 2008, see Background, page 714.

Getting around

Bangkok has the unenviable reputation of having some of the worst traffic in the world. The **Skytrain** – an elevated railway – along with the newer and still sparkling **Metro** have made things a lot easier for those areas of the city they cover. Plentiful **buses** travel to all city sights and offer the cheapest way to get around. There is an endless supply of metered **taxis**. A taxi for a trip within the centre of town should cost ฿50-100. All taxis now have meters although some drivers may refuse to switch them on. If this happens either insist they put the meter on or just get out of the car – most drivers will turn it on at this point. Alternatively, just wait for another cab. Bangkok's taxi drivers will sometimes refuse to pick up fares at all, particularly if they feel your destination is troublesome. This can be frustrating but don't get angry with drivers as they can have a very aggressive streak and reputation for violence. **Tuk-tuk** (motorized three-wheeled taxi) numbers are dwindling and the negotiated fares often work out more expensive than a taxi. Riding in an open-sided tuk-tuk coats you in Bangkok's notorious smog by the time you arrive –

Arrival advice

All facilities at Suvarnabhumi Airport are 24 hours so you'll have no problem exchanging money, getting a massage, finding something to eat or taking a taxi or other transport into the city at any time.

Very few buses arrive in Bangkok at night as nearly all long-distance services are timed to arrive in the morning. Bus stations are well served by meter taxis and if you do arrive late jump into one these.

Mo Chit and Ekamai bus stations are also linked to the Skytrain (BTS) which runs from 0600-2400. Mo Chit bus station and Hualamphong train station are linked to the Metro (MBK) which also runs from 0600-2400.

As Bangkok is a relatively safe city it is usually alright to walk around even the most deserted streets at night. However, be sensible, as you would anywhere else and don't display valuables or appear lost. The best bet late at night, if you're unsure where to go, is to flag down one of the capital's ubiquitous taxis.

Note: At all times of day and night airport flunkies are on hand inside the airport to try to direct passengers to the more expensive 'limousine' taxi service; for the public service walk through the exit to the well-signposted and helpful taxi desk.

---

tuk-tuk drivers also target tourists and have a deserved reputation for rip-offs and scams. **Walking** can be tough in the heat and fumes, although there are some parts of the city where this can be the best way to get around. For an alternative to the smog of Bangkok's streets, you can hop on board one of the express **river taxis** – more like river buses – which ply the Chao Phraya River and the network of *khlongs* (canals) that criss-cross the city; it's often quicker than going by road (see box, page 98). ▸▸ *See Transport, page 155, for further information on local transport. For boat tours, see pages 153 and 160.*

Maps and addresses Traversing the city can be complicated, especially as there is no consistent Romanization of Thai road names and no familiar 'block-style' street planning. Roads often lead to dead ends and numbers can be confusing, with multiple slashes indicating streets and/or buildings off main roads, and street or house numbers which do not necessarily run consecutively. As a guide: main roads are known as *Thanon* (or *Th*) some of which, like Sukhumvit, span the entire city, so landmarks are useful. A *soi* is a street that runs off a main road, so Sukhumvit (Soi) 21 is the name of a smaller street off Sukhumvit Road. They may also have their own names, Sukhumvit 21 is also known as Soi Asoke, but the name would generally be written in brackets after the *soi* number. In addresses house and apartment numbers come first, so 123/1 Soi 1, Th Sukhumvit will be on Sukhumvit 1. If in doubt, ask hotel staff to write addresses out in Thai for taxi drivers.

As a guide to road names, multiple spellings to watch out for include Rachdamri Road (Rajdamri, Ratchadamri Rachdameri), Phetburi (Phetchaburi), Aree (Ari) and Rama I-VI also known as Phra I-VI. Wireless Road next to Lumpini Park is also known as Thanon Witthayu).

Asia Books (see Shopping, page 141) has a good selection of Bangkok maps and A-Zs. A very accurate map of Bangkok called *Bangkok, Central Thailand Travel Map*, is published by **Periplus Editions**. **Nelles** also publishes an excellent detailed map of the city centre including new roads, expressways and bus routes. The *Nancy Chandler Map of Bangkok* is an infamous city resource. An artistically created hand-drawn map with accompanying mini guidebook, it highlights plenty of unknown and quirky areas of interest, mainly shopping, eating and sightseeing, as well as all the main ones. The sections on Chinatown, the main strip of Sukhumvit and the Weekend Market are particularly detailed. If travelling by bus, a bus map of the city (such as Nelles Map, see above) is an invaluable aid.

Tourist information

Tourist Authority of Thailand (TAT) ① *main office at 1600 New Phetburi Rd, Makkasan, Ratchathewi, T02-250 5500, www.tourismthailand.org; also at 4 Rachdamnern Nok Av (intersection with Chakrapatdipong Rd), Mon-Fri 0830-1630; in addition there are 2 counters at Suvarnabhumi Airport, in the Arrivals halls of Terminals 1 and 2, T02-504 2701, 0800-2400.*

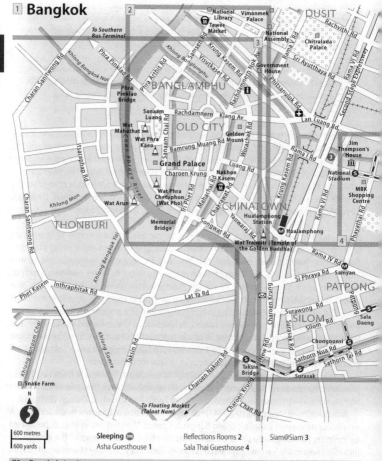

1 Bangkok

Sleeping
Asha Guesthouse **1**
Reflections Rooms **2**
Sala Thai Guesthouse **4**
Siam@Siam **3**

The two main offices are very helpful and provide a great deal of information for independent travellers – certainly worth a visit. For information, phone T1672 between 0800 and 2000 for the English-speaking **TAT Call Centre**. A number of good, informative English-language magazines provide listings of what to do and where to go in Bangkok. *BK Magazine* is a free weekly publication with good listings for clubs, restaurants and live acts. See also www.khao-san-road.com. ▶▶ *For listings, see pages 113-162.*

Background

The official name for Thailand's capital city begins Krungthepmahanakhon Amornrattana-kosin Mahintharayutthaya Mahadilokphop Noppharat Ratchathaniburirom Udomratchani-wetmahasathan Amonphiman Awatansathit Sakkathattiyawitsanukamprasit. It is not hard to see why Thais prefer the shortened version, Krungthep or the 'City of Angels'. The name used by the rest of the world – Bangkok – is derived from 17th-century Western maps, which referred to the city (or town as it then was) as *Bancok*, the 'village of the wild plum'. This name was only superseded by Krungthep in 1782, so the Western name has deeper historical roots.

➡ **Bangkok maps**
1 Bangkok, page 78
2 Old City, Banglamphu and Chinatown, page 90
3 Bangkok's rivers and khlongs, page 97
4 Siam Square and Ploenchit Road, page 102
5 Silom and Surawong, page 104
6 Sukhumvit Road, page 106

Bars & clubs ⬤
Club Culture **1**

In 1767, Ayutthaya, then the capital of Siam, fell to the marauding Burmese for the second time and it was imperative that the remnants of the court and army find a more defensible site for a new capital. Taksin, the Lord of Tak, chose Thonburi, on the Western banks of the Chao Phraya River, far from the Burmese. In three years, Taksin had established a kingdom and crowned himself king. His reign was short lived; the pressure of thwarting the Burmese over three arduous years caused him to go mad and in 1782 he was forced to abdicate. General Phraya Chakri was recalled from Cambodia and invited to accept the throne. This marked the start of the present Chakri Dynasty.

Bangkok: the new capital

In 1782, Chakri (now known as Rama I) moved his capital across the river to Bangkok (an even more defensible site) anticipating trouble from King Bodawpaya who had seized the throne of Burma (Myanmar). The river that flows between Thonburi and Bangkok and on which many of the luxury hotels – such as The Oriental –

are now located, began life not as a river at all, but as a *khlong* (canal). The canal was dug in the 16th century to reduce the distance between Ayutthaya and the sea by short-cutting a number of bends in the river. Since then, the canal has become the main channel of the Chao Phraya River. Its original course has shrunk in size, and is now represented by two *khlongs*, Bangkok Yai and Bangkok Noi; see the map of Bangkok's river and *khlongs*, page 97.

This new capital of Siam grew in size and influence. Symbolically, many of the new buildings were constructed using bricks from the palaces and temples of the ruined former capital of Ayutthaya. However, population growth was hardly spectacular – it appears that outbreaks of cholera sometimes reduced the population by a fifth or more in a matter of a few weeks. An almanac from 1820 records that "on the seventh month of the waxing moon, a little past 2100 in the evening, a shining light was seen in the northwest and multitudes of people purged, vomited and died".

Venice of the East

Bangkok began life as a city of floating houses; in 1864 the French explorer Henri Mouhot wrote that "Bangkok is the Venice of the East (making it one of several Asian cities to be landed with this sobriquet) and whether bent on business or pleasure you must go by water". In 1861, foreign consuls in Bangkok petitioned Rama IV and complained of ill-health due to their inability to go out riding in carriages or on horseback. The king complied with their request for roads and the first road was built in the 1860s – Charoen Krung ('New Road'). It was not until the late 19th century that King Chulalongkorn (Rama V) began to invest heavily in bridge and road building; notably, Rachdamnern Avenue ('the royal way for walking') and the Makawan Rungsun Bridge, which both link the Grand Palace with the new palace area of Dusit. This avenue was used at the end of the century for cycling (a royal craze at the time) and later for automobile processions which were announced in the newspapers.

In the rush to modernize, Bangkok may have buried its roots and in so doing, lost some of its charm. But beneath the patina of modern city life, Bangkok remains very much a Thai city, and has preserved a surprising amount of its past. Most obviously, a profusion of wats and palaces remain. In addition, not all the *khlongs* have been filled in, and by taking a long-tailed boat through Thonburi it is possible to gain an idea of what life must have been like in the 'Venice of the East'.

Bangkok is built on unstable land, much of it below sea level, and floods used to regularly afflict the capital. The most serious were in 1983 when 450 sq km of the city was submerged. Each year the Bangkok Metropolitan Authority announced a new flood prevention plan, and each year the city flooded. The former populist Bangkok governor, Chamlong Srimuang, was perhaps the first politician to address the problem of flooding seriously. His blindingly obvious approach was to clear the many culverts of refuse, and some people believe that at last serious flooding is a thing of the past. This may be over-optimistic: like Venice, Bangkok is sinking by over 10 cm a year in some areas and it may be that the authorities are only delaying the inevitable.

Population

In 1900 Bangkok had a population of approximately 200,000. By 1950 it had surpassed one million, and by the end of 1999 it was, officially, 5,662,499. This official figure considerably understates the true population of the city – 14 million would be more realistic. Many people who live in the capital continue to be registered as living upcountry, and the

24 hours in the city

Jetlag pending, head down to the closest park or patch of green around dawn to watch Bangkok rise and shine in typical style. Heading out between 0500 and 0700 you'll find foodstalls firing up their charcoal grills as saffron-clad monks make alms rounds. But it's in parks like Lumpini where Bangkok's day really kicks into action with spandex-clad folk pulling synchronized moves to hi-energy Thai pop. Aside from aerobics, other early morning activities include jogging, tai chi and early morning picnicking/snacking on chickens' feet. Gourmet tourists may want to sample a more *farang*-friendly bowl of 'jok' or rice porridge flavoured with chicken or pork – the hearty breakfast choice of Bangkok. Swilled down with a cup of bright amber Thai tea packed with caffeine and sugar, you should be ready to face Bangkok's bustling charms.

As the day's heat starts to take hold, jump in an aircon taxi to check out the unmissable opulent splendour of the Grand Palace and Wat Phra Kaew.

The nearby temple of **Wat Pho** and its famous massaging monks is the next stop: have every jetlagged crease and knot pummelled from your limp body. Then, on to nearby Chinatown for lunch. Wander the tiny alleys of the **Thieves' Market**, not forgetting to indulge in the endless throng of tasty street kitchens before walking to the **Chao Phrayo River**.

Climb aboard one of the numerous river taxis and head south to the Saphan Taksin pier where Bangkok's futuristic elevated Skytrain – awaits. Zoom through Silom's glass and concrete to **Siam Square**. Bring a big budget credit card as Siam is now Bangkok's busiest shopping district and is awash with weird fashions and expensive shopping centres.

As the evening kicks in take your pick of the city's endless entertainments, either by splashing your cash on fantastic-value extravagance, or seeking out more traditional treasures.

Sample some high-society pre-dinner drinks at Sirocco's Sky Bar at the Dome State Tower for the ultimate in city views and head for dinner at Celadon, in the Sukhothai Hotel, for one of the finest spreads of Thai goodies in the city.

For a more down-to-earth alternative take in a traditional puppet show at Joe Louis Theatre then sample the multiple foodstalls at the Lumpini night bazaar followed by **Lumpini Boxing Stadium** where you'll get a chance to watch the ancient art of Muay Thai (Thai boxing) and the frantic exhortations of the numerous gamblers who pack the ringside terraces.

Finally, join the beautiful people at the **Bed Supper Club** one of Asia's hippest night spots, or head to Silom for some lively street action and a Khatoey cabaret.

physical extent of the capital has long overrun its administrative boundaries. By 2010, analysts believe Bangkok will have a population of 20 million. As the population of the city has expanded, so has the area that it encompasses: in 1900 it covered a mere 13.3 sq km; in 1958, 96.4 sq km; while today the Bangkok Metropolitan Region extends over 1600 sq km.

Bangkok dominates Thailand in cultural, political and economic terms. All Thai civil servants have the ambition of serving in Bangkok, while many regard a posting to the poor northeast as (almost) the kiss of death. Most of the country's industry is located in and around the city, and Bangkok supports a far wider array of services than other towns in the country.

Sights

Wats and palaces, markets and shopping, traditional dancing and Thai boxing, glorious food, tuk-tuks and water taxis fill Bangkok. Get over the pace and pollution and you'll have a ball in Bangkok. This is one of the most engaging cities on the planet and its infectious, amiable energy soon wears down even the staunchest tree-hugger. Begin your sojourn in the bejewelled beauty of the **Old City**. Here you'll find the regal heart of Bangkok at the stupendous Grand Palace. The charming **Golden Mount** is a short hop to the east, while to the south are the bewildering alleyways and gaudy temples of Bangkok's frenetic **Chinatown**. Head west over the Chao Phraya River to the magnificent spire of **Wat Arun** and the *khlongs* of **Thonburi**. To the north sits the broad, leafy avenues of **Dusit**, the home of the Thai parliament and the king's residence. Carry on east and south and you'll reach modern Bangkok. A multitude of mini-boutiques forms **Siam Square** and the Thai capital's centre of youth fashion; **Silom** and **Sukhumvit roads** are vibrant runs of shopping centres, restaurants and hotels while the **Chatuchak Weekend Market** (known to locals as JJ), in the northern suburbs, is one of Asia's greatest markets.

Old City

Filled with palaces and temples, this is the ancient heart of Bangkok. These days it is the premium destination for visitors and controversial plans are afoot to change it into a 'tourist zone'. This would strip the area of the usual chaotic charm that typifies Bangkok, moving out the remaining poor people who live in the area and creating an ersatz, gentrified feel.

Wat Phra Chetuphon (Wat Pho)
ⓘ *The entrance is on the south side of the monastery, www.watpho.com. 0900-1700. ฿50. From Tha Tien pier at the end of Thai Wang Rd, close to Wat Pho, it is possible to get boats to Wat Arun (see page 95).*

Wat Phra Chetuphon, or Wat Pho, is the largest and most famous temple in Bangkok. 'The Temple of the Reclining Buddha' – built in 1781 – houses one of the largest reclining Buddhas in the country; the soles of the Buddha's feet are decorated with mother-of-pearl displaying the 108 auspicious signs of the Buddha.

The bustling grounds of the wat (see also box, page 740) display more than 1000 bronze images, mostly rescued from the ruins of Ayutthaya and Sukhothai, while the *bot* contains the ashes of Rama I. The *bot* is enclosed by two galleries, which house 394 seated bronze Buddha images. They were brought from the north during Rama I's reign and are of assorted periods and styles. Around the exterior base of the bot are marble reliefs telling the story of the *Ramakien* (see box, page 86) as adapted in the Thai poem *Maxims of King Ruang*. They recount only the second section of the *Ramakien*: the abduction and recovery of Ram's wife Seeda.

There are 95 *chedis* of various sizes scattered across the 8-ha (20-acre) complex. To the left of the bot are four large *chedis*, memorials to the first four Bangkok kings. The library nearby is richly decorated with broken pieces of porcelain. The large top-hatted stone figures, the stone animals and the Chinese pagodas scattered throughout the compound came to Bangkok as ballast on the royal rice boats returning from China. Rama III wanted Wat Pho to become known as a place of learning, a kind of exhibition of all the knowledge of the time, and it is regarded as Thailand's first university.

One of Wat Pho's biggest attractions is its role as a respected centre of **traditional Thai massage** (see box, page 151). Thousands of tourists, powerful Thai politicians, businessmen and military officers come here to seek relief from the tensions of modern life. The Burmese destroyed most medical texts when they sacked Ayutthaya in 1776. In 1832, to help preserve the ancient medical art, Rama III had what was known about Thai massage inscribed onto a series of stones which were then set into the walls of Wat Pho. If you want to come here for a massage then it is best to arrive in the morning; queues in the afternoon can be long. ▸▸ *See Activities and tours, page 151.*

Grand Palace and Wat Phra Kaeo

① *The main entrance is the Viseschaisri Gate on Na Phralan Rd, T02-222 0094, www.palaces.thai.net. Admission to the Grand Palace complex costs ฿500 (ticket office open daily 0830-1130, 1300-1530 except Buddhist holidays when Wat Phra Kaeo is free but the rest of the palace is closed). The cost of the admission includes a free guidebook to the palace (with plan) as well as a ticket to the Coin Pavilion, with its collection of medals and 'honours' presented to members of the Royal Family, and to the Vimanmek Palace in the Dusit area (see page 99). No photography is allowed inside the bot. The Royal Pantheon is only open to the public once a year on Chakri Day, 6 Apr (the anniversary of the founding of the present Royal Dynasty). All labels are in Thai. Free guided tours in English throughout the day. There are plenty of touts offering to guide tourists around the palace. Personal audio guides, ฿100 (2 hrs), available in English, French, German and some other languages. Decorum of dress means no shorts, short skirts, no sleeveless shirts, no flip flops or sandals. There are plastic shoes and trousers for hire near the entrance. Close to the Dusit Hall is a small café selling refreshing coconut drinks and other soft drinks.*

The Grand Palace is situated on the banks of the Chao Phraya River and is the most spectacular – some might say 'gaudy' – collection of buildings in Bangkok. The complex covers an area of over 1.5 sq km and the architectural plan is almost identical to that of the Royal Palace in the former capital of Ayutthaya. It began life in 1782.

The buildings of greatest interest are clustered around **Wat Phra Kaeo**, or the **Temple of the Emerald Buddha** (see box, page 85). The glittering brilliance of sunlight bouncing off the coloured glass mosaic exterior of Wat Phra Kaeo creates a gobsmacking first impression for visitors to the Grand Palace. Built by Rama I in imitation of the royal chapel in Ayutthaya, Wat Phra Kaeo was the first of the buildings within the Grand Palace complex to be constructed. While it was being erected the king lived in a small wooden building in one corner of the palace compound.

The **ubosoth (1)** is raised on a marble platform with a frieze of gilded *garudas* holding *nagas* running round the base. Mighty, bronze *singhas* (lions) act as door guardians. The inlaid mother-of-pearl door panels date from Rama I's reign (late 18th century) while the doors are watched over by Chinese door guardians riding on lions. Inside the temple, the Emerald Buddha peers down on the gathered throng from a lofty, illuminated position above a large golden altar. Facing the Buddha on three sides are dozens of other gilded Buddha images, depicting the enlightenment of the Buddha when he subdues the evil demon Mara, the final temptation of the Buddha and the subjugation of evil spirits.

Around the walls of the shaded **cloister**, which encompasses Wat Phra Kaeo, is a continuous mural depicting the *Ramakien* – the Thai version of the Indian *Ramayana* (see box, page 86). There are 178 sections in all, which were first painted during the reign of King Rama I but have since been restored on a number of occasions.

To the north of the *ubosoth* on a raised platform are the **Royal Pantheon (2)**, the **Phra Mondop (3)** (the library), two gilt stupas, a **model of Angkor Wat (4)** and the **Golden Stupa (5)**. At the entrance to the Royal Pantheon are gilded *kinarees*. On the same terrace there are two gilt stupas built by King Rama I in commemoration of his parents. The Mondop was also built by Rama I to house the first revised Buddhist scriptural canon. To the west of the Mondop is the large Golden Stupa or *chedi*, with its circular base. To the north of the Mondop is a model of Angkor Wat constructed during the reign of King Mongkut (1851-1868) when Cambodia was under Thai suzerainty.

To the north again from the Royal Pantheon is the **Supplementary Library** and two viharns – **Viharn Yod (6)** and **Phra Nak (7)**. The former is encrusted with pieces of Chinese porcelain.

To the south of Wat Phra Kaeo are the buildings of the **Grand Palace**. These are interesting for the contrast that they make with those of Wat Phra Kaeo. Walk out through the cloisters. On your left is the French-style **Boromabiman Hall (8)**, which was completed during the reign of Rama VI. The **Amarinda Hall (9)** has an impressive, airy interior, with chunky pillars and gilded thrones. The **Chakri Mahaprasart (10)** – the Palace Reception Hall – stands in front of a carefully manicured garden with topiary. It was built and lived in by Rama V shortly after he had returned from a trip to Java and Singapore in 1876, and it shows: the building is a rather unhappy amalgam of colonial

Wat Phra Kaeo & Grand Palace

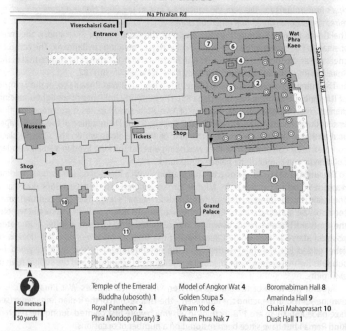

Temple of the Emerald Buddha (ubosoth) 1	Model of Angkor Wat 4	Boromabiman Hall 8
Royal Pantheon 2	Golden Stupa 5	Amarinda Hall 9
Phra Mondop (library) 3	Viharn Yod 6	Chakri Mahaprasart 10
	Viharn Phra Nak 7	Dusit Hall 11

The Emerald Buddha

Wat Phra Kaeo was specifically built to house the Emerald Buddha, the most venerated Buddha image in Thailand. It is carved from green jade (the emerald in the name referring only to its colour), a mere 75 cm high, and seated in an attitude of meditation. It is believed to have been found in 1434 in Chiang Rai, and stylistically belongs to the Late Chiang Saen or Chiang Mai schools. Since then, it has been moved on a number of occasions – to Lampang, Chiang Mai and Laos (both Luang Prabang and Vientiane). It stayed in Vientiane for 214 years before being recaptured by the Thai army in 1778 and placed in Wat Phra Kaeo on 22 March 1784.

The image wears seasonal costumes of gold and jewellery; one each for the hot, cool and the rainy seasons. The changing ceremony occurs three times a year in the presence of the king.

Buddha images are often thought to have personalities. The Phra Kaeo is no exception. It is said that such is the antipathy between the Phra Bang image in Luang Prabang (Laos) and the Phra Kaeo that they can never reside in the same town.

and traditional Thai styles of architecture. King Chulalongkorn (Rama V) found the overcrowded Grand Palace oppressive and after a visit to Europe in 1897 built himself a new home at Vimanmek (see page 99) in Dusit where the present king, Bhumibol, lives in the Chitralada Palace. The Grand Palace is now only used for state occasions. Next to the Chakri Mahaprasart is the raised **Dusit Hall (11)**, a cool, airy building containing mother-of-pearl thrones. Near the Dusit Hall is a **museum** ① *0900-1600, ฿50*, which has information on the restoration of the Grand Palace, models of the palace and many more Buddha images. There is a collection of old cannon, mainly supplied by London gun foundries.

Turn left outside the Grand Palace and a five-minute walk leads to **Tha Chang pier and market**. The market sells fruit and food, cold drinks and the like. There is also a small amulet (lucky charm) and second-hand section. From Tha Chang pier it is possible to get a boat to Wat Arun for about ฿150 return; alternatively take a water-taxi.

Sanaam Luang

To the north of the Grand Palace, across Na Phralan Road, lies the large open space of the Pramane Ground (Royal Cremation Ground), better known as Sanaam Luang. This area was originally used for the cremation of kings, queens and important princes. Later, foreigners began to use it as a race track and as a golf course. Today, Sanaam Luang is used for the annual **Royal Ploughing Ceremony**, held in May. This ancient Brahmanistic ritual, resurrected by Rama IV, signals the auspicious day on which farmers can begin to prepare their rice paddies, the time and date of the ceremony being set by Royal Astrologers. Bulls decorated with flowers pull a red and gold plough, while the selection of different lengths of cloth by the Ploughing Lord predicts whether the rains will be good or bad.

Sanaam Luang has several other claims to fame. It is the place in Bangkok to eat charcoal-grilled dried squid and have your fortune told. Regarding the latter, the *mor duu* ('seeing doctors') sit in the shade of the tamarind trees along the inner ring of the southern footpath. Each *mor duu* has his 'James Bond case' – a black briefcase –

Thai Ramayana: the Ramakien

The *Ramakien* – literally the "Story of Rama" – is an adaptation of the Indian Hindu classic, the *Ramayana*, which was written by the poet Valmiki about 2000 years ago. This 48,000-line epic odyssey – often likened to the works of Homer – was introduced into mainland Southeast Asia in the early centuries of the first millennium. The heroes were simply transposed into a mythical, ancient, Southeast Asian landscape. In Thailand, the *Ramakien* quickly became highly influential, and the name of the former capital of Siam, Ayutthaya, is taken from the legendary hero's city of Ayodhia in the epic. Unfortunately, these early Thai translations of the *Ramayana* were destroyed following the sacking of Ayutthaya by the Burmese in 1767. The earliest extant version was written by King Taksin in about 1775, although Rama I's rather later rendering is usually regarded as the classic interpretation.

In many respects, King Chakri's version closely follows that of the original Indian story. It tells of the life of Ram (Rama), the King of Ayodhia. In the first part of the story, Ram renounces his throne following a long and convoluted court intrigue, and flees into exile. With his wife Seeda (Sita) and trusted companion Hanuman (the monkey god), they undertake a long and arduous journey. In the second part, his wife Seeda is abducted by the evil king Ravana, forcing Ram to wage battle against the demons of Langka Island (Sri Lanka). He defeats the demons with the help of Hanuman and his monkey army, and recovers his wife. In the third and final part of the story – and here it diverges sharply from the Indian original – Seeda and Ram are reunited and reconciled with the help of the gods (in the Indian version there is no such reconciliation). Another difference with the Indian version is the significant role played by the Thai Hanuman – here an amorous adventurer who dominates much of the third part of the epic.

There are also numerous sub-plots which are original to the *Ramakien*, many building upon events in Thai history and local myth and folklore. In tone and issues of morality, the Thai version is less puritanical than the Indian original. There are also, of course, differences in dress, ecology, location and custom.

and having your fortune told costs around ฿30-60, or ฿100 for a full consultation. At the northeast corner of Sanaam Luang, opposite the **Royal Hotel**, is a statue of the **Goddess of the Earth** erected by King Chulalongkorn to provide drinking water for the public.

Lak Muang

ⓘ *Open daily, 24 hrs; there is no entrance charge to the compound although touts sometimes insist otherwise; donations can be placed in the boxes within the shrine precincts.*

In the southeast corner of Sanaam Luang, opposite the Grand Palace, is Bangkok's Lak Muang, housing the City Pillar and horoscope, originally placed there by Rama I in 1782. The shrine is believed to grant people's wishes, so it is a hive of activity all day. In a small pavilion to the left of the main entrance, Thai dancers are hired by supplicants to dance for the pleasure of the resident spirits – while providing a free spectacle for everyone else.

Wat Mahathat
① *Daily 0900-1700.*
North along Na Phrathat Road, on the river side of Sanaam Luang, is Wat Mahathat (the Temple of the Great Relic), a temple famous as a meditation centre; walk under the archway marked 'Naradhip Centre for Research in Social Sciences' to reach the wat. For those interested in learning more about Buddhist meditation, contact monks in section five within the compound. The wat is a royal temple of the first grade and a number of Supreme Patriarchs of Bangkok have based themselves here.

At No 24 Maharaj Road a narrow *soi* (lane) leads down towards the river and a large daily **market** selling exotic herbal cures, amulets, clothes and food. At weekends, the market spills out onto the surrounding streets (particularly Phra Chan Road) and amulet sellers line the pavement, their magical and holy talismen carefully displayed, see box, page 94.

Thammasat University
Further north along Na Phrathat Road is Thammasat University, the site of viciously suppressed student demonstrations in 1973. Sanaam Luang and Thammasat University remain a popular focus of discontent, the last being mass demonstrations in May 1992 demanding the resignation of Prime Minister General Suchinda which led to a military crackdown. In the grounds of Thammasat, there is a new monument to the victims of 1973, 1976 and 1992.

National Museum and Buddhaisawan Chapel
① *Wed-Sun 0900-1600, tickets on sale until 1530, ฿50, together with a skimpy leaflet outlining the galleries. Good information is lacking and it is recommended that interested visitors buy the Guide to the National Museum, Bangkok', or join a tour. For English-, French-, German-, Spanish- and Portuguese-speaking tour information call T02-224 1333. The tours are free and start at 0930, lasting 2 hrs (usually on Wed and Thu).*
Next to Thammasat lies the National Museum, reputedly the largest museum in Southeast Asia and an excellent place to visit before exploring the ancient Thai capitals, Ayutthaya and Sukhothai. The galleries contain a vast assortment of arts and artefacts divided according to period and style.

The Buddhaisawan Chapel, to the right of the ticket office for the National Museum, contains some of the finest Bangkok period murals in Thailand. The chapel was built in 1795 to house the famous Phra Sihing Buddha. Legend has it that this image originated in Ceylon and when the boat carrying it to Thailand sank, it floated off on a plank to be washed ashore in southern Thailand, near the town of Nakhon Si Thammarat. The chapel's magnificent murals were painted between 1795 and 1797 and depict stories from the Buddha's life.

National Theatre and National Art Gallery
① *National Theatre programmes can be checked by calling T02-2241342, Mon-Fri 0830-1630. National Art Gallery, Tue-Thu, Sat and Sun 0900-1600, ฿40.*

Next to the National Museum, on the corner of Na Phrathat and Phra Pinklao Bridge roads, is Thailand's National Theatre. Thai classical drama and music are staged here on the last Friday of each month at 1730 as well as periodically on other days.

Opposite the National Theatre is the National Art Gallery on Chao Fa Road. It exhibits traditional and contemporary work by Thai artists.

Banglamphu and Khaosan Road

Northeast of the National Art Gallery is the district of Banglamphu and the legendary Khaosan Road, backpacker haunt and epi-centre of Bangkok's travellers' culture. It all began when the **Viengtai Hotel** opened in 1962, giving the area a reputation for budget accommodation. Local families began to rent out rooms to travellers and by the mid-1970s the Khaosan Road we love/hate was firmly established. Much has been said and written about the strip. Thai purists look down their noses at it while many locals like the money it brings in but feel threatened by the loose Western culture it brings to the capital. For some younger Thais, it's a hip, liberal hang-out, a space and place apart from the constrictions of traditional Thai culture. There is no doubting Khaosan Road's sustained popularity, though the quality of food, accommodation, goods and services are easily surpassed in other parts of the city. As well as the expensive Thai food being of a very low standard, souvenirs are overpriced, while the minibuses that take unsuspecting backpackers to the popular beaches and islands tend to be falling apart and driven by Red Bull-fuelled maniacs. Taking public buses from the respective bus stations tends to be cheaper and safer. So why stay here? If you're travelling on a budget and it's your first time in Asia there are few better places to connect with other travellers and get into the swing of things. More seasoned travellers may find Khaosan Road a homogeneous spread of tie-dyed, penny-pinching backpackers and every bit as challenging as staying in a packaged resort.

Phra Arthit Road

Running north from the National Theatre, following the river upstream, is Phra Arthit Road. The community here is recognized to be one of the most cohesive in Bangkok, and a centre for artists and intellectuals as well as traditional shop owners. The nearby addition of a park and Thai *sala* on the river has created a pleasant place to sit and watch the boats. There are interesting shops and restaurants, many of which extend out on the water. The street is quite narrow and traffic is relatively sedate compared with other parts of the city.

Wat Indraviharn

Wat Indraviharn (see map, page 90) is rather isolated from the other sights, lying just off Visutkaset Road (not too far north of Phra Arthit Road and the traveller nexus of Banglamphu). It contains a 32-m standing Buddha encrusted in gold tiles that can be seen from the entrance to the wat. The image is impressive only for its size. The topknot contains a relic of the Buddha brought from Ceylon.

Golden Mount and around

This is where ancient Bangkok begins to give way to the modern thrust of this engagingly bewildering city. Apart from the obvious sights listed below there's little reason to hang around here but with its history of demonstrations and cries for democracy it beats a defining pulse in the hearts of most Thais. ▶▶ *See Old City map, page 90.*

Democracy Monument

ⓘ *Daily 0800-1800, ₿10. Refreshments available.*

The Democracy Monument is a 10- to 15-minute walk from the north side of Sanaam Luang, in the middle of Rachdamnern Klang Avenue. Completed in 1940 to commemorate the establishment of Siam as a constitutional monarchy, its dimensions signify, in various ways, the date of the 'revolution' – 24 June 1932. For example, the 75 buried cannon which surround the structure denote the Buddhist year (BE – or Buddhist Era) 2475 (AD 1932). In May 1992, the monument was the focus of the anti-Suchinda demonstrations, so brutally suppressed by the army. Scores of Thais died here, many others fleeing into the nearby **Royal Hotel** which also became an impromptu hospital to the many wounded.

Golden Mount

From the Democracy Monument, across Mahachai Road, at the point where Rachdamnern Klang Avenue crosses Khlong Banglamphu, the Golden Mount can be seen (also known as the Royal Mount), an impressive artificial hill nearly 80 m high. The climb to the top is exhausting but worth it for the fabulous views of Bangkok. On the way up, the path passes holy trees, memorial plaques and Chinese shrines. The construction of the mount was begun during the reign of Rama III who intended to build the greatest *chedi* in his kingdom. The structure collapsed before completion, and Rama IV decided merely to pile up the rubble in a heap and place a far smaller golden *chedi* on its summit. The *chedi* contains a relic of the Buddha placed there by the present king after the structure had been most recently repaired in 1966.

Wat Saket

ⓘ *Daily 0800-1800.*

Wat Saket lies at the bottom of the mount, between it and Damrong Rak Road – the mount actually lies within the wat's compound. Saket means 'washing of hair' and Rama I is reputed to have stopped here and ceremonially washed himself before being crowned King in Thonburi (see Festivals and events, page 140). The only building of real note is the *hor trai* (library) which is Ayutthayan in style. The door panels and lower windows are decorated with wood carvings depicting everyday Ayutthayan life, while the window panels show Persian and French soldiers from Louis XIV's reign.

Loha Prasat

ⓘ *Daily 0830-1600.*

Also in the shadow of the Golden Mount but to the west and on the corner of Rachdamnern Klang Avenue and Mahachai Road, lies Wat Rachanada and the Loha Prasat, a strange-looking 'Metal Palace' with 37 spires. Built by Rama III in 1846 as a memorial to his beloved niece, Princess Soammanas Vadhanavadi, it is said to be modelled on the first Loha Prasat built in India 2500 years ago. The 37 spires represent the 37 Dharma of the Bodhipakya. The monks who look after the building have had problems with homeless men and woman who use the Prasat's many nooks and crannies as handy places to sleep: they are turfed out (in a suitably meritorious manner) by the monks before the place opens each morning.

Wat Rachanada

ⓘ *Daily 0600-1800.*

Next to the Loha Prasat is the much more traditional Wat Rachanada. The principal Buddha image is made of copper mined in Isaan – the ordination hall also has some

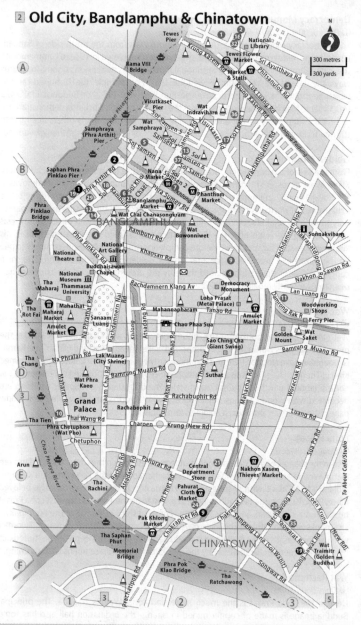

N

300 metres
300 yards

Tewes Pier
Krung Kasem Rd
National Library
Tewes Flower Market
Sri Ayutthaya Rd
Market & Stalls
Luk Luang Rd
Phitsanulok Rd
Krung Kasem Rd
Khlong Padung

Rama VIII Bridge

Chao Phraya River

Visutkaset Pier
Wat Indraviharn
Samsen 7
Visutkaset Rd
Prachathipathai Rd

Samphraya (Phra Arthit) Pier
Wat Samphraya
Samsen 5
Sol Samsen 3
Sol Samsen 6
Nana Market
Ban Phanthom Market

Saphan Phra Pinklao Pier
Phra Arthit Rd
Samsen 4
Banglamphu Market
Phra Sumen Rd
Chakrabongse

Phra Pinklao Bridge
Phra Pinklao Rd
Chakri
Wat Chai Chanasongkram
BANGLAMPHU
Rambutri Rd

Phra Pinklao Pier

Wat Bowonniwet
Rachdamnern Nok Av
Sonnakviham

National Theatre
National Art Gallery
Khaosan Rd

Tha Maharaj
National Museum
Buddhaisawan Chapel
Thammasat University
Rachdamnern Klang Av
Democracy Monument
Nakhon Sawan Rd
Lan Luang Rd

Tha Rot Fai
Mahathat
Maharaj Market
Amulet Market
Rachdamnern Nai Rd
Loha Prasat (Metal Palace)
Mahannapharam
Tanao Rd
Amulet Market
Chao Phaa Sua
Woodworking Shops
Ferry Pier
Damrong Rak Rd

Tha Chang
Lak Muang (City Shrine)
Sao Ching Cha (Giant Swing)
Golden Mount
Wat Saket
Bamrung Muang Rd

Na Phralan Rd
Wat Phra Kaeo
Bamrung Muang Rd
Suthat
Ti Thong Rd
Mahachai Rd

Maharat Rd
Grand Palace
Sanaam Chai Rd
Rachabuphit Rd
Fuang Nakhon Rd
Luang Rd

Tha Tien
Thai Wang Rd
Rachabophit
Charoen Krung (New Rd)

Phra Chetuphon (Wat Pho)
Chetuphon

Chao Phraya River
Arun
Pahurat Rd
Central Department Store
Nakhon Kasem (Thieves' Market)

Tha Rachini
Atsadang Rd
Pahurat Cloth Market
Chakrawat Rd
Charoen Krung
Yaowarat Rd

Pak Khlong Market
Chakraphet Rd
Sampeng Lane (Sol Wanit)
Ratchawong Rd
Songwat Rd

Tha Saphan Phut
Memorial Bridge
Phra Pok Klao Bridge
CHINATOWN
Song Sawat Rd
Wat Traimitr (Golden Buddha)

Prachathipok Rd
Tha Ratchawong

haosan Road detail

fine doors. What makes the wat particularly worth visiting is the **Amulet Market** (see box, page 147) to be found close by, between the Golden Mount and the wat. The market also contains Buddha images and other religious artefacts.

Wat Mahannapharam and Chao Phaa Sua

West of the Democracy Monument on Tanao Road is Wat Mahannapharam in a large, tree-filled compound. A peaceful place to retreat to, it contains some good examples of high-walled, Bangkok-period architecture decorated with woodcarvings and mother-of-pearl inlay. Just south of here is the bustling Chao Phaa Sua, a Chinese temple with a fine tiled roof surmounted with mythological figures.

Giant Swing

A five-minute walk south of Wat Rachanada, on Bamrung Muang Road, is the Sao Ching Cha (Giant Swing), consisting of two tall red pillars linked by an elaborate cross piece, set in the centre of a square. The Giant Swing was the original centre for a festival in honour of Siva. Young men on a giant 'raft' would be swung high into the air to grab pouches of coins, hung from bamboo poles, between their teeth. Because the swinging was from east to west, it has been said that it symbolized the rising and setting of the sun. The festival was banned in the 1930s because of the injuries that occurred; prior to its banning, thousands would congregate around the Giant Swing for two days of dancing and music.

Wat Suthat

ⓘ *0900-1700; viharn only opens on weekends and Buddhist holidays.*
The magnificent Wat Suthat faces the Giant Swing. The wat was begun by Rama I in 1807, and his intention was to build a temple that would equal the most glorious in Ayutthaya. The wat was not finished until the end of the reign of Rama III in 1851.

Surrounded by Chinese pagodas, the *viharn*'s six pairs of doors are each made from a single piece of teak, deeply carved with animals and celestial beings. Inside is the bronze Phra Sri Sakyamuni Buddha, while just behind is a very fine gilded stone carving from the Dvaravati period (second-11th centuries AD), 2.5 m in height and showing the miracle at Sravasti and the Buddha preaching in the Tavatimsa heaven. The bot is the tallest in Bangkok and one of the largest in Thailand.

Wat Rachabophit
① *Daily 0800-1700.*
The little-visited Wat Rachabophit is close to the Ministry of the Interior on Rachabophit Road, a few minutes' walk south of Wat Suthat down Ti Thong Road. It is recognizable by its distinctive doors carved in high relief with jaunty-looking soldiers wearing European-style uniforms and is peculiar in that it follows the ancient temple plan of placing the Phra Chedi in the centre of the complex.

The 43-m-high gilded *chedi*'s most striking feature are the five-coloured Chinese glass tiles which encrust the lower section. The ordination hall has 10 door panels and 28 window panels each decorated with gilded black lacquer on the inside and mother-of-pearl inlay on the outside showing royal insignia.

Pahurat Indian market 'Little India' and Pak Khlong market
From Wat Rachabophit, it is only a short distance to the Pahurat Indian textile market on Pahurat Road. Here you'll find a mesmerizing array of spangly fabrics and Indian trinkets as well as plenty of Indian restaurants/foodstalls (see **Royal India**, page 126). Tucked down an alley off Chakraphet Road is **Sri Guru Singh Sabha**, supposedly the second largest Sikh temple outside of India. To get to Pahurat, walk south on Ti Thong Road which quickly becomes Tri Phet Road. After a few blocks, Pahurat Road crosses Tri Phet Road. **Pak Khlong Market** is to be found a little further south on Tri Phet Road at the foot of the Memorial Bridge. A charming, authentic market specializing in fresh flowers, it is best visited between 2200 and dawn for an alternative, but still bedazzling taste of Thai nightlife. The market ends by 1000.

Chinatown

Chinatown covers the area from Charoen Krung (or New Road) down to the river and leads on from Pahurat market; cross over Chakraphet Road and immediately opposite is the entrance to Sampeng Lane. Few other places in Bangkok match Chinatown for atmosphere. The warren of alleys, lanes and tiny streets are cut through with an industrious hive of shops, temples and restaurants. Weird food, neatly arranged mountains of mechanical parts, gaudy temple architecture, gold, flowers and a constant frenetic bustle will lead to hours of happy wandering. This is an area to explore on foot, getting lost in the miasma of nooks and crannies. A trip through Chinatown can start at the Thieves' Market or at Wat Traimitr, the Golden Buddha, to the southeast.

Nakhon Kasem (Thieves' Market)
Nakhon Kasem, strictly speaking Woeng Nakhon Kasem (Thieves' Market), lies between Charoen Krung and Yaowarat Road, to the east of the *khlong* that runs parallel to Mahachai Road. Its boundaries are marked by archways. As its name suggests, this market used to be the centre for the fencing of stolen goods. It is not quite so colourful today, but

there remain a number of second-hand and antique shops that are worth a browse – such as the **Good Luck Antique Shop**. Items commonly for sale include musical instruments, brass ornaments and antique coffee grinders.

Yaowarat Road

Just to the southeast of the Thieves' Market are two roads that run parallel with one another: Yaowarat Road and Sampeng Lane. Yaowarat Road, a busy thoroughfare, is the centre of the country's gold trade. The trade is run by seven shops, the **Gold Traders Association**, and the price is fixed by the government. Sino-Thais often convert their cash into gold jewellery. The jewellery is bought by its 'baht weight' which fluctuates daily with the price of gold.

Sampeng Lane

The narrower Sampeng Lane, also called Soi Wanit, is just to the south of Yaowarat Road. This road's history is shrouded in murder and intrigue. It used to be populated by prostitutes and opium addicts and was fought over by Chinese gangs. Today, it is still an interesting commercial centre, although rather less illicit. There is not much to buy here – it is primarily a wholesale centre specializing in cloth and textiles although it is a good place to go for odd lengths of material, buttons of any shape and size, costume jewellery, and such like.

Wat Traimitr (Temple of the Golden Buddha)
① *Daily 0900-1700, ฿20.*

The most celebrated example of the goldsmiths' art in Thailand sits within Wat Traimitr (Temple of the Golden Buddha) which is located at the eastern edge of Chinatown, squashed between Charoen Krung, Yaowarat Road and Traimitr Road (just to the south of Bangkok's Hualamphong railway station). The Golden Buddha is housed in a small, rather gaudy and unimpressive room. Although the leaflet offered to visitors says the 3-m-high, 700-year-old image is 'unrivalled in beauty', be prepared for disappointment; it's featureless. What makes it special, drawing large numbers of visitors each day, is that it is made of 5½ tonnes of solid gold. Apparently, when the East Asiatic Company was extending the port of Bangkok, they came across a huge stucco Buddha image, which they obtained permission to move. However, whilst being moved by crane in 1957, it fell and the stucco cracked to reveal a solid gold image within. During the Ayutthayan period it was the custom to cover valuable Buddha images in plaster to protect them from the Burmese, and this particular example stayed that way for several centuries. In the grounds of the wat there is a school, crematorium, foodstalls and, inappropriately, a money changer. Gold beaters can still be seen at work behind Suksaphan store.

Between the river and Soi Wanit 2 there is a warren of lanes, too small for traffic – this is the Chinatown of old. From here it is possible to thread your way through to the River City shopping complex which is air-conditioned and a good place to cool off.

Thonburi, Wat Arun and the khlongs

Thonburi is Bangkok's little-known alter ego. Few people cross the Chao Phraya to see this side of the city, and if they do it is usually only to catch a glimpse from the seat of a speeding *hang yaaw* (long-tailed boat) and then climb the steps of Wat Arun. But Thonburi, during the reign of King Taksin, was once the capital of ancient Siam. King Rama I believed

Magic designs and tokens: tattoos and amulets

Many, if not most, Thai men wear *khruang* (amulets). Some Thai women do so too. In the past tattooing was equally common, although today it is usually only in the countryside that males are extensively tattooed. In the case of both tattoos and amulets the purpose is to bestow power, good luck or protection on the wearer.

Amulets have histories: those believed to have great powers sell for millions of baht and there are several magazines devoted to amulet buying and collecting. Vendors keep amulets with their takings to protect against robbery and put them into food at the beginning of the day to ensure good sales. An amulet is only to be handled by the wearer – otherwise its power is dissipated and might even be used against the owner.

Amulets can be obtained from spirit doctors and monks and come in a variety of forms. Most common are amulets of a religious nature, known as *Phra khruang*. These are normally images of the Buddha or of a particularly revered monk. (The most valuable are those fashioned by the 19th-century monk Phra Somdet – which are worth more than their weight in gold).

Khruang rang are usually made from tiger's teeth, buffalo horn or elephant tusk and protect the wearer in very specific ways – for example from drowning. *Khruang rang plu sek*, meanwhile, are magic formulas which are written down on an amulet, usually in old Khmer script (*khom*), and then recited during an accident, attack or confrontation.

Tattooing is primarily talismanic: magic designs, images of powerful wild beasts, texts reproduced in ancient Khmer and religious motifs are believed to offer protection from harm and give strength. (The word tattoo is derived from the Tahitian word *tattau*, meaning

'to mark'. It was introduced into the English language by Captain James Cook in 1769.) Tattoos are even believed to deflect bullets, should they be sufficiently potent. A popular design is the takraw ball, a woven rattan ball used in the sport of the same name. The ball is renowned for its strength and durability, and the tattoo is believed to have the same effect on the tattooed.

The purpose of some tattoos is reflected in the use of 'invisible' ink made from sesame oil – the talismatic effects are independent of whether the tattoo can be seen. Most inks are commercial today (usually dark blue) although traditionally they were made from secret recipes incorporating such ingredients as the fat from the chin of a corpse (preferably seven corpses, taken during a full moon).

The tattooist is not just an artist and technician. He is a man of power. A master tattooist is highly respected and often given the title *ajarn* (teacher) or *mor phi* (spirit doctor). Monks can also become well known for their tattoos. These are usually religious in tone, often incorporating sentences from religious texts. The tattoos are always beneficial or protective and always on the upper part of the body (the lower parts of the body are too lowly for a monk to tattoo). Tattoos and amulets are not only used for protection, but also for attraction: men can have tattoos or amulets instilled with the power to attract women; women, alternatively, can buy amulets which protect them from the advances of men. *Khruang phlad khik* ('deputy penis') are phallic amulets carved from ivory, coral or rare woods, and worn around the wrist or the waist – not around the neck. Not surprisingly, they are believed to ensure sexual prowess, as well as protection from such things as snake bites.

the other side of the river – present-day Bangkok – would be more easily defended from the Burmese and so, in 1782, he switched river banks. ▸▸ *See Bangkok's river and khlongs map, page 97. For boat tours, see page 153.*

Long-tailed boat tours, the Floating Market and Snake Farm

One of the most enjoyable ways to see Bangkok is by boat – and particularly by the fast and noisy long-tailed boats or *hang yaaws*: powerful, lean machines that roar around the river and the *khlongs* at breakneck speed. There are innumerable tours around the *khlongs* of Thonburi taking in a number of sights, which include the Floating Market, Snake Farm and Wat Arun. Boats go from the various piers located along the east bank of the Chao Phraya River. The journey begins by travelling downstream along the Chao Phraya, before turning 'inland' after passing beneath Krungthep Bridge. The route skirts past laden rice-barges, squatter communities on public land and houses overhanging the canals. This is a very popular route with tourists, and boats are intercepted by vendors selling everything from cold beer to straw hats. You may also get caught in a boat jam; traffic snarl-ups are not confined to the capital's roads. Nevertheless, the trip is a fascinating insight into what Bangkok must have been like when it was still the 'Venice of the East', and around every bend there seems to be yet another stunning wat. On private tours the first stop is usually the **Talaat Nam (Floating Market)**. This is now an artificial, ersatz gathering which exists purely for the tourist industry. The nearest functioning floating market is at Damnoen Saduak (see page 109). One of the largest floating markets in Thailand, it is chock full of tourists by 0900, but well worth a visit.

Next stop is the **Snake Farm** ① ฿70, *shows every 20 mins, refreshments available*, where visitors can pose with pythons and poisonous snakes are incited to burst balloons with their fangs, 'proving' how dangerous they are. There is also a rather motley zoo with a collection of crocodiles and sad-looking animals in small cages. The other snake farm in Central Bangkok (see page 105) is, appropriately, attached to the Thai Red Cross and is cheaper and more professional.

On leaving the snake farm, boats enter Khlong Bangkok Yai at the site of the large **Wat Paknam**. Just before re-entering the Chao Phraya itself, the route passes by the impressive **Wat Kalaya Nimit**.

To the south of Wat Kalaya Nimit, on the Thonburi side of the river, is **Wat Prayoon Wong**, virtually in the shadow of the Saphan Phut bridge. The wat is famous for its **Khao Tao (Turtle Mountain)** ① 0830-1730. This is a concrete fantasy land of grottoes and peaks, with miniature *chedis* and *viharns*, all set around a pond teeming with turtles. These are released to gain merit and the animals clearly thrive in the murky water. This wat, which can be reached by taking a cross-river shuttle boat from Tha Saphan Phut (฿4), is rarely visited by tourists but its large white *chedi* is clearly visible from Bangkok. A five-minute walk upstream from here is **Santa Cruz Church**. Cross-river shuttles run between here and Tha Rachini, close to the massive Pak Khlong fresh produce market, facing the river. The church, washed in pastel yellow with a domed tower, was built to serve the Portuguese community.

Wat Arun

① 0830-1730, ฿20. *Climbing the wat is not permitted. The men at the pier may demand ฿20 to help 'in the maintenance of the pier'. It is possible to get to Wat Arun by water-taxi from Tha Tien pier (at the end of Thai Wang Rd near Wat Pho), or from Tha Chang (at the end of Na Phralan near Wat Phra Kaeo) ฿3.50.*

Facing Wat Pho across the Chao Phraya River is the famous Wat Arun (Temple of the Dawn). Wat Arun stands 81 m high, making it the highest *prang* (tower) in Thailand. It was built in the early 19th century on the site of Wat Chaeng, the Royal Palace complex when Thonburi was briefly the capital of Thailand. The wat housed the Emerald Buddha before the image was transferred to Bangkok and it is said that King Taksin vowed to restore the wat after passing it one dawn. The *prang* is completely covered with fragments of Chinese porcelain and includes some delicate gold and black lacquered doors. The temple is really meant to be viewed from across the river; its scale and beauty can only be appreciated from a distance. The best view of Wat Arun is in the evening from the Bangkok side of the river when the sun sets behind the *prang*.

Royal Barges National Museum
ⓘ *0830-1630, ฿30, children free, extra for cameras and video cameras.*
After visiting Wat Arun, some tours then go further upstream to the mouth of Khlong Bangkok Noi where the Royal Barges are housed in a hangar-like boathouse. These ornately carved boats, winched out of the water in cradles, were used by the king at Krathin (see **Ok Phansa festival**, page 51) to present robes to the monks in Wat Arun at the end of the rainy season. The ceremony ceased in 1967 but the Royal Thai Navy restored the barges for the revival of the spectacle, as part of the extensive celebrations for the 60th anniversary of the king's succession to the throne in June 2006. The oldest and most beautiful barge is the *Sri Supannahong*, built during the reign of Rama I (1782-1809) and repaired during that of Rama VI (1910-1925). It measures 45 m long and 3 m wide, weighs 15 tonnes and was created from a single piece of teak. It required a crew of 50 oarsmen and two coxswains, along with such assorted crew members as a flagman, a rhythm-keeper and singer. Its gilded prow was carved in the form of a *hansa* (or goose) and its stern, in the shape of a naga (a mythical serpent-like creature).

Wat Rakhang
ⓘ *Daily 0500-2100, ฿20. The river ferry stops at the wat.*
Two rarely visited wats are Wat Suwannaram, see below, and Wat Rakhang. The royal Wat Rakhang is located just upstream from Wat Arun, almost opposite Tha Chang landing, and is identifiable from the river by the two plaster sailors standing to attention on either side of the jetty. Dating from the Ayutthaya period, the wat's **Phra Prang** is considered a particularly well proportioned example of early Bangkok architecture (late 18th century). The **Ordination Hall** (not always open – the abbot may oblige if he is available) was built during the reign of Rama III and contains a fine gilded Buddha image. The beautiful red-walled wooden **Tripitaka Hall** (originally a library built in the late 18th century), to the left of the *viharn*, was the residence of Rama I while he was a monk and Thonburi was still the capital of Siam. Consisting of two rooms, it is decorated with faded but none-theless highly regarded murals of the *Ramakien* (painted by a monk-artist), black and gold chests, a portrait of the king, and some odd bits of old carved door.

Wat Suwannaram
Wat Suwannaram is a short distance further on from the Royal Barges National Museum on Khlong Bangkok Noi, on the other side of the canal. The main buildings date from Rama I's reign (late 18th century), although the complex was later extensively renovated by Rama III. There was a wat on this site even prior to Rama I's reign, and the original name, Wat Thong (Golden Wat), remains in popular use. On the right-hand wall, as you

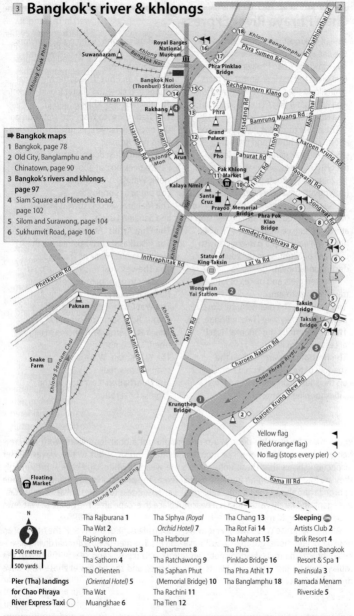

Bangkok maps
1 Bangkok, page 78
2 Old City, Banglamphu and Chinatown, page 90
3 Bangkok's rivers and khlongs, page 97
4 Siam Square and Ploenchit Road, page 102
5 Silom and Surawong, page 104
6 Sukhumvit Road, page 106

Yellow flag ◀
(Red/orange flag) ◀
No flag (stops every pier) ◇

N
500 metres
500 yards

Pier (Tha) landings for Chao Phraya River Express Taxi ○

Tha Rajburana **1**
Tha Wat Rajsingkorn
Tha Vorachanyawat **3**
Tha Sathorn **4**
Tha Orienten (Oriental Hotel) **5**
Tha Wat Muangkhae **6**

Tha Siphya (Royal Orchid Hotel) **7**
Tha Harbour Department **8**
Tha Ratchawong **9**
Tha Saphan Phut (Memorial Bridge) **10**
Tha Rachini **11**
Tha Tien **12**

Tha Chang **13**
Tha Rot Fai **14**
Tha Maharat **15**
Tha Phra Pinklao Bridge **16**
Tha Phra Athit **17**
Tha Banglamphu **18**

Sleeping 🛏
Artists Club **2**
Ibrik Resort **4**
Marriott Bangkok Resort & Spa **1**
Peninsula **3**
Ramada Menam Riverside **5**

Chao Phraya River Express

One of the most relaxing – and one of the cheapest – ways to see Bangkok is by taking the Chao Phraya River Express. Rua duan (boats) link almost 40 piers (tha) along the Chao Phraya River from Tha Rajburana (Big C) in the south to Tha Nonthaburi in the north.

The entire route entails a journey of about 1¼-1½ hours, and fares are ฿9-15. At peak periods, boats leave every 10 minutes, off-peak about every 15-25 minutes. Boats flying red/orange (downriver) or yellow (upriver) pennants are Special Express boats which only run 0600-0900, 1200-1900 and do not stop at every pier (see map, page 97). Also, boats will only stop if passengers wish to board or alight, so make your destination known.

Selected piers and places of interest, travelling upstream:

Tha Sathorn The pier with the closest access to the Skytrain (Taksin Bridge, S6).
Tha Orienten By the Oriental Hotel; access to Silom Road.
Tha Harbour Department In the shadow of the Royal Orchid Hotel, on the south side and close to River City shopping centre.

Tha Ratchawong Rabieng Ratchawong Restaurant; access to Chinatown and Sampeng Lane.
Tha Saphan Phut Under the Memorial Bridge and close to Pahurat Indian Market.
Tha Rachini Pak Khlong Market.
Tha Tien Close to Wat Pho; Wat Arun on the opposite bank; and, just downstream from Wat Arun.
Tha Chang Just downstream is the Grand Palace peeking out above whitewashed walls; Wat Rakhang with its white corn-cob *prang* lies opposite.
Tha Maharaj Access to Wat Mahathat and Sanaam Luang.
Tha Phra Arthit Access to Khaosan Road.
Tha Visutkasat Just upstream is the elegant central Bank of Thailand.
Tha Thewes Just upstream are boat-sheds with royal barges; close to the National Library.
Tha Wat Chan Just upstream is the Singha Beer Samoson brewery.
Tha Wat Khema Wat Khema in large, tree-filled compound.
Tha Wat Khian Wat Kien, semi-submerged.
Tha Nonthaburi Last stop on the express boat route.

enter from the riverside door, is a representation of a boat foundering with the crew being eaten by sharks and sea monsters as they thrash about in the waves. Closer inspection shows that these unfortunates are wearing white skull-caps – presumably they are Muslims returning from the *haj* to Mecca. The principal image in the *bot* is made of bronze and shows the Buddha calling the Earth Goddess to witness. Wat Suwannaram is elegant and rarely visited and is a peaceful place to escape after the bustle of Wat Arun and the Floating Market.

Almost opposite Wat Suwannaram, on the opposite bank of the river, is the home of an unusual occupational group – Chao Phraya's divers. The men use traditional diving gear – heavy bronze helmets, leaden shoes, air pumps and pipes – and search the bed of the murky river for lost precious objects, sunken boats, and the bodies of those who have drowned or been murdered.

Dusit, the present home of the Thai Royal family and the administration, is an area of wide tree-lined boulevards – the rationalized spaces more in keeping with a European city. It is grand but lacks the usual bustling atmosphere found in the rest of Bangkok. ▶▶ *See map, page 78, for sights in the Dusit area.*

Vimanmek Palace

① *T02-281 1569, www.palaces.thai.net, 0900-1600 (last tickets sold at 1500), ฿100. Visitors are not free to wander, but must be shown around by one of the charming guides who demonstrate the continued deep reverence for King Rama V (tour approximately 1 hr). Note that tickets to the Grand Palace include entrance to Vimanmek Palace. Dance shows are held twice a day at 1030 and 1400. Visitors to the palace are required to wear long trousers or a long skirt; sarongs available for hire (฿100, refundable). Refreshments available. Buses do go past the palace, but from the centre of town it is easier to get a tuk-tuk or taxi (฿50-60).*

The Vimanmek Palace, just off Rachvithi Road, to the north of the National Assembly, is the largest golden teakwood mansion in the world, but don't expect to see huge expanses of polished wood – the building is almost entirely painted. It was built in 1901 by Rama V, who was clearly taken with Western style. It seems like a large Victorian hunting lodge and is filled with china, silver and paintings from all over the world (as well as some gruesome hunting trophies). The photographs are fascinating – one shows the last time elephants were used in warfare in Thailand. Behind the palace is the Audience Hall, which houses a fine exhibition of crafts made by the Support Foundation, an organization set up and funded by Queen Sirikit. Also worth seeing is the exhibition of the king's own photographs and the clock museum.

Amporn Gardens area

From Vimanmek, it is a 10- to 15-minute walk to the Dusit Zoo, skirting around the **National Assembly** (which before the 1932 coup was the Marble Throne Hall and is not open to visitors). In the centre of the square in front of the National Assembly stands an equestrian statue of the venerated King Chulalongkorn. To the left lie the Amporn Gardens, the venue for royal social functions and fairs. Southwards from the square runs the impressive **Rachdamnern Nok Avenue**, a Siamese Champs Elysées. Enter the **Dusit Zoo** ① *0800-1800, ฿100, ฿50 children*, through Uthong Gate, just before the square. A pleasant walk through the zoo leads to the Chitralada Palace and Wat Benchamabophit. Animal lovers might want to avoid the zoo which, like almost every other attempt to house animals in Thailand, is appalling. There is a children's playground, a handful of restaurants and pedal-boats can be hired on the lake.

From the Dusit Zoo's Suanchit Gate, a right turn down the tree-lined Rama V Road leads to the present King Bhumibol's residence – **Chitralada Palace**. It was built by Rama VI and is not open to the public. Evidence of the king's forays into agricultural research may be visible. He has a great interest and concern for the development of the poorer, agricultural parts of his country, and invests large sums of his own money in royal projects. To the right of the intersection of Rama V and Sri Ayutthaya roads are the gold and ochre roofs of Wat Benchamabophit – a 10-minute walk from the zoo.

Wat Benchamabophit

ⓘ *0800-1700, ฿20.*

Wat Benchamabophit (the Marble Temple) is the most modern of the royal temples and was only finished in 1911. Designed by Rama V's half brother, Prince Naris, it is an unusual display of carrara marble pillars, a marble courtyard and two large *singhas* guarding the entrance to the *bot*. The interior is magnificently decorated with crossbeams of lacquer and gold, and in shallow niches in the walls are paintings of important stupas from all over the kingdom. The door panels are faced with bronze sculptures and the windows are of stained-glass, painted with angels. The cloisters around the assembly hall house 52 figures – a display of the evolution of the Buddha image in India, China and Japan.

Government House and Wat Sonnakviharn

ⓘ *Government House only open on Wan Dek – a once-yearly holiday for children on the 2nd Sat in Jan; Wat Sonnakviharn open daily.*

Government House is south of here on Nakhon Pathom Road. The building is a weird mixture of cathedral Gothic and colonial Thai. The little-visited Wat Sonnakviharn is on Krung Kasem Road, located behind a car park and schoolyard. Enter by the doorway in the far right-hand corner of the schoolyard, or down Soi Sommanat. It is peaceful, unkempt and rather beautiful, with fine gold lacquer doors and a large gold tile-encrusted *chedi*.

Siam Square area

Shop, shop and then shop some more. Head for Siam Square if you want to be at the apex of Thai youth culture and the biggest spread of shopping opportunities in the city. From the hi-tech market at Panthip Plaza, the massive MBK complex, the host of upmarket stores at one of Southeast Asia's largest malls, Siam Paragon and neighbour Siam Discovery, pure silk at Jim Thompson's House or the warren of tiny boutiques in Siam Square, you should leave with a big hole in your bank account.

Suan Pakkard Palace (Lettuce Garden Palace)

ⓘ *352-354 Sri Ayutthaya Rd, south of the Victory Monument, 0900-1600, ฿100 – including a fan to ward off the heat; all profits go to a fund for artists.*

A beautiful, relaxing spot. The five raised traditional Thai houses (domestic rather than royal) were built by Princess Chumbhot, a great granddaughter of King Rama IV. They contain her collection of fine, rare but badly labelled antiquities. The rear pavilion is lovely, decorated in black and gold lacquerwork panels. Prince Chumbhot discovered this temple near Ayutthaya and reassembled and restored it here for his wife's 50th birthday.

Jim Thompson's House

ⓘ *Soi Kasemsan Song (2), opposite the National Stadium, www.jimthompson.com, Mon-Sat 0900-1630, ฿100, children ฿50 (profits to charity). There is a sophisticated café as well as a shop. Shoes must be removed before entering; walking barefoot around the house adds to the appreciation of the cool teak floorboards; compulsory guided tours around the house and no photography allowed. Take the Skytrain to National Stadium; the house is well signposted from here. Alternatively, take a bus along Rama I Rd, taxi or tuk-tuk, or take a public canal boat (www.jimthompson house.com features a printable map for taxi drivers). To get to the jetty from Jim Thompson's, walk down to the canal, turn right and along to the jetty by the bridge. Boats travelling to the Grand Palace will be coming from the right.*

Jim Thompson's House is an assemblage of traditional teak northern Thai houses, some more than 200 years old (these houses were designed to be transportable, consisting of five parts – the floor, posts, roof, walls and decorative elements constructed without the use of nails). Bustling Bangkok only intrudes in the form of the stench from the *khlong* that runs behind the house. Jim Thompson arrived in Bangkok as an intelligence officer attached to the United States' OSS (Office of Strategic Services) and then made his name by reinvigorating the Thai silk industry after the Second World War. He disappeared mysteriously in the Malaysian jungle on 27 March 1967, but his silk industry continues to thrive. Jim Thompson chose this site for his house partly because a collection of silk weavers lived nearby on Khlong Saensaep. The house contains an eclectic collection of antiques from Thailand and China, with work displayed as though it was still his home.

The head office of the **Jim Thompson Silk Emporium**, selling fine Thai silk, is at the northeast end of Surawong Road and there are numerous branches in the top hotels around the city. This shop is a tourist attraction in itself. Shoppers can buy high-quality bolts of silk and silk clothing here (from a pocket handkerchiefs to suits. Prices are top of the scale.

Siam Square

A 10-minute walk east along Rama I Road is the biggest, busiest modern shopping area in the city. Most of it centres on a maze of tiny boutiques and covered market area known as Siam Square. Thronged with young people, Siam Square plays host to Bangkok's burgeoning youth culture: cutting-edge contemporary and experimental fashions, live music, pavement craft markets, Thai-style fast food and dozens of urban stylists keep the kids entertained. Needless to say, it epitomizes older Thais' fears about the direction their country is taking – young people aping Western mores and irreverent modern values. Despite this, the area is distinctly Thai, albeit with a contemporary face and the groups of vibrant, self-confidently style-conscious youth will unsettle visitors who'd prefer Bangkok to remain a museum of teak villas and traditional temples. Just across Rama 1 are the shiny bright shopping centres of the enormous Siam Paragon, Siam Centre and Discovery – an elevated walkway connects Siam with Chitlom further down Rama 1.

On the corner of Rama 1 and Phayathai Road is MBK, Bangkok's largest indoor shopping area. Crammed with bargains and outlets of every description this is one of the Thai capital's most popular shopping spots. Opposite MBK is the newly opened **Bangkok Art and Culture Centre** ① *939 Rama I Rd, T02-214 6630, T02-214 6631, www.bacc.or.th, Tue-Sun 1000-2100*, worth visting for contemporary arts and cultural activities.

Chulalongkorn University

This is the country's most prestigious university. While Thammasat University on Sanaam Luang is known for its radical politics, Chulalongkorn is more conservative. Just south of Siam Square, on the campus itself (off Soi Chulalongkorn 12, behind the MBK shopping centre; ask for *sa-sin*, the houses are nearby) is a collection of **traditional Thai houses**. Also on campus is the **Museum of Imaging Technology** ① *Mon-Fri 1000-1530, ฿100*. To get to the museum, enter the campus by the main entrance on the east side of Phaya Thai Road and walk along the south side of the playing field, turn right after the Chemistry 2 building and then right again at the entrance to the Mathematics Faculty; the museum is at the end of this walkway in the Department of Photographic Science and Printing Technology, with a few hands-on photographic displays. The Art Centre on the seventh floor of the Centre of Academic Resources (central library) next to the car park, hosts regular exhibitions of contemporary art and discussions in English and Thai.

Erawan Shrine

East of Siam Square is the Erawan Shrine, on the corner of Ploenchit and Rachdamri roads, at the Rachprasong intersection. This is Bangkok's most popular shrine, attracting not just Thais but also large numbers of other Asian visitors. The spirit of the shrine, the Hindu god Thao Maha Brahma, is reputed to grant people's wishes. In thanks, visitors offer garlands, wooden elephants and pay to have dances performed for them accompanied by the resident Thai orchestra. The shrine is a hive of activity at most hours, incongruously set on a noisy, polluted intersection tucked into a corner, and in the shadow of the Zen Department Store.

Panthip Plaza

Sited on Phetburi Road (parallel to Rama I, 800 m to the north), Panthip Plaza, otherwise known as 'geek's paradise', is home to one of the best hi-tech computer markets in Asia.

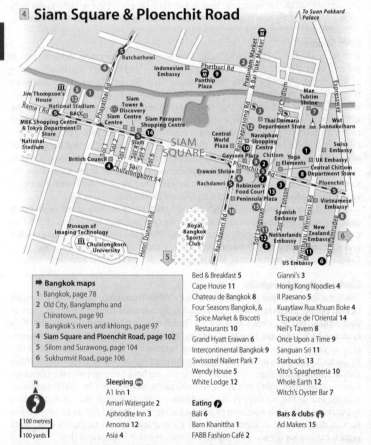

4 Siam Square & Ploenchit Road

Sleeping
A1 Inn 1
Amari Watergate 2
Aphrodite Inn 3
Arnoma 12
Asia 4
Bed & Breakfast 5
Cape House 11
Chateau de Bangkok 8
Four Seasons Bangkok, &
  Spice Market & Biscotti
  Restaurants 10
Grand Hyatt Erawan 6
Intercontinental Bangkok 9
Swissotel Nailert Park 7
Wendy House 5
White Lodge 12

Eating
Bali 6
Barn Khanittha 1
FABB Fashion Café 2
Gianni's 3
Hong Kong Noodles 4
Il Paesano 5
Kuaytiaw Rua Khuan Boke 4
L'Espace de l'Oriental 14
Neil's Tavern 8
Once Upon a Time 9
Sanguan Sri 11
Starbucks 13
Vito's Spaghetteria 10
Whole Earth 12
Witch's Oyster Bar 7

Bars & clubs
Ad Makers 15

Captive elephants in tourism

The Asian elephant is an endangered species, with fewer than 30,000 left in the world, and just 3000-4000 in Thailand (2700 in captivity). Since the banning of logging in 1989, captive elephants have been forced to walk the streets of Thailand's major cities in order to make a living. It has been estimated that around 35% of Thailand's captive elephants are now employed in the tourist industry. Pressure groups trying to protect the interests of elephants in Thailand maintain that those animals found on the streets or in shopping malls suffer from poor diet, stress due to polluted air, dehydration, loneliness, impaired hearing, and damage to their sensitive feet. They also argue that tourism is complicit in the elephants' predicament: unwitting tourists, seeing a 'cute' baby elephant, pay to have their photos taken with the animal. They are used, in effect, as begging bowls.

However, the arguments are not all one-way: tourism can benefit captive elephants, as they are seen to have 'value' if they are a tourist attraction. There are some elephant camps in Thailand where breeding programmes are successful and the animals are treated with respect.

Two elephant welfare groups operating in Thailand are the **Elephant Help Project** (**EHP**) and the **Jumbo Express**. The former was founded by two companies based in Phuket. Its objective is to raise funds primarily from tourism and use these funds to support elephant welfare and conservation in Phuket and southern Thailand. To contact its office in Phuket, call T076-280116, or email elephant help@siamsafari.com. **Jumbo Express** operates throughout northern Thailand, its office is at 29 Charoen Prathet Road, Soi 6, Chiang Mai, T053-272855, www.thaifocus.com/elephant.

Motherboards, chips, drives and all manner and make of devices are piled high and sold cheap over six floors. You'll be constantly hustled to buy copied software, DVDs, games, most of which make excellent and affordable alternatives to the real thing. There's a great foodhall on the second floor while several amulet shops on the ground floor remind you that even this most contemporary of Thai spaces is still governed by ancient beliefs. Many of the named-brand goods are cheaper back home so shop around.

Silom area

Hi-tech, high-rise and clad in concrete and glass, Silom is at the centre of booming Bangkok. Banks, international business and many media companies are based in this area as is the heart of Bangkok's gay community on Patpong 2, one of two infamous *sois*. Patpong 1 now houses a famous night market and is largely recognized as the eponymous home of Bangkok's notorious girly shows. Stylish, tacky and sweaty, head down the length of Silom for a slice of contemporary Bangkok life. ▸▸ *See Silom and Surawong map, page 104.*

Patpong
① *Catch the Skytrain to the Sala Daeng station.*
The seedier side of Bangkok life has always been a crowd-puller to the Western tourist. Most people flock to the red-light district of Patpong, which runs along two lanes

(Patpong 1 and 2) linking Silom to Surawong. These streets were transformed from a street of 'tea houses' (brothels serving local clients) into a hi-tech lane of go-go bars in 1969 when an American entrepreneur made a major investment. Patpong 1 is the larger and more active of the streets, with a host of stalls down the middle at night; Patpong 2 supports cocktail bars, pharmacies and clinics for STDs, as well as a few go-go bars. There are also restaurants and bars here. Expats and locals (gay and straight) in search of less sleazy surrounds, tend to opt for the middle ground of Patpong 4, still essentially a gay enclave but more sophisticated than seedy, see Bars and clubs, page 133. Patpong is also home to a night market infamous for its line in copied designer handbags, some of which are better made than the originals.

5 Silom & Surawong

➡ Bangkok maps
1 Bangkok, page 78
2 Old City, Banglamphu and Chinatown, page 90
3 Bangkok's rivers and khlongs, page 97
4 Siam Square and Ploenchit Road, page 102
5 Silom and Surawong, page 104
6 Sukhumvit Road, page 106

Sleeping
Banyan Tree 1 *B4*
Charlie's House 5 *B5*
Dusit Thani 2 *B4*
Heritage Baan Silom 10 *C2*
Honey House 7 *C5*
Malaysia 6 *C5*
Metropolitan 20 *B4*
Moon House 14 *C5*
New Road Guest House 3 *B1*
Oriental 8 *B1*
Pinnacle 18 *B5*
River View Guesthouse 13 *A1*
Royal Orchid Sheraton 11 *B1*
Shangri-La 12 *C1*
Siri Sathorn Executive
  Residence 4 *B4*
Sofitel Silom 15 *B2*
Sukhothai 16 *B4*
Tower Inn 19 *B2*

Eating
Anna's Café 1 *B4*
Banana House 14 *B3*
Banana Leaf 2 *B3*
Ban Krua 3 *B3*
Batavia 4 *B3*
Bobby's Arms 26 *B3*
Bua 5 *B3*
Bussaracum 6 *B3*
Dome at State Tower 23 *C*
Eat Me 8 *B3*
Himali Cha Cha 9 *B1*
Indian Hut 10 *B1*
Just One 27 *C5*
Kio Lio Nang 28 *B2*

Lumpini Park

ⓘ *Take a Skytrain to Sala Daeng station or Metro to Lumpini station.*

Lumpini Park, or 'suan lum' as it is known affectionately, is Bangkok's oldest, largest and most popular public park. It lies between Wireless Road and Rachdamri Road, just across from the entrance to Silom and Sathorn roads. Activity at the park starts early with large numbers of elderly and not so elderly Thais practising t'ai chi under the trees at dawn and dusk. This is also the time to join in the free en-mass aerobics sessions, jog along with the colourful crowds or lift some weights with the oiled beefcakes at the open-air gyms – all of which make great spectator sports too. Lumpini also has a lap pool, but it's for members only. At the weekend, it is a popular place for family picnics. In the evening, couples stroll along the lake and people jog or work out along the paths. Lumpini is also the site of the Bangkok Symphony Orchestra concerts that run during the cool season (November to February). Check the *Bangkok Post* for performances. Across the road is Bangkok's only official night bazaar, the **Suan Lumpini Night Bazaar**. Modelled on the very successful night bazaar of Chiang Mai, there is a good range of shops selling all manner of clothes, tourist trinkets, and handicrafts plus dozens of eateries and bars surrounding a large stage. This is also the place to catch a traditional puppet show at the **Joe Louis Puppet Theatre** (see Thai Perfoming Arts, page 139.

Thai Red Cross Snake Farm

ⓘ *Within the Science Division of the Thai Red Cross Society at the corner of Rama IV and Henri Dunant roads. Mon-Fri 0830-1630 (shows at 1100 and 1430), weekends and holidays 0830-1200 (show at 1100). ฿200.*

The Snake Farm of the Thai Red Cross is very central and easy to reach from Silom or Surawong roads (see map, left). It was established in 1923 and raises snakes for the production of serum, which is distributed worldwide. The farm also has a collection of non-venomous snakes. During showtime (which lasts a mesmerizing half an hour) various snakes are exhibited, venom extracted and visitors can fondle a python. The farm is well maintained. The construction of an adjoining museum is also underway.

e Basil 2 *B3*
e Bouchon 11 *B3*
e Café
de Paris 21 *B3*
eppers 24 *A5*
de Walk 12 *C2*
lom Village 13 *B2*
orrento 7 *C3*
haniya Garden 14 *B3*

Three On
Convent 29 *B3*
Whole Earth 25 *A5*
Zanotti 15 *B4*

Bars & clubs ⏺
Brown Sugar &
70s Bar16 *A4*
Delaney's 17 *B3*

Music Café 19 *B3*
Noriega's 20 *B3*
Radio City 22 *B3*
Tapas 18 *B3*

Sukhumvit Road

With the Skytrain running its length, Sukhumvit Road has developed into Bangkok's most vibrant strip. Shopping centres, girly bars, some of the city's best hotels and awesome places to eat have been joined by futuristic nightclubs. The grid of *sois* that run off the main drag are home to a variety of different communities including Arab, African and Korean as well as throngs of pasty Westerners. Sordid and dynamic, there's never a dull moment on Sukhumvit Road.

Siam Society

ⓘ *131 Soi Asoke, T02-6616470 for information on lectures, info@siam-society.org, Mon-Sat 0900-1700, ฿100.*

Just off Sukhumvit Road, sited in the **Kamthieng House**, a 120-year-old northern Thai building, is the Siam Society, a learned society established in 1904. Donated to the society in 1963 the house was transported to Bangkok from Chiang Mai and then reassembled a few years later. It now serves as an ethnological museum, devoted to preserving the traditional technologies and folk arts of northern Thailand. It makes an interesting contrast to the fine arts displayed in Suan Pakkard Palace and Jim Thompson's House. The Siam Society houses a library, organizes lectures and tours and publishes books, magazines and pamphlets.

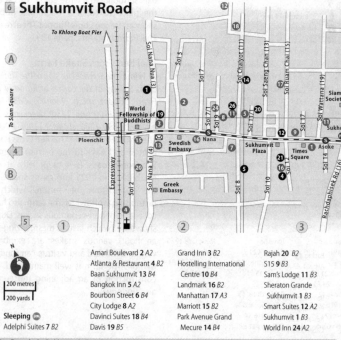

6 Sukhumvit Road

Sleeping 🛏
Adelphi Suites **7** *B2*
Amari Boulevard **2** *A2*
Atlanta & Restaurant **4** *B2*
Baan Sukhumvit **13** *B4*
Bangkok Inn **5** *A2*
Bourbon Street **6** *B4*
City Lodge **8** *A2*
Davinci Suites **18** *B4*
Davis **19** *B5*
Grand Inn **3** *B2*
Hostelling International
  Centre **10** *B4*
Landmark **16** *B2*
Manhattan **17** *A3*
Marriott **15** *B2*
Park Avenue Grand
  Mecure **14** *B4*
Rajah **20** *B2*
S15 **9** *B3*
Sam's Lodge **11** *B3*
Sheraton Grande
  Sukhumvit **1** *B3*
Smart Suites **12** *A2*
Sukhumvit **1** *B3*
World Inn **24** *A2*

Science Museum and Planetarium
ⓘ *Tue-Sun 0900-1600, closed public holidays, ฿40, ฿20 children. Skytrain to Ekkamai.*
The Science Museum and Planetarium is just past Sukhumvit Soi 40, next to the Eastern
bus terminal. As well as the planetarium, there are aeroplanes and other exhibits, but don't
expect many of them to work. As one recent report put it, there are lots of interactive
buttons, but nothing much happens when you press them. ►► *For information on the
newer and much better National Science Museum, see page 110.*

Bangkok suburbs

Chatuchak Weekend Market
ⓘ *At the weekend, the market is officially open from 0800-1800 (although some shops open
earlier around 0700, some later around 0900). It's best to go early in the day or after 1500.
Beware of pickpockets. The head office and information centre along with the police, first aid,
banks and left-baggage facilities can all be found opposite Gate 1 off Kampaengphet Rd. The
clock tower serves as a good reference point should visitors become disoriented. Take a
Skytrain to Mo Chit station. Or a/c buses Nos 3, 26, 27, 29, 34, 39, 59, 77, 96, 112, 134, 136, 138,
145, 502, 503, 509, 510, 512, 513 go past the market.*

North of Bangkok, the Chatuchak Weekend Market is just off Phahonyothin Road, opposite
the Northern bus terminal, near the Mo Chit Skytrain and Chatuchak Park and Kampaeng
Phet Metro stations. Until 1982 this market was held at Sanaam Luang in central Bangkok,

➡ **Bangkok maps**
1 Bangkok, page 78
2 Old City, Banglamphu and Chinatown, page 90
3 Bangkok's rivers and khlongs, page 97
4 Siam Square and Ploenchit Road, page 102
5 Silom and Surawong, page 104
6 Sukhumvit Road, page 106

Eating 🍴	Crêpes & Co 21 *B3*	L'Opera 9 *B5*	Bars & clubs 🍸
Akbar 1 *A2*	Gourmet Gallery 6 *A5*	Mrs Balbir's 20 *A3*	Bull's Head 16 *B3*
Ambassador Food	Kuppa 39 10 *B4*	Nasir al-Masri 19 *A2*	Cheap Charlie's 11 *A2*
Centre 12 *B3*	Larry's Dive 15 *B4*	Rang Mahal at Rembrandt	Jools 13 *B2*
Barn Khanittha 3 *A4*	Le Banyan 5 *B2*	Hotel 27 *B4*	Log Home 25 *A6*
Bed Supper Club 14 *A3*	Le Dalat Indochine 7 *A4*	Señor Pico at Rembrandt	Narcissus 17 *A4*
Bei Otto 23 *B4*	Lemon Grass 8 *B5*	Hotel 27 *B4*	Q 18 *A2*
Cabbages & Condoms 4 *B3*	Les Nymphéas 24 *B4*	Tapas Café 26 *A2*	

but was moved after it outgrew its original home. Chatuchak is a huge conglomeration of around 15,000 stallholders spread over an area of 14 ha, selling virtually everything under the sun, and an estimated 200,000 to 300,000 people visit the market each day. There are antique stalls, basket stalls, textile sellers, shirt vendors, carvers and painters along with the usual array of fishmongers, vegetable hawkers and butchers. A huge number of bars and foodstalls have also opened to cater for the crowds, so it is possible to rest and recharge before foraging once more. Also here, in the north section of Chatuchak Park adjacent to Kamphaeng Phet Road, is the **Railway Museum** ① *0900-1800, free*, with a small collection of steam locomotives as well as miniature and model trains.

Around Bangkok

If the heat and sprawl becomes too much then do what any self-respecting Bangkokian does and get the hell out. You don't have to travel far to see ancient palaces, dreamy rivers and bizarre museums. Travel a little further and you'll be taking in sweeping green vistas amid thick forests and dipping your toosties into warm sand.

Muang Boran (Ancient City) → Colour map 3, B4.
① *T02-2241057, 0800-1700, ฿300, ฿200 children. Take a city bus No 25, 45, 142, 145, 508, 511, 513 or 536 to Samut Prakarn and then a short songthaew ride. Alternatively, you can take a bus from the Eastern terminal to Samut Prakarn, or go on one of the innumerable organized tours (see Tours and tour operators, page 152).*
The Ancient City lies 25 km southeast of Bangkok in the province of Samut Prakarn and is billed as the world's largest outdoor museum. It houses scaled-down constructions of Thailand's most famous wats and palaces (some of which can no longer be visited in their original locations) along with a handful of originals relocated here. Artisans maintain the buildings while helping to keep alive traditional crafts. The 50-ha site corresponds in shape to the map of Thailand, with the wats and palaces appropriately sited. Allocate a full day for a trip out to the Ancient City.

Samut Prakarn Crocodile Farm and Zoo → Colour map 3, B4.
① *T02-7034891, 0700-1800, ฿300, ฿200 children. Croc combat and elephant show-time is every hour Mon-Fri 0900-1600 (no show at 1200), Sat, Sun and holidays every hour 0900-1700. Take bus No 142, 508, 513 or 536 to Samut Prakarn; or a tour (see Tours and tour operators, page 152), 1 hr, depending on traffic.*
The Samut Prakarn Crocodile Farm and Zoo claims to be the world's oldest crocodile farm. Founded in 1950 by a certain Mr Utai Young-prapakorn, it contains over 50,000 crocs of 28 species. Thailand has become, in recent years, one of the world's largest exporters of farmed crocodile skins and meat. Never slow in seeing a new market niche, Thai entrepreneurs have invested in the farming of the beasts – in some cases in association with chicken farms (the old battery chickens are simply fed to the crocs – no waste, no trouble). The irony is that the wild crocodile is now, to all intents and purposes, extinct in Thailand (there are said to be two left alive, unfortunately living in different areas. It is tempting to speculate that recent floods may have added to those numbers as captive crocodiles have frequently escaped from some of the less well-designed farms. While this has generated some understandable concern in the areas near the farm, most, if not all, escapees have eventually been captured or killed. The show includes the 'world famous' crocodile wrestling. The farm also has a small zoo, train and playground.

Damnoen Saduak Floating Market → Colour map 3, B3.

ⓘ Catch an early morning bus (No 79) from the Southern bus terminal in Thonburi – Damnoen Saduak opens early, from pre-dawn, aim to get there as early as possible, as the market winds down after 0900, leaving only trinket stalls. The trip takes about 1½ hrs. A/c and non-a/c buses leave every 40 mins from 0600 (a/c ฿80) (T02-435 5031 for booking). The bus travels via Nakhon Pathom (where it is possible to stop on the way back and see the Great Chedi). Ask the conductor to drop you at Thanarat Bridge in Damnoen Saduak. Then either walk down the lane (1.5 km) that leads to the market and follows the canal, or take a river taxi for ฿10, or a minibus, ฿2. There are a number of floating markets in the maze of khlongs – Ton Khem, Hia Kui and Khun Phithak – and it is best to hire a long-tailed boat to explore the backwaters and roam around the markets, about ฿300 per hr (agree the price before setting out). There is a tourist office here which can arrange tours and transport. Most tour companies also visit the Floating Market.

Damnoen Saduak Floating Market, in Ratchaburi Province, 109 km west of Bangkok, is (almost) the real thing. Sadly, it is becoming increasingly like the Floating Market in Thonburi (see page 95) and is one of the most popular day trips from the capital. Much of it is geared towards tourists these days but if you take time to explore the further-flung khlongs you should stumble across something more authentic. Most visitors arrive and depart on a tour bus, stopping only for a photo opportunity and the chance to buy overpriced fruit from the canny market sellers. Avoid the crowds by staying at a nearby guesthouse and arriving around sunrise. ▶ See Sleeping, page 125.

Rose Garden → Colour map 3, B3.

ⓘ Daily 0800-1800; the cultural show is at 1445 daily, ฿300. Bangkok office: 195/15 Soi Chokchai Chongchamron Rama III Rd, T02-2953261. Daily tour from Bangkok, half day (afternoons only).

A Thai 'cultural village' spread over 15 ha of landscaped tropical grounds, 32 km west of Bangkok. Most people go for the cultural show: elephants at work, Thai classical dancing, Thai boxing, hilltribe dancing and a Buddhist ordination ceremony. The resort also has a hotel, restaurants, a swimming pool and tennis courts, as well as a golf course close by.

Thai Human Imagery Museum

ⓘ T034-332109, Mon-Fri 0900-1730, Sat, Sun and holidays 0830-1800, ฿200. Take a bus (a/c and non-a/c) from the Southern bus terminals towards Nakhon Pathom; ask to be let off at the museum.

Situated 31 km west of Bangkok on Pinklao-Nakhon Chaisri highway, the Thai Human Imagery Museum is the Madame Tussauds of Bangkok. 'Breathtaking' sculptures include famous monks, Thai kings, and scenes from Thai life; the museum is probably more interesting to Thais than foreigners.

Nonthaburi → Colour map 3, B4.

ⓘ Take an express river taxi (45 mins) to Tha Nonthaburi or a Bangkok city bus (Nos 32, 64, 97 and 203). A day trip, including lunch, costs ฿500. Or take the Chao Phraya River Express Sunday Cruise T02-281 5564, (฿300-390) which departs from Tha Maharat at 0800. It is also possible to stay here, see Sleeping, page 125.

Nonthaburi is both a province and a provincial capital immediately to the north of Bangkok. Accessible by express river taxi from the city, the town has a provincial air that contrasts sharply with the overpowering capital: there are saamlors in the streets (now banished from Bangkok), plenty of temples, and the pace of life is tangibly less frenetic. About half an hour's walk away are rice fields and rural Thailand. A street market runs from the pier inland past the *sala klang* (provincial offices), selling clothes, sarong lengths and dried fish. The buildings of the *sala klang* are early 19th century, wooden and decayed. Note the lamp posts with their durian accessories – Nonthaburi's durians are renowned across the kingdom. Walk through the *sala klang* compound (downriver 100 m) to reach an excellent riverside restaurant, Rim Fung. Across the river and upstream (five minutes by long-tailed boat) is **Wat Chalerm Phra Kiat**, a refined wat built by Rama III as a tribute to his mother who is said to have lived in the vicinity. The gables of the bot are encrusted in ceramic tiles; the *chedi* behind the bot was built during the reign of King Mongkut or Rama IV (1851-1868). It is also possible to take interesting day trips along the canal by boat here and Klong Bang Khu Wiang houses an authentic floating market for early risers. Also see the sweet making demonstrations in traditional houses at Klong Khanom Wan and the large public and botanical park, Suan Somdet Phra Sinakarin, off Nonthaburi Pathum Thani Rd.

Koh Kret

① *Catch the express river boat to Nonthaburi then get a long-tailed boat to the island. The Chao Phraya Express offers tours to Koh Kret every Sun from Tha Sathorn at 0900 and Tha Maharat at 0930, T02-623 6143, ฿300.*

Koh Kret – an island in the middle of the Chao Phraya River, just past Nonthaburi – has a sleepy village that specializes in pottery production. A small meditation centre **Baan Dvara Prateep** (T02-538 4212, www.baandvaraprateep.com) is currently the only place to stay. Often referred to as a 'step back in time' this interesting little island is most famous for its production of traditional earthenware. During the late 16th century, the ancestors of the Mon families who still live here took refuge on the island to escape political instability. More recently it's become a popular weekend destination for Bangkok residents escaping the bustle of city life. Cars are not allowed on the island, only motorbikes and bikes. A walkway rings the island and it is possible to walk around in two or three hours. Old wooden buildings line both sides of the raised walkway and the surrounding forest's verdant foliage provides plenty of shade. Monks in saffron robes stroll in quiet temple courtyards in villages that give way to banana and coconut plantations. It is lined with pottery shops and quaint eateries with small, covered wooden porches jutting over the water.

National Science Museum

① *T02-577 9999 ext 1833, www.nsm.or.th, Tue-Sun 0930-1700, ฿60, free for children and students. In neighbouring Pathum Thani province, the Thai name for the museum is Ongkaan Phiphitiphan Withayasaat Haeng Chaat (or Or Por Wor Chor), but even if you manage to say that the chances are that the taxi driver will not know where you mean, so get someone from your hotel to make sure. Take the Chaeng Wattana-Bang Pa In expressway north and exit at Chiang Rak (for Thammasat University's new out-of-town campus). Continue west on Khlong Luang Rd, over Phahonyothin Rd, and follow your nose over khlong 1 to khlong 5 (canals) until the road ends at a T-junction. Turn right and the NSM is 4 km or so down here on the left. Bus 1155 goes direct from Future Park Rangsit to the museum on the hour.*

The National Science Museum (NSM), north of town, past the old airport, opened in Pathum Thani province in 2000. It is part of the Technopolis complex which, when completed, will consist of the Science and Natural History Museum (already open) as well as an IT museum and Bioworld.The money for the project – a cool one billion baht –

My kingdom for a durian

To many Thais, durians are not just any old fruit. They are Beaujolais, grouse and Dolcellate all rolled into one stinking, prickly ball. The best durian in Thailand – the cognoscenti would say the whole world – come from Nonthaburi, north of Bangkok. The best varieties are those like the *kan yao* durian.

The problem is Nonthaburi has been taken over by factories and housing estates. Durian orchards are disappearing as development proceeds and many of the most famous orchards are now under concrete. In early 2000 there were just 3000 rai of orchards left in the province (less than 500 ha). Such is the scarcity of these fruit that wealthy Thais reserve their fruit on the tree – each of which sells for ฿1200-1500. Nor is it just a case of land being redeveloped. Durian trees are said not to like thundering traffic and the fumes that go with Nonthaburi's industrialization. The sensible things just refuse to fruit or produce second-class offerings.

was allocated before the economic crisis. Air-conditioned buildings, internet centre, and lots of hands-on exhibits to thrill children (and adults) is the result. The exhibits are labelled in English and Thai and the recorded information is also in both languages. It is very good, well designed and with charming student helpers for that human touch. The cafeteria needs some more thought though.

Bang Sai → *Colour map 3, B4.*
ⓘ *Take a bus from the Northern bus terminal or a boat up the Chao Phraya.*
The **Royal Folk Arts and Crafts Centre** ⓘ *T035-366252, www.bangsaiarts.com, Tue-Sun 0830-1600, ฿50, ฿30 children,* is based north of Bangkok in the riverside workshops of Amphoe (district) Bang Sai, around 24 km from Bang Pa In. It covers an area of nearly 50 ha. Local farmers are trained in traditional arts and crafts such as basketry, weaving and wood carvings. The project is funded by the royal family in an attempt to keep alive Thailand's traditions. Visitors are offered a glimpse of traditional life and technologies. All products – artificial flowers, dolls, silk and cotton cloth, wood carvings, baskets and so on – are for sale. Other attractions at Bang Sai include a freshwater aquarium and a bird park.

Bang Pa In → *Colour map 3, B4.*
ⓘ *0830-1630, ฿50 (guidebook included). Currency exchange facilities are also available here. Regular bus connections from Bangkok's Northern terminal (1 hr) and 3 train connections each day from the capital's Hualamphong station, or long-tailed boat from Tien Pier (see map, page 97).*
Bang Pa In became the summer residence of the Ayutthayan kings of the 17th century. King Prasat Thong (1630-1656) started the trend of retiring here during the hot season, and he built both a palace and a temple. The palace is located in the middle of a lake that the king had created on the island. It is said that his fondness for Bang Pa In was because he was born here.

After the Thai capital was moved to Bangkok, Bang Pa In was abandoned and left to degenerate. It was not until Rama IV stopped here that a restoration programme was begun. The only original buildings that remain are those of Wat Chumphon Nikayaram, outside the palace walls, near the bridge and close to the railway station. Start at the

Varophat Phiman Hall, built by Chulalongkorn in 1876 as his private residence, and from here take the bridge that leads past the Thewarat Khanlai Gate overlooking the Isawan Thipaya-at Hall in the middle of the lake. Facing the gate and bridge is the Phra Thinang Uthayan Phumisathian, and though designed to resemble a Swiss chalet, it looks more like a New England country house. Behind the 'chalet', the Vehat Chamroon Hall, built in 1889, was a gift from Chinese traders to King Chulalongkorn. It is the only building open to the public and contains some interesting Chinese artefacts. In front stands the Hor Vithun Thasna, a tall observation tower. Another bridge leads to a pair of memorials. The second commemorates Queen Sunanda, Rama V's half-sister and favourite wife who drowned here; it is said her servants watched her drown because of the law that forbade a commoner from touching royalty. South of the palace, over the Chao Phraya River, is the Gothic-style Wat Nivet Thamaprawat, built in 1878 and resembling a Christian church. Boat trips around the wat run daily on the hour from Bang Pa In pier, 0900-1500.

Safari World
ⓘ *T02-518 1000, www.safariworld.com, daily 0900-1700, ฿700, ฿450 (children). Take bus Nos 26, 71, 60, 96 or 501 to Minburi where a minibus service runs to the park.*
Safari world is a 120-ha complex in Minburi, 9 km northeast of Bagnkok's city centre, with animals, a marine park and an amusement park. Most of the animals are African – zebras, lions, giraffes – and visitors can either drive through in their own (closed) vehicles or take one of the park's air-conditioned coaches. The marine park features dolphin and sea lion shows as well as a small aviary, restaurant and landscaped gardens.

Siam Park City
ⓘ *101 Sukhapibarn 2 Rd, Bangkapi, T02-919 7200, www.siamparkcity.com. Mon-Fri 1000-1800, Sat and Sun 1000-1800, ฿200. Take bus Nos 26 or 27 from the Victory Monument, 1 hr or 30 mins by car.*
Siam Park City is Water World – with artificial surf, fountains, waterfalls and chute – theme park, zoo, botanical gardens and fair all rolled into one.

Chachoengsao → *Colour map 3, B5.*
ⓘ *Trains leaves from Hualamphong station between 0510 and 1805 and the journey takes 1 hr 40 mins. The train station is to the north of the fruit market, an easy walk to/from the chedi. Buses depart from both the Mo Chit and Ekkamai terminals but it is quickest from Ekkamai – about 2 hrs, depending on the traffic. A/c buses also stop to the north of the fruit market, and there are regular connections (every 15 mins) with Bangkok's Southern bus terminal, 1-2 hrs.*
Chachoengsao lies just 1½ hours from Bangkok by train or bus making it a nifty day excursion from the capital – and offering an insight into 'traditional' Thailand. This is the country's mango capital, with thousands of hectares of plantations (March being the best month for mango fans to visit). It is also famous for Irrawaddy and Indo-Pacific dolphin watching, possible between November and February. Two- to three-hour trips are available from Tha Kham, or call the district office for details T038-573 411.

Chachoengsao lies on the Bang Pakong River, to the east of the capital, and has almost been engulfed by fast-expanding Bangkok. Nonetheless, old-style shophouses and restaurants, as well as some evidence of a much more rustic past, remain. The old heart of the town is near the confluence of the Bang Pakong River and Khlong Ban Mai, on Supakit Road. **Ban Mai market** is worth exploring not for its wares– the main market has moved into the centre of the new town – but for its traditional architecture. A concrete footbridge over Khlong Ban Mai links the two halves of the old market. A Chinese clan house reveals the largely Chinese origin of the population of the market area; most arrived before the outbreak of the Second World War. **Wat Sothorn Woramahavihan** is the town's best-known monastery and it contains one of the country's most revered images of the Buddha, Luang Por Sothorn. The monastery is a little over 2 km south of Sala Changwat (the Provincial Hall), on the banks of the Bang Prakong. A public park opposite Chach-aengsao Fortress on Maruphong Road offers good floating restaurants along the river bank.

◉ Bangkok listings

Hotel and guesthouse prices

LL over US$200	**L** US$151-200	**AL** US$101-150
A US$66-100	**B** US$46-65	**C** US$31-45
D US$21-30	**E** US$12-20	**F** US$7-11
G US$6		

Restaurant prices

₩₩₩ over US$12	₩₩ US$6-12	₩ US$6

◉ Sleeping

From humble backstreet digs through to opulent extravagance, Bangkok has an incredibly diverse range of hotels, guest-houses and serviced apartments. The best-value bargains are often to be had in the luxury sector; you'll find some of the best hotels in the world here, many of which offer rooms at knock-down prices. The boutique boom has also seen an explosion of stylish independent guesthouses which often offer exceptional style and comfort at reasonable prices. The guesthouses of Khaosan are cheapish but often more expensive than what you'll find in other parts of the country. Possibly the biggest bargains to be had are with long-stay options or serviced apartments. These are lavish flats, most of which come with all the amenities (pool, gym, maid and room service) you'd expect from a 4- or 5-star hotel, but at half the price. Terms of leasing are generally weekly or monthly and a deposit of 1-3 months is usually required. Officially, apartments are required to demand a minimum stay of a week; however, telephone negotiation of these terms is not uncommon and many allow nightly stays.

Many of the more expensive places to stay are on the **Chao Phraya River**. As well

as river transport, the Skytrain provides excellent transport from this part of town. Running eastwards from the river are **Silom and Surawong roads**, in the heart of Bangkok's business district and with Skytrain and Metro connections. The bars of **Patpong** link the 2 roads. Not far to the north of Silom and Surawong roads, close to Hualamphong (the central railway station and Metro stop), is **Chinatown**. There are a handful of hotels and guesthouses here – but it remains very much an alternative location. A well-established accommodation centre is along **Sukhumvit Rd**. The Skytrain runs along Sukhumvit's length and it is intersected by the Metro at Soi Asoke. The bulk of the accommodation here is in the **A-B** range and the *sois* are filled with shops, bars and restaurants of every description. Note, that the profusion of go-go bars in Soi Nana (Sois 3 and 4) and Soi Cowboy (off Soi 23) can be off-putting. In the vicinity of Siam Sq are a handful of de luxe hotels and several 'budget' establishments (especially along Rama 1 Soi Kasemsan Nung). **Siam Sq** is central, has a good shopping area and excellent Skytrain connections, easy bus and taxi access to Silom and Sukhumvit roads and the Old City. The main concentration of guest-houses is along and around **Khaosan Rd** (an area known as Banglamphu). There is a second, smaller and quieter cluster of guesthouses just north of Khaosan Rd, at the northwest end of **Sri Ayutthaya Rd**. A third concentration of budget accom-modation is on **Soi Ngam Duphli**, off Rama IV Rd.

Advertisements in the *Bangkok Post, The Nation* and hotels' own websites may provide some heavily discounted rates in some more upmarket hotels. Also see www.sabaai.com and www.bangkok-apartment.com to view and book serviced apartments online.

Airport

Those needing to stay near the new airport can book in at **AL** Novotel Suvarnabhumi Airport Hotel (Moo 1 Nongprue Bang Phli, Samutprakarn, 10540 Bangkok, T02-131 1111, www.novotel.com), which has 600-plus rooms, 2 bars, 4 restaurants, a pool, fitness centre and spa.

Banglamphu and Khaosan Road
p88, map p90

The *sois* off the main road are often quieter, such as Soi Chana Songkhran or Soi Rambutri. Note that rooms facing on to Khaosan Rd tend to be very noisy.

The reliable **Sawasdee Chain** has several guesthouses in the area all with attractive, clean interiors and large Thai-style communal areas. See www.sawasdee-hotels.com.

Sri Ayutthaya offers an alternative for travellers who want to stay close to the old city but avoid the chaos of the Khaosan Rd. It's a gradually developing tourist enclave with restaurants, foodstalls, a couple of travel agents/internet shops and even a 7-11. The area, known as Tewes, is also known for its bustling flower market. The handily located Tewes Pier sits behind the morning market and temple and commuters feed the fish while waiting for the river taxis. One family runs 4 of the guesthouses; this means that if one is full you will probably be moved on to another. One problem is getting here by taxi, Sri Ayutthaya is a long road and the tricky pronunciation of Tewes (try Tay-wet) can complicate matters. Pick up a card with directions from your guesthouse.

LL-AL Royal Princess, 269 Lan Luang Rd, T02-281 3088, www.royalprincess.com.

A/c, restaurants, pool, gorgeous 4-star hotel, part of the quality-stamped Dusit chain of hotels with excellent facilities and a fantastic location. All rooms have balconies overlooking the old city.

L-A Viengtai, 42 Soi Rambutri, Banglamphu, T02-228 05434, www.viengtai.co.th. A/c, restaurant, pool. A perennial favourite in the mid-range category, rooms here are spacious and reliably smart, if a little conservative on the design front. Helpful well-informed management and a slightly more civilized location on the street parallel to the Khaosan.

AL Aurum River Place, 394/27-29 Soi Pansook, Maharaj Rd, www.aurum-bangkok.com. A swish modern hotel a little further afield in a beautiful colonial building overlooking the river and a stone's throw from Wat Pho. The more expensive rooms overlook the river but there are also some great views from the (rather basic) rooftop garden. Stylish café downstairs that spills out into a small garden. Neat hotel-style rooms with good facilities.

A Baan Chantra Boutique, 120/1 Samsen Rd, T02-628 6988, www.khaosanroad.com/baan_chantra/home.htm. Around the corner from the Khaosan there are just 7 rooms in this exquisite boutique guesthouse. A restored antique Thai wooden house with romantically furnished interiors, pretty balconies and a strict no-smoking policy. Homely ambience and excellent service and attention to detail.

A Phranakorn Nornlen Hotel, T02-628 8188, www.phranakorn-nornlen.com. A little gem of an independent hotel with incredible attention to detail. Airy Thai-style rooms with artistic design are as homely as an artfully crafted doll's house. Wooden shutters, a garden café, beautiful rooftop views and an intimate, relaxed atmosphere. The small team of amicable staff includes an informative 'City Guide' who can help with bookings, etc. Daily cookery classes and other creative pursuits. Recommended.

A-B Buddy Lodge, 265 Khaosan Rd, T02-629 4477, www.buddylodge.com. One of the more upmarket options around the Khaosan Rd area and one of the first to use the now ubiquitous term 'boutique', **Buddy Lodge** actually deserves the title with rooms featuring relatively plush modern interiors and chic fittings as well as home comforts like a fridge and TV. De luxe balcony rooms are worth the extra ฿500. There is also a Japanese restaurant, coffee shop and pool.

A-B New World Lodge Apartments and Guesthouse, 2 Samsen Rd, T02-281 5596, www.newworldlodge.com. Popular with long-stay guests and with a cute community feel. A good location for the Old City yet away from the hurly-burly of Khaosan Rd. Rooms have fan or a/c, some are fairly spacious and have satellite TV for a higher price. Some overlook the canal. Safety boxes are free for guests, as is the use of a small gym.

A-B Trang Hotel, 99/1 Visutkaset Rd, T02-282 2141, www.tranghotelbangkok.com. A/c, restaurant, pool. Friendly, attractive hotel that is well priced and popular with families and return visitors. Set around a relaxing courtyard a little away from the action and major sights.

C Diamond House, 4 Samsen Rd, T02-629 4008, www.thaidiamondhouse.com. Twin rooms have bunk beds which make them feel like a ship's cabin. Fridge, TV, a/c in all rooms and very nice bathrooms. Call ahead to avoid paying inflated walk-in rates.

C-D D&D Inn, 68-70 Khaosan Rd, T02-629 0526, www.khaosanby.com. Large, very popular and well-priced but fairly characterless purpose-built hotel with lift, neat if slightly soulless a/c rooms, and hot showers. The small swimming pool and bar on the roof offers a fine view. Very centrally located. Due to the rapid turnover of guests use of the hotel's safety deposit boxes is recommended.

C-E Sawasdee Bangkok Inn, 126/2 Khaosan Rd, T02-2801251, www.sawasdee-hotels.com. Good value, clean, fair-sized rooms with wooden floors and some with a/c right at the centre of the action. A vibrant, popular bar and friendly staff. Free safety deposit and left luggage.

D Lamphu House, 75 Soi Rambutri, T02-629 5861, www.lamphuhouse.com. Undoubtedly one of the best budget options on offer. Situated down a very quiet soi. Clean, modern, very pleasantly decorated rooms with a/c and very comfy beds, the superior rooms have a large balcony and are the best value. Great restaurant downstairs and an extremely professional spa on the roof terrace. Highly recommended.

D Mango Lagoon, 30 Soi Rambutri, T02-281 4783. A relative newcomer with more than a modicum of charm and comfort. Light and airy rooms look out over the garden café in the courtyard out front.

D-E Sawasdee Krungthep Inn, 30 Praathi Rd, T02-629 0079, www.sawasdee-hotels.com. A lively communal atmosphere. Clean and simple rooms, all with cable TV. Family rooms available with 2 double beds.

D-F Sawasdee Khaosan, Chakrapong Rd T02-629 2340. Probably the pick of the Sawasdee bunch due to its modern style and location just around the corner from the Khaosarn towards Sanaam Luang. This one has its own bakery and popular cocktail bar looking out onto the street.

D-F Siam Oriental, 190 Khaosan Rd, T02-629 0312, siam_oriental@hotmail.com. Fine, clean rooms (some a/c), smart tiled corridors, and very friendly staff. Internet facilities downstairs, along with a very popular restaurant. Free safety deposit box.

E Shambara, 138 Khaosan Rd, T02-282 7968, www.shambarabangkok.com. 9 rooms ranging from fan to a/c, singles to twins. Individually designed with lots of characters. A lot of thought has gone into making these rooms comfortable. Restaurant and tours. Good value.

E Shanti Lodge, Sri Ayutthaya Rd, Soi 16, Si Tewet, T02-281 2497. Double rooms with a/c or fan and a dorm. The obvious pick of the budget bunch in a picturesque old wooden house with a pretty garden restaurant complete with resident turtle. The food (mostly vegetarian) is excellent, atmospheric rooms are beautifully decorated and the bohemian atmosphere harks back to halcyon days of the hippy era. There's a breezy space for yoga and Thai massage and a small shop selling crafts and clothing. The all-female staff including the intimidatingly efficient lead lady Yuan, take a while to crack, but are well worth the effort and offer a wealth of no-nonsense information on Bangkok pursuits. Travel agent and internet café.

E Tuptim Bed and Breakfast, 82 Soi Rambutri, T02-629 1535, www.tuptimb-b.com. Recommended budget option with some a/c and en suite shower, but even the shared facilities are exceptionally clean, breakfast included. Very friendly staff.

E-F Chai's House, 49/4-8 Chao Fa Soi Rongmai, T02-281 4901. Another reliable budget option, **Chai's** occupies the last house down Soi Rambutri, away from the competition. Some a/c, friendly and family-run. Traditional Thai-style rooms with wood panelling vary in size but are clean and the a/c ones are good value. Balconies and orchid-filled restaurant make it a quiet and relaxing place. Recommended.

E-F Chart Guest House, 62 Khaosan Rd, T02-282 0171, www.khaosanroad.com/chartguesthouse/index.htm. Very clean airy rooms, cosmopolitan feel, with winding staircase and retro-style bar with movies. Friendly, English-speaking staff.

E-F Home and Garden, 16 Samphraya Rd (Samsen 3), T02-280 1475. Away from the main concentration of guesthouses, down a quiet *soi* (although cockerels mean an early start for light sleepers). This small house in a delightful leafy compound has a homely atmosphere. The rooms are a fair size with large windows, some face onto a balcony. Friendly owner and excellent value.

E-F Orchid House, Rambutri St, T02-280 2691. Fan and a/c rooms with attached showers on this slightly sleepier *soi*, cosy clean and safe with pretty interior touches in the rooms and communal areas. The ground floor terrace restaurant is a nice quiet spot

for reading or people watching. Internet café and travel agent. Recommended.

E-F Pra Suri Guesthouse, 85/1 Soi Pra Suri (off Dinso Rd), T/F02-280 1428. 5 mins east of Khaosan Rd, not far from the Democracy Monument. Fan, restaurant, own bathrooms (no hot water), clean, spacious and quiet, very friendly and helpful family-run travellers' guesthouse with all the services to match. If you really can't face the shlep to the Khaosan from the airport bus (which stops close to the Democracy Monument). Recommended.

E-F Sawasdee Smile Inn, 35 Soi Rongmai, T02-629 2321, www.sawasdee-hotels.com. Large, spacious sitting area at the front under a gaudy looking green Thai-style roof. Restaurant and 24-hr bar, so ask for a room at the back if you want an early night. Rooms are clean and simple, all with cable TV. Free safety boxes available.

E-F Taewaz Guesthouse, Sri Ayutthaya Rd. T02-280 8856. New place with wooden floors and cosy but very clean rooms – a/c rooms are a bargain. Internet access, friendly staff.

E-F Tavee, 83 Sri Ayutthaya Rd, Soi 14, T02-282 5983. Restaurant, a quiet, relaxed and respectable place with a small garden and a number of fish tanks. Friendly management – a world away from the chaos of Khaosan Rd. The Tavee family keep the rooms and shared bathrooms immaculately clean and are a good source of information for travellers. This place has been operating since 1985 and has managed to maintain a very high standard.

F Backpackers Lodge, 85 Sri Ayutthaya Rd, Soi 14, T02-282 3231. Very similar to its neighbour, **Tavee** (whose owner is brother of the **Backpackers'** manager). The rooms are a little small but the service is friendly and there is an intimate feel to the place. It's back off the road so is a little quieter than the others.

F-G Bangkok Youth Hostel, 25/2 Phitsanulok Rd (off Samsen Rd), T02-282 0950. North of Khaosan Rd, away from the bustle, the dorm beds are great value (฿120) being newly furnished and with a/c. Other rooms are clean, small and basic but still a bargain for those who don't mind a few hardships. If you don't have a valid YHA membership card, it will cost an extra ฿50 per night.

F-G The River Guesthouse, 18 Samphraya Rd (Samsen 3), T02-280 0876. A small, family house with a homely and friendly communal atmosphere. Small but clean rooms with shared bathrooms.

Phra Arthit Road p88

B-D Pra Arthit Mansion, 22 Phra Arthit Rd, T02-280 0744. Leafy though slightly dated hotel, popular with German tour operators. Rooms are huge, carpeted and good value with vast comfy beds and all the trimmings including a/c, fridge, TV and even bath tubs. Quite a bargain in this price range, discounts for over 3 nights stay. Well run with helpful management. Linked to the fabulous Ricky's Coffee Shop downstairs (see Eating, page 127). Recommended.

C Bhiman Inn, 55 Phra Arthit Rd, T02-282 6171, www.bhimaninn.com. Another of the boutique boomer crowd but again a stylish title-holder with lots of character. Small pool, a/c rooms with fairly thin mattresses raised on platforms, chic interior design and small plant-filled balconies. Minibar and TV. Restaurant attached. Recommended.

E-F Baan Sabai, 12 Soi Rongmai, T02-629 1599, baansabai@hotmail.com. A large, colonial-style building with a green pillared entrance in front. Although not very expensive, it is not the typical backpacker scene. Rooms are simple but large and airy. Storage is available at ฿10 per bag/suitcase. Occasionally local Thai bands are invited to play here.

E-F My House, 37 Phra Arthit Soi Chana Songkram, T02-282 9263. Another reliable budget option with helpful and friendly management. Rooms are basic but exceptionally clean and comfortable, the attractive traditional-style entrance leads to a spacious lounge and restaurant. Popular travel service with minibus to the airport every hour.

Thonburi, Wat Arun and the khlongs p93, map p97

There's presently very little accommodation on the Thonburi side of the river. This is a shame as the *khlongs*, particularly to the north, make it one of the most beautiful parts of the city. However, this may all soon be set to change with the extension of the Skytrain route over the river at Saphan Taksin, which has been heavily delayed but is due to open by the end of 2009.

LL-L Peninsula, 333 Charoen Nakorn Rd, Klongsan, T02-2861 2888, www.bangkok. peninsula.com. Sited just across the river from Taksin Bridge, the 39-storey **Peninsula** has a commanding riverfront position providing spectacular city views. The large rooms are luxurious and a full range of leisure facilities are on offer, while 4 restaurants provide a variety of (mostly Asian) cuisine. Recommended.

LL-AL Marriott Bangkok Resort and Spa, 257/1-3 Charoen Nakorn Rd, T02-476 0021, www.marriot.com. Luxury hotel set beside the canal in spacious surroundings with more than 4 ha of grounds. A little downstream from the main action but free shuttle-boat services run every 30 mins between hotel and River City piers. Attractive, low-rise design with Thai-style ambience. A good place to escape from the fumes and frenzy after a day sightseeing or shopping – the soothing Mandara garden spa is here too. Recommended.

LL-AL Ramada Menam Riverside, 2074 Charoenkrung Rd, T02-688 1000, www.menamriverside-hotel.com. Decent enough 5-star high-rise pile beside the river. Rooms are standard contemporary Thai, with silks and soft lighting but nothing too fabulous. Nice location in a rootsy part of the city. Caters to a lot of hi-end Chinese guests and, consequently, is home to one of the best Chinese restaurants in town, the **Ah Yat Abalone**.

AL Ibrik Resort, 256 Soi Wat Rakang, Arun-Amarin Rd, Thonburi, T02-848 9220, www.ibrikresort.com. Just 3 beautifully designed rooms in this bijou little resort. A hidden gem worth seeking out for its romantic location, river views and chic oriental interiors. No pool though.

B-G The Artists Club, 61 Soi Tiem Boon Yang, T02-862 0056. Run by an artist, this is a guesthouse-cum-studio-cum-gallery buried deep in the *khlongs* with clean rooms, some a/c. It makes a genuine alternative with concerts, drawing lessons and other cultural endeavours, although the accommodation is very simple. Call for directions.

Chinatown *p92, map p90*

LL-L Royal Orchid Sheraton, 2 Charoen Krung Rd Soi 30 (Captain Bush Lane), T02-266 0123, www.royalorchidsheraton.com. Sited beside the river just outside the steamy narrow lanes of Chinatown, this hotel, while offering some of the best accommodation in this part of town, is not a patch on its sister **Sheraton** on Sukhumvit Rd. Having said that, the management is making a huge effort to spruce things up with newly renovated 'Tower' suites offering excellent value. The gardens are also a great spot to laze. Its biggest flaw is service, which is poor for this price range.

LL-AL Grand China Princess, 215 Yaowarat Rd, T02-2249977, www.grandchina.com. Centrally located with balconies over the river and a revolving restaurant up top, this dramatic high-rise with its magical views over the city mainly caters to the Asian market, with choice of Asian cuisine, business facilities, fitness centre and pool. The interior grandeur is a bit faded but still holds a certain chaotic charm.

L-B White Orchid, 409-421 Yaowarat Rd, T02-226 0026, www.whiteorchidhotelbkk. com. Decent enough hotel, although the cheaper rooms are dark and pokey. Everything is a/c, with hot water and en suite facilities. It offers a great alternative to Bangkok's usual accommodation due entirely to its great location in the heart of dynamic Chinatown.

D River View Guesthouse, 768 Songwad Soi Panurangsri, T02-234 5429, benjapak@ ksc.co.th. Some a/c, the restaurant/bar is on the top floor and overlooks the river, the food is average but the view spectacular. Some rooms have balconies overlooking the river (as the name suggests). It receives mixed reviews, perhaps due to the prioritizing of character over cleanliness, but is worth considering for its location away from the bulk of hotels, close to the Harbour Department boat pier and Chinatown. Recommended.

E Moon Hotel, Mahachai Rd, T02-235 7195. A rabbit warren of cellular a/c rooms joined by damp corridors. Excellent value however.

E-F Golden Inn Guesthouse, Mahachai Rd, no telephone. Excellent situation in the heart of Chinatown. Dark rooms and very noisy, but then this is Chinatown.

Siam Square area *p100 map p102*

LL Amari Watergate, 847 Phetburi Rd, T02-653 9000, www.amari.com. Lots of marble and plastic trees, uninspired block, good facilities and good value, great views from the upper floors on the south side of the building. Restaurants include the excellent **Thai on 4** (see Eating, page 128), fitness centre, squash court and pool.

LL Intercontinental Bangkok, 973 Ploenchit, T02-253 0444, www.ichotel group.com. In its former incarnation as Le Meridien, the hotel held the title of one of the more distinguished luxury hotels in Bangkok (it opened in 1966). Not much has changed since the takeover however, with the tranquil atmosphere, excellent service and opulent surrounds still in place. Lovely rooftop pool and gardens, spa, gym, stylish modern rooms and picture-perfect views.

LL Swissotel Nailert Park, 2 Witthayu Rd, T02-253 0123, www.swissotel.com. An excellent hotel and vast tropical oasis bang in the centre of the city. Set in lush canal-side gardens with running track and a stunningly designed tropical lagoon-like pool. Good service, excellent restaurants, attractive rooms all with beautiful views. Also the site of the much-visited phallic Chao Mae Tubtim shrine.

LL-L Arnoma, 99 Rajdamri Rd. T02-255 5555, www.arnoma.com. The opulence of the foyer isn't continued into the bedrooms, which are rather dated and lacking. There's a gym, pool and restaurant as you might expect. Internet bookings receive 50% discount. Possibly overpriced.

LL-L Four Seasons Bangkok, 155 Rachdamri Rd, T02-250 1000, www.fourseasons.com. A/c, restaurants (including **Spice Market** and the well-known **Biscotti** for fine Italian cuisine, see Eating, page 127), excellent reputation and ambience. Show-stoppingly stylish and postmodern in atmosphere with arguably the best range of cuisine in Bangkok as well as a Swiss Perfection spa. Recommended.

LL-L Grand Hyatt Erawan, 494 Rachdamri Rd, T02-254 1234, www.bangkok.grand.hyatt.com. A towering structure with grandiose entrance and an artificial tree-filled atrium plus sumptuous rooms and every facility. The **Spasso Restaurant/Club** here is very popular and very pricey. On the other hand, the bakery, which has a fantastic range of really sinful and delicious cakes, and the noodle shop, **You and Mee** – which are both also on the lower ground floor – are reasonably priced. Service is excellent and friendly, and this hotel does not charge for drinking water! Makes a great escape from Siam Water Park the traffic and pollution for lunch or afternoon tea even if you're not staying here.

LL-AL Chateau de Bangkok 29 Ruamrudee Soi 1, T02-651 4400. Owned by the **Accor** hotel chain, these serviced apartments have great amenities including private jacuzzis and designer furniture and are centrally located sharing a lovely rooftop pool and gym. Excellent value monthly rates. Restaurant and room service available.

AL Cape House, 43 Soi Langsuan, T02-658 7444, www.capehouse.com. Excellent serviced apartments in a great location. Each apartment comes with DVD, stereo, free Wi-Fi, cable TV, a/c and kitchenette. Has a rooftop pool, library, decent Italian and Thai restaurant, sauna and gym. Recommended.

AL Siam@Siam Design Hotel and Spa, 865 Rama 1 Rd, T02-217 3000, www.siam atsiam.com. Noteworthy interior design, mixing industrial with post-modernism. Textures and materials compliment each other superbly, the rooms are as far removed from the commonplace, boring hotel room design as possible. Facilities include restaurant, swimming pool. Recommended.

A Aphrodite Inn, 59-65 Ratchadamri Rd, T02-254 5999, www.aphroditeinn.com. A new addition to the area. The 30 rooms in this hotel are comfortably decorated with colourful touches such as throws and wall hangings. A/c, TV, safety box, spotlessly clean. Recommended at this price.

B Asia, 296 Phayathai Rd, T02-215 0808, www.asiahotel.co.th. A/c, several restaurants, 2 pools. A package deal and travel agent's favourite due to its handy location, excellent internet deals and impressively ostentatious lobby. However, although the entrance implies a certain degree of grandeur, rooms, aside from the recently upgraded superior suites, are fairly frills-free and the hotel is on a noisy thoroughfare. The walkway straight to the Skytrain station makes for easy access to the city sights. Good jewellers on site and the home of the infamous **Calypso** cabaret shows.

C Wendy House, 36/2 Soi Kasemsan Nung (1), Rama I Rd, T02-2162436. A/c, spotless but small rooms, eating area downstairs, hot water.

E A1 Inn, 25/13 Soi Kasemsan Nung (1), Rama I Rd, T02-215 3029, www.aoneinn.com. A/c, well-run, intimate hotel, very popular so book ahead. Recommended.

E Bed and Breakfast, 36/42 Soi Kasemsan Nung (1), Rama I Rd, T02-215 3004. A/c, efficient staff, clean but small rooms, good security, price includes basic breakfast. A good budget option.

E White Lodge, 36/8 Soi Kasemsan Nung (1), Rama I Rd, T02-216 8867, pnktour@hotmail. com. A/c, hot water, airy, light reasonably sized rooms and an outdoor patio.

Silom area p103, map p104

Of all Bangkok, this area most resembles a Western city, with its international banks, skyscrapers, first-class hotels, shopping malls, pizza parlours and pubs. It is also home to one of the world's best-known red-light districts – **Patpong**.

Soi Ngam Duphli to the east was the pre-Khaosan backpacker area and now mostly caters for long-stay guests on a tight budget. The rather racy after-hours' scene here is a draw for some and an unwanted distraction for others.

LL Banyan Tree, 21/100 South Sathorn Rd, T02-679 1200, www.banyantree.com. Glittering sumptuous surrounds immediately relax the soul here. Famous for its divine luxury spa and literally breathtaking rooftop **Moon Bar**, all rooms are suites with a good location and set back from busy Sathorn Rd.

LL Dusit Thani, 946 Rama IV Rd, T02-236 0450, www.bangkok.dusit.com. The holiday home of royalty, rock stars and other visiting dignitaries and one of the top of the luxury crop, what the **Dusit** lacks in unique design it more than makes up for in comfort and facilities. Ideally located adjacent to Lumpini park. A/c, 9 restaurants, 3 bars, pool, gym, excellent service and attention to detail. Its **Deverana Spa** is one of the finest in the city. Recommended.

LL Metropolitan, 27 South Sathorn Rd, T02-625 3333, www.metropolitan.como.bz. Designer chic at its most extravagantly stylish. From its fashionable members'/guest-only bar through to the beautiful contemporary rooms and the awesome restaurants (**Glow** and **Cy'an** – see Eating, page 129) this is one of Bangkok's hippest hotels. Suites come complete with kitchenette and excellent views while terrace rooms have enticing outdoor showers. Recommended.

LL Oriental, 48 Soi Oriental, Charoen Krung, T02-236 0400, www.mandarinoriental.com. A cut above the competition, at over 100 years old and host to some of history's most infamous literary figures, The **Oriental** is both a Bangkok legend and one of the finest

hotels in the world. A fairy-tale like interior of grandiose proportions, beautiful position overlooking the river and incomparable individual service (despite its 400 rooms). The older Author's wing is the place for high tea and each room is named after a famous guest/author from Somerset Maughan to Barbara Cartland. The Garden wing offers similar levels of nostalgic luxury. The modern River wing and Tower feature more contemporary design and river terraces. Recommended.

LL Shangri-La, 89 Soi Wat Suan Plu, Charoen Krung, T02-236 7777, www.shangri-la.com. Another of the top-end luxury hotels commanding excellent riverside views, the **Shangri-La** is preferred by some to the **Oriental** probably due to its more modern aesthetics and facilities, picturesque verdant grounds and first-class service. A frequent award winner it also houses one of the city's most celebrated spas, **Chi** (see Therapies page 151). Recommended.

LL Siri Sathorn Executive Residence, 27 Sala Daeng Soi 1, T02-266 2345, www.sirisathorn.com. Gleaming minimalist tower block with dozens of serviced apartments bang in the centre of Silom. Rooms are large, the upper floors have great views, amenities are top rate and it has a superb location. Recommended.

LL-L Sofitel Silom, 188 Silom Rd, T02-238 1991, www.sofitel.com. Stark and gleaming hi-tech high-rise with excellent facilities including the infamous **V9** wine bar on the 37th floor. Rooms are elegantly designed but vast comfy beds command the standard room size, so claustrophobics should opt for a more spacious suite. Sunbathers take note, the bijou pool is a little pokey and mostly shaded. Good seasonal promotions.

LL-AL Sukhothai, 13/3 South Sathorn Rd, T02-287 0222, www.sukhothai.com. A competitor for the **Metropolitan**'s crown as the sleekest, chicest place to sleep in the city. Stunning, modern oriental interiors set in huge landscaped gardens complete with decadent pool area, all modelled on the Sukhothai period make it a fashionable traveller's dream location. Several celebrated restaurants including **Celadon** (Thai) and **La Scala** (Italian). Recommended.

A Heritage Baan Silom, Soi 19, T02-236 8388, www.theheritagehotels.com. Contemporary style rooms exude comfort; some rooms have a Cotswolds cottage feel, all are finished to a very high standard. Facilities include Mini-bar, plasma TV and a/c. Recommended for the design appeal.

A Tower Inn, 533 Silom Rd, T02-237 8300, www.towerinnbangkok.com. A/c, restaurant, pool, simple but comfortable hotel, with large rooms and an excellent roof terrace, great value but room standards vary so ask to view first if possible.

A-B Pinnacle Hotel, 17 Soi Ngam Duphli, T02-287 0111, www.pinnaclehotels.com. A small, clean, attractive hotel that is part of a large chain and a pleasant surprise in this rather down-at-heel area. Rooms with all mod cons, helpful staff, pool, restaurant, gym and rooftop spa.

D New Road Guest House, 1216/1 Charoen Krung Rd, T02-237 1094. This Danish-owned riverside place provides a range of accommodation from decent budget rooms to hammocks on the roof. A restaurant serves inexpensive Thai dishes and there's a free fruit buffet for breakfast and tea- and coffee-making facilities. A bar provides a pool table and darts and there's a small outdoor sitting area.

D-E Malaysia Hotel, Soi Ngam Duphli, Rama IV Rd, www.malaysiahotelbkk.com, T02-679 7127. The centrepoint of the Soi Ngam Duphli gay cruising scene, this hulking hotel offers good value for money with pool, a/c, restaurants, travel service and all-night coffeeshop which is popular with after-hours' party goers. Superior rooms also come fully equipped with fridge, TV and DVD.

E Charlie's House, Soi Saphan Khu, T02-679 8330, www.charliehousethailand.com. A/c and TV. Helpful owners create a friendly atmosphere and the rooms are carpeted and very clean. This is probably the best of

the budget bunch. There is a restaurant and coffee corner downstairs with good food at reasonable prices. Recommended.

E Honey House, 35/2-4 Soi Ngam Duphli, T02-286 3460. An interesting building architecturally, but set off a noisy road. Big and clean rooms with attached bathrooms, some with small balconies. Tends to cater more for long-stay guests.

E-G Sala Thai Guesthouse, Soi Saphan Khu, off Soi Sri Bamphen, Rama IV, T02-287 1436. At end of peaceful, almost leafy *soi*, clean rooms have seen better days but it's family-run and has a cute roof garden. Shared bathrooms. Popular with teachers and long-stay guests. Recommended.

F Moon House, 2/10-11 Soi Sribamphen, T02-287 1756. Very good value a/c rooms with private bathroom. Stairwells and hallways are rather dark but then for this price should easily be forgiven.

Sukhumvit Road *p106, map p106*

Sukhumvit is one of Bangkok's premier centres of tourist accommodation and is a great place for restaurants and nightlife with several good bars and clubs. This is also a good area for shopping for furniture: antique and reproduction. Note also that the profusion of expatriate condominiums and hotels in the area between Sukhumvit Soi 18 and Sukhumvit Soi 24 attracts swindlers and petty thieves, particularly purse/bag snatchers and sex tourist-savvy tuk-tuk drivers.

LL Amari Boulevard, 2 Sukhumvit Rd, Soi 5, T02-255 2930, www.amari.com. Great location in the heart of Sukhumvit, good rooms, adequate fitness centre, small pool with terraced Thai restaurant. Popular with European visitors.

LL Park Avenue Grand Mecure Hotel, 30 Soi 22, www.accorhotels.com/asia. Modern, clean rooms all with a/c, TV, minibar and bathtub. The rooms are on the small side and feel a little cramped. Swimming pool, gym and restaurant. There's also a couple of rooms adapted for wheelchair users. Rates depend on occupancy and can be discounted by up to 50%. Professional staff.

LL Sheraton Grande Sukhumvit, 250 Sukhumvit Rd, T02-649 8888, www.luxurycollection.com/bangkok. A superbly managed business and leisure hotel well known for its impeccable service, food and facilities. The rooftop garden is an exotic oasis and the spa offers some of the best massage in town. **Basil** (Thai) and **Rossini** (Italian) see Eating, pages 131 and 132) are also top class and **The Living Room** is renowned for its classy jazz brunches. Great location and, if you can afford it, the best place to stay on Sukhumvit. Recommended.

LL-L Davis, 88 Sukhumvit, Soi 24, T02-260 8000, www.davisbangkok.net. A pioneer in the boutique market and a total treat of a hotel, **Davis** offers the ultimate in chic and unique interiors with a pool, gym, restaurants and a spa. Luxury traditional Thai accommodation is also available in the neighbouring Baan Thai compound tucked away in a quiet garden surrounding a small pool. Recommended.

LL-L Landmark, 138 Sukhumvit Rd, T02-2540404, www.landmarkbangkok.com. Used to be one of the most glamorous hotels in the area now aimed at the travelling family market. Excellent facilities, 12 restaurants, pool, health centre, smart shopping plaza and business facilities. Terrific views from the 31st floor. Some features need upgrading and renovating.

LL-L Marriott, 4 Sukhumvit Soi 2, T02-656 7700, www.marriott.com. Elegant, design, 4 restaurants, pool, health club and spa. More business-like than the **Marriott** hotel on the river but still luxuriously comfortable.

LL-L Rembrandt, 15-15/1 Sukhumvit Soi 18, T02-261 7100, www.rembrandtbkk.com. Lots of marble but limited ambience for this businesslike hotel, the usual top-end facilities including a pool and restaurants. The Indian **Rang Mahal** restaurant is recommended (as you might expect, given that the hotel is Indian-owned) although it is quite pricey.

AL S15, 217 Sukhumvit Rd, T02-651 2000, www.S15hotel.com. From the moment you enter, welcoming and professional staff signify that this hotel is something special. Plush and richly decorated hallways lead to extremely comfortable rooms, which come complete with free Wi-Fi, a/c, fridge, minibar, flat screen TV and DVD player. The bathrooms have walk-in showers and bathtubs. Its one minor shortcoming is that there isn't a pool, but there is a spa and gym. There have been reports of faulty showers. Recommended.

AL-A Davinci Suites, 3/8-10 Soi 31, T02-260 3939, www.davincilespa.com. Brand new boutique hotel down a very quiet soi, but still centrally located. Stylish black and white decor. Very comfortable rooms all with a/c, fridge, flat screen TV. Restaurant.

A Adelphi Suites, 6 Soi 8, T02-617 5100, www.adelphisuites.com. These swish rooms represent incredible value, coming equipped with stereo, flat screen TV, DVD player, a/c which can be enjoyed from the room's lounge area. There's also a pantry-style kitchen with fridge freezer and hob. For the facilities and price, recommended.

A Bangkok Inn, 12-13 Sukhumvit Soi 11/1, T02-254 4884. Friendly and informative German management, clean, basic rooms, with a/c, TV and attached shower.

A City Lodge, Sukhumvit Soi 9, T02-253 7710, www.amari.com/citylodge. Impressively smart, small hotel with bright rooms and a personal feel. Good discounts available for internet bookings. Trendy **Pasta n Noodles** restaurant (see Eating, page 133).

A Manhattan, 13 Sukhumvit Soi 15, T02-255 0166, www.hotelmanhattan.com. Smart hotel with 3 good, but expensive restaurants, pool. Lacks character but rooms are reliably comfortable. Tours available and tri-weekly cabaret.

A-B Grand Inn Hotel, 2/7-8 Soi 3, T02-254 9021, www.grandinnthailand.com. Recently renovated hotel. The rooms have a slightly hip, modern feel and are comfortable and clean. A/c, TV, fridge and bathtub. Wi-Fi is available at a charge.

A-B Smart Suites, 43/17 Sukhumvit Soi 11, T02-254 6544, www.smartsuites11.com. A boutique hotel suitable for both short and long stays.

B Baan Sukhumvit, 392/38-39 Soi 20, T02-258 5622, www.baansukhumvit.com. Small rooms with imitation dark teak furniture. Good facilities including a/c, TVs and DVD players in all the rooms. Free Wi-Fi. Restaurant downstairs. Weekly and monthly rates available. Friendly staff. Recommended.

B Rajah, 18 Sukhumvit Soi 2, T02-255 0040. Rather dated but ever-popular hotel. Attractive pool, good-value restaurant, travel agents and craft shop. The atrium is reminiscent of the former Eastern bloc. Good value.

B-C Bourbon Street, 29/4-6 Sukhumvit Soi 22 (behind Washington Theatre), T02-259 0328, www.bourbonstbkk.com. A/c, a handful of comfortable carpeted rooms with TV, attached to a good Cajun restaurant.

B-E Hostelling International Centre, Soi 25, T02-259 4900, www.thailandhostel.com.

From dorm rooms to private en suite. All rooms have a/c, TV and fridge. Rooms are rather uninspiring but the location is excellent.

C World Inn, 131 Sukhumvit Soi 7/1, T02-253 5391. Basic rooms with the standard TV, mini-bar and en suite bathroom. Coffee shop with Thai and Western food.

C-D Atlanta, 78 Sukhumvit Soi 2, T02-252 1650, www.theatlantahotel.bizland.com. With personality in abundance the **Atlanta**'s rooms are at best basic, although a/c and family rooms are available. The amazing art deco interior is often used by Thai filmmakers and there's a large pool surrounded by hammocks and sunbeds – a real treat for this price range. A sign above the door requests that "Oiks, lager louts and sex tourists" go elsewhere and staff can be sniffy with late-nighters and rule breakers (there is a long list at reception). Excellent restaurant (see Eating, page 133). Entertaining staff and a magical days-of-yore travellers ambience. Book early. Recommended.

E Sam's Lodge, 28-28/1 Sukhumvit 19 (upstairs), T02-253 6069, www.samslodge. com. Budget accommodation with modern facilities and roof terrace. English-speaking staff. Close to the Skytrain.

Bangkok suburbs *p107*
AL-B Reflections Rooms, 244/2-18 Pradi-pat Rd, T02-270 3344, www.reflections-thai. com. Travellers seeking out an off-beat but truly hip boutique boudoir need look no further. Words can not really do justice to this uber-kitsch creation in the midst of one of Bangkok's more stylish snooty suburbs, so see the website for full glorious details. Each of the 30 quirky rooms was designed independently by 30 guest artists. Themes range from a maharajah's palace to a huge post-industrial loft space. Excellent on-site restaurant serving Thai and Japanese food, cute pool, garden and spa. Ideally located on the Skytrain line and close to Chatuchak.

Downsides include some paper-thin walls and a lack of room service but otherwise service is good. Book early. Recommended.
B-F Greenery House, 260 Soi Ladprao 62 (64), Ladprao Rd, T02-5306 0979, www.greeneryhouse.com. Brilliant serviced apartment complex buried deep in a quiet residential suburb only a 5-min taxi ride from the Suthisan metro station. Apartments/ rooms can be rented nightly or monthly. There's Wi-Fi, a/c, full cable, swimming pool and a gym. It's very friendly and management speak German, French and English. Due to **Greenery**'s location you'll get an authentic slice of Thai life if you stay here – the *sois* in this area are filled with shophouses, great street food and a friendly vibe. Highly recommended.
E Asha Guesthouse, Soi 3 Suttisan Rd, T02-271 1417, www.ashaguesthouse.com. Down a quiet street very near to Chatuchak Market, this family run guesthouse offers a

wealth of facilities for a bargain price including free washing machines and Wi-Fi. There's also a small pool and a gym. Excellent value.

Around Bangkok p108

Damnoen Saduk Floating Market p109
E Ban Suchoke, T032-254 301. The one guesthouse of note here, **Ban Suchoke** offers simple but comfortable bungalows with wooden verandas overlooking the canal.

Nonthaburi p109
B Thai House, 32/4 Moo 8, Tambon Bang Meuang, Bang Yai, T02-903 9611, www.thai house.co.th. The area's most attractive accommodation option, this traditional Thai house by the river provides a picturesque pastoral escape from Bangkok's urban jungle. Rooms are cosy and attractively decorated and prices include breakfast.

🍴 Eating

Bangkok is one of the greatest food cities on earth. You could spend an entire lifetime finding the best places to eat in this city that seems totally obsessed with its tastebuds. The locals will often eat 4 or 5 times a day, each and every one of them able to pinpoint their favourite rice, noodles, *kai yang* (grilled chicken), *moo yang* (grilled pork), *som tam* (spicy papaya salad), *tom yam* (sour, spicy soup) and Chinese eateries. Endless runs of streetfood, steak houses, ice cream parlours, Italian diners, seafood specialists and trendy nouvelle cuisine restaurants vie for your attention. In fact, if you really want to see life as the Thais do, then spend your every waking moment in Bangkok thinking about, finding and eating every conceivable gourmet delight the city has to offer. The Thai capital is fanatical and infatuated with eating.

Many restaurants (especially Thai ones) close early (between 2200 and 2230). most of the more expensive restaurants listed here accept credit cards. Hotels and upmarket restaurants often offer excellent lunchtime buffets. Note that while there are some old timers among Bangkok's hundreds of restaurants, many more have a short life.

Bangkok has a large selection of fine **bakeries**, many attached to hotels like the **Landmark**, **Dusit Thani** and **Oriental**. There are also the generic 'donut' fast-food places although few lovers of bread and pastries would want to lump the 2 together. The bakeries often double as cafés serving coffee, sandwiches and such like. There are also increasing numbers of **coffee bars** such as **Starbucks** and its local equivalent, **Black Canyon Coffee**.

Streetfood can be found across the city and a rice or noodle dish will cost ฿25-40 instead of a minimum of ฿50 in the restaurants. Service is rough and ready and there are unlikely to be menus as most stalls specialize in 1 or 2 dishes only. Judge quality by popularity and don't be afraid to point out what you want if your Thai is lacking. All in all, the experience is quintessential Bangkok and the street is where the majority of locals eat. Some of the best streetfood can be found on the roads between **Silom** and **Surawong Rd**, **Soi Suanphlu** off South Sathorn Rd, down **Soi Somkid**, next to Ploenchit Rd, or opposite, on **Soi Tonson**.

Banglamphu and Khaosan Road
p88, map p90
Travellers' food such as banana pancakes and muesli is available in the guesthouse/travellers' hotel areas (see Sleeping, above). The Thai food along Khaosan Rd is some of the worst and least authentic in town, watered down to suit the tastebuds of unadventurous backpackers. However, head down nearby **Soi Rambutri** and on to **Phra Arthit** and you've suddenly stumbled on a gourmet oasis, one that also stays open a little later than most others in town.
🍴🍴🍴 **Teketei**, 202 Khaosan Rd, same entrance as **Nana Plaza Inn**, T02-629 0173. Open 1130-0100. Stakes its own claim as the only authentic Japanese restaurant on

the Khaosan. Good sushi, sashimi and vegetarian dishes but fairly pricey.

¶¶ D'Rus, Khaosan Rd. Open 0700-2400. A typical big-screen sports and sofas Khaosan place, but the Thai/Western food is decent and cheap and the coffee freshly brewed.

¶¶ Tom Yam Kung, Khaosan Rd (first Soi on the right after **Gulliver's**), T02-629 1818. Open 1500-0200. A real surprise just off the Khaosan, excellent Thai food in romantic surrounds that attracts locals and visitors.

¶¶-¶ Chabad House, 96 Soi Rambutri, Mon-Thu 1000-2200, Fri 1000-1500. For falafel fans who want to take a step up from the Khaosan's undeniably delicious streetstall pitta stuffers, **Chabad** offers fine Israeli food in fantastic surrounds. Kosher shop and bakery also on site.

¶¶-¶ Hemlock, 56 Phra Arthit Rd, T02-282 7507. Open 1730-2330. Probably the pick of the run of cool boutique Thai restaurants on this strip for its mouthwatering menu of Royal Thai dishes alone. The chic interior attracts a glamorous gaggle of off-beat literati from the nearby university.

¶¶-¶ Ricky's Coffee Shop, 22 Phra Arthit Rd. Daily 0800-2400. A civilized spot for breakfast, good coffee or a quick, typically Thai, 1-dish meal. Excellent Thai and Western snack food from cheese and olives to yellow curry. The charming wooden interior and small pavement seating area offer plenty of ambience. Sit upstairs for a view of the efficient chefs and spotless tiny kitchen and take in the framed pictures of Peking in the 1920s.

¶¶-¶ Royal India, 95 Soi Rambutri. Open 1130-2400. Sister branch of the infamous Pahurat branch (see page 131). For some reason the standards aren't quite up to scratch here but the excellent service, presentation and sweet leafy surrounds set back off the street almost make up for it.

¶ Bai Bau, 146 Soi Rambutri. Tasty Thai food in a quiet corner; best bet for a relaxed authentic meal in a friendly environment. Good value.

¶ Kaloang, 2 Sri Ayutthaya Rd, T02-281 9228. 2 dining areas, one on a pier, the other on a boat on the Chao Phraya River, attractive atmosphere, delicious Thai food.

¶ May Kaidee, 117/1 Tanao Rd, Banglamphu, www.maykaidee.com. Open 0800-2300. This tiny, simple vegetarian restaurant is a Khaosan institution. Take the *soi* down by Burger King and it's the 1st on the left. Delicious, cheap Thai vegetarian dishes served at tables on the street. Super-cheap cooking classes also held.

¶ No Name. Down a dead end *soi* off Chakra-pong Rd, after the police station. This non-descript, no frills pizza restaurant only has outdoor seating with tables on the road, but the staff are friendly staff and the pizzas decent.

¶ Roti Mataba, 136 Phra Arthit Rd. Mon-Sat 0700-2100. Unmissable for curry fans, **Roti Mataba**'s tiled chip-shop-style interior is piled high with the circular pancake-type breads, which come stuffed with meat or egg and vegetables or dipped into a range of point-and-choose curry pots. Sweet tooths can finish with a condensed milk or honey topping.

Chinatown *p92, map p90*

The street food in Chinatown is some of the best in Thailand. You'll find everything from fresh lobster through to what can only be described as grilled pig's face. Everything is very cheap so just look for the more popular places and dive in. There are also plenty of restaurants selling highly expensive birds' nest soup (see box, page 535) or, more controversially, shark fin soup. Both of these specialities might be – in both budgetary and culinary terms – out of many visitors' reach.

¶¶ Hua Seng Hong Restaurant, 371-372 Yaowarat Rd, T02-222 0635. The grimy exterior belies the fantastic restaurant within. Dim sum, noodles, duck and grilled pork are all awesome, staff brisk yet efficient. Perfect spot. Highly Recommended.

¶ The Canton House, 530 Yaowarat Rd, T02-221 3335. Hugely popular dim sum canteen set on the main drag. The prices – ฿15 – for a plate of dim sum are legendary and this has to be one of the best value places to eat in town. The food is OK but nothing exceptional while the frenetic,

Food courts

If you want a cheap meal with lots of choice, then a food court is a good place to start. They are often found along with supermarkets and in shopping malls.

Buy coupons and then use these to purchase your food from one of the many stalls – any unused coupons can be redeemed. A single-dish Thai meal like fried rice or noodles should cost around ฿25-30. The more sophisticated shopping malls will have stalls servings a wider geographical range of cuisines including, for example, Japanese and Korean.

There are food courts in the following (and many more) places:

Mah Boon Krong (MBK), Phaya Thai Rd (west of Siam Square, BTS Siam station).
Panthip Plaza, Phetburi Rd.
United Centre Building, 323 Silom Rd (near intersection with Convent Rd, BTS Sala Daeng station).
Central Chitlom Food Loft (see Eating, page 128), Ploenchit Rd (access from Chit Lom BTS station).
Elsewhere you will find more upmarket food courts:
The Emporium, 622 Sukhumvit Rd (corner of Soi 24).
Siam Discovery Centre, Rama 1 Rd (BTS Siam station).
Siam Paragon Rama 1 Rd (access from Siam BTS station).

friendly atmosphere is 100% Chinatown. Recommended.

Siam Square area *p100, map p102*
Siam Sq has a large number of shark's fin soup specialists. Those who are horrified by the manner in which the fins are removed and the way fishing boats are decimating the shark populations of the world should stay clear. Siam Sq also has 2 great noodle shops, side-by-side on Siam Sq Soi 10.

ﾊﾟ **Biscotti**, Four Seasons, 155 Rachdamri Rd, T02-255 5443. Italian 'fusion', a second superb restaurant at this top-class hotel. Very popular, book ahead.

ﾊﾟ **Gianni's**, Soi Tonson. An excellent Italian restaurant in the area with light airy decor and excellent pasta and main courses, not to mention very polished service and a good wine list.

ﾊﾟ **Il Paesano**, 96/7 Soi Tonson (off Soi Langsuan), Ploenchit Rd, T02-252 2834. Italian food in friendly atmosphere. This long-established restaurant has a loyal following and is very popular with *farangs* and Westernized Thais.

ﾊﾟ **L'Espace de l'Oriental**, main floor, Paragon Centre, T02-610 9840, www.mandarin oriental.com. Only in Bangkok can opulent dining take place in a shopping mall. Despite its location, **L'Espace** serves fine international and Thai cuisine.

ﾊﾟ **Ma Maison**, Nailert Park Hotel, 2 Witthayu Rd, T02-253 0123. Mon-Sat lunch and dinner, Sun dinner only. Classic French cuisine from duck Escoffier to wild mushroom soup and great soufflés, set in a traditional Thai teak house. Pricey.

ﾊﾟ **Once Upon a Time**, 32 Phetburi Soi 17 (opposite Panthip Plaza), T02-252 8629. Open Tue-Sun for lunch and dinner. Upmarket and inventive Thai cuisine including seafood soufflé in coconut and more traditional dishes like a delectable duck curry.

ﾊﾟ **Pho**, 2F Alma Link Building, 25 Soi Chitlom. Open daily for lunch and dinner. Supporters claim this place (there are 3 other branches) serves the best Vietnamese food in town even though the owner is not Vietnamese herself. Modern trendy setting, non-smoking area.

Spice Market, Four Seasons,
155 Rachdamri Rd, T02-251 6127. Open
daily for lunch and dinner. Westernized Thai,
typical hotel decoration, some of the city's
best Thai food and an excellent set menu.

Thai on 4, Amari Watergate Hotel, 847
Phetburi Rd, T02-653 9000. Classy, modernist
restaurant on the 4th floor of this hotel. The
food is excellent, pricey for Thai but good
value for a hotel restaurant (the lunchtime
buffet is the best value) with high standards.

Witch's Oyster Bar, 20/10 Ruamrudee
Village. Open 1100-2300. Bangkok's first
and only oyster bar, run by an eccentric
Thai, one of the few places where you
can eat late, good salmon fishcakes,
international cuisine.

Bali, 20/11 Ruamrudee Village, Soi
Ruamrudee, Ploenchit Rd, T02-250 0711.
Mon-Sat lunch and dinner, Sun dinner
only. Authentic Indonesian food, friendly
proprietress and a charming old-style
house with garden.

Ban Khun Mae, Siam Sq Soi 8/9,
T02-265 84112. Good Thai food and
friendly service in stylish surroundings.

Barn Khanittha, Ruamrudee Rd.
Beautifully designed Thai restaurant
particularly well known for dishes
made with soft-shelled crabs.

China, 231/3 Rachdamri Soi Sarasin.
Bangkok's oldest Chinese restaurant,
serving a full range of Chinese cuisine.

FABB Fashion Cafe, ground floor, Mercury
Tower, 540 Ploenchit Rd. Don't be put off by
the name, this international restaurant serves
well-priced Italian-meets-Thai food to high-
society Thais in swanky surrounds.

Kobune, 3rd floor, Mahboonkhrong (MBK)
Centre, Rama 1 Rd. Japanese, sushi bar and
tables, very good value.

Neil's Tavern, 58/4 Soi Ruanrudee,
Ploenchit Rd, T02-256 6875. Mon-Sat
1130-1400, 1730-2230. International
food, very popular with great steaks and
named after Neil Armstrong – it opened
the day he stepped on the moon. There's
another branch at 24 Sukhumvit Soi 21.

Peppers, 99/14 Soi Langsuan, T02-254
7355. Mon-Sat 1000-1700. Small restaurant
with just 20 seats serving home-cooked
Italian food and international dishes, friendly
atmosphere, wholesome, tasty food. Great
for a lunch stop.

Vito's Spaghetteria, Basement, Gaysorn
Plaza, Ploenchit Rd (next to **Le Meridien
Hotel**). Bright pasta bar, make up your own
dish by combining 10 types of pasta with
12 sauces and 29 fresh condiments, smallish
servings but good for quick lunches.

Whole Earth, 93/3 Soi Langsuan, Ploenchit
Rd. Open daily for lunch and dinner. Bangkok's
best-known vegetarian restaurant. A bit of a
stick in the mud compared to its newer
competition but it still has its charms. Good
Thai classics minus the meat and somewhat
worthy, if healthy takes on Indian familiars.

Central Chitlom Food Loft, Central
shopping Centre Chitlom. Don't be put off
by the shopping centre location, for a 1-stop
food centre/shopping stop **Central Food
Loft** is as stylish as they come. Wonderful
view, chic ambience and fine food from all
over the globe in the multiple concessions,
from sushi to pie and mash.

Hong Kong Noodles, Siam Sq Soi 10.
Usually packed with university students and
serves stupendously good *bamii muu deang
kio kung sai naam* (noodle soup with red
pork and stuffed pasta with shrimp).

Kuaytiaw Rua Khuan Boke, Siam Sq Soi 10.
Very popular. More expensive than most
noodle shops, but worth the extra few baht.

Sanguan Sri, Wireless Rd (diagonally
opposite the British Embassy). Exquisite
Thai food – but open only during the day.

Cafés and bakeries

Au Bon Pain, ground floor, Siam Discovery
Centre, Rama 1 Rd. Excellent bakery and
coffee shop with French pastries, croissants,
muffins, cookies and great sandwiches
as well as salads and some other dishes.

Basket of Plenty, Peninsula Plaza, Rachdamri
Rd (another branch at 66-67 Sukhumvit
Soi 33). Bakery, deli and trendy restaurant,

very good things baked and a classy (though expensive) place for lunch.

La Brioche, Novotel Hotel (ground floor) Siam Sq Soi 6. Good range of French patisseries.

Starbucks, centre of Soi Langsuan. One of the huge takeover chain and terribly over-priced, nevertheless this large branch in a faux-Thai teak house with its own garden, small library and free wireless internet access attracts the creative all-day-on-a-coffee crowd and makes for a great city escape.

Silom area *p103, map p104*

There are 4 or 5 Indian restaurants in a row on Sukhumvit Soi 11.

¶¶¶ Angelini, Shangri-La Hotel, 89 Soi Wat Suan Plu, T02-236 7777. Open 1130-late. One of the most popular Italian restaurants in town – a lively place with open kitchens, pizza oven and the usual range of dishes. Menu could be more imaginative.

¶¶¶ Anna's Café, 118 Silom Soi Sala Daeng, www.annascafes.com. Daily 1100-2200. Great Thai-cum-fusion restaurant in a villa off Silom Rd named after Anna of *King & I* fame. Some classic Thai dishes like *larb*, *nua yaang* and *som tam* along with fusion dishes and Western desserts such as apple crumble and banoffee pie. Nice outdoor eating area.

¶¶¶ Bua Restaurant, Convent Rd (off Silom Rd). Classy, postmodern Thai restaurant with starched white table linen and cool, mini-malist lines. Refined and immaculately prepared food.

¶¶¶ Bussaracum, 139 Pan Rd (off Silom Rd), T02-266 6312. Changing menu, popular, up-market Thai restaurant with prices to match.

¶¶¶ Cy'an, Metropolitan Hotel, 27 South Sathorn Rd, T02-625 3333, www.metro politan.como.bz. With a menu concocted by one of Asia's leading chefs, Amanda Gale, **Cy'an** is a scintillating dining experience, the like of which is not matched in the entire Thai capital. This is international cuisine of the highest order: the almond-fed serrano ham and Japanese *wagyu* beef are highlights in a stunning menu. Strangely ignored by wealthy Thais, this is a restaurant at the cutting edge of Bangkok eating, miles ahead of the competition.

¶¶¶ The Dome at State Tower, 10555 Silom Rd, T02-624 9555. Dine in ultimate style on top of the city in one of its highest skyscrapers. An array of restaurants to try but the super-stylish **Sirocco** has views, an ambience and a price list that all take the breath away. Well worth splashing out on for a special occasion.

¶¶¶ Eat Me, 1/6 Phipat Soi 2 (off Convent) T02-238 0931. Open 1800-0100. Join Bangkok's creative gourmet crowd at this super-chic art café and restaurant. The stylish interior borrows art from various Bangkok galleries and the fabulous fusion food is about as far from the 'spicy spaghetti' set as you can get. Slightly pricier than your average cool café but worth every mouthwatering baht. Small, leafy outdoor eating area.

¶¶¶ Glow, Metropolitan Hotel, 27 South Sathorn Rd, T02-625 3333, www.metropolitan.como.bz. An organic lunch bar created by Amanda Gale with a constantly evolving menu that has its ever-eager reviewers salivating. Feast on spirulina noodles and tuna sashimi, all washed down with fresh beetroot and ginger juice.

¶¶¶ Le Bouchon, 37/17 Patpong 2, T02-234 9109. Daily 1100-0200. French country cuisine (Provence), family-run, reasonable prices and well patronized by Bangkok's expat French community.

¶¶¶ Le Normandie, Oriental Hotel, see Sleeping, page 120. Mon-Sat open for lunch and dinner and Sun for dinner. **La Normandie** maintains extremely high standards of French cuisine and service (with guest chefs from around the world), jacket and tie required in the evening but the service is still not overbearing – set lunch and dinner menus are the best value.

¶¶¶ Lord Jim's, Oriental Hotel, see Sleeping, page 120. A fine restaurant, offering great views and stunning international food.

¶¶¶ Papa Alfredo's, ground floor, U Chu Liang Building, Rama IV Rd, T02-632 4043. Open for lunch and dinner. Italian café with Sicilian chef, recommended for its ambience, food and the size of the portions.

₩₩₩ Ristorante Sorrento, 66 North Sathorn Rd (next to the **Evergreen Laurel Hotel**), T02-234 9841. Excellent Italian food along with imported steaks.

₩₩₩ Thaniya Garden Restaurant, Thaniya Plaza, 3rd floor, Room 333-335, 52 Silom Rd, T02-231 2201. Mon-Sat 1100-2200. Excellent Thai food and enormous portions.

₩₩₩ Trader Vic's, Marriott Bangkok Resort, 257/1-3 Charoen Nakorn Rd, T02-476 0021. Open 1200-1400, 1800-2230. Bangkok's only restaurant serving Polynesian food, which is seafood based and takes inspiration from Chinese culinary traditions.

₩₩₩ Vertigo, 61st floor, The Banyan Tree Hotel, 21/100 South Sathorn Rd, T02-679 1200. As the name suggests this stunningly located restaurant commands some dizzying views which are best seen at sunset. The excellent service and elegantly presented food can occasionally be a bit 'style over substance' for these prices. Also see the **Moon Bar**, in Bars and clubs, page 135.

₩₩₩ Zanotti, Sala Daeng, Soi 2 (off Silom Rd), T02-636 0002. Open daily for lunch and dinner. Extremely popular, sophisticated restaurant serving authentic Italian cuisine including wonderful Italian breads and salads, pizzas, risotto and exceptional pasta dishes.

₩₩₩-₩₩ Kio Lio Nang, 152/6-7 Silom Rd, T02-635 6536. Open from lunch until 0500. This excellent Chinese restaurant is popular with Mandarin speaking patrons, although menus are also available in English.

₩₩ Banana Leaf, Silom Complex, basement, Silom Rd, T02-321 3124. Excellent Thai restaurant with some unusual dishes, including *kai manaaw* (chicken in lime sauce), *nam tok muu* (spicy pork salad, Isaan style) and fresh spring rolls 'Banana Leaf', along with excellent and classic *larb kai* (dishes such as minced chicken Isaan style). Booking recommended for lunch.

₩₩ Ban Krua, 29/1 Sala Daeng Soi 1, Silom Rd. Simple decor, friendly atmosphere, a/c room, traditional Thai food.

₩₩ The Barbican, 9/4-5 Soi Thaniya, Thaniya Plaza, Silom Rd, T02-234 3590. Open 1100-0200. Chic café-bistro in this stylish expat pub with duck, steaks, sophisticated sandwiches and fish. DJ on Thu, Fri and Sat evenings.

₩₩ Batavia, 1/2 Convent Rd, T02-266 7164. 'Imported' Indonesian chefs, good classic dishes like saté, *gado-gado* (vegetable with peanut sauce and rice) and *ayam goreng* (deep-fried chicken).

₩₩ Bobby's Arms, 2nd floor, car park building, Patpong 2 Rd, T02-233 6828. English pub and grill, open 1100-0100 with jazz on Sun from 2000. Roast beef, fish and chips, pies and mixed grill.

₩₩ Celadon, Sukhothai Hotel, 13/3 South Sathorn Rd, T02-287 0222. Exceptional contemporary Thai cuisine in stunning classical surrounds – one of the finest dining options in town. Booking highly recommended.

₩₩ Gallery Café, 1293-1295 Charoen Krung Rd, T02-234 0053. Reasonable Thai food in an artistic environment extending over 4 floors.

₩₩ Himali Cha Cha, 1229/11 Charoen Krung, T02-235 1569. Good choice of Indian cuisine, mountainous meals for the very hungry, originally set up by Cha Cha and now run by his son – "from generation to generation" as it is quaintly put. Another branch on Soi Convent, across the road from Patpong.

₩₩ Indian Hut, 311-2-5 Surawong Rd (opposite the **Manohra Hotel**), T02-237 8812. Long-standing and resolutely popular north Indian restaurant; well priced, good service.

₩₩ Just One, 58 Soi Ngam Duphli, T02-679 7932. Outside seating under a huge tree lit with fairy lights. Mix of Thai and *farang* customers nibble on Thai dishes. Raw prawns 'cooked' in lime and garlic is a speciality.

₩₩ Le Basil, Silom Complex, basement, Silom Rd, T02-231 3114. Recommended. Favourite among Bangkok's expat population. Serves some of the best Vietnamese food in the city.

₩₩ Le Café de Paris, Patpong 2 Rd, T02-237 2776. Open for lunch and dinner, daily. Traditional French food from steaks to pâté.

⑪ Sara Jane's, 55/21 Narathiwat Ratchana-kharin Rd, Sathorn, T02-679 3338. Great Thai salad and good duck. The Isaan food is yummy – excellent value. Very foreigner friendly, this is a fine place for finding your Thai-food 'feet', before heading out to sample the street food. Another branch in the Sindhorn Building at 130-132 Witthaya Rd.

⑪ Side Walk, 855/2 Silom Rd (opposite Central Dept Store). Grilled specialities, also serves French food.

⑪ Silom Village. There are several excellent Thai restaurants in this shopping mall, on Silom Rd (north side, opposite Pan Rd), excellent range of food from hundreds of stalls, all cooked in front of you, enjoyable village atmosphere.

⑪ Sweet Basil, 1 Silom Soi Srivieng (opposite Bangkok Christian College), T02-238 3088. Open daily for lunch and dinner. Vietnamese food in an attractive 1930s house with live music.

⑪ Three On Convent, 3 Convent Rd, T02-233 6721. Much of the cooking at this restaurant is done on a BBQ in a partially enclosed patio. An indoor eating area, similar to a country inn is also available. International food of a good quality although desserts aren't up to much.

⑪ Whole Earth, 71 Sukhumvit Soi 26, T02-258 4900. Open daily for lunch and dinner. Slightly swisher of the 2 Whole Earth vegetarian restaurants (the other branch is on Soi Langsuan). Both offer the same eclectic menu from Thai to Indian dishes, live music, *lassis* and coffee.

⑨ Banana House, Silom Rd/Thaniya Rd, 2nd floor, T02-234 9967. Very good and reasonably priced Thai food; few tourists here but lots of locals.

⑨ Royal India, 392/1 Chakraphet Rd, Pahurat, T02-221 6565. A little off the beaten track in Little India (Pahurat) but this infamous restaurant is well worth seeking out. A favourite haunt of Thai politicians and expats, Royal India serves delicious Indian dishes and thalis in simple red-brick surrounds.

⑨ Tamil Nadu, 5/1 Silom Soi (Tambisa) 11, T02-235 6336. Good, but limited South

Indian menu, cheap and filling, *dosas* are recommended.

Cafés and bakeries

The Authors' Lounge, Oriental Hotel, see Sleeping, page 120. Classy and relaxed atmosphere with impeccable service. For an extravagant treat, the high tea is unmissable.

Dusit Thani Hotel library, Rama IV Rd. For afternoon tea go to sip a cuppa in the Dusit's hushed 'library'.

Folies, 309/3 Soi Nang Linchee (Yannawa) off south end of Soi Ngam Duphli, T02-286 9786, www.folies.net. French expats and bake-o-philes maintain this bakery makes the most authentic pastries and breads in town. Coffee available, a great place to sit, eat and read.

Harmonique, 22 Charoen Krung, T02-237 8175 Small, elegant coffee shop with good music, fruit drinks and coffee, great atmosphere.

Sukhumvit Road *p106, map p106*

Nana is also known as 'Little Arabia' for its plethora of Middle Eastern and Muslim eateries. Only a few of these places sell alcohol but sheesha cafés (often in upstairs lounges) are plentiful and generally welcoming. For vegetarian food, see **Atlanta Hotel**, page 123 and Govinda, page 133.

⑪⑪ Basil, Sheraton Grande Sukhumvit, T02-653 0333. One of the best Thai fine-dining experiences in town. Legendary for its durian cheesecake – a gentle introduction to the complexities of enjoying this bizarre fruit.

⑪⑪ Beccassine, Sukhumvit, Soi Sawatdee. English and French home cooking.

⑪⑪ Bed Supper Club, 26 Sukhumvit Soi 11, T02-651 3537, www.bedsupperclub.com. Daily 2000-0200. Fabulous futuristic inter-national dining at its most upliftingly laid back (see Bars and clubs, page 137). Recline and dine on comfy padded platforms filled with plump cushions, funky beats and beautiful people. The food is exceptional too, and prices reflect this. Make early bookings for weekends/holidays and be on time. Bring a passport as ID for entry.

Kuppa 39, Sukhumvit Soi 16, T02-663 0495. Closed Mon. Coffee house with pale-wood interior and an upstairs art gallery. An expensive range of Thai and international dishes. Attracts a distinctly fashionable Thai crowd. Also has a trendy cookery school.

Le Banyan, 59 Sukhumvit Soi 8, T02-253 5556. Mon-Sat dinner only. Classic French food from foie gras to crêpes suzette, expensive with tougher dress code than most places. Highly regarded food, but a bit stuffy.

Les Nymphéas, Imperial Queen's Park Hotel, Sukhumvit Soi 22, T02-261 9000. An excellent restaurant (the interior theme is Monet's *Waterlillies* – hence the name) in an over-large and inconveniently located (unless you are staying here!) hotel. But don't be put off, it serves probably the best 'modern' French cuisine in Bangkok.

L'Opera, 55 Sukhumvit Soi 39, T02-258 5606. Italian restaurant with Italian manager, conservatory, good food (excellent salted baked fish), professional service, lively atmosphere, popular, booking essential.

Rang Mahal, Rembrandt Hotel, Sukhumvit Soi 18, T02-261 7107. Some of the finest Indian food in town, award-winning and very popular with the Indian community. Spectacular views from the rooftop position, sophisticated, elegant and expensive.

Rossini, Sheraton Grande Sukhumvit, Sukhumvit Rd, T02-653 0333. This hotel-based Italian restaurant is open for lunch and dinner. A tantalizing array of dishes and excellent bread. One of the best Italian places in town. Consistently excellent.

Seafood Market, Sukhumvit Soi 24, www.seafood.co.th. A deservedly famous restaurant which serves a huge range of seafood: "if it swims we have it". Choose your seafood and have it cooked to your own specifications.

Akbar, 1/4 Sukhumvit Soi 3, T02-253 3479. Open for lunch and dinner. Indian, Pakistani and Arabic. This is one of the first Indian restaurants to open outside the Pahurat enclave; food is pretty standard.

Bane Lao, Naphasup Ya-ak I, off Sukhumvit Soi 36 (it is No 49), T02-258 6096. Laotian open-air restaurant offering haphazard but friendly service and some good food. Popular, so best to book – especially at weekends.

Barn Khanittha, Sukhumvit Soi 23. The original branch of this popular Thai restaurant. Recently renovated it attracts clients of all nationalities – the food is of a consistently high standard and service is excellent.

Bei Otto, 1 Sukhumvit Soi 20, T02-262 0892. Thailand's best-known German restaurant, sausages made on the premises, good provincial food, large helpings, attached deli next door for takeaway. Also males very good pastries, breads and cakes.

Bourbon Street, 29/4-6 Sukhumvit Soi 22 (behind Washington Theatre), T02-259 4317. Open 0600-2400. Cajun specialities including gumbo, jambalaya and red fish, along with steaks, Mexican dishes (Mexican buffet every Tue) and pecan pie, served in a/c restaurant with central bar – good for breakfast, excellent pancakes.

Crêpes and Co, 18/1 Sukhumvit Soi 12, T02-653 3990. Open 0900-2400. The name says it all, a really popular place that specializes in crêpes but also serves good salads. Mostly Mediterranean but some local culinary touches, like the *crêpe mussaman* (a Thai-Muslim curry).

Gourmet Gallery, 6/1 Soi Promsri 1, between Sukhumvit Soi 39 and 40, T02-2600603. Interesting interior, with art work for sale, unusual European and American food.

Larry's Dive, 8/3 Sukhumvit Soi 22, T02-663 4563. American bar that bills itself as the 'only private beach restaurant in Bangkok'. Burgers, nachos, ribs, chicken wings.

Le Dalat Indochine, 47/1 Sukhumvit Soi 23, T02-661 7967. Open daily for lunch and dinner. Reputed to serve the best Vietnamese food in Bangkok. Not only is the food good, but the ambience is satisfying too.

Lemon Grass, 5/1 Sukhumvit Soi 24, T02-258 8637. Open daily for lunch and dinner. Thai food and Thai-style house. Recommended and popular, so best to book.

Mrs Balbir's, 155/18 Sukhumvit Soi 11, T02-253 2281, www.mrsbalbir.com. North Indian food orchestrated by Mrs Balbir, a Malay-Indian, serving succulent chicken dishes. Also runs cookery classes.

Nasir al-Masri, 4-6 Sukhumvit Soi Nana Nua, T02-253 5582. Reputedly the best Arabic food in Bangkok, falafel, tabhouleh, hummus, frequented by large numbers of Arabs who come to Sayed Saad Qutub Nasir for a taste of home.

Señor Pico, Rembrandt Hotel, 18 Sukhumvit Rd, T02-261 7100. Daily 1700-0100. Pseudo-Mexican decor, large, rather uncosy restaurant, average cuisine, live music.

Tapas Café, 1/25 Soi 11, T02-651 2947, www.tapasiarestaurants.com. Stylishly converted townhouse serving excellent tapas. Attentive staff, happy hour 1700-1900.

Ambassador Food Centre, Ambassador Hotel, Sukhumvit Rd. A vast self-service, upmarket hawkers' centre with a large selection of Asian foods at reasonable prices: Thai, Chinese, Japanese, Vietnamese, etc.

Cabbages and Condoms, Sukhumvit Soi 12 (around 400 m down the *soi*). Population and Community Development Association (PDA) restaurant so all proceeds go to this charity, eat rice in the Condom Room, drink in the Vasectomy Room, good *tom yam khung* and honey-roast chicken, curries all rather similar, good value. Very attractive courtyard area decorated with fairy lights.

Govinda, 6/5/6 Sukhumvit Soi 22. T02-663 4970. Vegetarian restaurant serving a range of excellent pizzas, risottos and salads created by an Italian chef serving up plenty of 'fake' meat substitutes. Attractive outdoor seating area.

New Korea, 41/1 Soi Chuam Rewang, Sukhumvit Sois 15-19. Excellent Korean food in small restaurant.

Pasta n Noodles, attached to **City Lodge**, Sukhumvit Soi 9. A trendy Italian and Thai restaurant, a/c, spotless open-plan kitchen.

The Restaurant, Atlanta Hotel, see Sleeping, page 123. Excellent Thai food in fantastically quirky surrounds. The highlight is the 1930s art deco interior, but don't expect tablecloths and candelabra – it's more about rickety tables and lively entertainment from the Fawlty Towers-style staff. Still, the food is great with some excellent vegetarian options.

Wannakarm, 98 Sukhumvit Soi 23, T02-259 6499. Well-established, very Thai restaurant, grim decor, no English spoken, but rated food.

Cafés and bakeries

The Bakery Landmark Hotel, 138 Sukhumvit Rd. Popular with expats, wide range of breads and fine cakes.

Cheesecake House, 69/2 Ekamai Soi 22. Rather out of town for most tourists but patronized enthusiastically by the city's large Sukhumvit-based expat population. As the name suggests, cheesecakes of all descriptions are a speciality.

Around Bangkok *p108*

Chachoengsao *p112*

The best restaurants in town are along Marupong Rd, which runs along the bank of the river. Specialities are prawn (this is a centre of production) and fish dishes. The **Koong Nang Restaurant** is one of the best known.

⬤ Bars and clubs

Bangkok's raunchy nightlife took a bit of a plunge when the former PM Thaksin Shinawatra introduced a midnight closing time, which is still largely enforced; extended licence clubs also still adhere to the 0200 curfew. A noise pollution law also prevents loud nightclubs, bars and karaokes from pumping out late-night sounds. Couple this with the (now less frequent) forced urine testing that goes on at some nightspots – special police units arrive and take urine tests from all guests in the search for drug use, a process that takes all night, leading to arrests and clubs being closed – and Bangkok is losing its reputation as Asia's hottest nightlife destination.

Don't let this put you off too much. Thais love to party and have just juggled their love of food and fun accordingly, combining the 2 into earlier nights out and more subdued after-hours' drinking. The city also has plenty of fantastic venues – everything from boozy pubs through to uber-trendy clubs. You can listen to decent jazz and blues or get into the achingly hip Thai indie scene or even hear local and big-name overseas DJs spinning the hippest beats.

The best source of all Bangkok nightlife knowledge can be found at www.bangkok recorder.com, the city's sassiest online listings magazines. Also check Bangkok listing magazines and newspapers (especially on Fri) for the latest information on who's spinning and what's opening. Groovy Map's *Bangkok by Night* (฿120) includes information on bars and dance clubs, the city's gay scene, as well as music venues and drinking spots.

Note ID is required for entry into all official nightclubs; carry a photocopy (preferably colour and laminated) at all times.

Old City *p82, map p90*
Boh, Tha Tien, Chao Phraya Express Boat Pier, Maharat Rd. Open 1900-2400. A popular student hang-out with good sunset views over Wat Arun.

Banglamphu and Khaosan Road
p88, map p90
Ad-Here, 13 Samsen Rd. Turn right at the temple end of Khaosan, walk for 10 mins and eventually you'll stumble across one of Bangkok's worst-kept secrets with saxophone sounds drifting out onto the pavement. This tiny place packs in magical live blues bands and a lively crowd of all ages and nationalities. Open all day but the bands arrive around 2200.

Brick Bar at Buddy Lodge, 265 Khaosan Rd, T02-629 4477. A relatively recently refurbished upmarket and pleasant venue overlooking Khaosan Rd, competitive prices and a mixed crowd of travellers and hip young locals looking to test out their English skills. Worth a trip, great live bands at night, open all day.
Café Democ, 78 Rachdamnern Klang. A happy hop and a skip from the Khaosan and sitting right under the shadow of the Democracy monument sits this trendy little bijou bar with its fun, fashionable clientele. The turntables turn one corner into an oft impromptu dance floor but look out for special events featuring familiar guest DJs. Wannabe DJs should head here on Tue when the cheeky 'Club Professionals' nights offer everyone a 5-set slot.
Cinnamon Bar, 106 Rambuttri Rd, T02-629 4075. Look for the water feature from the main road. Chic modern interior using glass and steel. Bar and club, the cocktails do the trick.
Gazebo, 44 Chakrapong Rd, T02-629 0705. Open 2000-late. A venue popular with both Thais and *farangs*. Roof top setting complete with (over-priced) Arabic sheesha pipes, soft, languid furnishings, and home to reasonable live bands. The indoor area plays more up-beat dance music. Friendly, relatively relaxed and hugely popular with young Thais.
Lava Club, 249 Khaosan Rd, T02-281 6565. Open 2000-0100. Playing the ubiquitous Bangkok mixture of hip-hop and house, this large cavernous and slightly scary venue looks not unlike a heavy metal club, decked out as it is in nothing but black with red lava running down the walls and floors. Lots of skimpily attired women, baggy-clothed boys and badly attired travellers.
Silk Bar, 129-131 Khaosan Rd, T02-281 9981. The wide decked terrace is a great place to sit and people watch. Live DJs in the evenings.
Susie's Pub, turn right between **Lava Club** and **Lek GH**. Open 2000-0200. This is the place for a more alternative Thai experience than clubbing down Khaosan; it's always

heaving, more with locals than travellers. Top decibel thumping local tunes and all sorts of flashing neon outside announce its presence, but while it might be easy to find, it's not always so simple to get in, as there's a seething mass of bodies to negotiate from relatively early on right up until closing.

Gay and lesbian

See also the Gay and lesbian section in Essentials, page 58.

Dog Days, 100/2-6 Phra Arthit Rd, Banglamphu. Cute art-bar serving a limited menu of decent food and drinks. Open daily 1000-1500, 1700-2400. A favourite of *tom-dees* (lesbians).

Golden Mount and around *p88, map p90*

Saxophone, 3/8 Victory Monument, Phayathai Rd. Open 1800-0300. **Saxophone** has a long-standing and well-deserved reputation for delivering live music. Great food and ambience, get there early for decent seats or join the dancing masses round the band. The nightly alternating house bands include jazz, blues, reggae and soul players, along with local ska sweethearts (and Glastonbury aficionados) T-Bone.

Siam Square area *p100, map p102*

Royal City Av is where Bangkok comes to party. The huge strip of glamorously fashionable bars stretches as far as the eye can see and is packed with a young and sassily attired crowd every night of the week. Bring your passport as ID, buy your bottle and mixers Thai style and settle in for prime people-watching opportunities.

Club Astra, Royal City Av (RCA), between Phetburi and Rama IX roads, T02-622 2572, www.club-astra.com. **Astra** took the local club scene by storm when it arrived in 2005 and it has since taken the crown as the hip modern music-lovers' venue of choice. The cavernous interior with its state of the art sound system has been host to a long list of huge-name DJs from breakbeats king Goldie

to Hot Chip. Music-wise anything goes but all stops are pulled out to supply the Bangkok crowd's love of house and hip hop. See the website for details of events.

Silom area *p103, map p104*

Ad Makers, 51 Soi Langsuan, T02-652 0168. A typically Thai pub that attracts a lot of expats and travellers. Excellent atmosphere and live bands in the evenings. The Thai menu is tasty and inexpensive.

Bamboo Bar, Oriental Hotel, see Sleeping, page 120, T02-236 0400. Sun-Thu 1100-0100, Fri-Sat 1100-0200. One of the best jazz venues in Bangkok, classy and cosy with good food and pricey drinks – but worth it if you like your jazz and can take the hit.

Big Echo, 140 Wireless Rd, T02-627 3071. Karaoke fans take note. This swish hotel-sized interior houses hundreds of plush private karaoke rooms serving great food and alcohol. Songs in English, Japanese, Chinese and Thai. Fantastic for parties or groups and an experience not to be missed.

Brown Sugar, 231/20 Sarasin Rd (opposite Lumpini Park). Mon-Fri 1100-0100, Sat and Sun 1700-0200. 5 regular bands play excellent jazz, in these smart swinging surrounds. A great menu of Thai and inter-national food with particularly good goulash. Jazz jam sessions on Sun. The hip **70s Bar** next door attracts a slightly younger, more fashionable crowd, here for the retro sounds.

Met Bar, 27 South Sathorn Rd, T02-625 3333, www.metropolitan.como.bz. Daily 1800-0100. This members- and hotel guests-only bar spins great tunes, serves good cocktails (try a *tomyumtini*) and has an excellent cigar menu.

Moon Bar at Vertigo, 61st floor of the **Banyan Tree Hotel**, 21/100 Sathorn Tai (South) Rd, T02-679 1200. Super-sophisticated roof-top bar with a breathtaking view of Bangkok. The best place for swanky sundown cocktails in the city. See Eating, page 130.

Oriental Hotel, see Sleeping, page 120. A particularly civilized place to have a beer and watch the sun go down is on the veranda, by the banks of the Chao Phraya River. Expensive, but romantic (strict dress code of no backpacks, flip-flops or T-shirts).

V9, 37th floor, **Sofitel Silom**, Silom Rd, T02-238 1991. A wine bar that's a cut above the rest due to its magnificent views, stunning design and startlingly affordable wine list. Good special offers, a menu designed to match the magnificent wine list and a nightly DJ to keep the quaffers in full flow.

Gay and lesbian

See also the Gay and lesbian section in Essentials, page 58. The hub of Bangkok's gay scene can be found on Silom sois 2 and 4, with clubs, bars and restaurants.

Balcony, 86-8 Silom Soi 4. Daily 1700-0200. Cute bar where you can hang out on the terraces watching the action below.

DJ Station, Silom Soi 2, www.dj-station.com. Daily 2200-0200, ฿100 admission. This is the busiest and largest club on a busy *soi*. 3 floors of pumping beats and flamboyant disco. Essential and recommended.

The Expresso, 8/6-8 Silom Soi 2. Daily 2200-0200. Good place to relax, with subdued lights and a lounge atmosphere.

Freeman, Silom Soi 2. Worth seeking out to find one of Bangkok's funniest *katoey* cabarets; it's mostly in Thai but the visual references leave little to the imagination. There's a dance floor on the top floor but it's a little dark and seedy.

Sphinx and Pharoah's, Silom Soi 4. Mon-Thu 1700-0100, Fri 1700-0200, Sat and Sun 1900-0200. Sited at the end of the *soi* this comfy little restaurant serves excellent food, including great *larb*. There's a karaoke bar upstairs.

Telephone, 114/11-13 Silom Soi 4. Daily 1800-0200. Western-style gay bar where phones at the tables allow you to call other guests.

Patpong *p103*

The greatest concentration of bars is to be found in the red-light districts of Patpong (between Silom and Surawong roads). Dancing queens of every gender and sexual preference should head to Silom Soi 4. For more hi-energy beats, the slick pick-up joints and cabaret bars on Silom Soi 2 offer glam surrounds and heaving crowds (See Gay and lesbian bars, above).

Delaney's, opposite Patpong, along Convent Rd. Daily 1100-0200. An Irish pub with draft Guinness from Malaysia (where it is brewed) and a limited menu, good atmosphere and well-patronized by Bangkok's expats – sofas for lounging and reading (upstairs). Limited and predictable menu – beef and Guinness pie, etc.

Music Café, Patpong 1. Open 2000-0200. A large open-plan, clean bar, with bags of atmosphere and frequented mainly by drinkers, rather than dancers.

Noriega's Bar, 106/108 Soi 4, Silom Rd, T02-233 2814. Open 1800-0200. Words like minimalist and Zen spring to mind in this relatively quiet watering hole on an otherwise bustling strip. Live acts on Sat, Sun and Mon nights help cater for the guys, gays and gals this place targets with its promise of booze, broads, bites and blues.

O'Reilly's, corner of Silom and Thaniya. Open 0800-0200. Another themed Irish pub, run by a Thai (Chak) but with all the usual cultural accoutrements – Guinness and Kilkenny, rugby on the satellite, etc.

Radio City, Patpong 1. Open 2000-0100. A must-see for Elvis fans. This airy bar opens right onto the road and is one of the most popular joints in the area. A slightly more mature crowd of both locals and Westerners come to break down the door to see the alternating Elvis impersonators and the fabulous Thai Tom, the local answer to Tom Jones.

Tapas, 114/17 Silom Soi 4, T02-234 4737. A very popular, sophisticated bar with contagious beats and atmosphere. Attracts a friendly mix of expats and locals. The bar upstairs caters for the dancing crowds at the weekends with live drumming sessions and guest DJs.

Sukhumvit Road p106, map p106

The strip of bars that run the length of Sukhumvit Rd are mostly populated by bar girls and their admirers. These watering holes generally pump out bad music and serve awful German food and tepid lager. Delve a bit further into Sukhumvit's *sois* and backstreets and you'll find a happening, urban nightclub scene, the equal of anything in Asia. If you want to indulge in more than just alcohol, take note of the notorious urine tests (see introduction to Bars and clubs, page 133); the nightclubs in this area are particular targets.

Bed Supper Club, 26 Sukhumvit Soi 11, T02-651 3537, www.bedsupperclub.com. Daily 2000-0200. Bangkok's hottest designer nightspot. A futuristic white pod filled with funky beats, awesome cocktails, superb food, groovy designer fittings and hordes of beautiful people. Check the website for the changing nightly music policy and guest DJs.

The Bull's Head, Sukhumvit Soi 33/1, T02-259 4444, www.greatbritishpub.com. Its title as the most authentic British pub in town might not attract every thirsty traveller but its famous comedy nights attract some big-name UK comedians.

Cheap Charlie's, 1 Sukhumvit Soi 11. Open 1500 until very late. Very popular with expats, backpackers and locals. Lively, cheap and unpretentious open-air bar in kitsch faux-tropical surrounds.

Jools Bar, 21/3 Nana Tai, Sukhumvit Soi 4. Open 0900-0100. A favourite watering hole for Brits. Also serves classic English food.

Log Home, Thonglor Soi 18, Sukhumvit 55, T02-714 7810. Formerly **Log Cabin**. A large and vibrant bar well known for its excellent live music and happy hour (1730-1900). The attached eatery is possibly a little too 'travel lodge' for Western patrons' taste.

The Londoner Brew Pub, Basement, UBC II Building, Sukhumvit 33. Open 1100-0200. A large pub, now brewing its English-style ales and as well as selling the usual lagers.

Narcissus, 112 Sukhumvit Soi 23, T02-258 2549. Open 2100-0200. Classy, art deco nightclub. The music here is trance, house and techno and the clientele are office types trying to hold on to their youth.

Q Bar, 34 Sukhumvit Soi 11, T02-252 3274, www.qbarbangkok.com. Housed in a modern building, it is the reincarnation of photographer David Jacobson's bar of the same name in Ho Chi Minh City. Good beats, great drinks menu and sophisticated layout. Despite the name the dance floor often heaves at the weekend and the music policy centres around house, hip-hop and R'n'B. See website for guest DJs and events.

Riva's, Sheraton Grande Sukhumvit Hotel, Sukhumvit Rd. Great jazz, often with leading US performers, makes this one of the best and most sophisticated jazz spots in town. Also serves great food.

Zanzibar, 139 Sukhumvit Soi 11, T02-651 2700. Open 1730-0200. Bistro-style bar/ restaurant with comfortable armchairs and a relaxing atmosphere. Plenty of glass walls, plants and trees give it that half-inside, half-outside feeling. Music is usually chilled jazz and blues and it regularly has live Thai bands.

Gay and lesbian

See also the Gay and lesbian section in Essentials, page 58.

Kitchenette, Duchess Plaza, Sukhumvit Soi 55. Mon-Sat 1700-2400. Chilled bar with an older *tom-dee* (lesbian) scene. Live folk music Fri and Sat.

Bangkok suburbs p107

Club Culture, 346/29 Sri Ayutthaya Rd, T02-653 7216. Popular and successful dance club with many excellent visiting guest DJs playing dubtech, electra and just plain old house. The nearest Skytrain stop is Phayathai.

Parking Toys, Kaset Nawarmin, T02-907 2228 (next to **Neverland**). This long party strip of Thai pubs, bars and clubs offers endless authentic Thai-style entertainment. Keeping a low profile next to the well-signposted **Neverland** is this bijou hidden talent. With a low-key interior filled with retro collectibles and artfully crafted slapdash design, PTs attracts an almost exclusively hip suburban crowd of cultural creative types. The secret is in the music, with owner Khun Wat's fine tuning of Bangkok's best bands who play a mix of modern hits and quirky takes on old-school classics.

Viva Bar, Section 26, Chatuchak Weekend Market. Sat and Sun only. An unmissable Bangkok institution, thirsty shoppers stop at **Viva** for a smoothie in the chi-chi surrounds but by night (1900-2100) the bar becomes a heaving mass of tambourine banging bodies downing bottled beers and icy jugs of margaritas. Consistently brilliant Bangkok bands play to a friendly mixed crowd. Not far from the MRT station.

☻ Entertainment

Bangkok *p82, maps p78, p90, p102, p104 and p106*

Art galleries and cultural centres

Listings of current shows and exhibitions are provided in the monthly *Bangkok Metro*. For films, books and other Anglocentric entertainment, check the local press, especially both *The Bangkok Post* and *The Nation*'s Fri and Sun supplements. Probably the best source of information about the Bangkok/Thai arts scene can be found at www.rama9art.org.

About Café/About Studio, 402-8 Maitri Chit Rd, T02-623 1742. Daily 1900-2400. A creative arts centre buried deep in the heart of Chinatown. You'll find everything from performances through to works hanging in the toilets. There are DJs, a bar, poetry readings, live music and lots of retro furniture.

Alliance Française, 29 South Sathorn Rd. Great place for showcasing French culture and movies.

Bangkok University Art Gallery, 3rd floor, building 9, Kluaynam Thai Campus, Rama IV Rd, T02-671 7526. Daily 0900-1700. Important though tiny space that mainly showcases future stars at the students' shows.

British Council, 254 Chulalongkorn Soi 64 (Siam Sq), T02-6116830.

Chulalongkorn Art Centre, T02-218 2911, 7th floor, Central Library Building, Phayathai Rd, Chulalongkorn University, www.car.chula.ac.th/art. Mon-Fri 0900-1900, Sat 0900-1800. Another important university space, though you'll find more than just student work here, with international artists regularly exhibiting.

Goethe Institute, 18/1 South Sathorn Rd, Soi Atthakan Prasit, T02-287 0942, www.goethe. de/so/ban. Everything from classical music to art exhibitions. International and Thai.

Siam Society, 131 Soi 21/Asoke Sukhumvit, T02-258 3494. Open Tue-Sat. Stages performances of music, dance, and drama; and hosts lectures and exhibitions.

Space Contemporary Art, 582/9 Ekkamai Soi 6, Sukhumvit, T08-1904 6306 (mob). Mon-Sat 1000-1700. Edgy, alternative contemporary art in an unusual gallery space. Hit and miss, but you will often find some unusual work here.

Cinemas

Remember to stand for the national anthem, which is played before every performance.

Bangkok cinemas are on the whole hi-tech, ultra luxurious and a great escape from the heat of the city. Most cinemas have daily showings in English (Thai subtitles) and Thai (English subtitles) at 1200, 1400, 1700, 1915 and 2115, with a 1300 matinee on weekends and holidays. Tickets cost from ฿100, while so-called 'love seats' will set you back upwards of ฿200, and for excessive comfort and waitress snack service opt for the ฿500 VIP seats. Details of showings from English-language newspapers and www.movie seer.com. There are also 2 excellent international film festivals held every year in the city and numerous smaller events/viewings are held by foreign cultural clubs such as the Goethe Institute and Alliance Française.

Easily accessible cinemas with English soundtracks include **Siam Paragon Cineplex**,

Rama I Rd, T02-515 5555; **EGV**, 6th floor, Siam Discovery Centre (Siam Tower), Rama I Rd (opposite Siam Sq), T02-812 9999; **SFX Emporium**, Sukhumvit Soi 24, T02-260 9333; and **SFX Mahboonkrong** (MBK shopping centre), T02-260 9333. The rather old-school **Scala**, Siam Sq Soi 1, T02-251 2861, and nearby **Lido Multiplex**, 256 Rama I Rd, Siam Sq, T02-252 6498, both show regular art movies and world cinema. Bangkok's only independent art house cinema is **House**, www.houserama.com, T02-641 5177.

Kitefighting and takraw

Sanaam Luang, near the Grand Palace, is a good place to sample traditional Thai sports. From late Feb to mid-Apr a traditional Thai Sports Fair is held here. It is possible to watch kite fighting and *takraw* (the only Thai ball game). A *takraw* ball is made of rattan, 12-15 cm in diameter; players hit the ball over a net, using their feet, head, knees and elbows – but not hands – and the ball should not be touched by the same team member twice in succession. Regions of Thailand tend to have their own variations; *sepak takraw* is the competition sport with a nationwide code of rules).

Muay boxing (Thai boxing)

Thai boxing is both a sport and a means of self-defence and was first developed during the Ayutthaya period, 1351-1767. It differs from Western boxing in that contestants are allowed to use almost any part of their body. Traditional music is played during bouts. There are 2 main boxing stadiums in Bangkok: **Lumpini**, T02-251 4303, Rama IV Rd, near Lumpini Park, and **Rachdamnern Stadium**, T02-281 4205, 1 Rachdamnern Rd (near the TAT office). At Lumpini boxing nights are Tue and Fri (1700-2000) and Sat (2030-2400), ฿1500 for a ringside seat, cheaper seats cost ฿500-800. At Rachdamnern Stadium boxing nights are Mon, Wed and Sun (1800-2230) and Sat (1700 and 2230), seats cost ฿500-1500. Bouts can also be seen occasionally at the **National Stadium**, Rama I Rd (Pathuwan)

and at **Hua Mark Stadium**, Khlong Ton Rd, near Ramkhamhaeng University. Or you can just turn on the television – bouts are often televised live, see www.muaythaionline.org.

If you want to learn more about the sport contact the **World Muay Thai Council**, T02-369 2213, www.wmcmuaythai.org.

Thai performing arts

Classical dancing and music is often performed at restaurants after a 'traditional' Thai meal has been served. Many tour companies or travel agents organize these 'cultural evenings'.
College of Dramatic Arts, near the National Theatre, T02-224 1391.
College Siam Thai Classical Dance and Restaurant Theatre, 496 Sukhumvit Rd, between Soi 22 and 24, T02-259 5128. 2 shows per evening at 1930 and 2100.
Joe Louis Puppet Theatre, 1875 Rama IV Rd, T02-252 9683. Office open Mon-Fri 0930-2130, Sat and Sun 0100-2100. Shows daily 1900-2045. Book before 1400. Tickets ฿900, ฿300 for children and free for under 7s. Classical stage productions with beautiful puppets based on traditional Thai masked dancers that magically come to life to tell whimsical tales. Arrive by 1800 to take the cultural tour of the puppet gallery.
National Theatre, Na Phrathat Rd, T02-2214885, for programme. Thai classical dramas, dancing and music on the last Fri of each month at 1730 and periodically on other days.
Patravadi Theatre, Soi Wat Rakhang, Thonburi, T02-412 7287, www.patravadi theatre.com. An open-air theatre with a cutting-edge programme of shows and events including classical and contemporary dance and innovative theatre.
The Thailand Cultural Centre, Thiam Ruam Mit Rd, T02-247 0028 (ext 8 for English), www.thaiculturalcenter.com. Performances from visiting ballet and theatre groups as well as Bangkok Symphony Orchestra and special Thai Productions.

☸ Festivals and events

Bangkok *p82, maps p78, p90, p102, p104 and p106*

See Essentials, page 50 and www.tourism thailand.org for a full calendar of exact dates.

January-February
Bangkok International Film Festival
Talent from both Thailand and overseas compete for the independent cinematic crown, www.bangkokfilm.org.
Red Cross Fair (movable) Held in Amporn Gardens next to the Parliament. Stalls, classical dancing, folk performances, etc.
Chinese New Year (movable) Chinatown's businesses close down, but Chinese temples are packed and dragons roam the packed streets to the sound of a million firecrackers.

March-April
Kite Flying (movable, for 1 month) Every afternoon and evening at Sanaam Luang there is kite fighting.
International Kite Festival (Mar) Kite fighting and demonstrations by kite-flyers take place at Sanaam Luang.
Tattoo Festival (movable, Sat near the last full moon before Songkran) Annual tattoo festival at the Wat Bang Phra temple just outside Nakhon Chaisi. Thousands of devotees come to be tattooed by the monks or to have the their existing tattoos 're-empowered'. A day trip from Bangkok.
Songkran Prepare for a drenching as the city heat gets washed away by a constant flow of water and sacred paste. See Festivals and events in Essentials, page 50. The Khaosan Rd and Patpong/Silom are the places to head/avoid depending on your chaos tolerance levels.

May
Royal Ploughing Ceremony (movable)
This celebrates the official start of the rice-planting season and is held at Sanaam Luang. It is an ancient Brahman ritual and is attended by the king (see page 85).

September
Swan-boat races (movable) Races on the Chao Phraya River.

October
Vegetarian Festival Look out for the yellow flags on foodstalls and in restaurants. Not as colourfully gruesome as the celebrations down south, but just as tasty. Chinatown offers some of the best gourmet opportunities as well as lively street theatre.

November
Loy Krathong A beautiful spectacle as the city's waterways are set alight by a flotilla of magical *krathong's* (floating miniature caskets of candles and incense) to honour the water spirits. Firework displays also take place along the Chao Phraya River.
Golden Mount Fair (movable) Stalls and theatres set up all around the Golden Mount and Wat Saket. Candles are carried in procession to the top of the mount.
Marathon Fortunately this road race takes place at one of the coolest times of year.
Fat Festival Bangkok's biggest independent music festival held by FAT104.5 radio station. This is where the city's hip creatives gather to take in the latest sounds from the region.

December
Trooping of the Colour (movable)
The elite Royal Guards swear allegiance to the king and march past members of the royal family. It is held in the Royal Plaza near the equestrian statue of King Chulalongkorn.
New Year Celebrations (31 Dec) Fireworks at Sanaam Luang and hotels along the river and a mass countdown at Siam Square, Central World Plaza and Silom.

◑ Shopping

Bangkok *p82, maps p78, p90, p102, p104 and p106*

After eating, the next big love for many Bangkok residents is shopping. From energetic all-night flower and fruit markets through to original (and fake) Louis Vuitton, Bangkok has the lot, though branded, Western goods are often cheaper back home. It is also wise to do your shopping at the end of your trip rather than the beginning. That way you'll have had a chance to gauge the real value of things and avoid being overcharged. Most street stalls will try and fleece you, so be prepared to shop around and bargain hard. The traditional street market is now supplemented by other types of shopping. Some arcades target the wealthier shopper, and are dominated by brand-name goods and designer wear. Others are not much more than street side stalls transplanted to an arcade environment. Most department stores are fixed price, though you can still ask for a discount. Shops do not generally open until 1000 or 1100.

Sukhumvit Rd and the *sois* to the north are lined with shops and stalls, especially around the **Ambassador** and **Landmark** hotels. Many tailors and made-to-measure shoe shops are to be found in this area. Higher up on Sukhumvit Rd particularly around Soi 49 are various antique and furnishing shops.

Nancy Chandler's *Map of Bangkok* is the best shopping guide. See Essentials, page 52, for further shopping information.

Antiques

Permission to take antiques out of the country must be obtained from the **Fine Arts Department** on Na Phrathat Rd, T02-221 4817. Shops will often arrange export licences for their customers. Buddha images may not be taken out of the country – although many are.

In Bangkok you will find Chinese porcelain, old Thai paintings, Burmese tapestries, wooden figures, hilltribe art, Thai ceramics and Buddhist art. Be careful of fakes – go to the well-known shops only. Even they, however, have been known to sell fake Khmer sculpture which even the experts find difficult to tell apart from the real thing.

Serious shoppers should consult Robin Brown's *Guide to buying antiques and arts*

and crafts in Thailand (1989, Times Books: Singapore).

Jim Thompson's, Surawong Rd, www.jimthompson.com. A range of antiques, wooden artefacts, furnishings and carpets.

L'Arcadia, 12/2 Sukhumvit Soi 23. Burmese antiques, beds, ceramics, doors, good quality and prices are fair. The affable owner Khun Tum is helpful and informative.

NeOld, 149 Surawong Rd. Good selection of new and old objects, but it's pricey.

Paul's Antiques, 41 Sukhumvit Soi 19 (behind the **Grand Pacific Hotel**). Mostly high-quality furniture from Thailand and Burma (Myanmar).

River City, a shopping complex next to the **Royal Orchid Sheraton Hotel**, houses a large number of the more expensive antique shops and holds monthly auctions, an excellent place to start. Reputable shops here include **Verandah** on the top floor, **The Tomlinson Collection Room** 427-428 and **Acala Room** 312 for Tibetan and Nepalese art.

More antique shops can be found in **Gaysorn Plaza** on Ploenchit Rd (particularly the much celebrated **Triphum** for its well-priced wall hangings) and at the **Jewellery Trade Centre**, 919/1 Silom Rd in the shopping mall on the ground floor called the **Galleria Plaza** or **Silom Galleria**.

Books and maps

Aporia Books, Tanao Rd, Banglamphu. At the bottom of the Khaosan Rd near Burger King this excellent little shop has a well-organized selection of new and second-hand books from literature to religion and philosophy.

Asia Books, 3rd floor of **Emporium Shopping Centre**, Sukhumvit Soi 24. Excellent for books on Asia but less comprehensive than **Kino-kuniya Books**. There are 10 other branches including at 221 Sukhumvit Rd, between Sois 15 and 17; 2nd floor, Peninsula Plaza, Rachdamri Rd; 3rd floor, Thaniya Plaza, Silom Rd; 2nd floor, Times Square, Sukhumvit Rd; and 3rd floor, Central World Plaza, Rachdamri Rd.

Chatuchak Weekend Market (see page 107 and page 146). Second-hand books are available in sections 22 and 25, 1 and 27.

Chulalongkorn University Book Centre, not on campus but in a more convenient location in Siam Sq, next to the British Council. Good for academic, business and travel books.

Dasa Book Café, 710/4 Sukhumvit (between Sois 24 and 26), T02-661 2993. Daily 1000-2100. A bookworm's browsing dream, **Dasa** offers 2 floors of high-quality new and second-hand books, a lovely quiet interior and a coffee shop with some of the best chocolate cake in Bangkok.

Elite Used Books, 593/5 Sukhumvit Rd, near Villa Supermarket and with a branch at 1/2 Sukhumvit Soi Nana Nua (Soi 3). Good range of second-hand books in several languages.

Kinokuniya Books, on the 3rd floor of the Emporium Shopping Centre on Sukhumvit Soi 24 (BTS Phrom Phong Station). Has the best selection of English-language books in town (there is another branch on the 6th floor of the **Isetan Department Store**, Central World Plaza, Rachdamri Rd).

White Lotus, 26 Soi Attakarnprasit, Sathorn Tai Rd, for collectors' books on Southeast Asia and reprints of historical volumes under their own imprint (also available from many other bookshops).

Maps

Asia Books (see above) sells a wide range of street maps and A-Zs. See also Getting around, page 76.

Old Maps and Prints, 4th floor, River City Complex, www.classicmaps.com. Has a wide range of historical carts and engravings, mostly of Asia.

Department stores and shopping malls

Visitors to Bangkok no longer have to suffer the heat of the market stall – the city is fast becoming another Singapore or Hong Kong with shopping malls springing up all over the place. The huge number of department stores and shopping centres feature endless retail, eating and entertainment opportunities. Where else in the world could you find a 'knowledge park' (**Central World Plaza**), aquarium (**Siam Paragon**), 'cultural design centre' (**Emporium**) or water park (**Central Bang Na**) atop a shopping mall?

Central Department Store, linked to the **Central World Plaza** (formerly known as the World Trade Centre) by the Skytrain station at Chitlom. Other outlets are on Silom Rd, Bang Na (north off the Northern bus station), Pinklao (close to the southern bus station) and Chinatown. This is the largest chain of department stores in Bangkok, with an enormous range of top-end Thai and imported goods at fixed prices; credit cards are accepted.

The Emporium, Sukhumvit Soi 24 (directly accessible from BTS Phrom Phong Station). An enormous place, dominated by the **Emporium Department Store** but with many other clothes outlets as well as record and bookshops, designer shops and more. The ground and 1st floors are monopolized by the big names in fashion – **Kenzo**, **Chanel**, **Versace**, are all there – along with some expensive-looking watch and jewellery shops. For the slightly less extravagant there are a number of trendy clothes shops on the 2nd floor, namely **Greyhound** and **Soda**. The 3rd floor has the more prosaic offerings in the way of shops including **Boots the Chemist**. **Exotique Thai** occupies the space between the escalators on the 4th floor. Here you can find a nice selection of decorative items for the home while the 5th floor is dedicated to household goods along with a large food hall.

Mah Boonkhrong Centre (MBK), corner of Phayathai and Rama 1. Long-established, downmarket and packed full of bargains with countless small shops/stalls.

Peninsula Plaza, between the **Hyatt Erawan** and **Regent** hotels, is considered one of the smarter shopping plazas in Bangkok.

Pratunam Market, north along Rachprasong Rd, crossing over Khlong Saensap, at the intersection with Phetburi Rd. Good for fabrics and clothing.

Robinson's, corner of Silom and Rama IV roads, Sukhumvit (near Soi 19) and Rachadapisek roads. A smaller, slightly less upmarket department store than **Central**.

Siam Centre, Rama 1, opposite Siam Sq. Mostly fairly young and funky fashion chain stores including surf/sportswear specialists on the top floor. Plenty of restaurants from fast food to 'boutique' bakeries.

Siam Discovery Centre (Siam Tower), 6 storeys of high-end fashion across the road from Siam Sq and MBK. All the top designers, both Thai and international names, have a presence here.

Siam Paragon, Rama 1 Rd, next to Siam Centre, www.siamparagon.co.th. The latest addition (opened 2006) and the undisputed holder of the title of most ostentatious shopping experience in town. This multi-billion-baht project houses exclusive and high-end retail, dining and entertainment opportunities beyond the dreams even the most die-hard shopaholic. Its endless designer wares from couture to cars could bust the budget of a billionaire. A constant calendar of events and entertainment includes an ocean world, theatre and opera.

Siam Square, at the intersection of Phayathai and Rama I roads. For teenage trendy Western clothing, bags, belts, jewellery, bookshops, some antique shops and American fast-food chains.

Tokyu, MBK Tower on Rama I Rd.

Zen, Central World Plaza, corner of Rama I and Rachdamri roads. Recently relaunched as a 'lifestyle megastore' with a fashionable new image, mostly clothing with some housewares.

Fashion

Bangkok has set its sights on becoming the fashion capital of Southeast Asia and is certainly a bustling centre of creativity when it comes to both cutting-edge home-grown couture and smaller independent labels. The previous government's **Fashion City Project** has raised the bar for major-league players like labels **Greyhound**, **Fly Now** and **Stretsis** while Siam Square, Chatuchack Weekend

Market and even the once-hippy/fake-label haven of the Khaosan Rd all rock with young designers' more daring wares.

Cheap designer wear with meaningless slogans and a surfeit of labels (on the outside) are available just about everywhere and anywhere, and especially in tourist areas like Patpong and Sukhumvit. Imitation Lacoste and other garments are less obviously on display now that the US is pressurizing Thailand to respect intellectual copyright laws but they are still available. Note that the less you pay, the more likely that the dyes will run, shirts will shrink after washing, and buttons will eject themselves at will.

Fly Now, 2nd floor, Gaysorn Plaza, Ploen-chit Rd. Directional but wearable designs blending Thai-style femininity and flair with current Western influences. As seen at London Fashion Week.

Greyhound, 2nd floor, Emporium, Sukhum-vit, www.greyhound.com. Chic streetwear for the modern, style-savvy urban casual, a look the Thais carry off with aplomb.

Issue, 266/10 Siam Sq, Soi 3. Daily 1200-2100. A small boutique making big waves on the international fashion circuit with its cool casual blend of fabulous fabrics, ethnic influences and modern shapes.

Kai Boutique, 187/1 Bangkok Cable Building, Thanon Rachdamri, www.kaiboutique.com. One of Bangkok's longest-standing high-fashion outlets, **Kai Boutique** sells its own effortlessly stylish creations alongside other newer names on the design scene. This flagship store also offers evening wear and cutting edge bridal creations.

Playground!, 818 Soi Thonglor, T02-714 7888, Daily 1030-2400. A vast modern store on this hip city strip which houses a creative cornucopia of design-savvy products from cutting-edge fashion to art books, home-wares, music and magazines. Pricey but inspirational products. Plenty of fashion able eating opportunities on site too.

Sretsis, 2nd floor, Gaysorn Plaza, Ploenchit, www.sretsis.com. A much-loved local label created by a trio of Thai sisters who are the darlings of the design scene. The influences of one of the trio's internship at Marc Jacobs is apparent in these exquisitely feminine yet fantastically funky creations.

Also see shopping malls such as **Siam Paragon**, **Siam Discovery**, **Siam Centre**, **Central**, **Zen** and **Emporium** as well as **Siam Square** for further branches of these boutiques alongside numerous others.

Tailoring services

Bangkok's tailors are skilled at copying anything; either from fashion magazines or from a piece of your own clothing, however aggressive sales methods and below-par results are also not uncommon. Always request at least 2 fittings, inspect the shop's finished garment for stitching quality, ask for a price in writing and pay as small a deposit as possible. Cheap package deals are best avoided. Tailors are concentrated along Silom, Sukhumvit and Ploenchit roads and Gaysorn Sq.

Ambassador & Smart Fashion, 28-28/1 Sukhumvit Soi 19, T02-253 2993, www.ambassadorfashion.com. Bespoke tailors. Free pick-up available from your hotel, T02-255 4516.

N and Y Boutique, 11 Chartered Bank Lane (Oriental Av), near the **Oriental Hotel**. Ladies' tailored clothes.

New Devis Custom Tailors, 179/2 Sukhumvit Rd, Soi 13. Recommended.

Rajawongse, 130 Sukhumvit Rd (near Sukhumvit Soi 4). Recommended.

Furniture and interior design

Between Soi 43 and Soi 45, Sukhumvit Rd, is an area where rattan furniture is sold. For stylish modern furniture visit the shopping mall attached to the **Hilton Hotel** on Witthayu Rd or **Home Place**, a shopping mall on Sukhumvit Soi 55 (Thonglor) at sub-*soi* No13. See also Markets, below.

Corner 43, 487/1-2 Sukhumvit Rd (between Soi 25-27).

Jim Thompson's Factory Outlet, 153 Sukhumvit Soi 93. Daily 0900-1800. Sells Jim Thompson's famous brand of home furnishings at slightly more affordable prices. A short taxi ride from On Nut Skytrain station.

Rattan House, 795-797 Sukhumvit Rd (between Soi 43 and 45).

Siam Discovery Centre (Siam Tower) has some great interior design shops, including **Habitat** and **Anyroom**, on the 4th floor.

Gold and bronzeware

Gold is considerably cheaper than in the USA or Europe; there is a concentration of shops along Yaowarat Rd (Chinatown), mostly selling the yellow 'Asian' gold. Price is determined by weight (its so-called 'baht weight').

Thai bronzeware, or the less elaborate Western designs, are available in Bangkok. There are a number of shops along Charoen Krung, north from Silom Rd, eg **Siam Bronze Factory** at No 1250, also at 714/6-7 Sukhumvit Rd between Sois 26 and 28. The cutlery has become particularly popular and is now even available at the big department stores.

Handicrafts

Cocoon, 3rd floor, Gaysorn Plaza. Here, traditional Thai objects have been trans-formed by altering the design slightly and using bright colours. Great for unusual and fun gifts.

State Handicraft Centre (**Narayana Phand**), 127 Rachdamri Rd, just north of Gaysorn. A good place to view the range of goods that are made around the country. Cheap but generally poor quality.

Suan Lumpini Night Bazaar, across the road from Lumpini Park (which is between Wireless and Ratchdamri roads), is rather contrived but nonetheless has a good range of shops and stalls selling clothes, tourist trinkets, and handicrafts.

Doi Tung (Mae Fah Luang Foundation). Has a large headquarters/wholesale and retail outlet at the Night Bazaar. There is another branch on floor 4 of the Siam Discovery Centre. **Doi Tung** is one of the Royal Initiatives set up by the Princess Mother (the king's mother) to help support and sustain the livelihoods of villagers previously involved in drug crop production. Products include beautiful handwoven fabrics, cushions, rugs, fashions and pottery.

The Thai Craft Museum Shop, top 2 floors of **Gaysorn Plaza**, is a collection of stalls which has a bit more style than Narayana Phand (above) and feels less like a tour bus shopping stop.

Chitralada Shop, Suan Chitralada, Dusit Palace (Ratchawithi Gate). Open 0900-1600. This shop sells products produced under the auspices of 'The Support Foundation of Her Majesty Queen Sirikit', an initiative that encourages rural people to produce original handicrafts indigenous to their region. Silks, basketware, crocheted tablecloths, fashion accessories and toys. The rather strict dress codes of the palace grounds apply (see Sights, page 83). There are also branches at the **Grand Palace** and at **Oriental Plaza**.

Celadon (ceramics)

Distinctive ceramics, originally produced during the Sukhothai period (from the late 13th century) have recently been revived. **Thai Celadon House**, 8/8 Rachdapisek Rd, Sukhumvit Rd (Soi 16), also sells seconds, or from **Narayana Phand** (see above).

Pottery

There are several pottery 'factories' on the left-hand side of the road on the way to the Rose Garden, near Samut Sakhon (see page 109). Also see Koh Kret (page 110).

Woodwork

There are lots of woodworking shops along Worachak Rd where it crosses Khlong Banglamphu. **Bua Thong** is recommended, although the sign is only in Thai. These are good places to buy bracelets, curtain rings and trinkets made from tropical hardwoods.

Jewellery

Thailand has become the world's largest gem-cutting centre and it is an excellent place to buy both gems and jewellery, although not for the uninitiated (see box, oppsite). The best buy of the native precious stones is the sapphire. Modern jewellery is well designed and of a high quality. Always insist on a certificate of authenticity and a receipt.

Ban Mo, on Pahurat Rd, north of Memorial Bridge, is the centre of the gem business although there are shops in all the tourist areas particularly on Silom Rd near the intersection with Surasak Rd, eg **Rama Gems**, 987 Silom Rd. **Uthai Gems**, 28/7 Soi Ruam Rudi, off Ploenchit Rd, just east of Witthayu Rd, is recommended, as is **P Jewellery** (Chantaburi), 9/292 Ramindra Rd, Anusawaree Bangkhan, T02-522 1857.

For Western designs, **Living Extra** and **Yves Joaillier** are to be found on the 3rd floor of the Charn Issara Tower, 942 Rama IV Rd. **Jewellery Trade Centre** (aka Galleria Plaza), next door to the **Holiday Inn Crowne Plaza** on the corner of Silom Rd, and Surasak Rd, contains a number of gem dealers and jewellery shops on the ground floor. **Tabtim Dreams**, at Unit 109, is a good place to buy loose gems.

Markets

The markets in Bangkok are an excellent place to get a real taste of the city: browse, take photographs and pick up bargains. Part of the lifeblood of Bangkok, the encroachment of more organized shops and the effects of the redeveloper's demolition ball are inimical to one of Bangkok's finest traditions, though such is their stronghold that impromptu markets still thrive and multiply on every bare piece of land in the city, however temporary. Below are some of the more established pick of the bunch. Nancy Chandler's *Map of Bangkok*, available from most bookshops, is the most useful guide to the markets of the capital.

Banglamphu Market, Chakrapong and Phra Sumen roads, close to the backpackers' haven of Khaosan Rd. Stalls here sell cheap clothing, shoes, food and household goods.

Chatuchak Weekend Market is the largest and is at Chatuchak Park (see page 107).

Flashlight Market (**Talat Fai Chai**), in the Chinatown area, between Luang and Charoen Krung roads, off Mahachak Rd. Part of the charm of this flea market is its after-dark ambience, enhanced by the fact that shoppers bring their own flashlights as many stalls can't afford lighting. Great for bargain-hunters, the market offers everything secnd hand imaginable, from vintage clothes to unwanted furnishings.

Khaosan Rd Market, close to Banglamphu Market on the infamous backpackers' strip. Much more geared to the needs and desires of the foreign tourist: counterfeit CDs, DVDs designer clothing and footwear, cheap noodles and falafel, rucksacks, leather goods, jewellery, souvenirs and so on. After sunset it steps up a gear in the fashion stakes with students and young designers touting their creative wares. Not necessarily as cheap as other markets but open late (1100-2200) and very convenient.

Nakhon Kasem, known as the **Thieves' Market**, is in the heart of Chinatown, see page 92. It's not what it used to be but aside from the mainstay of hardware items, the market houses a few 'antique' shops selling brassware, old electric fans and wood-carvings (tough bargaining is needed and don't expect everything to be genuine). Fun and fairly frantic.

Naraiphan Shopping Centre and **Narayana Bazaar**, Rachdamri Rd (opposite Central World Plaza). An indoor market/shopping centre affair (concentrated in the basement)

Buying gems and jewellery

More people lose their money through gem and jewellery scams in Thailand than in any other way – 60% of complaints to the Tourism Authority Thailand (TAT) involve gem scams. **DO NOT** fall for any story about gem sales, special holidays, tax breaks – no matter how convincing.

NEVER buy gems from people on the street (or beach) and try not to be taken to a shop by an intermediary. Any unsolicited approach is likely to be a scam. The problem is perceived to be so serious that in some countries Thai embassies are handing out warning leaflets with visas.

Rules of thumb to avoid being cheated: Choose a specialist shop in a relatively prestigious part of town (the TAT will recommend shops).
Note that no shop is authorized by the TAT or by the Thai government; if they claim as much they are lying. It is advisable to buy from shops which are members of the Thai Gem and Jewellery Traders Association.

Avoid touts.
Never be rushed into a purchase.
Do not believe stories about vast profits from reselling gems at home.
Do not agree to have items mailed ('for safety').
If buying a valuable gem, a certificate of identification is a good insurance policy. The Department of Mineral Resources (Rama VI Rd, T02-2461694) and the Asian Institute of Gemological Sciences (919/1 Silom Rd, T02-6743257, www.aigs laboratory.com) will both examine stones and give such certificates.
Compare prices; competition is stiff among the reputable shops; be suspicious of 'bargain' prices.
Ask for a receipt detailing the stone and recording the price.

For more information (and background reading on Thailand) the *Buyer's Guide to Thai Gems and Jewellery*, by John Hoskin can be bought at Asia Books (see page 141). For up-to-date information on all scams in Thailand, visit www.bangkokscams.com.

---

geared to tourists and selling fixed-price clothes, handbags, jewellery shoes, souvenirs, etc.
Or Tor Kor, Kampaengphet Rd, opposite the Weekend Market. One for the foodies, run by the Agricultural Market Organisation (OTK). Offers quality produce including takeaway delights such as locally produced curry pastes, jams and coffee, alongside a gourmet's dream of prepared sweets and savouries to sample. Come hungry.
Pahurat Indian Market (see page 92). A small slice of India in Thailand, with mounds of sarongs, batiks, buttons and bows; venture deep inside the maze of stalls to get a real taste of this market's treasures.

Pak Khlong Market, near the Memorial Bridge. A wholesale market selling fresh produce, orchids and cut flowers. It's an exciting place to visit at night when the place is a hive of activity (see page 92).
Patpong Market, arranged down the middle of Patpong Rd, linking Silom and Surawong roads. Opens at about 1700. Geared to tourists, selling counterfeit CDs and DVDs, handicrafts, T-shirts, leather goods, fake watches. Some welcome additions include such items as binoculars and all-in-one pliers. Bargain hard.
Penang Market, Khlong Toey. This portside market is situated under the expressway close to the railway line. It specializes in electronic equipment from hi-fis to computers, with

a spattering of other goods as well. Watch out for pickpockets. Next door is a market selling specialities from northeast Thailand and a general food market.

Phahonyothin Market, opposite the Northern bus terminal, close to the Weekend Market, is the city's largest plant market.

Pratunam Market, spread over a large area around Rachprarop and Phetburi roads. Famous for cut-price clothing and fabrics. Both indoor and outdoor stalls are a bit soulless but many of the mass-produced tourist items can be found here at much lower prices. Venture behind the outdoor stalls to find a maze of tailors whipping up everything from school uniforms to sequined showgirl/boy creations.

Sampeng Lane (see page 93), close to the Thieves' Market. A particularly busy market packed with stalls specializing in bulk buys of everything from fabric, ceramics, hair accessories and Chinese lanterns, to stationery, arts and crafts materials, clothes and household goods. The atmosphere is chaotic and exciting with plenty of steaming foodstalls. You can also buy individual items.

Stamp Market, Charoen Krung, next to the General Post Office. Open Sun only. Collectors come here to buy or exchange stamps.

Suan Lumpini Night Bazaar, across the road from Lumpini Park. This market has tried to emulate the success of Chiang Mai's night bazaar, and as a consequence is rather contrived. It has become more popular with art students and young designers recently, though, so alongside all the tourist trinkets, handicrafts and upmarket interior shops are some funkier fashion shops and art outlets.

Tewes Market, near the National Library. A photographers' dream; a daily market, selling flowers and plants.

West Silom/Charoen Krung (New Road). Antiques, jewellery, silk, stamps, coins and bronzeware. Stalls set up here at 2100.

Music

CDs and music DVDs can be bought from many stalls in tourist areas, although the choice is fairly limited. Cheap copies are harder to come by these days; as the genuine article is just ฿350-500 for a CD, it makes sense to buy the real McCoy.

CD Warehouse, branches in the Siam Discovery (5th floor), as well as in the Emporium and Central World Plaza. Offers a very good selection of CDs and DVDs as well as listening posts, with both international and local releases and a limited selection of vinyl.

Do Re Me, 274 Siam Sq, at the foot of the Skytrain steps opposite the Siam Centre. This hip little music store is a Bangkok institution. New and more obscure releases abound in every category (aside from Thai). Browsing the piles is welcomed but the owner is a renowned font of all musical knowledge.

Spectacles

Glasses and contact lenses are a good buy in Bangkok and can be made up in 24 hrs. Opticians can be found throughout the city.

Supermarkets

The city is now littered with the Brit-Thai **Tesco Lotus** supermarket chain, although those familiar with the brand may be surprised to see that the budget 'Basics' range features fish sauce rather than baked beans.

Central Department Store (see Department stores and shopping malls, above). Features a well-stocked 'international' supermarket, usually in the basement.

Isetan (Central World Plaza), Rachdamri Rd. Japanese ingredients, has a great bakery.

Villa Supermarket, 595 Sukhumvit Rd, Phrom Phong (and branches elsewhere in town, see www.villamarket.com). Caters for homesick expats and is the best place to go to for imported mainstays such as Marmite or cheese. The branch on Sukhumvit Rd is open 24 hrs and has a wine 'loft' upstairs.

Textiles

See also Handicrafts, above.

Prayer Textile Gallery, 197 Phayathai Rd. Good range of excellent-quality traditional and Laotian textiles.

Silk

Beware of 'bargains', as the silk may have been interwoven with rayon. It is best to stick to the well-known shops unless you know what you are doing. Silk varies greatly in quality. Generally, the heavier the weight the more expensive the fabric. 1-ply is the lightest and cheapest (about ฿200 per m); 4-ply the heaviest and most expensive (about ฿300-400 per m). Silk also comes in 3 grades: grade 1 is the finest and smoothest and comes from the inner part of the cocoon. Finally, there is also 'hard' and 'soft' silk, soft being rather more expensive. Handmade patterned silk, especially *matmii* from the northeast, can be much more expensive than simple, single-coloured industrial silk – well over ฿10,000 per piece. There are several specialist silk shops at the top of Surawong Rd (near Rama IV) and a number of shops along the bottom half of Silom Rd (towards Charoen Krung) and in the Siam Centre on Rama I Rd.

Anita's Thai Silk, 294/4-5 Silom Rd. Slightly more expensive than some, but the extensive range makes it worth a visit.

Cabbages and Condoms (also a restaurant, see page 133) Sukhumvit Soi 12 and Raja Siam, Sukhumvit Soi 23. Village-made silks.

Chatuchak Weekend Market, see page 107, sells lengths from Laos and northeast Thailand.

Home Made (HM) Thai Silk, 45 Sukhumvit Soi 35. Silk is made on the premises, good-quality *matmii* silk.

Jagtar, at 37 Sukhumvit Soi 11. Some lovely silk curtain fabrics as well as cushion covers in unusual shades and other accessories made from silk. Originality means prices are high.

Jim Thompson's, top of Surawong Rd, www.jimthompson.com. Daily 0900-2100. Famous silk shop which is expensive, but has the best selection. See also Jim Thompson's House, page 100.

Khompastr, 52/10 Surawong Rd, near Montien Hotel. Distinctive screen-printed fabric from Hua Hin.

Shinawatra on Sukhumvit Soi 31. Factory (industrial) silk available.

▲ Activities and tours

Bangkok *p82, maps p78, p90, p102, p104 and p106*

Facilities for sports such as badminton, squash or tennis are either available at the 4- and 5-star hotels or are listed in Bangkok's *Yellow Pages* and the monthly publications *Metro* and Bangkok *Timeout*.

Bowling

Bowling has really taken off in the city and bowling alleys are available in almost every shopping centre. You may need to book ahead on weekends.

Cosmo Bowl, 7th floor, Central Rama III, Mon-Fri 1100-0100, Sat and Sun 1000-0200. 36 lanes. Price depends on day and time.

Major Bowl, Central World Plaza, T02-255 6590. Features moonlight bowling sessions with disco lights and luminous balls.

PS Bowl, The Mall, Bangkapi, Lard Prao Rd, T02-734 1329. Mon-Thu 1000-0100, Fri-Sun 1000-0200.

Cookery courses

Blue Elephant, 233 Thanon Sathorn Tai, Bangrak, T02-673 9353, www.blue elephant.com. One of the most famous cooking schools with an innovative menu and beautiful, impeccably equipped surrounds in the former Thai-Chinese Chamber of Commerce. A 1-day course is ฿2800.

May Kaidee, 111 Tanao Rd, T02-281 7137, www.maykaidee.com. A vegetarian restaurant with its own veggie cooking school. At ฿1200 for 10 dishes it's also one of the best budget options.

Mrs Balbir's Cooking School, 155/18 Sukhumvit Soi 11, T02-651 1303, www.mrsbalbir.com. Closed Mon. Individual and group classes held at different venues.

Oriental Hotel, T02-437 6211 (see Sleeping, page 120).Organizes an intensive 4-day course, with different areas of cuisine covered each day, 0900-1200. ฿4000 per class or ฿20,000 for 6 classes. The classes take place in an old teak house on the other bank of the Chao Phraya – student gastronomes are ferried across from the hotel. For US$2500 it is possible to combine the course with staying at the hotel, breakfast and a jet lag massage.

UFM Baking and Cooking School, 593/29-39 Sukhumvit Soi 33, T02-259 0620, www.ufmfc.com. A large well-equipped cookery school with a variety of classes held Mon-Sat, in groups of 4-10.

Wandee's Culinary School, 294/16 Samsen-nai, T02-237 2051, www.wandeethai cooking.com. 5-day, 40-hr course from Mon-Fri for ฿15,900. Successful students emerge with a certificate and reeking faintly of chillies and *nam plaa*.

Diving

Larry's Dive, 8/3 Sukhumvit Soi 22, T02-663 4563, www.larrysdive.com. Attached to the popular Mexican bar and restaurant of the same name. Offers beginners' courses with theory and pool lessons in Bangkok and dive trips to Pattaya.

Golf

Most courses open at 0600 and play continues till dusk but early booking is imperative. Green fees start at roughly ฿500. Weekday green fees are two-thirds or less of the weekend fees. Most also have clubs for hire (as well as shoes) and players are expected to use caddies. See www.thaigolfer.com for advice on courses, equipment and competitions. There are a number of golf practice/driving ranges off New Phetburi and Sukhumvit roads.

Bangpoo Country Club, Km 37 191 Moo 9, Praksa Muang, T02-324 0320, www.bangpoo golf.com. 18-hole course designed by Arnold Palmer; oddly set within an industrial estate on the outskirts of Bangkok.

Muang-Ake, 34 Moo 7, Phahonyothin Rd, Amphoe Muang, Pathum Thani, T02-535 9335. 40 mins from city centre. Club hire. Phone to check regulations for temporary membership. Its sister course next door offers floodlit night golfing.

Royal Dusit, Royal Turf Club, 183 Phitsanulok Rd, T02-281 1330. Small 18-hole course

competing with the racetrack for space; no golf during race days (check the *Bangkok Post* or *Nation*).

Health clubs

Expensive hotels have fitness centres and health clubs, many allow day membership.

California Wow, Liberty Sq, Silom Rd (near corner of Soi Convent), T02-631 1122, www.californiawowx.com. Mon-Sat 0600-0100, Sun 0800-2200. You can't miss this several-storey building with the motivating sounds of its dance and fitness bouncing onto the pavement. It's all about the body beautiful here with everything from glossy hi-tech machines to hot yoga. No pool though. ฿800 for a day pass. Also at Siam Paragon.

Clark Hatch Physical Fitness Centre. 10 outlets throughout the city, see www.clarkhatchthailand.com.

National Stadium Pathumwan, Rama I Rd at the Skytrain's National Stadium stop, T02-215 1535. Gym, tennis courts, soccer and swimming pool. Day passes cost ฿30-100.

Phillip Wain International (women only gyms), 8th floor, Pacific Place, 140 Sukhumvit Rd, T02-254 2544. Mon-Sat 0700-2200.

Horse racing

At the **Royal Turf Club** and **Royal Sports Club** on alternate Sun 1230-1800. Each card usually consists of 10 races. Check newspapers for details. See also Lumpini Park, page 105.

Kite flying

Kites are sold at Sanaam Luang for ฿15-20 on Sun and public holidays from late Feb to mid-April.

Swimming

Department of Physical Education, Rama I Rd (next to Mahboonkrong Shopping Centre). Tue-Fri 1500-1800, Sat and Sun 0900-1800. ฿20 per hr. A reasonably priced and central pool.

SASA International House, north end of Chulalaongkorn University, 254 Soi Chula-longkorn 12, Phayathai Rd, T02-216 3880.

Traditional Thai massage

While a little less arousing than the Patpong-style massage, the traditional Thai massage (*nuat boraan*) is probably more invigorating, using methods similar to those of Shiatsu, reflexology and osteopathic manipulation. It probably has its origins in India and is a form of yoga. It aims to release blocked channels of energy and soothe tired muscles.

The thumbs are used to apply pressure on the 10 main 'lines' of muscles, so both relaxing and invigorating the muscles. Headaches, ankle and knee pains, neck and back problems can all be alleviated through this ancient art (a European visitor to the Siamese court at Ayutthaya 400 years ago noted the practice of Thai massage). Centres of massage can be found in most Thai towns – wats and tourist offices are the best sources of information. In Bangkok, Wat Pho is the best-known centre and murals on the temple buildings' walls help to guide the student. For Thais, this form of massage is as much a spiritual experience as a physical one – hence its association with monasteries and the Buddha (see page 83).

Tennis

Many hotels have courts.
Aree Golf and Tennis, Sukhumvit Soi 26, T02-259 8425. Public courts open daily 0630-2230, ฿120 per hr (0630-1730), ฿170 (1730-2230), 4 courts, racket hire, coaching, food available.
Santisuk Courts, Sukhumvit Soi 38, T02-391 1830. Daily 0700-2200, ฿80-100 per hr, 6 courts, racket hire, cash only.

Theme parks

For **Safari World** and **Siam Water Park**, see page 112.
Dream World, 10 mins' drive from Don Muang Airport at Km 7 on the Rangsit-Ong Kharak Rd, T02-533 1152, www.dream world-th.com. Mon-Fri 1000-1700, Sat and Sun 1000-1900. ฿450. To get there, take bus No 39, 59 or 29 to Rangsit and then a local bus. Fairground fantasy land-cum-historical recreation.

Therapies
Meditation

Also see the *Bangkok Post* and *Nation* newspaper listings for details of courses and meditation events. The website www.dham mathai.org also provides information on meditation centres in Bangkok and beyond.

Wat Bowonniwet in Banglamphu on Phra Sumen Rd (see map, page 90).
Wat Mahathat, T02-222 6011, facing Sanaam Luang. Bangkok's most renowned meditation centre (see page 87). Anyone interested is welcome to attend the daily classes. The centre is located in Khana 5 of the monastery. Classes in English are held on the 2nd and 4th Sat of each month, 1600-1800.
World Fellowship of Buddhists, Sukhumvit Sois 22-24, behind Benjasiri Park, T02-661 1284, www.wfb-hq.org. Contact the centre for details on meditation for Westerners. Practice sessions with talks and sitting/walking meditation in English held every 1st Sun of the month.

Traditional Thai massage

For further information, see page 25. The city overflows with massage services with everything from top-end spas to the somewhat seedier massage parlours. Competition means that even the swankiest of spas often offer great traditional massage at surprisingly low costs, and you're less likely to be propositioned by your masseuse. Other signals of a non-sexual service include the word 'traditional' or 'health' massage on the sign, or a depiction of meridian lines.

Large shopping centres often have reliable traditional massage shops. A tip for the tight-muscled: 'jet' is the polite Thai equivalent of 'ouch!' or try squeaking out a 'bao bao' ('gently'). The following centres offer quality massages by trained practitioners:

The Chi Spa at the Shangri-La Hotel, www.shangri-la.com/bangkok, T02-236 7777. For blow-the-budget-style pampering the Shangri-La's Chi Spa is part of the largest and arguably most attractive hotel on the river and houses what is widely considered to be the finest spa in Bangkok. Inspired by the Himalayan healing arts, the interior instantly casts a magical spell over visitors with its candle-lit niches and wooden screens; the multi-therapy 'journeys' also involve an element of Eastern mysticism that enhance the dreamlike ambience.

Healthlands, 96/1 Sukhumvit Soi 63, Ekamai, T02-392 2233, www.healthlandspa.com. Open 0900-2400. A no-nonsense chain of massage specialists offering what Thais refer to as 'real' massage, opposed to the softly-softly spa equivalent. For connoisseurs of Thai massage or those with slight masochistic tendencies this is the real deal – note the well-developed shoulder muscles of the otherwise tiny masseuses. The 'health' side is taken seriously here but spa treatments are also available. Other branches in Sathorn, Srinakarin, Pinklao and Pattaya.

Ruen Nuad, 42 Soi Convent (off Silom Rd close to the Skytrain exit). Highly recommended bijou boutique spa and massage centre inside a beautiful, peaceful wooden house in the centre of the city. Restaurant/café also on site. Expect to pay a little more than average but the reasonable prices still belie the magical ambience and attention to detail. Thai, aromatherapy and herbal massage.

Wat Pho, T02-221 2974, www.watpho.com (see page 82). The centre is located at the back of the wat, on the opposite side from the entrance. For details, the school offers body massage with or without herbs and foot massage. The service is available from 0800-1700 and costs from ฿250 for a

30-min body massage to ฿350 for a 1-hr body massage with herbal compress. A foot massage is ฿250 for 45 mins. For Westerners wishing to learn the art of traditional Thai massage, special 30-hr courses can be taken for ฿8,500, stretching over either 15 days (2 hrs per day) or 10 days (3 hrs per day). There is also a foot massage course at ฿6,500, 30 hrs over 5 or 10 days.

Yoga

Iyengar Yoga Studio, Sukhumvit Soi 55, www.iyengar-yoga-bangkok.com, T02-714 9924.

Rasayana Retreat, 41/1 Soi Prommitr, Soi Sukhumvit 39, T02-662 48035, www.rasayana retreat.com. A detoxification and rejuve-nation centre offering detox programmes, colonic irrigation, pilates and yoga classes and an excellent raw food café and spa.

Sunee Yoga Centre, 78/4 Rachprarop Rd, T02-245 0269. Mon-Sat 1000-1200, 1700-1900.

Yoga Elements Studio, 23rd floor, Vanissa Building, Soi Chitlom, T02-655 5671, www.yogaelements.com. Vinyassa and Ashtanga yoga and meditation as well as various workshops and a superb standard of guest teachers and speakers from across the globe. The beautifully designed studio commands stunning sunset views of the city. Reduced introductory rates.

Tours and travel agents
City tours

Bangkok has innumerable tour companies that can take visitors virtually anywhere. If there is not a tour to fit your bill – most run the same range of tours – many companies will produce a customized one for you, for a price. Most top hotels have their own tour desk and it is probably easiest to book there (arrange to be picked up from your hotel as part of the deal). Most will also book airline, bus and train tickets and hotel rooms.

The tour itineraries given below are the most popular; prices per person are about ฿400-800 for a half day, ฿1000-2000 for a full day (including lunch).

Half-day tours Grand Palace Tour; Temple Tour to Wat Traimitr, Wat Pho and Wat Benjamabophit; Khlong Tour around the *khlongs* (canals) of Bangkok and Thonburi, to Floating Market, Snake Farm and Wat Arun (mornings only); Old City Tour; Crocodile Farm Tour; Rice Barge and Khlong Tour (afternoons only); Damnoen Saduak Floating Market Tour.

Full-day tours Damnoen Saduak and Rose Garden; Thai Dinner and Classical Dance, eat in traditional Thai surroundings and consume toned-down Thai food, ฿250-300 (1900-2200). Pattaya, the infamous beach resort; River Kwai, a chance to see the famous bridge and war cemeteries, as well as the great *chedi* at Nakhon Pathom; Ayutthaya and Bang Pa In.

Bicycle, bus and walking tours
Amazing Bike Tours/Real Asia, T02-712 9301, www.realasia.net. Fun half-day cycling and walking tours around the city's 'greenbelt' including the less-explored riverside areas of Bang Kra Jao and Phra Padaeng.
Bangkok Tourist Bureau, 17/1 Phra Arthit Rd, under Phra Pinklao Bridge, T02-225 7612, www.bangkoktourist.com. Open 0900-1900. Offers every imaginable tour of Bangkok by river, bike and even bus. Knowledgeable and reliable. Their white booths are found in popular tourist areas and are easy to spot. 2-hr bicycle tours around Rattanakosin Island cover Sanaam Luang, Wat Pho, The Giant Swing, etc.

Boat tours Either book a tour at your hotel, one of the tour operators recommended above, or go to one of the piers and organize your own trip.

The most frequented piers are located between the Oriental Hotel and the Grand Palace or under Taksin Bridge (which marks the end of the Skytrain line). The pier just to the south of the **Royal Orchid Sheraton Hotel** is recommended. Organizing your own trip gives greater freedom to stop and start when the mood takes you. It is best to leave in the morning (0700). For the trip mentioned above under half-day tours

(excluding Wat Rakhang and Wat Suwannaram), the cost for a long-tail which can sit up to 10 people should be about ฿1000 per hr depending on the stops, distance and duration. 2 hrs for ฿2000 is a recommended starting point for a decent trip. If visiting Rakhang and Suwannaram as well as the other sights, expect to pay about another ฿200-300 for the hire of a boat. Be sure to agree the route and cost before setting out.

There are more than 30 boats (in addition to long-tails and regular ferries) offering cruises on the Chao Phraya. The *Ayutthaya Princess* operates from the **Shangri-La Hotel** pier or the **Royal Sheraton** pier. The *Ayutthaya Princess* is a 2-level vessel resembling a royal barge. Leaving at 0800 daily, there are cruises to Bang Pa In, an a/c bus tour around Ayutthaya, returning to Bangkok by coach at 1730. You can also do the reverse: coach to Ayutthaya and then a boat back to Bangkok, arriving at 1730, ฿1550, including buffet lunch on board. Kian Gwan Building, 140 Wireless Rd, T02-255 9200.

Cheaper are the day boat tours to Bang Pa In via Queen Sirikit's handicraft centre at Bang Sai and the stork sanctuary at Wat Phai Lom operated by the **Chao Phraya Express Boat Company**, T02-281 5564. Tours leave on Sun only from the Maharaj and Phra Athit piers at 0800, returning 1800, ฿400. Another company offering a professional cruise service is **Pearl of Siam**, T02-861 0255, www.grandpearlcruis.com, which operates 3 'yachts'. Like other companies, it offers passengers either a bus trip up to Ayutthaya and a cruise down, or vice versa (฿1700). In the evenings the company also offers dinner cruises for ฿1400. **Cruise Asia Ltd**, 133/14 Rajthevee Rd, T02-6401400, www.cruiseasia.net, runs 4- and 7-day trips on the River Kwai on the *RV Kwai*.

Dinner cruises Chao Phraya, T02-541 5599; Loy Nava, T02-437 4932, Tha Siphraya (1800-2000), charming old rice barge. **Wanfah Cruise**, www.cruise-thailand.com. ฿700. **Ayutthaya Princess**, T02-255 9200,

Sun dinner cruises for ฿1200. **Manohra**, www.manohracruises.com, T02-476 0021, a restored rice barge owned by the Bangkok Marriott, offers dinner cruises (1930-2230) and shorter sunset cocktail cruises (1800-1900). Luxury 3-day cruises to Ayutthaya stopping at Ko Kret are also available. A free 15-min river taxi runs from Tha Sathon (close to Saphan Thaksin Skytrain station).

Thailand tours

For further information on travelling by private bus, see page 158.

Asian Trails, 9th floor SG Tower, 161/1 Soi Mahadlek Luang 3, Rajdamri Rd, Lumpini, Pathumwan, T02-626 2000, www.asian trails.net. Specialists in Southeast Asia travel and tours.

Bike and Travel, 802/756 River Park, Moo 12, Kookot, Lamlookka, Prathumthani, 121330, T02-990 0274. A useful website is www.cyclingthailand.com.

Cruise Asia Ltd, 133/14 Ratchaprarop Rd, Makkasan, Rajthevi, 10400, T02-640 1400, www.cruiseasia.net.

Discover Asia, 19/9 Soi Suk Chai, Sukhumvit 42, Prakhanong, Klongtoey, T02-381 7742, www.asiantraveladventures.com. Oct-Jun day trips and longer tours around Thailand's marine parks and islands.

Magic Eyes Chao Phraya Barge Programme, T02-439 4746, www.magic eyes.or.th/barge. A non-profit organization offering educational day- and week-long trips on an antique rice barge for groups interested in exploring the river's history, arts, ecology and culture.

Responsible Ecological and Social Tour (**REST**) project, run by the **Thai Volunteer Services' (TVS)**. One of the best options, TVS is an NGO with links to other upcountry NGOs. People visit and stay in rural villages, go trekking and camping, are shown round local development projects and are encouraged to participate in community activities. See www.responsibletravel.com.

State Railway of Thailand. Organizes day trips to Nakhon Pathom and the bridge over the River Kwai, and to Ayutthaya. Trips run on weekends and holidays. The latter tour leaves Bangkok at 0630 and returns from Ayutthaya by boat along the Chao Phraya River.

Travel agents

For those wishing to travel to Vietnam, Laos, Cambodia and Burma (Myanmar), specialist agents are recommended as they are usually able to arrange visas – for a fee. **Asian Holiday Tour**, 294/8 Phayathai Rd, T02-215 5749. **Asian Trails**, 9th floor SG Tower, 161/1 Soi Mahadlek Luang 3, Rajdamri Rd, T02-626 2000, www.asian trails.net. **Banglamphu Tour Service**, 17 Khaosan Rd, T02-281 3122. **Dee Jai International Travel**, 2nd floor, 491/29 Silom Plaza Building, Silom Rd, T02-234 1685. **Diethelm Travel**, Kian Gwan Building II, 140/1, Witthayu Rd, T02-255 9150, F256 0248. **Dior Tours**, 146-158 Khaosan Rd, T02-282 9142. **East-West**, 46/1 Sukhumvit Soi Nana Nua, T02-253 0681. **Exotissimo**, 21/17 Sukhumvit Soi 4, T02-253 5240, and 755 Silom Rd, T02-235 9196. **Fortune Tours**, 9 Captain Bush Lane, Charoen Krung 30, T02-237 1050. **GM Tour & Travel**, 273 Khaosan Rd, T02-282 3979. One of the more efficient operations, with impartial flight information. **Guest House and Tour**, 46/1 Khaosan Rd, T02-282 3849. **MK Ways**, 57/11 Witthayu Rd, T02-255 5590. **Patco Chiang Mai**, Hualamphong Railway Station tourist office, organizes treks in the north, recommended. **Pawana Tour and Travel**, 72/2 Khaosan Rd, T02-267 8018. **Roong Ruang Tour Travel Centre Co**, 183-185 Samsen Rd, T02-280 1460. **Siam Wings**, 173/1-3 Surawong Rd, T02-253 4757. **Skyline Travel Service**, 491/39-40 Silom Plaza (2nd floor), Silom Rd, T02-233 1864. **St Louis Travel**, 18/7 Soi St Louis 3, Sathorn Tai Rd, T/F02-212 1583. **Thai Travel Service**, 119/4 Surawong Rd, T02-234 9360. **Top Thailand Tour**, 61 Khaosan Rd, T02-280 2251. **Tour East**, Rajapark Building, 10th floor, 163 Asoke Rd, T02-259 3160. **Transindo**, Thasos Building (9th floor), 1675 Chan Rd, T02-287 3241. **Vieng Travel**, branch on the ground floor of the Trang Hotel, 99/8 Wisutkaset Rd, T02-280 3537. **Vista Travel**, 244/4 Khaosan Rd, T02-280 0348. **Western Union**, branch in the foyer of Atlanta Hotel, 78 Sukhumvit Soi 2, T02-255 2151. Good all-round service.

⊖ Transport

Bangkok *p82, maps p78, p90, p102, p104 and p106*

Bangkok lies at the heart of Thailand's transport network. Virtually all trains and buses end up here and it is possible to reach anywhere in the country from the capital. Bangkok is also a regional transport hub, and there are flights to most international destinations. See Essentials, page 34, for international transport. For Getting around Bangkok, see page 76.

Air

The airport website www.bangkokairport online.com, offers excellent up-to-date information on transport services.

When working out your connecting schedule, try to arrange your onward flight from the same airport; you can reach all the same destinations from Suvarnabhumi as you can from Don Muang. Having said that, getting between the new and old airports, while a pain in the rear, is relatively easy: there are regular airport buses and taxis won't cast the earth (฿250-300). The journey can take between 1 hr and 3½ hrs, allow for the longest tranfer time.

Suvarnabhumi International Airport, is around 25 km southeast of the city. There are regular connections to many of the provincial capitals on THAI or any of the budget airlines (see Essentials, page 37). Tickets can also be bought at most travel agents. Bangkok Airways flies to **Koh Samui**, **Hua Hin**, **Phuket**, **Sukhothai**, **Chiang Mai** and **U-Tapao (Pattaya)**.

Don Muang Airport, 25 km north of the city at Don Muang, re-opened in Mar 2007 after Suvarnabhumi replaced it as Bangkok's premium airport in 2006. From here, 3 airlines – **Nok**, **1-2-Go** and **Thai** – fly to a handful of domestic routes. It is worth considering Don Muang as your primary choice for domestic routes as there will be fewer queues, it's easier to transit and connections to the city are just as good. There is a shortage of gates and Suvarnabhumi and you can often find your domestic flight stuck miles down the runway followed by a 10-min bus journey to reach the terminal.

Airline offices Air France, Vorawat Building, 20th floor, 849 Silom Rd, T02-635 1199. **Air India**, SS Building, 10/12-13 Convent Rd, Silom, T02-235 0557. **Air Lanka**, Ground floor, Charn Issara Tower, 942 Rama IV Rd, T02-236 9292. **Alitalia**, SSP Tower 3, 15th floor, Unit 15A, 88 Silom Rd, T02-634 1800. **American Airlines**, 518/5 Ploenchit Rd, T02-251 1393. **Asiana Airlines**, 18th floor, Ploenchit Centre, 2 Sukhumvit 2 Rd, T02-656 8610. **Bangkok Airways**, 99 Mu 14, Vibhavadirangsit Rd, Chom Phon, Chatuchak, T02-265 5678 (ext 1771 for reservations centre), www.bangkokair.com. **British Airways**, 14th floor, Abdulrahim Place, 990 Rama 1V Rd, T02-636 1747. **Canadian Airlines**, 6th floor, Maneeya Building, 518/5 Ploenchit Rd, T02-251 4521. **Cathay Pacific**, 11th floor, Ploenchit Tower, 898 Ploenchit Rd, T02-263 0606. **Continental Airlines**, CP Tower, 313 Silom Rd, T02-231 0113. **Delta Airlines**, 7th floor, Patpong Building, Surawong Rd, T02-237 6838. **Eva Airways**, Green Tower, 2nd floor, 425 Rama IV Rd, opposite Esso Head Office. **Finnair**, 6th floor, Vorawat Building, 849 Silom Rd, T02-635 1234. **Gulf Air**, 12th floor, Maneey Building, 518 Ploenchit Rd, T02-254 7931. **Japan Airlines**, 254/1 Ratchadapisek Rd, T02-692 5151. **KLM**, 19th floor, Thai Wah Tower 11, 21/133-134 South Sathorn Rd, T02-679 1100. **Korean Air**, Ground floor, Kong Bunma Building (opposite Narai Hotel), 699 Silom Rd, T02-635 0465. **Lao Airlines**, 491 17 ground floor, Silom Plaza,

Silom Rd, T02-236 9822. **Lufthansa**, 18th floor, Q-House (Asoke), Sukhumvit Rd Soi 21, T02-264 2400. **MAS (Malaysian Airlines)**, 20th floor, Ploenchit Tower, 898 Ploenchit Rd, T02-263 0565. **Myanmar Airways**, 23rd floor, Jewellery Trade Centre, Silom Rd, T02-630 0334. **PBAir**, T02-261 0220, www.pbair.com. **Qantas**, 14th floor, Abdul-rahim Place, 990 Rama IV Rd, T02-636 1747. **SAS**, 8th floor, Glas Haus I, Sukhumvit Rd Soi 25, T02-260 0444. **Singapore Airlines**, 12th floor, Silom Centre, 2 Silom Rd, T02-236 5295/6. **Swiss**, 21st floor Abdulrahim Place, 990 Rama 1V Rd, T02-636 2160. **THAI**, 485 Silom Rd, T02-234 3100, and 89 Vibhavadi-Rangsit Rd, T02-513 0121. **Vietnam Airlines**, 7th floor, Ploenchit Centre, 2 Sukhumvit 2 Rd, T02-656 9056.

Airport–city transport
Bus From **Suvarnabhumi International Airport**, an a/c **airport bus service** operates every 15 mins, 0500-2400, ฿150 to Silom Rd (service AE1), Khaosan Rd (service AE2), Wireless/Sukhumvit Rd (service AE3) and Hua Lumphong train station (service AE4). Each service stops at between 12 and 20 popular tourist destinations and hotels. The airport offers full details at the stop located outside the Arrivals area on the pavement. Some of the more popular stops on each line are: **Silom service (AE1)**: Pratunam, Central World Plaza, Lumpini Park, Sala Daeng, Patpong, Sofitel Silom. **Khaosan service (AE2)**: Pratuman, Amari Watergate Hotel, Asia Hotel, Royal Princess Hotel, Democracy Monument, Phra Artit, Khaosan Rd. **Wireless Rd service (AE3)**: BTS (Skytrain) On Nut, BTS Thonglor, Rex Hotel, Emporium Shopping Centre Sukhumvit 24, Novotel Sukhumvit, Westin Hotel, Amari Boulevard, Majestic Grande, Central Silom and Nana. **Hua Lumphong service (AE4)**: Victory Monument, BTS On Nut, Asia Hotel Ratcha-thewi, Siam Centre, MBK/National Stadium, Hua Lumphong train station.

Many visitors will see the ฿150 as money well spent (although if there are 3-4 of

you travelling together then a taxi is just as cheap, or cheaper). However, there will still be the hardened few who will opt for the **regular bus service**. This is just as slow as it ever was, 1½-3 hrs (depending on the time of day), prices for a/c buses linking the airport to the city are now a flat rate of ฿35. The public bus station or 'public transportation centre' is linked to the airport by a free shuttle bus service which picks up passengers at the Arrivals area. Public buses are crowded during rush hours and there is little room for luggage. However, the new bus station is well signposted and organized with some English-speaking information services. Local bus services to Pattaya and Nong Khai are also available.

From **Don Muang Airport**, Thai Airways operates a **City Air Terminal bus** from just outside the terminal to Lad Prao metro (0400-2000, every 20 mins); the service is free if you are flying with THAI and takes between 30 mins and 1 hr. Buses to the airport leave from opposite the metro station; you can also check in here, 3 hrs before your flight leaves.

Courtesy car Many upmarket hotels will meet passengers and provide free transport to town. Check before arrival or contact the **Thai Hotels Association** desk in the terminal.

Taxi It takes 30-60 mins to get to central Bangkok from both airports, depending on the time of day, the state of the traffic and how insane the driver is. There is an official taxi booking service in the Arrivals hall. There are 3 sets of taxi/limousine services. First, **airport limos** (before exiting from the restricted area), next **airport taxis** (before exiting from the terminal building), and finally, a **public taxi counter** (outside, on the slipway). The latter are the cheapest. A public taxi to downtown should cost roughly ฿300-400. Note that tolls on the expressways are paid on top of the fare on the meter and should be no more than ฿40 per toll. If taking a metered taxi, the coupon from the booking desk will quote no fare – ensure that the meter is turned on or you may find that the trip costs ฿900 instead of ฿300. There is a ฿50 airport surcharge on top of the meter cost. Keep hold of your coupon – some taxi drivers try to pocket it – as it details the obligations of taxi drivers. Only official taxis are allowed to serve airport visitors and are required to use their meter, but drivers often try to make an opportunistic buck from new arrivals in town. Don't be surprised if your driver decides to feign that he does not know where to go; it's all part of being a new boy/girl in a new town. If in doubt, call your guesthouse or hotel and ask them to speak to the driver. Also be wary of scams like turning the engine off on arrival so that the meter price disappears; politely ask for the engine to be turned on again and it will reappear. Regular airport visitors also recommend going up to the Departures floor and flagging down a taxi that has just dropped passengers off. Doing it unofficially like this this will save you around ฿50 and possibly a long wait in a taxi queue. Secure an agreement to use the meter before you get in – many drivers refuse, in which case you'll have to negotiate a fare.

There have been cases of visitors being robbed in unofficial taxis. To tell whether your vehicle is a registered taxi, check the colour of the number plate. Official airport limousines have green plates, public taxis have yellow plates – a white plate means the vehicle is not registered as a taxi.

Train Construction of a 28-km overhead city rail link between downtown Bangkok and the airport is underway. Travel time between the airport and the city centre is expected to take around 15 mins on the Express service and 27 mins on the Commuter service. Currently scheduled to be completed in 2009, the Commuter service will connect Suvarnabhumi Airport with city air terminals along the East rail track including Phayathai, Ratchaprarop (Skytrain interchange), Makkasan/Asoke (MRT/underground interchange), Ramkam-

haeng, Huamak, Bantubchang and Ladkrabung. The Express service will be a direct MRT link at Makkasan/Asoke station. See the airport website for up-to-date details.

You can still get the old overground train from Don Muang to either Hualamphong in downtown Bangkok or north to Ayutthaya and beyond. It's cheap but very slow and trains are often late.

Bus
Local
A routes map is indispensable. Good maps are available from bookshops as well as hotels, travel agents or tour companies. Major bus stops have maps of routes in English. Also see the **Bangkok Mass Transit Authority (BMTA)** website, www.bmta.co.th, for detailed information on all bus routes and tourist destinations in English and Thai.

The cheapest way to get around town, although more people have their belongings stolen on city buses than almost anywhere else. There is a range of buses, including a/c and non-a/c, micro and expressway. All run 0500-2300, apart from the limited all-night bus service, which runs 2300-0500.

Regular cream and red non-a/c buses cost ฿7; regular non-a/c white and blue buses cost ฿8.50; Expressway cream and red buses cost ฿8.50; cream and blue a/c buses cost ฿10-25 depending on the distance; yellow and orange Euro II buses cost ฿10-30 depending on the distance; night buses cost ฿10. Beware of pickpockets on these often-crowded buses. There are also smaller a/c minibuses which follow the same routes but are generally faster and less crowded because officially they are only meant to let passengers aboard if a seat is vacant. They charge ฿15-30, but their signs are often in Thai only.

Long distance
For bus routes and fares, see page 39. There are 3 main bus stations in Bangkok.

The **Northern bus terminal** (also known as Mo Chit Mai, New Mo Chit or Mo

Khao San Road Mystery Tours

More than one traveller has been duped by the mystery rogue bus journeys sold by the travel agents along Khao San Road which lure customers with offers of cheap all-nighters to far-flung destinations in the kingdom.

Theft, coercion and painfully slow or cramped services are not uncommon, with the luxurious VIP bus promised when you buy your tickets transforming into a beaten up jalopy when it comes to departure time. The buses often stop at expensive restaurants for a long wait or finish their journey in the middle of the night emptying guests into the 'only available' hotel. Worse still are thefts and scams. Over the years dozens of travellers have had their valuables stolen – sometimes even by the bus crew themselves who have, on occasion, been known to disappear into the night leaving travellers stranded and penniless.

Travellers should opt for the safe, inexpensive and relatively luxurious government-approved VIP buses from the public bus stations. Those cheap packages often to turn out too good to be true and are often more expensive than simply buying the ticket yourself.

For up-to-date information on all scams in Thailand, and especially Bangkok, visit www.bangkokscams.com.

Chit 2), is at the western side of Chatuchak Park on Kamphaeng Phet 2 Rd, T02-936 3659. It serves all destinations in the north and northeast as well as towns in the central plains that lie north of Bangkok like **Ayutthaya** and **Lopburi**. Non-a/c buses Nos 77, 134, 136 and 145 and a/c buses Nos 3, 8, 12, 134, 136 and 145 all pass the terminal.

The **Southern bus terminal** is on Phra Pinklao Rd, T02-434 7192, near the inter-section with Route 338. Buses for the west for places places like **Kanchanaburi** and the south leave from here. A/c town bus No 7 travels to the terminal. A/c buses to the south and west leave from the terminal on Charan Santiwong Rd, near Bangkok Noi Train Station in Thonburi, T02-435 1199.

The **Eastern bus terminal**, Sukhumvit Rd (Soi Ekamai), between Soi 40 and Soi 42, T02-391 2504, serves **Pattaya** and other destinations in the eastern region. To travel into Bangkok from this bus terminal by local bus, walk out of the terminal, turn left and enter the local bus terminal. Bus Nos 77 and 159 will travel down to the Siam Sq area.

Buses leave for most major destinations throughout the day, and often well into the night. There are overnight buses on longer routes – **Chiang Mai, Hat Yai, Chiang Rai, Phuket, Ubon Ratchathani**. Even small provincial towns such as **Mahasarakham** have de luxe a/c buses from Bangkok.

In addition to the government-operated buses, many companies run **private tour buses**, which run to most of the major tourist destinations. Tickets bought through travel agents will normally be for these private buses, which leave from offices all over the city as well as from the public bus terminals. Shop around as prices may vary. Note that although passengers may be picked up from their hotel/guesthouse – therefore saving the cost (and inconvenience) of getting out to the bus terminal – the private buses are generally less reliable and less safe. Many pick up passengers at Khaosan Rd and are notoriously cramped and unreliable (see box, above).

Car hire

See page 40 for general advice on driving in Thailand. Given the driving conditions in Bangkok it's often advisable (and sometimes cheaper) to hire a car with driver is approx

₿3000 for 8 hrs excluding fuel. Approximate cost for car hire only is ₿1500-2200 per day, ₿7000-11,000 per week; Hertz and Avis charge more than the local firms, but have better insurance cover. Both also have branches at the airport. Avis, 2/12 Witthayu Rd, T02-255 5300; Budget, 19/23 Royal City Av, New Phetburi Rd, T02-203 9200, www.budget.co.th; Central Car Rent, 115/5 Soi Ton-Son, Ploenchit Rd, T02-251 2778; Hertz, 420 Sukhumvit Soi 71, T02-390 0341; Highway Car Rent, 1018/5 Rama IV Rd, T02-235 7746.

Metro (MRT) and Skytrain (BTS)

With the opening of the **Metro** (**MRT**) in 2004 and extensions planned for 2009, Bangkok is steadily developing an efficient transport system. The MRT line, which loops through 18 stations, connecting Hualamphong with Lumpini Park, Sukhumvit Rd and Chatuchak Market and also intersects with the Skytrain, is a shining example of Thai modernity. The entire network is a/c, the comfortable trains run regularly and stations are well lit and airy. Nonetheless, it has been beset with problems: many Thais are nervous about travelling underground and a major crash in early 2005 did little to allay these fears. Another issue is a lack of integration with the Skytrain – separate tickets are needed and interchanges are awkward and badly planned. At present, fares for the metro are cheap – ₿15-39. For full details visit www.bangkokmetro.co.th.

The **Skytrain** (**BTS**) runs on an elevated track through the most developed parts of the city – it is quite a ride, veering between the skyscrapers. There are 2 lines, which cross at Siam Station (Siam Sq): one runs from Mo Chit on Phahonyothin Rd (close to the Chatuchak Weekend Market, to the north of the city centre) to On Nut. The 2nd line runs from the National Stadium on Rama I Rd to Taksin Bridge (Saphan Taksin) at the end of Silom Rd in the heart of the business district. The Skytrain covers a large chunk of the tourist, business and shopping areas so is very useful. It is also quick and cool – although the tramp up to the stations can be a drag and the open stations themselves are not a/c. The tracks over the river at Taksin are now built and the line extends into Thonburi but nobody seems to know when services will begin – hopefully by early 2009. Trains run from 0600-2400, every 3-5 mins during peak periods and every 10-15 mins out of the rush hour. Fares are steep by Thai standards but worth it for most overseas visitors: ₿15 for one stop, ₿40 for the whole route. Multi-trip tickets can also be purchased, which makes things slightly cheaper. For up to date information T02-617 7300, www.bts.co.th.

Motorcycle taxi

These are usually used to run up and down the long sois that extend out of the main thoroughfares. Riders wear numbered vests and tend to congregate at the end of the busiest sois. The short-hop fare down a *soi* is usually ₿10 though there is usually a pricelist (in Thai) at the gathering point. Some riders will agree to take you on longer journeys across town and fares will then need to be negotiated – expect to pay anything from ₿25-100, dependent on your negotiating skills and knowledge of Thai. A ride through Bangkok's hectic traffic with a Red Bull-fuelled motorcycle taxi driver is one you are likely never to forget – if you make it back alive.

River transport

Water taxi This is the cheapest way to travel on the river. There are 3 types of water taxi. The **Chao Phraya Express River Taxi** (*rua duan*) runs between Nonthaburi in the north and Rajburana (Big C) in the south. Fares are calculated by zone. At peak hours boats leave every 10 mins, off-peak about 15-25 mins. **Standard Express Boats** operate daily 0600-1840, ₿10-14. **Special Express Boats** run Mon-Fri 0600-0900 and 1200-1900, ₿12-32, to serve the commuter market (see map, page 97 for piers, and box page 98). The journey from one end of the route to the other takes 75 mins. Special Express Boats, flying either a red/orange or a yellow pennant, do not stop at all piers; boats without a flag are the Standard Express Boats and stop at all piers. Also, boats will only stop if passengers wish to board or alight, so make your destination known. Be warned that Thais trying to sell boat tours will tell you Special Express Boats are not running and will try to extort grossly inflated prices from you. Walk away and find the correct pier.

Ferries These slower, chunkier boats ply back and forth across the river, between Bangkok and **Thonburi**, and cost ฿4.

There are also a number of other boat services linking Bangkok with stops along the *khlongs*, which run off the main Chao Phraya River and into Thonburi. These are a good, cheap way of getting a glimpse of waterside life. Services from **Tha Tien pier** (by Wat Pho) to **Khlong Mon**, daily 0630-1800 (every 30 mins), ฿6; from **Memorial Bridge** pier to **Khlong Bang Waek**, daily 0600-2130 (every 15 mins), ฿12; from **Tha Chang pier** (by the Grand Palace) to **Khoo Wiang** Floating Market (market operates 0400-0700) and **Khlong Bang Yai**, daily 0615-2000 (every 20 mins), ฿12; and from **Nonthaburi's Phibun Pier** (north of the city) to **Khlong Om**, daily 0400-2100 (every 15 mins).

To **Ayutthaya**, boats leave from Tha Tien pier daily at 1000. Boat trips around the river from the pier cost ฿600 per trip for up to 12 people. The *Benjarang* boat does a tour south along the Chao Phraya River, stopping at Wat Chai Wattanaram, Wat Phutthaisawan and Wat Phanam Choeng for ฿180 per person. See boat tours, page 153.

Khlong or long-tailed boats (*hang yaaw*) can be rented for ฿1000 per hr, or more (see Tours and tour operators, page 152). See the *khlong* trips outlined on page 98 for information on what to see on the river. A good map, *Rivers and Khlongs*, is available from the **TAT** office (see page 78).

Taxi
Taxis are usually metered (they must have a/c to register) – look for the 'Taxi Meter' illuminated sign on the roof. Check that the meter is 'zeroed' before setting off.

Fares are ฿35 for the first 2 km, ฿4.50 per km up to 12 km, and ฿5 per km thereafter. Most trips in the city should cost ฿40-100. If the travel speed is less than 6 kph – always a distinct possibility in the traffic choked capital – a surcharge of ฿1.25 per min is automatically added. Passengers also pay the tolls for using the expressway. Taxi drivers sometimes refuse to use the meter despite the fact that they are required to do so by law. This is particularly the case in tourist areas like Patpong and Banglamphu. If a driver refuses to use the meter simply get out and hail another – there are usually scores around. It's also best to make sure you have sufficient 20s and 100s to pay as drivers rarely have change; tollways make good places to break big notes. Taxi drivers make a poor living on long hours in Bangkok and tipping, though not expected, is much appreciated. It is usual to round fares up or down to the nearest ฿5. Remember that Bangkok's taxis are some of the cheapest in the world and their drivers some of the worst paid. For most tourists the arrival of the metered taxi has lowered prices as it has eliminated the need to bargain. To call a taxi: **Siam Taxis**, T1661 or **Radio Taxi**, T1681, charge ฿20 plus the fare on the meter. They also offer long-distance/all-day hire from ฿1500. Note that taxi drivers are not renowned for their knowledge of Bangkok. Many are upcountry boys and who speak little English, so it's handy to have a rough idea of where you want to go, as well as a business card, telephone number of your location and/or an address written in Thai.

Train
See page 42 for more information on Thailand's railways. For train timetables, routes and fares, see page 43.

Bangkok has 2 main railway stations. **Hualamphong**, Rama IV Rd, T02-223 7010/20, is the primary station, catering for most destinations; condensed railway timetables in English can be picked up from the information counter on the main concourse. The exceptionally enthusiastic staff at the tourist information table at the main entrance offer efficient and reliable advice.

Bangkok Noi (Thonburi station), on the other side of the Chao Phraya River, is where trains to **Nakhon Pathom** and **Kanchanaburi** depart/arrive.

Tuk-tuk

The formerly ubiquitous motorized *saamlor* is rapidly becoming a piece of history in Bangkok, although they can still usually be found near tourist sites. Best for short journeys, they are uncomfortable and, being open to the elements, you are likely to be asphyxiated by car fumes. Bargaining is essential and the fare should be negotiated before boarding, though most tuk-tuk drivers try to rip tourists off and taking a metered taxi will be less hassle and cheaper. Expect to pay in the region of ฿30-100 for a short hop across town. Tuk-tuk drivers also have a reputation for hustling in other ways and perpetrate all kinds of scams. The general advice is to try a tuk-tuk once for the novelty value and then avoid.

⊙ Directory

Bangkok *p82, maps p78, p90, p102, p104 and p106*

Banks

There are countless exchange booths in all the tourist areas open 7 days a week, mostly 0800-1530, some 0800-2100. Rates vary only marginally between banks, although if changing a large sum, it is worth shopping around. ATMs abound in Bangkok and most can be used with credit cards and bank cards. They are open 24 hrs a day.

Embassies and consulates

Australia, 37 South Sathorn Rd, T02-287 2680. Mon-Fri 0830-1230, 1330-1630. **Burma (Myanmar)**, 132 Sathorn Nua Rd, T02-233 2237. **Cambodia**, 185 Rachdamri Rd, T02-254 6630, 0900-1100. **Canada**, 15th floor Abdulrahim Place, 990 Rama 1V Rd, T02-636 0541. Mon-Thu 0730-1615, Fri 0730-1300, visas Mon-Fri 0800-1200. **Denmark**, 10 Sathorn Tai Soi Attakarnprasit, T02-213 2021. Mon-Thu 0900-1530, Fri 0900-1230. **France**, 35 Customs House Lane, Charoen Krung, T02-266 8250. Mon-Thu 0800-1700, Fri 0800-1600, visas Mon-Fri 0800-1200 (there is also a French consulate at 29 Sathorn Tai Rd, T02-285 6104). **Germany**, 9 Sathorn Tai Rd, T02-287 9000. Mon-Fri 0830-1200, visas 0830-1100. **Israel**, 25th floor, Ocean Tower II, 75 Soi Wattana, Sukhumvit 19, T02-204 9200. **Italy**, 399 Nang Linchi Rd, T02-285 4090. **Japan**, 1674 New Phetburi Rd, T02-252 6151. Mon-Fri 0830-1200, 1330-1600. **Laos**, 502/1-3 Soi Ramkhamhaeng 39, T02-539 6667. Mon-Fri 0800-1200, 1300-1600. **Malaysia**, 33-35 Sathorn Tai Rd, T02-6792190. **Netherlands**, 6 Wireless Rd, T02-254 7701. Mon-Fri 0900-1200. **New Zealand**, 93 Wireless Rd, T02-254 2530. Mon-Fri 0730-1200, 1300-1600, visas 0900-1200, 1300-1500. **Singapore**, 129 Sathorn Tai Rd, T02-286 2111. **South Africa**, 6th floor, Park Place, 231 Soi Sarasin, Rachdamri Rd, T02-253 8473. **Spain**, 7th floor, Diethelm Building, 93 Wireless Rd, T02-2526112. Mon-Fri 0900-1430, visas 0830-1200. **Sweden**, 20th floor, Pacific Place, 140 Sukhumvit Rd, T02-3020360. Mon-Fri 0800-1200. **Switzerland**, 35 Wireless Rd, (GPO Box 821, Bangkok 10510, T02-254 6855. Mon-Fri 0900-1200. **UK**, 1031 Wireless Rd, T02-253 0191/9. Mon-Thu 0800-1100, 1300-1530, Fri 0800-1200. **USA**, 95 Wireless Rd, T02-205 4000. Mon-Fri 0800-1100, 1300-1500. **Vietnam**, 83/1 Wireless Rd, T02-251 7202. Open 0800-1130, 1330-1630, 2 photos required, normally takes 3 working days, same-day visas available at a price (฿2700).

Internet

There are literally thousands of internet cafés scattered around the entire city. Most offer high-speed access and away from the tourist areas will cost from ฿10 per hr while along Khaosan and Sukhumvit prices are ฿30-60 per hr. The majority of shops congregate around the Khaosan Rd, Silom and Siam Sq and even in the furthest outposts you'll find net shops choc-a-bloc with game-playing pre-teens. In addition most hotels and guesthouses offer the service. For the BYO laptop crowd, coffee shops and cafés from **Starbucks** to the local corner coffee shop now offer free or paid Wi-Fi services.

True, www.trueinternet.co.th, one of Bangkok's premier providers, now has over 20 **True Lifestyle** stores in and around Bangkok, all of which offer modern coffee shop surrounds and extensive services. The flagship **True Urban Park** in Siam Paragon is a space-age sight to behold with, armchair seating, personal iPod bubbles dangling from the ceiling and a wall of images streamed direct from Paragon's huge aquarium. The more upbeat Thonglor branch invites live bands to play at the weekends. The peaceful Khaosan Rd branch offers a pleasant escape from the crowds.

Immigration

Bangkok's immigration offices are at Sathorn Tai Soi Suanphlu, Silom district, T02-287 3101.

Language schools

Bangkok has scores of language schools. The best known is the **AUA** school at 179 Rachdamri, T02-252 8170. See the local English-language press for information on language schools.

Libraries

British Council Library, 254 Chulalongkorn Soi 64 (Siam Sq). Tue-Sat 1000-1930, membership library with good selection of English-language books. **National Library**, Samsen Rd, close to Sri Ayutthaya Rd. Daily 0930-1930. **Neilson Hays Library**, 195 Surawong Rd, T02-233 1731. Mon-Sat 0930-1600, Sun 0930-1230. A small library of English-language books housed in an elegant building dating from 1922. It is a private membership library, but welcomes visitors who might want to see the building and browse; occasional exhibitions are held here. **Siam Society Library**, 131 Sukhumvit Soi 21 (Asoke). Tue-Sat 0900-1700. Membership library with excellent collection of Thai and foreign-language books and periodicals (especially English) on Thailand and mainland Southeast Asia.

Medical services

Bangkok Adventist Hospital, 430 Phitsanulok Rd, Dusit, T02-281 1422, T02-282 1100. Efficient vaccination service and 24-hr emergency unit. **Bangkok General** Hospital, New Phetburi Soi 47, T02-318 0066. **Dental Hospital**, 88/88 Sukhumvit 49, T02-260 5000, F02-2605026. Good but expensive. **Clinic Banglamphu**, 187 Chakrapong Rd, T02-282 7479. **Dental Polyclinic**, New Phetburi Rd, T02-314 5070. **St Louis Hospital**, 215 Sathorn Tai Rd, T02-212 0033.

Post

Central General Post Office (Praysani Klang for taxi drivers): 1160 Charoen Krung, opposite the Ramada Hotel. Mon-Fri 0800-2000, Sat, Sun and holidays 0800-1300. The money and postal order service is open Mon-Fri 0800-1700, Sat 0800-1200. Closed on Sun and holidays. 24-hr telegram and telephone service (phone rates are reduced 2100-0700) and a packing service. There are small post offices in most districts and many shopping centres.

Tourist police

24-hr hotline T1155, 4 Rachadamnoen Nok Av, Dusit.

Contents

Border crossings

Thailand–Burma (Myanmar)
Saam Ong–Payathonzu (Three
Pagodas Pass), see page 187
Mae Sot–Myawady, see page 223

Central Thailand

At a glance

◉ **Getting around** Buses, trains
and bicycles (if you have the energy).

◉ **Time required** A week for the
main sites, a month if you want to
take in the nooks and crannies.

☽ **Weather** Much like Bangkok,
Dec and Jan, when it's cool and
dry, are the most bearable months.

✖ **When not to go** Floods are
common in monsoon season;
watch out during Sep and Oct.

The entire central plain – cutting a 100-mile-wide swathe 250 miles upcountry from Bangkok – forms the cradle of Thai civilization. Ruined cities, temples and fortresses, museums filled with antiquities, and the remains of several great civilizations await the visitor. The abandoned capital of Ayutthaya is here, as is Sukhothai – the ancient city the Thais consider represents their 'Golden Age' – while the exquisite ruins of Si Satchanalai nestle nearby. Take time out to explore the forests of Sukhothai and Si Sat and you'll discover revered Buddhas and *chedis* lost amongst thick foliage. Don't forget the diamond citadel of Kamphaeng Phet, built to protect Sukhothai from attack, the assortment of monkey-colonized ruins of Lopburi and the spiritually uplifting, living temple of Wat Phra Sri Ratana Mahathat in Phitsanulok. The vast plain finally gives way to ridges of forested hills. These are relatively remote areas with trekking centres in the affable western towns of Mae Sot and Umphang.

Head north and west from Bangkok to the frontier with Burma (Myanmar) and Thailand's history takes on a different complexion. It was through this thin slice of western Thailand that the Japanese built their infamous 'death railway'. It's not only this dramatic history that attracts visitors to the region and its hub, Kanchanaburi. Add wonderful cave complexes, jungle trekking, waterfalls, river trips, elephant rides, raft houses and a host of national parks and you have an important centre of ecotourism. Venture north of Kanchanaburi towards the Burmese border and you'll reach Sangkhlaburi and the Three Pagodas Pass. Ethnically, this is an incredibly diverse area with minority peoples, such as Karen, Mon, Burmese, Indian and Chinese all living side by side. It is a wild natural forested area with fantastic trekking and rafting and it is also possible, when the Thai and Burmese authorities are on good terms, to enter Burma.

Ayutthaya and around

→ Colour map 2, C1.

The ancient, venerable capital of the Kingdom of Siam, Ayutthaya, had a population of 150,000 during its heyday and was the equal of any city in Europe. It was at the epicentre of an empire that controlled more than 500,000 sq km and all the wealth of this great kingdom gravitated to the capital city. These days a large portion of the city is a bustling modern Thai conurbation with little to remind the visitor of its halcyon days – in typical Thai fashion traffic is heavy and city planning chaotic. Amid all this concrete are several ancient sites and you may find yourself walking past them without even realizing they are there.

If you head west from this urban setting you will soon begin to pick up more traces of the old city of Ayutthaya, until it opens up into a series of broad spaces, littered with atmospheric ruins. Arrive when the setting sun illuminates the deep red-brick ruins and it is not hard to imagine the grandeur of this place which so amazed early European visitors. Here is a stunning complex of palaces, shrines, monasteries and chedis. The historical park, which was made a UNESCO World Heritage Site in 1991, covers some 3 sq km. Rama V (1868-1910) was the first person to appreciate the value of the site, both in terms of Thailand's national identity and in terms of its artistic merit. The historic city of Lopburi, known for its kleptomaniac monkeys, lies to the north. ▸▸ *For listings, see pages 176-179.*

Ins and outs

Getting there

Most people get here by bus from Bangkok's Northern bus terminal. It is an easy 1½-hour journey, making a day trip from Bangkok possible. The bus station in Ayutthaya is centrally located on Naresuan Road. Another option is to arrive by ferry, which takes a leisurely three hours from Tha Tien pier in Bangkok (see page 160). You can also take the train from Bangkok's Hualomphong station – it takes about 1½ hours. Local trains leave regularly and charge a fraction of the cost of the express services, yet don't take much longer. The train station in Ayutthaya is just off Rojana Rd, across the Pasak River. A *songthaew* to the old city costs around ฿7. Alternatively, take the small track facing the station down to the river; from the jetty here ferries cross over to the other side every five minutes or so (฿2), just off Uthong Road. Most of the guesthouses are a short walk from here. ▸▸ *See Transport, page 178, for further information.*

Getting around

The wats are spread over a considerable area, too large to walk around comfortably, so the best way to cover quite a bit of ground is to hire a *saamlor* by the hour. That way, you can decide your route and instruct accordingly. Long-tailed boats are available to transport people around the perimeter of the town, in order to visit the outlying sites. Many of the guesthouses hire out bicycles. A tuk-tuk around town costs ฿50-60. *Songthaews* charge a flat fare of ฿7 for trips around town and can be chartered for about ฿300 per day.

Tourist information

TAT ① *Si Sanphet Rd, next to Chao Sam Phraya Museum (temporary office), T035-246 076,* offers information on Ayutthaya, Ang Thong, Suphanburi and Nonthaburi. Ayutthaya is one of the most popular day tours from Bangkok (see page 154), but for those with an interest in

King Naresuan the Great of Ayutthaya

King Naresuan of Ayutthaya (1590-1605) was one of only five of Thailand's great kings to have posthumously been awarded the sobriquet 'the Great'. In 1569 the Burmese had taken Ayutthaya and placed a puppet monarch on the throne. The great kingdom appeared to be on the wane. But Naresuan, who in American historian David Wyatt's words was "one of those rare figures in Siamese history who, by virtue of dynamic leadership, personal courage, and decisive character, succeed in Herculean tasks that have daunted others before them", proceeded to challenge the Burmese. He confronted their forces in 1585, 1585-1586 and in 1586-1587, defeating armies that grew larger by turn. Finally, at the beginning of 1593, the decisive battle occurred at Nong Sarai, to the northwest of Suphanburi. The Burmese had assembled an army of monumental proportions. During the initial skirmish, Naresuan saw the Burmese crown prince mounted on his war elephant and, according to the chronicles, shouted across the battlefield: "Come forth and let us fight an elephant duel for the honour of our kingdoms". When the Burmese prince lunged with his lance, Naresuan ducked beneath the blow to rake, and kill, his opponent with his sword. The battle was won and Ayutthaya was once again in a position to flourish.

ruins or Thai history, there is more than enough to occupy a couple of days. The average day trip only allows about two hours. Ignore tour operators who maintain there is no accommodation here, it is perfectly adequate. A number of companies run boat tours up the Chao Phraya to Ayutthaya. River tours around Ayutthaya can also be arranged through various guesthouses.

Background

"In 712, a Year of the Tiger, second of the decade, on Friday, the sixth day of the waxing moon of the fifth month, at three nalika and nine bat after the break of dawn, the capital city of Ayutthaya was first established." So recorded the Royal Chronicles of Ayutthaya. In translation this is widely accepted to mean Friday 4 March 1351, at about 0900. It is said that Prince Uthong (later King Ramathibodi I) and his court were forced here following an outbreak of cholera and, after a brief interlude at the nearby Wat Panancherng, founded the city.

Ayutthaya's name derives from 'Ayodhya', the sacred town in the Indian epic, the *Ramayana*. It became one of the most prosperous kingdoms in the Southeast Asian region, and by 1378 the King of Sukhothai had been forced to swear his allegiance. Ultimately, the kingdom stretched from Angkor (Cambodia) in the east, to Pegu (Burma) in the west. In 1500 it was reported that the kingdom was exporting 30 junk loads (10,000 tonnes) of rice to Malacca (Malaysia), each year while also being an important source of animal skins and ivory.

The city is situated on an island at the confluence of three rivers: the Chao Phraya, Pasak and Lopburi. Ayutthaya's strong defensive position proved to be valuable as it was attacked by the Burmese on no less than 24 occasions. Recent research on changes in sea level indicates that in 1351 the coastline was much further north and so the city was considerably closer to the sea. Ayutthaya, therefore, would have been able to develop as a trading port unlike the previous Thai capitals of Sukhothai and Si Satchanalai.

One of Ayutthaya's most famous kings was Boromtrailokant (1448-1488), a model of the benevolent monarch. He is best known for his love of justice and his administrative and legislative reforms. This may seem surprising in view of some of the less than enlightened legal practices employed later in the Ayutthaya period. A plaintiff and defendant might, for example, have had to plunge their hands into molten tin, or their heads into water, to see which party was the guilty one.

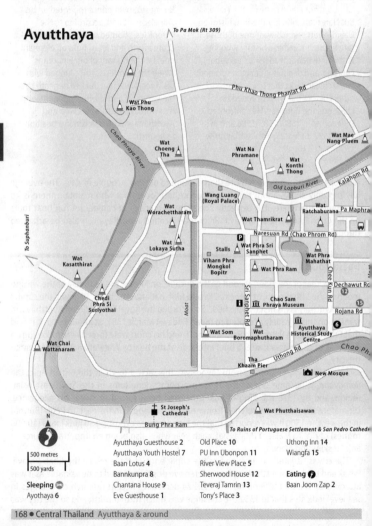

Ayutthaya

To Pa Mok (Rt 309)

Phu Khao Thong Phanlat Rd

Chao Phraya River

Wat Phu Kao Thong

Wat Mae Nang Pluem

Wat Choeng Tha

Wat Na Phramane

Wat Konthi Thong

Old Lopburi River

Kalahom Rd

Wang Luang (Royal Palace)

Wat Worachettharam

Wat Ratchaburana

Pa Maphra

To Suphanburi

Wat Thamrikrat

Naresuan Rd (Chao Phrom Rd)

Wat Phra Sri Sanphet

Stalls

Wat Lokaya Sutha

Viharn Phra Mongkol Bopitr

Wat Phra Ram

Wat Phra Mahathat

Chee Kun Rd

Dechawut Rd

Wat Kasatthirat

Chedi Phra Si Suriyothai

Sri Sanphet Rd

Chao Sam Phraya Museum

Rojana Rd

Moat

Wat Chai Wattanaram

Wat Som

Wat Boromaphutharam

Ayutthaya Historical Study Centre

Chao Phr

Tha Khaam Pier

Uthong Rd

New Mosque

St Joseph's Cathedral

Wat Phutthaisawan

Bung Phra Ram

To Ruins of Portuguese Settlement & San Pedro Cathedral

N

500 metres

500 yards

Sleeping
Ayothaya 6

Ayutthaya Guesthouse 2
Ayutthaya Youth Hostel 7
Baan Lotus 4
Bannkunpra 8
Chantana House 9
Eve Guesthouse 1

Old Place 10
PU Inn Ubonpon 11
River View Place 5
Sherwood House 12
Teveraj Tamrin 13
Tony's Place 3

Uthong Inn 14
Wiangfa 15

Eating
Baan Joom Zap 2

A succession struggle in the mid-16th century led to 20 years of warfare with the Burmese, who managed to seize and occupy Ayutthaya. It wasn't long before the hero-king, Naresuan (1590-1605), recaptured the city and led his country back to independence. Under King Narai (1656-1688), Ayutthaya became a rich, cosmopolitan trading post. Merchants came to the city from Portugal, Spain, Holland, China, Arabia, Persia, Malaya, India and Japan. In the 16th century Ayutthaya was said to have 40 different nationalities living in and around the city walls, and supported a population larger than London's.

The city was strongly fortified, with ramparts 20 m high and 5 m thick, and was protected on all sides by waterways: rivers on three sides and a linking canal on the fourth creating an oriental Venice. The cosmopolitan atmosphere was evident on the waterways where royal barges rubbed shoulders with Chinese junks, Arab dhows and ocean-going schooners. Visitors found endless sources of amusement in the city. There were elephant jousts, tiger fights, Muay Thai (Thai boxing), masked plays and puppet theatre.

It was said that the King of Ayutthaya was so wealthy that the elephants were fed from gold vessels. Indeed, early Western visitors to Ayutthaya often commented on the king's elephants and the treatment they received. One of the earliest accounts is by Jacques de Countres, a merchant from Bruges who resided in the city for eight months in 1596 (during Naresuan's reign). His son later recorded his father's experiences: "The palace is surrounded by stables where live the favourite elephants ridden by the king. Each one had its silk cushion, and they slept on it as if they were small dogs. Each one of them had six very large bowls of gold. Some contained oil to grease their skins; others were filled with water for sprinkling; others served for eating; others for drinking; others for urinating and defecating. The elephants were indeed so well trained that they got up from their beds when they felt the urge to urinate or defecate. Their attendants understood at once and handed them the bowls. And they kept their lodges always very sweet-smelling and fumigated with benzoin and other fragrant substances. I would not have believed it if I had not actually seen it." (Smithies, Michael *Descriptions of Old Siam*, Kuala Lumpur, 1995, OUP.)

Da Ivo 7
Moon Café 7
Nai Pun 6
Phae Krung Kao 5
Ruan Thai Mai Suay 8
Tea & Coffee House 7

Bars & clubs
Cocohut 9
Jazz Bar 4
Wo Gun-T 3

One European became particularly influential: King Narai's Greek foreign affairs officer (and later prime minister), Constantine Phaulcon (see box, page 173). It was at this time the word '*farang*' – to describe any white foreigner – entered the Thai vocabulary, derived from 'ferenghi', the Indian for 'French'. In 1688, Narai was taken ill and at the same time the French, who Phaulcon had been encouraging, became a serious threat, gaining control of a fortress in Bangkok. An anti-French lobby arrested the by now very unpopular Phaulcon and had him executed for suspected designs on the throne. The French troops were expelled and for the next century Europeans were kept at arm's length. It was not until the 19th century that they regained influence in the Thai court.

In 1767 the kingdom was again invaded, by the Burmese, who, at the 24th attempt, were finally successful in vanquishing the defenders. The city was sacked and its defences destroyed, but, unable to consolidate their position, the Burmese left for home, taking with them large numbers of prisoners and leaving the city in ruins. The population was reduced from one million to 10,000. Ayutthaya never recovered from this final attack, and the magnificent temples were left to deteriorate.

Sights

The modern town of Ayutthaya is concentrated in the eastern quarter of the old walled city, and beyond the walls to the east. Much of the rest of the old city is green and open, interspersed with abandoned wats and new government buildings.

The sights described below take in the most important wats. Ayutthaya's other fine ruins are described in the second half of this section. The sheer size of the site means that the considerable numbers of tourists are easily dispersed among the ruins, leaving the visitor to wander in complete tranquillity among the walkways, *chedis* and trees.

Wat Ratchaburana
ⓘ ฿30.
This wat was built by King Boromraja II in 1424 on the cremation site of his two brothers (princes Ai and Yo), who were killed while contesting the throne. The Khmer-style *prang* (which has been partially restored) still stands amidst the ruins of the wat. Some of the most important treasures found in Ayutthaya were discovered here in 1958: bronze Buddha images, precious stones and golden royal regalia, belonging, it is assumed, to the two brothers.

Wat Phra Mahathat
ⓘ ฿30.
Across the road from Wat Ratchaburana sits the Monastery of the Great Relic. It was founded in 1384, making it one of the earliest *prangs* in Ayutthaya, and was the largest of all Ayutthaya's monasteries, built to house holy relics of the Buddha (hence its name). It is said that King Boromraja I (1370-1388) was meditating one dawn when he saw a glow emanating from the earth; he took this to mean that a relic of the Buddha lay under the soil and ordered a wat to be founded. Only the large base remains of the original Khmer-style *prang*, which collapsed during the reign of King Song Tham (1610-1628). When the Fine Arts Department excavated the site in 1956, it found a number of gold Buddha images as well as relics of the Buddha inside a gold casket, now exhibited in the National Museum, Bangkok.

Ayutthaya Historical Study Centre
ⓘ *Wed-Fri 0900-1630, Sat-Sun 0900-1700, ฿100.*
Further south, on Rojana Road, this museum and research centre is housed in a surprisingly sensitively designed modern building, proving there are some creative architects in the country. The museum tries to recreate Ayutthaya life and does so with some excellent models.

Chao Sam Phraya Museum
ⓘ *Wed-Sun 0900-1200, 1300-1600 (except public holidays). ฿30.*
Located on Rojana Road, this museum was opened in 1961. Votive tablets excavated from Wat Ratchaburana were auctioned off to raise funds for its construction. It houses many of Ayutthaya's relics, in particular the Mongkol Buddha.

Wat Phra Sri Sanphet
ⓘ *฿30.*
Within the extensive grounds of Wang Luang (Royal Palace), this was the largest and most beautiful wat in Ayutthaya – the equivalent of Wat Phra Kaeo in Bangkok. Three restored Ceylonese-style *chedis* dominate the compound. They contain the ashes of King Boromtrailokant (1448-1488) and his two sons (who were also kings of Ayutthaya). There are no *prangs* here; the three central *chedis* are surrounded by alternate smaller *chedis* and *viharns*. Remains of walls and leaning pillars give an impression of the vastness of the wat. In 1500 it is alleged that a 16-m standing Buddha was cast by King Ramathipodi II (1491-1529), using a staggering 5,500,000 kg of bronze and covered in 340 kg of gold leaf. The image's name, Phra Sri Sanphet, later became the name of the wat. When the Burmese invaded the city in 1767 the image was set on fire in order to release the gold, in the process destroying both it and the temple.

Viharn Phra Mongkol Bopitr
South of Wat Phra Sri Sanphet stands this 'new' *viharn*, built in 1956 and modelled on the 15th-century original which was razed by the Burmese. It houses one of the largest bronze Buddhas in the world, at 12.5 m high. This black image, which is made of sheets of copper-bronze fastened onto a core of brick and plaster, probably dates from the 16th century.

Wat Na Phramane
ⓘ *฿20. Note the image cannot always be viewed.*
Travel back past Wang Luang to the main road, turn east and after 250 m the road crosses the Old Lopburi River. From the bridge one can see Wat Na Phramane, which dates from 1503 and is one of the most complete examples of Ayutthayan architecture. It is reputed to have been built by one of King Ramathibodi's concubines, Pra Ong, at which time it was known as Wat Pramerurachikaram. A treaty to end one of the many wars with Burma was signed here in 1549. More than two centuries later in 1767, the Burmese used the position to attack the city once again, and it is said that the King of Burma suffered a mortal blow from a cannon which backfired during the initial bombardment. Perhaps because of this, the Burmese – unusually – left the wat intact. Even without the helping hands of the Burmese, the wat still fell into disrepair and was not restored until 1838. The lovely early Ayutthayan *bot* is the largest in the city and contains an impressive crowned bronze Buddha image.

Wat Thamrikrat

South over the bridge that crosses a small tributary of the Old Lopburi River, again, a short distance east along Kalahom Road, is Wat Thamrikrat (Monastery of the Pious Monarch), with *singha* (stucco lions) surrounding an overgrown *chedi*. Scholars are not sure exactly when it was built, but they are largely agreed that it predates the reign of King Boromtrailokant (1448-1488).

Wat Choeng Tha

Also on the north bank of the river, not far from the confluence of the Chao Phraya and Old Lopburi rivers, is this wat. It is not known when it was originally built – it has been restored on a number of occasions – but it is said to have been constructed by a man whose daughter ran away with her lover and never returned; it was known as Wat Koy Tha (Monastery of Waiting). The Ayutthaya-style *prang* is in reasonable condition, as is the *sala kan parian*, although the *bot* and *viharn* are both in poor condition.

Wat Yai Chai Mongkol

① ฿30.

Southeast of the town is Wat Yai Chai Mongkol, or simply Wat Yai (Big Wat), built by King Uthong, also known as King Ramathibodi I, in 1357, for a group of monks who had studied and been ordained in Ceylon. The imposing 72-m-high *chedi* was built in the Ceylonese style (now with a rather alarming tilt) to celebrate the victory of King Naresuan over the Prince of Burma in 1592, in single-handed elephant combat. The *viharn* contains a massive reclining Buddha image. It is unusual because its eyes are open; reclining images traditionally symbolize death or sleep, so the eyes are closed.

Elephant kraals

① Take a saamlor from Chee Kun Rd northwards over the Old Lopburi River to reach the kraal. If coming from Wat Phu Kao Thong, cross the Pa Mok Highway and drive for 3.5 km.

Northeast of the city, on the banks of the Old Lopburi River, are the only remaining elephant kraals in Thailand. The kraals were built in the reign of King Maha Chakrapat in 1580 to capture wild elephants. The kraals are square-shaped enclosures with double walls. The inner walls are made of teak posts fixed to the ground at close intervals. The outer walls are made of earth, faced with brick, and are 3 m high. The kraals have two entrances: one to allow the decoy elephant to lure the herd into the enclosure, and the other to lead them out again. The outer wall on the west side is slightly wider to provide a platform from which the king, seated in a pavilion, could watch the elephant round-up. The last round-up of wild elephants occurred in May 1903, to entertain royal guests during King Chulalongkorn's reign. The kraal has been extensively restored and is rather clinical as a result.

River tours of outlying wats

The extensive waterways of Ayutthaya (more than 50 km of them) are a pleasant way to see some of the less accessible sights. Long-tailed boats can be taken from the landing pier opposite Chandra Kasem Palace, in the northeast corner of the town (see Transport, page 178). During the dry season, it is not possible to circle the entire island; the Old Lopburi River becomes unnavigable. The usual route runs south down the Pasak River and round as far as Wat Chai Wattanaram on the Chao Phraya River. The following wats can also be visited by road.

Constantine Phaulcon: Greek adventurer, Siamese minister, Roman Catholic zealot

Constantine Phaulcon (1647-1688) was a Greek adventurer who became, for a short time, the most influential man in Siam barring the king. He arrived in Ayutthaya in 1678 with the English East India Company, learnt Thai and became an interpreter in the court. By 1682 he had worked his way up through the bureaucracy to become the Mahatthai, the most senior position. But it was also at this time that, in retrospect, he sealed his fate. Phaulcon acted as interpreter for a French mission led by Monsignor Pallu. An avid Roman Catholic, having recently been converted by Jesuit priests, Phaulcon was enthralled by the idea of converting King Narai and his subjects to Christianity. He discussed with Narai – who was the King's most trusted adviser – the superiority of Roman Catholicism versus Buddhism, and seemed to be representing the interests of the French in negotiations, rather than those of Siam. Phaulcon made many enemies among powerful Siamese, who doubted his integrity and his intentions. By 1688, Phaulcon's activities were becoming increasingly unacceptable, and he was also linked by association with the excesses of French and British troops, with the proselytizing of priests, and with the effect that foreign traders were having upon the interests of local businessmen. A plot was hatched to kill the foreigner on the king's death. In March 1688, when Narai fell seriously ill, Phra Phetracha – a claimant for the throne – had Phaulcon arrested, tried and convicted for treason, and then executed on 5 June.

Situated close to the junction of the Pasak and Chao Phraya rivers, **Wat Phanan Choeng** is the first wat to be reached by boat, travelling clockwise from the Chandra Kasem pier. The 19-m-high seated Buddha image in the *viharn* (immediately behind the bot) is mentioned in a chronicle as having been made in 1324, some 26 years before Ayutthaya became the capital. It is likely that the wat was founded at the same time, making it the oldest in Ayutthaya. The Buddha is made of brick, plaster and is gilded. This image is said to have wept tears when Ayutthaya was sacked by the Burmese in 1767.

Wat Chai Wattanaram ① *β30*, sits on the west bank of the Chao Phraya River, to the west of the city. A decapitated Buddha sits overlooking the river in front of the ruins, while the large central *prang* is surrounded by two rows of smaller *chedis* and *prang*-like *chedis*, arranged on the cardinal and sub-cardinal points of the cloister that surrounds the central structure. The wat was built by King Prasat Thong (1630-1656) in honour of his mother and the complex has a Khmer quality about it. Relatively few tours of Ayutthaya include Wat Chai Wattanaram on their itineraries, which is a great shame as this is a marvellous site. It is also possibly the best restored of all the monasteries, avoiding the rather cack-handed over-restoration that mars some of the other sites.

North of here is **Wat Kasatthirat**. This wat represents the end of a river tour unless the Old Lopburi River is navigable in which case Wat Na Phramane (see page 171) can also be reached, returning, full circle, to the Chandra Kasem pier.

Most of the guesthouses will run river tours on long-tailed boats. You can expect to pay somewhere between β200-300 per person for a two-hour tour.

San Pedro Cathedral

Lying 11 km south outside the city, this was the site of the original Portuguese settlement in Ayutthaya, dating from 1511. At one point as many as 3000 Portuguese and their mixed-blood offspring were living here, although with the sacking of Ayutthaya by the Burmese in 1767 the community was abandoned. Since the mid-1980s the Fine Arts Department, with financial support from Portugal, has been excavating the site and the cathedral itself is now fully restored. It was opened to the public in 1995.

Lopburi ●❶❷❸❹ ⟩⟩ pp176-179.

→ Colour map 2, C1.

To the west of Lopburi is the old city with its historical sights. To the east is the new town with its major military base. Inevitably, most visitors will be attracted to the palace, museum, monasteries and *prangs* of the old city. This part of town is also teeming with Lopburi's famous monkeys, which clamber from one telegraph pole to another, laze around the temples (particularly Sam Phra Karn), feast on the offerings left by worshippers, and grasp playfully at the hair of unwitting tourists. They have a penchant for stealing sunglasses or spectacles: be warned. Don't try and feed them, as you are likely to provoke a monkey riot.

Background

Lopburi has been seemingly caught between competing powers for more than 1000 years. The discovery of Neolithic and Bronze Age remains indicate that the site on the left bank of the Lopburi River was in use in prehistoric times. The town became a major centre during the Dvaravati period (sixth-11th century), when it was known as Lavo (the original settlers were the 'Lavah', related to the Mon). In AD 950 Lopburi fell to the expanding Khmers who made it a provincial capital; in Thailand, the Khmer period of art and architecture is known as 'Lopburi' because of their artistic impact evident in the town and surrounding area (see page 736). By the 14th century, Khmer influence had waned and the Thais reclaimed Lopburi. In 1351 King Uthong of Ayutthaya gave his son – Prince Ramesuan – governorship of the town, indicating its continued importance. It fell into obscurity during the 16th century, but was resuscitated when King Narai (1656-1688) restored the city with the assistance of European architects. With Narai's death in Lopburi, the town entered another period of obscurity but was again restored to glory during Rama IV's reign.

Ins and outs

There are regular bus connections from Bangkok's Northern bus terminal and Ayutthaya, as well as destinations in the north. The bus station is in the new town, 2 km from the old town, close to the roundabout where Routes 311 and 3016 cross (Wongwian Sra Kaeo). It's also possible to arrive by train from Bangkok's Hualamphong station or Ayutthaya. Frequent buses and *songthaews* ferry passengers between the old and new towns. ⟩⟩ See Transport, page 179, for further information.

Sights

The **Narai Ratchaniwet Palace** ① Wed-Sun 0830-1200, 1300-1630, ฿30, represents the historical heart of Lopburi, encased by massive walls and bordered to the west by the Lopburi River. King Narai declared Lopburi his second capital in the 17th century, and, between 1665 and 1677, built his palace, which became his 'summer' retreat. The main gate is on Sorasak Road, opposite the **Asia Lopburi Hotel**. The well-kept palace grounds are divided into three sections: an outer, middle and an inner courtyard.

The outer courtyard, now in ruins, contained the 'functional' buildings: a tank to supply water to the palace, transported down terracotta pipes from a lake some distance away; storage warehouses for hides and spices; and elephant and horse stables. There was also a Banquet Hall for royal visitors, and, on the south wall, an Audience Hall (Tuk Phrachao Hao). The niches that line the inner side of the walls by the main gates would have contained oil lamps, lit during festivals and important functions.

An archway leads to the middle courtyard. On the left are the tall ruins of the Dusitsawan Thanya Mahaprasat Hall, built in 1685 for audiences with visiting dignitaries. Next to this is the Phiman Mongkut Pavilion, now the King Narai Museum, housing a fine collection spanning all periods of Thai art, but concentrating, not surprisingly, on Lopburi period sculpture. To the north, the Chantra Paisan Pavilion, looking like a wat, was one of the first structures built by King Narai and served as his audience hall until the Suttha Sawan Pavilion was completed. Behind these buildings were the Women's Quarters, again built by Rama IV. One of them has been turned into a Farmer's Museum displaying traditional central plains farming technology and other implements used in rural life, for pottery and iron production, weaving and fishing. The other buildings in the women's quarters are in the process of being restored.

The inner courtyard contains the ruins of King Narai's own residence, the Suttha Sawan Pavilion. It is isolated from the rest of the complex and was surrounded by gardens, ponds (where the king took his bath under huge canopies) and fountains. King Narai died in this pavilion on 11 July 1688 while his opponents plotted against him.

North of Vichayen Road, next to the railway line, is **Wat Phra Prang Sam Yod** (Wat of Three Prangs), a laterite and sandstone shrine whose three spires originally represented the three Hindu deities: Brahma, Vishnu and Siva. The south *prang* has remnants of some fine stucco friezes and naga heads; also note how the stone door frames are carved to resemble their wooden antecedents. The temple is also home to a large troupe of cute, vicious monkeys who are best left well alone. It's also here where the locals hold, in late November, an annual feast to honour the monkeys. Tables are laid out with fruit, nuts and various monkey treats; the result is a a giant monkey food-fight with nasty spats breaking out over monkey favourites – thousands of Thais turn out to watch.

West along Vichayen Road is the Khmer **Prang Khaek**. Built in the late eighth century, this, like Prang Sam Yod, was also originally a Hindu shrine. The three brick spires represent the oldest Khmer *prangs* found in the Central region of Thailand. It was restored in the 17th century, but today lies in ruins.

Further along Vichayen Road are the remains of **Vichayen House** ① ฿30, better known as Constantine Phaulcon's House, the influential adviser to King Narai (see box, page 173). The house, European in style, was constructed for Chevalier de Chaumont, the first French ambassador to Thailand who lived here in 1685. Later, it was used by the Greek Prime Minister, Phaulcon, as his residence.

Opposite the railway station is the entrance to **Wat Phra Sri Ratana Mahathat**, ① ฿30, the oldest and tallest wat in Lopburi. The laterite *prang* is slender and elegant and thought to be contemporary with Angkor Wat in Cambodia (12th century).

Wat Phra Buddhabat

① *24 km south of the old city in the town of Phra Buddhabat, take Route 1 south and after 23 km turn onto Route 310, or catch a Saraburi bus from the bus station; passengers are let off on the main road, from where it's 1 km to the shrine.*

This wat is founded on the site of a large footprint of the Buddha – the most renowned in the country. A short stairway, flanked by two well-wrought many-headed nagas, leads up to a cluster of shrines, *salas*, *chedis* and pavilions set at different levels. The ornate tile-encrusted *mondop*, built to cover the footprint, was constructed during Rama I's reign. It has four pairs of exquisite mother-of-pearl doors. The footprint itself, which is a natural impression made in the limestone rock (depending on one's beliefs), was first discovered in the reign of King Song Tham (1610-1628). It is 150 cm long, edged in gold and set down below floor level. The print must be special: pilgrims not only rub gold leaf onto it, but also rain down coins and banknotes, hence the protective grill. It is said that King Song Tham ordered officials to search for the footprint, having been told by Ceylonese monks that one might be found in Thailand. A hunter stumbled across it while trailing a wounded deer – which was miraculously healed of its injury – and the site was declared a shrine.

◉ Ayutthaya and around listings

For Sleeping and Eating price codes and other relevant information, see pages 44-49.

◉ Sleeping

Ayutthaya *p166, map p168*
A-C Uthong Inn, 210 Rojana Rd, Amphoe Phra Nakhon Si, T035-242236, www.uthong inn.com. Inconveniently located a couple of kilometres east of town, but a strikingly attractive 100-room hotel, primarily aimed at the business market. Some a/c. Japanese restaurant and pool.
C River View Place Hotel, T035-241444, www.riverviewplace.com. Originally designed as a condominium the well-appointed rooms are massive, all with balconies and kitchenettes. Most come with views over the river to Wat Phanan Choeng and beyond. Nice terrace, swimming pool, reasonable food and good, quiet location make this the best hotel in the old city. Service, while friendly, is soporific at best. Recommended.
D Ayothaya Hotel, Naresuan Rd (Chao Phrom Rd), T035-232855. Average hotel with OK rooms and pool.
D Teveraj Tamrin Hotel, 91 Moo 10, Tambon Ka Mung, T035-243139. Close to the train station (turn left), with views

over the River Pasak. Pleasant rooms with good Western bathrooms. **Floating Restaurant** (see Eating, below).
E Ayutthaya Youth Hostel, 2 Rojana Rd, T035-210941. Very friendly, well-run hostel with pleasant gardens and clean rooms. All are en suite and are the usual mix of fan, a/c and hot/cold water. No dorms. Rates include breakfast. Recommended.
E Eve Guesthouse, 11/19 Moo 2, Tambon Morrattanachai, T08-1294 3293 (mob). Very cute and well-maintained guesthouse set in a purpose built brick cottage. Located on a quiet back *soi* this place is also sited in a small garden. Rooms are mix of a/c and fan, hot water and cold. Very friendly owner, Eve, is a local lawyer. Recommended.
E Wiangfa Hotel, 1/8 Rojana Rd, T035-241353. Old-school Thai hotel set in a small compound just off a busy road. Some rooms have funky tiling while the upstairs ones have hot water – all have a/c, TV and en suite facilities. Friendly, breakfast on request.
E-F Baan Lotus, Pa-Maphrao Rd, T035-251 988. This wonderful, crumbling old school-house, complete with massive gardens and huge lotus pond, is one of the most interesting places to stay in Ayutthaya – despite becoming more and more run-down.

Run by the engaging English-speaking Khun Kosoom – a retired female medical scientist who keeps a huge supply of medicines to help out travellers – the rooms are large and en suite with either fan or a/c. Often full, you will probably need to book ahead. Recommended.

E-F Bannkunpra, 48 Uthong Rd, T035-241978, www.bannkunpra.com. An atmospheric teak house set by the river, each room is furnished with antiques and rickety 4-poster beds. There's a great terrace overlooking the Pasak River but bring earplugs as the tugs pulling the barges upstream do so at full volume. Other drawbacks are that the rooms are slightly overpriced, the staff barely interested in their guests and the food is very average.

E-F Chantana House, 12/22 Soi 8, Nareasuan Rd, T035-323200. Friendly little guesthouse with small garden and homely feel. Clean rooms, some have a/c.

E-F The Old Place, 102 Uthong Rd, T035-211162, www.theoldplaceguesthouse.com. Friendly enough place set by the river. Rooms are clean, some have river view and a/c. Restaurant popular with local Thais – always a good sign. Small coffee shop out front.

E-G Ayutthaya Guesthouse, 12/34 Soi Thor Kor Sor, Naresuan Rd (Chao Phrom Rd), T035-232658. Some a/c rooms, some fan-cooled. The communal facilities in this attractive teak house are kept spotless. Dorm beds also available.

E-G PU Inn Ubonpon, 20/1 Soi Thor Kor Sor, Naresuan Rd, T035-251213, www.puguesthouse.com. Cute little guesthouse in the backstreets. Rooms are adequate, some a/c and en suite, and the owner is friendly. Good place to hang out, attracting a decent crowd.

E-G Tony's Place, 12/18 Soi 8 Nareasuan Rd, T035-252578. A generic, well-run, backpacker hang-out with all the facilities you'd expect: toned-down Thai food, internet, tours. Rooms, some a/c, are fine and location is sound.

F Sherwood House, 21/25 Dechawut Rd, T08-6666 0813 (mob). Ask for rooms at the back of this small, well-run guesthouse –

the road out front is very busy. The main draw is the small swimming pool (non-guests ฿45), which makes this place a real bargain. You can also sample great cheddar cheese sandwiches and excellent coffee here.

Lopburi p174
Most people only stop off in Lopburi for a few hours and the standard of accommodation reflects this. Those listed below are rarely full.

B-D Lopburi Inn, Phahonyothin Rd, T036-411625. Slightly overpowering monkey theme employed in this hotel's decor and it is also a long way out of town. Nevertheless, it's the smartest in the area with good facilities including a gym and a large pool.

E-F Asia Lopburi, 28/9 Narai Maharat Rd, T036-411625. Fairly clean rooms, friendly and great location. Good option.

F-G Nett, 17/1-2 Rachdamnern Soi 2, T036-411738. Clean, central and quiet, with attached shower rooms, the best of the cheaper hotels.

🍴 Eating

Ayutthaya p166, map p168
Restaurants in Ayutthaya are good places to sample Chao Phraya river fish like *plaa chon*, *plaa nam ngen* and snake head.

Ψ Baan Joom Zap (the sign is in Thai), Uthong Rd. Daily 1000-2200. Riverside restaurant, set back from the road and in between the **Bannkunpra** and **Old Place** guesthouses. This great Thai restaurant specializes in excellent Isaan food – it even offers a unique deep-fried *somtam* (spicy papaya salad) and Thai style herbal soups with seafood and glass noodles. The friendly owner, Wee, a retired lawyer and political activist, speaks English and offers all his dishes *pet nit noi* (just a little bit spicy) if you can't handle eating local.

Ψ Da Ivo, 10/28 Naresuan Rd. Offers decent enough pizza for this part of the world but don't expect anything too authentic.

Ψ Floating Restaurant, at the Teveraj Tamrin, on the Pasak River. This pleasing restaurant is divided into a/c and open-air sections. It serves sushi and a very large choice of Thai and Western food.

¶¶ Nai Pun, corner of Chee Kun and Uthong roads. A friendly little Thai restaurant with a homely atmosphere and a/c should the heat be getting to you. The fantastic green curry is a must.

¶¶ Phae Krung Kao, 4 Uthong Rd. Floating restaurant to the south of Pridi Damrong bridge, excellent Chao Phraya river fish – try the *plaa chon* and the tasty deep-fried snake head (actually a fish) with chillies.

¶¶ Ruan Thai Mai Suay (Thai House), 2 km or so south of the city on Route 3059. Worth the effort of getting here, this restaurant offers good Thai food in a traditional open wooden house typical of the central plains. Very popular with wealthier locals.

Cafés

¶¶ Moon Café, Soi Thor Kor Sor, Naresuan Rd (Chao Phrom Rd). A general watering hole serving tea, coffee and alcohol, the Moon Café's reputation has been tarnished of late with reports of bad service, poor food and high prices. A good spot for people watching.

¶¶ The Tea and Coffee house, next door to Moon Café. Offers a fine array of hot beverages and good Western and Thai breakfasts. Recommended.

Foodstalls

There is a **night market** with cheap foodstalls in the parking area in front of Chandra Kasem Palace; stalls are also concentrated at the west end of Chao Phrom Rd and in the market at the northeast corner of the city on Uthong Rd. The covered **Chao Phrom Market** is also an excellent place for cheap food.

Lopburi *p174*

The orchards around Lopburi are reputed to produce the country's finest *noi naa* (custard apples). Lopburi has a good selection of Chinese-Thai restaurants, especially along Na Phrakan Rd and Sorasak Rd. The market between Rachdamnern Rd and

Rue de France provides the usual range of stall foods, as do the stalls along Sorasak Rd. The best places to eat in the evening are at the stalls along Na Phrakan Rd in the Old City.

¶¶ Chulathip, corner of Na Phrakan and Rachdamnern roads. Nothing to do with the hotel, this 24-hr open-air restaurant is good value. Recommended.

⃝ Bars and clubs

Ayutthaya *p166, map p168*
Cocohut, corner of Naresuan and Makhan Rang roads. Daily 1400-2400. New bar selling a range of good cocktails at good prices. Sounds are typically lounge, chill-out and world music. Bar snacks available along with affable, English-speaking owner.
Jazz Bar, Naresuan Rd, opposite Tony's Place. Open 1400-late. Lively, friendly bar offering good atmosphere and some decent sounds.
Wo Gun-T, next to Baan Lotus on Pa Maphrao Rd. Small bar in a well-maintained shack serving snacks, massive selection of non-alcoholic and alcoholic cocktails. The only place in town serving ice cold Heineken on draft.

✾ Festivals and events

Ayutthaya *p166, map p168*
Nov Loi Krathong (Festival of Lights)
See Essentials, page 51.

⊖ Transport

Ayutthaya *p166, map p168*
Bicycle and motorbike
Kan Kitti Travel, next to the Jazz Bar on Soi Naresuan. Offers reliable bikes (฿30 for 24 hrs) and motorbikes (฿250 for 24 hrs) for hire. It also organizes train and bus tickets.

Boat
Long-tailed boats can be hired at the jetty opposite the Chandra Kasem Palace in the

northeast corner of town. Expect to pay ฿250 for 1 hr (boats can take 10 people). The **Ayutthaya Guesthouse** and several other guesthouses also arrange boats.

Private boats can be hired from the pier opposite Chandra Kasem Palace in Ayutthaya, the most popular destination being the Summer Palace at **Bang Pa In** (see page 111), ฿250-300 one-way, ฿400 return (3 hrs).

Bus
Regular a/c and non-a/c connections with **Bangkok**'s Northern bus terminal (1½ hrs) and stops north including **Lopburi** (2 hrs), **Phitsanu lok**, **Chiang Mai** and **Sukhothai** (5 hrs).

Train
There are 9 connections daily with **Bangkok**'s Hualamphong station (1½ hrs, Express ฿245, local train ฿15), and with all stops north to **Chiang Mai** (12 hrs).

Lopburi p174
Bus
Regular connections with **Bangkok**'s Northern bus terminal (2-3 hrs) and with **Ayutthaya** (1 hr). Buses from **Kanchanaburi** via **Suphanburi** and **Singburi** (6 hrs), and destinations north.

Train
Regular connections with **Bangkok**'s Hualamphong station (2¾ hrs), **Ayutthaya** (1 hr) and destinations to the north.

ⓘ Directory

Ayutthaya p166, map p168
Banks Most of the banks are either on Uthong Rd or Naresuan Rd (Chao Phrom Rd) and change TCs and have ATMs. Bangkok, Uthong Rd (next to Cathay Hotel). Siam City, Uthong Rd (close to Uthong Hotel). Thai Military, Chao Phrom Rd. Thai Farmers, Chao Phrom Rd. **Internet** Log On, Makham Rang Rd, offers excellent bandwidth on new machines for ฿15 per hr – it's the best place in town by a mile though a little walk from the main backpacker area. A number of internet cafés have opened up on Naresuan Rd and Soi Thor Kor Sor. **Post office** Uthong Rd (south from the Chandra Kasem Palace). International calls available here. **Tourist Police**, across the street from the TAT office, Si Sanphet Rd, T035-242352.

Lopburi p174
Banks Krung Thai, 74 Vichayen Rd. Thai Military, corner of Sorasak and Rachdamnern roads. **Medical services** Hospital, Phahonyothin Rd. **Post office** On road to Singburi, not far from Prang Sam Yod. There's a 2nd post office near the bus station.

Kanchanaburi and the west

The wonderful forests, hills and melange of different peoples of this western tract of Thailand
are overshadowed by a terrible history – during the Second World War thousands of prisoners
of war and local labourers died at the hands of their Japanese captors building a railway line
through almost impassable terrain. This piece of history was made famous in David Lean's
1957 Oscar-winning epic, Bridge on the River Kwai. Today, the bridge, sited at the town of
Kanchanaburi, and the war museums and memorials associated with it, has helped turn the
region into a tourist mecca. Most come not only to visit the famous bridge but also to relax by
Kanchanaburi's elegant Kwai Noi River.

    The more adventurous head into the national parks and hills further west. Awaiting here are
the evocatively named Three Pagodas Pass (Saam Ong), miscellaneous indigenous groups, the
resort town of Sangkhlaburi and the Burmese border. ▸▸ For listings, see pages 190-195.

Kanchanaburi and around ●●●●●●▲●● ▸▸ pp190-195.

→ Colour map 3, B3.

Famous for the Bridge on the River Kwai, Kanchanaburi is surrounded by a vast area of
great natural beauty making it a good base to visit national parks, sail down the Kwai
River or travel to one of a number of waterfalls and caves. Over the years, with the languid
river providing a charming backdrop, the town has become one of Thailand's biggest
tourist destinations, for both foreigners and Thais. The main run of Kanchanaburi's
backpacker hang-outs, internet cafés and insipid food, along Mae Nam Kwai Road, is
reminiscent of Khao San in Bangkok – there's very little local flavour left here. Head out of
the backpacker ghetto and large parts of the rest of the town are filled with markets,
shophouses and memorials to those who died in the Second World War. Apart from
tourism, the province's wealth is derived from gems mined at the Bo-Phloi mines, teak
trading with Burma and sugar cane plantations. It was from here that the Japanese set
Allied prisoners of war to work on the construction of the notorious 'death railway',
linking Thailand with Burma during the Second World War (see box, page 184).

Ins and outs

Getting there There are regular connections by train and bus with Bangkok. The journey
from Bangkok takes around 2½ hours by train while any of the numerous buses take
two hours. There are also bus connections with Nakhon Pathom (1½ hours), Suphanburi
and onwards to Sangkhlaburi. Unfortunately, there are no direct bus connections
with Ayutthaya – you must connect with a slow local service at Suphanburi. This is
something local tour operators in Kanchanaburi have taken advantage of, cramming
rickety minibuses with backpackers willing to pay inflated prices; you're better advised to
travel via Bangkok.

    Non-air-conditioned buses arrive at the station in the market area, behind Saengchuto
Road. Air-conditioned buses run to the corner of Saengchuto Road, opposite Lak Muang
Road. Take a songthaew from the bus station to the guesthouse area, but beware of over-
charging (it should cost ฿60). The train station is 2 km northwest of town on Saengchuto
Road, not far from the cemetery, T034-511285. Left-luggage available. ▸▸ See Transport,
page 194, for further information.

Kanchanaburi

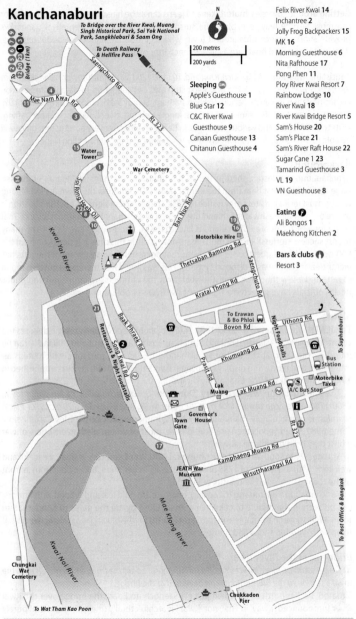

N

200 metres

200 yards

To Bridge over the River Kwai, Muang
Singh Historical Park, Sai Yok National
Park, Sangkhlaburi & Saam Ong

To Death Railway
& Hellfire Pass

Saengchuto Rd

Mae Nam Kwai Rd

Rt 323

Soi Rong Heeb Oil

Water
Tower

War Cemetery

Ban Nue Rd

Motorbike Hire

Thetsaban Bamrung Rd

Kwai Yai River

Kratai Thong Rd

Baak Phraek Rd

Song Kwai Rd
Restaurants & Night Foodstalls

To Erawan
& Bo Phloi
Bovon Rd

Prasit Rd

Khumuang Rd

Night Foodstalls

Uthong Rd

To Suphanburi

Bus
Station

Motorbike
Taxis

A/C Bus Stop

Lak Muang Rd

Lak
Muang

Pol

Town
Gate

Governor's
House

Kamphaeng Muang Rd

JEATH War
Museum

Wisuttharangsi Rd

To Post Office & Bangkok

Rt 323

Mae Klong River

Kwai Noi River

Chungkai
War
Cemetery

To Wat Tham Kao Poon

Chukkadon
Pier

Sleeping

Apple's Guesthouse 1
Blue Star 12
C&C River Kwai
 Guesthouse 9
Canaan Guesthouse 13
Chitanun Guesthouse 4
Felix River Kwai 14
Inchantree 2
Jolly Frog Backpackers 15
MK 16
Morning Guesthouse 6
Nita Rafthouse 17
Pong Phen 11
Ploy River Kwai Resort 7
Rainbow Lodge 10
River Kwai 18
River Kwai Bridge Resort 5
Sam's House 20
Sam's Place 21
Sam's River Raft House 22
Sugar Cane 1 23
Tamarind Guesthouse 3
VL 19
VN Guesthouse 8

Eating

Ali Bongos 1
Maekhong Kitchen 2

Bars & clubs

Resort 3

Getting around Bicycles, motorbikes and jeeps can all be hired in Kanchanaburi and offer the most flexible way to explore the surrounding countryside. Alternatively, *saamlors* provide short-distance trips around town while tuk-tuks are handy for longer journeys. Rafts and long-tailed boats are available for charter on the river.

Tourist information TAT ① *Saengchuto Rd, T034-511200 (walk south, towards Bangkok, from the market and bus station)*, is a good first stop and can supply up-to-date information on accommodation in Kanchanaburi, Nakhon Pathom, Samut Sakhon and Samut Songkhram. Most tour operators offer similar excursions: jungle trekking, elephant rides, bamboo rafting, visits to Hellfire Pass and various waterfalls. In Bangkok, virtually every hotel or tour office will be able to offer a day tour (or longer) to Kanchanaburi and the surrounding sights.

Background
Kanchanaburi was established in the 1830s, although the ruins of Muang Singh (see page 184) to the west date from the Khmer period. On entering the town (called Muang Kan by most locals), visitors may notice the fish-shaped street signs. The fish in question is the yisok, a small freshwater fish and the symbol of Kanchanaburi. Another slice of Thai fauna for which this area of Thailand is known is Kitti's hog-nosed bat. As with so many tourist success stories, Kanchanaburi has its downside. In this case, it is pollution from the 900-odd raft-based guesthouse and restaurant operations. Almost none of the rafts has water treatment or waste disposal systems. This was fine when there were just a handful of rafts and a few thousand tourists a year. Now the numbers are far greater and public health officials have detected a significant rise in water pollution.

Sights
The **JEATH War Museum** ① *0830-1800, ฿30 (no photographs)*, whose name denotes the countries involved – Japan, England, America, Australia, Thailand and Holland – can be found by the river, at the end of Wisuttharangsi Road. The museum, which holds an interesting and harrowing display of prisoners working on the railway, was established in 1977 by the monks of Wat Chanasongkhram.

The **Kanchanaburi War Cemetery (Don Rak)** ① *Saengchuto Rd, 1.5 km out of town, 0800-1700, or you can always look over the gates, walk, hire a bicycle (฿20 a day) or take a saamlor*, is immaculately maintained by the Commonwealth Cemeteries Commission. Some 6982 Allied servicemen are buried here, most of whom died as prisoners of war whilst they built the Burma railway.

Situated 2 km south of town, the **Chungkai (UK) War Cemetery** is small, peaceful and well kept, with the graves of 1750 prisoners of war. To get there, take a boat from in front of the town gates, or go by tuk-tuk or bicycle.

Kanchanaburi's **lak muang** (city pillar), encrusted in gold leaf and draped with flowers, can be seen in the middle of Lak Muang Road. Close by are the gates to Kanchanaburi town. Walk through the gates and turn right (north) for the old and most attractive part of town with wooden shops and houses.

Bridge over the River Kwai
① *Take a saamlor, hire a bicycle, catch a songthaew or board the train, which travels from the town's station to the bridge. Boats can be rented at the bridge.*
Situated 3-4 km north of the town just off Saengchuto Road, the bridge over the Kwai River (pronounced 'Kway' in Thai, not 'Kwai') is architecturally unexciting and is of purely

historical interest. The central span was destroyed by Allied bombing towards the end of the war, and has been rebuilt in a different style. Visitors can walk across the bridge, visit the **Second World War Museum and Art Gallery** ① *0900-1630, ฿30*, or browse in the many souvenir stalls. The museum is an odd affair with some displays relating to the bridge and the prisoners of war who worked and died here, along with a collection of Thai weaponry and amulets, and some astonishingly bad portraits of Thai kings.

Death Railway and Hellfire Pass

① *No admission fee, but donations requested (most visitors leave ฿100). Two trains leave Kanchanaburi daily at 1045 and 1637, with return trains at 0525 and 1300, approximately 2 hrs. From the Nam Tok station, it is another 14 km to the Hellfire Pass and Museum, for which you need a songthaew (฿400 return, 20 mins one way). To reach the pass by road take a northbound bus about 80 km on Route 323 to a Royal Thai Army farm at the Km 66 marker. A track here leads through the farm to a steep path to the pass. There are numerous organized tours to Hellfire Pass.*

Only 130 km of the 'death railway' remain, from Nong Pradook station in the neighbouring province of Ratchaburi through to the small town of Nam Tok. From Kanchanaburi to Nam Tok the railway sweeps through a tranche of dramatic scenery stopping at the ancient Khmer site of Muang Singh en route (see page 184). The name for the pass was bestowed by one of the prisoners of war who, looking down on his comrades working below at night by the glow of numerous open fires, remarked that the sight was like "the jaws of hell". Australian Rod Beattie, with the support of the Australian government, has developed the pass as a memorial cutting a path through to the pass and building a museum. Clear, well-written wall panels surrounded by photographs, along with some reproduction objects, provide a very moving account of the cutting of the pass. From here it is possible to walk a fair distance of the railway route (the rails no longer exist); sturdy shoes are recommended. There are two routes: the Konyu Cutting or the full 4.5-km circuit that ends at Hellfire Pass itself.

Wat Tham Kao Poon

① *5 km southwest of town, a few kilometres on from the Chungkai Cemetery. No entrance fee to the caves, but visitors are encouraged to make a contribution to the maintenance of the monastery (฿10-20). Hire a bicycle or tuk-tuk or charter a boat from in front of the town gates.*
Wat Tham Kao Poon is a rather gaudy temple with caves attached. Follow the arrows through the cave system. There is a large Buddha image at the bottom of the system (and smaller ones elsewhere), as well as *kutis* (cells) in which monks can meditate. Intrepid explorers will find they emerge at the back of the hill. Early in 1996 this cave wat was the site of the murder of British tourist, Johanne Masheder (the cave where the murder took place is permanently closed), by a drug-addicted Thai monk. The crime shook Thailand's religious establishment and the abbot of the monastery was suspended for neglect.

Wat Tham Sua and Wat Tham Kao Noi

① *Hire a motorbike or charter a tuk-tuk/songthaew.*
Wat Tham Sua and Wat Tham Kao Noi lie 20 km southeast of Kanchanaburi. The main temple is a strange, pagoda-like affair perched on a hilly outcrop, and can be seen from afar. At the base of the hill is a Chinese temple, and a short walk further is the steep dragon-lined staircase that leads up the hill to the wat itself. The pagoda is a weird amalgam of Chinese and Thai, new and old.

The death railway

The River Kwai will be forever associated with a small bridge and a bloody railway.

For the Japanese high command during the Second World War, the logic of building a rail link between Siam and Burma was clear – it would cut almost 2000 km off the sea journey from Japan to Rangoon making it easier to supply their fast-expanding empire. The problem was that the Japanese lacked the labour to construct the line through some of the wettest and most inhospitable land in the region. They estimated that it would take five to six years to finish. The solution to their dilemma was simple: employ some of the 300,000 POWs who were being unproductively incarcerated in Singapore.

Work began in June 1942. More than 3,000,000 cu m of rock were shifted, 15 km of bridges built and 415 km of track laid. The workforce, at its peak, numbered 61,000 Allied POWs and an estimated 250,000 Asians. Work was hard; a prisoner, Naylor wrote: "We started work the day after we arrived, carrying huge baulks of timber. It was the heaviest work I have ever known; the Japs drove us on and by nightfall I was so tired and sore that I could not eat my dinner and just crawled on to the bed and fell asleep. The next day was spent carrying stretchers of earth, also heavy work and incredibly monotonous. The hours were 0830 to 1930 with an hour for lunch."

The Japanese, but particularly the Korean overseers, adopted a harsh code of discipline – face slapping, blows with rifle butts, standing erect for hours on end, and solitary confinement for weeks in small cells made of mud and bamboo. By 1943, after years of torturous work combined with poor diet, most of the men were in an appalling state.

Phu Phra Caves, Wat Tham Kun Phaen and Kanchanaburi Cultural Centre
① *Take bus 8203 or hire a motorbike or songthaew/tuk-tuk.*
Phu Phra Caves and Wat Tham Kun Phaen are about 20 km north of town, just off Route 323 to Sangkhlaburi. The wat and its associated caves nestle in foothills which rise up towards Burma. Back on Route 323 is the Kanchanaburi Cultural Centre, with a collection of handicrafts, artefacts and historical exhibits.

Muang Singh Historical Park
① *45 km west of Kanchanaburi, open 0800-1700, ฿4. Hire a tuk-tuk/songthaew or motorbike, or take the train to Thakilen station – it is about a 1.5-km walk.*
This ancient Khmer town, the 'city of lions', is situated on the banks of the Kwai Noi River. Built of deep red laterite, Muang Singh reached its apogee during the 12th-13th centuries when it flourished as a trading post linking Siam with the Indian Ocean. The city represents an artistic and strategic outlier of the great Cambodian Empire, and it is mentioned in inscriptions from the reign of the Khmer King Jayavarman VII.

Khao Phang and Sai Yok Noi waterfall
① *60 km northwest of Kanchanaburi on Route 323. Take bus 8203 from Kanchanaburi town (1 hr). Buses leave every 30 mins between 0645 and 1800. It is 1 km to the falls and 2 km to the caves (the sign for the falls is in Thai only, so follow signs to the cave which are in English).*

In Colonel Toosey's report of October 1945, he wrote: "On one occasion a party of 60, mostly stretcher cases, were dumped off a train in a paddy field some two miles from the Camp in the pouring rain at 0300 hours. As a typical example I can remember one man who was so thin that he could be lifted easily in one arm. His hair was growing down his back and was full of maggots; his clothing consisted of a ragged pair of shorts soaked with dysentery excreta; he was lousy and covered with flies all the time. He was so weak that he was unable to lift his head to brush away the flies which were clustered on his eyes and on the sore places of his body. I forced the Japanese Staff to come and look at these parties, which could be smelt for some hundreds of yards, but with the exception of the Camp Comdt they showed no signs of sympathy, and sometimes merely laughed." (Quoted in Peter Davies, *The man behind the Bridge*, 1991:116).

The railway was finished in late 1943, the line from Nong Pladuk being linked with that from Burma on 17 October. For the POWs it was not the end, however; even after the Japanese capitulated on 10 August 1945, the men had to wait for some while before they were liberated. During this period of limbo, Allied officers were worried most about venereal disease, and Colonel Toosey radioed to Delhi for 10,000 condoms to be dropped by air – an incredible thought given the physical condition of the former POWs. In all, 16,000 Allied prisoners lost their lives and Kanchanaburi contains the graves of 7000 of the victims in two war cemeteries. Less well known are the 75,000 Asian forced labourers who also died constructing the railway. Their sufferings are not celebrated.

Khao Phang and Sai Yok Noi waterfall are only impressive in the wet season (July-September), and swimming in the pools below the waterfall is also best during this season. Close by are the **Vang Ba Dalh Caves**.

Sai Yok National Park

ⓘ *104 km northwest of Kanchanaburi. Boats can be hired from Pak Saeng pier in Tambon Tha Saaw, 50 km north of Kanchanaburi town. A boat (10-12 people) to the park (including the Lawa caves and Sai Yok Yai waterfall), should cost ฿1200 per boat (or go on a tour); the trip will take 2½ hrs upstream and 1½ hrs down. There are also buses from Kanchanaburi to the park, 1 hr. The best time of year to visit is May-Dec.*

The main attraction of Sai Yok National Park is the **Sai Yok Yai Waterfall**. Also near Sai Yok Yai are the **Daowadung Caves** (30 minutes north by boat from the falls and then a 3-km walk). Tigers and elephants still inhabit this wild region of stunning scenery, stretching to the Burmese border.

Erawan National Park

ⓘ *65 km north of Kanchanaburi, open 0600-1800, ฿200 entrance fee to the park. Regular buses (No 8170) every 50 mins from 0800 onwards from Kanchanaburi (1½-2 hrs, ฿26). The last bus back to Kanchanaburi leaves Erawan at 1600. The best time to visit the falls is during the rainy season. It is a 35-min walk from the bus station to the first of the series of 7 falls. There are also plenty of places to eat Thai food next to the bus stop. If you want to make like* the locals it is considered the done thing to combine *ahan Isaan* (Isaan food), such as *som tam* (spicy papaya salad), *kai yang* (grilled chicken) and *khao niaow* (sticky rice) with *nam tok* (waterfall).

Without doubt this is an area of great natural beauty, covering 550 sq km and containing the impressive **Erawan Falls**. Split into seven levels the first is popular with swimmers and picnickers. Level three is very beautiful, and level seven is well worth the steep climb with refreshing pools awaiting any intrepid trekker who makes the precarious climb up. The impressive **Phrathat Caves**, with huge and stupendous stalactites and stalagmites, are located about 10 km northwest of headquarters, a good hike or easy drive.

Arguably the most striking waterfalls are those at **Huay Khamin**, some 108 km northwest of town. The falls are awkward to reach independently but tour companies will provide arranged trips. The **Thung Yai** and **Huai Kha Khaeng wildlife sanctuaries**, where the falls are based, were once threatened by a proposed dam that would have destroyed rare stands of riverine tropical forest that exist here. Public pressure ensured that the plans were shelved, representing the first significant victory for environmentalists in Thailand. In 1992 the two sanctuaries were declared Southeast Asia's first Natural World Heritage Site by UNESCO, vindicating the environmentalists' stand.

Bo Phloi
① *Take bus No 325 from Kanchanaburi bus station, 1½ hrs.*
Bo Phloi, 50 km north of town, is one of Thailand's main gem-mining areas. Here are eight opencast mines – extracting sapphires, onyx and semi-precious stones – and a number of polishing plants. Local production techniques are displayed.

Tham Than Lot National Park
① *There are regular connections between Kanchanaburi and Nong Pru. The road to the park cuts off left from Route 3086 shortly before entering Nong Pru; the park entrance is 22 km from this turn-off. During the week it is usually necessary to charter a motorcycle or songthaew to the park, but at weekends there is a public service from Nong Pru.*
The park encompasses a portion of the Tenasserim range of mountains that form the border between Thailand and Burma and includes small populations of Asiatic black bear, white-handed gibbon and elephant. There is even talk that there may be tigers here. The highest peak is Khao Khampaeng, which rises to 1260 m. Within easy walking of park headquarters (where there is a visitor centre) is **Than Lot Noi Cave**, after which the park was named. The cave reaches around 300 m into the mountain side. A trail leads from here for around 2 km to another cave, **Than Lot Yai**, where there is a small Buddhist shrine.

Sangkhlaburi and Saam Ong (Three Pagodas Pass) ●❼▲❶❻
▶▶ *pp190-195.*

→ *Colour map 3, A2.*
The route to Sangkhlaburi, or 'Sangkhla', and Saam Ong (Three Pagodas Pass) from Kanchanaburi, a total of some 240 km, follows the valley of the Kwai. The scenery soon becomes increasingly rugged with the road passing through remnant forests and expanses of deep red tropical soils used to grow cassava, tamarind, mango and cotton. Roughly three hours from Kanchanaburi sits the market town of Thong Pha Phum and the eastern edge of the massive Khao Laem reservoir. From here, the road begins to wind through a steep hills and dense forest. Just before Sangkhlaburi the road skirts the reservoir;

Border essentials: Thailand–Burma (Myanmar)

Three Pagodas Pass (Saam Ong–Payathonzu)

The border between Burma and Thailand (open 0600-1800) is periodically closed due to political conflict. It is therefore well worth checking the situation before arrival; there is a tourist police office at the pass if you encounter problems. At the border, visitors can pay a US$10 immigration fee to cross into Burma and visit the village of Payathonzu (meaning 'Three Pagodas'). Motorbike taxis can transport you to the market area of Payathonzu (฿25 from the *songthaew* drop-off point). The last *songthaew* back to Sangkhlaburi leaves at about 1630; check on arrival.

Beyond the village, there is another border post, beyond which visitors are forbidden to go. Note that it is illegal to cross the border anywhere other than at a checkpoint. Similarly, do not go beyond Payathonzu without permission of the Burmese army.

a strange landscape of submerged (now dead) trees and what appear to be raft-houses. This upland area is also home to several different ethnic groups: Karen, Mon and Burmese.

Towards Sangkhlaburi

Thong Pha Phum is a small, lively market town situated in a beautiful position on the southern shores of the Khao Laem Reservoir, 74 km south of Sangkhlaburi. Many of the inhabitants of the town are Mon and Karen. There are regular bus connections with Kanchanaburi's bus terminal (three hours) and onwards north to Sangkhlaburi. Around Thong Pha Phum are a small number of lakeside resort hotels and raft operations, mainly geared to Thai weekenders from Bangkok. Comparatively few *farangs* make it up here, which is evident in the Thai-only signage at the local hotels. The Khao Laem Reservoir was created in 1983 when the Electricity Generating Authority of Thailand built the Khao Laem Dam and flooded the valley. About a dozen villages were inundated as a result and submerged tree-trunks still make navigation hazardous in the lake's shallows. It's possible to hire expensive long-tailed boats or go fishing and swimming. There are also numerous walks and trails to explore, and various waterfalls and caves.

Although the 1500-sq-km **Khao Laem National Park** has been heavily logged, parts of it still play host to small populations of leopard, gibbon and macaque, as well as lesser mammals such as civets and mongoose. The most pristine habitats can be found towards the northeast and the small Thung Yai wildlife sanctuary, which abuts the park. Park headquarters are close to the main road (Route 323) to Sangkhlaburi. Thong Pha Phum has regular bus connections with Kanchanaburi's bus terminal (three hours) and onwards north to Sangkhlaburi.

Sangkhlaburi

On the hill just above Sangkhlaburi, next to the main road, rests a massive gold-painted reclining Buddha followed by a collection of other enormous golden Buddha statues. This ostentatious display reveals little of the lethargic town down below. Situated on the edge of the huge Khan Laem Reservoir, which was created in 1983 with the damming of three rivers, Sangkhlaburi is a great place to wile away the hours in peaceful surroundings. The town is also a centre for wood and drugs smuggling. There's a remarkably diverse population of Karen, Mon, Burmese, Indians and Chinese.

The morning market here provides a range of textiles and various Burmese goods. A 400-m wooden bridge across the lake, leads to an atmospheric Mon village (Waeng Kha). There are also stunning views of the surrounding hills from the bridge.

Around Sangkhlaburi

To Moulmein (70 km)
Kroeng Tho Waterfall

Road Closed
Three Pagodas Pass (Saam Ong)   Payathonzu
                                 Burmese Temple

MYANMAR   Timber Factory
                          2 km   Gate
                                 Wang Bandan Cave
                          5 km

THAILAND   Thai   9 km
                          7 km   Army
                                 Small Temple
                                 Entrance to Thung Yai
                   Forest   Wildlife Sanctuary
                   Department   Takien Thong
                                  Waterfall
          Ban Songkaria
                                 Songkaria River
Songkaria River   Ban Sane Pong
                                  (Karen Village)
                                   Thung Yai Wildlife
                          6 km   Sanctuary
                   Immigration   Entrance & HQ
                                 Steep
                                 Road
To Huay Malai (20 km)   8 km
          Supermarket Minibus   Gold
                       Station   Buddhas
                                 Karen Village   To Umphang (200 km)
                   Immigration
Wat Wang   Sangkhlaburi 4 km
Wiwekaram   1.5 km
         Wooden
Mon   Footbridge
Village &
Market   Tambon Nong Loo
                                  8 km
Mon Temple
& Handicraft   Gong Mong Tha
Market   (Karen Village)
                   Entrance to Thung Yai
Beeklee River   Wildlife Sanctuary 10 km

Khao Laem
Reservoir   4 km

Wat Saam Prasop   Runtee River
(Old temple of
former Sangkla)   To Kanchanaburi (220 km)

N
Not to scale

Sleeping
Burmese Inn 1
P Guesthouse 3
Phornphailin 4

Pornpailin Riverside 2
Sam Prasob Resort 6
Three Pagodas Resort 8

Eating
Baan Unrak 1

The 8000 inhabitants are mainly displaced Burmese who cannot get a Thai passport and can only work around Sangkhla. From 1948 onwards refugees have fled Burma for the relative safety of Thailand. Most of them will never be allowed a visa or resident's permit. In 1983 the old town of Sangkhlaburi was flooded by the dam and these refugees were again left with no homes or land. The abbot of the flooded Wat Sam Prasop, the spires of which can be seen – so it is said – protruding above the lake waters during the dry season, was able to acquire land for a new wat and helped 500 households to re-establish themselves. These people are not wanted by the Thai government and there have been several raids by the army to round up Mon people without identity cards. Over the years they have been protected by the monks living here, but there is no guarantee this will continue and their existence in Thailand is uncertain to say the least.

Wat Wang Wiwekaram is situated across the lake from Sangkhlaburi on a hill. It was built in 1982 to replace the revered temple Wat Sam Prasop, which was submerged by the reservoir. The *chedi* is said to be modelled on the Mahabodhi stupa in Bodhgaya, India, with the *viharn*, allegedly constructed with black market profits, providing a fine example of nouveau gauche temple architecture. To the east of the wat is a **Burmese handicraft market**, where sarongs, silk, cloth, lacquerware and silver jewellery are all for sale. Avoid the 'gems', though, since they are almost certainly fakes.

Saam Ong (Three Pagodas Pass) → *Colour map 3, A2.*

This is an unexciting spot, 20 km northwest of Sangkhlaburi, with a tacky market in a makeshift shelter, which sells a few Burmese goods (teak, umghi, seed pearls) and a lot of Chinese imports (the 'gems' here will also be fake). The pagodas, wrapped in red, saffron and white cloth, are tiny and truly unremarkable. This was the traditional invasion route for Burmese soldiers during the Ayutthayan period (see pages 167 and 690).

On the border lie the remains of the Burmese/Thai/Japanese railway. The market in **Payathonzu** is marginally more interesting than at Saam Ong, with a range of handicrafts, jewellery, jade, amulets, Burmese blankets, and an alarming amount of teak furniture. There is also a handful of Thai restaurants and noodle stalls and an Indian-run bakery.

Control of this area has vacillated between the Burmese army and Mon and Karen rebels. At present it is firmly in the hands of the Burmese authorities and posters declare "Love your Motherland" and "Respect the Law". If you're undecided about visiting Burma due to its human rights' record then check the facts on Amnesty International's website (www.amnesty.org). The only place to stay at Saam Ong is the **Three Pagodas Pass Resort**, see Sleeping, page 193.

Note Malaria is common in this area, particularly in the jungle, so take precautions and try to avoid being bitten.

Around Saam Ong

The Mon village of **Ban Songkalia** lies 6 km north from the turn-off to Three Pagodas Pass. It was once the headquarters for the Mon army.

One of the three local entrances to **Thung Yai Wildlife Sanctuary** lies 15 km northeast of Sangkhla, in the Karen village of Ban Sane Pong. Within the park is the **Takien Thong Waterfall**, with big pools for swimming. The falls lie 26 km from Sangkhla, north of Ban Sane Pong, but are only accessible by taking the main road north for 13 km from the turn-off to Three Pagodas Pass, and then taking a right turn down a dirt road for 9 km, which is possible to drive down on motorbikes. Until recently this route was only negotiable during the dry season, but with the new all-weather road access should now be possible year-round.

Wang Bandan Cave ⓘ *no entrance fee, but the monks may try to charge ฿50 to guide visitors through the cave*, lies 18 km north from the turn-off to Three Pagodas Pass, 2 km down a track to the right of the road. Monks used to live in the cave until a few years ago, but (it is said) due to the effects of increasing tourism in the area, from both Thais and foreigners, they have moved to small houses at the bottom of the hill. The entrance and exit are different.

Huay Kha Khaeng Wildlife Sanctuary ⓘ *0800-1700, ฿200 including accommodation in one of the three very basic fan huts; larger groups should seek prior approval from the Wildlife Conservation Division of the Royal Forest Department, 61 Phaholyathin Ladyao Jatujak, Bangkok, T02-561 4292, webmaster@forest.go.th; take the Uthai Thani route to Lan Sak, and turn off about 30 km before you get to Lan Sak, follow this turn-off 14 km to Huay Kha Khaeng; public transport available*, is a World Heritage Site and one of the largest wildlife sanctuaries in Southeast Asia. If you're looking for the best of Thailand's free ranging wildlife species, including an enormous range of birdlife, it is unmissable. It borders the Tak and Kanchanaburi Provinces and is a haven for animals with its virgin deciduous forests, prairies, mountains and many streams. Hidden among the fronds are some of Thailand's largest remaining wild elephant herds, the last remaining herds of wild water buffalo, rare gibbons, three otter species and the large gaur and banteng wild cattle species. Also watch out for tigers, clouded leopards and sun bears. The sanctuary is, as yet, underdeveloped and it is advised not to stray too far from the bungalows both because of the danger of the resident animals, and that of getting lost. If the staff have enough time on their hands, they will lead short walks around the area, but they speak little English. There is a nature trail for small groups of visitors but additional services are limited.

ⓖ Kanchanaburi and the west listings

For Sleeping and Eating price codes and other relevant information, see pages 44-49.

ⓢ Sleeping

Kanchanaburi and around *p180, map p181*

Most of the budget accommodation is lined up along busy Mae Nam Kwai Rd. There are also a few raft-type places along the quieter Ron Heeb Oil Rd. Disco boats on the river can cause noise pollution but they are only really active at weekends and usually stop at 2000. Most places will pick you up from the bus/train stations if you book in advance.

A-C Felix River Kwai Hotel, 9/1 Moo 3 Thamakhom, north of the bridge on the west bank of the river, T034-515061. This, rather rambling hotel is the most luxurious in town, with 255 rooms and all the facilities you'd expect from a 1st-class establishment.

B-C River Kwai Bridge Resort, River Kwai Rd, T034-514522, www.riverkwaibridge resort.com. Well appointed bungalows and rooms all with hot water, a/c, TV, located in fine gardens beside the river in a quiet part of town near the bridge. A good choice.

C-D River Kwai Hotel, 284 Saengchuto Rd, T02-677 6240 (Bangkok reservation office). Bog-standard hotel, with generic rooms, a/c, en suite, small gym and pool. The food is awful.

C-D River Kwai Jungle House, 96/1 Moo 3, Amphoe Sai Yok, 40 km from Kanchanaburi, near Muang Singh Historical Park, T034-561052, www.banrimkwae.com/eng/welcome.htm. Rattan bungalows afloat on the river.

D Inchantree, T034-624914, www.inchan treeresort.com. Tucked away in a tiny back road just past the River Kwai Bridge, this is a serene place with sleek, well-designed, contemporary Thai-style rooms. There's a natural swimming pool, terrace with views over to the bridge and a good restaurant.

All rooms have a/c, TV and huge beds – a bargain for the rate. Highly recommended.

D-E Ploy River Kwai Resort, Mae Nam Kwai Rd, T034-515804, www.ploygh.com. Central guesthouse in good location next to the river. Rooms have outdoor showers. Friendly. Excellent value. Free bus/train station pick-up. Recommended.

D-E Rainbow Lodge, 48/5 Soi Rong Heeb Oil, T034-518683, www.seethailand.com. Friendly place with good, split-level mini-bungalows and large a/c VIP rooms, all en suite. Good river views and best of the bunch in this part of town. Recommended.

D-F Chitanun Guesthouse, 47/3 Mae Nam Kwai Rd, T034-624785. Great little guesthouse on the opposite side of Mae Nam Rd from the river. Without a riverside location you get more for your baht and these well-designed rooms, offering a mix of fan and a/c and hot/cold water, are good value. Friendly, quiet, with nice gardens. Another branch, **Chitanun Mansion** will soon be opening on the main Bangkok road. Recommended.

D-F Pong Phen Guesthouse, Soi Bangladesh, Mae Nam Kwai Rd, T034-512981, www.pongphen.com. With a decent-sized swimming pool (non-guests ฿100) and riverside terraces, **Pong Phen** does a lot with a small space. The rooms vary in quality, facilities and price but all are clean and not too old. Friendly and business-like.

D-F Sam's House, 14/1 Mae Nam Kwai Rd, T034-515956, sams_guesthouse@hotmail.com. Good wooden huts with toilets, and balconies on the mangrove-esque edge of the Kwai. Good value.

D-F Sugar Cane 1, 22 Soi Pakstan, Mae Nam Kwai Rd, T034-624520. This secluded spot provides a pleasant retreat in a good location. Spotlessly clean with friendly staff. The restaurant commands fantastic views over the river. Tours organized.

D-G Tamarind Guesthouse, 29/1 Mae Nam Kwai Rd, T034-518790. Probably the best value on the river front – you can get a spotless a/c river-view room with balcony for less than ฿500 here. There are plenty of

terraces and a decent little bar. Owners are friendly. Also have raft rooms. Recommended.

E-F Apple's Guesthouse, 293 Mae Nam Kwai Rd, T034-512017, www.applenoi-kanchanauri.com. An extremely good guest-house, with very clean, comfortable mattresses and private showers, run by a very friendly female couple. This is one of the few locally owned businesses on this stretch and the owners also speak excellent English. The restaurant (see Eating, below) serves awesome Thai food. Free pick-up from bus/train station available. Some of the touts might tell you it is closed – ignore them. Recommended.

E-F MK, 277/41 Saengchuto Rd, T034-621 143. Clean, a/c motel-style rooms with good mosquito screens, TV and shower room. Beauty salon, golf shop and laundry. More expensive rooms are airy with great views.

E-G Blue Star, 241 Mae Nam Kwai Rd, T034-512161. This extremely friendly place, which offers guests a free cookery course, boasts rooms in a variety of styles, notably the 'tarzan stilt houses', some of which have rooftop terraces overlooking the river.

E-G Jolly Frog Backpackers, 28 Mae Nam Kwai Rd, T034-514579. Popular, well-established guesthouse, with attractive garden overlooking the river and local tour information. Wide range of vegetarian, Thai and European food in an affordable restaurant.

E-G Morning Guesthouse, 337 Mae Nam Kwai Rd, T08-1634 3507 (mob). Run by a very friendly Thai woman. This collection of bungalows down the end of a remote *soi*, has a vibe all of its own. Rooms have the usual mixed facilities but have enough pretty details to make them feel more homely.

E-G Sam's Place 7/3 Song Kwai Rd, T034-513971, sams_guesthouse@hotmail.com. Very average rooms, set next to a concrete road bridge. Friendly.

E-G Sam's River Raft House, Soi Rong Heeb Oil, T034-624231, www.samsguesthouse.com. Friendly and attractive, basic guesthouse. Offers great views of the river and mountains.

E-G VN Guesthouse, 44 Soi Rong Heeb Oil, T034-514082, vnguesthouse@yahoo.com.

Well-run clean guesthouse with good river view rooms. Some rooms a/c, all en suite.
F VL, 18/11 Saengchuto Rd, T034-513546. Some a/c, small restaurant, 3-storey block. Quiet, cool, spacious and secluded rooms (with bathrooms) set back from the busy road.
F-G C & C River Kwai Guesthouse, 265/2 Mae Nam Kwai Rd, T034-624547. Rough and ready though very friendly small collection of bungalows and rooms in this backpacker resort. Has some a/c rooms. Also run a huge amount of tours and day trips.
F-G Canaan Guesthouse, 63 Taopoon Soi 2, T034-62995. Conveniently situated behind the bus station. Offers a wonderful family atmosphere, which makes up for the bland rooms. Great home-cooked food, dorms and some a/c en suite rooms.
G Nita Rafthouse, 27/1 Pakprak Rd, T034-514521. Very basic and cheap, though friendly. Good choice if you're on a tiny budget.

Sai Yok National Park p185
The following places are all near the waterfall.
A Panthawee Raft, T034-512572. Has a few rafts in the upmarket category.
A-D Rom Suk Saiyok Yai Raft, 231/3 Moo 7, T034-516130. Has a wide range of rooms and camping facilities.
B See Pee Nong Raft, T034-2156224. Has a few rafts.
B-C Ranthawee Raft. Only has 4 rooms.
B-E Kwai Noi Rafthouse, T034-591075. Has a small collection of floating rooms.

Erawan National Park p185
Park bungalows, designed for groups, can be rented, and it's possible to pitch a tent. There are 2 bungalow operations outside the park boundaries, before the entrance gates: **Erawan Resort Guesthouse** and **Phu Daeng Resort**.

Tham Than Lot National Park p186
There are bungalows in the park and it is also possible to camp. Alternatively, stay a night at the only hotel in the neighbouring town of Nong Pru (฿100 for fan and attached bathroom) – cheaper than staying in the park.

Towards Sangkhlaburi p187
None of the accommodation in Thong Pha Phum has English signage.
C-E Somjaineuk, Thong Pha Phum, T034-599067. New wing with a/c rooms and en suite hot water bathrooms; older part of hotel with basic, but clean, rooms.
D-E Boonyong Bungalows, Thong Pha Phum, T034-599049. The best of the cheaper places. Set away from the road, rooms are clean and reasonably peaceful, with a/c or fan.
D-E Si Thong Pha Phum Bungalows, Thong Pha Phum, T034-599058. Spacious bungalows, some with a/c.

Camping
Camping is possible on a site 2-3 km from Khao Laem National Park headquarters.

Sangkhlaburi p187, map p188
B-D Pornpailin Riverside, T034-595322, www.ppailin.com. Nice location, friendly staff. Mostly geared to Thai weekenders. The cheaper rooms are a bit dark while the more expensive ones are huge airy affairs with large balconies overlooking the lake. Restaurant.
B-D Sam Prasob Resort, overlooking lake, by the wooden bridge, T034-595050, www.samprasob.com. A/C, good restaurant, individual bungalows, small rooms with bathroom, not much English spoken.
E-F Phornphailin T034-595039. Some a/c rooms in this rather run-down hotel near the market; not as picturesque as the lakeside guesthouses. Lively karaoke bar.
E-G Burmese Inn, 52/3 Tambon Nong Loo, T034-595146, www.sangkhlaburi.com. Decent restaurant and friendly atmosphere. The cheaper rooms are very basic, the more expensive are en suite and a/c. Boat and motorbikes available for hire. Tours can also be booked from here.
E-G P Guesthouse, 81/1 Tambon Nong Loo, T034-595061, www.pguesthouse.com. Good restaurant (with honesty system), little stone bungalows with an attractive position over-looking the lake. It's well set up for travellers, the helpful owner will organize tours and

trekking (see Tour operators, page 194) and rent canoes (฿100 per hr). Recommended.

Saam Ong (Three Pagodas Pass) p189, map p188

D-F Three Pagodas Resort, 1.5 km before pass on right-hand side, T034-590098. Wooden bungalows in a peaceful setting.

❷ Eating

Kanchanaburi and around p180, map p181

† **Ali Bongos**, opposite Sam's Guesthouse, Mae Nam Kwai Rd. Good shakes and decent Indian food.

† **The Brew House**, Soí India Thamakham, Mae Nam Kwae Rd. Outstanding value for money. Tasty Thai food and cheap beer served at this friendly open-air establishment.

† **Jolly Frogs Restaurant**, 28 Mae Nam Kwai Rd. Wide range of Western and Thai grub, tourist information plastered on the walls.

† **Kala Kala**, Song Khwae Rd. Excellent Thai food at very good prices.

† **Krathom Thais Restaurant**, Apple's Guesthouse, see Sleeping, above. Excellent Thai food – the banana flower fritters and grilled pork salad are delicious. Very friendly English-speaking staff. Also run a very good cookery school and cater for vegetarians. Highly recommended.

† **Maekhong Kitchen** (Thai signage), Song Kwai Rd. Faces onto the river along with other food-stalls. Offers an excellent array of Thai food and specializes in noodles, specifically ones served in a 'blood' soup. Recommended.

† **Prasopsuk Restaurant**, 677 Saengchuto Rd. A large, clean restaurant serving a wide range of dishes. Good cheap Thai food. Attached to the hotel of the same name. Recommended.

† **Sugar Canes Restaurant**, 22 Soi Pakistan, Mae Nam Kwai Rd. The menu is limited but the restaurant has a beautiful view of the river.

† **Woof**, Mae Nam Kwai Rd. An exclusively vegetarian restaurant serving mainly Thai food at reasonable prices.

Foodstalls and bakeries

Numerous stalls set up along the river in the afternoon and evening – the best spot is by Song Kwai Rd – and there is also an excellent night market with a wide range of food in the vicinity of the bus station. Recommended.

Aree Bakery, Baak Phraek Rd. Delicious ice creams and breakfasts.

Sii Fa Bakery, by bus the terminal. Good range of pastries.

Sangkhlaburi p187, map p188

There are many inexpensive restaurants around the Central Market, some serving good Burmese food. In the high season (Nov-Feb) there are also a few places open along Tambon Nong Loo serving up some Western and Thai food.

† **Baan Unrak**, Tambon Nong Loo. This small coffee shop, open all year, serves up vegetarian food, fresh coffee and a variety of freshly baked cakes and cookies. It is mostly staffed by Burmese refugees and is a sustainable project run by a nearby orphanage. Recommended.

❻ Bars and clubs

Kanchanaburi and around p180, map p181

Several karaoke joints along the riverfront.

4Nines, Saengchuto Rd, opposite River Kwai Hotel. Open 1600-2400. Good for British meat pies, whisky and rock 'n' roll. Can be seedy.

Bar (no name), round the corner from Sugar Cane guesthouse (Mae Nam Kwai Rd). Run by friendly British expats, serving huge portions of chips and good Thai food.

Brew House, Mae Nam Kwai Rd (Soi India Corner, near the King Naresuan statue). Good-value beer in a place run by a UK-educated Thai.

RK Cowboy Bar, just in front of River Kwai Hotel. Hosts live Thai music, serves beer by the gallon and BBQ meat by the plateful.

Resort Bar, Mae Nam Kwai Rd. Open 1100-1300. A great place to relax, set in a huge, old villa and gardens you'll find cheesy live music, good snacks and a big range of drinks. Popular with stylish, younger Thais this place has a cool, lounge vibe. Recommended.

🎉 Festivals and events

Kanchanaburi and around *p180, map p181*

Nov/Dec River Kwai Bridge Week (movable). The festival starts with an evening ceremony conducted by dozens of monks followed by a procession from the city Pillar Shrine to the bridge. There's also a very realistic re-enactment of the destruction of bridge by the Allies in 1945. Other events include longboat races, exhibitions, steam train rides and cultural shows.

🛍 Shopping

Kanchanaburi and around *p180, map p181*

Baak Phraek Rd is a pleasant shopping street. Blue sapphires, onyx and topaz are all mined at Bo Phloi, 50 km from Kanchanaburi. Good prices for them at shops near the bridge or in the market area of town.

🔺 Activities and tours

Kanchanaburi and around *p180, map p181*
Fishing
On the Kwai River, Khao Laem and Srinak-harin reservoirs. Travel agents will help organize expeditions.

Tours and tour operators
It's not very easy to organize your own raft and boat trips; it is probably better to go through a tour operator.
AS Mixed Travel, T034-514958, www.apple noi-kanchanaburi.com. Run by the same people who own **Apple Guesthouse**. One-stop shop offering a variety of great little tours, some trekking trips, flight reservations, bus and train tickets. Recommended.

BT Travel Co Ltd, T034-624630, bttravel_centre@hotmail.com. Organizes raft trips to Chungkai Cemetery, together with fishing and swimming on the River Kwai Noi. Also arranges a/c minibus tours to Muang Singh Historical Park, Ban Kao, Sai Yok Noi and elsewhere.
Good Times Travel Service, T034-624441, good_times_travel@hotmail.com. Offers similar excursions to **BT Travel Co Ltd**, and notably the opportunity to bathe with elephants. Recommended.
State Railways of Thailand, Railway Advance Book Office, Hualamphong Station in Bangkok, T02-2256964, or Kanchanaburi Train Station, T034-511285. Thailand's **State Railways** offers an all-day tour from Bangkok to Kanchanaburi on weekends and holidays leaving Thonburi station at 0615, stopping at Nakhon Pathom, the River Kwai Bridge, arriving at Nam Tok at 1130. A minibus connects Khao Pang/Sai Yok Noi waterfall and the train leaves Nam Tok at 1430, arriving in Kanchanaburi at 1605 for a brief stop, arriving in Bangkok at 1930. There are also a number of other tours, with overnight stays, rafting and fishing. Advance booking recommended.
Toi's Tours, T034-514209, toistours@yahoo.com. Offers a wide range of excursions ranging from half-day excursions to 2-day tours, all at reasonable prices.

Sangkhlaburi *p187, map p188*
Tour operators
P Guesthouse and **Burmese Inn** both organize trips around Sangkhlaburi. They include visits to Karen village by boat, a 2-hr elephant ride through the jungle, swimming and bamboo whitewater rafting. The **Burmese Inn** may be able to organize a visit to a Karen camp.

🚌 Transport

Kanchanaburi and around *p180, map p181*
Bicycle
A good way to get around town and out to the bridge. Reliable bikes can be hired for

฿30-40 per day from **Green Bamboo** on the Mae Nam Kwai Rd, or ask at guesthouses.

Boat

Noisy, long-tailed boats roar up and down the river; tickets are available at guesthouses. A more peaceful option is to hire canoes. **Cruise Asia Ltd**, www.cruiseasia.net. Runs 4- and 7-day trips on the River Kwai. **Safarino**, on the Mae Nam Kwai Rd. Rents out canoes for ฿280 per 3 hrs.

Bus

Non-a/c buses leave from the station in the market area, behind Saengchuto Rd. A/c buses leave from the corner of Saengchuto Rd, opposite Lak Muang Rd. Regular twice hourly connections with **Bangkok**'s Southern bus terminal (a/c bus No 81), 2 hrs, or non-a/c bus, 3-4 hrs. Also connections with **Nakhon Pathom** (1½ hrs, ฿15) from where there are buses to the floating market at **Damnoen Saduak** (see page 109).

Jeep

Several places rent out jeeps along Mae Nam Kwai Rd.

Motorbike and scooter

Yankee, Mae Nam Kwai Rd. Rents out motorbikes and scooters from ฿150 per day. As well as the usual 125cc step-throughs it also has 200cc chopper-style Phantoms.

Saamlor, songthaew and tuk-tuk

A *saamlor* charter for 2-3 hrs should cost about ฿100 for a trip to the Kwai bridge, JEATH museum and the cemetery.

A *songthaew*/tuk-tuk is most useful for out-of-town trips.

Train

Regular connections with **Nakhon Pathom** and on to Hualampong Station. Weekends and holidays, special service (see Tours and tour operators, above). It is possible to take a local train between Kanchanaburi and **Nam Tok**, stopping off along the way.

Sangkhlaburi *p187, map p188*
Bus

Regular connections on non-a/c bus with **Kanchanaburi** (5-6 hrs, ฿90). A/c minibus runs 3 times a day (3½ hrs, ฿130). Larger, more comfortable buses with a/c depart 3 times a day (฿151). At time of writing there was still no way of getting north directly to **Umpang**; to get there you must go from Sangklaburi to Suphanburi and then north via Mae Sot.

Motorbike and scooter

Baan Unrak (see Eating, above) and P Guesthouse can help arrange motorbike hire, from ฿250 per day.

Saamlor, songthaew and tuk-tuk

Flat rate charge of ฿10 to almost everywhere, but ฿30 to the Mon monastery and market. *Songthaews* to **Saam Ong**, leave every 40 mins from the bus station, 30 mins (฿30).

ⓓ Directory

Kanchanaburi and around *p180, map p181*
Banks There are a number near the bus station, most with ATMs. Bangkok, 2 Uthong Rd. Thai Farmers, 160/80-2 Saengchuto Rd. Thai Military, 160/34 Saengchuto Rd. **Internet** There are several along Mae Nam Kwai Rd. **Laundry** A few line Mae Nam Kwai Rd (฿15-20 a kilo). **Medical services** Hospital Saengchuto Rd, close to Saengchuto Soi 20. **Police** Corner of Saengchuto and Lak Muang roads. **Post office** Corner of Lak Muang Rd and Baak Phraek Rd (not far from Sathani Rot Fai Rd), some distance out of town towards Bangkok.

Sangkhlaburi *p187, map p188*
Banks Siam Commercial Bank offers exchange services but no ATM. **Internet** Baan Unrak (see Eating, above) runs the adjoining internet café. **Medical services** Hospital and malaria centre in town. **Post office** Opposite 7-11 store.

Sukhothai and the north central plains

→ *Colour map 1, C3. Population 28,000.*

The modern conurbation of Sukhothai reveals little of Thailand's ancient capital. Head west about 12 km, keeping an eye on the surrounding landscape, and the ruined brick foundations of ancient religious structures appear in the rice fields, interspersed between wooden shophouses until the road pierces the ramparts of Old Sukhothai.

Officially, the Old City and its surroundings are a national historical park covering 640 ha, which opened in 1988 after a total of 192 wats were restored. The metal lamp posts, concrete-lined ponds and horrible hedgerows of the central area evince overbearing sterility. Head out beyond the city walls and you'll discover dozens of crumbling wats, Buddhas and chedis among the surrounding woodlands.

If you want to stay amid ancient surroundings there is some excellent accommodation in the Old City but choice is limited. Staying here gives you a chance to explore the atmospheric outer ruins in the fresh early-morning mist. There's more accommodation available in the new town, a pleasant enough spot to stay while exploring the glories of Old Sukhothai. Guesthouses here are generally of a high standard, there is good street food at the night market on Ramkhamhaeng Road, a fresh day market off Charodwithithong Road and a useful range of tourist amenities.

Phitsanulok, to the east, houses one of the most striking and most important Buddhist shrines in Thailand – Wat Phra Sri Ratana Mahathat (Wat Yai). Si Satchanalai, north of Sukhothai, now a historical park and once linked to Sukhothai by a 50-km highway, is full of Ceylonese-style bell-shaped chedis, Khmer prangs and Sukhothai-era buildings.

The region to the west of Sukhothai is little visited and all the better for it. Just 80 km southwest of the ancient Thai capital sits Kamphaeng Phet. This antiquated city is also a historical park and UNESCO World Heritage Site. ▸▸ *For listings, see pages 213-219.*

Ins and outs

Getting there

Sukhothai airport is owned by **Bangkok Airways**, which has flights from Bangkok and Chiang Mai once daily. **THAI** flies from Phitsanulok, an hour away. Most people arrive by bus and there are regular connections with Bangkok, Chiang Mai, Phitsanulok and Khon Kaen, as well as other major towns in the north and central plains. There are also two buses a day from Bangkok's northern Mo Chit bus terminal direct to Old Sukhothai.
▸▸ *See Transport, page 218.*

Getting around

Most people come to Sukhothai to see the ruins of the former capital. Regular buses (every 10 minutes) and *songthaews* ply the route between old and new cities or it is easy to hire a motorcycle. The ruins themselves are spread over a considerable area.
▸▸ *See page 199 for details on getting around the park.*

Best time to visit

This part of Thailand is one of the hottest. If visiting Sukhothai Old City during the hot or rainy seasons (roughly March to October), it is best to explore either early in the morning or at the end of the day. The best time to visit is November to February.

Background

If you ask a Thai about the history of Sukhothai, he or she will say that King Intradit ('Glorious Sun-King') founded the Sukhothai Kingdom in 1240, after driving off the Khmers following a single-handed elephant duel with the Khmer commander. King Intradit then founded Wat Mahathat, the geographical and symbolic heart of the new kingdom. Revisionist historians and archaeologists reject this view, regarding it as myth-making on a grand scale (see page 198). They maintain that Sukhothai evolved into a great kingdom over a long period and find the big bang theory ultimately unconvincing.

Like Angkor Wat in Cambodia, until comparatively recently Sukhothai was a 'lost city in the jungle'. It was only in 1833 that the future King Mongkut discovered the famous Inscription No 1 and not until 1895 that the French scholar Lucien Fournereau published an incomplete description of the site. The key date, though, is 1907 when crown Prince Maha Vajiravudh made an eight-day visit to Sukhothai. It was his account that laid the foundations for the Sukhothai 'myth': a proud, glorious and civilized past for a country that was on the verge of being submerged by an alien culture. What is remarkable is that Prince Vajiravudh's account, based on a cursory visit, was accepted for so long and by so many. It has only been since the mid-1980s that people have begun to question the conventional history.

Sukhothai became the first capital of Siam and the following 200 years (until the early 15th century) are considered the pinnacle of Thai civilization. There were nine kings during the Sukhothai Dynasty, the most famous being Ramkhamhaeng, whose reign is believed to have been 1275-1317. He was the first ruler to leave accounts of the state

Sukhothai New City

To Wat Thai Chumphon (300m)
& Si Satchanalai (56 km)

To Tak

To Phitsanulok (56 km)

To Post Office (400m)

➡ Sukhothai maps
1 Sukothai New City, page 197
2 Sukothai Old City, page 200

N

200 metres
200 yards

Sleeping	River House 15	Eating
Ban Thai 1	Sukhothai Guesthouse 14	Art's Fresh Coffee & Beer 1
J&J Guesthouse 4	Sukhothai Lotus Village 13	Chinnawat 2
Ninety Nine Guest House 5	Sukhothai Orchid 6	Dream Café 3
No 4 7		Rainbow Café 2

Sukhothai: a 'Golden Age' or mother of invention?

At the beginning of March 1989, several hundred people assembled at the Bangkok Bank's headquarters on Silom Road to debate an issue that threatened to undermine the very identity of the Thai people. Some archaeologists had begun to argue that famous Inscription No 1, on which the interpretation of King Ramkhamhaeng's reign is based (see page 688), was a forgery. They maintained that the then Prince Mongkut's remarkably timely 'discovery' of the inscription in 1833 served Siam's political purposes – it showed to the expansionist British and French that the country was a 'civilized' kingdom that could govern itself without outside interference. Along with certain literary and artistic anomalies, this led some commentators to maintain that King Mongkut created King Ramkhamhaeng – or at least his popular image – to protect his kingdom from the colonial powers.

Before Mongkut stumbled upon Inscription No 1, knowledge of Sukhothai's history was based upon myth and legend.

The great king Phra Ruang – who was believed to have hatched from the egg of a *naga* (serpent) and to be so powerful that he could make trees flower – was clearly the stuff of imagination. And some scholars also argued the same was true of King Ramkhamhaeng.

Since the meeting of 1989, academic opinion has swung back to viewing Mongkut's discovery as genuine. For most Thais, of course, who have been raised to believe that Sukhothai was Thailand's Golden Age and Ramkhamhaeng its chief architect, this is beyond reproach. However, this does not detract from the fact that Inscription No 1 – and the other inscriptions – are fanciful portrayals of history carved to serve the interests of an elite, not to reflect 'reality'. As Betty Gosling writes in *Sukhothai: its history, culture and art* (1991), "... the controversy emphasizes the need to consider Sukhothai inscriptions ... Not in the golden afterglow of Thai mythology, but in the harsh daylight of objective research".

inscribed in stone (now displayed in the National Museum in Bangkok). These provide a wealth of information on conquests, taxation and political philosophy. Ramkhamhaeng created the Thai script, derived from Mon and Khmer, and the Inscription No 1 of 1292 is regarded by many as the first work of Thai literature (see page 688).

At its peak Ramkhamhaeng's kingdom encompassed much of present-day Thailand, south down the Malay Peninsula and west into Lower Burma, though the northern kingdom of Lanna Thai, Lopburi and the Khorat Plateau were still controlled by the waning Khmer Empire.

Ramkhamhaeng was an absolute monarch, but one who governed his people with justice and magnanimity. If anyone wanted to lodge a complaint, he or she would ring a bell at the gate and the king would grant them an audience. King Ramkhamhaeng was responsible for the introduction of Theravada Buddhism, when he brought Ceylonese monks to his kingdom – partly intended to displace the influence of the Khmers. He displayed considerable diplomatic powers and cultivated good relations with his northern neighbours in order to form an alliance against the Khmers. In addition, he opened relations with China, establishing both economic and cultural links. The fine pottery produced at Sukhothai and Si Satchanalai is thought by some scholars to have developed only after the arrival of expert Chinese potters, with their knowledge of advanced glazing techniques.

The Sukhothai period saw a flowering not just of ceramic arts, but of art in general (see page 737). The Buddha images are regarded as the most beautiful and original to have ever been created in Thailand, with the walking Buddha image being the first free-standing Buddha the country produced.

King Ramkhamhaeng's son, Lo Thai (1327-1346), was an ineffectual leader, over-shadowed even in death by his father, and much of the territory gained by the previous reign was lost. By the sixth reign of the Sukhothai Dynasty, the kingdom was in decline, and by the seventh, Sukhothai paid homage to Ayutthaya. In 1438 Ayutthaya officially incorporated Sukhothai into its realm; the first Thai kingdom had succumbed to its younger and more vigorous neighbour.

Old City ⬤🕐 ↦ pp213-219.

The Old City is 1800 m long and 1400 m wide, and was originally encompassed by triple earthen ramparts and two moats, punctuated by four gates. Within the city there are 21 historical sites; outside the walls are another 70 or so places of historical interest. At one time the city may have been home to as many as 300,000 people, with an efficient tunnel system to bring water from the mountains and a network of roads. It was an urban centre to rival any in Europe. Within the city are monuments of many different styles – as if the architects were attempting to imbue the centre with the magical power of other Buddhist sites: there are Mon *chedis*, Khmer *prangs* and Ceylonese *chedis*, as well as monuments of clearly Sukhothai inspiration.

Park essentials
The park is open daily 0600-1800. A new entrance has also been created about 250 m from its original location towards Namo Gate. It is divided into five zones, each with an admission charge: ฿40 for the central section, and ฿30 for each of the north, south, east and west sections. If you intend to visit all the zones, then it makes sense to purchase the 'Total' ticket which costs ฿150, thus saving ฿10. This 'all in' ticket also includes entrance to the Si Satchanalai Historical Park, the Ramkhamhaeng National Museum, the Sangkaloke Kiln Education and Preservation Center (45 km outside Sukhothai) and the Sawankha Woranayok National Museum (at Sawankhalok)– you could end up saving more than ฿100. The Total ticket is valid for 30 days (each site can only be visited once within this time). There are additional charges: ฿50 per car, ฿10 per bike, ฿20 per motorcycle. If you want to explore the outer ruins, such as Wat Chetuphon and Wat Saphan Hin no ticket is needed and entrance is free.

Getting around Travelling the 12 km between the new and old cities is easy enough; the open-sided buses leave every 10 minutes (0600-1730, ฿10) from the station on Charodwithithong Road or from the main bus station (buses from the Old City to Sukhothai stop operating at 1800). Tuk-tuks cost no more than ฿100 (they congregate on Nikhon Kasem Road). Alternatively, go on a tour (see Tour operators, page 217), hire a motorbike (฿250) or charter a tuk-tuk for the trip there and back, along with trips around the site (฿200-250 for three hours). When you arrive in the Old City hire a bicycle (฿20 per day) or moped (฿250 per day) from the entrance gate close to the museum, or take the little yellow trolley bus that tours the major sights (฿20). Don't forget a bottle of water if you're cycling.

Kamphanghek Gate (a) and Ramkhamhaeng National Museum (b)

ⓘ *T055-612167, 0900-1600, ฿30 or with Total ticket, see Park essentials, above.*
Situated just inside the Kamphanghek ('broken wall') Gate entrance is the Ramkhamhaeng National Museum – a good place to begin a tour. The museum contains a copy of some wonderful Buddha images, along with explanatory information. It also houses a range of household goods giving an indication of the sophistication of Sukhothai society.

Wat Mahathat (c)

The centre of the Sukhothai Kingdom was Wat Mahathat and the royal palace – the earliest example in Thailand. This was both the religious and the political centre of the kingdom and is usually regarded as the first truly 'Sukhothai' monument. The complex was begun by King Intradit, expanded by King Ramkhamhaeng and finally completed by King Lo Thai in 1345, or thereabouts.

The principal building is the central sanctuary, which King Lo Thai is said to have rebuilt in the 1340s to house the hair and neckbone relics of the Buddha which had been brought back from Ceylon. The central tower is surrounded by four smaller *chedis* in Srivijaya-Ceylonese style, alternating with four Khmer *prangs*. The entire ensemble is raised up on a two-tiered base with a stucco frieze of walking monks in relief.

Sukhothai Old City

➡ Sukhothai maps
1 Sukhothai New City, page 197
2 Sukhothai Old City, page 200

Sleeping 😴	Old City ○	
Old City Guesthouse 1	Kamphanghek Gate a	Wat Trapang Ngoen f
Orchid Hibiscus 5	Ramkhamhaeng	Wat Trapang Thong g
Paylin 2	Museum b	Wat Sra Sri h
	Wat Mahathat c	King Ramkhamhaeng's
Eating 🍴	Royal Palace d	statue i
Coffee Cup 1	San Da Pa Deng e	Wat Sri Sawai j

Some original Buddha images still sit among the ruins. Particularly unusual are the two monumental standing Buddhas, in an attitude of forgiveness, on either side of the central sanctuary, enclosed by brick walls, with their heads protruding over the top.

Royal Palace (Phra Ruang Palace) (d)

Little remains of the original Royal Palace. It was here that King Mongkut, while he was still the Crown Prince, found the famous Inscription No 1 of King Ramkhamhaeng, the Manangsilabat stone throne, and the stone inscription of King Lithai in 1833. All three objects – which became talismans for the Thai people – were carted off to Bangkok. Whether the Royal Palace really was a palace is a subject for conjecture. The site appears rather too small and, although it has revealed a mass of objects, some scholars believe it was the site of a royal pavilion rather than a royal palace. To the north of Wat Mahathat is **San Da Pa Deng (e)**, the oldest existing structure from the Sukhothai era. It is a small Khmer laterite *prang* built during the first half of the 12th century.

Wat Trapang Ngoen (f) and Wat Trapang Thong (g)

Wat Trapang Ngoen – Temple of the Silver Pond – contains a large lotus-bud *chedi*, similar to that at Wat Mahathat. One passage from Inscription No 1 refers to this wat: "In the middle of this city of Sukhothai the water of the Pho Si Pond is as clear and as good to drink as the river of the Khong [Mekong] in the dry season". Wat Trapang Thong sits on an island, after which the monastery is named. It is approached along a rickety bridge. Particularly fine are the stucco reliefs, of which perhaps the most beautiful is that on the south side of the *mondop*. It shows the Buddha descending from the Tavatimsa Heaven with the attendant Brahma on his left and Indra on his right and is considered the finest piece of stucco work from the Sukhothai period.

Wat Sra Sri (h) and King Ramkhamhaeng's statue (i)

Wat Sra Sri, to the north of Wat Trapang Ngoen, is a popular photo-spot, as the *bot* is reflected in a pond. A Ceylonese-style *chedi* dominates the complex, which also contains a fine, large, seated Buddha image enclosed by columns. To the east of here is King Ramkhamhaeng's statue, seated on a copy of the stone throne (the Phra Thaen Manang Silabat) that was found on the site of the Royal Palace and which is now in the Wat Phra Kaeo Museum in Bangkok. The statue was erected in 1969 and the high-relief carvings depict famous episodes from the life of the illustrious king.

Wat Sri Sawai (j)

To the southwest of Wat Mahathat is Wat Sri Sawai, enclosed within laterite walls. It was built during the time that Sukhothai was under Khmer domination. The *prang* is in the three-tower style, with the largest central *prang* (rather badly restored) being 20 m tall. The stucco decoration was added to the towers in the 15th century, as were their upper brick portions. The lower laterite levels are the original sections, built under Khmer influence. It must originally have been a Hindu shrine, as carvings of Vishnu and other Hindu divinities have been found on the site.

Wats outside the Old City walls

The main reason to see the monasteries outside the Old City walls is to get a better idea of what Sukhothai was like before it became a historical park and was cleared of undergrowth.

Some of the lesser-known monasteries are still in the forest. **Note** Try cycling to these wats during the morning when it is cooler as they are far apart. Alternatively, hire a tuk-tuk.

Wat Sri Chum

Take the northwest gate out of the city to visit the impressive Wat Sri Chum. A large *mondop*, with a narrow vaulted entrance, encloses an enormous brick and stucco seated Buddha image. The temple was probably built during the seventh reign of the Sukhothai Kingdom (mid-14th century) and is said to have caused a Burmese army to flee in terror, such is the power of its withering gaze. The large Buddha seems almost suffocated by the surrounding walls, which must have been added at a later stage. There is a stairway in the *mondop* which leads up to a space behind the head of the image (closed since 1988). Here, there are line carvings recounting the Jataka tales, covering the slate slab ceiling. Each slab depicts one story, skilfully carved with free-flowing lines – which originally would have been enlivened with paint. These are the finest and earliest (circa 1350) to be found in Thailand (there are examples from Wat Sri Chum in the National Museum, Bangkok). The image here is said to have talked on a number of occasions – although the back stairs provide a useful hiding place for someone to play a practical joke.

Wat Phra Pai Luang

East of Wat Sri Chum is Wat Phra Pai Luang, the Monastery of the Great Wind, interesting for the remains of three laterite *prangs*. Built during the reign of King Jayavarman VII (a Khmer king who ruled 1181-1217) it dates from the Khmer period that preceded the rise of Sukhothai. Its Khmer inspiration is clearly evident in the square base and indented tiers. To the east of the *prang* is a later stupa, with niches on all four sides containing damaged Buddha images. Further east still is a ruined *mondop* with the remains of large stucco Buddha images, standing, walking and reclining. In total, Wat Phra Pai Luang contains over 30 stupas of assorted styles. It is thought that not only was it originally a Hindu shrine, but that it was also the site of an earlier Khmer town.

Wat Saphan Hin

Take the northwest road 3 km beyond the city walls where a large, standing Buddha image is located at the top of an ancient staircase. Sited at the top of a hill amid languorous woodlands Wat Saphan Hin has one of the most beautiful locations in Sukhothai. Many Thais still come here, offering prayers and incense. It is also a perfect spot to watch a tropical sunrise, though you'll need to get up early if you want to reach here in time.

Wat Khao Phrabat Noi

Not far away from Wat Saphan Hin are the remains of two other monasteries. Wat Khao Phrabat Noi lies about 2.5 km northwest of the city walls and it is approached along a stone-lined footpath. The *chedi* here is unusual in that it is not really Sukhothai in style and it is presumed that it was remodelled during the Ayutthaya period. Four Buddha footprints were found here, but these have been removed to the National Museum in Bangkok.

Wat Chang Rob

South from this group of three monasteries is the better-known Wat Chang Rob (Monastery Encircled by Elephants). In Buddhist mythology, elephants – the holiest of beasts – support Mount Meru, the centre of the universe.

Wat Chedi Ngam

Continuing south to Route 12 is the impressive, at least in size, Wat Chedi Ngam (Monastery of the Beautiful Chedi). The large *chedi*, pure and simple in its form, has been well preserved. Also here are the remains of a large viharn with some standing columns, and what is thought to have been a *kuti* (monks' quarters) or place for bathing.

Wat Mangkon and Wat Phra Yuen

On the north side of Route 12 is Wat Mangkon (Dragon Monastery). A relatively large complex, the *bot*, surrounded by large leaf-shaped boundary stones, has an unusual slate-tiled brick base. To the west of the *bot* is the base of a pavilion or *sala*, and to the north the remains of a Ceylonese-style bell-shaped *phra chedi*. Wat Phra Yuen is around 200 m from Wat Mangkon and 1500 m from the city walls, just to the south of Route 12. The remains of a *bot* can be identified by the *bai sema* (boundary stones) that surround it and a *mondop* houses a large standing Buddha image.

Wat Ton Chan and Wat Chetuphon

There are also a series of monasteries to the south and east of the city. Travel 1 km from the city by the south gate and you'll find Wat Ton Chan (Sandalwood Tree Monastery). Although large, the monastery is nothing special, although it is moated and has a bathing pool along with the usual array of *viharn* and *chedi*. Far more impressive is Wat Chetuphon, one of Sukhothai's more important monasteries. The building materials are more varied than the usual brick and stucco; stone, slate and brick have also been used in its construction. However, archaeologists and art historians suspect that the monastery was renovated and expanded on a number of occasions, so how much of the structure is Sukhothai, is a source of conjecture.

Wat Chedi Si Hong

About 500 m from Wat Chetuphon is Wat Chedi Si Hong. The most notable feature of this wat is the fine stucco work depicting *devas* (heavenly beings), humans and *garudas* riding elephants on the base of the *viharn* and *chedi*.

Around Sukhothai ● ⇒ pp 213-219.

Ramkhamhaeng National Park

ⓘ *Public transport is limited – take a local bus along Route 101 towards Kamphaeng Phet, getting off at the road to the national park (Uthayaan Haeng Chart Ramkhamhaeng); it's 16 km from here. Motorcycle taxis are sometimes available at the turn-off.*

Ramkhamhaeng National Park, 30 km southwest of New Sukhothai in Amphoe Khiri Mat, covers 341 sq km. The highest peak here, **Khao Luang** – after which the park is also sometimes known – rises to nearly 1200 m. Highlights of the park include the 100-m-high **Sai Rung Waterfall**, several caves, and an ancient dam which fed the canals of Sukhothai city.

Phitsanulok and around ●●●●▲●● ⇒ pp213-219. Colour map 2, B1.

Phitsanulok, attractively positioned on the banks of the River Nan, with houseboats lining the steep banks, is home to one of the most striking and important Buddhist shrines in Thailand: Wat Phra Sri Ratana Mahathat (Wat Yai). The rest of this friendly, bustling city is non-descript with most of its old wooden buildings destroyed in a disastrous fire in the 1960s. Phitsanulok is also an important transport hub, linking the central plains with the north and northeast and it is a convenient base from which to visit nearby Sukhothai and Si Satchanalai.

Ins and outs

Getting there The bus terminal is not central, it's on the road east to Lom Sak (Route 12), 2 km out of town, T055-242430, but bus No 10 travels between the local bus station and the terminal every 10 minutes (and takes 30 minutes). The journey from Bangkok takes five to six hours. If the bus travels through town en route to the bus terminal, ask the driver to let you off at the more convenient Swiss chalet-style train station. There is a

Phitsanulok

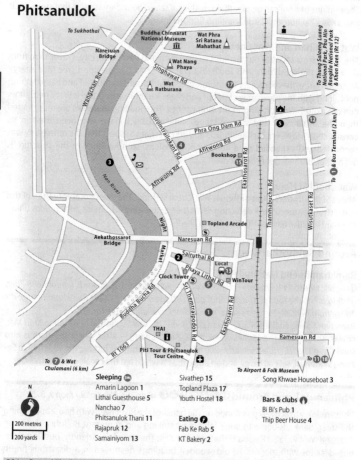

Sleeping
Amarin Lagoon 1
Lithai Guesthouse 5
Nanchao 7
Phitsanulok Thani 11
Rajapruk 12
Samainiyom 13

Sivathep 15
Topland Plaza 17
Youth Hostel 18

Eating
Fab Ke Rab 5
KT Bakery 2

Song Khwae Houseboat 3

Bars & clubs
Bi Bi's Pub 1
Thip Beer House 4

N
200 metres
200 yards

steam locomotive parked outside and it's on Ekathosarot Road, T055-258005. If you arrive by train and are heading straight to Sukothai, take a tuk-tuk the 4 km to the bus station. It is possible to fly to Phitsanulok, with plenty of daily connections to Bangkok and also with other northern towns. The airport is just out of town on Sanambin Road, T055-258029, to get to town take *songthaew* or there are buses that run to the city bus centre near the railway station every 10 minutes (฿4-6). ⟩⟩ See Transport, page 218, for further information.

Getting around Phitsanulok is a good walking city with the main site of interest, Wat Yai, being in the northern part of town while an evening stroll along the river allows you to take in the night market at full swing.

Tourist information TAT ⓘ *209/7-8 Surasi Shopping Centre, Boromtrailokant Rd, T055-252742, tatphs@loxinfo.co.th, open 0830-1630.* Helpful and informative, with good maps of the town and surrounding area. There's also a small office next to **Wat Yai** ⓘ *0900-1600*, which will furnish you with a photocopied map and little else.

Background

Phitsanulok was the birthplace of one of the heroes of Thai history: King Naresuan the Great of Ayutthaya, who reigned 1590-1605 (there is a shrine to the king on the west side of the river facing Wat Mahathat). Shortly after his birth, the young Naresuan was bundled off to Burma as a guarantor of his father's – King Thammaracha – good behaviour. He did not return to Phitsanulok until he was 16, when he was awarded the principality by his father. Here he developed the military and political skills which were to stand him in good stead when he assumed the throne of Ayutthaya 19 years later in 1590 (see box, page 167). For the short period of 25 years, during the reign of King Boromtrailokant of Ayutthaya (1448-1488), Phitsanulok was actually the capital of Siam, and over the four centuries prior to the fall of Ayutthaya to the Burmese in 1767 it was effectively the kingdom's second city.

Wat Phra Sri Ratana Mahathat

ⓘ*0800-1700, donation of ฿50 recommended.*
One of the most venerated temples in Thailand – this is no musuem-like relic but a thriving place of worship – the Monastery of the Great Relic, known as Wat Yai, 'Big Wat' – is to be found on the east bank of the Nan River, close to the Naresuan Bridge. It was built in the reign of King Lithai (1347-1368) of Sukhothai, in 1357. The *viharn* contains one of the most highly regarded and venerated Buddha images in Thailand – the Phra Buddha Chinaraj. Through the centuries, successive Thai kings have come to Phitsanulok to pay homage to the bronze image and to make offerings of gifts. The Buddha is a superlative example of late Sukhothai style and is said to have wept tears of blood when the city was captured by the Ayutthayan army in the early 14th century. The three-tiered *viharn* was built during the Ayutthaya period and shows a fusion of Ayutthayan and Lanna (northern) Thai architectural styles. The low sweeping roofs, supported by black and gold pillars, accentuate the massive gilded bronze Buddha image seated at the end of the nave. The entrance is through inlaid mother-of-pearl doors, made in 1756 in the reign of King Boromkot to replace the original ones of carved wood. The small *viharn* in front of the main building houses another significant Buddha image, known as the 'Remnant Buddha' because it was cast from the bronze remaining after the main image had been produced. The 36-m-high *prang* in the centre of the complex has stairs leading up to a niche containing relics of the Buddha but access is often locked. Also in the wat

compound is the **Buddha Chinnarat National Museum**, with a small collection of Sukhothai Buddhas and assorted ceramics. Wat Yai is a very popular site for Thai tourists/ Buddhists. Most buy lotuses and incense from a stall at the gate to offer to the Buddhas. There's also a large antique, food and trinket market next door to the compound plus rows of lottery ticket sellers; the trick is you gain favour by supplicating yourself to the Buddha and then get lucky.

Folk museum and Buddha image factory
① Wisutkaset Rd, Folk Museum Tue-Sun 0830-1200, 1300-1630; factory Mon-Sat 0800-1700.
The Folk Museum exhibits items from everyday rural life, in particular agricultural implements and tools, children's games, festival and ceremonial items, and other bits and pieces. Across the street, and run by the same man, is a factory (the door is always shut; open it and go in), casting Buddha images. These are produced using the lost wax method and range in size from diminutive to monstrous. It is usually possible to see at least some of the production process.

Wat Chulamani
① Catch bus No 5 which leaves from the City bus (local) centre, near the railway station on Ekathosarot Rd, every 10 mins (takes 20 mins).
Wat Chulamani, 6 km to the south of Phitsanulok on Route 1063, was probably the original town centre. During the Khmer period Phitsanulok was known as Muang Song Kwae ('Two River Town'), as it lies between the Nan and the Kwae Noi rivers. The wat was built by King Boromtrailokant in 1464 and houses the remains of an ornate Khmer *prang* which pre-dates the Sukhothai period: note the fine stucco work of the *prang*.

Phu Hin Rongkla National Park
① Catch a bus towards Loei and get off at Nakhon Thai (3 hrs, ฿35), and then a songthaew to the park (฿15-25).
Phu Hin Rongkla National Park covers 5000 sq km over three provinces: Phitsanulok, Phetchabun and Loei. The park, 120 km east of Phitsanulok, off Route 2113, which links Phitsanulok with Loei, has been partly deforested. It was a stronghold of the Communist Party of Thailand (CPT) until the early 1980s, and hundreds of disaffected students fled here following the Thammasat University massacre of 1976. The government encouraged farmers to settle in the park to deny the guerrillas refuge; but now that the CPT has been vanquished, the same farmers have been told they are illegal squatters and must move. The buildings used by the CPT for training and indoctrination (3 km southwest of the park headquarters) have been preserved and have now become sights of historical interest to the Thais, particularly former students who joined the movement after the student demonstrations of 1973-1976. The base supported a political and military school – with printing press and communications centre, a small hospital, cafeteria and air-raid shelter.

Rising to 1780 m, the park has a pine forest on the upper slopes and many orchids and lichens. Wildlife includes small numbers of tiger, bear, sambar deer and hornbills.

Thung Salaeng National Park
① The park office is at Km 80 on the Phitsanulok–Lomsak Highway; regular buses run between Phitsanulok and Lomsak.
On the road between Phitsanulok and Lomsak, Highway 12, is the Thung Salaeng National Park and a number of waterfalls and resort hotels. The **Sakunothayon Botanical Gardens**

is located off the road at the Km 33 marker. To get there take one of the regular buses running between Phitsanulok and Lomsak. A 500-m-long access road leads to the gardens, which are best known for the picturesque, 10-m-high Waeng Nok Aen Waterfall.

The Thung Salaeng Luang National Park, consisting of forest and grasslands, covers more than 1250 sq km of Phitsanulok and Phetchabun provinces, rising from 300 m to more than 1000 m. There's a huge variety of birdlife (190 recorded species), including hornbills, the Siamese fireback pheasants, eagles and owls. Of the park's 17 mammal species the most notable is the park's small population of elephants; tigers are also said to inhabit the park, but are rarely seen. The best time for trekking is between November and March.

Si Satchanalai and around ⊖❶❷❸❸ ⋙ *pp213-219. Colour map 1, B3.*

Si Sat nestles languidly on the west bank of the Yom River about 50 km to the north of Sukhothai. It remained undiscovered by tourists until 1987, when a grant was provided to prepare the town for 'Visit Thailand Year'. The site has been 'cleaned up', though not to the extent of Sukhothai and still retains a lot of charm. Si Satchanalai makes a fascinating side trip from Sukhothai with examples of Ceylonese-style bell-shaped *chedis*, Khmer *prangs* and Sukhothai-era buildings. There is no modern town here; the whole area has become a 'historical park' and is littered with monuments.

Ins and outs
Getting around Si Satchanalai is compact and the main monuments can be seen on foot. To reach Chaliang and the sights outside the city walls it is best to hire a bicycle (฿30 per day) at the admission gate.

Tourist information The Si Satchanalai Historical Park Information Centre is just outside Ram Narong Gate, to the southeast. There's not much information here, just a scale model and map of the park and a few books for sale. Admission fee to Si Satchanalai: ฿40, ฿50 for a car, ฿30 for a motorbike and ฿10 for a bicycle. See the admission information under the entry for Sukhothai for details on the 'Total' ticket, page 199, which provides entry to both Si Sat and Sukhothai.

Background
During the fourth reign of Sukhothai, Si Sat became the seat of the king's son and the two cities were linked by a 50-km-long road, the Phra Ruang Highway. Bounded by a moat 10 m wide and by thick town walls, during its heyday it was the equal of Sukhothai in splendour, and probably superior in terms of its defences. Protected by rapids, swamp and mountains, not to mention a triple moat filled with barbed spikes, Si Sat must have seemed immensely daunting to any prospective attacker.

Critical to Si Sat's vitality was the ceramic industry based at Ban Pha Yang and Ban Ko-noi, to the north of the city. With the technical assistance of Chinese potters these villages produced probably the finest of all Thai ceramics. These were not just for local consumption; Sangkhalok ware has been found as far afield as Java, Borneo and the Philippines.

Sights
Wat Chang Lom lies in the heart of the old city and is the most sacred wat in Si Satchanalai. The principal *chedi* was built between 1285 and 1291 to contain sacred relics of the Buddha, which King Ramkhamhaeng dug up, worshipped for a month and six days

and buried; he then had a *chedi* built over them, which took three years to complete. The Ceylonese-style *chedi* is the earliest example of its kind in Thailand and became the prototype for many others. Stairs take the pilgrim from the lower, earthly levels, upwards towards the more spiritual realm of the Buddha. The *chedi* is enclosed by 50-m-long laterite walls, and in front of it are the ruins of a large *viharn*, together with another smaller stupa and *viharn*.

Wat Chedi Jet Thaew (30 m south of Wat Chang Lom) stands within a ditch and two rows of laterite walls pierced by four gates. The wat contains the remnants of seven rows of lotus-bud *chedis*, some 34 in total, which house the ashes of members of the Si Satchanalai ruling family.

South of here is **Wat Suan Kaeo Utthayanyai** and the southernmost wat within the walls, **Wat Nang Phaya** (Monastery of the Queen). The latter is enclosed by single walls of laterite, with four gateways. A Ceylonese-style *chedi* dominates the compound. The fine stucco floral motifs (now protected by a shed) on the west wall of the large laterite *viharn* are early Ayutthayan in style (15th century), and are the best preserved of any such decoration in either Sukhothai or Si Sat.

Wat Khao Phanom Phloeng lies on a 20-m-high hillock on the north side of the town and is reached by a laterite staircase of 144 steps. It comprises a Ceylonese-style *chedi*, a large seated Buddha and some stone columns. Recent excavations at this site have revealed an early animist shrine, the **Sala Chao Mae Laong Samli**, which pre-dates both

Si Satchanalai & Chaliang

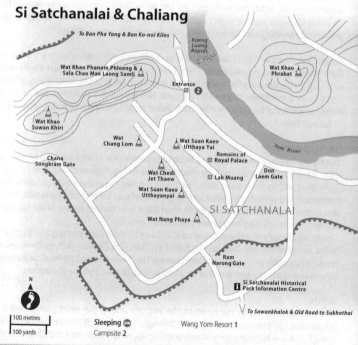

the Khmer and Tai periods, showing that Si Sat was occupied – and of significant importance – long before the rise of the Sukhothai Kingdom. To the west of Wat Khao Phanom Phloeng and linked by a path and staircase, on a higher hillock, are the remains of **Wat Khao Suwan Khiri**.

Chaliang

ⓘ *Get off at the pink archway on Route 101, 2 km before Route 1201, which leads to a suspension footbridge crossing the Yom River to Chaliang.*

To the southeast, 2 km outside the Si Satchanalai city walls, is the area known as Chaliang. The first wat you come to along the road to Chaliang is **Wat Kok Singh Karam**, on the right-hand side, which includes three *chedis* on the same base. In front of these stupas are a *viharn* and *bot*.

Wat Chom Chuen (Monastery of Prince Chan) contains a *prang* built in the time of the Khmer King Jayavarman VII (1181-1217). It seems that Chaliang was chosen by the Khmer as the site for one of its outposts at the far extremity of the Khmer Empire because of its defensive position. Next to this wat is an **Archaeological Site Museum** ⓘ *free*, a great building set into the riverbank with a grass roof. The excavations revealed 15 inhumation burials. The bodies were buried during the Dvaravati period (sixth to 11th centuries). Grave goods devoted to the dead comprise glass beads, iron tools and clay paddles. Head orientation is to the west.

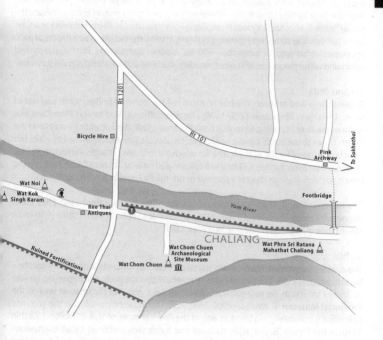

Positioned on the banks of the Yom River is **Wat Phra Sri Ratana Mahathat Chaliang** (or Wat Phra Prang), an impressive laterite *prang* originally built in the mid-15th century. Its origins are older still, as the *prang* is thought to have been built on top of an earlier Khmer *prasat*. In front of the *prang* are the ruins of a *viharn* which houses a large seated Sukhothai Buddha image, with long, graceful fingers 'touching ground'. Even more beautiful is the smaller walking Buddha of brick and stucco to the left. It is thought to be one of the finest from the Sukhothai period displaying that enigmatic 'Sukhothai smile'. The wat also contains a number of other interesting Buddha images.

Ban Pha Yang and Kan Ko-noi

North of the city, at Ban Pha Yang and Ban Ko-noi, remains of ceramic kilns have been discovered, dating from the 1350s. The pottery produced from here is known as 'Sangkhalok', after the early Ayutthaya name for the district (there is a town of the same name to the south). The kilns of Ban Pha Yang lie 500 m north of the old city walls, and so far 21 kilns have been found, all of the closed-kiln variety. It is thought that they produced architectural and high-quality ceramics.

Kamphaeng Phet ⬤🅰🅕🅖🅒 ➡ *pp213-219. Colour map 1, C3.*

It is possible to wander through the ruined monasteries and forts of Kamphaeng Phet, many overgrown with verdant trees, without meeting a single person. The town was originally built by King Lithai in the 14th century as a garrison to protect and consolidate the power of the Sukhothai Kingdom (Kampheng Phet translates as 'Diamond Wall') at a time when surrounding states were growing in threat. In total, the old city, now a historical park, encompasses an area of more than 400 ha. Modern Kamphaeng Phet is sleepy and easygoing with a proportion of its older, wooden, shuttered and tiled buildings still surviving.

Ins and outs

Getting there and around The bus terminal is 2 km from the bridge, some way out of town. The city is open daily 0800-1630. The ticket office is next to Wat Phra Kaeo and north of the river. It costs ฿40 to visit both the area within the ancient city walls and the forested area to the north, known as Aranyik. It is possible to walk within the city walls, but vehicles are useful for the Aranyik area, for which the following charges are levied: ฿10 for a bike, ฿20 for a motorbike, ฿30 for a tuk-tuk and ฿50 for a car. It's possible to walk around the site though you can charter a *saamlor* or tuk-tuk for roughly ฿150 for one hour.

Tourist information There's a badly run tourist office in the **Kamphaeng Phet Local Handicraft Centre**, Thesa Road (near Soi 13), which should open between 0800-2000 and a Tourist Information Centre next to Wat Phra Kaeo.

Sights

The massive 6-m-high defensive walls still stand – earthen ramparts topped with laterite – beyond which is a moat to further deter attackers. Within the walls, encompassing an area of 2.5 km by 500 m, lie two old wats, Wat Phra Kaeo and Wat Phrathat, as well as the **Provincial Museum** ① *Wed-Sun 0900-1600*, ฿30. The museum contains, in the entrance hall, what is commonly regarded as one of the finest bronzes of Siva in Thailand. Cast in 1510, in the Khmer 'Bayon' style, its head and hands were removed by an overzealous German visitor in 1886. Fortunately, he was intercepted, and the limbs and head were reunited with the torso. The museum contains some good examples of Buddha images found in the locality.

From the museum, walk west to **Wat Phrathat** (Monastery of the Great Relic). Not much remains except a *chedi* and a well-weathered seated Buddha (of laterite) sitting in the *viharn*. Immediately north, **Wat Phra Kaeo** was probably the largest and most

Kamphaeng Phet

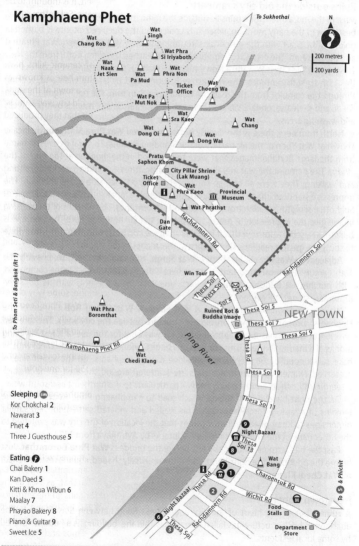

200 metres
200 yards

To Sukhothai

N

Sleeping 🛏
Kor Chokchai **2**
Nawarat **3**
Phet **4**
Three J Guesthouse **5**

Eating 🍴
Chai Bakery **1**
Kan Daed **5**
Kitti & Khrua Wibun **6**
Maalay **7**
Phayao Bakery **8**
Piano & Guitar **9**
Sweet Ice **5**

important wat in Kamphaeng Phet. It was initially built during the Sukhothai period and then extensively remodelled in the Ayutthaya period. Just beyond the ticket office is Kamphaeng Phet's **Lak Muang** (City Pillar Shrine). Many *saamlor* drivers ring their bells when passing the shrine in recognition of the power of the spirits that reside here.

Ruins outside the old city's ramparts

Most of the more interesting ruins lie outside the ramparts, to the north of town. They are best seen in the early morning, when it is cooler and the deep red laterite is bathed in golden light. Start with the outer ruins, returning to view Wat Phra Kaeo, Wat Phrathat and the museum. The first wat of significance to be reached travelling north from the New Town to the Old City is **Wat Phra Non** which, like many of the structures here, dates from the 15th to 16th centuries. The monastery is surrounded by laterite walls and, walking through the complex from the road the buildings are, in turn, the *bot*, *viharn*, the main *chedi*, and then a secondary *viharn*. There are also the remains of monk's quarters, wells and washing areas.

North from here, there is the slightly better-preserved **Wat Phra Si Iriyaboth**, locally known as Wat Yuen or the Monastery of the Standing Buddha. This wat derives its name from the large Buddha images that were to be found in the *mondop* at the end of the *viharn*. The name of the wat literally means 'four postures' – standing, reclining, sitting and walking. They were all in high stucco relief, one on each side of the *mondop*. The impressive standing image is the only one in reasonable repair and is a good example of Sukhothai sculpture, dating from the 14th to 15th centuries. The remains of the walking image give the impression of grace, so typical of the Sukhothai period. The *viharn* was built on a raised platform so that it is higher than the *bot*. It is thought that this was done to show the greater religious significance of the images in the *viharn*.

Adjacent to Wat Phra Si Iriyaboth is **Wat Singh**, again built in the 15th, possibly the 16th, century. The most important structure here is the stupa at the back of the compound, with porches for Buddha images on each side. In front is the bot, with its *bai sema* (boundary stone) still evident.

Walking through the forest behind Wat Singh is **Wat Chang Rob** (Shrine of the Elephants), probably the most impressive structure outside the city walls. The forested position of this monastery is appropriate for it was built for the use of forest-dwelling monks of a meditation sect. This consists of a huge Ceylonese-style laterite *chedi* with its base surrounded by 68 elephants. Only one row of elephants, on the south side, is preserved. Numerous other minor wats are scattered around the area, some in thick undergrowth, others amidst paddy fields – particularly to the northeast and southwest.

On the right-hand side of the approach road to Kamphaeng Phet (Route 1) are the remains of a laterite fort, **Phom Seti**. This walled and moated settlement had similar dimensions to Khamphaeng Phet. It seems that the location of the city was switched to the other bank of the Ping after successive attacks by Ayutthaya from 1373.

Past the bus terminal and on the left before the bridge is **Wat Phra Boromthat**. Just before the bridge, on the right-hand side, is the unusually shaped, square, restored *chedi* of **Wat Chedi Klang**.

New town sights

A **ruined bot** in the heart of the city is on Thesa Road between Sois 6 and 8. The abandoned brick structure has fallen into ruin; within the 'building' is a Buddha revered by some local residents.

As with any Thai town, Kamphaeng Phet has its share of markets. On Thesa Road, opposite the tourist information centre, is a small **fresh market**; a little further south, also on Thesa Road, is a **night bazaar**, a good place to eat stall food in the evening (near Soi 13). But the main **day market** occupies a large area sandwiched between Wichit and Charoensuk roads.

◉ Sukhothai and the north central plains

For Sleeping and Eating price codes and other relevant information, see pages 44-49.

● Sleeping

Sukhothai New City *p196, map p197*
There are some excellent guesthouses in Sukhothai's newer city. Beware: the tuk-tuk drivers at the bus station may be on commission with certain guesthouses/hotels and refuse to take you or try and charge exorbitant rates (it should cost ฿30-40). Call your guesthouse if in doubt – many offer a free pick-up.
C-D Sukhothai Orchid, 43 Singhawat Rd, T055-611193. Large, airy hotel with spacious, cool reception area and restaurant. Rooms are clean and smart with a/c, hot shower, en suite and cable TV.
C-F Sukhothai Lotus Village, 170 Rachthani Rd, T055-621484, www.lotus-village.com. The large, leafy compound is scattered with several ponds, has a number of attractive teak houses and several spotless bungalows, some with a/c. Tastefully decorated, clean, peaceful, and managed by an informative Thai/French couple. It also serves tasty Western breakfasts of toast, yoghurt, fresh juice and fresh coffee. Beds are very hard. Highly recommended.
D-F Sukhothai Guesthouse, 68 Vichien Chamnong Rd, T055-610453, www.thai.net/sukhothaiguesthouse. Some a/c rooms, hot water showers, restaurant. A well-maintained establishment, with attractive teak balconies. Friendly and informative owners. Also runs informal cookery classes and offers a range of tours, free bikes, free pick-up at the bus station and internet. Highly recommended.
E-F Ban Thai, 38 Prawert Nakhon Rd, T055-610163, www.geocities.com/guesthouse_banthai. Overlooking the

Yom River, an assortment of clean, well-kept rustic bungalows and rooms in a large natural-style house. Excellent en suite bungalows and small rooms and clean shared toilets. The friendly English-speaking management offers lots of free maps to surrounding area, recycle as much plastic and paper as possible and offers bicycle tours through surrounding villages (from ฿150).
E-F J&J Guesthouse, just before you come to No 4, T055-620095, jjguest@hotmail.com. Attractive bungalows, some with a/c and en suite, hot showers, all spotless. Small restaurant attached, well-kept gardens. Friendly, informative English-speaking management. Bakery and bar attached.
E-F No 4, 140/4 Soi Maerampan Jarodwitheethong Rd, T055-610165, no.4guesthouse@thaimail.com. Very friendly English-speaking lady owner rents out spotless bamboo bungalows, tucked into a small compound in a wonderfully secluded location. Well kept, clean, cute en suite rooms. Excellent Thai food in the restaurant. She also runs cookery classes. Tours organized from here. Good value. Highly recommended.
F-G Ninety Nine Guest House, 234/6 Soi Panichsan, off Charodwithithong Rd, T055-611315, ninetynine_gh@yahoo.com. A very clean family-run guesthouse in a wooden house with a friendly sitting room area for relaxation. Very helpful owner who runs cookery courses. Other services include local information and history, tour guide and traditional Thai massage. Recommended.
F-G River House, Khuha Suwan Rd. Peaceful location by river, rooms with fan and shared shower. Friendly and helpful management. Recommended.

Sukhothai Old City *p199, map p200*

A-C Paylin, Charodwithithong Rd, about 4 km from the Old City on the road leading to Sukhothai, T055-613310. A monster of a hotel stuck out on the road between the old and new cities. This is the most luxurious place to stay, but lacks character and the restaurant has an awful reputation.

C-E Orchid Hibiscus, T/F055-633284, orchid_hibiscus_guest_house@hotmail.com. Run by the engaging Paolo – an Italian from Rome – and his Thai wife, Pinthong, this is one the nicest guesthouses in Thailand. Rates may be a little high for the average backpacker hostel but the gorgeous en suite, a/c bungalows, swimming pool, gardens, tropical birds and wonderful breakfasts (beware of the highly addictive coconut pudding smothered in fresh, wild honey) certainly make it excellent value. Paolo is a font of local knowledge and knows the outer temples so well he can even tell you the best spots for sunrise and sunset. Highly recommended.

D-E Old Sukhothai Cultural Centre (aka Thai Village House), 214 Charodwithithong Rd, Muang Kao, T055-612275. A/c, run-down, en suite teak bungalows set on a semi-island, almost surrounded by water. Large, clean and simply decorated rooms.

D-G Old City Guesthouse, 28/7 Charodwithithong Rd, in front of the National Museum, north of the entrance to the park, T055-697515. Offers a range of rooms from tiny to enormous, from fan and shared bathroom to en suite, a/c and cable TV, all spotless. Friendly management. Outstanding value and highly recommended.

E-G Vitoon Guesthouse, 49/3 Charodwithithong Rd, at the bend in the road, T055-697045. Not as peaceful as the Old City Guesthouse, but rooms are spotless, 8 with a/c and hot showers, and 12 with fan, and immaculate Western toilets attached. Bicycle hire. Good value, despite noise pollution.

Ramkhamhaeng National Park *p203*

B-C There are bungalows near the park headquarters and tents for hire.

Reservations can be made by contacting either Ramkhamhaeng National Park, PO Box 1, Amphoe Kirimas, Sukhothai, 64160, or by phoning the **Royal Forest Department** on T0-2579 4842. Some guesthouses in the New City (for example **Ban Thai**) are beginning to organize trips here.

Phitsanulok *p203, map p204*

A-B Amarin Lagoon Hotel, 52/299 Phra Ong Khao Rd, out of town centre, T055-213149, amarin@psnulok.loxinfo.co.th. A/c, restaurant, pool, this soulless 305-room hotel on a 10-ha site is really a business hotel. The management provides a shuttle service, and the hotel is well run, with courteous and efficient staff, superb views from the back over the lagoon and open countryside to the far hills.

B-C Phitsanulok Thani Hotel, 39 Sanambin Rd, T055-211065, www.phitsanulok thani.com. A/c, restaurant, pub, pool, luxury hotel, one of the Dusit chain, so standards are high. The room rate includes breakfast and there are a few pleasant garden restaurants just across the road. A little out of town, but within walking distance.

B-C Topland Plaza Hotel, 68/33 Ekathosarot St, T055-247800. A/c, restaurant, well-run multi-storey hotel, with good views over the city from the upper floors. A real bargain but it has a very noisy disco at weekends that will keep even the deepest sleeper awake.

B-D Rajapruk, 99/9 Phra Ong Dam Rd, T055-258788. A/c, restaurant, inviting pool. Comfortable and clean with helpful and friendly staff. Recommended.

D-E Nanchao, 242 Boromtrailokant Rd, T055-244702. A/c, modern hotel with views from the upper floors, good value. Recommended.

F Lithai Guesthouse, 73/1 Phaya Lithai Rd, T055-219626, maka@loxinfo.co.th. Some fan, some a/c, satellite TV, en suite rooms. Views of either dirty rooftops or busy streets below. Still, good value for money.

F Samainiyom Hotel, 175 Ekathosarot Rd, T055-258575. All rooms a/c, satellite TV and clean en suite bathrooms for those willing to pay a little bit more. Reasonable prices.

F Sivathep Hotel, 110/21 Ekathosarot Rd, T055-219146. Some fan, some a/c, all rooms en suite with satellite TV.
F-G Youth Hostel, 38 Sanambin Rd, T055-242060. Southeast of the railway, slightly out of town. This has become the travellers' hang-out, so it is very popular. Relaxing atmosphere in an attractive wooden building, large, clean rooms with some a/c and some style, helpful owner, dorm beds available, breakfast included, bicycles for rent. Outdoor sitting area for hammocks. The best option in town for those on a budget. Recommended.

Phu Hin Rongkla National Park *p206*
B-C Bungalows are available at park head-quarters (book in advance, T055-579 5734). 2 restaurants (take own food if self-catering) and money changer.

Camping
Camping ground (tents for hire, ฿40).

Thung Salaeng National Park *p206*
There are guesthouses and a dormitory block at the headquarters and 4 campsites. Tents are available for hire. A more comfortable alternative is to stay in one of the resort hotels along Highway 12.
B-C Rainforest Resort, at Km 44, T055-241185. Overlooks the Khek River and offers wooden bungalows with a/c. recommended.

Si Satchanalai *p207, map p208*
B Wang Yom Resort, off Route 101 to Sawankhalok, T055-611179. It has overpriced, tatty bungalows. Attached restaurant serves Thai food (♔).

Camping
You can rent tents (฿80) at the main gate into the park – there's a small campsite in a nice spot overlooking the river, a toilet/shower block and 24-hr security.

Kamphaeng Phet *p210, map p211*
All hotels are situated in the new town. There is a distinct lack of budget accommodation.

C-D Nawarat, 2 Soi 15, Thesa 1 Rd, T055-711106. A/c, TV (Thai only), restaurant. Reasonable, clean rooms have thin walls, making it potentially noisy. The upper floors have good views.
C-D Phet Hotel, 189 Bumrungraj Rd, T055-712810, phethtl@phethotel.com. The most comfortable hotel in town. A/c, small pool (open to non-residents), restaurant serves Thai and international food, snooker club. Good value for money with breakfast included.
E-F Kor Chokchai, 7-31 Rachdamnern Soi 6, T055-711247. Some a/c, some fan. Large, clean rooms and bathrooms, Western toilets, though aimed at Thai businessmen.
E-F Three J Guesthouse, 79 Rachavitee Rd, T055-720384, charin.sri@chaiyo.com. Chintzy, clean bungalows, some a/c, some fan. The cutesy decor might leave you feeling dizzy but this is one of the friendliest places in town. Recommended.

🍴 Eating

Sukhothai New City *p196, map p197*
♔ **Art's Fresh Coffee and Beer**, by the bus station for the Old City on Charodwithithong Rd, is a good place for a mug of early morning coffee while waiting in the chill for the bus.
♔ **Chinnawat**, 1-3 Nikhon Kasem Rd. A/c restaurant with satellite TV and reasonable food, it offers the rather novel option of small and large portions – the latter are for the very hungry.
♔ **Dream Café**, Singhawat Rd, near Sawatdipong Hotel. Thai and international dishes in cool interior, with a great collection of bric-a-brac, good for breakfasts.
♔ **Rainbow Café**, off Nikhon Kasem Rd (near night market). Good breakfasts and sometimes patrons can watch CNN or BBC *World News* (when it isn't set on Thai TV), although the road is a bit noisy. Also serves international food.
♔ **Sukhothai Coca**, 56/2-5 Singhawat Rd. Thai food and sandwiches.

Coffee shops
DK Coffee, opposite the River View Hotel, attached to **DK Books**. Serves good coffee.

Foodstalls
Night market (*talaat to rung*), on Ramkhamhaeng Rd, off Nikhon Kasem Rd, opposite the cinema, for good stalls. Open 1800-0600. Other stalls open up at about the same time along the walls of Wat Rachthani.

Sukhothai Old City *p199, map 200*
A number of stalls and small restaurants sell simple Thai dishes in the Old City. There's a collection of good Thai eateries in the compound just outside the new main entrance and, during the evening, dozens of stalls spring up along the main road selling everything from spicy papaya salad to freshly roasted chicken.

The Coffee Cup, opposite the National Museum. A small, friendly café with drinks, snacks and internet facilities.

Vitoon Guesthouse, 49/3 Charodvithithong Rd, T055-697045. Excellent breakfasts and coffee for early risers arriving from Sukhothai.

Phitsanulok *p203, map p204*
There is a good choice of excellent restaurants, mostly concentrated in the centre of town around Naresuan, Sairuthai and Phaya Lithai roads. Check out Phitsanulok's 2 famed specialities: *kluay thaak* (sweet bananas) and *thao mai luai* (morning glory). This vegetable is flash-fried in a wok with a great burst of flame and then tossed onto the plate (the dish is usually known as *phak bung loi fan*). 'Flying vegetable' artistes can be seen at work in the night market and at a few restaurants. Not to be missed! Several houseboat restaurants are to be found along Buddha Bucha Rd, near Naresuan Bridge.

Song Khwae Houseboat, Buddha Bucha Rd. Nice place to hang out on the river. Serves Chinese food.

Fab Ke Rab Phra Ong Dam Rd, 80 m east of the level crossing. Muslim restaurant,

friendly staff, good food and very well priced. Recommended. The other Muslim restaurant on the same road (adjacent to the level crossing) hasn't had a very good press.

Poon Sri, Phaya Lithai Rd. A great little Thai restaurant where you can get a good meal for ฿50 a head. Recommended.

Sor Lert Rod, 4/5 Boromtrailokant Rd, near **Phailyn Hotel**. Great location for this good Thai eatery. Recommended.

Tiparot, 9 Soi Lue Thai Rd. In the heart of town, serves up authentic and delicious Chinese food.

Viroys, 99/18-19 Phra Ong Dam Rd. Excellent Chinese food, with morning glory for the uninitiated.

Bakeries
KT, Phaya Lithai Rd. Excellent range of cakes and pastries.

Foodstalls
The **riverside night market** is open from 1800-2400, selling Thai and Chinese food. Thai desserts such as *khao niaw sangkayaa* (sticky rice and custard) can be bought from the foodstalls on Phaya Lithai Rd in the evening. **Basement of Topland Arcade**, Boromtrailokant Rd, has a good selection of clean, well-presented foodstalls.

Si Satchanalai *p207, map p208*
Several bus loads of tourists arrive each day at Si Sat and most of them eat at the run of overpriced, though decent enough, Thai restaurants on the same stretch of road as the **Wang Yom Resort**. By the main gate (next door to the campsite) is a whole heave of cheap Thai stalls selling the usual fried rice, noodles, ice cream and drinks.

Kamphang Phet *p210, map p211*
Piano and Guitar, Thesa Rd. This restaurant, serving Thai food, has a charming interior.

Kitti and **Khrua Wibun**, 101 and 102 Thesa Rd (near Thesa Soi 2). Excellent Thai restaurants serving *khao muu daeng* (red pork and rice), *khao man kai* (chicken and rice) and most simple rice and noodle dishes. Recommended.

Maalay, 77 Thesa Rd. Look out for the rice baskets hanging outside, serves excellent Isaan (Lao) food, traditional. Recommended.

Bakeries, coffee shops and ice cream parlours

Chai Bakery, Rachdamnern Rd (near intersection with Charoensuk Rd).
Kan Daed, Thesa Rd. Coffee house inside an attractive wooden shophouse.
Phayao Bakery, Thesa Rd (near Charoensuk Rd).
Sweet Ice, Thesa Rd, near Thesa Soi 7, and **Tasty**, Thesa Rd, near Thesa Soi 2 (sign in Thai only). 2 a/c ice cream parlours.

Foodstalls

In the evening the best selection of foodstalls can be found at the night bazaar on Thesa Rd. Another group of stalls on Wichit Rd.

🍷 Bars and clubs

Sukhothai *p196, maps p197 and p200*
Several pubs are scattered along the bypass such as **Focus Bar** and **Top Country Pub**; rather out of the way for an evening drink unless you have your own transport. Also **Chopper Beer Bar** on Charodwithithong Rd, about 20 m after the bridge, on the left.

Phitsanulok *p203, map p204*
Most bars are near expensive hotels.
Bi Bi's Pub, Sithamtripidok Rd (down *soi* near **Thep Nakhon Hotel**). Cocktails and a wide range of drinks in an a/c 'chalet'.
Thip Beer House, Boromtrailokant Rd. Ice-cold beer in an open bar.

🎉 Festivals and events

Sukhothai *p196, maps p197 and p200*
Oct/Nov Loi Krathong is very special and Sukhothai is reputed to be the 'home' of this

most beautiful of Thai festivals. It is said that one of the king's mistresses carved the first *krathong* from a piece of fruit and floated it down the river to her king. Today, the festival symbolizes the floating away of the previous year's sins, although traditionally it was linked to the gift of water. The Thai word for irrigation, *chonprathaan*, literally means the 'gift of water', and the festival comes at the end of the rainy season when the rice is maturing in the paddy fields.

🛍 Shopping

Phitsanulok *p203, map p204*
Gold shops line the streets throughout town. Some jewellery and ornaments are hand-made locally, with their designs taken from ruins and remains in the Sri Satchanalai area.
Hat Tim, 1/1 Sithamtripidok Rd. For antiques and handicrafts.
Mondok Thai, 10 Sithamtripidok Rd. Also for antiques and handicrafts.
Night market, Buddha Bucha Rd, on the river. Sells everything from handicrafts, clothes and toys to amulets (see page 94); something Phitsanulok has a reputation for.
Topland Arcade,Boromtrailokant Rd. A large a/c shopping centre.
Topland Plaza, Singhawat Rd, near the **Topland Plaza Hotel**. Similar to **Topland Arcade**.

Si Satchanalai *p207, map p208*
Ree Thai Antiques, a small quaint Walt Disney-style house selling antiques.

⛰ Activities and tours

Sukhothai *p196, map p197*
Tours and tour operators
Many hotels and guesthouses arrange tours to the Old City, Kamphaeng Phet and Si Satchanalai. Expect to pay ฿300 for a tour to the Old City and ฿500 for Si Satchanalai.

Phitsanulok *p203, map p204*
Tour operators
Able Group Company Ltd, 55/45 Sri Thammatripidok Rd, T055-243851. Runs sightseeing and trekking tours and rents cars.
Piti Tour and Phitsanulok Tour Centre, 55/45 Surasri Trade Centre, 43/11 Borom-trailokant Rd, T055-242206. Organizes city tours and tours to Sukhothai and Si Satchanalai by private car.

⊖ Transport

Sukhothai *p196, maps p197 and p200*
Air
Bangkok Airways provides daily connections with **Bangkok** and **Chiang Mai**. Sukhothai Airport, T055-647224 is privately owned by Bangkok Airways.
    Airline offices Bangkok Airways, 99 Moo 4, Klongkrajong, Sawankaloke, T055-647225/6, www.bangkokair.com.

Bicycle and motorbike hire
Bikes in the new town, ฿50 per day from many guesthouses. There are several places in the old town where a bike costs ฿20 a day. Motorbikes are ฿250-300 per day from many guesthouses.

Bus
For regular connections with **Bangkok** (7 hrs), **Phitsanulok** (1 hr), **Chiang Mai** (6 hrs) and **Lampang** (5 hrs), the station is about 2 km west of town on the bypass road. There are 2 direct buses a day from the Old City to **Bangkok**'s Northern terminal – at 0900 and 2100, ฿256. You can buy tickets from **The Coffee Cup** (see Eating, above). The Chiang Mai bus from the New City also goes through the Old City and you can wait on the main road outside the old entrance and flag one down. Buses for other parts of the kingdom leave from offices at assorted points. For **Tak** and **Mae Sot**, buses leave from Ban Muang Rd; for **Si Satchanalai** from the corner of Raj Uthit and Charodwithithong roads.

Tuk-tuk
For town trips and for excursions further afield, tuk-tuks congregate on Nikhon Kasem Rd, opposite the **Chinnawat Hotel**.

Phitsanulok *p203, map p204*
Air
THAI has multiple daily connections with **Bangkok**. There are also connections with **Loei**, **Tak**, **Lampang**, **Chiang Mai** (daily), **Mae Hong Son**, **Mae Sot** and **Nan**.
    Airline offices THAI, 209/26-28 Boromtrailokant Rd, T055-280 0060.

Bus
Local Both a/c and non-a/c (฿10-20).
Long distance Regular connections with **Bangkok** from the Northern bus terminal (5-6 hrs), **Kamphaeng Phet** (2 hrs), **Uttaradit** (2 hrs), **Nan** (5 hrs, via Uttaradit), **Phrae** (3 hrs), **Udon Thani**, **Sukhothai** (every 30 mins), **Pattaya**, **Tak** (3 hrs), **Mae Sot** (5 hrs), **Chiang Mai** (5-6 hrs), **Lampang** (4 hrs), **Korat** (6 hrs) and **Chiang Rai** (6-7 hrs).

Car hire
Able Group Company Ltd, see Tour operators, above.

Train
A copy of the timetable in English is available from the TAT office, see page 205. Regular connections with **Bangkok**'s Hualamphong station (6 hrs), **Lopburi** (5 hrs), **Ayutthaya** (5 hrs) and **Chiang Mai** (6-7 hrs).

Si Satchanalai *p207, map p208*
Bus
Regular connections 0600-1800 with **Sukho-thai** from Raj Uthit Rd, 54 km, 1 hr. Ask to be dropped off at the Muang Kao (Old City).

Kamphaeng Phet *p210, map p211*
Bus
The terminal is 2 km from the bridge, some way out of town. Regular connections with **Bangkok**'s Northern terminal (5 hrs) and with **Phitsanulok**, **Chiang Mai**, **Tak** (2 hrs),

Nan, **Phrae** and **Chiang Rai**. Win Tour, Kamphaeng Phet Rd, and corner of Thesa Rd, operates a/c tour buses to Bangkok.

Songthaew

Songthaews to local destinations depart from the main market (the municipal or Thetsabarn) for the bus station. They run from the bus terminal to the market in town (฿5); and from Kamphaeng Phet Rd, at the roundabout by the bridge.

❶ Directory

Sukhothai *p196, maps p197 and p200*
Banks Bangkok, 49 Singhawat Rd. Bangkok Bank of Commerce, 15 Singhawat Rd. Thai Farmers, 134 Charoen Withi Rd. There is also a currency exchange booth by the Ramkhamhaeng Museum in the Old City – open daily 0830-1200. **Internet** A number of cafés have opened up in both the Old City and Sukhothai; some guesthouses provide internet services. **Medical services** Sukhothai Hospital, Charodwithithong Rd,

T055-611782, about 4 km out of town on the road towards the Old City. **Police** Nikhon Kasem Rd, T055-611010. **Post office** Nikhon Kasem Rd. There is also a sub post office and overseas telephone service in the Old City.

Phitsanulok *p203, map p204*
Banks Bangkok, 35 Naresuan Rd. Krung Thai, 31/1 Naresuan Rd. Thai Farmers, 144/1 Boromtrailokant Rd, TCs and ATM. **Internet** A couple of places just over the Aekathossarot Bridge. More internet cafés are opening. **Medical services** Hospital Sithamtripidok Rd, T055-258812. **Post office and telephone centre** Buddha Bucha Rd. **Tourist police** Boromtrailokant Rd, next to TAT office, T055-251179.

Kamphaeng Phet *p210, map p211*
Banks Thai Farmers, 233 Charoensuk Rd, and Bangkok Bank both have ATMs. **Internet** There are an increasing number of internet cafés in town, mainly situated on Thesa Rd. **Post office** Corner of Thesa Rd and Thesa Soi 3. Also has fax and overseas telephone facilities.

Mae Sot and the Burmese border

West of Sukhothai is Tak – a town built on the trade of various nefarious goods that pass through from nearby Burma. Pressed right up against the Burmese border, Mae Sot has a reputation for bandits and smuggling, though the town authorities are eager to build on its burgeoning reputation as a trekking centre. From Mae Sot it's possible to cross the Moei River for a day trip into the Burmese town of Myawadi. Follow the Burmese border further north from Mae Sot to reach Mae Sariang and Mae Hong Son or head south to the rugged forests of Umphang. ▶ *For listings, see pages 224-228.*

Tak ⊜❼❶⊜❻ ▶ *pp224-228. Colour map 1, C1.*

Sprawling along the east bank of the Ping River, Tak was once a junction in the river trade but is now better known as a smuggling centre; drugs, teak and gems from Burma are exchanged for guns and consumer goods from Thailand. The Phahonyothin Highway is often lined with logging lorries carrying timber from Burma, a trade that has the political and commercial support of the Thai army. Still small and distinctly provincial, Tak has managed to retain some of its traditional architecture: wooden houses with tiled roofs are scattered amongst the ubiquitous concrete shophouses. Christian missionaries have been active in Tak Province and there is a large Roman Catholic Church on the Phahonyothin Highway.

Sights
A source of local pride is the long, slender and rather unusual **suspension bridge** for motorcycles and pedestrians north of the **Viang Tak 2 Hotel**. As in any other town, Tak has its share of markets and wats. There is a large general market between Chompon and Rimping roads, and a food market opposite the **Viang Tak Hotel** on Mahatthai Bamrung Road. TAT ① *193 Thaksin Rd, T055-514341, daily 0830-1630.*

Lan Sang National Park
① *฿200, car ฿20; the park is 3 km off the Tak–Mae Sot Highway (No 105) between Km 12 and Km 13; it's easy enough to alight the bus at the main road and walk the final 3 km or hitch a lift on a motorbike.*
The Lan Sang National Park supports small populations of leopard, deer and bear; much of the wildlife has been decimated over years of (usually illegal) hunting. There are a number of trails leading to waterfalls, together with the **Doi Musur Hilltribe Development and Welfare Centre**. It covers just over 100 sq km. Hilltribe products are for sale at Km 29 on the Tak–Mae Sot highway.

Mae Sot and around ⊜❼❶⊜▲⊜❻ ▶ *pp224-228. Colour map 1, C2.*

Mae Sot lies 5 km from the Burmese border, near the end of Route 105, which swoops its way through hills and forest from Tak to Mae Sot and the Moei River Valley. The town has developed into an important trading centre and just about every ethnic group can be seen wandering the streets: Thais, Chinese, Burmese, Karen, Hmong and other mountain peoples. Although Mae Sot has quietened down over the last few years, it still has a reputation as being one of the more lawless towns in Thailand. With a flourishing, and sometimes illicit, trade in teak and gems and drugs – this is perhaps unsurprising.

The importance of teak has grown since the Thai government imposed a ban on all logging in Thailand, and companies have turned instead to concessions just across the border in Burma to secure their wood. Whether the army and police force are protecting the forests or are making a tidy profit out of the industry is never quite clear. Over the last few years the Burmese army have made intermittent incursions into Thailand near Mae Sot pursuing Karen rebels. There have also been several assassinations of high-profile anti-Burmese rebels – Mae Sot's reputation as a slightly 'dangerous' frontier town is still well deserved. The Thai-Burmese border in this area is strewn with anti-personnel mines and many local people refuse to graze their cattle because of the danger.

The authorities in Mae Sot are now trying to diversify the town's economy and build a reputation as a tourist destination and trekking centre. They have had some success and there is now a modern, Western-style hotel on the outskirts of the town – the **Mae Sot Hill**, see page 224.

Sights

Wat Moni Phraison, on Intharakit Road, has an unusual *chedi* in which a golden central spire is surrounded by numerous smaller *chedis* rising in tiers, behind each of which is a small image of the Buddha. **Wat Chumphon**, also on Intharakit Road but on the western side of town, is worth visiting. Many of Mae Sot's older wooden shophouses are still standing, especially on Intharakit Road. There is a busy morning market between Prasat Withi and Intharakit roads in the town centre that attracts many Burmese eager to sell their produce. Burmese day migrants can be identified by their dress (many wear *longyis*, Burmese-style sarongs), their language and the pearl-coloured powder called *tanaka*, which often covers the faces of women and children.

Trekking and tours

Mae Sot offers some of the best trekking in northern and western Thailand. However, its potential as another Mae Hong Son or Pai has not gone unnoticed. Its popularity is increasing and in the immediate future there are likely to be new or improved bus services, as well as more guesthouses, trekking companies and associated services. It's also possible to cross the border into Burma, for an immigration fee of approximately US$10 (which goes straight to the Burmese military government). Treks tend to either go south to Umphang or north towards Mae Sariang, and incorporate visits to caves, waterfalls and mountain villages. The usual array of rafting trips and elephant rides are available, in addition to straightforward trekking. ▸▸ *See Trek operators, page 227.*

Towards the Burmese border

A visit to the border makes for an interesting day trip, even if you don't actually cross into Burma. There is a modern, covered market at the border selling Burmese goods (hats, blankets, gems, silver, baskets and agricultural produce like dried mushrooms), with gun-toting Thai rangers, powder-covered Burmese girls and a few restaurants.

Around 1 km from the bridge, back along the road to Mae Sot, is **Wat Thai Wattanaram**. This monastery is notable mainly for the massive, recently built, Burmese-style reclining Buddha in the rear courtyard. Also here is a gallery of over 25 smaller sitting Buddhas.

No refuge

Thailand's beautiful and rugged north-west is rightly famous with travellers for its excellent trekking and friendly mountain peoples. What few visitors realize is that this region is also home to between 500,000 and 2 million Burmese refugees. From Mae Hong Son to the Golden Triangle, Burmese political activists and economic migrants, having fled their country's repressive regime, are living together in squalid and cramped conditions in huge camps. Surprisingly, Thailand is not a signatory to the UN 1951 Convention Relating to the Status of Refugees, and any Burmese living outside any of the nine official camps are considered illegal aliens, subject to arrest and deportation. These 'illegal' refugees face a wide array of problems arising from their status, ranging from no access to either education, safe housing or healthcare through to ruth-less exploitation and harassment. Many of the street-children, sexworkers, and sweatshop workers in Thailand's north-west are Burmese illegals and all are potential victims of corrupt Thai businesses and officials – deaths are not uncommon.

In late-2008 the international press highlighted the appalling treatment of several hundred Burmese Muslim Rohingya refugees at the hands of the Thai military and thus brought their plight back into the limelight. For further information, see Background, page 716.

Following these reports, the UN requested access to Rohingya living in Thailand, which the Thai government initially denied. With growing pressure from the international press, they relented by January 2009 and the UN were allowed to visit the camps where Rohingya were being kept. Their treatment appears to have improved.

Until Burma becomes democratic, these refugees will continue to live lives at the mercy of whoever comes across them. In trying to improve their situation many Burmese are working within the pro-democracy movement.

For more information on the plight of Burmese refugees in Thailand see BWU at www.bwunion.org, BVP at www.geocities.com/maesotesl, or the Irrawaddy at www.irrawaddy.org.

Umphang and around ○○▲○○ ▶▶ pp224-228. Colour map 3, A2.

The 164 km of road that twists and turns its way from Mae Sot to Umphang is one of the most dramatic in the country with vast, jaw-dropping views across into the ranges of hills that lie along the Burmese border. Along this route are also several Karen refugee communities – vast holding pens with the inhabitants not allowed beyond the surrounding area. The Karen, who'd fought the Burmese dictatorship for decades and held most of the border region until the late 1990s, have also been, in many cases, ruthlessly exploited by their Thai hosts. Mae Sot town is filled with sweatshops staffed by Karen refugees who get paid wages as low as ฿20 for a 16-hour day. The struggle by the Karen to secure a decent life is ongoing and a visit to one of the local Karen villages can certainly put paid to the lie that Thailand is the 'Land of Smiles'.

Umphang is one of the least developed regions in western Thailand, its rugged terrain and large expanses of forest, including the Khlong Lan National Park, making it ideal for trekking. Although an organized trek is the best way to see and experience the area's

Border essentials: Thailand–Burma (Myanmar)

Mae Sot–Myawady

The border lies 5 km west of Mae Sot, and runs down the middle of the Moei River. The construction of the 420-m Friendship Bridge across the river, directly linking Mae Sot with the Burmese town of Myawady, was completed in 1997. Thai and Burmese nationals can cross the border freely. Regular blue *songthaews* to the Moei River and the Burmese border leave from the west end of Prasat Withi Road, not far from the Thai Airways office (฿10), here though overseas visitors are limited to one-day visas, which can be purchased at the border. It is also possible to extend your Thai visa at the immigration office here. Thai and Burmese relations are such that border crossings close and reopen with regularity. As the situation is subject to frequent change it is a good idea to check on the status of the border at your hotel/guesthouse or at the Mae Sot Travel Centre (see page 227) before making your journey.

beauty (see page 221, or arrange a trek through one of the Umphang guest houses), it is possible to explore the area on one's own. Umphang town is not much more than an oversized village and the majority of its population are Karen.

Many of the trekking companies in Mae Sot head this way, with the guesthouses, tour companies and resorts in Umphang offering similar packages. See Tour and trek operators, page 227. (Treks arranged from Umphang rather than Mae Sot usually work out considerably cheaper, although you'll have to suffer the five-hour journey from Mae Sot in a *songthaew* rather than a comfortable 4WD.)

Another reason to visit Umphang is to see the Thi Lo Su waterfall – widely recognized as the most beautiful in the country. Set on a massive limestone escarpment in the middle of the jungle, the 500-m-wide fall drops almost 250 m through a series of pools. To reach the waterfall is difficult and you'll probably need to hire a car or *songthaew* from Umphang as it's a 45-km journey along dirt tracks requiring a 3-km walk at the end to reach the falls. Its remoteness also means that it is not overrun with tourists. Set off early from Umphang and don't forget to pack your swimming kit. The road here is often closed during the wetter months and visit here is best planned from November to May.

If travelling to Umphang in your own transport, leave early in the morning as there are quite a number of worthwhile stops en route, including waterfalls and Karen villages. The **Thara Rak waterfall** is 25 km from Mae Sot. Turn off the road after the Km 24 marker.

Khlong Lan National Park

The park covers around 300 sq km with its highest point at 1440-m-high Khun Klong Lan. Wildlife includes sambar deer, wild pig and macaques. There are also a number of waterfalls, including the **Khlong Lan Waterfall** which cascades over a 100-m-high rock face. Khlong Nam Lai Waterfall is good for swimming.

Mae Sot to Mae Sariang ⬤ ➔ *pp224-228.*

On most maps, this road – Route 105 – appears as if it is no more than a track. In fact, the entire 230-km road is in excellent shape. Police checkpoints are interspersed along its length; you might be asked to produce your passport. Travelling south to north, the road is fast to the district town of Tha Song Yang. It then follows the Moei River and the Burmese border. The road becomes slower and the landscape more wild, mountainous and less populated with each kilometre, making for a beautiful, if uncomfortable, six-hour journey.

● Mae Sot and the Burmese border listings

For Sleeping and Eating price codes and other relevant information, see pages 44-49.

● Sleeping

Tak *p220*
Hotels are limited, with no guesthouses that can be recommended for budget travellers.
B-D Viang Tak 2, 236 Chomphon Rd, T055-511910. The best hotel in Tak, overlooking the Ping River. Well run and well maintained with clean a/c rooms. There's a pool, coffee shop, snooker, nightclub, shopping plaza with 24-hr supermarket. Significant discounts available during low season. Recommended.
E-F Racha Villa, 307/1 Pahonyothin Rd, T055-512361. On the outskirts of town, this hotel is more like a motel. Facilities include a/c, TV and Western toilet. The rooms are large and clean, if a little tatty.

Lan Sang National Park *p220*
Limited accommodation is available in the park (T02-579 0529 to book) and camping is permitted.

Mae Sot *p220*
C-D Mae Sot Hill, 100 Asia Rd, T055-532601. Facilities, including a pool, snooker room, gym, bar and decent lakeside restaurant are excellent, though the rooms are a bit worn. The management do the best they can with what they have.
D-E DK Hotel, 298/2 Intharakit Rd, T055-542648. Built by the Duang Kamol publishing group, the lower floor is a large Thai-language bookshop. A/c and fan rooms available. The quality of the rooms differs dramatically between fan and a/c and the hotel is only good value if you get an a/c room. No double beds available. Friendliness of the staff is variable.

E-F Baan Thai Guesthouse, 740/1 Intharakit Rd, T08-1366 5882, banthai_mth@hotmail.com. An oasis of sorts, Baan Thai Guesthouse consist of one large and some smaller teak buildings nestled in a lush garden. Rooms are large, attractive and clean. A/c, fan, daily laundry, Wi-Fi available. Book in advance as this guesthouse quickly fills up. Highly recommended.
E-F First Hotel, 444 Sawat Withi Rd, T055-531233. Some a/c, large, clean rooms, some character. Friendly staff.
E-F No 4 Guesthouse, 736 Intharakit Rd, T/F055-544976, no4guesthouse@yahoo.com. This large teak building is set back on a big plot to the west of town on the road to the Moei River (about 10-15 mins' walk from the bus station). Rooms are large, airy and basic with mattresses on wooden floors, rather dirty shared toilets, but hot showers. Seating area with Thai TV, and a few books and magazines. Eco-trekking is run from here (see Trekking and tours, page 221).
F-G Mae Sot Guesthouse, 208/4 Intharakit Rd, T055-532745. Teak house in largish garden compound. Small simple rooms in main house, bigger rooms with attached cold-water bathrooms and a/c in 'motelese' bungalow (dorm beds available). It's full of grime and not great value. Situated opposite a karaoke bar, and it can be very noisy. Attractive dining and seating area in a large airy teak barn on the side of the house, with satellite TV and lots of information. Extremely friendly owner speaks fantastic English – but he's not always around. The guesthouse organizes trekking tours and collects unwanted clothing and medicines to distribute to Burmese refugees in the area.

Umphang and around *p222*
For the budget traveller the accommodation here is good value for money, but if you are

looking for the minibar and executive lounge experience, expect to be disappointed. In fact, hardly any of the guesthouses have a/c, although the cool weather usually makes this unnecessary.

C-D Huai Namyen Resort, on the road to Palatha, T055-561092. This place is hard to find despite being signposted from the road: just keep bearing left after the turn-off and you'll get to 3 houses, each made up of 2 rooms and sizeable veranda, overlooking nearby cornfields. Advance booking is essential. A peaceful and rustic choice.

D-F Umphang Hill Resort, Palata Rd, T055-561063, www.umphanghill.com. Big resort, set on a hillside, it caters mostly to group tours and is a bit impersonal though friendly enough. Some rooms have fan, some a/c and all are en suite.

D-G Garden Huts, 106 Palata Rd, T055-561093. Cute bamboo and wood bungalows some with beds on raised platforms and some with Western toilets. More expensive rooms have a river view and a small sitting area. The complex is set in a pretty location on the banks of the river. Very friendly management with a little English. Recommended.

E-G Tu Ka Su, Palata Rd, T/F055-561295, T08-1825 8238 (mob). Attractive setting, wood and bamboo en suite bungalows. Very clean and pleasant atmosphere. Bicycles for rent (฿200 per day). Recommended.

E-G Um Phang House, Palata Rd north of the bridge, T055-561073. Range of rooms with attached facilities, some separate bungalows. Basic, with mattresses on raised wooden platforms. Cheaper rooms have squat toilets, bungalows (2-3 people) have Western toilets. There are also a few rooms in the main house. Friendly, nice views to the surrounding forests.

Khlong Lan National Park *p223*
B-C Bungalows. There are 9 bungalows sleeping 5-12, and a campsite near park HQ.

Mae Sot to Mae Sariang *p223*
G Mae Salid Guesthouse, 121 km from Mae Sariang, 109 km from Mae Sot. Almost where

the road stops following the river and climbs into the hills is this grubby little guesthouse. The owner is a very friendly Karen who'll do everything possible to make you feel welcome. Facilities are very basic here.

⑦ Eating

Tak *p220*
There is a limited number of restaurants, although simple Thai eateries are scattered throughout the town, particularly along **Phahonyothin Rd**. For even cheaper options there are stall food available from the market on **Mahatthai Bamrung Rd**.

Mae Sot *p220*
Several small restaurants have recently opened along the western part of **Intharakit Rd**; notable are the Burmese restaurants at the southern end of **Tang Khim Chiang Rd**.
♚♚♚ Baan Chay Nam, at the Mae Sot Hill hotel. Mon-Fri 1700-2230 and Sat and Sun 1100-2230. Charmingly set beside a small lake on a floating pontoon and with axe pillows for seats, this place serves up a good array of excellent northern Thai fare. The Western food, though, is not so good. Recommended.
♚ Aiya Restaurant, 533 Intarakhiri Rd, T08-9706 2329. Arguably the best Burmese restaurant in town, Aiya cooks up beautifully tasting food. Highly recommended.
♚ Bai Fern Restaurant, 660/2 Intharakit Rd. Serves Thai, Western and Burmese food, with a range of pizzas and vegetarian options. Pleasant indoor area with wonderful decor. Popular with travellers and medical interns.
♚ Borderline Teashop, 674/14 Intarakhiri Rd, T05-554 6584, www.borderlinecollective.org. Everything from the presentation of the dishes to the taste of the food impresses. For breakfast, try the flatbread with chickpeas or the ginger salad. Portions are generous and the coffee fresh and strong. Highly recommended.
♚ Canton (Kwangtung), 2/1 Soi Sriphanich. Locals say that this place serves the best Chinese food in town.

Casa Mia, Don Kuaw Rd, T08-720 44701. Home-cooked authentic Italian food, Burmese and Thai dishes as well as Western desserts such as brownies and pumpkin pies. Friendly. Recommended.

Krua Canadian, 3 Sri Phanit Rd, T055-534659. 0700-2100/2200. Smallish café with Canadian owner, Dave, serving good-value Thai and Western dishes with a menu in English. North American breakfast is the best in town. Truly mouth-watering steaks, excellent curries. Takeaway service. Hilltribe coffee is sold. Dave is also an excellent source of information. Recommended.

Neung Nuk, Intharakit Rd. Garden restaurant serving up great Thai grub.

Foodstalls
There are 2 excellent stall restaurants by the Chiang Mai bus stop on Intharakit Rd. One specializes in superb *phat thai* (fried noodles), the other in seafood. The **night market**, just off Prasat Withi Rd, is a good place to eat cheaply in the evening.

Umphang and around *p222*
Almost all guesthouses and resorts have their own restaurants using cheap Thai food.

Dot.com, Palata Rd, near the bridge. Daily 0800-2400. The friendly English-speaking owner, Pradit, serves up decent breakfasts, drinks and some Thai food. You can also find Wi-Fi here (฿30 per hr). Recommended.

Nong Koong, on the corner of Palata Rd, opposite BL Tours. Local place serving simple Thai dishes (use your phrasebook to order).

Phudoi Restaurant, Palata Rd, north of the river. Extensive menu in English and a nice wooden interior. Good food, reasonable prices.

Bars and clubs

Mae Sot *p220*
Walking along Intharakit Rd, you will find a bewildering array of bars catering to all sorts of tastes. Near Baan Thai Guesthouse there is **Cool Bar**, mostly frequented by Thais.

Near Borderline, there's **Kung's Bar**, a newly renovated and nicely decorated bar, run by music-lover Kung. A little further along, **Thaimes Bar** is located, a laid-back relaxed place popular with NGO's working in Mae Sot.

Shopping

Mae Sot *p220*
Books
DK Bookstore, under the DK Hotel. A large range of English-language Penguin classics.

There is also a second-hand bookshop with a small selection of English-language books on Intharakit Rd.

Burmese goods
On sale in the market on the Moei River and in the market behind the **Siam Hotel**. For better-quality objects, try the Burmese lacquerware shop on Prasat Withi Rd, almost opposite the *songthaew* stop for the Moei River.

Gems
A good buy; most of the jewellery shops are concentrated on **Prasat Withi Rd** around the Siam Hotel.

Handicrafts
Borderline Teashop (see Eating, above). Sells everything from passport-holders, book covers and shoulder-bags to scarfs and traditional Karen and Burmese clothes. Profits go to the women, all from marginalized Burmese ethnic groups, who make the handicrafts.
WEAVE, Intharakit Rd, www.weave-women.org. Women's collective selling hand-woven handicrafts made by women fleeing civil strife and economic hardship in Burma.

Activities and tours

Mae Sot *p220*
Art galleries
Aiya (see Eating, above). Showcases art by local Burmese artists on the walls of the

restaurant. The gallery is upstairs, showing mostly watercolour work by local artists. **Borderline Teashop** (see Eating, above) hosts regular exhibitions, held on the first weekend of every month in the gallery above the shop.

Casa Mia, (see Eating, above). Home to the **Burma Border Children Arts Project**, with exhibits paintings by Burmese children on the walls of its restaurant.

Cookery courses

Borderline Teashop (see Eating, above). Offers a 1-day Burmese, Shan, and Karen cookery course. From ฿450 per person. Drop in at the café or visit the website for more details.

Tour and trek operators

Approximate rates are ฿3500 for a 3-day/2-night trek, ฿4500 for 4 days/3 nights, dependent upon whether raft trips and elephant rides are part of the deal. With all tours it's worthwhile confirming precisely what's included in the price.

Mae Sot Conservation Tour, 415/11 Intrarakhiri Rd, T055-532818, premat@ ksc15.th.com. Runs educational and 'soft' adventure tours for families and the elderly.

Mae Sot Travel Centre (aka **SP Tours**), 14/21 Asia Rd, T055-531409. The main office is out of town, but it can be contacted at the Mae Sot Hill and the Siam Hotel.

Max One Tours (opposite DK Hotel), T055-542942, www.maxonetours.com. Runs day trips around Mae Sot (waterfall, gibbon sanctuary, hot spring, temple and Thai-Burmese border market, ฿1500 per person) as well as longer treks.

Weaving courses

At the **Borderline Teashop** (see Eating, above) you can participate in a week-long natural dye weaving course.

Umphang and around *p222*

Most of the tour companies (aside from those arranged by guesthouses) are on Palata Rd.

Be aware that only a handful of outfits have English-speaking guides. The more sophisticated operations include: **The Ecotourist Center**, T055-561063; **Boonchay Camping Tour**, 360 M 1 Tambol, T055-561 020; **BL Tours**, T055-561021. Guides are Burmese and speak English, although their local knowledge isn't perhaps quite equal to that of the guides from **Umphang Hill Resort** or **The Trekker Hill**.

The Trekker Hill, 620 Prawesphywan Rd, T055-561090. Run by Mr T whose guides speak English and Danish, and who offers a 'service guarantee' whereby if clients aren't satisfied he'll return a portion of the cost.

Umphang Hill Resort, Palata Rd, T055-561 0634, www.umphanghill.com. Guides speak English, French, German, Japanese and Chinese.

⊖ Transport

Tak *p220*
Bus

Non-a/c and a/c buses leave from the station on Route 12 near crossroads of Phahonyothin Rd. There are connections with **Bangkok**'s Northern bus terminal (7 hrs), **Chiang Mai** (4 hrs), **Mae Sot** (1½ hrs), **Kamphaeng Phet** (1 hr, departures hourly), **Sukhothai** (1-1½ hrs, departures hourly), **Chiang Rai**, **Mae Sai**, **Lampang** and elsewhere in the northern and central plains regions.

Saamlor, songthaew and tuk-tuk

Tuk-tuks, *saamlors* and motorcycle taxis are available. Local *songthaews* also leave from this station.

Mae Sot *p220*
Bus

A/c and non-a/c buses for **Chiang Mai** (6½ hrs) leave at 0600 and 0800. **Tak** (1½ hrs), **Lampang** and **Mae Sai** (12 hrs) leave from the bus terminal.

Motorbike hire

Prasat Withi Rd (close to the Bangkok Bank), ₿160 per day.

Songthaew

Several *songthaews* a day connect Mae Sot with **Umphang**. The first leaves around 0700, the last at about 1400 (4-5 hrs, ₿200).

Songthaews for **Mae Sariang** leave in the morning from the road running past the police station, off Intharakit Rd (6 hrs from 0600-1200).

Umphang and around *p222*
Songthaew and motorbike

Several *songthaews* a day connect Umphang with **Mae Sot**. They leave Umphang for Mae Sot at 0700, 0800, 0900, 1300, 1400 and 1500, although the number of departures per day seem to be subject to demand. It is also possible to go by motorbike – but a scooter will not be powerful enough due to the steep inclines.

● Directory

Tak *p220*
Banks Krung Thai, Taksin Rd (corner of Soi 9). Siam City, 125 Mahatthai Bamrung Rd. Thai Military, 77/2 Mahatthai Bamrung Rd.

Internet There are now several internet access facilities in town, mostly concentrated on Mahatthai Bamrung Rd. **Post office** Off Mahatthai Bamrung Rd in the north of town.

Mae Sot *p220*
Banks Siam Commercial, 544/1-5 Intharakit Rd. Thai Farmers, 84/9 Prasat Withi Rd. Bangkok Bank, Prasat Withi Rd. **Internet** A few internet cafés have opened up at the western ends of Prasat Withi Rd and Intharakit Rd. **Post office** Intharakit Rd (opposite DK Hotel). The main post office is also on Intharakit Rd, but past the No 4 Guesthouse about 1 km out of town on the road to the Moei River. **Telephone and fax** Overseas service at post office on Intharakit Rd, as well as in some of the internet cafés on Intharakit Rd. **Tourist police** On Intharakit Rd (next to No 4 Guesthouse), T055-533523.

Umphang and around *p222*
Banks No banks in Umphang – make sure you bring plenty of money. **Internet and telephone** Dot.com on Palata Rd (see, page 226). Several terminals here, including a wireless connection should you have your own laptop. At ₿30 per hr, also very cheap. **Police** T055-561112.

Contents

Footprint features

Border crossings

Thailand–China
Chiang Saen–Jin Hang, see page 306

Thailand–Laos
Chiang Khong-Ban Houei Xai,
see page 308

Thailand–Burma (Myanmar)
Mae Sai–Tachilek, see page 310

At a glance

⊖ **Getting around** There are flights,
buses and trains. Alternatively, rent
a motorbike and get everywhere.

◉ **Time required** 10 days for
a trek, city and Golden Triangle
tour. A month to really explore.

☀ **Weather** In Mar and Apr, this
can be one of the hottest places
in Thailand.

✖ **When not to go** Landslides are
common from Aug-Oct. Songkran
festival (Apr) in Chiang Mai is not
for the fainthearted.

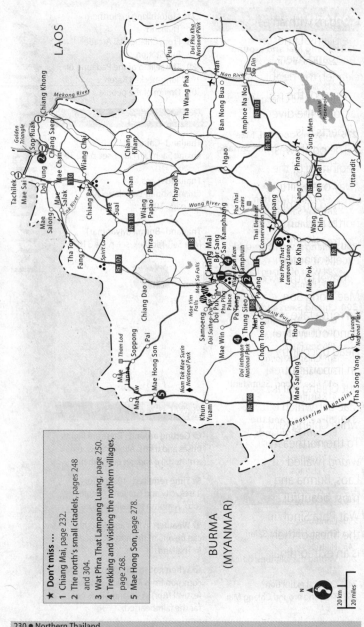

LAOS

BURMA (MYANMAR)

Golden Triangle

Mekong River

Tachilek
Mae Sai
Sop Ruak
Chiang Khong
Chiang Saen
Mae Chan
Doi Tung
Wiang Chai

Mae Salong
Mae Salak
Chiang Rai
Kok River
Phan
Wiang Chai

Mae Suai
Wiang Papao

Tha Ton
Spirit Cave
Fang
Phrao

Chiang Dao

Mae Hong Son
Tham Lod
Pai
Soppong
Mae Lana

Mae Aw

Nam Tok Mae Surin
National Park

Mae Sariang
Khun Yuam

Doi Inthanon
National Park

Mae Win
Thung Sieo
Mae Chaem

Samoeng
Doi Suthep-Pui
Phu Ping
Palace
Doi Pui

Mae Yim
Falls
Mae Sa Falls

Chiang Mai
Ban Sang
San Kamphaeng
Wat Ton Kam
Wat Chedi Liam
Pa Sang
Lamphun

Thai Elephant
Conservation Centre

Lampang

Wat Phra That
Lampang Luang

Ko Kha
Mae Pok

Wang Chin

Den Chai
Uttaradit

Phrae
Sung Men

Rt 101
Amphoe Na Noi
Sirikit
Reservoir
Sao Din

Nan River
Ban Nong Bua
Nan

Tha Wang Pha
Pua
Doi Phu Kha
National Park

Wang River
Ngao
Phayao

Pha Thai
Caves

Rt 103

Rt 11

Rt 1

Rt 106

Rt 108

Rt 107

Rt 118

Rt 110

Rt 111

Hod
Ping River

Chom Thong
Doi Luang
National Park

Tha Song Yang

Tenasserim Mountains

20 km
20 miles

N

★ Don't miss ...
Chiang Mai, page 232.
1 The north's small citadels, pages 248
   and 304.
2 Wat Phra That Lampang Luang, page 250.
3 Trekking and visiting the nothern villages,
   page 268.
4 Mae Hong Son, page 278.

It begins with an easing of the dusty, overwhelming heat of the plains. Limestone hills draped with calming verdant forest, roads and rivers twisting into endless switchbacks. The air seems cleaner, the people and pace gentler. After the raucous intensity of most of the rest of Thailand, the north feels like another country; factor in the diverse array of the tribal hill peoples, and in many respects it is.

The north wasn't incorporated into the Thai nation until the beginning of the 20th century. For centuries local lords held sway over shifting principalities, the most significant being centred on Chiang Mai. This city remains the largest in the north, and a magnet for thousands of tourists. With its walled centre, serene and ancient temples, bustling markets and excellent accommodation it's easy to understand why.

Travel to the west of Chiang Mai and you'll find beautiful Mae Hong Son, encircled by hills and often cloaked in mist. En route take in Pai; set in a stunning location this is a travellers' hang-out with all the banana pancakes you could ever consume. Head upcountry and you'll reach the venerable city of Chiang Rai, an important trekking centre. Most of its history has been lost but Chiang Rai is still a friendly and proud place. Further north is Mae Sai, which offers the opportunity for excursions into Burma, while Chiang Khong, on the Mekong, is a crossing point into Laos. To the northeast is Chiang Saen, an early 14th-century fortified *wiang* (walled city) and the infamous Golden Triangle, where Laos, Burma and Thailand meet. Finally, some of Thailand's most beautiful and peaceful monasteries are found in the north. Wat Phra Singh in Chiang Mai, Wat Phumin in Nan and, perhaps the finest of them, Wat Phra That Lampang Luang, in Lampang, is an extraordinary display of temple craft.

Chiang Mai and around

→ *Colour map 1, B2.*

When Reginald Le May wrote about Chiang Mai back in 1938, this was, in his view, one of the loveliest cities imaginable. Life, as they say, has moved on since then. But while old Thailand hands may worry about lost innocence, Chiang Mai is still worth visiting.

While in Chiang Mai don't forget to climb Doi Suthep, the city's revered mountain, which rises 1000 m above the city and is crowned with an important temple. While this temple has succumbed to money-grabbing practices, it is still a beautiful setting and worth the effort. A visit to the tribal museum, just to the north of the city centre, is essential to understanding the region's indigenous peoples while to the south rests the handsome remains of a ruined city, Wiang Kum Kam.

The city's monasteries are the most beautiful in the north; there is a rich tradition of arts and crafts, and the moated old city still gives a flavour of the past. It is the unofficial 'capital of the north', there are also some good practical reasons to base yourself here. It is an important transport hub, there is an excellent range of hotels and restaurants, the shopping is the best in the north, and there are also scores of trekking and other companies offering everything from whitewater rafting to elephant treks.

The nearby historical towns of Lamphun and Lampang provide handsome, striking temples – some say they are the best in the whole country. Both can be reached as day excursions from Chiang Mai though Lampang, with its laid-back riverside vibe, warrants a little more attention.
▶▶ *For hilltribes and trekking, see pages 243 and 268, for all listings, see pages 252-275.*

Ins and outs

Getting there

The quickest way of getting to Chiang Mai is by air, and a number of airlines offer flights from Bangkok as well as links to other provincial centres. The **airport** ① *T053-270222, www.chiangmaiairportonline.com*, is 3 km southwest of town and has banks, currency exchange booths, a hotel booking counter, post office, Avis rent-a-car counter, tourist information counter, Pizza Hut, coffee shops and a snack bar. Taxis to town cost ฿90 (fixed price from the taxi booking counter). THAI operates a shuttle bus service between the airport and its office in town (but you can get off anywhere in town) for ฿40.

There are several trains a day from Bangkok (12 hours) including the splendid sleeper service. The overnight Special Express train (first- and second-class sleepers only, fan or air-conditioned, T02-491 1193) leaves Bangkok at 1800 and arrives in Chiang Mai at 0710, whilst the Sprinter (second-class air-conditioned carriage only) leaves at 1925 and arrives at 0720; the Nakornping Special Express (first- and second-class sleeper only, T02-611 1193) leaves at 1940, arriving at 0905, and the Rapid Train (second- and third-class only, T02-161471) leaves at 2200 and arrives in Chiang Mai at 1305. For more information on trains from Bangkok, see page 43. The station is in the east of the town, on Charoen Muang Road, across the Ping River. To get to town, there are frequent *songthaews* and tuk-tuks, or take city bus No 1, 3 or 6 which stop outside the station.

Scores of buses arrive from all over Thailand – from super-luxury VIP buses through to the bone-shaking ordinary variety. The long-distance bus station is at the Chiang Mai Arcade, on the corner of the 'super highway' and Kaew Nawarat Road, northeast of town, T053-242664. Tuk-tuks and *songthaews* wait at the station to take passengers into town. **▶▶** *See Transport, page 272, for further information.*

Getting around

Much of the central part of the city can be easily covered on foot. *Songthaews* (converted pick-ups) operate as the main mode of public transport, ferrying people around for a fixed fare of between ฿15-20 per person. Just flag one down and pay them at the end – they vary their routes but they'll normally take you anywhere in central Chiang Mai for this price. If you go out of the central area, expect to pay more. There are also tuk-tuks, some taxis, and a good number of car, motorbike and bicycle hire companies. Tuk-tuks charge a minimum of ฿30 per trip, ฿60-100 for longer journeys. *Saamlors* charge ฿8-10 within city, ฿20 for longer distances.

Tourist information

TAT ① *105/1 Chiang Mai-Lamphun Rd, T053-248604, www.tatchiangmai.org, daily 0830-1630*, is very helpful and informative with good English spoken and a good range of maps and leaflets, including information on guesthouses and guidelines for trekking. **Chiang Mai Municipal Tourist Information Centre** ① *corner of Tha Phae and Charoen Prathet roads, Mon-Fri 0830-1200, 1300-1630*, is the only one of its type in Thailand, supplying good maps and some other handouts, but it's not yet up to TAT standard. In addition to these tourist offices, there are also various free, tourist-oriented magazines, namely: *Trip Info, Chiang Mai This Week, Le Journal* (in French), *Guidelines Chiang Mai, Chiang Mai Newsletter, What's On Chiang Mai* and *Good Morning Chiang Mai*. These have good maps but are mostly based on advertising so don't expect objective information. The *Chiang Mai Newsletter* has the most informed articles. The website www.chiangmainews.com is also useful. ▸▸ *See Activities and tours, page 267.*

Background

Around 1290 King Mengrai annexed the last of the Mon kingdoms at Lamphun and moved his capital from Chiang Rai to a site on the banks of the Ping River called Nopburi Sri Nakawan Ping Chiang Mai. It is said he chose the site after seeing a big mouse accompanied by four smaller mice scurry down a hole beneath a holy Bodhi tree. He made this site the heart of his Lanna kingdom.

Mengrai was a great patron of Theravada Buddhism and he brought monks from Ceylon to unify the country. Up until the 15th century, Chiang Mai flourished. As this century ended, relations with up-and-coming Ayutthaya became strained and the two kingdoms engaged in a series of wars with few gains on either side.

While Chiang Mai and Ayutthaya were busy fighting, the Burmese eventually captured the city of Chiang Mai in 1556. King Bayinnaung, who had unified Burma, took Chiang Mai after a three-day battle and the city remained a Burmese regency for 220 years. There was constant conflict during these years and by the time the Burmese succeeded in over-throwing Ayutthaya in 1767, the city of Chiang Mai was decimated and depopulated. In 1775, General Taksin united the kingdom of Thailand and a semi-autonomous prince of the Lampang Dynasty was appointed to rule the north. Chiang Mai lost its semi-independence in 1938 and came under direct rule from Bangkok.

Modern Chiang Mai

Today, Chiang Mai is the second largest city in Thailand, with a population of roughly 500,000; a thriving commercial centre as well as a favourite tourist destination. TAT estimates that 12% of Thailand's tourists travel to Chiang Mai. Its attractions to the

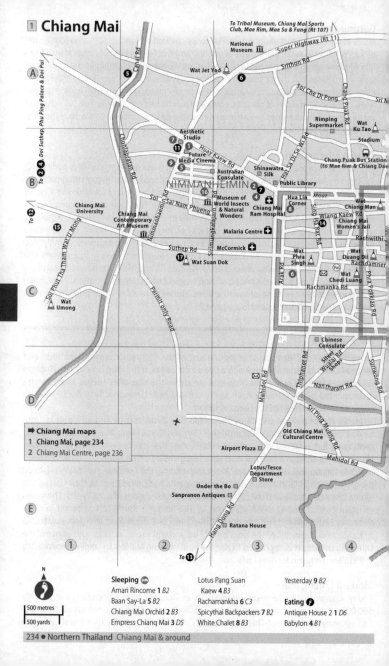

Chiang Mai

Chiang Mai maps
1 Chiang Mai, page 234
2 Chiang Mai Centre, page 236

Sleeping
Amari Rincome 1 B2
Baan Say-La 5 B2
Chiang Mai Orchid 2 B3
Empress Chiang Mai 3 D5
Lotus Pang Suan
Kaew 4 B3
Rachamankha 6 C3
Spicythai Backpackers 7 B2
White Chalet 8 B3
Yesterday 9 B2

Eating
Antique House 2 1 D6
Babylon 4 B1

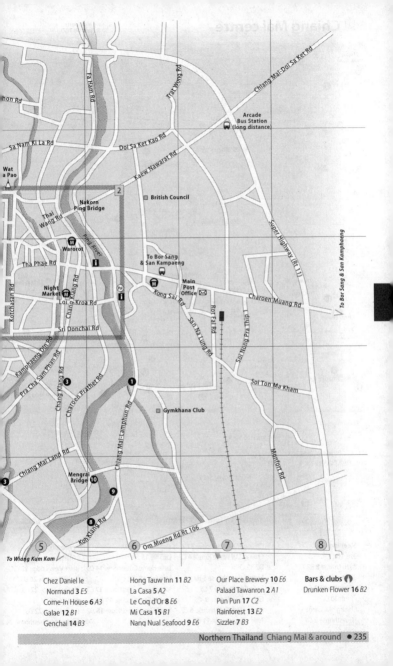

Chez Daniel le Normand **3** *E5*
Come-In House **6** *A3*
Galae **12** *B1*
Genchai **14** *B3*

Hong Tauw Inn **11** *B2*
La Casa **5** *A2*
Le Coq d'Or **8** *E6*
Mi Casa **15** *B1*
Nang Nual Seafood **9** *E6*

Our Place Brewery **10** *E6*
Palaad Tawanron **2** *A1*
Pun Pun **17** *C2*
Rainforest **13** *E2*
Sizzler **7** *B3*

Bars & clubs 🍸
Drunken Flower **16** *B2*

2 Chiang Mai centre

Sleeping
3sis **10** *C1*
Baan Orapin **8** *B7*
Bang Jong Come
 Guesthouse **1** *C4*
Chedi **20** *D7*
Chiang Mai Garden
 Guesthouse **2** *D1*

Chiang Mai Kristi House **3** *C2*
Chiang Mai White House **4** *C2*
D2 **32** *C6*
Eagle II Guesthouse **5** *B2*
Fang Guesthouse **7** *C5*
Galare Guesthouse **9** *C5*
Johnny Boy Guesthouse **6** *C5*
Julie's Guesthouse **11** *D2*

Kim House **12** *D7*
Lai Thai **13** *E3*
Little Home Guesthouse **14** *D3*
Montri's **15** *C3*
Namkhong Guesthouse **17** *C5*
Orchid Guest House **19** *C4*
Panda Tour Guesthouse **18** *D2*

Rendezvous
 Guesthouse **21** *C2*
River View Lodge **23** *C7*
Royal Princess **26** *D6*
Rydges Tapae **27** *C3*
Sarah's **28** *D4*
Smile House **22** *D3*
Somwang Guesthouse **24** *L*

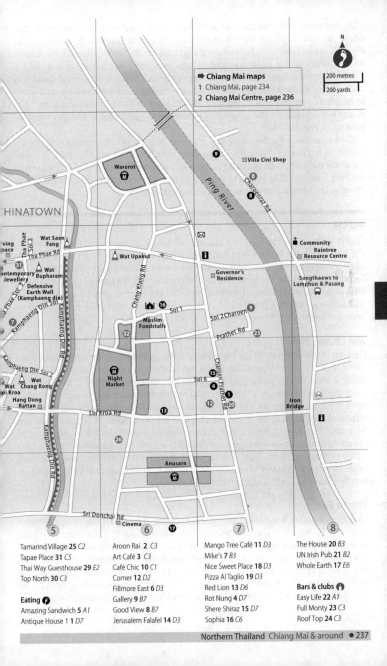

Chiang Mai maps
1 Chiang Mai, page 234
2 **Chiang Mai Centre, page 236**

200 metres
200 yards

Villa Cini Shop

HINATOWN

Warorot

Ping River

Charoen Rd

Wat Saen
Fang

Tha Phae Rd

Wat
Bupharam

Community
Raintree
Resource Centre

Songthaews to
Lamphun & Pasang

Contemporary
Jewellery

Defensive
Earth Wall
(Kamphaeng din)

Wat Upakut

Chiang Klang Rd

Governor's
Residence

Soi 1

Muslim
Foodstalls

Soi 2 Charoen

Prathet Rd

Kamphaeng Din Soi 1

Kamphaeng Din Soi 2

Wat
Chang Kong

Soi Kroa

Hang Dong
Rattan

Night
Market

Charoen Prathet Rd

Soi 6

Iron
Bridge

Loi Kroa Rd

Pol

Kamphaeng Din Rd

Anusarn

Sri Donchai Rd

Cinema

Tamarind Village **25** *C2*
Tapae Place **31** *C5*
Thai Way Guesthouse **29** *E2*
Top North **30** *C3*

Eating 🍴
Amazing Sandwich **5** *A1*
Antique House 1 **1** *D7*

Aroon Rai **2** *C3*
Art Café **3** *C3*
Café Chic **10** *C1*
Corner **12** *D2*
Fillmore East **6** *D3*
Gallery **9** *B7*
Good View **8** *B7*
Jerusalem Falafel **14** *D3*

Mango Tree Café **11** *D3*
Mike's **7** *B3*
Nice Sweet Place **18** *D3*
Pizza Al Taglio **19** *D3*
Red Lion **13** *D6*
Rot Nung **4** *D7*
Shere Shiraz **15** *D7*
Sophia **16** *C6*

The House **20** *B3*
UN Irish Pub **21** *B2*
Whole Earth **17** *E6*

Bars & clubs 🍸
Easy Life **22** *A1*
Full Monty **23** *C3*
Roof Top **24** *C3*

visitor are obvious: the city has a rich and colourful history, still evident in the architecture of the city, which includes more than 300 wats; it is manageable and still relatively 'user friendly' (unlike Bangkok); it has perhaps the greatest concentration of handicraft industries in the country; and it is also an excellent base from which to go trekking and visit the famous hilltribe villages in the surrounding highlands. Chiang Mai has developed into a major tourist centre with a good infrastructure, including excellent hotels and restaurants in all price categories. Some long-term visitors argue that the city has lost some of its charm in the process: traffic congestion, pollution and frantic property development are now much in evidence.

On a clear day at the start of the cold season, or after the rains have begun towards the end of the hot season, Chiang Mai's strategic location becomes clear. Mountains surround the city to the north, west and east, enclosing a large and rich bowl of rice fields drained by the Ping River. With Doi Suthep to the west clothed in trees and the golden *chedi* of Wat Phrathat Doi Suthep glittering on its slopes, it is a magical place.

Sights

Chiang Mai is centred on a square moat and defensive wall built during the 19th century. The four corner bastions are reasonably well preserved and are a useful reference point when roaming the city. Much of the rest of the town's walls were demolished during the Second World War and the bricks used for road construction. Not surprisingly, given Chiang Mai's turbulent history, many of the more important and interesting wats are within the city walls which is – surprisingly – the least built-up part. Modern commercial development has been concentrated to the east of the city and now well beyond the Ping River.

Wat Chiang Man

Situated in the northeast of the walled town, Wat Chiang Man is on Rachpakinai Road within a peaceful compound. The wat is the oldest in the city and was built by King Mengrai soon after he had chosen the site for his new capital in 1296. It is said that he resided here while waiting for his new city to be constructed and also spent the last years of his life at the monastery. The gold-topped *chedi* Chang Lom is supported by rows of elephants, similar to those of the two *chedis* of the same name at Si Satchanalai and Sukhothai. Two ancient Buddha images are contained behind bars within the *viharn*, on the right-hand side as you enter the compound. One is the crystal Buddha, Phra Sae Tang Tamani (standing 10 cm high). The second is the Phra Sila (literally, 'Stone Buddha'), believed to have originated in India or Ceylon about 2500 years ago. Wat Chiang Man is an excellent place to see how wat architecture has evolved.

Wat Pa Pao

To the northeast of Wat Chiang Man, just outside the city walls, is the unique Burmese Shan, Wat Pa Pao, which was founded more than 400 years ago by a Shan monk. A narrow *soi* leads off the busy road through an archway and into the wat's peaceful and rather ramshackle compound. The *chedi* is a melange of stuccoed animals from *singhas* to *nagas*, while the flat-roofed *viharn*, with its dark and atmospheric interior, contains three Buddha images. The monks at the wat are Shan – most having come here from Burma over the last few years – and it continues to serve Chiang Mai's Shan community.

Wat Phra Singh

Wat Phra Singh (Temple of the Lion Buddha) is situated in the west quarter of the **old city** and is impressively positioned at the end of Phra Singh Road (see map, page 234). The wat was founded in 1345 and contains a number of beautiful buildings decorated with fine woodcarving. Towards the back of the compound is the intimate Lai Kham Viharn, which houses the venerated Phra Buddha Singh image. It was built between 1385 and 1400 and the walls are decorated with early 18th-century murals. The **Phra Buddha Sihing** is said to have come from Ceylon by a rather roundabout route (see page 675) but, as art historians point out, is Sukhothai in style. The head, which was stolen in 1922, is a copy. Among the other buildings in the wat is an attractive raised *hor trai* (library), with intricate carved wood decorations, inset with mother-of-pearl.

Wat Chedi Luang and city pillar

On Phra Pokklao Road, to the east of Wat Phra Singh, is the 500-year-old ruined *chedi* of Wat Chedi Luang. It's a charming place to wander around, set in a sizeable compound with huge trees at the boundaries. Judging by the remains, it must have once been an impressive monument. Only the Buddha in the northern niche is original; the others are reproductions. To the west of the *chedi* is a reclining Buddha in an open pavilion.

Chiang Mai's rather dull city pillar is found in a small shrine close to the large *viharn*, at the western side of the monastery compound. This is the foundation stone of the city and home to Chiang Mai's guardian spirits. These must be periodically appeased if the city is to prosper.

Wat Duang Dii

Just north of the intersection of Rachdamnern and Phra Pokklao roads, is peaceful Wat Duang Dii. The compound contains three northern Thai wooden temple buildings, with fine woodcarving and attractively weathered doors; note the small, almost Chinese, pagoda-roofed structure to the left of the gate with its meticulous stucco work. Behind the *viharn* and *bot* is a *chedi* with elephants at each corner, topped with copper plate.

Wat Suan Dok

Outside the walls, Wat Suan Dok lies to the west of town on Suthep Road (Chiang Mai map, page 234). Originally built in 1371 but subsequently restored and enlarged, the wat contains the ashes of Chiang Mai's royal family, housed in white, variously shaped, mini-*chedis*. Much of the monastery was erected during the reign of King Kawila (1782-1813). The large central *chedi* is said to house eight relics of the Lord Buddha.

The *bot* is usually open to the public and has a large, brightly lit, gilded bronze Buddha image in the Chiang Saen style. The walls are decorated with lively, rather gaudy, scenes from the Jataka stories. Above the entrance is a mural showing the Buddha's mother being impregnated by a white elephant (highly auspicious), while on the left-hand wall is depicted (along with several other episodes from the Buddha's life) the moment when, as a prince (note the fine clothes and jewellery), he renounces his wealth and position and symbolically cuts his hair.

Wat Umong

ⓘ *Take a songthaew or bus (Nos 1 and 4) along Suthep Rd and ask to be let off at the turning for Wat Umong. It is about a 1-km walk from here (turn left almost opposite the gates to CMU, just past a market travelling west).*

The wat was founded in 1371 by King Ku Na (1355-1385) who promoted the establishment of a new, ascetic school of forest-dwelling monks. In 1369 he brought a leading Sukhothai monk to Chiang Mai – the Venerable Sumana – and built Wat Umong for him and his followers. Sumana studied here until his death in 1389. Although the wat is at the edge of the city, set in areas of woodland, it feels much more distant. There are tunnels which house several Buddha images. The wat was abandoned in the 19th century and the *chedi* pillaged for its treasures some years later. It became a functioning wat again in 1948. From the trees hang Thai proverbs and sayings from the Buddhist texts, extolling pilgrims to lead good and productive lives.

Chiang Mai Contemporary Art Museum

ⓘ *Corner of Nimmahaemin and Suthep roads, T053-933833, Tue-Sun 0930-1700, ฿50.*
The Chiang Mai Contemporary Art Museum (see map, page 234) in a large modern structure, displays modern fine art including paintings, sculpture, installation works and prints by mostly Thai artists. There are occasional temporary exhibitions of work by non-Thais. Other activities include concerts and puppet shows. It is interesting for displaying the progress of Thai fine art, but hardly world class. The small but chic attached Art Café and shop (selling books and ceramics) is classier than the works displayed.

Wat Jet Yod

The beautiful Wat Jet Yod (literally, 'seven spires') is just off the 'super highway' at the intersection with Ladda Land Road, northwest of the city and close to the National Museum (see map, page 234). It was founded in 1453 and contains a highly unusual square *chedi* with seven spires. These represent the seven weeks the Buddha resided in the gardens at Bodhgaya, after his enlightenment under the Bodhi tree. According to the chronicles the structure is a copy of the 13th-century Mahabodhi temple in Pagan, Burma, which itself was a copy of the famous temple at Bodhgaya in Bihar (although it is hard to see the resemblance). On the faces of the *chedi* are an assortment of superbly modelled stucco figures in bas-relief, while at one end is a niche containing a large Buddha image – dating from 1455 – in an attitude of subduing Mara (now protected behind steel bars). The stucco work represents the 70 celestial deities and are among the finest works from the Lanna School of Art.

National Museum

ⓘ *Wed-Sun 0900-1600, ฿30. Take bus No 6.*
The National Museum (see map, page 234) lies just to the east of Wat Jet Yod on Highway 11 and has a fine collection of Buddha images and Sawankhalok china downstairs, as well as some impressive ethnological exhibits upstairs.

Other wats

Wat Ku Tao (see map, page 234), to the north of the city off Chotana Road, dates from 1613. It is situated in a leafy compound and has an unusual *chedi*, shaped like a pile of inverted alms bowls. Others worth a fleeting visit for those not yet 'watted out' include: **Wat Chetawan**, **Wat Mahawan**, **Wat Saen Fang** and **Wat Bupharam** – all on Tha Phae Road (see map, page 236) – between the east walls of the city and the Ping River. Wat Mahawan displays some accomplished woodcarving on its *viharn*, washed in a delicate yellow, while the stupa is guarded by an array of *singhas* (mythical lions) – some with bodies hanging from their gaping jaws. Wat Bupharam has two old *viharns* a small *bot* and a stupa.

Markets and Chinatown

The night market dominates the west side of Chang Klang Road (see map, page 234). It comprises a number of purpose-built buildings with hundreds of stalls, selling a huge array of tribal goods as well as clothing, jewellery and other tourist goodies (see Shopping, page 266). For a completely different atmosphere, walk through Chiang Mai's Chinatown which lies to the north of Tha Phae Road, between the moat and the river. Small work-shops run by entrepreneurial Sino-Thais jostle between excellent small restaurants serving reasonably priced Thai and Chinese food. Near the river, and running two or three streets in from the river, is the **Warorot Market** (east of the Old City map, see page 236), the city's largest. It starts on Praisani Road, close to the river, as a flower market, but transforms into a mixed market with fruit, vegetables, dried fish, pigs' heads and trotters, great dollops of buffalo flesh, crabs, dried beans and deep-fried pork skin. There are several large covered market areas with clothes, textiles, shoes, leather goods, stationery and baskets.

Chiang Mai is famous for its **Sunday Walking Street** ① *1700-midnight, year-round*, a street market which closes the southwest part of the city to all but pedestrians. It's the social event of the week for many locals, and stalls sell everything from hand-made clothes and souvenirs to plants and goldfish. The wats along Rachdamern and Phra Pokklao Road open their space up to foodhawkers and massage therapists. **Wualai Saturday Night Market** ① *late afternoon until 2300*, is smaller than the Sunday market and runs along Wualai Road south of the city. It sells clothes, food and the silver this street is famous for.

Museum of World Insects and Natural Wonders

① *West of town at 72 Nimmanhaemin Soi 13 (near Sirimungkalajarn 3), T053-211891, insects_museum@hotmail.com, open 0900-1630, ฿100, ฿50 children.*

Established in 1999 by Manop and Rampa Rattanarithikul, this eccentric couple take pleasure in showing you around their house which has become a mausoleum for thousands of insectoid beasties (see map, page 234). Rampa's specialism is mosquitoes; there are 420 species of mosquito in Thailand (all on show here), 18 of which she personally identified and categorized, travelling to London to check the type specimens in the Natural History Museum. There are interesting collections of shells, fossils, petrified wood and, of course, case after case of bugs including beetles, moths, roaches and butterflies.

Around Chiang Mai ●❼❶⊛○▲⊕❶ ➤ *pp252-275.*

Doi Suthep

① *Songthaew from Mani Noparat Rd, by Chang Puak Gate or take bus No 3 to the zoo and then change onto a minibus. A songthaew from outside the zoo is ฿20. A taxi should cost about ฿200 return. The temple is closed after 1630. Entry fee is for foreigners only.*

Overlooking Chiang Mai, 16 km to the northwest, is Doi Suthep (Suthep Mountain) a very popular pilgrimage spot for Thais, perched on the hillside and offering spectacular views of the city and plain below. A steep, winding road climbs 1000 m to the base of a 300-step *naga* staircase, which in turn leads up to **Wat Phrathat**. Initially, you'd be forgiven for thinking you'd arrived at a tacky theme park rather than a revered site, such is the proliferation of overpriced souvenir stalls. And, where foreign tourists are concerned, everybody seems to be on the make, from the tuk-tuk drivers to the temple staff who ensure no foreigner enters without their ฿30 ticket. Some Thais have complained that Doi Suthep is becoming degraded by the influence of tourism, yet the same critics have failed to address the fact that the temple guardians themselves have adopted commercial practices.

Chiang Mai Night Safari

Before it had even officially opened its doors to the public in early 2006, the Chiang Mai Night Safari was mired in controversy. In place was a bizarre plan to serve up its own wild animals for dinner in the zoo's restaurant. Not surprisingly, this 'exotic buffet' of imported giraffe, crocodile, snake, elephant, tiger and lion meat drew a storm of criticism, both in Thailand and abroad, with protesters camping outside the zoo. Even more bizarre was the zoo's supposed aim to promote education and conservation. For once, the government recognized the incongruity, and killed the plan for the restaurant though allowed the safari to open for business. But complaints are still lingering – locals living near the zoo have been forced to give up land without receiving any compensation, the camp's animals are reportedly mistreated and the abundance of musical fountains and cheap shopping zones are tacky and tasteless. As if this wasn't enough, local activists have filed complaints concerning the management's lack of transparency. People without any previous management experience but with close ties to the zoo's director Mr Plodprasop have been given extremely well-paid executive positions. The Thai authorities have shrugged off these complaints, claiming the zoo is not only "the most nature- friendly in the world", but also "the best" (Reuters).

If you don't fancy the climb take the cable car (฿20). A white elephant is alleged to have collapsed here, after King Ku Na (1355-1385) gave it the task of finding an auspicious site for a shrine to house a holy relic of the Lord Buddha. The 24-m-high *chedi* has a number of Buddha images in both Sukhothai and Chiang Saen styles, arrayed in the gallery surrounding it. The compound is surrounded by bells (which visitors can no longer ring).

Phu Ping Palace
ⓘ *Fri-Sun and public holidays 0830-1630 when the royal family is not in residence. Songthaews from Doi Suthep to Phu Ping, ฿20.*
The winter residence of the King, Phu Ping Palace, is 5 km past Wat Phrathat. The immaculate gardens are open to the public when the family is not in residence.

Doi Pui
ⓘ *Charter a songthaew; alternatively take a minibus from Mani Noparat Rd, by Chang Puak Gate, and then take a songthaew from Doi Suthep, ฿50 one way.*
Rather commercialized, Meo village, 4 km past Phu Ping Palace, is only worth a visit for those unable to get to other villages. There are two second-rate museum huts, one focusing on opium production, the other on the different hilltribes. On the hillside above the village is an **English flower garden** ⓘ ฿8, which is in full bloom in January.

Tribal Museum
ⓘ *T053-221933, www.chmai.com/tribal/museum/index.html, Mon-Fri 0900-1600; a slide and video show is screened at 1000 and 1400. An informative book on hilltribes can be bought here, ฿35. A songthaew from the city is ฿50. It's a 15-20 min walk to the museum.*
The Tribal Museum, attached to the **Tribal Research Institute**, overlooks a lake in Rachamankha Park, 5 km north of town off Chotana Road. The building itself looks like a

Hilltribes

A visit to a hilltribe village is one of the main reasons why people travel to the north of Thailand. The hilltribe population (Chao Khao in Thai – l'Mountain People') numbers about 800,000, or a little over 1% of the total population of the country.

These 800,000 people are far from homogenous: each hilltribe (there are nine recognized by the government), has a different language, dress, religion, artistic heritage and culture. They meet their subsistence needs in different ways and often occupy different ecological niches. In some respects they are as far removed from one another as they are from the low-land Thais.

As their name suggests, the hilltribes occupy the highland areas that fringe the northern region, with the largest populations in the provinces of Chiang Mai (143,000), Chiang Rai (98,000), Mae Hong Son (83,000) and Tak (69,000). These figures are a few years old, but the relative balance between the provinces has not changed significantly. Although this guide follows the tradition of using the term 'hilltribe' to describe these diverse peoples, it is in many regards an unfortunate one. They are not tribes in the anthropological sense, derived as it is from the study of the peoples of Africa. For information on all the people, see Background page 716. For information on trekking and choosing a trek operator, see Activities and tours, page 272.

cross between a rocket and a *chedi* and it houses the fine collection of tribal pieces that were formerly held at Chiang Mai University's Tribal Research Centre. Carefully and professionally presented, the pieces on show include textiles, agricultural implements, musical instruments, jewellery and weapons. The museum is particularly worth visiting for those intending to go trekking (see page 268).

Wiang Kum Kam

ⓘ *Accessible by bicycle, motorbike or tuk-tuk. Take Route 106 south towards Lamphun; the ruins are signposted off to the right about 5 km from Chiang Mai – but only in Thai – from where it is another 2 km. Look out for a ruined chedi on the right and ask along the way for confirmation. To get to Wat Kan Thom, follow the yellow sign to the left about 800 m from the main road. It's about a 10- to 15-min walk from the main road. For Wat Chedi Liam, follow the land all the way to the river road (Koh Klang Rd), about 2 km or so, and turn left. The wat is about 200 m down here, on the left – impossible to miss.*

Wiang Kum Kam is a ruined city, 5 km south of Chiang Mai, which was established by the Mon in the 12th or 13th centuries and abandoned in the 18th century. The gardens and ruins are beautiful and peaceful, dotted with bodhi trees. Today, archaeologists are beginning to uncover a site of about 9 sq km which contains the remains of at least 20 wats. It was discovered in 1984 when rumours surfaced that a hoard of valuable amulets were found. Treasure seekers began to dig up the grounds of the Wat Chang Kham monastery until the Fine Arts Department intervened and began a systematic survey of the site to reveal Wiang Kum Kam. The most complete monument is Wat Chang Kham, which has a marvellous bronze *naga* outside. In front of the wat is the spirit chamber of Chiang Mai's founder, King Mengrai. Nearby are the ruins of Wat Noi and two dilapidated *chedis*. Perhaps the most impressive single structure is the renovated *chedi* at

Visiting the hilltribes: house rules

Etiquette and customs vary between the hilltribes. However, the following are general rules of good behaviour that should be adhered to whenever possible.

→ Dress modestly and avoid undressing/changing in public.

→ Ask permission before photographing anyone (old people and pregnant women often object to having their photograph taken). Be aware that hill people are unlikely to pose out of the kindness of their hearts – don't begrudge them the money; for many, tourism is their livelihood.

→ Ask permission before entering a house.

→ Do not touch or photograph village shrines.

→ Do not smoke opium.

→ Avoid sitting or stepping on door sills.

→ Avoid excessive displays of wealth and be sensitive when giving gifts (for children, pens are better than sweets).

→ Avoid introducing Western medicines.

Wat Chedi Liam. This takes the form of a stepped pyramid – a unique Mon architectural style of which there are only a handful of examples in Thailand.

Bor Sang and San Kamphaeng circuit

A pleasant 75-km day trip takes you east of the city, visiting craft centres a couple of interesting wats, some incredible caves and a hot spring. Almost immediately after leaving the city along Route 1006 (Charoen Muang Road), kilns, paper factories and lacquerware stalls start to appear, and continue for a full 15 km all the way to Bor Sang.

Bor Sang is famous for its handmade, painted paper umbrellas. The shaft is crafted from local softwood, the ribs from bamboo, and the covering from oiled rice paper. The **Umbrella Festival** in January is a colourful affair. Beyond Bor Sang is San Kamphaeng, another craft village, which has expanded and diversified so that it has effectively merged with Bor Sang – at least in terms of shopping. If you make it as far as San Kamphaeng, there is a good Muslim restaurant at the intersection with the main road (left hand, near side) serving chicken biryani, other Indian dishes, ice creams and cappuccino.

For **Wat Pa Tung**, which is 10 km on from San Kamphaeng, take a right-hand fork onto Route 1147. At the junction with Route 1317, cross over the road (signposted towards the Chiang Mai-Lamphun Golf Club). Where the road takes a sharp right (with another signpost for the golf club), continue straight ahead on the minor road. About 3 km on is Wat Pa Tung. This wat is a lively and popular modern wat, set amongst sugar palms and rice fields. Its popularity rests on the fact that the revered Luang Phu La Chaiya Janto (an influential thinker and preacher, highly regarded for his asceticism) lived here to the ripe old age of 96. When he died in 1993 his rather diminutive body was entombed in a sealed glass coffin, which was then placed in a specially built stilted modern *kuti* where it still resides today.

From Wat Pa Tung, return to Route 1317 and turn right. After about 10 km, on the left, you will see a rocky outcrop with flags fluttering from the top; this is the only marker for the **Muang On Caves** ① *open daily during daylight hours, ฿10*; take a left turning (no sign in English) and wind up a lane, past a forest of ordained trees, to the car park. From here there are around 170 steps up a *naga* staircase to the entrance to the caves, with great

Cultural extinction?

Much of the concern that has been focused upon the hilltribes dwells on their increasingly untenable position in a country where they occupy a distinctly subordinate position. Over a number of years, the government has tried culturally and economically to assimilate the hilltribes into the Thai state (read, Tai state). Projects have attempted to settle them in *nikhom* (resettlement villages) and to 'instill a strong sense of Thai citizenship, obligation and faith in the institutions of Nation, Religion and Monarchy ...' (Thai Army document). This desire on the part of the government is understandable, when one considers the hilltribes occupy strategically-sensitive border areas.

There are a number of factors that have lent weight to this policy of resettlement and integration: the former strength of the Communist Party of Thailand (CPT), the narcotics problem (it has been estimated that as recently as 30 years ago, 45% of hilltribe households were engaged in the cultivation of the poppy), the more recent concern with the preservation of Thailand's few remaining forests, as well as the simple demographic reality that the population is growing. However, in many respects the most significant process encouraging change has been the commercialization of life among the hilltribes: as they have been inexorably drawn into the market economy, so their traditional subsistence

systems and ethics have become increasingly obsolete. This process is voluntary, spontaneous and profound.

Although tourists may feel they are somehow more culturally aware and sensitive than the next man or woman and therefore can watch and not influence, this is of course untrue. As people, and especially monetized Westerners, push their way into the last remaining remote areas of the north in an endless quest for the 'real thing', they are helping to erode that for which they search. Not that the hilltribes could ever remain, or ever have been, isolated. There has always been contact and trade between hilltribes and the lowland peoples.

Their 'Westernization' or 'Thai-ization' is popularly seen as a 'bad thing'. This says more about our romantic image of the Rousseauesque tribal peoples of the world than it does about the realities of life in the mountains. Certainly, it is impossible selectively to develop the hilltribe communities. If they are to have the benefits of schooling and medical care, then they must also receive – or come into contact with – all those other, and perhaps less desirable, facets of modern Thai life. And if culture is functional, as anthropologists would have us believe, then in so doing they are experiencing a process of cultural erosion. To dramatize slightly, they are on the road to cultural extinction.

---

views over the valley. The entrance to the caves is tricky and the steps very steep, with low overhangs of rock. But it is worth the sweating and bending; the cave opens up into a series of impressive caverns with a large stalagmite wrapped with sacred cloth and a number of images of the Buddha. There are drink stalls at the car park.

At the foot of the hill (before returning to the main road), take a left turn for the back route (2.5 km) to the **Roong Arun Hot Springs** ① ฿20, ฿10 children, public baths ฿60. Here, sulphur springs bubble up into an artificial pond, where visitors can buy chicken or quail eggs to boil in wicker baskets hung from bamboo rods. The springs reach boiling point; if you want a dip head for the public baths, where the water is cooled. A full range of massages, mud baths, saunas and herbal treatments are also available. Return to Chiang Mai by way of Route 118 – about a 20-minute drive.

Mae Sa Valley – Samoeng circuit

ⓘ *Buses and songthaews run along this route, but it would be much more convenient to do the round-trip by hire car or motorbike.*

The 100-km loop from Chiang Mai along the Mae Sa Valley to Samoeng and then back along Route 1269 is an attractive drive that can easily be accomplished in a day. Travel north on Route 107 out of town and then turn west onto Route 1096, in the district town of Mae Rim. From here the road follows the course of the Mae Sa River. Just past Mae Rim are a couple of exclusive shops selling 'antiques'. Also here is the **Sai Nam Phung Orchid and Butterfly Farm** ⓘ *0800-1600*. It has the best selection of orchids in the area as well as a small butterfly enclosure and unusual jewellery for sale. At the Km 5 marker is the sign for the **Tad Mok Waterfalls**, which lie 9 km off the main road to the right. These are less popular than the Mae Sa Falls a couple of kilometres on from here (see below), but still worthwhile.

Continuing west on the main road, there are two more orchid gardens: **Suan Bua Mae Sa Orchid** ⓘ *between the Km 5 and Km 6 markers, 0800-1600*, and **Mae Rim Orchid and Butterfly Farm** ⓘ *at the Km 6 marker, 0800-1600, ฿20*. The orchids are beautiful, the butterflies even more so (watch them emerge from their chrysalises), but the food is average and overpriced.

Mae Sa Waterfall ⓘ *0800-1800, ฿3, ฿20 per car*, is located in the **Doi Suthep-Pui National Park**, 1 km off Route 1096 (to the left) and about 1 km beyond the orchid farm. The waterfall is in fact a succession of mini-falls – peaceful, with a visitor centre and stalls.

But the most popular destination of all in the valley, 3 km further on from the waterfall, is the **Elephant Training Camp** ⓘ *T053-297060, elephant rides available 0700-1400, ฿80; 2 shows a day at 0800 and 0940 and an additional show at 1330 during peak periods*. Around 100 elephants are well cared for here (with a number of babies, which must be a good indicator of their happiness). Visitors can see the elephants bathing, feed them bananas and sugarcane and then watch an elephant show.

Queen Sirikit Botanical Gardens ⓘ *www.welcome-to.chiangmai-chiangrai.com/ queensirikitgarden.htm, 0800-1700, ฿20, ฿10 child, ฿50 car*, was established in 1993 on the edge of the Doi Suthep-Pui National Park, 12 km from the Mae Rim turn-off. The great bulk of the gardens was designated a conservation area before 1993, and there are a number of large trees. It is Thailand's first botanical gardens and a truly impressive enterprise. There are three marked trails (rock garden and nursery plus waterfall, arboreta and climber trail), a museum and an information centre. But the highlight of the gardens is the glasshouse complex. The largest features a waterfall and elevated boardwalk, and there are also glasshouses for desert flora, savannah flora and wetland plants.

Mae Sa Craft Village ⓘ *T053-290052*, is a leafy resort spread over a hillside, with immaculately kept gardens of brightly coloured annual flowers. There are dozens of great activities to get involved in. ▸▸ *See Sleeping, page 256, and tours and tour operators, page 271.*

Continuing further on along Route 1096 there are, in turn, the **Mae Yim Falls** (17 km), **Doi Sang** – a Meo village (25 km) – and the **Nang Koi Falls** (34 km). At the furthest point in this loop is **Samoeng**, the district capital. There's little to do here unless you arrive for Samoeng's annual **strawberry festival** held in January or February.

Continuing on from Samoeng, the road skirts around the heavily forested **Doi Suthep-Pui National Park**. The winding road finally descends from the hills and comes out by the north-south irrigation canal at the village of Ban Ton Khwen. Just before you reach the canal is a turning to the right and, a little further along, the bare brick walls of **Wat Inthrawat**. The entrance at the back is by a cluster of sugar palms. This spectacular *viharn* was built in 1858 in Lanna style. Its graceful roofs and detailed woodcarving are a fine sight. Return to Chiang Mai by way of the canal road (turn left at the junction) or on Route 108 (the Hang Dong road), which is a little further to the east of the canal road.

Chiang Dao Elephant Training Centre

ⓘ *฿60, ฿30 children. Numerous companies offer tours to the centre from Chiang Mai, although it is easy enough to get here by public transport as it is on the main road; catch a bus or songthaew from the Chang Puak bus station.*

This elephant training centre at Chiang Dao is 56 km from Chiang Mai on the route north to Fang, about 15 km south of Chiang Dao. Elephant riding and rafting is available. A second elephant camp 17 km south of Chiang Dao, the **Mae Ping Elephant Camp**, is not as good.

Chiang Dao

ⓘ *As Chiang Dao is on the main Chiang Mai–Fang road, there are numerous buses and songthaews from the Chang Puak bus station.*

Chiang Dao, a district town 70 km north of Chiang Mai, is a useful stopping-off point for visitors to the Chiang Dao Caves (see below). The surfaced road running east from the town leads to a series of hilltribe villages: Palong, Mussur, Lahu and Karen. Most of these are situated on public forest reserve land and many of the inhabitants do not have Thai citizenship. They have built simple huts where tourists can stay (฿20 a night) and a number of trekking companies in Chiang Mai begin or end their treks in the villages here. The town has a number of good restaurants; of particular note is the locally renowned **Bun Thong Phanit** (on the left-hand side, travelling north, in a wooden shophouse), which serves excellent *khao kha muu* (baked pork with rice).

Chiang Dao Caves

ⓘ *฿5 to go as far as the electric light system extends; ฿60 to hire a guide with lamp for a 40-min tour deeper into the caves (guides congregate 100 m or so into the caves where a rota system ensures an equal share of business). Catch a bus to Fang from the Chang Puak bus station on Chotana Rd and get off at Chiang Dao. Songthaews take visitors the final 6 km from the main road to the caves. A taxi to the caves and back should cost about ฿1000 (1½ hrs each way). It is also possible to hire motorbikes and bicycles in Chiang Dao itself – from the 'tourist corner' on the left-hand side of the main road, shortly before reaching the turn-off for the caves (turn left in the town of Chiang Dao, just after the Km 72 marker; it is clearly signposted).*

These caves, 78 km north of Chiang Mai on Route 107, penetrate deep into the limestone hills and are associated with Wat Chiang Dao. They are among the most extensive in Thailand and are a popular pilgrimage spot for monks and ordinary Thais. There is a profusion of stalls here, many selling herbal remedies said to cure most ailments. The caverns contain Buddha and hermit images, as well as impressive natural rock formations. Electric lights have been installed, but only as far as the **Tham Phra Non** (Cave of the Reclining Buddha), where a royal coat of arms on the cave wall records Queen Sirikit's visit to the caves. To explore further it is necessary to hire a guide.

Lamphun

ⓘ *Most people visit Lamphun from Chiang Mai and regular (blue) songthaews run along the old Lamphun–Chiang Mai Rd, leaving Chiang Mai just over the Nawarat Bridge, near the TAT office (30-40 mins, ₿7). They can be picked up by the National Museum too. The train station is 2 km north off Charoenrd Rd, 5 daily connections with Bangkok and Chiang Mai. If travelling to Lamphun from Chiang Mai it is worth taking the old road, which, for a 10-km stretch, is lined with an avenue of Yang trees. Only the action of activist monks, who ordained the trees, saved them from felling.*

This quiet, historic city lies 26 km south of Chiang Mai, and is famous for its *longans* (small tropical fruit) – there's a **Longan Fair** every August with a contest to judge both the best fruit and to select the year's Miss Lamyai (*longan*). It is also a venerated place of Buddhist teaching at **Wat Phra That Haripunjaya**. This famous temple has a 50-m-tall *chedi* crowned by a solid gold nine-tiered honorific umbrella (weighing, apparently, 6498.75 g). Another renowned temple is **Wat Chama Devi**, which lies 1 km west of the moat on Chama Devi Road. It is said that Princess Chama Devi selected the spot by having an archer shoot an arrow to the north from town – her ashes are contained within the main *chedi*. Built in 1218, this square-based *chedi* of brick and stucco has five tiers of niches, each containing a beautiful standing Buddha.

Lamphun, which was founded in AD 600, is sited on the banks of the Ping River and was formerly the capital of the Haripunjaya Kingdom. The moat and parts of the old defensive walls are still present and it was a powerful centre of the Mon culture until King Mengrai succeeded in taking the city in 1281.

Lampang → *Colour map 1, B3. Phone code: 054.*

ⓘ *Regular buses from Nawarat Bridge or from the Arcade terminal and trains connect with Chiang Mai (2 hrs) while local transport is provided by the town's horse-drawn carriages.*

An atmospheric provincial capital complete with horse-drawn carriages, soothing riverside hang-outs and the sumptuous temple of Wat Phra That Lampang Luang, Lampang makes a great day or overnight trip from Chiang Mai. A tour around town in a horse-drawn carriage costs ₿80-120. They generally take two routes, the cheaper one takes about 20 minutes, the more expensive one 45 minutes or alternatively ₿120 per hour. There's some decent accommodation and a chance to indulge in a leisurely lunch at one of the great riverside restaurants. The **tourist office** ⓘ *Boonyawat Rd, in the front of the police station, 1st floor, T054-218823,* has good maps and brochures. The airport is on the south edge of town, off Prabhat Road, and the bus station is on Route 1, just east of the railway line (a 15-minute walk to the town centre). The railway station is on the west side of town, at the end of Surain Road. *Saamlors* charge ₿10 for trips around town or ₿50 per hour to hire. *Songthaews* run routes around town (although these are flexibly interpreted); the *rop muang* or *rop wiang* ('around town') are the most useful (₿10 anywhere in town).

Established in the seventh-century Dvaravati period, Lampang prospered as a trading centre, with a wealth of ornate and well-endowed wats. Re-built in the 19th century as a fortified *wiang* (a walled city), it became an important centre for the teak industry with British loggers making this one of their key centres. The influence of the Burmese is reflected in the architecture of some of the more important wats – a number still have Burmese abbots.

Wat Phra Kaeo Don Tao ⓘ *₿10,* and its 'sister' **Wat Chadaram** are to be found on Phra Kaeo Road, north across the Rachada Phisek Bridge. Wat Phra Kaeo housed the renowned Emerald Buddha (the Phra Kaeo – now in Wat Phra Kaeo, Bangkok) for 32 years during the

15th century. This royal temple is said to be imbued with particular spiritual power and significance, largely because of its association with the Phra Kaeo. The ceilings and columns of the 18th-century *viharn* are carved in wood and are intricately inlaid with porcelain and enamel. In the compound, there is also a Burmese-style chapel (probably late 18th century) and a golden *chedi*. Next door, Wat Chadaram contains the most attractive building in the whole complex: a small, intimate, well-proportioned, wooden *viharn*.

Wat Chedi Sao ① *0800-1700*, the 'temple of the 20 chedis', is 3 km northeast of the town, 1 km off the Lampang–Jae Hom road at Ban Wang Moh. A large white *chedi* is surrounded by 19 smaller ones, and a strange assortment of concrete animals and monks. The most important Buddha image here is a gold, seated image cast in the 15th century. Its importance stems both from its miraculous discovery – by a local farmer in his rice field in 1983 – and from the fact that it is said to contain a piece of the Lord Buddha's skull in its head. To reach the wat, walk over the bridge to the junction of Jhamatawee and Wangkhon roads and hail a *saamlor* there for ฿5.

Wat Sri Chum ① *Tippowan Rd (aka Sri Chum Rd), 0700-1830, ฿10*, is a beautiful wat, constructed 200 years ago and regarded as one of the finest Burmese-style wats in Thailand. Tragically, the richly carved and painted *viharn*, was destroyed by fire in 1993. The compound exudes an ambience of peaceful meditation, although it is in urgent need of funds to complete restoration.

Lampang

Not to scale

Sleeping 🛏	Eating 🍴	Terrace 2
Asia Lampang 1	Cha-ba Pub 1	
Lampang Wiengthong 2	Krua Thai 3	**Bars & clubs 🍸**
Pin 3	Oey Thong Café 4	Relax 7
Siam 4	Riverside 6	

Wat Phra That Lampang Luang

ⓘ *0900-1200, 1300-1700, donation. Take a songthaew to Ko Kha and then a motorbike taxi the last 2.5 km to the wat. Songthaews for Ko Kha run regularly along Phahonyothin Rd. Alternatively, charter a songthaew from Lampang (฿150-200). If travelling by private transport from Lampang, drive along Route 1 towards Ko Kha. In Ko Kha pass through the town, over the bridge, and then turn right at the T-junction onto Route 1034. The wat is 2.5 km away – just off Route 1034 (the chedi can be seen rising up behind some sugar palms). From Chiang Mai, turn right off Route 11 just past the Km 80 marker, signposted to Ko Kha.*

The monastery stands on a slight hill, surrounded by a brick wall – all that remains of the original fortressed city which was sited here more than 1000 years ago. Sand and tiles, rather than concrete, surround the monuments. While the buildings have been restored on a number of occasions over the years, it remains beautifully complete and authentic.

Originally this wat was a fortified site, protected by walls, moats and ramparts. Approached by a staircase flanked by guardian lions and *nagas*, visitors enter through an archway of intricate 15th-century stone carving. The large, open central *viharn*, **Viharn Luang (a)**, houses a *ku* – a brick, stucco and gilded pyramid peculiar to northern wats – containing a Buddha image (1563), a collection of thrones and some wall paintings. The building, with its intricate woodcarving and fine pattern work on the pillars and ceiling, is dazzling.

Behind the *viharn* is the principal **chedi (b)**, 45 m high it contains three relics of the Buddha: a hair and the ashes of the Buddha's right forehead and neck bone. Made of beaten copper and brass plates over a brick core, it is typically Lanna Thai in style and was erected in the late 15th century. The **Buddha Viharn (c)** to the left of the *chedi* is thought to date from the 13th century and was restored in 1802. Beautifully carved and painted, it contains a seated Buddha image. Behind this *viharn* is a small, raised building housing a **footprint of the Buddha (d)** (only men are permitted). This building houses a camera obscura; at certain times of day (from late morning through to early afternoon) the sun's rays pass through a small hole in the wall, projecting an inverted image of the *chedi* and the surrounding buildings onto a sheet.

To the right of the main *viharn* are two more small, but equally beautiful, *viharns*: the **Viharn Nam Taem (e)** and the **Viharn Ton Kaew (f)**. The former is thought to date from the early 16th century, and may be the oldest wooden building in Thailand. It also contains some old wall paintings, although these are difficult to see in the gloom. Finally within the walls are the **Viharn Phra Chao Sila (g)**, built to enshrine an image of Buddha.

Outside the walls, through the southern doorway, is an enormous and ancient **bodhi tree (h)**, supported by a veritable army of crutches. Close by is a small, musty and rather unexciting **museum (i)**. Next to this is a raised scripture library and a *viharn*, within which is another revered **Emerald Buddha (j)** –

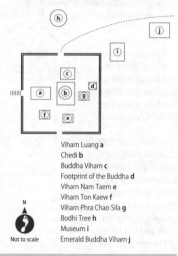

Wat Phra That Lampang Luang

Viharn Luang **a**
Chedi **b**
Buddha Viharn **c**
Footprint of the Buddha **d**
Viharn Nam Taem **e**
Viharn Ton Kaew **f**
Viharn Phra Chao Sila **g**
Bodhi Tree **h**
Museum **i**
Emerald Buddha Viharn **j**

N

Not to scale

heavily obscured by two rows of steel bars. It is rumoured to have been made from the same block of jasper as the famous Emerald Buddha in Bangkok.

Thai Elephant Conservation Centre

① *T054-227051, www.thaielephant.com. Bathing sessions daily at 0945, 'shows' daily at 1000 and 1100, with an additional show at 1330 at weekends and holidays, ฿150. Elephant rides ฿150 for 10 mins, ฿400 for 30 mins, ฿800 for 1 hr. There is also a small restaurant, souvenir shop and toilets. The ECC also runs English-language mahout training courses – contact them directly for details. Take an early morning bus towards Chiang Mai; get off at the Km 37 marker (ask the bus driver to let you off at the Conservation Centre). From the road it is a 1.8-km walk by road or take a short cut through the forest; alternatively charter a songthaew from town for ฿350 return. You can stay at the camp; see the website for details.*

The recent fate of the Thai elephant has been a slow inexorable decline. Numbers are dwindling and the few that do remain are mainly used as tourist attractions (see page 103). Many of the places that offer chances to interact with elephants are poorly run, treating their charges with contempt. Not so the excellent Thai Elephant Conservation Centre, which lies 33 km northwest of Lampang near Thung Kwian, on the road to Chiang Mai (Highway 11). Here elephants are trained for forest work, others are released back into the wild, there are elephant musicians, elephant artists and elephant dung paper. There's even an elephant hospital and rescue centre. All in all there are about 100 animals here.

Pha Thai caves

① *The first 400 m of the cave is open to the public but the great majority of the system is off-limits. Take Route 1 from Lampang towards Ngao and 19 km before Ngao turn left.*

The Pha Thai caves are some of the most spectacular in Thailand; the cave system is one of the country's deepest too, extending more than 1200 m. The caves are renowned not only for their length but also for the snakes that have taken up residence here. From the arrival point to the cave entrance visitors have to climb 283 steps. As with many caves, it has acquired religious significance and the cave is associated with a wat. A white *chedi* stands like a sentinel outside the mouth of the cave and a large gilded Buddha fills the entrance.

Jai Sorn (Chae Sorn) National Park

① *Take the road from Lampang towards Wak Nua and then turn left at the Km 58-59 marker. Continue along this road for another 17 km.*

The park, Lampang's only protected area, has hot volcanic springs in the waterfall pools – the Chae Son Waterfall and Chae Son Hot Spa Park, which are just 1 km apart. The waterfall tumbles seven levels and during the wet season is spectacular. The springs bubble out at 75-80°C, are mixed with cold water from the waterfall and channelled into 11 bathrooms.

Doi Inthanon National Park → *Colour map 1, B2.*

① *0600-1800, ฿200, ฿100 children. ฿30 car, ฿10 motorbike, ฿50 songthaew and minibus. Best time to visit: just after the end of the rainy season, in late Oct or Nov. By Jan and Feb the air becomes hazy, not least because of forest fires. Buses, minibuses and songthaews for Hang Dong and Chom Thong leave from the Chiang Mai Gate. Take a yellow songthaew for the 58 km from Chiang Mai Gate to Chom Thong (฿10). From Chom Thong market, take another yellow songthaew to the Mae Klang Falls (฿5) or the Wachiratan Falls (a10). To reach Mae Ya Falls and Doi Inthanon summit, a songthaew must be chartered (this will seat 10 people); ฿350 and ฿500 respectively. From Hang Dong there are songthaews to Doi Inthanon.*

Located off Route 108, on Route 1009, Doi Inthanon is Thailand's highest peak at 2595 m. The mountain is a national park and the winding route to the top is stunning, with terraced rice fields, cultivated valleys and a few hilltribe villages. The park covers 482 sq km and is one of the most visited in Thailand. Although the drive to the top is dramatic, the park's flora and fauna can only really be appreciated by taking one of the hiking trails off the main road. The flora ranges from dry deciduous forest on the lower slopes, to moist evergreen between 1000 m and 1800 m, and 'cloud' forest and a sphagnum (moss) bog towards the summit. There are even some relict pines. Once the habitat of bears and tigers, the wildlife has been severely depleted through over-hunting. However, it is still possible to see flying squirrel, red-toothed shrew, Chinese pangolin and Pere David's vole, as well as an abundance of butterflies and moths. Although the mountain, in its entirety, is a national park, there are several thousand Hmong and Karen living here and cultivating the slopes.

Just beneath the summit, in a spectacular position, are a pair of bronze and gold-tiled *chedis*, one dedicated to the king in 1989 and the other dedicated to Queen Sirikit at the end of 1992. Both *chedis* contain intricate symbolism and have been built to reaffirm the unity of the Thai nation. The ashes of Chiang Mai's last king, Inthawichayanon, are contained in a small white *chedi* on the summit – the ultimate reflection of the idea that no one should be higher than the king, in life or in death.

There are a number of waterfalls on the slopes: the **Mae Klang Falls** (near the Km 8 marker and not far from the visitor centre), **Wachiratan Falls** (26 km down from the summit and near the Km 21 marker, restaurant here) and **Siriphum Falls** (3-4 km off the road near the Km 31 marker and not far from the park headquarters), as well as the large **Borichinda Cave** (a 2-km hike off the main road near the visitor centre at the Km 9 marker). Note that it is a tiring climb up steep steps to the Mae Klang and Wachiratan falls. The **Mae Ya Falls** in the south of the park are the most spectacular, plunging more than 250 m (they lie 15 km from park headquarters and are accessible from Chom Thong town). Ask for details at the visitor centre a few kilometres on from the park's entrance.

Ob Luang National Park
① *Take Route 108 to Hot, then take the Mae Sariang road. After Km 17 you will reach the park's headquarters. Entry ฿200, tents available for hire.*
The park is just over 100 km southwest of Chiang Mai, and makes a good weekend trip. It's famous for its gorge, through which the Mae Chaem River flows, and there are waterfalls, caves, hot springs and marked trails for trekking. It you follow the trail by the Mae-Bua Come Waterfall, you will pass the 'Land of Prehistoric Human', where archeologists have found remains and artefacts dating back to the Stone Age.

◉ Chiang Mai and around listings

For Sleeping and Eating price codes and other relevant information, see pages 44-49.

● Sleeping

Chiang Mai *p232, maps p234 and p236*
Chiang Mai has a huge range of places to stay, mostly concentrated to the east of the old walled city, although there is a significant group of guesthouses to be found west of Moon Muang Rd, south of Tha Phae Gate. It is rare for visitors to have to pay the set room (rack) rate. Booking online is one way to get a bargain – try www.chiangmai-online.com. Backpacker places can put pressure on guests to book tours through them – be aware before checking in. A guesthouse may run very good tours, but it does limit your options.

Old City

Within the old city walls and the moat is the greatest concentration of guesthouses, plus 1 or 2 small(ish) mid-range places. Most are to be found in the eastern half. The old city is relatively quiet and tree-filled and away from the main centre of commercial activity. It's a 15-min walk to the night market, although there are bars, restaurants, tour operators, laundries, and motorbike/jeep rental outfits.

LL-AL Rachamankha, 9 Phra Singh Rd, T053-904114, www.rachamankha.com (see Chiang Mai map, page 234). This oasis of calm is an inspired boutique hotel with a designer's eye for detail, all built using traditional techniques. The a/c rooms can be a bit small and dark but are filled with sumptuous antiques. Service is definitely a bit ropey for the price range. Also has pool, decent library (free internet) and restaurant.

LL-AL Tamarind Village, 50/1 Rachadamnern Rd, T053-418896, www.tamarindvillage.com. Great location in the heart of the old city. Slightly worn and overpriced Lanna-style hotel that caters mostly to package tourists. The gardens and pool are quite pretty, though the Lanna boutique vibe is a bit hackneyed.

A-B Montri's, 2-6 Rachdamnern Rd, T053-211 070. Good central position near Tha Phae Gate, but on an intersection so tends to be very noisy. Large clean rooms, sparsely furnished, some with a/c. The restaurant, **Zest**, is one of Chiang Mai's most popular.

A-B Top North, 41 Moon Muang Rd, T053-279623. Modern hotel in a good location, with pool and decent food. Overpriced.

B-C 3sis, 1 Soi 8, Prapokklao Rd, T53-273243, www.the3sis.com. This airy, Lanna-style guesthouse consists of 2 buildings and is just across from Wat Chedi Luang. Staff speak excellent English, rooms are large with a/c, en suite and TV. Also has Wi-Fi.

B-C Chiang Mai Kristi House, 14/2 Rachdamnern Soi 5, T053-418165. A largish place with over 30 rooms, down quiet *soi*. Rooms are well kept and a good size, with very clean attached bathrooms and hot water. Great views from the rooms at the back.

B-C Chiang Mai White House, 12 Rachdamnern Soi 5, T053-357130, www.chiang maiwhitehouse.com. A 3-storey block with 18 cosy rooms (some a/c), an immaculate garden and very high standard of cleanliness.

B-C Smile House, 5 Rachmanka Soi 2, T053-208661, smile208@mail.cscoms.com. 32 spotless, but rather bare, rooms, some with a/c and hot water showers. Breakfast available, bikes for rent, tours and trekking organized. Small sauna in the garden.

B-C White Chalet, 9/1 Arak Rd, T053-326188, www.chiangmaiwhitechalet.com. Newly-built modern guesthouse. Everything is white, from the chairs in the lobby to the bedcovers. Fresh-looking, standard-sized a/c rooms with double bed, flat screen TV and en suite. Earplugs are recommended as the street outside is busy day and night.

D-E Chiang Mai Garden Guesthouse, 82/86 Rachmanka Rd, T053-278881. Good food, very clean large rooms with bathroom. The owner is exceptionally knowledgeable about the area and speaks excellent English, German and French. Popular.

D-E Eagle II Guesthouse, 26 Rachwithi Rd, Soi 2, T053-210620, www.eaglehouse.com. Dorms for ฿60. Friendly staff, rooms are clean but a little worn with a/c and some attached bathrooms. Excellent food (it is also possible to take cookery courses here). Also organizes treks. Attractive area to sit, efficient and friendly set up. Recommended.

D-E Johnny Boy Guesthouse (JB House), 7/3 Rachdamnern Soi 1, T053-213329. Small restaurant, hot water, clean, quiet and friendly – runs good treks.

D-E Rendezvous Guesthouse, 3/1 Rachdamnern Soi 5, T053-213763. Some a/c, situated down a quiet *soi*, good rooms with clean bathrooms, hot showers, cable TV and some rooms with fridge. Relaxing plant-filled lobby, satellite TV, books and comfy chairs, good value. Very popular with travellers so worth booking in advance.

E Panda Tour Guesthouse, 130/1 Rachamanka Rd, T053-206420. This wonderfully friendly, family-run business of over 12 years' standing is a real gem. The stable-like block has meticulously clean, well-equipped rooms with fans, tiled floors and white-washed walls. Buzzing little restaurant with exceptional food. Also runs one of the best tour companies in Chiang Mai, with long-standing guides whose knowledge of the surrounding area is phenomenal. Recommended.

E Somwang Guesthouse, 2 Rachmanka Soi 2, T053-278505. Large clean rooms in a rather basic setting, but still excellent value for the level of facilities provided. Very friendly and informative owner who speaks good English. Recommended.

E-F Julie's Guesthouse, 7/1 Phra Pokklao Soi 5, T053-274355, wwww.julieguesthouse.com Swiss-run. Basic fan rooms, some with their own bathroom and hot water. Friendly atmosphere with lots of communal space for chilling out, including a rooftop. Thai and Western food, treks organized. Recommended.

E-F Thai Way Guesthouse, 63A Bamrung-buri Rd (by Chiang Mai Gate), T053-206316. Formerly the **Chiang Mai Youth Hostel**. Good-value accommodation, friendly. The garden and restaurant are a little scruffy, but the place is busy and is frequently fully booked with young Japanese tourists.

Between the eastern city wall and Chang Klang Rd

This area of town includes 2 sections of hotels and guesthouses. On **Chang Klang Rd** and close by are a number of large, upmarket hotels. The area is busy and noisy (although the hotels need not be), with a good range of restaurants. West of here, down the *sois* or lanes between **Loi Kroa** and **Tha Phae** roads, are a number of guesthouses and small mid-range hotels. This area, though quiet and peaceful, is still close to many restaurants and the shops and stalls of Chiang Klan Rd.

L-AL Royal Princess (formerly **Dusit Inn**), 112 Chang Klang Rd, T053-253 3900, www.dusit.com. Central and quite noisy (on the main road). With 200 rooms, the hotel makes an effort to be more Thai than Western in image and style. Service is of a high standard and there's a restaurant, small pool and gym. Of the top-range hotels in town, this is recommended.

L-A D2, 100 Chang Klang Rd, T053-999999 www.d2hotels.com. Owned by the **Dusit Thani** chain the D2 attempts to create a designer hotel in the heart of Chiang Mai but doesn't quite pull it off. The rooms, while nicely designed, are small and the orange-everything is off-putting. However, the food is great and the location, right in the heart of the night market, can't be beaten.

AL Rydges Tapae Hotel, 22 Chaiyaphum Rd, T053-251531, www.rydges.com. All the facilities you'd expect from a top range hotel, but not quite up to the standard of other hotels in this price bracket. Staff are friendly enough, small pool, pleasant lobby.

B-D Lai Thai, 111/4-5 Kotchasan Rd, T053-271725, www.laithai.com. A cross between a north Thai house and a Swiss chalet. Spotless rooms, some with a/c, free baby cots. Popular and professional set-up, good facilities, attractive surroundings, tours, trekking and motorbike rental. Restaurant, good clean pool. Note that the cheaper rooms at the back are noisy, so expect an early wake-up. Nonetheless, recommended.

C Tapae Place Hotel, 2 Tha Phae Soi 3, T053-270159. Small mid-range hotel, refined and surprisingly stylish for a place in this price category. Good central location but set off the busy Tha Phae Rd. A/c, restaurant next to Wat Bupharam. Room rate includes breakfast.

C-D Bang Jong Come Guesthouse, 47 Tha Phae Soi 4, T053-207043, www.namkhong travel.com. Larger than most guesthouses, almost like a small hotel. Rooms are light and airy with hot water showers and some with a/c. Attached restaurant. Trekking available.

C-D Fang Guesthouse, 46-48 Kamphaeng Din Soi 1, T053-282940. Quiet place in a good central location, rooms are very clean although a little dark, good attached bathrooms (some with hot water). A/c rooms are especially good value. Restaurant.

D Little Home Guesthouse, 1/1 Kotchasan Soi 3, T/F053-206939. More like a small hotel than a guesthouse, but don't be put off; it is peaceful, down a quiet *soi* within a leafy compound. Rooms are clean and the management has insisted on no TV, videos or music. Professionally run and popular, with cheaper package tours. Recommended.

D Sarah's, 20 Tha Phae Soi 4, T053-208271, www.sarahguesthouse.com. 12 basic but clean rooms, with attached bathrooms and shared hot water showers. Trekking, tour services and cookery courses available. Very popular, well-established guesthouse in the heart of the guesthouse area. Recommended.

D-E Namkhong Guesthouse, 55 Tha Phae Soi 3, T053-215556. Friendly guesthouse. All 44 rooms are a little small and can be hot, but they are clean with reasonable attached bathrooms. Treks arranged, restaurant attached, well run and popular.

D-E Orchid Guest House, 4 Tha Phae Soi 5, T053-275370. Some a/c, hot water, rooms with bathrooms, clean and quiet. Lots of travellers' information here.

Near the river

This area includes a number of mid- and upper-range hotels on the river that are within easy walking distance of many restaurants and the shops of Chang Klang Rd.

LL-AL The Chedi, 123 Charoen Prathet Rd, T053-253333, www.ghmhotels.com. Stunningly designed property built around the restored 1920s British consulate – itself a historical treat – has been created here by the river. The rooms are minimalist, with huge tubs and plasma screens while the lobby is spacious and relaxed. Pool, sundeck and great food complete the picture. Expensive but the best in town. Highly recommended.

L-AL Empress Chiang Mai, 199/42 Chang Klang Rd, T053-270240, www.empress hotels.com (see map, page 234). Restaurants, pool and fitness centre. 375 spacious, attractive rooms with silk wall panelling and decorated with local products. Recommended.

A River View Lodge, 25 Soi 2 Charoen Prathet Rd, T053-271109, www.riverviewlodg ch.com (see map, page 234). Tucked away

down a narrow *soi*. A/c, small, family-run, riverside hotel with wonderful gardens, a pool and a friendly vibe. Rooms are overpriced, there's a noisy bar just across the river and service can sometimes be snooty.

A-C Baan Orapin, 150 Charoenrat Rd, T053-243677, www.baanorapin.com. One of the most popular places in Chiang Mai. A run of well-maintained bungalows surround a central teak house, all set in quiet gardens on a road on the east side of the river. The owner speaks great English and is friendly, though can be hard to find. Email or call ahead as it's often booked solid. Highly recommended.

B Galare Guesthouse, 7 Soi 2 Charoen Prathet Rd, T053-818887, www.galare.com. A/c, restaurant, small hotel in leafy compound, lovely position on the river. Rooms are rundown though service is good and the open-air restaurant serves simple, tasty food.

C-D Kim House, 62 Charoen Prathet Rd, T/F053-282441. Small hotel in leafy compound down a secluded *soi*, with clean rooms (some a/c) and hot showers. Friendly, welcoming atmosphere. Recommended.

West of the city

With Nimmanhaemin now firmly established as Chiang Mai's artist quarter a few excellent guesthouses have sprung up. There are also a number of large hotels on Huay Kaew Rd.

AL Ayatana Hamlet and Spa, 99/9 Moo 14, Suthep Rd, T053-811388, www.ayatana-resort.com. Boutique hotel and spa tucked away at the base of Doi Suthep. Pool, yoga lessons and private outdoor showers. A/c rooms with en suite and TV. Restaurant offers a 'weight watcher menu' cooked in 'special northern spices'.

L-A Amari Rincome, 1 Nimmanhaemin Rd, T053-221130, www.amari.com. A/c, restaurant (Italian), pool, tennis court and 158 rooms. Located west of the town centre, this hotel remains popular with tour groups. Friendly and professional service puts it ahead of some of the glitzier newer places.

L-A Chiang Mai Orchid, 23 Huay Kaew Rd, T053-222099, www.chiangmaiorchid.com.

Situated right next to the large Kad Suan Kaew shopping complex. Attractive hotel recently expanded, a/c, restaurants, pool, health club, efficient service, relatively peaceful, very good Chinese restaurant. Low-season discounts of up to 50%.

L-A Lotus-Pang Suan Kaew Hotel, 99/4 Huay Kaew Rd, T053-224333. Massive hotel which is ugly from the outside but makes up for it with competitive rates and large, luxurious rooms. A/c, restaurants, pool, gym. Recommended.

C-D Yesterday, 24 Nimmanhaemin Rd, T053-213809, www.yesterday.co.th. Opened by the friendly and laid-back owners of **Baan Sal-La**, this beautiful teak house boasts 28 individually designed rooms with a/c, en suite and TV. Also offers 2 small houses, free Wi-Fi and airport transfers. There's a small garden. Recommended.

D-E Baan Say-La, 4-4/1 Nimmanhaemin Rd, Soi 5, T053-894229, baansayla@gmail.com. In an old colonial-style house, this is one of Chiang Mai's best bargains. The tasteful rooms are well designed, some have balconies, while everyone has access to the cool air on the roof terrace. The friendly vibe stems from the half-Thai, half-Spanish owner, Rodney. Its location right in the heart of hip Nimmanhaemin means that you can escape most of the other tourists. The only drawback is noisy nightclub next door. Recommended.

E-G Spicythai Backpackers, 4/80 Nanthawan Village, Nimmanhaemin Rd, T053-400 444, www.spicythaibackpackers.com. Set in a small, very quiet compound of houses, a well-managed hostel with dorm rooms (2 a/c rooms available). The owner also supplies a range of trips and activities as well as free coffee, tea and internet. You need to be prepared for communal living if you want to stay here – it is slightly reminiscent of the Big Brother house. The dorms are quite pricey.

Mae Sa Valley–Samoeng circuit *p246*
A number of resorts (**B**) have been established along the road around the Doi Suthep-Pui National Park. Most cater for Thais. The largest

and most luxurious are **Suan Bua**, in the village of Ban Don, 22 km from Samoeng, T053-365 2709, www.suanbua.com, set in attractively landscaped gardens; and **Belle Villa**, 19 km from Samoeng, www.bellevillaresort.com, where there are cottages for longer-term rental as well as some hotel accommodation, T053-365318, belle_villa@hotmail.com.

B Mae Sa Craft Village, T053-290052. Non a/c rooms. Has an average restaurant (avoid non-Thai food) and a smallish swimming pool. There are dozens of great activities to get involved in, from ceramic painting to batik dyeing and *sa* paper-making. There is also a working farm where visitors can help with the rice cultivation, a Thai cookery school and a health centre for massage and relaxation.

B Samoeng Resort, northwest of Samoeng town, T053-487072. Restaurant, pool, hot water showers, in spacious gardens set in an isolated spot.

Chiang Dao Caves *p247*
D-F Malee's Nature Lovers Bungalows, 144/2 Moo 5, Chiang Dao, 1 km from the caves, T08-1961 8387 (mob), www.malee nature.com. Bungalows and dorm beds, restaurant, good for trekking and walking. Can be cold between Nov and Feb.

Lamphun *p248*
D Suphamit Hotel, Chama Devi Rd (opposite Wat Chama Devi), T053-534865. The one decent place to stay with simple rooms in a good location.

Lampang *p248, map p249*
Lampang is 2 hrs from Chiang Mai.
A Lampang Wiengthong Hotel, 138/109 Phahonyothin Rd, T054-225801. A/c, pool, restaurant, 250 rooms in this, the smartest and largest of Lampang's hotels. Easily the most luxurious place to stay in town.

A-B Lampang River Lodge, 330 Moo 11 Tambon Chompoo, 6 km south of Lampang on the banks of the Wang River, T054-224 1173. A/c, restaurant, 60 Thai-style bungalows on stilts, in an attractive position.

B-C Pin, 8 Suan Dok Rd, T054-221509. A/c, fridge, satellite TV, some rooms with attached bathrooms, squeaky clean and quiet.

C-D Asia Lampang, 229 Boonyawat Rd, T054-227844. A/c, restaurant, large, clean rooms with TV. Good value. Friendly staff and with the added bonus of the 'Sweety Room' for "the romantic of your ambience moods". Recommended.

D Siam, 260/29 Chatchai Rd, T054-217472. A 4-storey block with bare rooms, some a/c. Friendly management, restaurant has live music and dancing.

D-E Riverside Guesthouse, 286 Talad Kao Rd, T054-227005. Some a/c, restaurant overlooking the Wang river. Beautiful and unique rooms individually decorated by the friendly Italian owner. Room include dorms, family-sized room and suites. Highly recommended.

Jai Sorn (Chae Sorn) National Park *p251*
B-C Bungalows at the park, T054-229000.

Doi Inthanon National Park *p251*
There is a camping ground at the Km 31 mark (฿5 per person). Small tents (฿50 per night) and blankets are available for hire.

A-C Bungalows, Km 31, out-station on the route up the mountain. To book, T02-579 0529 or write to the Superintendent, Doi Inthanon National Park, Chom Thong District, Chiang Mai 50160. Advance reservation recommended as this is a very popular park. A relatively new Karen eco-resort has been set up by 4 villages with support from the National Parks Authorities. The bungalows, sleeping 4-30 people, have been built in the traditional style and the location is fantastic. The resort organizes treks, teaches about medicinal plants, introduces visitors to Karen dance, etc. The resort is on the road to the summit, before the second checkpoint.

● Eating

For listings of where to go for a northern Khantoke meal plus cultural show, see Entertainment, page 262. Some of the best Thai food, particularly seafood, is served from numerous restaurants, large and small, and countless stalls, in the **Anusarn market** area (see map, page 236). This is the best place to see what is on offer in a small area; food is available all day, but best at night when there is a cacophony of talking, frying and chopping. Note some bars and pubs also serve food, see page 261.

Chiang Mai *p232, maps p234 and p236*
Old City

♦♦♦ The House, 199 Moon Muang Rd, T053-419011. Open 1200-2400. Set in a funky 1930s colonial house, this is an attempt to serve upmarket international cuisine. It largely succeeds though it is a bit hit and miss.

♦♦♦ Rachamankha, 9 Phra Singh Rd, T053-904 114, www.rachamankha.com. The restaurant at this stunning hotel serves a tasty menu of Thai and Asian fusion dishes. It is expensive but is a great choice for a romantic splurge.

♦♦ Café Chic, 105/5 Phra Pokklao Rd, T053-814651. Thu-Tue 1000-2000. A great little place serving a limited menu of Thai and Western food, its strength lies in its great range of cakes, coffees and teas. A small shop here sells a range of products, artfully displayed and therefore probably overpriced. Recommended.

♦♦ Jerusalem Falafel, 35/3 Moon Muang Rd, T053-270208. Sat-Thu 0900-2200. This place doesn't look much from the outside, but don't be put off – it's a cracking little eatery, and the only one of its kind serving a wide variety of very freshly prepared Middle Eastern food. Recommended.

♦♦ UN Irish Pub, 24/1 Rachwithi Rd. Lamb chops, Irish stew, steaks, pasta, lasagne, etc. Pretty good fare in a pub atmosphere. See Bars and clubs, page 261.

♦ The Amazing Sandwich, 252/3 Phra Pokklao Rd, T053-218846. Mon-Sat 0900-2030. Only 4 tables in this sandwich bar (and a couple more outside), which makes it feel a little cramped. However, the sandwiches are very high quality (good bread too).

Also serves a typical English breakfast. Take-away and limited delivery service available.

The Corner, Rachmanka/Moon Muang Rd. Range of classics and some vegetarian dishes. Also a popular place for breakfast.

Genchai, 54/1 Sing Ha Rat Rd. Excellent and very popular Isaan and Thai restaurant mostly frequented by locals. Good for sticky rice, grilled catfish and chicken. English menu. Recommended.

Nice Sweet Place, 27/1 Moon Muang Rd. A/c restaurant with attached bakery, good pastries, serves breakfast.

Pizza Al Taglio, Rachmanka Soi 2. Very good value pizzas cooked by the friendly Italian owner and his Thai wife.

Zest, Montri Hotel, Tha Phae Gate and in the Chiang Inn Plaza, Chang Klang Rd. Good breakfasts and sandwiches. Nice spot.

Between the eastern city wall and Chang Klang Rd

Moxie, D2 Hotel, 100 Chang Klang Rd, T053-999999, www.d2hotels.com. Great food in this designer restaurant. An oasis of calm in the scrum of the night market this makes a great pit stop. The international and Thai menus are both extensive.

Antique House 1, 71 Charoen Prathet Rd (next to the Diamond Riverside Hotel). Open 1100-2400. Well-prepared Thai and Chinese food in a wonderful garden with antiques and an old teak house, built in 1870s (and listed as a National Heritage Site), very nice candlelit ambience, tasty but small servings and rather slow service, live music. Busy road can be intrusive.

Antique House 2, 154/1 Chiang Mai/Lamphun Rd, T053-240270 (see map, page 234). Open 1600-0200. A terraced restaurant overlooking the River Ping, live music.

Aroon Rai, 43-45 Kotchasan Rd. Open 0900-2200. Very big restaurant, good-value Thai food, north Thai specialities, very popular. Tables on the open-air upper floor are quieter.

Art Café, 291 Tha Phae Rd (on the corner facing Tha Phae Gate) T053-206365. Open 0700-2300. In a great position for trade,

this place serves Italian specialities including pizzas and pasta, as well as Thai and Mexican favourites. Fairly expensive.

The Fillmore East, 15/7 Loi Kroa Rd. Super Angus beef, imported from the US, served up to DVD 'concerts'. Excellent burgers, kebabs and salads. A popular house dish is the home-made mashed potato. Pool table, friendly staff, happy customers. Recommended.

The Gallery, 25-29 Charoenrat Rd, T053-248601. Quiet and refined Thai restaurant, in a century-old traditional Thai house, superb food, highly recommended for a special night out, art gallery attached, either sit in a leafy veranda (under an ancient makiang tree) overlooking the river, or inside. Recommended are the fish dishes, including steamed sea bass with lime and deep-fried *plaa chon*.

The Good View Bar and Restaurant, 13 Charoenrat Rd, T053-249029. Not open for lunch. Situated on the Ping River, outdoor or a/c dining available. Good live music and bar and very reasonably priced. The atmosphere is more modern than its long-established neighbour, the Riverside Restaurant.

Mango Tree Café, 8/2-3 Loi Kroa Rd, T053-208292. Popular with expats for its famed roast lamb Sun lunches and northern Thai, international and fusion cuisine.

Mike's, corner of Chang Moi and Chaiyaphum Rd. Daily 1200-2400. Created by an American expat, Mike's serves up the best home-made burgers, fries and shakes you'll find this side of Brooklyn. You can sit at the retro road-side bar or take away. Highly recommended.

Whole Earth, 88 Sri Donchai Rd. Open 1100-2200. Indian food served in a traditional Thai house. Very civilized, with unobtrusive live Thai classical music. Recommended.

Red Lion, 123 Loi Kroa Rd. Not a bad imitation of an English pub – sausages and mash, beans on toast, fish and chips, as well as a range of salads and sandwiches.

Rot Nung, Charoen Prathet Rd (opposite the Diamond Riverside Hotel). Excellent *kway tiaw* (Thai noodle soup) in a restaurant almost entirely frequented by Thais.

West bank of the river off Charoen Prathet Rd

¶¶¶ The Restaurant, The Chedi, 123 Charoen Prathet Rd, T053-253333, www.ghmhotels.com. Great traditional northern Thai specialities and innovative Pacific Rim cuisine complemented by an extensive wine list served in what was once the British consulate. Expensive but recommended.

¶ Shere Shiraz, 23-25 Charoen Prathet Soi 6, T053-276132. Popular Indian restaurant with good tandoori.

¶ Sophia, Charoen Prathet Soi 1 (down a narrow *soi* between the night market and the river road). Cheap and very popular Muslim restaurant, this *soi* also usually supports a number of stalls, serving Malay/Muslim dishes from roti to mutton curry.

West of the city

¶¶¶ La Casa, Chonlapratan Rd T053-215802, just north of Huay Kaew Rd. Good range of authentic Italian cuisine (heavy on the garlic), apparently a popular restaurant with the Queen of Thailand. Fairly pricey.

¶¶¶ Mi Casa, 60/2 Moo 14, Soi Wat Padaeng, Suthep Rd, T053-810088, www.micasachiangmai.com. Mediterranean food served in a homely setting. The good selection of tapas, wine and vegetarian dishes makes this a favourite with the hip local crowd.

¶¶¶ St Germain des Pres, 4/1 Ratwithi Rd, T053-289557. Open Tue-Sun. New French restaurant. Rooftop bar offers a selection of colourful cocktails and French wine. Good service, friendly staff and excellent food. A little pricey but well worth the money.

¶¶ Babylon, Huay Kaew Rd (about 100 m past the entrance to the university, on the right travelling out of town). Open lunch and dinner. Long-established Italian restaurant with an Italian owner. Pasta, pizza, salads, steaks, veal – unpretentious and reasonable food.

¶¶ Hong Tauw Inn, 95/16-17 Nimmanhaemin Rd (opposite **Amari Rincome Hotel**), T053-400039. Elegant restaurant with an antique clock collection, relaxed, friendly service, northern Thai specialities from regional

sausage to crispy catfish, plus ice-cold beer. Slightly more expensive than the average Thai restaurant. Recommended.

¶¶ Khun Churn, Soi 15, 136/28 Nimmanhaemin Rd. Beautiful Thai vegetarian food in a nice, realxed setting. All-you-can-eat lunch buffet. Recommended.

¶¶ Maze Café, 8/11 Nimmanhaemin Rd, T053-894879. New, modern restaurant and café. Serves Asian fusion dishes and cocktails, as well as cakes and coffee. Frequented by Thai students and office workers. Free Wi-Fi.

¶¶ Sizzler, Kad Suan Kaew, Huay Kaew Rd. For slap-up steaks, this place is pretty good. Its 'all-you-can-eat' salad bar is extremely good value. Perhaps a bit too generic.

¶¶ Tsunami Sushi Bar, Huay Kaew Rd, opposite Lanna Condo II, T08-7189 9338. Open 1730-2330. Highly affordable, tasty Japanese food. Very popular with students, so come early or you might not get a seat.

¶ Nong Bee, 28 Nimmanhaemin Rd. Home-cooked Burmese and Shan food: fermented tea-leaf salad and tomato-fried rice. Excellent value for money and open all day

¶ Pun Pun, in the grounds of Wat Suan Dok, Suthep Rd, www.punpunthailand.org. Thai vegetarian restaurant, serving organic food made from produce sourced from nearby cooperative farms. Beautiful setting, popular with monks and the local expat crowd. Highly recommended.

Elsewhere in the city

¶¶¶ Chez Daniel Le Normand, 255/18 Mahidol Rd, near Ormuang 'superhighway', T053-204600. Normandy-style food – home-made charcuterie, wide choice of French wine. Daniel has cooked for the Queen of Thailand and members of the royal family.

¶¶¶ Le Coq d'Or, 68/1 Koh Klang Rd, T053-282024. A long-established international restaurant. Over-zealous waiters anticipate your every need. High standard of cuisine (including mouth-watering steaks), choice of wines, not heavily patronized, pricey.

¶¶ Come-In House, 79/3 Srithon Rd, T053-212516, Chang Puak, down a *soi* opposite

Wat Jet Yod. Set in a traditional teak house and pleasant garden, not easy to locate.

Our Place Brewery and Restaurant, 411 Charoen Prathet Rd. Large and popular open-air bar and restaurant, with a long menu covering European, Thai and Chinese and dishes. Live music in the evenings from a revolving stage, range of cocktails.

Ta-Krite Thai Restaurant, Samlarn Rd Soi 1 (down the road that runs along the southern wall of Wat Phra Singh). Excellent Thai restaurant in an attractive, plant-filled house. Good atmosphere.

Nang Nual Seafood, 27/2-5 Koh Klang Rd. On the east bank of the Ping River, just south of **Westin Hotel**. Serves Chinese and international food, popular with tour groups.

Around Chiang Mai *p241*

Anusarn Market, southeast of night market has foodstalls. These are mostly open at night, but a smaller number are open throughout the day, they're cheap (฿10-15 single-dish meals), lively and fun. **Chang Klang Rd** has stalls selling delicious pancakes, ฿3-7; **Somphet Market** (see page 236), Moon Muang Rd, is good for takeaway curries, fresh fish, meat and fruitl; and north of **Chang Phuak Gate**, outside the moat, is another congregation of good foodstalls. **Warorot Market**, north of Chang Klang and Tha Phae roads, is good for foodstalls at night.

If you need a/c comfort, then there are some excellent food courts in the basement of the **Airport Plaza** and **Kad Suan Kaew** (aka Central), Huay Kaew Rd. The former is quieter and slightly less frenetic than Kad Suan Kaew, which is a bit like eating in a crowd of pedestrians. Buy coupons (any you don't spend can be redeemed) and then browse the stalls: wide range of noodle and rice dishes, drinks, *kanom*, Korean, Japanese and some other Asian cuisines, along with cold drinks including bottled and draft beer.

Palaad Tawanron Restaurant, Suthep Rd (near university), T053-217073, www.palaad tawanron.com. On the lower parts of the Doi Suthep mountain near a large waterfall and amid thick forest, this is an award-winning

restaurant with some of the best Thai food in Chiang Mai. Book a terrace table at the back and you'll secure an awesome view to go with your sundowner. Highly recommended.

Rainforest, 181 Chiang Mai-Hot Rd, T053-441908. Rather out-of-the-way Thai restaurant, only really worth considering for those with their own transport. Set around a lake about 8 km out of town. Good seafood and northern specialities.

Galae, 65 Suthep Rd, T053-278655. In the foothills of Doi Suthep on the edge of a reservoir, west of the city, Thai and northern Thai dishes in garden setting.

The Tea Shop, Huay Kaew Rd, on south side, near Chiang Mai University. A tiny place, easy to miss, just beyond the **Black Canyon Coffee Shop**. Delightful place for a coffee, with a good range of desserts. Limited menu of spaghetti and lasagne. Recommended.

Lamphun *p248*

There are some reasonable foodstalls around Wat Phra That Haripunjaya while on the road running down the south wall of the monastery is **Lamphun Ice**, an a/c place good for ice cream, coffee and a 16-page menu with delicacies such as pig's knuckle and chicken tendon. On the road running down the north wall is vegetarian restaurant **Yota**, popular with locals and monks, and a seedy looking bar called **Pan Stand in the Room and the Garden**, which has a/c and menus in English. For Kuaytiaw fans, there is a tremendous **Duck Noodle Soup Shop** on Inthayongyot Rd, just south of Wat Phra That Haripunjaya. **Buds Ice-Cream Bar** is next to the tourist information centre west of the monastery.

Lampang *p248, map p249*

For a cheap meal, try one of the Thai pavement cafés along Ropwiang Rd between the clock tower and the **Lampang Guesthouse**. There are foodstalls near the railway station and around the market.

Krua Thai, Phahonyothin Rd (near Lampang Wiengthong Hotel). Good Thai food in an immaculate a/c restaurant.

¶ Terrace Restaurant, Tipchang Rd.
Reasonable food overlooking the river;
a great place for a drink and/or a meal.

¶ Cha-ba Pub and Restaurant, off Tipchang
Rd. Pleasant open-air seating area and while
the food is nothing remarkable, the ambience
just about makes up for it.

¶ Oey Thong Café, Tipchang Rd (near the
bridge), good Thai food in cosy surroundings.

¶ Riverside (Baan Rim Nam), 328 Tipchang
Rd. Wooden house overlooking the river,
attractive ambience, reasonable Thai and
international food. Recommended.

Doi Inthanon National Park *p251*
A small park shop at the Km 31 mark will
serve meals. There are no stalls on the
summit, although there is a restaurant
near the *chedis* close to the summit.

☉ Bars and clubs

Chiang Mai *p232, maps p234 and p236*
Chiang Mai has a reasonable bar scene but is
fairly subdued compared to Bangkok – there
is the usual run of go-go bars along **Loi Kroa
Rd**. If nothing grabs you from the list below
there is a smattering of usually short-lived hip
bohemian hang-outs scattered throughout
the Old City particularly along **Rachdamnern**
and **Rachwithi** roads. The area around **Tae
Pae Gate** also has a high concentration of
watering holes. There are quite a few pubs at
the western end of **Loi Kroa Rd**. A younger,
hipper Thai crowd – and a few *farang* – hang
out at various generic nightspots along
Nimmanhaemin Rd. However, you'll need
to search the back sois to find the best places.
See also Entertainment, below.

Apocalypse Mexican Cantina, 80/2 Loi Kroa
Rd, T053-284288. Located on a busy street,
this place usually pulls in a bit of a crowd, and
boasts a pool table, lots of wooden picnic
tables and large swivel stools around the bar.

Baritone, 96 Praisani Rd. Live jazz from 2100.

Bubble, Pornping Tower Hotel, Charoen
Prathet Rd, T053-270099. Popular disco.

Drunken Flower, Soi 17 Nimmanhaemin Rd,
T053-212081. Alternative politics, art and
music mingle in this ramshackle though
engaging bar-cum-restaurant.

Early Times, Kotchasan Rd. Open air with
live heavy metal music.

Easy Life, 65 Seepoom Rd, east of Chang
Puak Gate. Showing sport, movies and
world news. The friendly owner, Noi, speaks
reasonable English, and this place is never
that busy, so it's worth knowing that if you
buy a drink or food you get free use of the
internet – when it works, that is.

The Full Monty, 29/3 Kotchasan Rd, T08-
9167 0879 (mob). Small but popular with
good happy hour deals and the latest music.

Khan-Asa, 87 Sriphum Rd, T053-213037.
Arty little bar and restaurant with live bands
and DJs. Good for music lovers.

Monkey Club, Soi 9, 7 Nimmanhaemin Rd,
T053-226997. Open 1730-0200. Dance club,
restaurant and bar. Very popular with
students. Crowded, hot and loud.

Rasta Café, off Rachpakinai Rd, near the
intersection with Rachwithi Rd. Hang-out of
choice for the toking traveller set. Lots of Bob
Marley, interesting garden but hardly original.

The Red Lion, 123 Loi Kroa Rd. Open
1200-0100. An English pub (and restaurant,
see Eating, above) with satellite sports TV.

Riverside Bar and Restaurant, 9-11
Charoenrat Rd. Assorted music from blues
to Thai rock, the owner is a big Beatles fan.

Roof Top, Kotchasan Rd, just down from
Tha Phae Gate, and accessed through the
Tribal Hemp Connection shop. A seriously
laid-back setting, the roof pulls back to
create a breezy atmosphere, where countless mats, cushions and low tables play host
to a merry band of travellers. Very popular.

True Blue Bar and Restaurant, Moon
Muang Rd. Australian owned, serves a
wide variety of Western food, including
Vegemite on toast. Happy hour 1700-1900.
Recommended for its relaxed atmosphere.

UN Irish Pub, Rachwithi Rd. Open 0900-2400.
Good atmosphere and cheap food available
(see Eating, above). The name speaks for

itself – management (which is Australian) help to organize the (small) annual St Patrick's Day parade. Quiz nights, live music and occasionally English Premiership football.
Warm-up Café, 40 Nimmanhaemin Rd, T053-306253. Open 1800-0100. Popular club, bar and restaurant. Attracting a young crowd of trendy Thai students and expats. Live music and DJs.

Lampang *p248, map p249*
Relax, Tipchang Rd (next to **Riverside Restaurant**). Modern-style bar overlooking the river. Cold beer and open-air veranda.
Riverside (see Eating, above). Live music most nights, ranging from Rock and Roll to romantic Thai ballad groups.

⊙ Entertainment

Chiang Mai *p232, maps p234 and p236*
Cinema
Airport Plaza, Highway 1141 (on the way to the airport), 4th floor, T053-283939. Big complex, showing American blockbusters and latest Thai films. Discounts on Tue.
Chiang Mai Museum, see Sights. Shows free foreign independent films on Sat evenings.
Future Media, Nimmanhaemin Rd, south of **Amari Rincome** hotel on same side of road. Possible to rent a room to watch movies on big TV screens. ฿200. Good choice.
Lotus Kad Suan Kaew, Huay Kaew Rd. Top floor, 3 screens, latest blockbusters, changes every Fri. ฿70. Call 'Movie line' for information, T053-262661. This complex hosts the EU Film festival, which runs for 10 days every year. Ask at the cinema for more information. Across the road, 12 Huay Kaew, also shows English-language movies, ฿90.

Cultural centres
Alliance Française, 138 Charoen Prathet Rd, T053-275277. French cultural (some northern Thai) activities. French films with English sub-titles shown on Tue (1630) and Fri (2000). Non-members, students ฿10, public ฿20.

American University Alumni (AUA), 24 Rachdamnern Rd, T053-278407. Library Mon-Fri 1200-1800, Sat 0900-1200. English and Thai classes; films and other shows.

Cultural shows and Khantoke dinners
These traditional northern Thai meals get a lot of coverage. Average food is served at low tables by traditionally dressed women while diners sit on the floor. In addition to those listed below, **Diamond Riverside Hotel**, Charoen Prathet Rd, and the **Galare Food Centre**, in the night bazaar, Chang Klang Rd, also organize Khantoke dinners, 1900, ฿180.
Khun Kaew Palace, 252 Phra Pokklao Rd (north end), next to **Vista Hotel**, T053-210663. Admission ฿180 (book in advance),.
Old Chiang Mai Cultural Centre, 185/3 Wualai Rd, T053-275097. Admission ฿180 (book in advance), Khantoke dinner, followed by hilltribe show, daily 1900-2200.

Muay Thai (Thai boxing)
Dechanukrau boxing ring, south of San Pakoi market, on Bumrungrat Rd. Matches every weekend at 2000 (฿20/70).
Kawila boxing stadium, near Nawarat Bridge. Matches start at 2000 every Fri. For ฿400 you can see 10 matches between foreign and Thai boxers. Tickets can be bought at the stadium or at a travel agents in town.

⊙ Festivals and events

Chiang Mai *p232, maps p234 and p236*
Jan Chiang Mai Winter Fair, 10-day festival held late Dec/early Jan, based in the Municipal Stadium. Exhibitions, Miss Beauty Contest, musical performances.
1st Fri-Sun of Jan Flower Festival. This is a great festival and is centred on the inner moat road, at the southwest corner of the Old City. Small displays of flowers and plants arranged by schools, colleges and professional gardeners and garden shops from across the north. There are also, as you would expect in Thailand, lots of foodstalls as well

as handicrafts. If you have ever felt the urge to grow a papaya tree then this is the place to get your seeds. The highlight is a parade of floral floats along with the requisite beauty contest. If you want to avoid the crowds, come Fri evening.

Mid-Jan Bor Sang Umbrella Fair (outside Chiang Mai) celebrates traditional skills of umbrella-making, and features contests, exhibitions and stalls selling umbrellas and other handicrafts. Miss Bor Sang, a beauty contest, is also held.

13-16 Apr Songkran, traditional Thai New Year (public holiday) celebrated with more enthusiasm in Chiang Mai than elsewhere. Boisterous water-throwing, particularly directed at *farangs*; expect to be soaked to the skin for the entire 4 days.

Mid-Nov Yi Peng Loi Krathong, a popular Buddhist holiday when krathong (boats) filled with flowers and lit candles are floated down the river. Fireworks at night, and small hot-air balloons are launched into the sky.

1st week Dec Nimmanhaemin Arts Festival. Pleasant Soi 1 is closed to traffic and given over to the best of Chiang Mai's designers in what is rapidly becoming on northern Thailand's premium arts festivals.

Lampang *p248*
Feb (movable) Luang Wiang Lakon, 5 important Buddha images are carried through the streets in procession. There is traditional dancing and a light show at Wat Lampang Luang.

O Shopping

Chiang Mai *p232, maps p234 and p236*
Chiang Mai is a shoppers' paradise. It provides many of the treasures of Bangkok, in a compact area. The craft 'villages' on the San Kamphaeng and Hang Dong (Ban Tawai) roads are a popular jaunt of the coach tour, whilst the night market, with its array of handicrafts, antique shops and fake designer shirts, continues to pack the tourists in night

after night. A quieter, less frequented spot, is the group of sophisticated shops, cafés and bars, that have opened up near the Amari Rincome hotel, on Nimmanhaemin Rd, mostly patronized by trendy Thai students and expats. Soi 1 and Soi 4 in particular (where Nimman Promenade is located) are both great little alleys featuring small design boutiques, galleries and coffee shops. Tha Phae Rd is an old favourite and is smartening up its act, with the likes of **Living Space** and **Contemporary Jewellery** opening up. Two department stores at Kad Suan Kaew on Huay Kaew Rd and the Airport Plaza, south of town near the airport, provide focal points for a vast array of shops, including plenty of cheap clothes outlets. The area around Tha Phae Gate becomes pedestrianized on a Sun afternoon and evening to make way for hundreds of food and souvenir stalls and buskers.

If you want to ship your goodies back home **UPS** has a walk-in office at **S&M Parcel Express**, 9 Soi 7 Rajdamnoen Rd, T053-416351, Mon-Sat.

Antiques and lacquerware
There are a number of shops on **Tha Phae Rd**. Another good road to wander along is **Loi Kroa**, which supports a many antique and hilltribe handicraft shops. **Hang Dong Rd** has several places worth a browse, as does the **San Kamphaeng Rd**, towards Bor Sang (take a tuk-tuk or a bus from the north side of Charoen Mang Rd). Beware of fakes. Cheaper lacquerware is available from the night bazaar.
Gong Dee, Soi 1, Nimmaneheiman Rd, T053-225032, www.gongdeegallery.com. Laquerware and handicrafts, famous for the gold leaf decorating their products. Hosts exhibitions by local artists. Recommended.
Masusook Antiques, 263/2-3 Tha Phae Rd. Lacquerware.
Sanpranon Antiques, west side of Hang Dong Rd, about 4 km from Airport Plaza. It's a huge place well worth a visit just to rummage. There's an overwhelming amount of stock (from lacquerware to ceramics to wood-carvings), much of which is not antique.

Art Galleries

There is a vibrant art scene in Chiang Mai. Read the local papers, such as *Chiang Mai City Life* (www.chiangmainews.com) and check out the sois around Nimmanheimin and Charoenrat Rd for news about exhibitions and small new galleries.

Art Space, 7 Sirimankalajarn Rd, Soi 7, artspacecm@gmail.com. The ground floor of this building houses regular exhibitions, whilst the upper floors host drawing classes, music classes and school holiday workshops.

La Luna, 190 Charoenrat Rd, on the eastern side of the river, www.lalunagallery.com. One of a growing number of contemporary art galleries opening up in Chiang Mai. This airy, open-plan space houses abstract works and photography from throughout Southeast Asia. Aso sell a range of high-quality prints.

Suvannabhumi Art Gallery, 116, Chareonrat Rd, T08-1031 5309, www.suvburma-art.com. Art gallery featuring the work of prominent artists from Burma. Not to be missed.

Bookshops

Book Zone, 318 Tha Phae Rd, part of **Asia Books**. Open 0900-2130. This small store sells Thai coffee-table books, a good range of guidebooks, some English-language novels, children's books, magazines and maps.

Gecko Books has opened a 3rd branch on 2 Rachamanka Rd. The other 2 branches are near Thae Pae Gate on 2/6 Chang Moi Kao Rd, and 2 Thae Pae Gate Rd. Big selection of new and used books in English, Dutch, German, French, Swedish, Danish and Norwegian.

Suriwong Book Centre, 54/1-5 Sri Donchai Rd. Most extensive collection of books in English on Thailand in Chiang Mai.

Ceramics and terracotta

Beautiful celadon-glazed ceramics can be found in proliferation in Chiang Mai. San Kamphaeng Rd is as good a place as any to see a number of set-ups. Several of the establishments on this road are selling outlets for small factories on the same site, which are open to visitors. One such place is:

Baan Celadon, 7 Moo 3, Chiangmai-Sankamphaeng Rd, T053-338288. A good range of ceramics for sale from simple everyday bowls to elaborate vases.

Ban Phor Liang Muen, 36 Phra Pokklao Rd. Huge range of terracotta plaques, murals, statues and pots at in outdoor display garden.

Mengrai Kilns, 79/2 Arak Rd, T053-272063. A showroom only, with a good range of celadon-ware. Seconds at reasonable prices.

Siam Celadon, 38 Moo 10, Sankampaeng Rd, T053-331526. Award-winning designs though it is a little far from town.

Clothes

A huge assortment of T-shirts, cotton clothing and tribal clothing can be found in the 3 night markets on **Chang Klang Rd**. See page 728, for more detailed information on the various styles of clothing. Other shops along **Tha Phae Rd** or for more contemporary styles, the 2 shopping centres (**Kad Suan Kaew** on Huay Kaew Rd and **Airport Plaza**) have a good range. The former has some bargains on both the top and basement floors. If you want to have clothes made to measure, see Tailors, below. See also Silk, lace and textiles.

Chabaa, 14/32 Nimman Promenade, Nimmanhaemin Rd, T08-1886 8689 (mob). Tiny shop selling beautiful clothes of the owner's design. A little expensive, worth a look.

Ginger Shop, 199 Moon Muang, T053-419 011. Wide range of clothes and accessories for both men and women. Chic and beautiful, but expensive and somewhat exclusive.

Kad Suan Kaew, Huay Kaew Rd. This is the place to come for cheap clothes. Lots of small shops and stalls mostly concentrated on the top floor, with a few more in the basement and scattered through the complex.

Computers and software

Panthip Plaza, 152/1 Changklan Rd. The Chiang Mai version of the Bangkok classic. Mounds of hardware and mountains of software. Pick up the latest PC and Mac programme copies at a fraction of the cost.

Furniture and rattanware

If you are prepared to ship furniture home, Chiang Mai is an excellent place. For locally made products, **Hang** Dong Rd is your best bet, with plenty of choice (and they can make furniture to order too). There are several shops on the main north–south road, but the best area to look is to the east of Hang Dong – turn left at the junction. There is a strip of shops along here selling an excellent range of furniture, both old and new. The road to Bor Sang (the **San Kamphaeng Rd**, to the northeast of town) is also worth a visit. There are also quite a few shops selling furniture imported from the region. For rattanware there is a good range of cheaper stalls strung out along Route 108 towards Hang Dong, about 10 km south of town.

Hang Dong Rattan, Loi Kroa Rd (near intersection with Kamphaeng Din Rd). High-quality rattan products.

Under the Bo, 22-23 Night Bazaar, also has a shop on the west side of Hang Dong Rd, about 4 km south of the **Airport Plaza**. Fascinating mixture of Indonesian, Bhutanese, Afghan and Pakistani pieces. Worth a visit.

Handicrafts

Chiang Mai is the centre for hilltribe handicrafts. There is a bewildering array of goods, much of which is of poor quality (**Tha Phae Rd** seems to specialize in a poorer range of products). Bargain for everything. The **night market** on Chang Klang Rd also has a lot on offer; but better pieces can be found at the more exclusive shops on **Loi Kroa Rd**.

Chakhriya, 14/7 Nimman Promenade, Nimmanhaemin Rd, T08-1952 5773 (mob). Small boutique selling everything from candle holders and frames to bowls and ashtrays.

Co-op Handicraft, Tha Phae Rd, next to Thai Farmer's Bank.

Thai Tribal Crafts, 208 Bumrungrat Rd, near McCormick Hospital – run by Karen and Lahu church organizations on a non-profit basis. Good selection, quality and prices.

Interior design

Undoubtedly the best place outside Bangkok to find good-quality 'decorative items' and contemporary furniture for your home. Probably the best concentration of shops of this kind is on **Nimmanhaemin Rd**, west of town, opposite the Amari Rincome hotel, but **Charoenrat Rd** is also well worth a visit.

Aesthetic Accessories, 50-60 Rachmanka Rd, opposite **Anodard Hotel**, T053-278659. Not to be confused with the other Aesthetic opposite **Amari Rincome** hotel, this is a great little place selling beautiful small-scale 'accessories'. Quite pricey by Thai standards.

Aesthetic Studio, 95/12 Nimmanhaemin Rd, opposite **Amari Rincome** hotel, T053-222026, shop@aesthetic-studio.com. Fabulous little place with some really interesting pieces from clocks to lamps to glass and ceramics.

In Bloom, 14/27 Nimman Promenade, Nimmanahaemin Rd. A small shop offering funky and alternative home accessories, ranging from doors mats and coffee table books to bright pink Buddha money banks.

King's Kid, 14/10 Nimman Promenade, Nimmanhaemin Rd, T053-217340. Specializes in handmade decorations and toys for children. Also offer a small variety of furniture.

Villa Cini, 30, 32 and 34 Charoenrat Rd, T053-244025. Beautiful range of textiles and antiques, high-quality products displayed in sophisticated surroundings makes for inflated prices, but it's fun to browse here. Also has a small restaurant in the courtyard.

Jewellery and silverwork

Chiang Mai now offers some contemporary designed jewellery. A good starting point is **Tha Phae Rd**, where there is a strip of about 5 shops near the Thai Farmers Bank.

For more traditional, Thai-style silverwork, make your way to **Wualai Rd** which runs off the southern moat road. There are quite a number of shops and workshops down here on both sides of the road.

Bijoux, 145 Changkan, A Muang, T08-1764 9419 (mob), near the night bazaar. Range of beaded handcrafted jewellery and gems.

Old Silver, 59/3 Loi Kroa Rd, and **Sipsong Panna Silver**, 95/19 Nimmanhaemin Rd. Sell traditional and modern silver jewellery. **Shiraz Jewelry**, 170 Tha Phae Rd, T053-252382. A long-established gem shop.

Night markets
Situated on the west and east sides of Chang Klang Rd, Chiang Mai's multiple night markets are now a major tourist attraction and consist of 2- or 3-storey purpose-built structures containing countless stalls. It is an excellent place to browse and, along with a wide range of tribal handicrafts, it is possible to buy T-shirts, watches, cheap CDs, leather goods, children's clothes and Burmese 'antiques'. In addition, there are some better-quality shops selling jewellery, antiques and silks (both ready-made and lengths) on the 1st floor of the Viang Ping Building. Most stalls and shops open at about 1800 and close around 2300.
Huay Kaew Rd night market, north of Nimmanhaemin Rd. Daily 1800-2300. Caters mainly to students and offers cheap clothes, shoes, accessories, and food.
Mae Jo, 287 Chiang Mai-Mae Jo Rd. Sells fresh food, plants and household items.
Warorot Market, north of Tha Phae Rd. Clothing, fabric, sportswear, handicrafts.
Wualai Rd, south of the moat, turns into a walking street on Sat 1700-2300. Here you can find everything from cheap clothing and home-made jewellery to art, make-up and kitchenware. Popular with locals.

Paper products
There is now a proliferation of shops selling handmade paper products. The best place to find paper is along San Kamphaeng Rd, where there are many small-scale operations making paper. Take the lane to the west just before Chiang Mai Sudaluck, and before the Bor Sang junction, signposted to Preservation House. If you are stuck in town, then try **HQ Paper Maker**, 3/31 Samlarn Rd, behind Wat Phra Singh.

Silk, lace and textiles
For a good range of textiles, it is worth walking down Loi Kroa Rd, east of the city wall.
Chatraporn, 194 Tha Phae Rd. For silks, cotton and made-up garments.
Classic Lanna Thai, night bazaar, upper floor, far right-hand corner. Fabulous range of well-designed jackets, dresses and blouses. Also sells antique silk. Will make to measure.
The Loom Textile Gallery, 90 Rajchiang Sean Rd, T053-278892. Wooden Thai house with a good range of textiles, old and new.
Nandakwang, 6/1-3 Nimmanhaemin Rd, opposite **Amari Rincome** hotel, T053-222261, also 3rd floor, **Chiang Inn Plaza**, Chiang Klan Rd, T053-281356. Loose-weave cotton 'homespun creations', ranging from napkins to cushion covers to bedspreads to made-up clothing. Attractive range of colours. Also some ceramics (brightly coloured coffee cups).
Pothong House, 4 Moon Muang Soi 5. For Khmer, Lao and hilltribe fabrics.
Sarapee Handmade Lace, 2 Rachwithi Rd. Claims to be the only lace workshop in Southeast Asia using silk thread.
Shinawatra Silk, Huay Kaew Rd (opposite **Chiang Mai Orchid Hotel**). For the usual array of silk products: specs cases, silk frames, ties, scarves, and endless bolts of fabric. Hardly funky, but a good stop for stocking fillers.

Supermarkets and department stores
Central Department Store, in the Kad Suan Kaew shopping complex on Huay Kaew Rd. The largest department store; there is a Tops supermarket in the basement.
Lotus/Tesco, Hang Dong Rd, about 3 km south of **Airport Plaza**. Household goods, clothing, electrical goods and a big super-market, with a good range of fresh fruit and vegetables, and some Western foods.
Rimping Supermarket, 171 Chotana Rd, by **Novotel**. One of the better small central supermarkets for Western foods (including good cheeses, salads, cold meats and pâtés).
Robinsons department store and **Tops** supermarket provide good selection of clothing, household goods and Western food.

Tailors
Big Boss, 99/8 Loi Kroh Rd, T053-818953. Friendly staff and a fantastic range of silks.
Far Mee, 66 Square U Pakut, Tha Phae Rd. Many of the stalls in and around Warorot Market will make up clothes. Walk north along Vichayanon Rd from Tha Phae Rd.

Woodcarving
Many outlets along Tha Phae Rd sell carved wooden trinkets.
Ban Tawai, a woodcarving centre about 3 km east of Hang Dong. This place began life as a wood-carving village, and has been colonized and now overgrown by shops and stalls selling everything from frogs to grandiose sculptures. Packing services available.
Ratana House, 284 Chiang Mai-Hang Dong Rd, east side, T053-271734. Huge range of goods from Burmese lacquerware to wood products of all descriptions, from chests and cupboards tocandlesticks and wooden frogs.

Lampang *p248, map p249*
Ceramics
Lampang is famous for its ceramics. There are more than 50 factories in and around the town; a number are to be found to the west along Phahonyothin Rd (eg, **Chao Lampang** and **Ceramic Art** at 246/1) and Route 1 towards Ko Kha (eg, **Art Lampang**). International outlets selling seconds very cheaply can also be found near Lampang; ask at the TAT office in Chiang Mai for details.

Handicrafts
Lampang Plaza, on Ropwiang Rd near the clock tower, stalls sell an assortment of knick-knacks like wind chimes, shells and ceramics.
Northern Handicraft Hilltribe Shopping Centre, not as grand as it sounds.

▲ Activities and tours

Chiang Mai *p232, maps p234 and p236*
Latest information on sports is listed in most free newspapers and newsletters, available from many shops, hotels and guesthouses. See the **Mae Sa Craft Village**, page 246, for its activities.

Boat trips
Evening departures from the **Riverside Restaurant** on Charoenrat Rd for trips on the Ping River. ฿50 a head, minimum 2 people.

Bungee jumping
Jungle Bungey Jump, T053-298442.

Cookery courses
Baan Thai, 11 Rachdamnern Rd, T053-357 339, info@cookinthai.com. All day, hands-on lesson for ฿700. Provides free transportation to and from your guesthouse.
Chiang Mai Thai Cookery School, book through 47/2 Moon Muang Rd, T053-206388, www.thaicookeryschool.com. One of the best. Runs a variety of courses from ฿990 for one day. Contact Samphon and Elizabeth Nabnian. Course take place at **The Wok**, 44 Rachmanka Rd, although some sessions are in a charming rural location outside town.
Eagle II Guesthouse, (see Sleeping, above). Run recommended cookery courses.
Siam Kitchen, Rachdamnern Soi 4, beside Gap House, T053-213415, siam-kitchen@ bangkok.com. Attractively laid out with pleasant seating areas to relax in after slaving over a hot stove.
Thai Kitchen Cookery School, 25 Moon Muang Rd, Soi 9, T053-219896. Run by Prathuang (Tim) Impraphai, who speaks good English (having worked as a chef in Canada for 3 years), a full day's course with a recipe book costs ฿700 – a good deal.
Tom Yam Cookery School, Lake View Park II, Maejo Rd, T053-844877. 15 mins from Chiang Mai (free pick-up, swimming pool available at lunchtime). Book (and more information) at 2 Rachmanka Rd.
You Sabai Home, Baan Thai Project, Mae Teang, T08-6096 6439, www.yousabai.com/ index.html. Run by Yao and her husband, both English-speakers. Offer 4-day organic vegetarian cookery course at their farm.

Trekking around Chiang Mai

There are scores of trekking companies in Chiang Mai and hundreds of places selling trekking tours. Competition is stiff and most companies provide roughly the same assortment of treks, ranging from one night to over a week. Not many places actually organize the trek themselves and it is rare to meet the guide – or other people in the group – before leaving for the trek. The quality of the guide rather than the organizing company usually makes the trip successful or not and the happiest trekkers are often those who have done their homework and found a company with long-term, permanent staff who they can meet beforehand.

For further information, see Background, page 716. See also Tour operators, page 271.

Like many other areas of tourism, trekking is suffering from its own success. Companies organizing treks are finding it increasingly difficult to present their products as authentic get-away-from-it-all adventures when there is such a high probability of bumping into another group of tourists. As numbers increase so travellers are demanding more authenticity in their trekking experiences. The answer is to avoid the environs of Chiang Mai and trek in less pressured areas like Mae Hong Son, Nan and Pai. Many trek operators – like those along Moon Muang Road – are advertising special non-tourist routes, although these so-called special routes are virtually indistinguishable from established routes. Some companies even claim to offer a money-back guarantee should they come into contact with other trekkers.

The TAT office distributes a list of recommended trekking operators and a leaflet on what to look out for when choosing your trip. The Tribal Research Institute (see page 242), situated at the back of the Chiang Mai University campus on Huay Kaew Rd, provides information on the various hilltribes, maps of the trekking areas, and a library of books on these fascinating people. You can also download a useful pdf file from their website, www.chmai.com/tribal/content.html.

When to trek The best time to trek is during the cool, dry season between October and February. In March and April, although it is dry, temperatures can be high and the vegetation is parched. During the wet season, paths are muddy and walking can be difficult.

What to take Trekkers who leave their cards for safekeeping in their guesthouses have sometimes found that a large bill awaits them on their return. A safety deposit box hired at a bank is the safest way to leave your valuables ((banks on Tha Phae Road have safety deposits and charge about ฿200 per month).

Stay in simple earthen huts, participate in breakfast yoga and enjoy the stunning scenery. Phone for prices. Recommended.

Fitness and sports centres
Hash House Harriers. The hashes are fortnightly, Sat evening for men and women, Mon for men. Contact either David or Martin on T053-278503, or John on T053-271950, or the **Domino Bar**, T053-278503.

Hillside Fitness Centre, 4th floor, Hillside Plaza 4, Huay Kaew Rd, T053-225984. Fitness centre, sauna and herbal steam rooms, beauty treatment.

Huay Kaew Fitness Park, Huay Kaew Rd, at the bottom of Doi Suthep, near the zoo.

Trekking companies should advise on what to take and many provide rucksacks, sleeping bags, first-aid kits and food. However, the following is a checklist of items that might be useful: good walking shoes; bed sheet (blanket/sleeping bag in the cold season November-February); waterproof (July-October); insect repellent; toiletries (soap, toothpaste, toilet papre); small first-aid kit (including antiseptic, plasters, diarrhoea pills, salt tablets); sun protection (suncream/sun hat); photocopy of passport (if venturing into border area); and water bottle (to cut down on the plastic bottles accumulating in the hills in the north). Remember to take protection against mosquitoes; long trousers and long-sleeved shirts are essential for the night-time.

Choosing a trekking company When choosing a guide for the trip, ensure that he or she can speak the hilltribe dialect as well as good English (or French, German etc). Guides must hold a 'Professional Guide Licence'. Treks must be registered with the Tourist Police; to do this the guide must supply the Tourist Police with a photocopy of the Identity page of your passport and your date of entry stamp. You can check on a company's reputation by contacting the police department. Note that the best guides may move between companies or work for more than one.

Health precautions By living in hilltribe villages, even if only for a few days, the health hazard is amplified significantly. Inoculation against hepatitis and protection against malaria are both strongly recommended. Particular dietary care should be exercised: do not drink unboiled or untreated water and avoid uncooked vegetables. Although the hilltribe population may look healthy, remember that the incidence of parasitic infection in most communities is not far off 100%.

Costs It does not take long to work out the going price for a trek – just ask around. For a basic walking trek, costs are ฿250-500 per day, the cheaper end of the the range relating to trekking companies that specialize in the backpacking market; if rafting and elephant rides are also included, the cost rises to ฿500-1000 per day. Many trekking companies and some guesthouses take donations to help support the hill people, and in particular the many thousands of displaced refugees from Burma.

Opium smoking For some, one of the attractions of trekking is the chance to smoke opium. It should be remembered that opium smoking, as well as opium cultivation, is illegal in Thailand. It is also not unusual for first-time users to experience adverse physical and psychological side effects. Police regularly stop and search tourists who are motorcycle trekking. Be careful not to carry any illicit substances.

Go-karting

Chiang Mai Speedway, 8 km out of town on Route 108, T053-430059. Racing every Sat and Sun afternoon, daily 0930-1900.
Chiang Mai Gokart, San Kamphaeng Rd, near Bor Sang intersection.

Golf

Information on golf in Thailand can be found at www.thailandamazinggolf.com.
Lanna Public Golf Course, Chotana Rd (at Nong Bua, 4 km north of the city). A woodland course. Green fee ฿500, ฿700 at weekends, club hire ฿300. Open 0600-1930. There is also a driving range here.

Gymkhana Club, Chiangmai–Lamphun Rd, 9-hole course, green fees ฿100 weekdays, ฿400 weekends.

Horse riding
Lanna Sports Centre, Chotana Rd (north of town), ฿250 per hr, call Janet, T053-217956.

Meditation, t'ai chi and yoga
Holstic Self-Empowerment Center, 46 Tewan Rd, T053-406007, h_s_empower@ hotmail.com. Meditation for people of all ages.
Khun Wai, Huay Kaew Rd. Mon-Sat 0800-1800. Yoga ฿100 per hr.
Raja Yoga Meditation Centre, 218/6 Chotana Rd, T053-214904.
T'ai Chi, T08-1706 7406 (mob), www.taichi thailand.com. Classes start on the 1st and 16th day of each month.

Organic Farms
Pun Pun, Ban Mae Joe, Mae Taeng, T08-147 0461, www.punpunthailand.org. Run by Jo and his American wife Peggy, a seed-saving operation and sustainable living and learning centre based about 50km north of Chiang Mai. They offer internships, overnight stays and short courses. A great place to get away from the city for a couple of days.

Spas
Oasis Spa, 102 Sirimangkalajan Rd, T053-815 000. Luxurious day spa, offering massages, aromatherapy and herbal scrubs and steams.
RarinJinda, 14 Chareonraj Rd, T 053-247000, www.rarinjinda.com. Guava foot polisher and Tibetan sound therapy. Yoga and aerobics studio, gym, pools, sauna, steam rooms and a whirlpool with chromotherapy. Pricey.
Sinativa Spa, 22/1 Nimmanheimen Rd, T053-217928, www.sinativaspaclub.com. Packages including herbal baths and steams, Swedish, Thai and Shiatsu massages, and facials.
Tao Garden Health Resort, 274 Moo 7, Luang Nua Doi Saket, T053-495596, www.tao-garden.com. An expensive alcohol- and smoke-free retreat organized around ancient Chinese Tao practices. Treatments

begin with a Chinese medical check-up, after which you can access massages, detox methods and aromatherapies. Guests can also attend courses in order to learn more about Taoist shamanism or nutrition, and participate in daily yoga and meditation.

Swimming
700 Stadium, Canal Rd. Olympic-sized pool built for the 1997 ASEAN games. ฿50.
Chiang Mai University, west of town, see map, page 236. You will need an annual membership card (฿300) to swim here. Good if you're staying a while.
Lotus-Pang Suan Kaew Hotel, see Sleeping. Has a big rooftop pool, 0900-2100 (฿70).
The Real Centre of the Universe, T08-1473 0746, www.therealcentreoftheuniverse.com. Saltwater pool, set in a quiet garden north-west of town. ฿200.

Tennis
Amari Rincome Hotel, Anantasiri Courts, 'super highway' (near the National Museum). Fees are about ฿100 per hr; rackets for hire.

Therapies
Massage There are umpteen places in town offering massage. They tend to charge around the same amount (฿200 per hr). Many masseuses seem to have had rudimentary training and the massage rooms consist of mattresses laid on the floors of upper rooms. The experience may be pleasant enough, but don't expect your sinuses to clear or your lower colon to sort itself out. For a traditional Thai massage, it is best to avoid the places geared to tourists around Tha Phae Gate.

In an unusual rehabilitation initiative, **Chiang Mai's women's jail**, sited on Ratch-awithi Rd in the middle of the old city, has opened a spa (T08-1706 1041) staffed entirely by female prisoners. Here, the paying public can get body and foot massages, herbal steam and a variety of beauty treatments. Almost all of the money goes directly to the masseuse, helping them to get ready for when they are released.

Motorbiking in Northern Thailand

Renting a motorbike to explore Thailand's north is fast-becoming one of the most popular ways to tour this part of the kingdom. Bike rental and fuel is relatively cheap, with everything from 50cc automatic mopeds through to giant 1200cc BMWs on offer in Chiang Mai.

If you plan to ride a bike then your first port of call should be the Golden Triangle Rider's website and forum, www.gt-rider.com. Put together by David Unkovich, an Australian expat with over 25 years' experience of riding in northern Thailand, you'll find everything you need right down to road surfaces, suggestions for the best food and accommodation, reviews of Chiang Mai's different rental outlets and even safety tips. Unkovich also produces a set of essential maps that cover the north of Thailand in great detail and include some off-road trails. These maps are on sale in many outlets in Chiang Mai – the more expensive laminated one is almost indestructible.

"If you have a week, the best route is to head for the far north," says Unkovich. "Head north from Chiang Mai to Doi Ang Khang, a mountain-top high above the Burmese border, before carrying on up to Tha Ton and Mae Salong. Pass through Doi Tung towards Mae Sai, through the Golden Triangle and along the Mekong to Chiang Khong. Nearby is Phu Chi Fah, where a dramatic mountain road edges along the Laos border. From there swing south to Nan on the 1148 – bikers' paradise – and from Nan it's a few hours back to Chiang Mai. Just rent a bike and get on with it. You won't need a guide."

Let's Relax, Chiang Mai Plaza (basement), Chang Klang Rd, T053-818498, and **Chiang Mai Pavilion Plaza** (2nd floor, above McDonald's), both branches, in the night market, offer a more upmarket experience: foot, hand and back massage in clean, a/c surroundings, and the masseuses seem to know a bit more about what they are doing. More expensive at around ฿250 for 45 mins.
Wat Umong, a couple of kilometres west of the city centre. If visited at the weekends you will have to wait your turn, it's very popular with locals for a traditional Thai massage. Cheap at ฿99 for 1 hr and very good.
Massage courses For those who want to find out more about Thai massage, a number of courses are available.
ITM (Institute of Thai Massage), 17/7 Morokot Rd, T053-218632. Offers 5- to 10-day courses in basic, intermediate and advanced Thai massage, 0900-1600; courses begin on Mon and cost ฿1500 – the 'Master Teacher' Chongkol Setthakorn is well qualified.

Moh Shivagakomarpaj Foundation, Old Chiang Mai Traditional Hospital, 238/8 Wuolai Rd, T053-275085, www.thaimassage school.ac.th. Courses last 11 days (fee ฿2770) from the beginning and middle of the month.

Tours and tour operators
See also Trekking, below. Many of the larger tour companies and travel agents arrange visas and tours to Burma, Cambodia, Laos and Vietnam. Laos, US$30 on arrival or US$20 pre-arranged (30 days); Burma, ฿1500 (30 days); Vietnam, ฿2600 (30 days). Visas take 3-7 days.

A range of day tours run from Chiang Mai. Prices seem to vary between companies; examples of tours include: Wat Phrathat Doi Suthep, the Phu Ping Palace and a Meo village (฿600-800); the Mae Sa Valley to visit a waterfall, orchid farm and elephants at work (฿800); Doi Inthanon National Park (฿900-1300); Bor Sang (the Umbrella village) and San Kamphaeng (฿100-200); Chiang Rai and the Golden Triangle (฿750); the Sukhothai Historical Park over 200 km south (฿1500). A ride on an elephant, bamboo rafting and a visit to an orchid farm cost ฿800.

Make sure you know exactly what is included in the price; some travellers have complained of hidden costs such as road tolls, tips for guides, entrance fees, etc. It is advisable to shop around to secure the best deal. Most tour operators are concentrated around Tha Phae Gate, Chang Klang and Moon Muang (near Tha Phae Gate), so this process is not as time consuming as it may seem. Most operators will also book air, train and bus tickets out of Chiang Mai.

The TAT recommends that services should only be bought from companies that register with the tourist Business and Guide Registration Office. It provides a list of all such companies. As noted in the trekking section, we have decided not to list or recommend companies because standards vary between tours (and guides) within individual outfits, and because these standards can change rapidly. Word of mouth is the best guarantee. Exceptions are:
Chiang Mai Green Tour and Trekking, 29-31 Chiang Mai-Lamphun Rd, A Muang, Chiang Mai 50000, F053-247374, cmgreent@ chiangmai.a-net.net.th. A notable operator that tries to provide eco-friendly and culturally sensitive tours. However, the motorbike treks can hardly be described as eco-friendly.
Click and Travel Ltd, www.clickandtravel online.com. A young 'Soft Adventure Company' specializing in bicycle tours.
North Pearl Travel, 332/334 Tha Phae Rd, T/F053-232976.

Trekking companies
Many companies are concentrated along Tha Phae, Chaiyaphum, Moon Muang and Kotchasan roads. Standards change so very rapidly that recommending companies is a dangerous business, but the safest bet is to find somewhere with permanent, long-term staff, such as: **Chiang Mai Garden Guesthouse**, 82-86 Rachamanka Rd, T053-278881, and

Panda Tour Guesthouse, 130/1 Rachmanka Rd, T053-206420, www.pandatour.com.

Prices for treks are variable with 2-day trips costing between ฿1600-1800, 3-day treks ฿1700-2000 and 4 days ฿2000-2400. Be aware that the better trips do usually cost more, either because they're more off the beaten track and therefore further away, or because the company is paying for one of the better guides, who are worth their weight in gold. If you find a trek for a price that seems too good to be true, it probably is.

Lampang *p248, map p249*
Massage
Northern Herbal Medicine Society, opposite Wat Prakaew Don Tao. Traditional Thai massage – good value at ฿150 per hr, 108 herbs available for the full treatment.

⊖ Transport

Chiang Mai *p232, maps p234 and p236*
Air
The situation with the different airlines is very fluid, with budget operators appearing for a short period and then going bust. At the time of writing numerous airlines – THAI, Air Asia, SGA, Nok, 1-2 Go, PB and Bangkok Airways – connect Chiang Mai with various domestic and regional destinations, including **Bangkok** (all), **Phuket** (THAI), **Mae Hong Son** (Nok, THAI), **Kuala Lumpur** (Air Asia), **Sukhothai** (Bangkok Airways), **Pai** (SGA), **Udon Thani** (Nok). Air Mandalay fly to **Mandalay** and **Rangoon** (Burma), Silk and Tiger Air fly to **Singapore**, China Airlines fly to Taipei (Taiwan), HK Express fly to **Hong Kong**, Bangkok Airways fly to **Chang Rung** (Burma), **Luang Prabang** and **Vientiane** (Laos). THAI also fly to **Kunming** (China), **Chittagong** (Bangladesh), **Frankfurt** (Germany) and **Tokyo** (Japan).

Airline offices Air Mandalay (Skybird Tour), 92/3 Sri Donchai Rd, T053-818049. Bangkok Airways, Chiang Mai International Airport, T053-922258.

From Chiang Mai Arcade Bus Station

Fares are guidelines and include the range from standard to air-conditioned.

Destination	Journey time	Distance	Price (baht)
Bangkok	10-12 hrs	726 km	200-800 (VIP)
Chiang Rai	3 hrs	194 km	70-145
Chiang Saen & Golden Triangle	5 hrs	265 km	90-160
Mae Sai	4.5 hrs	256 km	90-160
Mae Hong Son	8 hrs	359 km	130-270
Pai	4 hrs	137 km	65-120
Chiang Khong	6 hrs	337 km	90-160
Phrae	4 hrs	216 km	75-130
Nan	6 hrs	338 km	130-250
Lampang	2 hrs	97 km	40
Mae Sot (via Tak)	6 hrs	393 km	130-250
Phitsanulok	6 hrs	428 km	120-250
Sukhothai	5 hrs	373 km	125-180
Udon Thani	12 hrs	712 km	220-400
Nakhon Ratchasima	12 hrs	756 km	230-410
Ubon Ratchathani	15 hrs	1055 km	320-600
Rayong/Pattaya	15 hrs	990 km	300-600

Bicycle

Available from Chang Phuak Gate, southern end of Moon Muang Rd, ฿50 per day, or on Nakhon Ping Bridge, plus some guesthouses. **Bike & Bite**, 23/1 Sri Phum Rd, T053-418534. A deposit or your passport will probably be required. Mountain bikes should be locked. **The Wild Planet Adventure**, Charoen Prathet Rd, T053-277178.

Bus

The long-distance bus station is northeast of town, and most companies provide a transfer service: pick-up points are Anusarn Market, Narawat Bridge, Sang Tawan Cinema and Chiang Inn Hotel Lane. There is an information desk in the main terminal building, with times and prices. **Bangkok**'s Northern bus terminal (9-12 hrs), **Phitsanulok** (6 hrs), **Sukhothai** (5 hrs), **Chiang Rai** (3-4 hrs, see below), **Mae Sariang** (4-5 hrs), **Mae Hong Son** (8-9 hrs), **Pai** (4 hrs), **Nan** (6 hrs) and other northern towns. A number of tour companies organize coaches to the capital; these are concentrated in the Anusarn Market area and usually provide transport to the Arcade terminal, from where the buses depart. Buses to closer destinations (such as **Mae Rim, Phrao, Chiang Dao, Fang, Tha Ton** and **Lamphun**) go from Chotana Rd, north of Chang Puak Gate. For **Pasang**, there are direct buses from the Arcade Bus Station, or catch a bus to Lamphun (1 hr, ฿12) and then a connecting bus to Pasang (45 mins, ฿15). For **Bor Sang** and **San Kamphaeng** take a red bus running along the north side of Charoen Muang Rd, opposite the San Pa Khoi Market east of the Narawat Bridge, or take a bus from Chiang Puak Gate.

To **Chiang Rai**, buses taking the *sai kao* (old route) leave from the Old Lamphun Rd, near Narawat Bridge; those on the *sai mai* (new route) leave from Arcade bus station, northeast of the city on the 'super highway'. The old route is via Lampang and Phayao (6 hrs); the new route takes Route 1019, via Doi Saket, Wiang Papao hot springs (4 hrs).

Car or jeep hire

Rates start at ฿800-1800 per day, ฿6000 per week. Many guesthouses will arrange rental or there are outfits along Chaiyaphum and Moon Muang roads. **National** and **Avis** are slightly more expensive, but are more reliable. **Avis**, Royal Princess Hotel, T053-281033, or the airport, T053-201574.

North Wheels, 127/2 Moon Muang Rd, T053-216189, www.northwheels.com. Some cars have seen better days. Competitive.

SMT Rent-a-car (aka **National**), Amari Rincome hotel, smtcar@samart.co.th.

Motorbike hire

Wearing helmets is compulsory (but you wouldn't know it) and you are supposed to have a valid motorbike licence. If you don't have these things, you may have to pay ฿200 baht upwards if stopped by the traffic police.

Motorbike hire is available along Chaiy-uphum Rd, Moon Muang Rd and at many guesthouses. Rates start at about ฿150-200 for a Honda Dream and rise up to ฿1200 for a chopper or sports bike. Insurance is not available for small bikes and most policies only protect you from 50% of the repair costs. **Mr Mechanic**, 4 Soi 5 Moon Muang Rd; 135/1 Ratchaphakhinai Rd, T053-214708, T08-1882 4402 (mob), T08-1530 8518 (mob), www.mr-mechanic1994.com. Motorcycle rentals for on- and off-road. GT Rider recommended.

Train

Ticket office is open 0500-2100. Information, T053-244795; reservations T053-242094. Left luggage 0600-1800, ฿5 per bag for first 5 days, ฿10 per bag from then on.

Bangkok's Hualamphong station and towns along the route (11-15 hrs).

Lampang p248, map p249

Air

Daily flights to **Bangkok** via **Phitsanulok**.

Airline offices THAI, 314 Sanambin Rd, T054-217078.

Bus

Bangkok's Northern bus terminal (9 hrs), **Chiang Mai** (2 hrs), **Chiang Rai**, **Sukhothai**, **Tak** and **Phitsanulok**. Buses from Chiang Mai leave from the Old Chiang Mai–Lamphun Rd, near the tourist office. Buses also go east to **Phrae** (2½ hrs) and on to **Nan**; 1 every hr.

Train

Bangkok (12 hrs) and **Chiang Mai** (2 hrs).

❶ Directory

Chiang Mai *p232, maps p234 and p236*
Banks Tha Phae Rd; exchange services along Chang Klang and Tha Phae roads. Exchange booths open daily 0800-2000. Most banks offer a safety deposit service, about ฿200 per month. Good rates at SK, 73/8 Charoen Prathet Rd. **Consulates** Australia, 165 Sirimungklajarn Rd, T053-213473. French Honorary Consulate, 138 Charoen Prathet Rd, T053-281466. India, 304 Charoenrat Rd, T053-243066. Japan, Suite 104-107, Airport Business Park, 90 Mahidol Rd, T053-203367. People's Republic of China, 111 Changlor Rd, T053-200525, F053-274614. Sweden, Green Valley, Mae Rim, T053-298632. UK,198 Bumrungrat Rd, T053-263015. USA, 387 Vichayanon Rd, T053-252629. **Emergencies** T191. **Immigration office** Fang Rd, 300 m before the entrance to the airport, T053-277 510. Mon-Fri 0830-1200, 1300-1630 (visa extensions possible, see page 71). **Internet** Dozens of internet places around town, ฿1-2 per min in tourist areas. **Language schools** AUA, 73 Rachdamnern Rd, T053-278407. For a more serious look at the Thai language, AUA teaches in 60-hr modules, also offers some conversation classes. CEC, Nimmanhaemin Rd, west side, T053-895202. Open 0800-2100, private tuition here for around ฿200 per hr. Watana Language Centre, Phra Pokklao Rd, T053-278 464, 0900-2000, ฿20 per hr and learn about Thai culture. **Libraries** 21/1 Rachmanka Rd,

Soi 2. Mon-Sat, advice on routes, books on Thailand and novels available; AUA (see above) has a small but nice library; Chiang Mai University's **Tribal Research Institute** is a useful information source for people going trekking – see pages 268 and 269. **Raintree Resource Centre**, Charoenrat Rd (by Nawarat Bridge), small English-language lending library, daily 1000-1200. **Medical services** Chiang Mai's medical services have a good reputation. The most popular expat hospital is **Ram**, open 24-hrs, with English-speaking doctors. **Chiang Mai Ram Hospital**, Boonruangrit Rd, T053-224851/224881. McCormick Hospital, Kaew Nawarat Rd, T053-241010, **Malaria Centre**, Boonruangrit Rd, north of Suan Dok Gate. Out-patient fees ฿100-140, emergency fees are not exorbitant. Dentist: **Dr Pramote's Clinic**, 206 Vichayanon Rd, T053-234453. Ram Hospital also has a good dental clinic. **Police** Corner of Phra Singh and Jhaban roads. **Tourist Police**: in the same building as the TAT office on the Chiang Mai-Lamphon Rd, T053-248974, at the Arcade Bus Station, the night market and at the airport. **Post office** General Post Office, Charoen Muang Rd, 24 hrs, T053-241 056; **Mae Ping Post Office** Praisani Rd, packing service, more conveniently situated than the GPO, offers international telephone facility; **Phra Singh Post Office**, near Wat Phra Singh; **Sriphum Post Office**, Phra Pokklao Rd; **Night Bazaar Post Office**; in the basement of the bazaar, Chang Klang Rd, open until 2300; **Rachdamnern Post Office** , convenient for many guesthouses on Moon Muang Rd, packing service available, daily 0830-2200. **Telephone** International calls can be made from the post offices on Charoen Muang and Praisani roads and at the airport. Travel agents in town offer overseas call and fax services.

Lampang *p248, map p249*
Banks Siam Commercial, Chatchai Rd; Thai Farmers, 284/8 Chatchai Rd; Thai Military, 173-75 Chatchai Rd. **Medical services** Khelang Nakom Hospital, Phahonyothin Rd, T054-217045. **Post office** Surain Rd.

Western loop: Pai, Mae Hong Son, Mae Sariang

Some of the most spectacular scenery in Thailand lies to the west of Chiang Mai, where the Tenasserim range divides Burma from Thailand. Travelling northwest from Chiang Mai on Route 107, then Route 108, the road passes through the Mae Sa Valley to the popular backpacker and trekking town of Pai, a distance of 140 km. From Pai to Soppong is more stunning scenery, then onto the hill town of Mae Hong Son, a centre for trekking and home to fine Burmese-style wats. Due south to Mae Sariang (160 km from Mae Hong Son), close to the Burmese border, there is some more excellent trekking, then the road follows narrow river valleys to Doi Inthanon, one of the country's most famous peaks and national parks. ▸▸ For listings, pages 282-289.

Pai ○○○○▲○○ ▸▸ pp282-289. Colour map 1, A2.

The road from Chiang Mai winds its way through scintillating landscapes and thick forest until the view unfolds into a broad valley. In the middle, encircled by handsome, high

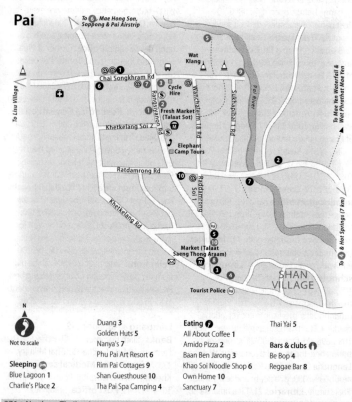

Not to scale

Sleeping ○
Blue Lagoon 1
Charlie's Place 2
Duang 3
Golden Huts 5
Nanya's 7
Phu Pai Art Resort 6
Rim Pai Cottages 9
Shan Guesthouse 10
Tha Pai Spa Camping 4

Eating ○
All About Coffee 1
Amido Pizza 2
Baan Ben Jarong 3
Khao Soi Noodle Shop 6
Own Home 10
Sanctuary 7
Thai Yai 5

Bars & clubs ○
Be Bop 4
Reggae Bar 8

ridges, sits Pai. Over the last 25 years this small mountain village has transformed itself into one of Northern Thailand's most popular destinations. These days, with its organic eateries and reggae bars Pai could be considered a travellers' oasis. Even hip young city dwellers from Bangkok are slowly catching onto the area's beauty, facilities, hot springs and diversity – Lisu, Karen, Shan, Red Lahu, Kuomintang-Chinese are all represented. But in January 2008 Pai's idyllic charms were somewhat shattered by the shooting of two, young Canadian backpackers by a drunk, off-duty Thai policeman.

However, Pai's tourist trade appears robust enough to survive such events. There's excellent trekking, superb rafting, a plethora of places to get massaged and pummelled, some great food and the town still manages to retain a sense of charm. The range of accommodation is also huge – everything from boutique spa resorts through to cheap and nasty huts populated with wasted travellers. All this makes Pai seductive to the visitor who likes to consume their experience rather create it. Don't come here thinking you're going to get an authentic slice of Thai life. This is a generic, contrived Khaosan Road-style experience, though, admittedly, in very pleasant surroundings. Helping to cement Pai's growing status, an airstrip has opened just to the north of town with a couple of flights a day linking Pai with Chiang Mai.

There are two markets in town – the *talaat sot* (fresh market) on Rangsiyanon Road and the *talaat saeng thong araam* on Khetkelang Road. The finest monastery in town is Thai Yai-style **Wat Klang** near the bus station. There's another monastery, **Wat Phrathat Mae Yen**, about 1.5 km east of town, on a hill. Head a further 3 km east and you'll arrive at Pai's famous **hot springs**. The sulphurous water bubbles up through a systems of streams – bring a towel and jump in. There's also a campsite here.

Lisu, **Shan**, **Red Lahu** and **Kuomintang-Chinese villages** are all in the vicinity. Most guesthouses provide rough maps detailing hilltribe villages, hot springs, caves, waterfalls and other sights. For further information on hilltribes and trekking, see Chiang Mai page 268 and Background page 716. For activities such as rafting, elephant safaris, cookery and aromatherapy classes, see Activities and tours, page 287.

Soppong ⊖❼⊖❻ ▶ *pp282-289. Colour map 1, A2.*

Soppong, or Phang Ma Pha, is a small way station between Pai and Mae Hong Son. It is slowly metamorphosing into an alternative to Pai – there's no real backpacker 'scene' here, though there a few great guesthouses offering a decent array of trekking services. Many people come here to trek and explore the surrounding countryside. Most of the guesthouses organize treks and this is one of the best bases hereabouts. Local villages include Lisu, Black and Red Lahu, and Shan. This is also a good place to escape to if what you want to do is nothing. The journey from Pai to Soppong is stunning with magnificent views. The road winds through beautiful cultivated valleys and forest.

Around Soppong

Guesthouses provide maps of the surrounding countryside and villages, with tracks marked. The main sight is **Lod Cave (Tham Lod)** ① *0800-1700*, about 10 km from town. The cave (in fact a series of three accessible caves) has been used for habitation since prehistoric times and is a small part of what is presumed to be one of the largest cave systems in northern Thailand. To explore the accessible areas of the cave system takes around two hours; guides hire out their services – and their lamps – to take visitors through the cave, which has a large stream running through it. Rafts are available to traverse the stream. In the nearby village you'll find **Cave Lodge** (see page 283), an excellent guesthouse, which offers trips through the caves and serves great coffee and food.

Mae Lanna is a quiet, highland Shan village/town 16 km northwest of Soppong, off Route 1095. The area offers limestone caves, good forest walks and stunning limestone scenery. To get there, take a bus towards Mae Hong Song and get off at the turn-off for Mae Lanna, about 10 km west of Soppong. Pick-ups run the steep 6 km up to the village – or walk. Guesthouses in Soppong provide sketch maps of the area, with hiking trails marked.

Mae Hong Son ⊖⊙⊕⊛⊗▲⊖⊙ ⤻ *pp282-289. Colour map 1, A1.*

Mae Hong Son lies in a forested valley, surrounded by soaring verdant hills and just about lives up to its claim of being the 'Switzerland of Thailand'. The road from Pai is continuous switchback, cutting through spectacular scenery and communities of diverse ethnicities. On a clear day, the short flight from Chiang Mai is breathtaking – the plane crosses a range of high hills before spiralling down into a tight series of continuous banks, depositing its passengers almost in the middle of the town.

An excellent centre for trekking, the town is changing rapidly (some would say has changed) from a backpackers' hideaway to a tour centre, with the construction of two major hotels and a proliferation of 'resort'-style hotels. Despite this, Mae Hong Son still manages to retain peaceful, upland vibe.

Ins and outs

Getting there and around There are regular flights from Chiang Mai. You can easily walk from the airport to the town. The airport is to the north of town on Niveshpishan Road. It has an information counter and currency exchange booth, and *songthaews* are also available for hire. The bus station is at the northern end of town on Khunlum Praphat Road; there are plenty of connections with Chiang Mai, other destinations in this area of western Thailand and Bangkok's Northern bus terminal. It's a short walk to town and most guesthouses from the bus station. Mae Hong Son is small enough to walk around and tuk-tuk journeys around town cost ฿10-20. It is a friendly, accessible and amenable place. ⤻ *See Transport, page 289, for further information.*

Best time to visit During the cool season (December to February), when the days are warm and clear and the nights are fresh, you'll need a sweater as evening temperatures can get as low as 2°C.

Tourist information There is a poor tourist information booth at the night market.

Background

Mae Hong Son Province is about as far removed from 'Thailand' as you are likely to get, with only an estimated 2% of the population here being ethnic Thais. The great majority belong to one of the various hilltribes: mostly Karen, but also Lisu, Hmong and Lahu.

Mae Hong Son has always been caught between the competing powers of Burma and Siam/Thailand. For much of recent history the area has been under the (loose) control of various Burmese kingdoms. The influence of Burmese culture is also clearly reflected in the architecture of the town's many monasteries.

Mae Hong Son also has a murky reputation for illegal logging; this area has some of the richest forests in the country. At the beginning of 1998, revelations surfaced about an alleged massive bribe to officials of the Royal Forestry Department, to overlook logging in the Salween conservation area.

Sights

Most postcards of the town picture the lake, with **Wat Jong Klang**, a Burmese wat, in the background. It is particularly beautiful in the early morning, when mist rises off the lake. Wat Jong Klang started life as a rest pavilion for monks on pilgrimage, with a wat being built by the Shans living in the area between 1867 and 1871. The monastery contains some 50 carved Burmese *tukata* (wooden dolls) depicting characters from the Jataka stories, as

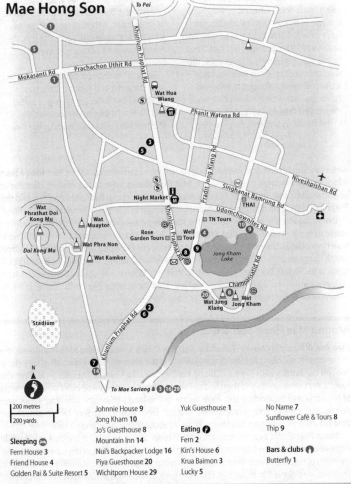

Mae Hong Son

To Pai

Mokasanti Rd

Prachachon Uthit Rd

Khunlum Praphat Rd

Wat Hua Wiang

Phanit Watana Rd

Pradit Jong Klang Rd

Niveshpishan Rd

Singhanat Bamrung Rd

THAI

Night Market

Udomchownites Rd

TN Tours

Wat Phrathat Doi Kong Mu

Wat Muaytor

Doi Kong Mu

Wat Phra Non

Rose Garden Tours

Well Tour

Wat Kamkor

Jong Kham Lake

Chamonsanid Rd

Chamonsanid Rd

Stadium

Wat Jong Klang

Wat Jong Kham

N

To Mae Sariang & 3 16 29

200 metres
200 yards

Sleeping
Fern House **3**
Friend House **4**
Golden Pai & Suite Resort **5**

Johnnie House **9**
Jong Kham **10**
Jo's Guesthouse **8**
Mountain Inn **14**
Nui's Backpacker Lodge **16**
Piya Guesthouse **20**
Wichitporn House **29**

Yuk Guesthouse **1**

Eating
Fern **2**
Kin's House **6**
Krua Baimon **3**
Lucky **5**

No Name **7**
Sunflower Café & Tours **8**
Thip **9**

Bars & clubs
Butterfly **1**

The Selling of the Padaung or 'long-necked Karen'

The Padaung, a Burmese people from the state of Kayah, are better known as the 'long-necked Karen' or, derogatorily, as the 'giraffe people'. Forced out of Burma, they have become refugees in Thailand and objects of tourist fascination. Their name says it all: female Padaung 'lengthen' their necks using brass rings, which they add from the age of five. An adult Padaung can have a neck 30 cm long and be weighed down with 5 kg, or more, of brass. Their heads supported by the brass coils, the women's neck muscles waste away – if the coils were removed they would suffocate. The women claim that while they take a little longer to get dressed in the morning and they have to sleep

with a supportive bamboo pillow, they are otherwise able to lead full and productive lives.

Some Padaung claim that the brass rings arose from the need to protect from tiger attack. Another explanation is that the practice deliberately disfigured Padaung women so they would not be taken to the Burmese court as concubines or prostitutes. A third reason relates to a mythical Padaung dragon; the lengthening mimics the dragon's long and beautiful neck.

Sadly, Thai entrepreneurs, in allegiance with the army and Karen rebels, have exploited the Padaung's refugee status and their relative commercial naivety. Most tourists who take tours to the two

well as a series of mediocre painted glass panels. In the same compound is **Wat Jong Kham**, which contains a large seated Buddha. **Wat Hua Wiang**, next to the market, contains an important Burmese-style brass Buddha image – the Phra Chao Phla La Khaeng. It is said that the image was cast in nine pieces in Burma and brought to Mae Hong Son along the Pai River.

Doi Kong Mu, the hill overlooking the town, provides superb views of the valley and is home to the Burmese-style **Wat Phrathat Doi Kong Mu**, constructed by the first King of Mae Hong Son in the mid-19th century. At the foot of Doi Kung Mu Hill is **Wat Phra Non**, which contains a 12-m-long Burmese-style reclining Buddha. The main fresh **market** in town is on Phanit Watana Road, next to Wat Hua Wiang. The usual commodities from slippery catfish to synthetic clothing are sold here, together with some produce from Burma. ▶▶ *For tours and trekking see page 287.*

Around Mae Hong Son ●●●● ▶▶ *pp282-289.*

Mae Aw, officially known in Thailand as Ban Rak Thai, is a Hmong and KMT (Kuomintang – the remnants of Chiang Kai Shek's army) village in the mountains, 22 km north of Mae Hong Son, on the border with Burma. (Chiang Kai Shek was the Chinese Republican leader who fought the Communists and then fled to Taiwan when the latter were victorious. Remnants of his army and supporters also took refuge in Thailand.) There are stunning views over Burma and the trip here is worthwhile in itself. From Mae Hong Son, take a *songthaew* (two hours) from Singhanat Bamrung Road (at about 0800), or arrange a trek.

Tham Plaa (Fish Cave), 16 km northeast of town off Route 1095, is another worthwhile excursion, which can be combined with a trip to Mae Aw. The name of the cave refers to the numbers of carp that live in the cave pools – several hundred, some exceeding 1 m in length. The carp are believed to be sacred. From the gate, a path leads across a river to the cave.

refugee camps (paying ฿250 to enter the villages) in Mae Hong Son Province leave disgusted at the 'selling' of these people in what can only be called a human display.

Even more tragic and contemptible is the case of a village near Tha Ton, where a small group of Padaung were held against their wishes on land controlled by the Thai army. At the end of 1997, journalist Andrew Drummond quoted from a tape smuggled out by these kidnapped people: "Please come now. Things cannot be any worse...I feel so sorry when foreigners come and ask about our children's schooling. They won't let us take our children to school. We cannot eat the food they give us. They shout and scream if we do not make the foreigners [tourists] happy." (Bangkok Post, 8.11.98).

Notwithstanding this particularly tragic and repugnant case, the hard fact is that the Padaung have little else to sell. Most are paid the paltry figure of ฿1000 a month simply to pose for tourist photographs. Like so many other indigenous peoples in Southeast Asia, the Padaung find themselves caught in a web of poverty, oppression, exploitation and powerlessness. The great irony is that a custom, which had almost died out, has been revived. Every young girl is now bedecked with coils, parents hoping to cash in as unscrupulous tourists search for the exotic.

Khun Yuam and Muang Pon

ⓘ *Buses plying the Mae Hong Son to Mae Sariang road will pass through both towns – Khun Yuam is about 90 mins south of Mae Hong Son, Maung Pon is 15 mins further. Homestays at Muang Pon can arrange pick-ups from Khun Yuam, Mae Hong Son and Mae Sariang.*
Roughly halfway between Mae Sariang and Mae Hong Son is the bustling market town of Khun Yuam. The town itself has few attractions yet it is an engaging and friendly place to stop off for a couple of days if you want to make a slow meander through this part of the country. Most of the people who live here are Karen, Shan or Hmong. There is a pretty Hmong/Burmese-style temple 5 km to the west at **Wat To Phae**, which is worth a look; it houses a 150-year-old tapestry just to the side of the main altar. There is also a **War Museum** ⓘ *on the main road near the town centre, Tue-Sat 0930-1200, 1400-1600, ฿50,* which focuses on the plight of Japanese soldiers during World War Two. Thousands died here as Khun Yuam was home to a Japanese army hospital. The museum houses a collection of poignant artefacts left behind by the dying soldiers.

The nearby Shan village of Muang Pon, about 15 km to the south of Khun Yuam on the road to Mae Sariang, hosts an excellent homestay programme that is run, managed and owned by local people. Stay here for a few days and you'll get a chance to engage in a genuine encounter with local people a million miles from the usual intrusions of a 'hilltribe' trek. Nearby you'll find hot springs, mountain walks and a small hilltop temple.

Mae Sariang ●❷❻▲❸❻ ⤻ *pp282-289. Colour map 1, B1.*

The capital of Amphoe district, Mae Sariang is a small market town on the banks of the Yuam River, and a good departure point for trekking. The road from Chom Thong runs up the Ping Valley, before turning west to follow the Chaem River, climbing steadily through beautiful dipterocarp forest, the Op Luang National Park (17 km from Hod), and into the mountains of western Thailand. There is little to draw people here, except as a stopping-off point for Mae Hong Son or as a starting point for trekking. The town is small and leafy, with many of the houses still built of wood – a comparative oasis after the dusty urban centres. The bus station is on Mae Sariang Road in the centre of town, five minutes' walk from the Riverside Guesthouse, next to Wat Jong Sung.

There are a handful of unremarkable wats. Wat Utthayarom, known locally as Wat Chom Soong, is Burmese in style but also displays two Mon-inspired white *chedis*. Other monasteries include Wat Sri Bunruang (in town) and Wat Joom Thong (on a hill, over-looking town). The latter has a large and recently constructed white seated Buddha image surveying the valley below. The town also has a better stock of wooden shophouses than most Thai towns – that is on Laeng Phanit Road (the river road). The morning market operates from a plot on Sathit Phon Road and there is also an evening market – good for stall food – at the end of Wiang Mai Road.

Trekking, rafting, cave and waterfall visits and elephants rides are also possible, see Activities and tours, page 287. See also Background, page 716.

◉ Western loop: Pai, Mae Hong Son and Mae Sariang listings

For Sleeping and Eating price codes and other relevant information, see pages 44-49.

● Sleeping

Pai *p276, map p276*

The accommodation here is constantly changing. The selection here is a cross section of what's available.

A-B Phu Pai Art Resort, 5 km north of town, T053-065111, www.phupai.com. Beautiful resort in a gorgeous location. Rooms are huge, with all the modern facilities you'd expect. Service is a bit patchy, but it's still good value.

A-E Rim Pai Cottages, 3 Chai Songkhram Rd, T053-699133. Good position on the river, small A-frame huts which are clean and cosy. Spotless Western toilets, a little overpriced but discounts available in the low season.

C-D Tha Pai Spa Camping, 2 Mai Hee Rd, T053-693267, www.thapaispa.com. Decent bungalows with their own hot springs, aimed more at Thai guests.

D Blue Lagoon, on main road in centre of town, T053-699824. Clean and well run with decent rooms, swimming pool and excellent disabled facilities.

F-G Duang, 3 Rangsiyanon Rd, T053-699101. Opposite the bus station, noisy at night.

Clean, friendly English-speaking family-run guesthouse. Cheap, clean rooms with shared hot-water showers, good restaurant (excellent coffee and French bread), trekking organized. Foreign exchange, bicycles for hire and maps provided.

F-G Nanya's, 1 Rangsiyanon Rd, T053-699 051. Offer 7 clean rooms in 2-storey building set back from the road, upstairs rooms share hot water showers, those on the ground floor have attached clean Thai-style bathrooms, rather overgrown small garden, well run. Treks organized through **Perm Chais Trekking**.

F-G Shan Guesthouse, 4 Wiangtai Rd, T053-699162. On the edge of town, quiet, with great views, but rather exposed. Raised wooden bungalows, with 'leaf' roofs and good balconies, set around a pond, with a Burmese pagoda-esque restaurant in the middle.

G Charlie's Place, 3 Wiangtai Rd, T053-699 039. One of the larger places in town, with a range of accommodation from dormitory beds to more expensive and less run-down brick bungalows with attached bathrooms, all set in a largish garden. Good trekking organized from here.

G Golden Huts, T053-699949. Very quiet, beautiful out-of-the-way location on the riverbank. Quiet and relaxing atmosphere,

French owner provides a friendly service. Small but adequate restaurant with good food and great views. Recommended.

Soppong p277

B-C Baan Cafe Resort, next to main road, T053-617081. Nicely laid-out rooms and bungalows, some with terraces overlooking a river. Pleasant gardens, friendly, good food. Shop selling local produce. Recommended.

B-E Little Eden, on main road, T053-617053, www.littleeden-guesthouse.com. Wide selection of bungalows and a river-view house. Rooms are fresh and well-kept, a/c, hot water and en suite available. Attractive gardens and swimming pool. Recommended.

B-E Soppong River Inn, 500 m from village centre towards Mae Hong Son, T053-617107, www.soppong.com. Range of great huts, some with verandas, overlooking a small gorge. Also offers trekking service, massage and fresh coffee. Friendly and recommended.

D-E Northern Hill Guest House, main road, just before the village, T053-617136, www.northernhillgh.com. There's a nice view from the small bungalows dotted around a pleasant garden, some a/c and with hot water/en suite. But they are a little overpriced.

E Jungle House, 500 m out of Soppong towards Mae Hong Son, T053-617099. Simple huts, hot water, garden and attractive restaurant. Organizes treks.

F Kemarin Garden, a short way down a lane 200 m up the hill towards Pai. 4 bungalows, peaceful rural position with views over the hills, hot-water showers. Huts and showers are surprisingly clean. Friendly management (but no English spoken). Recommended.

Around Soppong p277

There are several places to stay in Mae Lanna.

E Mae Lanna Guesthouse, T08-6911 7086 (mob). Closed Jul-Aug. Good base from which to explore the surrounding countryside. The guesthouse is run by a French woman who is an excellent source of information and advice.

E-G Cave Lodge, T053-617203, www.cave lodge.com. Set up 24 years ago, Cave Lodge

is a labour of love for its Aussie owner, John Spies. A cluster of small bungalows cling to a steep rock face, which leads down to a small glade and stream. Facilities are basic but include everything from en suite rooms with hot water to dorms, and even a home-made sauna. Excellent Western, Thai and local cuisine available. The owner has an incredible local knowledge of the nearby cave systems, trekking routes and different ethnic groups. From Soppong, a motorbike taxi costs ฿200-300, or walk the 6.5 km from the villlage. One of the best guesthouses in the country. Highly recommended.

Mae Hong Son p278, map p279

A-D Golden Pai and Suite Resort, 285/1 Ban Pang Moo, T053-061114, www.golden pai.com. 33 modern yet traditional Shan-style chalets, well furnished, a/c, private terrace and 30 de luxe rooms. Set in landscaped gardens with 2 swimming pools, open-air restaurant overlooking Pai River. Tours organized. Very friendly though a little way out of town.

A-D Mountain Inn, 112 Khunlum Praphat Rd, T053-611802, www.mhsmountain inn.com. A/c rooms surround an atmospheric garden. Friendly management, serves good food (see Eating, below). Recommended.

B Fern House, 2 km from Highway 108 at the turn-off for Ban Nua Hum Mae Sakut Village (5 km from town), T053-611374, ferngroup@softhome.net. Bungalows built on rice paddies in Shan style. Simple, comfortable and tasteful. Set in lovely grounds, friendly and helpful staff; eco-friendly place, good local walks.

D-G Sang Tong Huts, 250 Moo 11 T Pangmoo, T053-620680, sangtonghuts@hotmail.com. Secluded spot northwest of town), with great views. Range of huts, dining area with great food and hilltribe coffee. Friendly and helpful owners. Recommended.

E Piya Guesthouse, 1 Soi 3 Khunlum Praphat Rd, T053-611260. Garden setting next to the lake. Recently refurbished, 14 clean double or twin rooms with a/c and TV. The restaurant has a great view – a good place to sit and relax. Manager is extremely friendly.

E Wichitporn House, 54 Pang Lor Nikom Rd, T053-612163. 2 longhouses set around a nice garden. 10 clean twin rooms, with hot shower.
E-F Prince's Guesthouse, 37 Udomchaonitet Rd, T053-611136, princesguesthouse@ gmail.com. A/c and fan, some rooms overlooking the lake. Wi-Fi available. Rooms are simple but clean, good value for money.
F-G Friend House, 21 Pradit Jong Kham Rd, T053-620119. Set back from the road. 10 very clean rooms (shared showers even cleaner), upstairs rooms have a view of the lake. Well managed and carefully maintained, small café downstairs, laundry service. Recommended.
F-G Johnnie House, 5/2 Udomchownites Rd, T053-611667. Peaceful position on the lakeside, 7 spotlessly clean and simple rooms, shared hot-water showers. Breakfast menu, laundry facilities. Friendly and quiet.
F-G Jo's Guesthouse, 3 Chamnansatid Rd, T053-612417. Small personal place, 6 small clean rooms with mattresses on the floor and fans in an old teak house. More expensive rooms have own hot shower.
F-G Yuk Guesthouse, 14 Sri Mongkol Rd, T053-611532. Tucked away behind a wat, this is a great place. Very clean and comfortable with a peaceful little garden. Small restaurant with good food. Free transport to and from the bus station and airport.
G Jong Kham, 7 Udomchownites Rd, T053-611420. Lakeside, run-down bungalows with 'leaf' roofs. Some cheaper rooms in the main house, largish garden, very popular.
G Nui's Backpacker Lodge, 152/1 Makasanti Rd on corner before **Mae Hong Son Guest House** (no phone). 5 concrete and bamboo huts with shower and double bed. Laundry service and some food. Nui speaks English.

Khun Yuam and Muang Pon *p281*
B-D Baan Farang Guesthouse, 499 Moo 1 Khun Yuam Rd, T053-622086. Decent, clean and friendly set of bungalows and rooms available here. Set just outside Khun Yuam town off the main road towards the north.
E The Muang Pon Homestay, T053-684644, kunlaya_mall@hotmail.com. Several houses

in this appealing Shan village take part in a very well-run homestay programme. You'll be treated as one of the family and introduced to the eccentricities of village life and Shan cuisine. Rates includes breakfast and dinner. The villagers run excursions to nearby temples, villages, mountains and hot springs. Call or email to book and you'll be allocated your family. Transfers from Mae Hong Son and even Chiang Mai can be arranged for a fee. One of the best examples of low-impact, fair trade tourism. Highly recommended.

Mae Sariang *p281*
There are several reasonable guesthouses, most are 5-15 mins' walk from the bus station.
C Komolsarn Hotel, Mae Sariang Rd, T053-681524. Reasonably priced hotel with good facilities and several en suite rooms.
C River House Hotel, Laeng Phanit Rd (next to **Riverside**, see below). Clean and inviting rooms with great views from the balconies and good facilities. There is an excellent restaurant with riverside seating.
D-E Riverside, 85/1 Laeng Phanit Rd, T053-681188. A 5-min stroll from the bus station, this attractive building has large, clean rooms by the river and wonderful views from the breakfast/seating area. A popular choice for travellers and is a good source of information.
E North West Guest House, 87/1 Laeng Phanit Rd, T053-332464, info@faz.co.th. A spick-and-span guesthouse under the same management as **River House Hotel** across the road. Recommended.
E See View, 70 Wiang Mai Rd (across the river, on the edge of town), T053-681556. Good-sized rooms in stone bungalows, smaller wooden rooms available, with shared facilities. Quiet and peaceful but shabby. Owner speaks English and is very helpful.

🍴 Eating

Pai *p276, map p276*
There are some very good noodle places in town: by the post office on Khetkelang Rd

is an excellent restaurant specializing in duck noodle soup; at the corner of Khetkelang and Chai Songkhram roads, you can find superb *khao soi* (spicy northern noodles).

¶ The Sanctuary, Ratdamrong Rd, just before the river, www.thesanctuarythailand.com. Nice decor and riverside location make this a standout effort. However, the food doesn't really match the price. Good wine list.

¶ Amido Pizza, Ratdamrong Rd. Just over the bridge on way to the hot springs. Awesome pizza, pasta and lasagne.

¶ Baan Ben Jarong, edge of town, on the way to Chiang Mai. High-class Thai cuisine – exceptional and one of the best places to eat in the area. Highly recommended.

¶ Own Home Restaurant, Ratdamrong Rd. Some Thai dishes, along with travellers' fare including tortillas, banana porridge, shakes, pizzas, moussaka and sandwiches.

¶ Thai Yai, Rangsiyanon Rd, not far from Shan Guesthouse. Thai and international, good quiche, wholemeal bread, etc.

Bakeries

All About Coffee, Chai Songkhram Rd. An arty café, with huge open chicken and cashew sandwiches and a range of coffees and teas.
Oy Bakery, in front of day market. Good bread, cheese and other provisions.

Foodstalls

There are only a handful of stalls, but good pancakes and other food is available.

Soppong *p277*

There are noodle stalls on the main road but if you want something more upmarket most of the guesthouses serve reasonable food. Cave Lodge, 6.5 km away (see Sleeping, above), makes a great lunch spot.

Mae Hong Son *p278, map p279*

The largest concentration of restaurants is on Khunlum Praphat Rd; the cheapest place to eat is in the night market.

¶ 99 Restaurant, on the road out of town near the stadium. Thai dishes at reasonable prices, set breakfast, barbecue, curries and salads. Open-air roadside place.

¶ Baby Corn Restaurant, Khunlum Praphat Rd (at the traffic lights). Thai rice and noodles, small menu but very cheap. Good shakes.

¶ Fern Restaurant, 87 Khunlum Praphat Rd. Large restaurant on road towards Mae Sariang. Smart, unpretentious and affordable, mostly Thai dishes including good frog, spicy salads and crispy fish, also ice cream.

¶ Kin's House, 89 Khunlum Praphat Rd (past Fern Restaurant). Selection of traditional and local Thai cuisine and Western food. Plesasant decor, café/bar atmosphere.

¶ Krua Baimon, Khunlum Praphat Rd. Good-value Thai food, often shows Western films.

¶ Lucky Restaurant, 5 Singhanat Bamrung Rd. Excellent restaurant in wooden house. Good atmosphere and choice of Thai and Western dishes. Specialities include deep-fried catfish and steaks, also serves breakfast.

¶ Mountain Inn, 112 Khunlum Praphat Rd, (see Sleeping, above). Serves great Thai grub in its romantic garden.

¶ Paa Dim, Khunlum Praphat Rd (near the 7-11). Popular with locals, varied but small selection of Thai dishes, good portions, cheap.

¶ Reaun Pap Restaurant, Singhanat Bamrung Rd. International food, good atmosphere, decor and music. Real coffee and good orange juice.

¶ Restaurant (no name), next to **Mountain Inn**. Offers very authentic hilltribe dishes that are extremely popular with locals. The owner will let you taste before you buy.

¶ Salween River Restaurant, 3 Singhanat Bamrung Rd, T053-612050. British, Burmese, Shan and Thai dishes available. Generous portions and home-made bread. Sells books and maps, and has free Wi-Fi and plenty of information on treks and homestays.

¶ Sunflower Café and Tours, 2/1 Khunlum Praphat Soi 3, T053-620549, sunctmhs@cscoms.com. Cosy café run by an Australian/Thai couple, popular with *farangs*. Good spot for breakfast and the best bread in town, good coffee, internet access, organizes tours and is a great source of information.

♥ Thip Restaurant, Pradit Jong Klang Rd
(next to the lake). A newer touristy restaurant
with upstairs balcony overlooking the lake.
Reasonable prices and reasonable food.
♥ Ton Restaurant, Pradit Jong Klang Rd
(near the lake). Great little local roadside
restaurant run by Ton. Good Thai dishes
(especially red and green curries), sticky rice,
salads and soups. Extensive, cheap and tasty.

Bakeries and cafés

Baan Tua Lek, Chamnansatid Rd, T053-620
688. Cosy with friendly staff and free Wi-Fi.
Sells coffee, tea, smoothies, home-made
sandwiches and cookies. Recommended.
KK Bakery, near Pen Porn House. Fresh-
baked cakes and bread, small selection of
Thai dishes, set breakfasts, snacks and drinks.

Foodstalls

Night market on Khunlum Praphat Rd. For
Shan salads and different kinds of excellent
noodle soups, try the morning market.

Khun Yuam and Muang Pon *p281*

Khun Yuam has a decent collection of rice
and noodle shops and stalls on the main road
towards the southern end of town. In Muang
Pon the homestay progamme should meet
most needs, though there are a few lunchtime noodle stalls and a bakery to be found
in the village centre.

Mae Sariang *p281*

♥ Inthira Restaurant, Wiang Mai Rd. Tasty
dishes and good prices, probably the best
Chinese/Thai restaurant in town.
♥ River House Restaurant, Laeng Phanit Rd.
Excellent range of food at reasonable prices
in superb surroundings.
♥ Ruan Phrae, down the *soi* to Wat Sri
Bunruang, off Wiang Mai Rd. Thai and
Chinese. Recommended.

Foodstalls

At the night market on Wiang Mai Rd
(about 1 km from the centre of town).

◑ Bars and clubs

Pai *p276, map p276*
Be Bop, Rangsiyanon Rd. Live music most
nights, extremely popular with travellers.
Great atmosphere, serves Western spirits.
Reggae Bar, Rangsiyanon Rd. If you like
sitting around a fire playing bongos and
comparing how little money you spent on
your gap year travels, this is the place for
you. It is also home to the now annual **Pai
Reggae Festival**, www.paifestival.com.
Satang Bar, next to the bus stop. Sells Thai
herbal whisky (฿8 a shot), which is allegedly
medicinal, claiming to increase blood
circulation, improve your health, increase
bodily strength, relieve backache, aid
sleep and also act as a poor man's Viagra.

Mae Hong Son *p278, map p279*
Butterfly, at the crossroads on the way
to **Mae Kong Son Guesthouse**, the best bar
in town. A swanky Thai lounging bar with
karaoke, big 1970s-style kitsch chairs, live
music and open as long as you care to drink.
Chilli Bar, 29 Phaditchongkham Rd. Friendly
staff, international and Thai dishes and
strong drinks.
Crossroads, at the crossroads of Sinahanat
Bamrung Rd and Khunlum Praphat Rd.
Expensive drinks, limited bar menu, free pool.
Waterbar, Khunlum Praphat Rd. Slightly out
of place, this bar has faux-designer sofas, a
flatscreen TV and waitresses in plastic outfits.

Mae Sariang *p281*
Black and White Bar. Some live music.

❀ Festivals and events

Mae Hong Son *p278, map p279*
Early Apr Poi Sang Long, young novices
(10-16 years old) are ordained into the monkhood. Beforehand, they are dressed up as
princes and on the following day there is a
colourful procession through town starting
from Wat Kham Ko.

O Shopping

Pai *p276, map p276*
Bookshops
Back Trax Tour and Trekking, 67/1
Rangsiyanon Rd. Rents, sells and exchanges
English-language books.

Mae Hong Son *p278, map p279*
A number of places along Khunlum Praphat Rd
as well as in the morning and night markets
sell locally-made tea and coffee.

Bookshops
Asia Books, Khunlum Praphat Rd (next to
Panorama Hotel). English-language novels
and magazines.

Handicrafts
Several places on Singhanat Bamrung Rd. The
morning market near Wat Huan Wing sells
Burmese fabric, bags and clothes. Look for
the sewing machine at the southern end
of the market and you can have your fabric
sewn into wearable *longyis* for about ฿30.
Chokeadradet, 645 Khunlum Praphat Rd.
Antiques and handicrafts. Recommended.
Thai Handicraft Centre, Khunlum Praphat Rd.

Supermarkets
A 24-hr 7-11 and 2 good supermarkets, both
near the crossroads in the town centre.

▲ Activities and tours

Pai *p276, map p276*
Rafting
Thai Adventure Rafting, just past the bus
station, T053-699111, www.activethailand.
com/rafting. The oldest whitewater rafting
company in Thailand. It runs unforgettable,
professional 2-day expeditions down the Pai
River and beyond. It is run by Guy, a friendly
Frenchman who has lived in Pai for 17 years.
The river is only high enough Jul to end of
Jan, trips start at ฿2200 and include everything from insurance to food/drinks. There

are other companies organizing similar (and
cheaper) rafting trips in the area though none
are as good. Avoid nearby **Pai Adventure
Rafting** who are a poor copy of the real thing.

Therapies
Traditional massage Opposite the **Rim
Pai Cottages**, 68 Rachdamrong Rd, excellent
massage (฿100-150 per hr) and friendly. Also
available at several other places, including
the **Foundation of Shivaga Kommapaj**.

Tour operators
Many of the guesthouses run treks and there
are plenty of companies offering a choice of
treks and rafting trips. Shop around and talk
to people who have recently returned.
Back-Trax Tour and Trekking, 67/1
Rangsiyanon Rd. Organizes treks with Khun
Chao, a TAT-registered guide. Offers cookery
courses and lessons in aromatherapy massage.
Duang Trekking (at Duang Guesthouse, see
page 282). Basic trekking with all-inclusive
prices of ฿1000-2000.
Karen Tours and Trekking, Rangsiyanon Rd.
Lisu Tours and Trekking Rangsiyanon Rd,
next to the market. Also recommended.
Average prices are ฿800-1000 per day.
1- to 4-day treks available.
Pai Elephant Camp Tours, 5/3 Rangsiyanon
Rd, T053-699286. One of several companies
offering elephant rides. Khun Thom, the
owner, runs a professional set-up and treats
her animals with respect. Her elephant camp
is out of town towards the hot springs.
Recommended – you can even swim with
the elephants in the river or ride bareback.
Perm Chais, contact Nunyas or the office
along Raddamrong Rd. Will organize rafting
and elephant safaris.

Mae Hong Son *p278, map p279*
Therapies
Traditional massage and herbal steam bath
is a Mae Hong Son speciality; particularly
welcome for those just back from treks.
Tubtim Thai Massage, next door to the
Lakeside Bar, T053-620553, and above

Sunny Supermarket, Khunlum Praphat Rd. Has been recommended (฿100-150 per hr). **Ban Thai Massage and Spa**, 28 Singhanat-bamroong Rd, T053-620441, banthaispa@ yahoo.com. Great service, friendly staff and amazing massages. Highly recommended.

Tours operators

There are various day tours to sights such as Pha Sua Waterfall, Pang Tong Summer Palace, the KMT village of Mae Aw, Tham Plaa (Fish Cave) and Tham Nam Lot (Water Cave). A number of companies also advertise trips to the 'long-necked' Padaung, which involves a bumpy 1-hr trip to the 2 villages where they live. Many people deplore this type of tourism (see box, page 280). Most guesthouses will organize treks ranging from trips down the Salween River to the Burmese border to Mae Sot, elephant treks and rafting on the Pai River. Treks usually last 1 day to 1 week; the average price is ฿800 per day for a group of at least 4 people (this does not include rafting and elephant rides). There are dedicated trekking companies, and trekking outfits attached to guesthouses: **TN Tours**, Pradit Jong Kham Rd; **Rose Garden Tour**, 86/4 Kunlum Praphat, T/F053-611577; **Sawasdee Tour**, Khunlum Praphat Rd (by bus station); **Well Tour**, Khunlum Praphat Rd.

Friend Tour at Friend Guesthouse, T053-620 119. Trekking, bamboo rafting, elephant rides, boat trips.

Rose Garden Tours, 86/4 Khunlum Prapaht Rd, T053-611577. Cultural and ecological tours. French also spoken.

Sunflower Tours, Sunflower Café. Eco-conscious birdwatching and nature treks.

TN Tour, 10 Udom Chuannithet Rd, T053-620059. Trekking, jeep adventure, rafting, licensed guides.

Mae Sariang p281
Tour operators

Baan Nam Ngao. Specialist birdwatching and star-gazing trips, as well as treks. **Chan trekking company**, operates through the Roj Thip Restaurant at 661 Wiang Mai Rd.

Kanchana, T019-522167, kanchanakosai@ yahoo.com. Friendly, organizes bike tours around the Thai–Burma border. **Riverside** (see Sleeping, page 284). Treks through **Salawin Tours**, including rafting, elephant rides, visits to caves, waterfalls and Karen villages or to the Burmese border. **See View** (see page 284). Organizes treks.

⊖ Transport

Pai p276, map p276
Air

SGA (one of Thailand's smallest airlines) has twice daily flights in tiny 12-seater Cessnas between Pai and **Chiang Mai**. Tickets (฿1450 single, ฿2900 return) are available via their website, www.sga.co.th, or call their Pai (T053-698207) or Chiang Mai (T053-280444) offices.

Bicycle

Mountain bike hire from ฿50 per day from the shop adjoining the **Duang** guesthouse (see page 282), or from **Nunya's**. **Pai Tai Bike Society**, opposite the bus station, which has information on routes and sights.

Bus

The bus stop is on Chai Songkhram Rd, near the centre of town. 4 buses run to **Mae Hong Son** daily (3 hrs) and 4 to **Chiang Mai** (4 hrs) for ฿80. There are 5 connections a day to **Fang** (2½ hrs) via **Mae Ma Lai**. Some Fang buses continue to **Tha Ton**.

Motorbike

Hire costs ฿80-250 per day from several guesthouses and shops in town. The pick of the bunch is next door to **Thai Adventure Rafting** with gearless scooters through to dirt bikes – it also offers daily insurance.

Soppong p277
Bus

There are 6-7 buses each day (1 a/c) in each direction – west to **Mae Hong Son** (2 hrs), east to **Pai** (1 hr) and **Chiang Mai** (5 hrs).

Introduction

There's no doubt that Thailand likes to party. At times, the whole country appears to be engaged in squeezing as much *sanuk* – a word that loosely translates as fun or pleasure – into the day as possible. But it is during Thailand's festivals when the locals really let go, and the range of events is as staggering as the joyous and sometimes bizarre celebrations that ensue. The three festivals described below should prepare you for some of Thailand's wildest moments.

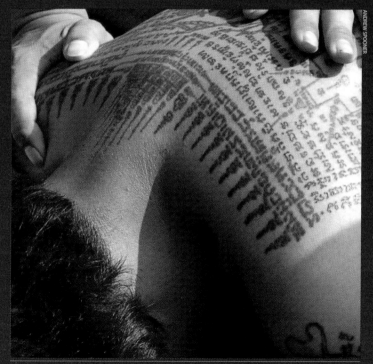

ANDREW SPOONER

Previous page: Many of the devotees at the Wat Bang Phra tattoo festival believe they are possessed by the protective animal spirits inculcated into their tattoos. **Above**: Thai temple tattoos have a spiritual significance. **Opposite page**: The possessions can often seem like performances.

Tattoo festival

There's a roar from deep within the throng. A man, stripped to his waist, is standing, dripping with sweat, head thrown back, arms outstretched and his mouth grimaced wide as he emits a wild animalistic noise. He is covered in tattoos – reams of esoteric cabalistic Khmer lettering and symbols spreading over his shoulders, chest and back.

The scream gets louder and louder, his expression more intense, eyes rolling into the back of his head. Then, suddenly, he starts sprinting through the packed crowd. People scramble in the dirt to get out of his way, yet, at full speed, he clips a bystander and lands face first, his body belly-flopping into the gravel. Without skipping a beat the tattooed man leaps to his feet, lets out a roar and carries on with his screaming charge.

His target is a large plinth where a number of Buddhist monks are sitting and chanting. Surrounding the monks is a phalanx of khaki-clad soldiers. As the deranged running man reaches their ranks several soldiers grab him and lift him off the ground. Curiously, one of the soldiers gently rubs the tattooed man's ears. The spell is broken and the man instantly returns to 'normal'. He quietly returns to his place in the crowd, nimbly avoiding other onrushing, entranced devotees.

The annual tattoo festival at the Wat Bang Phra temple, just outside the western Thai town of Nakhon Chaisi, is one of the strangest gatherings in a nation famed for the arcane. Every year, on a Saturday near the last full moon before Songkran (Thai New Year), thousands of devotees come to be tattooed by the monks or to have the their existing tattoos 're-empowered'. These devotees, many of whom work as soldiers, policemen, hitmen, mobsters and even motorcycle taxi drivers, have their bodies adorned with what they deem to be protective symbols or spells.

Often the tattoos represent animals (monkeys, tigers and buffaloes) and the devotees will become possessed with the spirits of these beasts: you might witness someone galloping like a monkey, scraping their knuckles and screeching simian calls; or see a tiger standing enraged, growling, slavering, clawing at the sky, until it bounds through the crowd; or the buffalo, far slower but huge and equally ferocious, will lumber forward, stopping for nothing.

The end of the festival comes when the monks spray the crowd with water jets – a symbolic act of cleansing and re-empowerment. When they begin there is normally a mass storming of the plinth, as by this point the crowd is on the point of hysteria with the intensity of the heat and collective possession reaching a powerful crescendo.

FACTS

Foreign visitors are welcome to attend, photograph and film the festival but should be aware of the dangers – the author was knocked over twice while researching this book. It's a good idea to bring water, a sun hat and suncream. The date is movable but the festival usually occurs in mid-March (the 2010 and 2011 dates were not available at time of publication but can easily be found with a Google search nearer the time).

To get there, take a bus from Bangkok's Southern Terminal towards Nakhon Pathom. Ask to be let out at Ha Na and take a *songthaew* to Nakhon Chaisi, where Wat Bang Phra is located.

Songkran

Travel to Thailand in April and you're likely to be bowled over by the heat. This is the hottest month in a hot country and there's little chance of cooling rains providing respite – April is the driest time of year. Yet if you're in the kingdom a week either side of 14 April, be warned that you're likely to receive a complete and utter drenching; probably with ice cold water.

Songkran (Thai New Year) is one of the kingdom's most famous festivals. At times it can resemble a giant, out-of-control water fight, complete with buckets, hoses, water pistols and tubs. Some people even go to the length of placing giant ice blocks into huge barrels of water to provide icy ammunition for the ensuing battle. Others bring water supplies on the back of pick-up trucks, creating snaking convoys of giggling water-throwers. People set up stereo systems on the street, pumping out thumping beats or nasal Thai pop. Impromptu bars spring up beside the road, further soaking the already saturated masses with copious amounts of alcohol. Bright gaudy colours are de rigueur and some even go to the trouble of attiring themselves in full costumes. If you're there then you're fair game; either stay inside or be prepared to take part.

The roots of Songkran are widely spread throughout Southeast Asia with the festival being celebrated in different forms in different countries. In Laos it is called *Pi Mai Lao*, Cambodians call it *Chaul Chnam Thmey* and the Burmese, *Thingyan*. The Dai people in Yunnan (China) celebrate a festival on the same day as do the Assamese and Bengali.

Before it became the riotous, wild festival it is today, Songkran was traditionally used as a time to pay respects to elders, including family members, friends and neighbours. Elements of this practice still exist and some people will attend temples for prayer

Left: Dressing up is part of the fun. **Right**: Everyone wants to interact with you, particularly if you're a foreigner.

Get ready to be drenched.

and to give gifts to the monks. Buddha images, from both homes and temples, will be ritually cleansed by dousing them in water – in Chiang Mai some images are paraded through the streets to be collectively 'washed'. Much like in the West, people will make New Year resolutions to refrain from 'bad' behaviour such as smoking or drinking and some families will give their homes a thorough Songkran clean.

FACTS

Chiang Mai is famed for hosting the wildest Songkran celebrations. In some parts of southern Thailand the festival is not as prominent and may be far more low-key.

The dates in Thailand when Songkran is held are now fixed from 13-15 April, but the date was originally dependent on complicated astrological calculations involving the sun's movement into the Aries zodiac. Even these dates are not uniformly followed throughout Thailand, with some regions and cities hosting the day of water-throwing up to a week apart.

Vegetarian Festival

Getting your ears pierced is a relatively straightforward and widely accepted practice in the West. It is also almost entirely painless – a quick spray of antiseptic and a stud is fired into your lobe in an instant.

But imagine several skewers pushed through your neck-skin or an ice cream parasol spiked through your cheek – that's going to take time and effort. Or how about a sword through your tongue and a giant chain through your lip? It's got to hurt.

For the devotees of the Chinese deity *Mazu* – the Taoist goddess of the sea and queen of heaven – spikes, swords, skewers and even ice cream parasols hold no fear. Once a year they gather for the festival of the Nine Emperor Gods to mark the gods' return from heaven to earth where they are embodied, as one, in *Mazu*. More commonly known in Thailand as *Tesagan Gin Je*, or the Vegetarian festival, the most famous site for celebration is Phuket, where thousands of devotees slash, pierce and undergo gruesome acts of endurance in one of the kingdom's most spectacular festivals.

This festival doesn't just take place in Phuket but is widespread throughout Thailand in varying degrees and formats. Where there is a Chinese community (which is pretty much everywhere in Thailand) you might find the Vegetarian festival.

An excellent and low-key place to experience *Tesagan Gin Je* is in the southern Thai town of Trang (see page 559). A large Hainan Chinese community has resided here for over 100 years and the festival takes place at the same time of year as it does in Phuket.

Much like its better-known neighbours, the Trang festival involves large numbers of *Mah Song* – pure, unmarried devotees who invite the spirits of gods to possess their bodies and then perform acts of flagellation and self-mutilation – parading the streets in bright costumes and letting off extremely loud firecrackers.

During the entire festival all participants and the local community will abstain from eating meat, poultry, seafood and dairy products – hence the name Vegetarian Festival. In Trang you might find yourself invited by locals for a free vegetarian lunch in any one of a number

The bigger the object the more devoted the devotee.

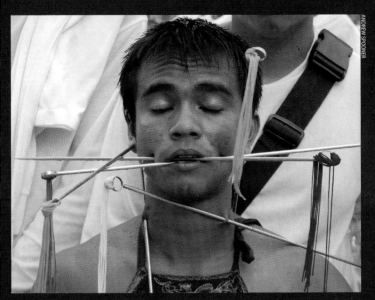

Above: Fireworks and meat skewers are de rigeur. **Next page:** Elaborate cabalistic spells are tattooed in ancient Khmer scripts.

of temporary kitchens set up for the event. Accepting the offer of lunch is a good way to get involved in festivities that, thankfully, involves no suffering.

FACTS

The Vegetarian Festival takes place from the eve of the ninth moon of the Chinese year, until the climax on the ninth day of the ninth moon, usually September or October. The exact dates for the 2009 or 2010 festivals had yet to be decided when this book went to press, so visit www.phuketvegetarian.com for the confirmed dates.

Motorbike/scooter
Most guesthouses can arrange hire, or try the the shop close to the bus stop.

Mae Hong Son *p278, map p279*
Air
Daily connections on **SGA** and **Nok Air** with **Chiang Mai** (35 mins). Mar-Apr, flights may be cancelled or delayed because of smoke.

Bus
2 routes to **Chiang Mai**: the northern, more gruelling route via Pai, or the route to the south, via Mae Sariang. Buses leave throughout the day in both directions – in total there are 7 each way, most non-a/c. The first via **Pai** is at 0700 (to Pai, 3-3½ hrs, ฿48-100; to Chiang Mai, 8 hrs, ฿94-180). The first via **Mae Sariang** is at 0600 (to Mae Sariang, 4 hrs, ฿69-124 ; to Chiang Mai, 9½ hrs, ฿133-240 to Chiang Mai). **Bangkok**, 12½ hrs.

Car
Avis, airport, T053-620457. From ฿1400 a day.

Motorbike and jeep
Motorbikes from ฿150-180 per day (couple of places at the southern end of Khunlum Praphat Rd), jeeps ฿800-1000 per day.

Mountain bike
Mountain bikes are available for hire from 22 Singhanat Bamrun Rd, ฿100 per day.

Mae Sariang *p281*
Bus
7 buses daily to **Chiang Mai** and **Mae Hong Son** (4 hrs) and several a/c and non-a/c a day to **Bangkok**. The road south to **Mae Sot**, following the Burmese border, though slow (6 hrs), is mainly in good repair, see page 223.

Songthaew
Songthaews to local destinations, congregate at the morning market on Sathit Phon Rd.
 Songthaews depart 4 times a day from the bus station for **Mae Sot** (6 hrs, ฿150).

❶ Directory

Pai *p276, map p276*
Banks Krung Thai Bank, Rangsiyanon Rd, (largest building in town). Mon-Fri 0830-1530. **Internet** Many internet cafés, mainly on Chi Song- khram Rd. **Post office** Khetkelang Rd. **Medical services** Pai Hospital, Chai Songkhram Rd (about 500 m from the town centre). **Telephone** Overseas calls can be made from Rangsiyanon Rd.

Soppong *p277*
Banks The nearest bank with exchange facilities is 1 hr away in Pai. **Post office** By the Lemon Hill Guesthouse, towards Pai. **Telephone** Domestic calls can be made from the restaurant at the bus stop.

Mae Hong Son *p278, map p279*
Banks 6 in town, 4 with ATMs, all on Khunlum Praphat Rd: Bangkok Bank, Bank of Ayydhya, Kasikorn Bank and Thai Farmers. Thai Military Bank, at intersection with Panit Wattana Rd. **Immigration** Khunlum Praphat Rd (northern end of town. **Internet** Sunflower Café, Mae Hong Son Computer (80 Khunlum Praphat Rd), Reaun Pap Restaurant and in an office over the bridge near the immigration office (the cheapest place). **Medical services** Clinic, Khunlum Praphat Rd; Hospital, at the eastern end of Singhanat Bamrung Rd. **Police** Tourist Police: 1 Rachathampitak Rd, T053-611812 (claim 24 hrs service). **Post office** Southern end of town, corner of Khunlum Praphat Rd/ Soi 3, Mon-Fri 0830-1630, Sat-Sun 0900-1200. **Telephone** In new building behind Paa Dim Restaurant, Mon-Sat 0830-1630.

Mae Sariang *p281*
Banks Thai Farmers, 150/1 Wiang Mai Rd; Krung Thai Bank, Laeng Phanit Rd; Thai Military Bank, Wiang Mai Rd (ATM). **Internet** Large internet access point on Mae Sariang Rd. **Post office and telephone** 31/1 Wiang Mai Rd.

Chiang Rai and around

Given the ancient roots of Chiang Rai, the capital of Thailand's most northerly province, there's little here in the way of historical interest, with modern shophouse architecture predominating. What Chiang Rai lacks in sights it makes up for with a dose of rootsy, friendly charm and some great accommodation. It also makes a perfect base for trekking and to visit the towns further to the north.

West of the city are Ta Thon, a centre for rafting down to Chiang Rai and another good base for trekking. Fang, south of Ta Thon, has some good examples of shophouses, and is an opium trafficking centre. ▸▸ *For listings, see pages 295-303.*

Ins and outs → *Colour map 1, A3.*

Getting there Chiang Rai's airport is 8 km north of the city. There are daily connections with Bangkok and Chiang Mai, and some talk of flights to international destinations in the region. The bus station is in the centre of town (but a fair walk from most of the guesthouses), and there are regular connections with Bangkok, most northern towns including Chiang Mai, and with assorted destinations in the northeast and central plains. Boats ply the Kok River, upstream from Tha Ton and downstream from Chiang Khong.

The new road to Chiang Rai from Chiang Mai cuts through forests and is fast and scenic. There are rather novel European-style country cottages along the way and some good resort-style hotels (see Sleeping, page 295). **Mae Suai**, with a hilltop monastery, is at the junction where roads lead south to Chiang Mai, north to Chiang Rai, west to Fang and southeast to Phayao. ▸▸ *See Transport, page 302, for further information.*

Getting around Chiang Rai is a sprawling town and, while walking is fine in the morning and evening, during the day many locals choose to travel by *saamlor* or *songthaew*. Most of the area's attractions lie in the surrounding countryside, and there are ample vehicle hire shops offering bicycles, cars, motorbikes and jeeps.

Tourist information TAT ① *448/16 Singhaklai Rd (near the river, opposite Wat Phra Singh), T053-744674.* Well-run office with useful town maps and information on trekking and accommodation. Areas of responsibility are Chiang Rai, Phayao, Uttaradit, Phrae and Nan.

Chiang Rai ☺☻♪♫♀☂♣☯ ▸▸ *pp295-303.*

Chiang Rai was founded in 1268 by King Mengrai, who later moved his capital here. The city became one of the key *muang* (city states), within the Lanna Kingdom's sphere of control – until Lanna began to disintegrate in the 16th century. Although it is now Thailand's most northerly town, at the time of its foundation Chiang Rai represented the most southerly bulwark against the Mons. It was later conquered by the Burmese and only became part of Thailand again in 1786.

Today, Chiang Rai has ambitious plans for the future. Lying close to what has been termed the 'Golden Rectangle', linking Thailand with Laos, Burma (Myanmar) and southern China, the city's politicians and businessmen hope to cash in on the opening up of the latter three countries. Always searching for catchy phrases to talk up a nascent idea, they even talk of the 'Five Chiangs strategy' – referring to the five towns of Chiang Tung (or Kengtung in Burma), Chiang Rung (in China), Chiang Thong (in Laos), and Chiang Mai and Chiang Rai (both in Thailand). Roads linking the five are being planned and an EU-style free trade area discussed. Talk, as they say, is cheap; a mini-EU in this peripheral part of Asia seems a distant dream, despite a noticeable increase in cross-border activity.

Getting there and around
The international airport is 8 km north of the city, just off the main Chiang Rai–Mae Sai Highway and the central bus station is just off Phahonyothin Road, T053-711224. The local *songthaew* stand is near the morning market on Uttarakit Road. *Songthaews* run on set routes around the city and each journey costs ฿2.

Sights
The city's finest monastery is **Wat Phra Kaeo**, at the north end of Trairat Road. The wat is thought to have been founded in the 13th century when it was known as Wat Pa-Year. Its change of name came about following divine intervention in 1434 when, local legend recounts, the stupa was struck by lightning to reveal the famous Emerald Buddha or Phra Kaeo, now in residence in Bangkok's Temple of the Emerald Buddha. With this momentous discovery, the wat was renamed Wat Phra Kaeo and was elevated to the status of a royal wat in 1987.

The finest structure here is the *bot* (straight ahead as you pass through the main gates on Trairat Road) featuring accomplished woodcarving, a pair of fine *nagas* flanking the entrance way and, inside, a 13th-century image of the Buddha calling the earth goddess to witness. Presumably slightly peeved that the Phra Kaeo itself had been carted off to Bangkok, a rich local Chinese businessman – Mr Lo – commissioned a Chinese artist to carve a replica image from Canadian jade. The work was undertaken in Beijing to mark the 90th birthday of the Princess Mother and she gave it the gargantuan name Phraphuttaratanakorn Nawutiwatsanusornmong-khon, or The Lord Buddha is the source of the Three Gems of Buddhism. The image was kept in the monastery's *bot* until a new building, specially designed to house it, had been completed and the image installed in a consecration ceremony held in 1991. The Chiang Rai Phra Kaeo Shrine is behind the *bot*, with two ponds filled with turtles (set free by people to gain merit) in front of it.

Above Wat Phra Kaeo, perched at the top of a small hill, is **Wat Ngam Muang**, unremarkable except for the views it offers of the city and surrounding countryside. However, historically it is important, as the stupa here contains the ashes of the great King Mengrai (1259-1317). The edifice is currently being renovated and will have a statue of the king placed in front of his *ku*.

Further northwest still is **Wat Phrathat Doi Chom Thong**, built at the top of a small hill. The wat contains the *lak muang* (city pillar).

Wat Phra Singh (dating from 1385) is an important teaching monastery on Singhaklai Road, in the north of town. Note the finely wrought animal medallions below the windows of the *bot* – rats, elephants, tigers, snakes and other beasts – and the gaudy but vivacious murals that decorate the interior. Also unusual is the Bodhi tree, surrounded by images of the Buddha in each of the principal *mudras*.

South of Wat Phra Singh is **Wat Mung Muang**, notable for its corpulent image of the Buddha, which projects above the monastery walls. The image is not at all Thai in style, but appears Chinese with its sausage-like fingers spinning the wheel of law. The area around Wat Mung Muang supports a daily **market** and, in the mornings from 0600, vegetable hawkers set up along the monastery walls, providing a wonderful contrast in colour and texture with the golden Buddha image. *Songthaews*, *saamlors* and tuk-tuks

Chiang Rai

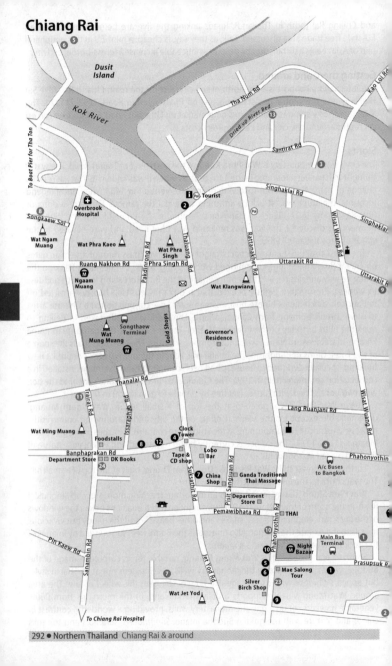

Dusit Island

Kok River

To Boat Pier for Tha Ton

Tha Num Rd

Dried up River Bed

Santirat Rd

Singhaklai Rd

Kao Loi Rd

Tourist

Overbrook Hospital

Songkaew Soi

Wat Ngam Muang

Wat Phra Kaeo

Wat Phra Singh

Phra Singh Rd

Thalung Rd

Pakdinong Rd

Ruang Nakhon Rd

Ngaam Muang

Wat Klangwiang

Rattanakhet Rd

Uttarakit Rd

Singhaklai

Wisat Muang Rd

Uttarakit R

Wat Mung Muang

Songthaew Terminal

Gold Shops

Governor's Residence

Thanalai Rd

Talat Rd

Lang Ruanjani Rd

Wat Ming Muang

Foodstalls

Issaraphap Rd

Clock Tower

Lobo Bar

Phahonyothin

Wisat Wuang Rd

Banphaprakan Rd

Department Store

DK Books

Tape & CD shop

Suksathit Rd

China Shop

Ganda Traditional Thai Massage

A/c Buses to Bangkok

Pibit Sangsuan Rd

Department Store

Pemawibhata Rd

THAI

Pln Kaew Rd

Sanambin Rd

Jet Yod Rd

Phahonyothin Rd

Night Bazaar

Main Bus Terminal

Prasupsuk R

Wat Jet Yod

Silver Birch Shop

Mae Salong Tour

To Chiang Rai Hospital

To 12 16 19, Wat Rong Khun & Chiang Mai

Sleeping 😴
Akha Guesthouse **13**
Baan Wararbordee **2**
Boonbundan
 Guesthouse **7**
Charin Garden Resort **19**
Chat House **8**
Chiang Rai Inn **9**
Chian House **14**
Diamond Park Inn **17**
Dusit Island **6**
Golden Triangle Inn **4**
International (YMCA) **25**
Legend Chiang Rai **25**
Lek House **11**
Little Duck **12**
Mae Hong Son **3**
Mantrini **16**
North **1**
Pintamorn Guesthouse **15**
Sukniran **18**
Wangcome **10**

White House **22**
Wiang Inn **23**
Ya House **24**

Eating 🍴
Aye's Place **5**
Baan Chivitmai **1**
Cabbages & Condoms **2**
Chum Cha **2**
Doi Chaang **4**
Funny House Café **6**
Haw Naliga **8**
La Cantina **7**
La Vinci **10**
Muang Thong **9**
Ratburi **12**

N

100 metres
100 yards

wait to transport market-goers back to their houses and villages. In the east of town, at the so-called *haa yaek* (five-way junction) on Phahonyothin Road, is the new statue of King Mengrai, Chiang Rai's most illustrious king.

Building on the success of Chiang Mai's night bazaar or market, Chiang Rai opened its own **night bazaar** off Phahonyothin Road a few years back. It has since expanded tremendously and sells the usual range of hilltribe handicrafts, carvings, china products, wooden boxes, picture frames, the Thai equivalent of beanie babies, catapults and so on. In many ways it is a nicer place to browse than the Chiang Mai night bazaar. It is more open, less frenetic, friendlier, and there is live music and open-air restaurants.

About 10 km south towards Chiang Mai stands one of the north's newest and most popular temples, **Wat Rong Khun** ① *Mon-Fri 0800-1730, Sat and Sun 0800-1800, free*. Crafted by a local artist, this temple looks like it has been frosted white by a freezing Arctic storm – the entire construction is built in concrete, inlaid with mirrors and then whitewashed. Some might think the result is daring beauty – others could come to the conclusion it is kitsch trash dressed up as art. The general populous seems to love the place and at weekends queues of camera-phone-wielding Thais eagerly take snaps of their loved ones in front of this startling structure. If you want to judge for yourself take a *songthaew* (every 30 minutes) from the centre of Chiang Rai to Mae Lao and get off at the temple (฿30). Alternatively hire a tuk-tuk for a half-day excursion (฿300-400).

The **Hilltribe Education Center** ① *620/25 Thanalai Rd, 1300-1330, or on request, for a small fee, in English, Thai, French or Japanese*, is one of the more interesting attractions in the town, with a small, informative **hill-tribe museum** ① *0830-2000; admission to museum ฿20, CRPDA@hotmail.com*, and an audiovisual presentation on hilltribe life. It is run by the Population and Development Association's (PDA), which is better known for its family planning and AIDS work. With this project, it is attempting to provide hill-tribe communities with additional income-earning opportunities, as the pressures of commercial life increase. The museum has recently been expanded and refurbished. Attached to the museum is a branch of the **Cabbages and Condoms** chain of restaurants (see Eating, page 299).

Ban Du is a paper-making village, 8 km north of Chiang Rai off Route 110. Paper is produced from the bark of the sa tree, which is stripped off, air dried, soaked in water, boiled in caustic soda and finally beaten, before being made into paper.

West of Chiang Rai ⊖⊘▲⊖⊙ ⇥ pp295-303.

From Chiang Rai a road winds westwards over the mountains towards Tha Ton where boats and rafts can be hired to travel down the Kok River to Chiang Rai. Beyond Tha Ton on Route 107 is the former strategic town of Fang.

Tha Ton → Colour map 1, A3.

Tha Ton lies on the Mae Kok and is a good starting point for trips on the Kok River to Chiang Rai, and for treks to the various hilltribe villages in the area. It is a pleasant little town with good accommodation and a friendly atmosphere. It also makes a good base for exploring this area of the north. Rafts travel downstream to Chiang Rai, while by road it is possible to head towards Doi Mae Salong, Mae Sai and Chiang Saen. Remember to alight at the junction of Routes 1095 and 107 and then catch one of the regular buses heading north to Fang.

Wat Tha Ton overlooks the river, not far from the bridge. A stairway leads up to this schizophrenic monastery. On the hillside is a rather ersatz Chinese grotto, with gods, goddesses and fantastic animals including Kuan Yin, the monkey god and entwined dragons. From this little piece of China, the stairway emerges in the compound of a classic, but rather ugly, modern Theravada Buddhist monastery. There is a restaurant, souvenir stall and more to show that Wat Tha Ton has truly embraced the pilgrim's dollar (or baht).

The boat trip to and from Chiang Rai takes 2½-3½ hours on a long-tailed boat, which is noisy and uncomfortable (฿200). A more relaxing form of transport is a gentle drift (at least in the dry season) on a bamboo raft. The rafts dock in Chiang Rai and the trip takes two days and a night (฿6000). Most guesthouses will arrange raft trips and many will include a trek and/or elephant ride in various combinations, plus stops at hot springs, hilltribe villages and elephant camps. ⇥ See Activities and tours, page 301, and Transport, page 302.

The regular boat down the Kok River stops at riverside villages, from where it is possible to trek to hilltribe communities. (See Background, page 718.) **Louta**, 14 km east of Tha Ton and 1.5 km off the main road between Tha Ton and Doi Mae Salong/Chiang Rai, is a well-off, developed Lisu village. It's also possible to get here by yellow pick-up (14 km), then take a motorbike taxi the remaining 1500 m uphill.

Other nearby villages include: **Tahamakeng**, one hour from Tha Ton (Lahu and Lisu villages within easy reach); **Ban Mai**, 45 minutes on from Tahamakeng (Lahu, Karen and Akha villages); and Mae Salak, further on still (Lahu, Lisu and Yao villages). ⇥ See Activities and tours, page 301.

Fang → *Colour map 1, A3.*

Fang was once a lawless centre for the trafficking of opium. Though it is not a major tourist destination, it retains a distinctive frontier feel, cut off by a ring of distant rising hills, the rows of whisky bars and karaoke clubs attesting to its unruly element.

It was founded by King Mengrai in the 13th century, although its strategic location at the head of a valley means it has probably been an important trading settlement for centuries. The government has had some success in encouraging the predominantly Yao hilltribes to switch from opium production to other cash crops such as cabbages and potatoes. Some of the old drug business persists but compared to years gone by it is relatively marginal. The valley surrounding Fang is particularly fertile and is used for rice, fruit and vegetable cultivation. The Fang Oil Refinery, on Route 109, also provides employment.

There is a good smattering of traditional wooden shophouses in town. The bus station is on the main road in the centre of town. Wat Jong Paen, on Tha Phae Road at the northern edge of town, is Burmese in style. The best day to be in Fang is Wednesday – market day – when colourful hill peoples come to town to sell crops, textiles and more. The market winds down from 1300.

Chiang Dao Caves (see page 247) is a large cave complex, 90 km south of Fang off Route 107 towards Chiang Mai. To get there, take a bus to Chiang Mai and get off in **Chiang Dao** – the town, sited beneath a dramatic peak – which offers a charming collection of old wooden shophouses and is well worth a visit. *Songthaews* transport passengers the final 6 km to the caves.

The *bor nam rawn* or **hot springs** can be found 12 km west of Fang, near Ban Muang Chom. To get there, turn left shortly after leaving the town on the road north to Tha Ton.

◉ Chiang Rai and around listings

For Sleeping and Eating price codes and other relevant information, see pages 44-49.

◉ Sleeping

Chiang Rai *p290, map p292*
Accommodation in Chiang Rai is of a high standard. Guesthouses, in particular, are quiet, with large and generally clean rooms – a welcome change from some places in Chiang Mai. Most are concentrated in the quieter northern part of the city, some on the 'island' between both branches of the Kok River.
LL-AL Dusit Island, 1129 Kraisorasit Rd, T053-607999, chiangrai.dusit.com. Overblown, fairly ostentatious hotel, just north of town on an 'island' in the river, set in lavish grounds. 271 a/c rooms and suites, and every facility including restaurant, fitness centre, tennis courts, pool and spa.
L-AL The Legend Chiang Rai, 124/15 Kohloy Rd, T053-910400,

www.thelegend-chiangrai.com. A boutique hotel on the banks of the Mae Kok River.
L-C Wangcome Hotel, 869/90 Pemawibhata Rd, T053-711800, www.wangcome.com. Reasonable hotel in a great central location. Each room is a/c and en suite with minibar and TV. Restaurant, bar and karaoke on site. Huge suites if you can afford them.
AL-A Mantrini, on the main road a couple of kilometres from the centre, T053-755226, www.mantrini.com. One of the few genuine design hotels in this part of Thailand. The lobby is cool, understated and relaxed, the pool is surrounded by gardens while the rooftop is a perfect spot to watch the sunset. Rooms are smallish, but well appointed. Free Wi-Fi, bar, restaurant and breakfast included in the rate. Recommended.
A Little Duck, 4 Phahonyothin Rd, 2 km south of town, off main road to Chiang Mai, T053-715637. Large and impersonal but professionally run. With all amenities,

including a/c, restaurant, pool and its own department store. Price includes breakfast.

A Wiang Inn, 893 Phahonyothin Rd, T053-711533. The original 'luxury' hotel in town, renovated in 1992-1993 and still holding its own. Competitively priced, central location but set back from the main road so comparatively peaceful, stylish lobby. Rooms are fairly standard, but perfectly adequate with satellite TV. A/c, restaurant, small pool, The buffet breakfast and lunch (with dim sum) are very good value. Recommended.

A-D Diamond Park Inn, 74/6 Moo 18, Sanpanard Rd, T053-754960, www.diamond parkinn.com. Good-value hotel down the end of a quiet *soi* a short walk from the night bazaar. All rooms are en suite with a/c. The larger 'de luxe' rooms are the best value. Also has a restaurant.

C Chiang Rai Inn, 661 Uttarakit Rd, T053-712673. A/c hotel in modern interpretation of northern Thai architecture. Large, spotless but plain rooms, immaculate bathrooms, hot water. Discounts available, good value.

C Golden Triangle Inn, 590 Phahonyothin Rd, T053-711339. A/c, restaurant. This is a great little hotel on a tree-filled plot of land, rooms are clean and stylish with hot water. Good treks, friendly atmosphere, breakfast included in room rate. Recommended.

C The International (YMCA), 70 Phahonyothin Rd, 6 km on the main highway towards Mae Sai, past the handicraft centre, T053-713785, ymcawf@loxinfo.co.th. Clean and well kept, but some rooms are noisy due to passing traffic. A/c, pool, restaurant (good-value Thai, Chinese and European food), handicraft shop, health centre, playground and conference rooms. Dorm rooms available. As with YMCA Chiang Mai, all profits go to support rural development projects.

C Sukniran, 424/1 Banphaprakan Rd, T053-711955. Some a/c, good position close to clock tower, airy lobby and rooms facing a courtyard away from the main road, so not too noisy.

C-E Boonbundan Guesthouse, 1005/13 Jet Yod Rd, T053-717040. Quiet leafy compound near the centre of town.

Professionally managed, good range of services, clean rooms with hot water although becoming shabby. Some a/c, outdoor eating area. Recommended, including the tours.

D Charin Garden Resort, Mae Suay on main road to Chiang Mai, 40 km south of Chiang Rai, T053-918628, www.chiangraiprovince.com/htl/charin. If you get a chance to spend a night at the Charin it's worth it just for the cake – one of the best bakeries in Northern Thailand. The location is also gorgeous, set beside a sweeping river. Bungalows are adequate, with a/c and en suite but nothing to write home about. Friendly owners. Recommended.

D-E Chat House, 3/2 Trairat Soi Songkaew (near Wat Phra Kaeo), T053-711481. In a quiet, leafy compound down a narrow *soi*, and away from the main concentration of guesthouses. Reasonably clean but basic rooms and attached bathrooms with hot showers. A run-down feel about the place, although friendly people and great potential. Dorm beds available, good food and satellite TV. Trekking and motorbike hire available.

D-E The North Hotel, small *soi* between the market and night bazaar, T053-719873, www.thenorth.co.th. A funky little hotel with library, roof terrace, bar and restaurant – one of the coolest places to stay in town. Charming a/c rooms with TV and en suite. Owner is friendly and speaks English. Recommended.

D-F Chian House, 172 Sriboonruang Rd, on the island, T053-713388. Clean and friendly – the large bungalows are especially good value. Peaceful atmosphere and good food. Also organizes treks and tours and has internet.

D-F Pintamorn Guesthouse, 199/1-3 Moo 21 Singhaklai Rd, T053-714161. Some a/c, a quiet and friendly guesthouse in a peaceful area of town. Rooms are large and well maintained, the 'VIP' room is a real bargain. Trekking and motorbike and jeep rental can be arranged. A friendly place with lots of atmosphere and good value. Recommended.

E Baan Wararbordee, 59/1 Moo 18, Sanpanard Rd, T053-754888. Delightful little guesthouse tucked away on a quiet *soi*. Very friendly, helpful owner, free coffee, tea and internet. Rooms on the upper floors are better lit – all have TV, en suite, hot water and a/c. There's a garden as well. Recommended.

E-F Mae Hong Son, 126 Singhaklai Rd, T053-715367. Friendly Dutch-run guesthouse at the end of a very quiet *soi*. The traditional wooden house has clean rooms with shared bathrooms; newer rooms have en suite but are more expensive. Treks (recommended, with a great guide), jeep and motorbike hire, good source of information. Peaceful and good value. Tasty food. Recommended.

E-F The White House, 789 Phahonyothin Rd, T053-713427. Set back off Chiang Rai's main road in a leafy compound. A recent coat of paint has rendered rooms bright and clean. A pool and jacuzzi have also been added which is pretty good for a place this cheap (for use by non-residents, ฿20).

E-G Akha Guesthouse, 423/25 Moo 21 Soi1 Kohloy, T053-715084, www.akha.info. Pleasant location in gardens next to a small stream in a quiet part of town. Run by local Akha people, all rooms – from en suite a/c bungalows through to single, fan rooms with shared facilities – are excellent value and clean. Small restaurant with Akha and Thai dishes. Also runs a homestay programme in a nearby Akha village. Free pick-up from bus station. Recommended.

F Lek House, 95 Thanalai Rd, T053-713337. Well-organized, friendly place, with a bar and food and satellite TV. Hires motorbikes.

F Ya House, down a *soi* at the western end of Banphaprakan Rd, T053-717090. Attractive wooden building with a quiet garden and reading library makes this a good place for backpackers to chill out. Clean rooms, some with hot water shower, breakfast and evening food provided.

Tha Ton *p294*

There is a good range of accommodation here, from basic guesthouses through to comfortable small hotels.

A Thaton River View Resort (Comfort Inn), T053-459289, www.thaton-riverview-resort.th66.com. Probably the most attractively positioned of all the places to stay in Tha Ton. Small bungalows scattered along the riverbank, at the confluence of the Mae Kok and a tributary, overlooking fields and mountains. Rooms are comfortable and clean with satellite TV. Airy restaurant (cheap) with extensive Thai menu and a smattering of Western dishes, small library. Well-run with friendly atmosphere. Rates are negotiable and include buffet breakfast.

B Thaton Chalet, 192/1 Moo 14, T053-373155, www.thatonchalet.com. A/c, restaurant, 4 storeys, right by the bridge and overlooking the river with chalets of sorts. Rooms are clean and very comfortable with hot-water showers (baths in the de luxe rooms), minibar and satellite TV. Riverside bar.

B-E Garden Home, T053-373015. Away from the main bustle, this peaceful resort has bungalows set in a large tree-filled orchard garden on the river's edge. Rooms range widely in price from guesthouse level up to hotel quality: some rooms have fan and squat toilets, others have Western toilets, a/c and hot-water showers. All rooms are spotlessly clean. Quiet and friendly, no restaurant. Recommended.

D Tha Ton Garden. Easily confused with the nearby **Garden Home**. Riverside location, garden compound, well maintained, hot water and a/c.

D-E Apple Restaurant and Guesthouse. There are 2 **Apples**. The first, 2 streets south of the river is reminiscent of an Austrian ski chalet, and has quite good clean fan rooms with bath, hot water and Western toilets. The airy restaurant downstairs has an extensive menu of Western and Thai dishes, but management are unhelpful. The 2nd **Apple** is the guesthouse about 100 m away. Peaceful, in a large garden compound, but with no river view.

F-G Naam Waan Guesthouse, Soi Udomphon, T053-459403. Small, clean, simple rooms set around a courtyard. Friendly.

Fang *p295*

A-B Angkhang Nature Resort, 40 km west of Fang, on Route 1249, 1/1 Moo 5 Baan Koom, Tambon Mae Ngon, T053-450110, www.amari.com/angkhang. Situated high in the cool mountains very close to the border with Burma, the resort was developed under the auspices of the Royal Project Foundation. It consists of 72 well-appointed rooms with all mod-cons.

B Chiang Dao Hill Resort, on the main road north to Fang, 24 km from Chiang Dao and 52 km south of Fang, T053-232434, www.chiangdaohillresort.com. Only really worth visiting for those with their own transport (or on a tour). Bavarian-style building with comfortable rooms, hot water, overlooked by limestone pinnacles.

C-D Tangerine Ville Hotel, 117 Moo 2 Sansai, T053-882600. Decent enough hotel a couple of kilometres south of town on the road to Chiang Mai. Rooms offer the standard TV, hot water and a/c facilities you'd expect while not much character. Rate also includes breakfast.

D Cheap Cheap Guesthouse, 500 m off the main road towards the southern edge of the town (towards Chiang Mai), T053-453265. Its real name is **Fang Academic Centre (FAC)**. Quiet location overlooking rice fields. ฿200 for a dorm bed with fridge, TV and fan and cold water shower. Free laundry. Food available if ordered in advance.

D Baan Sa-Bai Hotel, 88 Moo 9, Wieng Fang. Set almost behind the new Tesco Lotus in a very quiet *soi*, this is very relaxed place to stay. Rooms are simple, spotless and well-kept, all with TV, hot showers, a/c etc. Good choice if you need a rest.

D-E Chok Thani, 425 Chotana Rd, just off the main road, T053-451252. Some a/c, clean if functional rooms.

E Baan Fanh Hotel, 49 Moo 3 Tapae Rd. T053-451281. Small hotel set back from the main road. Friendly with a stylish feel. All rooms are a/c with en suite and hot water. Free Wi-Fi and a basic, self-service breakfast. Good value and recommended.

E New Poo Guesthouse, off main road, just past **Chok Thani Hotel** down a dirt rack, T053-453210. Very small block with only 4 rooms, clean with fan and cold-water shower and Thai toilet. Restaurant and snooker table, a quiet place and friendly management.

E Uang Kham (Ueng Khum), 227 Tha Phae Rd Soi 3, T053-451268. Clean bungalows, hot water. Recommended.

E Wiang Kaew, just off Tha Phae Rd (over the bridge, north of the town centre). A friendly place that has kept good standards long-term. Simple clean rooms, hot water.

Chiang Dao

D-F Chiang Dao Rainbow Guesthouse, 344 Ban Tunglakorn, T084-8038116. This is a great little guesthouse located just outside Chiang Dao (call for directions). 3 rooms in the main house, a couple of small bungalows and a larger house in the village. The food is also excellent. Recommended.

E-F Mon and Kurts, 78 Moo 15 Baandon, T053-388011, www.chiangdao.org. Friendly roadside guesthouse a little way from the town centre. Rooms are average, with a/c with en suite and hot water. Also serves a good mix of Thai and Western food.

🍴 Eating

Chiang Rai *p290, map p292*
The greatest variety of restaurants is to be found in the streets around the **Wangcome Hotel**, from Mexican to French to cheap Thai and Chinese. Many of the tourist-oriented restaurants serve the same range of dishes: wiener schnitzel, lasagne, pizza, burgers, fried rice. Having said that, the food is quite good. In the evenings, the night bazaar off Phahonyothin Rd is good for stall food; there is an excellent range of places here where you can choose from spring rolls, wonton, pancakes, kebabs, noodles, rice dishes, even deep-fried beetles and grubs – and then sit at a table and listen to live music – great atmosphere.

¶¶¶ **La Vinci**, 879/4-6 Phahonyothin Rd, opposite entrance to the night bazaar. Decent enough, if overpriced, wood-fired pizzas and passable attempts at Italian food provide something for those bored of spicy food.

¶¶ **Chiangrai Island Restaurant**, 1129/1 Kraisorasit Rd (part of Dusit Island Hotel). Northern Thai specialities, also serves international food.

¶¶ **Haw Naliga**, 401/1-2 Banphaprakan Rd (west of Ratburi and Phetburi restaurants). Country setting, rather expensive but good food, although the quality is highly variable.

¶¶ **La Cantina**, Soi Punyodyana (near Wangcome Hotel, off Phahonyothin Rd by the clock tower). The manager and cook is Italian so the food is pretty authentic, including some unusual regional dishes.

¶¶ **Ratanakosin**, T053-740012. Open 1600-2400. Highly recommended for quality of food and atmospheric decor. Faces onto the night bazaar, so you can feel part of the action, and dine from the upstairs balcony, whilst watching the Thai dancing below.

¶ **Aye's Place**, Phahonyothin Rd, opposite entrance to Wiang Inn, T053-752535. Spacious restaurant open for breakfast (though not very early), lunch and dinner, extensive Thai and international menu. The baguettes are particularly good.

¶ **Cabbages and Condoms**, 620/25 Thanalai Rd (attached to the Hilltribe Museum). Run by the PDA, a non-governmental organization (see page 301), all proceeds go to charity. Good northern food including *larb* (spicy minced meat – really a northeastern delicacy), northern spicy sausage, duck curry and chicken in banana leaves. Eat inside or outdoors (rather noisy on the road), reasonably priced.

¶ **Chum Cha**, Singhaklai Rd (next to TAT office). Clean, new place for coffee and ice cream, with some simple noodle and rice dishes.

¶ **Funny House Café**, Phahonyothin Rd, opposite Wiang Inn. German-run, this diminutive place is popular and has the same menu as many of the other 'international' restaurants on this strip.

¶ **Golden Triangle Café**, Golden Triangle Inn (see Sleeping, above), 590 Phahonyothin Rd. International food. Recommended.

¶ **Muang Thong**, Phahonyothin Rd (just south of Wiang Inn). A serious restaurant where Chinese/Thai food is served, with little pretence, on plastic plates. Especially good vegetable dishes, recommended by locals who make up the bulk of the clientele.

¶ **Ratburi**, Banphaprakan Rd, opposite Sukniran Hotel. Large selection of curries, eat in or takeaway, ฿15 per dish.

Bakeries

¶¶-¶ **Baan Chivitmai**, just opposite the bus station. Run by a Swedish Christian charity, this is a perfect spot to gather your thoughts, chomp on a yummy cake and sup on a decent coffee before setting off around town. Great breakfasts and good juices keep this place full but it's a little pricey.

¶¶-¶ **Doi Chaang**, Banphapraken Rd. An outlet for a community-controlled coffee-growing project that is well worth supporting if only for the fact that they serve a great cup of the brown, roasted stuff. Decent cakes as well.

Foodstalls

There are dozens of stalls at night around the night market off Phahonyothin Rd (by the bus terminal). One trader does a great roti with stupendous banana, strawberry, orange and other pancakes – he usually sets up near the entrance to the night market. There are stalls on the alley leading from Phahonyothin Rd into the night market. Another group can be found near Wat Ming Muang, at the intersection of Trairat and Banphaprakan roads.

Tha Ton *p294*

There are a number of attractive riverside restaurants.

¶ **Khao Soi Restaurant**, right by the river and bridge, and next to Thip's Travellers House. Friendly place serving *khao soi* (of course) and the usual rice and noodle dishes.

¶ **Riverside Thai Restaurant**, by the river. A nice place to eat, open for breakfast, lunch

and dinner. Thatched riverside affair with
good fish dishes – watch out for mozzies
in the evening.

¶ Sonay Chainam Restaurant, on the
north side of the bridge by the riverside.
Thai and European food. Long wait for
average food.

¶ Thaton Chalet Restaurant, riverside
restaurant on the veranda of the hotel.
Thai and Chinese food.

Fang *p295*
¶ 'Homemade Coffee and Cake', on main
road to Chiang Mai, past the Tesco Lotus.
The big sign outside this place states exactly
what you will get. Sticky mini-donuts will
help cure any sugar cravings.
¶ JJ's Bakery, opposite Wat Chedi Ngam on
the main road. Cakes, Thai and international.
¶ Muang Fang, on the main road, next
to the Bangkok Bank. Typical Thai food.

🍸 Bars and clubs

Chiang Rai *p290, map p292*
There's now a burgeoning bar scene in
Chiang Rai – many can be found in and
around Phahonyothin Rd, near the
crossroads with Banphaprakan Rd.
Easy House Bar and Restaurant,
Permaviphat Rd (opposite **Wangcome**
Hotel). Cocktails, beers, live music, self-
consciously hip.
Lobo Bar, down a narrow private *soi* off
Phahonyothin Rd, near the clock tower.
A lively place.

🎭 Entertainment

Chiang Rai *p290, map p292*
Music
Night market, close to the bus terminal
off Phahonyothin Rd. Live music shows
are held periodically.

⭕ Shopping

Chiang Rai *p290, map p292*
Books
DK Book Store, along Barnphaprakan Rd.
Sells guidebooks of the region in English.
Pho Thong Book Store, Thanalai Rd (close
to the intersection with Trairat Rd). Mostly in
Thai, but some English books and magazines.

China
China shop, Pisit Sangsuan Rd. Thai-
decorated seconds for US and UK shops (such
as **Whittards**), on sale here at rock-bottom
prices. Mugs, bowls, plates and teapots.

Department stores
Edision department store, on the corner of
Banphraprakan and Sanambin roads. Also an
a/c department store near the **Wangcome**
Hotel, on the corner of Phahonyothin and
Pemavipat roads.

Handicrafts, silver and textiles
Many shops in town around the **Wangcome**
Hotel plaza area and on Phahonyothin Rd
sell hilltribe goods, silver, textiles and woodcarvings. See also Night market, below.
Chiang Rai Handicrafts Centre,
3 km out of town on road to Chiang Saen.
Ego, 869/81-82 (next to **Wangcome** Hotel),
for Burmese and hilltribe antiques, beads,
jewellery, carvings, textiles, reasonable
prices. Recommended.
Hilltribe Education Center, 620/25 Thanalai
Rd. Sells genuine hilltribe textiles and other
goods, all profits go back to the communities.
Silver Birch, 891 Phahonyothin Rd, near
Wiang Inn. For unusual woodcarvings and
silverware, more expensive but finely crafted.

Music
There is a great little music shop near the
clock tower at the northern end of Jet Yod Rd.

Night market
There is a night bazaar just off Phahonyothin Rd, close to the bus terminal.

The stalls and shops sell a range of goods, including hilltribe handicrafts, silverware, woodcarvings, T-shirts, clothes, pin cushions, Burmese bags and leatherware. Foodstalls and bars open in the evening.

▲ Activities and tours

Chiang Rai *p290, map p292*
Sports clubs
Pintamorn Sportsclub, 115/1-8 Wat Sribo-onruang Rd. Sauna, exercise room, pool table.

Therapies
There are several places in the network of streets near the Wangcome Hotel.
Ganda Traditional Thai Massage, 869/59-63 Pisit Sangsuan Rd. Recommended.
Mue Thong Thai Massage, Inn Come Hotel, 172/6 Ratbamrung Rd, T053-717850.
Yogi massage and sauna centre, at the Royal Princess Hotel. The most luxurious place for a Thai Massage. (฿900 for 2-hr massage and 30-min sauna).

Tours and trekking
Most treks are cheaper if organized through guesthouses and they are usually also more adventurous. Guesthouses that organize treks include: Boonbundan, Chat House, Chian House, Golden Triangle Inn, Mae Hong Son (recommended) and Pintamorn (see Sleeping, above). The usual range of **elephant rides** and **boat trips** as part of a trek are also offered. A 2- day/1-night **raft trip** costs ฿800-1100 per person, 4-day/3-night **trek** about ฿1500-2000. Day tours to visit **hilltribe villages** such as Sop Ruak and the Golden Triangle, Mae Sai, Mae Salong and Chiang Saen, are organized by most of the tour/trekking companies listed below (฿600). Tours that include an elephant ride and boat trip, plus visits to hilltribe villages, cost about ฿700. Before embarking on a trek, it is worth-while visiting the Hilltribe Education Center. Tribes in the area include Karen, Lisu, Lahu and Akha. See also Background, page 716.

Motorcycle tours are becoming increasingly popular, and many guesthouses provide rental services and information on routes to take for a day's excursion.

There are several trekking companies and tour operators around the **Wangcome Hotel** plaza area, along Phahonyothin and Premwipak roads (a *soi* off Phahonyothin). The **TAT** office produces a list of companies with average prices and other useful advice.
Chiangrai Agency Centre, 428/10 Banpha-prakan Rd, T053-717274.
Chiangrai Travel and Tour, 869/95 Premwipak Rd, T053-713314.
Far East North Tours Chiang Rai, 402/1 Moo 13, Phahonyothin Rd, T053-715690.
Golden Triangle Tours, 590 Phahonyothin Rd, T053-711339 (attached to the **Golden Triangle Hotel**). Recommended.
Mae Salong Tour, 882/4 Phahonyothin Rd, T053-712515. Recommended treks, also organizes river cruises on the Mekong including Laos, China and Thailand.
PDA, 620/25 Thanalai Rd, T053-719167. Primarily a charity, working to improve the lot of the hilltribes but also runs treks – all profits are ploughed back into the charity. Treks introduce clients to the PDA's community development projects; guides tend to be very knowledgeable about hilltribe customs. Advance booking recommended.
PD Tour, 834/6 Phahonyothin Rd, T053-712829.

Ta Thon *p294*
Most guesthouses in Tha Ton will help you to organize trekking or raft/boat trips, or take the scheduled daily boat from the pier. Treks cost around ฿1500 for 1 night/2 days including rafting. A 1-day trip on an elephant will set you back ฿950, and a trip to Mae Sai and across the border into Burma costs ฿1250 (including visa, car and guide). Tour operators include: **Tha Ton Tours**, T/F053-373143, and **Thip Travel** (attached to **Thip's Travellers House**), T053-459312. Both arrange raft trips although we have received a negative comment on **Thip Travel**

with regards to poor camping equipment and lack of care. A 2-day raft trip to Chiang Rai costs around ฿6000.

⊙ Transport

Chiang Rai p290, map p292
Air
THAI, 1-2Go and Air Asia provide Regular connections with **Chiang Mai** (40 mins) and **Bangkok** (1 hr 25 mins). The runway has been lengthened to take wide-bodied jets, and there is some talk of the possibility of international connections in the near future with other Asian destinations.
   Airline offices THAI, 870 Phahon-yothin Rd, T053-711179.

Bicycle
Guesthouses offer hire for ฿20-40 per day.

Boat
Long-tailed boats leave from the new pier, 2 km northwest of the centre; follow Trairat Rd north, past the entrance to the **Dusit Island Resort**, to the T-junction with Winitchakun Rd. Turn right and continue past the golf course to the bridge over the Kok River. The pier is on the far side of the river. Boats for **Tha Ton** depart daily at 1030 (฿350). Boats can be chartered for ฿300 per hr or for ฿1600 to Tha Ton, ฿500 to Rim Kok, ฿1500 to Chiang Khong. A boat takes a maximum of 8 passengers, the pier is open daily 0700-1600 (see page 294).

Bus
Regular connections with **Chiang Saen** every 15 mins (1½ hrs) and **Mae Sai** every 15 mins (1 hr 40 mins), **Chiang Mai** (3 hrs), **Phayao** (1 hr 40 mins), **Phrae** (4 hrs), **Nan** (6 hrs), **Chiang Kham** (2 hrs), **Chiang Khong** (3 hrs), **Lampang** (5 hrs), **Phitsanulok** via Sukhothai (6 hrs), **Khon Kaen** (12 hrs), **Nakhon Ratchasima** (13 hrs), **Bangkok** (12 hrs), **Fang, Mae Suai, Nakhon Sawan, Sukhothai, Nakhon Phanom, Udon Thani** and **Pattaya**.

To **Chiang Mai**, buses taking the *sai kao* (old route) go via Phayao (6 hrs) and Lampang; buses taking the new road along Route 1019, go via Wiang Papao hot springs (4 hrs) and Doi Saket. A/c and VIP buses to **Bangkok** leave from the office on Phahon-yothin Rd, opposite the **Golden Triangle Inn**.

Car
Hire can be arranged through one of the many tour and travel companies around the **Wangcome Hotel**, or from **Budget**, based at the **Golden Triangle Inn**.
   Jeep hire is ฿800 per day from many guesthouses, eg Bowling Guesthouse, Chian House, Pintamorn, Mae Hong Son Guesthouse and many tour companies.

Motorbike
Motorbike hire costs ฿150-200 per day, from most guesthouses and tour companies. **ST Motorcycle**, Banphaprakan Rd. One of the best motorcycle rental services in Northern Thailand, and one of the only places that will allow you (after a large deposit has been taken) to cross into Laos and Burma. The owner, Khun Seksit, is friendly and straight talking. In addition to the ubiquitous step-throughs, he also has a fleet of well-maintained 250-600cc off-road bikes for the more serious motor-cyclist. Highly recommended if biking is your thing.

Tha Ton p294
Boat
The boat to **Chiang Rai** departs at 1230 and takes 2½-3½ hrs, depending on the state of the river (฿250). **Tha Ton Boat Office**, by the river, T053-459427, is open 0900-1500.
   It's possible to hire an entire boat (seating up to 8 people) for ฿1700, or ฿1400 if hired through one of the tour operators, see above. See Tours and trekking, page 301, for details of organizing a raft trip to Chiang Rai. Before leaving Tha Ton by boat, travellers must sign out at the tourist police box next to the pier.

Bicycle

Bicycle hire is available from **Apple Guest-house** and **Thaton River View Resort**.

Bus

Regular connections with **Bangkok**, most leaving in the evening. Buses run to **Chiang Mai** (4 hrs), or take a minibus to **Fang** (45 mins), which has more frequent connections with Chiang Mai (40 mins). Regular connections with **Chiang Rai** (2½ hrs), **Mae Sai** (1½ hrs), **Chiang Saen** (1½ hrs), **Chiang Khong** (2½ hrs) and **Mae Salong** (2½ hrs). It is also possible to get to **Pai/Mae Hong Son** without going through Chiang Mai: from Tha Ton, catch a bus through Fang heading for Chiang Mai and get off at Ban Mae Malai, at the junction with Route 1095. Then, pick up a bus heading for Pai/Mae Hong Son.

Songthaew

Connections with **Fang** every 15 mins.

Fang *p295*
Bus

Regular connections with **Chiang Mai** from the Chang Puak bus station on Chotana Rd, 3 hrs. Minibuses run on the hour through the week from next to the hospital to Chiang Mai (฿80).

Songthaew

Regular connections with **Tha Ton** (40 mins). There are 2 routes to Chiang Rai: either take the *songthaew* from Fang to Mae Suai (40 mins), then catch a bus to **Chiang Rai** (95 km), or take a *songthaew* from Tha Ton up to Doi Mae Salong, then to Mae Chan, then on to Chiang Rai (114 km).

❶ Directory

Chiang Rai *p290, map p292*
Banks There is a profusion of exchange booths and banks on Thanalai and Phahon-yothin roads. Many open 7 days a week and in the evening. **Internet** An abundance of internet cafés around the Wangcome Hotel, ฿30 per hr. **Medical services** Overbrook, opposite Chat House, Trairat Rd, T053-711 366. Provincial, on Sanambin Rd. Chiang Rai Hospital, Sathorn Payabarn Rd, T053-711403, T053-711119. **Police** Police Station, Rattanakhat Rd, T053-711444. Tourist Police, Singhaklai Rd (below the TAT office, opposite Wat Phra Singh), T053-717779, and a booth at the night market. In an emergency call T1155 (24 hrs). **Post office** On Uttarakit Rd at the northern end of Suksathit Rd.

Tha Ton *p294*
Police Tourist Police emergency telephone number, T1155 (24 hrs). **Telephone** Ngam Muang Rd, near Wat Phra Kaeo.

Fang *p295*
Banks A number on the main road close to the clock tower. **Post office** Past the bus station, not far from the Bangkok Bank on the main road.

Chiang Saen and the Golden Triangle

Chiang Saen, northeast of Chiang Rai on the banks of the mighty Mekong River, was once the evocative capital of an ancient kingdom. Follow the meandering Mekong downstream and the road reaches the small outpost of Chiang Khong, home of the giant catfish and a crossing point into Laos. Meanwhile, 11 km upstream from Chiang Saen, is the infamous Golden Triangle, the meeting point of Laos, Thailand and Burma. This was once a lawless area filled with smugglers and drug lords. These days it's home to the tourist village of Sop Ruak and the compelling Opium Museum. Still further upstream, 61 km north of Chiang Rai, Mae Sai is Thailand's most northerly town and a busy border trading post with Burma. A new road runs off Route 110 to the hill town of Mae Salong, from where a poor track continues west to Tha Ton. ▸▸ *For listings, see pages 312-318.*

Chiang Saen ☺🕐🕐🕐☺ ▸▸ *pp312-318. Colour map 1, A3.*

Chiang Saen is an ancient capital on the banks of the Mekong River, the last village before the famed 'Golden Triangle'. Today, with the impressive town ramparts still very much in evidence, it is a charming one-street market town. The city walls run along three sides of the town and are pierced by five gates. The fourth 'wall' is formed by the Mekong River. Quiet, with wooden shophouses and a scattering of ruins lying haphazardly and untended in the undergrowth, it has so far managed to escape the uncontrolled tourist development of other towns in northern Thailand.

Ins and outs

Getting there and around Buses arrive regularly from Chiang Rai (one hour 20 minutes), Mae Sai and Chiang Khong. Long-tailed boats ply the Mekong River connecting Chiang Saen with Sop Ruak, Chiang Khong and Jin Hang in China. Motorized *saamlors* congregate by the bus stop and offer trips around the sights. ▸▸ *See Transport, page 317, for further information.*

Tourist information TAT① *Phahonyothin Rd, opposite the National Museum, 0830-1630*, is attached to the sensitively designed Bureau for the Restoration and Conservation of the Historic City of Chiang Mai.

Background

Chiang Saen was probably established during the early years of the last millennium and became the capital of the Chiang Saen Kingdom, founded in 1328 by King Saen Phu, the grandson of King Mengrai. Captured in the 16th century by the Burmese, the town became a Burmese stronghold in their constant wars with the Thais. It was not recaptured until Rama I sent an army here in 1803. Fearing that the Burmese might use the town to mount raids against his kingdom in the future, Rama I ordered it to be destroyed. Chiang Saen remained deserted for nearly 100 years. King Mongkut ordered the town to be repopulated, but it still feels as though it is only part-filled, its inhabitants rattling around in the area's illustrious history. The ancient city is a gazetted historic monument managed by the Thai Fine Arts Department, and in total there are 75 monasteries and other monuments inside the city walls and another 66 outside.

In September 1992, a 120-tonne ship, with 60 Chinese delegates aboard, made the 385-km trip down the Mekong from Yunnan. Since then, links with China – as well as Laos – have developed apace. Cargo boats unload apples and other produce from China, and the market in Chiang Saen is stocked with low-quality manufactured goods. Anticipating a trade boom, two new piers were built (one of which was promptly washed away) as well as a luxurious business centre south of town – demonstrating how much money there is around as people try to cash in on the 'Golden Quadrangle' (Thailand, Burma, Laos and China).

The economic crisis in Thailand changed things. Before mid-1997 Thai tourists were rushing upriver to visit their ethnic brethren in Yunnan. With the crash of the baht in July 1997, the flow reversed; Thais stayed at home, no longer able to travel abroad, while Chinese tourists from Yunnan suddenly found a trip to Thailand within their grasp.

Chiang Saen

400 metres
400 yards

Sleeping
Chiang Saen Guesthouse 1
Chiang Saen River Hill 2

Eating
Danang Vietnam Kitchen 1

Nameless 2

Bars & clubs
Pub & Karaoke 3

Transport
To Chiang Rai 1
To Mae Sai 2
To Chiang Khong 3

Sights

Entering the town from Chiang Rai, the ruins of **Wat Phrathat Chedi Luang** can be seen on the right-hand side shortly after passing through the city's ancient ramparts. Built by King Saen Phu in 1331, this wat was established as the main monastery in the city. The *chedi*, resting on an octagonal base, is 60 m tall, but has fallen into disrepair over the centuries and is now clothed in long grass. The *viharn* is in a similar state of decrepitude and is protected by a jury-rigged corrugated-iron roof.

Just to the west of Wat Phrathat Chedi Luang is a small branch of the **National Museum** ① *Wed-Sun 0900-1200, 1300-1600, ฿10.* It contains various Buddha images and other artefacts unearthed in the area, as well as a small display of hilltribe handicrafts including clothing and musical instruments. Of the Buddha images, the most significant are those in the so-called Chiang Saen style, with their oval faces and slender bodies. They are regarded by art historians as being among the first true 'Thai' works of art.

West of town, just outside the city ramparts, is the beautiful **Wat Pa Sak** ① *฿30,* or 'Forest of Teak Wat' – so-called because of a wall of 300 teak trees, planted around the wat when it was founded. The monastery was founded in 1295 during the reign of Ramkhamhaeng of Sukhothai and actually predates the town. The unusual pyramid-

Chiang Saen–Jin Hang

Regular boat services ply the Mekong between Chiang Saen and Jin Hang. A weekly slow boat takes three days and the ฿1500 fare includes food and accommodation. This is an unofficial service and you are not allowed to leave the boat en route. The other service, a speedboat, takes about six hours and costs ฿4000. The **Chiang Saen Guesthouse** (see page 312) sells tickets for these services.

Visas Be aware that you require the correct visa to enter China via the Mekong and you may get turned away from the border. You'd be wise to contact the Chinese embassy in Bangkok before attempting this route.

---

shaped *chedi*, said to house a bone relic of the Lord Buddha, is the main building of interest here. Art historians see a combination of influences in the *chedi*: Pagan (Burma), Dvaravati, Sukhothai, and even Srivijaya. The niches along the base contain alternating *devatas* (heavenly beings) and standing Buddha images – poorly restored – the latter in the mudra of the Buddha 'Calling for Rain' (an attitude common in Laos but less so in Thailand). Much of the fine stucco work, save for fragments of *nagas* and *garudas*, has disappeared (some can be seen in the Chiang Saen Museum). The Spirit House at the entrance, by the ramparts, is also worth a little more than a glance.

On a hill 2.5 km north of Wat Pa Sak, following the ramparts, is **Wat Phrathat Chom Kitti**, which may date from as early as the 10th century. A golden-topped stupa is being restored, but there is little else save for the views of the river and surrounding countryside. **Wat Chom Cheung**, a small ruined *chedi*, lies close by on the same hill. If visiting on foot, the stairs start about 150 m from the city walls and come first to Wat Chom Cheung. A highly decorated new wat has recently been completed here.

Strung out along the riverbank, the market sells plenty of unnecessary plastic objects and is a good place to watch hilltribe people (Karen and Lua among others) browsing through the goods. Since trade with China and Laos has expanded, it is also possible to pick up cheap – but poorly made – products from 'across the water'.

Wat Phrathat Pa Ngao, lies 4 km from Chiang Saen, along the road that follows the Mekong downstream. Perched on a hill, it provides views of the river and countryside. For Sop Ruak and the Golden Triangle take the same road upstream, 11 km from town (see below). Take a *songthaew* or long-tailed boat; boats can be hired from the jetty below the **Salathai Restaurant** and will also take passengers to riverside villages (bargain hard).

Sop Ruak ●●▲●● ▸▸ pp312-318. Colour map 1, A3.

This small 'village', 11 km north of Chiang Saen at the apex of the Golden Triangle, where Burma, Laos and Thailand meet, has become a busy tourist spot on the basis (largely unwarranted) of its association with drugs, intrigue and violence. It's actually rather dull, with rows of tacky stalls selling hilltribe handicrafts and Burmese and Laotian goods, and a succession of maps and marble constructions informing visitors they are at the Golden Triangle. Two first-class hotels have been built to exploit the supposed romance of the place.

For those searching for something else to experience, **Wat Prathat Phukaeo** provides good views of the Golden Triangle. The **Opium Museum** ① *just outside town opposite the*

Chiang Khong

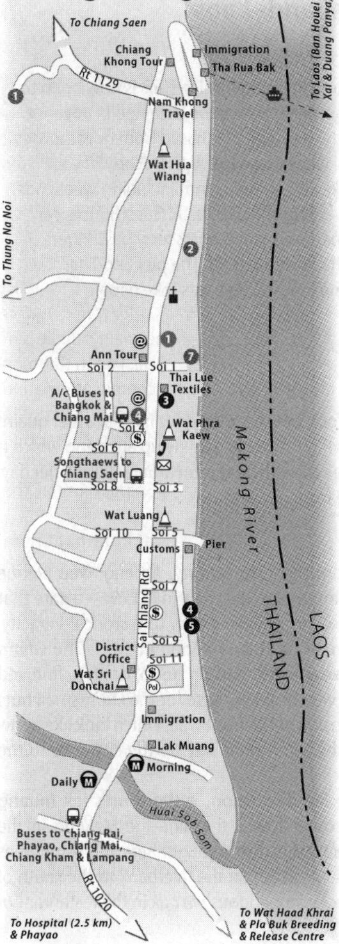

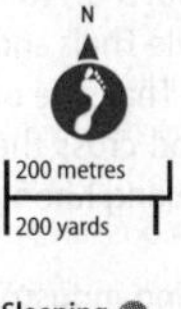

Sleeping 🛏
Baan Golden Triangle 1
Bamboo Riverside 2
Ban Tam Mi La 7
Green Tree Guesthouse 4
Ruan Thai Sophaphan
  Resort 7

Eating 🍴
Nong Kwan 3
Rimkhong 4
Rim Naam 5

Bars & clubs 🍸
999 1

gate to the Anantara, 0700-1800, ₿20, charts the rise of the international opium trade – largely put in place by 19th-century British business men with the backing of the British government – and the contemporary effects of the narcotics trade.

Wanglao, 4 km west towards Mae Sai, is a rice-farming community. It is sometimes possible to buy handicrafts here. *Song-thaews* run through here on the (longer) back route to Mae Sai.

Boats can be chartered from the river-bank opposite the Opium Museum for trips downstream to Chiang Saen (₿400 for five people, 30 minutes), or further on still to Chiang Khong (around ₿1500-1700, 1½ hours). Alternatively they can be chartered just to explore the Golden Triangle area. Boats are also available from the riverbank opposite the **Delta Golden Triangle Hotel**.

Chiang Khong 🚌🌐🏠🛏🍴🍸
>> *pp312-318. Colour map 1, A4.*

This border settlement, on the south bank of the Mekong, is really more a collection of villages than a town: Ban Haad Khrai, Ban Sobsom and Ban Hua Wiang were all originally individual communities – and still retain their village monasteries. For such a small town, it has had a relatively high profile in Thai history. In the 1260s, King Mengrai extended control over the area and Chiang Khong became one of the Lanna Thai Kingdom's major principalities. Later, the town was captured by the Burmese.

The area is growing in popularity and becoming increasingly more tourism-orientated, due mainly to the opening of a border crossing into Laos – just the other side of the river. Boats from the Laos town of Huay Xai, the Laos settlement on the opposite side, travel downriver to the ancient Laos city of Luang Prabang. Aside from that, Chiang Khong has a relaxed atmosphere making it an attractive spot to unwind.

Border essentials: Thailand–Laos

Chiang Khong–Ban Houei Xai

The border crossing from Chiang Khong into to Ban Houei Xai in Laos is now open to foreigners. Visas are not available in at this border and must be obtained in advance. Most people opt for a 30-day visa (฿1200) which can be purchased from guesthouses or tour operators in Chiang Khong or Mai Sai (see page 316). A photocopy of your passport is needed. The process normally takes 24-48 hours (not including weekends) as travellers' passports are taken to the Laos embassy in Bangkok. Guesthouses can also provide transport and organize boat trips. Long-tailed boats ferry passengers across the Mekong to Ban Houei Xai, from Tha Rua Bak (฿20). The pier and Thai immigration are 1 km or so north of town, and long-tailed boats take people across for ฿20.

Getting around

Chiang Khong is small enough to explore on foot, but the town does have a rather quaint line in underpowered motorized rickshaws, which struggle gamely up anything which is not billiard-table flat. Tour companies provide cars with drivers for around ฿1200 per day. Bicycles and motorbikes are available for hire from guesthouses.

Sights

Wat Luang, in the centre of town, dates from the 13th century. An engraved plaque maintains that two hairs of the Buddha were interred in the *chedi* in AD 704 – a date that would seem to owe more to poor maths or over-optimism than to historical veracity. However, it was reputedly restored by the ruler of Chiang Khong in 1881. The *viharn* sports some rather lurid murals. **Wat Phra Kaew**, a little further north, has two fine, red guardian lions at its entrance. Otherwise it is very ordinary, save for the *kutis* (small huts that serve as the monks' quarters) along the inside of the front wall, which look like a row of assorted Wendy houses, and the *nagas* which curl their way up the entrance to the *viharn*, on the far side of the building.

Further south, at the track leading to the Pla Buk Resort, is the town's **lak muang** (foundation pillar). Like Nong Khai and the other towns that line the Mekong in the northeastern region, the rare (and delicious) *pla buk* catfish is caught here. It is sometimes possible to watch the fishermen catching a giant catfish on the riverbank to the south of town. If that is a no go, there are some pictures of stupendous *pla buk* in the restaurant of the Ruan Thai Sophaphan Resort.

The town's illegal traffic can be seen in action either at the pier end of Soi 5 or, to a greater degree, at Tha Rua Bak – 1 km or so north of town. For some years, while Thais and Laos could make the crossing to trade, foreigners had to stay firmly on the Thai side of the river. This has now changed and it is easy enough to arrange a visa and cross the Mekong to another country – and another world. It is also possible to use Chiang Khong as an entry point into Laos (see box, above).

There are **hilltribe villages** within reach of Chiang Khong, but the trekking industry here is relatively undeveloped. Ask at the guesthouses to see if a guide is available. Tour operators cater mainly for those travelling on to Laos.

Opium of the people

The Golden Triangle is synonymous with the cultivation of the opium poppy. It is a favourite cash crop of the Lahu, Lisu, Mien and Hmong (the Karen and Akha only rarely grow it) and the attractions are clear: it is profitable, can be grown at high altitudes (above 1500 m), has low bulk (important when there is no transport) and does not rot. This explains why, though cultivation has been banned in Thailand since 1959, it has only been since the 1980s that the Thai government, with US assistance, has significantly reduced the poppy crop. Today, most opium is grown in Burma and Laos. In 2001 the UN estimated opium production in the Golden Triangle amounted to a total of 1260 tonnes of which 1087 tonnes was produced in Burma, 167 tonnes in Laos and just six tonnes in Thailand. This latter figure is not even sufficient for opium consumption by the hill peoples themselves.

The opium poppy is sown in September/October (the end of the wet season) and 'harvesting' stretches from the beginning of January through to the end of March. The petals then drop off and the remaining 'pod' is then carefully scoured with a sharp knife. The sap oozes out, oxidizes into a brown gum – raw opium – which is scraped off, rolled into balls and wrapped in banana leaves. It is now ready for sale.

Though profitable, opium has not benefited the hilltribes. In the government's eyes they are criminals, and opium addiction is widespread – up to 30% in some areas. Efforts to change the ways of the hilltribes have focused upon crop substitution programmes and simple intimidation.

Mae Sai ⊖🕖🕒⚠⊖❶ ↠ pp312-318. Colour map 1, A3.

Marking Thailand's northernmost point, Mae Sai is a busy trading centre with Burma and has a rather clandestine and frenetic frontier atmosphere. The area around the bridge is the centre of activity, with stalls and shops selling gems and an array of Burmese and Chinese goods, from knitted hats and Burmese marionettes to antiques and animal skulls. There is also an abundance of Burmese hawkers (selling Burmese coins and postage stamps) and beggars (particularly children) stretching about 1 km down the road, away from the border and towards Mae Chan. The main bus station is 5 km out of town, just off the main road running to Mae Chan and Chiang Rai. *Songthaews* and motorcycle taxis take passengers from town to the terminal and vice versa.

The town of Mae Sai is rather drab, but the movement of peoples across the border makes this an interesting place to visit. **Wat Phrathat Doi Wao** sits on a hill overlooking the town, off Phahonyothin Road, not far from the **Top North Hotel**. The wat is not particularly beautiful and was reputedly built in the mid-1960s in commemoration of a platoon of Burmese soldiers killed in action against a KMT (Kuomintang – the Chinese Republican Army) force.

Around Mae Sai

Luang Cave (Tham Luang) is an impressive cave with natural rock formations, 3 km off Route 110 to Chiang Rai, 7 km from town. After the initial large cavern, the passage narrows, over the course of 1 km, to a series of smaller chambers. Guides with lamps wait

Border essentials: Thailand–Burma (Myanmar)

Mae Sai–Tachilek

The border with Burma opens and closes periodically depending on the state of Thai-Burmese relations. When open, tourists, as well as Burmese and Thais, are permitted to cross the bridge that spans the River Sai and leads to the quiet Burmese town of Tachilek. Here, foreigners with day visas are free to roam within a 5-km radius of the town, but not to stay overnight. The border is open daily 0800-1800, border fee US$10 (US dollars only), passports to be lodged with Thai customs, two photocopies of passport required; take a photocopy of your passport and Thai visa (there are photocopy shops close to the border.

Tour companies are keen to encourage the Burmese government to loosen their regulations and allow foreigners to venture further afield – and to stay longer. It has been suggested that tourists may also be given 'visas on arrival' to visit Mandalay; see Dits Travel in Sop Ruak, page 316, and Tour operators in Mae Sae, page 316, for contacts.

The Burmese will also allow individuals and tour groups with the correct visas to travel the 167 km along a haphazardly upgraded road (six to eight hours) to **Kengtung**, known in Thailand as **Chiang Tung**. The long journey to Kengtung is through remote, wild forest, giving a good impression of what northern Thailand must have been like 50 years ago. Kengtung itself is a historic Tai Yüan community, almost perfectly preserved. The town is a gem compared with raucous Mae Sai.

A three-night/four-day visa costs US$18, plus a transport fee of US$10 at Tachilek (the trip into Burma does not count as an exit/re-entry for single-entry Thai visas and the Thai immigration authorities keep hold of visitors' passports until they return). Visitors are also required to change US$100 into FECs at the official (and very low) rate of exchange. The 'visa' is either for a four-day/three-night or three-day/two-night visit, and all-inclusive tours cost US$260 per person for a party of four for the three-day/two-night trip, or US$320 for four days and three nights.

outside the cave to lead visitors – for a fee – through the system. To get there take a regular *songthaew* to the turn-off; ask for 'Tham loo-ang'.

Doi Tung is a 2000-m-high hill village, almost 50 km south of Mae Sai. The road snakes its way past Akha, Lahu and KMT villages, as well as former poppy fields, before reaching Wat Phrathat Doi Tung, some 24 km from the main road. The road is now surfaced to the summit, although it is still quite a stomach-churning journey and the road can deteriorate after heavy rain. The twin *chedis* on the summit are said to contain the left collarbone of the Buddha and to have been initially built by a king of Chiang Saen in the 10th century. The views from the wat are breathtaking. A few years ago the king's mother built a palace here, a vast Austrian/Thai chalet with fantastic views over what was, at the time of construction, a devastated and deforested landscape. (Depending on who you talk to, the culprits were either shifting cultivators growing opium or big business interests logging protected land.) With the king's mother's influence, the hills around the palace were reforested. These days Doi Tung is very popular with Thai day-trippers and there's an overpriced restaurant, some gardens and a café. To get there, travel south on Route 110 from Mae Sai for 22 km to Huai Klai and then turn off onto Route 1149. Or take a bus heading for Chiang Rai and ask to be let off in Ban Huai Klai, at the turn-off for Doi Tung.

From there, *songthaews* run to Doi Tung. Now that the road is upgraded the *songthaew* service is rather more regular – but check on return journeys if you intend to make it back the same day; it is easiest to explore the area by rented motorbike.

Mae Salong (Santikhiri) 🏨🍴🛵🛍️🚌🏧 ↠ *pp312-318. Colour map 1, A3.*

Mae Salong is situated at an altitude of over 1200 m, close to the border with Burma. It is like a small pocket of China. After the Communist victory in China in 1949, remnants of the nationalist KMT (Kuomintang) sought refuge here and developed it as a base from which they would mount an invasion of China. This wish has long since faded into fantasy and the Thai authorities have attempted to integrate the exiled Chinese into the Thai mainstream. A paved road now leads to the town which is easily accessible. It is also an alternative place to trek from.

Despite the attempts to Thai-ify Mae Salong, it still feels Chinese. The hillsides are scattered with Japanese sakura trees, with beautiful pink blossom, whilst Chinese herbs and vegetables are grown in the surrounding countryside and sold at the morning market. Many of the inhabitants still speak Chinese, Yunnanese food is sold on the streets, and there are glimpses of China everywhere. One of the reasons why Mae Salong has remained so distinctive is because a significant proportion of the KMT refugees who settled here became involved in opium production and trade. This put the inhabitants in conflict with the Thai authorities and created the conditions whereby they were excluded from mainstream Thai society. Mae Salong's remoteness – at least until recently – also isolated the town from intensive interaction with other areas of the country.

Tea growing has now become a massive industry in and around Mae Salong and the hills are filled with endless tea terraces while the village is now home to dozens of tea-houses. The local brew is subtle and tasty – the variety of Oolong is particularly good. Less nuanced and completely tasteless are attempts to build a weird **tea visitor centre** just outside of town. Here massive gold and silver tea pots (soon to have fountains pouring from the spouts) sit beside giant Chinese dragons as surreal, gaudy evidence of someone with too much money and not enough sense.

The **morning market** is worth a visit for early risers (0530-0800), as this is where hilltribe people come to sell their produce. **Wat Santakhiri** is situated in a great position, with views of the hills on the road up to the impressive shrine to the Princess Mother. It is a Mahayana Buddhist monastery with images of Kuan Yin and Chinese-style *salas*.

Around Mae Salong

Thord Thai (Toerd Thai) is a small Shan village about 20 km north towards the Burmese border. It was here that Khun Sa, the legendary leader of the Shan state and notorious opium warlord, lived for a while. You can visit the house where he stayed and see a collection of photographs and other artefacts. There are a few signs for **Khun Sa House**, just ask around; there are no fixed opening hours, so aim for early afternoon when it's more likely the family across the road who hold the key will be there. To get to the village, you'll need to arrange your own transport or rent a motorbike.

Pha Dua is a Yao village, 15 km from Mae Salong. It was founded by Yao tribespeople escaping from the Communist Pathet Lao 45 years ago, and during the 1960s it became a centre for the trade in opium. With the opium trade curtailed by the government, the inhabitants have turned to food crops such as cabbages and strawberries, and to tourism, to earn a living. Handicrafts from Burma, Nan (in the eastern highlands) and even Nepal are sold from stalls, while women and children parade the streets in their traditional indigo costumes. If you wish to spend the night here, ask the village headmen if anyone can accommodate you.

Treks to **Akha**, **Hmong**, **Shan** and other hilltribe villages are arranged by the Sinsane guesthouse, among others (see Sleeping, page 314). It also organizes pony trekking to local hilltribe villages.

◉ Chiang Saen and the Golden Triangle listings

For Sleeping and Eating price codes and other relevant information, see pages 44-49.

▣ Sleeping

Chiang Saen *p304, map p305*
Accommodation is poor; many of the guest-houses have closed and only the **Chiang Saen Guesthouse** seems to be doing a reasonable trade. Most people visit the city as a day trip from Mae Sai or Chiang Rai.
B-D Chiang Saen River Hill Hotel, Phahonyothin Soi 2 (just inside the southern city walls), T053-650826, chiangsaen@ hotmail.com. The best hotel in town with 60 rooms and 4 storeys. It's nothing flash, but management are friendly and rooms are comfortable, with attached showers (very clean), minibar and TV. A/c, restaurant.
G Chiang Saen Guesthouse, Rimkhong Rd. Cheaper rooms in the guesthouse are basic and not very clean, with a shared bathroom; they are also noisy, being close to the road and the river (long-tailed boats). The bungalow is a better option, with private bathroom, and pleasant views of the river. Good restaurant for Thai food and breakfast. The guesthouse also offers tickets for a boat ride up the Mekong to Jin Hang in China (speed boat ฿4000, slow boat ฿1500) though you may encounter visa problems when trying to enter China.

Sop Ruak *p306*
Like Chiang Saen, Sop Ruak's popularity as a tourist destination has declined. The upmarket hotels have low occupancy rates and almost all the cheaper guesthouses have closed. Most people come here on a day trip

from Mae Sai or Chiang Rai. The **Golden Triangle Paradise Resort** (the casino on the island) has an office on the main road through the town. There are claims that some new ruins have been unearthed nearby in Laos – whether these will be accessible or even worthwhile visiting remains to be seen.
LL-AL Anantara Golden Triangle, 1 km north of Sop Ruak, T053-784084. Relatively peaceful location, with wonderful evening views. 'Traditional' architecture has been taken to the limit and it's a bit of a blot on the landscape for this timeless area of Thailand. However, the hotel is very well run with good service and facilities (including pool, tennis and squash courts, gymnasium, pétanque and sauna). It also runs an excellent Elephant Camp in conjunction with the Thai Elephant Conservation Centre near Lampang (see page 251).
A-B Imperial Golden Triangle Resort, 222 Golden Triangle, T053-784001. It is rather a surprise coming upon a hotel like this in what should be a quiet corner of Thailand. 73 plush and tasteful a/c rooms, restaurant, pool. Well run and attractive but probably ill-conceived, as they seem to have difficulty filling the rooms. Large discounts available, especially in low season.

Chiang Khong *p307, map p307*
There are now about 30 guesthouses here.
C-D Baan Golden Triangle, on top of a hill to the north of town, T053-791350. This is a stab at a 'back-to-nature' resort, with wooden bungalows, garden and cart wheels. The rooms are fine, with attached bathrooms and hot water. Great views, too, over a tiny rice valley to the Mekong and Laos.

C-D Ruan Thai Sophaphan Resort, Tambon Wiang Rd, T053-791023. Big wooden house with a large raised veranda. Rooms are large and clean with en suite and hot water. The upstairs rooms are better and have more natural light. There are also bungalows for 2-4 people. Good river views, very friendly, restaurant, self-service drinks, price negotiable out of season. Recommended.

D-E Ban Tam Mi La, 8/1 Sai Klang Rd, down a side street (northern end of town), T053-791234. Set in an attractive rambling garden along the riverside. Cheaper rooms are very basic with mosquito net and shared bathroom; more expensive rooms have private bathrooms; bungalows have river views. Restaurant serves good food. Friendly and helpful, although some recent visitors have said that it is overpriced.

D-F Bamboo Riverside, Sai Khlang Rd, T053-791621. Generally a higher standard of huts to the rest of the places in this category. Rooms have balconies overlooking the river, with clean, hot showers. Friendly owners speak good English and are full of information. The restaurant has superb views over the river to Laos and serves great Mexican food and freshly baked bread.

E-F Green Tree Guesthouse, Sai Khlang Rd. Extremely friendly owner with exceptional English. Pleasant yet basic rooms with shared hot-water showers. Nice shady restaurant. Lots of information and tours available. Recommended.

Mae Sai *p309*

Most of Mae Sai's guesthouses are concentrated along Sawlomgchong Rd, which follows the Sai River and the Burmese border upstream (west). Sawlomgchong Rd used to be quiet and relatively peaceful but there has been a good deal of new development and it is now rather dusty, noisy and busy. There aren't many decent places to stay and most people just consider Mai Sai as a stop-off point.

A-B Wang Thong, 299 Phahonyothin Rd, T053-733388. Set back from the road in the centre of town, this new high-rise hotel gets rather overrun by tour groups. 150 small a/c rooms with rather over-the-top decor, restaurant and pool. There's also a disco for those (to quote their brochure) "who prefer more turmultuous jollity". Non-guests can use the pool for ฿50. Low-season discounts.

C-D Top North, 306 Phahonyothin Rd, T053-731955. From the outside this place doesn't look very promising, but in fact it is well run with large, cleanish rooms, some a/c. It's reasonably quiet as the hotel is some way back from the main road over a river. The restaurant in the lobby serves fairly cheap Thai food.

E KK (King Kobra) Guesthouse, 35/5 Sawlomchong Rd, next door to **Mae Sai Plaza Guesthouse** restaurant, T/F053-733055. Rooms are a bit tatty, and attached bathrooms leave a lot to be desired despite hot water. Pleasant eating area with videos screened most evenings. 'Kobra Joe' speaks very good English and runs trekking tours to the area west of Mae Chan. He also organizes trips to Burma and can arrange visas for Laos.

E Mae Sai Plaza Guesthouse, 386/3 Sawlomchong Rd, T053-732230. Good position overlooking river, with views to Burma from the verandas of the huts, but rooms are liable to get damp during the wet season. Shared showers and outside sinks give the place a 'back-to-nature' feel which may not be to everybody's liking. Also available are rooms with attached bathroom and hot water, very popular, good source of local information.

E Yeesun Hotel, 816/13 Sawlongchong Rd, T053-733455. Decent small hotel aimed mainly at Thais but still a good deal and one of the best of the bunch. Rooms are a/c with hot showers and cable TV. Recommended.

E-F Mae Sai Guesthouse, 688, Moo 1, Sawlongchong Rd, T053-732021. Nice spot beside the river right at the end of the road. Owner is grumpy and bungalows a bit dark and grim. Worth it if you like to be away from the crowds. Some rooms a/c and en suite.

E-F Monkey Island, Sawlongchong Rd, T053-734060. British-owned guesthouse by the river offering food and lots of other facilities to travellers. Rooms are ok but characterless. Bar and internet (Wi-Fi).

F-G Bamboo Guesthouse, T08-6916 1895 (mob), Sawlongchong Rd. Run-down but friendly and in a good location, this place has seen better days but is an ok option if you're on a budget. Some rooms en suite, all with fan.

Around Mae Sai *p309*
Accommodation is limited. The following are good sources of information on the surrounding area.

D-E Khwan Guesthouse, Doi Tung, 2 km along Route 1149. A-frame huts.

F Akha Guesthouse (in the Akha village of Ban Pakha), 7 km along the road. Officially closed but some rooms still available.

Mae Salong (Santikhiri) *p311*
There's now an excellent range of places to stay in Mae Salong, making it a great base to explore the local hills. Discounts can be negotiated in the low season.

L-E Mae Salong Flower Hills Resort, T053-765496, www.maesalongflowerhills.com. This large resort looks out of place with its over-coiffured lawns and gardens but it actually offers surprisingly good value and a very friendly welcome. The rooms and bungalows are cast over a steep hillside with spectacular views and all are a/c, en suite and have cable TV. There's even a pool. Recommended.

C-D Mae Salong Resort, set in a small village of its own, on the hill in a pine forest, T053-765014. With individual though basic bungalows. Chinese/Thai restaurant and several stalls and shops sell trinkets and Chinese products (such as tea).

D-E Golden Dragon Guesthouse, T053-765009. Rooms are clean and quiet with private bathroom, hot water and Western toilets. No English spoken.

D-E Mae Salong Farmstay, T08-4611 5608 (mob), www.maesalongfarmstay.com. Down the end of a dusty track just before you enter town from the north (the owner will collect you from the town). A collection of fine bungalows, each with a/c and en suite, though luxury increases with price. There's also restaurant, bar and free Wi-Fi. The giant teapots are in walking distance and the owners very friendly. Recommended.

E Mae Salong Central Hills Hotel, opposite 7-11, T053-765113, www.maesalongcentral hills.com. Decent enough small hotel in the centre of the village. The rooms are all en suite, a/c and offer great views.

E-F Little Home Guesthouse, next to Sinsane, T053-765389, www.maesalonglittle home.com. One of the friendliest and best-run small guesthouses in this part of Thailand. The owner, Somboon (an ex-child soldier with the KMT) and his family go out of their way to be hospitable. Rooms in the teak house at the front are basic but spotless and there are a couple of bungalows for rent at the back. Food, drinks and internet available. Highly recommended.

F-G Sinsane. Basic, grubby and noisy. Friendly atmosphere and the food is good.

G Akha Guesthouse, next door to Sinsane. Clean, basic, big rooms with shared bathrooms. A bit noisy but friendly management. Trekking organized by Dan Hill Tribe Tours from here. The restaurant outside is concrete, but the interior is all wood.

🍴 Eating

Chiang Saen *p304, map p305*
The areas out of town towards Sop Ruak and the Golden Triangle have better riverside restaurants selling good Thai food, eg **Rim Khong** (2 km north of the city walls) and the **Mekong River Banks** (3 km).

🍴 Danang Vietnam Kitchen, Rimkhong Rd, near the **Chiang Saen Guesthouse**. Good Vietnamese food and noodles.

Nameless restaurant, corner of Rob Wiang and Phahonyothin roads. Clean and well-run place serving simple dishes, coffee, ice cream, etc.

Riverside, close to the **Chiang Saen Guesthouse**. Probably the best restaurant in town.

Foodstalls

There are a number of cheap *kwaytio* stalls along the riverbank and on Phahonyothin Rd.

Chiang Khong *p307, map p307*

In town, along the main road, there are a number of noodle and rice stalls. The more interesting places are along the river road, or down one of the *sois* leading to the Mekong.

Bamboo Riverside Guesthouse, Sai Khlang Rd (see Sleeping, above). Great views over the Mekong to Laos and excellent Mexican food. Recommended.

Nong Kwan, Sai Khlang Rd. Serves great Thai food at reasonable prices. The chicken and cashew dishes are recommended.

Ruan Thai Sophaphan Resort, see Sleeping, above. Very comfortable with wicker chairs, cold beer, a great view and good food.

Rimkhong, in the centre, and **Rim Naam**, next door, are good value but the fish dishes are rather limited and hardly memorable.

Mae Sai *p309*

Restaurants in Mae Sai tend to be serious eating establishments with little character. There are numerous places along Phahonyothin Rd and the market area is good for cheaper stall food. Most guesthouses have restaurants serving Thai food. You'll find a run of small shophouses selling excellent Chinese-style roast port and rice on the road to Chiang Rai about 2 km from the border. There's also a great noodle place right next to **Bamboo Guesthouse** (see Sleeping, above).

Daw Restaurant, couple of doors down from the **Bamboo Guesthouse**. Serves up delicious Thai grub. Highly recommended.

Melting Pot, next door to **Monkey Island**. Serves decent international and Thai food.

Monkey Island. Decent Western food; the English breakfasts are worth a go.

Coffee Heart, on the main road to Chiang Mai about 1 km from the border. Good coffee, cake and snacks.

Mae Salong (Santikhiri) *p311*

Mae Salong is a good place to eat Yunnanese food. There are expensive restaurants at the **Mae Salong Villa** and **Mae Salong Resort**, and there is also a restaurant housed in a conservatory-type shelter on the roof of the **Mae Salong Central Hills Hotel**, next to the bus stop (fairly priced and great views). It is also worth sampling the excellent Chinese-style chicken noodle soup, which is sold from numerous roadside stalls.

Sweet Mae Salong. A new café serving probably the best chocolate brownies in the whole country. The friendly owners speak great English and offer a range of Thai/Western food and excellent coffee. It's a little pricey but the quality/value is very high, and there's free internet for customers. There's a great little balcony overlooking the hills and magazines to browse. Recommended.

Little Home Guesthouse, see Sleeping, above. Great noodle and Thai dishes.

Salima Restaurant, 300 m past **Sinsane** guesthouse (see Sleeping, above). This Muslim restaurant is probably the best place to eat in town. The owners are very friendly, speak almost no English and are slightly eccentric. Memorable and recommended.

🍸 Bars and clubs

Chiang Saen *p304, map p305*
Pub and Karaoke, Sai 1 Rd (off Phahonyothin Rd, not far from the post office). Reasonable place for a cold beer.

Chiang Khong *p307, map p307*
If you're looking for a place for an evening drink most of the riverside restaurants are

worth contemplating. For dedicated bars try either the **Bam-Boo Bar** (which has the added advantage of a free pool) or **999 Bar**. Both are popular.

O Shopping

Sop Ruak p306
Most people come to Sop Ruak for the shopping, which is interesting but hardly spectacular. Goods from China, Laos and Burma, as well as hilltribe handicrafts, are on sale from countless stalls. The range of goods – and what vendors have decided people would wish to buy – is sometimes perplexing: crocheted hats, nylon hammocks, animal skulls, weaver bird nests. There are also some more expected items such as gems, traditional textiles and T-shirts.

Chiang Khong p307, map p307
Thai Lue Textiles, main road, just north of Wat Phra Kaew. Chiang Khong is not the obvious place to come shopping, but this place sells traditional textiles, woodcarvings, handicrafts and other items.

Mae Sai p309
Most people come to Mae Sai for the shopping, although the market is rather disappointing and items are of poor quality. There are scores of stalls and shops selling Burmese, Chinese, Lao and Thai goods. The Burmese products are the most diverse and the best buys: puppets, cheroots, gemstones, 'antiques' and lacquerware. **Mandalay Shop**, 381/1-4 Phahonyothin Rd, for Burmese jade, sapphires and rubies (see box, page 147).

Mae Salong (Santikhiri) p311
There's not a lot to buy in Mae Salong but there are a lot of tea shops, which also stock a huge variety of very tasty dried fruit. Probably the best are the 10 varieties of dried cherries, all sourced locally. Visiting these places for tea tasting is recommended, however, if

you just expect repeated handouts the locals will soon get annoyed.

▲ Activities and tours

Sop Ruak p306
Tour operators
Dits Travel, Baanboran Hotel, T053-716678. Organizes tours to Burma.

Chiang Khong p307, map p307
Tour operators
There are a growing number of tour companies in Chiang Khong. **Ann Tour**, 6/1 Sai Klang Rd, T/F053-791218, is recommended. **Chiang Khong Tour** and **Nam Khong Travel**, north of town, by the pier, get most of their business arranging visas for Laos. For further information on visas, see page 70.

Mae Sai p309
Tour operators
The **Mae Sai Plaza Guesthouse** and the **Northern Guesthouse** both organize treks for about ฿300 per day. See also Background, page 716. Visas for Laos can be arranged in town either through one of the tour companies or through 'Kobra Joe' at the **KK Guesthouse**, Kkmaesai@ chmai.loxinfo.co.th.
Ananda Tour, 22 Phahonyothin Rd, T053-731038.
Mandalay Tour, 382-83 Phahonyothin Rd (next to **Mandalay Shop**). Or book in Bangkok with **Diethelm Travel**, Kian Gwan Building, 140/1 Wittayu Rd, T053-2559150. A 3-day/2-night tour to Burma costs ฿6500-8000 for a 4-day/3-night tour (minimum 4 people).

Mae Salong (Santikhiri) p311
Somboon at **Little Home Guesthouse** (see Sleeping, above) can help arrange tours or put you in contact with the right people. He also has motorbikes for hire.

🚌 Transport

Chiang Saen *p304, map p305*
Boat
Long-tailed boats can be hired from the riverbank at the end of Phahonyothin Rd. A boat downstream to **Chiang Khong** should cost around ฿1200-1500 and can take 8 people (1 hr 20 mins). To **Sop Ruak**, upstream (30 mins), should cost ฿400 for a boat.

Bus
There are regular connections with **Chiang Rai** (1 hr 20 mins), **Mae Sai** (1 hr) and **Chiang Khong** (2 hrs).

Motorbike and bicycle
Bikes can be hired from **SK Hire** on Soi 1 Rd and from a shop on Phahonyothin Rd close to Soi 2, ฿150 per day for a Honda Dream. SK Hire also has vehicles for hire.

Sop Ruak *p306*
Boat
Boats leave from the pier for trips to **Chiang Saen** (฿400 per boat) and on to **Chiang Khong** (see below for details).

Car
Avis, at the Golden Triangle Hotel.

Songthaew
Regular connections with **Mae Sai** (40 mins) and **Chiang Saen** (10 mins, ฿10). Just flag one down on the road – they run through Sop Ruak about every 40 mins.

Chiang Khong *p307, map p307*
Boat
These can be chartered to make the journey to **Chiang Saen** (about ฿150 per head or ฿1200-1500 to charter an entire boat).

For transport to Laos, see box, page 308.

Bus
There are hourly connections with **Chiang Rai** (3 hrs). A/c and non-a/c connections with

Bangkok and **Chiang Mai** (6½ hrs), as well as **Lampang** and **Phayao**. A/c buses leave from the office on the main road near Wat Phra Kaew. Non-a/c buses depart from the bus station, just over the Huai Sob Som on the south edge of town. Non-a/c buses for **Chiang Saen** leave from 0600, and take the attractive river road following the Mekong and the Thai-Lao border (2 hrs).

Songthaew
Regular connections with **Chiang Saen** and from there on to **Sop Ruak**, **Mae Sai** and **Chiang Rai**. *Songthaews* leave from opposite the army post next to the post office, but can be flagged down as they make their way north through Chiang Khong.

Mae Sai *p309*
Bus
Regular connections with **Bangkok**'s Northern bus terminal (13-15 hrs), **Chiang Mai** (5 hrs), **Chiang Rai** (1 hr 20 mins), and **Mae Chan** (45 mins-1½ hrs).

Motorbike
Many of the guesthouses that used to rent out motorbikes have stopped because of the number of accidents. However, there are still a couple of places hiring out bikes, and most guesthouses will find a machine if required. Prices start at ฿150 per day for a Honda Dream.
Batman Motorbike, Sawlomgchong Rd.
Thong Motorbike Rental, Sawlomgchong Rd.

Songthaew
Connections with **Chiang Saen**, **Sop Ruak** and the **Golden Triangle**, every 30-40 mins. *Songthaews* leave from Phahonyothin Rd, near the centre of town. *Songthaews* for **Mae Chan** and **Chiang Rai** also leave from town, saving a journey out to the bus terminal.

Mae Salong (Santikhiri) *p311*
Bus and songthaew
To get to **Chiang Rai** take the a Mae Sai-bound bus and get off at Mae Chan.

From there, *songthaews* run 6 times daily 0600-1400 (1½ hrs). From Mae Salong to **Tha Thon** there are 5 *songthaews* a day (2 hrs) 0730-1530. **Little Home Guesthouse** has the full timetable.

ⓓ Directory

Chiang Saen *p304, map p305*
Banks Siam Commercial, 116 Phahon-yothin Rd (exchange service). ATM on Phahonyothin Rd. **Post office** Phahon-yothin Rd. There's a small internet shop on Phahonyothin Rd, Soi 2.

Sop Ruak *p306*
Banks There are money changers by the Opium Museum, a **Thai Farmers Bank** and a small branch of the **Siam Commercial Bank**. Open daily 0900-1600.

Chiang Khong *p307, map p307*
Banks Siam Commercial, Sai Khlang Rd, opposite the district office, has a currency

exchange service. **Thai Farmers**, 416 Sai Khlang Rd. **Internet** There are several places with internet access at the northern end of Sai Khlang Rd. **Post office** On main road next to the army post. **Telephone** International calls can be made form the post office.

Mae Sai *p309*
Banks A number of banks with money-changing facilities, some open daily 0830-1700. **Bangkok Metropolitan Bank**, Phahonyothin Rd. **Krung Thai**, Phahonyothin Rd. **Thai Farmers**, 122/1 Phahonyothin Rd. **Internet** Internet access can be found next door to the Wang Thong Hotel. **Post office** Phahonyothin Rd (2 km from bridge towards Mae Chan). **Telephone** Next door to the post office.

Mae Salong (Santikhiri) *p311*
Banks There are also a couple of banks with ATMs in the village. **Internet** There's internet at both the **Little Home Guesthouse** and at the **Sweet Mae Salong Café**.

Phrae, Nan and the Eastern Highlands

The Eastern Highlands, an area of outstanding natural beauty with a relaxed vibe and an intriguing history, is still off the main tourist and backpacker routes. The lack of development adds to its charm: the area's burgeoning tourist industry is easily integrated into a genuine slice of Thai rural life. The provincial capital, Phrae, is an attractive and friendly town with good accommodation and restaurants, situated in a narrow rice valley on the banks of the Mae Yom River, flanked by mountains to the east and west. Nan is a province to be explored for its natural beauty. Fertile valleys are chequered with paddy fields, teak plantations, hill-tribes and fast-flowing rivers. It was not until 1931 that the central authorities managed to overcome the area's inaccessibility and bring Nan under Bangkok's direct control. Ever since then, there have been periods – most recently in the 1970s when Communist insurgency was a problem – when the army and police have treated the province as a no-go area virtually, and it still exudes an atmosphere of other-worldliness and isolation. In addition, the area boasts rarely visited national parks, some of the finest forest in the country, weaving villages and excellent trekking in the hills. ►► *For listings, see pages 323-326.*

Phrae ⊖🟢🟡🟠🟤● ►► pp323-326. Colour map 1, B4.

Phrae was founded in the 12th century – when it was known as Wiang Kosai or Silk Cloth City – and is one of the oldest cities in Thailand. It still has its own 'royal' family and was an independent Thai *muang* (city state) until the early 16th century, when it was captured by an army from Ayutthaya. When Ayutthaya's power began to wane in the 18th century, Phrae – like many other northern principalities – came under the sway of the Burmese. It was finally incorporated into the Siamese state in the 19th century.

Phrae's ancient roots can still be seen in the city walls and moat, which separate the old city from the new commercial centre. On Charoen Muang Road, there are a handful of attractive wooden Chinese shophouses, although the scourge of uncontrolled development is gradually gnawing away at the remnants of old Phrae.

Ins and outs

Phrae is not a large place and the town is pleasant enough to stroll around. The main bus terminal is a 15-minute walk from most of the accommodation. It's 7 km northeast of the centre off Yantaeakitkoson Road, opposite the Maeyom Palace Hotel. The airport is 7 km southeast of town. The nearest train station to Phrae is at Den Chai, 24 km southwest of town. Regular buses and *songthaews* run from the train station into town.

Sights

The Burmese-style **Wat Chom Sawan** ① *on the edge of town, 1 km northeast of the centre, on the road to Nan, admission by donation,* was commissioned by Rama V (1868-1910) and designed by a Burmese architect. Like most Burmese (Thai Yai) wats, the *bot* and *viharn* are consolidated in one elaborate, multi-roofed towering structure, with verandas and side rooms. It has survived relatively unscathed; the wooden roof tiles have not been replaced by corrugated iron, and the rich original interior decoration of mirror tiles upon a deep red ground is also intact. Ask one of the monks to point out the rare Buddhist texts carved on sheets of ivory, and the bamboo and gold Buddha 'basket'.

Wat Luang ⓘ *admission by donation*, is a few minutes' walk from Wat Sri Chum, near the city wall and moat. The wat was founded in the 12th century, although continuous renovation and expansion has obscured its ancient origins. The wat also supports an impressive museum which houses valuable Buddha images, swords, coins, burial caskets, Buddhist texts, old photographs (one of a decapitation), betel boxes and jewellery. An old northern house, with all the accessories of traditional life, is also part of the collection. Finally, the wat is also notable for its fine well pavilion on the west wall and the individual monk's *kutis*, or cells, like small bungalows, along the south wall.

Around Phrae
Wat Phrathat Chor Hae, a hilltop wat, 8 km southeast of town, probably dates from the 12th to 13th centuries. Its 28-m-high *chedi* is said to contain a hair of the Lord Buddha, brought here by the Indian emperor, Asoka. The *chedi* is surrounded by a small cloister and linked to this is an ornate, high-ceilinged *viharn*, with bold murals depicting episodes from the Buddha's life. The name of the wat is the same as that of a particularly fine cloth woven by the people of the area and in which the *chedi* is shrouded each year. Also here, at the foot of the hill, are a number of souvenir stalls. To get here, take a *songthaew* from

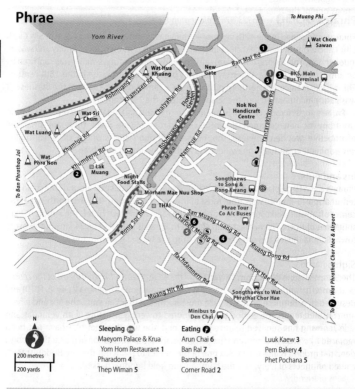

Phrae

Sleeping 🛌
Maeyom Palace & Krua
  Yom Hom Restaurant **1**
Pharadorn **4**
Thep Wiman **5**

Eating 🍴
Arun Chai **6**
Ban Rai **7**
Barrahouse **1**
Corner Road **2**

Luuk Kaew **3**
Pern Bakery **4**
Phet Pochana **5**

Charoen Muang Road, near the intersection with Yantarakitkoson Road, ฿10; there are few return *songthaews* in the afternoon, so it is best to make the trip in the morning.

Muang Phi, the City of Ghosts, is an area of strange, eroded rock formations, about 15 km northeast of town. Turn right after 9 km off Route 101 to Nan, and onto Route 1134; the turning for the canyon is 6 km along Route 1134 and lies about 2 km off the road. It's easiest to get there by chartering a *songthaew* (about ฿200). Alternatively, take a bus towards Nan and get off at the intersection with Route 1134, which is signposted to Muang Phi. From here, catch another *songthaew* (not regular) and get off after 6 km to walk the final 2 km or so to Muang Phi.

Nan 🏠🍴🏨❋🛏️⛰️🚌🛍️ ➤➤ *pp323-326. Colour map 1, B4.*

A charming, friendly town with a historical ambience, Nan occupies a small valley in the far north of the Eastern Highlands – about 50 km from the border with Laos. The airport is on the northern edge of town (5 km from the centre). It is thought the earliest settlers arrived from Laos in 1282, establishing a town 70 km north of Nan. According to legend, the Buddha himself was trekking here, picking out auspicious sites for wats, over 2500 years ago. The 13th-century inscriptions of King Ramkhamhaeng of Sukhothai named Nan as one of the *muang* whose 'submission he received', although it would be more accurate to view the royal house of Nan ruling autonomously until the 15th century, when Lanna established suzerainty over Nan. Even then, the turbulent politics of the area, with the Burmese, Lao, Siamese and the *muang* of the area all vying with one another, coupled with Nan's location, afforded it considerable independence.

Sights

The **National Museum** ① *Phakong Rd, daily 0900-1200, 1300-1600, ฿30*, once the home of the Nan royal family, houses an impressive collection, including beautiful wood and bronze Buddha images, ceramics, textiles, jewellery and musical instruments. There's a decent ethnographic display offering an insight into the lives of the local ethnic groups and a collection of stone-age tools. On the second floor, protected in a steel cage, is a 97-cm-long black elephant tusk that once belonged to the Nan royal family and is reputed to have magic powers. This is a great little museum and well worth a visit; exhibits are well displayed with English explanations throughout.

Just opposite the National Museum is **Wat Phumin** ① *Phakong Rd*. Built in 1596 it was restored between 1865 and 1873. The cruciform *bot*-cum-*viharn* is supported by the coils of two magnificent *nagas* (mythical serpents). The head forms the buttress of the north entrance, and the tail the south. Inside, there are some of the finest murals to be found in the north. Painted at the end of the 19th century – probably in 1894 – they depict the tale of the Sihanadajataka, but also illustrate aspects of northern Thai life: hunting, weaving, lovers, musicians, elephants, courtiers, a starving *farang* clasping a tool for pre-masticating food (eastern wall, top) and people with over-sized testicles. The naive style of the murals – large areas of empty space, figures of various sizes – distinguish them from the sophisticated art of Bangkok.

Wat Chang Kham, on the diagonally opposite corner to Wat Phumin, features a *chedi* supported by elephant buttresses (caryatids), similar to those at Sukhothai. The *viharn* was built in 1547 and contains three Sukhothai-style Buddha images: two walking and one standing. There's a large seminary here and the temple compound is often filled with dozens of friendly, shaven-headed novices.

Wat Ming Muang ① *Suriyaphong Rd*, contains the city of Nan's **lak muang** (city pillar), liberally draped in garlands. Wat Hua Chang, on the corner of Phakong and Mahaphrom roads, features a two-storey stone and wood *tripitaka*, or scripture, library, a square-based *chedi* with four Buddhas in raised niches and a fine *bot* (with *bai sema*). Gaudy **Wat Hua Wiang Tai** ① *Sumonthewarat Rd, just north of Anantavoraritdet Rd*, has *nagas* running along the top of the surrounding wall and bright murals painted on the exterior of the *viharn*. Other wats in the town include **Wat Suan Tan**, in Tambon Nai Wiang, which has a *prang* – unusual for the area – and a 15th-century bronze Buddha image named Phra Chao Thong Thit. A fireworks display takes place at the wat during Songkran.

Around Nan
Wat Phrathat Chae Haeng, 3 km southeast of town across the Nan River, is a 30-minute walk (or rent a bicycle or motorbike). Built in 1355, the 55-m-high, gold-sheeted *chedi* is Lao in style, and the *bot* has an interesting multi-tiered roof. A fair with fireworks and processions is held here on the full moon day of the first lunar month). Also notable are the fine pair of *nagas* that form the balustrade of the approach stairway to the monastery.

Nan

Sleeping	Eating	Transport
Amazing Guesthouse 1	Chokchai 1	Buses to Chiang Mai
Dhevaraj & Dhervee	Hot Bread 4	& Chiang Rai 1
Restaurant 2	No Name 3	BKS Terminal for Phrae,
Doi Phukha Guesthouse 3		Bangkok, Phitsanulok
Nanfa 4	Bars & clubs	& South 2
Nan Guesthouse 5	Laanchang Pub 2	Songthaews to North 3

Sao Din, in Amphoe Na Noi, lies about 30 km south of Nan, off Route 1026. It is a heavily eroded canyon with tall earth pillars and deeply eroded earth, reminiscent of Muang Phi outside Phrae. It's also the site of some of the prehistoric finds in Nan's museum. To get there, either catch a local bus to Amphoe Na Noi and then charter a motorcycle taxi, or charter a *songthaew* from town.

Tha Wang Pha, 40 km to the north of Nan on Route 1080, is the district capital and famous for its Tai Lue weaving. The Tai Lue were forced out of Yunnan in southern China by King Rama I (1782-1809); they settled in Nan province, turned to farming and are now peacefully assimilated into the Thai population. However, they still retain some cultural distinctiveness: the skilled weavers wear a tubular *pha sin* of bright stripes and a black jacket, decorated with multicoloured embroidered stripes and silver jewellery. Tai Lue textiles and jewellery are available in town. To get to Tha Wang Pha from Nan, take a regular local bus or *songthaew* from the stand on Sumonthewarat Road, just north of Anantavoraritdet Road.

En route to Tha Wang Pha, about 35 km north of Nan, is the turn-off for Ban Nong Bua and the fine **Wat Nong Bua**. (Ask the bus driver to drop you off at the turn-off, from where it's a 2-km walk). The monastery is Tai Lue in design and features fine murals, executed by the same Tai Lue artists who are thought to have decorated Wat Phumin in Nan (see above). Tai Lue textiles are also available in this small town.

Doi Phu Kha National Park ① *70 km north of Nan, Park HQ, PO Box 8, Tambol Phu Ka, Amphur Pua, Nan Province 55120, T08-1224 0789 (mob)*, is one of northern Thailands largest and newest protected areas and it offers good trekking. The mountainous park covers more than 1700 sq km and is named after a 1980-m peak, which offers good views. The limestone mountain ranges also offer an abundance of waterfalls, caves, crags and grottoes. The deciduous and evergreen forest provides a home for a range of hilltribes and various rare and near extinct flora– notably the pink-flowered Chomphu Phukha (*Bretschneidera ninensis hems 1*). Check at Park HQ for details on trekking. The best time to visit is between November and February, but it is cold so take warm clothes. The rainy season here is May to October. To get to the park, catch a bus to Pua (one hour from Nan); then from Pua, *songthaews* run from 0800 to 1200 up to the Park HQ (฿20); outside those times they have to be chartered (฿350).

◉ Phrae, Nan and the Eastern Highlands listings

For Sleeping and Eating price codes and other relevant information, see pages 44-49.

● Sleeping

Phrae *p319, map p320*

A-C Maeyom Palace, 1 km from the centre, 81/6 Yantarakitkoson Rd, T054-521028. The best hotel in town, with large rooms, professional service, a/c, restaurant and pool (non-guests ฿45). Organizes tours to hilltribe villages and home industries, Discounts available, especially in low season. Bikes for hire (฿100 per day).

E-G Pharadorn, 177 Yantarakitkoson Rd, T054-511540. Rooms are spacious and clean, a/c rooms benefit from carpets and hot water. Some a/c, restaurant, karaoke bar. Good value.

G Thep Wiman, 226-228 Charoen Muang Rd, T054-511003. Typical Chinese hotel, friendly.

Nan *p321, map p322*

AL-C City Park, 99 Moo 4 Yantarakitkoson Rd, Tambon Tuu Tai, T054-741343. Motel/resort-style hotel on a 4-ha plot outside town with restaurant and a large pool. All rooms have TV, minibar and a/c.

Peaceful, but inconvenient for exploring the city.

A-F Dhevaraj (pronounced – *thewarat*), 445 Sumonthewarat Rd, T054-757577. Range of good, if bland, hotel rooms, some a/c, some fan, all en suite. Clean and well run, pool, spa and excellent restaurant. Recommended.

D-E Nan Guesthouse, 57/16 Mahaphrom Rd, T054-771849. Nice guesthouse in quiet backstreet. More expensive rooms are en suite. Clean, friendly. Recommended.

E-F Nanfa Hotel, 438-440 Sumonthewarat Rd, T054-710284. A 100-year-old teak building. Rooms are run down but large with en suite and TV.

F-G Amazing Guesthouse, 25/7 Rattam-nuay Rd, T054-710893. Homely atmosphere with simple rooms and shared bathrooms with hot showers. English spoken, friendly and clean. The owner will pick you up from the bus station if you phone upon arrival. Recommended.

F-G Doi Phukha Guesthouse, 94/5 Sumon-thewarat Soi 1, T054-771422. An old teak house set in leafy compound. Quiet, clean rooms with shared Western toilets, dorm beds available, lots of trekking and excursion information, sells books and a good map of Nan. Very friendly, good atmosphere.

Around Nan *p322*
Doi Phu Kha National Park
Two government houses rent out rooms in the park when officials are not staying. Pay by donation. There are also 14 bungalows with shared toilets (฿200 per night) and 2 campsites (one at HQ and one at the star-gazing area (฿100 per night). The cook at HQ will prepare meals for you if you call ahead of arrival (T054-731362); breakfast (฿60), lunch (฿80), dinner (฿120).

❶ Eating

Phrae *p319, map p320*
There is a series of good little restaurants and foodstalls stretching along Charoen Muang

and Robmuang roads and there are several bars on Rachdamnern Rd.

❚❚ Krua Yom Hom, Maeyom Palace Hotel, Yantarakitkoson Rd. Expensive Thai, Chinese and European food, but the live music and seafood barbecue in the evening makes it worth it.

❚ Arun Chai, Charoen Muang Rd. Good food.

❚ Ban Rai, Yantarakitkoson Rd. 2 km south of town. Large outdoor garden restaurant.

❚ Barrahouse, 45 Ban Mai Rd (1 km from town on road to Nan). Friendly owners, good food, clean and welcoming, coffee and ice cream, along with usual Thai/Chinese dishes.

❚ Corner Road, corner of Lak Muang and Khumderm roads. Serves ice cream, clean, friendly and pleasant atmosphere.

❚ Luuk Kaew, Yantarakitkoson Rd (opposite Maeyom Palace Hotel). Only open in the evening. Excellent Thai and Chinese food, succulent satay. Highly recommended.

❚ Phet Pochana, Yantarakitkoson Rd (next to Maeyom Palace Hotel). Open-air restaurant, also serves Chinese dishes.

Bakeries
Pern Bakery, 347 Charoen Muang Rd. Cakes, pastries, coffee and ice cream.

Nan *p321, map p322*
❚ Chokchai, Mahayot Rd. Good food, friendly.

❚ Dhervee, Dhevaraj Hotel, see Sleeping, above. Serves up a large range of excellent Thai food. It also has a tasty lunchtime buffet (daily 1100-1400) for ฿59, including coffee, soft drinks and dessert – a great deal for the quality. Recommended.

❚ Hot Bread, 38/2 Suriyaphong Rd. Good veggie menu, freshly baked pitta bread, great coffee and friendly English-speaking owner.

❚ Restaurant (no name) 38/1 Suriyaphong Rd (next to Wat Ming Muang/opposite the museum). Excellent spicy *kwaytio khao soi* (egg noodles in curry broth).

Foodstalls
There is a small night market at the inter-section of Phakong and Anantavoraritidet

roads, lots of decent noodle shops along Sumonthewarat Rd and an excellent daytime food market just opposite the **Dhevaraj Hotel** (see Sleeping, above).

🍸 Bars and clubs

Nan *p321, map p322*
62 Bar and Restaurant, Sumonthewarat Rd. Serves excellent coffee, especially espresso.
Laanchang Pub, Sumonthewarat Rd. Wild ornamentation including leopard skins and hanging vines. Good place for an evening drink, occasional live music.
Pin Pub, Nanfa Hotel (see Sleeping, above). Plays live country music (adds to the Wild West ambience) most nights. Cheap Thai food.

✸ Festivals and events

Nan *p321, map p322*
Mid Oct-mid Nov Boat races, at the end of the Buddhist Lent. These races are thought to have started about a century ago, when they were part of the Songkran celebrations. The boats are hollowed-out logs, painted in bright designs. There is a lively fair in the weeks before (and during) the races.

🛍 Shopping

Phrae *p319, map p320*
Morhom Mae Nuu, 60-62 Charoen Muang Rd. Phrae is a centre of *morhom* production – the traditional blue garb of the northern farmer. Available all over town, but **Morhom Mae Nuu** is recommended. A simple tunic costs ฿60-100.
Nok Noi Handicraft Centre, 6/3 Yantara-kitkoson Trok (Soi 2). Woodcarvings, some clothing, baskets and hats.

Nan *p321, map p322*
Ban Fai, Kha Luang Rd. Basketry, textiles and woodcarving.

Big D Supermarket, along the Sumon-thewarat Rd (opposite the Thai Payap Development Association).
Nan Silverware, corner of Sumonthewarat and Anantavoraritidet roads, for locally produced jewellery.
Nara Department store, Sumonthewarat Rd, north of intersection with Anantaroraritdet Rd.
Thai Payap Development Association. A co-op selling hilltribes' handicrafts.

🏔 Activities and tours

Nan *p321, map p322*
Tour operators
Fhu Travel Service, 453/4 Sumonthewarat Rd, T054-710636. The best tour company in town. Mr Fhu rents out bicycles and motorbikes and arranges treks to see local hilltribes, the Doi Phu Kha National Park, provincial sites and boat tours up the Nan River. Prices from ฿600 per day upwards – given the quality of the service provided this is good value for money.

The **Dhevaraj**, **Nan Guesthouse**, **Doi Phukha** and **Nanfa** also organize tours.

⊖ Transport

Phrae *p319, map p320*
Air
Daily connections on THAI with **Bangkok** (1 hr 20 mins). THAI lays on transport from town to the airport.
   Airline offices THAI, Rachdamnern Rd, T054-511123.

Bus
Regular connections with **Bangkok**'s Northern bus terminal (8¼ hrs), **Uttaradit**, **Chiang Mai** and other towns in the north (hourly connections with Nan, 2-2½ hrs). A/c tour buses for **Bangkok** leave from **Phrae Tour**'s offices at 141/6 Yantarakitkoson Rd at 2030 and 2100.

Songthaew

Songthaew is the main form of local transport. *Songthaews* running north to **Song** and **Rong Kwang** leave from outside the Piriyalai School on Yantarakitkoson Rd; those running south to **Den Chai** (for the nearest train station) depart from Yantarakitkoson Rd near the intersection with Muang Hit Rd (by the petrol station).

Train

The nearest train station to Phrae is at **Den Chai**, 24 km southwest of town. Connections south to **Bangkok** (8½ hrs) and north to **Chiang Mai** (4½ hrs). To get to Den Chai, pick up a bus on Yantarakitkoson Rd near the intersection with Muang Hit Rd (by the petrol station).

Nan *p321, map p322*
Air

Connections on **PB Air** with **Bangkok** (2 hrs 10 mins). For ticket information contact Fahthanin Travel Agency, T054-711223.

Airline offices PB Air, at the airport.

Bicycle and motorbike

Hire is available from **Fhu Travel Service, Oversea Shop, Nan** and **Rob Muang** guesthouses and Laanchang Pub.

Bus

Nan has 2 bus terminals. Buses for towns to the north and west, including **Chiang Rai, Chiang Mai** (6½ hrs, ₿117), **Lamphun, Lampang, Phrae** and **Den Chai**, leave from the station off Anantavoraritdet Rd about 1 km west of the town centre. Buses running north to **Chiang Rai** take 2 routes: either a trip west and northwest on routes 1091 and 1251 to Phayao and then north to Chiang Rai, or by first running south to Phrae and then north to Phayao and Chiang Rai.

Buses serving destinations to the south, including **Bangkok**'s Northern bus terminal (9½-10 hrs), **Phitsanulok, Uttaradit, Nakhon Sawan, Kamphaeng Phet** and **Sukhothai**, leave from the BKS terminal, 500 m to the north of the city centre on Kha Luang Rd. VIP and a/c buses go to major destinations. Bus times and costs are displayed on boards at the **Nan** and **Doi Phukha** guesthouses. The information officers at the terminals speak English.

🟦 Directory

Phrae *p319, map p320*
Banks Several on Charoen Muang Rd. **Internet** Internet café on Yantarakitkoson Rd. **Post office** Charoen Muang Rd (in the old city), with telephone. **Telephone** 163/2 Yantarakitkoson Rd.

Nan *p321, map p322*
Banks Thai Farmers and Bangkok on Sumonthewarat Rd. **Internet** Internet café on Anantavoraritidet Rd. **Post office** Mahawong Rd (with international telephone, fax facilities). **Telephone** 345/7 Sumonthewarat Rd.

Contents

Border crossings

Thailand–Laos
Chongmek–Pakxe, see page 352
Travel to Laos from Isaan, see page 361
Friendship Bridge, see page 386

At a glance

◉ **Getting around** Very flat so good for cycling. Extensive bus network.

◉ **Time required** 2 weeks to sample the Mekong towns and Phnom Rung. More time and you'll begin to develop a taste for Isaan life.

☽ **Weather** Very hot in Mar and Apr, wet through to Nov then cool for a couple of months.

✖ **When not to go** The rains can be incredibly intense, so avoid the monsoon months.

Northeastern Thailand

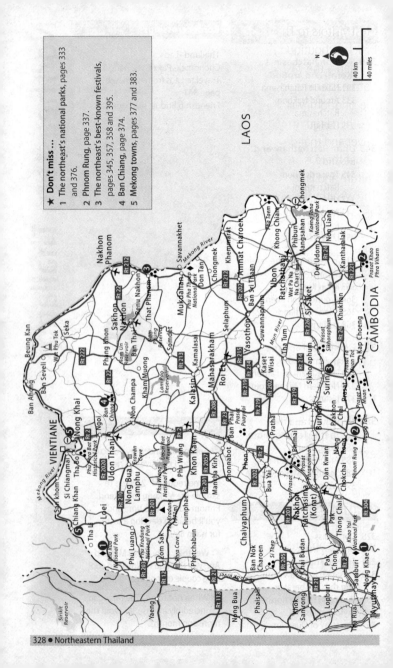

★ **Don't miss …**
1 The northeast's national parks, pages 333 and 376.
2 Phnom Rung, page 337.
3 The northeast's best-known festivals, pages 345, 357, 358 and 395.
4 Ban Chiang, page 374.
5 Mekong towns, pages 377 and 383.

LAOS

CAMBODIA

N

40 km
40 miles

Most visitors to Thailand, eager for the hackneyed image of beaches, boutique hotels and floating markets never make it to Isaan – the vast plain of land that makes up Thailand's northeastern region. The same visitors, wherever they end up in the kingdom, will have experienced Isaan culture in some form or other. From the bellboy at your hotel to the taxi or tuk-tuk driver and that delicious street food you've just scoffed, likelihood is that there is an Isaan connection. So distinct are Isaan's people, culture and language that many barely consider them Thai at all. The wealthy whiter Thais of the central plain certainly look down their noses at this region and that's their loss, as Isaan is the friendliest part of a friendly country. The locals, tired of being labelled country bumpkins by the sophisticates of Bangkok, are delighted to see visitors taking an interest in their region. However, there's more than this. At Ban Chiang, a village east of Udon Thani, some of the world's earliest evidence of agriculture has been uncovered, dating back 5000 to 7000 years. The region once formed an integral part of the magnificent Khmer Empire based at Angkor. The impressive ruins at Phimai, Phnom Rung, Muang Tham and Prasat Khao Phra Viharn clearly show that Isaan – the Thai name for the northeast – has not always been devoid of 'civilized' life, whatever those in Bangkok might like to think. There's a rich, contemporary Isaan culture too: check out the exotic temple fairs and wild rocket festivals; the fine handwoven textiles and unique celebrations of Buddhist lent; aromatic *kai yang* (grilled chicken) and fiery *som tam* (papaya salads); while Isaan pop musicians, nasal to the max, are among the highest sellers in the country. And don't forget national parks, mountain walks, elephant treks, tubing on the Mekong and the best bicycling in the country.

Nakhon Ratchasima (Korat) and around

Most visitors to the northeast only travel as far as Nakhon Ratchasima, more commonly known as Korat, the largest town in the northeast and an important provincial capital. The city has made huge strides to become a pleasant place to visit and there are nice shady parks and promenades circling the city moat. It's the main base for visiting the magnificent Khmer monuments of Phimai, Phnom Rung and Muang Tham.

Korat was established when the older settlements of Sema and Khorakpura were merged under King Narai in the 17th century. During the Vietnam War, Korat provided an important US airbase. The warplanes that set out from here bombed the Ho Chi Minh Trail – the infamous Vietcong supply. Today, Korat is a thriving town, with a lively, friendly atmosphere. Nothing really remains of its ancient roots – dating from the 8th century – and Korat appears to be on the cusp of becoming a booming, modern metropolis. A stop-off here makes a great introduction to Isaan life.

The ancient sanctuary of Phimai lies to the northeast of Korat; Ban Khwao, famed for its silk weaving, lies to the northwest; the popular Khao Yai National Park is situated to the southwest; and the remarkable Phnom Rung, the finest Khmer Temple in Thailand, lies to the southeast.
▶▶ For listings, see pages 339-344.

Nakhon Ratchasima (Korat)

Sleeping

Iyara 1
Korat 2
Korat Doctor's Guesthouse 7
Potong 8
Royal Princess Korat 9
San Sabai 3
Sima Thani 10
Siri 11

Ins and outs

Getting there The city's airport is 5 km south of town on Route 304. There are daily connections with Bangkok, 256 km away. There are three bus terminals serving Bangkok, as well as many other destinations in the north, northeast and central plains. The railway station is west of the town centre and provides links with Bangkok and other destinations in the northeast. ▶ *See also Transport, page 343.*

Getting around Korat is a large town. A city bus system (bus maps with routes marked are available from the tourist office), along with a plentiful supply of fixed route songthaews (฿8 per person), tuk-tuks (฿40-60) and *saamlors*, provide transportation. Local buses cost ฿4-6 and are infrequent during rush hour.

Tourist information TAT ⓘ *2102-2104 Mittraphap Rd, T044-213666, 0830-1630*, on the western edge of town, is inconveniently located (although town bus No 2 runs out here) next door to the **Sima Thani Hotel**. Good town maps available, along with a fair amount of other information on Korat and the northeastern region. It's worth coming here if you have time.

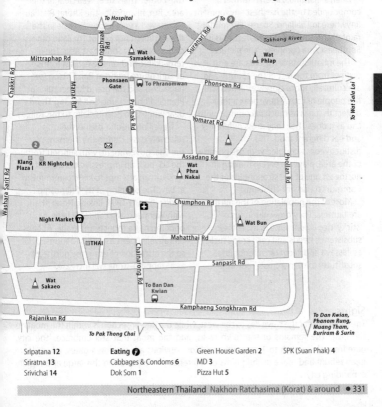

Sripatana **12**
Sriratna **13**
Srivichai **14**

Eating 🍴
Cabbages & Condoms **6**
Dok Som **1**

Green House Garden **2**
MD **3**
Pizza Hut **5**

SPK (Suan Phak) **4**

One-way traffic

Isolated from the rest of the country by a string of mountains, the northeast has always been at the periphery of the Thai kingdom. The epic poem, *Nirat Nongkhai*, written during a military campaign of the 1870s, recounts the two months, 170 elephants and 500 oxen it took to proceed up a thickly forested trail from Bangkok to Korat (Nakhon Ratchasima). With his men dying all around him from malaria and food poisoning, and finding it difficult to procure supplies, the army's commander managed to miss the vital battle and returned to Bangkok having never confronted the enemy.

Isaan's marginalization is further compounded by the harshest environment anywhere in Thailand. Sparse, intermittent rainfall and some of the poorest soils in Southeast Asia completes the picture.

The inhabitants of the area are also distinct from the rest of the country and are culturally more closely affiliated with the people of Laos. They speak a thick dialect that has as much in common with Lao as it does Thai; they dress differently and eat different food. This distinctiveness, coupled with the poverty of the area, played a part in making the northeast one of the strongholds of the Communist Party of Thailand.

Most of the population of the northeast are farmers. They grow glutinous or 'sticky' rice (*khao niaw*) to meet their subsistence needs and cash crops such as cassava and *kenaf* (an inferior jute substitute) to earn a crust. They also migrate to Bangkok in their thousands: most of the capitals' servants and labourers, tuk-tuk and taxi drivers, prostitutes and bar girls are poor Isaan folk. Some villages are so depopulated that they seem to consist of only the very old and the very young. It is easy to see why they leave. In the northeast the daily rate for back-breaking agricultural work is only ฿50; in Bangkok the official minimum wage is more than ฿150 per day.

With the heat, the poverty, the perceived threat of communism, and the general backwardness of the northeast, most other Thais steer well clear of the area. But, historically, the Khorat Plateau has played a very important role in the development not just of Thailand but of the whole of Southeast Asia. The remarkable finds of the earliest forms of agriculture found at Ban Chiang (see page 374) and the grand Khmer ruins at Phimai, Phnom Rung and Muang Tham bear witness to Isaan's claim to this role.

Travelling around the northeast is relatively easy. During the Vietnam War the Thai government, with support from the US, built an impressive network of roads, in an attempt to keep communism at bay. The opening of the Friendship Bridge in early 1994, linking Nong Khai with Vientiane, the capital of Laos, is bringing more tourists and trade. As Laos tentatively opens its doors to tourists, so the attraction of using the northeast as a stepping-stone will increase.

Sights

The older part of the town lies to the west, while the newer section is within the moat, to the east. The remains of the town walls, and the moat that still embraces the city, date from the eighth to 10th centuries. More obvious are the town gates, which have been rebuilt and make useful points of reference while exploring this large and rapidly expanding city.

Mahawirawong Museum ① *Rachdamnern Rd, Wed-Sun 0930-1530, ฿10, a ฿100 combination ticket gives access to the museum as well as Prasat Phranomwan, Phimai and Muang Khaek, saving ฿40 if all are visited*, in the grounds of Wat Sutchinda just outside the city moat, is an informative museum housing a small collection of Khmer art.

Thao Suranari Shrine is in the centre of town, by the Chumphon Gate. This bronze monument erected in 1934 commemorates the revered wife of a provincial governor, popularly known as Khunying Mo, who in 1826 saved the town from an invading Lao army. Legend has it that she and some fellow prisoners plied the over confident Lao soldiers with alcohol and then, having lulled them into a drunken stupor, slaughtered them. Traditional Isaan folk songs are performed at the shrine and in late March and early April a 10-day festival honours the heroine (see Festivals, page 342).

Just outside the northeast corner of the city moat (walk or take bus No 5) is **Wat Sala Loi**, a modern wat, with an ubosoth resembling a Chinese junk. It was built in 1973 and is meant to symbolize a boat taking the faithful to nirvana. It is one of the few modern wats with any originality of design in Thailand (the majority repeat the same visual themes) and it has won numerous architectural awards. The ashes of the local heroine Thao Suranari are interred here.

The **night market** ① *Manat Rd, between Chumphon and Mahatthai roads, daily from 1800*, has lots of foodstalls, as well as some clothes and handicraft stalls. The **general market** ① *Suranari Rd*, is opposite Wat Sakae.

Around Nakhon Ratchasima ●❷❻❽✱▲●❻ ▶▶ pp339-344.

Khao Yai National Park → *Colour map 2, C2.*

① *The park turning is at the Km 165 marker on Route 2, 200 km from Bangkok, 2-3 hrs by car. There are 2 entrances to the park. One from the north, near Pak Chong, the other from the south, near Prachinburi. Access from the south is mostly by hired or private vehicle; all buses go to the north entrance. ฿200, children ฿100 and cars ฿ 30. The tourist office and visitors' centre at Khao Yai provide maps and organize guides on an intermittent basis. The centre is also probably the closest you will get to rare wildlife, but it is pickled or stuffed. If you intend to trek, tell someone before you leave and let them know your intentions. During the wet season, liberally apply insect repellent and take along water and food. The best time to see wildlife is weekday mornings and late afternoons – at weekends the park is inundated with visitors. Spotlight safaris can be organized up until 2100, ฿300-600, although recent visitors have suggested that these are a 'waste of time' because of the number of noisy pick-ups with searchlights keeping the animals, sensibly, out of sight. See also Sleeping, and Activities and tours, pages 340 and 344.*

Khao Yai National Park, one of the country's finest, covering an area of 2168 sq km, encompasses the limestone Dangrek mountain range, a large area of rainforest, waterfalls and a surprisingly wide selection of wildlife. Visitors may be lucky enough to see Asiatic black bear, Javan mongoose, slow loris and tiger. Two notable species are the white-handed (or lar) gibbon and the pileated gibbon. There may be as many as 200 elephants in the park. Having said this, recent reports have indicated a distinct lack of any wildlife, and you may travel long distances for little reward and unfortunately, because of the park's easy accessibility from Bangkok, it is overrun with visitors and its environmental integrity is at risk.

Short trails are marked in the park; for longer hikes, a guide is usually needed. The 50 km of trails are the most extensive and best marked of any national park; it was the first

Trails in Khao Yai

Trail 1: Kong Kaew to Haew Suwat Starts behind visitors' centre, marked in red, 6 km, 3-4 hours' walking – transport back to headquarters should be arranged. One of the most popular trails, offering opportunities to observe gibbons.

Trail 2: Kong Kaew to Elephant Salt Lick 2 Starts behind visitors' centre, marked in blue, 6 km, 3-4 hours. Not well marked, over grassland to salt lick – guide advisable. Frequented by elephants.

Trail 3: Kong Kaew to Pha Kluai Mai Starts behind visitors' centre, marked in yellow.

Trail 4: Pha Kluai Mai to Haew Suwat Starts on far side of campsite, marked in red, 3 km. Popular trail along Lam Takhong riverbank. Good trail for orchids and birdlife (blue-eared kingfishers, scarlet minivets, cormorant, hornbills – both wreathed and great). Probable sightings of gibbon, macaques and elephants.

Trail 5: Haew Suwat to Khao Laem grassland Starts across the Lam Takhong River from the parking area. Difficult trail to follow, not much wildlife but good views of Khao Laem mountain.

Trail 6: HQ to Nong Phak Chi Watchtower Starts across road from Wang Kong Kaew restaurant, south of Park Office, marked in red, 6-km round-trip. Popular and easy to follow until last 500 m. The tower makes a good viewing spot at dawn or dusk. White-headed gibbon frequently seen. Clouded leopard has been seen occasionally, herds of wild pig, and even tiger.

Trail 7: HQ to Wang Cham Pi Starts in the same place as 6, marked in blue, 4.5-km round-trip, 2-3 hours, good for ornithologists, gibbons and macaques easily seen.

Trail 8: Headquarters Looping Trail Marked in yellow, 2.5 km.

Trail 9: Headquarters to Mo Singto Marked in blue, starts in the same place as 6, ends at a reservoir close to headquarters, 2 km. A favourite haunt for tigers.

park to be founded in Thailand in 1962. **Kong Kaeo Waterfall** is a short walk from the visitors' centre. Six kilometres east is the **Haew Suwat Waterfall** (three to four hours' walk). There are 'rest areas' near Haew Suwat and Haew Narok waterfalls, providing drink and simple Thai food. Waterfalls are at their best between June and November, wildlife is best seen during April and May, although August and September are good months to see the **hornbills** (of which there are four species here). Night-time is good for animal observation, when you might be able to see sambar and barking deer, porcupine, gibbon, pig-tailed macaques, mongoose, civet cats and elephants.

The closest town to the national park is **Pak Chong**, where there are numerous *songthaews* to take you to the park. While there is some accommodation in the park itself, most of the commercial hotels and guesthouses are situated here and it is a good place to base yourself. Cars can be hired and tours booked. There is little to see here, apart from the markets on the north side of Mittraphap Road. The main road through town is the Bangkok-Korat (Friendship Highway). There's a bus from Bangkok to Pak Chong (2½ hrs), or alternatively you can take a train. Trains runs to Pak Chong from Bangkok (3½-4 hours) and Ayutthaya.➤➤ *For more information on reaching Pak Chong from Nakhon Ratchasima, see Transport, page 343.*

Phimai → *Colour map 2, C3.*

ⓘ *Regular services from Korat, the last bus leaves at 2000. Phimai is a very small town. Saamlors are available and there are bicycles for hire from guesthouses. The Bai Teiy Restaurant, see Eating, page 342, acts as an informal tourist information centre.*

The ancient town of Phimai, northeast of Korat, lies on the Mun River – a tributary of the Mekong and one of the northeast's major waterways. The town itself is small and rather charming; it has only two hotels and one major attraction to offer the visitor: the magnificent Khmer sanctuary of Phimai, around which the new town has grown.

The Phimai sanctuary was important even prior to the arrival of the Khmers; excavations have revealed burnished blackware pottery from as early as AD 500. The Mun River formed a natural defensive position and the site also benefited from an extensive area of rich, arable land. These twin advantages of security and nutrition meant this area was occupied almost continuously for more than seven centuries up to the establishment of the Khmer sanctuary, for which Phimai is known.

Dating from the reign of the Cambodian King Jayavarman VII (1181-1201), Phimai was built at the western edge of his Khmer Kingdom, on a Hindu site. A road ran the 240 km from his capital at Angkor to Phimai, via Muang Tham and Phnom Rung. Unlike other

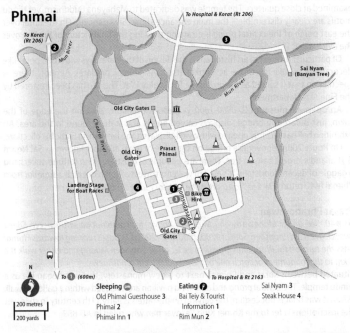

Phimai

To Korat (Rt 206)

To Hospital & Korat (Rt 206)

Mun River

Mun River

Sai Nyam (Banyan Tree)

Chakrai River

Old City Gates

Old City Gates

Prasat Phimai

Night Market

Landing Stage for Boat Races

Bike Hire

Chomsudasadet Rd

Old City Gates

N

To ① (600m)

To Hospital & Rt 2163

200 metres
200 yards

Sleeping
Old Phimai Guesthouse 3
Phimai 2
Phimai Inn 1

Eating
Bai Teiy & Tourist
Information 1
Rim Mun 2

Sai Nyam 3
Steak House 4

Khmer monuments which face east (towards the rising sun), Phimai faces southeast; probably so that it would face Angkor, although some scholars have postulated it was due to the influence of Funan – the earliest so-called 'Indianized' state of Southeast Asia which existed in Cambodia from the first to the sixth centuries AD.

The **original complex** ⓘ 0730-1800, ฿40, lay within a walled rectangle 1000 m by 560 m, set on an artificial island. There are four gopuras, which have been placed in such a way that their entrances coincide with the sanctuary entrances. The **Pratu Chai (Victory Gate)** faces southeast and was built with the purpose of accommodating elephants. Shortly before the gate is the **Khlang Ngoen (Treasury)**, where important pilgrims were lodged. Within the compound are three *prangs*: the largest, **Prang Prathan**, is made of white sandstone; those on either side are of laterite (**Prang Phromathat**) and red sandstone (**Prang Hin Daeng**). The central and largest *prang* is a major departure for Khmer architecture. Though similar to Phnom Rung in plan, the elegant curving *prang* probably became the model for the famous towers at Angkor.

Another unusual feature of Phimai is the predominance of Buddhist motifs in the carvings that adorn the temple. The lintel over the south gateway to the main sanctuary shows the Buddha meditating under a protective naga, the naga's coiled body lifting the Buddha above the swirling flood waters. Another scene, magnificently carved on the corridor leading into the south antechamber, depicts the Buddha vanquishing the evil forces of Mara. On the west side of the building is a lintel showing the Buddha preaching – both hands raised.

To the right of the gateway is a 'homeless lintels' park where the Khmer artistry can be examined at close quarters. The temple was dedicated to Mahayana Buddhism, yet Hindu motifs are clearly discernible – the main entrance shows Siva dancing. On the lintel over the east porch of the central *prang* is a carving showing the final victory of Krishna over the evil Kamsa.

Of particular interest to art historians is the design of the gateways with their petal-like decorations, similar to those at Angkor itself. As Phimai predates Angkor, there is speculation that it served as the prototype for Angkor Wat. The site has been restored by the Fine Arts Department.

An **open-air museum** ⓘ 0900-1600, guidebook available, ฿60, on the edge of the town, just before the bridge, displays carved lintels and statues found in the area. An exhibition hall has recently opened with a well-displayed and labelled (in English) collection.

On Route 206, just over the bridge on the edge of town at a spot known as **Sai Ngam** is Thailand's largest banyan tree. There are a couple of crusty-looking fortune-tellers and a gaggle of decent foodstalls. It's a 2-km walk northwest of town or catch a *saamlor* from Phimai (฿40 return). ▶▶ *See Transport, page 344, for further information.*

Prasat Phranomwan

ⓘ ฿40. See under Mahawirawong Museum, above, for combination entry ticket. Direct buses leave from Phonsaen Gate at 0700, 1000 and 1200 (฿7). Buses running towards Phimai pass the turn-off for Phranomwan; ask to be let off at Ban Saen Muang and either walk the 4 km to the monument or catch one of the irregular local songthaews.

Situated between Korat and Phimai, next to a new monastery, this wat began life as a Hindu temple. The central *prang* and adjoining pavilion are enclosed within a galleried wall. When it was built is not certain: the carving on the lintels is early 11th century in style, yet the inscriptions refer to the Khmer King Yasovarman who ruled in AD 889.

Ban Prasat
① *Take a bus towards Phimai. The site is 2 km off the main road and 45 km from Korat city, on the left-hand side, before the turning for Phimai.*

This is a prehistoric site dating back about 5000 years. The dig has been converted into an open-air museum, much like Ban Chiang outside Udon Thani (see page 374). Indeed, there seem to be close cultural links between Ban Prasat and Ban Chiang. Similar high-quality, red-slipped and burnished trumpet-rimmed pots have been discovered at both sites. Rice was eaten as the subsistence crop, domestic animals raised, and the technology of bronze casting understood. The examination of skeletons unearthed at the site reveals a high infant mortality rate, and a relatively short lifespan of only 34 to 36 years.

Chaiyaphum → *Colour map 2, B2.*
The few people who do stop off at this small provincial capital are mainly here for the famed silk-weaving at the nearby village of Ban Khwao. However, Chaiyaphum offers an authentic slice of Isaan life, away from other tourists, that can be sampled in a couple of nights. The bus station is on the northeast edge of town about 1 km from the centre.

The name Chaiyaphum means site of victory, a reference to Pho Khun Lae's (the town's first governor) success in thwarting an attack from an invading Lao army during the reign of Rama III. A statue and shrine to his memory are situated 3 km west of town and a festival is held in his honour each January.

The only real point of interest is **Prang Ku**, a 12th-century Khmer sanctuary tower built entirely of laterite blocks, 2 km east of the town centre on Bannakaan Road. Though scarcely matching the Khmer monuments to be found elsewhere on the Khorat Plateau the local people consider it an important holy site. Within the *prang* is a Dvaravati Buddha, highly revered by the townspeople. The statue is ritually bathed on the day of the full moon in April.

Ban Khwao ① *guesthouses will help arrange tours to silk-weaving villages or simply catch a songthaew from Nornmuang Road (near the intersection with Tantawan Road), close to the centre of town, to Ban Khwao, 14 km west of Chaiyaphum (on Route 225), is well known for the quality of its silk. Like Surin, Chaiyaphum is a centre for silk production and weaving.*

Ban Dan Kwian
① *Take a songthaew towards Chokchai from the south city gates on Kamphaeng Songkhram and Chainarong roads, 30 mins, ฿6.*

Ban Dan Kwian, 15 km to the southeast of Korat on Route 224, is famous for producing rust-coloured clay ceramics. The ruddy clay – taking its reddish hue from its high iron content – is drawn from the local river and is used to make vases, pots, wind chimes, water jars, ceramic fish and other objects. Countless stalls and shops line the main road. Unfortunately, most of the items are too big to transport home, although some local producers are beginning to branch out into new products, designed to appeal to foreigners.

Phnom Rung
① *0730-1800. ฿40. Take a Surin-bound bus from Terminal 2 and get off at Ban Tako. From Ban Tako motorcycle taxis wait at the bus stop and charge ฿250 to visit Phnom Rung and Muang Tam. From Phnom Rung it is a short trip – 8 km – on to Muang Tam (see below). The route to the site is well signposted. See also Transport, Buriram, page 360. The best way to visit Phnom Rung and Muang Tam is to go on a tour (see Activities and tours, page 343).*

Phnom Rung, the finest Khmer temple in Thailand, was built in sandstone and laterite over a period of 200 years between the 10th and early 13th centuries. It stands majestically at the top of Rainbow Hill, an inactive volcano overlooking the Thai-Cambodian border. The name Phnom Rung means 'Large Hill'. It was built on a grand scale – the approach is along a 160-m avenue of pink sandstone pillars (nang riang). Lying 112 km southeast of Korat and 64 km south of Buriram, Phnom Rung is similar in layout to Phimai and both monuments are believed to have been prototypes for Angkor Wat.

The monumental staircase is reached via a five-headed naga bridge; this 'bridge' is one of Thailand's Khmer treasures. The style is 12th century and the detail is superb: crowned heads studded with jewels, carefully carved scales and backbones and magnificent rearing bodies. The naga bridge represented a symbolic division between the worlds of mortals and gods. From here the pilgrim climbed upwards to the sanctuary, a divine place of beauty and power.

The Prasat Phnom Rung (central Hindu sanctuary) is of typical Khmer design, being symmetrical, of cruciform plan, with four gopuras leading to antechambers. It was probably built between 1050 and 1150, most likely by the Khmer King Suryavarman II. The outstanding stone carvings on the central *prang* illustrate scenes from the Hindu epics, the *Ramayana* and the *Mahabharata*. The Reclining Vishnu Lintel on the main east porch was discovered in the Art Institute of Chicago in 1973, and after repeated requests from the Fine Arts Department in Bangkok, it was returned to Thailand in 1988. It can now be seen in its original position. The pediment of this same eastern face portrays Siva cavorting in his dance of creation and destruction. The central hall of the shrine would probably have had a wooden floor – visitors now have to step down below ground level. The quality of the carving at Phnom Rung is regarded by some as being the finest of the Angkor period. Lunet de Lajonquiere, who first surveyed the site in 1907, wrote "in plan, execution and decoration it is among the most perfect of its kind".

The Busabong Festival is held here every April. The only place to eat near the site is at the Phnom Rung Park, an assemblage of small restaurants and stalls serving cold drinks

Phnom Rung

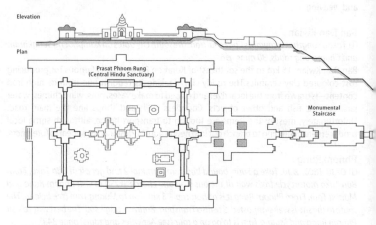

Elevation

Plan

Prasat Phnom Rung
(Central Hindu Sanctuary)

Monumental
Staircase

and good Isaan food, including *kai yang* (grilled chicken), *som tam* (spicy papaya salad) and *khao niaw* (sticky rice).

Muang Tam
ⓘ *Daily 0730-1800. ฿40. Catch a Surin bus to Prakhon Chai on Route 24. From there, song-thaews leave for Muang Tham. If combining the trip with a visit to Phnom Rung, it is necessary to charter a motorcycle taxi or hitch from Phnom Rung – there is no public transport yet (see Phnom Rung, above, for details). See also Transport, Buriram, for access from there, page 360.*

The smaller, intimate Muang Tam, or 'Temple of the Lower city', is found 8 km from Phnom Rung and dates from the 10th-11th century. It is thought to have been the palace of the regional governor of the area. It is surrounded by colossal laterite walls pierced by four gopuras, at the four points of the compass. Three still retain their sculpted lintels. Nagas decorate the L-shaped ponds, which lie within the walls and are stylistically different from those at Phnom Rung: they are smooth-headed rather than adorned with crowns. Historians believe this prasat pre-dates Phnom Rung by some 100 to 200 years. Many regard these nagas as unparalleled in their beauty: lotuses are carved on some of their chests, jewels stream from their mouths and garlands adorn them.

⦿ Nakhon Ratchasima (Korat) and around listings

For Sleeping and Eating price codes and other relevant information, see pages 44-49.

⬤ Sleeping

Nakhon Ratchasima *p331, map p330*
Most hotels are geared to Thais, not *farangs* and particularly not backpackers. The cheap

end of the market is poor quality although middle range accommodation is good value.
B Royal Princess Korat, T044-256629, F044-256601. A/c, restaurant, pool, 200-room hotel and the best in the city, tennis courts, situated north of town across the Takhong River off Suranari Rd and about 2 km from the town centre.

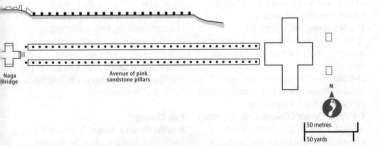

Naga Bridge

Avenue of pink sandstone pillars

N

50 metres
50 yards

B-C Sima Thani Hotel, 2112/2 Mittraphap Rd, T044-213100, www.simathani.co.th. West of town next to the TAT office. This place houses a huge complex of restaurants (food recommended at the **Nai-Ruen**), swimming pool, health club, various gift shops and over 130 rooms. Rooms here are all a/c but tend to be a little worn around the edges, though it is still good value. Location, on the edge of town, is a bit of a drawback.

B-E Iyara Hotel, 497/1 Chompon Rd, T044-268777. The glitzy façade gives way to a huge soulless barn with badly maintained rooms. The views of brick walls and pipes offer a slice of gritty realism but that's probably not what you are in Thailand for. All en-suite, with a/c and colour TV.

C-D Srivichai, 9-11 Buarong Rd, T044-241284. Some a/c, breakfast and drinks available, friendly place with pleasant rooms and a good central location. Recommended.

C-E Korat Hotel, 191 Asdang Rd, T044-341345, www.korathotel.com. Set back from the road, this is another very basic, badly maintained local hotel. Staff are friendly though and the café isn't bad. All rooms have a/c, colour TV and are en suite. The 'suites' are like weird retro museum collections the furniture is so old.

D-E Siri, 167-8 Phoklang Rd, T044-242831. Recently renovated, the rooms here are clean, functional and comfortable. Probably the best deal in town, though the location is a little distant from the town centre. Management a bit diffident, The **Veterans of Foreign Wars Café** – a legacy of the years when Korat was a US airforce base during the Vietnam War – is based here. Recommended.

D-E Sripatana, 346 Suranari Rd, T044-251652, www.sripatana.com. Average a/c rooms. Restaurant, pool and excellent 24-hr coffee shop.

D-E Sriratna, 7 Suranari Rd, T044-243116. Average rooms – best of the cheapies. Those on the front street are a bit noisy.

E-F Korat Doctor's Guesthouse, 78 Suebsiri Rd Soi 4, T044-255846. West of centre, towards TAT. More like a homestay than a

guesthouse, the furnishings and fittings are long past their sell-by date and this once-charming place has begun to decay. It still provides an excellent source of information and is quiet and welcoming, but some may find the rooms a little depressing.

E-F San Sabai, 335 Suranaree Rd, T08-1547 3066. This small hotel-cum-guesthouse is a real find amongst the bustle of Korat city centre. The owner, a kindly middle-aged English-speaking Thai woman called Tim, has created the best place by far to stay in Korat. There are spotless budget fan rooms (all with colour TV), some with balconies while the newer, massive a/c rooms have wooden floors and are nicely decorated. Every room is en suite with hot water. There's a small café/bar and even a court-yard to relax in. Food is available to guests and there are plans for Wi-Fi as well. Excellent value, great location and highly recommended.

G Potong, 652-8 Rachdamnern Rd, T044-242084. Grim fan rooms and this is, with good reason, the cheapest place in town. Central location. Don't leave your valuables in your room.

Khao Yai National Park *p333*

There is a campsite near the Kong Kaeo Waterfall and tents can be hired. Permission to camp must be obtained from the park office. Special permission is required from HQ if you want to stay at outstations.

D-E National Park Lodges, T044-7223579. Book at the National Park Accommodation Office, T044-5614292-3. Price includes bedding and bath facilities. Diverse range of accommodation from dormitories to individual bungalows. Booking highly recommended at weekends.

G Ya Wachon Camp, 2 km from park HQ. Dormitory accommodation and hard floors (bring your own bedding).

Pak Chong

B Juldis Khao Yai Resort, Thannarat Rd, Km 17 (15-25 mins north of the northern gate to the park), T044-2352414. A/c, restaurant, pool, tennis courts and golf available at this resort-style hotel, with both bungalows and larger blocks.

F Happy Trails Tour and Guesthouse, facing the train station. Run by a Thai with good English who has returned from the US. Simple rooms that could do with sprucing up, but the owner is also a guide in the park so has a good knowledge of the area.

F Jungle Guest House, 752/11 Kongwaksin Rd (off Soi 3), south of the Friendship Highway, T044-312877. A backpackers' haunt with enthusiastic staff and basic, overpriced rooms. Also over-enthusiastic in pressing guests to use their tours. Popular.

F Phubade, 781 Thetsaban Rd, just off Friendship Highway, T044-311979. 49 rooms in one of the few central hotels in town, otherwise known as Phubet, most mod cons but no frills.

Phimai *p335, map p335*

E Lamai Homestay, 23/1 Moo 3, Ban Ko Phet, Bua Yai, T08-6258 5894 (mob), www.thailandhomestay.com. Lakeside accommodation in an Isaan rice village. Silk-weaving and basket-making tours offered.

E Phimai Hotel, 305/1-2 Haruethairome Rd, T044-471306, www.korat.in.th/phimaihotel/index.htm. Some a/c, comfortable but plain rooms. Front rooms are noisy, but it's good value and has a good collection of tourist information.

E Phimai Inn, 33/1 Bypass Rd, T044-287228. Easily the best accommodation in Phimai. All the rooms are excellent value in this medium-sized, modern hotel, with TV, shower, a/c and hot water. There is also a very nice, large swimming pool, gardens, good restaurant and cheap internet facilities. Only drawback is that it is about 2 km west of the town. Highly recommended.

E-G Old Phimai Guesthouse, alley off Chomsudasadet Rd, T044-471918. Atmospheric, old wooden house set in a calm *soi*. This place has seen better days but is still a good budget choice. There's a

library and lots of information on local sites and how to reach them. Has one a/c room, a small dormitory and very thin walls.

Chaiyaphum *p337*

E-F Letnimit, 14 Niwarat Rd, T044-811522. A/c, dull hotel opposite the bus station, with equally dull rooms, interesting for the insight it offers into the Thai travelling businessman.

E-F Sirichai, Nornmuang Rd, T044-812848. Some a/c, another dull Sino-Thai hotel in the centre of town.

F-G Yin's Guesthouse, off Niwarat Rd (directly opposite the bus station, 150 m down a dirt track and facing a small lake). Partitioned rooms in raised wooden house, basic but friendly, run by a Norwegian and Thai, bicycles lent gratis and tours to local silk-weaving villages arranged.

❶ Eating

Nakhon Ratchasima *p331, map p330*

Good Thai and Chinese food to be found by the west gates, near the **Thao Suranari Shrine**, for example. A number of bars and restaurants are to be found on **Jomsurangyaat Rd**. Good *kwaytio* restaurant, close to the corner of Buarong and Jomsurangyaat roads. The **night market** on Manat Rd, open from 1800, has a good range of cheap Thai/Chinese cafés and excellent foodstalls.

❢❢ Cabbages and Condoms, 1030-2200 Suebsiri Rd. near **Doctor's House**. Good mix of Thai food. This project's profits go to promote sexual health. Free condoms but prices are little high, though your conscience will also get fed.

❢❢ Nai-Ruen, Sima Thani Hotel, 2112/2 Mittraphap Rd (slightly out of town near the TAT office). Wonderful Thai/Chinese fresh food, and an 'all you can eat and drink' experience to boot. Recommended.

❢ Dok Som Restaurant, 130-142 Chumphon Rd, across the street from the **Potong Hotel**. Very pleasant restaurant with covered terrace area, Thai and Western food. Recommended.

The Emperor Mittraphap Rd (in the **Sima Thani**). Good Chinese restaurant, but eclipsed by the **Seow Seow** in terms of quality; prices to match.

Green House Garden, 50-52 Jomsurang-yaat Rd (next to the post office). Delicious Thai and Isaan grub set in a sheltered 'garden'.

MD Restaurant, Klang Plaza, Jomsurang-yaat Rd. Lots of choice, good, clean restaurant.

Pizza Hut, next to the museum on Rachdamnern Rd.

Seow Seow (pronounced She She), just off Mahatthai Rd. Inexpensive Chinese restaurant. Huge menu, excellent service, seats 250 diners. Recommended.

SPK (Suan Phak), 196 Chumphon Rd. Hang-out for the Korat trendies, good food, also serves cakes.

Veterans of Foreign Wars Café, Siri Hotel, 167-8 Phoklang Rd. Restaurant serving a range of Western dishes along with simple Thai food, a good place for breakfast.

Khao Yai National Park *p333*
The best place to eat in Pak Chong is at the **night market**, which begins operation around 1700 and continues through to shortly before midnight. There are also a fair number of restaurants in town – this, after all, is on the main Bangkok–Korat highway.

Mr Die, 200 m up the road from the **Garden Lodge**, next to a blue 'Bonanza' sign. A small restaurant – unnamed but run by Mr Die – serving good food. Mr Die is also an excellent source of information, being an ex-guide. Recommended.

Phimai *p335, map p335*
The best food is served at the **night market** near the southeast corner of the prasat, open 1800-2400.

Bai Teiy, off Chomsudasadet Rd. Open 0800-2200. Has a good range of Isaan and Chinese/Thai food and ice cream. Recommended.

Rim Mun, north of the town overlooking the river (as the name suggests). For Isaan

food eaten aboard a floating raft, reported to be safe as long as the irrigation canals are not flooded.

Rot Niyom, off Chomsudasadet Rd. Serves good Isaan food.

Sai Nyam, north of the town, near the banyan tree (see map; hence the name). A 'garden restaurant' serving tasty Isaan food.

Steak House, on main road (see map). Excellent little steak house serving up very cheap and hearty meals. Recommended.

Chaiyaphum *p337*
The best food in town is to be had at the **night market** on Taksin Rd. During the day, a good place for Isaan specialities like *kai yaang* (grilled chicken) and *somtam* (spicy papaya salad) is the group of stalls on Bannakaan Rd, opposite the hospital.

Bars and clubs

Nakhon Ratchasima *p331, map p330*
KR Nightclub (described as 'The One American Dance Club') T044-248944, opposite the **Korat Hotel** on Assadang Rd.
London Tavern, 176 Mahatthai Rd. UK-style pub where local football fans congregate.

Chaiyaphum *p337*
Relax Beerhouse, Nonthanakorn Rd (near the intersection with Bannakaan Rd), ice-cold beer, relaxing as the name suggests.

Festivals and events

Nakhon Ratchasima *p331, map p330*
Mar-Apr (end of month) Thao Suranari Fair, a 10-day fair commemorating the local heroine Thao Suranari who helped defeat an invading Lao army. Exhibitions, parades, bazaars, beauty contests and *likay* perfor-mances, along with thousands of participants and onlookers, make this one of Thailand's most vibrant festivals.

Phimai *p335, map p335*
Nov (2nd weekend) Phimai Boat races held on the Phlaimat River, competition of decorated boats, various stalls.

Phnom Rung *p337*
Apr Busabong Festival, see page 338.

O Shopping

Nakhon Ratchasima *p331, map p330*
Books
DK Books, Chumphon Rd.

Handicrafts
Korat is the centre for *matmii* (handwoven cloth), both silk and cotton **Korat Craft Centre** is located behind the Sala Changwat (Provincial Hall).

There are a number of shops around the central square: **Thusnee Thai Silk**, 680 Rachdamnern Rd (opposite Thao Suranari Shrine); **Today Silk**, Rachdamnern Rd; **Klang Plaza I**, Assadang Rd, and **Klang Plaza II**, on Jomsurangyaat Rd.

▲ Activities and tours

Nakhon Ratchasima *p331, map p330*
Tour operators
Hill Top Tour, 516/4 Friendship Rd, Pak Chong, T044-311671.
Prayurakit, 40-44 Suranari Rd, T044-252114.

Khao Yai National Park *p333*
Tour operators
Pak Chong guesthouse representatives meeting visitors off the bus sometimes give the impression that theirs are the only tours to the park; there are many on offer.
KH Tours, on the Friendship Highway, T044-515709, promises to show you 'bird with ear – mouse with wings', in their 2-day tour and slightly cheaper programme (₿650). Bikes for rent, ₿300 per day.

Khao Yai National Park and Wildlife Tours, which operates out of **Khao Yai Garden Lodge**, has been recommended. A 1½-day tour is charged at ₿950 per person, but it also operates tours up to 7 days long.

Phimai *p335, map p335*
See under **Lamai Homestay**, Sleeping.

☺ Transport

Nakhon Ratchasima *p331, map p330*
Air
Daily connections with **Bangkok** (30 mins).
Airline offices THAI, 14 Manat Rd, T044-257211.

Bus
The a/c bus terminal for **Bangkok** is on Mittraphap Rd, west of the town centre. Connections with Bangkok's Northeastern bus terminal (4-5 hrs). There are 2 more long-distance bus terminals for other destinations in Thailand: Terminal 2, which is 2 km northwest of town on Route 2 to **Khon Kaen** and serves most northeastern destinations, as well as places in the east, such as **Rayong** (useful for Koh Samet), **Chantaburi** and **Pattaya**. Terminal 1, off Burin Rd, closer to the centre of town, serves **Khon Kaen**, **Chiang Mai** and **Chiang Rai**.

4 buses leave Korat for **Pak Chong** in the morning (₿20), or it is possible to catch a Bangkok-bound bus and get off in Pak Chong.

Motorbike hire
Virojyarnyon, 554-556 Phoklang Rd. Charge ₿150-200 per day.

Train
The station is on Mukamontri Rd, in the west of town (T044-242044). Connections with **Bangkok**'s Hualamphong station (5-6 hrs) and with **Ubon**, close to the Laos border.

Khao Yai National Park *p333*
Train
The trains from **Bangkok** (3½-4 hrs) and **Ayutthaya** travel onward to Ubon Ratchathani.

Phimai *p335, map p335*
Bicycle hire
฿20 per day from the small shop on Chomsudasadet Rd.

Bus
Regular connections with **Korat**'s main bus station on Suranari Rd (1½ hrs), last bus leaves Phimai for Korat at 1800. Hourly service to **Bangkok** between 0830 and 2300 (5 hrs). To travel north, take a local bus to **Thalat Khae** and then catch a bus travelling north.

Chaiyaphum *p337*
Bus
Regular bus connections with **Bangkok**'s Northeastern bus terminal (7 hrs), and with **Phitsanulok**, **Chiang Mai** and towns in the northeast leave from the bus station on the northeast edge of town. A/c buses (VIP and standard) to Bangkok leave from the offices of Air Chaiyaphum at 202/8-9 Nornmuang Rd, just to the north of the Sirichai Hotel in the town centre.

For a/c buses to **Chiang Mai** and **Ubon Ratchathani**, the terminal is on Nornmuang Rd, south of the post office.

ⓓ Directory

Nakhon Ratchasima *p331, map p330*
Banks There are a number of banks offering foreign exchange services on Mittraphap and Chumphon roads. Bangkok, Jomsurangyaat Rd, close to the post office. **Internet** At the internet café next to Klang Plaza II. **Medical services** Maharaj Hospital, near the bus station on Suranari Rd, T044-254990. **Police** Sanpasit Rd, T044-242010. **Tourist Police** 2102-2104 Mittraphap Rd (on western edge of town, next to the TAT office), T044-213333. **Post office** Main office on Assadang Rd, between Prachak and Manat roads; a more convenient branch is at 48 Jomsurangyaat Rd, next to Klang Plaza II. **Telephone** Telecom centre, Jomsurangyaat Rd, next to the post office.

Phimai *p335, map p335*
Banks Currency exchange service opposite the entrance to the Phimai Historical Park. Thai Farmers Bank, Chomsudasadet Rd.

Chaiyaphum *p337*
Banks Banks with exchange facilities are located on Uthittham Rd (eg **Krung Thai**) and Hot Thai Rd (eg **Thai Farmers Bank**). **Post office** Intersection of Bannakaan Rd and Nornmuang Rd (telephone and fax facilities available).

Ubon Ratchathani and around

Head into the far eastern corner of Isaan and you'll find one of the region's most important cities – Ubon Ratchathani. Administrative capital and transport hub, it is a friendly stop-off point while investigating the more impressive sights of this far-flung corner of Thailand. With the border crossing fully open at Chongmek this also now forms an important land route into Laos – there are regular bus connections between Ubon and the Laos city of Pakxe though you will need a visa before commencing your journey if you want to travel straight through (see box, page 361, for details of links to Laos).

Surin is famous for its annual Elephant Round-up and the nearby Suay people, who have a unique relationship with these huge beasts. If you want the spectacular, Yasothon hosts a yearly skyrocket festival. Some of these mammoth fireworks weigh hundreds of kilos and are suitably blessed by Buddhists monks before being fired into the heavens. Elsewhere there are the rapids of Tana and Kaen Sapu, and the obscure river cliffs of Pha Taem, while Phra Viharn – one of the most spectacular Khmer temples ever built – nestles just across the Cambodian border (see page 350 for the current situation here). ▸▸ For listings, see pages 353-362.

Towards Ubon Ratchathani ●❼❶❀❺▲❸❶ ▸▸ pp353-362.

Buriram → Colour map 2, C4.
Buriram is small, unassuming and, in all senses, provincial. However, a new airport has recently opened in Buriram (30 km northeast of town). It makes a good base to visit the Khmer ruins at Phnom Rung and Muang Tam, yet few people stay here, preferring to travel from the larger city of Korat. Pink buses criss-cross the town (฿5 for any distance) and there are tuk-tuks (฿10-20) if you need to get around. The railway station can be found at the end of Romburi Road, near the centre of town.

There's not much to see, though the **Isaan Cultural Centre** ① *Jira Rd, sporadic opening hours*, at the Buriram teachers' college, supports a museum, stages dance, music and drama performances, and hosts exhibitions of folk art. The small collection is labelled in Thai. The town's fresh market is off Soonthonthep Road, not far north of Buriram's largest wat, the peaceful but otherwise plain **Wat Klang**.

Khao Krudong is a 300-m volcanic cinder cone 8 km southeast of town. To get there take a *songthaew* in the morning from the station near the market, off Sriphet Road. The hill, rising up from the surrounding rice plain, is a holy place and is crowned by a white 20-m-high statue of the Buddha. The views from the summit are best at sunset (although public transport is limited in the afternoon).

Surin and around → Colour map 2, C4.
Surin is a silk-producing town, best known for its **Elephant Round-up**, held in the third week of November at the Surin Sports Park. The forested Thai/Cambodian border has long been the domain of a tribe of elephant catchers called the Suay. At the beginning of the 20th century there were 100,000 domesticated elephants in Thailand. The Suay were much in demand to look after the working population and catch wild elephants. With the advent of other transport the need for elephants fell; today, there are about 4000 working elephants.

During the festival, 40,000 people come to watch the Suay practise their skills with at least 200 elephants. They take part in parades and mock battles. There are also demonstrations of Thai dance and an unusual game of soccer played by elephants and their mahouts. The bus station is off Chitbamrung Road, special air-conditioned buses are laid on by tour companies and major hotels for the Elephant Round-up. The railway station is at the north end of Tanasarn Road, with a statue of three elephants outside. The overnight air-conditioned express leaves Bangkok at 2100 and arrives in Surin at 0424. Tickets must be booked two weeks in advance for travel during November when the Elephant Round-up is under way. The TAT organizes a special train during this period.

For the rest of the year Surin becomes a backwater: the only reason to stay here is to visit the numerous Khmer temples that are to be found in this southern part of the northeast.

The **Surin Museum** ① *Chitbamrung Rd, Wed-Sun*, displays many of the accessories used by the Suay to capture wild elephants, including the magical talismans that are worn to protect men from injury. A bustling morning **market** lies between Thetsabarn and Krungsi-Nai roads and a there's very small **museum** ① *Chitbamrung Rd, Mon-Fri 0830-1630*, at the south edge of town.

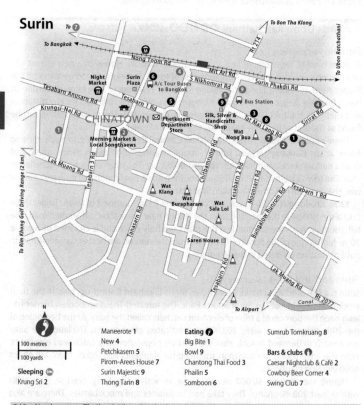

Surin

Sleeping		Eating 🍴		Bars & clubs 🍸
Krung Sri 2	Maneerote 1	Big Bite 1	Sumrub Tornkruang 8	
	New 4	Bowl 9		Caesar Nightclub & Café 2
	Petchkasem 5	Chantong Thai Food 3		Cowboy Beer Corner 4
	Pirom-Arees House 7	Phailin 5		Swing Club 7
	Surin Majestic 9	Somboon 6		
	Thong Tarin 8			

Ban Tha Klang is a Suay settlement, 58 km north of Surin, near the town of Tha Tum. There's an hourly bus from the terminal in Surin (two hours). The Suay are said to have filtered into Thailand from central Asia during the ninth and 10th centuries, becoming the first people of the area to tame elephants for human use. The village is sometimes called Elephant Village because of the close association the population has with the art and science of capturing and training pachyderms. Outside the official Elephant Round-up festival period, it is sometimes possible to see training in progress here. It is best to come in the weeks just prior to the round-up (see Festivals and events, page 357), when the villagers are intensively preparing for the festival, or try to make your visit coincide with the elephant feeding schedule. Even if you don't see any elephants, the village is worth a visit.

Prasat Ta Muan Tot and **Prasat Ta Muan** lie just 100 m apart in Kab Choeng District, Surin Province, about 60 km due south of Surin on the Thai-Cambodian border. It's not possible to get there on public transport. However, the site is close to Phnom Rung and Muang Tam and could be included in a tour of these better known Khmer sites. Alternatively, hire a car or *songthaew*. Built in the 11th century during the reign of Khmer King Jayavarman VII, the prasats are situated on the road that linked Angkor Wat with Phimai. These were once fine complexes, although they have been extensively damaged in recent years – largely during a period of occupation by Khmer Rouge troops. Prasat Ta Muan Tot was built as a hospital to minister to weary and sick travellers while Prasat Ta Muan was a chapel. There is an impressive 30-m-long staircase leading down into Cambodian territory, a central sanctuary and associated minor *prangs* and buildings.

Prasat Sikhoraphum (aka **Prasat Ban Ra-ngaeng**) ① ₿20, can be found at the Km 34 marker from Surin to Si Saket, Route 226. Four small *prangs* sit on a laterite base, surrounding a larger central *prang*. A 12th-century Khmer temple, Sikhoraphum began life as a Hindu shrine. The central *prang* retains some beautiful carvings on the lintels (dancing Siva) and door jambs (door guardians and floral designs).

Si Saket → *Colour map 2, C5.*

Si Saket is a good base from which to visit the lesser-known Khmer sites in the lower northeast such as Prasat Sikhoraphum (see above), which is located on Route 266, 34 km before reaching Surin and 69 km from Si Saket. The town is a small provincial capital with few sights – the daily market off Khukhan Road can be entertaining – though it is an enjoyable place to absorb authentic Isaan culture. The bus terminal is on the south side of town, off Khukhan Road and the railway station is in the centre of town on Kaanrotfai Road.

Ubon Ratchathani ◒◗ⓕⓝ⊗◓▲⊖◗ » *pp353-362. Colour map 2, C5.*

The 'Royal City of the Lotus' is an important provincial capital on the Mun River. Like a number of other towns in the northeast, Ubon was a US airbase during the Vietnam War and as a result houses a good selection of Western-style hotels, as well as bars and massage parlours. The money that filtered into the town during the war meant that it became one of the richest in the region: this can still be seen reflected in the impressive, although slowly decaying, public buildings. Like Udon Thani and Korat, there is still a small community of ex-GIs who have married local women and are living out their days here.

Ins and outs

Getting there The airport is a longish walk from the city centre, on the north side of town. It is just about possible to walk if it's cool, there's a following breeze and you have

Ubon Ratchathani

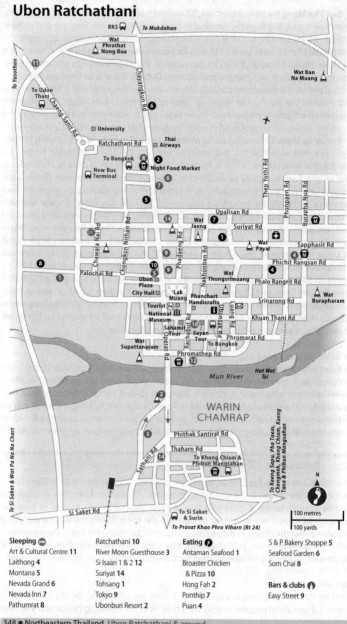

Sleeping 🛏
Art & Cultural Centre **11**
Laithong **4**
Montana **5**
Nevada Grand **6**
Nevada Inn **7**
Pathumrat **8**

Ratchathani **10**
River Moon Guesthouse **3**
Si Isaan 1 & 2 **12**
Suriyat **14**
Tohsang **1**
Tokyo **9**
Ubonburi Resort **2**

Eating 🍴
Antaman Seafood **1**
Broaster Chicken
& Pizza **10**
Hong Fah **2**
Ponthip **7**
Puan **4**

S & P Bakery Shoppe **5**
Seafood Garden **6**
Som Chai **8**

Bars & clubs 🍸
Easy Street **9**

light bags. A taxi service is available: ฿70 to the town centre, ฿120 to the railway station at Warin Chamrap, south of town. Bigger hotels pick up guests gratis. Buses Nos 2 and 6 run into town from the railway station but most people arrive in Ubon by bus. The main bus terminal is north of town (too far to walk), but many tour buses drop off in the city centre. ▶▶ See also Transport, page 360, for further details.

Getting around Ubon is a large town. The TAT provides a map marking city bus routes – there are 13 routes across town. There are also lots of *saamlors* and tuk-tuks, as well as cars and motorbikes for hire.

Tourist information TAT ① *264/1 Khuan Thani Rd (facing the Srikamol Hotel), T045-243770, 0830-1630*, provides a map of Ubon with bus routes and other handouts. It's a useful first stop, though not particularly efficient. Areas of responsibility are Ubon Ratchathani, Si Saket and Yasothon.

Sights

There is a good archaeological, historical and cultural **museum** ① *Khuan Thani Rd, Wed-Sun 0900-1600, ฿30*, the Ubon branch of the National Museum in Bangkok. It is housed in a panya-style (southern Thai architectural style) building, erected in 1918 as a palace for King Vajiravudh (Rama VI). The collection includes prehistoric artefacts collected in the province, as well as pieces from the historic period, including Khmer artefacts, and cultural pieces such as local textiles and musical instruments. The star of the collection is a large, bronze Dong-son drum.

Wat Phrathat Nong Bua ① *500 m west off Chayangkun Rd travelling north to Nakhon Phanom*, is not far past the army base. Take town bus No 2 or 3, or go by tuk-tuk. It is a large, white angular *chedi* built in 1957 to celebrate the 2500th anniversary of the death of the Lord Buddha. It is said to be a copy of the Mahabodhi stupa in Bodhgaya, India. It is certainly unusual in the Thai context. Jataka reliefs and cloaked standing Buddhas in various stances are depicted on the outside of the *chedi*.

Wat Thungsrimuang, on Luang Road, and named after the *thung* (field) by the provincial hall, is a short walk from the TAT office. It is notable for its red-stained wooden *hor trai* (library) on stilts, in the middle of a stagnant pond. The library contains Buddhist texts and rare examples of Isaan literature, but is usually locked. The monastery was built during the reign of Rama III (1824-1851) and there is a fine late Ayutthayan-style bot, graciously decaying.

At the west end of Phromathep Road, **Wat Supattanaram** is pleasantly situated overlooking the Mun River. It was built in 1853 and supports monks of the Dharmayuthi sect (a Theravada Buddhist sect best known for its meditation practices). It is significant for its collection of lintels which surround the bot, commemorating the dead. One of the sandstone lintels is Khmer and is said to date from the seventh century. Also here is a massive, suspended wooden gong, said to be the largest in the country.

The large sandbank (**Hat Wat Tai**) in the middle of the Mun River is linked by a rope footbridge to Phonpaen Road (take bus No 1, then walk south along Phonpaen Road). The residents of Ubon come here for picnics during the low water summer months, between March and May. Foodstalls set up in the evening and on weekends. It is possible to swim here. There is a bustling fruit and vegetable market between the river and Phromathep Road, east of the bridge.

Prasat Khao Phra Viharn and the October War

In 2008 a longstanding application for Preah Vihear to be placed on the UNESCO World Heritage Site list came to fruition. Initially the Thai government supported the move, even though this meant accepting the contested areas were inside Cambodian territory. The thinking at the time was that the site could now benefit both nations.

With huge pressure coming to bear on the Peoples' Power Party (PPP) from the extreme nationalists of the Peoples' Alliance for Democracy (PAD), Thailand withdrew its support for UNESCO status and reneged on its promise to finally recognize Cambodia's claims. Nonetheless, UNESCO declared Preah Vihear a World Heritage Site on 8 July 2008.

Much sabre rattling ensued, with shots fired and military units mobilized. Thai nationalists were arrested by the Cambodians as they tried to plant a Thai flag in the Preah Vihear's grounds and bizarre black magic rituals were claimed to have been enacted by both sides. With the Thai foreign minister forced to resign and Thailand completely entrenched, a conflict seemed inevitable.

In October 2008 the fighting started in earnest with a mini-battle taking place that left several soldiers on both sides dead or injured. Thai nationals were advised to leave Cambodia by the Thai government and war seemed imminent. Fortunately, after intervention by the international community, both sides saw sense and pulled back from the brink.

As this book goes to press, the situation is still tense although it seems unlikely it will escalate into a conflict again – at least for now. Unfortunately this means that one of Southeast Asia's most dramatic sites is off limits to travellers trying to reach it from the Thai side of the border.

It is recommended that readers avoid Phra Viharn until the situation is more stable.

Warin Chamrap, a busy town, is 3 km south of Ubon over the Mun River. Warin still possesses some architectural charm including a number of gently decaying wood, brick and stucco shophouses. There is also a good mixed market near the main bus station. The main reasons to come here are either to catch a public bus from one of the bus terminals or to reach the train station. Town buses Nos 1, 2, 3, 6 and 7 all link Warin with Ubon.

Around Ubon Ratchathani ⊖⊘⊛⊖⊖❶ ➠ *pp353-362.*

Wat Pa Na Na Chart
ⓘ *Take a local bus or songthaew running towards Surin from the station in Warin Chamrap to the south of town, over the Mun River. Get to Warin Chamrap by town buses Nos 1, 2 or 6.*
This is a forest wat 14 km from Ubon, on Route 226 towards Surin. The wat is a popular meditation retreat for *farangs* interested in Buddhism. The abbot is Canadian and most of the monks are non-Thais. English is the language of communication and both men and women are welcomed.

Prasat Khao Phra Viharn ➔ *Colour map 3, C5.*
The 'Holy Monastery' of Prasat Khao Phra Viharn, known in Cambodian as **Preah Vihear**, lies south of Ubon, perched on a 500-m-high escarpment on the border between Thailand

and Cambodia, a couple of hours drive west of Ubon. It is a magnificent Khmer sanctuary, in one of the most spectacular positions of any monument in Southeast Asia. Yet it's recent history has been the source of huge antagonism between the two countries.

It lies close to a disputed section of the Cambodian border; 30 years ago the international court in The Hague ruled that it lay inside Cambodian territory. The Thai authorities reacted angrily to this and never fully recognized Cambodia's claim to what could potentially be one of the most lucrative tourist sites in Southeast Asia. Thai maps often mark the sanctuary as lying within Thai territory. The Cambodian side of the area was controlled by the Khmer Rouge until the end of December 1998. With the demise of the Khmer Rouge, Prasat Phra Viharn re-opened and until 2008 was on its way to becoming a required stop on any tour of the northeast. In July 2008, Preah Vihear was declared a UNESCO World Heritage Site but in October fighting broke out between Thai and Cambodian forces (see box, opposite). Travel to Prasat Phra Viharn is currently not recommended, check locally for details on the current situation.

Kaeng Sapu
① *Take town bus Nos 1, 3 or 6 to Warin Chamrap. From here buses run regularly to Phibun Mangsahan, 1 hr. The rapids are 1 km from town; walk or take a saamlor.*

A series of rapids on the Mun River, 1 km outside the district town of Phibun Mangsahan and about 45 km from Ubon, Kaeng Sapu do not compare with the rapids at Kaeng Tana National Park (see below), but are much easier to reach. Inner tubes can be hired to float downriver and there is a small market with foodstalls and poor quality handicrafts. **Wat Sarakaew** is close by, with a viharn showing some colonial influences.

Chongmek
① *Catch town buses Nos 1, 3 or 6 from Ubon Ratchathani to Warin Chamrap and then take a 2nd bus from the station in Warin Chamrap to Phibun Mangsahan, about 45 km (1 hr). From Phibun Mangsahan there are converted trucks (large songthaews) to Chongmek, 44 km away (1½ hrs). You can also get buses direct from Ubon to Pakxe, negating the need to even stop in Chongmek. See page 361 for details on negotiating the border.*

Chongmek is an interesting border town east of Ubon with an extraordinary attempt at post-modern architecture in the form of the frontier station – giant purple juxtaposed slabs extend into the sky. There is a large Thai-Lao market selling food (including baguettes), baskets, clothes and basic manufactured goods, as well as some 'antiques' and wild animal products from Laos. Check out the plethora of army surplus stalls here making it a good place to pick up bargain strides and T-shirts. Even those without entry visas for Laos are allowed to cross the Thai border and mosey around the market.

Kaeng Tana National Park
① *The park is about 75 km to the east of Ubon off Route 217, where the park office is located. It is easiest to visit on a tour (see Tour operators, page 359) or by private car/motorcycle. There is no easy way to reach the rapids on public transport. The nearest town is Khong Chiam, which is reached by changing bus at Warin Chamrap.*

The Kaeng Tana – the Tana rapids – after which the park is named, are found at a point where the Mun River squeezes through a rocky outcrop before flowing into the Mekong. In the dry season the rocks present an almost lunar landscape of giant ossified bones, jumbled together into a heap of eroded boulders. It is possible to chicken leap across the river to midstream. The controversial Pak Mun Dam, completed in 1994 and designed

Border essentials: Thailand–Laos

Chongmek–Pakxe

It is possible to enter Laos east of Ubon at Chongmek (for details on Chongmek, see page 351). There are now four direct connections a day from Ubon to Pakxe in Laos. The fare is ฿200 and the journey takes about three hours. If you want to take advantage of this easy, through connection you should get your visa before travel – the bus will not wait at the border for you to sort out your paper work if you are planning visa on arrival (see box, page 361, for information on travel to Laos).

to generate hydropower and irrigate land, can be seen from the rapids. Bungalow accommodation is available here or in Khong Chiam (see Sleeping, page 355).

Khong Chiam → *Colour map 2, C6.*

ⓘ *To get here, catch town bus Nos 1, 3 or 6 from Ubon Ratchathani to Warin Chamrap; and from there to Khong Chiam via Phibun Mangsahan.*

This attractive district town at Thailand's easternmost point is situated on the Mekong, close to the confluence of the Mun and Mekong, the so-called two-coloured river or Maenam Song Sii, because of the meeting of the red-brown Mekong and the deep blue Mun. Boats take visitors out to the point of confluence to view the ripple effect at close hand, which is best towards the end of the dry season in March to May. There is accommodation here and some excellent restaurants. Inner tubes can be hired to swim in the Mekong and it makes an alternative and much quieter place to stay than Ubon. It has also been reported that visitors can cross the Mekong to visit the town on the other bank for the day, although this cannot be used as an entry point to Laos. In addition, Khong Chiam can be used as a base to visit the other sights in this easternmost area of Thailand, eg Pha Taem, Kaeng Sapu and Kaeng Tana National Park. In the town, a morning market operates between 0600 and 0830. Boats can be hired anywhere along the riverbank.

Pha Taem

ⓘ *It's quite difficult to reach on public transport. First take an Ubon town bus to Warin Chamrap (Nos 1, 3 or 6), and from there to Khong Chiam via Phibun Mangsahan (where accommodation is available, see Sleeping, below). There are also some direct buses to Khong Chiam from Ubon. From Khong Chiam charter a tuk-tuk for the last 20 km to the cliff (฿150 return). Chongmek Travellers and Takerng Tour organize boat trips there (see Tour operators, page 359), or hire a motorbike or car.*

In Khong Chiam district, 94 km northeast of Ubon, is a sandstone cliff overlooking a wide, deep gorge that cuts through the Mekong. Views from this clifftop across the Mekong to Laos are spectacular. Ochre prehistoric paintings, about 3000 years old, of figures, turtles, elephants, fish and geometric forms stretch for some 400 m along a cliff set high above the Mekong. A trail leads down and then along the face of the cliff, past three groups of paintings now protected by unsightly barbed wire. Two viewing towers allow the images to be viewed at eye level.

Two kilometres before the turn-off for Pha Taem is **Sao Chaliang**, an area of strange, heavily eroded sandstone rock formations.

Yasothon → Colour map 2, B5. Population: 34,000.

This small provincial capital is situated northwest of Ubon and there is really only one reason to visit: to see the famous **bun bang fai** (**skyrocket festival**), which is held annually over the second weekend in May. Once a regionwide festival, Yasothon has made it its own (see box, page 358).

In the centre of Yasothon, on Withdamrong Road, is a daily market which, though not geared to tourists, does sell functional handicrafts: Isaan pillows and cushions, and baskets and woven sticky-rice containers. The bus station is at the northeastern edge of town, an easy walk from the centre. Wat Mahathat Yasothon, just off the main road, is said to date from the foundation of the city. The Phra That Phra Anon Chedi, within the monastery's precincts, is said to date from the seventh century and contains the ashes of the Lord Buddha's first disciple, Phra Anon (better known outside Thailand as Ananda).

ⓔ Ubon Ratchathani and around listings

For Sleeping and Eating price codes and other relevant information, see pages 44-49.

ⓔ Sleeping

Buriram p345

Buriram is a reasonable option as a base for exploring Phnom Rung and the other assorted Khmer temples.

C-E Vongthong Hotel, 512/1 Jira Rd. A/c rooms have fridge and TV and there are hot-water bathrooms. Gaudy Isaan-inspired lobby and theme provides atmosphere and there's an authentic massage place attached and a large snooker hall and bar. The suites are enormous. Recommended.

D-E Paradise Resort, unnamed *soi* off Injandranarong Rd, T044-602288. Brand new, motel style set-up with good a/c rooms, all very clean and complete with cable TV. Not much English spoken but friendly enough.

E Thai, 38/1 Romburi Rd, T044-611112, F612461. Some a/c, the best of the town centre hotels (which isn't, admittedly, saying much). Clean but plain and a safe bet given the limited competition in this category. All rooms have hot water, but some have no windows.

E Thepnakorn, Moo 3, Isan Rd (edge of town, off continuation of Jira Rd), T044-613400, F613400. Reasonable, mid-range hotel.

E-F Serm Sunnee, unnamed *soi* off Bulamduan Rd, look for giant sign saying 'guesthouse', T044-614026. Good, clean cheap rooms with balconies, all en suite. You can opt to have the a/c switched off and get a lower rate. No English spoken and more akin to an apartment block than a guesthouse, so no food, information or much atmosphere. Nonetheless, excellent value and recommended.

Surin p345, map p346

Some good mid-range options here – and if they're beyond your budget Surin is also home to one of the nicest guesthouses in the region. All accommodation during the Round-up booked up and expensive.

B-D Surin Majestic, 99 Chitbamrung Rd, T044-713980, www.surinmajestic.net. Brand new hotel complex next to the bus station. A well-run, friendly hotel with good, large a/c, en suite rooms complemented by balconies. Free internet for guests, fitness centre, pool and English movie channels. Recommended.

B-E Petchkasem, 104 Chitbamrung Rd, T044-511274, pkhotel@cscoms.com. A/c, restaurant, pool, coffee shop, snooker and nightclubs. 162 smart, average rooms, 30% discounts available during the off-season.

B-E Thong Tarin, 60 Sirirat Rd, T044-514281, www.thongtarinhotel.com. A/c, restaurant, pool. The 200 plus rooms look a bit worn and need renovating. Close to bus station.

The cheapest rooms are good value for money.

D-E New Hotel, 22 Tanasarn Rd, T044-511341, F511971. Some a/c, large hotel of 100 rooms with worn and dirty prison-like corridors, but rooms are suprisingly clean, no hot water and bolshy management, close to train station; hardly 'new'.

E Maneerote, 11/1 Soi Poytango, Krungsi-Nai Rd, T044-539477, www.maneerotehotel. Nice clean rooms in sparkling, new block. All have a/c and balconies and are en suite. The so-called VIP rooms are better value. Rate includes breakfast. Recommmended.

E-F Krung Sri, 185 Krungsi-Nai Rd, just off the market, T044-511037. Basic, clean, light rooms, some with a/c, squat toilets, en suite showers.

G Pirom – Arees House, 55, 326 Soi Arunee, T044-513234. Cute little guesthouse set down a rural *soi* about 1.5 km out of town (a tuk-tuk costs ฿50/60). The owners, Pirom and Aree, are very friendly and a gold mine of info on local Isaan culture and the Khmer ruins. Some of the smaller rooms are very basic with thin walls while the larger rooms have good views over the surrounding countryside. Shared facilities, some nice areas to lounge in and gardens make this a great spot to relax. Pirom also runs tours of the Khmer antiquities (from ฿1200). Highly recommended.

Si Saket *p347*

There's not a great range of accommodation in Si Saket.

C-E Ketsiri Hotel, 1102-5 Khukhan Rd, T045-614006, F614008. Surprisingly luxurious for a small town with 11th-floor rooftop pool, satellite TV in lobby (not in rooms), coffee shop serving excellent food, starched linen, a/c and a marble foyer. Spotless, cooperative and very friendly staff. A good base.

F Si Saket Hotel, 384/5 Si Saket Rd, T045-611846. Some a/c, the best budget hotel within easy reach of the railway station, although that is not much of a recommendation given the competition.

Ubon Ratchathani *p347, map p348*

B-D Laithong Hotel, Phichit Rangsan Rd, T045-264271. Very attractive hotel with all facilities including pool, restaurant, karaoke, night club and bars.

B-D Pathumrat, 337 Chayangkun Rd, T045-241501, F242313. North of town centre, near the market bus station, a/c, restaurant, pool, built during the Vietnam War to meet US military demand, it still exudes 1970s kitsch.

B-D Tohsang Hotel, 251 Palochai Rd, T045-245531, www.tohsang.com. Good rooms in an interesting location. They aspire to be a contemporary boutique hotel but don't quite pull it off. Decent food.

B-D Ubonburi Resort and Hotel, 1 Srinmongkol Rd, T045-266777, www.ubonburihotel.com. Best hotel in town with a lovely lakeside setting – only drawback is the location; it's not very near the town centre. Pool, good restaurant and a variety of accommodation options – the excellent lakeside cottages represent the best value. Recommended.

C-D Art and Cultural Centre, Jangsanit Rd, T045-352031. This massive pagoda-style concrete edifice out by the university hosts not only a mediocre Isaan arts centre but also several dozen massive rooms. Each is en suite, with a/c, balconies and cable TV. A slightly bizarre choice but all the better for it. Recommended.

D-E Nevada Grand Hotel, Chayagkul Rd, T045-280999. A/c, TV, pleasant, spacious rooms, a more de luxe version of the **Nevada Inn** (see below) which is located next door.

D-F Montana Hotel, 179/1 Uparat Rd, T045-261752. A/c, 40 comfortable rooms and friendly staff, central location close to town square, room rate includes breakfast. Very popular. Recommended.

D-F Nevada Inn, 436/1 Chayagkul Rd, T045-313355, F313350. A/c, TV, some rooms with good views. Divides its karaoke-goers into 'very' VIPs, VIPs and the normal karaoke rooms for riff-raff. Featureless restaurant, attached to a cinema complex with internet.

D-F Ratchathani, 229 Khuan Thani Rd, T045-244388, F243561. Some a/c, all rooms with TV and hot water, clean and generally well run, comfortable beds in spacious rooms, competitively priced.

D-F Si Isaan 1 and 2, 62 Rachabut Rd, T045-754204, service@sriisanhotel.com. Some a/c, open airy and clean hotel with very friendly management. Rooms have tea- and coffee-making facilities and room service at very reasonable prices. A delightful place to stay, free transport to train and bus stations.

E-F Suriyat, 47/1-4 Suriyat Rd, T045-241144. Some a/c, TV. Clean, simple, pleasant rooms.

E-G Tokyo Hotel, 360 Operat Rd, T045-241 739. Opt for the good-value a/c rooms in the newer building. The cheaper rooms have the seedy feel of fleeting visits for short-time pleasure. Still one of the better budget choices.

G River Moon Guesthouse, 43 Sisaket Rd, T045-286093. Set just over the river in the neighbouring town of Warin Chamrup (Ubon's railway station is also here), this guesthouse has seen better days and is run down. It is very cheap, friendly and OK for those on a tight budget.

Chongmek *p351*

F-G Hotel Phiphunkit Song, T040-396639. Set in the tiny village of Nikom Song, 8 km from the border at Chong Mek and marked with a sign saying 'Hotel' in English, this place serves good Thai food and has some decent a/c and fan rooms. This is the nearest accommodation to the frontier with Laos.

Khong Chiam *p352*

B-C Araya Resort, Pukumchai Rd, T045-351191. Large, attractive bungalows situated in a beautiful spot on a landscaped rocky hill-garden above the river. A/c, TV, hot water, fridge. The associated restaurant, **Araya Raft**, floats down below on the Mekong, and is justly known for its fish dishes.

B-C Khong Chiam Marina Resort, T045-361011. Range of bungalows some with a/c, good restaurant.

B-D Khiang Nam Resort (Ban Kiang Nam), Klaepradit Rd, T045-351374/5. Beautiful bungalows in neat little gardens. A/c, hot water, TV and peaceful surroundings.

B-D Rim Khong Resort, Klaepradit Rd, T045-351101, close to Mekong River. Luxurious, big timber bungalows, some with balconies overlooking the river. A/c, TV, fridge, and wonderful garden-like private bathrooms. There is also a restaurant, and you can take day trips to Pha Taem from here.

D-E Khong Chiam Hotel, Pukumchai Rd, T045-351160, F351074. Some a/c and hot water, private bathrooms, quiet location, good source of information.

D-G Mongkhon Guesthouse, 595 Klaepradit Rd, T045-351352, T08-1312 0249 (mob). A very friendly guesthouse with English-speaking management on edge of town, close to the bus stop. Large, spacious, clean rooms, some with a/c, internet, bicycle and motorbike hire. Recommended.

D-G Sibae Guesthouse, 380 Ratsadonbumrung Rd, T045-351068. This is a wonderfully clean and friendly guesthouse. Range of rooms, fan, a/c and en suite shower. Great location next to the river and near the ferry to Laos. Recommended.

E Pakmool Guesthouse, Pukumchai Rd, T045-351052. Great location and decent rooms spoiled by bad windowless design which is bizarre given the awesome riverside setting. There is a nice terrace. No English spoken.

G Apple Guesthouse, 267 Klaepradit Rd, T045-351160. Clean, some rooms with attached showers, fans, a bit small and dark.

Yasothon *p353*

E-F Yod Nakhon, 143 Uthairamrit Rd, T045-711481, F711476. Some a/c, large, featureless but comfortable enough, with, so it is claimed, a 24-hr coffee shop, a/c rooms have TV but no hot water.

F-G Surawit Watthana, 128/1 Chaeng Sanit Rd, T045-711690. Fan rooms with attached bathrooms.

🍴 Eating

Buriram *p345*

Buriram is famous for its fiery papaya *pok pok* salad, similar to the more widely available Isaan dish, *somtam*.

🍴 Be My Guest, next door to **Vongthong Hotel**. Good array of steaks, smoothies and Western food.

🍴 Book n Bed, opposite **Vongthong Hotel**. No beds here but good coffee, English-language papers and magazines, freindly owner, steaks and good breakfasts.

🍴 Beer House, Romburi Rd. Open-air bar and restaurant specializing in ice-cold beer and chargrilled seafood. Recommended.

🍴 Lung Chaan Restaurant, Romburi Rd (near **Thai Hotel**). Excellent cheap Thai/Chinese food, with superb *kwaytio* and other simple dishes.

🍴 Nong Kai Restaurant, Romburi Rd (south end). Pleasant, shady open-air noodle house with excellent noodle soup specialities.

🍴 Thippawan Cafe, Jira Rd, next to the railway tracks on edge of town. Excellent noodles and fresh fruit.

Surin *p345, map p346*

🍴 Big Bite, on the side road up to the **Thong Tarin Hotel**. Open 1000-0200. Serves a vast range of Thai, Chinese and European food in a relaxing atmosphere. Many varieties of whisky and brandy.

🍴 The Bowl, opposite the **Petchkasem Hotel**. Good fresh coffee, ice cream, cakes, Isaan and Thai food and even the internet are available in this a/c diner.

🍴 Chantong Thai Food, Tat Mai Lang Rd, T045-515599. Open 1000-2400. Smart place with fine food – and very good value too.

🍴 Cocaa, Soi Thetsabarn 2 Rd. Open 1000-2300. This simple restaurant has Thai and Chinese dishes, with some excellent seafood. Recommended.

🍴 Indochine Restaurant, 168-170 Sapphasit Rd (not far from Wat Jaeng). Closes at 1800. Vietnamese food in basic but attractive restaurant, good value and great food.

🍴 Phailin Restaurant, 174 Tanasarn Rd. Open-air restaurant with excellent cheap Thai and Lao food.

🍴 Somboon Restaurant, Krungsi-Nai Rd. Good, cheap Thai food.

🍴 Sumrub Tornkruang, Tat Mai Lang Rd. Good Thai and Lao food and mediocre European, in sophisticated a/c restaurant. Attractive decor and well run, good value for the ambience. Recommended.

Foodstalls

There are foodstalls around the train station in the evening. The night market is also highly recommended for its wide range of food, good prices and great atmosphere.

Si Saket *p347*

There is a collection of good Lao/Chinese/Thai restaurants strung out along Khukhan Rd.

🍴 Mr Hagen, Ubon Rd. Small a/c restaurant serving a range of Western dishes; a pleasant stop-off and foot-rest.

Foodstalls

The **night market** off Ratchakan Rotfai 3 Rd is the best place for stall food.

Ubon Ratchathani *p347, map p348*

🍴 Hong Fah Restaurant, Chayangkun Rd (opposite **Pathumrat Hotel**). Expensive but great Chinese in sophisticated a/c restaurant.

🍴 Seafood Garden, Chayangkun Rd (about 1 km north of the bus station on the opposite side of the road). Large sea-food restaurant, barbecue fish and prawn specialities, a/c room, but tables on roof are by far the best in the evening.

🍴 Antaman Seafood, Sapphasit Rd (opposite the Caltex garage, not far from Wat Jaeng). Barbecue seafood including *gung pao* (prawns), *maengda* (horseshoe crabs), sea and river fish and crabs.

🍴 Ponthip, Suriyat Rd, on corner of Soi16, 0800-1800. This is allegedly the best grilled chicken and *som tam* place in town and is often packed. The friendly owner speaks some English. Recommended.

¶ Broaster Chicken and Pizza, Upparat Rd.
The name says it all; brash a/c restaurant
selling fried chicken, pizzas and fries, etc.
¶ Khai Di Restaurant, 24/20 Sapphasit Rd
(not far from Wat Jaeng). A rather grubby-
looking place serving delicious *muhan* or
barbecue suckling pig.
¶ Phon, Yutthaphan Rd, opposite fire station.
Thai and Chinese food. Recommended.
¶ Puan Restaurant, Phichit Rangsan Rd.
One of the most popular restaurants
with locals serving traditional Isaan food.
Recommended.
¶ Restaurant with no name, Khuan Thani Rd,
30 m west of the **Chio Kee Restaurant**.
Clean and friendly cafeteria-style vegetarian
restaurant, eat all you like.
¶ Som Chai, Palochai Rd – can't be missed
as it has 2 giant concrete chickens outside.
Open 0900-1900. Excellent grilled chicken,
spicy salads and cat fish curries in this large,
popular, down-to-earth establishment.
Recommended.

Bakeries

¶ Jiaw Kii, Khuan Thani Rd. A good place
for breakfast with bacon and eggs, coffee
and toast, as well as more usual Thai
morning dishes.
¶ S & P Bakery Shoppe, 207 Chayangkun Rd.
Pastries, ice cream and pizzas in pristine a/c
Western-style surroundings; a little piece of
Bangkok in Ubon.

Foodstalls

Ubon has a profusion of foodstalls. A good
range can be found on Chayangkun Rd, just
south of the **Pathumrat Hotel**, including stalls
selling *kanom* (sweets and pastries), seafood
dishes and fruit drinks.

Khong Chiam *p352*

There are 4 karaoke restaurants as well as
several floating barges that double up as
restaurants moored around the peninsula.
These can hold hundreds of people. All
serve similar Thai dishes (cheap) and there
is little to choose between them – they

make a pleasant place to sit and watch the
sun go down.
¶ Araya Raft, below **Araya Resort**, Santirat Rd,
T045-351015. Overlooking the Mekong, a
beautiful and breezy place to eat, with
Mekong River fish specialities, including *yisok*.

O Bars and clubs

Surin *p345, map p346*

There are a good number of clubs and
bars in Surin, although none is really geared
to overseas visitors; rather, it's karaoke,
Thai crooners in overblown dresses, and
heavy drinking.
Caesar Nightclub and Cafe, below the
Thong Tarin Hotel. Open 2100-0200.
Cowboy Beer Corner, Sirirat Rd, which
reflects this part of Thailand's enthusiasm
for all things Western.
Swing Club, Sirirat Rd. Open 1730-0130.
Food, bar and karaoke.

Ubon Ratchathani *p347, map p348*
Easy Street, Chayangkun Rd. 1800-0100.
Raucous den of iniquity and Thai whisky.
Rough and ready.

⊛ Festivals and events

Buriram *p345*
Nov Annual boat races at Satuk, 40 km
north of Buriram on the Mun River, with
contestants coming from all over Thailand
to compete. The event opens with an
elephant parade, and festivities, beauty
pageants and dancing fill the evenings.
Dec Kite festival, held early in the month
at Huai Chorakee Mak Reservoir, just south
of Buriram. Processions of vehicles decorated
with kites, and a beauty pageant.

Surin *p345, map p346*
Nov (3rd week) Elephant Round-up,
see page 345. Contact the TAT in Bangkok
for full information on the festival.

Bun bang fai: the northeast's skyrocket festival

Perhaps the northeast's best-known festival is the *bun bang fai* or skyrocket festival. This is celebrated across the region between May and June, at the end of the dry season, though most fervently in the town of Yasothon. The festival was originally linked to animist beliefs, but became closely associated with Buddhism. The climax of the festival involves the firing of massive rockets into the air to ensure bountiful rain by invoking the rain god Vassakarn (or, as some people maintain, Phya Thaen), who also has a penchant for fire.

The rockets can be over 4 m long and contain as much as 500 kg of gunpowder. As well as these *bang jut* rockets, there are also elaborately constructed *bang eh* rockets which are just for show. Traditionally, the rockets were made of bamboo; now steel and plastic storm pipes are used while specialist rocket-makers, have taken over from the amateurs of the past.

The rockets are mounted on a bamboo scaffold and fired into the air with much cheering, shouting and exchanging of money. Gambling has become part and parcel of the event with bets laid on which rocket will reach the greatest height. The festival is preceded by a procession of monks, dancing troupes and musicians. There is even a beauty contest, *Thida bang fai ko*, or the Sparkling daughters of the skyrockets.

In the past, *bun bang fai* was a lewd and wild festival more akin to Rio de Janeiro than Isaan. Men wearing phallic symbols would parade through the village, drunken groups would dance wildly imitating sexual intercourse. At the same time, young boys would be ordained and monks blessed. The governor of Yasothon has banned the use of phallic symbols, regarding them as unfitting for a national event, although he has had a more difficult time trying to outlaw drunkenness.

Ubon Ratchathani *p347, map p348*
Jul (movable, for 5 days from the 1st day of the Buddhist Lent) **Candle Festival.** Enormous sculpted beeswax candles, made by villagers from all over the province, are ceremoniously paraded through the streets before being presented to the monks. The festival seems to have been introduced during the reign of Rama I. The Buddha is said to have remarked that the monk Anurudha, in a previous life, led his people out of darkness using a candle – the festival celebrates the feat and is also associated with learning and enlightenment. Candles are given to the monks so that they have light to read the sacred texts during the Buddhist Lent.

Yasothon *p353*
May Bun bang fai (skyrocket festival), celebrated most fervently here in Yasothon (see box, above).

O Shopping

Surin *p345, map p346*
Silk
Surin is a centre of silk production, with villages in the area producing fine matmii silk and cotton ikat cloth. There are a number of shops on Chitbamrung Rd, near the bus station, including **Surinat**, 361-363 Chitbamrung Rd, and **Nong Ying** (close to Phetkasem Hotel). In the same area are numerous tailors. There are also 2 shops selling silk and cotton cloth near the Phetkasem Hotel: **Net Craft** and **Mai Surin**.

Saren Handicrafts and Travel Ltd,
Saren House, 202/1-4 Thetsaban 2 Rd,
T045-540176, F513599. This place offers a
good range of silk and other handicrafts
and also organizes tours of the area (see
Tour operators).

Silverware
Silverware is also a traditional product of
the area and many shops selling cloth also
have small displays of local silverware.

Si Saket *p347*
Crafts
There is a reasonable craft shop on a lane
running off Khukhan Rd to the southeast
of the **Kessiri Hotel**, selling a range of
products including Isaan axe pillows.

Ubon Ratchathani *p347, map p348*
Baskets
On Luang Rd, near the intersection with
Khuan Thai Rd, is a short strip of shops
specializing in basketwork.

Department stores
Ubon Plaza, Uparat Rd. A/c department
store and supermarket selling all necessities.

Handicrafts
Peaceland, Luang Rd. Provides a wide
range of cultural artefacts and a few trinkets.
Phanchart, 158 Rachabut Rd. Selection
of antiques and northeastern handicrafts,
including an excellent range of matmii silk.

Yasothon *p353*
Handicrafts
Baskets are available from the market
in the town centre. Near the market on
Chaeng Sanit Rd, is a shop selling axe
pillows, northeastern textiles and some
baskets. Yasothon is renowned in Thailand
for the quality of its triangular, colourful
axe pillows or *mon khit*.

▲ Activities and tours

Surin *p345, map p346*
Tour operators
Petchkasem Hotel (see Sleeping, above)
also organizes day trips and overnight tours.
Pirom – Arees House (see Sleeping, above).
Mr Pirom organizes tours to the temples
at weekends, as well as tours of silk-weaving
villages in the area. Highly recommended.
Saren Handicrafts and Travel Ltd,
Saren House, 202/1-4 Thetsaban 2 Rd,
T045-540176, sarentour@yahoo.com.
Located opposite the police station on
Lak Muang Rd, the friendly staff provide
good information on excursions and
overnight tours of the area, starting at
฿600 per person.

Ubon Ratchathani *p347, map p348*
Tour operators
Chongmek Travellers, Srikamol Hotel, 26
Ubonsak Rd, T045-255804, organizes tours
along the Mekong River, taking in a Blu Meo
village and the Pha Taem cave paintings, with
a night in a fishing village. ฿1340 per person,
minimum 3 people for trip. Tours to Prasat
Phra Viharn are also now available from
companies in Ubon.
State Railways of Thailand, T045-2256964,
or visit the advance booking office at
Hualamphong Station, Bangkok. Offers a
weekend trip to Prasat Phra Viharn leaving
at 0925 on Sat and returning 0535 on Mon,
including accommodation in Ubon and
all transport.
Takerng Tour, 425 Phromathep Rd,
T045-255777, organizes tours to the Kaeng
Tana Rapids and Pha Taem (approximately
฿1000 per person).
  Other operators include: **Chi Chi Tour**,
Chayangkun Rd, T045-241464; **Sakda
Travel**, 150/1 Kartharalak, Warin,
T045-323048, Thai agent; **Ubonsak
Travel**, Chayangkun Rd, T045-311028.

⊖ Transport

Buriram *p345*
Bus
The bus station is on the west side of town off Bulamduan and Thani roads. Regular a/c and non-a/c connections with **Bangkok**'s Northeastern bus terminal (6½ hrs) and with **Pattaya**, **Chantaburi** and **Trat**, as well as many towns in the northeast including **Khon Kaen**, **Mahasarakham**, **Ubon**, **Si Saket** and **Surin**.

To get to **Phnom Rung** (page 337) and **Muang Tham** (page 339) from Buriram by bus from the station off Thani Rd towards Prakhon Chai. Get off at Ban Tako, before Prakhon Chai; for details thereafter, see page 337.

Songthaew
The *songthaew* terminal is near the market off Sriphet Rd. There are also several morning *songthaews* from Buriram's central market to **Dong Nong Nae**, which meet up with local *songthaews* that run direct to the ruins at **Phnom Rung** (page 337) and **Muang Tham** (page 339).

Train
Connections with **Bangkok**'s Hualamphong station and all stops between Bangkok and **Ubon Ratchathani**. It's better to take the train as the rail route is much more direct between Buriram and either Korat or Ubon.

Surin *p345, map p346*
Bicycle
For hire from **Pirom – Arees House** (see Sleeping, above), ฿30 per day.

Bus
Regular a/c and non-a/c connections with **Bangkok**'s Northeastern bus terminal (6-7 hrs). A/c tour buses to **Bangkok** leave from the offices of Kitikarn Ratchasima near the Surin Plaza. Connections with **Korat**, **Ubon** and from other northeastern towns, and also with **Chiang Mai**.

Songthaew
Songthaews leave from the market area off Thetsabarn 3 Rd (near the clock tower) to surrounding villages, mostly in the morning. Drivers will also charter their vehicles out – expect to pay about ฿500 per day. Vehicles can be rented through the **Tharin Hotel**.

Train
Connections with **Bangkok**'s Hualamphong station (8 hrs), stops en route between Ubon and Bangkok.

Si Saket *p347*
Bus
The terminal is on the south side of town off Khukhan Rd. Regular connections with **Bangkok**'s Northeastern bus terminal (8-9 hrs) and with other northeastern centres.

Train
Regular connections with **Bangkok**'s Hualamphong station and stations en route between Bangkok and Ubon.

Ubon Ratchathani *p347, map p348*
Air
Regular daily connections with **Bangkok** (1 hr).

Airline offices THAI, 292/9 Chayangkun Rd, T045-254431.

Bus
The recently renovated BKS station for non-a/c buses is some distance north of town, not far from Wat Nong Bua at the end of Chayangkun Rd. Get there by town bus No 2 or 3. The station for a/c and non-a/c buses to **Bangkok** is at the back of the market on Chayangkun Rd, south of the Pathumrat Hotel. Regular connections with Bangkok's Northeastern bus terminal (8 hrs), **Nakhon Phanom** (5½-7 hrs), and less frequently with other northeastern towns – eg there are 2 bus companies which service **Surin** regularly (4 hrs); a/c and non-a/c tour buses to Bangkok also leave from Khuan Thani Rd, opposite the TAT Office; Sahamit Tour, on

Border essentials: Travel to Laos from Isaan

With the number of visitors travelling to Laos increasing and connections improving, reaching Laos from Thailand has never been easier. At the moment there are direct bus connections from **Udon Thani** and **Nong Khai** to **Vientiane**. You can take a bus from **Ubon Ratchathani** to **Pakxe** via **Chongmek** and the recently opened bridge at **Mukdahan** will undoubtedly lead to new services being introduced.

If you do want the convenience of a through bus connection to Laos you will need a visa before travel – the bus won't wait at the border while you deal with immigration. However, if you are quick you can sometimes collect your visa at the border before the rest of the passengers are processed. If you don't want to risk this, you can pick up visas from the Laos Embassy in Bangkok and the consulate in Khon Kaen.

In Bangkok the price for UK, USA and most EU citizens is ฿1400 (payable in Thai baht only). You'll need a couple of photos and leave a day for processing the visa. Australians and New Zealanders pay a little less and Canadians a little more, add ฿200 for the express one hour service. Visit www.bkklaoembassy.com, for full details. The Khon Kaen consulate also offers visas for similar rates, though you may need to wait a little longer. If you want to get your visa at the border you can still travel via Isaan though you will often have to cobble together local tuk-tuks, taxis and buses to make this work; an easily viable option. A visa on arrival costs US$35 or ฿1400 – this works out at ฿40 per US$1 while the usual rate is less than ฿35 per US dollar so you're better changing into dollars before you reach the frontier. Visa charges also vary at the boder depending on nationality (see above).

Khuan Thani Rd near the National Museum, runs buses to **Udon Thani** via **Mukdahan**, **That Phanom** and **Nakhon Phanom**; Sayan Tour, near the Ratchathani Hotel, runs buses to **Udon Thani** via **Yasothon**, **Roi Et**, **Mahasarakham** and **Khon Kaen**. VIP buses to Bangkok leave from the station on the south side of the Mun River, north of Warin Chamrap on the left-hand side of the road, heading north. Night bus leaves at 2130, arriving in Bangkok at 0600. Reservations recommended.

Car and motorbike hire

Car drivers often wait on Rachabut Rd and near the TAT office. A car and driver for the day, including petrol, will cost about ฿1000. There are several car/motorbike rental places on Chayangkun Rd.
Chaw Watana, 39/8 Suriyat Rd, T045-242202. Costs ฿250 for a motorbike, ฿1000-1200 for a car). Seems to rent out anything with wheels.

Saamlor and tuk-tuk

Saamlors and tuk-tuks also available (at breakneck speed); map from the TAT office (fare ฿3).

Train

There are connections with **Bangkok** and stops along the southern northeastern track. It is also possible to enter Laos from Ubon, via Chongmek.
Regular connections with **Bangkok**'s Hualamphong station (10 hrs) and all stations in between.

Yasothon *p353*
Bus

Non-a/c buses to **Ubon**, **Udon**, **Roi Et**, Mahasarakham and **Khon Kaen**, as well as with **Bangkok**'s Northeastern bus terminal (10 hrs). A/c buses leave from offices close to the station for Bangkok (10 hrs) and Ubon.

❶ Directory

Buriram *p345*
Banks Bangkok Bank of Commerce, corner of Thani and Romburi rds. **Thai Farmers**, 132 Soonthouthep Rd. **Post office** Intersection of Romburi and Niwat rds, by the railway station. Card phones available.

Surin *p345, map p346*
Banks Thai Farmers, 353 Tanasarn Rd. **Medical services** Hospital, T045-511757. **Police** Lak Muang Rd, T045-511007. **Post office** Corner of Tanasarn and Thetsabarn 1 roads.

Si Saket *p347*
Banks Thai Farmers Bank, 1492/4 Khukhan Rd. **Post office** Chaisawat Rd.

Ubon Ratchathani *p347, map p348*
Banks Bangkok, 88 Chayangkun Rd. Thai Farmers Bank, 356/9 Phromathep Rd. Thai Military, 130 Chayangkun Rd. **Siam Commercial**, Chayangkun Rd. All have ATMs.

Immigration Phibun Mangsahan Rd, T045-441108 (in Phibun Mangsahan). **Internet** Cafés at 323 Suriyat Rd and on Uparat Chayangkun and Srinarong roads. Email next door to the telephone office and above the Nevada Hotel. **Police** Tourist Police, Corner of Srinarong and Upparat roads, T045-243770. **Medical services** Rom Kao Hospital, Upparat Rd (close to the Mun River), is said to be the best in the city. There is another hospital on Sapphasit Rd, T045-254906. **Post office** Corner of Srinarong and Luang Rd. **Telephone** Office at the back of the post office.

Khong Chiam *p352*
Banks Krung Thai Bank, Santirat Rd (exchange facilities available). **Post office and telephone** Store opposite the Apple Guesthouse. An international phone and fax is available here and also next door.

Yasothon *p353*
Banks Thai Farmers Bank, 289 Chaeng Sanit Rd.

Khon Kaen and the Isaan Heartland

The centre of the Khorat Plateau provides the heartland of northeast culture. Here, you'll find the dusty provincial towns of Mahasarakham and Roi Et. This is an agricultural area far off the tourist trail yet it encapsulates completely the ambience of Isaan. The larger, booming city of Khon Kaen marks a return to modernity and is an excellent transport hub for the whole region. ▸▸ *For listings, see pages 368-371.*

Khon Kaen 🏛🚉🛍🏊🌙⛰🍴🎭 ▸▸ *pp368-371. Colour map 2, B3.*

Khon Kaen is an important commercial and administrative centre which houses the largest university in the northeast. Selected by the government as a 'growth pole' during the 1960s to help facilitate the development of the region, Khon Kaen was also home to a US airforce base during the Vietnam War. It has a good selection of hotels, cinemas, restaurants and bars. Because Khon Kaen is one of the principal transport hubs of the northeast, tourists may find that they need to spend a night here en route elsewhere.

Khon Kaen

Sleeping 🛏		Eating 🍴
Bussarakam **3**	Khon Kaen **4**	Best Place **1**
Cactus Resort **10**	Kosa **5**	Diamond Garden **4**
Charoen Thani	Roma **6**	Kham Hom **5**
Royal Princess **1**	Saen Samran **11**	Pizza & Bake **2**
Kaen Inn **2**	Sofitel Raja Orchid **8**	Vietnamese **6**
	Suksawad **9**	

Ins and outs

Getting there The airport is 6 km from town, with multiple daily flights from Bangkok. The railway station is a 15- to 20-minute walk from the centre on Station Road, southwest of town. The air-conditioned and non-air-conditioned bus terminals are both reasonably central, with bus services from Bangkok, Chiang Mai and many other destinations in the northeast, north and central plains. The non-air-conditioned bus station is south of the town centre on Somtawin Road. ▸▸ *See also Transport, page 370.*

Getting around Khon Kaen is a large town. *Songthaews* provide the main and cheapest mode of public transport and run along 12 fixed routes (maps available from tourist office). The fare is usually around ฿4. There are also *saamlors* and tuk-tuks and local buses to out-of-town destinations.

Tourist information TAT ① *Prachasamoson Rd, T043-244498, F043-244497.* New and helpful branch of the TAT, with good maps and details on accommodation and attractions in and around Khon Kaen (with a heavy emphasis on the dinosaurs; see below for more information).

Sights

Khon Kaen supports an excellent branch of the **National Museum** ① *intersection of Kasikhon Thungsang and Lungsun Rachakhan roads, Wed-Sun 0900-1200, 1300-1600, ฿30,* at the northeast edge of the city. It contains, among other things, a good collection of Ban Chiang artefacts and beautiful Dvaravati boundary stones. Also worthy of note is the **Bung Kaen Nakhon** at the southern edge of the city, reaching a maximum extent at the peak of the rainy season of nearly 100 ha. On the northern shore of the *bung* (pond) is the Lao-style **Wat That**, with the characteristic lotus bud-shaped *chedi* of the Lao. The lake is used by local residents for walks and picnics and there are also a number of open-air restaurants.

Around Khon Kaen

Phu Wiang National Park

① *It is easiest to get here on a tour. By road, take the route from Khon Kaen towards Chumphae and turn right at the Km 48 marker onto Route 2038. Continue along this road for 38 km to the national park. It is also possible to get here by public transport: take a bus from the public bus terminal to Phu Wiang district town. From the town take a songthaew or tuk-tuk to the national park, about ฿200.*

This park, which consists of a central plain encircled by low hills, sprung to modest fame in the mid-1990s when it was discovered that the area had one of the world's largest **dinosaur graveyards**. The first dinosaur fossils were unearthed here in 1978 and by 1991 nine sites had been uncovered. In 1996 the remains of a new family of carnivorous thunder lizards were unearthed here and were appropriately called *Siamotyrannus isaanensis*. The importance of the find is that while the animals are considerably smaller than their well-known North American and Chinese cousins, the Thai tyrannosaur is much older: 120-130 million years as opposed to 65-80 million years. The dinosaur remains are concentrated in the northern part of the park and it is possible to walk from site to site.

Ban Kok

ⓘ Ban Kok is 50 km from Khon Kaen. Take the Khon Kaen–Chumpae road past the airport and turn left at Ban Thum Then onto Route 2062. Continue along this road to the Km 40 marker and turn onto a road by the Shell petrol station. The village is a short way from main road. By public transport, take a bus to Mancha Kiri district town (there is said to be a bus at 0600 and a return bus at 1830); from here it is just another 4 km to Ban Kok.

Also known as **Tortoise Village**, Ban Kok harbours a rather confusing tale about tortoises that means that these creatures are regarded as sacred by the inhabitants of Ban Kok and surrounding villages. There are 2000 of the animals wandering about, unmolested, eating every piece of greenery in sight. Be warned: anyone hurting the tortoises has been afflicted with all sorts of strange maladies.

Chonnabot

ⓘ Take a local bus from the station on Prachasamoson Rd (1 hr). Note that the last song-thaew back to town leaves Chonnabot around 1600.

The villages around here are well known for the quality and variety of their matmii silk and cotton cloth. Much of the silk and cotton cloth from here is sent to Bangkok. There is a handicraft centre where local cloth is sold, or lengths can be bought direct from weaving households – just wander through the village; looms can be seen under the houses. Note that cloth is bought by the *phun*. A normal sarong length will be about two phun, so prices will rarely relate to the whole piece of cloth. However, English is not widely spoken, so it either takes modest Thai or skilful hand signals to secure a deal. Chonnabot town, the capital of the district, lies 12 km off Route 2, travelling south towards Korat (turn-off near Km 399 marker onto Route 2057).

Prasat Puaynoi

ⓘ Take the main Khon Kaen-Korat Highway (Rte 2) and turn off at Ban Phai onto Route 23. After 23 km, turn off again onto Route 2297. This leads to the temple, which is situated at the entrance to a village.

This is a recently renovated 10th-century Khmer temple, about 80 km southeast of Khon Kaen. The four buildings that comprise the structure make it similar to the far better known Pimai – but smaller in scale. There is some sculpture.

Isaan Heartland ◐⦿❀◉◐◖ ⇢ *pp368-371.*

Mahasarakham → *Colour map 2, B4.*
Known locally as Sarakham, Mahasarakham is a quiet, provincial capital, situated right in the centre of the Khorat Plateau known as a centre for northeastern handicrafts.

The **Research Institute of Northeastern Art and Culture** *ⓘ Mon-Fri, ½-day on Sat*, has a small permanent exhibition of textiles, metal casting, music, basketry and other handicrafts. It is located behind the main lecture building of the university, 2 km west of town on the road to Khon Kaen. The **Isaan Cultural and Art Centre** *ⓘ in the Rajabhat Institute*, has an exhibition of Isaan history and handicrafts and arts including textiles and palm-leaf manuscripts. There is a daily fresh market on the corner of Nakhon Sawan and Worayut roads, in the centre of town.

Tambon Kwao, 5 km from Mahasarakham, is a centre of pottery production. Around 100 households here produce simple, traditional pottery products including water pots and various food containers. East of Mahasarakham off Route 208 towards Roi Et, the turn-off for the village is 4 km along Route 208 and then 1 km down a laterite track. Take one of the regular local buses from the station on Somtawin Road.

Roi Et → *Colour map 2, B4.*

ⓘ *The main bus station is to the west of town, off Jaeng Sanit Rd (Rte 23 towards Mahasarakham). The a/c bus terminal is at the southeast corner of town.*

Roi Et is the capital of a province encompassing one of the poorest agricultural areas in Thailand. The **Tung Kula Rong Hai** is a large, dry, salty and infertile plain that covers much of the province. The name means the 'Weeping Plain of the Kula', and millions of baht have been invested in projects to improve the land and productivity of agriculture. Although there have been some successes, the incidence of circular migration – the movement of young men and women to Bangkok and elsewhere in a seasonal search for work – illustrates the inability of the land to support rapidly rising needs and expectations.

Roi Et is built around an artificial lake – the Bung Phlan Chai. The island in the centre, linked by footbridges, contains the town's **lak muang** (foundation pillar) and a large Sukhothai-style walking Buddha. This, the moat which surrounds the city and several well-stocked gardens, creates an airy, well-planned town; something of a novelty in Thailand. Paddle boats can be hired on the lake, and the island is a popular spot with locals for walking and feeding the fish.

Wat Phung Phralaan Chai, at the southwest corner of the lake, is ancient but vigorous rebuilding has obliterated the old, with the exception of the *bai sema* (boundary stones) which surround the new bot. The concrete high-relief morality tales which surround the three-storeyed, moated mondop are enjoyable. Roi Et's most obvious 'sight' (if size is

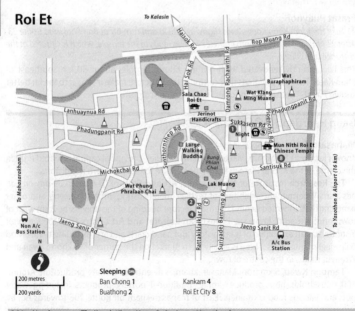

Roi Et

To Kalasin

Haisok Rd
Hai Sok Rd
Rop Muang Rd
Damrong Rachawithi Rd
Wat Buraphaphiram
Sala Chao Roi Et
Wat Klang Ming Muang
Jerinot Handicrafts
Lanhuaynua Rd
Phadungpanit Rd
Sukkasem Rd
Ploenchit Rd
Phadungpanit Rd
Night
Mun Nithi Roi Et Chinese Temple
Sunthornthep Rd
Large Walking Buddha
Bung Phlan Chai
Santisuk Rd
Michokchai Rd
Lak Muang
Wat Phung Phralaan Chai
Bamrung Rd
To Mahasarakham
Rattakikiaikar Rd
Suriyade Rd
Jaeng Sanit Rd
Non A/c Bus Station
Jaeng Sanit Rd
A/c Bus Station
To Yasothon & Airport (16 km)

200 metres
200 yards
N

Sleeping
Ban Chong 1
Buathong 2
Kankam 4
Roi Et City 8

The story of Quan Am

Quan Am was turned onto the streets by her husband for some unspecified wrongdoing and, dressed as a monk, took refuge in a monastery. There, a woman accused her of fathering, and then abandoning, her child. Accepting the blame (why, no one knows), she was again turned out onto the streets, only to return to the monastery much later when she was on the point of death to confess her true identity. When the Emperor of China heard the tale, he made Quan Am the Guardian Spirit of Mother and Child, and couples without a son now pray to her. Quan Am's husband is sometimes depicted as a parakeet, with the Goddess usually holding her adopted son in one arm and standing on a lotus leaf (the symbol of purity).

anything to go by) is the massive 59-m (sometimes 68-m, but who's counting?) standing **Buddha of Wat Buraphaphiram**, on the east side of town near Rop Muang Road. The Buddha is known as Phra Phutta Ratana Mongkhon Maha Mani. It is possible to climb up the side of the statue for a view over the town.

On Ploenchit Road is the **Mun Nithi Roi Et Chinese Temple**. In classic Chinese style, the ground floor is a trading business; the temple is on the first floor. Three altars face the room: to the left is one dedicated to the corpulent 'laughing' Buddha; in the centre, to the historic Buddha and various future Buddhas (or Bodhisattvas); to the right, to Kuan Yin or Quan Am, the Chinese Goddess of Mercy (see box, above). The pagoda pragmatically combines Theravada and Mahayana Buddhism (see page 750), and Daoism and Confucianism. Despite Thailand's large Chinese population – around 15% – it is relatively rare to see Chinese pagodas and temples. This is partly because the Chinese have assimilated so seamlessly into Thai society and become good Theravada Buddhists. Another reason is a wish to blend in, in order to reduce any chance of persecution. At times of economic nationalism – 'Thailand for the Thais' – the Chinese have been discriminated against. Another, smaller, Chinese pagoda is the **Sala Chao Roi Et** on Phadungphanit Road, not far from the lake.

The market on and between Phadungphanit and Hai Sok roads sells Isaan handicrafts and fresh foods, including insects. On the roadside, women market the ingredients for betel 'nut'.

Ku Phra Kona, a Khmer sanctuary, is not far north of Ku Kasingh. Like Ku Kasingh it consists of three *prangs*, one of which has been remodelled (in 1928) into a tiered 'stupa', rather like Wat Phrathat Haripunjaya in Lamphun. A *baray* (reservoir), 300 m from the site, was probably linked by a naga bridge. The sanctuary is Baphuon in style and probably dates from the mid-11th century. To get there, take Route 215 and then 214 south towards Suwannaphum and Surin – buses leave for Surin from the station on Jaeng Sanit Road; Ku Phra Kona is at Ban Ku, about 12 km south of Suwannaphum.

For Sleeping and Eating price codes and other relevant information, see pages 44-49.

⊜ Sleeping

Khon Kaen *p363, map p363*

A-D Hotel Sofitel Raja Orchid, 9/9 Prachasamoson Rd, T043-322155, F322150. A/c, restaurant, pool, health club and gym. Efficient with a good range of facilities and the 3 restaurants cover just about the entire Asian region.

B-D Charoen Thani Royal Princess, 260 Sri Chand Rd, T043-220400, F220438. A/c, restaurant, pool with a great view of the city (open to non-residents), 320 rooms in high-rise block, a little piece of Bangkok in Khon Kaen, central location and good rates available, including discounts in the wet season.

B-D Kaen Inn, 56 Klang Muang Rd, T043-237744, F239457. A/c, restaurant, well run but rather characterless, with all 'business' facilities.

B-D Kosa, 250-252 Sri Chand Rd, T043-225014, F225013. A/c, restaurant, pool, the original 'Western' hotel, comfortable rooms, massage parlour, live music. The Kosa is linked to the Charoen Thani hotel by a walkway, and they share an entertainment complex. Excellent service.

C Roma, 50/2 Klang Muang Rd, T236276. Some a/c, the poor cousin to the Khon Kaen. Bare, functional rooms in bare functional block which looks as though it has been made out of Lego – but very reasonable for a/c and hot water and the best-value place in town. Recommended.

C-D Bussarakam, 68 Phimphasut Rd, T043-333666, bussarakamhotel@yahoo.com. This decent, friendly, new mid-range hotel, has agreeable en suite, a/c rooms. There's a tasty Chinese/Thai restaurant, it's in a good central location and they provide free wireless internet in the lobby. Recommended.

C-E Khon Kaen, 43/2 Phimphasut Rd, T043-237711, F242458. A/c, restaurant, geared to Thai businessmen with bars and massage parlours, comfortable – no more.

E Cactus Resort and Hotel, 171/38-39 Prachasamoson Rd, T043-244888. Attempts to be a contemporary Ikea-style hotel but still has enough rough edges to give it an Isaan vibe. The rooms are simple and spotless. The location 2 km from the town centre, almost opposite the Laos consulate makes it perfect if your only reason for stopping in Khon Kaen is to pick up a visa. The low price also represents exceptional value. Recommended.

F-G Suksawad, 2/2 Klang Muang Rd, T043-236472. Wooden building down *soi* off main road, so relatively quiet, rooms are shabby but clean, friendly, attached bathrooms, 3-min walk from the tourist office.

G Saen Samran Hotel, 555-59 Klang Muang Rd, T043-239611. Cheap and cheerful. For the very low prices this place represents good value. The rooms are clean and basic, complete with a private, cold shower and toilet – the ones upstairs at the back are the quietest and have the best light. Best low-budget option.

Mahasarakham *p365*

D-F Wasu, 1096/4 Damnoen Nat Rd, T043-723075, F721290. Clean a/c rooms and excellent value. Part of a complex of pubs and clubs.

E-F Sunthon Hotel, 1157/1 Worayut Rd, T043-711201. Some a/c, small hotel in town centre with 30 rooms, a/c rooms have attached bathrooms, basic.

Roi Et *p366*

B-D Roi Et City Hotel, 78 Ploenchit Rd, T043-520387, F520401. 167 rooms on 6 floors, a good pool, gym and business centre. It is undoubtedly the most luxurious place in the area and professionally run.

F Ban Chong, 81-83 Suriyadej Bamrung Rd, T043-511235. Simple but good-value and reasonably clean rooms with attached facilities.

F Kankam Hotel, 12-14 Rattikiklaiklar Rd, T043-511508. Some a/c with hot water, well managed and maintained, the best of the Chinese-style hotels in Roi Et.

F-G Buathong, 6 Rattikiklaiklar Rd, T043-511142. Some a/c, best rooms on top floor where windows allow a breeze in, squat loos, no hot water, no frills but friendly.

🍴 Eating

Khon Kaen p363, map p363

The best selection of cheaper Chinese/Thai restaurants is on Klang Muang Rd, between the **Kaen Inn** and **Suksawad Hotel**. Head out to Bungkaen Nakhon, a small lake 2 km south of the town centre, and there's a good array of Thai eateries.

Kham Hom, Na Muang Rd. 1000-2300. Good Thai food served up in this Isaan entertainment joint popular with the locals.

Best Place, Klang Muang Rd (near **Kaen Inn**). Rather sanitized a/c restaurant, serving pizzas, burgers and other similar dishes.

Diamond Garden (Beer Garden), Sri Chand Rd, near the Fairy Plaza. Thai food.

Pizza and Bake, Klang Muang Rd. Pizzas, burgers and various Thai dishes, good place for breakfast and Western food if needed.

Vietnamese. A small local eatery next to the **Saen Samran Hotel**. Good selection of Vietnamese and Thai grub.

Foodstalls

Usual array of foodstalls to be found on the streets. A good selection near the a/c bus terminal, off Sri Chand Rd.

Mahasarakham p365

There is a row of good restaurants, bars and bakeries on **Nakhon Sawan Rd**, about 1 km from the town centre near the Mahasarakham University. **Night market** or **Talaat tor rung**, south of town behind the bus station, best place to eat (0600-2100), selling Isaan specialities like *kai yang* (barbecue chicken), *somtam* (hot papaya

salad) and *larb* (minced meat with herbs), as well as rice and noodles.

M and Y, Nakhon Sawan Rd (about 1 km from town centre). Seafood restaurant, tables in garden, excellent chargrilled prawns. Recommended.

Maeng Khian, behind the bus station. A/c restaurant in ranch-house style with live music, Thai food, with good Isaan specialities.

Somphort Pochana, Somthawin Rd (near intersection with Warayut Rd). Good Chinese and Thai dishes, excellent value.

Roi Et p366

Excellent evening **food market** by the post office, from dusk until 2100, best choice of food in town including Isaan specialities. There are also a collection of pleasant open-air garden restaurants situated around the central lake.

🎭 Entertainment

Khon Kaen p363, map p363

Along with the high density of karaoke bars and massage parlours, there is also a **cinema** on Sri Chand Rd not far from the Kosa Hotel.

🎉 Festivals and events

Khon Kaen p363, map p363

Late Nov to early Dec (movable) Silk Fair and Phuk Siao (friendship) Festival. Wide variety of silks on sale and production processes demonstrated. People tie threads around each other's wrists to symbolize their friendship, known as *phuk siao* (*siao* means 'friend' in Lao). Folk culture performances. The festival is centred on the Sala Klang Changwat or Provincial Hall on the north side of town.

Roi Et p366

May Bun bang fai (skyrocket festival), celebrated most fervently in Yasothon (see page 358), but a more traditional

example is held in the district town of
Suwannaphum, south of Roi Et. Get there
by regular bus from the station on Jaeng
Sanit Rd.

O Shopping

Khon Kaen *p363, map p363*
There is a general market area, opposite
the bus station on Prachasamoson Rd, and
a larger market on Klang Muang Rd. Villagers
hawk textiles on the street. Local products
include spicy pork sausages, which can be
seen hanging in many shops.

Books
Smart Books, Klang Muang Rd. Some English
books and a good range of stationery.

Silk
Good-quality matmii silk and other traditional
cloth can be found in Khon Kaen. **Heng
Hguan Hiang**, 54/1-2 Klang Muang Rd (near
intersection with Sri Chand Rd). Sells textiles,
axe pillows, Isaan food and other handicrafts.
Prathamakant, 79/2-3 Ruanrom Rd. Silk,
cotton and handicrafts.
Rin Thai, 412 Na Muang Rd, T043-221042.
A long-established silk shop selling silk,
cotton, local handicrafts, souvenirs and
ready-to-wear clothes.

Roi Et *p366*
Handicrafts
Roi Et is a centre for production of silk and
cotton ikat cloth. It is sold by the phun and
can range from ฿100 per phun for simple
cotton cloth to ฿3000 for a piece of finest
quality silk. Go to **Jerinot**, 383 Phadungphanit Rd, or **Phaw Kaan Khaa**, 377-379
Phadungphanit Rd, to see a wide selection
and to gauge prices.

Also sold along this road and in market
stalls are axe cushions, baskets, *khaens* (a
northeastern reed pipe) and other handicrafts.

▲▲ Activities and tours

Khon Kaen *p363, map p363*
Tour operators
Air Booking and Travel Centre Co,
4 Sri Chand Rd, T043-244482.
Northeast Travel Service, 87/56 Klang
Muang Rd, T043-244792, F243238. At
the a/c bus terminal.

⊖ Transport

Khon Kaen *p363, map p363*
Air
3 flights a day to **Bangkok** (55 mins) on THAI.
    Airline offices THAI, 183/6 Maliwan
Rd, T043-236523.

Bus
The vast non-a/c bus station is on
Prachasamoson Rd; a/c buses leave from the
terminal just off Klang Muang Rd. Regular
connections with **Bangkok**'s Northeastern
bus terminal. Buses, both a/c and non-a/c,
run to most other northeastern towns and
to **Chiang Mai**, **Chiang Rai**, **Phitsanalok**,
Tak, **Rayong** (for Pattaya).

Car hire
R Rent Service, T043-243543, ฿1500
per day.

Train
Regular connections with **Bangkok**'s
Hualamphong station (8 hrs), **Korat** and
other stops en route north to **Nong Khai**
(3 hrs on the morning stopping train).

Mahasarakham *p365*
Bus
Regular departures from the non-a/c bus
station to **Bangkok**'s Northeastern bus
terminal (7 hrs) and other northeastern
towns. A/c buses leave from various offices
around town.

Roi Et *p366*
Air
PB Air, flies 3 times a week to Bangkok.

Bus
The main bus station is to the west of town, off Jaeng Sanit Rd (Rte 23 towards Mahasarakham). Non-a/c buses to **Bangkok** (8 hrs), **Khon Kaen**, **Ubon**, **Udon**, **Nong Khai**, **Mahasarakham**, **Buriram**, **Surin** and **Korat**. A/c bus connections with **Bangkok**'s Northeastern terminal (8 hrs).

❶ Directory

Khon Kaen *p363, map p363*
Banks Bangkok, Sri Chand Rd (near the Kosa Hotel). Krung Thai, 457-461 Sri Chand Rd. **Siam Commercial**, 491 Sri Chand Rd. Thai Farmers, 145 Prachasamoson Rd. **Embassies and consulates** Lao PDR Consulate, 123 Photisan Rd, T043-223698. Tourist visas available for US$30, open 0800-1200, 1300-1600 – bank on it taking a day to get your visa, though the sitiuation

often changes and you can sometimes secure them within an hr. Also provides leaflets detailing 'How to enter Laos/Vietnam'. Vietnamese Consulate, 65/6 Chatapadung Rd, T043-241586. **Medical services** Hospital: Sri Chand Rd, T043-236005. **Police** Klang Muang Rd, T043-211162 (near post office). **Post office** Klang Muang Rd (near the intersection with Sri Chand Rd), T043-221147.

Mahasarakam *p365*
Banks Thai Farmers Bank, Worayut Rd. Thai Military Bank, Padongwithi Rd. Both with currency exchange. **Internet** KK Internet, just south of the river. **Post office** Facing the clock tower on Nakh on Sawan Rd.

Roi Et *p366*
Banks Thai Farmers Bank, 431 Phadung-phanit Rd. Thai Military Bank, Ploenchit Rd (near intersection with Sukkasem Rd). **Post office** Suriyadejbamrung Rd (at intersection with Santisuk Rd). **Telephone** Overseas calls can be made from the post office.

Udon Thani and the northern Mekong route

Udon is a frenetic place, or as close to frenetic as it is possible to get in this part of Thailand. The palm-fringed roundabouts provide a tropical Riviera feel amidst the bustle and the city has a reputation of being one of Thailand's cleanest provincial capitals. Most tourists only stay here because of its proximity to the outstanding prehistoric site at Ban Chiang. Like Khon Kaen, Udon was a boom-town during the Vietnam War, so it retains reminders of that time: massage parlours, bars, coffee shops and fully air-conditioned hotels. It is said that about 60 former US servicemen have married Thais and settled here. There is even an Udon branch of the US Veterans of Foreign Wars Association, along with a relay station of Voice of America Radio.

The Mekong forms the border between Thailand and Laos for several hundred kilometres in the northeastern region. A good starting point is Loei, a provincial capital 50 km south of the Mekong and within easy reach of a number of fine national parks in the Phetchabun hills, including the popular Phu Kradung National Park. The nearby riverside town of Chiang Khan provides a peaceful base with atmospheric accommodation. Travelling downstream, the beautiful river road passes through Pak Chom, Sangkhom and Si Chiangmai, before reaching the provincial capital of Nong Khai.
▶▶ For listings, see pages 378-382.

Udon Thani and around ⊖🅿🅾🔺🅰🅸 ▶▶ pp378-382. Colour map 2, A3.

Ins and outs

Getting there The airport is 2 km south out of town (off Route 2), with multiple daily flights from Bangkok. The train station is just to the east of the town centre, off Lang Sathanirotfai Road. Udon's two bus terminals, one centrally placed (BKS 1) and the second slightly out of town (BKS 2), provide connections with Bangkok, Chiang Mai, Chiang Rai and most destinations in the northeast. Bangkok passengers can get from BKS 2 by yellow town buses (No 23), which run into the centre. Buses also run from the more central BKS 1.
▶▶ *See Transport, page 381, for further details.*

Getting around A profusion of *saamlors* and tuk-tuks (a typical journey will cost ฿40-50) provide the main mode of city transport, with buses and *songthaews* linking the town with local out-of-town destinations. There are also plenty of places hiring cars and motorbikes.

Tourist information TAT ⓘ *Thesa Rd, facing Nong Prachak Silpakhorn, T042-325406, F042-325408, 0830-1630.* Limited resources but maps of Udon available.

Background

With the border crossing to the north now becoming a growth factor in this part of Thailand, Udon Thani is well placed to springboard to wealthier times. Despite this, poverty, much like in the rest of Isaan, still persists and compared to Thai towns nearer Bangkok Udon can appear rundown. Another growth factor for the local economy has been the arrival of 100s of expat middle-aged men, moving here with their 'girlfriends' or wives. Girlie bars, many owned by expats, have sprung up in town and even though several of them have been shutdown an atmosphere of sex-tourism is beginning to pervade Udon. It's easily avoided, although for single men, the endless cries of 'mista mista' can get a bit tiresome.

Precha Market

① Daily 1800-2200.

Set in huge area just to the west of the railway station, Precha market is one of the highlights of visiting Udon. Endless runs of stalls sell awesome Isaan and Thai food – everything from sweet, sticky cakes through to spicy *larb moo* (a minced pork dish famous in Isaan) and the ubiquitous *som-tam* (spicy papaya salad). One of the market's specialities is salted, barbequed fish – it's served with salad and various condiments, including handfuls of fresh herbs. There are also lots of clothes stalls, with some real

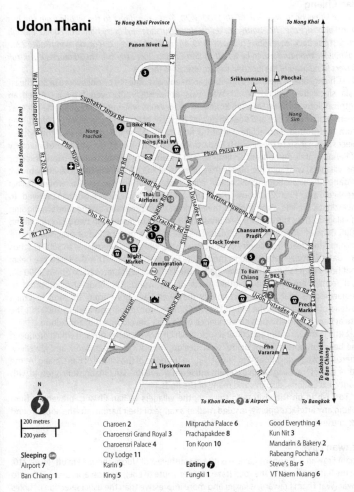

Udon Thani

To Nong Khai Province
To Nong Khai ▲

Panon Nivet △

Rt 2

Srikhunmuang △ △ Phochai

Wat Phothisompom Rd

Suphakit-Janya Rd

Nong Prachak

Bike Hire

Buses to Nong Khai

Nong Sim

To Bus Station BKS 2 (2 km)

Pho Niyom Rd

Rt 2024

Phon Phisai Rd

Athibadi Rd

Wattana Nuwong Rd

To Loei
Rt 2139

Pho Sri Rd

Thai Airlines

Chansunthon Pradit △

Udon Dutsadee Rd

Clock Tower

Night Market

Immigration

To Ban Chiang

BKS

Ranosan Rd

Sri Suk Rd

Udon Dutsadee Rd

Precha Market

Rt 22

Pho Vararam △

To Sakhon Nakhon & Ban Chiang

△ Tipsuntiwan

N

200 metres
200 yards

To Khon Kaen, 🍴 & Airport
To Bangkok ▼

Sleeping 🛏
Airport **7**
Ban Chiang **1**

Charoen **2**
Charoensri Grand Royal **3**
Charoensri Palace **4**
City Lodge **11**
Karin **9**
King **5**

Mitpracha Palace **6**
Prachapakdee **8**
Ton Koon **10**

Eating 🍴
Fungki **1**

Good Everything **4**
Kun Nit **3**
Mandarin & Bakery **2**
Rabeang Pochana **7**
Steve's Bar **5**
VT Naem Nuang **6**

bargains available. If you want to watch English Premier League football (now a national pastime in Thailand) there is a giant screen set in the middle of the market, surrounded by Thai bars and eateries.

Nong Prachak Park

In the northwestern quarter of town is Nong Prachak Park, a municipal park set around a large lake. There are a number of reasonable garden restaurants here and it is one of the more attractive places to come for an evening meal.

Ban Chiang

ⓘ *The site is open Wed-Sun 0830-1700. ฿20. Buses run direct to the village from the bus stand opposite the Thai-Isaan market on Udon Dutsadee Rd every hour from 0600, though the last one back leaves Ban Chiang at 1400. Alternatively, take a bus going along Route 22 to Sakhon Nakhon and ask to be let off at Ban Chiang (just after the Km 50 marker). Tuk-tuk drivers hang around the junction to take visitors to the site.*

Ban Chiang, one of the most important archaeological sites to be uncovered in Southeast Asia since the Second World War, was accidentally discovered by an American anthropology student, Stephen Young, in 1966. While walking in the village he fell over the root of a kapok tree and noticed dozens of pieces of broken ancient pottery protruding from the ground. Appreciating that his find might be significant, he sent the pottery pieces for analysis to the Fine Arts Department in Bangkok and then later to the University of Pennsylvania. Rumours of his finds spread and much of the area was then ransacked by the villagers, who sold the pieces they unearthed to collectors in Bangkok and abroad. Organized excavations only really commenced during the 1970s, when a Thai archaeologist, Pisit Charoenwongsa and an American, Chester Gorman, arrived to investigate the site. Even though their task was compromised by the random digging of villagers, they still managed to unearth 18 tonnes of material in two years, including 5000 bags of sherds and 123 burials. The site spans a time period of over 5000 years. Perhaps the greatest discovery is the **bronzeware**, which has been dated to 3600 BC, thus pre-dating bronzeware found in the Middle East by 500 years. This shattered the belief that bronze metallurgy had developed in the Tigris and Euphrates basin about 3000 BC, and from there diffused to other parts of the world. The finds also indicated to archaeologists that bronze technology may well have gone from Thailand to China instead of vice versa as the oldest known Chinese bronzes only go back to 2000 BC. The site at Ban Chiang also provides evidence of an early development of agriculture.

Little is known of the agricultural society which inhabited the site and which produced the beautiful pots of burnt ochre 'swirl' design, sophisticated metalwork and jewellery. There are two burial pits at Wat Pho Si Nai, on the edge of the village of Ban Chiang. At the other side of the village is an excellent **museum** where the Ban Chiang story is retold with clarity, exceptional displays and many of the finds.

To cash in on the visitors to the site, the villagers of Ban Chiang, prevented from selling any artefacts openly, instead market a range of their handicrafts in shops around the museum.

Erawan Cave

Tham Erawan – 'Elephant Cave' – is 40 km southwest of Udon, about 2 km off Route 210, on the left-hand side of the road (take a bus en route to Loei). The cave, as usual, linked to a wat (Wat Tham Erawan), is larger and more impressive than the usual selection of holes in the ground that pass as caves in Thailand; it is a vast cavern with very fine stalactites and stalacmites. There's a route through, with steps that emerge near the mountain top, providing spectacular views of the surrounding countryside.

Northern Mekong route ⏺️🚍🚲🏠🛏️ → pp378-382.

Loei → Colour map 2, A2.

This frontier settlement, known as Muang Loei, has dusty streets and seedy-looking shophouses, and is situated on the Loei River. Most tourists visit Loei either as a stop-off on the way to Chiang Khan (see page 377) or to sample the remarkable scenery of the area; there are no city sights as such. There is an airport 5 km south of town, and the bus terminal is on Maliwan Road (about 1 km south of town). Motorized *saamlors* run around town, ฿10-20. An important cotton-growing area, it is known for its warm cotton quilts, available in many shops around town.

Of all the provinces of the northeast, Loei has managed to preserve the greatest proportion of its forests and the surrounding area was a haven for the communist guerrillas until the early 1980s. There are a number of national parks in the province, of which the most famous is the Phu Kradung National Park (see below). Also accessible is

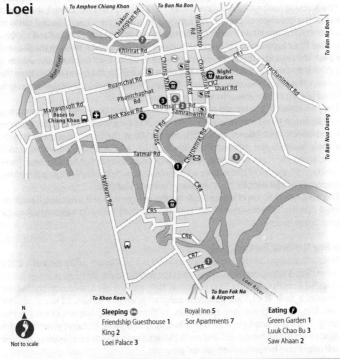

Loei

To Amphoe Chiang Khan
To Ban Na Bon
Sakon Chiangkran Rd
Wisuthithep Rd
To Ban Na Bon
Khirirat Rd
CR1
Prachaniimmit Rd
Man River
Ruamchai Rd
Chiang Khan Rd
Ruamchit Rd
Charoenrat Rd
Night Market
CR2
Usari Rd
Phanichaphat Rd
Chumsai Rd
To Ban Nua Duang
Maliwansoli Rd
Buses to Chiang Khan
Nok Kaew Rd
Samrahwithit Rd
Soi 21 Rd
Tatmai Rd
Charoenrat Rd
Maliwan Rd
CR5
CR6
CR7
CR8
Loei River
To Khon Kaen
To Ban Fak Na & Airport

N
Not to scale

Sleeping 🛏️
Friendship Guesthouse 1
King 2
Loei Palace 3
Royal Inn 5
Sor Apartments 7

Eating 🍴
Green Garden 1
Luuk Chao Bu 3
Saw Ahaan 2

the Phu Hin Rongkla National Park, an area formerly used as a sanctuary by the communists, and the Phu Rua National Park (see below).

Tham Paa Phu, a Buddhist meditation cave, is 11 km from town on the road to Tha Li. Kutis (monks' cells) are arranged along a steep cliff. It is a peaceful place. To get there, take a bus towards Tha Li or go by tuk-tuk.

Phu Kradung National Park

ⓘ *The park is 82 km south of Loei, 8 km off Route 201 on Route 2019. Sep-May 0700-1400 (closed during the rainy season Jun-Aug), ฿200. The park station at Sithan (at the foot of the mountain) has an information centre, restaurants and porters. Porters will carry luggage for ฿10 per kg. Trekking maps are available. There is also a cable car – the source of considerable friction between environmentalists and the park authorities – for those who want the easy option. Bus from Loei to Phu Kradung town, 1½ hrs (the Khon Kaen bus, leaving every 30 mins); from here there are motorcycles, songthaews and tuk-tuks to cover the final 8 km to the park office. From the south, catch a bus via Chumphae to Pa Nok Kao. From there, local buses leave for Phu Kradung town (8 km) and then motorcycles or charter cars are available for the trip to the park.*

The best time to visit is February to April to see wild flowers, or November to December to see the waterfalls at their most impressive. It is a very popular spot with Thais, so can be crowded at weekends during the dry season, especially December to mid-January.

Phu Kradung National Park is named after Phu Kradung ('Bell Mountain'), the highest point in the province of Loei at 1571 m and is one of the most beautiful parks in the country. The mountain is in fact a plateau, which lies between 1200 m and 1500 m. There are three explanations of origin of its name: the first is that it refers to the shape of the peak; the second is that it refers to the wild bulls which used to inhabit the area; and the third is that on Buddhist holy days the noise of a bell can be heard issuing from the mountain. It is one of the coolest areas in Thailand; temperatures sometimes fall to near freezing point from November to January, so come prepared.

The park covers 348 sq km and supports a range of vegetation types: tropical evergreen forest, savannah forest and even some trees typical of temperate locations, for example oak and beech. Wild flowers are particularly prolific in the park – especially orchids. Mammals found in the park include wild pig, Asian wild dog and the white-handed gibbon, along with rarer elephants, Asiatic black bears and sambar barking deer. There are at least 130 species of bird in the park. Residents include the brown hornbill, maroon oriole, large scimitar babbler and the snowy-browed flycatcher.

There are nearly 50 km of marked trails for the keen trekker and naturalist, though be warned that this is a strenuous climb, with the last third being up near-vertical metal ladders (three hours each way).

Phu Rua National Park

ⓘ *Regular buses from Loei to Nakhon Thai (Route 203), 1 hr. The turn-off for the park is at the Km 48 marker. A laterite road leads for 4 km to the park entrance.*

Phu Rua National Park, literally 'Boat Mountain' National Park because of a cliff shaped like the bow of a junk, lies 1.5 km outside the district town of Phu Rua, 50 km southwest of Loei. The highest point here approaches 1500 m and temperatures can fall below freezing. There is a good network of marked trails and some fantastic views over the lowlands from the higher ground and north to Laos. Eroded sandstone boulders perched on cliff edges give the park added natural presence.

Chiang Khan and around → *Colour map 2, A2.*

ⓘ *Buses from Loei stop at the western end of town; a 10-min walk to the main area of hotels and guesthouses, or take a tuk-tuk.*

This is a place to visit for people who enjoy slow, lazy days watching a river, in this case the mighty Mekong, drifting by. There are no bars or discos here, few obvious sights, and basic, characterful accommodation. The town marks the beginning (or end) of the Mekong River route. Chiang Khan is strung out for 2 km along the river and consists of just two parallel streets, linked by some 20 *sois*. The riverfront road, Chai Khong Road, is quieter, with much of the original wooden shophouse architecture still standing; the inland road is the relatively busy Route 2186, linking Loei and Nong Khai.

The monasteries in town, like several settlements along the Mekong in this part of Thailand, show a French influence in their shuttered and colonnaded buildings. An example is **Wat Tha Khok** at the east edge of town near Soi 20 and overlooking the Mekong. The interior of the viharn displays some attractive murals. On the west edge of town, is **Wat Sri Khun Muang**. It is notable for its Lao-style *chedi* and the gaudy, vibrant murals on the exterior of the viharn. Other wats in town, all dating from the late-19th century, are **Wat Santi** and **Wat Pa Klang**. The oldest monastery is **Wat Mahathat**, where the bot is thought to date from the mid-17th century.

Kaeng Kut Kou, a series of rapids, lie 4 km downstream from Chiang Khan. There is a park here with restaurants, souvenir shops and vendors selling spicy Isaan food. It is very popular; coachloads of Thai tourists stop off here. In the dry season it is possible to walk down to the river and eat at the riverside. Most hotels and guesthouses will arrange boat trips to the rapids, ฿150-250 for the journey, depending on the number of people. Most people visit the rapids as a day trip; however, there is accommodation available.
▸▸ *See Sleeping, page 379 for more information.*

Sangkhom and around → *Colour map 2, A3.*

This place is little more than a village, but with four riverside guesthouses and attractive surrounding countryside, it has become something of a laid-back backpackers' refuge. As one visitor recently put it, "the only thing to worry about is finding something to worry about".

Two kilometres west of Sangkhom, is **Wat Hai Sok**, beautifully positioned overlooking the Mekong. The bananas grown in the surrounding countryside are highly regarded, and are cured, sweetened and then sold across the country as *kluay khai*.

There are several good walks in the vicinity of Sangkhom. One of the most interesting is to the hilltop monastery on **Patakseua Cliffs** ⓘ *walk east to the Km 81 marker (about 4 km) and then climb up to the monastery*, which offers superb views over the Mekong to Laos.

Guesthouses arrange boat and fishing trips on the Mekong (฿50-60 per person). Inner tubes are available free of charge from most guesthouses to languidly float down the Mekong (out of the rainy season). Guesthouses have suggested itineraries for those intending to explore the surrounding countryside; best by bicycle or motorcycle.

The turn-off for the **Than Thip Falls** is a short distance east of Sangkhom between the Km 97 and 98 markers, and 3 km off the main road. The falls are enclosed by forest and there are a series of pools good for swimming. Another set of falls are the **Tharn Tong Falls**, 15 km from Sangkhom. For detailed information on directions to these two places, ask at one of the guesthouses.

Wat Hin Mak Peng is about 30 km east of Sangkhom and is superbly positioned on the Mekong with great views up and downstream. The former abbot of this monastery was the highly revered Phra Thute, so much so that the King of Thailand came to the cremation when he died in 1998. The audience hall is one of Thailand's finest. There is a museum devoted to Phra Thute's life. A peaceful, clean and beautiful place.

Si Chiangmai → Colour map 2, A3.
ⓘ *It is 40 km from Sangkhom. There are regular bus connections with Nong Khai (45 mins) and Udon Thani. Less regular connections are west along the river road to Loei, via Sangkhom and Chiang Khan.*

A small, rather dusty town, Si Chiangmai is best known as a centre of spring roll wrapper production; not a lot else seems to take place. Spring roll wrappers are made from rice flour and can be seen drying on racks in the sun in villages all around the town. The main road is noisy and unattractive, but the riverside road is quiet and peaceful with restaurants built over the Mekong. The town's proximity to Laos is reflected in the availability of baguettes, which are freshly baked each day. There is also a large Lao and Vietnamese population in town; the latter are said to control the spring roll wrapper industry. Boat trips and cookery classes can be taken. See Sleeping, below.

⦿ Udon Thani and the northern Mekong route listings

For Sleeping and Eating price codes and other relevant information, see pages 44-49.

⬤ Sleeping

Udon Thani *p372, map p373*
B-D Charoensri Grand Royal, Prachak Rd, next to the main shopping complex, T042-343555, F3435502. A/c, a decent, popular 250-room high-rise with all the usual amenities.
B-E Airport Hotel, 14 Moo 1, Udon-Nongbualamphu Rd, T042-346223, F346514. 114 rooms, set in a garden plot with all mod cons, really only useful for those looking for a place to stay before or after catching a flight.
B-E Ban Chiang, Mukhamontri Rd, T042-327911, F223200. Attractive, centrally located with 149 rooms and friendly staff. The hotel offers a luxurious spa, gym and pool complex as well as an in-house bakery, coffee shop, restaurant and karaoke bar.
B-E Charoen, 549 Pho Sri Rd, T042-248155, F241093. A/c, restaurant, bar and nightclub, pool, good value.
D-E City Lodge, 83/14-15 Wattananuwong Rd, T08-1049 4816 (mob). Good location near the railway station. Lots of expats stay here with their girlfriends but it is a well-run

and decent hotel. All rooms a/c, en suite and with colour TV. The Western food is pretty good (see Eating, below) and the room price includes breakfast and free Wi-Fi. Recommended.
D-E Karin Hotel, 37 Wattana Nuwong Rd, T042-320515. Good-value rooms in this large hotel. Restaurant attached, all rooms a/c, en suite and with colour TVs. Block out the back has the pricier, bigger and nicer rooms. Has a reputation for thefts so watch your valuables.
D-F Charoensri Palace, 60 Pho Sri Rd, T042-242611, F222601. A/c, clean spacious rooms with fridge and TV. Although a little dated, a good-value option. Recommended.
E-F Mitpracha Palace, 271/2-3 Prachak Rd, T042-344184. Just 46 a/c rooms in this pleasant little hotel, good value.
E-F Prachapakdee, 156/8 Sulpakorn Rd, T042-221804. Functional rooms with clean bathrooms. Receptive staff, reasonable rates, in a convenient central location.
E-F Ton Koon Hotel, 50/1 Mak Khaeng Rd, T042-326336, F326349/50. A/c, restaurant, 115 rooms. A very comfortable Western-style hotel with polite and friendly staff.
F-G King Hotel, 57 Pho Sri Rd, T042-241444. Some a/c, TV, clean and serviceable rooms much as you would expect for the price.

Ban Chiang *p374*
F Lakeside Sunrise Guesthouse,
T042-208167. With simple but clean
rooms close to the museum.

Loei *p375, map p375*
A-D Loei Palace Hotel, 167/4 Charoenrat Rd,
T042-815668, F815875. A/c, comfortable
rooms, 2 excellent restaurants, karaoke
bar, pool, gym, sauna, Thai massage and
acupuncture. Palatial and elegantly
designed hotel set in attractive gardens,
with friendly staff.
B-D King Hotel, 11/9-12 Chumsai Rd,
T042-811701, F811235. Open 0700-2300.
Comfortable hotel, central location, good
value. Restaurant with excellent range of
food available, popular with locals. The hotel
also has the **Queen Bar**, open 1000-2400.
C-E Royal Inn, off Chumsai Rd, T042-830
178. Plush renovation of average buildings,
large rooms, all amenities and comfortable
although the rooms at the front of the hotel
can be a little noisy: a good-value option.
D-E Sor Apartments, also located in the
northern part of the city, T042-833644.
Some a/c and en suite facilities, good-sized
rooms, clean and airy, no English spoken.
F-G Friendship Guesthouse, 257/41 Soi
Bunchareon Rd, T042-832408, north of wat,
200 m left off main road. Large rooms,
shared facilities and huts on riverside.

Phu Kradung National Park *p376*
Tents can be hired (฿50) and camping is
permitted at the summit (฿5). There are
also cabins of various sizes and prices (**E**),
T02-5790529, and stalls selling food and
basic necessities.
  Outside the national park are a number
of guesthouses (a couple of kilometres from
the entrance).
C-D Phu Krudung House, T042-811449. A
large number of bungalows with hot water.

Phu Rua National Park *p376*
C-E There are 8 bungalows at the visitors'
centre and a camping ground part way up

the mountain. It is necessary to book:
T042-5790529.
  In addition, there are 2 'back-to-nature'
resorts, 2 km north of Phu Rua town, on
the road to Loei: **C-D Phu Rua Chalet**,
T042-899012, and the **C-D Phu Rua
Resort**, T042-899048.

Chiang Khan and around *p377*
Chiang Khan has a good selection of
atmospheric guesthouses; hardly luxurious,
but they make a change from the usual dull
Thai hotels.
C-D Chiang Khan Hill Resort, T042-821285.
Has bungalows near the rapids, but is overrun
by tourists.
E Cootcoo Resort, T042-821248, Kaeng Kut
Kou, has quiet huts on offer during the dry
season only.
E-G Ton Khong Guesthouse, 299/3 Chai
Khong Rd, T042-821547, tonkhong@
hotmail.com. Attractive location with clean
rooms and excellent food. A bit noisy. Like
all other guesthouses here, can organize
Thai massage and boat trips on the Mekong.
F-G Chiang Khan, 282 Chai Khong Rd,
T042-821691, pimchiang@hotmail.com.
Opposite end of town from the Loei bus
stop, very clean and attractive rooms, with
friendly management. Attractive riverside
position and excellent cheap restaurant.
F-G Nong Sam, 1.25 km west of town,
T042-821457. English-run, quiet and
atmospheric, with floral surroundings,
spacious rooms, good home-cooked food
and river views. Motorbikes for hire, ฿200,
0600-1800.
F-G Poonsawat, 251/2 Chai Khong Rd,
Soi 9, T042-821114. Attractive wooden
hotel, clean rooms, friendly management,
shared bathrooms, small book collection to
help while away the hours. Recommended.

Sangkhom *p377*
E-G Mama's (aka **TXK**), Rim Khong Rd,
T042-441462. Basic bamboo huts overlooking the river with 2 new villas with
wooden floors and shutters. 'Mama',

the maternal owner, has – as ever – big plans and is very proud of her Thai and Lao food.
E-G River Huts. Pleasant open area with well-kept gardens, some of the buildings have been renovated. Friendly owners, a good choice.
F-G Bouy, Rim Khong Rd, 1 km west of the centre, T/F042-441065. Nice bungalows overlooking the river. The attached restaurant serves good food in large portions. Probably the best choice here.

Si Chiangmai p378
C-D Maneerat Resort, T042-451311. Very swish but under occupied, Thai cookery courses run if there is demand. Nice restaurant with good views.
E-F Tim Guesthouse, 553 Moo 2 Rim Khong Rd, T042-451072. Some dorm beds, attractive, quiet huts on the riverfront, the front rooms are brighter and have better views. Swiss management, good source of information, motorcycles, bicycles and boats for hire. Western, Isaan and Thai food available, as well as French liqueurs and custard in various flavours! Boat trips organized.

🍴 Eating

Udon Thani p372, map p373
You can still find fresh-baked baguettes in Udon Thani though they are getting more difficult to locate. There's some pretty good Western food available as well and if you can't find anything to eat at the Prechar market you should maybe think about either going home or to KFC.
🍴 City Lodge, see Sleeping, above. Great British breakfasts, they even have good sausages and HP sauce, and some stonking desserts, the apple crumble with cream is essential. Also do a mean roast. Recommended.
🍴 Good Everything, Pho Niyom Rd. Open 1100-2200. Cute, friendly little café/restaurant with engaging garden and near the Nong

Prachak lake. Serve set lunches, pasta, lamb, steaks, delicious Thai food, home-made cakes, fresh coffee and juices. Recommended.
🍴 Mayfair, Charoen Hotel, 549 Pho Sri Rd. Perhaps the best Thai/Chinese restaurant in town, pricey for northeast Thailand but worth splashing out on.
🍴 Fungki Restaurant, Pho Sri Rd. Excellent range of Thai/Indochinese food at a range of prices.
🍴 Kun Nit, Udon Dutsadee Rd, T042-246128. Delicious, good-value, traditional, Isaan food such as chargrilled chicken and spicy salads.
🍴 Mandarin Restaurant and Bakery, 225-7 Mak Khaeng Rd. Specializes in fish dishes, quiet with touches of contemporary design, attached bakery. Recommended.
🍴 Rabeang Pochana, 53 Saphakit Janya Rd, T042-241515 (beside the lake). Locals continue to recommend this restaurant as the best in town. Highly recommended.
🍴 Steve's Bar and Restaurant, 254/26 Pra-chak Rd, T042-244523. Open 0900-2300. Full Thai and English menu, friendly place recently opened with an extensive spirit and wine selection, wide-screen TV and golf, bridge, cribbage and darts club. Also has a book exchange – worth a visit.
🍴 VT Naem Nuang, Pho Sri Rd, T042-348740 (next to the market). Open 0600-2100. A little out of town but worth the trip for Vietnamese food and drink.

Loei p375, map p375
The best place for stall food is at the **night market** on the corner of Ruamchai and Charoenrat roads.
🍴 Green Garden Restaurant. Vegetarian Thai/Chinese food.
🍴 Luuk Chao Bu, Sathorn Chiang Khan (near the clock tower). Good Thai dishes with generous portions.
🍴 Nang Nuan, 68 Sathorn Chiang Khan Rd. Attractive, well-run outdoor restaurant with *nua yaang* speciality – cook-it-yourself barbecue. Recommended.
🍴 Saw Ahaan, Nok Kaew Rd. Extensive Thai menu, attentive staff and open-air setting.

Bakeries

King Hotel Coffee Shop, 11/9-12 Chumsai Rd. Good for ice cream sundaes in a/c splendour.

Chiang Khan *p377*

Isaan food is excellent in Chiang Khan; a local speciality is live shrimps, fished straight from the Mekong River, served squirming in a spicy marinade of lemon and chilli (*kung ten*) – not for the faint-hearted. There are several riverside restaurants – the best places to eat – with views over to Laos.

♦ **Mekong Riverside**, Chai Khong Rd (opposite Soi 10). Quiet veranda, views over the Mekong, good food, especially fish dishes.

♦ **No Name**, Chai Khong Soi 9 (opposite Poonsawat Hotel). Very popular restaurant serving large portions of freshly wokked rice and noodle dishes.

♦ **Prachamit**, 263/2 Si Chiang Khan Rd (near Soi 9). Frequented by locals, no riverside position but good food.

♦ **Rabiang Rim Khong**, Chai Khong Rd (opposite Soi 10). Small restaurant overlooking the Mekong, good food, generous portions.

♦ **Sook Somboon Hotel**, 243/3 Chai Khong Rd. Wonderful position overhanging the Mekong, excellent fish dishes, including succulent sweet and sour fish.

O Shopping

Udon Thani *p372, map p373*
Robinson's Plaza, off Pho Sri Rd. Shops, cafés and Western-style eating places.

▲ Activities and tours

Udon Thani *p372, map p373*
Tour operators
Aranya Tour, 105 Mak Khaeng Rd, T042-243182. Also arranges visas for Indo-China.
Kannika Tour, 36/9 Srisatha Rd, T042-241378, F241378. Tours in the northeast and to Laos, Cambodia and Vietnam.
Toy Ting, 55/1-5 Thahaan Rd, T042-244771.

⊙ Transport

Udon Thani *p372, map p373*
Air
Regular connections with **Bangkok** (1 hr), 4 times daily, on THAI. Budget airlines **Air Asia** and **Nok Air** fly direct to Bangkok daily. Nok also fly to **Loie** and **Chiang Mai** twice a week. **Silk Air** offer twice-weekly flights to Singapore. Note that these budget airline routes are subject to change at short notice.

Airline offices Air Asia, www.air asia.com; Nok Air, www.nokair.com; Silk Air, www.silkair.com; THAI, 60 Mak Khaeng Rd, T042-246697.

Bicycle
There's a small place renting bikes by the Nong Prachak lake on Suphakit Janya Rd, ฿10 per hr.

Bus
Udon has 2 main bus stations. BKS 2 is on the northwestern edge of town, about 2 km from the centre along Pho Sri Rd. Buses leave here for **Chiang Mai** and **Chiang Rai** in the north, **Nakhon Phanom** and **Nong Khai** in the northeast, **Phitsanulok**, and **Bangkok**. Bangkok passengers can get to/from BKS 2 by yellow town buses (No 23) which run into the centre. Buses also run from the more central BKS 1 on Sai Uthit Rd, just off Pho Sri Rd to **Korat**, **Nakhon Phanom**, **Ubon**, **Khon Kaen**, **Roi Et**, **Sakhon Nakhon** and **Nong Khai**.
International connections There are also several buses a day from BKS1 to **Vientiane** in Laos (see box, page 361, for details of travel to Laos).

Car hire
Parada Car Rent, 78/1 Mak Khaeng Rd, T042-244147; **VIP Car Rent**, 824 Pho Sri Rd, T042-223758.

Train
Regular connections with **Bangkok**'s Hualamphong station (10 hrs) and all

stops en route – **Ayutthaya**, **Saraburi**, **Korat**, **Khon Kaen** and on to **Nong Khai**.

Loei *p375, map p375*
Air
Airline offices THAI, next to Royal Inn Hotel, T042-812344.

Bus
Regular connections to **Bangkok**'s Northeastern bus terminal (10 hrs), **Udon Thani** (4 hrs), **Khon Kaen** and **Phitsanulok** (4 hrs). Note that some buses travel via Lom Sak to Phitsanulok and others via Nathon Thai. For **Chiang Khan** (1 hr, ฿18) and other stops along the Mekong River route downstream (east), buses leave from the junction of Maliwan and Ruanchai roads.

Songthaew
Songthaews for out of town trips.

Chiang Khan *p377*
Bus
Rather unreliable buses (in fact, converted trucks) travel to **Loei** (1 hr) and east towards **Pak Chom**, **Sangkhom**, **Si Chiangmai** and on to **Nong Khai**. To travel to Sangkhom take the bus to Pak Chom (1½ hrs) from opposite the Shell petrol station and from there change to the bus to Nong Khai (2 hrs). For Pak Chom, it may be quicker to join up with other travellers and hire a *songthaew*.
A/c bus connections with **Bangkok** from the station on Soi 9 (inland from Si Chiang Khan Rd).

Sangkhom *p377*
Bicycle
Hire is ฿50 per day.

Bus
Connections west to **Loei** via Chiang Khan, and east to **Nong Khai** via Si Chiangmai.

Motorcycle
฿250 per day for hire from **River Huts Guesthouse**; the best way to explore the backroads.

❶ Directory

Udon Thani *p372, map p373*
Banks Bangkok Bank, Pho Sri Rd. Krung Thai, 216 Mak Khaeng Rd. Thai Farmers, 236 Pho Sri Rd. **Medical services** Pho Niyom Rd, T042-222572. **Police** Sri Suk Rd, T042-222285. **Post office** Wattana Nuwong Rd (near the Provincial Governor's Office).

Loei *p375, map p375*
Banks Siam Commercial, 3/8 Ruamchai Rd. Thai Farmers, Ruamchai Rd – both banks have exchange facilities. **Medical services** Hospital: corner of Nok Kaew and Maliwan roads, T042-811806. **Police** Phiphatmongkhon Rd, T042-811254. **Post office** Charoenrat Rd (southern end), telecom office on top floor.

Chiang Khan *p377*
Banks Thai Farmers (exchange facilities), 444 Si Chiang Khan Rd. **Immigration** Immigration office, next to post office. Visa extension possible. **Post office** Chai Khong Rd (eastern edge of town).

Nong Khai and the southern Mekong route

The last stop before the Friendship Bridge and communist Laos, Nong Khai is a charming laid-back riverside town: the sort of place where jaded travellers get 'stuck' for several days, doing nothing but enjoying the romantic atmosphere of the place. There are a number of wats to visit and from here, while supping on a cold beer, you can look across to Tha Dua in Laos and imagine the enormous and rare pla buk catfish – weighing up to 340 kg – foraging on the riverbed.

From Nong Khai, Route 212 follows the Mekong River 137 km to the riverside town of Beung Kan and from there another 175 km to the provincial capital, Nakhon Phanom. Swing 75 km westwards away from Nakhon Phanom and the Mekong and you'll reach Sakhon Nakhon and the sacred stupa, Phrathat Cheong Chum. Continuing southwards from Nakhon Phanom on the river road for another 50 km, Route 212 reaches That Phanom, the site of one of the most revered chedis in Thailand: Wat That Phanom. This area is also a centre of traditional textile production, particularly around the town of Renu Nakhon. From That Phanom, Route 212 heads 50 km south to the newly created provincial capital of Mukdahan finishing its journey 170 km away at Ubon Ratchathani.
▸▸ *For listings, see pages 391-398.*

Nong Khai ⊙⊘∅⊛⊙▲⊙❶ ▸▸ *pp391-398. Colour map 2, A3.*

Nong Khai, with good access to Laos and its capital Vientiane, has become increasingly popular. The town is one of the most attractive in the region, with French-style colonial architecture.

Ins and outs
Getting there Nong Khai is situated at the end of Route 2, the Friendship Highway, and on the banks of the mighty Mekong. Currently, visitors to Laos have to cross the Mekong by road; visas are available on arrival in the country. The bus station is on the east side of town on Praserm Road and there are connections with Bangkok and destinations in the northeast. This is as far as it is possible to travel on the northeastern rail line from Bangkok and although the track now continues across the bridge into Laos there are no plans for passenger trains. The station is 3 km from town, west on Kaeo Worawut Road. Nong Khai also happens to be the logical place to start or end a tour of the Thai towns which line the Mekong River. ▸▸ *See Transport, page 396, for further information.*

Getting around *Saamlors* or tuk-tuks provide the main means of local transport; the town is strung out along the river, so it is quite a hike getting from one end to the other. Some guesthouses hire out bicycles and motorbikes. Local buses link Nong Khai with out-of-town destinations.

Background
Nong Khai, as the flow of tourists and trade into Laos increases, is slowly transforming itself from a sleepy provincial backwater into a bustling border town. The Australian-financed Friendship Bridge at Tambon Meechai, 2 km from town, the first bridge across the lower reaches of the Mekong River, was officially opened on 8 April 1994, leading to a boom in development. Fortunately for the preservation of Nong Khai's charming core, many of the ugliest new constructions are concentrated along Highway 2, which leads to the bridge. The riverfront has now been redeveloped into a 'promenade' for visiting

tourists and it makes for quite a pleasant stroll with the setting sun as a backdrop. The riverside market is now almost fully covered – with the steamy Isaan heat this can make for welcome relief. Most of the goods on sale in the market are imported stuff from China and not of particularly good quality.

Sights

The influence of the French in Indochina is clearly reflected in the architecture of Meechai Road, which runs parallel with the river. The most impressive building is the 1920s French colonial style Governor's Mansion. It's now disused – the last governor left in April 2007 – but it is beautifully preserved. There are plans to open it to the public, the tiling and interiors are very typical of the period, but for now you can just walk through the grounds.

Notable among the wats are the important teaching wat, **Wat Sisaket**, and, towards the east of town past the bus station, **Wat Pho Chai** – with its Lao-style viharn and venerated solid gold-headed Buddha (the body is bronze), looted from Vientiane by the future Rama I. The bot contains murals showing how the image is reputed to have got to Nong Khai: Rama I loaded the image onto a raft to cross the Mekong, but while negotiating the river the raft capsized and the image was lost. It then resurfaced (this is a common theme in the lost Buddha image genre), to be retrieved and placed in Wat Pho Chai. (Or, less miraculously, it was dredged from the river 25 years later.)

A third religious building, or rather what remains of it, is **Phrathat Nong Khai**, better known as **Phrathat Klang Nam** (Phrathat in the Middle of the River). In Henri Mouhot's

Nong Khai

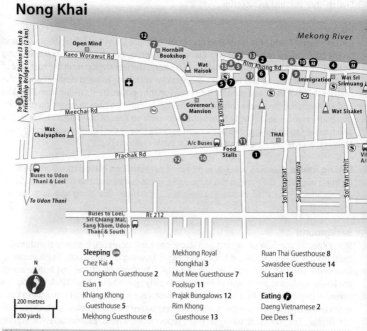

account of his trip up the Mekong in 1860, the 'discoverer' of Angkor Wat, described upon arrival in 'Nong Kay' a "Buddhist tat or pyramidal landmark ... that has been washed away from the shore, and now lies half submerged, like a wrecked ship". The phrathat is only visible during the dry season, when it emerges from the muddy river and is promptly bedecked with pennants. To see it, walk east along Meechai Road for about 2 km from the town centre, and turn left down Soi Paa Phrao 3. On the riverfront Rim Khong Road, there is a daily **market** selling goods from Laos.

Around Nong Khai ▸ pp391-398.

Wat Phrathat Bang Phuan
ⓘ *Most Sangkhom bound buses stop at Phrathat Bang Phuan or at the nearby village of Ban Bang Phuan.*

The wat, 22 km southwest of Nong Khai, contains an Indian-style stupa, similar (it is presumed) to the original Phra Pathom Chedi in Nakhon Pathom. Its exact date of construction is unknown, but it is believed to date from the early centuries AD. The newer *chedi*, which was built on the sight in 1559, toppled over in 1970 and was restored in 1978. As a result, the unrestored Lao *chedis* in this compound are now of greater historical interest. The site is only worth visiting en route to or from Udon or Nong Khai.

Phu Phra Bat Historical Park
ⓘ *0830-1700. There is a reception centre, with a historical exhibition and a small café. Guides are also available here. To see all the main sites allow at least 3 hrs. The park is just about equidistant from Nong Khai and Udon Thani, almost 70 km. Catch a bus to Ban Phu (there is a very simple hotel here should visitors need to stay), the town where Routes 2020 and 2021 meet, a journey of about 2½ hrs. From there (it is signposted), the park is another 15 km by songthaew towards Ban Tiu (quicker to take a motorcycle taxi from here).*

Encompassing an area of 650 ha in the Phu Phan hills, the Phu Phra Bat Historical Park has been a site of almost continuous human habitation since prehistoric times. There are prehistoric cave paintings, Dvaravati boundary stones (seventh-10th centuries), Lopburi Bodhisattvas (10th-13th centuries), Lang Chan Buddha images (14th-18th centuries), and a stupa built in 1920 to shelter a Buddha footprint. The terrain consists of rocky outcrops, bare sandy soil and savannah forest, and it is easy to imagine why people, for thousands of years, have regarded the area as a magical place.

Duck & Pork Shophouse **5**
German Bakery **7**
Hadda **4**
Khun Daeng **6**
Nagarind **12**
Nem Nuang Deng **3**
Steak House **8**

Udom Rot **10**

Bars & clubs 🍸
Thasadej Café **9**
Warm Up **13**
Winner Pub **11**

Border essentials: Thailand–Laos

Friendship Bridge

The Friendship Bridge at Tambon Meechai, 2 km from Nong Khai, offers a road link across the Mekong. The bridge is open daily 0600-2200. Visas are available upon entry to Laos. The price is US$35 and a passport photograph is required.

To get to the Friendship Bridge, take a tuk-tuk to the last bus stop before the bridge and from there catch a bus to Thai immigration. See also box, page 361.

In early March 2009, the railway line over the Friendship Bridge from Nong Khai to the station at **Tha Na Lang** (Laos) finally opened to the public, with a full service presumed to be starting in the very near future. At present details are sketchy and it is not even sure if the rail crossing is open to non-Thai/Lao citizens. Travellers would be best advised to check locally before travelling. Plans are afoot to run a direct service from Bangkok into Laos and there are rumours about extending the line into Vientiane.

Sala Kaew Ku

① 0830-1800, ฿20. Take a songthaew heading towards Beung Kan (Rte 212) or go by tuk-tuk. Turn right after the Km 4 marker where there is signpost to Sala Kaew Ku. To cycle from town, it is best to take the riverside road as far as Wat Sirimahakatcha, then turn right and travel south. A return tuk-tuk, including 1 hr's wait, should cost ฿120.

Also known as **Wat Khaek** ('Indian' Wat) and **Sala Kaew Ku**, the clumsily named **Wat Phutthamamaka-samakhom**, which houses bizarre giant sculptures too weird to miss, was established in the late 1970s and lies 4.5 km east of Nong Khai on Route 212 to Beung Kan. The sculpture park – recently renovated – was set up by a Laotian artist named Luang Poo Boun Leua Sourirat, who died in 1996 at the age of 72. Luang Poo saw himself as part holy man, part artist and part sage. He studied under a Hindu rishi in Vietnam and formed his own synthesis of Buddhist and Hindu philosophy, which is displayed in his work here. He established a similar bizarre concoction of concrete figurines near Tha Deua in Laos (not far from Vientiane), but was ejected from the country shortly after it became communist in 1975, probably on the grounds that he was simply too weird. A wealthy man, he bought a small slice of Thailand and started again.

Reflecting Luang Poo's beliefs, the wat promotes a strange mixture of Buddhism and Hinduism and is dominated by a vast array of strange brick and cement statues. Some are clearly of Buddhist and Hindu inspiration. Others are rather harder to interpret: for example, a life-size elephant being attacked by a large pack of dogs, four in a jeep – apparently a symbolic representation of Luang Poo (the elephant) being attacked by his critics. The 'Life and Death' grouping is especially interesting. And there's an assortment of figures: a baby, a businesswoman, soldier and beggar. The series concludes with two couples holding hands, one pair skeletonized and standing next to a coffin on a pyre.

By far the most surreal site is the array of gaudy effigies and representations of Hindu gods contained within the enormous, domed temple. Climb to the top floor and you'll find Luang Poo's mausoleum, complete with all the worldly goods he owned at the time of his death – there's even a photograph of the blood he coughed up in his final moments.

At the back of the mausoleum, surrounded by a kitsch horde of plastic flowers, fairy lights and even a computer screen running images of an aquarium, lies the shrouded corpse of Luang Poo, his mummified head sticking out of orange sheets. Here you'll see many Thais, who consider Luang Poo to be a holy man, praying and lighting incense.

Southern Mekong route 🏛️🚌🌸🏠▲🚗🚤 ➼ pp391-398.

Beung Kan ➼ Colour map 2, A4.
A much more scenic and adventurous way to reach Nakhon Phanom is by taking the river road east from Nong Khai. This road follows the Mekong for nearly 320 km. The only logical place to break the journey is in the small district town of Beung Kan, 137 km from Nong Khai and 175 km from Nakhon Phanom. There are regular connections with both places. Beung Kan is one of the more difficult Thai town names to pronounce: it's best to hold your nose to get the required nasal inflexion.

Wat Phu Tok
① Take an early morning songthaew to the village of Ben Seveli (1 hr). From there, either charter a tuk-tuk or motorcycle taxi to the wat, which is about 20 km away, or there are a few public songthaews.
Wat Phu Tok, also known as **Wat Chedi Ya Khiri Viharn**, is a cave wat situated in an area of breathtaking limestone scenery, about 140 km east of Nong Khai. The wat was established by Phra Acaan Juen in 1968, and it is now a sprawling monastery with meditation grottoes and *kutis* (monks' cells) spread among the honeycombed mountain. Climbing up the mountain is an exhausting business, but the spectacular views of the plain below make it all worthwhile. The wat itself is at the foot of the hill. From here, vertiginous steps lead up through a series of levels, marked by shrines. Part way up the path divides: left is a bit of a scramble; right is spectacular and not for the faint-hearted, because the stairway (attached to the rock face) is 1.8 m wide with a fall of several hundred feet! At the end of this is an almost sheer rock face, with a rope to help the adrenaline junkies who want to climb the last 18 m. It is possible to stay the night at the wat, although some recent visitors have reported that the monks are not terribly welcoming (take some donations if intending to stay). Visitors should also expect only very basic facilities. There are a couple of acceptable guesthouses in **Seveli** village and it is also possible to camp in the area.

Ban Ahong
① Buses making the journey between Nong Khai and Bueung Kan all pass through Ban Ahong.
Ban Ahong is around 25 km west of Beung Kan on Route 212 (at the Km 115 marker) to Nong Khai. Close by is Wat Paa Ahong and its abbot and lone monk, Luang Phor Phraeng. The monastery is a strange oasis of shrubbery and plants. Luang Phor is renowned for his medicinal skills and is reputed to have magical powers of healing. It is possible to swim in the Mekong at this stretch of the river's course during the dry season.

Nakhon Phanom ➼ Colour map 3, B3.
There is little to do in Nakhon Phanom except admire the view of the majestic Mekong River as it sweeps its way past the distant mountains of Laos. Like Nong Khai, sipping a beer or eating catfish curry overlooking the river does have a certain romantic appeal. There are several striking French colonial buildings scattered along the riverfront – particularly along the northern stretch – and the town's tree-lined streets create a pleasing atmosphere. Unfortunately most people only visit Nakhon Phanom en route to Phra That Phanom Chedi, the northeast's most revered religious shrine (50 km to the south).

Nakhon Phanom is the closest town with adequate hotels to the wat. The TAT tourist office is housed in an attractive building on the corner of Salaklang and Suthorn Vichit roads.

Nakhon Phanom's limited sights include **Wat Sri Thep** on Srithep Road (which boasts a statue of Luang Pu Chan, a revered northeastern holy man) and **Wat Mahathat** (with a lotus-bud *chedi*), at the southern end of Sunthon Vichit Road. The former monastery has some exuberant murals depicting episodes from the Buddha's life (the Jataka tales). Otherwise you can simply wander along the riverfront, past handicraft shops and a Chinese temple. There is a morning **market** on the river. Just south of the **Grand View Hotel**, south of town, is an area of beach, **Hat Sai Tai Muang**, which local people use to lounge on in the evening while stalls sell Thai snacks. During the dry season the exposed area of sand expands considerably. Across the river is the Lao town of Thakhek and foreigners with visas are allowed to cross the border here.

Some 88 km west of Nakhon Phanom, **Wat Phrathat Narai Chengweng** (Phrathat Naweng) is a Khmer *prang* dating from the 11th or 12th century. Despite being reconstructed in what appears to be a remarkably haphazard fashion, this small sanctuary is very satisfying and displays finely carved lintels: the east lintel above the entrance to the sanctuary shows Siva dancing; the north face, Vishnu reclining on a naga. To get there, take Route 22 to the junction with Route 223 (it is signposted); walk through a green archway, and the wat is 500 m along a dirt track. There is a good, cheap Thai restaurant on the other side of the road from the wat, beyond the inter-section on the way to Udon Thani (about 200 m); take a bus travelling towards Sakhon Nakhon from the bus station near the market.

Sakhon Nakhon → *Colour map 2, A5.*

This ancient town was one of the Khmer Empire's more important provincial centres in the northeast; it's now one of the region's smaller provincial capitals. Along with a revered monastery, Sakhon Nakhon also has a reputation in Thailand as a centre of dog-meat consumption. Most famously though, Sakhon Nakhon is home to the second most sacred Lao-style stupa in Thailand: the Phrathat Choeng Chum (the most sacred is That Phanom, see below).

Phrathat Choeng Chum, a 24-m-tall, white, angular, lotus-bud *chedi* has become

Nakhon Phanom

200 metres
200 yards

N

Sleeping 🛏
Grand 2

Nakhon Phanom
River View 1
Nam Khong Grand View 4

Eating 🍴
Ban Chom Chol 2
Cafe Bon 3
Golden Giant Catfish 1

an important pilgrimage spot for Thais. The *chedi* is built over a laterite Khmer *prang* dating from the 11th or 12th century, and to reach the *chedi* it is necessary to walk through the viharn. The *chedi* is surrounded by ancient images of the Buddha captured during raids into Laos and Cambodia. Behind the stupa is an entrance through which pilgrims walk to make offerings to two revered Buddha images. The older, and finer, image is set behind a newer one, and is easy to miss. The wat next to Wat Prathat Choeng Chum is a popular teaching monastery.

Another important religious site in town is **Wat Pa Suthawat** ① *0800-1800*, opposite the town hall. This is important not for any artistic merit, but because one of Thailand's most revered monks lived and died here: Phra Acaan Man Bhuritatto, better known as Luang Pho Man (1871-1949). A chapel in his memory has been constructed and his (few) possessions are kept on display.

The Phu Thai ethnic group inhabit the area around Sakhon Nakhon, and the **Wax Castle Ceremony** is associated with them (see Festivals and events, page 395).

The 32-sq km **Nong Han Lake** is close to town beyond the beautiful and peaceful Royal Park. Boats can be hired to visit the islands on the lake (not as easy as it sounds, and needs to be done a day in advance), and it is a popular place at weekends. Do not swim in the lake, as it is infected with liver flukes. It is also said to be the largest natural inland water body in Thailand.

Phrathat Narai Chenweng is situated 5 km west of town in the village of Ban Thai. The 11th-century monastery was built as a Hindu shrine. The name *cheng weng* is Khmer for 'with long legs' and this is thought to refer to the carving of Vishnu on the northern pediment of the laterite prasat, still standing in the monastery's precincts. The four-armed Vishnu holds his head up with one hand while two of the other three hands hold a lotus and a baton.

That Phanom → *Colour map 2, B5.*
The small town of That Phanom is a scruffy riverside settlement with one attraction: Wat That Phanom, the most revered temple in the northeast and the second most revered by the people of Laos (the most revered being That Luang in Vientiane). It also holds an annual temple festival. There is no bus terminal as such. Buses stop on Chaiyangkun Road (the main Route 212, north to Nakhon Phanom and south to Ubon), an easy walk to the river and guesthouses.

Wat That Phanom is dominated by an impressive 52-m white and gold Lao-style *chedi*. Legend has it that it was originally constructed in 535 BC to house a breastbone of the Buddha, eight years after his death. Since then it has been restored no less than eight times, most recently in 1995 by the Thai Fine Arts Department with a major restoration taking place in 1977, following the *chedi*'s collapse after heavy rains in 1975. A legend said that should the *chedi* fall, then so too would the Kingdom of Laos; shortly afterwards, the communist Pathet Lao took Luang Prabang and Vientiane, and ousted the American-backed government. The 1995 restoration gave thieves the opportunity to climb the scaffolding and prise out the diamonds studded into the finial. The *chedi* is surrounded by Buddha images that thousands of pilgrims have covered in gold leaf. During festivals and religious holidays, the wat is seething with people making offerings of flowers and incense.

On Monday and Thursday from around 0800 until 1200, a Lao **market** is held upstream from town, when hoards of Laotians cross the Mekong to market their wares. They arrive laden with pigs, wild forest products and herbal remedies, returning home with cash and

Thai consumer goods. The market winds down soon after midday, although the shops near the ferry pier sell excellent-quality goods very cheaply every day of the week. Laotians and Thais spend the day being ferried back and forth across the river to trade, and the border here is now open for non-Thai and Laotian nationals too.

Renu Nakhon, a traditional weaving and embroidery centre, is almost 15 km northwest of That Phanom. On Wednesdays and fair days, the central wat of the village is home to hundreds of market stalls selling a wide selection of local and Lao textiles, as well as Isaan axe pillows. Outside the wat compound, there are permanent shops selling a similar selection of cloth and local handicrafts throughout the week. Cloth is sold by the phun and there are about two phun in a sarong length. Prices quoted therefore do not usually relate to the piece. For simple cotton cloth, expect to pay ฿100-200 per phun; for the best silk, up to ฿3000. To get to Renu Nakhon, travel 8 km north of That Phanom on Route 212, and then left onto Route 2031 for another 6.5 km; if the bus drops you off at the junction, there are *songthaews* for the final stretch.

Mukdahan → *Colour map 2, B5.*

ⓘ *Arriving by bus, you may be dropped off at the junction of Muang Mai Rd and Route 212. Tuk-tuks wait here and ฿20 is the usual rate into town.*

The capital of one of Thailand's newer provinces, Mukdahan's greatest claim to fame is as the home town of one of Thailand's best-known leaders, General Sarit Thanarat (see page 700). As one of the gateways to an emerging Laos, and a new bridge recently opened 5 km north of the town centre, Mukdahan is quickly becoming a boom town. There are still a few old-style wooden houses, but they are fast disappearing. Mukdahan is also something of a riverside resort town for Thai tourists who come to eat Mekong fish and repose beside the river. It also lies directly opposite the important Lao town of Savannakhet.

Because of its location, Mukdahan has become an important trading centre with goods from Laos, like gems, timber, cattle and agricultural commodities, being exchanged for Thai consumer goods. There is a Lao and Thai market, the so-called **Talaat Indochine**, held daily opposite the pier where boats from Laos land. It is best to get to the market in the morning. Along with Thai consumer goods, Lao silk and cotton cloth (see Shopping), good French bread, china, axe cushions, *khaens* (a local, bamboo pan pipe) and baskets are also sold. Near the pier and opposite Wat Si Mongkhon Tai is a Bodhi tree where numerous traditional soothsayers ply their trade.

Wat Sri Sumong, on Samran Chai Khong Road, the river road, is interesting for the colonial architectural elements – arches over the windows and veranda – reflected in the bot. A little further north on the river road, **Wat Yod Kaew Sriwichai** also has Lao lotus-bud *chedis* and a large, gold Buddha spinning the Wheel of Law.

The **Space Needle** (**Hor Kaew Mukdahan**) ⓘ *0800-1800, ฿20*, is 2 km south of town. Looking rather like an air traffic control tower, the building houses a costume museum, a display of local artefacts, a gallery of Buddha images and a viewing gallery with exceptional views of Laos.

For good views of the river and surrounding countryside, climb **Phu Manorom**, a small hill 5 km south of town. Take Route 2034 south towards Don Tan and after 2 km turn right. The summit is another 3 km from the turn-off.

Phu Pha Thoep National Park (also known as **Mukdahan National Park**), covering a modest 54 sq km, lies 15 km south of Mukdahan, off Route 2034. The principal forest type here is dry dipterocarp savannah forest and there is a succession of oddly shaped rock outcrops, easily accessible from park headquarters. The environment almost feels prehistoric, and fossils and finger paintings have been found amidst the boulders. Cut into the cliff face that rises above the headquarters, is an interesting cave packed with Buddha images. To get to the park, catch a *songthaew* travelling south towards Don Tan; the turning for the park is between the Km 14 and 15 markers and it is a 2-km walk from there to the park headquarters; camping is permitted.

◉ Nong Khai and the southern Mekong route listings

For Sleeping and Eating price codes and other relevant information, see pages 44-49.

● Sleeping

Nong Khai *p383, map p384*
Guesthouses in Nong Khai are of a high standard (but avoid **Pantawee** – it has a reputation both as a centre of sex tourism and for doubling the rate for *farang* guests).

B-C Mekong Royal Nongkhai, 222 Jomanee Rd, west of railway station out of town, T042-420024, www.holidayinnhotels.co.th. A/c, restaurant, pool, tennis, 8-storey block, with nearly 200 rooms overlooking Mekong with all facilities, best in town.

D-E Chongkonh Guesthouse, 649 Rim-khong Rd, T042-460548, F412229. French-run with 14 large, clean fan rooms, some with TV. Tranquil location overlooking the river.

D-E Prajak Bungalows, 1178 Prachak Rd, T042-412644. A quiet place with good facilities for the price. Clean and well run, surprisingly underutilized.

D-F Mut Mee Guesthouse, 1111/4 Kaeo Worawut Rd, F042-460717, mutmee@ nk.ksc.co.th. Restaurant, large rooms and bungalows, nice garden by the river, very friendly English/Thai management, good source of information on Laos, bikes for rent, widely regarded as the best place in town. The rooms are well maintained and mostly en suite. Also serves food, though if you want authentic Thai you'll do better eating on the **Nagarina** (see Eating, below). Having said that, the bread, cheese and ham are excellent. Owner can also help set up longer-term rentals. Highly recommended.

E Mekong Guesthouse, 519 Rim Khong, T042-412320, naga_tour@hotmail.com. Clean, cute wooden rooms, on the river with a good veranda for sundowners and information. Restaurant next door and internet café attached (฿ 30 per hr). But noisy from the road.

E-F Suksant Hotel, 1164 Prachak Rd, T042-411585. Some a/c, large clean airy rooms but rather featureless.

F Chez Kai, 1160 Soi Samosorn, T042-460 968. Clean airy rooms, some with balcony, restaurant downstairs with lots of vegetarian food, all very cheap.

F Khiang Khong Guesthouse, 541 Rim-khong Rd, T042-422870. Outstanding value, spotless a/c, en suite rooms, some with river-view balcony available in this brand new 5-storey high establishment. Recommended.

F Poolsup, 843 Meechai Rd, T042-2202031. Chinese-style hotel with OK rooms and charming proprietress – try her cool rainwater.

F Ruan Thai Guesthouse, 1126/2 Rim Khong Rd, T042-412519, www.ruanthai house.com. Amiable wooden house, near the river with a/c and fan en suite rooms. English spoken, lots of local information. Rooms are a little dark, though cooler for it.

F Rim Khong Guesthouse, Rim Khong Rd. Shared bathrooms, clean rooms with fans, friendly staff, wooden house with river views. Small bar/restaurant providing drinks and breakfast.

F Sawasdee Guesthouse, 402 Meechai Rd, T042-412602, F420259. Old wooden house with inner courtyard brimming with plants. Some with a/c, clean rooms and immaculate bathrooms, complimentary coffee, friendly, good source of information, fan, hot water. Recommended.

F-G Esan, 538 Soi Srikunmuang. Meechai Rd, T042-412008. Cute little guesthouse set in a quiet *soi* near the river. The owner, Den, is very friendly and the clean, stylish cheaper rooms (fan and shared facilities), set in an authentic teak villa are probably the best bargain in town. They also have a small selection of rooms with a/c, TV and private bathrooms. Recommended.

Beung Kan *p387*
Only basic accommodation is available, but all are centrally located and have a certain provincial charm.

F Neramit, Prasatchai Rd, north of the bus station, towards the river, and opposite the Santisuk. Has the only international phone in town.

F Santisuk, Prasatchai Rd. Some a/c, reasonable rooms at reasonable prices.

Nakhon Phanom *p387, map p388*
A good variety of accommodation is available here, the best place to base yourself to visit That Phanom.

B-D Nakhon Phanom River View, 9 Nakhon Phanom–That Phanom Rd, T042-522333, www.northeast-hotel.com. A/c, restaurant, pool, fitness centre. Good food, friendly atmosphere and standard rooms with balconies facing directly on the Mekong make this the best place in Nakhon Phanom.

B-E Nam Khong Grand View, 527 Sunthorn Vichit Rd, T042-513564, F511037. A/c, restaurant, modern hotel with 114 impressive rooms, but very average and the worst of the upmarket places.

F-G Grand Hotel, 210 Sri Thep Rd, T042-511526, F513788. Some a/c, very clean and the best budget option – friendly owners, central location and near the river.

F-G Windsor Hotel, 272 Bamrungmuang Rd, T042-511946. Good rooms, some a/c, some fan, all clean, well presented and en suite. Recommended.

Sakhon Nakhon *p388*
A-C MJ Hotel, Kumuang Rd, located slightly outside town. The newest hotel in town, big and brash and certainly not beautiful, but the rooms are spacious, immaculate and good value.

C Imperial, 1892 Suk Khasem Rd, T042-713 320. Some a/c, 180 rooms and a snooker parlour, rooms in the newer wing are considerably smarter, although the a/c rooms in the old wing are a good deal.

E Araya I, 1432 Prempreeda Rd, T042-711224. Some a/c, 50 simple rooms.

E Araya II, 345 Prempreeda Rd, T042-711054. Cheapest in town and it shows; run-down, but sufficient for a night's stopover. Some rooms with bathrooms attached.

That Phanom *p389*
There is very little accommodation in That Phanom, though there is one very friendly guesthouse. When the temple fair is on during the Feb full moon (see Festivals and events, page 395), it is often impossible to find a room.

D Kaeng Pho Resort, Highway 212 (3 km south of town), T042-541412. Some a/c, the better of Nakhon Phanom's 2 resort-style hotels, but even so this is hardly an example of rustic splendour – attractive gardens.

D That Phanom Resort, south of the town, T042-541047. Some a/c, basic and boring rooms with the only plus that they are clean.

F-G Chaiwan, 34 Phanom Phanarak Rd. A small Chinese-style hotel with dark run-down rooms.

G Niyana's Guesthouse, 65 Moo 14, Soi Weetheesawra, T042-540580. Rooms in traditional country house, in a peaceful leafy compound. Has seen better days, though the very helpful and friendly owner – Niyana – makes the place. She can help guests visit nearby villages and take part in the local community. Also very cheap for tours and motorbike and cycle rental. Recommended.

Mukdahan p390

AL-D Ploy Palace, 40 Pitakpanomkhet Rd, T042-631111, www.hotelthailand.com/ mukdahan/ploypalace. A sauna, swimming pool and great views compliment this well-run hotel. Rooms are large, a/c and en suite – some have DVD players and all have TVs.

B-D Mukdahan Grand, 78 Song Nang Sathit, T042-612020, F612021. A/c, restaurant, comparatively plush with nice rooms and good views. The local crooners hang out here at the **Zubano Karaoke Bar** and **MG Snooker Club**. Good food and good value. Recommended.

D-E Kieng Piman Hotel and Spa, 26 Damrongmongdo Rd, T042-615284. Brand new place in the south of the town. The rooms are all a/c, en suite and have English-language TV channels. Very clean and well run with a friendly English-speaking owner. Recommended.

F-G Hua Nam, 36 Samut Sakdarak Rd, T042-611137. Central location on corner with Song Nang Sathit Rd, rooms are large, clean and well maintained. Some a/c with TV and hot water. Set around a courtyard, so relatively quiet despite central crossroads location. Also has internet, and bicycles for rent. Recommended.

G Sansuk Bungalow, 136 Phithak Santirat Rd, T042-611294. Some a/c, near town centre, clean rooms, friendly management, the best of the cheaper accommodation.

● Eating

Nong Khai p383, map p384

In the evening a whole run of excellent grilled chicken stalls now set up along Prachak Rd.

ᵀᵀ Nagarina. Floating restaurant that operates on both a tethered raft and boat just outside Mutmee. They offer a good range of tasty affordable Thai food. The boat also sets sail at 1700 for a sundown cruise (฿100).

ᵀᵀ Nem Nuang Deng, Soi Thepbanterng opposite **Thasadej Café**, near the river. Open 1000-2200. Good Vietnamese food,

including delicious Vietnamese-style spring rolls. Eat in or takeaway. Recommended.

ᵀᵀ-ᵀ Dee Dees, Prachak Rd. One of the most popular places in town with the locals, and deservedly so. Huge array of Thai and Isaan food served up in this large, spotless road-side diner. Recommended.

ᵀ Banya Pochana, 295 Rim Khong Rd. Chinese, Thai and Lao food, fish dishes particularly good.

ᵀ Chez Kai, 1160 Soi Samosorn, T042-460 968. This guesthouse has a restaurant downstairs specializing in vegetarian food.

ᵀ Daeng Vietnamese, on the riverside, Rimkhong Rd. With a nice terrace and an upmarket feel which belies its rock-bottom prices. Food is just above average but location is the big seller.

ᵀ Duck and pork shophouse, on the corner of Meechai Rd and Haisok Rd. Have your duck or pork with either rice or noodles. Cheap, clean, quick and non-spicy but oh-so-tasty. Makes for a great Thai-style pit stop. Awesome.

ᵀ German Bakery, right next door to the the duck and port shophouse (see above). Good bread and other assorted goodies.

ᵀ Hadda, Rim Khong Rd, between the immigration office and the market, T042-411543. Wide-ranging menu, including a selection of fish dishes. Fantastic setting with river views and very popular with locals. Recommended.

ᵀ Happy Kitchen, 1164 Prachak Rd. Restaurant attached to the **Suksant Hotel** (no English sign for the restaurant). Excellent fish dishes, recommended.

ᵀ Khun Daeng, 521 Rim Khong Rd, just west from Udom Rot and the immigration office. Views over the Mekong River, seafood and superb Isaan specialities.

ᵀ Steak House, Meechai Rd (next to **Sawasdee Guesthouse**). Predictably selling steaks, very tasty and good value.

ᵀ Udom Rot, 193 Rim Khong Rd. Views over the Mekong River, great seafood as well as some Lao and Vietnamese dishes. Recommended.

Coffee shops

The Coffee Shop, Rim Khong Rd. Attractive rustic design.

Beung Kan p387

There is a night market situated near the a/c bus terminal on Bumrungrad Rd, plus the usual street-side Thai eating houses.
♥ **Santisuk**, Prasatchai Rd (see Sleeping). Has a good and cheap restaurant.

Nakhon Phanom p387, map p388

Restaurants along the river road all serve the same broad range of dishes. Mekong catfish cooked in a variety of ways – curried, stir fried, deep fried, in soups – is a local speciality.
♥♥ **Ban Chom Chol**. Open 1100-1400, 1600-2200. Restaurant and pub set by river in sleek, modern Thai villa. You can sit in the garden or in the a/c restaurant. Serves good river fish and Thai fare.
♥ **Cafe Bon**, Rim Khong Rd, north of town centre. A small rustic fresh coffee shop with nice river views.
♥ **Golden Giant Catfish**, Sunthorn Vichit Rd. Serves *pla buk*, the famed giant Mekong catfish, in a variety of guises. Recommended.
♥ **Nawt Laap Phet**, 464 Aphibarn Bancha Rd. An Isaan restaurant serving Lao specialities, including the usual grilled chicken and spicy salad, along with great *larb*.

Sakhon Nakhon p388

Just north of Sakhon Nakhon is a dog market which sells, slaughters and serves dog meat. There are 2 **night markets** in town. One is close to the Charoensuk Hotel, at the roundabout at the junction of Charoenmuang and Jaiphasuk roads. The other is at the inter section of Charoenmuang and Suk Khasem roads.
♥ **Best House Suki**, Prem Prida Rd. Excellent Isaan food served here, seafood specialities.
♥ **Sook Kasen**, Kamchatpai Rd. Thai food.

Bakeries

Greencorner, Ratphattana Rd. Pleasant a/c bakery with good breakfast and usual food selection.

That Phanom p389

Foodstalls and restaurants can be found on the riverfront and along Rachdamnern Rd; try the That Phanom Pochana or Somkhane, both fish restaurants close to the triumphal arch. Lao-style French fare is also available, including good, strong fresh coffee and baguettes. The **night market** sells Thai dishes.

Mukdahan p390

The best places to eat are along the river.
♥♥ **Enjoy Restaurant**, 7/1 Samut Sakdarak Rd. Bright and cheerful restaurant with Lao specialities, a few Vietnamese dishes and river fish and prawns.
♥♥ **Sky Lounge**, Ploy Palace (see Sleeping, above). Open 1600-0200. Great views over to Laos from this top-floor restaurant-cum-lounge bar. Whisky and live music mixes with Thai food, steaks and Isaan grub. Recommended.
♥ **Phai Rim Khong** (Riverside), Samran Chai Khong Rd, south of town. Good Thai dishes in attractive location with good views.
♥ **River View**, Samran Chai Khong Rd. Chalet-style restaurant with tables overlooking Mekong, average Thai and Lao food, spectacular setting.

Bakeries

Bakery, opposite Ploy Palace Hotel. Good cakes, coffee and ice cream.
Phit Bakery, 709 Phithak Santirat. Good breakfasts, coffee, cakes and ice creams, friendly. Recommended.

Foodstalls

There's a night market on Song Nang Sathit Rd, near the bus station. Best place for cheap Isaan dishes and Vietnamese stall food.

◑ Bars and clubs

Nong Khai p383, map p384

There is a nascent sex tourism scene developing in Nong Khai and some places seem to get periodically taken over by bargirls.

Gaia, located on Nagarina restaurant boat (see Eating, above) and attached to the Mut Mee Guesthouse (see Sleeping, above). Open 1700 till late. This is a genuine travellers' bar. Live music, beer and cocktails.

Surreal, Rim Khong Rd. Opening times vary but usually 1200-late. Cool little riverside bar, playing good sounds and serving up Western-style snacks. Popular with both Thai students and *farang* travellers, also has a free pool table, comfy seating and a terrace. Good hang-out spot. Recommended.

Thasadej Cafe, 387/3 Soi Thepbanterng, T042-412075. Open 0830-0100, food all day till 2300. A fun place to go, very clean with a good selection of spirits and draft beer. Free coffee refills, under friendly German management.

Warm Up, Rimkhong Rd. A small bar selling beer, playing good tunes and offering decent bar snacks. It has a terrace overlooking the river and nice relaxed lounge vibe.

Winner Pub, Prachak Rd. Open 2100-0100. Live easy listening or pop music, the place to go if you want a night out. Also serves a selection of traditional Thai food.

⊛ Festivals and events

Nong Khai *p383, map p384*
Mar (2nd week) Nong Khai Show.
May (2nd week) Rocket Festival (*Bun bang fai*). See page 358.
Jul Candle Festival (the beginning of the Buddhist Lent or Khao Phansa). See Ubon Ratchathani, page 358.
Oct (movable) Boat races on the Mekong. Naga-powered canoes with up to 40 oarsmen race along the river, with a great deal of cheering and drinking from the onlookers that line the bank.

Nakhon Phanom *p387, map p388*
Oct (9-13th, end of Buddhist Lent) Ok Phansa. 4-day celebrations with long-boat races, and the launching of illuminated boats onto the Mekong.

Sakhon Nakhon *p388*
Oct Wax Castle Ceremony, celebrated at Ok Phansa (the end of the Buddhist lent), when elaborate and intricately detailed models of wats are moulded out of bees-wax in order to gain merit. Images of the Buddha are placed inside these temporary edifices, and they are paraded through town accompanied by northeastern music, singing and dancing. Boat races take place at Nong Han Lake at the same time.

That Phanom *p389*
Jan/Feb (full moon) Phra That Phanom Chedi Homage-paying Fair, the northeast's largest temple fair, when thousands of pilgrims converge on the wat and walk around the *chedi* in homage. Dancing, bands and other entertainments; perhaps the most vivid display of northeastern regional identity. The entire town is engulfed by market stalls, selling a vast array of goods for the week of the festival, day and night.

○ Shopping

Nong Khai *p383, map p384*
The best area to browse is down Rim Khong Rd, which runs along the riverbank. Here, northeastern and Lao handicrafts are sold together with Chinese, Soviet and East European goods. It is possible to come away with a (former) Soviet military watch, an Isaan axe pillow, and 'French' sandalwood soap made in Laos.

Village Weaver Handicrafts, 1151 Soi Chitapanya, Prachak Rd, T042-411236, village@udon.ksc.co.th. This outlet sells cloth, in particular *mut mee*, produced by a self-help project, which aims to provide women with an income-earning activity and so prevent the city-ward drift of young people. Better quality than those along the riverbank.

Hornbill Bookshop, near the Mut Mee Guesthouse, is an excellent bookshop and book exchange. It also has email and fax.

Mukdahan p390
Antiques

Sa-aat, 77 Samut Sakdarak Rd. Small collection of antiques for sale including Chinese ceramics, old irons, Buddhist alms bowls and amulets.

Handicrafts

Mukdahan is a good place to buy Lao or Isaan handicrafts like baskets, axe cushions and textiles. Cloth is sold in phuns; a sarong length is normally 2 phuns with cotton cloth costing ฿100 per phun and silk several times more. The textiles with the elephant motif are distinctively Lao, although much of the cloth is now woven in Thailand. Textiles and other handicrafts can be bought in the daily Talaat Indochine riverside market (see page 390). There are also permanent shops on Samut Sakdarak Rd.

▲ Activities and tours

Nong Khai p383, map p384
River tours with dinner

The **Mut Mee Guesthouse** run Morning Pearl boats at 1700 just outside Mut Mee – price ฿100 for the 1-hr cruise. Food can be ordered before you set sail.

Therapies

Alternative Centre, next to the **Mut Mee Guesthouse** on Kaeo Worawut Rd. Daily yoga sessions; reiki, t'ai chi and astrology readings are some of the courses on offer.
Massage Excellent traditional massage centre on Meechai Rd, opposite Nong Khai general hospital. There's also highly skilled massage available with **Sarama Massage** (contact via Mut Mee or by mobile T08-962 2455), who offer a ฿500 endless massage designed to end when all your knots have been smoothed out.

Tour operators

There are plenty of bog-standard tour operators to be found along Meechai

or Prachak roads – **Rapport Travel Services** have a good reputation.

Voluntary work/holidays

Nong Khai is also home to the **Open Mind**, 1039/3 Kaeworawut Rd, who run non-profit programmes for volunteer workers in several eco, fairtrade tourism projects in Thailand and Laos. As well as working in the local community you are expected to pay a fee (€350 per month) to cover rent and food. This is so that the projects are financed without the intrusion of big business or government sponsorship. Highly recommended.

Mukdahan p390
Tour operators

There are 4 small tour offices opposite Wat Si Mongkhon Tai, at the north end of Samran Chai Khong Rd: **TAR Tour**, **Mukdahan Tour (Thailand)**, **Sompong Tour** and **Sakonpasa Department Store**. They are mainly oriented towards Thai tourists travelling to Laos and Vietnam. However, now that non-Thais can cross the border into Laos at this point, they have branched into providing services for *farangs*. Visa services and tours to Laos available.

⊙ Transport

Nong Khai p383, map p384
Air

The nearest airport is in Udon Thani and a shuttle bus takes passengers there.

   Airline offices THAI, 453 Prachak Rd, T042-2202530. **Air Asia** also fly to Udon, www.airasia.com.

Bicycle

Hire from **Mut Mee Guesthouse**, see Sleeping, above.

Bus

Regular connections with **Bangkok**'s Northeastern bus terminal (9-11 hrs) and **Khon Kaen**, **Udon Thani** and other northeastern towns. There is also a service to **Rayong** on the eastern seaboard. There are several direct buses to **Vientiane** – see box page 361, for Laos visa details.

VIP buses for Bangkok leave from 745 Prachak Rd. A/c buses from the corner of Haisok and Prachak roads. A/c buses also depart from the BKS station.

Motorcycle
Hire from the **International Meeting Place**, 1117 Soi Chuanjit, ฿200 per day, and from opposite the entrance to Mut Mee Guesthouse.

Train
Regular connections with **Bangkok**'s Hualamphong station (11 hrs) and all stops northeast: **Ayutthaya**, **Saraburi**, **Korat**, **Khon Kaen** and **Udon**.

Tuk-tuk
Note that tuk-tuk drivers have taken to hounding *farangs* and charging exorbitant rates for journeys. For example, don't pay more than ฿50 to get to or from the bridge. There is a small tuk-tuk rank next to the temple, on the riverbank, next door to the side entrance of **Mut Mee** – they have a price list in English displayed.

Also try looking for tuk-tuks hosting adverts for **Mut Mee Guesthouse** – they are part of a voluntary scheme to charge *farang* a fair rate. In the unlikely event you get ripped off by one, report them to **Mut Mee**.

Nakhon Phanom *p387, map p388*
Air
Daily connections on THAI with **Bangkok**.

Boat
Foreigners can cross the Mekong to Laos using a ferry service.

Bus
The station for local buses and *songthaews* is near the market, opposite the **Nakhon Phanom Hotel**. There is another bus terminal

2 km southwest of town. Buses to **That Phanom** come back into town at the southern clock tower and then head south. Connections with **Nong Khai** and **Sakhon Nakhon**. Tour buses running south to **Ubon** leave every 2 hrs during the day from near the **Windsor Hotel** (4½ hrs).

Songthaew
Songthaews to **That Phanom** leave from the local bus station.

Sakhon Nakhon *p388*
Air
One flight a day on THAI to **Bangkok**.
   Airline offices THAI, 1446 Yuwa Phattana Rd, T042-712259.

Bus
Regular connections with **Bangkok**'s Northeastern bus terminal (11 hrs) and with other northeastern centres.

That Phanom *p389*
Bus
Regular connections with **Nakhon Phanom**, **Mukdahan**, **Sakhon Nakhon**, **Udon Thani** and **Ubon Ratchatani**. Buses for **Bangkok** leave from the southern end of Chayang-kun Rd.

Mukdahan *p390*
Boat
Ferries to **Savannakhet** and Laos leave from the pier near Wat Si Mongkhon Tai. Foreigners can cross from Thailand to Laos here.

Bus
The bus terminal for non-a/c and some a/c buses to **Ubon**, **Nakhon Phanom**, **That Phanom**, other northeastern towns, and **Bangkok** is at the western end of Song Nang Sathit Rd, about 2 km from the centre (a ฿20 motor *saamlor* ride). A/c buses leave from close to Bangkok Bank on Song Nang Sathit Rd. Buses across the new bridge are in the offing – check when you arrive in Mukdahan or before you travel.

▲ Directory

Nong Khai *p383, map p384*
Banks Bangkok, 374 Sisaket Rd; Krung Thai, 102 Meechai Rd; Thai Farmers, 929 Meechai Rd, are but a few. **Embassies and consulates** The closest Lao consulate is in Khon Kaen, although travel agents in Nong Khai will also arrange visas, for a fee (see Tour operators, above). **Immigration** Sisaket Rd, T042-2202154. **Internet** Hornbill Bookshop has internet connections international phone and fax (F042-460717) available. **Medical services** Hospital: Meechai Rd, T042-220 2504. **Police** Meechai Rd, T042-2202020. **Post office and telephone** Meechai Rd (opposite Soi Prisnee), there is an international telephone office upstairs.

Beung Kan *p387*
Banks There is a Thai Farmers Bank here.

Nakhon Phanom *p387, map p388*
Banks Bangkok, Srithep Rd; Thai Farmers, 439 Aphibarn Bancha Rd. **Immigration** Sunthorn Vichit Rd, T042-51147.

Internet Windsor Hotel (see Sleeping, above) and opposite Grand Hotel. **Medical services** Sunthorn Vichit Rd, T042-511422. **Police** Sunthorn Vichit Rd (northern end). **Post office** Sunthorn Vichit Rd (northern end). **Telephone** Off Fuang Nakhon Rd.

That Phanom *p389*
Banks Thai Military, on the main road into town (Rte 212), north of Wat That Phanom (amongst others). **Immigration** Rachdamnern Rd, by the river, T042-541 090. **Post office** North of the Thai Military Bank. No English spoken here, there is a phone available if you can make yourself understood.

Mukdahan *p390*
Banks Bangkok Bank, Song Nang Sathit Rd; Thai Farmers, Song Nang Sathit Rd. **Immigration** Samran Chai Khong Rd, T042-611074. **Post office** Phithak Santirat Rd (on the roundabout), be prepared for a steep ascent to the front desk.

Contents

Footprint features

Border crossings

Eastern Thailand

At a glance

⊖ **Getting around** Served by trains and buses.

◉ **Time required** 1 week if you don't visit Koh Chang, longer if you find that perfect hammock.

☀ **Weather** Cooler from Nov-Jan. Koh Samet has some of the best year-round conditions.

✖ **When not to go** Some travellers think that there is never a good time to visit gaudy, sinful Pattaya.

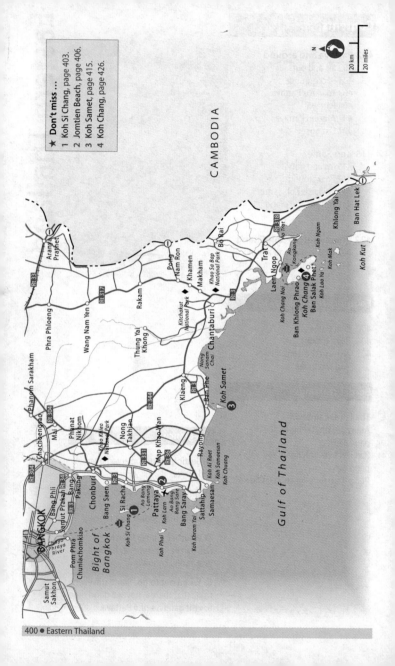

★ Don't miss ...
1 Koh Si Chang, page 403.
2 Jomtien Beach, page 406.
3 Koh Samet, page 415.
4 Koh Chang, page 426.

CAMBODIA

Gulf of Thailand

Bight of Bangkok

Head east from Bangkok into a region that blends trashy gaudiness and gorgeous beaches. Add to the mix some remote forested islands, gem markets and oddball idiosyncrasy and you won't look back.

On the enigmatic island of Koh Si Chang there are weird abandoned palaces, sacred Chinese temples and platoons of monkeys. Next stop is Pattaya. Even a mere utterance of this name sends anti-tourism activists apoplectic. Polluted waters, bad planning and an endless supply of worn-out bargirls clutching, fat, 50-something *farang* men, has done little to endear Pattaya to the more discerning traveller but amid the neon and fleshpots, it has some of the best hotels in the country and there is no better place in Southeast Asia to dig ironic kitsch. A little further east is Koh Samet, a national marine park. Samet used to be a sleepy island surrounded by azure seas and crested with crystalline beaches. These days it has been transformed into the weekend destination of choice for Bangkok's younger, trendier and wealthier crowd – at times it can be seem completely overrun with drunk, Thai students. Chantaburi is worth a stopover for its gem market, traditional architecture and cathedral. As for Koh Chang: the traveller's idyll of isolated, white-sand beaches secreted away from the machinations of contemporary consumer society is quickly disappearing. Parts of the coast are slowly turning into a run of homogenous resorts. Girlie bars and sex tourists are proliferating and prices are rocketing. However, if you look hard enough, there are still some wonderful spots to lounge about in, losing yourself in the alluring sunsets, swimming in the calm, clear waters. Koh Chang's interior is also largely untouched, filled with waterfalls, jungle tracks and a colourful, noisy population of tropical birds and forest beasties.

Pattaya and around

→ Colour map 3, C4.

Brash and brazen, Pattaya ('Southwest wind') is argued by some to be Thailand's premier beach resort, yet only 35 years ago it was a little-known coastal village frequented by fishermen, farmers and a handful of weekenders. There are now two schools of thought: School 1 – it is the type of tourist resort Thailand should be thinking of bulldozing: environmentally unsound, crass, criminal and encourages sex tourism. School 2 – it is a great commercial success: the hotels are well run and very competitive, there is an enormous variety of excellent restaurants, and the sea sports are diverse and professionally managed. Somewhere in the middle is Jomtien – a beach just to the south of Pattaya's main strip where you can find a much more low-key atmosphere, some good accommodation and some nice sand.

Si Racha, with its excellent seafood restaurants, is a stepping stone for Koh Si Chang, an easy weekend getaway for Bangkok residents. The coast after Pattaya – running past the town of Rayong – has been developed into an elongated run of resorts that are aimed at the mass domestic tourist market. The beaches and hotels are decent enough: think of the Costa del Sol and give it an Asian twist. ►► *For listings see pages 407-414.*

Ins and outs

Getting there
Route 3 from Bangkok follows Thailand's eastern seaboard to the Cambodian border. The first 130 km (on Highway 34) are an ugly ribbon of industrial development that takes in once-sleepy Si Racha, now a jump-off point for the nearest island to Bangkok, eccentric Koh Si Chang. Travel a little further and you'll reach the renowned beach resort of Pattaya. There is an airport at U-Tapao, south of Pattaya. This is gradually expanding and is now receiving some international scheduled arrivals. THAI runs a service from the airport to the Royal Cliff Beach Resort, ฿250 and there is also a public bus leaving every two hours, 0700-1700. Pattaya railway station is off the Sukhumvit Highway, 200 m north of the intersection with Central Pattaya Road. ►► *See Transport, page 413, for further information.*

Getting around
Koh Si Chang is visited by taking a boat from Si Racha, they run hourly from daily 0700-1900. Pattaya itself is simple to get around consisting of one long, straight seafront road running the length of the beach (Pattaya Beach Road), linked to another parallel road (Pattaya 2 Road) by innumerable sois packed with bars, restaurants and hotels. Local transport is abundant; *songthaews* run regularly between all the tourist centres and there are also scores of people hiring out bikes, motorbikes and jeeps. *Songthaews* charge ฿5 for short trips around Pattaya Bay (although it is not uncommon for visitors to be charged ฿10), ฿10 between Naklua and Pattaya Beach and ฿20 to Jomtien. To avoid being charged more than the standard fare, present the driver with the correct fare – do not try to negotiate the price, as the driver will expect you to hire the vehicle as a taxi.

Tourist information
TAT ① *382/1 Beach Rd, Pattaya, T038-428750, F038-429113*, has helpful staff and lots of information. There are several free tourist magazines and maps available. For information on Koh Si Chang check out the excellent www.ko-sichang.com.

Background

Pattaya began to metamorphose when the US navy set up shop at the nearby port of Sattahip (40 km further down the coast). As the war in Vietnam escalated, so the influx of GIs on 'R & R' grew and Pattaya responded enthusiastically. Today, it provides around 36,000 hotel rooms and supplies everything you could ever need from a beach holiday – except, arguably, peace and quiet. Given its origins in the Vietnam War, it is hardly surprising that Pattaya's stock in trade is sex tourism and at any one time, about 4000 girls are touting for work around the many bars and restaurants.

While Pattaya's official population is 60,000, there are between 200,000 and 300,000 staying in town at any one time, whether international tourists or migrant workers. This has inevitably led to environmental problems with a lack of water treatment facilities leading to polluted seas and beaches. With the recent opening of good sewerage plants things are now starting to improve and it shouldn't take long for the seas to be as clean here as almost any other place on the Gulf coast.

Pattaya – according to official statements at least – is going out of its way to play down its go-go bar image and promote a 'family' resort profile. This emphasis on wholesome family fun is hard to reconcile with reality. But still the effort continues, with some notable success to the south in Jomtien (see page 406). The busiest and noisiest area is at the southern end of town (South Pattaya or 'The Village'); from about Soi 11 to Soi Post Office (with Pattayaland 1, 2 and 3 being the gay areas of town). There must be one of the highest concentration of bars, discos, massage parlours, prostitutes and transvestites of any place in the world. Many people find this aspect of Pattaya repugnant. However, there is no pretence here – either on the part of the hosts or their guests. This is a beach resort of the most lurid kind.

Pattaya may be infamous in the west as a city of sin, but there is more to the resort than this perception might indicate. It is also popular with watersports lovers: there is sailing, parasailing, windsurfing, ski-boating, snorkelling, deep-sea fishing and scuba-diving.

Towards Pattaya ●❼●● ➠ pp407-414.

Si Racha → Colour map 3, C4.

Si Racha, some 100 km from Bangkok, is home to a famous hot chilli sauce (*nam prik Si Racha*), usually eaten with seafood. The town also has a reputation for its profusion of excellent seafood restaurants; the most enjoyable are built on jetties by the harbour. Westerners usually visit Si Racha in order to reach Koh Si Chang (see below), but the town has character and is worth more than a cursory wander.

A short distance to the north of town, built on a rocky islet, is the gaudy and enjoyable **Sino-Thai Wat**. The monastery commemorates a devout monk and boasts a Buddha footprint as well as an image of the Chinese Goddess of Mercy, Kuan Yin. On Choem-chomphon Road, the waterfront road, almost opposite Soi 16, is the **Jaw Phor Samut Dam** Chinese temple. Up the road towards the clock tower at the southern end is a large covered **market**. Keep an eye out for Si Racha's overpowered, chariot-like motorized *saamlors*.

Koh Si Chang → Colour map 3, C4.

Koh Si Chang is one of those places that had a moment in the spotlight – King Rama V built a palace here – and then history moved on. It does make for an entertaining, idiosyncratic short break and is relatively easy to reach from Bangkok, making it a popular spot for weekenders from the capital. There's Rama V's ruined palace, a popular Chinese temple, a handful of reasonable beaches and, like Si Racha, some truly stupendous motorized *saamlors*. There are a number of massive motorized *saamlors* and, given the state of the roads, they must be among the most overpowered taxis in the world. A tour of all the sights should be no more than ฿200 – in chariot-like splendour (the owner of No 38, Nerng, speaks reasonable English and distributes free maps).

Koh Si Chang used to be the trans-shipment point for both cargo and passenger vessels before the Chao Phraya River was dredged sufficiently to allow ships to reach Bangkok. Even though many vessels now bypass Si Racha, the surrounding water is still chock-a-block with ships at anchor (normally about 50, but sometimes as many as 100 ships), their cargoes being unloaded into smaller lighters and barges. The island's main trade is now as a service base for the freighter crews. Their visas often do not allow them to disembark, so all R & R is taken to them by the varied residents of Koh Si Chang. The island also has a reputation as a sanctuary for criminals. The drugs trade is reportedly rife and corruption within the police force endemic. This activity shouldn't impact on travellers.

At the northern edge of the town, set up on a hill overlooking the town, is **Chaw Por Khaw Yai**, a Chinese temple. From its assortment of decorated shrines and caves there are great views of the island and town. It's a very important temple for Thailand's Chinese community and particularly popular at Chinese New Year when over 5000 people visit the shrine each evening, doubling the island's population. Not far away to the south, and overlooking the town, is a **Buddhist retreat** set among limestone caves. A large, yellow-seated Buddha image looks out over the bay. On the east coast, south of the retreat, are the **ruins of a palace** built by Rama V. It was abandoned in 1893 when the French took control of the island during a confrontation with the Thais. Not much remains – most of the structure was dismantled and rebuilt in Bangkok. Rather eerie stairways, balustrades and an empty reservoir remain scattered across the rocky hillside. The only remaining building of any size is **Wat Atsadangnimit** ① *0800-1800,* a revered monastery that still attracts a surprising number of pilgrims largely because King Chulalongkorn used to meditate here.

The island also has a number of **beaches** with reasonable swimming and snorkelling. The quietest beach with the best coral and swimming is **Tham Phang** on the western side of the island; easier to reach are **Tha Wang** (next to the palace) – a rocky beach and not suitable for swimming – and **Hat Sai Kaew** (over the hill from the palace). While it is possible to swim, note that at certain times of year the currents can wash all sorts of rubbish onto the beach. There are plans to build a nature trail from Tham Phang to Si Phitsanu Bungalows.

Pattaya ○○○○○▲○○ ➤➤ *pp407-414. Colour map 3, C4.*

There are few sights in Pattaya, though most visitors do make their way to the **Big Buddha** on the hill at the southern end of the beach. There are good views over the resort from the vantage point and the monks based here are usually willing to talk to interested visitors. The main Buddha image is surrounded by smaller images representing each day of the week.

The infamous **Walking Street**, is where you'll find the highest concentration of bars, brothels, pole-dancers, ladyboys, drunken sexpats, street robberies and bad food, and it is

Pattaya

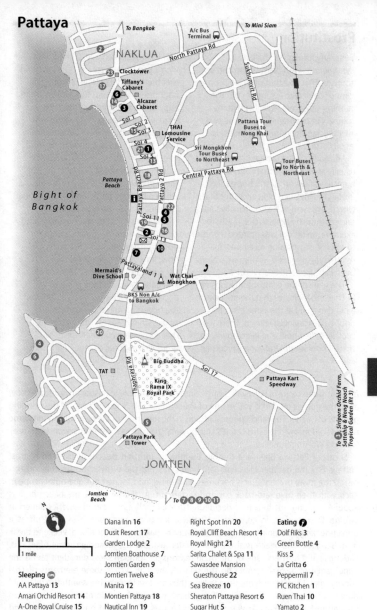

To Bangkok
To Mini Siam
A/c Bus Terminal

NAKLUA

North Pattaya Rd

Clocktower
Tiffany's Cabaret
Alcazar Cabaret

Soi 1
Soi 2
Soi 3
THAI Limousine Service
Soi 4
Soi 5

Pattana Tour Buses to Nong Khai

Sri Mongkhon Tour Buses to Northeast

Tour Buses to North & Northeast

Pattaya Beach

Pattaya Beach Rd
Pattaya 2 Rd

Central Pattaya Rd

Bight of Bangkok

Soi 11
Soi 13

Pattayaland 1

Mermaid's Dive School

Wat Chai Mongkhon

BKS Non A/c to Bangkok

TAT

Big Buddha
King Rama IX Royal Park

Soi 17

Pattaya Kart Speedway

To Sriporn Orchid Farm, Sattahip & Nong Nooch Tropical Garden (Rt 3)

Pattaya Park Tower

JOMTIEN

Jomtien Beach

To 7 8 9 10 11

N

1 km
1 mile

Sleeping
AA Pattaya **13**
Amari Orchid Resort **14**
A-One Royal Cruise **15**
Birds & Bees Resort **1**

Diana Inn **16**
Dusit Resort **17**
Garden Lodge **2**
Jomtien Boathouse **7**
Jomtien Garden **9**
Jomtien Twelve **8**
Manita **12**
Montien Pattaya **18**
Nautical Inn **19**
Ocean Marina Yacht Club **3**

Right Spot Inn **20**
Royal Cliff Beach Resort **4**
Royal Night **21**
Sarita Chalet & Spa **11**
Sawasdee Mansion
  Guesthouse **22**
Sea Breeze **10**
Sheraton Pattaya Resort **6**
Sugar Hut **5**
Woodlands Resort **23**

Eating
Dolf Riks **3**
Green Bottle **4**
Kiss **5**
La Gritta **6**
Peppermill **7**
PIC Kitchen **1**
Ruen Thai **10**
Yamato **2**

Prostitution

For many foreigners Thailand is synonymous with prostitution and sex tourism. That prostitution is big business cannot be denied: estimates put the number of women employed in the industry at between 120,000 and two million, and the number of brothels at 60,000.

Although the growth of prostitution is usually associated with the arrival of large numbers of GIs on 'Rest & Recreation' during the Vietnam War, and after that with the growth of sex tourism, it is an ancient industry here. In the 1680s, for example, an official was granted a licence to run the prostitution monopoly in Ayutthaya, using 600 women who had been captured and enslaved.

The scale of the prostitution industry in Thailand indicates that the police turn a blind eye and at the same time, no doubt, gain financial reward. There is a brothel or 'tea house' in every town, no matter how small. One survey recorded that 95% of all men over 21 had slept with a prostitute. Some people maintain that the subordinate role of women in Buddhism means that there is less stigma attached to becoming a prostitute. In some villages, having a daughter who has 'gone south', as it is euphemistically termed, is viewed as a good thing. Asia Watch belives there is "clear evidence of direct involvement in every stage of the trafficking process". There are also women working in the trade from Yunnan (South China), Laos and Cambodia.

Prime Minister Chuan Leepkai tried to clean up the prostitution business and put some new laws on the books: it is now, for example, illegal for men to have sex with girls aged under 18 years old, and parents selling their children will also face prosecution. The problem for the government is that prostitution is so ingrained into the Thai way of life that combating commercial sex work requires a national change of attitude.

now considered one of Pattaya's 'sights'. Some might be able to raise at an ironic eyebrow at all the goings on and if you're one of them, make sure you don't forget the grinding poverty of Isaan – Thailand's poorest region in the northeast of the country and the home to most of Pattaya's prostitutes. It's this poverty that drives most of the women to seek work on Walking Street.

South of Pattaya Bay, past the Big Buddha, is **Jomtien Beach**. At the end nearest Pattaya Bay the gaudier elements still hold sway but the further you head along this beach the more presentable it becomes. Charming, mid-range boutique hotels appear, each with their own laid-back bar and restaurant. At the far end – the beach here is about 4 km long – it becomes decidedly tranquil with a number of eateries aimed at visiting Thai tourists. In contrast to Pattaya, Jomtien could even pass itself off as a bona fide family destination and would certainly make a good spot for a weekend break from Bangkok. The beach is also much quieter, without the tiresome throng of jet skis, wideboys and hustlers. One of the main reasons for Jomtien's less decadent feel is the appearance of a small temple on the beachfront road. While some elements of Thai society may struggle with man-made laws they are less likely to mess with the rules laid down in the spiritual dimension. If you have time while on Jomtien, take a trip up the 240-m **Pattaya Park Tower** ① *T038-251201, ฿200*, situated on the headland and providing spectacular views of the surrounding area.

Pattaya Beach is the central sweep on the main seafront, **Naklua** is further north. This is the quieter end of town, although it still has its fair share of clubs and bars. Both Pattaya Beach and Naklua are pretty similar – a long run of high-rise concrete, interspersed with go-go bars and eateries. Both beaches have a long narrow run of sand, backing onto a promenade and main road, and are overrun with beach brollies.

The **Siriporn Orchid Farm** ① *235/14 Moo 5, Tambon Nong Prue, T038-429013, 0800-1700, ฿10*, displays an array of orchids (some are for sale).

Mini Siam ① *T038-421628, 0700-2200*, is a cultural and historical park where 80 of Thailand's most famous 'sights' – including Wat Phra Kaeo and the Bridge over the River Kwai – are recreated at a scale of 1:25. The park lies 3 km north of Pattaya Beach, on the Sukhumvit Highway (Route 3) at the Km 143 marker.

The **Nong Nooch Tropical Garden** ① *T038-42932, 0900-1800, ฿20, ฿200 for the cultural show, or take a tour from Pattaya for ฿250, T038-238063*, is a 200-ha park containing immaculate gardens with lakes (and boating), an orchid farm, family zoo, Thai handicraft demonstrations and a thrice-daily (1015, 1500 and 1545) 'cultural spectacular' with Thai dancing, Thai boxing and an elephant show. The garden is 15 minutes from Pattaya town, 3 km off the main road, at the Km 163 marker.

Around Pattaya ●●● ➤ *pp407-414.*

Koh Larn → *Colour map 3, C4.*

① *Tickets from the booth next to the Sailing Club. Boats leave at 0930 and 1130, returning at 1600 (45 mins, ฿250). Boats can be chartered for ฿1500 per day. A shared sailing junk ฿250 (inclusive of lunch and coral reef viewing), or a chartered sailing junk costs ฿3000 per day.* When Pattaya gets too much, many people retire to one of the offshore islands for rest and recreation. The largest island (and the only one with accommodation) is Koh Larn, which has good snorkelling and scuba-diving. Glass-bottomed boats are available for touring the reef and the island even has an 18-hole golf course.

Rayong → *Colour map 3, C5.*

Rayong makes an alternative stop-off point to Pattaya if you want a rest while travelling to the eastern reaches of Thailand. Apart from a passable beach and some decent seafood, there's little to keep you occupied.

◉ Pattaya and around listings

For Sleeping and Eating price codes and other relevant information, see pages 44-49.

● Sleeping

Si Racha *p403*

Like Si Racha's restaurants, the town's most atmospheric hotels are built on extended jetties on the waterfront – many are well run and clean with attached restaurants.

A-E Laemthong Residence Hotel, 135/9 Sukhumvit Rd, T038-322886, F312651. A/c,

restaurant, pool, tennis. Modern hotel lacking the character of the others listed here, but the closest thing to a starred establishment. Central location.

D-E Grand Bungalow, 9 Choemchomphon Soi 18, south end of town, T038-311079. A range of bungalows built off a jetty. Better for larger groups or families rather than couples.

E-G Bungalow Sri Wattana, 35 Choemchomphon Rd, Soi 8, T038-311037. Wooden hotel constructed on a jetty, friendly and clean with great atmosphere and enthusiastic service. Good restaurant attached.

E-G Sri Wichai, 38 Choemchomphon Rd, Soi 8, T038-311212. Wooden hotel, much like the **Sri Wattana**, just a shade pricier. Friendly, good attached restaurant, clean and classy. Recommended.

F Samchai, 3 Choemchomphon Rd, Soi 10, T038-311800. Some a/c, wooden hotel, clean rooms, good atmosphere, great food.

Koh Si Chang *p403*

Camping is possible, but bring your own equipment; at weekends Thais from the mainland camp in large numbers.

B-D Rim Talay, 250 m north of entrance to Rama V Palace, T038-216116. Mix of rooms and eccentric bungalow/barge affairs (up to 7 people can sleep in 1) that come complete with seaviews. All rooms have TV, a/c and are en suite. Cheapest rooms have cold water only.

B-F Tew Phai, 8 Moo 2 Thewawong Rd, T038-216084, T08-1947 0573 (mob). Some a/c, restaurant (pricey), and welcoming management.

C House of Dreams, back road 200 m before **Pan and David**'s restaurant (see Eating, below), T08-4348 8317 (mob). A 2-bedroom homestay in a brand new property. The larger room has a balcony and bathtub, both have en suite facilities, TV and a/c. Excellent views across the sea to the mainland and friendly English-speaking owners make this one of the nicest spots to stay on the island. Recommended, though book ahead.

C-D Sichang View Resort, west coast of the island, T038-216210. Great location, set along the Khao Khaad cliffs in a remote corner of the island. The nice gardens make great spot for sundowners and the huge rooms are well kept, with en suite facilities, a/c and TVs. Good food in the restuarant.

C-E Si Chang Palace, 81 Atsadang Rd, T038-216276. A/c, restaurant, pool. This hideous building seems very out of place and is overpriced. Its redeeming feature is that is has great views (and a pool).

C-E Sripitsanu Bungalows, Hat Tham, T038-216024. Bungalow operation that is built into the cliff-face overlooking the sea. Range of rooms and bungalows available not far from Hat Tham. Little English spoken.

E Benz, T038-216091. Some a/c, unusual stone bungalows, clean and well kept, close to the sea.

Pattaya *p404, map p405*

The high season is Nov-Mar. Pattaya has the largest selection of hotels outside Bangkok and, while there is little for the budget traveller (rooms start at ฿350), there are some excellent-value mid-range places.

There are 3 distinct areas of accommodation. At the northern end of the beach is Naklua. Pattaya Beach, busier and noisier with the bulk of the cheaper accommodation, is at the southern end of the beach. Jomtien, to the south, has a better beach, less nightlife and is certainly more relaxed.

All **A** accommodation has a/c, restaurant, pool, and prices are exclusive of tax. Except at weekends and high season, rates should be reduced. Check out hotels on www.hotel thailand.com/pattaya/.

Jomtien

LL-L Royal Cliff Beach Resort, 353 Moo 12 Pratamnak Rd, South Pattaya, T038-250421, www.royalcliff.co.th. A/c, restaurants, pool, every imaginable facility. A favourite with conference and incentive groups. Set high up on the south end of the beach.

LL-L Sugar Hut, 391/18 Thaphraya Rd, T038-251686, F251689. A/c, restaurant, 2 pools, overgrown gardens with rabbits and peacocks. Thai-style bungalows not on the beach, but in very attractive grounds. Recommended.

LL-AL Ocean Marina Yacht Club, 274/1-9 Moo 4, Sukhumvit Highway, T038-237310, F237325, www.oceanmarinayachtclub.com. Massive high-rise hotel linked to the marina. With choice of restaurants, tennis and squash courts, fitness centre, 25-m pool. Extensive business facilities.

LL-AL Sheraton Pattaya Resort, 437 Phra Tamnak Rd, T038-259888, www.sheraton. com/pattaya. Superbluxury resort next to the **Royal Cliff**. Great breezy location perched up on the cliffs adds to the stunning rooms and bungalows. Possibly the best luxury resort in town. Fantastic spa, bar and restuarants. Recommended

LL-A Birds and Bees Resort, 366/11 Moo 12 Phra Tamnak Rd, T038-250556, www.cab bagesandcondoms.co.th. Wonderful resort with pool, gardens, children's play area and awesome cliff-top location – a path leads to a secluded beach. Run by the Cabbages and Condoms not-for-profit AIDs awareness organization that has a restaurant in Bangkok, this resort is irreverent with subversive flourishes (check out the paths to Communism and Capitalism that both end up in the same place – by a pond filled with frantic, hungry fish which are called 'Greedy Politicians') and some real charm. It is slightly pricey, though rooms are cheaper in low-season. The suites offer best value with balcony jacuzzis and sea-views. Highly recommended.

L-B Sarita Chalet ad Spa, 279/373 Jomtien Beach Rd, T038-233952, www.saritachalet. com. Relaxed, professional small hotel in nice part of Jomtien. Stylish rooms, all en-suite, with a/c and TV. There's a small pool and spa. Some rooms face the beach. Often booked out. Breakfast included. Recommended.

A-B Sea Breeze, 347/5 Jomtien Beach Rd. T038-231056, www.seabreezehotelpattaya. com. Decent enough hotel set back a little from the beach road. Rooms are clean and simple, with en suite, TV and a/c. There are a couple of pools and breakfast is included.

B-C Jomtien Garden Hotel and Resort, 31/71 Moo 12, Jomtien Beach Rd, T038-756523, www.jomtiengarden.com. Friendly, family orientated resort with pool, spa and other facilities. Rooms have en suite facilities, a/c and TV but could do with freshening up – they look a bit tired.

B-C Jomtien Twelve, 240/13 Moo 12, Jomtien Beach Rd. T038-756865, www.jomtientwelve.com. Brand new,

great little hotel right on the beach road in a very quiet part of Jomtien – perfect for a short weekend break. All rooms are well designed with nice touches and an eye for the aesthetic. En suite facilities, cable TV and a/c. The rooms at the front have decent-sized beach-facing balconies. Breakfast included. Best deal on this stretch of beach. Recommended.

C-D Jomtien Boathouse, 380/5-6 Jomtien Beach Rd, T038-756143, www.jomtien-boathouse.com. Great budget option located in lively part of Jomtien. Rooms at the front have balconies and all have TV, a/c and are en suite. The bar downstairs can be a bit noisy – bring earplugs.

Pattaya Beach

LL-A Amari Orchid Resort, 240 Moo 5 Beach Rd, North Pattaya, T038-428161, www.amari.com. A/c, restaurants, Olympic-sized pool, tennis, mini golf, watersports. 230-room hotel on a tranquil, 4-ha plot of lush gardens at the northern end of the beach, away from most of the bars and discos.

LL-A Montien Pattaya, 369 Moo 9 Beach Rd, T038-428155, www.montien.com. Central location, extensive gardens, excellent hotel, despite its age and size. Good value.

L-A Dusit Resort, 240/2 Beach Rd (north end), T038-425611, www.dusit.com. Excellent hotel with 474 rooms, good service and all facilities. Health club, tennis, squash courts, children's pools, table tennis and a games room, watersports, shopping arcade, and a disco.

AL-A A-One Royal Cruise, 499 Beach Rd, near Soi 2, T038-259500, www.hotelthailand. com/pattaya/theroyalcruise/. Novel design – the hotel looks like a cruise liner – rooms (or 'cabins') are average though rates good.

A-B Manita, T038-489490, www.manita hotel.com. Slightly pretentious though friendly small 'designer' hotel set in a strange location just down the hill from the main TAT office overlooking an overpass. Rooms are nice enough with flat screen TVs, a/c and pleasing bathrooms – there's also a garden and a pool.

C-D Nautical Inn, 10 Moo 10 Beach Rd, T038-428110, F038-428116. A/c, restaurant, pool, rather dated, low-rise hotel in the centre of town but has more character than most.

C-E AA Pattaya, 182 Beach Rd and Pattaya 2 Rd, T038-420894, F038-429057. In the midst of bar-land, attractive 4th-floor pool, well-equipped rooms. Recommended.

D-E Diana Inn, 216/6-9 Pattaya 2 Rd, between Sois 11 and 12, T038-429675, F038-424566, www.dianapattaya.co.th. A/c, restaurant, pool, on busy road but rooms have good facilities for price, modern, well run, friendly and popular. Recommended.

F Right Spot Inn, 583 Beach Rd, South Pattaya, T038-429629. Clean and quiet, with an excellent restaurant.

F Royal Night Hotel-bungalow, 362/9 Pattaya Beach, Soi 5, T038-428735. Quiet hotel halfway down Soi 5. Small shaded pool, good rooms, hot water, popular.

F-G Sawasdee MansionGuesthouse, 502/1 Pattaya 2 Rd, Soi 10, T038-425360. Some a/c, one of the cheapest places in town in a high-rise block down a built-up soi, but the decent rooms are clean.

Naklua

LL-A Woodlands Resort, 164/1 Pattaya–Naklua Rd, T038-421707, F425663 www.woodland-resort.com. On the edge of Pattaya and Naklua. Has tried to recreate a colonial lodge-type atmosphere. Quiet, leafy and airy with pool and landscaped gardens.

D Garden Lodge, 170 Moo 5 Naklua Rd, T038-429109, F421221, www.gardenlodge pattaya.com. A/c, pool, bungalow rooms looking onto gardens, quiet and excellent value. Recommended.

Koh Larn p407

E Koh Larn Resort, Pattaya office at 183 Soi Post Office, T08-1996 3942 (mob). Decent bungalows set alongside a nice beach, price includes the boat fare and transfer

to the bungalows. Watch out for annoying jet-skiers.

Rayong p407

Resort and bungalow developments line the coast from Rayong to Ban Phe. Few foreigners stay here – these resorts are geared to Thais.

AL-B Kanary Bay, 50 Beach Rd, Muang T038-804844, www.kanarybay.com. A few kilometres west of Rayong facing the beach. Well-run, serviced apartments, good for long-term stay or lazy weekends. A/c cable TV, pool, Italian and Thai restaurant.

C-D Rayong President Hotel, T038-611307, in an alley just of Sukhumvit Rd near Rayong bus station. Quiet and simple rooms.

● Eating

Si Racha p403

Si Racha is known for its excellent seafood. Mussels and oysters are good, and many of the dishes come with Si Racha's famed chilli sauce. The town is now famous for its large Japanese community and there are a huge number of Japanese restaurants in and around Nakhorn Rd 3.

Ⅲ Cherinot, Choemchomphon Rd, Soi 14 (pier). Superb seafood – watch your catch come in from the pier location.

Ⅲ Chua Li, Choemchomphon Soi 10. Most expensive of the seafood restaurants in town with an established, and well-deserved reputation for quality victuals.

Ⅲ Hua Huat, 102 Choemchomphon Rd. More delicious seafood.

Ⅲ Jaw Sii, 98 Choemchomphon Rd. Incredibly fresh seafood at this great restaurant.

Ⅲ Si Racha Seafood, Choemchomphon Rd (near the bus stop). Large array of Thai-style seafood.

Koh Si Chang p403

Ⅲ-Ⅰ Pan and David, 167 Asdang Road, 200 m before Rama V Palace, next to

Marine Police, T038-216 075. Mon-Fri 1100-2130, Sat and holidays 08302200, Sun 0830-2030. Reservations recommended at the weekends. Fantastic place to eat, run by long-term Si Chang residents. Pan cooks up superb steaks, Isaan grub and fresh seafood. David is an American expat who can tell you pretty much anything you need to know about Si Chang. Highly recommended.

† **Lek Naa Wang** and **Noi**, beside the road to the palace, a 10-min walk out of town. These are famed for serving up the island's best seafood.

† **Si Chang Palace Coffee Shop**, at the palace. An a/c refuge offering a range of coffee and cakes.

Pattaya p404, map p405

Pattaya has the greatest choice of international cuisine outside Bangkok. By Thai standards prices tend to be high. The best seafood is on Jomtien Beach or at the southern end of Pattaya Beach.

††† **Buccaneer**, Beach Rd. Seafood and steaks in rooftop restaurant above the **Nipa Lodge**.

††† **Dolf Riks**, Regent Marina Complex. Speciality Indonesian, some international, one of the original Pattaya restaurants.

††† **Empress**, Dusit Resort. Large Chinese restaurant overlooking Pattaya Bay. Good dim sum lunches.

††† **Green Bottle**, Pattaya 2 Rd. Ersatz English pub with exposed 'beams', grills, seafood.

††† **La Gritta**, Beach Rd. Some people maintain this restaurant serves the best Italian in town. Pizzas, pasta dishes and seafood specialities.

††† **Lobster Pot**, 228 Beach Rd, South Pattaya. On a pier, known for very fresh seafood.

††† **Mex**, at **Sheraton**, see Sleeping, above. Mon-Sat 1830-2230. This is an excellent restaurant and quite possibly one of the best hotel diners in the country. Playful blends of tastes, textures and aromas – from Asia and beyond – are accompanied by an eye for the finest and freshest ingredients available. Pricey but this is somewhere really worth the splurge.

††† **Peppermill**, 16 Beach Rd, near Soi Post Office. First-class French food.

††† **PIC Kitchen**, Soi 5. 4 traditional Thai pavilions, Thai classical dancing in garden compound, good food. Recommended.

††† **Ruen Thai**, Pattaya 2 Rd, opposite Soi Post Office. Very good Thai food and not excessively overpriced. Recommended.

††† **Yamato**, Pattaya Beach Soi 13. Japanese sushi bar (฿100), also serves sukiyaki, sashimi and tempura, all excellent.

†††-†† **Jomtien Twelve**, see Sleeping, above. Good spot to stop for coffee, breakfast, lunch and dinner. Cocktails and beer.

†† **Dream Bakery**, 485/3 Pattaya 2 Rd. English breakfasts and Thai food.

†† **Italiano Espresso**, 325/1 Beach Rd. Traditional Italian food and some Thai dishes.

†† **Kiss**, Pattaya 2 Rd, between sois 11 and 12, next to **Diana Inn**. Good range of Western and Thai food at low prices. An excellent place to watch the world go by.

†† **Nang Nual**, 214/10 Beach Rd, South Pattaya, on the waterfront. Recommended for seafood. There is another **Nang Nual** restaurant in Jomtien).

† **Aussie Ken's Toast Shop**, 205/31 Pattaya 2 Rd. Fish and chips, sandwiches, cheap beer.

◑ Bars and clubs

Pattaya p404, map p405

The majority of Pattaya's bars are concentrated at the south end of the beach, between Beach Rd and Pattaya 2 Rd. They are mostly open-air and lined with stools. The men-only bars are around Pattayaland Soi 3, and the karaoke bars are along Pattaya 2 Rd.

Jomtien Boathouse, see Sleeping, above. You'll find a highly amusing Elvis impersonator performing twice a week (call for details) at this well-run Jomtien bar. Also have a giant screen for sports.

Latitude Lounge, at Sheraton, see Sleeping, above. Get away from the Beach Rd and head to this very relaxed, cool, bar-cum-lounge. Beautifully designed and in a breezy location, spend all evening here supping cocktails, the contemporary sounds add to the ambience.

🎭 Entertainment

Pattaya *p404, map p405*
Pattaya comes to life as dusk approaches – it is a beach version of Bangkok's Patpong. Music blares out from the bars, discos and massage parlours, which are concentrated in South Pattaya, referred to as 'The Strip'.

Cabaret
Mostly performed by members of Pattaya's legendary *ka-toey* (transexual) population, a night at the cabaret is essential. The biggest and best are **Alcazar** and **Tiffany's**, both found on the northern end of Pattaya 2 Rd. Shows at Tiffany's are daily at 1900, 2030 and 2200, T038-429642 for reservations – prices starts at ฿400. (There's also a gun range in the basement at Tiffany's – from ฿200 – should you want to arm yourself after the show.)

Traditional Thai dance
PIC Kitchen, Soi 5. Wed 1930, ฿100;
Ruen Thai, Pattaya 2 Rd, opposite Soi PO.
Recommended. ฿120.

🛍 Shopping

Pattaya *p404, map p405*
There are hundreds of stalls and shops on Pattaya 2 Rd selling jewellery, fashion, handicrafts, leather goods, silk, and a good selection of shopping plazas where most Western goods can be purchased. In the evenings South Pattaya Rd is closed to traffic.

🔺 Activities and tours

Pattaya *p404, map p405*
Prices, times and locations of sport activities in and around Pattaya are listed in the free magazines that are available all over the city. In addition to the watersports listed in more detail below, the following are on offer: badminton, bowling, bungee jumping, fishing, fitness, golf, go-karting, helicopter rides, motor racing, paintball, parasailing, horse riding, sailing, shooting, snooker, speedboat hire, squash, swimming, tennis, waterskiing and windsurfing.

Diving and snorkelling
A lot of work has been done to revitalize Pattaya's diving – dynamite fishing has been outlawed and coral beds protected. Marine life, after years of degrading, is slowly returning to normal with stunning coral, sea turtles, rays and angelfish all making an appearance. There are even a couple of wrecks within easy reach as well as the best dive schools in the country. This makes Pattaya an excellent place to learn to dive. There are more than 10 dive shops here.

Snorkelling day trips to the offshore islands can be organized through the dive shops.
Seafari, Soi 12, opposite Lek Hotel, T038-429060, www.seafari.co.th. A 5-star PADI resort. A PADI Open Water course costs ฿14,000, including all equipment (except course manuals), dives and boat fees. Certified divers can do a day's diving (all equipment, 2 dives, boat fees, lunch and soft drinks) to the nearby islands and wrecks for ฿3200. Recommended.

Other operators include **Aquanauts**, 437/17 Soi Yodsak, T038-361724, aquanautsdive.com; **Dave's Divers Den**, Pattaya-Naklua Rd, T038-420411 (NAUI); and **Mermaid's Dive School**, Soi Mermaid, Jomtien Beach, T038-232219.

Game fishing
There are 4 or 5 game-fishing operators in Pattaya. Commonly caught fish include shark, king mackerel, garoupa and marlin.
The Fisherman's Club, Soi Yodsak (Soi 6). Takes groups of 4-10 anglers and offer 3 different packages (including overnight trip).

Martin Henniker, at **Jenny's Hotel**, Soi Pattayaland 1. Recommended.

Pattaya Sports Supply shop, opposite **Regent Marina Hotel** (North Pattaya). Equipment is available from Alan Ross.

Tours and tour operators

There are countless tours organized by travel agents in town: the standard long-distance trips are to Koh Samet, the sapphire mines near Chantaburi, Ayutthaya, Bangkok, the Floating Market, Kanchanaburi and the River Kwai Bridge (2 days). Prices for day tours (meal included) range from ฿600-1200.

⊖ Transport

Si Racha *p403*
Boat
Ferries for **Koh Si Chang** depart from the pier at the end Jermjomphon Rd, Soi 14, 0700-1900, 40 mins, ฿30.

Bus
Connections every 30 mins or so with **Bangkok**'s Eastern bus terminal (2-3 hrs), as well as with **Pattaya**, 29 km south, 45 mins.

Train
While just about everyone leaves here by bus, there are a handful of trains each day to Hualamphong station in **Bangkok**. Cheap, slow but considerably more attractive than the bus journey (3 hrs 15 mins, around ฿100 1st class).

Koh Si Chang *p403*
Bicycle/motorbike hire
Sripitsanu Bungalows, see Sleeping, above. Can organize mountain bike hire (฿50 per day), motorbike hire (฿250 per day) and boat trips to nearby islands.

Pattaya *p404, map p405*
Air
There are daily connections on **Bangkok Airways** with **Koh Samui**, 1 hr. Pre-flight

check-in is available at the **Royal Cliff Beach Resort**.

Airline offices Bangkok Airways, 75/8 Moo 9, Pattaya 2nd Rd, T038-412382; **Kuwait Airways**, 218 Beach Rd, T038-410 493; **THAI**, T038-602192.

Bicycle/motorbike/jeep/car hire
Along Beach Rd (bargaining required), bicycles ฿100 per day or ฿20 per hr, jeeps ฿500-700 per day (jeeps are rarely insured), motorbikes from ฿150 per day.

Avis at Dusit Resort, T038-425611; and the **Royal Cliff Beach Resort**, T038-250421.

Limousine service THAI operates a service from Don Muang airport, T038-423140 for bookings from Pattaya. A chauffeur-driven car from travel agencies in Bangkok should cost about ฿1600.

Boat
Charter from along Beach Rd, ฿700-1500 per day (seats 12 people).

Bus
A/c buses stop at the a/c bus terminal on North Pattaya Rd, near to the intersection with the Sukhumvit Highway. Regular connections with **Bangkok**'s Eastern bus terminal, next to Ekamai Skytrain station. There are bus connections direct with Don Muang Airport.

Non-a/c buses to **Bangkok** leave from the BKS stop in front of Wat Chai Mongkhon, near the intersection of Pattaya 2 and South Pattaya roads. The main terminal (non-a/c) for buses to other Eastern region destinations is in Jomtien, near the intersection of Beach and Chaiyapruk roads. If staying in Pattaya City, it is possible to stand on the Sukhumvit Highway and wave down a bus. Tour buses to the north (**Chiang Mai**, **Mae Hong Son**, **Mae Sai**, **Phitsanulok**, etc) leave from the station on the Sukhumvit Highway, near the intersection with Central Pattaya Rd. Nearby, buses also leave for **Ubon** and **Nong Khai**.

Train
The Pattaya–**Bangkok** train leaves at 1330 (3½ hrs).

Rayong *p407*
Bus
Regular connections direct to **Bangkok's** Eastern bus terminal and to **Pattaya** (1 hr).

Songthaew
From Rayong to **Ban Phe** *songthaews* stop outside Tesco Lotus on Sukhumvit Rd, ฿20.

ⓘ Directory

Si Racha *p403*
Banks Bangkok Bank of Commerce, Surasak Rd.

Koh Si Chang *p403*
Banks Thai Farmers, 9-9/1-2 Coast Rd. There's an ATM here. **Internet** There are a couple of places down near the pier.

Pattaya *p404, map p405*
Banks There are countless exchange facilities both on the beach road and on the many sois running east–west, many stay open until 2200. **Emergencies** Sea rescue, Beach Rd, next to the TAT office, T038-433752. **Internet** There are many facilities around town. **Medical services** Pattaya International Clinic, Soi 4, Beach Rd, T038-428374; Pattaya Memorial Hospital, 328/1 Central Pattaya Rd, T038-429422, 24-hr service; Dr Olivier Clinic, 20/23 Moo 10, South Pattaya Rd (opposite the Day-Night Hotel), T038-72352. There are plenty of pharmacies on South Pattaya Rd. **Police** Tourist police, T038-429371, or T1699 for 24-hr service.

Rayong *p407*
Banks There are several ATMs and banks on Sukhumvit Rd.

Koh Samet

→ Colour map 3, C5.

Until the early 1980s, Koh Samet, a 6-km-long, lozenge-shaped island, just a short boat trip from the mainland, was home to a small community of fishermen and was visited by a few intrepid travellers. Even less than five years ago it was still reasonably low-key, but the massive influx of wealthy, weekending, mostly drunk Bangkok students and the arrival of mains electricity has transformed Samet. Much like other popular destinations in Thailand it has now evolved into a brash, badly planned place with terrible damage being done to the local environment and unsightly resorts and karaoke bars lining the beach. What's even more surprising to outsiders is that Samet's superb beaches are all part of a national park and should be protected, but the park rangers who man the entrance points to the island seem more content squeezing cash out of visitors than doing their jobs and Samet seems well on its way to ecological meltdown.

However, there is no doubt the island retains some beauty and if you can find a quiet spot to watch the sun rise or set – it's easy to walk from the western to eastern side of the island – then it can still be an affable place. The famous 19th-century Thai romantic poet Sunthorn Phu retired to this beautiful island and, suitably inspired, proceeded to write his finest work, the epic Phra Aphaimani. The poem recounts the story of a prince, banished by his father to live with a sea-dwelling, broken-hearted giantess. Escaping to Koh Samet with the help of a mermaid, the prince kills the pursuing giant with his magic flute and marries the mermaid. ⊷ *For listings, see pages 418-421.*

Ins and outs

Getting there

Take a bus to Ban Phe, see page 417, about 3½ hours from Bangkok, and then one of the regular boats, another 40 minutes or so. The price is normally ฿50 each way but the sales people at the ticket desk usually force you to buy a return. All visitors also pay an entrance fee (฿200 for foreign adults, ฿100 for children – five times the rate for locals). Many visitors land at the main Na Dan Pier in the northeast of the island (it is becoming commonplace for bungalow operators to run boats directly to their beaches from Ban Phe). There are also a number of other boats and speedboats offering their services to Samet's various beaches, but schedules change frequently. The rough rule is that there are three a day.

Getting around

As Koh Samet is only 6 km long and 3 km wide it is possible to walk everywhere – the beach walk from end to end is a good adventure. If exploring on foot though take plenty of water. There are rough tracks, some suitable for *songthaews*, others for motorbike (฿300-400 a day). There is now a Koh Samet taxi union operating a fleet of green *songthaews* on the island. Their fares, both for rental of the entire vehicle and for one person in a shared vehicle (they normally travel when full, though do operate to a rough timetable as well), are posted on a notice board at the main pier. ⊷ *See Transport, page 421, for further information.*

Best time to visit

Samet is a dry island (1350 mm rain per year – Chantaburi has 3164 mm per year) and a good place to pitch up during the rainy season. However, between May and October

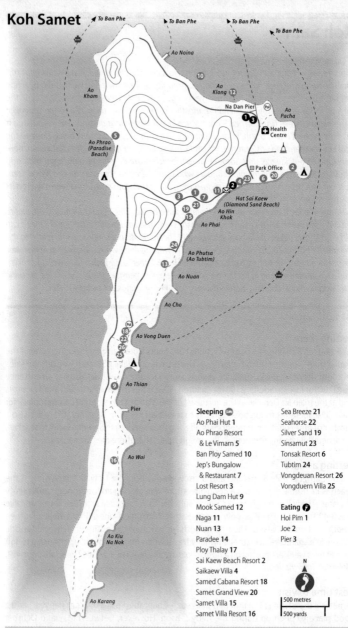

Koh Samet

To Ban Phe · To Ban Phe · To Ban Phe · To Ban Phe

Ao Noina

Ao Kham

Ao Klong

Na Dan Pier

Ao Pacha

Health Centre

Ao Phrao
(Paradise
Beach)

Park Office

Hat Sai Kaew
(Diamond Sand Beach)

Ao Hin
Khok

Ao Phai

Ao Phutsa
(Ao Tubtim)

Ao Nuan

Ao Cho

Ao Vong Duen

Ao Thian

Pier

Ao Wai

Ao Kiu
Na Nok

Ao Karang

Sleeping
Ao Phai Hut **1**
Ao Phrao Resort
  & Le Vimarn **5**
Ban Ploy Samed **10**
Jep's Bungalow
  & Restaurant **7**
Lost Resort **3**
Lung Dam Hut **9**
Mook Samed **12**
Naga **11**
Nuan **13**
Paradee **14**
Ploy Thalay **17**
Sai Kaew Beach Resort **2**
Saikaew Villa **4**
Samed Cabana Resort **18**
Samet Grand View **20**
Samet Villa **15**
Samet Villa Resort **16**

Sea Breeze **21**
Seahorse **22**
Silver Sand **19**
Sinsamut **23**
Tonsak Resort **6**
Tubtim **24**
Vongdeuan Resort **26**
Vongduern Villa **25**

Eating
Hoi Pim **1**
Joe **2**
Pier **3**

N

500 metres
500 yards

there can be strong winds and rough seas, while heavy rains can be a problem between July and September. During this period rates are cut and the island is less crowded. It is best to visit during the week; at weekends and public holidays it is popular with Thais and can be full with visitors camped out on every square metre.

Background

It is unlikely Sunthorn Phu would find the necessary quiet today; over the past decade, Koh Samet has become very popular with young Thai holiday makers and foreign visitors.

In 1981 Samet became part of the Khao Laem Ya National Park (hence the admission fee). Authorities have ostensibly insisted that all accommodation remains limited to bungalows set back behind the tree line of the beach. This is difficult to reconcile with the scale and pattern of development that has occurred. The park authorities have threatened to shut the island down on the basis that every bungalow owner is breaking the law. Indeed, they have closed the island to tourists on a couple of occasions, only to reopen it after protests from bungalow owners, many of whom were making a living on the island prior to 1981 when it was declared a national park.

Rubbish created by tourism is becoming an environmental threat on the island. It seems that however hard the park authorities, the TAT and the environmentalist pressure groups try to protect Samet, they are fighting a losing battle; people continue to visit the island in their thousands and yet more bungalows are being built.

Towards Koh Samet ●●● » pp418-421.

Ban Phe → Colour map 3, C5.

A further 25 km along the coast from Rayong is Ban Phe, once a small fishing village with a national reputation for its fish sauce and now a way station for visitors heading for Koh Samet. There are regular connections from Bangkok's Eastern bus terminal to Ban Phe. It is also possible to catch a bus to Rayong or Pattaya and then a connecting *songthaew* to Ban Phe. Alternatively, a private car from Bangkok should cost around ฿2200 (three hours).

It has many food and handicraft stalls, but few people stay any longer than it takes to catch the boat. Around the village are a number of mediocre beaches lined with bungalows and resorts – **Hat Ban Phe**, **Hat Mae Ram Phung** (to the west), **Laem Mae Phim**, **Suan Son** and **Wang Kaew** (all to the east), which are largely used by Thai tourists.

Around the island ●●▲●● » pp418-421.

There has been a settlement on Koh Samet for many years; while it is now a fishing settlement-cum-tourist service centre, junks from China used to anchor here to be checked before the authorities would allow them to sail over the sandbar at the mouth of the Chao Phraya River and north to Bangkok.

Ao Klong is a stretch of sand that runs to the west of the Na Dan pier. Apart from watching the boats moving around the island there's little else to do here, though there are a few 'floating' guesthouses/seafood restaurants built on wooden stilts in the bay.

Hat Sai Kaew (Diamond or White Sand Beach) is a 10-minute walk southeast from Na Dan Pier, and remains the most popular place to stay. This is still a beautiful spot, even if it has been disfigured by uncontrolled development. Bars, restaurants, and shops all vie for attention and during the evening sound systems blare out a continual cacophony of thumping beats. Despite the crowded, bustling atmosphere, the beach remains clean and it has a sandy bottom. Just south along the coast from Hat Sai Kaew is **Ao Hin Khok** where Koh Samet's one and only sight is to be found: a rather tatty statue depicting the tale of *Phra Aphaimani* (see page 415). A short distance further south still is **Ao Phai**, which is less developed and more peaceful.

About 2.5 km from Ao Phai, past the smaller **Ao Tubtim**, **Ao Nuan** and **Ao Cho**, is **Ao Vong Duen**. This crescent-shaped bay has a number of more upmarket resort developments and a good range of facilities: water-skiing, diving, boat trips, and windsurfing. Continuing south from Ao Vong Duen is **Ao Thian**, **Ao Wai** and **Ao Kiu Na Nok**. These are the most peaceful locations on Koh Samet, and the island's finest coral is also found off the southern tip of the island. **Ao Phrao**, (Paradise Beach), 2 km from Sai Kaew, is the only beach to have been developed (so far) on the west side of the island. There is a dive shop here. Hire a fishing boat (or go on a tour), take a picnic, and explore the **Kuti** and **Thalu islands**.

⊙ Koh Samet listings

For Sleeping and Eating price codes and other relevant information, see pages 44-49.

🛏 Sleeping

Ban Phe *p417*
D-E Diamond Phe, 286/12 Ban Phe Rd, T038-615826. A/c, east of Ban Phe near the pier for Koh Samet, plain and rather kitsch but comfortable and convenient.
E Christie's, 280/92 Soi1, opposite main pier, T038-651976. OK guesthouse in good location. Rooms are en suite, with hot water, a/c and colour TV. Great breakfasts.

Around the island *p417, map p416*
Koh Samet now offers some of the worst value, most overpriced and unfriendliest accommodation in Thailand. In some places during high-season weekends you can be charged ฿4500 for a basic resort room (the same price of a 5 star hotel room in Bangkok) and ฿800 for a fan bungalow with shared facilities. Many places are now staffed by surly teenagers so don't expect any kind of service.

Because the island is a national park, it is permissible to camp on any of the beaches or anywhere else on the island. The best area is on the west coast, which means a walk on one of the many trails of not more than 3 km.

Ao Klong
L Ban Ploy Samed, T038-644188, www.banploysamed.com. Set on wooden stilts in the middle of the bay (ring the bell by the road and a winched dinghy is sent over to pick you up) Ban Ploy Samed is in all likelihood the most overpriced place in Thailand. The place is largely staffed by comatose teenagers, its clientele tend to be drunken Thai students and the rooms are basic affairs with a/c, hot water and little else. The seafood restaurant isn't bad though.
A Mook Samed, T038-644165. Nearer to Na Dan, and similarly laid out to **Ploy Samed** – you have to cross a precarious tangle of planks to reach it. Rooms are en suite with a/c and TV. Outrageously overpriced.

Hat Sai Kaew
If you like to be where the action is, then this is the place to head for. All bungalows have attached restaurants.
L-AL Sai Kaew Beach Resort, www.koh sametsaikaew.com. Wide range of neat bungalows, some facing onto the beach. It also has de luxe bungalows, in a tranquil spot just over the headland. All with a/c and cable TV.
L-A Samet Grand View, T038-644220, www.grandviewgroup.net. This would be a nice resort – the rooms are well put together with some nice touches, all en suite, with TV

and a/c – but the grumpy owners and teen staff don't do it justice. Overpriced.

L-A Tonsak Resort, T038-644314, www.tonsak.com. Very friendly and well run resort though the rooms are pretty average. All with a/c, en suite and TV. Somewhat overpriced.

A-D Ploy Thalay, T08-1302 5223 (mob). Overrated and overpriced beachfront bungalows and rooms, some have a/c. Also home to a PADI dive school.

A-D Saikaew Villa, T038-644144, www.saikaew.com. Some decent, simple wooden rooms set back from the beach and a few nicer bungalows on offer here. Cheaper ones come with cold water and fan. Tourist fatigued owners. Not a bad deal, but still overpriced.

C-D Sinsamut, T038-644134, www.sinsamut-kohsamed.com. Tiny rooms, some with fans, some with a/c. Friendly.

Ao Hin Khok

AL-E Jep's Bungalow and Restaurant, T038-644112, www.jepbungalow.com. Good-value rooms, the restaurant has a large range of tasty dishes. Probably one of the best deals on the island and often booked up. Recommended.

D-E Lost Resort, T038-644041, www.thelostresort.net. Set by the road just behind the beach this is one of Samet's only proper guesthouses. Friendly English owner but the rooms (some with a/c and hot water) look a bit tired. Probably best budget option.

D-E Naga, T08-9939 9063 (mob). English-run and friendly, offers home-baked cakes, bread and pastries. The only post office on Koh Samet is located here. Basic huts, some with fans, all have shared, if rather smelly, bathrooms. Naga is also a popular nightspot on the island.

Ao Phai

B-E Ao Phai Hut, T038-644278. Some a/c, friendly, clean operation, with wooden huts higher up behind the tree line. Mosquitoes prevalent. This place has a library and organizes minibuses to Pattaya.

C-E Samet Villa, T038-644094, F644093. This clean and friendly Swiss-run establishment

offers some of the best-value accommodation on Samet, all rooms have fans and attached bathrooms and electricity is on round the clock. It organizes a number of trips and excursions to neighbouring islands and rents out snorkelling equipment. Recommended.

C-F Silver Sand, T08-1996 5720 (mob). Good-value bungalows, popular restaurant (0930-2200) offering a wide range of dishes, large selection of recent videos, discos at weekends.

E-F Sea Breeze, T038-644124. Bungalows (some with a/c) are fairly cheap but are located facing the back wall of the restaurant and are fairly grotty inside and out. Restaurant also poorly located, set back from the sea beside the path. On the plus side, the seafood is good and the staff friendly and helpful.

Ao Tubtim

C-E Tubtim, T038-644025, tubtimresort@yahoo.com. The more expensive huts have their own showers, some have a/c. We have received reports of dirty rooms.

Ao Nuan

B-D Nuan, the only place on this tiny beach. Great location, the bungalows are spread out along the beach and over the headland, but this is undone by the ripoff rates and the grumpy owners. Airless huts with a mattress and a net – you'd be better in a tent.

Ao Vong Duen

This beach is coming a close second to Hat Sai Kaew in terms of action, though it's not as cramped. Several guesthouses run boats to Ban Phe. Can get overrun with Thai students.

LL-B Samed Cabana Resort, T038-644320, www.samedcabana.com. Newish, concrete and wooden bungalows on a noisy part of the beach. All mod-cons but and vaguely luxurious but, once again, overpriced.

AL-A Vongdeuan Resort, T038-644171, www.vongdeuan.com. Typical bad service in this very average resort. Rooms are OK but the prices are ridiculous.

AL-C Vongduern Villa, T038-644260, www.vongduernvilla.com. One of the better run places on the island. Homely little cabins are spread out through the trees and face onto the quieter end of this busy beach. The more expensive rooms come with DVD players, all have hotwater, TVs and a/c. Good food and friendly service. Recommended.
C-D Seahorse, T08-1323 0049 (mob). Some a/c, friendly and popular with 2 restaurants and a travel agency, but the cheaper rooms in a longhouse aren't up to much.

Ao Thian
E-F Lung Dam Hut, T038-651810. Basic wood and bamboo huts with grass roofs, or try their treehouse just a fewmetres from the sea. Some huts have fans, some their own bath.

Ao Wai
A-E Samet Villa Resort, can book through the boat Phra Aphai at Ban Phe, T08-1321 1284 (mob). The only accommodation on this beach – good bungalows but quite expensive. A peaceful and attractive location, but lacks places to sit with sea views.

Ao Kiu Na Nok
LL Paradee, www.kohsametparadee.com. Super luxurious 5-star bungalows, most of them with private pools, set in a gorgeous location with a beach each side of the resort. This is one of the most expensive places on the entire eastern seaboard.

Ao Phrao
A more peaceful experience on this side of the island, with the added bonus of sunsets.
LL-AL Ao Phrao Resort and **Le Vimarn**, T02-4389771, www.kohsametaoprao.com and www.kohsametlevimarn.com. Both run by the same company, offer excellent luxurious and expensive accommodation. Ao Phrao has a family atmosphere while Le Vimarn is more stylish and comes complete with an excellent spa. Both resorts run their own boat service from Ban Phe, where they have an office.

⊘ Eating

Ban Phe *p417*
♯-♱ Christie's, just opposite the main pier, T038-651976. Irish owned bar and café. Great breakfasts and Western food. Perfect pit stop after you've got off the ferry. Friendly and good place to people watch. Also serves tasty Thai fare. Recommended.

Around the island *p417, map p416*
Just about all the resorts and guesthouses on Koh Samet provide the usual Thai dishes and travellers' food. The following places have a particularly good reputation for their food.
♱ Bamboo Restaurant, Ao Cho. Open through the day, reasonable food and one of the island's few restaurants.
♱ Hoi Pim, opposite the main pier. A/c restaurant providing another good pit stop and some decent Western food.
♱ Joe Restaurant, Hat Sai Kaew, on the beach. Food and service are passable. Good hang-out spot, with a nice low terrace.
♱ Miss You, just before the park's main entrance, north end of the island. Samet's best coffee and great ice cream sundaes.
♱ Naga, Ao Hin Khok, see Sleeping, above. Home-baked cakes, bread and pastries, and a popular nightspot.
♱ Nuan Kitchen, Ao Nuan, see Sleeping, above. Very good food.
♱ The Pier, opposite the main pier. New coffee shop that does a mean cappuccino. Good stop when you're catching the ferry. The croissants are sometimes a bit stale.
♱ Sea Breeze, Ao Phai, see Sleeping, above. Good seafood.
♱ Vongduean Resort, Ao Vong Duen, see Sleeping, above. A vast range of Thai and Western dishes.

Foodstalls
♱ Stall inbetween **Le Vimarn** and **Ao Phrao Resort**, set up by the resort owners mainly to feed their own staff. Sells a variety of excellent Thai and Isaan dishes in a breezy beach-side location. Recommended.

▲ Activities and tours

Around the island p417, map p416
The major beaches offer sailing, windsurfing, snorkelling and waterskiing. However, many of the bungalows display notices requesting visitors not to hire jetskis because they are dangerous to swimmers, damage the coral and disrupt the peace. Some of the jet-ski operators are notorious rip-off artists and the whole activity is best avoided. You can also scuba-dive here but the diving isn't great and you'd be better saving your money to dive in other parts of the country.

Ao Wong Duan has the best watersports and the best snorkelling is to be found at Ao Wai, Ao Kiu Na Nok and Ao Phrao. **Samet Villa**, at Ao Phai, runs an adventure tour to Koh Mun Nok, Koh Mun Klang and Koh Mun Nai for ฿500 per person, trips to Thalu and Kuti for ฿300, and trips around the island for ฿200 per person.

⊖ Transport

Ban Phe p417
Boat
To **Na Dan** from Ban Phe Pier throughout the day departing when full (30-40 mins, ฿50) – most are now forced to stick to a rough timetable, with the last boat leaving at 1700. Also many boats to various beaches from **Nuanthip Pier** and **Seree Ban Phe Pier**, which lie just to the west of the main pier. Most of these boats are run by bungalow operators and they tend to cost ฿40-50. It may be difficult to find out which boat is going where; boat operators try hard to get visitors to stay at certain bungalows. It is best not to agree to stay anywhere until arrival on the island whereupon claims of cleanliness and luxury can be checked out. Travel agents on Khaosan Rd, Bangkok, also arrange transport to Samet.

Bus
There is a daily bus from Ban Phe to **Koh Chang**, ฿250 with tickets on sale at several places on Samet.

Car
A private car from Bangkok to **Ban Phe** should cost around ฿2200 and take 3 hrs.

Motorbike hire
Can be hired for ฿300-400 per day.

Songthaew
These are the main form of public transport. Rates are posted on a board at the main pier. To **Hat Sai Kaew** from the main pier its ฿10 per person in a shared vehicle and ฿100 to hire the whole thing; to **Ao Vong Duen** its ฿30/฿250 and to **Ao Kiu** at the end of the island its ฿60/฿550. Don't negotiate, just pay the set rate at the end of your journey.

⊙ Directory

Ban Phe p417
Banks Krung Thai, a short distance west of the pier.

Around the island p417, map p416
Banks The island has no banks but a couple of ATMs near Hat Sai Kaew and one at Ao Vong Duen. So for the best rates, change money on the mainland. Many of the bungalows and travel agents do offer a money-changing service but take a 5% fee. **Medical services** Koh Samet Health Centre, a small, public health unit, is situated on the road south from Na Dan to Hat Sai Kaew. **Post office** Situated inside **Naga Bungalows** at Hin Khok between Hat Sai Kaew and Ao Phai (Poste Restante). Mon-Fri 0830-1500, Sat 0830-1200. **Telephone and internet** Many places offer international calls for about ฿30 per min while internet charges should be ฿2 per min. **Miss You** coffee shop by the National Park office at Hat Sai Kaew has new machines and a fast connection.

Chantaburi to Koh Chang

Head east from Koh Samet and you'll soon reach Chantaburi, famed for its trade in precious stones. Unless you fancy your chances on picking up a bargain in the gemstone market – most farang fair badly against the hard-nosed sapphire and ruby traders – travel down the coast to Trat and the increasingly popular island of Koh Chang. This is Thailand's second largest island and is part of a national marine park which includes 50-odd islands and islets covering 650 sq km. Despite the 'protection' that its national park status should offer, Koh Chang is developing rapidly, with resorts and bungalows springing up along its shores. It is Thailand's last tropical island idyll – at least of any size – to be developed and it has excellent beaches, sea, coral and diving. There are treks, waterfalls, rivers and pools, villages, mangroves, three peaks of over 700 m, and a rich variety of wildlife.

The healing waters of Nam Tok Kratang waterfall are 30 km northwest of town. The border market at Aranya Prathet is the chief attraction here. ▸▸ *For listings, see pages 430-440.*

Chantaburi and around ⬤❶❷⬤▲⬤❶ ▸▸ *pp430-440. Colour map 3, C6.*

Chantaburi is not a popular destination for international visitors to Thailand; most pass it by en route to Trat and the island of Koh Chang. But it deserves more attention, if only because it is an unusual town with its large population of ethnic Vietnamese, a strong Catholic presence, well-preserved traditional shophouses, excellent restaurants, and some of the finest durian in Thailand. Chantaburi has built its wealth on rubies and sapphires with many of the gem mines being developed during the 19th century by Shan people from Burma, who are thought to be among the best miners in the world. It is also becoming a jump-off point for entry into Cambodia via Pong Nam Ron, about 60 km to the north (see box, page 425, for details).

Getting there

If coming from Koh Samet, get a boat to Ban Phe, *songthaew* to Rayong (฿20) and then a bus to Chantaburi – buses leave every hour, the journey takes two hours and costs ฿30. There are less regular bus connections with destinations in the northeast including Korat. ▸▸ *See Transport, page 438, for further information.*

Sights

Muang Chan – as it is locally known – has a large Chinese and Vietnamese population, lending the town an atmospheric run of narrower streets, shuttered wooden shophouses, Chinese temples and an industrious air. This atmosphere is most palpable along Rim Nam or Sukhaphiban Road. The French-style **Catholic Cathedral** of the Immaculate Conception was built in 1880 and is the largest church in Thailand. Architecturally uninspiring, it is significant for its presence. The cathedral was built to serve the many Vietnamese Catholics who fled their homeland and settled here. The Vietnamese part of town is north of the cathedral, on the opposite side of the river.

Apart from gems, Chantaburi is also highly regarded as a source of some of the best durians in Thailand, which flourish in the lush climate. The finest cost several hundred baht (more than a week's wages for an agricultural labourer), a fact which can seem astonishing to visitors who regard the fruit as repulsive.

Tears of the gods: rubies and sapphires

Major deposits of two of the world's most precious stones are found distributed right across mainland Southeast Asia: rubies and sapphires. They are mined in Thailand, Burma, Vietnam, Cambodia and Laos. The finest of all come from Burma, and especially from the renowned Mogok Stone Tract, which supports a town of 100,000 almost entirely upon the proceeds of the gem industry. Here, peerless examples are unearthed, including the rare 'pigeon's blood' ruby. One Thai trader was reported to say that "Asking to see the pigeon's blood is like asking to see the face of God".

Although the Burmese government tries to keep a tight grip on the industry, many of the gems pass into the hands of Thai gem dealers, often with the connivance of the Thai army. Corruption, violence, murder, arson and blackmail are all part and parcel of the trade. Through fair means and foul, Bangkok has become the centre of the world's gem business and Thailand is the largest exporter of cut stones – indeed, it has a virtual monopoly of the sapphire trade. Those who try to buck the system and bypass Bangkok risk having a contract taken out on their lives.

Rubies and sapphires are different colours of corundum, the crystalline form of aluminium oxide. Small quantities of various trace elements give the gems their colour; in the case of rubies, chromium and for blue sapphires, titanium. Sapphires are also found in other colours including green and yellow. Rubies are among the rarest of gems, and command prices four times higher than equivalent sized diamonds. The Burmese call the ruby *ma naw ma ya* or 'desire-fulfilling stones'.

The colour of sapphires can be changed through heat treatment (the most advanced form is called diffusion treatment) to 1500-1600°C (sapphires melt at 2050°C). For example, relatively valueless colourless geuda sapphires from Sri Lanka, turn a brilliant blue or yellow after heating. The technique is an ancient one: Pliny the Elder described the heating of agate by Romans nearly 2000 years ago, while the Arabs had developed heat treatment into almost a science by the 13th century. Today, almost all sapphires and rubies are heat treated. The most valued colour for sapphires is cornflower blue – dark, almost black, sapphires command a lower price. The value of a stone is based on the four 'C's: Colour, Clarity, Cut and Carat (1 carat = 200 milligrams). Note that almost all stones are heat treated to improve their colour. For more on buying gems in Thailand, see page 147.

If you're a diehard beach bum there is a decent stretch of sand about 20 km to the east of Chantaburi at **Laem Sim**, though public transport is very hit and miss. Take a bus along Route 3 about 15 km to the Laem Sim turn-off and then try and pick up a *songthaew* to take you the final 6 km to the beach. Laem Sim is also home to a small fishing fleet and several makeshift fish restaurants line the beach road.

Nam Tok Krating
ⓘ *Regular public songthaews run past the entrance to the park on Route 3249; from here it is a 15-min walk to the park HQ. There is accommodation available in the park.*
The waterfall of Nam Tok Krating is in the **Kitchakut National Park** (along with a few caves), about 30 km northwest of town. The water is believed to have healing powers.

The park is one of the smallest in the country, covering less than 60 sq km, and was established in 1977. The falls are within hiking distance of the park headquarters. It is also possible to walk to the summit of the **Phrabat Mountain**, so-called because there is an impression of a footprint of the Buddha. Allow four hours to reach the top.

Aranya Prathet and the Cambodian border

Aranya Prathet, a bit more than a day trip, has gained some measure of notoriety because of its location close to the border with Cambodia (see box, page 425) and its growing use as an alternative route to Siem Reap. The journey to Siem Reap takes around six hours by truck – a bone-jarring experience – sometimes much longer in the wet season. It is best to cross the border early so that you do not have to stay overnight in the cross-border town of Poipet. There have been reports of bandit attacks on trucks. The highlight of Aranya Prathet itself is the **Talat Rong Klua** (border market), around 7 km from town (a moto costs around ฿40-50), a mêlée of frantic activity selling textiles, shoes, leather goods, handicrafts, fish, wickerwork, electronics, sunglasses, wild animals and agricultural products.

Trat and Khlong Yai

Trat is the provincial capital and the closest Thai town of any size to Cambodia. Like Chantaburi, Trat is a gem centre and with peace in Cambodia it has flourished as a centre of cross-border commerce. Most people visit Trat en route to beautiful Koh Chang, not staying any longer than they need to catch a bus or boat out of the place. Tourist offices ① *Soi Sukhumvit, not far from the market*, are helpful and informative. A new bus station has been built a couple of kilometres northeast of the town past the post office.

If you do decide to stay longer in Trat you'll have the chance to sample the diverse selection of excellent guesthouses. There's also a bustling **covered market** on Sukhum vit Road offering a good selection of food and drink stalls. On the same road, north of the shopping mall, there is a busy **night market**. **Wat Buppharam**, also known as **Wat Plai Klong**, dates from the late Ayutthaya period. It is notable for its wooden viharn and monk's kutis, and is 2 km west of town, down the road opposite the shopping mall.

Trat

To Bangkok

Soi Sukhaphibun 5
Soi Sukhaphibun 5

Wiwatthana Rd

To Wat Buppharam

Sukhumvit Rd

Thatmai Rd

Night Market

Wat Klang

Trat Department Store

Municipal Market

City Pillar

Soi Sukhumvit

Tak-Mai Rd

Rot Amnon Rd

Lak Muang Rd

Tratosphere Bookshop

Than Charoen Rd

To Laem Ngop Pier

Canal

To Bus Station, GPO & Trat River

To

N

100 metres
100 yards

Sleeping 🛏
Ban Jai Dee 1
Basar 2
Guy Guesthouse 6
NP Guesthouse 8
Sawadee Guesthouse 3

Eating 🍴
Baibuo 6
Cool Corner 2
Isaan Shophouse 4
Joys 5
Krua Rim Klong 1
Nam Chok 3
Pier 112 Restaurant & Bar 7
Vegetarian 8

Border essentials: Thailand–Cambodia

In 2008 Thailand and Cambodia came close to full-blown conflict. While the situation in January 2009 was relatively calm, underlying tensions persist. Land borders would likely be the first to close if sabre rattling – or worse – resumed. If you are planning an overland journey from Thailand to Cambodia pay attention to the political developments before you travel.

It is possible to cross into Cambodia from several points along Thailand's eastern border. Visas can be obtained at each for US$20 or ฿1000 – you'll need one recent photo. Be aware that some border posts insist on being paid in baht others in US dollars, so take both. These border crossings are also in constant flux, and opening times and other details can change at short notice; for the most recent information check locally. The following are the most useful entry points:

Aranya Prathet–Poipet

This remains the most popular border crossing with good bus and train connections to Bangkok. It is the best entry point if you want to visit Siem Reap and the ruins at Angkor Wat. Be advised that the road on the Cambodian side of the border is often in an appalling state and journey times to Siem Reap can be lengthy. The border is open daily 0800-2000. Sometimes tourists are asked for an International Vaccination Certificate; this is a means by which local immigration officers boost their income (if you don't have one they demand US$5). The certificate is not legally required; if the border guards insist ask for a receipt and the name of the commanding officer – this usually dissuades them. A tuk-tuk from Aranya Prathet train or bus station to the border (7 km from town) should cost around ฿60-80.

Ban Hat Lek–Koh Kong

South of Trat and just past the town of Khlong Yai, this is the best entry point if you want to visit Sihanoukville and the southern Cambodian town of Kampot. The border is open 0800-2000. Minibuses (฿100) and *songthaews* (฿40) run from Trat direct to Hat Lek (one hour). After crossing the border at Hat Lek you'll arrive on the Cambodian island of Koh Kong. From there a daily boat (departs 0800 – you may need to spend the night on Koh Kong) will take you direct to Sihanoukville (three to four hours). The alternatives are minibuses and taxis that depart when full (six hours).

Pong Nam Ron–Pailin

Open 0900-1700, this is the best crossing if you want to reach Battambang – it could also be used as an alternative route to Siem Reap. Take a Khorat-bound bus from Chantaburi to the small town of Pong Nam Ron (one hour, ฿30). Just by the clearly marked turning to the border is a small market – *songthaews* from here to the border should cost ฿60 (30 minutes). Shared taxis await in Pailin to take you to Battambang (four hours).

Khlong Yai is the southernmost town on this eastern arm of Thailand and an important fishing port. Take a *songthaew* from the back of the municipal market (฿25) or shared taxi from the front of the market (฿35 each). The journey there is worthwhile for the dramatic scenery with the mountains of Cambodia rising to the east and the sea to the west. Khlong Yai is also a pretty and bustling little port, well worth the trip. There are several Cambodian markets and the seafood is excellent. The border crossing at Hat Lek (see page 425) is a short journey south of Khlong Yai.

Laem Ngop → *Colour map 3, C6.*

This sleepy fishing village – in fact the district capital – has a long pier lined with boats, along with good seafood and a relaxed atmosphere. As Koh Chang becomes Thailand's next island beach resort to hit the big time, expect things to get busier – at present there's a handful of guesthouses and a few waterside restaurants. The **TAT office** ① *Mon-Fri 0830-1630*, is at 100 Moo 1 Trat, Laem Ngop Rd, T039-597255.

Koh Chang National Park ●◉◕◔◐▲●◉ ►► *pp430-440.*

→ *www.ko-chang.info/index.htm.*

As you set sail from the mainland across the glittering seas, Koh Chang (Elephant Island), covered in thick, verdant forest and with a vivid, sweeping skyline, rises up to meet you. This 40-km-long and 16-km-wide island is Thailand's second biggest (after Phuket), and the teeming wildlife, rustic appeal and wonderful beaches have long attracted the more adventurous traveller.

Things are changing. Koh Chang has now been earmarked as Thailand's next big destination. Hotel chains and tour operators are moving in and the beaches are now almost entirely colonized by Thai and European package tourists. It's not all upmarket; odious 'monkey schools' (where monkey's are forced to perform degrading tricks) and that definitive marker of tourist saturation, the 'girlie bar', have now made their home on Koh Chang. Any recent visitor has to work harder to find the best parts of the island.

Elephant Island also forms the fulcrum of the Koh Chang National Park – an archipelago of dozens of smaller islands that stretch to the south. Many of these are also being taken over by mass tourism/backpackers and the recently pristine environment is suffering. If you do visit these outlying islands be very aware of your impact, some of them are overwhelmed with mountains of plastic water bottles and other detritus.

Ins and outs → *Colour map 3, C6.*
Getting there With regular flights from nearby Trat (see page 439), Koh Chang is getting easier to reach. From Bangkok catch a bus from the Eastern bus terminal (Ekkamai) or Northern bus terminal (Mo Chit) to Trat (to avoid having to charter a taxi, once you arrive on Koh Chang you should leave no later than 1100), or fly (see page 439); from Trat, there are regular *songthaews* to Laem Ngop. During the high season (November-May) boats leave every hour from Laem Ngop for Koh Chang. But during the low season departures are much more intermittent. Beware of Sea Horse, who reputedly run minibuses to Laem Ngop and drive deliberately slowly to miss the last ferry, so they get to choose where you stay (and take a commission). If you arrive on Koh Chang after 1700, there may not be enough people to fill a taxi, so you might have to charter one, which costs ฿1000.
►► *See Transport, page 439, for further information.*

Getting around Koh Chang's best beaches are on the western side of the island – Hat Sai Kaew (White Sand), Hat Khlong Phrao and, on the southern coast, Hat Bang Bao. These can be reached either by jeep taxi from Ao Sapparot (prices range from ฿50-100, depending on destination and whether you manage to fill up the taxi) or by boat from Laem Ngop. There is a paved road up the east coast and down the west coast as far south as Bang Bao. If you need to travel later in the day there are lots of pick-up trucks that you can catch a lift with. However, it is still not possible to travel between Bang Boa and Salak Phet. In addition to *songthaews* there are also motorbikes (around ฿200 per day) and mountain bikes for hire. For walkers, there is a path crossing the middle of the island from Ban Khlong Phrao to Than Ma Yom but it is a strenuous day-long hike and locals recommend taking a guide.

Tourist information There are several places claiming to be official tourist information offices on the island – all are agents trying to get you to buy day trips.

Best time to visit For snorkelling and diving the best time to visit is November to May, when visibility is at its best. The best spots are off the islands south of Koh Chang. This is also the best time to visit from the weather point of view. Koh Chang is a wet island with an annual rainfall of over 3000 mm (the wettest month is August). Mosquitoes (carrying malaria) and sandflies are a problem on Koh Chang and surrounding islands, so repellent and anti-malarials are essential. Take a net if camping.

Koh Chang

Khlong Son, near Koh Chang's northern tip, is the largest settlement on the island. Even so, there's not much here: a health clinic, a few small noodle shops, a monastery, a post office and a school. Many of the other islands within the national park have villages and a fair amount of land, particularly around the coast, has been cleared for agriculture – mostly coconut plantations.

Koh Chang is now well on its way to being another 'international resort island' similar to Phuket. Local tourism operators have expressed their enthusiasm for the plans, tempered with concern that this type of centrally planned development may only benefit big businesses from Bangkok, etc. All of the outer islands have now experienced some sort of development with numerous luxury resorts appearing where before there might have been just the occasional cluster of bamboo bungalows. Some of the islands are very small, so it does raise the question of where the resorts get their water supply from and how long the demands of five-star resort guests can be satisfied.

Ao Khlong Son is at the northern tip of the island. Further south on the western side is **Hat Sai Kaew** (White Sand Beach), a *songthaew* to this beach costs ฿50 from the pier. **Hat Khlong Phrao**, 5 km south of Hat Sai Kaew, and 2 km long, is spread out each side of the mouth of the Khlong Phrao canal and is a beautiful beach but the water tends to be shallow.

At **Ao Khlong Makok** there is almost no beach at high tide and just a couple of bungalow operations which are virtually deserted in the low season, see Sleeping, page 433. **Ao Kai Bae** is the southernmost beach on the west coast. It is beautiful but swimming is tricky as the water is very shallow and covered with rocks and dead coral in places.

Haad Tha Nam (Lonely Beach) is an attractive stretch of coastline and much more quiet and relaxed than the more accessible northern stretches. However, most of the well-run, cheap operations have been pushed out to be replaced with awful bungalows or dull generic resorts – it may be best to pass this beach by. If you do want to visit though, *songthaews* from the pier cost approximately ฿80. A short *songthaew* ride south of Lonely beach is **Bailan Bay**, another relaxing, peaceful spot where people come to get away from it all. *Songthaews* from the pier cost about ฿100.

Ao Bang Bao and **Ao Bai Bin** are lovely beaches on the south coast of the island. The bay dries out at low tide and it is virtually inaccessible in the low season when the accommodation tends to shut down.

Although there is a scattering of bungalow operations on the east coast, very few people choose to stay here even in the high season. The only beach is at **Sai Thong**.

Than Ma Yom Waterfall is on the east side of the island. King Chulalongkorn (Rama V) visited this waterfall on no less than six occasions at the end of the 19th century, so even given the Thai predilection for waterfalls of any size, it counts as an impressive one (in fact there are three falls). To prove the point, the king carved his initials (or had them carved), on a stone to mark one of his visits. Rama VI and VII also visited the falls, although it seems

Koh Chang

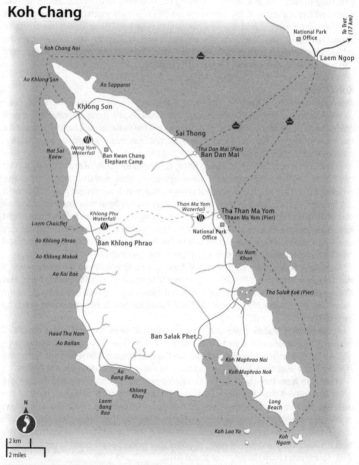

that they didn't get quite so far – they left their initials inscribed on stones at the nearest of the falls. The falls are accessible from either Ban Dan Mai or Thaan Ma Yom, both on the east coast and getting to the first of the cascades involves a walk of around one hour; it is around 4 km to the furthest of the three falls.

Khlong Phu Falls, at Ao Khlong Phrao, are perhaps even more beautiful than Than Ma Yom waterfall. There is a good pool here for swimming as well as a restaurant and some bungalows. Because this is a national park it is also possible to camp. To get here, it's a 10-minute taxi or motorbike ride from Hat Sai Kaew; you can also travel to it from the road by elephant for ฿200 or for free by walking just 3 km.

Koh Chang's forest is one of the most species-rich in the country and while the island's coast may be undergoing development, the rugged, mountainous interior is still largely inaccessible and covered with virgin rainforest (around 70% is said to be forested). There is a good population of birds, including parrots, sunbirds, hornbills and trogons, as well as Koh Chang's well-known population of wild boar, although the chances of seeing any are slim. It is advisable, however, to take a guide for exploring – **Jungle Way** bungalows (see page 431) organizes guided hikes for ฿450 including lunch.

Around Koh Chang
While the waters around Koh Chang are clear there have been some reports of a deterioration in water quality connected with coastal gem mining on the mainland. Nonetheless, hard and especially soft corals are abundant. Fish are less numerous and varied than on the other side of the Gulf of Thailand or in the Andaman Sea. During the wet season visibility is very poor, due to high seas, which also makes diving dangerous. The months between November and March are best for diving. Generally, diving is better in the waters to the south of the island. Notable are the wrecks of two Thai warships, the *Thonburi* and *Chonburi*, sunk here in an engagement with seven French ships and the loss of 36 lives on 17 January 1941. One Thai ship escaped unharmed, the *Songkhla*. A memorial tablet (in Thai) has been erected on the beach and the wrecks are marked with buoys off the southeasternmost point of Koh Chang. The raised coral reefs seen around parts of the island extends out into the sea, where soft and hard corals, including massive, columnar and stags' horn varieties can be seen. The best diving is between 5 m and 25 m where blue-tipped rays, moray eels, trigger fish, grouper and batfish can be seen. There is a fantastic vertical dive but even more adventurous dive sites are found off Koh Man Nok and Hun Sarn Soa. If you are lucky it is possible to spot turtles and whalesharks.

Islands off Koh Chang
Koh Kood is the next largest island after Koh Chang. This island has lovely beaches, especially on the west side, and a number of small fishing villages linked by dirt roads. So far it has managed to escape the ravages of development; there aren't any 7/11s, banks or girly bars, making this an ideal place to escape and relax. There is an impressive waterfall and the coral is also said to be good. For further information, see www.kohkood.com.

During high season, speedboats (฿550, 1½ hrs) leave daily at 0800, 0830 and 0900 from Dankao Pier in Trat, you should tell the driver where you are staying so you are dropped off at the correct pier on the island. A slow boat (฿300, five hours) also leaves from Dankao pier at 1000. *Songthaews* leave for the pier from opposite KFC in Trat, Note that it's ฿100 for the *songthaew*, not per person. Additional speedboats leave from Laem Sok pier at 1300 and Coral beach at 1400, both cost ฿550.

Koh Mak is the third largest island in the archipelago after Koh Chang and Koh Kood. It is privately owned by a few wealthy local families and a little over half of the island has been cleared for coconut plantations. There is still a reasonable area of forest and the coral is also good. The best beach is on the northwest shore. It is said that many of the prime pieces of shorefront have been sold to Bangkok-based developers, so it remains to be seen what happens to Koh Mak. Boats leave daily (฿450), from Klom long Chumporn pier in Laem Ngop for Koh Mak during the high season (November to May); departures may be suspended during the low season.

Koh Kham, a tiny island, is well known for its swallows' nests and turtle eggs, as well as good coral and rock formations for divers. Boats leave from Laem Ngop (3½ hours, ฿150); Koh Kham Resort offers a boat service from Laem Ngop Pier to Koh Kham (departs at 1500 and arrives at 1800).

Koh Ngam, two hours from Laem Ngop by boat, is a very small island with lush vegetation and beautiful beaches. It has two upmarket resorts. See Sleeping, below.

Koh Whai has two resorts but these are better value than those at Koh Ngam. There's a daily ferry from Laem Ngop at 0800, returning at 1500 (฿130).

Many of the more sophisticated bungalow operations on Koh Chang organize day trips to **Koh Lao Ya, Koh Phrao, Koh Khlum, Koh Kra Dad** (which has exceptionally beautiful beaches and lush vegetation) and **Koh Rayang Nok** during the high season, when the seas are calmer, the visibility greater and there is generally more demand. In the low season few boats go between these islands and either Koh Chang or the mainland and most of the accommodation closes down.

◉ Chantaburi to Koh Chang listings

For Sleeping and Eating price codes and other relevant information, see pages 44-49.

● Sleeping

Chantaburi p422

A-B Maneechan River Resort and Sport Club, 110 Moo 11 Plubpla Rd, T039-343777, www.maneechanresort.com. Very good hotel with a good range of amenities including mod cons and decent sports facilities. Excellent pool, good Thai food and free Wi-Fi. Recommended.
B-E Eastern, 899 Tha Chalaep Rd, T039-323 220. Pool, all rooms have a/c, TV and bath tub. Larger rooms have fridges and are almost twice the price, smaller rooms are good value.
D-E Kasemsarn 1, 98/1 Benchama Rachuthit Rd, T039-311100. Some a/c, large, clean rooms in big hotel, some can be noisy. Well run.
F-G Arun Sawat, 239 Sukhaphiban Rd, T039-311082. Situated in the most attractive part of town. The rooms are dark and small.

Nam Tok Krating p423
There is accommodation (**D-E**) near the park headquarters, T02-579 0529, T02-579 4842 (Bangkok).
B-D Mermaid Hotel, 33 Tanavitee Rd, T039-223655. Some a/c. Close to the bus and train stations in the northwest part of town. Comfortable with clean rooms.

Aranya Prathet and the Cambodian border p424
E-F Thupthongkum Hotel, just over 1 km from the bus station (turn left on exiting the bus station), T037-231550. The best place to stay in this price bracket, clean rooms.

Trat and Khlong Yai p424, map p424
E-G Guy Guesthouse, Than Charoen Rd, Trat, T039-524556. Range of rooms from very basic through to en suite with TV and a/c.
F Basar, 87 Thana Charoen Rd, Trat, T039-523 247. Beautifully restored Teak house, with a modern funky touch. All rooms have

bathroom and mosquito net. There's a small restaurant on the ground floor. Recommended.

F Suksamlan Hotel, 623/1 Mung Kiri Rd, Khlong Yai, T039-581109. Tucked away in back streets near the market, this is an old-school Thai/Chinese hotel with basic fan rooms, some en suite.

F-G Ban Jai Dee, Chaimongkon Rd, Trat, T039-520678. The best of the bunch, very friendly English-speaking owners. Rooms have fan, shared bathrooms. Recommended.

F-G NP Guesthouse, 1-3 Soi Luang Aet, Lak Muang Rd, Trat, T039-512564. Clean, friendly, well-run, converted shophouse, with a bright little restaurant, shared bathroom, hot showers, dorm beds, internet facilities. Recommended.

F-G Sawadee Guesthouse, 90 Lakmuang Rd, Trat, T039-530063. Basic but very clean fan rooms have nice finishing touches. Shared bathroom. Internet. Run by young Thai family.

Laem Ngop p426
There are a number of guesthouses on the main road into the village.

D Koh Chang Tour B&B, Anusornsathorn Rd, opposite the immigration building, T039-538 265, www.kohchangtourco.com. Rooms with a/c, hot shower and TV. Near the pier.

E-F Laem Ngop Inn, T039-597044. Sonthiciri Rd. Decent enough rooms, some a/c.

E-F Paradise Inn, T039-597031. Some a/c.

F Siri A Neak Place, at the start of Centre Point pier. Basic fan rooms. Ideal for catching the first boat to Koh Chang.

F-G Chut Kaew, T039-597088. Good source of information, friendly, with basic rooms.

Koh Chang p426, map p428
The backpacker heaven that was once very evident on Koh Chang with endless runs of cheap bungalows is slowly being replaced by generic, 4- and 5-star, upmarket operators. There are still a few cheaper options left, especially when you head further south away

from White Sand beach, though their lifespan may be limited. If you're staying in a basic bamboo hut be careful with valuables. Rapid develop- ment means the accommodation below may date very quickly. The best source of information is at the **Tratosphere** bookshop in Trat (see page 438). Almost all the budget accommodation consists of simple wood-slat bungalows. Some of the accommodation closes during the low season so check before you travel. The TAT office in Laem Ngop (see page 426) also holds reasonably up-to-date lists of accommodation. As popularity increases Koh Chang's prices are rising, particularly during the very busy months (Dec and Jan) and during Songkran.

Ao Khlong Son
Few budget travellers choose to stay here anymore but head instead for the beaches on the west or south coasts.

LL-AL Aiyapura Resort & Spa, T039-555 111, www.aiyapura.com. Luxury and very expensive development of huge villas built into the hillside and nicely shaded with trees. Good views. The villas are well furnished but not particularly elegant. Pool and all the other facilities you'd expect for the price.

E-F Jungle Way, about 2 km from the coastal road into the interior (there's a big sign in Khlong Son pointing the way), T08-9247 3161 (mob), www.jungleway.com. Open Oct-May. Simple bungalows in jungle location, next to bubbling stream. Run by an Englishwoman and her Thai husband. Yoga and reike courses available.

Hat Sai Kaew (White Sand Beach)
The most-developed stretch on the island with lots of mid-range resorts, shops, bars and burgeoning sex tourism. There are about 40 different places to stay on this stretch. Cheaper options can be found behind the beach in the village.

L-A Koh Chang Kacha Resort, 88-89 Moo 4. T039-551223, www.kohchangkacha.com. Exceptionally well-designed villas and bungalows set in a luscious garden with a beautiful pool. Deluxe villas have huge bath. Friendly management. Recommended.

AL-A Lagoon Resort, next to Mac Bungalows, T039-551201, www.kohchang lagoonresort.com. Average hotel rooms and bungalows. All are en suite with a/c. Comfortable resort with a decent seafood beach barbecue.

AL-A Mac Bungalow, T08-1864 6463 (mob). A very popular, centrally located resort with some hotel rooms available in addition to the bungalows. Possibly overpriced. The restaurant is probably the best on the beach and has fantastic barbecues and breakfasts.

AL-C KC Grande Resort 1/2 Moo 4, T039-552111, www.kcresortkohchang.com. Clean huts arranged along the seafront in a very good location, quiet but not too secluded. Friendly restaurant and staff.

A-B Cookies Hotel, T039-551107, www.koh changcookieshotel.com. Non descript resort-style rooms, some overlooking the pool area and beach. Good location and a restaurant.

A-C Plaloma Cliff Resort, 1/2 Moo 4, T039-551119, www.plalomacliff.com. German/Swiss-run operation on the southern tip of the bay, some bungalows with a view over the sea. No beach here, but the restaurant is very good. Small library.

B White Sand Beach Resort, further up the beach from Rock Sand, T08-6310 5553 (mob), www.whitesandbeachresort.net. On the quietest and least developed stretch of White Sand Beach. Nicely designed bungalows all with a/c, fridge and TV. Most have great sea views.

C-E Rock Sand, northern end of the beach, T08-1863 7611 (mob). Tired looking rooms are a little hit and miss, although the location is superb. Some a/c and en suite.

D-F Apple Bungalow, T039-551228. Slightly smarter huts than other places in this price category. These are great huts for the price and location.

E Tonsai Home, next to Palm Garden Hotel, T09-895 7229 (mob), muser@loxinfo.co.th. Tastefully designed wooden bungalows with fan, mosquito net and bathroom. Set back from the road in a small garden. 2 mins' walk from the beach. Best of the cheap options. Great restaurant. Highly recommended.

Hat Khlong Phrao

LL-AL Aanna Resort & Spa, Klong Praow, 19/2 Moo 4, T09-551539, www.aana resort.com. Set back quite a distance from the beach. The most interesting style of accommodation at this luxury resort and spa, are the villa rooms. Built on stilts, the individual huts are connected by elevated wooden walkways. All rooms have a/c, TV, DVD player and fridge. There are 2 pools and a restaurant that overlooks the river. A boat transfers guests to the beach.

LL-AL Amari Emerald Cove, T039-552000, T02-2552588 (central reservations), www.amari.com. The island's first 5-star resort has wonderful rooms, great restaurants (the best veggie selection on the island) and all the amenities you'd expect. The layout, though, is very dull – a uniform arc of hotel rooms facing onto the pool.

LL-AL Koh Chang Resort, T02-2775256, www.kohchangresortandspa.com. Expensive and not particularly spacious a/c bungalows with bamboo interiors and clunky furniture. The garden setting houses a pool and spa and is quite pleasant with shading coconut palms.

L-C Magic Resort, 34 Moo 4, www.koh-chang.com/magicresort/index.htm. Rather characterless rooms in concrete huts all have a/c and are reasonably spacious. Possibly overpriced.

A-B Coconut Beach Bungalow, 17/2 Moo 4, T08-1861 2458 (mob), www.koh-chang.com/coconutbeachresort/index.htm. Wooden huts with shared bath, well built, mosquito nets provided, set above the beach. Rather unfriendly management.

A-C Boutique Resort and Spa, T02-3250927, www.boutiqueresortandhealthspa.com. Brilliant pixie-like huts with beautiful interiors. A health spa is attached where you you can fine-tune your yoga positions.

B Royal Coconut Resort, T08-1781 7078 (mob), www.koh-chang/theroyalcoconut resort/index.htm. Newly built hotel with a/c, friendly staff and fantastic views down the beach. Lovely individual floating dining areas.

B-E KP Huts, 51 Moo 4, T08-4099 5100 (mob). Amongst coconut palms, these wood cabins are basic but clean. There are a range of options from fan with bathroom outside, to a/c huts on stilts right on the beach with huge balconies.

E-F Tiger Huts, 13/16 Moo 1, T08-4109 9660 (mob). Although these bamboo huts, some with bathroom, have seen better days and could be cleaner, the peaceful location, right on the beach, can't be faulted. There is also a restaurant serving reasonable Thai and Western food.

Ao Khlong Makok

D Mai Pen Rai Guest House, 30/50 Moo 4, T039-557115. Rooms in a newly built building, all with a/c and TV. Good value if you don't mind being a 10-min walk from the beach.

E Chok Dee Resort, 38 Moo 4. T08-1910 9052 (mob). Basic concrete bungalows with bathroom and fan. Good value for what they are. Quiet spot very near the beach. Also has a restaurant.

Ao Kai Bae

LL-A Koh Chang Cliff Beach, T08-1868 1840 (mob), www.kohchangcliffbeach.com. Strangely designed resort resembling a caravan park. A wide range of rooms are available, pleasant grounds and attractive pool, although still overpriced.

LL-A Sea View Resort, 10/2 Moo 4, T08-1830 7529 (mob), www.seaviewkoh chang.com. Very comfortable bungalows set on a steep hill in a landscaped garden.

A Siam Bay Resort, southern end of the beach, T08-1859 5529 (mob), www.siambay resort.in.th. Spacious modern bungalows with TV, a/c and seaview. Secluded spot at the foot of jungle covered cliffs. Swimming pool and restaurant.

D-F Porn Bungalows, offer huts on the beach, they're basic and rather run-down, but reasonable.

Haad Tha Nam (Lonely beach)

A-E Warapura Resort, next to Sunset Hut, T08-1824 4177 (mob). Swish and very modern,the seaview bungalows have a lounge area, equipped with a flat screen TV and a huge balcony right on the water's edge. At the time of writing, cheaper fan cottages are being built a little way back from the sea. There's no sandy beach here, that's a 10-min walk away. Recommended.

D-E Kachapura, 40/20 Moo 1, T08-6050 0754 (mob), www.kachapura.com. These new, beautifully designed bungalows are incredible value. A/c or fan they come with roofless bathrooms and are set in a landscaped garden. The beach is a 5-min walk. For the price, it's highly recommended.

D-E Siam Hut, T08-6609 7772(mob). Basic cheap and cheerful huts. Great if you fancy undisturbed peace and quiet.

E Paradise cottage, 104/1 Moo 1, T039-558 121, y_yinggg@hotmail.com. Laid-back vibe, with plenty of chill-out areas. These new bungalows (fan only) are basic but well designed and have been built using natural materials, On a rocky part of the beach. Internet, bar and restaurant. Recommended.

F Treehouse, take the turning before Kachapura Resort. Hippy village feel. Very basic bamboo huts with bathroom outside and no fan, although with the sea breeze, it's not needed. Raised platform over the sea, houses the bar and restaurant which serves up tasty wraps. Buckets, shots and DJ ensure a party atmosphere.

Bailan Bay

D-E Bai Lan Hut, next to Bai Lan Beach Resort, T08-7028 0796 (mob), info@bailanhuts.com. Basic bamboo huts available with either fan of a/c, both with bathroom. Although the beach is rocky here, it is extremely peaceful. Restauarant serves Thai and Western food.

D-E Rock Inn, 4/7 Moo 1, T039-558126, Gerhard@rockinn-kohchang.com. These huts, with bathroom and fan are set in a nice garden about 5 mins' walk from a sandy beach. They are all individually designed and have lots of character. There is a restaurant serving quality Thai and Western food. Long- term rates available.

E-F Bailan Family Bungalows, T08-9051 2701 (mob), www.bailanfamilybungalow. com. Typical basic bamboo huts set on a gentle slope that leads to the beach. Fan and a/c rooms. Restaurant serves Thai and European food.

Ao Bang Bao and Ao Bai Bin

LL-AL Nivana, 12/4 Moo 1, T039-5580614, www.nivanaresorts.com. On a very secluded part of the beach. Large, well appointed rooms with somewhat chunky furniture. Recommended for its peaceful location. There is a fresh water and salt water swimming pool.

A Bang Bao Sea Hut, 28 Moo 1, T01-285 0570. At the very end of the pier, each of these spacious wooden huts are on stilts on the water. Stunning location, all have a/c, TV, fridge and a balcony. Prices include breakfast. Recommended.

C-D Buddha view, 28 Moo 1, T03-9558157. Nicely decorated log-cabin-style rooms at the end of the pier, some en suite, others with shared bathroom, all with a/c.

F Paradise, 27 Moo 1, T08-9934 8044 (mob). Very basic, small, wooden huts, mid-way along the pier, have just a mattress on the floor and a fan. Shared bathroom.

Islands off Koh Chang *p429*

Nearly all the islands in the Koh Chang archipelago are part of a national park (Koh Kood, the largest, is outside the park) and any accommodation built on them shouldn't really be there. Most of the resorts are all-inclusive and of the mid-range, 3- to 4-star variety – the best value come from package deals. As this is a national park you

can camp anywhere. Also remember that all beaches in Thailand are public.

Koh Kood

For the latest impartial advice and for help with booking accommodation, contact Koh Kood Happy Days Infocentre, T08-7144 5945 (mob). The majority of cheaper backpacker options are found on and around Ao Klong Chao, a peaceful sandy beach.

L-AL Koh Kood Island Resort, T039-511 824, www.sawadee.com/thai/koodisland. Has 2 styles of room – one resembling traditional southern-style houses constructed on stilts over the water; the other in among the hills. Both are very tastefully designed, using natural materials.

L-C Away Resorts, 43/8 Moo 2, Laem Khlang Chao, T02-6968239, www.awayresorts.com. Well-designed bungalows with TV, a/c and hot water. The safari-style tents are the most interesting and fun option. With 25 sq m and en suite bathrooms with hot water, these are not your usual camping tents. Great views across the bay. The beach is either a 10-min walk or a 1-min transfer by kayak. Professional, friendly and helpful management. Excellent and very reasonably priced restaurant. Recommended.

B Hindard Resort, 162 Moo 2, Ao Ngam Kho, T039-521359, www.hindardresort.com. Bright and airy wooden huts on a small rise with stunning seaviews. Fan and a/c. The beach is a 2-min walk through a landscaped garden. Maybe overpriced.

B Koh Kood Resort & Spa, 45 Moo 5, Ao Bang Bao, T01-8297751, www.kohkood resortandspa.com. Spacious wooden bungalows in a tropical garden that leads to a secluded beach. All of the bungalows have lots of natural light, mosquito nets, a/c and a huge bathroom.

C-D Mangrove Bungalows, along the road from **Mark House**, Ao Klong Chao. Further back from the beach, about a 5 min walk, these clean a/c and fan bungalows overlook the mangroves of the Klong Jao River, a serene spot. There is a restaurant that serves good Thai and Western food and the room price includes breakfast. There are kayaks for rent so you can explore the river.

C-D Mark House Bungalows, 43/4 Moo 2, Ao Klong Chao, T08-6133 0402 (mob), www.mark housebungalow.com. These comfortable and clean wooden bungalows, fan and a/c, are a 5 min walk from the beach. Set in a small garden.

C-E Happy Days Guesthouse & Restaurant, next to the Koh Kood Post Office, Ao Klong Chao, T08-7144 5945 (mob), kaikoh kood@yahoo.com. Spotlessly clean fan and a/c rooms, all with bathroom. 2 family bungalows available. 1 min walk from the beach. Extremely helpful and knowledgeable owners speak English, Thai and German. Motorbikes for hire (฿300). Highly recommended.

C-E Siam Beach Resort, 49 Moo 4, Ao Bang Bao, T08-1899 6200 (mob). Tired-looking bungalows that have seen better days and rude management. However, the location right on a long stretch of sandy beach is superb. Both a/c and fan available.

C-F Baan Din, near the Siam Beach Resort, Ao Bang Bao, T08-6052 2929 (mob). These individually designed huts have lots of character. On the edge of the jungle so mosquitoes might be a problem. The beach is a short walk away.

D-F Baan Klong Jao Homestay, next to Mark House Bungalows, Ao Klong Chao, T08-7075 0943 (mob). Clean and homely a/c and fan rooms, with shared bathroom. This is a traditional Thai teak house on stilts overlooking the river. The Thai food in the restaurant comes recommended.

E Ngamkho Resort, next to the Hin Dat Resort, Ao Ngam Kho, T08-18257076 (mob), www.kohkood-ngamkho.com. Beautiful huts on a gentle slope that leads to the beach. Made using natural materials, all bungalows have a mosquito net, hammock, bathroom and fan. For the price these are exceptional value. Highly recommended.

F Seaview Bungalows, 43/5 Moo 2, Ao Klong Chao, T08-7908 3593 (mob). Cheap,

cheerful and clean huts with fan and bathroom (although most have a squat toilet). Garden setting, 2 mins from the beach. Friendly staff. There is also an excellent shop selling fresh fruit and vegetables. The restaurant comes recommended.

Koh Mak
AL-A Ban Laem Chan, T08-1914 2593 (mob). 7 wooden cottages with seaview, attached bathrooms and 'club house'.

AL-E Koh Maak Resort, T039-501013, www.kohmakresort.com. Old-style bungalows. Claims to have a private beach – all beaches have full public access in Thailand. A/c, TV and fan. Possibly overpriced.

B-E Ao Khao Resort, T039-501 000. Average bungalows in an OK location. All a/c and clean though, once again, they're overpriced.

D-E TK Hut Bungalow, T08-7134 8435 (mob). Affordable, clean bungalows in a decent location. Free Wi-Fi and pick-up from the pier.

Koh Kham
B-D Koh Kham Resort, T08-1303 1229 (mob), www.kohkhamisland.com. Average bungalow operation with en suite fan rooms in nice enough location. They offer packages that includes transfers from Trat, and food. Overpriced.

Koh Ngam
B-C Royal Paradise Koh-Ngam Resort. Simple bungalows on stilts arranged in a row, simply furnished. Pricey, paying for the location. Also has a restaurant.

B-C Twin Island Resort. Similar to Royal Paradise. Has a restaurant.

Koh Whai
C-E Koh Wai Pakarang (Coral), www.kohwaipakarang.com, T08-4113 8946 (mob). Open Oct-May. Your standard basic bungalow with beachside location. Rooms come with fan or a/c, all en suite. There are also some rooms in a concrete block.

F-G Koh Wai Paradise, 9/5 Moo 6. T08-1762 2548 (mob). Tiny, very basic and cheap bungalows set beside a gorgeous beach. When visited, mountains of plastic bottles were dumped in the forest behind the huts and on surrounding beaches.

🍴 Eating

Chantaburi *p422*

Most restaurants are on Tha Chalaep Rd. Where the road runs along the eastern side of King Taksin Lake, there is a profusion of pubs, bars and ice cream parlours. Good places to eat seafood on Tha Chalaep Rd include: **Phikul Phochana Thalchaleb** (53 Moo 9), **Suan Poo Thachaleb** (134 Moo 9), and **Thachaleb Seafood** (all 🍴🍴).

🍴🍴 **Bangon's**, Sukhaphiban Rd. Open 0800-2200. Smaller in size than **Luong-toy's**, which is next door, and with a more limited menu, but equally cheerful.

🍴🍴 **Luongtoy's**, Sukhaphiban Rd. Open 1200-2200. Relaxed and friendly riverside restaurant with a great range of Thai food served in an attractive location under thatched roofs (free rice and fruit). Traditional music in the evenings on Tue, Thu and Fri.

🍴🍴 **Meun-ban** ('Homely' restaurant), Saritdet Rd, next to the bus terminal. Probably the best mid-rang restaurant in town offering a multitude of Thai dishes (including a huge vegetarian selection and ice creams). The owners speak good English and are a helpful source of local information. It is also in an ideal location if you arrive tired and hungry after a long bus journey and need some refreshment. Recommended.

🍴🍴 **San Chandra** (Chantaburi Rice and Noodle House), Saritdet Rd. Another sparklingly clean and friendly restaurant offering delicious Thai food and ice creams. Recommended.

Aranya Prathet and the Cambodian border *p424*

There are several night markets scattered around town selling the usual dishes.

Steak and Bakery, situated in the centre of town in a redeveloped shopping precinct. Not much steak but recommended for its Thai food.

Trat and Khlong Yai *p424, map p424*

🍴 **Cool Corner**, 21-23 Than Charoen Rd, Trat. Serves excellent coffee, cake, Thai and veggie food. Recommended.

🍴 **Joys**, Than Charoen Rd, opposite **Guy Guesthouse**, Trat. A French-run pizzeria, that does delicious thin-bases.

🍴-🍴 **Baibuo**, take a right after Pier 112, it's on the left over the bridge, Trat. Korean style BBQ where you grill your own meat at the table.

🍴-🍴 **Orchid restaurant**, 92 Lakmuang Rd, Trat. Wide range of tasty Thai and European food.

🍴 **Isaan shophouse restaurant**, Than Charoen Rd, next door to **Ban Jai Dee**, Trat. If your tastebuds are crying out for *som tam*, *larb moo* and sticky rice this is an excellent choice.

🍴 **Krua Rim Klong**, on the corner of Thanacharoen Rd and Soi Rimklong, Trat, T039-524919. This modern restaurant/bar, with courtyard garden, serves a superb range of food and drink.

🍴 **Nam Chok**, corner of Soi Butnoi and Wiwatthana roads (off Thatmai Rd), Trat. Good local food served outdoors.

🍴 **Pier 112**, 132 Thanachareon Rd, Trat. Laid-back restaurant and bar set in large garden area. Good range of Western and Thai food, including vegetarian. Serves cocktails.

🍴 **Vegetarian restaurant**, tucked away down Soi Tat Mai, take the first *soi* on the left after Ban Jai Dee, Trat. Serves delicious and incredibly cheap Thai veggie food. Just point at the dish you want.

Foodstalls

The municipal market has a good range of stalls to choose from – good value and delicious. Other markets which sell food include the night market next to the a/c bus station.

Koh Chang p426, map p428
Hat Sai Kaew (White Sand Beach)
₩₩₩-₩₩ Texas Steak House. Tasty steaks in pleasant surroundings, sea views from the balcony, just.

₩ 15 Palms, offers a wide range of delicious Thai and Western food.

₩ The Fisherman's, between Patthai and Cookie. Good fresh fish.

₩ India Hut. Next to the post office on the main road. Authentic Indian food.

₩ Mac Bungalows. A must for barbecues.

₩ The Taxi Stop. Recommended for a great steak sandwich with cheese and decent bread.

₩ Thor's Palace. Excellent restaurant of the variety where you sit on the floor at low, lamp-lit tables, good Thai curries, very friendly management and popular, library.

₩-₩ Tapas Bar, next to Koh Chang Lagoon Resort. Funky beachfront bar serving pizza and baguettes.

₩-₩ Tonsai Restaurant, across the road, opposite Sangtawan Bungalows. This restaurant is built around a 'Tonsai' tree and is a magical place to enjoy lunch, dinner or some cocktails. Friendly staff serve delicious Thai food. Highly recommended.

₩ A Biento Coffee, on the main road, opposite Kacha Spa & Resort. Coffee and sandwiches in a/c café, offering respite from the heat.

₩ Cookies, south of Patthai. Good selection of Thai and travellers' food, popular and cheap.

Hat Khlong Prao
₩₩-₩ Crust Bakery, 19/5 Moo 4. Bakery, deli, restaurant and bar. Fantastic range of gourmet food: truffles, Bavarian beer and bread, salami … the list goes on. The baguettes are delicious.

Bailan Bay
₩ Rock Inn, 4/7 Moo 7. The Western food is recommended.

₩ Sundown Terrace. Superb location overlooking the bay. Reasonable Thai food.

Ao Bang Bao
₩ Little Havana, Bang Bao Pier. Cuban restaurant serving tapas and cocktails in cool and breezy surroundings.

₩ Blue Café, Bang Bao Pier. Good hearty breakfasts and sandwiches.

Islands off Koh Chang p429
Koh Kood
₩ Away Restaurant, 43/8 Moo 2. Professional chef serves delicious Thai and Western food. Cocktails and fresh coffee are also available. Restaurant overlooks the bay.

₩ Baan Klong Jao Homestay, Baan Klong Jao. Serves tasty spicy Thai food. Remember to order your food not spicy if you can't handle the chillies.

₩ Mangrove. Excellent Thai food dished up on the bank of the River Klong Jao

₩ Sunset Restaurant & Bar. Good range of Thai and Western food, also serve cocktails. They occasionally have beach BBQs.

⊙ Bars and clubs

Koh Chang p426, map p428
Dolphin Divers Bar, Klong Prao, opposite the turning for Chok Dee Bungalows. Small open bamboo huts serve drinks at bargain prices. Happy hour 1800-2000 (buy 1 get 1 free).

No Name Bar, next to Kai Bae Hut Resort, Ao Kai Be. Another good place to spend an evening.

Sabay Bar, Hat Sai Kaew, just next to the Sabay Resort. A night-time location where you can either relax on cushions on the beach or dance the night away inside – the buckets are a must try.

White Sands Cat Bar, Hat Sai Kaew, opposite Best Garden Resort. A friendly, little, well-stocked bar and an excellent source of information as well as a good place to hire motorbikes.

O Shopping

Chantaburi p422
Si Chan Rd, or 'Gem St', has the best selection of jewellery shops and gem stores. However, you are unlikely to pick up a bargain. On Fri, Sat and Sun a gem street market operates along Krachang Lane. Chantaburi is regarded as one of the centres of fine rattan work in Thailand. Available from numerous shops in town.

Trat and Khlong Yai p424, map p424
Tratosphere bookshop, 23 Rimklong Soi, Trat. The French- and English-speaking owner is exceptionally helpful and knowledgeable about everything to do with Trat, Koh Chang and surrounding islands. Pop in here for the latest, up-to-date information.

▲▲ Activities and tours

Trat and Khlong Yai p424, map p424
Tour operators
Koh Chang TT Travel, Sukhumvit Rd, Trat, T039-531420. For trustworthy travel advice and bookings.

Koh Chang p426, map p428
Canopying
Tree Top Adventure Park, Aow Bai Lan, T08-4310 7600 (mob). Obstacle course in the jungle, test your skill and daring by walking along platforms suspended from trees. ฿700.

Diving
Dolphin Divers, T07-0281627, www.dolphin kohchang.com. This Swiss-owned outfit has its main office on Khlong Phrao and offers all PADI courses from Open Water (฿13,500) through to Instructor. It runs dive trips (2 dives) around the Koh Chang archipelago starting at ฿2300, inclusive of equipment and food.
Koh Chang Divers, Hat Sai Kaew. A Swiss-run diving school, which offers PADI and snorkelling; no credit cards accepted.

Elephant trekking
Ban Kwan Chang elephant camp, near Khlong Son, www.jungleway.com. Was set up to look after elephants that were no longer working in northern Thailand, rescuing them from a lifetime of walking the streets of Bangkok. It is a project set up in conjunction with the **Asian Elephant Foundation** to provide a natural environment for elephants and their keepers. To fund the project it runs elephant treks ranging from ฿500-900. The price includes transport, food and drink, and a trek. If you want to go elephant trekking this is a great place to do it, as the keepers are very friendly and the elephants are well looked after.

Islands off Koh Chang p429
Diving
The only resort on the **Koh Kood** with PADI Certified instructors is **Away Resorts**, T08-4466 5554 (mob), for more information.

Watersports
On **Koh Kood**, the Happy Days Infocentre rents snorkelling equipment (฿150 per day) and kayaks.

⊖ Transport

Chantaburi p422
Bus
Regular connections with **Bangkok**'s Eastern bus terminal. Also buses to **Pattaya**, **Rayong**, **Ban Phe** and other eastern seaboard towns.
    There are roughly 8 buses a day from Chantburi to **Aranya Prathet**'s bus terminal, 3 hrs.

Aranya Prathet and the Cambodian border p424
Bus
From Aranya Prathet's bus terminal (1.5 km northwest of the town centre), there are connections with **Korat** (Nakhon Ratchasima) and **Bangkok** (4 hrs).

Train

Trains also link Aranya Prathet with **Bangkok**: just 2 trains a day in each direction with 3rd-class, non-a/c trains only.

Trat and Khlong Yai *p424, map p424*
Air

Bangkok Airways, www.bangkokair.com, runs twice daily flights from Trat to **Bangkok**, fares start at about ฿2200.

Boat

Boats leave for **Koh Mak** from Klom Long Chumporn pier at 0930, 1000, 1400 and 1600, ฿450, 1 hr.

Speedboats for **Koh Kood** leave from Dankao pier at 0800, 0830 and 0900; Laem Sok pier at 1300; and Coral beach at 1400. All cost ฿550 and take approximately 1½ hrs. A slow boat, ฿300, 5 hrs, leaves from the Dankao pier at 1000.

Bus

฿ 40 by *songthaew* to the bus station in Trat, where there are regular connections with **Bangkok**'s Eastern bus terminal (฿250B, 5½ hrs). There are also regular connections to **Bangkok**'s Northern bus terminal, all stopping at Savanahubuni International airport (฿258, 5½ hrs); **Pattaya** (3½ hrs); and **Chantaburi** (1 hr 40 mins).

Songthaew

To **Laem Ngop** from outside the municipal market, opposite KFC, on Sukhumvit Rd (30 mins, ฿40). To Dankao pier, ฿100 (charter, not per person) There are also regular connections to **Khlong Yai** (฿60) and **Hat Lek**. First take a *songthaew* to Khlong Yai and then another to Hat Lek (฿20).

Regular departures during daylight hours. After dark, *songthaews* must be chartered.

Laem Ngop *p426*
Boat

Boats leave daily for the various beaches from one of the 3 piers in Laem Ngop hourly between 0600-1900. This service is reduced

to every 2 hrs in the wet season. The ferry costs about ฿100 one way or ฿160 return and takes 1 hr. The main pier is right at the end of the road from Trat, before you fall into the sea. The other 2 piers are several kilometres west of Laem Ngop and service the more expensive resorts.

To **Koh Chang**, regular, hourly, departures from the Centre Point pier. Boats to **Khlong Son Beach** take 1 hr; to **Than Ma Yom Pier**, 50 mins; to **Dan Mai Pier**, 35 mins. During peak season (Nov-May) there are almost hourly departures, some to **Than Ma Yom Pier** (east coast), others to the west coast.
Car ferry A car ferry leaves from Laem Ngop's third pier, at Ao Thammachat on Rte 3156 – 5 departures daily.

Koh Chang *p426, map p428*

When leaving the island it is advisable to get immediately into a *songthaew* to Trat (if that is where you want to go) rather than hanging around because if you miss the one which meets the boat you may have to wait hours for the next one or have to charter one.

See pages 429-430 for details on getting to the smaller islands of Koh Kood and Koh Mak.

Bicycle

Some of the guesthouses now have mountain bikes for hire (around ฿100 per day).

Boat

In bad weather ring the Laem Ngop tourist office, see page 426, or the national parks office on Koh Chang, T039-586056, T08-1758 2145 (mob), Mon-Fri 0800-1700, for information on ferry schedules.

There are boats from 0730 from **Than Ma Yom Pier** (pick-ups leave from Hat Sai Kaew). Between Jun and Oct – the low season – boats are more irregular and some routes do not operate at all because of rough seas combined with limited demand.
Car ferry Car ferries leave from Koh Chang Centrepoint Pier, northwest of Laem Ngop, 12 times daily. Another vehicular ferry leaves

from Laem Ngop's third pier, at Ao Thamma-chat on Route 3156 – 5 departures daily.

Motorbike
Hire available from many of the guesthouses – can be a much cheaper option if you intend on travelling around the island. ฿200 for 24 hrs.

Taxi
There are no cars, but there are motorbike and jeep taxis. These are pretty expensive (about ฿20-40 per 5 km). The usual rule of not getting into an empty one without checking the price first applies of course. The high prices date back to the days when the roads were poor and the machines had a very short lifespan but there is really no excuse for it now that the roads have been improved.

Islands off Koh Chang p429
Boat
Ferryboat Departs from Sapannamlook (Koh Kood) for Dankao pier at 1100, ฿350.
Slowboat Sapannamlook (Koh Kood) to Dankao pier, ฿250, 5 hrs.
Speedboat Speedboats depart Koh Kood 1st for Koh Mak (฿300)and then Trat, Laem Sok pier (฿550) at 1000 and 1300 daily in high season. The price to Laem Sok includes transfer to the town centre or bus station. Additional speedboats (also ฿550) depart at 0900 for Coral beach and Dankao pier at 1300. Speedboat to Koh Chang departs 0900, via Koh Mak ฿400, direct ฿900.

Motorbike
Motorbikes can be hired from several guesthouses in Koh Kood, including **Happy Days Guesthouse** (฿300 per day). It's not recommended that you learn how to ride a bike here.

❶ Directory

Chantaburi p422
Banks Bangkok, 50 Tha Chalaep Rd; Thai Farmers, 103 Sirong Muang Rd. **Post office**

At the intersection of Amphawan and Si Chan roads.

Aranya Prathet and the Cambodian border p424
Banks There are a few banks, including the Siam City Bank, with ATM facilities. **Internet and post office** There are a few internet cafés and a post office.

Trat and Khlong Yai p424, map p424
Banks On Sukhumvit Rd. **Post office** Tha Reua Jang Rd on northeast side of town.

Laem Ngop p426
Banks Mobile exchange service at the pier, 0900-1600. Exchange rates on Koh Chang are poor. **Medical services** Malaria Centre, on main road, opposite Laem Ngop Inn. It gives the latest information on malaria and can help with treatment.

Koh Chang p426, map p428
Banks Koh Chang now has several ATMs located at Hat Sai Kaew and Khlong Phrao – there is also a Siam Bank branch at Khlong Phrao – opposite Boutique Resort offering an exchange service, 1000-1800. **Internet, post office and telephone** There are now dozens of phoneboxes and internet cafés (฿2 per min) throughout the island and a post office at the southern end of Sai Kaew beach. **Medical services** Bangkok Hospital, T039-551555. There are doctors in Ao Khlong Son and in Ao Khlong Phrao near Hobby Hut. For more serious injuries patients are transferred to Laem Ngop. **Police** There are 6 policemen permanently at the station in Khlong Son. Thefts should be reported immediately so that if there are suspects, the next boat to the mainland can be intercepted by the mainland police.

Islands off Koh Chang p429
Medical Services Hospital, Koh Kood, T08-6836 4177 (mob), English speaking staff.
Post office There is one next to Happy Days Guesthouse, Koh Kood.

Contents

Footprint features

Border crossings

Thailand–Malaysia
Sungei Golok–Rantau Panjang,
see page 560
Satun–Kuala Perlis, see page 577

At a glance

⊖ **Getting around** Cheap flights,
and trains, buses and boats.

◉ **Time required** Stay longer than
the 2 weeks and you'll discover more.

☀ **Weather** The intense Indian
monsoon hits from Jul-Oct.

✖ **When not to go** Try to avoid
monsoon season.

Andaman Coast

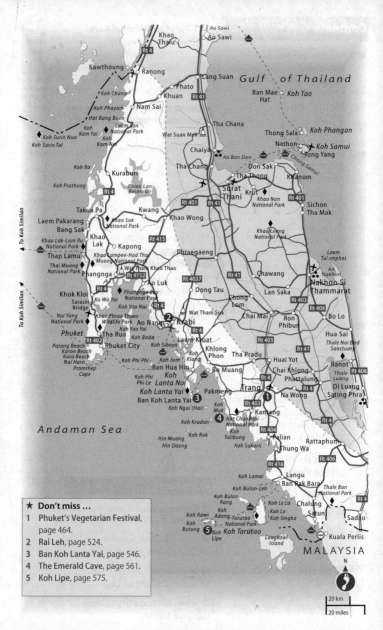

★ Don't miss ...
1 Phuket's Vegetarian Festival, page 464.
2 Rai Leh, page 524.
3 Ban Koh Lanta Yai, page 546.
4 The Emerald Cave, page 561.
5 Koh Lipe, page 575.

The Andaman coast presents a startling cultural mosaic, from Ranong's cheroot-smoking Burmese in the north to the south's strident Muslims, along with the numerous Chao Le sea gypsies and Chinese traders. On Ranong's rain-drenched islands, bare-knuckle boxing matches between Burmese and Thai re-enact an age-old rivalry while a growing separatist movement continues to spread through the hotly contested deep South that was part of Malaysia a little over a century ago. Meanwhile, indigenous sea gypsies who escaped the tsunami persist in animist practices, including offerings of human hair to the spirits of the treacherous Andaman. Travellers will find many pleasures along this coast, from the Similan islands' world-famous diving sites, including Richelieu Rock, to Phuket's beaches including *katoey* paradise Patong and jetset Pansea.

Further down the coast are Phangnga's sea cave paintings and the magical floating fishing village of Koh Panyi. Off Krabi – where giant prehistoric human skulls were found – are eerie towering limestone karsts revered by climbers. Deeper south reveals Koh Lanta's white-sand coral-rimmed beaches while the brooding ex-prison island of Tarutao, reputed to be haunted, offers dense and terrifying untouched jungle populated by wild boar, barking deer and poisonous snakes. And the Adang-Rawi archipelago's tiny islands – unreachable during the monsoon – provide cosy homes for pythons and hornbills while only metres off shore snorkellers can find untouched sea life including shoals of barracuda. Finally, the whole of the coast is dotted with island retreats with no electricity or cars, among them Koh Muk with the nearby Emerald Cave and the tropical idyll Koh Bulon-Leh.

Ranong to Khao Lak

A wild, untouched landscape begins to unfold, with waterfalls, lush rainforest and dense mountains all home to fantastical species like the largest flower in the world and insects the size of a man's hand. Ranong, on Route 4, is famous for both its hot springs and visa runs by expats and travellers who can cross the border into Burma by boat to renew their visas in a day. Like Mae Sot, its proximity to Burma fosters a border diaspora as Burmese workers – many illegal – hasten across, desperately searching for work in a country which traditionally has fought bitterly with the their own. In Ranong and the surrounding islands, the tribal Burmese clearly stand out with the men wearing sarongs and the women daubed with clay face paint smoking cheroots. There are often boxing competitions between the two nationalities which dramatically display another difference, between the fighting style of the highly ritualistic Thai muay and compared frenzied freeform Burmese style.

From Prathong Island near Takua Pa (south of Ranong), right down to Phuket, virtually the entire western coast of Phangnga comprises great long sandy bays with the occasional peninsula or rocky headland. With the Thai Muang National Park to the south, the Khao Lak Lam Ru National Park bordering the Khao Lak area, and the Khao Sok National Park inland to the north, tourism operators along the coast of Phangnga are targeting those interested in 'getaway' and nature tours. Meanwhile Ranong's proximity to the Similan and Surin islands (the western coast resorts in Phangnga are also the closest departure points for the Similan Islands) makes it an ideal stopover for divers. Certainly, as the gateway to Richelieu Rock and the Mergul archipelago, it is hard to beat.
▶▶ *For listings, see pages 454-461.*

Ranong ⊜❷❼❺⊿❻❻ ▶▶ *pp454-461. Colour map 4, B2.*

Surrounded by forested mountains, Ranong is a scenic place to stay for a day or two. It is a small and unpretentious provincial capital and an important administrative centre. Increasingly, it is being eyed up as a spa/hot spring location but is currently still more popular with Southeast Asian tourists than those from further afield. The free municipal hot springs just outside the town are a charming spot, where the area's varied population gather day and night to get warm, floppy and relaxed in the ever hot water. It offers an excellent way to watch all levels of Thai society at their most lethargic while warming yourself after one of the town's many thunderstorms. There are waterfalls here, one of which, Punyaban, can be seen from the road as you approach the town. It is also the jumping-off point for a number of beautiful islands in the Andaman Sea. There is a small tourist office on Kamlungsab Road.

Getting there
The road journey from the north is arduous (eight hours at least) the last half of which is through mountains; not good for travel sickness sufferers. Consider taking the train from Bangkok to Chumphon and the bus from there (which takes the same time in total). The bus terminal is on the edge of town, Highway 4, near the Jansom Thara Hotel. However, the buses stop in town on Ruangrat Road before the terminal. From Bangkok, the ordinary buses are around ฿180 while second-class air-conditioned are around ฿280. VIP buses cost around ฿500. The air-conditioned bus departs only twice in the morning and three times in the evening, the last direct bus to Ranong departs at 2130. There is an airport 20 km south of town.

1941 Japanese invasion of Burma

On 8 December 1941, the Japanese military landed at Parkham Chumpon, to seize Burma. However, young Thais – mainly students and villagers – resisted the Japanese and many were killed on both sides. Following collaboration with the Thai government, the Imperial Army were able to halt any further resisters and by the end of December had captured Victoria Point in Burma. But when the infantry discovered that the terrain along Highway 4 – which followed Chumphon, Kra Buri, the La-un canal and Petchakasem – was virtually impassable, they decided to construct a railway parallel to the highway instead and set up headquarters at Khao Fachi village. Here they surveyed enemy approaches from the tops of two trees on the mountain while down below soldiers quarters were rapidly erected and underground prisons created to hold POWs – mainly Malay Indians and some Thai.

Used as slave labour, the POWs built roads and a complex of hospitals, kitchens, dining halls and a railway station along with a graveyard for fellow POWs. The Japanese needed more POWs in order to fulfill their obligations having signed an agreement to build the railway.

Consequently, in 1943, further POWs were brought by train from Chumpon railway station and marched the many arduous miles to the site, many dying en route or escaping to Petchaburi where they begged for food from villagers or were caught, to be returned and tortured.

The Japanese used the Chumphon–Kra Buri–La-un railway for 11 months until Allied forces heavily bombed the railway and base at Khao Fachi on 19 March 1945. On 10 August 1945, the Japanese surrendered. Today all that remains of the camp and railway are relics of guns, mortar bombs, samurai swords, tunnels, trenches and underground shelters while the railway is overgrown and filled with defunct and rusty sleepers. The well, built and used by the POWs and the guards at the camp, is now used by the villagers of Khao Fachi.

Background

The name Ranong is derived from *rae* (tin) *nong* (rich), and the town was established in the late 18th century by a family from Hokkien, China. Prosperous through its tin mines, Ranong relied heavily on slave labour. Indeed, when Khaw Soo Cheang, another Chinese émigré became governor of Ranong in the mid-1800s, he imported indentured Chinese labourers from Penang to work in the tin mines. The working conditions were so merciless that a popular Ranong saying at the time went: 'The Ranong pit is easy to get into, but it is impossible to get out of.' In 1876, when Khaw Soo Cheang went to China to pay an ancestral visit, 2000 Chinese labourers revolted but Kaw Soo Cheang, a self-made man from a poor background, was able to quell the mob on his return and was duly rewarded by the Thai monarch – Rama V – with the title of the rajah of Ranong. Among other gifts he received from the gracious King of Siam were a gold jug, gold table, gold spittoon and long-handled red umbrella with matching robes. A polygamous husband, in keeping with the standards of that time, Kaw Soo Cheang had a Thai wife and a Chinese one. Later in life, when one died, he replaced her with an 18-year-old beauty chosen by his family. Today you can see the legacy of Kaw Soo Cheang with Ranong still boasting a predominantly Sino-Thai population and a number of attractive 19th-century Chinese-style houses.

Ranong province is the first southern province bordering the Indian Ocean and it is Thailand's rainiest (often in excess of 5000 mm per year), narrowest and least populated province. Kra Buri, 58 km north of Ranong, is the point where the Kra Isthmus is also at its narrowest, and there has been debate for centuries about the benefits of digging a canal across the isthmus, so linking the Gulf of Thailand with the Andaman Sea and short-cutting the long hike down the peninsula to Singapore and north through the Melaka Strait.

Sights

The town contains excellent geo-thermal mineral water springs (65°C) at **Wat Tapotharam** ① *2 km east of the town and behind the Jansom Thara Hotel, free.* To get there, walk or take a *songthaew* along Route 2; ask for 'bor nam rawn' (hot water well). Surrounded by dramatic forested hills, the spa water bubbles out of the ground hot enough to boil an egg and cools sufficiently to allow the city's residents to enjoy a free hot bath and take refuge in its cosy depths during Ranong's frequent thunderstorms. The valley also has a luxurious hot spring and health club, offering a jacuzzi, gym, steam room, sauna and massages from ฿300, but it lacks the natural setting and village green feel of the municipal springs across the road. Around the park are several seafood restaurants and food stands. The springs also provide the **Jansom Thara Hotel** with thermal water for hot baths and a giant jacuzzi. There is a small park with a cable bridge over the river, a tiny cave containing a small Buddhist shrine and a number of municipal bathing pools. The wat here contains a footprint of the Buddha. Continuing along Route 2 for another 6 km or so, the road reaches the old tin-mining village of Hat Som Paen. **Wat Som Paen** is worth a visit to see the numerous giant carp, protected because of their supposed magical qualities. Deep in the hills, a few kilometres further up the road, is Ranong canyon, where city folk escape to recline in pretty shalas above the water, swim or feed countless hungry catfish.

Port of Ranong lies 3 km from town. Each morning the dock seethes with activity as Thai and Burmese fishing boats unload their catches. Boats can be hired, at a pontoon next to the dock, to tour the bustling harbour and look across the Kra River estuary to the Burmese border (approximately ฿400). Border officials can be touchy so carry your passport. Ranong is an important point of contact between Burma and Thailand. Like Mae Sot, there are more intensive searches and check points as you leave the area. Do not be surprised if the military come onto your bus up to three or four times on the way out to check documents. This intensifies in line with the guerrilla operations in Burma and the drug wars.

Laem Son National Park ⊜🕑🔺 »» pp454-461. Colour map 4, B1.

Ins and outs

① *T077-824224, free entry.*
Laem Son National Park is 45 km south of Ranong and includes islands in the Andaman Sea. Travel agents can organize day trips taking in a couple of the islands, but to get the most out of your money it's possible to take a *songthaew* (฿25) 43 km south of Ranong along Route 4. On the right, there's a 10-km turn-off that leads straight to the park (฿30 by motorbike taxi from the roadside). Taxi boats run from the island pier (Saphan Plaa) in Ranong out to Koh Chang four or five times a day in high season at 0900, 1000, 1200, 1400 and 1500. From May to October one boat runs daily at 1400 (฿120, one hour). Outside these hours you can charter speedboats from **Cashew Resort** ① *T077-820 116.* Taxi boats

for Koh Phayam leave the same pier at 0900 and 1400 (฿150, two hours), returning at 0830 and 1400. Speed boats leave at 0900 and return at 1300 (฿350, 40 minutes). In low season one taxi boat a day departs from Ranong at 1400 and from Phayam at 0830. The quickest and cheapest way to explore the smaller islands closer to Laem Son is to charter a long-tailed boat once almost in the national park. Negotiating directly with the fishermen operating from Hat Bang Baen (turn off left just before the park entrance) should cost about ฿1000, while **Wasana Resort** offers its guests a worthwhile day trip including food, frisbee, badminton and snorkelling for ฿1500 per boat. For trips to Koh Surin, see page 452 and Koh Similan, see page 453.

Beaches and islands

There are a number of notable beaches and islands in the neighbourhood of Ranong, many within the limits of the Laem Son National Park, such as Hat Bang Baen, Koh Khang Khao, Koh Khao Khwai, Koh Nam Noi, Koh Kam Yai, Koh Kam Tok, Koh Chang and Koh Phayam (pronounced pie-yam). The water here is warm and a pleasure to swim in, especially around the reefs. The park and the islands effectively lie at the outer limits of the Kra River estuary – so don't expect coral on all islands or excellent visibility. Mangroves fringe many of the islands and because of the high rainfall in the area the natural vegetation is tropical rainforest. This park did receive a cruel blow from the 2004 tsunami, which caused considerable damage to the mangrove forests. While the islands may not have the best snorkelling and water, they hide some wonderfully white sand and secluded beaches and they do have good birdlife (there are around 138 bird species in the park). The best birdwatching months are December to February with many migrating birds and optimum weather conditions.

Hat Bang Baen This is a delightful, relatively untouched, enormous beach lined by forest with lovely shells and fine sand. You can also organize boat trips here to nearby islands.

Koh Chang Unlike the larger Koh Chang on Thailand's east coast, Ranong's tiny Koh Chang has more to offer birdwatchers than beach lovers, but is best known for its distinctly laid-back ambience. Commonly sighted birds are kites, sea eagles and the endearingly clumsy hornbill. And, in the forest along the coast, monkeys and deer can be spied – and heard. The beaches here are mediocre at best and grim at worst, with streaks of black and dubious grey-yellow sand. The island also hibernates from June to mid-October when the monsoon rains lash down with even locals shifting to the mainland, leaving Koh Chang almost empty. But what this island lacks in beach bounty, it makes up for in the chill-out stakes. While there is a burgeoning backpacker tourist industry replete with yoga and dive schools, beach bars and tattooists, the economy still depends on fishing and plantations of rubber, palm and cashew nut. Self-generated electricity remains sporadic and there is no sign of cars, with most people getting around on motorbikes through tracks to the beaches. But, while the beaches are never going to be used in an ice cream advert, the swimmable Ao Yai on the west coast is well worth a visit. Split in two by a strip of a lagoon, from Ao Yai you can see the thuggish silhouette of Burma's mountainous jungle-covered St Matthew's Island which seems to take up most of the horizon. It is intriguing to know that St Matthew's remains a military hotspot because of a massive radar site with a direct satellite link to China. Koh Chang also sports a radar site – for the Thai navy.

Koh Chang survived the tsunami remarkably well, thanks to other islands acting as a breaker for the waves. Only its market was destroyed along with a few bungalows.

Koh Phayam Buffered by Koh Similan, Koh Phayam, along with Koh Chang, were the only inhabited islands on the Ranong coastline not to suffer any deaths from the tsunami. Only on Koh Phayam would there be both Full Moon Parties – albeit low-key ones – and a Miss Cashew Nut Beauty Competition (held during the Cashew Nut Festival). Koh Phayam has no cars and boasts only narrow rutted roads, many that are more like big lanes which run through the nut plantations. There are, however, a series of small tracks around the island for walking, cycling or motorbiking to make a change from lounging on the long and curving white-sand beaches at Ao Yai 'Sunset Bay' or Ao Khao Kwai 'Buffalo Bay'. These days, Koh Phayam has become a quiet hit for the laid-back diving and snorkelling set, see Activities and tours, page 459. This is partly because the island, sometimes called the 'muck divers playground,' offers such offshore delights as flat worms, ascidians, sponges, soft corals, nudibranchs and a variety of sea horses. If you are not the diving sort, the island is also home to wonderfully diverse wildlife with hornbills, while further inland away from the white sandy beaches are monitor lizards, boar, deer, monkeys and snakes. There is also a tiny fishing village on the east coast of the island and a sea gypsy settlement to the west. As for locals, Koh Phayam is populated by Burmese and Thai, 200 and 300 respectively, and there are even a handful of full-time *farang* but come May, this hardy bunch largely dribbles away. Though still a relatively sleepy island, Koh Phayam's guesthouses, especially on Buffalo Bay, have developed steadily since the tsunami, flourishing as the Koh Surin, which are easily accessible from Phayam, become ever more popular. The effects of this development on the island's idyllic status is a cause of concern as there are already serious problems with sewage and rubbish as ferries crossing between the islands and the mainland throw their discards into the sea. Ecological awareness is therefore high on the island agenda, recycling is common, as is solar power and conservative use of electricity (bring a torch). It is possible to hire motorbikes (฿200 per day) but be warned that the roads are sometimes treacherous, narrow and uneven.

Koh Khang Khao (25 minutes from Hat Bang Baen) is the stuff of dreams – it has a relatively small white-sand beach for sunbathing and rocks for picnics, sheltered by trees that continue to grow thick, fast and jungle-like up the steep mountainous slopes. A sandy shelf means there's about 7 m of shallow swimming – ideal for families – before the bed falls away to deeper, rockier territory with some reefs providing good snorkelling. The more adventurous can try to circumnavigate the island by clambering over the countless rocks that fringe the rest of the coastline.

Koh Khao Khwai (30 minutes from Khang Khao) is another beautiful island boasting a long stretch of beach and azure water, with lots of tiny crabs scuttling over the sand and the parched skeletons of long-dead trees lying further up the beach. The longer of the two beaches sweeps from the west along the southerly curve of the island. It's easy to walk from the west to the east side, or take a short path from the southern tip of the beach through the rich vegetation and into a dreamy cove, with white sands, set against the impressive backdrop of mountainous rainforest. The water is bath-like in temperature, but beware of the stony bottom. This cove is, however, overlooked by some national park bungalows, which have information leaflets.

Koh Kam Yai (15 minutes from Khao Khwai) has a western coastline which is all rocks and mountains, with just one short, quiet beach. Most of the beaches are along the northeast coast, with the biggest and most beautiful being at the northeasterly tip. Although fairly small, the beaches are secluded and there's enough space for plenty of people to feel they have the island to themselves. Near the shore there are some good reefs suitable for snorkelling.

Koh Kam Noi (10 minutes from Kam Yai), has only one small beach, with the seabed shelving sharply away after only a couple of metres. The sand is soft and white, but covered with washed-up driftwood, and the trees don't afford much cover from the sun.

South of Ranong ●▲● ₩ *pp454-461.*

Kuraburi
Between Ranong and Takua Pa, the small town of Kuraburi offers some adequate accommodation for a stopover to break up the journey. You can visit the town's attractive beach 12 km to the north, or use Kuraburi as a base to explore the surrounding forests or before a boat journey to the Surin or Prathong islands. Surin boats leave between 15 November and 15 May and cost ฿1100 for the slow boat (2½ hours), and ฿1700 for the fast boat (one hour and 10 minutes).

Koh Prathong
ⓘ *Accessible via Takua Pa on the mainland. Some a/c and non-a/c connections between the Southern terminal in Bangkok and Takua Pa (12 hrs). From Krabi and Phangnga, take a bus towards Phuket and change at Kochloi for a bus running north to Takua Pa. From Phuket take a local bus to Takua Pa. Local buses and songthaews provide transport between smaller communities.*
Prathong Island had one resort on the 11 km of beach – the **Golden Buddha Beach Resort** – and was well known for its environmental focus. The Chelon Institute carried out research on sea turtles here with the help of the resort, and also accepted volunteers. However, the resort did not escape the tsunami and the villages nearby endured terrific damage. Work continues on the **Golden Buddha Resort** and the island's villages. See www.ecoclub.com/goldenbuddha, for the latest updates.

Khao Sok National Park → *Colour map 4, B1.*
ⓘ *www.khaosok.com, entry ฿400.*
The closest town to Khao Sok National Park is Takua Pa (see Sleeping, page 457) but companies from Phuket, Phangnga, Krabi and Surat Thani operate day and overnight tours. An overnight tour is the best way to explore the park. If you want to get into the forest, take an overnight tour into the park with an experienced guide. Overnight stays by the lake, although spartan, are recommended, as the scenery is spectacular and the early morning calm is hard to beat. Tours are available from virtually all the guesthouses near the park (see Sleeping, page 456). Park rangers will also act as guides. Have a chat with your guide before you make up your mind to go so you can be sure you feel comfortable about the level of English (or other languages) they speak, familiarity with the park and knowledge of the environment and wildlife. Taking a guide is sensible as the treks take longer than a day and can be daunting, even for the more experienced walkers. Expect to pay from ฿300 per person for a guide to take you on a day trek, and around ฿2500 per person for an overnight trip to the reservoir (this includes accommodation and all meals), plus the ฿400 to enter the park. Prices vary depending on how many people are in the group. If visiting the park independently, take a local bus from Takua Pa to Phun Phin near

Surat Thani town, or vice versa, and ask the driver to stop at the Khao Sok National Park (*oo-tayaan-haeng-chart-khao-sok*). When you arrive at the stop there will usually be a number of bungalow operators waiting to whisk you off to their establishment; you can otherwise walk or take transport into the park. If you decide to walk take a small pack as it's quite a hike to some bungalows. The drive from Takua Pa to Panom (about halfway between Takua Pa and Surat) is very scenic with views of dramatic limestone karst, forested mountains and valleys. For further information, *Waterfalls and Gibbon Calls: Exploring Khao Sok National Park*, by Thom Henley, is available across southern Thailand, from the visitors' centre at the national park, and from many of the bungalows at Khao Sok.

Khao Sok National Park has limestone karst mountains (the tallest reaches more than 900 m), low mountains covered with evergreen forest, streams and waterfalls, and a large reservoir and dam. The impressive scenery alone would be a good enough reason to visit, but Khao Sok also has a high degree of endemism and an exceptionally large number of mammals, birds, reptiles and other fauna.

The list of 48 confirmed species of mammals include: wild elephants, tigers, barking deer, langur, macaques, civets, bears, gibbons and cloud leopards. Of the 184 confirmed bird species, perhaps the most dramatic include: the rhinoceros hornbill, great hornbill, Malayan peacock pheasant and crested serpent-eagle. The plants to be found here are also of interest. The orchids are best seen from late February to April. If you visit between December and February, the **rafflesia Kerri Meijer** is in flower. This parasitic flower (it depends on low-lying lianas) has an 80-cm bloom – the largest in the world – with a phenomenally pungent odour so that it can attract the highest number of pollinating insects. It also has no chlorophyll. Besides the astounding rafflesia, there are also at least two palms endemic to the Khao Sok area.

In the centre of the park is the **Rachabrapah Reservoir**. Near the dam there is a longhouse of sorts, and several houseboats. The best location for animal spotting is near the reservoir where grassland at the edge of the reservoir attracts animals.

In addition to camping, canoeing and walking tours, you can take elephant treks at Khao Sok. The routes taken must be outside the park, however, as elephant trekking is not permitted within the confines of the national park.

Like many of the wonders of nature in Thailand, Khao Sok does not come without a giant technological blot. In this case, it's a hydroelectric dam right next to Khao Sok that has formed a vast artificial lake that now comprises one border of the national park. This dam began in the 1980s and has since become the bane of the park, as it transformed hills and valleys into small islands, trapping the wildlife with rising tides. While there have been attempts to rescue the beleaguered wildlife, nothing has proved successful as yet. But Khao Sok is successfully capitalizing on its assets, including its association with the famous Canadian naturalist Thom Henley (see above).

Khao Lak

A few years ago, before the infamous 2004 Tsunami that killed 5000 here and before the construction boom that followed it, Khao Lak was a quintessential sleepy beach town. Palms swayed, locals served up food and beer, and the almost empty beaches provided an idyllic backdrop. Unfortunately, Khao Lak's original ambience seems to have all but disappeared now.

These days endless generic resorts, some illegally pouring concrete onto the beach, others building buttresses made of ugly sand-filled plastic bags, are destroying one of Thailand's nicest spots. The town itself is little more than a facsimile of every other dull

Tsunami

Obliterating miles of picture-perfect coastline and killing thousands, the tsunami of Boxing Day 2004, left the world reeling in shock. Among the dead were countless Burmese, Mon and Karen intinerant workers without papers, while those who escaped the tsunami fled into the dense hills and rubber plantations of Phangnga or to Phuket or Ranong to evade repatriation.

In the wake of the disaster, the dearth of tourists compounded the horrors as small businesses suffered bankruptcy while traditional sea gypsies remained in limbo, unable to return to their former coastal homes because they lacked property deeds and also because they feared another wave. Since those early days, the tourist industry has been rebuilt, most famously Patong Beach which now boasts the cleanest sands in years.

Fortunately, many of the dive sites, including the Similan Islands, Ko Bon, Ko Tachai, Surin and Richelieu Rock received only superficial damage. And, while it will be some time before Khao Lak returns to a lucrative holiday strip, much of the Andaman remains gloriously lush with an abundance of accommodation and rare sights.

For many locals, however, the nightmare is not yet over. Along with the tsunami came the hired hench men of the *nai toons* or money barons who descended on villages that had been devastated by the waves, demanding property deeds from impoverished and often illiterate villagers. All up and down the coast from Laem Pon in Ban Nem Khem to Ban Sangka-oo on Koh Lanta and Kamala in Ranong, the same story was told of villagers who had been evicted and even barred from searching for the bodies of their loved ones in their former villages, following the tsunami. However, while many were loath to speak out for fear of losing compensation administered by corrupt local administrators, others fought back by refusing to move into new homes far from their original coastal sites. The oft-disparaged sea gypsies, in particular the Moken at Ban Tung Wa and Ban Tap Tawan in Phangnga, turned out to be the most united in their fight and successful, returning to their homes to rebuild rather than move into the small concrete bungalows far from the sea. At the time, Hon Klatalay, leader of the Ban Tung Wa community said: "We are one big family and we speak and move as one."

---

resort town in Thailand serving up bad Thai and Western food and endless tourist trinkets. Pretty much all local atmosphere is disappearing – some suggest that the tsunami provided an opportunity for ruthless property speculators to clear out the locals and replace them with resorts.

Even the planned tsunami museum and memorial has been handled badly; a single statue tucked away on a scrub of land behind a row of shops is the supposed memorial, while the only effort to create a museum is a community-run single room known as the **International Tsunami Museum** ⓘ *on the main road, daily 0930-2030, suggested donation ฿100*, containing a few photographs.

There are, however, a few plus points – you should still be able to find some space on one of Khao Lak's long beaches – head to the far end of Khuk Kak beach or Bang Sak just to the north. Given its proximity to the Koh Similans, Khao Lak is now becoming something of a dive mecca and there are a few excellent dive operators based here. Note that many buses now travel on a new road which bypasses Khao Lak and goes straight to Phangnga town, and then on to Phuket. Check that your bus passes through Khao Lak if you want to get off here.

Khao Lak-Lam Ru National Park

Khao Lak-Lam Ru National Park stretches from a small bay just south of the main Khao Lak tourism area inland up into the hills. There is a tiered waterfall with walks from the main path at the top of the hill, and forest rangers can take trekkers through the hills. However, the level of English spoken leaves rather a lot to be desired and the trails are less trail and more trudge through seriously thick and scratchy jungle. This can be intensely rewarding but you need to dress properly.

Khao Lampee-Had Thai Muang National Park

ⓘ *Park Visitor Centre, Thai Muang District, Phangnga Province 8210 (along the coast past Ban Thai Muang along 14 km of beach, 6 km from Thai Muang town), T077-395025, ฿200 for entry for 3 days, children ฿100.*

This relatively small national park, 72 sq km, comprises two distinct geographical zones: the Thai Muang Beach and the Khao Lampee area. The western portion, **Thai Muang Beach**, has 14 km of undisturbed beach lined with casuarina trees. The park continues inland for about 1 km and includes mangrove forest along the edge of the sea inlet, some swamp forest (*pa samet*) and freshwater lagoons from the old mine works from which Thai Muang derives its name (*muang* in this case means mine). The inland eastern portion covers several waterfalls and surrounding forested hills. **Turtle Beach** ⓘ *entrance fee ฿20*, is a 20-km-long beach where turtles, including the giant leatherback, come ashore at night to nest from November to February. Young turtles can be seen hatching from March to July. Hawksbill and Olive Ridley turtles are currently being raised in ponds near the park headquarters. There is an office in the Khao Lampee area, but the park headquarters are based in the Thai Muang area near the entrance.

Koh Surin ⊖ ⇢ *pp454-461. Colour map 4, B1.*

ⓘ *Boats leave from Patong or Rawai on Phuket (10 hrs), from Ranong (through the Jansom Thara Resort), see page 460, or from the pier at Ban Hin Lat, 1 km west of Kuraburi (4-5 hrs, ฿500). Long-tailed boats can be hired around Koh Surin, ฿400 for 4 hrs. The national park office is at Ao Mae Yai, on the southwest side of Koh Surin Nua. Best time to visit: Dec-Mar. Koh Surin Tai may close to visitors during the full moon each March, when the Chao Le hold a festival.*

Five islands make up this marine national park, just south of the Burmese border, and 53 km off the mainland. The two main islands, **Koh Surin Tai** and **Koh Surin Nua** (South and North Surin respectively), are separated by a narrow strait which can be waded at low tide. Both islands are hilly, with few inhabitants; a small community of Chao Le fishermen live on Koh Surin Tai. The diving and snorkelling is good here and the coral reefs are said to be the most diverse in Thailand. However, overfishing has led some people to maintain that diving is now better around the Similan Islands. Novices will still find the experience both exhilarating and enchanting.

There have been concerns expressed regarding the detrimental effects of tourism on several marine national parks, including the Surin Islands Marine National Park. In 1991 the national parks department closed Mae Yai Bay to tourism to allow the coral the time and opportunity to recover. In Spring 2008 the bay remained closed except for a small dive site 20 m below the surface at the southern tip – the coral has mostly recovered but, for once, the Thais are taking conservation seriously and Surin's fragile eco-system should remain intact for another generation.

A local Thai woman, Daeng, has set up a good website for information on snorkelling and diving in and around Surin, see www.ko-surin-diving.com.

Koh Similan ⊕▲⊕ ➤ pp454-461. Colour map 4, A1.

ⓘ *Vessels depart from Thap Lamu pier, 20 km north of Thai Muang (3-5hrs) to the Similans, 40 km offshore. Boats also leave from Ao Chalong and Patong Beach, Phuket with Songserm Travel (T076-222570), Tue, Thu and Sat from Dec-Apr, 6-10 hrs. Boats also leave from Ranong. The best time to visit is Dec-Apr. The west monsoon makes the islands virtually inaccessible during the rest of the year; be warned that boats have been known to capsize at this time. Also, bear in mind that transport away from the islands is unpredictable and you might find yourself stranded here, rapidly running out of money. At the end of Mar/early Apr underwater visibility is not good, but this is the best time to see manta rays and whalesharks.*

The Similan Islands lying 80 km northwest of Phuket and 65 km west of Khao Lak are some of the most beautiful, unspoilt tropical idylls in Southeast Asia. The national park consists of nine islands (named by Malay fishermen, who referred to them as the 'Nine Islands' – *sembilan* is Malay for nine). The water surrounding the archipelago supports a wealth of marine life and is considered one of the best diving locations in the world, as well as a good place for anglers. A particular feature of the islands is the huge granite boulders. These same boulders litter the seabed and make for interesting peaks and caves for scuba divers. On the west side of the islands the currents have kept the boulders 'clean', while on the east, they have been buried by sand. The contrast between diving on the west and east coasts is defined by the boulders. On the west, currents sweep around these massive granite structures, some as large as houses, which can be swum around and through and many have fantastic colourful soft coral growing on them. A guide is essential on the west, as navigation can be tricky. The east is calmer, with hard coral gardens sloping from the surface down to 30-40 m. Navigation is straightforward here and can be done with a buddy, without the need for a guide.

Koh Miang, named after the king's daughter, houses the park office and some dormitory and camping accommodation. While water did sweep over Koh Miang, it is largely recovered and was the first place that Thailand's navy established a tsunami warning system. **Koh Hu Yong**, the southernmost island, is the most popular diving location. From some 16,000 tourists in 1994, the numbers visiting the Similan Islands has risen to more than 25,000. Anchor damage and the dumping of rubbish is a big problem, although buoys have now been moored.

For Sleeping and Eating price codes and other relevant information, see pages 44-49.

⊜ Sleeping

Ranong *p444*

AL-A Jansom Hot Spa Hotel 2/10 Petkasem Rd, T077-811 5103, www.jansomhotspa.com. In places this is a slightly shabby spa hotel with charming pretensions of grandeur. There have been some improvements over the years and the rooms, pool and a huge jacuzzi are all supplied with mineral water from the nearby hot-springs. The rooms remain a good deal with bathtubs, linen, fridge and TV. Breakfast included.

A-C Jansom Beach Resort, 135 Moo 5, T077-821611. A small block of rooms set in a scrub of jungle and beside an excuse of a beach about 10 km from Ranong Town. You'll find 30 rooms all with private balconies overlooking the Andaman Sea and Victoria Point (Burma). Pool and restaurant. Rooms have rather low ceilings and are somewhat busy with furniture, but still a great location and great service. Popular during Chinese New Year and Songkran.

A-C Khao Nanghong Resort and Spa, 123/6 Moo 5, T077-831088, www.khaonang hongresort.com. A beachside boutique resort with large, airy, luxury thatched villas set in gardens overlooking Burma's Victoria Point. Stylish design, spa and a romantic restaurant with sea views.

B-C Royal Princess Ranong, 41/144 Tamuang Rd, T077-835240-44, www.dusit.com. A 4-star hotel (part of the long-established Dusit chain) with excellent service, good facilities including a mineral spa, and comfortable. One of the best hotels in Ranong. Has a pool and offers babysitting. It also pumps mineral water into the jacuzzi. Still very corporate with a suburban feeling to the rooms.

D-F Rim Than Resort, Chon Rau Rd, T077-833792. A little out of town, just past the hot springs on the road up to Ranong Canyon, this small, eccentric family-run resort offers a range of simple, clean fan and a/c bungalows set in a pretty garden with balconies right over the river. The choice of en suite rooms includes cosy doubles and a large family villa with 2 bedrooms, bathtub, fridge, TV, veranda and private garden. Also has a restaurant. Recommended.

F Bangsan (TV Bar), 281 Ruangrat Rd, T077-811240. Super-cheap, very basic rooms with fan above the trendiest cocktail bar in town. Hip with the young Thai and backpacker crowd.

F The Springs Guesthouse, 1/2 Chon Rao Rd, T077-834369. On the road to the hot springs, a/c and fan rooms which are bright but basic with shared bathrooms. Good value if a little musty. Motorbikes for hire and tours to Burma organized.

Hat Bang Baen *p447*

D-E Wasana Resort, T077-828209. This Dutch/Thai operation is on the left before the main park entrance. It has 10 smart concrete bungalows tastefully decorated, attached Western toilets and verandas arranged around a pleasant garden with a badminton net, ping-pong table, children's pool and good restaurant. The proprietors are helpful, friendly and arrange day trips.

E Andaman Peace Bungalows, T077-820239. A handful of smart concrete bungalows at the northern end of the long beach with fridge, fan and TV on slightly sparse land beyond the beach. Although it isn't a white- sand beach, trips to nearby paradise isles are popular and the excellent restaurant is the best in the area. Commands fantastic sunset views and attracts a mainly Thai clientele.

Koh Chang *p447*

While Koh Chang has retained its reputation as a bit of a hippy hideaway, the number of guesthouses on the island has more than doubled over the past couple of years. Most are in the budget range. As Koh Chang is largely covered by rainforest, it is difficult to see many resorts from the boat because they are camouflaged in the foliage. The majority of the resorts (around 15) are at **Ao Yai beach** on the west (Ao Yai is roughly 2 km wide and 5 km long). There is also a scattering of secluded beachfront and cliffside operations in **Ao Tadaeng** and **Ao Siad** to the south. Beware of the island's many wild boar. Many guesthouses shut down during the monsoon season so you do need to check. Prices start from around ฿100-150 per night for fan bungalows with shared bathroom. There is limited electricity in most resorts. Many can be booked through travel agents in Ranong.

E-F Cashew Resort, T077-820116. The granddaddy of the resorts and the largest with a variety of bungalows, pool table, travel services, credit card facilities, money exchange and attached yoga school. The resort has its own boat for fishing and trawling.

E-F Koh Chang Resort, T077-820176. Restaurant and sturdy wooden huts with attached bathrooms tucked among the trees. Snorkelling and fishing can be organized from here.

E-F Lae Tawan, T077-820179. Tucked away in a slightly out-of-the-way spot this cosy little place is one of the few open all year round. Thai restaurant. Recommended.

F Contex Resort, Ao Yai, T077-820118. Popular, simple place run by a Thai family with around 15 bungalows and a decent restaurant on an idyllic beach at the northern tip of Ao Yai.

G Sabai Yai T08-6278 4112 (mob). Swedish and Thai owned with good Western food, excellent service and well-kept rooms including dorms and bungalows. Home-baked bread.

G Sunset, T077-820171. This small family-run operation has clean, airy bungalows and a friendly atmosphere. It shares its boat with Cashew Resort.

Koh Phayam p448

Koh Phayam has around 30 guesthouses, with the most recent arrivals seen on **Ao Kao Kwai (Buffalo Bay)**, which was previously the sleepier of the 2 large beaches.

C-D Ao Yai Bungalows, Ao Yai, T077-821 753, gilles_phatchara@hotmail.com. The original operation on this strip, this pretty, immaculately kept place in a secluded spot is run by a French/Thai couple, Gilles and Phatchara, who know the island intimately and have a range of wood and concrete bungalows on stilts. Some are surrounded by lovely gardens and set among pine and coconut trees. West facing, it makes for an ideal spot to watch the wildlife and the sunsets. Tasty restaurant.

C-G Bamboo Bungalows, Ao Yai, T077-820012, www.bamboo-bungalows.com. A beach-side idyll and probably the most popular place on Ao Yai – booking is recommended during high season – although it is one of the few operations open year round. Bungalows range from new luxurious wooden villas with sprung mattresses, sofas, marble floors, sliding balcony doors and woven gables, through to pretty A-frame shell-covered bungalows. All have romantic outdoor bathrooms. There are also a few cheaper bamboo huts. The landscaped communal areas, large dining table, small yoga space, beach campfires and volleyball sessions create a community vibe. The excellent restaurant with huge portions and home-baked bread attracts visitors from neighbouring bungalows. Kayaks, surfboards and snorkelling equipment are available.

D-F Hornbill Hut, Ao Yai, T077-825543, hornbill_hut@yahoo.com. Fantastically friendly family-run place with a great reputation and several styles of basic bamboo bungalows with concrete bathrooms set among the trees, along with a few excellent-value concrete vill as with high ceilings and windows which allow the sea breeze to whistle through. Recommended.

E Jansom Bungalow, Buffalo Bay, T077-835 3179. A retreat set above Buffalo Bay with great views. It belongs to the **Jansom Beach Resort** in Ranong and has simple, clean wooden huts with vast tiled bathrooms and a traditional Thai outdoor restaurant overlooking the boulder-strewn expanse of sand.
E-F Baan Suan Kayoo Cottage, Ao Yai, T077-820133, www.gopayam.com. At the northern tip of the beach, with cottages and large restaurant set in a charming tropical garden – '*suan kayoo*' means cashew nut garden in Thai. A choice of sturdy wooden superior en suite cottages with king-size beds and up-market interior or budget thatched cottages with attached Thai-style toilet. Mosquitoes can be a problem.
E-F Vijit Bungalows, Buffalo Bay, T077-834082, www.kohpayam-vijit.com. Another of the island's original operations, this place is popular and renowned for its laid-back ambience.
F Uncle Red's, turn left from the Phayam village pier, over the small bridge. 4 basic but clean and well-kept en suite bungalows just over a bridge from the pier. An alternative option to the bigger beaches on a secluded strip of sand presided over by the picturesque wooden skeleton of a marooned boat. Close to the village shops and morning ferry off the island. The similarly basic operation which has opened next door looks promising and there are plans to open a campsite with communal kitchen on the beach.

Kuraburi *p449*
E Boon Piya Resort, T08-1752 5457 (mob). Has 20 spotless modern a/c bungalows squeezed in next to the main road. Well decorated and with TVs, it is the best place to stay in town but has less character than the **Tarar Inn**. The English-speaking owner Panich can organize boat and jungle tours.
E-F Tarar Inn, 076-491789. Has en suite bungalows with TVs and balconies overlooking the river. There are quaint bamboo huts, more substantial concrete constructions and an attractive waterside restaurant.

Khao Sok National Park *p449*
Tourism is well developed around Khao Sok, and visitors have a considerable choice in how they travel to the park and where they stay. There are several excellent bungalow operations near the park headquarters and new businesses sprout up every year. Be aware that colourful, deadly snakes occasionally invade the resorts and visitors should tread carefully. Prices range from ฿200-1200.
A-D Art's Riverview Lodge, T08-6470 3234 (mob), artsriverviewlodge@yahoo.co.uk, or write to Art's Riverview Jungle Lodge, PO Box 28, Takua Pa, Phangnga 82110. **Art's** is long-running, stylish and popular so book ahead. Its 30 rooms include substantial lodges with balconies overlooking the river, solid furniture and many rooms have a spare bedroom and small dining room. There is no hot water. The restaurant is beside the river near a swimming hole with a rope providing endless entertainment. Impertinent monkeys congregate at sunset to be fed bananas by residents.
A-E Our Jungle House, T08-9909 6814 (mob), ourjunglehouse@yahoo.de. At the end of bumpy track, this riverside resort run by a Thai/German couple offers some of Khao Sok's most comfortable rooms. The family bedroom (฿1200) has a delightful mezzanine floor. The 12 polished teakwood bungalows are well spaced and tastefully decorated.
C Khao Sok Green Valley Resort, T077-395145. Run by the friendly Eit, this is a great little resort with 8 spotless bungalows, all with hot water and a/c. Recommended.
C Khao Sok River Lodge, T077-395165, reservation@phukettrekkingclub.com. This surprisingly cheap government-run resort was apparently forced to reduce its prices because of lack of interest. The 15 exclusive rooms are immaculately kept and stylishly fitted, with balconies overlooking the river, making it the area's best-value resort. An elevated bamboo walkway leads from the charming wooden restaurant to the more

solid concrete bungalows. Villagers complain that, like that of many of the larger resorts, the construction led to the removal of so many large trees that it left the area exposed to flooding.

C Khao Sok Treehouse Resort, T08-99703353 (mob), khaosok_treehouse@ yahoo.com. Sandwiched between 2 rivers, the 8 treehouses offer a quirky night's sleep with huge trees crashing through their floors and ceilings. The rooms, which have fresh linen, hot water and bathrooms filled with plants, are slightly cramped compared with other Khao Sok rooms. An aged hornbill is a regular visitor to the resort. The owner, Sakda, sold his business in Koh Samui in 2004 to escape the island's commercialization and now sleeps in a suspended bamboo shack above the restaurant.

C-E Morning Mist Resort, T08-9971 8794 (mob). Spread next to the river with 16 bungalows of varying quality. The larger, more expensive rooms have hot water, fridges, flat concrete floors and a balcony with a bamboo boat hammock with the water rushing beneath. Some of the resort's paths are poorly lit at night.

D-F Bamboo House, T08-1787 7484 (mob), bamboo_khaosok@yahoo.com. 13 new bungalows built above the riverbank, suspended on ridiculous concrete stands, fashioned to look like trees while the stumps of the trees cleared for the development are visible below. An ugly suspended concrete path leads to the rooms, which are modern and comfortable with smart bathrooms.

E-F Nung House, T077-395147, nunghouse 2002@hotmail.com. Popular with backpackers, Nung's 12 spacious and comfortable bungalows are good value, starting at just ฿150, and its restaurant is the place to meet trekking companions.

F Khao Sok Valley Lodge, T08-6283 9933 (mob), khaosok@hotmail.com. Has 5 basic, concrete-mounted, en suite bungalows. Although the rooms could do with a little more furniture, the English-speaking owner Bao is an expert on the park and leads tours

using his park ranger father to enhance his trips, which cost between ฿300 and ฿2500.

Takua Pa

C-F Extra Hotel, just behind the Esso garage next to the town's main road, across the river from the bus station, T076-421026. If visitors are forced to spend a night in Takua Pa, this is the best option. It has a new building with sparkling modern rooms and smart en suite bathrooms, and a dingy old block with musty sheets and grimy bathrooms.

Khao Lak *p450*

Prices out of season can be very low – the price ranges below reflect this.

LL-L Le Meridien Khao Lak Beach and Spa Resort, 9/9 Moo 1, Khuk Kak beach, T076-427500, www.starwoodhotels.com. Huge, well-managed resort beside a beautiful stretch of sand about 8 km north of Khao Lak town. It has superb kids play area, complete with a scarily large teddy bear, and all the usual spa and swimming pool facilities you'd expect, plus a range of accommodation from standard rooms through to stunning villas complete with private pools. The food is also top-notch. Recommended – if you can afford it.

LL-L Mukdara Beach Villa and Spa, T076-429999, www.mukdarabeach.com. The bungalows had to be rebuilt after the tsunami but the 3-storey block survived the tragedy. It offers the services that would be expected considering the price tag of up to ฿26,000 per night. There are 6 restaurants and 148 rooms.

AL-C Nangthong Bay Resort, T076-485 088, www.nangthongbayresort.de. One of the first beachside resorts to reopen after the tsunami, this exclusive hotel has a pool, spotless seaside restaurant and superior beach bungalows with outdoor slate-fitted shower rooms. The rooms are elegant, if a little modern, characterless and squashed along the prized coastline.

A-D Khao Lak Palm Hill Resort and Spa, 4/135 Moo 7, Khuk Kak, T076-485138, www.khaolakpalmhill.com. Friendly, well-run small resort set on a back soi, 5 mins' walk from the beach. The rooms are large, cooling affairs all backing out onto a large pool. Decent food make this place one of the nicest away from the beach. Recommended.

C-D Khao Lak Youth Club, 5/55 Moo 7, Khuk Kak Beach, T076-485900. Owned by the same people as **Tony's Lodge**, this place offers a cluster of tiny bungalows crammed together on a slope overlooking a small shopping arcade. The rooms are nice enough, with hot water, a/c and cable TV. There's a dorm (฿200) if you want company.

C-D Krathom Khao Lak, T076-485149, krathom_khaolak@hotmail.com. Set in a lush garden that leads to the beach, the spacious a/c bungalows are considerably more comfortable than their bamboo, fan-cooled counterparts.

C-D Motive Cottage, 21/16 Moo 5, Khuk Kak, T076-486820, www.motivecottage resort.com. Elegant minimalist rooms, each with their own little balcony and surrounding a bijou pool make this an uplifting place to stay. All rooms have a/c, en suite facilities and hot water. Set beside the main road it's a 5-min walk from the beach – recommended.

C-D Tony Lodge, T076-420073, www.tony lodge.com. With space clearly at a premium, this 4-storey building is home to 22 swish new rooms with hot water and a/c. The English-speaking owner, Tony, is very friendly and owns more places nearby.

C-E Khao Lak Banana Bungalow, 4/147 Moo 7, Khuk Kak, T076-485889, www.khao lakbanana.com. Eccentric collection of bungalows set back from the road at the end of a quiet soi. Friendly owners provide a range of cramped-together bungalows which differ in range and price. Small pool.

D-F Father and Son Bungalow, T076-48527. The friendly Nom family are planning to add to their 10 fan bungalows spread around a charming, shaded garden where the road is barely audible. The more expensive en suite rooms are good value at ฿500.

Khao Lampee-Had Thai Muang National Park *p452*

Accommodation is available in 4 fan-cooled bungalows in the Thai Muang part of Khao Lampee-Had Thai Muang National Park. Prices range from ฿800 for a 6-person bungalow to ฿1000 for a bungalow for 10 people. Bookings can be made at the central **Forestry Department** office in Bangkok (Reservations office, Marine National Parks Division, Royal Forest Department, Chatuchak, Bangkok, 10900 – T02-5797047/8) or at the park HQ in Thai Muang. Call ahead to see if the bungalows are in operation. Camping is allowed and food and drinks can be purchased at the canteen.

Koh Similan *p453*

E-F Bungalows are now available on Koh Ba Ngu by the time of publication. Reservations can be made at the **Similan National Park Office**, Thai Muang, or at Tap Lamu Pier, T076-411 914. Camping may also be possible on Koh Ba Ngu. Bring your own tent.

🍴 Eating

Ranong *p444*

The markets on **Ruangrat Rd** offer some of the best eating opportunities in town with specials worth sampling including the roast pork and duck. Also worth seeking out for its famously delicious dahl lunches is the Muslim roti shop (no English sign) on Rungruat Rd, opposite TV Bar and guesthouse. Look for the roti/pancake stand outside.

♥♥-♥ Gad Jio Pub/Restaurant, centre of town on Ruangrat Rd. Pizzas cooked in a wood oven along with steaks, salads and burgers. A pretty stone and wood interior. Look out for the wooden façade.

♥♥-♥ Shinjuku Boutique Bar, Ruangrat Rd next to D&D. A chic little Japanese pub with indoor and outdoor seating, and draught Asahi and Chang beer.

¶¶-¶ **Somboon Restaurant**, opposite the Jansom Thara Hotel. Delicious Thai and Chinese seafood much of which is displayed in tanks at the front.

¶ **D&D coffee**, Ruangrat Rd. Where Ranong's café society congregate to discuss the day's issues, eat delicious Thai dishes over rice and sample a wide selection of good coffees.

¶ **J&T Food and Ice**, also centrally located on Ruangrat Rd. Excellent and serves a range of delicious but very reasonably priced Thai food and ice creams; popular place with locals and visitors, friendly owners.

¶ **Taxi Restaurant and Pizzeria**, opposite the cinema with balcony seating overlooking Ruangrat Rd. Inexpensive Thai, Italian and fusion dishes of a surprisingly good standard.

Koh Phayam *p448*

Most guesthouses have cheap restaurants and guests have been known to be asked to leave resorts during the high season if they fail to eat where they are staying. There are 3 other restaurants to bear in mind:

¶ **Middle Village**, on the road to Ao Yai. Renowned for its excellent Isaan (northeastern Thai) dishes and rowdy karaoke nights.

¶ **Oscar's Bar**, also in the village, turn right from the pier. Run by the infamously affable Englishman Richard, a self-proclaimed food buff who offers a wealth of information about the island and its politics. The bar serves great, unexpected Western and Thai dishes to a sociable crowd.

¶ **Pom's Restaurant**, in the village by the pier. Its sign, "Thai food, cheap and delicious" sums it up.

Khao Lak *p450*

There are plenty of *farang* orientated restaurants on the main drag, though most of them aren't very special. Most resorts and guesthouses will also offer food of some kind.

¶¶¶-¶¶ **Pizzeria**, main road, next to **Siam Commercial Bank**, T076-485271, Open 1200-2300. Passable pizzas, pasta and other Italian dishes.

¶¶ **Discovery Cafe**, main road near Nang Thong Beach, T08-1425 6236 (mob). Open 0930-midnight. Tasty cheeseburgers on offer here along with some good Thai food.

¶¶ **The Dome**, north end opposite Town Plaza. Pies, beer, Thai and international food.

¶¶ **La Dolce Vita**, 4/10-11, Moo 7, Sawasdee Plaza, T076-485480. Wood-fired pizzas, Italian pasta and Argentinian grill.

¶¶ **Sun Star Siam**, 26/27 Moo 7, Khuk Kak, T076-485637. Friendly, homely Thai-Swiss run place serving up excellent Thai food.

O Shopping

Ranong *p444*

Ranong's retail opportunities have expanded along with the tourist industry and cater for the crowds, with camping and outdoors shops lining Ruangrat Rd, ideal for pre-island purchases of tents, hammocks, mosquito nets and sturdy combat clothing. There are fashion boutiques and even a hip 60s-style hairdressers, **Dichun Hair**.

Khao Lak *p450*

There are lots of the usual stalls selling axe pillows and buddha figures to tourists in Khao Lak. There are a couple more stylish shops opposite the Khao Lak Youth Club (see Sleeping, above) including the well-stocked **Book Tree** bookshop which also sells a great range of international magazines and newspapers.

▲ Activities and tours

Ranong *p444*
Diving

A-One-Diving, has branches at 256 Ruangrat Rd as well as a dive school on Koh Phayam (opposite the pier), www.a-one-diving.com, T077-832984. Organizes trips all over the Andaman Sea including the Similans, Surin and Burma.

Tour operators

Pon's Place Travel Agency, by the new market on Ruangrat Rd, T077 823344. Run by the affable Mr Pon who is an excellent source of information on the islands and areas surrounding Ranong and can help with tours, travel information, guesthouse/ hotel bookings, and car and bike rental.
Ranong Travel, 37 Ruangrat Rd. Probably a better source of information than the tourist information office. It can book bungalows on Koh Chang, arrange fishing trips and advise on visiting Burma.

Koh Phayam p448
Diving
A-One-Diving, see Ranong, above.

Khao Lak p450
Diving

Diving operations, including live-aboard boats, day trips and courses, are still widely available from various operators, including **Seal-Asia**, see page 493. Dive sites along the coast, including the Similan Islands, Koh Bon, Koh Tachai, Koh Surin and Richelieu Rock as well as the Mergui Archipelago, received minimal damage during the tsunami although there have been some changes around Island Number Nine in the Similans that you will need to check. The best way to enjoy the Surin Islands is to join one of the daily dive trips from coastal towns. The dive sites in the Mergui Archipelago were left unscathed while the islands escaped topside damage or destruction. Contrary to reports, there are still Moken sea gypsies living in the Mergui Archipelago.
Khao Lak Scuba Adventures, 13/47 Moo 7, Khuk Kak, T076-485602, www.khaolakscuba adventures.com. Well-run 5-star PADI dive resort located in central Khao Lak, offering all the usual PADI courses and live-aboard trips to the Koh Similans.
Sea Dragon, 9/1 Moo 7, T Khuk Kak, T076-420420, www.seadragondivecenter.com. A well-established operation organizing day trips or liveaboards to Richelieu Rock,

Similan and Surin Islands. Teaches PADI dive courses. European-managed.

Tour operators
Khao Lak Oasis Tour, just down the road from **Khao Lak Scuba Adventures**, T076-485501, T08-7271 4326 (mob). One of the best and most affordable tour operators in Khao Lak. The owner, Su, works hard to keep her customers and has a lot of returnees. Private cars, minibus tickets, train and flight reservations and packages for Khao Sok can all be arranged here. Recommended.

Koh Similan p453

Hotels and tour operators organize boat and dive trips and most dive companies in Phuket offer tours to the Similan Islands (see page 492). See also Bangkok tour operators, page 154. Although it is possible to visit the Similan Islands independently, it can be an expensive and/or time-consuming business; it is far easier to book onto a tour. See also under Khao Lak, above, for further information.

⊖ Transport

Ranong p444
Air
Budget airline **Air Asia**, www.airasia.com, flies once a day between **Ranong** and **Bangkok**. Be aware that budget airlines chop and change schedules at very short notice, so check the website before travelling.

Bus
The bus terminal is on the edge of town, Highway 4, near the **Jansom Thara Hotel**. There are regular a/c and non-a/c connections with **Bangkok**'s Southern bus terminal near the Thonburi railway station. Also connections with **Chumphon**, **Surat Thani** and **Phuket** (304 km south).

Khao Lak *p450*
There are some a/c and non-a/c connections
with the Southern terminal in **Bangkok**.

Directory

Ranong *p444*
Banks On Tha Muang Rd there are branches
of Bank of Ayudya, Siam Commercial Bank,
Thai Farmers Bank and Thai Military Bank,
all with ATMs and/or exchange facilities.
Medical services Hospital: At the junction
of Permphon Rd and Kamlungsab Rd.

Post office Chon Rao Rd, near the junction
with Dap Khadi Rd. There is also a Poste
Restante service. **Telephone** Office on
Ruangrat Rd. There is a regional branch
of the Tourist Police on Petkasem Rd.

Khao Lak *p450*
All the usual facilities are now back online
in Khao Lak. **Banks** There are plenty of
exchange booths and ATMs. The main
banks, Siam Commercial and Thai Farmers
both have offices on the main road. **Post
office** Next to the police station a little
way north of town on the main road.

Phuket Island

→ Colour map 4, C1.

Known as 'the Pearl of Thailand' because of its shape, Phuket lies on the west coast of the Kra Isthmus in the warm Andaman Sea and is connected to the mainland by the 700-m-long Sarasin causeway. It is a fully developed resort island with hundreds of hotels including some that are world renowned. The name Phuket is derived from the Malay word bukit, meaning crystal mountain, and it is Thailand's only island to have provincial status. It is about the same size as Singapore (550 sq km), making it Thailand's largest island. While its wild monkeys, rhinos, elephants and tigers disappeared around the beginning of the 19th century, there is still tropical rainforest to be found on Phuket at Khao Phrao Thaeo National Park. ▸▸ *For listings, see pages 476-498.*

Ins and outs

Getting there

Phuket is nearly 900 km south of Bangkok. Getting to the island is easy. Phuket International Airport is in the north of the island, about 30 km from Phuket City, but rather closer to many of the main beaches and hotels. It's next to a beautiful beach and there are numerous pleasant restaurants on the airport road. There are international connections and multiple daily connections with Bangkok as well as with Koh Samui, Chiang Mai and Hat Yai and daily connections to Krabi. Thai Airways appears to have a virtual monopoly on transport from the airport (unless being picked up by your hotel). They run an **airport bus** ① *T076-232371, www.airportbusphuket.com*, into town and this is the cheapest way to get from the airport. The fare is between ฿10 and ฿85 (foreigners are sometimes overcharged). The first bus from the airport is 0630; the last bus is at 2045. There are three main companies that service the airport with metered taxis, cars (known as limousines) and vans. The ongoing squabbles between these groups generally don't affect passengers. To get to the metered taxis, turn right as you exit the airport and walk down to the kiosk. Despite being metered, the taxis will usually insist you agree on the fare beforehand. As you leave the airport, hordes of limousine drivers will try and usher you into their vehicles. Travel from the airport is expensive, but you can usually talk the price down a little. A taxi from the airport to Phuket City shouldn't cost more than ฿500. The service put on by the minivans has improved over the years. The drivers have been ordered to stop hassling tourists about their choices of accommodation. A trip from the airport to Phuket City by minivan should cost about ฿150.

Cheaper ways into Phuket City are either to walk or catch a *songthaew* the 5 km to the main north–south road, Route 402, and pick up a public bus or alternatively, walk out of the airport gate and wait for a motorcycle taxi dropping someone off (฿30), they cannot pick up fares at the airport itself. Buses take passengers to Patong, Kata and Karon beaches for ฿100, or by private taxi for ฿400.

The main **bus terminal** ① *Phangnga Rd, T076-211480*, is in Phuket City and there are regular connections with Bangkok (14 hours) as well as destinations in the south. In Bangkok, many buses for Phuket leave from Khaosan Rd. Be careful with these and don't economize as thieves have been known to board the Khaosan buses, which have a suspicious habit of 'breaking down'. The southern railway line doesn't come to the island. However, it is possible to take a train to Phun Phin near Surat Thani and then catch a connecting bus (six hours). ▸▸ *See Transport, page 496, for further information.*

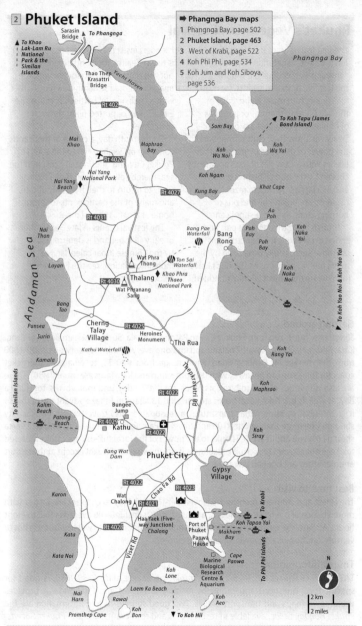

➡ **Phangnga Bay maps**

Phuket's Vegetarian Festival

The first four days of the Ngan Kin Jeh (Chinese Vegetarian Festival) are comparatively ordinary. It is during the last five days that events, for most foreigners, turn really weird. Each of the five Chinese temples or pagodas of Phuket City arranges a procession. Devotees show their commitment and the power of the gods by piercing their bodies with an array of objects apparently chosen by the gods. The processions end in a large field where razor ladders, cauldrons of boiling oil and pits of burning coals await the supplicants.

Tourists have tried to take part and ended up severely injured but locals say those successfully possessed by the spirits feel no pain, unless the gods leave them while the object is still embedded.

Islanders insist the festival's real message is to eat healthy food and do good deeds but this is often hard to square with the image of people strolling down the street with a chair, model battleship, miniature Eiffel Tower or potted plant through their cheek.

On the ninth day, a crowd of thousands converge on Saphan Hin to the south of Phuket City and offerings are cast into the sea, thereby allowing the Nine Emperor Gods to return to their heavenly abode, and many of the participants to return home and eat a meal of meat.

The festival occurs in late September or early October and is determined by the Chinese lunar calendar. For more information, see the Festivals colour section.

Getting around

Songthaew buses run from Phuket City to Patong, Kamala, Surin, Makham Bay, Nai Yang, Kata, Karon, Nai Harn, Rawai, Thalang and Chalong every 30 minutes between 0600-1800 from the market on Ranong Road. Fares range from ฿20-25, to whatever the ticket collector thinks he can get away with (to both Karon and Kata fares are usually ฿30). There are also numerous places to hire cars/jeeps, for ฿900 a day, and motorbikes, for ฿200 a day, as well as tuk-tuks. Local buses stop around 1800; tuk-tuks take advantage of this so it is essential to know what constitutes a reasonable fare: travel within Phuket City shouldn't be more than about ฿100 and travel to Patong from Phuket City and vice versa should cost you about ฿450. Thanks to the power of the local tuk-tuk operators, metered taxis are not allowed to pick up passengers from anywhere in Phuket except at the airport or unless they are booked privately.

Best time to visit

The driest and sunniest months are November to April. May to October are wetter with more chance of overcast conditions, although daily sunshine still averages five to eight hours. August is when the monsoon begins and red flags appear to warn swimmers not to venture out because of powerful and fatal currents.

Tourist information

TAT ① *73-75 Phuket Rd, T076-212213, tathkt@phuket.ksc.co.th, 0830-1630*, is good for specific local questions and problems relating to Phuket and Phangnga. It provides useful town maps and transport details. Two good sources of free information are the *Phuket Holiday Guide*, available in resorts, bars and restaurants, and the *Phuket Gazette*, www.phuketgazette.net, a newspaper/magazine which costs ฿25 and has quirky local human-interest stories and community updates. There are many tour companies offering a range of excursions and tours, see Activities and tours, page 490.

Background

Phuket was first 'discovered' by Arab and Indian navigators around the end of the ninth century, although it is rumoured that the island appears on charts as early as the first century. The first Europeans (Dutch pearl traders) arrived in the 16th century. Always a rich island – known for its pearls, fish and fruits – Phuket proved irresistible to the Burmese who carried out a surprise attack in 1785 after having already captured Ayutthaya, the old capital of Thailand. But, while the governor of Phuket had just died, he had left behind his wily young widow Chan and her equally clever sister Mook. The resourceful pair immediately disguised all the women of the town as men and had them pose as soldiers along the walls of Thalang – then capital of Phuket. Fearing the worst from the fierce-looking ranks, the Burmese retreated. Chan and Mook were honoured for their bravery and today, on the road to the airport, you can see the Heroines' Monument to the two sisters. But Phuket had not seen the last of the Burmese who destroyed Thalang and other parts of the island 40 years later, forcing the inhabitants to flee to the mainland. Twenty years after that, the Burmese threat receded and the islanders returned, founding Phuket Town in the southeast to replace the scarred and battered Thalang.

Much of Phuket's considerable wealth derived from tin and the island was dubbed 'Junk Ceylon' in the mid-16th century – a name thought to have been bestowed on the island by early European visitors. In 1876, during the reign of King Rama III – the older brother of King Mongkut who was the model for *The King and I* – Chinese workers flooded the island to work in the mines. The slave conditions that ensued later led to rebellion and pillage that was only halted at Wat Chalong. Labour conditions improved moderately and, in 1907, modern tin-mining methods were introduced by the Englishman Captain Edward Miles with elephants transporting ore from the mines to the smelting works. Phuket Town became so wealthy that paved roads and cars appeared around 1910. Today, Phuket remains the centre of tin production in Thailand although it is largely offshore with very few open tin mines left. Now, tourism is the big earner, with rubber, coconut and fisheries also contributing to the island's wealth. The population has shifted again, and a third of the island's 200,000 population now lives in Phuket City. While around 30% of these are Chinese descendents, the rest are indigenous Thais, Sikhs, Hindus, Malay Muslims and Chao Le sea gypsies. As for the elephants, these days they transport tourists along the beaches or on ersatz 'jungle treks' into the interior, which is seeing a rapid spread of Tesco Lotus supermarkets and malls. While the average Thai cannot afford to shop at such places, a new pastime has sprung up – window-shopping with the extended family – at Tesco on the weekend. The main attraction is rumoured to be the air-conditioning.

The tsunami of 26 December 2004 hit Phuket at a peak time for tourism, with the infamously raucous Patong Beach suffering tremendous loss of life. Indeed, much of the televised footage came from Patong. Phuket's beaches have now largely recovered with the grand sweep of Patong touted as a minor miracle. Of Phuket's other beaches, Bang Tao, Kamala, Kata, Karon, Nai Harn and Phuket Fantasea all suffered damage. Land grabs by developers in the wake of the disaster forced out many small businesses.

On the whole, the island has bounced back in terms of tourism and visitor numbers are now higher than ever.

Phuket City was given city status in 2004, although most islanders still call it "Phuket Town". This upgrade came as a surprise to many who still regard it as a sleepy provincial hub, hardly big or bustling enough to merit the city crown. Treated largely as a stopover by divers en route to the Similan or Surin islands and beach junkies headed further up the coast, Phuket City is now anxious to revamp its image and pull in a more sophisticated crowd. So, in addition to its Sino-Portuguese architectural heritage, which is reminiscent of Georgetown in Malaysian Penang – a leftover of the wealthy Chinese tin barons of the 19th century – there is a burgeoning arts and literary scene and even a foreign film festival once a year. It seems to be working as, increasingly, the city's incomers include weary Bangkok urbanites hankering for a business by the sea and expat foodies attracted by the city's excellent restaurant reputation. But Phuket City is still small enough and swamped enough by the glory of the beaches, to be down the pecking order. Not that this matters to the old-timers who can still remember when the town was surrounded by virgin forest. This is, perhaps, the card up Phuket City's sleeve – a subtle confidence underneath the tourist glitter, especially in the old town, and a feeling that another chapter is unravelling in this prosperous settlement. A cooler, hipper Phuket could easily emerge if the arts scene gets beyond the cottage industry feel and allows itself to be injected by that incoming Bangkok and expat buzz. But they will need to ward off the bland cloned high streets that have taken over so many of the beaches west of the city. What will aid Phuket City is that there are still some old and grand buildings left, rare in Thailand, and a magnet for those with an eye for architecture.

At the end of the 19th century, Phuket Town, one of the richest settlements in the country, saw a flowering of Sino-Portuguese mansions built by tin-barons revelling in their wealth. In Old Phuket you'll still find houses and shops in styles similar to that of Penang and Macao and dating back 100 to 130 years. Featuring complex latticework, Mediterranean coloured ceramic tiles, high ceilings and gleaming wooden interiors, these architectural dreams, remain cool in the summer and free of damp during the monsoon. While the style is commonly called Sino-Portuguese, many were actually built by Italian workers who imported materials straight from their homeland. Once a year at the end of the Old Phuket Town Festival in mid-December, these houses are open to the public. The best examples are along Thalang, Yaowarat, Ranong, Phangnga, Krabi, Dibuk, Rassada, Soi Romanee and Damrong roads.

A particularly notable example of one of Phuket's finer older buildings is the **Government House**, which stood in as the 'American Embassy' in Phnom Penh in the classic film – *The Killing Fields*. Preservation orders have been placed on all buildings in Old Phuket. Among the finer ones are the **Chartered Bank THAI office** ① *Ranong Rd opposite the market*, and the **Sala Phuket** ① *Damrong Rd*. You will notice that there is a police station right opposite the bank. Apparently the expatriate community involved in the lucrative tin trade demanded a police station to tackle raiders after they had a bank built. Less grand, but quietly elegant, are the turn-of-the-20th-century **shophouses** on, for example, Thalang Road. There has been considerable renovation of buildings on Dibuk, Thalang and Krabi roads but nearby there are still side streets with some lovely examples of traditional shophouses. **Soi Romanee**, the island's former red-light district, in particular is such a street with traditional merchant houses on both sides of the road, a few with fading paintwork on the walls. Some of the renovation has introduced smart new restaurants, cafés, art galleries and antique shops. Notably, **The Loft**, which sells expensive Southeast

Phuket City

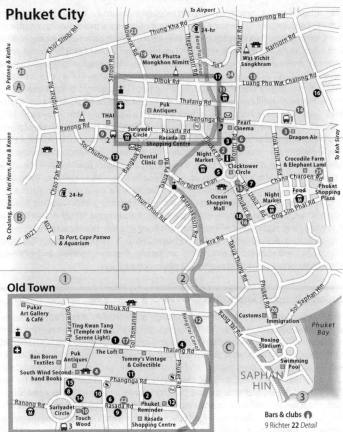

Old Town

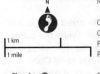

1 km
1 mile

N

Sleeping
Baan Suwantawe **11** *A2*
Bhukitta **14** *A3*
Crystal Guest House **1** *B3*
Crystal Inn **15** *B3*
Forty-three **17** *Detail*
Imperial **2** *B2*
iPavilion Phuket **5** *A1*
Nana Chart Mansion **6** *B3*
Novotel Royal Phuket
   City **3** *A3*
On On **4** *Detail*
OT Guesthouse **8** *Detail*
Phuket 346 **16** *B3*
Phuket Backpacker
   Hostel **9** *A1*
Raya Thai Cuisine **12** *Detail*
Sino House **13** *A3*
Taste Phuket **10** *Detail*
Thalang Guesthouse **7** *A1*

Eating
Baan Talang **1** *Detail*
Bondeli Café &
   Internet **2** *Detail*
Ka Jok See **10** *Detail*
Kanda Bakery **6** *Detail*
Khai Muk **12** *Detail*
Khanom Jee Vendor **16** *A3*
Koh Lao Luat Mu **8** *Detail*
Kow-Tom-Hua-Pla **4** *Detail*
La Gaetana **18** *B3*
Lai-An Lao **9** *Detail*
Lemon Grass **17** *A2*
Natural **13** *B1*
Roak Ros **5** *B2*
Salvatore's **14** *Detail*
Santana Coffee **3** *B2*
Siam Indigo **15** *Detail*
Vegetarian **7** *B3*
Venus Chinese **11** *Detail*

Bars & clubs
9 Richter **22** *Detail*
Balé **26** *C3*
Barzah **21** *B2*
Blue Marina **23** *A2*
Kor Tor Mor **25** *B3*
Oasis **20** *A1*
O'Malley's **24** *A2*
Timber Hut **19** *A2*

Transport
Long distance bus terminal
   to destinations beyond
   Phuket (Bor Kor Sor) **1** *A3*
Songthaew to Rawai and
   Nai Harn **3** *Detail*
Local buses to beaches,
   Thalong, Sarasin Bridge
   & turn off for airport **2** *A1*

Asian antiques and Chinese porcelains and received an award for its efforts in conserving traditional architecture. At the same time there are still plenty of more traditional hardware stores, small tailors, stationery shops and the like, that clearly cater to the locals. Another sight worth visiting in the old town is the **Temple of the Serene Light** ① *Phangnga Rd, entrance is marked in English and Thai*. Although it feels a little strange to take the narrow alleyway and to go into the temple, there are signs telling the story of the place in English, which is reassuring for Western visitors. Believed to be 110 years old, this is a small Taoist temple, filled with paintings and religious artefacts, that was rebuilt following a fire. It is the oldest Taoist temple in Phuket and is dedicated to the Goddess of Mercy, see page 367.

There are **night markets** on Ong Sim Phai and Tilok Uthit 1. These are excellent places to buy spicy rolls and other street foods on a nocturnal prowl through the old town. Khao Rang Viewpoint is a romantic spot atop a large hill in Phuket City. Although the view isn't quite as stunning as at Promthep Cape, Khao Rang is a cool place to watch over the whole of the city. There's also a fitness park up here if you feel like a bit of exercise. There are a few reasonable Thai restaurants around that offer the same great views. To reach Khao Rang, you need to make your way up the hill by either travelling from Yaowarat Road on to Soi Vachira, turning right at the end of the *soi* and following the hill up; or take the turn up to Khao Rang at the point where Thung Kha Road and Mae Luan Road meet.

A few kilometres south of Phuket City is **Phuket Zoo** ① *23/2 Moo 3, Soi Palai, Chao Fa Rd, T076-381227, www.phuketzoo.com*. There are regular elephant, monkey and crocodile shows here but the place screams, 'tourist photo opportunity'.

Phuket's beaches and sights ⊜❼❶❺❺❶ ➠ *pp476-498.*

The gorgeous 3-km-long sweep of sand and coconut palms of Patong Beach (see below) that attracted backpackers in the 1970s is now a dim memory. While the towering palms went down with the buildings when the tsunami came in, new ones have been planted, but the beach is still somewhat devoid of shade and balance. Other changes include the beach road, which has been moved, and the smaller side roads or soi, which have been praised for their cleanliness. Initially, there were hopes that Phuket would go for less development the second time around but this proved a fantasy. For less hedonistic, smaller beaches that still have charm, you can go south of Patong. Here you will find the twin, horseshoe-shaped Karon and Kata beaches. **Karon Beach** is around half the size of Patong, less densely developed, and with a general atmosphere that is more laid-back and family friendly. **Kata Beach**, however, is like a mini-Patong, with hotels, restaurants and shops chaotically jostling for space.

At Phuket's southern end is **Nai Harn**, a pretty white beach favoured by Thais, with a small number of more expensive hotels and limited amenities. While the bamboo restaurants at the back of the beach received only water damage, the restaurants at the entrance to the main hotel here – the luxury **Royal Meridien Phuket Yacht Club** – were completely wiped out. However, the hotel itself received only superficial damage and is fully operational. In the middle of this charming beach, the **Samnak Song Monastery** acts as an unexpected bodyguard against major developers.

The east coast of Phuket is only thinly developed from a tourist point of view. Much of it is rocky and the beaches that are to be found here do not compare with those on the west coast. There are some excellent hotels, but these are largely stand-alone establishments; don't expect a great wealth of facilities.

Ladyboys

Katoeys, transvestites or, as they tend to be known by *farang* in Thailand, 'ladyboys', are larger in number than one might expect. They are also part of a long tradition of transvestites in Southeast Asia. Many bars and clubs will have *katoeys* working for them, whether as bar 'girls' or in shows of one sort or another.

They are often very beautiful and extraordinarily difficult, if not impossible, to tell apart from the real thing. In Bangkok there are also groups of *katoeys* who have been known to surround and pick-pocket *farang* men on the street – particularly on the Landmark side of Sukhumvit Road and along sois 5-11.

Kamala Beach, north of Patong, was severely affected by the tsunami, with a harsh death toll and much of the landscape left distraught. The next beach north is **Surin**, home to Phuket's first golf course more than 60 years ago, during the reign of King Rama VII. The course is largely in disuse now except as a park and the beach is patronized mostly by Thais – especially on Sundays when they picnic here. Choppy water – particularly during the monsoon – and a steep incline keep the beach from being developed. While there are a few exclusive resorts close by, the guests here only rarely venture beyond their hotels. You can camp on the beach for free.

Surin and **Bang Tao**, further north, are similar in that the resorts are widely spaced with no centre for shops. Bang Tao was formerly used for tin mining which turned the landscape into a desert. **Nai Ton** and **Layan** are small bays with exclusive resorts. Finally, at the northern end of the island, is **Nai Yang Beach** and the **Nai Yang National Park**, a 9-km casuarina-lined beach with a few resorts and some park bungalows.

Patong Beach

Patong began to metamorphose from a hippy paradise into a commercial centre during the 1970s. It is now a mass of neon signs advertising hotels, massage parlours, restaurants, straight bars, gay bars, nightclubs and the plain peculiar. While families may not be able to avoid vulgarity, they will be able to bypass ladyboys and devious side-street deals by choosing from a range of excellent family hotels. Patong tourists are a mixed lot – a Butlins overspill, shameless beer boys and plump retirees. Increasingly, Russians are also turning up, both for business and revelry.

Take Patong for what it is: an overdeveloped mass of cheap booze, expensive restaurants, mediocre beaches and odd characters. For a night out, it's fun, but otherwise, there's little point in basing your holiday around a stay in Patong. Many visitors to Phuket spend all of their time in Patong and then leave with a negative view of the island as a whole. Don't be one of them, there is so much more to Phuket.

Patong does, however, offer the widest selection of watersports on Phuket and, in spite of hotel development, it is still possible to snorkel on the reef at the southern end of the bay.

Driving towards Karon from Patong you will come to **Tri Trang Beach**, a charming little beach located in front of the Merlin Beach Resort. The area is spotless with very few disturbances but the water is full of rocks and not suitable for swimming during low tide. There is decent snorkelling here and very few tourists ever make it out this way. From Tri Trang Beach it's possible to charter a long-tailed boat to picturesque **Freedom Beach**, you can't get to there by road, where the water and sand are beautiful.

Shake, Rattle and Roll

Clad in enough rhinestones to sink the Titanic, numerous Thai Elvis impersonators can be fawned over at Phuket theme nights or while munching BBQ ribs at the Karon Sea Sands Resort in Karon Road.

The enduring popularity in Thailand of the former trucker from Memphis, Tennessee, is largely down to a chance meeting in 1960 between the King of Siam and Elvis. Captured in a tinted photograph, on the set of *GI Blues* in Hollywood, are the two kings – Elvis in pressed army fatigues.

Consequently the king of Memphis, who never visited Thailand, became an enduring icon on cigarette packets, TV adverts and clothes brands. But the best time to catch the king is either on Elvis' birthday (January 8) or the anniversary of his death (August 17). That's when bands like The President Band and Elvises named Lek (little) Elvis or Yaowarat Elvis come out to croon. For the truly Elvis obsessed, there are even Elvis conferences, attracting hundreds of imitators.

Karon and Kata beaches

The horseshoe-shaped Karon and Kata beaches south of Patong are divided by a narrow rocky outcrop. Karon started tourist life as a haven for backpackers; it is now well developed, with a range of hotels and bungalows and a wide selection of restaurants. Although there is a tiny hippy/alternative corner at the southern end of the beach, tipped off by a reggae bar, on the whole, prosperous Scandinavians dominate now. Some places bear mini Swedish flags and it is usually these establishments that are guaranteed to make you feel as if you never left the aeroplane. This can prove tedious and an air of predictability and safety pervades the beach. Karon's major drawback, physically, is the overly exposed beach despite its cosy curve. Nonetheless, there are good mid-range places to stay, and the slower pace of life here will appeal to many.

Kata consists of two beaches: **Kata Yai** (Big) and **Kata Noi** (Little), divided by a cliff. Both bays are picturesque with rocks along the edges and sweeping fine pale yellow sands in the centre. Descending a winding hill, Kata Noi comes as a pleasant surprises, offering an adorable little bay with a small and perfect beach. Although it is dominated by the **Amari Kata Thani Hotel**, on the whole it feels much like a hidden seaside harbour, and even the tourist infrastructure of souvenir shops, guesthouses, laundries and restaurants are made up of a pleasant jumble of locally owned businesses. There are also cheapish bungalows here. The snorkelling is good at the south end of Kata Noi and around Koh Pu, the island in the middle of the bay which looks like a squashed bowler hat. Kata Yai, just the other side, is a sprawling mass of development: hotels, souvenir shops and roadside restaurants abound. It provides excellent facilities for the holidaymaker. including numerous options for watersports and a lot of choices for nightlife down the rambling streets running inland from the coast. Despite this, the huge hotels on the beach over-whelm the bay with umbrellas and sunbeds spread across almost the entire beach. The beautifully painted and cared-for tour boats with their smart wooden benches and umbrellas are a far cry from the traditional fisherman's longboats, on which they are obviously modelled.

Nai Harn and Promthep Cape

Nai Harn, a small, gently sloping beach – home to the prestigious **Phuket Yacht Club** – is one of the island's most beautiful locations, renowned for its spectacular sunsets. The slopes of the bay are steep so, to reach most accommodation, you'll need to climb numerous steps. From Nai Harn it is possible to walk to **Promthep Cape**, the best place to view the sunset. Near the highest point there is a shrine covered in gold leaf and surrounded by wooden elephants.

Rawai → *14 km south of Phuket City.*

To the north of Promthep Cape, up the eastern side of the island, the first beach is Rawai, which was 'discovered' by King Rama VII in the 1920s. This crescent-shaped beach is now relatively developed although not to the same degree as Patong or Karon, being more popular with Thai and Southeast Asian tourists, particularly during Chinese New Year and Songkran. Many Thais go to Rawai for the cheap restaurants, although prices are going up. The bay is sheltered and it is safe to swim throughout the year, but the beach, although long and relatively peaceful, is rather dirty and rocky. Rawai is more of a jumping-off point for offshore trips to Koh Hae (Coral Island), Koh Bon and Koh Lone. At Rawai's northern end there is also a sea gypsy village, **Chao Le**.

Koh Kaew Pisadarn

ⓘ *Take a long-tailed boat from Rawai Beach; negotiate with one of the boat owners, take a picnic and arrange to be picked up.*

Koh Kaew Pisadarn can be seen from Promthep Cape and is a 15-minute boat ride from Rawai Beach. The island is the site of three footprints of the Buddha. Two are among the boulders and stone on the upper shore; the third is just below the low watermark. For many years important Buddhist festivals were celebrated here because of the island's supposed spiritual power and significance. Then, about 40 years ago, these religious pilgrimages stopped. Sam Fang, who researched a story on the island for the *Bangkok Post*, discovered a tragedy had occurred about that time. Some rowing boats en route to the island had sunk during a storm, which was blamed on a sea serpent that had become enraged by continual trespassing. Between 1952 and 1967, attempts to construct a Buddha on the island were continually thwarted by bad weather and high seas. The island quickly gained the reputation of being cursed. Only in 1994 were attempts at erecting a Buddha image renewed and, defying superstition, a 1.5-m-high concrete statue now stands on the northeastern side of the island, overlooking Promthep Cape. The statue, about a 10-minute walk along a laid path from the boat landing, is surrounded by two protective nagas that slither over the top of the encircling balustrade. Steps lead down to the footprints on the shore beneath the Buddha. In 1995 the celebration of Loi Krathong at Koh Kaew Pisadarn was reintroduced.

Laem Ka and Chalong beaches

The next beaches up the east coast and south of Phuket City are Laem Ka and Chalong. Ao Chalong is 1 km off the main road. There is not much here for the sun and sea worshipper and the beach is filthy. Offshore tin dredging is said to have ruined it. From Chalong's long pier boats can be caught to the offshore islands for game fishing, snorkelling and scuba-diving. There are also a few reasonable seafood restaurants from which you can watch the dozens of working and pleasure boats gather off the pier in the harbour. The rest of the east coast is of limited interest for tourists because of a rocky coast.

Shark's fin soup

Throughout Asia, wherever there are large populations of Chinese, shark's fin soup is on the menu of the more expensive or traditional restaurants. Anyone tempted to partake should be aware of the consequences of dramatically increased demand for shark products.

Sharks play a key role in marine systems such as coral reefs and are critical to maintaining a natural balance in the marine world. Taking away the sharks will lead to an increase in numbers of parrot fish and other species which graze on coral, thus leading to excessive grazing and later destruction of the reef system.

The biology of the shark, unlike other fish, does not lend itself to large-range exploitation. Sharks are at the very top of the food chain. In direct contrast to most commercially fished species they live for a long time and produce few young, most of which will survive to adulthood. Little is known about many shark species which are highly migratory. Therefore, the impact of this increase in fishing of sharks is not known. Nor is it possible to say whether any species of shark is currently threatened by this fishing. But experience in shark fisheries does not bode well. To date every fishery directed at sharks has collapsed as the populations have been ravaged.

Until we know more about the impact of our desires for shark products, please take stay clear of shark's fin soup. In June 2000, responding to passenger concern, THAI Airways took it off its menu.

(Statistics taken from the TRAFFIC Southeast Asia report on species in danger: *Managing Shark Fisheries: Opportunities for International Conservation*, by Michael L Weber and Sonja V Fordham).

Tin is what first attracted people to Phuket and chronicling that history is the **Royal Pewter Showroom** ⓘ *61/16 Moo 6, Soi Baan Nai Trok, T076-281001, www.phuketroyal pewter.com*, in Chalong. There are displays of some of the items made from pewter (a combination of tin and copper). You can buy items from the showroom, but there is also the opportunity to make something out of tin yourself under the watchful eyes of an instructor (฿350). Most people don't get much further than hammering out some sort of bowl-shaped item, but as a souvenir, it's pretty cool. You can learn everything there is to know about tin mining in Phuket and children will enjoy the hands-on element here.

About 6 km south of Phuket City, just north of Chalong junction, is the ostentatious Wat Chalong, best known for its gold-leaf encrusted statues of the previous abbots, Luang Pho Chaem and Luang Pho Chuang. The former was highly respected for his medical skills, which proved to be particularly valuable when Phuket's Chinese miners revolted in 1876. The halving of the international price of tin coupled with Bangkok's attempt to extract excessive taxes from the province inflamed the Chinese. Some 2000 converged on the governor's house and when they failed to take the building, they rampaged through the less well-defended villages. The spree of killing and looting was only brought to an end at Wat Chalong where the two respected monks talked the mob out of their fury. Visible from almost anywhere around the south of Phuket City is Phuket's own Big Buddha Statue. Your reward for scaling the enormous and steep Nakkerd Hill is a great view of Chalong Bay and an up-close glimpse of a 45-m seated Buddha. There is also a smaller Buddha statue. To get to the Buddha driving from Phuket City, go past Wat Chalong and look for the sign pointing out the right-hand turn to the statue.

Cape Panwa

South of Phuket City, down Sakdidej Road which becomes Route 4023, in the grounds of the **Cape Panwa Hotel**, is **Panwa House**, one of Phuket's finest examples of Sino-Portuguese architecture. Panwa House was formerly inhabited by a fishing family from Phuket and, later, by the hotel's official coconut catcher. The catcher's job was to remove coconuts from the trees so the guests would not be concussed. However, he was under orders not to take a coconut from the trees on the beach, and in all his years as official coconut catcher, he never disobeyed. The house is now filled with curious artefacts, like the coconut scraper in the shape of an otter. The first floor has attractive views of guests below at their meals, framed by swaying palms and beach and being serenaded by performers. At the tip of Panwa Cape is the **Marine Biological Research Centre and Aquarium** ① *T076-391126, 1000-1600, ฿20*. The air-conditioned aquarium is well laid out with a moderate collection of salt- and freshwater fish, lobsters, molluscs and turtles and some other weird species. This centre re-opened thanks to funding from the Danish government. There are regular public *songthaews* every hour (฿10) from the market on Ranong Road to the aquarium. Watching the sun set along the paved seafront is recommended. It is sublimely free of tourists and there are a few café/restaurants, all open to a view which always seems to include imposing Thai naval boats in the distance. It is possible to charter long-tailed boats from Cape Panwa to **Koh Hii** (฿600), and **Koh Mai Ton** (฿1200), or to go fishing (฿1200). See below.

Koh Tapao Yai, a small island off the cape, is home to a few hotels (see Sleeping, page 478) and around 200 hornbills. Baby brother of Koh Tapao Yai, **Koh Tapao Noi** is another small island, secluded and devoid of almost everything except flora, fauna and hornbills. There is also a lighthouse that was built in 1890. Other than that, enjoy the beach and the sea while you can. To get there, take a boat from Ao Makham Pier (6 km from Phuket City).

Koh Lone, Koh Mai Ton and other southern islands

There are places to stay on several of the islands off the east and southeast coasts of Phuket. All the resorts play on the desert island getaway theme. These places are hard to reach in the monsoon season and often shut for up to three months of the year. Koh Mai Ton, for instance, is a private island 9 km southeast of Phuket with little on it except the **Mai Ton Resort**. This fits the bill for 'deserted tropical island' holidays, except the resort seems rather out of place with mock classical pillars by the pool and rooms that could be on any tropical island.

Koh Maprao (Coconut Island)

Coconut Island is what Phuket was like before people started arriving en masse. To get there, make your way to Laem Hin Pier (15 minutes north of Phuket City, on the east coast, about ฿150 in a tuk-tuk), take a long-tailed boat (฿15) over to the island and a short motorcycle ride to the beach. There are only a few hundred people living on this tiny island and the locals get their electricity from solar panels. There are no shops, go-go bars or places to stay. All you have is a tropical island – let's hope it stays that way.

Koh Rang Yai

This small island off the east coast of Phuket has a focus on day trips, so you might feel like you're being herded in and out like cattle. It's a beautiful island, though, and worth a visit. The island has its own pearl farm and demonstrations are given along with a trip to a pearl shop. Bicycles are available, and there's a putting course. The beach is clean, although the water looks a bit murky and if you just fancy loafing about without many people around, this is a good place to do it.

Boats depart from Sapam Bay, which is about 15 km north of Phuket City, on the east coast. Expect to pay up to ฿300 for a tuk-tuk from Phuket City to Sapam Bay. Bungalows can be rented on the island (see Sleeping, page 481).

Kamala Beach

Kamala Beach, fringed by coconut trees, hosts a sedate Muslim fishing village where modest clothing should be worn. There is little tourist development with the north of the beach offering the best swimming as fishermen toss their nets into the surf and the occasional buffalo strolls down the sand.

Laem Sing

Between Kamala and Surin is a little-known beach by the name of Laem Sing. It's one of the less-crowded beaches on the island and the sand is clean and the water is clear. The only problem is the onslaught of jet skis that noisily zip around dangerously close to where people are swimming. Laem Sing is also where you'll find Soundwave Sundays, the most happening Sunday night party in Phuket. Local DJs spin house and electro until the early hours during high season.

Surin Beach and Pansea Beach → *West coast, north of Patong Beach.*

Surin Beach is quite dirty. It is lined with casuarina trees and open-air restaurants, patronized mostly by Thais. The seabed shelves away steeply from the shoreline and swimming can be dangerous. There is a short golf course but no hotels on the beach. Pansea Beach has soft sand in a steeply sloping bay just north of Surin, with two exclusive hotels.

Bang Tao Beach → *West coast, north of Patong Beach.*

The **Laguna Phuket** complex at the north of Bang Tao Beach consists of four expensive hotels built around a lagoon. Free tuk-tuks and boats link the hotels and guests are able to use all the facilities. There is a great range of watersports and good free provision for children. The **Canal Village** offers 40 or so shops and a lagoon-side café serving satay. The adjoining bakery serves good pastries and cakes. To the south of the **Laguna Phuket** are some other places to stay. The most recent additions to this southern section of the beach are all fairly small, stylish and intimate in design. This southern part of the beach is also one of the few areas where you will still see traditional boat builders and the boats themselves in operation, instead of the tourist variety used to take people on island tours.

Nai Thon and Layan

Between Bang Tao and Nai Yang are the isolated beaches of Nai Thon and Layan. These beaches have recently been developed with a luxury resort and spa at Layan occupying the whole bay and similarly expensive developments are moving into Nai Thon which only has a 400-m-long beach. South of Nai Thon is an exquisite cove, most easily accessible by boat.

Nai Yang and Nai Yang National Park

ⓘ *Entrance to beach ฿5 per car.*

Nai Yang is close to the airport and 37 km from Phuket City. To get there, take a bus from the market on Ranong Road in Phuket City. The attractive and often empty forest-lined beach of Nai Yang lies next to the airport and is part of the Nai Yang National Park. It is the ideal place to pass a few hours before an early evening flight. Further south, there is more activity, with a range of luxury hotels and bungalows. The park encompasses Nai Yang and **Mai Khao** beaches, which together form the longest beach on the island (13 km). The area was declared a national park in 1981 to protect the turtles which lay their eggs here from November to March. Eggs are collected by the Fisheries Department and young turtles are released into the sea around the second week of April (check on the date as it changes), on **Turtle Release Festival Day**. The north end of the beach (where there is good snorkelling on the reef) is peaceful and secluded. There is no accommodation in the national park, although camping is possible.

Mai Khao

This is Phuket's northernmost and largest beach – still with no proper development. Instead there is the village of Had Mai Khao and the Sirinath National Park. The village is dominated by shrimp nurseries which sell the grown shrimp on to numerous farms throughout the south of Thailand. These discharge waste to the sea off the Mai Khao beach, but not to the same levels as shrimp farms. Again, sea turtles nest on this beach, including the huge leatherbacks, and the Turtle Release Festival is in mid-April. The community effort to conserve the turtles involves collecting the eggs and keeping a hatchery. Details of this work can be found at the one low-budget bungalows on the beach – **Mai Khao Bungalows**. The beach is steeply shelved so swimming isn't recommended and it is unsuitable for children. The beach is lined with casuarina trees.

Heroines' Monument and Thalang National Museum

About 12 km north of Phuket City on Route 402, towards the airport, is the village of **Tha Rua**. At the crossroads there is a statue of two female warriors: **Muk** and **Chan**. These are the sisters who repelled an army of Burmese invaders in 1785 by dressing up all the women of the town as men, so fooling the Burmese. Rama I awarded them titles for their deeds and they are celebrated in bronze, swords drawn. The statue was erected in 1966 and Thais rub gold leaf on its base as a sign of respect and to gain merit. The **Thalang National Museum** ① *0900-1600, except national holidays, ฿30*, is just east of this crossroads on Route 4027. It has a well-presented collection on Phuket's history and culture.

Khao Phra Thaeo Wildlife Park

① *T076-311998, 20 km north of Phuket City, 0600-1800, Admission for foreigners is ฿200. Entry is ½-price for children.*

To get to this wildlife park turn east off the main road in Thalang and follow signs for Ton Sai Waterfall. The beautiful, peaceful road winds through stands of rubber trees and degraded forest. The park supports wild boar and monkeys and represents the last of the island's natural forest ecosystem. During dry season, a walk around the park is a lot of fun and not particularly gruelling. The primary nature trail has 14 stations where you can stop and learn a bit about the park. There isn't much wildlife to be seen, although you may come across a monitor lizard, gibbon or even wild boar. The main trail is about 2 km long. The park's two waterfalls, Bang Pae Waterfall and Ton Sai Waterfall, are not up to much during the dry season when there isn't any water. When there is water, visitors can paddle in the upper pool. There are bungalows, a lakeside restaurant and a number of hiking routes here.

Bang Pae Waterfall and Gibbon Rehabilitation Project

The road east from Ton Sai Waterfall becomes rough and can only be negotiated on foot or by motorbike; it leads to **Bang Pae Waterfall** ① *0600-1800*. Alternatively, the falls can be approached from the other direction, by turning off Route 4027 and driving 1 km along a dirt track. There is a beautiful lake, refreshment stands, forest trails, and bathing pools. Just south of the waterfall (follow signs off Route 4027) is a **Gibbon Rehabilitation Centre** ① *T076-260492, gibbon@samart.co.th, 1000-1600, free, donations welcome as it is run by volunteers*, funded from the US and apparently the only such initiative in Southeast Asia for these endangered animals.

Naka Noi Pearl Farm

① *T076-219870, 0900-1530, ฿500. Long-tailed boats can be chartered at any time, ฿700, and the driver will wait for you.*

Also off Route 4027, at Ao Poh, there is a long wooden jetty where boat tours leave for Naka Noi Island and Pearl Farm – Thailand's largest. At the farm, the owner asks you to wait half an hour while they prepare the oysters for the demonstration, which takes around 1½ hours. Ensure your visit is to Naka Noi, rather than Naka Yai, where the 'Pearl Farm' seems to be a fake.

◉ Phuket Island listings

For Sleeping and Eating price codes and other relevant information, see pages 44-49.

● Sleeping

Phuket has hundreds of places to stay, largely at the upper price end. During the low season (Jun-Oct) room rates may be as little as half the high season price. All rates quoted are peak season. Advance booking is recommended during high season (particularly at Christmas and New Year).

Phuket City *p466, map p467*
The hotels in town are rather uninspired: most people avoid staying here and head straight for the beaches, however, there are some good guesthouses in the old part of town.
AL-A Novotel Royal Phuket City Hotel, opposite the main bus station in town, T076-233333. Swimming pool, business centre and gym. Expensive but up to 50% discount in the wet season. Hints of Las Vegas with shimmering fountain out front. Rather out of place as it dominates the street.
A iPavilion Phuket, 133 Satool Rd, T076-210 445, www.islandpavilion.com. Almost groovy,

circular, high-rise. Nice rooms with an unusual layout. Pool and all facilities.
A The Taste Phuket, 16-18 Rassada Rd, T076-222812, www.thetastephuket.com. Decent hotel in a converted shophouse. On the upmarket side of Phuket City accommodation. Rooms come with hot-water rain shower, a/c, cable TV and large double bed. The expensive rooms have massive TVs, DVD players and gardens. The Taste is dubbed a 'lifestyle venue', which means it has a café and bar where you can chill while listening to jazz and drinking cocktails. The staff can offer advice on places to go in Phuket and organize bookings. Recommended.
A-B Bhukitta, 20, 22, 23, 26, 28 Phangnga Rd, T076-215712-3, www.bhukitta.com. Hidden away down a *soi* within walking distance of the bus station. A mid-range hotel with a bar, spa and great restaurant. Rooms have all mod cons and are large and modern. Wi-Fi is offered throughout the hotel. Rooms are spotless and well furnished. There's also a karaoke room, if that's your thing.
A-B Sino House, 1 Montri Rd, T076-221398, www.sinohousephuket.com. Another modern

hotel in town, this time with a Chinese twist. The rooms are large and all have Wi-Fi access, a fridge, a/c and cable TV. A decent breakfast is included. This hotel is located in a quiet area of town, opposite O'Malleys Irish bar if you fancy a drink. They also have a spa that comes highly recommended for massages.

A-D Imperial, 51 Phuket Rd, T076-212311, www.imperialphuket.com. Cooperative staff, good clean rooms, appropriately priced. Low-key corporate look – dreary front. Restaurant.

B-C Phuket 346, 346-348 Phuket Rd, T076-256128. Hip little guesthouse with only 3 rooms in a converted Sino-Portugese shophouse. There is lots of art around the place making it quaint and chilled. Rooms have high ceilings, comfortable beds, lovely linen and a/c. You'll feel more like you're in someone's home than a guesthouse. There's also a café and art gallery.

C Baan Suwantawe, 1/10 Dibuk Rd, T076-212879, www.baansuwantawe.co.th. Serviced apartments and hotel. The rooms are clean and comfortable and there is a large outdoor swimming pool. Breakfast is not included. Rooms have access to broadband and overlook the pool. The accommodation here really stands out from other choices in Phuket. Large beds, cable TV and a/c. The hotel is opposite **Lemongrass** restaurant.

C-D Raya Thai Cuisine, 48 Deebuk Rd, T076-218155. Offers 5 simple rooms in a 70-year-old Macao-style house set off the road. Part of the **Raya Thai Cuisine** restaurant (see Eating, below). Quirky in the nicest possible way. The rooms themselves are simply furnished and decorated, but the setting is romantic, with a bridge leading to the rooms from the restaurant. Friendly owners full of tales about Old Phuket. The food is also good. Recommended.

C-D Thalang Guesthouse, 37 Thalang Rd, T076-214225. A pleasant house with an old-world charm, large windows, wood floors, double-panelled doors and ceiling fans. 13 rooms on 3 floors. Varying prices and standards. Some rooms look onto a

brick wall. Rooms 3 and 21 are best, though a little more expensive – they have balconies overlooking the street. This is an excellent base to explore the old town. The owner, Mr Tee, has a good reputation with guests who are encouraged to leave notes and drawings on the landing. As well as Japanese customers, it attracts students, backpackers and divers. Recommended.

C-F Phuket Backpacker Hostel, 167 Ranong Rd, T076-256680, www.phuket backpacker.com. By day, Ranong Rd is home to a lively market, but by night, the street has a strange empty charm about it. The hostel may look gloomy from the outside, but inside it's everything you would expect from decent, budget accommodation. There are dorms and rooms with or without air conditioning. The standard rooms are a little pricey for true backpackers (฿900 or ฿1000), but they are clean and the lounge is a cool place to hang out. This place is dubbed a 'boutique hostel', if such a thing is possible.

D Crystal Inn Hotel, 2/1-10 Soi Surin, Montri Rd, T076-22 27756, www.phuket crystalinn.com. Comfortable, trendy rooms conveniently close to Surin Circle. There are 54 rooms in total and the hotel also has a lobby bar. Rooms come with twin beds or a large double bed. TV, a/c and artwork come as part of the package. Stylish accommodation at a reasonable price.

E Forty-three, 43 Thalang Rd, T076-258127. Tucked away on Thalang Rd is this gem. There are 4 room types, with the most snazzy having private gardens or balconies, as well as outdoor showers. Definitely worth a look if you're in Phuket City on a budget.

E-F Crystal Guest House, 41/16 Montri Rd, T076-222774-5. Does daily or monthly rent for decently sized a/c and fan rooms. Not much in the way of views. Glum staff. Rooms are clean though dispiriting.

E-F Nana Chart Mansion, 41/34 Montri Rd, T076-230041-2/230050 (extension 3). Spotless, sizeable a/c and fan rooms, although many are slightly airless. It is excellent value and the staff are helpful.

E-F OT Guesthouse, 42 Krabi Rd, T076-258 272, T08-1569 2519 (mob). Cheap, cheerful and basic. Not all rooms are en suite, not all have a/c. Prices include breakfast, which is served 0700-1000. The communal bathroom has a hot shower. Run by the same people behind **Thalang Guesthouse**.

F-G On On, 19 Phangnga Rd, T076-211154. Riding on its reputation as Phuket City's first hotel, this establishment, dating from 1929, is in the heart of the old town. It has a curious colonial feel with 49 sub-divided a/c and fan rooms with walls that shudder when you sneeze. Cold showers, strip lighting, dark, forbidding wardrobes and the bar down-stairs make for an uncomfortable, noisy night. A pity because there are hints, in the lovely worn staircase, that this was once a dignified establishment. Attached a/c coffee shop and good restaurant, plus an excellent tour desk run by the relaxed Woody.

Patong Beach *p469, map p463*

LL-L Merlin, 44 Moo 4, Thaweewong Rd, T076-340037-41, www.merlinphuket.com/patongmerlin/index.html. A/c, restaurant, 3 sculptured pools and a children's pool, large 4-storey hotel, attractively laid out with well-designed, spacious rooms. Watersports, fitness club and disabled facilities. Seaside restaurant, beauty salon, kids playground. Recommended.

LL-L Sunset Beach Resort, 316/2 Phrab-arame Rd, T076-342482, www.sunsetphuket.com. What better place to feel safe than a hotel with the tsunami warning tower on the roof? This is another mega-hotel with a double kidney-shaped pool snaking its way between terraced, balconied wings. From the upper floor rooms you can see the sea. There is also a decent spa and good but predictable meals. A 5-min tuk-tuk ride from Bangla Rd. Recommended.

LL-AL Holiday Inn, 52 Thaweewong Rd, T076-340608-9, www.holiday.phuket.com. This mega-hotel takes up a chunk of Patong. Pool-side rooms need to be reserved. This hotel is suited to couples and families and has all the comforts you would expect from a **Holiday Inn**.

LL-AL Safari Beach, 136 Thaweewong Rd, T076-341171, www.safaribeachhotel.com. A/c rooms only, restaurant attached. Small hotel set around pool in leafy compound just north of Soi Bangla. The location remains sought after as it is on the beach and the standard rooms are spacious and of a decent standard. Recommended.

LL-A Club Andaman, 2 Patong Rd, T076-340530, www.clubandaman.com. A/c, restaurant, pool, large new block and 53 older thatched cottages, set in large, spacious grounds. Fitness centre, tennis courts, watersports, children's games room.

LL-B Patong Villa, 152/1 Thaweewong Rd, T076-340132, www.patongvilla.com. Minimalist decor in the 72 rooms can be soothing after all the neon of Patong. A little like a US motel at the centre of the beach with restaurant and pool.

A Thavorn Beach Village, 6/2 Moo 6, Nakalay Bay (between Kamala and Patong beaches, on the Kao Phanthurat Pass, 5 km from Patong), T076-290334-42, www.thavornbeachvillage.com. Giant vulgar concrete Hindu cobras spring from the fountain in front of the reception at this otherwise attractively designed resort of Thai-style villas, with 4 rooms each (2 ground floor, 2 first) many with verandas beside the large lagoon-like pool. A secluded spot on a sparsely populated beach – Nakalay Bay (rocky at low tide). It also offers extras like Thai cooking courses and scuba-diving. The restaurant overlooks the sea.

B Smile Inn, 108/9 Thaweewong Rd, T076-776240/5. This is a small hotel in the centre of the Patong Beach with rooms painted bright enough to warrant dim light. However, it is only 2 mins from the beach and well maintained for the price.

C-D Beau Rivage, 77/15-17 Rat Uthit Rd, T076-340725. Some a/c, large rooms – some suites – with clean bathrooms, spacious and good value although like the other hotels on Rat Uthit Rd, it is some way from the beach.

Karon and Kata beaches *p470, map p463*
LL Boathouse Inn, T076-330015,
www.boathouse.net. Southern end of Kata
Beach, a/c, pool. This establishment, also
known as **Mom Tri's Boathouse**, is clearly a
labour of love. Its creator, Mom Tri Devakul,
is an architect and artist, and there's an art
gallery supporting local Phuket artists.
The villa also has a saltwater pool and a
professional health spa. Thai cookery classes
are offeredand there's even a customized
Boathouse Cookbook. The wine cellar is one
of the nicest surprises with over 400 wines –
a rarity in the land of whisky and beer.
Recommended.
LL Katathani Resort and Spa, 14 Kata
Noi Rd, T076-330124-26, www.kata
thani.com. Stunning location in this quiet
cove. All rooms have seafront balcony
and there are even louvered panels in the
bathroom that can be opened if you want
to gaze at the sea from your bath. For even
greater luxury, there is a natural rain shower
and bathtub in the Grand Suite while the
Royal Thani Suite has floor-to-ceiling
windows. Recommended.
LL Merlin Beach Resort, Tri-Trang Beach,
T076-294300, www.merlinphuket.com/
merlinbeach/resort/index.htm. A resort
and spa set in a private bay between Karon
and the southern end of Patong Beach.
This overly large hotel is in a lovely setting
but a hotchpotch of styles makes for an
unintentionally comical effect. The rooms
are, however, nicely done and not too over
the top.
LL-L Karon Beach Resort, 5/2 Moo 3 Patak
Rd, T076-330006-7, www.katagroup.com/
karonbeach. A/c, restaurant and simple pool
on the beach at the southern end of the bay.
All rooms with balconies overlooking beach
but not all have full views. Owned by
the **Kata Group**, the manager is an
English woman.
LL-L Kata Beach Resort, 5/2 Mue 2 Patak Rd,
T076-330530, www.katagroup.com/kata
beach/index.htm. Southern end, 262 rooms
in L-shaped block set around a free-form

pool. Run by an English woman married
to a Thai, this is a smoothly operated hotel,
paired with **Karon Beach Resort**, see below.
LL-L Marina Phuket (formerly Marina
Cottage), 47 Karon Rd, southern end of beach,
T076-330625, www.marina phuket.com. A/c,
2 good restaurants, beautiful secluded pool,
individual cottages in lush grounds set on a
hilltop. **Marina Divers** here, runs tours and
boat trips. Recommended.
LL-AL Centara Villa Phuket, 701 Patak Rd,
T076-286300/9, www.centralhotelsresorts.
com/ckt/ckt_default.asp. This luxury resort
and spa is perched almost on the highest
point overlooking Karon Bay (between Karon
and Patong). There's a **Centara Spas** offering
a range of services. The 72 villas are set on a
steep hill but there are converted tuk-tuks
to transport guests. While all villas are ocean-
facing not all have a good view of the beach.
There are 2 small swimming pools (that can
be crowded), a garden and walkway to the
beach. The resort itself lies on a rocky part of
the headland. The garden and spa are both
on the cliff edge – which makes for great
views. The bungalows are nicely decorated,
bathrooms are spacious and airy – some
with glass roofs. You can sunbathe on the
room balconies. Friendly staff.
LL-AL Hilton Phuket Arcadia Resort & Spa,
333 Patak Rd, Karon Beach, T076-396433,
www.phuketarcadia.com. Everything
you would expect from Hilton. A spa,
3 swimming pools, scuba lessons and
world-class accommodation. Each room
has a desk, internet access, balcony and
dining table.
LL-AL South Sea Resort, 36/12 Moo 1,
Patak Rd, T076-370888, www.phuket-
southsea.com. A/c, restaurant, pool, nearly
100 rooms in this low-rise, intimate boutique
resort. Rooms feature teak wood and Thai
silks and are cool and minimalist. Some
bathrooms need renovation. Attractive
central pool, gym could be better equipped.
You have to negotiate a busy street to reach
the beach although a security guard is there
to help nervous pedestrians across the road.

AL Kata Minta Resort, 156 Khok-Thanod Rd, T076-333283. A/c rooms, close to Kata Yai and Noi beaches. Typical Thai luxury look with pointed roof and stone Buddhas in the Elephant restaurant. Predictable and pleasant enough.

A Best Western Phuket Ocean Resort, 9/1 Moo 1, T076-396176, www.phuket-ocean.com. A/c, restaurant, pool, on a hillside, this establishment overlooks the Andaman Sea and Karon Lagoon. At the quieter, northern end of the bay, away from the beach, OK mid-range place to stay, no pretensions, comfortable. Get up early for the free breakfast or risk missing out.

A Felix Karon View Point (Swissôtel), 4/8 Patak Rd, T076-396666, www.felixhotels.com/karonphuket. A/c, restaurant, low-rise hotel with 125 rooms and a small pool, at the northern end of Karon, but away from the beach. The style is more Spanish than Thai, but nonetheless it is more attractive than most.

C Kata Noi Pavilion 3/71 Patak Road, near Kata Thani Hotel, T076-284346, jaspalt@loxinfo.co.th. Small rooms crowded into a tall building with TV, fridge, hot water and cheap furniture.

E-F P&T Kata House 104/1 Koktanod Rd, T076-284203. One of several cheap guesthouses at the southern end of Kata Beach set back a few hundred metres from the shore, past a 7-11, offering some of the island's cheapest rooms outside Phuket City. The rooms are clean with fresh linen and many overlook a garden, and are of similar quality to competitors which charge 3 times as much. There is no hot water but a/c rooms are available. The boss is friendly. Recommended.

Nai Harn and Promthep Cape *p471, map p463*

LL-AL Baan Krating Jungle Beach, 11/3 Moo 1, Witset Rd, T076-288264, www.baankrating.com/phuket/. Remote, attractive position, has a long and good track record. Accessible through Le Royal

Meridien Phuket Yacht Club, this is on Ao Sane Beach, which is nicknamed Jungle Beach for the foliage around it. There are 30 villas, all with sea views from the balconies and a pool overlooking Nai Harn Bay. The rooms have a slightly rustic Western feel, picked up again by the presence of a pool table and big screens in the relaxation area. If you like to explore, your own transport is a good idea here as it is an isolated spot.

D Ao Sane Bungalow, 11/12 Ao Sane Moo 1, Witset Rd, T076-288306. Also accessible through the yacht club's car park. Bungalows on a small rocky bay with coral. But this is a refreshingly secluded part of Phuket.

Laem Ka and Chalong beaches *p471, map p463*

LL Evason Phuket Resort and Spa, formerly Phuket Island Resort, 100 Witset Rd, Rawai Beach, T076-38010-7, www.six-senses.com/evason-phuket/. On the tip of Laem Ka with stunning views across to the nearby islands and over Chalong Bay. While the buildings are quite large, the rooms are exquisite with a cool, airy feel. There are tennis courts and a refined spa. To make up for the poor quality of the beaches on the main island, the resort has its own island in the bay – Koh Bon. Set in 26 ha of garden facing the Andaman Sea, this is definitely intended to be a place of escapism as the resort, though large – 285 rooms – is flanked by 2 inland lagoons and surrounded by extensive foliage.

Cape Panwa *p472, map p463*

LL The Bay Hotel, 31/11 Moo 8, Sakdidej Rd, T07-6391514, www.thebay-phuket.com. A seafront hotel 15 mins' drive from Phuket. Rooms have sofa and dining table, stereo and large balcony. There is a gym, 2 pools and a garden.

LL Sri Panwa, Cape Panwa, www.sripanwa.com. This luxury resort is definitely worth checking out if you feel like a splurge. The pool villas are spacious and located in a small community on a hillside overlooking the cape. Away from the tourist traps of the island, this is a resort for people who want a quiet time with the finer things in life. You could easily spend your entire holiday in your pool villa. They're enormous and stunningly decorated. **LL-AL Cape Panwa**, 27 Moo 8, Sakdidej Rd, T076-391123, www.capepanwa.com. Beautifully secluded, good variety of accommodation including bungalows for families or friends, tennis courts, fitness centre, beauty salon, flower arranging and Thai cookery courses. For a touch of exclusivity take the Mercedes electric tram down to the beach which can only be accessed through the hotel. There is also a coral reef 40 m offshore. Leonardo Di Caprio stayed here in Room E301 which has a double balcony and the best view of the sea and the bay. Other famous guests include Catherine Zeta Jones, Pierce Brosnan and Elizabeth Taylor. The choice of restaurants include Italian and Thai fusion and there's an excellent cocktail bar. Good breakfast buffet. While you may never wish to leave the hotel, there is also a shuttle service into Phuket Old Town. Recommended.

Koh Tapao Yai

This small island off the cape is home to a few hotels and around 200 hornbills. **A Phuket Paradise Resort**, T076-211935, www.phuketweb.com/pprh/index.html. The idiosyncratic ambience of this resort on Koh Tapao Yai is largely due to the presence of hornbills which can be seen between 0600 and 1800 as they fly around the hotel (dawn is the best time to catch the shy birds). In 1986 there were a mere handful of these colourful heavy-beaked birds, until hornbill fan and manager Khun Aroon insisted that everyone take care of the birds. There are now over 200 on Koh Tapao Yai. The rooms are set in the hillsides, some with a seaview. There is a free daily boat trip and car service to town and golf trips can be arranged.

Koh Lone, Koh Mai Ton and other southern islands p472, map p463
LL Maiton Island Resort, Koh Mai Ton, T076-214954, maitonislandresort@thai-tour.com.

A/c, restaurants, pools, 75 individual Thai pavilions withseparate sitting rooms, good sports facilities and beautiful white beaches with a decent coral reef.
L-A Coral Island Resort, Koh Hii, T076-281 060, www.coralislandresort.com. Around 70 snazzy a/c bungalows – poolside and beachfront. This place is named after Koh Hii's nickname – Coral Island. The resort is near perfect: white beaches with coral reefs fit for snorkelling. On the other side of the island, you can also visit pleasant secluded bays.
AL Baan Mai Cottages, 35/1 Moo 3, Koh Lone, T02-6730966, bannmai@tahi-tour.com. Bungalow/houses decorated with faux 19th-century Burmese furniture and Balinese-style bathrooms. Thai and French cuisine. Pool.

Koh Rang Yai p473
C Richy Island Phuket Co, T076-2398934, T076-2385656, www.rangyaiisland-phuket.com. Rang Yai is privately owned and as such everything on the island is run by one company. Bungalows can be rented for ฿1000 a night for overnight stays. There's no a/c, but electricity is provided 24 hrs. The bungalows are basic, with bedding on the floor and mosquito nets above. There is also the option of camping out. Hotel pickups can be arranged and boats depart from Sapam Bay. The food on the island is excellent. There is the option of taking your vows on Rang Yai if you fancy getting married on a tropical island. Full-day tours cost up to ฿2200 for adults, ฿1200 for children, without an overnight stay.

Kamala Beach p474, map p463
A-E Papa Crab Guesthouse, 93/5 Moo 3 Kamala Beach, T076-385315, www.phuket papacrab.com. 10 air-conditioned rooms and 3 bungalows at this unusually named guesthouse. Basic accommodation next to the beach. Has tour information and can arrange a taxi to the airport. Cosy little place. The rooms are simple, clean and with comfortable beds. Everything is very white, so it all looks a bit post-modern.

C-E Popeye's Place, 99/25 Moo 3, Soi 10, T076-385815, www.popeyes-place.com. Run by a Danish-Thai couple combo, there are 11 rooms, 5 bungalows and 1 luxury villa on offer. Also features a minimart, restaurant and internet access. A stay in the luxury villa will set you back ฿6500 a night, but the regular rooms are well priced, although a little sparse. Rooms are large, with a/c, TV, fridge and double bed. The bungalows have hot showers. Located 400 m from the beach.

Surin Beach and Pansea Beach p474, map p463
LL Amanpuri Resort, 118/1 Pansea Beach, T076-324333, www.amanpuri.com. A/c, restaurant, pool, the more expensive rooms are beautifully designed Thai pavilions, with attention to every detail. Superb facilities include private yacht, watersports, tennis and squash courts, fitness centre, private beach, library, undoubtedly the best on Phuket. Guests include political leaders. Surroundings, style and service incomparable.
LL Chedi Phuket (formerly Pansea Resort), 118 Moo3, T076-236550, www.phuket.com/chedi. South of Amanpuri. Chic, exclusive resort set into the hillside above a perfectly secluded sandy white beach. There is a range of beautifully designed traditional thatched Thai cottages sleeping 2-10 people, professional staff, superb facilities, including watersports, cinema, library, games room, a/c, restaurant, pool. Rooms can be somewhat small and monastic. The small pool appears almost black due to the dark stone used.
A Pen Villa Hotel, 9/1 Moo 3 Surin Beach, Srisootorn Rd, T076-271100. Bland red-roofed complex with decent pool and big clean rooms. Offers good Thai cookery course. Suitable for families. Free transfers to 2 local beaches – Surin and Laem Sing. The hotel also arranges daytrips, fishing and golf.

Bang Tao Beach p474, map p463
LL-L Dusit Laguna, T076-324320, www.lagunaphuket.com. A/c, restaurants, attractive pool, the quietest and most refined of the **Laguna Phuket** complex. Excellent service, beautifully laid out, unimposing hotel, tennis courts, watersports. Rooms can be a little small.
LL-L Sheraton Grande Laguna, T076-324101, www.lagunaphuket.com. A/c, 5 restaurants (with a good choice of cuisine),and a large pool with interlinked sections, including a sandy 'beach' and a sunken bar. Some of the accommodation is on stilts on the lagoon. Has tennis courts, a health centre, massage and a children's corner.
L Banyan Tree, T076-324374, www.banyantree.com/en/Phuket/index.html. Voted the 'World's Best Spa Resort' by Conde Nast Traveller and 'Best Resort Hotel in Asia' by Asian Wall Street Journal, this is luxury indeed. Spa pool villas with private pool, jacuzzi, sunken baths, outdoor showers and beds sheathed in silk that 'float' over lily ponds. The spa itself is similarly spectacular, the only drawback being the priority of privacy over space in terms of the grounds.
A-C Bangtao Lagoon Bungalow, 72/3 Moo 3, Tambon Cherng Talay, T076-324260. Some a/c, small pool, a bungalow development in a comparatively isolated position. Range of chalets from simple fan bungalows to 'de luxe' a/c affairs, the latter are small and featureless, but clean, family cottages also available.

Nai Thon and Layan p474, map p462
LL-L Layan Resort and Spa, T076-313412, www.layanresort.com. Set back from the beach, low-rise, open design with pleasant rooms, 2 pools, gym and lush gardens. Well-equipped spa with lots of open-air areas.

Nai Yang and Nai Yang National Park p474, map p463
LL Indigo Pearl, T076-327006, www.indigo-pearl.com. Built in 2006 in a stark, chic fashion with stand-alone bathtubs, marble and grey stone walls. The sprawling resort dominates the underdeveloped southern end of the bay.
LL-D Nai Yang Beach Resort, T076-328300, www.phuket.com/naiyangbeach. Well-built

bungalows with good facilities and simple decor. Some a/c. Set in large grounds with plenty of trees for shade. Friendly staff. A bit pricey at the upper end but excellent value at the lower end. Right next to the **Pearl Village** and a hop over the road to the beach.

C Garden Cottage 53/1 Moo 1, T076-327 293, gardencot@yahoo.com. 2 mins from the airport and walking distance from the beach, charming cottage-style bungalows, friendly owners willing to show you the island. Excellent value with a masseur and attractive restaurant and communal areas. Recommended.

Camping
In the national park, ฿60.

Mai Khao p475, map p463
L Marriott's Phuket Beach Club
T076-338000, www.marriott.com. Take the turn-off at the sign on the main road (402) travelling north from the airport. There are also airport pick-up services for the hotel. Over 200 rooms and 2 pools, spa, fitness centre, tennis courts, shops, gallery and playground. Brightly painted traditional boats (*korlae*) are dotted throughout the resort. Service is impeccable. The rooms are elegant and spacious. Sea turtle nesting grounds are close and the hotel has donated a large sum to the Thai World Wildlife Fund to start up a turtle conservation fund. Watersports are banned, and guests are asked to use the pools rather than the sea to avoid disturbing sea turtles.

A-E Mai Khao Beach Bungalows,
T08-05228392 (mob), www.mai-khao-beach.com. It's a good idea to contact the bungalow in advance to organize transport with their help. The bungalows are well signposted. Take the third turn-off heading north towards Phangnga to Mai Khao Beach (this should take you past fields of watermelons and head south); the sign and dirt track are on the right-hand side. Alternatively, take an earlier turn-off and go right through the village and head back towards the main

road, and the sign will be on your left once you start seeing the watermelon fields. This is quite a find for Phuket. Tucked away in a grassy clearing shaded by large casuarina trees and shrubs right on the beach. There are 2 ranges of bungalows, smaller bamboo and palm roof huts with shared bathrooms and larger en suite concrete and wood rooms. It is also possible to pitch a tent for ฿150. The owners seem to enjoy getting to know their guests and set up a regular campfire to chat during the night. Recommended.

Eating

Phuket City p466, map p467
There are quite a few reasonably priced Thai restaurants in the old town. The food in Phuket is highly rated throughout Thailand, for the range of dishes and the invigorating and sophisticated spices and herbs used in Southern Thai cuisine.

₦₦₦ Ka Jok See, 26 Takua Pa Rd, T076-217903. Excellent Thai restaurant. The success of the restaurant is leading to some pretty sharp pricing but the atmosphere, character, style and first-rate cuisine make it worth paying extra. Booking is essential.

₦₦₦ Kanda Bakery, 31-33 Rasada Rd. This spotlessly clean a/c restaurant with art deco undertones, serves breakfast, Thai and international dishes and good cakes like cinnamon rolls, croissant and chocolate brownies.

₦₦₦ La Gaetana, Phuket Rd, T076-250253, T08-1397 1227 (mob). The best Italian food in Phuket. Owners Gianni Ferrara and Chonticha Buasukhon offer impeccable service. There is also a decent wine list. Booking is recommended as the restaurant is rather small and fills up early.

₦₦₦ Le Café, Rasada Centre. Elegant café serving burgers, steaks, sandwiches, cappuccinos and milkshakes.

₦₦₦ Raya Thai Cuisine, see Sleeping, above. This restaurant is in a 70-year-old Macao-style house with a garden. It is well preserved with original tiling, windows, lighting and ceiling fans, and with a selection of photographs of old Phuket. The airy room upstairs is a pleasant place to eat. It serves Thai dishes and local specialities; if you like spicy food, try the *nam bu bai cha plu* (crab curry with local herbs served with Chinese rice noodles).

♥♥♥ Santana Coffee, 54/8-9 Montri Rd. A nicely decorated European-style café that serves Thai food, steaks and European food as well as an excellent selection of coffees. Brews range from Jamaica Pea to Kilamanjaro.

♥♥♥ Venus Chinese Restaurant, 34-38 Phangnga Rd. Classy establishment serving a variety of Chinese and Thai dishes.

♥♥ Bondeli Café, Thanon Rat Sada corner by the bridge and Thanon Phuket. Now an internet café with pastries and savouries including pizzas.

♥♥ Farang Restaurant, off Chaloem Kiat Rd, next to **Index**, T08-6946 3142 (mob). Amazing little restaurant that serves cheap, quality fusion dishes. Sausages, steaks, pasta, pizza, it's all here. There is also a second branch at 120/6 Cherngtalay, Thalang, T08-1620 7429 (mob).

♥♥ Kama Sutra, Takuapa Rd, T076-256192. If you're in Phuket City and feel like eating Indian, this is the place to go. The portions are generous, although the atmosphere is a little gloomy. The management and staff are a friendly bunch.

♥♥ Lai-An Lao, 58 Rasada Rd. Chinese restaurant with seafood specialities.

♥♥ Natural Restaurant, Soi Phutorn, T076-224287, T076-214037. A long-time favorite in Phuket City, with fish swimming in televisions and all manner of plants everywhere. The oysters are perhaps the best in Phuket. The sushi is average, but the Thai food is exceptional. Check out the range of curries for some spicy excitement.

♥♥ Roak Ros, opposite **Fresh Mart** on Phuket Rd and Soi Thalang Chan. Popular with locals. Spartan interior with stainless steel table-tops, and cutlery and plates in a plastic tray screwed into the wall above your table. The favourite here is clams in chilli paste. Shellfish can be small, though.

♥♥ Salvatore's, Rassada Rd, T076-225958, T08-9871 1184 (mob). A jolly little restaurant that looks and feels like a cliché but has some decent pasta dishes to choose from. A little expensive for what it is. Aimed at tourists.

♥♥ Shelter, down from the **On-On Hotel** on Phangnga Rd. Burgers, breakfast and Thai food, greasy café, popular with surfers.

♥♥ Siam Indigo, Phangnga Rd, T076-256697, T08-1892 4885 (mob). Reasonable restaurant with Thai dishes and a few international splashes here and there. Does a decent rack of lamb.

♥ Baan Talang Restaurant, 65 Thalang Rd. Tasty Thai and Islamic food (the lamb curry is excellent but hot). As with most places in this part of town, the walls are lined with photographs of old Phuket and there is an old-world feel.

♥ Fine Day, Chumphon Rd, www.fineday-phuket.com. Fine Day is an institution in Phuket. It's a hip hotspot where people hang out, eat and drink. Stays open until about midnight and is always busy. The staff are friendly and although there isn't a menu in English, there is always someone on hand to help out.

♥ Food Court, 4th floor, around the corner from the cinema, **Central Festival Phuket**. An excellent food court serving cheap Thai nosh. You can get everything from *kao man gai* (boiled chicken meat on a bed of rice and a side of spicy, ginger sauce) to noodles. Much better than most of the restaurants at Central Festival.

♥ Kow-Tom-Hua-Pla (Boiled Fish Rice) opposite **Caramba Bar and Restaurant** on Phuket Rd past Thalang Rd. Popular with locals, this simple noodle café is open 1700-2400 and is run by Chinese-Thai Mr Pinit. It serves an eclectic mix of noodles, including *Yen-ta-Foa* seafood noodles coloured a blood-red by a sweetish slightly hot sauce. Other noodle soups include fish skin and fish stomach noodles. Recommended.

♥ Lemon Grass, Dibuk Rd. Decent Thai food at a large, outdoor restaurant. A bit out of the way but worth the journey.

Lullaby, Soi Hongyok Utis, off Yaowarat Rd. Tucked away off the main road, this is a popular hangout with the locals. The outdoor restaurant serves up decent Thai grub in the evenings. Not a bad place to have a drink with friends.

Nong Jote Café, 16 Yaowarat Rd. This 100-plus-year-old building looks like a café in Lisbon with high ceilings, and, along one side, ceiling-to-floor antique glassed cabinets in teak. On the other side there are banners for English football clubs; it's a sociable spot to watch Premiership matches. Tables are large enough to read a newspaper on and the service is admirably unrushed. The owner lived in New Zealand and has excellent English. You can find some of the best southern Thai food here, certainly in Phuket. Try the *yum tour plu* but remember it is hot. Some dishes have a Chinese edge. Recommended.

P Pizza, Yaowarat Rd, next to Samkong Shrine. For cheap pizzas you can't go wrong, the rest of the menu is a bit hit and miss.

Vegetarian Restaurant, corner of Tilik Uthit 1 Rd and Chanacharoen Rd, near **Crystal Hotel**. Don't be fooled by the hemp leaf decorations everywhere. This place is filled with wholesome Scandinavian families eating somewhat bland food. Good for those with allergies.

Foodstalls

There is a late-night *khanom jeen* vendor on Surin Rd (towards Damrong Rd, just up the road from the Shell garage). While usually a breakfast dish, there is no better meal to have late at night when you get a case of the munchies then *khanom jeen*. Choose your curry, throw in a few condiments and enjoy some of the best Thai food on offer. Look for the large brown pots at the side of the road.

The best place to browse on the street is around the market on **Ranong Rd**. A good and cheap restaurant close by is **Koh Lao Luat Mu** (name only in Thai), on the round-about linking Ranong and Rasada roads,

which serves tasty noodle and rice dishes. Alternatively, **Khai Muk**, Rasada Rd (opposite the **Thavorn Hotel**) serves superb *kwaytio* (noodle soup). Just round the corner from Robinson on Ong Sim Phai Rd, is a lively collection of night-time street food vendors serving cheap Thai dishes to locals. There is a wide choice of food to choose from, much better than the nearby burgers and pizza.

Patong Beach *p469, map p463*
Many of the sois off Patong Beach Rd sell a good range of international food.

Da Maurizio, Kalim Beach, north of Patong, opposite **Diamond Cliff Hotel**, T076-344079. Italian food in an attractive setting.

Floyd's Brasserie, Burasari Resort, 18/110 Ruamjai Rd, T076-370000. Who better to open a restaurant in Phuket than acclaimed TV chef Keith Floyd? As you'd expect, the wine list is top class with 52 labels on the menu. There is some great food available, too. When Floyd is in town, the fun really begins, but even in his absence this is a restaurant worth checking out.

Hungry Tiger, intersection of Bangla and Second roads. Thai and Western dishes. In the words of one visitor, "they have the guts to serve [the food] unmoderated ... hot really means hot".

Patong Beer Garden, by K Hotel, 82/47 Rat Uthit Rd. Attractive garden setting, Viennese food cooked by Austrian chef.

White Box, 247/5 Prabaramee Rd, T076-346271, www.whiteboxrestaurant.com. A simple concept: it's white and it looks like a large box. The setting is ideal, far enough away from the madness of Patong, but with decent views over Patong Bay. The food is good, with a range of Mediterranean and Thai dishes. Children are welcome. Although not the cheapest place to drink (฿150 for a beer), there are usually parties at weekends with dancing until after midnight.

Lim's, Soi 7, Kalim Bay. This opened in a small house in 1999 and now has a vast dining room with high ceilings and outdoor courtyard. Also features bold abstract paintings by one of the owners, 'Gop'. Has a *Sex in the City* feel. The food concentrates more on the quality of the ingredients rather than overwhelming with spices. Suits an exhausted palate. Choices of dishes range from grilled pork ribs to Vietnamese spring rolls with, among other things, capsicum.

ꗠ Charlie's Restaurant, Soi Sansabai. Thai and Tex-Mex. BBQ every Fri from 2100. Good bar.

ꗠ Joe's Downstairs, 223/3 Prabaramee Rd, Kalim Beach, near Patong, T076-344254, T076-344927. A cool place to watch the sun set while sipping on a cocktail and enjoying the view of Kalim Bay. They have some great tapas here.

ꗠ Pavarotti's, Patong Resort Hotel, Rat Uthit Rd, good seafood BBQ with set price eat-as-much-as-you-like option.

ꗠ Rock Hard Café, 82/51 Bangla Rd. Garden, steaks, pizzas.

ꗠ-ꗢ Le Croissant, Soi Bangla. Thai/European restaurant/bakery. Good selection.

ꗢ Lai Mai, 86/15 Patong Beach Rd. Great Western breakfasts.

ꗢ Waikiki Dive Café, Soi Patong Resort. Food and pool and internet. A cool place to chill out, open until 0200, more a bar than a restaurant.

ꗢ Woody's Sandwich Shoppe, Aroonsom Plaza, T076-290468, www.khunwoody.com. Woody's Shoppe, run by local computer guru Woody Leonhard, is something of an institution in Phuket. For about ฿100 to ฿150, you can get a sandwich that puts Subway to shame. Woody also offers free Wi-Fi access.

Karon and Kata Beaches *p470, map p463*

ꗠ Al Dente, Beach Rd close to Karon Circle, T076-396569. You can't miss it, this is the traffic island decorated with mythical creatures. Try their meat and cheese fondues and Italian dishes while listening to classical music.

ꗠ JaoJong Seafood, 4/2 Patak Rd, Katanoi Beach, T076-330136. Unpretentious sea-shanty feel to this spacious open-fronted

seafood restaurant. Good selection of freshly caught seafood and well executed. The menu is illustrated with pictures – very useful. Low-key atmosphere. Reasonably priced. Recommended.

ꗠ Swiss Bakery, Kata beach, Bougainvillea Terrace House, 117/1 Patak Rd, T076-33139. 0800-2400. Open-air terrace, Swiss delicacies here include Bouguionne and Tartaren Hut. Also do burgers and sandwiches from ฿120.

Rawai *p471, map p463*

ꗠ Drunken Monkey, Viset Rd, T08-1787 1184 (mob). A favorite with Phuket's British contingent, Drunken Monkey does an awesome Sun roast as well as the best bangers and mash on the island.

ꗠ The Green Man, 82/15 Moo 4, Patak Rd, T076-281445, www.the-green-man.net. Claims to be the only Tudor-style pub in Asia. In terms of pub grub, it's all very British and it's all very tasty. They even have pickled eggs.

Laem Ka and Chalong beaches *p471, map p463*

ꗠ Kan Eang Seafood, on the beach. Good choice of seafood. Recommended.

Cape Panwa *p472, map p463*

ꗠꗠ-ꗠ Panwa House, Cape Panwa, on the beach. Everything is in place here for the perfect meal: the 2-storey Sino-Portuguese house perched on the edge of a beach with indoor and outdoor dining, the serenading guitarist and singer, excellent service and deliciously executed dishes. Try their spicy beef salad in lime juice or the lobster with shavings of caramelized shallot, palm sugar and tamarind. The desserts are superb too, for example the stuffed rambutan with vanilla custard. Recommended.

ꗠ Yaun Yen, 200 m from the aquarium. Reasonable food, seafood is best.

ꗢ Sawasdee Restaurant, 31/4 Sakdidej Rd. The food here is average and caters to a perceived Western taste which is bland, slightly sugary and somewhat slippery with oil. However, the set-up is fun. You sit at old Singer sewing tables in a brick rustic Thai-style bungalow with an open front and a great view of the ocean. The 80-year-old bricks were taken from the owner's home on the Malaysian border. A good place to snack.

Surin Beach and Pansea Beach *p474, map p463*

† Amanpuri, see Sleeping, above, T076-324394. Considered one of the best Thai restaurants on the island and the setting is sensational. At least 48 hrs advanced booking needed during peak season.

Bang Tao Beach *p474, map p463*

††† Lotus Restaurant, in front of Banyan Tree Beach, Moo 4, Cherng Talay, T076-3626256, T08-1797 3110 (mob). Slightly expensive, but the food is good and the vibe is unbeatable. Next to the sea. The live seafood is interesting to look at if you don't fancy singling out which creatures you'd like eat.

Nai Yang and Nai Yang National Park *p474, map p463*

†† Nai Yang Seafood, Nai Yang beach. One of several charming spots next to the empty beach, all of which serve excellent seafood.

Mai Khao *p473, map p463*

There is a full range of restaurants in the Marriott and a simple in-house restaurant at the Mai Khao Beach Bungalows.
††† Rivet Grill, Indigo Pearl Resort, www.indigo-pearl.com/dining-rivetgrill.html. Yes, it's expensive, but this is the restaurant to go to for the best steaks in Phuket and probably the whole of Southern Thailand. The restaurant is well designed with count-less touches that reflect the overall tin-mining theme at the resort.

○ Bars and clubs

Phuket's club scene has experienced some-thing of a resurgence and is now attracting the attention of DJs and promoters who have previously favored Koh Phangan and Ko Samui. International DJs such as Louie Vega, Judge Jules and Brandon Block have passed through. Whether you want house, electro, hip hop, rock, pop or reggae – you'll find somewhere to go in Phuket.

Phuket City *p466, map p467*

9Richter, Rassada Rd. This is a great place to hang out because very few foreigners make it inside. Stays open until about 0100, with the usual Thai songs sung by live bands and a DJ who isn't afraid to rupture eardrums with bizarre techno music. If you're lucky enough to catch a guest slot from some of Thailand's best indie bands (Modern Dog, Flure and so on) you'll be in for a treat. There's only a cover charge for special events.
Balé, Phuket Rd. While karaoke may not be top on your list of things to do, if you fancy screaming your lungs out in a small booth while drinking copious amounts of whisky, this is the place to do it. If you didn't bring your singing voice, there's a cool open-air beer garden that stays open reasonably late.
Barzah, Phun Pol Rd. Although Barzah is supposedly located in the 'bad' area of town, this extremely loud hip hop club is a fun place to drink and dance, often after other clubs have closed their doors. The locals are friendly and there is almost never any trouble.
Blue Marina, Phuket Merlin Hotel, 158/1 Yaowarat Rd, T076-212866-70. A long-standing favorite with the locals. Offers up standard Thai hits and other random treats from bands and DJs. Fri and Sat are always very busy.
Kor Tor Mor, Chana Charoen Rd, near Nimit Circle, T076-232285. Large, incredibly popular Thai club that gets ludicrously busy on Fri and Sat. Get there early or else you may be turned away. Buy a bottle of whisky, drink, kick back, dance and enjoy.
O'Malleys, 2/20-21 Montri Rd, T076-220170. An Irish-style pub that serves pints as well as a killer all-day breakfast (฿99). Upstairs there is free pool, darts, table football and some

PS2s. There are usually a few friendly faces around if you fancy a chat about football or island life.

Oasis, Mae Luang Rd. Oasis is quintessentially Thai and a lot of fun. It's a small venue that doesn't attract too big a crowd so you've always got a bit of space to drink and dance in. As usual, expect bands singing Thai favorites and the occasional Green Day number. The in-house DJ usually closes the night with blistering dance music. The Thais will be surprised to see you, but you'll be welcomed as long as you join in the fun.

Timber Hut, 118/1 Yaowarat Rd, T076-211839. Something of an institution in Phuket, Timber Hut has been around for about 20 years. The crowd is a mix of Thais and foreigners. Arrive early on Fri and Sat because once midnight comes, you won't be able to move. A standard selection of Thai songs and odd Western classics are the order of the night. It's fun, but there are better places to choose.

Patong Beach *p469, map p463*

Bars in Patong are concentrated along Rat Uthit Rd and Bangla Rd. The latter is throbbing with activity in the evening, as bars cater with gusto for all nationalities, persuasions and perversions.

Banana, on the beach road, T076-340306. A firm favorite with the locals. It's always very busy with a large number of tourists finding their way there. The club doesn't stay open very late and the drinks are reasonably priced. Expect to hear a range of rock music, hip hop and pop. As Phuket's longest-running nightclub, you can count on a decent night out. A few undesirable tourist characters lurk in the shadows.

BYD Lofts, Rat-U-Thit Road, **Club Andaman Resort**, T076-3430247, www.bydlofts.com. In Patong, but sufficiently away from the madness of Soi Bangla. This restaurant doubles as a bar. The food is average but for pre-club drinks it's a chilled affair.

Club Lime, on the beach road, T08-5798 1850 (mob), T08-5798 8511 (mob),

www.clublime.info. Past guest DJs here include Jo Mills and Barry Ashworth. The music ranges from electro and house to tribal and techno. Expect to pay a cover charge of up to ฿300 with 1 or 2 drinks included. Alcohol is priced on the expensive side for Patong, but the club has a really good vibe and you'll look out of place in sandals and a Beer Chang vest.

Crocodile Pub (formerly Le Crocodile), at the back of Soi Crocodile which is packed with bars down from Soi Bangla. 2200-0200. You can't miss this place with its funfair sign festooned with crocodile figures jamming in a rock band. It's a small disco, with ฿70 cover charge open late Mon, Wed and Sat with cabaret shows from Tiffany's Tiara. Show time is at 0130. For discount cocktails not such a bad place. Also do theme nights including Latino Party Time.

H20, Soi Post Office. Not the most exciting of clubs, but popular with an older crowd and there's usually karaoke.

Paradise Complex, Rat-U-Thit Rd. Paradise Complex is like the gay community's version of Soi Bangla. The complex is huge, comprising numerous gay bars, hotels, cafés and restaurants. The fun is hedonistic and there are endless cabaret shows to be watched. This is a popular, friendly area where all walks of life are accepted and celebrated. It can get pretty raunchy, but you won't come across any trouble. Visit www.gaypatong.com for info about the gay scene.

Rock City, 188/1 Thaweewong Rd, www.rockcity.cc. Get your rocks off at Rock City. This small club on the beach road is all rock 'n' roll. Cover bands steam through Bon Jovi, Metallica, Megadeath and even Bryan Adams. The place is usually packed on Fri and Sats. Beer is cheap, but the food is worth avoiding. The bands are pretty good and for a kind of nostalgic, 80s-themed night out, you can't go far wrong.

Safari, located on the hill between Patong and Karon. Where most people go after the other clubs have closed. There's a climbing wall that drunk tourists try to scale, not recommended if you've had a few. There are also opportunities to drench ladyboys by dunking them in large pools of water. You have to see it to believe it. The music is pumping and the people range from tired tourists through to drunk locals and every hanger-on in between.

Seduction Discotheque, Soi Bangla, www.seductiondisco.com. Has been around for a while and provides reasonably priced drinks and 2 floors of hip hop and dance beats. Doesn't get busy until later, but is worth a look if you fancy a dance. They sometimes have international guest DJs playing, but usually it's the residents taking you into the early hours of the morning. Happy hour is between 2300 and midnight.

Tai Pan, at the far end of Soi Bangla on the opposite side to the beach, www.taipan.st. A rowdy nightspot with live bands, cheap drinks, lots of shouting and dancers. Open late.

Tin Mine 21, Paradise Complex, 135/23 Rat Uthit Rd, T076-340666. 1900-0200. From here you can go up to the **Sky Lounge** for cocktails which is 24 floors above Patong. Tin Mine has 300 seats.

Karon and Kata Beaches *p470, map p463*
Deep Sea Video Theque on the ground floor of the **Hilton Phuket Arcadia Resort & Spa**. The DJ here does a cabaret show with a different theme every night. Semi-Butlins feel in this 700 capacity venue.

Ratri Jazztaurant, Kata Hill, T076-333538, www.ratrijazztaurant.com. The perfect spot for a romantic dinner or to kick back, have a few drinks and enjoy the view. As the name suggests, this place is all about jazz. It isn't the cheapest spot around, but it can't be beaten in terms of setting and ambience.

Nai Harn and Promthep Cape *p471, map p463*
Reggae Bar, Nai Harn Lake. Definitely worth a visit. This is about as real a reggae bar as you'll find in Thailand, complete with

Rastafarians. It's chilled and peaceful next to the lake. Usually stays open later than regular closing times.

Cape Panwa *p472, map p463*
Baba Dining Lounge, Sri Panwa, T076-371 006, www.sripanwa.com. Hip, happening and with killer views of the sea at sunrise and sunset. The food and drinks are priced at the upper end of the Phuket scale, but you expect quality when you're at a place like Baba. When they have special events the venue becomes a hive of nocturnal activity with lots of dancing. Requires a trip to the southernmost point of Phuket.
The Top of the Reef Bar, Cape Panwa Hotel, see Sleeping, above. Excellent house cocktails and a view of the sea on a wicker-chaired veranda. Even if you are not staying here, it is worth dropping in for the feeling of tropical indulgence and glamour. There's a jazz singer taking your requests. Dress for the occasion.

◑ Entertainment

Phuket City *p466, map p467*
Saphan Hin motor show, the parking lot at Saphan Hin. Earplugs at the ready. Every Sat night about 60 souped-up mean machines come with sound systems blazing and more neon lights than Chinese New Year. This weekly motor show is where car shops flaunt the latest technology on some seriously expensive car upgrades. The whole thing is a wonder in itself. It's not strictly official, but it's totally safe and beers and snacks can be bought from the onslaught of vendors scattered around the lot. The noise is unbelievable, but this is a rare chance to see what some of the local kids are into. Feel free to take pictures, but ask permission from the car owners before you do.

Patong Beach *p469, map p463*
Sphinx Restaurant and Theatre, Rat Uthit Rd. Gaining popularity among the gay scene, this upmarket set-up offers Thai classical

performances as well as Broadway hits and comedy. The food isn't bad – a mix of Thai and European cuisine.

Kamala Beach *p474, map p463*
Phuket Fantasea, 99 Moo 3, T076-385111, www.phuket-fantasea.com. For a long time, this has been a firm favourite with visitors. It's billed as the ultimate in nightlife entertainment. The entire complex is huge and includes a carnival village, a restaurant and Las Vegas-style shows involving lots of animals, lighting effects and acrobatics.

❀ Festivals and events

Phuket Island *p462, maps p463 and p467*
9-10 Feb Chinese New Year.
Feb Old Phuket Town Festival. During the first weekend of Feb, the locals close off Thalang Rd, Krabi Rd and Soi Rommanee to celebrate Old Phuket Town with foodstalls, music, plays and exhibitions.
Feb Phuket Blues Festival, www.phuket bluesfestival.com. One of the few music festivals held in Phuket. Great bands, a good crowd and lots of booze.
March Phuket Food Festival. Held every year in Saphan Hin over a period of about 10 days. Enjoy Thai food accompanied by the world's most out-of-tune brass band, some karaoke singing and carnival games where you can win fish.
13 Mar Thao Thep Kasattri and Thao Sisunthon Fair. Celebrates the 2 heroines who saved Phuket from the Burmese.
Apr Fish Releasing Festival timed to coincide with Songkran or Thai New Year. Baby turtles are released at several of Phuket's beaches.
Apr Bike Week at Patong Beach – during Songkran. Get your kicks with Harley and Co.
May Seafood Festival, in conjunction with the Marine Tourism Resources and Phuket Tourism. There's a parade, seafood stalls displaying regional cuisines, and demonstrations as well as cultural shows.

For keen foodies anxious to improve their repertoire.
End May Rugby Tournament, held at Karon Beach and Karon Municipal Stadium.
Between the 6th and 11th lunar month Chao Le Boat Floating Festival, involving the Rawai, Sapan, Koh Sire and Laem Ka. This festival is held at night as small boats are set adrift to ward off evil.
Jul Marathon (2nd week).
22 Aug-3 Sep Por Tor Festival, in Phuket City. This means 'hungry ghosts' and is a time when ancestors are honoured. Ghosts are supposedly released into the world for the whole month. To keep them quiet and reasonable, they are given food, flowers and candles at family altars. Bribes include cakes in the shape of turtles – the Chinese symbol of longevity.
Oct (movable) Chinese Vegetarian Festival, *Ngan Kin Jeh*, lasts 9 days and marks the beginning of Taoist lent. No meat is eaten, alcohol consumed nor sex indulged in (in order to cleanse the soul). Men pierce their cheeks or tongues with long spears and other sharp objects and walk over hot coals and (supposedly) feel no pain. The festival is celebrated elsewhere, but most enthusias-tically in Phuket, especially at Wat Jui Tui on Ranong Rd in Phuket City (see box, page 464). This must be one of the star attractions of a visit to Phuket. Visitors are made to feel welcome and encouraged to take part in the event. For more information, see the Festivals colour section.
Nov Patong Carnival welcomes in the tourist season.
5 Dec King's Cup Regatta is a yachting competition in the Andaman Sea, timed to coincide with the king's birthday (he is a yachtsman of international repute). The event attracts competitors from across the globe.
Dec Laguna Phuket Triathlon, 1000-m swim, 5-km bicycle race and 12-km run. For international athletes.

O Shopping

Phuket City *p466, map p467*
Most souvenirs found here can be bought more cheaply elsewhere in Thailand, and if travelling back to Bangkok, it is best to wait. Best buys are pearls and gold jewellery.
Weekend Market, located on the outskirts of Phuket City, just off Chao Fa West Rd, opposite Wat Naka. A sprawling mass of cheap T-shirts, shoes and knick-knacks. Definitely worth a visit. Sat-Sun from 1600.

Antiques

Antiques House, Rasada Centre. Central location and a limited stock of Thai and other Asian antiques.
Ban Boran Antiques, 39 Yaowarat Rd (near the circle), recently moved from Rasada Rd. This is arguably the best antique shop on Phuket; interesting pieces from Thailand and Burma especially; well priced.
Chan's Antiques, Thepkrasatri Rd, just south of the Heroines' Monument. Not many 'antiques', but a selection of Thai artefacts.

Food

Methee Cashew Nut Factory, 9/1-2 Tilok Uthit Rd, T076-219622/3. The factory offers tours so you learn just why cashew nuts are so damned expensive. The Methee experts have been around for over 40 yrs. Stock up on a weird and wonderful range of cashews, including garlic, chilli and palm sugar flavour.

Handicrafts

Dam Dam, Rasada Rd, interesting selection; **Rasada Centre**, Rasada Rd; **Prachanukhao Road**, numerous stalls leading to Karon which sell hand-painted copies of great artists, including Gauguin, Van Gogh and Da Vinci.

▲ Activities and tours

Phuket Island *p462, maps p463 and p467*
Information on sporting activities is provided in the free tourist magazines available from

hotels, restaurants and tour companies. In addition to those listed below, activities include paintballing, horse riding, sailing, mini-golf and herbal saunas.

Art galleries.

DGallery, 63/501 Moo 2, Thepkrasatri Rd, Koh Kaew, www.dgallery.co.th. Tue-Sat 1100-1900, Sun 1200-1800. Trendy gallery with regular exhibitions by Southeast Asian artists. Artwork can be bought if you fancy taking something different home with you.
Number 1 Gallery, 32 Yaowarat Rd, Phuket City, T076-214535, www.number1gallery. com. Tue-Sun 1030-1930. Large art gallery.
Sarasil Art Gallery, 121 Phangnga Rd, Phuket City, T076-224532. Daily 0800-2200. Original work by 5 local artists.
Vichen Gallery, Bzenter Mall, Saiyuand Rd, Rawai. Catch a glimpse of what Thai artists can do. There is usually an exhibition at the gallery.

Boating

Tour by glass-bottomed boat. 2-hr cruises in the Andaman Sea, ฿300 (or on a chartered basis for ฿5000 per 2 hrs). Yacht charter. From Nov-May boats can be chartered to sail around Phuket.
Seal Superyachts, 225 Rat Uthit Rd, Phuket City, T076-340406. This well-established outfit goes to the Similan and Surin islands and offers PADI courses. Contact Gordon Fernandes. Professional crews, fishing and snorkelling equipment.

Bungee jumping

Jungle Bungee Jump, Wichit Songkram Rd, Kathu, T076-321351, www.phuket bungy.com. Daily 0900-1800. Get your kicks with a bungee jump over a lagoon or try catapult bungeeing or trampoline bungeeing. There is also a bar in case you need to steady your nerves. Jumps are said to be to New Zealand standards.
Tarzan's Bungee Jump, Patong Beach, on road to Phuket City, 61/3 Moo 6, T076-321351.

Tarzan's Catapult, near Expat Hotel on Soi Sunset, Patong Beach, T08-1464 1581 (mob).

World Bungee Jumping, Soi Kebsab 2, Patong, T076-345185. Open daily 1000-1900. Jump above water. They claim the jumps are to Canadian standards.

Canoeing

Andaman Sea Kayak, T076-235353, www.andamanseakayak.com. Hires out 2-man canoes to explore the grottoes, capes and bays that line Phuket's coast, but which are often not accessible by road. Day trips cost about ฿2800-3300; 4-day expeditions, all-inclusive, ฿22,000.

John Gray's Sea Canoe Thailand, 124 Soi 1 Yaowarat Rd, Phuket 83000, T076-254505, T076-254506, www.johngray-seacanoe.com. John Gray has had over 20 years' experience and is the man for day trips and overnights with the advantage being the limited number of guests in the combo long-tail and kayak expeditions. Many people swear by the John Gray experience.

Santana, 222 Thaweewong Rd, Patong Beach, T076-294220, www.santanaphuket. com. River canoeing through the jungle as well as sea canoeing.

Canopying

Phuket Cable Jungle Adventure, 232/17 Bansuanneramit, Moo 8, Srisoon-thorn, Thalang, T076-527054, www.phuket-canopy.com. Some people get their kicks bungee jumping, others choose to zip through the jungle on cables. There are 8 stations about 20 m above the ground. The adventure costs ฿1600. They can pick you up from the pretty much anywhere on the island. Call for details.

Cookery courses

Many luxury spa resorts and 4-star hotels are now offering Thai cookery courses. Check out what dishes you want to learn and find out if they can teach them; these courses can often be tailored to your needs.

Boathouse Inn Cookery School, Kata Beach, T076-3300157, see Sleeping, page 479.

Diving

The greatest concentration of diving companies is to be found along Patong Beach Rd, on Kata and Karon beaches, at Ao Chalong and in Phuket City. Dive centres – over 25 of them – offer a range of courses (introductory to advanced), day trips and liveaboard – leading to one of the inter-nationally recognized certificates such as PADI and NAUI. For an open-water course the cost is about ฿7200-11,500. The course stretches over 4 days, beginning in a hotel pool and ending on a reef. An advance open-water diver course costs around ฿9500. A simple introductory dive, fully supervised, will cost ฿1500-2000 (1 dive) or ฿2000-2500 (2 dives). For those with experience there are a range of tours from single day, 2-dive outings to dive spots like Koh Raja Yai and Koh Raja Noi (south of Phuket), and Shark Point (east of Phuket) which cost ฿2500-3000 depending on the location, to 1-week expeditions to offshore islands such as the Similan and Surin islands. 5 days and 4 nights to the Similans costs around ฿20,000-25,000. Other liveaboards, depending on location and length of trip, vary from ฿18,000-30,000. Snorkelling is good on the outer islands; the waters around Phuket itself are mediocre. For the best snorkelling and diving it is necessary to go to the Similan Islands, see page 453.

All 4 Diving, 5.4 Sawatdirak Rd, Patong Beach, T076-344611. Offers a diving service with other dive operators and sells equipment.

Andaman Divers, 62 Prabaramee Rd, Patong Beach, T076-341126, www.andaman divers.com. 17 years in the business, this operation does liveaboards to the Similan Islands and PADI courses. Japanese-, English- and French-speaking instructors. Claims to offer the best rates.

Dive Asia, 121/10 Moo 4, Patak Rd, Kata Beach, T076-330598/284117. Established 18 years ago.

Fantasea Divers, Patong Beach, T076-340088. Instruction in English, French, German and Japanese.

Marina Cottage, Kata Beach, T076-381625.

Marina Divers, southern end of Karon Beach, T076-330272. PADI certified courses, professional set-up. Recommended.

Phuket International Diving Centre (PIDC), Le Meridien, Karon Noi Beach, T076-321480.

Phuket Scuba Club, Kata Noi Rd, Patong Beach, T076-284026, www.phuket-scuba-club.com. South African owned. Good reports of a Similans liveaboard with this outfit, which offers instructors of varying nationalities. Thai and English spoken. Single dives available from ฿1750.

Santana, 222 Thanon Sawatdirak Rd, Patong Beach, T076-294220, www.santana phuket.com. A prestigious 5-star PADI instructor training centre. This operation is the most experienced, having been 25 years in the business. It does liveaboards to the Similan Islands, Surin and Hin Daeng. Courses in English, German and Thai. It has even named dive sties such as Elephant Head.

Scuba Cats, 94 Thaweewong Rd, Patong Beach, T076-293120, www.scubacats.com. Also a 5-star PADI Instructor Development Centre offering liveaboards to the Similan Islands, Koh Bon, Koh Tachai and Richelieu Rock as well as fun dives around Phuket. Phuket's first **National Geograhic Dive Centre**, it is also a **Go-Eco** operator and is involved in marine clean-up. Finalist in Diver Training Award too.

Sea Bees Diving, Chalong Beach, T076-381765.

Seafarer Divers, Le Meridien Hotel, Karon Noi Beach, T076-321479, www.seafarer-divers.com.

Seal Asia, 225 Rat Uthit Rd, Patong Beach, T076-340406, www.seal-asia.com.

Siam Diving Centre, 121/9 Patak Rd, southern end of Karon Beach, T076-330936. Organizes diving expeditions to the Similan Islands (instruction in English and Swedish).

Elephant trekking
Kalim Elephant Trekking, Kalim Beach, T076-290056. 0800-1000.

Fitness
Fitness Club Centre, Holiday Inn, Patong Beach, T076-340608. Aerobics, sauna and body building. Mon-Sat 0900-2100, Sun 1200-2100. Daily, weekly and monthly membership available.

Game fishing
There are a number of operators on Patong Beach. Expect to pay ฿1500-2000 per day.
Dorado Big Game Fishing, 73/37 Praphuket Rd, T076-202679, dorado@phket.loxinfo.co. Offers Phuket's largest deep-sea fishing boat – a 60-ft hardwood timber cruiser with shaded deck, sundeck and lounge that is big enough for 12 passengers. Does day trips and sleeps 6-8 passengers for liveaboard safaris. The English owner is an ex-oilman. The company specializes in long-range liveaboard safaris to the Similan Islands.
Wahoo Big Game Fishing, Sea Center, 48/20 Moo 9, Soi Ao Chalong, T076-281510, www.wahoo.ws. Has been in business for over 18 years and knows the area inside-out.

Go-karting
Patong Go-Kart Speedway, 118/5 Moo 6, Pra Baramee Rd, Kathu, T076-321948, www.gokartthailand.com. Open daily. Go-karting is a popular activity for visitors to Phuket. Just turn up and drive. If you have 5 or more people you can race in a mini-grand prix. There are kids' karts and 2-seater karts available. There's also an off-road track if you're feeling a little more adventurous.

Golf
Blue Canyon Country Club, 165 Moo 1, Thepkrasatri Rd, Thalang, T076-328088, www.bluecanyonclub.com. The Canyon Course and the Lakes Course are here Top pros from around the world have walked the fairways at both. Blue Canyon has received numerous awards over the years.

Chalong beach, left of the narrow road to Ao Chalong from the main road. Daily 1000-2300. An 18-hole mini golf course.

Laguna Phuket Golf Club (formerly Banyan Tree Golf Club), 34 Moo 4, Srisoonthorn Rd, Cherng Talay, T076-270991/2, www.laguna phuket.com/golfclub. Located in the Laguna compound, this golf club offers some fine greens with a range of challenging hazards. Rated as one of the best courses in Thailand, golf pros like Nick Faldo have had good things to say about it.

Loch Palm Golf Club, 38 Moo 5 Wichit Songkram Rd, Kathu, T076-321929-34, www.lochpalm.com. The serene setting of this established course makes it a firm favourite on the island.

Mission Hills Phuket Golf Club Resort and Spa, 195 Moo 4 Pla khlok, Thalang, T076-310888, www.missionhillsphuket.com. Boasts a 9-hole night course.

Phuket Country Club, 80/1 Moo 7, Wichit Songkram Rd, Kathu, T076-319200, www.phuketcountryclub.com. Has been around for 20 years on a former tin-mining site. As with all of Phuket's golf courses, the scenery is stunning and the course is challenging.

Red Mountain Golf Course, Kathu, T076-3219 2934, www.lochpalm.com. This is the sister course of **Loch Palm**. It's billed as the most challenging course in Phuket.

Horse riding

Crazy Horse Club, rides on Laem Ka beach or along mountain trails (฿300 per hr). Good for families as it also offers ponies.

Kata Beach, next to shooting range, T076-381667. ฿600 per hr. 0700-1200, 1300-1830.

Phuket Riding Club, south of Chalong traffic circle, T076-288213. ฿500 per hr.

Lawn bowls

Kamala Lawn Bowling Club, 71/26 Moo 5, Kamala, T076-385912, www.lawnbowl phuket.com. Believe it or not, Phuket has its own dedicated lawn bowls club. Evening games can be fun with a group of friends

and a few cold beers. Afternoon games usually kick off about 1500 and you can be picked up from your hotel for a small fee. Tuition is available and there is an on-site bar.

Motorbike and jeep tours

In order to explore some of the sights it is best to hire a motorbike or jeep for the day. A suggested route might run north from Phuket City or east from Patong to Tha Rua, the Heroines' Monument and the National Museum at Thalang. Take a side trip to Ton Sai Waterfall and the national park, then continue north on Route 402, before turning left for Nai Yang Beach and the national park. Crossing Route 402, drive east through rubber plantations, taking in Bang Pae Waterfall, before returning to the main road at the Heroines' Monument.

Muay Thai (Thai boxing)

There are few better places than Phuket to see a Muay Thai fight and if you want to do more than watch, there is ample opportunity to train with some of the island's top fighters.

Bangla Boxing Stadium, 198/4 Rat-u-thit 200 Pee Rd, Patong, T08-6940 5463 (mob), T08-9724 1581 (mob), www.banglamuay thai.com/bangla_stadium.php. A decent place to watch a fight and down a few beers. Near enough to Patong's nightlife so that you can sneak out when you want and you're not in the middle of nowhere. They have some high-calibre fights here.

Patong Boxing Stadium, 140-22 Nanai Rd, Patong, T08-1719 5640. Boxing stadium where fights are held every Mon and Thu. Ring-side seats will set you back ฿1000.

Phuket Thai Boxing Gym, 82/5 Moo 4, Patak Rd, Kata, T076-281090, www.muay thaiphuket.com. Open Mon-Sat.

Rawai Muay Thai, Rawai Beach, T08-1476 9377 (mob), www.rawaimuaythai.com. Thai boxing and fitness training gym. Train 6 hrs a day with knowledgeable coaches. Beginners are welcomed. They also have accommodation available.

Saphan Hin Stadium, South Phuket Rd, T076-258393. Charge ฿350. Every Fri at 2000 (tickets available from 1600). Not one of the most popular places to watch Muay Thai.

Suwit Muay Thai Camp, Moo 1, Choa Fa Rd, Chalong, T076-38116715, www.bestmuay thai.com. This camp has been around for more than 15 years. Pick up a few tricks from boxing pros.

Tiger Muay Thai and MMA Training Camp, 7/6 Moo 5 Soi Tad-ied, Chalong, T076-367 071, T076-383107, www.tigermuaythai.com. One of the most famous camps in Phuket. Anyone, from beginners to advanced fighters, is invited to attend for some serious training. Walk-ins welcome.

Nature tours
Phuket Nature Tours, 5/15 Chao Fah Rd, Phiket City, T076-225522. There is not much 'nature' left on Phuket but nonetheless this company has managed to climb on board the ecotourism bandwagon and offers tours to forests, rice fields, villages, plantations, secluded beaches and so on.

Siam Safari, 45 Chao Fah Rd, Chalong, T076-280116, www.siamsafari.com. Offers eco nature tours, a similar set-up to the above.

Sea kayaking
Paddle Asia, 9/71 Moo 3, Thanon, Rasdanu-sorn, Ban Kuku, T076-216145, www.sea kayaking-thailand.com. Traditional kayaks taking tours around the marine parks, specifically for bird- and nature-lovers.

Sea Canoe Thailand, 367/4 Yaowarat Rd, T076-212172, www.seacanoe.net. Established watersports company offering day trips and longer tours from Phuket.

Shooting
The noise at shooting ranges is deafening and the price you pay to shoot is many times what the ammunition actually costs.

Kathu International Shooting Club, 86/3 Soi Kathu Waterfall, Wichit Songkram Rd, Kathu, T076-323996. Learn various tricks and techniques for firing rifles and handguns.

Tuition is provided along with all safety equipment. There is also the opportunity to shoot 357 Maxum Cowguns. Expect to pay up to ฿1000 to fire off 10 real bullets. Less people find their way here than **Phuket Shooting Range** so you may well have the place to yourself, but the staff are terminally bored.

Phuket Airsoft BB Gun, Rawai, T08-9592 1959 (mob). The game is similar to paintball, just without the paint. Getting shot still hurts, but when you are hit, you have to do the honorable thing and leave the game. Lots of fun can be had in large-scale battles, complete with full-camo outfits. All safety equipment, including masks, is provided. A day's outing costs upwards of ฿890. Teams must comprise between 2 and 10 players.

Phuket Shooting Range, 82/2 Moo 4 Patak Rd, Rawai, T076-381667. Standard shooting range where all manner of guns can be fired for a hefty price. Prices are up to ฿1000 for 10 bullets. There are revolvers and shotguns, but thankfully no machine guns. The staff are more into the whole experience than at the **Kathu Range**.

Surfing
There is a small but tight community of surfers in Phuket. Every year there are small-scale international surfing competitions held at Kalim, Kata-Karon and Kamala beaches. While Phuket is not the most renowned surfing destination, it is possible to catch a wave, especially during the wetter months. Boards in varying conditions can be rented from most of the beaches.

Patong Beach is generally considered the worst place to surf. Kamala and Karon are reasonable, while Kata is the most popular spot on the island. Nai Harn is quiet and often gets the best waves in Phuket.

Phuket Board Riders, 371-41 Yaowarat Rd, Talaad Yai, Phuket City, T08-1956 5854 (mob), www.phuketboardriders.com. Clued-up group of local surfers who are always willing to help visitors.

Saltwater Dreaming Surf Shop, 108/3 Moo 3, Cherng Thalay, Thalang, T076-271050, www.saltwater-dreaming.com. Keeps tabs on the surf is in Phuket and also has information about renting boards and where to go.

Therapies
Traditional Thai massage is available from countless (usually untrained) women and men on Patong Beach or from more permanent places. Check for a certificate from Wat Po.
Mai Khao Sand Spa, follow Thepkrastri Rd past the airport, turn left at Wat Mai Khao and then turn left at Mai Khao Village until you come to the 'spa', T08-1895 4833 (mob). This isn't a spa as such because it's out on the beach. There are some people in Phuket who are convinced that being buried in sand with all of your clothes on is good for you.

Tours and tour operators
Full-day tours usually cost ฿700-2000. To the **Similan Islands** (see page 453), **Phangnga Bay** and **Coral Island** (Koh Hii) including swimming, snorkelling and fishing.

Waterskiing
Phuket Waterski Cableways, 86/3 Moo 6, Soi Nam Tok Kathu, near Kathu Waterfall, T076-202525/7. Inland waterskiing course on a man-made lake. Skiers are pulled around an oval track at up to 30 kph by giant overhead cables.

⊖ Transport

Phuket Island *p462, maps p463 and p467*
Air
THAI run a minibus service from Phuket City to the airport for ฿80, it leaves from the city bus station on Phangnga Rd. Alternatively, motorcycle taxis wait at the intersection with Route 402 to ferry people to the terminal (฿30). Phuket's airport bus, T076-232371, www.air portbusphuket.com, is the cheapest way to get to the airport. The fare is between

฿10 and ฿85 (foreigners are sometimes overcharged). The bus departs from Phuket Bus Terminal and travels through Phuket City, along the bypass road, past Heroine's Monument and on to the airport. The first bus from Phuket City leaves at 0530; last bus is 1830. The bus has 'Airport Bus' plastered on its windshield, so give the driver a wave when you see him or else he won't stop.

For flight reservations call T076-3272307. Regular cheap connections with **Airasia** and **Nok Air** to **Bangkok** and with One-Two-Go and THAI to **Bangkok**, **Chiang Mai**, **Hat Yai**, **Nakhon Si Thammarat**, **Surat Thani** and **Trang**. Bangkok Airways also runs daily connections with **Koh Samui**. For a list of other airlines that fly between Bangkok and Phuket, see www.tourismthailand.org. There are also flights to **Beijing**, **Hong Kong**, **Penang** and **Kuala Lumpur** (Malaysia), **Singapore**, **Taipei**, **Tokyo**, **Munich** and **Dusseldorf**.

Airline offices Bangkok Airways, 158/2-3 Yaowarat Rd, T076-225033; Dragonair, 156/14 Phangnga Rd, T076-215734 (from Hong Kong); **Malaysia Airlines**, Merlin Hotel, T076-216675; Silk Air, 183/103 Phangnga Rd, T076-213891; THAI, 78/1 Ranong Rd, T076-211195; Tradewinds, 95/20 Phuket Rd, T076-213891 (from Singapore).

Boat
During the high season (Nov-May) there are 3 ferries a day to **Koh Phi Phi** at 0830, 1330 and 1430. The journey takes 90 mins and leaves from Rassada Pier on Phuket's east coast costing ฿500 or ฿750 return. Tourist offices sell tickets and can confirm boat times, which vary through the season.

There are many boats to **Koh Yao Yai**, ฿50, with vessels leaving from Laem Hin Pier at 1400, 1 hr 20 mins. From Tien Sin Pier at 1000 and 1400. From Rassada Port on Thu and Sun only at 1400 and Sat at 0600. Boats from the village of Bang Rong leave at 1230. 5 boats a day from Phuket to **Koh Yao Noi** leave Bang Rong Pier, 1 hr, ฿50.

There are currently no direct services to **Koh Lanta**, meaning it is best to catch one of the regular buses to Krabi to pick up a boat.

Long-tailed boats can be hired to visit reefs and more isolated coves, ฿600-1200 per day.

Bus

The station (*bor ko sor* – BKS) is on Phangnga Rd in Phuket City, T076-211480. It's cheaper to buy tickets here than through travel agents. The information desk usually has a timetable and fare list produced by the TAT detailing all departures as well as local transport.

Regular a/c and non-a/c connections with **Bangkok**'s Southern bus terminal (14 hrs). Regular morning connections with **Hat Yai** (8 hrs), **Trang** (6 hrs), **Surat Thani** (6 hrs) and **Satun** (7 hrs). Regular connections with **Phangnga** (2 hrs), **Takua Pa** (3 hrs), **Ranong** (6 hrs) and **Krabi** (4 hrs). Journey times for these buses will vary between 30 mins and 1 hr.

Car

Small outfits along most beaches, expect to pay ฿900-1200 per day, depending on the age of car, etc. It is worth picking up an updated map of the island from the TAT office in Phuket City as the roads in the north can be confusing. **Avis** has an office opposite Phuket airport, T076-311358, and desks at, the Holiday Inn, the Dusit Laguna (on Bang Tao Beach) and the Metropole (in Phuket City), ฿1200 per day, ฿7200 per wk. **Hertz**, at the airport, T076-311162, and at the Patong Merlin and Tara Patong; prices are similar to **Avis**. There are other companies down Rasada Rd in Phuket City.

Motorbike

As for car hire above, ฿200-350 per day. There are also several places on Rasada Rd in Phuket City. Some places insist on taking your passport as a deposit/collateral but it is best not to let it out of your hands if you can help it.

In Kata Noi Beach, a reliable agent is **Boy's Shop Travel and Tour**, 4/12 Moo 2, T076-284062, T01-8911910, which offers tours, car rental, international tickets and books hotels. Contact Kunakron Suthiprapa (aka 'Boy').

Motorbike taxi and tuk-tuk

Men (and a few women) with red vests will whisk passengers almost anywhere for a minimum of about ฿40. The motorbike taxis congregate at intersections.

Avoid tuk-tuks unless you can't resist the exotic factor. They are overpriced and as comfortable as a rickshaw with 1 wheel.

Taxi

Taxis will leave when they are full (usually with 5 passengers). For **Surat Thani**, they leave from the coffee shop opposite the **Pearl Cinema** on Phangnga Rd (฿150 per person).

Phuket City *p466, map p467*
Car and motorbike

Avis, Metropole Hotel, 1 Montri Rd, T076-215050, ฿950 per day; **Phuket Horizon Car Rent**, 235/4 Yaowarat Rd, T076-215200; **Pure Car Rent**, 75 Rasada Rd, T076-211002, ฿1000 per day.

Motorbikes are available from ฿150 per day.

Patong Beach *p469, map p463*
Jeep and motorbike

Jeeps from outlets along Patong Beach Rd, motorbikes on Rat Uthit Rd. **Avis** has desks at the Holiday Inn (T076-340608) and Phuket Cabana Hotel (T076-340138), **Hertz** is at the Merlin, T076-340037.

Songthaew and minibus

Regular departures from Ranong Rd, by the market in Phuket City, ฿25.

Tuk-tuk

Chartered tuk-tuk ฿450 one way, from Patong to **Phuket City** or vice versa.

Karon and Kata Beaches *p470, map p463*
Car
Avis has a desk at the Hilton Phuket Arcadia (T076-381038), Le Meridien (T076-340480) and Kata Beach Resort (T076-381530). Hertz has a desk at the Thavorn Palm Beach (T076-381034).

Directory

Phuket City *p466, map p467*
Banks Along Rasada, Phuket, Phangnga and Thepkrasatri roads there are branches of all the major banks, all with ATMs and currency exchange. **Sea Tour**, 95/4 Phuket Rd, T076-218417, American Express agent.
Immigration South Phuket Rd (close to Saphan Hin). Ask for the boxing stadium; the office is next door, T076-212108.
Internet Many hotels and guesthouses now offer internet services – check out the varying prices per hr and whether they are on broadband. **Medical services** Phuket City has the largest concentration of hospitals on the island, offering varied levels of treatment at varied prices, it also has the best medical facilities. Phuket has no centralized ambulance service, but most hospitals have their own vechicles that can be sent in emergencies. **Bangkok Hospital Phuket**, 2/1 Hongyokutis Rd, T076-254421, www.phukethospital.com, world-class treatment and facilities, can be a bit pricey, but you get what you pay for; **Phuket International Hospital**, 44 Chalermprakiat Ror 9 Rd, T076-249400, www.phuket-inter-hospital.co.th; **Phuket Ruampaet Hospital**, 340 Phuket Rd, T076-217964; **Vachira Hospital Phuket**, Yaowarat Rd, T076-212150,

www.vachiraphuket.go.th, not far from Bangkok Hospital. **Police** On corner of Phuket and Phangnga roads; **Marine Police** Division 5. Phuket Rd, T076-211883, T076-214368; **Muang District Police Station** (serves Phuket City), T076-216856, T076-212115, 1 Chumporn Rd; **Phuket Provincial Police Headquarters**, Yaowarat Rd, T076-212046, T076-212194; **Phuket Traffic Police Station**, Yaowarat Rd, T076-220919, T076-212115. **Tourist Police** Emergency T1699, alternatively T076-219878 (until 1630) or call T076-212046 to reach the police. **Post office** Montri Rd (at the corner of Thalang Rd). **Telephone** 122/2 Phangnga Rd, open 24 hrs. Overseas telephone and fax also available from the post office in town.

Patong Beach *p469, map p463*
Banks Banks and currency exchange booths are concentrated on Patong Beach Rd (Thaweewong Rd) but some have offices further away in the wake of the tsunami. **Medical services** Kathu Hospital on Rat Uthit Rd. **Police** Kathu Police Station, T076-342719, T076-342721; **Tourist Police**, Patong Beach Rd. **Post office** Patong Beach Rd (beachfront road), near Soi Permpong Pattana (aka Soi Post Office). **Telephone** International service next door to the post office on Patong Beach Rd. 0800-2300.

Nai Yang and Nai Yang National Park *p473, map p463*
Banks Mobile exchange van.

Mai Khao *p473, map p463*
Banks Exchange possible in the Marriott or at banks in Thalang.

Phangnga Bay

→ Colour map 4, C1.

Phangnga Bay is best known as the location for the 1974 James Bond movie The Man with the Golden Gun. Limestone rocks tower out of the sea (some as high as 100 m); boats can be hired to tour the area from Tha Don, the Phangnga customs pier.

Travelling from Phuket to Phangnga the road passes through limestone scenery. Much of the land looks scrubby and dry, punctuated by shrimp farms and scrappy farms. But en route, it is possible to watch rubber being processed by smallholders. Not long ago, over-mature rubber trees (those more than 25 years old) were cut down and processed into charcoal. Today, due to the efforts of an enterprising Taiwanese businessman, a rubber-wood furniture industry has developed.
▶▶ For listings, see pages 503-507.

Ins and outs

Getting there and around

Phangnga has no train station or airport – the only way here is by bus (or private transport). Buses leave through the day from Bangkok's Southern bus terminal, including overnight VIP coaches (15 hours). Phangna bus station is on Petkasem Road, near the centre of town. There are regular bus connections with Phuket, Krabi and towns south to the Malaysian border and north to Bangkok. Motorcycle taxis will wait at the bus station to take passengers further afield, ฿5. Cramped but rather extraordinary teak wood *songthaews* with unpadded seats constantly ply the main road, ฿5. They are the main form of transport around town (which is easy to cover on foot) and to surrounding villages.
▶▶ See Transport, page 506, for further information.

Phangnga town and around ◉❾▲⊖◐ ▶▶ *pp503-507.*

The poor relation to its neighbouring tourist hotspots of Phuket and Krabi, Phangnga is often overlooked by visitors. Its relaxed, authentic Thai feel, dramatic setting and interesting daytrips make it an excellent place to pass a few days. There is one main road that goes through the centre of town which nestles narrowly between striking limestone crags. If you want urban sophistication and multiple culinary options, then Phangnga may disappoint. It is a non-tourist Thai experience, and Phangnga folk come across as almost grumpy with tourists – a relief after the feigned jollity of so many Thailand's tourist-drenched resorts.

In the centre of town, behind the **Rattanapong Hotel** is the fresh produce and early morning market while along the main street near the **Thaweesuk Hotel** are some remaining examples of the **Chinese shophouses** that used to line the street.

Around Phangnga town

Due to the limestone geology, there are a number of caves in the vicinity. The most memorable, and by far the most disgusting, are at **Wat Thomtharpan Amphoe Muang**, the so-called 'Heaven and Hell Caves', around 2 km to the south of town on the road to Phuket. It's hard to see where Heaven is in this Buddhist depiction of Hell, designed to teach youngsters about the consequences of sinning. Cheap plaster models of human are burned on spits, chopped in half, sent through a mangle, torn apart by birds and gutted by dogs. Hideously distorted demons with metre-long tongues and outsized genitalia glare down on the visitor. Eat before you arrive at this eerily deserted compound. Just on the outskirts of town on Route 4 towards Phuket, on the left-hand side, is the **Somdet Phra Sinakharin Park**, surrounded by limestone mountains; it is visible from the road and opposite the former city hall. Within this park are **Tham Luk Sua** and **Tham Ruesi Sawan**, two adjoining caves with streams, stalactites and stalagmites. These watery, sun-filled caves have rather unsympathic concrete paths. At the entrance to the cave sits Luu Sii, the cave guardian, under an umbrella. **Tham Phung Chang** is a little closer into town on the other side of the road, within the precincts of **Wat Phraphat Phrachim Khet**. To get to the arched entrance to the wat, take a *songthaew* about 300 m past the traffic lights (themselves past the **New Lak Muang Hotel**). The cave is actually inside the symbol of Phangnga – a huge mountain that apparently looks like a crouched elephant called Khao Chang. It can be found behind Phangnga's former city hall. In this long dark cave, again dripping with stalactites and stalagmites, there is a spring, Buddha images and a small pool where boys swim. The wat is more visually interesting though not as quirky. It enjoys a fine position against the limestone cliff and set within a large compound.

Tham Suwan Kuha ① ฿10, is 12 km from Phangnga on Route 4 to Phuket, take a southwest-bound bus. A turning to the right leads to this cave temple. It is popular with Thais and is full of Buddhas. Stairs lead up to a series of tunnels, containing some natural rock formations. King Chulalongkorn visited the cave in 1890 and his initials are carved into the rock.

Several kilometres out of town, and a right turn off the Krabi road, the **Sra Nang Manora Forest Park** (probably best reached on a scooter) offers a delightful break from the midday heat. The forest is free to enter and offers an easy, shaded 90-minute walk past several caves and sheer limestone cliffs. Thai visitors congregate at the park entrance to picnic next to the gushing stream, but anyone prepared to walk for a few minutes will have the forest to themselves.

Wat Tham Khao Thao is 12 km from Phangnga on Route 4152 to Krabi, on the left-hand side of the road, under a cliff wall (buses travel the route). Views of the surrounding plain can be seen from a stairway up the cliff face. The road here passes through nipa palm which then becomes an area of mangrove. Aquaculture is an important sideline industry, and tiger prawns are raised in the brackish waters of the mangroves and in purpose-built ponds.

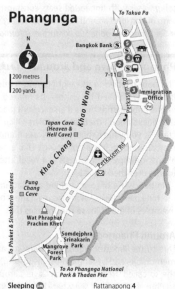

Phangnga

To Takua Pa

Bangkok Bank

7-11

Immigration Office

Tapan Cave
(Heaven &
Hell Cave)

Pung
Chang
Cave

Wat Phraphat
Prachim Khet

Somdejphra
Srinakarin
Park

Mangrove
Forest
Park

To Phuket & Sinakharin Gardens

To Ao Phangnga National
Park & Thadan Pier

Phangnga Bay National Park
⊜ ⦿ ⌂ ▲ ⊠ ⟩⟩ *pp503-507.*

① *Park entrance fee, ฿200 (check to make sure it is included in the tour price). To get there take a songthaew to the pier, ฿10, from*

Sleeping ⊜
Phangnga Guest House **2**
Phangnga Inn **3**

Rattanapong **4**
Thawesuk **5**

Phangnga town. 7 km along Route 4 there is a turning to the left (Route 4144 – signposted Phangnga Bay and the Ao Phangnga National Park Headquarters) and the pier is another 3 km down this road.

Relaxed, excellent-value boat tours of Phangnga Bay can be booked from one of the travel agents in the town's bus station. They cost up to ฿1100, and include the park entrance fee, accomodation, meals and a guided canoe tour, where someone does the paddling for you. The trips are just sightseeing tours as the boat drivers speak little English.

The standard tour winds through mangrove swamps, which act as a buffer between land and sea and nipa palm, and past striking limestone cliffs before arriving at **Tham Lod Cave**. This is not really a cave at all, but a tunnel cut into the limestone and dripping with stalagmites that look like petrified chickens hanging upside down. From Tham Lod, the route skirts past **Koh Panyi** – a Muslim fishing village built on stilts which extends out into the bay; its most striking feature being a golden mosque and the sheer peak rearing up behind it. Through the narrow lanes, the main transport is bicycle. There are also overpriced seafood restaurants in this village.

Other sights include **Khao Mah Ju**, a small mountain between Tha Dan and Koh Pnay which resembles a dog. There is also **Khao Khian** or 'Mountain of Writings' with ancient depictions of animals and sea life dating back more than 3000 years. These drawings include a cartoon-like dolphin which looks suspiciously contemporary. It is believed that seamen who used the place to escape from the monsoon, painted these vivid images. While all of these sights may seem highlights in themselves, it is the 'James Bond' island that is touted as the raison d'être for these tours. **James Bond Island** or **Koh Tapu** lies in the little bay of Koh Phing Kan or 'Leaning Mountain' which is a huge rock split into two parts with the smaller part having slid down so that the taller section appears to be leaning. The limestone karst stack that sticks up out from the sea just off this island is called **Koh Tapu** (Nail Island). The 'famous' rock, like a chisel, seems much smaller than it should be, and the tiny beach and cave are littered with trinket-stalls (refreshments available) and other tourists. Endless tour groups are spewed onto the small beach throughout the day to barge into each other as they wander past tatty souvenirs. There are few tackier sights in Asia. Recently, erosion of Koh Tapu caused by the wash from the hundreds of boats visiting the island has led to a declared intent to limit the numbers of visitors. However, the tsunami shifted the goalposts on this and there is no effort to enforce a limit at the moment. For details on the two large islands in the bay, Koh Yao Yai and Koh Yao Noi, see below.

Koh Yao Noi and Koh Yao Yai

Koh Yao Noi and Koh Yao Yai, equidistant from Krabi mainland and Phuket, are the two most important islands in the 44-strong cluster of islands known as Koh Yao, to the east of Phuket. They are so close to each other that it only takes around eight minutes by long-tailed boat to cross over from Koh Yao Yai to Koh Yao Noi.

Consistently untouched by tourism – due to a strong Muslim and Chao Le community who wanted to retain control over what could have become a rampaging beast – these islands have no banks, and Koh Noi has only very few restaurants and shops. Indeed, in 2002, Koh Yao Noi gained recognition from eco-tourists when it received the World Legacy Award for Destination Stewardship from **Conservation International** and *National Geographic Traveler* magazine jointly for its eco-friendly homestays. Eco-activities include rubber plantation and fishing demonstrations, kayaking, hiking and snorkelling. In keeping with the eco-theme, there are a few sensitively designed resorts on Koh Yao Noi, a project by the responsible tourism company REST, while most other operations are basic bungalows. Visitors need to remember that the locals prefer outsiders to dress modestly and not to drink alcohol outside resorts or restaurants.

Traditional ways and handicrafts still persist, as with the inventive 'fish-scale flowers' by the housewives of Koh Yao. These flowers – usually roses, geraniums and bougainvillea – are created from dried fish scales. The unusual rural heritage is seen in other ways too. Although expensive resorts are appearing on Koh Yao Yai, there are still wooden houses, rubber plantations and wandering buffalos. A partially paved road encircles Koh Yao Noi, with its village in the middle and huts scattered throughout the island. For little trips there are beautiful beaches, especially on Koh Nok, and a dreamy lagoon on Koh Hong.

Koh Yao Yai, the larger of the two islands, has better beaches for swimming but fewer places to stay, most of which tend to be overpriced. There's a spectacular view where the road ends on the west side of the island, overlooking Klong Son Bay. Koh Yao Noi is considerably more advanced than its bigger sister, with better facilities, including a hospital and internet shops. Mobile phones operate throughout both the islands. On the northern tip of this island and best reached by boat, is an enormous tree, the trunk of

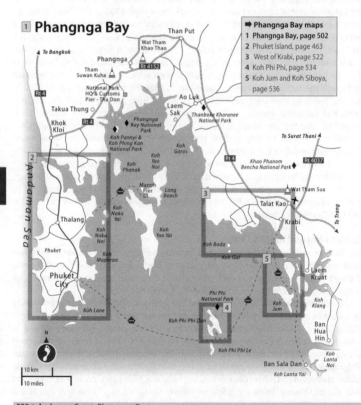

1 Phangnga Bay

➡ **Phangnga Bay maps**
1 Phangnga Bay, page 502
2 Phuket Island, page 463
3 West of Krabi, page 522
4 Koh Phi Phi, page 534
5 Koh Jum and Koh Siboya, page 536

which takes 23 men to span. Hire a bike for a delightful few hours taking in the beauty of the island while negotiating the (sometimes difficult) roads. The main attraction is the peace and quiet. It has become a bit of a hotspot for alternative traveller groups, who have bagged the place as good for retreats ranging from yoga to healing crystal workshops.

Phangnga to Krabi

From Phangnga to Krabi, the road passes mangrove swamps and nipa palm, more dramatic karst formations and impressive stands of tropical forest. For those travelling independently by car or motorbike, there is a lovely detour worth taking for about an hour. Look out for signs to **Tham Raird** or **Ban Bang Toei** and turn left down towards the towering karst formations. The road leads through a pass into a valley in the heart of the karst. It is a little like stepping back in time, and several Thai television commercials idealizing rural life have been filmed here. The backdrop of lush forest on towering karst, with a foreground of rice fields and small villages, is wonderful. Rainy season visitors will be well rewarded with mist and cloud on the peaks and a golden light on the wet paddy. Sadly, behind these wonderful, almost circular limestone crags there are several large limestone concessions blasting the mountains away. To the front there are similar scenes of rice farming against a backdrop of towering mountains, interspersed with the occasional village or temple.

⊚ Phangnga Bay listings

For Sleeping and Eating price codes and other relevant information, see pages 44-49.

⊜ Sleeping

Phangnga town *p499, map p500*
B-D Phangnga Inn, 2/2 Soi Lohakit, Petkasem Rd, T076-411963. A beautiful family house converted into a cosy hotel with a range of contrasting, immaculately clean en suite rooms. It is off the main road, and clearly marked by a purple sign. It is by far the quietest, most comfortable place to stay in town. There is a smart kitchen, spacious communal areas and the more expensive rooms have stylish furniture and elegant wooden floors. Recommended.
D-F Phangnga Guest House, 99/1 Petka-sem Rd, next to **Rattanapong**, T076-411358. Excellent-value fan and a/c, fastidiously clean small rooms, tiny sparkling café downstairs. Cantankerous staff that grow on you. Recommended.
E-G Rattanapong, 111 Petkasem Rd, T076-411247. In the town centre, this

5-storey building is a converted hospital. It is a friendly establishment with large, cleanish a/c and fan rooms. A few with balconies overlooking the market.
F Thawesuk, 79 Petkasem Rd, T076-412100. Clean rooms, thin walls, basic, run by an eccentric family. Mr Thawesuk is an amiable character with a sharp eye for anyone who's not a guest, so the security is excellent, despite having to walk through what feels like an open garage to get to the rooms. A narrow stone staircase leads to a roof terrace at the back of the building where you can view the surrounding limestone mountains. Rooms have been recently renovated. Recommended.

Koh Yao Noi and Koh Yao Yai *p501*
Koh Yao Noi
LL Six Senses Hideaway Yao Noi, 56 Moo 5, T076-418500, www.sixsenses.com. Over the last few years the luxury **Six Senses** resort chain have been developing their portfolio of properties in Thailand and this is probably their finest example to date. Set amid the

trees are 56 luxurious wooden villas, all complete with private pool, sunken tubs and sala. If you get one of the hill-top villas the sunrise will leave your jaw on the floor. Eating here is unforgettable as well – they have an in-house deli stocking the best cheeses and charcuterie you'll find anywhere in Thailand. The bakery is excellent and the spa probably the best on the island. Prices are high but you get a lot for your money. Six Senses also donate a percentage of their revenue to carefully selected local projects. Highly recommended.

LL-AL Koyao Island Resort, 24/2 Moo 5, T076-597474-6, www.koyao.com. Operated by a Frenchman. 15 villas incorporating traditional thatched Thai architecture mixed with the latest in French style. All villas are set around a garden in a coconut plantation, and look out onto an island-spotted stretch of the Andaman Sea and the only non-rocky beach on the island. Villas have small private gardens, satellite TV, phone and fax, minibar, etc. A largely outdoor spa offers sauna, jaccuzi and traditional Thai massage in a relaxed and airy setting.

C Long Beach Village Bungalows, T08-16077921 (mob). Not much to look at, but some of these 40 rooms are bigger than most options, though all need repairs. Clean and airy on the inside, all with attached Western toilet and nice views. Some a/c. Long-time manager, Suthup, is friendly.

C-E Sabai Corner Bungalows, T076-597 497, T08-1892 1827 (mob), www.sabai cornerbungalows.com. Run by an Italian woman and her Thai husband. 10 romantic bungalows set among cashew and coconut trees with magnificent views over Pasai Beach. Attached toilets. Motorbikes, mountain bikes and canoes for rent, and the restaurant serves up tasty fare. Between them the management speak Italian, Spanish, French, English, German and Thai. A popular option, often full so ring ahead.

D-E Ban Tha Khao Bungalows, T076-212 172. Several decently sized bamboo and wooden structures with chairs, table,

wardrobes, Western toilets and mini balconies. No a/c. Near a deserted cove up a rough road in the centre of the island so a bit of a hike. this is a picturesque choice and the Mut family who runs it can arrange for a pick-up by motorcycle taxi. The owners also manage the **Sea Canoe** company.

D-E Coconut Corner Bungalows, T076-597134. A handful of bungalows, all basic but charming, with attached toilets, presided over by the friendly and knowledge-able Mr Bean. The attached restaurant serves excellent food, and eating with the family is often the norm. Attracts returnees for the hospitality and Mr Bean's verve. Recommended.

Koh Yao Yai
The choice on Koh Yao Yai isn't as great as on its smaller neighbour, and much of it is overpriced, although the lack of visitors does make a degree of bargaining possible.

LL-L The Paradise Koh Yao Boutique Beach Resort and Spa, 24 Moo 4, T08-1892 4878, T08-1892 4879 (mob), www.theparadise.biz/. 48 superior studios, 16 de luxe studios and 6 pool villas on the beach in the north of Koh Yao Noi. Has its own passenger transfer boats and you can even get here by seaplane.

A-D Yao Yai Island Resort, Moo 7, Ban Lopareh, T08-94719110, www.yaoyai resort.com. Located on a beach that's decent even at low tide, this western facing resort means you'll actually get to enjoy the setting sun. Good bungalows complete with eccentric wood furnishings, everything is en suite though there is the choice of fan and a/c. If you can help it don't get suckered into taking the resort's overpriced transfer boat.

C-E Thiwson Bungalows, 58/2 Moo 4, Ko Yao Yai Rd, T08-1956 7582 (mob). Clean, little rooms in the usual bamboo and wood style, with bedside lights, Western toilets, deckchairs on the verandas and a pleasant garden over-looking one of the nicest beaches on the island, with Koh Yao Noi clearly visible. Restaurant. Recommended.

F Koh Yao Beach Bungalow, 65/2 Moo 3 Prunai, T08-9728 6280 (mob), kohyaobeach@ hotmail.com. 6 atmospheric bungalows stand in the middle of a marshy, flooded bog. At first glance it doesn't look attractive but the clean rooms are en suite and come complete with sea views. Rough and ready but certainly memorable.

🍴 Eating

Phangnga town p499, map p500
Cafés on Petkasem Rd, near the market, sell the usual array of Thai dishes, including excellent *khaaw man kai* (chicken and rice) and *khaaw mu daeng* (red pork and rice). There is also a good shop selling all manner of rice crackers, nuts and Thai biscuits on Petakasem Rd past **Thaweesuk Hotel**. Try the popular **Kha Muu Restaurant** opposite the **Thaweesuk Hotel**.

There is an early morning market behind **Rattanapong Hotel**, which begins as early as 0500. There are a couple very good cafés here that do traditional morning rice soup to perfection until around about 0900. This soup is a rice porridge with coriander, basil, ginger, spices, onion, lemon grass, pepper and minced pork. You can also get a fix of sweet tea. The market itself, though small, sells an astonishing array of foodstuffs, fish, meat, flowers for making garlands and lots of sarongs. Recommended.
🍴 Duang Seafood, 122 Petkasem Rd (opposite **Bank of Ayudhya**). Mediocre seafood restaurant if you go for the *farang* menu and Chinese specialities. But the Thai menu is completely different so the best move is to be emphatic and point to what the locals are eating.
🍴-🍴 Ivy's House, 38 Petkasem Rd, next door to a dental clinic. A tiny European-style café with a gas-fired oven for pizza, Italian wines and liquors and decent pastries. A little pricey but then the owner 'Ivy', who is from Switzerland, has to get all her imports from Phuket – including cheese from Italy.

All her food is to a high standard. For many years she had a business in Koh Phi Phi but got tired of 'smiling all the time', so came to Phangnga. Good source of information. Recommended.
🍴-🍴 Khru Thai (Thai Teacher), Petkasem Rd (opposite the post office). Clean and cheap place, where the dishes are openly displayed making selection easy.
🍴 Open-air cinema eaterie, Petkasem Rd and around Soi Bamrungrat. This no-name eatery (the sign in Thai script simply describes what it sells) is not to be missed. There is a 100-year-old-plus tree that grows through part of it and a gigantic screen that can be heard along Petkasem Rd as it blares Southeast Asian martial arts flicks and straight-to-video Western horror movies. Outside this open-air restaurant and cinema, nocturnal stalls also sell sweet pastries. The food is of good quality. Popular with the locals, this Cinema Paradiso is a magical treat. Recommended.
🍴 Ran Ja Jang, Soi Bamrungrat on a corner opposite another café. Superb seafood soup with egg and Tom Yee sauce swimming in tiger prawns and squid. This operation is run by 2 ladies wearing reassuring hair-nets as they bustle over an open kitchen. They also do home-made ices. Recommended.

Koh Yao Noi and Koh Yao Yai p501
Most people eat at the restaurant attached to their bungalows, although there is **Tha Khao Seafood** right next to the pier. Otherwise a good option is to pick your choice of fish from the fishermen's huts on Tha Tondo Pier to the northwest of the island, and take it to the local restaurant just by the pier for cooking while watching arguably the best sunset the island can offer.

For a local delicacy on Koh Yao Yai, it is worth trying/buying the *pla ching chang* dried anchovy paste which is used with rices and noodles to liven things up.

🎵 Bars and clubs

Koh Yao Noi and Koh Yao Yai p501
Koh Yao Noi
Reggae Bar, on the non-beach side of the road between **Sabai Corner** and **Long Beach Village Bungalows**. Offers beer and cocktails and consists of a few tables set outside.
Pyramid Bar, a nice beachfront bar offering beer and cocktails.

▲ Activities and tours

Phangnga town p499, map p500
Tour operators
The 3 main tour companies in town are **Sayan**, 209 Bus Terminal City, T076-430348, www.sayantour.com; **Kean**, bus terminal, T076-430619; and **MT Tours**, Muang Tong Hotel, 128 Petkasem Rd. All advertise widely, run very similar tours and charge the same (฿300 for ½-day, ฿750 for full day). The tours are worthwhile and good value. **Mr Hassim**, who operates **MT Tours** is an affable and endearing man who grew up in Koh Panyi and comes from a long line of fishermen. For an extra ฿250 he will put you up in his stilted Muslim village for the night and provide a seafood dinner. He is a very accommodating host who speaks relatively good English and who has quite a loyal following.

Phangnga Bay National Park
p499, map p502
Tour operators
Long-tailed boats can be chartered from the pier for a trip around the sights of Phangnga Bay for about ฿350-450 although it is cheaper for 1 person to take a tour with **Sayan**, **Kean** or Mr Hussein at **MT Tours** (see Phangnga town, above).

There are other ways of getting down to the bay and taking tours: as the road nears Phangnga, there are a number of roads down to the coast, from where tours to Phangnga Bay depart. Look out for signs and the next U-turn on this widened and

rather fast road. The first of these leads down a long winding road through rubber plantations and over hills to Khlong Khian pier. Although there are several tour operators here they are small-scale efforts. Most of the boatmen speak little English, but can take you to caves and islands you will never see on larger tours. They are also more flexible in terms of timing, and take no more than 8 people per boat.

Further down the road there are 2 more routes to the Phangnga Bay tours. The first is in Takua Thung town which has been partially bypassed by the main road to Krabi. Once in the town there is a well-marked narrow *soi* leading to a pier. At the pier, there are several restaurants and souvenir shops, and parking for tour buses. Independent travellers will find plenty of tour operators willing to book you a trip on a boat. The boats here are large, taking up to 20 passengers, and more reminiscent of Bangkok long-tailed boats than local fishing boats.

A similar scene is to be found on the last main turn-off to Phangnga Bay near the national park offices. the national park offices contain some interesting information on the bay and feature a mangrove interpretive walk, and some accommodation. Also, this last bay attracts smaller independent tour operators so it is possible to get away from the crowds in this location too.

Koh Yao Noi and Koh Yao Yai p501
Koh Yao Noi
Reggae Tour, next to **Reggae Bar**, see Bars and clubs, above. Rents a long-tailed boat (฿800 for ½-day, or ฿1200 for a full day), and kayaks (฿250 for ½-day, ฿500, full day).

🚌 Transport

Phangnga town p499, map p500
Bus
The bus station is on Petkasem Rd, a short walk from the **Thaweesuk** and

Lak Muang 1 hotels. Call T076-434119 for a/c bus information and T076-4345557 for non-a/c bus information. Buses to **Bangkok**'s Southern bus terminal, 15 hrs. 3 VIP buses leave in the evenings for Bangkok. Regular connections with **Phuket**'s bus terminal on Phangnga Rd, 2 hrs, and with **Krabi**, 2 hrs. Also buses to **Ranong**, **Takua Pa**, **Hat Yai** and **Trang**. You can wave down these buses if you catch them coming out of the station and pay on board.

Motorbike
Hire from the **Thaweesuk Hotel** and **MT Hotel** for ฿200 daily.

Koh Yao Noi and Koh Yao Yai *p501*
Boats
From Koh Yao Yai to **Phuket**: to Laem Hin Pier, 0800; to **Tien Sin Pier**, 0800 and 1500;

Rassada Port, Thu and Sun 0830, Sat 1430; to the village of **Bang Rong**, return at 0700, 1000 and 1500.

Boats from both Koh Yao Yai and Koh Yao Noi to **Krabi** and **Phangnga** usually depart from around 0700. Times vary; you need to check with your bungalow or resort.

❶ Directory

Phangnga town *p499*, map *p500*
Banks ATMs on Petkasem Rd. **Internet** In Kean tour company (at the bus station) and further along Petkasem Rd toward Thung Jadee School. **Post office** On Petkasem Rd, 2 km from centre on main road entering town from Phuket. Overseas phone service.

Krabi and around

→ *Colour map 4, C2*

Krabi is a small provincial capital on the banks of the Krabi river. It is fairly touristy and a jumping-off point for Koh Phi Phi (see page 533), Koh Lanta (see page 543), Ao Nang and Rai Leh and smaller islands like Koh Jum, Koh Bubu and Koh Siboya (see page 536 and 537). Krabi town itself is a shambling and amiable waterfront port with excellent, easily accessible tourist sites like the Tham Lod cave and Tiger Temple.

In the past, the town acquired the unfortunate reputation of being a haven for junkies and a place where you really shouldn't leave anything in your hotel room. But in recent years Krabi has attempted to cash in on its heritage in an idiosyncratic way. Hence, the kitsch iron statues on Muharat Road of four bearded prehistoric men carrying the traffic signals. This vision, best viewed at twilight with the jungle foliage behind, is meant to remind visitors that big human skulls were found in Tham Phi Hua To Cave, which means Big-Headed Ghost Cave. Aside from anthropological joys, Krabi town is a perfect place to either prepare for, or recuperate from, island-hopping, especially for those who have been on islands with limited electricity and luxuries. Here, you can stock up on bread – Krabi has excellent bakeries – fetch your newspapers and get a decent café latte before heading back to the nature reserve for some more hammock swinging.

Rock climbing, river trips, birdwatching, hiking at national parks and reserves, motorcycle treks and sea canoeing are all available and most tour companies also operate daily and overnight tours around Phangnga Bay (see page 506) often incorporating a visit to Wat Tham Suwan Kuha and other sights. ▸▸ *For listings, see pages 513-520.*

Ins and outs

Getting there and around

Krabi is well connected. The new Krabi International Airport, 15 km from town, offers seven daily flights from Bangkok. The taxi to town from the airport is around ฿400 and to Ao Nang ฿500. *Songthaews* offer a cheaper option. There are also boats to Koh Phi Phi – still worth a day-trip – and Koh Lanta, from the new pier on the outskirts of Krabi town. Free courtesy tuk-tuks from the old pier at Chao Fah to the new one may still be offered, so don't be too keen to flag down a taxi. Meanwhile, Chao Fah Pier continues to operate services to Rai Leh beach and there is a white minibus for ฿50 to Ao Nang from there as well.

There is no train station in Krabi but Phun Phin (the stop for Surat Thani) is a three-hour bus ride away. The overnight sleeper is met by buses for those going on to Krabi. Buses drop travellers at the tourist office in Krabi, where bookings for the islands can be made. Alternatively, travel to Trang or Nakhon Si Thammarat and take buses from there. Combination tickets from Bangkok via Surat Thani are available and can be booked through travel agencies. From the bus station, around 5 km from the centre in Talat Kao (Old Market), close to the intersection of Uttarakit Road and Route 4, there are regular connections with Bangkok's Southern bus terminal (16 hours) as well as with all major towns in the south. The VIP bus from Bangkok is a 12-hour overnight journey. However, do your homework and don't economize – Krabi hoteliers are now warning tourists of a rogue bus service (see box page 158) with contraband 'passengers'. For Koh Samui, companies offer combination bus/boat tickets. Motorcycle taxis also wait to ferry bus passengers into town. *Songthaews* are the main form of local transport, they drive through town stopping at various places such as Phattana Road, in front of **Travel & Tour**, for

Ao Phra Nang and in front of the foodstalls on Uttarakit Rpad for Noppharat Thara Beach. Red *songthaews* regularly run between the bus station and town, ฿20. Motorbikes are widely available for hire. ▶ *See Transport, page 519, for further information.*

Krabi

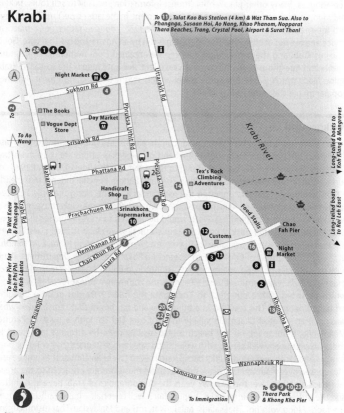

To **11**, Talat Kao Bus Station (4 km) & Wat Tham Sua. Also to Phangnga, Susaan Hoi, Ao Nang, Khao Phanom, Nopparat Thara Beaches, Trang, Crystal Pool, Airport & Surat Thani

50 metres
50 yards

Sleeping 🛏
A Mansion **1** *C2*
B&B House & Hostel **8** *B2*
Bai Fern Guesthouse **22** *C2*
Ban Chaofa **20** *C2*
Blue Juice **16** *B3*
Boon Siam **2** *A1*
City **4** *A1*
Europa Café &
  Guesthouse **5** *C1*

Grand Tower **6** *B2*
Hollywood **7** *B2*
K Guest House **13** *C2*
Khong Kha Guest
  House **9** *C3*
Krabi City Sea View **10** *C3*
Krabi Meritime **11** *A2*
Krabi River **3** *C3*
KR Mansion **12** *C2*
P Guesthouse **15** *C2*
Star Guest House **18** *C3*
Thai **21** *B2*
Thara Guesthouse **23** *C3*

Theparat Travel Lodge
  & Restaurant **24** *A1*
Up To You **14** *B2*

Eating 🍴
89 Café **5** *C2*
Boathouse **7** *A1*
Bolero **12** *B2*
Chao Sua **4** *A1*
Chawan **2** *C3*
Chok Dee **3** *B2*
I-Oon **9** *B2*
Kwan Coffee Corner **8** *B3*

May & Mark's **10** *B2*
Pizzeria Firenze **11** *B2*
Ruen Mai **1** *A1*
Seafood Restaurant **6** *A1*
Sea House **13** *B2*
Viva **15** *B2*

Transport 🚌
White Songthaews to
  Ao Nang & Nopparat
  Thara **1** *B1, B2*
Minibus to Talat Kao **2** *B2*

Tourist information

Small TAT office ① *Uttarakit Rd, across from Kasikorn Bank, 0830-1630*. For more information on Krabi, Ao Nang, Phra Nang, Rai Leh, Koh Phi Phi and Koh Lanta and some good articles, pick up the free guide, *Flyer* (www.yourkrabi.com/flyer), from various bars and guesthouses. Many other places offer 'tourist information', usually to sell tours, tickets and rooms, which can either be offensive or convenient. In the latter case, **Ibris Travel Tour and Internet Service Group** ① *23 Isara Rd, T075-630276*, do give rather good practical advice and are not at all pushy. The operation is run by an Aussie and his Thai wife. Good maps of Krabi and the surrounding area can be obtained from numerous shops, tour agents and guesthouses around town. An excellent, accurate map is the so-called Krabi Guide Map, which is free but some travel agents might try to charge for it. Another popular map is the *Frank Tour*.

Background

Krabi's economy used to be based on agriculture and fishing but since the mid- to late 1980s, tourism has grown although rubber and palm-oil plantations are still a mainstay. The tourism takeover in Krabi is all down to the growth in the late 1970s and 1980s of surfaced roads at Ao Nang, Ao Luk, Klong Tom and Panom Bencha. Indeed, in the early 1970s communists bandits operated the roadblocks at night, along the only surfaced road in Krabi – Highway 4 – which linked the town with Phangnga. Only those motorists who knew an ever-changing password would be allowed to travel while locals learned not to venture out after dusk. What scant tourists there were clung to their guesthouses, not that maps were even available for the more adventurous among them. Ever mindful of the possible spread of Communism, a watchful Royal Thai Survey Department along with the US Defence Mapping Agency in Washington, published a secret map of the area that no civilian was permitted to see. Then, as the communist threat receded, Ao Nang, which persisted with a dirt track to Krabi until the mid-1970s, got in on a budding asphalted network. This resulted in a bungalow and bar boom that transformed what was once an isolated beachside village into a Costa Del Sol with a twist of Patong. Meanwhile, Krabi town, on the beach route, steadily grew as a tourist layby and is, today, exceptionally well served with well-priced cafés and restaurants, catering for both tourists and locals and good quirky bars. There is even talk of an annual Thai reggae and Moken 'sea gypsy' summer music festival as more musicians are attracted to the area's laid-back nightlife. Over the past five years the demographics of Krabi have also shifted and the present burgeoning Muslim population – well over half – has clearly influenced the food. Along with hot Thai salads, halal meat, roti and Malaysian-Thai fusion cuisine are commonplace.

Krabi town ☺️🚻🏦🐘🏧⛰️🍽️ℹ️ ⇥ *pp513-520*.

There is a **general market** on Srisawat and Sukhon roads, and a **night market** close to the Chao Fah Pier. Chao Fah Pier at night is flooded with foodstalls frequented mainly by locals. The food is highly varied and cheap, although the cooking is quick-fire so you need to make sure everything is properly cooked. However, for a nocturnal nibble alfresco and a promenade walk, the pier is ideal, especially as the streets are thronged with people around twilight. Depending on how you feel about young elephants performing tricks for a cucumber, visitors can pay to feed the gentle beasts. There are also a handful of guesthouses, some shabby but intriguing, along the river and opposite the market if you want to be close to the action.

Around Krabi ◉🕐▲🕘🕓 ↠ *pp513-520.*

Wat Tham Sua (Tiger Cave Temple)
ⓘ *Wat Tham Sua is east along Route 4. Take a red songthaew from Phattana Rd in town for ฿20 to Route 4 (the songthaew is marked 'Airport/Fossil Beach'). From here either walk along Route 4 to the Cave Temple or take a motorcycle taxi (about ฿20). Walk to the cave from the main road.*

Wat Tham Sua is 8 km northeast of town just past Talat Kao down a track on the left and has dozens of *kutis* (monastic cells) set into the limestone cliff. Here, the monks still meditate in the forest. Tiger Cave is so called because once a large tiger apparently lived there and left his pawprints behind as proof, although some visitors have found this a dubious claim and grumble that the pawprints are not at all paw-like. Real wild creatures can be found in the surrounding rocky hillsides and mangrove forest. Here, trees that are hundreds of years old ensconce garrulous macaque monkeys. Walk behind the ridge where the bot is situated to find a network of limestone caves, which eventually lead back to the entrance. There is also a staircase on the left; 1237 steps leading to the top of a 600-m-high karst peak with fantastic views and meditation areas for the monks which are often occupied. This is a demanding climb as it is steep; it is best reserved for cool weather and early morning. Take water and a sunhat.

Tham Phi Hua To and Tham Lod
ⓘ *The caves of Tham Phi Hua To and Tham Lod can be reached by boat from a pier just down the road from Hat Nopparat Thara (take the first left as you exit towards Khlong Muang), or you can take one of many tours by boat or canoe to the same caves. It is also possible to visit these areas with companies offering sea canoeing. While generally more expensive than the trips via long-tailed boat (bear in mind that sea canoes cost upwards of US$350 each in Thailand), a more private trip is worth it, particularly when passing through the lush and mysterious limestone canyons. Then you can be assured that the main sounds will be eerie watery echos and the dipping of oars rather than tourist chatter.*

Phi Hua To Cave (Big-Headed Ghost Cave) is famous for the discovery there of ancient and unusually large human skulls as well as 70 paintings in red and black of people and animals, all of which upholds Krabi Province's claim to having hosted the oldest human settlements in Thailand. A large pile of shells was also discovered in the cave. There are two paths in the cave. Take the left for a cathedral-like cavern illuminated by a shaft of light and the right for a hall reputed to have been a shelter for prehistoric people.

Tham Lod Tai is a cavern in the limestone karst through which you can travel by boat along narrow passages filled with stalactites and stalagmites. Tham Lod Nua is a longer and larger cavern with more meandering passages. Both are passable only at low-tide. The boat ride to the caves passes mangroves and limestone karst outcrops.

Mangrove trips
ⓘ *Long-tailed boats can be hired for a trip into the mangroves at the Chao Fah Pier (rates are negotiable and depend on the time of year, length of time and number of passengers). For this trip it may also be possible to get a rua jaew –the traditional boat used in the Krabi area (including Koh Lanta). Paddles are used instead of a motor (though most now use both).*

Mangroves line the river opposite Krabi. This is a protected area although heavy logging has left most of the forest quite immature. It is worth visiting for the birds and other wildlife including several families of macaques, but ask the boatman to go slowly when in the mangroves so as not to startle the wildlife.

Thanboke Khoranee National Park
ⓘ *Entry is ฿400 (the same as for Phanom Bencha National Park and Khao Nor Chu Chi). Take Route 4 towards Phangnga; turn left down Route 4039 for Ao Luk after 45 km. About 2 km down this road there is a sign for the gardens, to the left. By public transport, take a songthaew from Krabi to Ao Luk, and then walk or catch a songthaew.*

Thanboke Khoranee National Park is a beautiful, cool and peaceful forest grove with emerald rock pools, streams and walkways. In the park, swimming is permitted in the upper pool which is near a small nature trail leading up into the limestone cliffs (sturdy shoes are advised).

Laem Sak
ⓘ *Turn left as you exit Thanboke Khoranee National Park and continue on Route 4039 into the town of Ao Luk and beyond down a small road to the end of the peninsula.*

Laem Sak juts out from the mainland just north of Ao Luk and makes a good trip before or after a visit to the Thanboke Khoranee National Park. Views back towards the mainland are impressive with a wall of limestone karst in the distance fringed by mangroves. Out to sea and to the west are a group of rocky islands. The fishing pier is working with plenty of activity and there are restaurants serving fresh seafood. This is a good place to watch the fishing boats pass by and eat reasonably priced fish.

Garos Island
ⓘ *A tour leaves from a pier down a rough dirt track which can be reached from Ban Thung. (Turn left at Ban Thung, drive about 500 m and take a right turn down the dirt track. There are signs to the pier after about 5 km, and the pier is about 12 km from the main road). Pre-arrange a tour by calling T076-649149. Mr Mos speaks reasonably good English. His partner (Mr Mudura), can also take the tour but speaks much less English, although he knows more about the area having lived there for most of his 60 years.*

Garos Island lies off the coast of mainland Krabi near Ban Thung (before Ao Luk). A day trip in a small long-tailed fishing boat will take you past mangroves and limestone karst islands to Garos, where you can see somewhat sinister prehistoric wall paintings and several caves used as traditional burial grounds for 'sea gypsies' (Chao Le). It's good for birdwatching and for seeing the traditional lifestyles of fishing communities. The tour, which provides a fantastic lunch cooked on a small island beach where you can also enjoy a swim, is operated by members of the community. Recommended.

Khao Phanom Bencha National Park
ⓘ *Take a motorcycle or other transport out on the main road going towards Trang (past Talat Kao). The turn-off comes before the exit for Wat Tham Sua. Motorcycle theft from the car park at Kho Panom Bencha happens regularly.*

Khao Phanom Bencha National Park provides a magnificent backdrop to the town with a peak rising more than 600 m above the surrounding land. Near the park entrance is the lovely **Huai To Waterfall** best seen between September and December after the monsoon. The drive to the waterfall is pleasant with a distinctly rural feel and the area around the park entrance has some charming trees and open grassland, good for picnics. Park rangers lead treks up to the peak and to a waterfall on the other side. The level of English spoken by rangers can vary – check that you feel comfortable with any potential guide before setting out. The trek takes more than a day as the climb is quite steep.

Khao Nor Chu Chi forest, Crystal Pool and hot springs

ⓘ *Tours can be arranged from most tour offices in town. For self-drive, the turn-off to Khao Nor Chu Chi is just after the major intersection in Khlong Thom town, it's marked. Once you get on to the road to the Crystal Pool and hot springs, you will find clear signposting.*

These sights are all in Khlong Thom district to the south of Krabi province. Khao Nor Chu Chi, which is in the middle of nowhere, is a mere parcel of rainforest surrounded by plantations. It has a forest trail and bungalow-style accommodation (**Morakot Resort**) that was initiated as part of an ecotourism project aimed at conserving the seriously endangered **gurney's pitta**, a bird believed to be extinct; it was re-discovered by the ornithologists Philip Round and Uthai Treesucon. Prince Charles, a keen ornithologist, has also endorsed the fight to save the comically named bird with its flashes of turquoise, red and brown. Gurney's pitta, which favours heavy forest, can be almost impossible to find and visitors have spent two days looking for a glimpse of this jewel-winged bird, which is listed as one of the top 50 endangered birds in the world. The ongoing fear now is that gurney's pitta will become extinct in the next 10 years as deforestation due to rubber and palm-oil plantations continues to dominate over ecological concerns. Tourism could save the day as the Tourist Authority of Thailand gets increasingly involved in the plight of gurney's pitta.

The **Crystal Pool** ⓘ *entrance ฿200*, is visited by the Queen and other royals annually and is so-called because of the exceptional clarity of the water and its emerald colour. The colour derives from mineral deposits that are visible through the water. The pool is shallow and the water buoyant. However, while the pool may look attractive enough, the deposits feel rather crunchy and not particularly pleasant under foot and the slopes leading to the pool are slippery.

A visit to hot springs (฿100) on a hot day may seem rather odd, but the temperature of the water is comfortable and it's a relaxing place to spend some time. The springs have been developed into Thai-style mineral baths with changing rooms, walkway to the original springs and landscaped gardens for the walk through to the river. There are eight of these springs, all with enticing names. They are **Nam Lod** (Water Passing Through), **Cheng Kao** (Valley), **Jorakeh Kao** (White Crocodile), **Nam Tip** (Heavenly Waters) **Nam Krahm** (Indigo Water), **Morakot** (Emerald Water), **Hun Kaeo** (Barking Deer) and **Noi** (Small).

◉ Krabi and around listings

For Sleeping and Eating price codes and other relevant information, see pages 44-49.

● Sleeping

Krabi *p508, map p509*
With the rising cost of accommodation at nearby beach resorts and the spectre of burgeoning 4-star complexes on Koh Lanta, Krabi has found a niche in providing low-cost but often friendly and imaginative accommodation for the lower-budget crowd. This has also meant a lot more guesthouses are cropping up, which has forced some of the original dross out.

Generally, the older guesthouses on Ruen-Ruedee Rd are cramped and stuffy; those up the hill and elsewhere in the town are more spacious, better maintained and often cheaper. Note that prices during the high season can double. Another good reason to give the nearby beaches a miss for overnight stays is the food. Krabi town boasts 2 night markets, a morning market, excellent restaurants offering an eclectic range of cuisines and fine cafés with good coffee, tea and pastries.

AL-A Krabi Meritime Hotel, 1 Tungfah Rd, T075-6200 2846. Krabi town's first luxury hotel, about 2 km from town, is off the road towards the bus station. Rooms are large and clean with balconies overlooking huge twin limestone outcrops. On the river overlooking the mangroves and limestone karst, they run a ferry service to a private beach and club and have a pool. Somewhat overpriced.

B-C Theparat Travel Lodge and Restaurant, 151-155 Maharaj Rd, T075-622048, www.thepparatlodge.com. This white 4-storey offers a/c and fan rooms with satellite TV and mini-bar. It does an extensive range of tours, including one to a King Cobra Show, and has a bakery. Not bad service and clean rooms. Worth checking out but you may find it lacking in atmosphere.

B-E City Hotel, 15/2-3 Sukhon Rd, T075-621 280, www.citykrabi.com. Some a/c, 3-storey hotel for which we have received mixed reports, rooms are clean with attached bathrooms, faces onto one of the quieter streets in town. Rooms can be hot and airless and staff unfriendly. Still, better value than the **Thai**.

C Boon Siam Hotel, 27 Chao Khul Rd, T075-632511-5. Prides itself on being de luxe. This 5-storey hotel block has a concrete exterior. Rooms are all a/c with hot water, spacious and comfortable, with satellite TV. A bit far out of the town, but still within walking distance of the centre. Does a brisk trade around Chinese New Year. Good value.

C-D Krabi River Hotel, 73/1 Khongkha Rd, T075-612321. Fairly new, 5-storey white-fronted hotel with splendid view of the river, the mangroves and the hustle and bustle of the boats. Rooms are bright and simply decorated if uninspiring. Concrete and tiles throughout. Spotless. Has all facilities and restaurant that is ideal for breakfast. There is

also a rooftop terrace. Good value, especially if you can get a room with a small veranda overlooking the river. Suitable for families. Recommended.

C-E Krabi City Sea View Hotel, 77/1 Khongkha Rd, T075-6228858, www.krabicityseaview.com. Hotel block on the promenade, down the road from the Immigration Department. Great views from the top storey, but the lower floor rooms have no view, although these small rooms have been recently upgraded with TVs and fridges. The restaurant at the top is a fine place for breakfast if you do not mind the sound of long-tailed boats that are initially part of the charm but soon become piercing.

C-E Thai, 7 Issara Rd, T075-6111474. Some a/c, large hotel with 150 rooms, grotty corridors and rooms that are run-down though large and clean, with reasonable bathrooms. The expensive rooms are better maintained. There is a pervasive smell of mildew in this dimly lit hotel. It all makes for a borderline acceptable mid-range establishment in immediate need of renovations. Discounts available in the low season.

D-E A Mansion, 12/6 Chao Fah Rd, T075-630 5113. Hotel-style facilities and prices. The rooms are all a/c and should have hot water. Rooms, though box-like, are clean and smell fresh. This is centrally located. It is possible to ask for a discount on the top-end price and staff can be swayed.

D-F Bai Fern Guesthouse, 24/2 Chao Fah Rd, T075-630339, www.baifern-mansion.com. Clean rooms in this well-run guesthouse Some attempt has been made to personalize the entrance with an aquarium by the stairs but overall the establishment craves a more intimate touch. However, it is safe, secure and clean with trustworthy family staff who try to help and, if you choose your room carefully, it is decent value. Excellent advice on tours and travel.

D-F Chan Chalay, 55 Uttarakit Rd, T075-620952/01-9788081, chanchalay@ hotmail.com. Pleasant white and blue building on Uttarakit Rd near the post office.

Reasonably priced, clean and airy rooms set back a little from the road. The best rooms at the back. Has a popular breezy café. Recommended.

D-F Thara Guesthouse, 79/3 Kongkha Rd, T075-630499. Next to the **Krabi City Sea View Hotel**. The rooms are bright and airy, they have fridges and TVs with some overlooking the river. The staff are considerate and everything is well maintained. In this price range – recommended.

E Ban Chaofa, 20/1 Chao Fah Rd, T075-630359. Mix of a/c and fan, 2-storey hotel edging to 2-star. Japanese/Ikea feel – clean, chic and minimalist. Rooms overlooking street have small balconies. The owner speaks fairly good English and has put care into his venture. Internet and laundry. Restaurant on ground floor. Reccommended.

E-F B&B House and Hostel, 98 Pleugsa Uthit Rd, T075-632315. Rooms are a little sterile and bleak but various options are available, from rooms with mattress on the floor with shared bathroom, to a/c rooms. The real bonus here is that there's free Wi-Fi access for all guests.

E-F Grand Tower Hotel, 9 Chao Fah Rd, T075-6214567, www.krabigrandtower.com. A long-standing average hotel, neither towering nor grand. The rooms are bare but clean, some with attached showers and a tendency to smell musty. Nonetheless, there is a popular bar.

E-F Hollywood, 26 Issara Rd, T075-620508. Offers 10 rooms above a restaurant, all with shared bathrooms (separate male and female). Rooms are large, well furnished, cool and clean with ceiling fans, some have a nice view. Largish restaurant and log cabin bar that resembles a red-neck honky-tonk. Serves Western and Thai food. Friendly staff but service can be slow and grudging.

E-F K Guest House, 15-25 Chao Fah Rd, T075-623166. Mainly fan rooms with mosquito nets. 2-storey building with a long wooden veranda balcony along the first floor. Views over town. Wonderful

potted foliage along the front intensifies the feeling of being in a hideaway. Wooden floor and ambient lighting. Get a room in the wooden part and not the airless ones with shared bathroom at the back. Restaurant, laundry service and internet. Good bargain. Recommended.

E-F Khong Kha Guest House, Khongkha Rd. Small guesthouse with great views over the mangroves, looking across to Koh Klang. To reach it, walk along the promenade past the pier to Phi Phi and away from the town. A converted house, all rooms have windows. Clean and simply furnished, most rooms are spacious with views over the water. One of the better locations in Krabi. Easy access to the night market and tour agency. Friendly, helpful owner. The only downside is the noise of long-tailed boats during peak season.

E-F KR Mansion, 52/1 Chao Fah Rd, T075-612761, www.kr-mansion.com. Some a/c, clean, bright and airy rooms, rooftop balcony for an evening beer and good views. At the quieter top end of town, a 10-min walk from most of the bars and restaurants. Visitors have complained of dud cocktails in the rooftop bar.

E-F P Guesthouse, Chaofa Rd, T075-630382. The rather garish colour scheme of lilac and lime green in the hallways, thankfully doesn't continue into the rooms, which are well appointed with TV and hot water showers. Good level of comfort for this price range. Internet and tours on the ground floor.

F Europa Café and Guesthouse, 1/9 Soi Ruamjit Rd, T075-620407, www.cafe europa-krabi.com. Under Thai and Danish management, the **Europa Café** has 5 rooms above the restaurant. All rooms are nicely decorated and clean but the smallest lack windows. Shared spotless bathroom with hot water. The restaurant is cosy and inviting, rather like a Danish café, and serves good-quality northern European food (imported meats and cheeses). The owners are entertaining sources of information – all speak excellent English, German and Danish. The guesthouse closes at 2300 and security is excellent. Recommended, although some may prefer a more laissez-faire approach.

F-G Blue Juice, 1/1 Chaofa Rd, T075-630679. Just before the pier, where the boats leave for Railay, this concrete building houses several different fan rooms. The cheaper ones have a shared clean bathroom, The teak floors and whitewashed walls makes this place bright and airy. There's a PADI dive shop and restaurant on the ground floor. Recommended.

G Star Guest House, Khongkha Rd, T075-630234. A charming wooden guesthouse over the top of a small convenience store and tour office, the 7 rooms are tiny, leaving little space for more than a bed, but there is a pleasant balcony with tables and chairs overlooking the night market and the river. Separate bathrooms are downstairs near a small bar in a garden at the back. Recommended.

G Up To You, 91 Uttarakit Rd, T075-611245. Rooms in this traditional teak shophouse are very basic with just a mattress on the floor, a mosquito net and shared bathroom. There is a restaurant and internet downstairs. Good budget option.

🍴 Eating

Krabi p508, map p509

🍴 **Bolero**, Oottahanahkit Rd. Italian restaurant run by 2 Thais. Good pizza and pasta. There's also a live band in the evening.

🍴 **Chao Sua**, on Maharaj Rd, along the road from the **Ruen Mai** (the sign, with a leopard on it, is in Thai). Considered by many locals to be one of the best restaurants in Krabi. The restaurant itself has a rambling feel and service is sometimes a little haphazard. Excellent Thai food. Barbecued seafood, crispy duck salad and virtually anything that is fried is especially good; the *pad pak pung* is delicious. An original menu with lots of house specialities, for example, the *chao sua* eggs are well worth trying – like a Thai scotch egg although the appearance may put one off.

🍴 **Pizzeria Firenze**, Khongkha Rd. No-nonsense decor, though not much atmosphere. Usual mix of Thai and Italian dishes. Perfectly acceptable when the taste buds have reached overload with one too many papaya salads. Unobtrusive staff.

🍴 **Ruen Mai**, on Maharaj Rd well beyond the **Vogue Department Store** up the hill on the left-hand side as you leave the town. Excellent Thai food in a quiet garden. Popular with locals, with good English-language menu and helpful staff. Has a number of southern specialities. Fish dishes are particularly good, as are the salads.

🍴🍸 **The Boathouse**, Soi Hutangkonn. A restaurant in a real wooden boat set in a garden with a fake moat around it. Even more bizarre, the street appears largely residential. What keeps the whole affair from looking like a theme restaurant nightmare is the skewered romantic glory of the gleaming golden boat with its chandeliers and perfectly executed main courses, like steamed bass and plum sauce. This is the perfect place for couples though it also popular for intimate business meetings. Recommended.

🍴🍸 **Europa Café**, 1/9 Soi Ruamjit Rd, T075-620407. A favourite with locals and expats. Serves tasty northern European food – including pickled fish and Danish pork. Excellent helpings and always fresh. Possibly the best Western breakfast in town. Leonardo Di Caprio ate here while filming *The Beach*. Japanese tourists are keen on sitting in the star's seat and scoffing the Leonardo Special which is a banana milkshake, meatballs with mashed potatoes, mixed salad and bread and a pancake with strawberry ice cream.

🍴🍸 **The Seafood Restaurant**, Sukhorn Rd, in front of the night market. Offers excellent cheap food but do get there early for the best selection.

🍴🍸 **Sea House**, Chao Fah Rd. Reasonable prices, menu includes freshly ground coffee.

🍴🍸 **Viva**, Phruksa-Uthit Rd, between Phattana and Issara roads. Serves a range of

Italian and Thai food and good fresh coffee (Lavazza). This is a hang-out for travellers having a break from the rigours of no-frills bungalow huts but unfortunately also for the British lager lout and his Thai bargirl travelling companion. The music is often loud. However, reassuring Italian favourites like bruschetta and pizza are good and the place has proper olive oil and grappa and other Italian liquors. Reasonable prices and portions.

† **89 Café**, Chaofa Rd. Very popular place that also serves reasonable thai and Western food. Nightly movies. Fresh coffees and herbal teas. Cheap Wi-Fi at ฿30 per hr.

† **Chawan**, 38 Khongkha Rd. Serves Thai food and the usual Western dishes (sandwiches, spaghetti, etc). The Thai food comes in generous portions but can be bland in its eagerness to cater to a Western palate.

† **Chok Dee**, Chao Fah Rd. Reasonable prices, some dishes are delicious, and good value for the quality and quantity. TVs with cable and a good selection of movies. Friendly management and staff.

† **I-Oon**, 7/3 Chao Fah Rd, near the **Grand Tower Hotel**. Excellent little café, with good breakfasts and special deals for dinners.

† **Kanchanee Bakery**, 12-14 Maharaj Soi 6, T075-630501. Spacious, bright and airy café, maybe a little too bright if you have a hangover but the pastries are good and the coffee is superb. Also has newspapers.

† **Kwan Coffee Corner**, Khongkha Rd, T075-611706, kwan_café_kbi@hotmail.com. Delicious fresh coffee, sandwiches, milkshakes, ice creams, cheap and tasty Thai food, good breakfasts of fruit and muesli, almost everything. A good place to acclimatize to Krabi, with chatty owners. **Kwan** has become so much of an institution that they have their own T-shirts for sale. Recommended.

† **May and Mark's Restaurant**, Ruen-Ruedee Rd. Good information, friendly atmosphere and attracts expats so the conversation goes beyond predictable backpacker chat. However, this tiny and well-loved hang-out seems to be resting on its laurels. It's not as clean as it could be and the much-touted bread needs to appear more often. Thai, Italian, Mexican and German food, along with the traveller usuals.

Foodstalls

A **night market** sets up in the early evening on Khlong Kha Rd, along the Krabi river, and serves good seafood dishes. Halal and Chinese dishes can be found here. Instead of opting for *banana roti* it's worth trying the *mataba* as a savoury dish. This is made in the area near the town – slightly spicy, sweet and with a pleasant taste of curry and vegetables. Tasty ice cream and good Thai desserts further up the hill. There should also be a stall selling *khao man kai* (Hainanese chicken with rice), red pork and soups with real ginger and soy sauce to go with the chicken.

A second **night market** is based in the parking lot near the Provincial Electricity Authority office on the road running between Uttarakit and Maharaj roads. This market sells fruit at night, at much cheaper prices than the market by the pier. Keep your eyes peeled for mango and sticky rice. It also has an excellent selection of halal stalls, *phat thai*, noodle soups, *khanom jeen* (noodles with sauces and vegetables) and desserts. There is a beer garden in the grounds plus clothes and cheap goods stalls. The hum begins in the early evening, continuing until 2200.

Stall food is also available from the **fresh market** between Srisawat and Sukhon roads, and from scattered places along Uttarakit Rd, facing onto the Krabi river. For a real treat, try the **morning market** on Soi 7 off Maharat Rd. In the middle aisles, are stalls selling extraordinarily complex salads that can be found for around ฿25. Order noodle soup and the stall-owner will set before you a series of tiny dishes that are variously pickled, shredded and dry, prawn-festooned plus baby aubergine salads. There will also be a plate of fresh herbs including mint, coriander, basil and lemon grass. The salads are eaten separately and the herbs added to your noodle soup. All the produce is fresh daily and there is constant dicing, chopping, washing and peeling. The market is packed with other vendors and the only place to eat is at long tables where elbows jostle for space so it is well worth getting up early. The fresh fish stalls are also impressive – if you are going back to a smaller island, you can purchase things like shellfish here and have it cooked back at your bungalow.

The **Vogue Department Store** on Maharaj Rd also has an a/c food court on the 3rd floor.

🌓 Bars and clubs

Krabi *p508, map p509*
Bar Chaofa Rd. A laid-back vibe with lots of comfy places to sit and chill. There are also numerous other bars alond this road worth checking out.
Kwan Fang Live Music, Sudmongkol Rd, next to **Mixer Pub**. For a sense of weirdness and longing, there is always Kwan Fang with its staple of country and western bands. This out-of-place haunt looks a little like a western saloon with some of the space out in the wide open air. An older crowd than **Mixer**.
Mixer Pub, 100 Sudmongkol Rd. Pulls in a solid local crowd. At **Mixer** they prepare your poison all night with your choice of mixer. Mischievous staff will also videotape you through the stages of drunkenness, table-top dancing and singing. Doubling the fun (or horror), this is later played on a screen, so not a place for shrinking violets. Suits a younger crowd. Great for anthropological viewing and for the brave – unparalleled for shameless exhibitionism.
Nyvhavn, across from **Europa**, Soi Ruamjit. Based on Nyhavn in Denmark. They only play jazz and sometimes have live performances. You also get sandwiches and baguettes with roast beef, imported cheese, salami, etc. It has a small garden too.

🎇 Festivals and events

Krabi *p508, map p509*
Boat races on the river can be thrilling, particularly when the Samsong is flowing.
Nov **Berg Fa Andaman Festival** in the gardens beyond the pier (coinciding with *Loi Krathong*) – a showcase for traditional dancing and singing from around Thailand. Also features Andaman handicrafts.

🛍 Shopping

Krabi *p508, map p509*
Books
Many of the guesthouses and tour companies also run book exchanges.
The Books, 78-80 Maharat Rd, next to **Vogue Department Store**.

Clothes and tailoring
There is a tailor on the corner of Issara and Khongkha roads. Lots of clothes stores on Phattana, Prachachuen and Uttarakit roads, mostly selling beachwear.

Department stores and supermarkets
Sri Nakhorn, opposite the Thai Hotel;
Vogue Department Store, Maharat Rd.

Souvenirs
Khun B Souvenir, and other souvenir shops on Khongkha and Uttarakit Rd, sell a range of souvenirs from all over Thailand and Southeast Asia.
Thai Silver, opposite Thai Hotel. Sells silverware mostly from Nakhon Sri Thammarat.

⛰ Activities and tours

Krabi *p508, map p509*
Canoeing tours
Europa Café, see Eating, above. Offers a mangrove/canoeing tour but with an English-speaking guide, which is necessary

if you wish to learn a little en route about local history and why mangroves are so important. The tour, which goes near Bor Thor village close to Ao Luk, takes in caves and allows for swimming.

Game fishing
Phi Phi Marine Travel Co, 201 Uttarakit Rd, T075-621297. It can arrange expeditions to catch marlin, sailfish, barracuda and tuna.

Golf
Krabi Golf, 12 Kongka Rd, T08-9871 1997 (mob), www.krabigolftours.com. Golf tours to courses in Krabi, Surat Thani and Phuket. Run by a knowledgable Aussie named Diane.

Tour operators
Tour operators are concentrated on Uttarakit and Ruen-Ruedee roads and close to the Chao Fah Pier. There are so many tour and travel agents, and information is so freely and widely available, that it is not necessary to list numerous outfits here. Prices and schedules are all openly posted and a 30-min walk around town will reveal all.
Krabi Somporn Travel and Service, 72 Khongkha Rd, opposite the old pier, T08-1895 7873 (mob). This is run by Mrs Tree. She is friendly and doesn't overcharge.

☉ Transport

Krabi *p508, map p509*
Air
The international airport is 17 km northeast of the town on Highway 4, T075-636546. It is served by **THAI**, **Airasia**, **Tiger** and **Singapore** airways with the vast bulk of flights going to Bangkok.

Boat
The monsoon season affects timetables as does the low season. The pier outside Krabi town is called Chao Fah Pier and services Koh Lanta and Koh Phi Koh. To **Koh Phi Koh**, 1000 and 1500, 1½ hrs, ฿350 (includes transfer

from guesthouse). There is also an additional 0900 boat going via Rai Leh Beach to Phi Phi, ฿390. It is also possible to take a long-tailed boat from Khong Pier ฿120 per person, leaves when full.

There is still a boat from Krabi to **Koh Lanta** via Koh Jum (1½ hrs). This runs from mid-Oct to mid-May, departing at 1100 for around ฿350. In the wet season, a minibus runs from Klong Chi Lard Pier and via 2 short car ferries across Lanta Noi and to Ban Sala Dan, 2 hrs, contact a tour operator for details.

There are boat connections with **Ban Hua Hin**, on the southern tip of Koh Klang. *Songthaews* also go to Ban Hua Hin

To **Phuket** there is one direct boat leaving at 1500 from Ao Nang Hat Naopparat Thara Pier, ฿550, 2 hrs.

There are also boats from Krabi to **Koh Yao Yai** and **Koh Yao Noi**, ฿350, 1 hr, leaving Thalane Pier at 1500, including transfer from guesthouse.

Bus
Numerous evening a/c, VIP and non-a/c connections with **Bangkok**'s Southern bus terminal, 16 hrs. There is also a service that departs for Bangkok's Khaosan Rd at 1600. Regular a/c and non-a/c connections with **Phuket**, 3 hrs via **Phangnga**, 1½ hrs. Minivan to Phuket, daily 1100, 1400, pick-up from guesthouse, ฿350. Regular connections with **Surat Thani**, 3 hrs and **Trang**, a/c minibuses to **Hat Yai**. Tickets and information about bus connection (both public buses and private tour buses) available from travel agents.

To Koh Samui (฿400) and Koh Phangnan (฿550), bus and boat, 1100 and 1600. One connection daily with Koh Tao at 1600, ฿850.

International connections with Malaysia and Singapore By a/c mini-bus to **Singapore**, 0700, ฿1000; **Kuala Lumpur**, 0700, ฿850 (there's also a VIP bus at 1100) and **Penang**, 0700 and 1200, 7-11 hrs, ฿600). Buses stop in **Hat Yai**, for passport checks. Some travel agents charge ฿10 'border service', avoid paying if possible.

Motorbike and jeep

Scooters cost ฿150-200 per day. Jeeps, ฿900-1200 per day.

Songthaew

Songthaew run regularly to the bus station at Talaat Kao, 5 km from town. White *songthaews* leave regularly 0600-1800 from Maharat Rd next to the 7-11 and from Phattana Rd stopping at both **Nopparat Thara** and **Ao Nang**, ฿50 from 0800-2200, and ฿80-100 after dark.

☉ Directory

Krabi *p508, map p509*
Banks Branches of all major banks with ATMs. **Immigration** Immigration office,

Uttarakit Rd, a little way up from the post office on the same side of the road. The office will extend 60-day visas by 30 days (฿1900) and provide free 14-day visas for people arriving by sailing boat. It will also provide re-entry permits for those travelling on longer-stay visas. Mon-Fri 0830-1200, 1300-1630. Photocopies can be made at a couple of shops just across the road in the row of wooden shophouses. **Internet** Lots of services available around the town, especially on Uttarakit Rd, Chao Fah Rd (towards the pier) and around Hollywood. **Post office** Uttarakit Rd (halfway up the hill, not far from the Customs Pier). It has a Poste Restante counter. **Telephone** Quite a way out of the town on the way to the **Krabi Meritime Hotel**. Alternatively, look for services in some tour offices on Uttarakit Rd.

West of Krabi

The road to the coast from Krabi winds for 15 km past limestone cliffs, a large reclining Buddha, rubber stands and verdant forest. Arriving at the coast in the evening, with the setting sun turning the limestone cliffs of Ao Nang a rich orange and the sea interspersed with precipitous limestone crags, is a beautiful first impression.

The coast west of Krabi consists of the beach areas of Ao Nang and Hat Nopparat Thara (which lie 18 km and 22 km respectively to the west of Krabi town), and also Ao Phra Nang, Ao Rai Leh East, Ao Rai Leh West and Ao Ton Sai. ▸▸ *For listings, see pages 525-532.*

Ins and outs

Tourist information
More than half the native population are now Muslim Thais, discreetly signalled by the absence of pork on restaurant menus, even though you will not hear the call of the muzzein at prayer times. Buying alcohol in public at a beach bar should be disallowed, but in typical Thai-style, bar staff are Buddhist in Muslim-run and owned operations, which nicely gets around that dilemma. It should be remembered that topless sunbathing is very definitely frowned upon. It is rare to see Thai women even in bikinis at the beach – due to modesty and also an abhorrence of tanning. But, while most sun-starved Westerners come to Thailand to sunbathe and indeed are encouraged, with ever-present deckchairs, cold towels and beach masseurs, it is still a good idea to cover up when you leave the beach for restaurants. These establishments will often be staffed by Thai-Muslims even if the bars aren't. If you get too hot and bothered by this option, there's always takeaway.

Ao Nang, Nopparat Thara and Khlong Muang ●🖼🖼🖼🖼🖼🖼
▸▸ *pp525-532.*

Ao Nang is neither sweeping nor glorious and has coarse dirty yellow sand intermingled with millions of broken shells that are unpleasant to walk on. One end of the beach is filled with kayaks and long-tailed boats for transporting tourists to nearby islands and it is these motorized long-tailed boats that punctuate the quiet with ferocious regularity. The concrete wall behind the beachfront, the construction of which initially excited much antagonism, saved Ao Nang from the greater force of the tsunami and is being rebuilt in parts. Behind this is the commercial outcrop of Ao Nang itself which has taken up the whole of the beach road and swarmed inland. The town itself is a generic collection of souvenir shops, small resorts and bad restaurants – it is mind-boggling to think that just 15 years ago, Ao Nang was a sleepy fishing hamlet. On the whole, there is little to do in today's Ao Nang, including eating. The food is dreadful; if you don't count the gas-oven pizzerias of which there are far too many, even something simple like a fruit salad or toast is substandard and often served grudgingly. The whole set-up utterly lacks the shameless exuberance of Patong or the charm of Kata Noi and the tourists reflect this. However, there are pleasant features in spite of all this, which makes the current development even more regrettable. The beachfront is lined with coconut palms and mango trees with limestone walls at one end and lovely views of the islands on the horizon. Ao Nang also is good at providing facilities including diving, windsurfing, fishing and tours to the surrounding islands. It is still relatively quiet and the beach water is fine for swimming, out of the monsoon season, with calm waters and beautiful limestone scenery. But it is really the surrounding beaches, coves, caves and grottoes that make the place bearable.

At **Hat Nopparat Thara**, about 3 km northwest of Ao Nang, is a deliciously long stretch of soft, pale beige sand covered in tiny seashells and lined with tall casuarinas at the beachside. To the back are paperbark forests. Locals used to call this place 'Hat Khlong Haeng' or dried canal beach because at low tide the canal dries up, leaving a long beach. Khlong Haeng is also the name of the village closest to the beach – around 900 m away. This 5-km-long beach is divided by a river with the side closest to Ao Nang being the most developed as it is bordered by a main road. The other side, which is lousy with sandflies, can only be accessed by boat or by a dirt track from the road to Khlong Muang.

Khlong Muang, a more remote stretch of average beach, is attracting ever-greater interest from upmarket developers who tout the hotels on the shore as having 'private beaches' (despite these being shallow and rocky) because there is only indirect public access to them once the hotels are up. Many of the bungalows here are closed during the

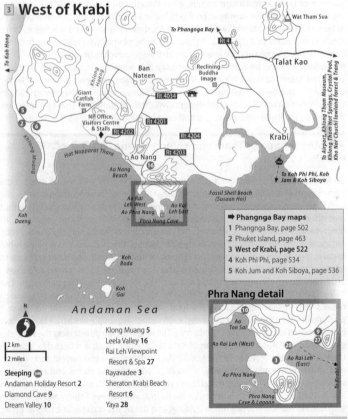

3 West of Krabi

Phangnga Bay maps
1 Phangnga Bay, page 502
2 Phuket Island, page 463
3 West of Krabi, page 522
4 Koh Phi Phi, page 534
5 Koh Jum and Koh Siboya, page 536

Phra Nang detail

2 km
2 miles

Sleeping
Andaman Holiday Resort 2
Diamond Cave 9
Dream Valley 10
Klong Muang 5
Leela Valley 16
Rai Leh Viewpoint
  Resort & Spa 27
Rayavadee 3
Sheraton Krabi Beach
  Resort 6
Yaya 28

monsoon season and there also appears to be ongoing construction at a boxing stadium so it is worth checking beforehand what the works are going to be like as it may be a noisy and dusty experience.

There are also a couple of interesting places on the road in from Ao Nang. The first is **Ban Nateen** – a Muslim village that has set up one the best homestay and activity programmes in southern Thailand. The village itself is just a small collection of housing that holds little attraction. The homestay programme itself is spread throughout the village or at a centre just off the main road. Here you can see a variety of traditional crafts and buy local produce. See Sleeping, page 528, and Tour operators, page 531. The other attraction on this stretch of road, about 8 km before Khlong Muang, is the **Giant Catfish Farm** ① *T075-644209, daily 0800-1800, ฿80.* Set up by Nina, an American expat and her Thai husband, Paichit, a visit here is a genuinely eccentric and fascinating experience. More like an adventure zoo than anything else – there are crocodiles, tarantulas, monitor lizards and ponds of huge catfish – the entire place is set up amid the jungle with gorgeous waterfalls and refreshing pools on hand should you require a dip. They also run a very popular restaurant.

Nopparat Thara has three distinct sections. The first is closest to Ao Nang and is where most of the bungalow and hotel developments have taken place and where most Western tourists wander. This area has limited shade. Further down the beach near the **Hat Nopparat Thara-Mu Ko Phi Phi National Park office** ① *0830-1630,* is the area where most Thai tourists congregate – this area is well shaded with picnic grounds under the casuarina trees. The final section is across the canal, adjacent to the national parks office and by the harbour used by local fishermen. This stretch of beach is home to affordable bungalow resorts, and has a completely different character to Ao Nang and the other parts of Nopparat Thara. These bungalows are accessible by boat across the canal and by road. Although it is a pleasant place to rest with great views and more peace and quiet than in Ao Nang, the water is very shallow, making swimming during anything except high tide next to impossible. Well inhabited with crustaceans and other sea creatures you never know what you might step on, so wear sandals if you decide to paddle in the shallowest waters. Some guests even wear shoes. But there are some sweet sights to be had here – monkeys, kingfishers and sea eagles at the west end of the beach – as well as caves to explore. At low tide it is also possible to walk out to some of the islands in the bay. In these ways, it is an ideal place for children. ▸ *See Activities and tours, page 530, for details on snorkelling, canoeing and kayaking.*

In the opposite direction, beyond the limestone crags, is drop-dead gorgeous Phra Nang, see page 524, and the beaches (and accommodation) of boho-chic Rai Leh, which has been visited by the likes of Mick Jagger, Colin Farrel, and Fatboy Slim who gave an impromptu set.

Susaan Hoi (Fossil Shell Beach)
① *Take the white songthaews from the corner of Phattana and Maharat Rd in Krabi. ฿50. Coincide your visit with low tide when more pavement is exposed.*

Susaan Hoi, literally 'shell cemetery', lies 20 km southwest of Krabi near the village of Laem Pho (not far from Ao Nang Beach) and 5 km east of Ao Nang. Great slabs of what looks like concrete are littered along the shoreline but on closer inspection turn out to be countless fossilized freshwater shells, laid down 40 million years ago. It is one of only three such cemeteries in the world; the others are in the US and Japan. It is an impressive and curious sight.

Koh Boda and Koh Gai

Koh Boda is 30 minutes by boat from Ao Nang. It is hugely popular with snorkellers for its wonderfully clear water. Round-trip excursions last five hours. The nearby Koh Gai is also a 30-minute boat trip from Ao Nang. Ao Thalen combines the curious and wonderful shapes of the mangrove, with extraordinary limestone crags, cave paintings, monkey troupes, and an overall sense of mystery in the gorges that is quite magical. ▸▸ *See Sleeping, page 528, and Activities and tours, page 531.*

Phra Nang and Rai Leh ☺▲☺ ▸▸ *pp525-532.*

Phra Nang is the peninsula to the south of Ao Nang. There are no roads on Phra Nang, which lends it a secret-hideaway ambience – albeit an exclusive one as all the land behind the beach is occupied by the **Rayavadee Resort**. The point consists of **Rai Leh West** and **Ao Phra Nang** on the west side and **Rai Leh East** on the east. Further west from Rai Leh West is **Ao Ton Sai**. Over the last few years Rai Leh has become something of a mecca for rock climbers. This is partly because limestone is porous so that the water cuts into it and makes the natural grips ideal for climbers. But, equally alluring, say climbers, is the combination of landscape, climate and rock, which rarely come together in such harmonious splendour.

The best beach is on the west side – a truly picture-postcard affair. However, the east coast beach is still amazing at low tide in a sci-fi end-of-the-world way as the landscape transforms into a 300-m stretch of sinister shining mud. When Rai Leh East is not a mudbath, there are still the mangroves lining the beach so that it is fairly impossible to get any swimming in here. Rai Leh East also acts as a pier for taxi boats to and from Krabi and you will often spy tourists slogging across the mud with luggage over their heads. Pretty Rai Leh West, also knows as 'Sunset Beach', is about 10 minutes' walk away from the other beach – this means there is no escaping the daytime noises of the long-tailed boats although the evenings are delightful. There is also good snorkelling and swimming in archetypal crystal-clear water. The limestone rock formations are spectacular, and there are interesting caves with stalagmites and stalactites to explore though they require patience and fortitude as the paths are not always straightforward nor easygoing. At the southern extremity of the bay is a mountain cave (**Outer Princess Cave**) on Phra Nang Beach that is dedicated to the goddess of the area and considered 'her summer palace'. Here, you may be delighted to find an abundance of wooden and stone penises, many in wonderful colours of candy pink, lime green and pillar box red. It is believed local fishermen put the penises there to bribe the goddess into granting them plenty of fish on the sea. Be that as it may, many non-sailors also like to drop by a penis or two and the cave is suitably endowed. Near the penis cave are lots of monkeys that are rather friendly and several beachside stalls selling trinkets, clothes, beer and snacks like barbecued corn on the cob. There is also one outrageously priced bar that looks totally out of place. If you feel you must make an effort, there is Sa Phra Nang (Princess Pool) to explore. This is a pond inside the cliff that can be accessed along a cave trail at the side of the mountain. You can get to the top of the mountain if you keep climbing. There's a walkway to Rai Leh east from Ao Phra Nang if you care to visit yet another Princess cave called the Inner Princess cave which is three caverns, one of which has a waterfall of quartz-like frozen amber.

There are several climbing schools (see Activities and tours, page 532), as the tower karst formations offer some truly outstanding climbing opportunities along with spectacular views.

Rai Leh is suffering from being too popular. The area available for development is small, sandwiched between limestone cliffs and crags, and already the bungalows are cheek-by-jowl in places. It is also going upscale with the recent appearances of superstars, so prices are starting to soar. On the whole, the entertainment here remains coffee houses/bars/bookshops during the day and low-key parties on the east side at night – still more reggae than rave. Everything on Rai Leh continues to be run by generators as there are no mains currents and there are still no banks. Foodies will be seriously disappointed as the closest and most patronized outpost for food is Ao Nang.

Ao Ton Sai, north of Ao Rai Leh West, largely appeals to climbers who can manage far more than five-minute walks. Climbing is the main activity here, followed by frisbee, volleyball and assorted refreshments à la *Big Lebowski*.

◉ West of Krabi listings

For Sleeping and Eating price codes and other relevant information, see pages 44-49.

● Sleeping

Ao Nang, Nopparat Thara and Khlong Muang *p521, map p522*
High-season (Nov-May) room rates may be as much as double (or more) the low-season (Jun-Oct) rates.

Accommodation in Ao Nang seems to have settled down into 2 broad groups – fairly faceless 4- to 5-star hotels with a pool or 2- to 3-star hotels without a pool. Since the difference is negligible and no one is there for the museums, the pool question does need to be considered – we've tried to list the best in each category. Most of the places here are populated with package tourists. Rates are slashed May-Oct.

Ao Nang
LL-L Pavilion Queen's Bay, 56 Moo 3, T075-637612, www.pavilionhotels.com/queensbay. This huge hotel of more than 100 rooms is certainly luxurious and has very friendly staff, but is hampered with some silly design flaws, and lack of attention to detail. International, Thai and Japanese restaurants (the last highly exclusive with top-class sushi on offer), very large spacious rooms but somewhat cramped bathrooms. Luxurious spa – one of the best features of the hotel and open to non-residents too.

All the other facilities expected from a hotel like this, including a 3-layered swimming pool. Good views. Big discounts online.
LL-AL Beach Terrace Hotel, 154 Moo 2, T075-637180, www.krabibeachterrace.com. All rooms have a/c, fridge and TV. The rooms without balconies have small windows and are a little dark. Some rooms need redecorating as do the hallways. Swimming pool and massage area. Overpriced.
LL-AL Golden Beach Resort, 254 Moo 2, T075-637870-4, www.goldenbeach-resort.com/beach. This has one of the best locations on the beach with good views across to the islands. Rooms are in cute green-roofed-white-bungalow style and low-rise hotel blocks. Pool and well-tended gardens. The Thai restaurant (**Thai Thai**) is probably the best in Ao Nang.
LL-AL Pakasai Resort, 88 Moo 3, T075-637777, www.pakasai.com. Has all the facilities that you would expect at this price range, including Wi-Fi. Nice design features such as a bathtub on the balcony in the Andora rooms.
LL-A Royal Nakara, 155/4-7 Moo 3, T075-661441, www.royalnakara.com. Built on the edge of a steep drop, the rooms are reached by descending several flights of stairs. All rooms are very light and spacious, with modern furniture, TV and DVD player. Premium rooms have pantry kitchen and dining area. Infinity pool. Interesting design. Very accommodating staff. Recommended.

LL-A Thai Village Resort, 260 Moo 2, T075-637710, www.krabithaivillage.com. This huge red-winged traditional Thai-roofed hotel shoots out of the forest in a rather predatorial way. 3 large swimming pools, pool bar and children's pool. Large dull buffets and unadventurous food. At night you can hear the crickets.

L-AL Princeville Resort, 164 Moo 2, T075-637971, www.aonangprinceville.com. The rooms are spacious and decorated in warm, rustic tones, all overlooking the swimming pool. De luxe rooms have a bathtub. Restaurant and massage areas are hidden in thick foliage.

L-AL Vogue Pranang Bay Resort and Spa, 244 Moo 2, T075-637635, www.vogue resort.com. One of the more appealing of the luxury hotels. Nestled into mountain foliage, this complex sprawls beautifully through landscaped gardens and has a very nice pool. It is especially good for honeymooners who like to go from the bath to the poolside.

AL-A Emerald Garden Beach Resort, 90 Moo 3, T075-637692. Italian-owned timeshare property that rents out 20 villa cottages. Up on the hill away from the beach in a quiet location with 2 pools, a gym and bar plus good facilities (excellent bathrooms with bidets). Variable decorations. A bit far from everything, but represents pretty good value for the facilities.

AL-A Lai Thai Resort, 25/1 Moo 2, T075-637281, www.laithai-resort.com. About 1 km from the beach, but with a free shuttle service. Family-run resort with great views of the mountains at the back of Ao Nang. The swimming pool is black-tiled. Rooms are spacious and very comfortable. Restaurant has a range of food including Mexican. Consistently good reports aobut service. Possibly overpriced.

AL-B Ao Nang Beach Resort, 142 Moo 2, T075-637766-9. Hotel-style accommodation in a white Costa del Sol block along the seafront. The entrance is set back from the front but the hotel lives up to its claim that many of the rooms have excellent sea views.

Clean, standard type of rooms, central location. Try to get a balcony though.

AL-C Phi Phi Don Resort, 1 Moo 7, Ao Nang, T075-6126 8126. Choice of garden view or seaview, fan or a/c. Concrete bungalows are dated and tired looking, but the staff are friendly and it's close to the action.

A Ao Nang Beach Home, 132 Moo 2, T075-695260, www.aonangbeachhome.com. Offers large, well appointed a/c rooms, with spacious bathrooms and nice touches such as beach mats in the rooms. Laminate teak furniture, modern and comfortable. Restaurant overlooking the beach. Recommended for price (includes breakfast) and location.

A-B Blue Village, 105 Moo 3, T075-637887, www.bluevillagekrabi.com. Ignore the goofy name, this is a fantastic lay-out with huts and palm trees growing through the roofs – beds on floor futon-style, sunken bathrooms. Run by a Canadian (Richard) a former diving instructor who has lived in Thailand for 19 years. Good cheap food. Impossible not to chill here. Recommended.

A-C Baan Pimphaka Bungalows, 115/2 Moo 3, T075-637562, www.baan pimphaka.com. Comfortable chalet-style rooms with hot water showers and large comfy beds. Homely restaurant and friendly staff. Discounts available for longer stays. Recommended.

B-C Ben's House, next to Royal Nakara, T075-661595. Various styles of rooms located over 6 floors, the rooms on the top floors have a sea cottage feel and are the best designed. For a modern hotel with swimming pool and a good range of facilities, it's not bad for the price.

B-D Ao Nang Village, 49/3 Moo 2, T075-637544. Quite a walk from the beach. Concrete fan bungalows and a/c rooms in a 2 storey building. Basic but very clean. Quiet garden setting. **Me Me** offers a similar set-up next door.

B-D PP October, 90 Moo 7, Ao Nang, T075-601193. Towards the end of the village, this building offers good quality a/c, en suite rooms; a little thought has gone a long way. One of the better accommodations on offer. Tour bookings and internet downstairs.

C Harvest House, 420/18-19 Moo 2, T075-695256, harvest-house@hotmail.com. Spanking new rooms, comfortably furnished with balcony, a/c, cable TV, bathtub. It is quite a walk to the beach from here but these rooms are very good value.

C-D Dream Garden House, 86/2 Moo 2, T075-637338, www.krabidir.com/dream gardenhostel. Some of the 16 rooms here have balconies which look onto walls so don't believe the advertorials. A/c also quite noisy but the service is good.

C-D Hill Side Village, 168/10 Moo 2, T075-637604, www.krabidir.com/hillside village. Opposite the Lai Thai Resort. Converted concrete row of a/c rooms. 19 rooms come in sets of 2 (double at back, twin at front) and would make good family rooms. Rooms to the back are smaller and cheaper, with shower only and no hot water. Rooms at the front are twin beds with a bath and hot water. All rooms come with TV (satellite) and a fridge. Friendly staff provide information on tours, and will take guests to and from the beach.

D-E Ao Nung Thara Lodge, 115/2 Moo 3, T075-637087. Basic bamboo bungalows in a garden setting a short walk from the beach. Old furniture but rooms come with TV and hot water shower. Both a/c and fan available.

D-F Leela Valley, 262/1 Ao Nang, T075-635673, www.krabidir.com/leelavalley. Some simple bamboo bungalows on the ground that need repairs, and some smarter fan and a/c houses on stilts with balconies, set in spacious grounds rather lacking in shade. Good views of the mountains. Rooms are clean. Discounts for long stays. Quite a distance from the sea, but excellent value.

Nopparat Thara

A-B Emerald Bungalow, catch a boat from Nopparat Thara pier across the estuary, westwards, T08-1892 1072 (mob). This place is very peaceful with around 40 large, fan bungalows and some a/c rooms. Restaurant. Location is the high point; it is south facing so you get a good sunset and there is also a river to swim in at the end of the beach. Can arrange transfers for you. Friendly staff.

A-B Jinnie's Place, 101 Moo 3, T075-621 042, aonangks@hotmail.com. The red brick a/c bungalows have bags of character and charm. The bathrooms are possibly the largest in Krabi and have bathtubs and even a garden. There's a children's pool and a main pool. Recommended.

B-D Lakeside Bungalow, 119 Moo 3, T075-637751, www.lakesideaonang.com. Typically designed bamboo huts in a very quiet area. Facilities include TV. A/c rooms are also available. Restaurant and lounge area where football matches are often shown.

B-E Cashew Nut Bungalows, 96 Moo 3, T075-637560. Concrete bungalows set amongst cashew trees (hence the name). Family run. Rooms range from fan and cold water, to a/c with hot water. Basic but clean. Very quiet. 5 mins from the beach.

B-E Na-Thai Resort, near Nopparat Thara and Phi Phi Island National Park Head-quarters and the Montessori School, T075-637752. It's 5-10 mins by motorbike or car from Hat Phra Ao Nang and Hat Nopparat Thara. Free pick up. Surrounded by oil palms and rubber trees, this is a husband and wife set-up – Gerard and Walee who have more of an eco-friendly approach to running things. There are 5 evenly-spaced bungalows set around a small pool that you can swim in at night and a restaurant where they can trot out Western favourites or excellent Thai food. Not the most imaginative bungalows but great attitude and good for a more isolated getaway. Prices depend on the month. Recommended.

C-E Nopparat Thara and Phi Phi Islands National Park Headquarters, PO Box 23, Muang District, Krabi 8100, T075-637436 or make reservations at the Royal Forestry Department in Bangkok, T02-5790529. Has some bungalows and camping facilities but you have to make reservations ahead of time.

Khlong Muang

New accommodation is springing up along this stretch of beach with some big players moving in.

LL-L Sheraton Krabi Beach Resort, 155 Moo 2, Nong Thale, T075-628000, www.sheraton.com/krabi. A large and luxurious resort. It's very well planned with nice gardens and good beach access. You can opt for either hotel rooms or bungalows – both are of a very high standard and include all the usual top-end trimmings. 2 large pools, kids play area, elephants and an excellent wood-fired pizza restaurant. Lots of other facilities, including a spa, gym, etc.

LL-A Andaman Holiday Resort, 98 Moo 3, T075-628300, www.andamanholiday.com. Large (too large really at 116 rooms) resort on a former rubber plantation which extends right down to the beach in a peaceful and semi-isolated spot. The pool is a bit small for the number of rooms. Rooms vary, with the more expensive thatched villas representing better value. There's a fitness centre, convention centre, tour counter. Overpriced for what it is and the food lets it down. The beach is also not good for swimming.

B-C Klong Muang, 36/13 Moo 3, Nong Thale, T08-9971 9938 (mob), www.klong-muang-inn.com. All rooms are clean and en suite in this small guesthouse – go for the rooms on the upper floors. Set about 200 m from the sea and run by German expat, Freddy.

Ban Nateen

C-D Home Stay Ban Nateen, Bannateen 4/2 Moo 4, T075-637390, www.homestay thai.info/homestay. Excellent programme, run and managed entirely by the friendly local Muslim villagers. You can choose to stay either in a small compound of bungalows or in other dwellings scattered throughout the village. Accommodation is basic but the rates include all meals plus one daily activity such as cooking, fishing, tuk-tuk tours. Awesome value and highly recommended.

Koh Boda and Koh Gai p524

There are bungalows available on the island. Book through the **Krabi Resort**, T075-611389, T02-2518094 (Bangkok). The bungalows are a good size, with restaurant, Western toilets and not particularly friendly staff. Camping is possible on the island

Phra Nang and Rai Leh p524

There is not much to distinguish between the various lower-end bungalow operations at Rai Leh. The cheapest rooms are found at Ao Ton Sai and Rai Leh East, which has no beach and faces out on mangroves and mudflats. The area has been turned into an unpleasant building site as some of the more quaint establishments are replaced by concrete chicken sheds. Rai Leh East is a short walk from the beaches at Phra Nang and Rai Leh West. Many of the owners have crammed too many structures onto too small an area, and others have grown too large (with 40 or more cottages) and service has consequently suffered. All have their own restaurants, bars and often minimarts, tour desks and telephones. Many also have exchange services often offering poor rates.

Rai Leh West

A beautiful beach but huts have been built too closely together, making for overcrowded conditions and basic (but not cheap) accommodation. To get here, take a boat from Ao Nang or Krabi town.

LL-B Railei Beach Club, T08-1464 4338 (mob), www.raileibeachclub.com. On its own section of beach (opposite end to the **Rayavadee**), is one of the most stylish places to stay at Rai Leh. Traditional Thai-style houses have been sold as holiday homes. Their owners let them whenever they are not in residence. Fully equipped with kitchens and bathrooms but no a/c. Electricity goes off after 2400. Prices vary depending on the size. Houses for 2 to 10 guests are available. Maid service can be provided as there is no restaurant.

Phra Nang headland

LL Rayavadee, T075-620740, www.raya
vadee.com. 98 2-storey pavilions and 5 villas
set amid luscious grounds studded with
coconut palms in this luxurious, isolated
getaway. Every service imaginable is provided
in the beautifully furnished pavilions,
including lovely, exclusive bathrooms and
bedtime chocolates. Some rooms have
private pools. The strikingly large main
pool faces Rai Leh beach. Restaurants include
the **Krua Phranang**, on the renowned Phra
Nang beach, where the Mieng Kana, small
parcels of kale leaves filled with lime, chilli,
shallots, ginger, cashew and shrimp, are to
be savoured. Indulge in the magnificent
spa and the **Rayavadee** signature massage,
including a hot herb compress. Excursions
are offered. Due to its location, bordering
3 beaches and caves, it feels more like an
adventure than just a hotel. Price includes
airport transfer. Recommended.

Rai Leh East

AL-A Diamond Cave, 36 Moo 1, T075-622
589, www.diamondcave-railay.com. Next to
a huge limestone outcrop. Almost monstrous
number (for the space) of solidly built and
clean concrete a/c bungalows set on a hill on
the sunrise side of Rai Leh peninsula. Pool,
massage and minimart. Clean and secure.
A-C Rai Leh Viewpoint Resort and Spa,
T075-621686-7, www.viewpointresort
66.com. Large upgraded resort. Friendly,
well run, clean and well-maintained rooms.
Good restaurant, minimart, internet and pool.
The least accessible of all the places at the far
end of Rai Leh East, but some of the best
bungalows, especially given the rates.
Cheaper ones are far from the water.
A-D Yaya, T075-611585, www.ya-ya.com.
Long-running with variable, relatively hellish
rooms set in 2-3 storey wooden blocks. Little
effort is made to keep the rooms clean and
many are rat-infested (little palm rats that
are more mouse-sized). It is loud with
well-muscled types strutting about, gazing
at their well-sculpted navels and comparing

climbs. The walls are paper-thin giving no
protection from the constant disco beats
and poorly strummed acoustic guitars. One
of the few places that offers fresh coffee.

Ao Ton Sai

Ao Ton Sai is a building site, transforming it
from a hippy hang-out into a large resort.
The restaurants here are generally poor,
even for the area, and most of the accommodation is a 5-min walk uphill behind
the sand.

Cheaper rooms can be found further up
the hill at **Andaman Nature, Krabi Mountain
View** and **Phoenix Bungalow** resorts.
C-E Dream Valley, T075-621772.
Revolutionized in recent years with a field
full of concrete, characterless a/c bungalows
that have hot water and patios where there
used to be a few bamboo huts.

🍴 Eating

Ao Nang, Nopparat Thara and
Khlong Muang *p521, map p522*
Food in Ao Nang and Rai Leh remains
dominated by sloppy Western and tourist
Thai restaurants with a silly number of
pizzerias. As one would expect, the best
food available at Ao Nang is fresh seafood.
Almost all the restaurants along the beachfront road, and then lining the path northwest towards the **Krabi Resort**, serve BBQ
fish, chilli crab, steamed crab, prawns and
so on. There is little to choose between these
restaurants – they tend to serve the same
dishes, prepared in the same way, in rather
lacklustre sauces; food does not come close
to the standards set by the better restaurants
in Krabi. Most lay their catches out on ice
for customers to peruse – snapper, shark,
pomfret, tiger prawns and glistening crabs.
Those concerned about conserving the
marine environment should avoid the shark
and coral fish which usually come at a much
higher price than the tag you see on the fish.
Evening is certainly the best time to eat, drink

and relax, with the sun illuminating the cliffs and a breeze taking the heat off the day.

₮₮₮ The Roof Restaurant, Ao Nang. Attractive building with a flower-filled dining room and setting, although not on the beach. Good extensive menu which offers organic steak and Swiss-German specialities as well as Thai dishes. Expensive, but worth it.

₮₮₮ Wanna's Place, Beach Front Rd, Ao Nang. Produces Swiss cuisine – veal escalopes, rösti and chicken and also serves wine, but the service is terrible or rather up to Ao Nang standards – unfriendly and slow – and the prices are steep for what's on offer.

₮₮₮-₮₮ Freddy and Jurgen, next to the **Klong Muang**, see Sleeping, above. Thai and German food, along with pizza and a massive array of beer should keep most people happy.

₮₮₮-₮₮ Giant Catfish Farm, 8 km before Khlong Muang, T075-644209. Great little restaurant nestling beside the eccentric adventure zoo set up by American expat, Nina. Combine a visit there with a meal here. Excellent, affordable Thai food. Recommended.

₮₮₮-₮₮ Lavinia restaurant, on the Beach Front Rd, next to **Encore Café** and **Kodak Shop**, Ao Nang. Great view of beach, good selection of bread but London prices for a sandwich. Service slow and scatty.

₮₮₮-₮₮ Sushi Hut and Grill, Ao Nang Beach Rd, Ao Nang. See if you can get *uni* (sea urchin) or *toro* (tuna belly). It also does tempura, miso soups, tofu steak in mirin, edamame and all the standards. Steak and Thai food also available.

₮₮ Azzurra, Beach Front Rd, ao Nang. Can become rather dusty during the drier months of Jan-Mar. Good unpredictable Italian fare with decent ingredients.

🍷 Bars and clubs

Ao Nang, Nopparat Thara and Khlong Muang *p521, map p522*

Plenty to choose from but they tend to open and close with great frequency. A 'bar-beer'

scene has opened up off the beachfront in Hat Nopparat Thara behind the front row of dive and souvenir shops and is complete with massage services, pink lights, cocktails, etc.

Fisherman Bar, Ao Nang. for a drink on the beach. Flexible closing hours.

Full Moon Bar, Ao Nang. Tried and trusty and right in the centre.

Irish Rover and Grill, 247/8 Moo 2, Ao Nang. Theme pub but still, sometimes, Guiness is good for you. Good selection of draughts and have cider too. Well run, with fairly high standard of bar food here too including chilli con carne, toasties, pies and chops. Does roast dinner but can be heavy for a tropical climate. Live sports. Recommended.

The Lost Pirate Bar, Beachfront Rd, down from **La Luna**, Ao Nang. Slightly more adventurous crowd – good information about parties and alternative scenes.

Luna Beach Bar, Hat Nopparat Thara, Ao Nang. Has fantastic cocktail prices (for Ao Nang anyway), and a very loose interpretation of closing hours. Can get raucous with Happy Hour becoming unhappy hours.

🛍 Shopping

Ao Nang, Nopparat Thara and Khlong Muang *p521, map p522*

Shops open on the beachfront at Ao Nang during the evening selling garments, leather goods, jewellery and other products made specifically for the tourist market. There isn't much that's unusual, except for batik 'paintings', usually illustrating marine scenes, which are made in small workshops here.

🏔 Activities and tours

Ao Nang, Nopparat Thara and Khlong Muang *p521, map p522*
Canoeing
Sea Canoe, T075-212252, www.seacanoe.net. Provides small-scale sea canoeing trips

(self-paddle), exploring the overhanging cliffs and caves, and the rocky coastline of Phra Nang, Rai Leh and nearby islands.

Other companies include **Sea World Kayaking**, T075-637334; **Mr Kayak**, T075-637500, **New Star Kayaking** and **Sea Kayak Krabi**, T075-630270, www.sea kayak-krabi.com, on the front. It is fairly difficult to choose between them.

Sea Canoe boasts about its strong environmental policies, including restrictions on the number of people per trip, and no foam or plastic-packaged lunches. Some of the other operators such as **Mr Kayak** have adopted these policies too, particularly in the Ao Thalen area where there is a small group of companies operating in amicable fashion. The best thing is probably to spend some time chatting to your prospective guide to see if you like the way they operate and whether you are happy with the level of English they speak. You should also try to get some guarantees on the number of people on the tour. In this regard **Mr Kayak** has been very good about taking very small groups but **Sea Kayak Krabi** has been known to promise no more than 10 participants but then take up to 30. Remember too that sea canoes in Thailand are open, so you should either wear a strong waterproof sun block or go for long trousers/sleeves and a hat.

Diving
Ao Nang Divers (PADI certification) at Krabi Seaview Resort, try Andre Gysin; **Aqua Vision Diving**, next to Beach Bungalows; **Calypso** (PADI certification); **Phra Nang Divers**, near the new guesthouses, on the beachfront road by La Luna and the Lost Pirate Bar, old-time expat Kyle Seymour is recommended; **Seafan Divers** (NAUI and PADI certification).

Muay Thai (Thai boxing)
There is a well-supported stadium for Thai boxing in the Ao Nang area. The old one was next to **Ao Nang Paradise**. This much larger stadium which attracts national standard

boxers is set back from Hat Nopparat Thara beach by about 300 m.

Rock climbing
King Climbers has an office down towards Phra Nang Inn.

Shooting
Ao Nang Shooting Range, 99/9 Moo 2, Ao Nang Rd, Ao Nang, T075-695555. You can fire shotguns, Berettas, semi-automatics and Magnums at this well-run shooting range. Prices start at around ฿890 for a full clip.

Therapies
Most luxury hotels are now offering spa facilities.
Tropical Herbal Spa, 20/1 Moo 2, Ao Nang, www.tropicalherbalspa.com. A glorious day spa, a little away from the beach but set in beautiful gardens and mostly open to the air.
Pavilion Queen's Bay, see Sleeping, above. Offers the best in-hotel spa. Others offer the services one might expect, but don't have that aura of peace and tranquillity that leads to a truly pampering experience.

Tour operators
The **Ban Nateen** homestay programme (see Sleeping, above) run a huge range of excursions, tours and activities.
Ao Nang Ban Lae Travel, close to Krabi Resort. Run boat tours to various islands and beaches, including Rai Leh and Phi Phi.
AP Travel, Beachfront Rd, T075-637642. Offer a range of tours to various temples and short 'jungle tours' – very helpful and friendly though not terribly exciting.

Koh Boda and Koh Gai *p524*
Canoeing and sea kayaking
Although the trips to areas like Koh Hong with its coral reefs are appealing, in some ways the trips to the limestone karst and mangroves along the mainland are more exotic and interesting. It's also worth remembering that coral reefs are only

really wonderful when you snorkel and are thus able to catch the sealife spectacle just inches below the water.

Phra Nang and Rai Leh *p524*
Rock climbing
Tex's Rock Climbing Adventure, Rai Leh Beach, www.molon.de/galleries/Thailand/Krabi/Climbing/. Mr 'Tex' is a bit of a local hero who also runs a children's overnight adventure camp just outside town for orphans and street children.

⊖ Transport

Ao Nang, Nopparat Thara and Khlong Muang *p521, map p522*
Boat
Regular long-tailed boats to **Rai Leh** during the high season (Oct-May), from the beach opposite Sea Canoe, 15 mins, around ฿100. The *Ao Nang Princess* links Ao Nang with Rai Leh and **Koh Phi Phi** daily during the high season 2 hrs, ฿390. Arrange a ticket for the boat trip through your guesthouse. The boat departs from Ao Nang at 0900 returning at 1630. This is subject to change and depends on the number of travellers.

Jeep and motorbike hire
Jeep hire (฿900-1200 per day) and motor-bike hire (฿250 per day) are available from travel agents and guesthouses.

Songthaew
Regular white *songthaew* connections with **Krabi**, 30 mins, ฿40, or ฿80 after dark. For Krabi, *songthaews* leave from the eastern end of the beach road, opposite Sea Canoe. The service runs regularly 0600-1800.

Phra Nang and Rai Leh *p524*
Boat
The *Ao Nang Princess* links **Phi Phi**, **Ao Nang** and **Rai Leh** during the high season, 2 hrs, ฿390.

❶ Directory

Ao Nang, Nopparat Thara and Khlong Muang *p521, map p522*
Banks Mobile exchange booths along Ao Nang beachfront and a more permanent place opposite the Phra Nang Inn, run by the **Siam City Bank**. Also a bank and exchange along from Vogue Phranang Bay Resort. **Thai Military Bank** booth next to AP Resort, 1000-1730. During low season (Jun-Oct) exchange booths may not open. **Internet** Now available at most guest houses, hotels and resorts. **Police** The station is halfway along the beach road; it is really just a police booth. **Tourist police** near the Ao Nang Bay Resort and Spa and another general police box near the Phra Nang Inn. **Telephone** Overseas telephone facilities available from numerous tour and travel. There is no official tourist information service. Agents along the beachfront road.

Islands south of Krabi

For most arrivals on Koh Phi Phi it seems like you've reached paradise. Anvil-shaped and fringed by sheer limestone cliffs and golden beaches, Koh Phi Phi – the setting for the Leonardo Di Caprio film The Beach – is stunning. However, a quick walk along the beach, heaving with masses of pink, roasting flesh, or through Ton Sai village, which is filled with persistent touts and standardized tourist facilities, soon shatters the illusion of Nirvana; the endless stream of boats spewing diesel into the sea doesn't help either. Ostensibly Phi Phi should be protected by its national park status but this seems to cut little ice with the developers who appear to be doing more irretrievable damage than the Asian tsunami which devastated the island on 26 December 2004. Whether Phi Phi can encourage enough sustainable tourism to survive the future is debatable – what is certain is that it has very quickly reached the same levels of development that existed pre-tsunami. ◆◆ *For listings, see pages 537-542.*

Koh Phi Phi ⊜🅿🅞⛰🅗🅖 ◆◆ pp537-542. Colour map 4, C2.

Kho Phi Phi was one of the sites worst-hit by the tsunami – there is a aerial photograph on display in the Amico restaurant in Ton Sai village which shows the apocalyptic dimensions of the devastation. Both Ton Sai and Loh Dalem Bay were almost wiped out by the impact of the killer waves overlapping simultaneously on either side of this thin stretch of island. Today, Phi Phi is back to rude health. Tourists are streaming in and the dive shops, hotels, restaurants, shops and bars are now fully up and running. It should also be pointed out that large parts of the island were also completely unaffected by the tsunami.

Phi Phi Le is a national park, entirely girdled by sheer cliffs, where swiftlets nest (see box, page 535). It found fame as the location for the film *The Beach* starring Leonardo Di Caprio and Tilda Swinton. It is not possible to stay on Phi Phi Le but it can be visited by boat. The best snorkelling off Phi Phi is at **Hat Yao** (Long Beach) or nearby Bamboo Island and most boat excursions include a visit to the **Viking Cave**, which contains prehistoric paintings of what look like Viking longboats, and the cliffs where birds' nests are harvested for bird's nest soup.

Getting there Phi Phi lies between Krabi and Phuket and can be reached from both, but the only way to get there is by boat. There are daily connections with Krabi, taking one hour on an express boat and 1½ hours on the normal service. Boats also run from the beaches of Ao Nang and Rai Leh close to Krabi (two hours). There are daily boats from Koh Lanta (one hour) and from various spots on Phuket (one to 1½ hours). The quickest way of getting to Phi Phi from Bangkok is to fly to Phuket and catch a boat from there. ◆◆ *See Transport, page 542, for further information.*

Best time to visit It is possible to travel to Koh Phi Phi all year round but during the rainy season (May to October), the boat trip can be very rough and not for the faint-hearted. The driest months are between June and September.

Beaches

Koh Phi Phi's beaches include **Loh Dalam**, which faces north and is on the opposite side to **Ton Sai Bay**, so is still under recovery. **Laem Hin** next to Ton Sai Bay, has beautiful

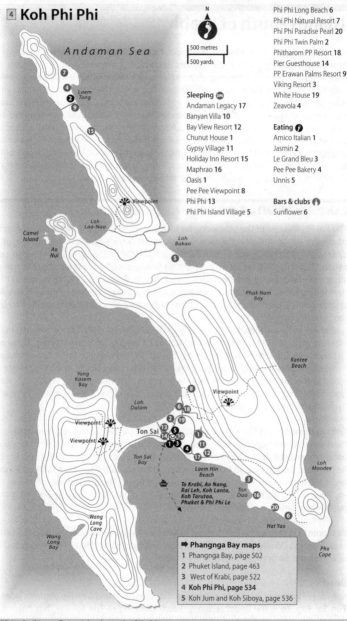

4 Koh Phi Phi

Andaman Sea

N

500 metres
500 yards

Sleeping
Andaman Legacy **17**
Banyan Villa **10**
Bay View Resort **12**
Chunut House **1**
Gypsy Village **11**
Holiday Inn Resort **15**
Maphrao **16**
Oasis **1**
Pee Pee Viewpoint **8**
Phi Phi **13**
Phi Phi Island Village **5**

Phi Phi Long Beach **6**
Phi Phi Natural Resort **7**
Phi Phi Paradise Pearl **20**
Phi Phi Twin Palm **2**
Phitharom PP Resort **18**
Pier Guesthouse **14**
PP Erawan Palms Resort **9**
Viking Resort **3**
White House **19**
Zeavola **4**

Eating
Amico Italian **1**
Jasmin **2**
Le Grand Bleu **3**
Pee Pee Bakery **4**
Unnis **5**

Bars & clubs
Sunflower **6**

Laem Tong

Camel Island

Ao Nui

Loh Laa-Naa

Viewpoint

Loh Bakao

Phak Nam Bay

Rantee Beach

Yong Kasem Bay

Loh Dalam

Viewpoint

Viewpoint

Ton Sai

Viewpoint

Ton Sai Bay

Laem Hin Beach

To Krabi, Ao Nang, Rai Leh, Koh Lanta, Koh Tarutao, Phuket & Phi Phi Le

Loh Moodee

Ton Dao

Hat Yao

Pho Cape

Wang Long Cave

Wang Long Bay

➡ **Phangnga Bay maps**
1 Phangnga Bay, page 502
2 Phuket Island, page 463
3 West of Krabi, page 522
4 Koh Phi Phi, page 534
5 Koh Jum and Koh Siboya, page 536

Bird's nest soup

The tiny nests of the brown-rumped swift (*Collocalia esculenta*), also known as the edible-nest swiftlet or sea swallow, are collected for bird's nest soup, a Chinese delicacy, throughout Southeast Asia.

The semi-oval nests are made of silk-like strands of saliva secreted by the birds which, when cooked in broth, softens and becomes a little like noodles. Like so many Chinese delicacies, the nests are believed to be an aphrodisiac and the soup has even been suggested as a cure for Aids.

The red nests are the most valued and the Vietnamese emperor Minh Mang (1820-1840) is said to have owed his

extraordinary vitality to his inordinate consumption of bird's nest soup. This may explain why restaurants serving it in Southern Thailand are usually also associated with massage parlours.

Collecting the nests is a precarious business and is only officially allowed twice a year – between February and April and in September. The collectors climb flimsy bamboo poles into total darkness, with candles strapped to their heads. In Hong Kong a kilogramme of nests may sell for US$2000 and nest concessions in Thailand are vigorously protected.

fine sand. **Ton Dao** beach is a small and relatively peaceful stretch to the east of Laem Hin, hemmed in with the usual craggy rocks and vegetation.

Hat Yao (Long Beach), post-tsunami, has become a day-trippers' destination as curious folk from the mainland resorts hit Koh Phi Phi to see where everything happened. However, it is gradually starting to attract overnighters. There are other reasons to stay here; the beach has excellent snorkelling offshore. Even before the tsunami, it was touted as having the cleanest water in Koh Phi Phi. Early in the morning (the best time being before 0930) black-tip sharks are a regular fixture here, before they swim further out to sea as the temperature rises. A walk to Hat Yao along the beach from the former Ton Sai Village takes about 30 minutes. You can also get a boat for around ฿100.

Loh Bakao is one of the larger of the minor beaches dotted around this island. **Phi Phi Island Village** is the only resort on this stretch of wide golden sand and is now fully operational. **Laem Tong** (Cape of God) boasts a wonderful sweep of white sandy beach that's relatively quiet and empty. There are only a few upper range resorts here, where many guests prefer poolside sunbathing, or the privacy of their own verandas, to the beach. The resorts also offer day trips, diving, snorkelling and cave-exploring expeditions. Increasingly, resorts are also conducting cultural workshops in skills such as Thai cookery, batik-painting and language courses.

Around the islands

Hire a long-tailed boat to take a trip around the island. Boats seat eight people, and cost ฿1000 per boat. A day trip snorkelling is well worthwhile (฿450 per person, including lunch, snorkels and fins), with Bamboo Island, Hat Yao and, on Phi Phi Le, Loh Samah and Maya Bay, being particularly good spots. Diving is also possible, with a chance of seeing white-tip sharks. Areas of interest include the Bida Islands, south of Phi Phi Le, where the variety of coral is impressive. There is a 50-m underwater tunnel here for more experienced divers. Wrecks can be found behind Mosquito Island – so-named for its mosquitoes, so do take repellent. The best visibility (25-40 m) is from December to April.

Trips can be taken to see the cliff formations at **Phi Phi Le**, the **Viking Cave**, **Lo Samah Bay** and **Maya Bay** (about ฿300 per person). Maya Bay was used in the filming of *The Beach* starring Leonardo Di Caprio.

Koh Jum, Koh Bubu and Koh Siboya 🌐📞🏕📧 ›› *pp537-542.*

These islands, south of Krabi, are places to escape the crowd. The beaches are not as divine as other Andaman Sea spots but they are quiet and somewhat away from the *farang* trail.

Koh Jum (Jam)
ⓘ *The boat from Krabi to Koh Lanta goes via Koh Jum, 1½ hrs, ฿350. There are also connections with Koh Phi Phi and with Laem Kruat, on the mainland.*

The island itself, with its beige-yellow beach and shallow waters, is not one of the most beautiful in the Andaman Sea, although it does have a magnificent pair of sea eagles who make regular appearances on the village side. Its main attraction is as an escape from the crowds on other islands, a slightly rough-hewn edge and enough variety in accommodation and restaurants to keep things interesting. Recently, the island, which only has around a couple of hundred residents – mostly Chao Le and Muslim fishing families – has seen a flourishing of cheap bungalows and there are now over 20 places to choose from. There is a fear that the resort side of the island is quickly running out of space, thus seriously hampering the privacy and quiet that travellers find here. Additionally, there are concerns that high-level developers will step in to create hermetically sealed resorts and drive out the smaller set-ups. But this still seems unlikely as the beach is not particularly attractive and there are no sites of note on the island to visit. So far, the operations on Koh Jum do not have pools – the only one that did had its opening day on Boxing Day 2004 and was promptly wiped out by the tsunami.

There is also still a sense of being in the jungle, with pythons making slithering debuts in resort kitchens from time to time. Koh Jum's real ace-in-the-hole for independent travellers continues to be that it does not have mains electricity, so that resorts depend on individual generators – most of the places only have electricity from 1800 to 2200/2300. The island also has a

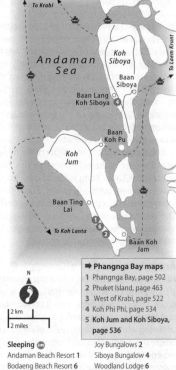

5 Koh Jum & Koh Siboya

To Krabi

Andaman Sea

Koh Siboya

Baan Siboya

Baan Lang Koh Siboya ④

To Laem Krunt

Baan Koh Pu

Koh Jum

Baan Ting Lai

To Koh Lanta

① ⑥
②

Baan Koh Jam

➡ Phangnga Bay maps
1 Phangnga Bay, page 502
2 Phuket Island, page 463
3 West of Krabi, page 522
4 Koh Phi Phi, page 534
5 Koh Jum and Koh Siboya, page 536

N

2 km
2 miles

Sleeping 🛏
Andaman Beach Resort 1
Bodaeng Beach Resort 6

Joy Bungalows 2
Siboya Bungalow 4
Woodland Lodge 6

undeniable quirky charm, both in terms of the locals and expats who have set up semi-permanent base here. There is a working fishing village with a mosque on the other side of the island from the resorts, which protects Koh Jum from being a toy island like the voluptuous Koh Ngai. The village has a superb restaurant with sophisticated seafood dishes that would not be out of place in a metropolis, general stores and clothes shops selling ubiquitous backpacker tat – fishermen trousers, hippy Alice bands and multi-coloured ashram muslin shirts. You can also watch fishermen at work here or have a cool beer away from the resorts. Finally, if you find that Koh Jum is not isolated enough for you, then take a day trip to Koh Bubu or Koh Siboya (see below).

Koh Siboya

ⓘ *During the high season (Nov-Apr), you can get a boat opposite Kasikorn Bank, Uttarakit Rd in Krabi where there is a small 'local pier', ฿150, leaving at 0800. Or you can take the hard way which is negligibly cheaper: you need the local bus from Krabi to Nua Klong for ฿30; then change bus and get one for Ban Lam Kruad for ฿40. From here there are 3 boats daily, 1230, 1400 and 1630, ฿30 to Koh Siboya. Or take a private long-tail from Koh Jum.*

Koh Siboya is a speck of an island with a population of about 1000 people, most of whom are Muslim and involved in rubber or fisheries. The beach is really just mud-flats that stretch for an astonishing length and bake and crack in the midday heat. However, it is the isolation of Koh Siboya that attracts returnee visitors – a mixture of hardcore travellers and middle-aged hippies. You will also find expats here who came for a couple weeks years ago and who have stayed on living in idiosyncratic and charming bungalows. There is not a lot to do and, from our reports, the main attraction/activity for visitors remains watching monkeys catch crabs on the beach, and freeform meditation.

⦿ Islands south of Krabi listings

For Sleeping and Eating price codes and other relevant information, see pages 44-49.

⦿ Sleeping

Koh Phi Phi *p533, map p534*
Developers are currently hoovering up the empty spaces created by the tsunami and are building endlessly replicating resorts.
LL-AL Holiday Inn Resort, Laem Tong, T075-627300, www.phiphi-palmbeach.com. 80 mostly low-rise bungalow-style buildings in 8 ha of garden setting right on the beach. Rooms are somewhat antiseptic and frumpy in the Holiday Inn way, though they do have wooden floors. 2 restaurants, 2 bars. Lots of activities on offer such as learning Thai cookery, batik painting, etc. Swimming pool, jacuzzi, tennis courts. Even provides picnic hampers for guests who wish to explore. One of the better equipped resorts on Phi

Phi. Lovely stretch of turquoise sea, very quiet beaches.
LL-AL Phi Phi Island Village, Loh Bakao, T075-215014, www.ppisland.com. Set alone to the north of the island this is the only resort on this stretch of beach. It relies on an individual generator for water and electricity. 84 traditional Thai bungalows set in immaculately tended gardens with a view of the beach. The rooms are extremely pleasant, with a/c, satellite TV, minibar, wooden flooring set off by bamboo and whitewashed walls and muted colours used for en suite bathrooms. Decent-sized verandas. There's a nearby diving centre, a pool and a resort speed-boat for quick journeys. Attached spa.
LL-AL Phi Phi Natural Resort, Laem Tong, T075-613010, www.phiphinatural.com. There's nothing natural about the huge signage outside this resort nor the endless

stream of boats that bring day-trippers to eat in their very average restaurant. It's a shame because the location on the northern stretch of Laem Tong beach is gorgeous. Around 70 bungalows with the de luxe options being built right on the hill over-looking the sea and Bamboo Island and incorporating a large area of decking from which to drink in the view. Beachside bar, coffee house and diving centre.

LL-AL PP Erawan Palms Resort, Moo 8, T075-627500, www.pperawanpalms.com. Decent-sized wooden bungalows with fresh-water swimming pool on the northern tip. Set in well-manicured paths. Beachside restaurant and nightly performances of Thai classical music, although not necessarily very good ones. Still entertaining and at times, edifying.

LL Zeavola, Laem Tong, T075-627000, www.zeavola.com. Set on the beachfront, close to the swimming pool or on the hillside among gardens of the flowering plant after which the resort is named (*Scaevola taccada*, in Thai the flower's name means Love the Sea). Some of the beautifully furnished wooden suites have outside showers and bathrooms with coloured ceramic sinks. Outside living areas with chairs and minibars are also a feature, although the mosquitoes can be horrific. The food is decidedly good though you can dine on the beach by candle-light or under the fabulous striped awning at the **Tacada** restaurant or enjoy Italian cuisine at **Baxil**, the covered restaurant. Excellent spa. There's a PADI dive centre and excursions are arranged. Staff are friendly, helpful and courteous. Transfers from Phuket ฿1750 and Krabi ฿ 1700 per person.

LL-B Pee Pee Viewpoint, 107 Moo 7, T075-622351. Around 60 airy a/c bungalows on stilts, surrounded by coconut trees. Big verandas. View of Loh Dalam Bay. Not all bungalows have good views and they are rather too close together.

LL-C Viking Resort, T075-819398, www.ppvikingresort.com. All of these huts have been individually designed

with Balinese influences. Most sit on the cliffside with seaviews, all have bags of character, with homely, warm touches such as floor rugs, paintings, lamps and 2 person hammocks. The cheapest share a bathroom and are possibly overpriced, the rest, for Phi Phi, are good value especially considering the attention given to creating a unique atmosphere. Very quiet and secluded sandy beach. Recommended.

AL-A Bay View Resort, 43/19 Moo 5, Laem Hin, T075-261360/4, www.phiphi bayview.com. Split-level bungalows on hill with views of Tonsai Cliffs and Phi Phi Ley. Pool.

A Banyan Villa, Ton Sai, T075-611233, www.phiphi-hotel.com. This is the sister resort of the **Phi Phi Hotel**. Its location is right in the centre of Ton Sai though its large gardens and pool create a secluded feel. Well run, though nothing too exciting, each room is en suite, with a/c and TV.

A-B Phi Phi Hotel, Ton Sai, T075-611233, www.phiphi-hotel.com. A decent enough, well-run hotel sited in a good location between and the beach and Ton Sai. All rooms are en suite, with balcony, TV and a/c.

A-C Maphrao, Ton Dao Beach, T075-622486. 3 grades of accommodation, the most expensive have own bathrooms. Restaurant, quiet, private beach, bungalows set on hill.

A-E Phi Phi Paradise Pearl, Hat Yao (Long Beach), T075-618050, info@ppparadise.com. Big, overpriced restaurant, quiet, 80 a/c bungalows with a range of rooms. Some have sea view. All clean. The cheaper ones have limited electricity and no fan, the more expensive ones are spacious. Tours are organized to Phi Phi Le, and kayaks, snorkels and fins are available for hire.

B Andaman Legacy, 1 Moo 7, T075-601106, www.phiphiandamanlegacy.com. Concrete bungalows arranged around a garden area with a swimming pool at its centre. Rooms are basic, with green pastel wallpaper. Only a short walk from the beach and there's a gym (฿150 per day) so guests can make sure they look buff before sunbathing.

B White House, 125/100 Moo 7, T075-601 300, www.whitephiphi.com. Rooms in this modern building are, you've guessed it, white. All come with a/c, hot water, cable TV. Cool, relaxing decor. The close proximity to the bars and restaurants might mean it's too noisy for some. Free Wi-Fi for guests.

B-C Chunut House, a little further up the path to **Oasis**, T075-601227. Bright, modern, airy and clean rooms in wooden huts arranged in a well kept garden. About a 10-min walk to Ton Sai Bay and Loh Dalum Bay.

C-D Phi Phi Twin Palm, Loh Dalum Bay, T075-601285. Simple bamboo huts, with fan, very near to the beach. More expensive ones have bathroom inside. Friendly staff.

C-E Phi Phi Long Beach, Hat Yao,T08-9973 6425 (mob). Very basic huts, good food, some private bathrooms, saltwater showers in dry season.

D Oasis, Phi Phi Don, after **Gypsy Village**. All 12 rooms, in this wooden building have fan and are en suite with hot water. Friendly management.

D-E Gypsy Village, Ton Sai Bay,T075-601045. Big stone bungalows on southeast side of island inland from former Phi Phi Resort. Bunglaows are spaced around nice open area. Big verandas. Quiet, but very tired looking. There are also bamboo bungalows that have seen better days, such as when the roof didn't leak, these are the cheapest option on the island.

D-E Pier Guesthouse, Ton Sai, T08-7002 4776 (mob). Decent little guesthouse in the heart of Ton Sai village. Rooms are mostly en suite and the more expensive ones have satellite TV and a/c as well. Good location and friendly vibe, though a little overpriced.

Koh Jum (Jam) *p536*

All of the accommodation on Koh Jum is listed on www.kohjumonline.com.There are around 20 bungalow operations on the tiny island. Prices vary according to the season but Koh Jum is generally very reasonably priced compared with some other island destinations although many of the bungalows

shut down for 6 months of the year so you do need to check. Accommodation is simple bamboo bungalows or other basic A-frame bungalows although more upmarket regimental set-ups are appearing. They are evenly spread along the beach.

B-F Joy Bungalows, T075-618199. Best known and most established resort; still the most imaginative in terms of variety. There are over 30 wooden family chalets with balconies on the beachfront, bamboo huts on stilts at back, wooden bungalows throughout, and treehouses – some of these set-ups even come with attached bathrooms (hot and cold water) and mosquito nets. Tour counter and an average restaurant. The bungalows at the back are not particularly well-kept and are too close together but the de luxe wooden chalet ones at the front are usually taken by families. **Joy Bungalows** also has hammocks slung along the beachfront which become more essential as the days wear on. There is a path which will take you to the Muslim and Chao Le village. Recommended.

C-D Andaman Beach Resort, T08-1693 1346 (mob). Around 20 modern A-frame chalets that look like pathological Wendy houses in mauve. They even have a fake balcony and 2nd floor. All are set facing each other in a square U-shaped plan on a rather bare site. These are different in ambience and style from other resorts and, one hopes, not a precursor to the homogenized bungalow barracks set-up seen on islands like Koh Lanta. Chalets have attached bathrooms with cold and hot-water showers and electricity from 1800-0500 (fans in rooms), which is a little more upmarket although some guests boasted of having electricity 24 hrs. This set-up is usually patronized by members of the Thai military or police when they need to stay on Koh Jum.

C-F Woodland Lodge, next to **Bodaeng Beach Resort**, T08-1893 5330 (mob), rayandsao@hotmail.com. Run by Englishman Ray and his Thai wife Sao, reliable concrete bungalow set-up. Some of the bungalows, which are nicely spaced from each other, can be too hot as they lack the necessary electricity for day-time fans. But they are kept clean and staff are very helpful. What makes this place stand out is a marooned Gilligan's Island feel as it acts as a meeting spot for expats on the island. The food is generally buffet but if you want anything special, Ray can fetch it at the markets in Krabi. Do be firm about how you want it cooked – in fact hover. One other thing, the establishment is next door to the Chao Le graveyard, apparently anathema to thieves. Recommended.

F-G Bodaeng Beach Resort, between Woodland Lodge and the Andaman Beach Resort. These are basic bamboo huts on stilts with shared bathroom. Some bungalows are on a terrifying tilt and really need to be taken down. Most are either on the beach or only a minute away. Attracts hardcore travellers and those seeking spiritual solace in physical discomfort. Excellent restaurant, however, the best of all the resorts. Entertaining owner with a roguish twinkle in her eyes and an outrageously contagious giggle. Do check the bills, however, as her maths needs a bit of work.

Koh Siboya p537, map p536
There are only 2 resorts on the island. Private houses can also be rented but it seems that most people who rent them are so attached to them that they stay for months and months. Friendly staff, good food and interesting residents.

A-E Thai West Resort, www.thai-west.com. A new resort offering a range of accommodation, from very basic bamboo huts to houses. Restaurant, and kayaks and mountain bikes for hire. Can also arrange tours.

C-F Siboya Bungalow, around 500 m south of Lang Koh Village on the west coast of Koh Siboya, T075-618026, T08-1979 3344 (mob), www.siboyabungalows.com. If you do plan on staying it is best to make arrangements for transportation after contacting their office in Krabi town or

on the island. Bungalows are simple bamboo affairs set in spacious gardens near the sea and vary in size and price.

🍴 Eating

Koh Phi Phi p533, map p534
Nearly all the food on the island is aimed at tourists and so few of the culinary delights found in the rest of the country are available here. There are some good Western restaurants though, and Ton Sai is packed with bakeries and all manner of seafood.

🍴 **Le Grand Bleu**, Ton Sai. French- and Thai-run restaurant near the pier. Excellent wine list and seafood make this one of the best places to eat on the island. Good atmosphere and friendly service.

🍴-🍴 **Amico Italian Restaurant**, Ton Sai, T08-1894 0876 (mob). Great little pizza and pasta place near the pier. Perfect pit stop if you're jumping on the ferry. Friendly with good, efficient service.

🍴 **Cosmic Pizza**, in a side street, Ton Sai. Recommended as serving the best pizza on the island.

🍴 **Unni's**, next to Plum's Rest, Phi Phi Don village. Tex-mex restaurant popular with the expat divers.

🍴-🍴 **Jasmin**, Laem Tong beach. A tiny little Thai eatery set next to the sea gypsy village. Tak (translates as grasshopper), the owner, is a friendly character who serves up excellent Thai food. The seafood is great and the beachside tables romantic. It is full every night with guests from the nearby luxury resorts. Highly recommended.

🍴-🍴 **Pee Pee Bakery**, Ton Sai. In the heart of Ton Sai this awesome little bakery and coffee house sells donuts, choc-chip cookies and anything else you need for a sugar rush.

Koh Jum p536, map 536
🍴 **Koh Jum Seafood**, on a mini pier next to the actual working pier. Choose fine fresh seafood directly from traps. Cooked to perfection with a sophisticated range of

ingredients – do not be surprised to find them cooking the shellfish in a broth of around 15 different ingredients. Having anything simply steamed would be a waste of their talents. Sweet views too – you can watch the birds following the boats for fish and all the activities of a working pier while taking in the islands opposite. It may seem expensive after the resorts but it is worth it.

¶ **Bodaeng Beach Resort**, see Sleeping, above. Excellent fare from the owner here, especially the salads and soups. But take a mosquito coil or repellent as the restaurant is open and set in a little from the beach. The best you will find among the resorts and the best price too. Recommended.

Foodstalls
You can also get simple noodle, chicken and rice dishes in the village street – particularly at **Mamas**. There is only 1 tiny street – the prices are slightly cheaper than the resorts with little difference in preparation or taste although more atmosphere.

🍸 Bars and clubs

Koh Phi Phi *p533, map p534*
Carlito's Bar, east from Ton Sai Bay. Well worth visiting just to get the real atmosphere of the island and its people. It used to cater to largely Swedish clientele but has since become more international.
Sunflower Bar, at the end of Loh Dalum Bay. This bar, made from flotsam and other debris, is a good place to chill out and enjoy a few cocktails. BBQ and live music.
Tiger Bar, next to Papaya Restaurant. Popular, if only for buy 1 get 1 free.

⛰ Activities and tours

Koh Phi Phi *p533, map p534*
As well as the activities listed below, kayaking can be arranged through resorts or tour

operators for about ฿700 per day; paddle boats can be rented for ฿150 per hr from the northern shore, where waterskiing is also possible; snorkelling is popular too, and snorkels and fins can be hired from most resorts and bungalows for ฿150 per day.

Diving
There are currently around 15 dive shops operating on Koh Phi Phi. Most of the dive shops charge the same with 2 local fun dives coming in at around ฿1800. Open Water courses start from ฿11,900. Alternatively, you can book with one of the many dive centres on Phuket.
Phi Phi Scuba Diving, main street in Ton Sai, T075-612665, www.phiphi-scuba.com; SSI (Scuba School International), offers a 5-day certificate course; **Visa Diving**, main street in Ton Sai, T076-618106, www.visa diving.com.

Fishing
Dang Dang Tour, T08-1894 2708 (mob). A full day is ฿8000 with gear for a maximum of 4 people, including food.

Rock climbing
The limestone cliffs here are known inter-nationally. There are 3 companies operating, including **Cat Climbers** and **Phi Phi Climbers**, www.krabidir.com/phiphiclimbers/index.htm. **KE Hang Out**, main street down from the pier at Ton Sai Bay. Probably the best, the most informative and the friendliest of the bunch. They are experienced climbers who have been here for 7 years. The funny and pleasant Mr Suthida is the owner. A ½-day costs ฿1000 for 4-5 hrs, ฿1500 for 8-9 hrs, and includes lunch, water and fruit. A 3-day course is ฿5000.

Therapies
Zeavola Spa, Zeavola, T075-627000. Open 0900-2100. It is definitely worth stopping by here for some wonderful treatments. The signature massage is the Zeavola Body Brush

Massage – a full-body brushing followed by a head massage then full-body massage with rice oil and lemongrass, kaffir lime and essential oils.

Tour operators
The North Star Travel, 125/101 Moo 7, T075-601279, northpole_nts@hotmail.com. Very helpful and friendly tourist information and booking centre. Not pushy, good level of English. Recommended.

Koh Jum *p536, map 536*
Tour operators
Koh Jum Center Tour, shop on the opposite side of Koh Jum Seafood and the pier at 161 Moo 3. Native Koh Jumian Wasana Laemkoh provides tickets for planes, trains, buses and boats. She will also change money, make overseas calls, and arrange 1-day boat trips. Her husband is a local fisherman so you may end up going with him. You can also rent motorbikes here. Honest and reliable.
Wildside Tours, along the road opposite Koh Jum Village School (signposted). This set-up, operated by a German lady, offers kayaking and snorkelling expeditions, and some trekking.

⊖ Transport

Koh Phi Phi *p533, map p534*
Boat
To **Krabi**, 2 services a day at 0900 and 1400, 1hr 45 mins, ฿350. Some of the resorts also offer private boat connections with Krabi.

Daily connections with **Ao Nang**, 1530, 2 hrs, ฿390; and **Rai Leh**, 1 hr 45 mins, ฿390 on the *Ao Nang Princess*. There are also boat connections with **Koh Lanta**, 1130, 1400 and 1500, 1 hr 15 mins, ฿350. Connections with **Phuket**, 0900 and 1430, 1 hr 45 mins, ฿350. There's a twice daily, seasonal service to Koh Lanta, Oct-Apr, ฿350.

① Directory

Koh Phi Phi *p533, map p534*
Banks Money may be exchanged at the resorts but for very poor rates indeed. It is best to change money in Ao Nang first. There are ATMs up and running on the island now. **Post office** Stamps can be bought and letters posted in the village.

Koh Lanta

➔ *Colour map 4, C2.*

It's not that long ago that Koh Lanta provided a genuine opportunity to get away from it all and have an authentic encounter with a unique local culture. There were no telephones, no electricity and the road that ran the length of the island was unpaved. Step off the boat at Sala Dan Pier today and into the rigorous grip of the resort ambushers with their private van service to one of more than 100 resorts and you can see that the island is in the grips of real estate mania.

But while three- to five-star resorts are pushing out bargain shoppers, there are still ฿300 backpacker bungalows towards the national park end of the island. Koh Lanta, with its 85% Muslim population increasingly attracts families and pensioners, mainly here for R&R although superb diving, including the world-famous Hin Daeng (Red Rock) and Hin Muong (Purple Rock), also pull in swashbuckling hardcore divers.

Beach overdevelopment aside, Koh Lanta's east coast is still underdeveloped with villagers dependent on wells and young people rejecting the traditional economy of rubber, cashew and fishing for the tourist industry. And, while it is worth a motorbike ride to see the east coast's rough and tumble hills with giant umbrella trees and the rare python sunning itself in the middle of the unfinished road, there are scant architectural gems apart from the Old Town, site of trade routes for China in the early 1900s and home to a sea gypsy village. The island was also affected by the tsunami of 2004 when several resorts were swamped and some tourists lost their lives – signs along the main road point to tsunami evacuation points, though even these have been misplaced, often resulting in conflicting directions. ▸▸ *For listings, see pages 549-557.*

Ins and outs

Getting there

The main access point to Koh Lanta is from Klong Chi Lard Pier, around 5 km out of Krabi Town to Sala Dan, via Koh Jum (two hours). The island largely shuts its tourist industry down during the wet season when unpredictable large waves make it too dangerous to cross (May to October). A minibus then takes visitors via two short car ferry crossings from Lanta Noi to Sala Dan (two hours). There are boat connections with Ban Hua Hin at the southern end of Koh Klang, and *songthaews* from Krabi to Ban Hua Hin. Minibuses also run from Trang and, during the high-season (November to March), boats run to and from Phi Phi. ▸▸ *See Transport, page 557, for further information.*

Getting around

Not one bay area accessible from the road has not been developed. To get to the resorts and bungalows, there is a road which stretches the length of the island from Sala Dan Pier to the national park end. It is now fully sealed making exploration of the Island easy. However the roads leading to resort land are seriously potholed, steep and after periods of dry weather covered with plumes of chronic red dust. Further down this road, as it approaches the national park and the sealed tarmac ends, accidents are common, it therefore makes sense to wear long trousers and sturdy footwear,

Songthaews are the main form of public transport around the island, though they are few and far between. Motorbikes and mountain bikes are available for hire from guest-houses, some shops and tour companies. Although the rental situation has improved greatly with most places renting out nearly new motorbikes, it is advisable to check the tyres, the brakes and the tank before you set off as most of the rental places expect you to sign a contract before you set off agreeing to pay for any damages incurred. A more reliable solution is to rent a jeep but these are considerably more expensive unless you find other people to share the costs. Long-tailed boats can be chartered for coastal trips. There are also a smattering of tuk-tuks in Sala Dan but prices are high – even for the shortest 2-km hop.

Koh Lanta

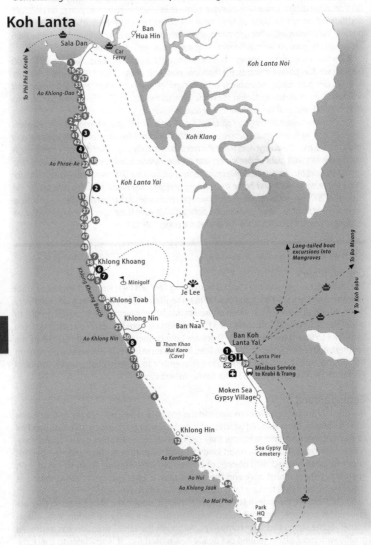

Background

Koh Lanta is packed with bungalows and resorts. Some of these set-ups are replete with internet, minimarts, souvenir shops, spas, restaurants, pools and bars so that guests need never leave. Meanwhile, on the main road, there is almost a total absence of cultural outposts like libraries, bookshops or music stores. Instead, the road is dominated by restaurants in shacks, garages, the occasional massage and tattoo parlour and general grocery shops along with *farang*- tailored bars that promise the latest football results and pub dinners. Still, in the evening when the fairylights are switched on and the dust clouds expand with Saharan girth, it is bearable – briefly.

There is a sizeable sea gypsy village to the southeast of the island, where the inhabitants continue with a lifestyle they have maintained for generations. The village comprises shacks – some awash with the flotsam and jetsam of a fishing life – from broken equipment to torn nets mixed in with today's ecologically nightmarish household rubbish. From the lack of any businesses set up to lure in tourists – even the most basic cafés – it is clear they have no wish to become yet another 'tourist attraction'. Walking through the chaotic layout of their living space, it is impossible not to intrude and, while the Chao Le are remarkably patient and gracious, it is perhaps better to resist curiosity about the 'indigenous lifestyle' unless invited. Yet local tour operators on the island and further afield are now including this village in their itineraries. If you have a concern about infringing on the rights of these communities, you should check with tour operators about the extent to which their wishes are respected, and the extent to which they receive benefits from the visits.

N

1 km
1 mile

Sleeping ●
Andaman Lanta Resort 2
Atcha Hut 50
Blue Marlin Resort 11
Blue Sky Resort &
    Restaurant 42
Chaba Bungalows &
    Art Gallery 24
Chaw Ka Cher Lanta
    Tropicana Resort 35
Costa Lanta 1
Dream Team 4
D R Lanta Bay Resort 29
Fisherman's Cottage 5
Freedom Estate 18
Golden Bay 6
Hans Restaurant &
    Bungalows 29
Holiday Villa 2
Khlong Jark Bungalows 34
Lanta Bee Garden 26
Lanta Coconut Green
    Field 7
Lanta Emerald Resort 47
Lanta Garden Home
    Resort 9
Lanta Island Resort 36
Lanta Long Beach 10
Lanta Marina Resort 11
Lanta Marine Park
    Resort 12
Lanta Mermaid Boutique
    House 37
Lanta Miami 13
Lanta Nature Beach
    Resort 14

Lanta Palace 15
Lanta Paradise 17
Lanta River Sand 19
Lanta Riviera Bungalow 20
Lanta Sand Resort & Spa 2
Lanta Sea House 21
Lanta Sunny House 22
Lanta Thip House 38
Mango House 39
Mook Lanta 45
Narima Bungalow
    Resort 23
Nice & Easy 48
Palm Beach Resort 42
Pimalai Resort 25
Rawi Warin Resort & Spa 40
Relax Bay 27
Royal Lanta 16
Sayang Beach 28
Sea Culture House 46
Somewhere Else 41
Southern Lanta Resort 33
Sri Lanta 30
Sun, Fun & Sea Resort 29
Thai House Beach Resort 43
Where Else Resort 49

Eating ●
Bulan Lanta 7
Cook Kai 8
Danny's 3
Green Leaf Café 6
Krue Lanta Yai 1
Mr Wee Pizzeria 4
Retro 2
Rom Thai 5

Around the island
● ● ▸▸ *pp549-557*.

Sala Dan
This dusty two-street town on the northern tip of the island is most arrivees' introduction

to Koh Lanta, as the majority of ferries and boats dock here. During the high season it can resemble the Village of the Damned with throngs of blond, blue-eyed Scandinavians mingling with the grumpy locals most of whom seem keen to fleece every dumb *farang* that passes through. To cut to the chase, Sala Dan is geared to emptying the pockets of tourists as quickly as possible. If you're used to the charms of sleepy rural Thailand, turning up here can fel like you're in a different country. Sala Dan does provide numerous facilities, including banks, ATMs, internet, bars and restaurants, though most are excessively overpriced, filled with *farang* and serving up weak examples of Thai food.

Ban Koh Lanta Yai

Blink and you miss it; Ban Koh Lanta Yai, the old administrative centre and port on Koh Lanta, now known as 'Ban Koh Lanta' or simply as 'nai talad' (in the market), is developing its own tourism niche. With stunning views across to the islands of Koh Bubu, Koh Po, Ko Kum and Koh Tala Beng, and most of its original old wooden shophouse/fishing houses still standing, this micro-town, which is actually only a couple of streets, has buckets of charm. Here, local entrepreneurs have opened galleries and souvenir shops, there are bed and breakfasts and the closest thing to family stays available on the island (see Sleeping, page 549). Ban Koh Lanta really comprises one main street that doesn't even go on for that long. The end of this road is indicated by an extraordinary ancient tree rather like a banyan and a tiny canal rivulet. There is a distinct Thai-Chinese ambience with rows of busy shophouses, each replete with its own exotically plumed bird in a wooden cage. Trade on this main street is largely fishing tackle shops and general goods stores, indicating the locals' overruling occupations. There are excellent restaurants offering either good working man's fare or more sophisticated seafood dishes.

Koh Bubu

Koh Bubu is a tiny uninhabited island in the Lanta group of Koh Lanta Yai which takes a mere 15 minutes to walk around. There is one resort, see Sleeping, page 550. People who have stayed here return to the mainland completely relaxed and detached from the world they left behind. There is a very pleasant walk around the island and lots of birdwatching opportunities.

Ao Khlong Dao

Ao Khlong Dao, which starts on the edge of Sala Dan, was one of the first bays to open to tourism in Koh Lanta and as little as eight years ago had only about six small bungalow resorts and a couple of independent restaurants, not to mention the occasional buffalo family going for a paddle in the sea. While it is a lovely bay with soft sand and pleasant views over to Deer Neck Cape, development here has been rapid and unplanned. The bay is now heavily developed with most resorts encroaching onto the beach, each separated by high walls. Khlong Dao itself is a relatively safe place to swim and good for families and with the number of 'proper' hotels, it is often booked via travel agencies offering package tours to Lanta.

Ao Phra-Ae (Long Beach)

Ao Phra-Ae, also known as Long Beach, is a lovely beach to stroll on with soft white sand and a very long, gently sloping stretch that allows for safe swimming at both low and high tides. In the late evening, as you splash your feet in the waves close to the shore, a magical phospheresence appears as if you are walking on a thin surface of stars.

This beach is catering increasingly to well-healed retirees and families, particularly the Scandinavians although there are still remnants of its earlier days as a backpacker haven with restaurants and bars like the **Ozone**. In its central area, near the **Opium Restaurant and Bar**, Ao Phra-Ae has several bars including the well-established, very popular and predictable **Reggae Bar**. While great for those who like to party all night and sleep all day, the newer lot of tourists have complained about the noise although everyone seems to like the by-now standard fire shows. The area around Lanta Sandy Beach has a slightly more laid-back character with late-night pizzerias and fairylight festooned beach bars. The resorts here are no longer owned by local families and the bungalow resorts make their most lucrative profits through restaurant and bar sales. To encourage their guests to 'stay at home', many of the resorts have created barriers that extend right down to the beach and may use barbed wire or natural borders like strategically planted palms to keep the tourists in. This has resulted in more independently minded travellers feeling trapped and resentful and has generated an atmosphere of comically poisonous competition between the resorts. Perhaps the only delightful upshot of the tsunami was that the waves destroyed many of these barriers, allowing 'rival' guests to almost forget they were actually still in a compound comprised of an endless number or resorts staggered to only one side of the island.

Hat Khlong Khoang

Hat Khlong Khoang is advertised by some as the 'most beautiful beach on Lanta'. But the beach is fairly steep down to the sea and the sand not as fine as that at Long Beach. The views along the bay are pleasant, but not spectacular. Behind many bungalow resorts is a canal which is treated as a dump for all sorts of waste from construction debris to coconut husks. In many parts of the beach it smells and is a mosquito trap and consequently best avoided if you are offered a room anywhere near. That said, there are a handful of establishments with real character and charm and, offshore, there are coral reefs that are increasingly attracting snorkellers and divers.

Khlong Toab

Khlong Toab, just beyond the Fisherman's Cottage and close to Khlong Toab village, supports two resorts in marked contrast to each other. It is a quiet area and the beach shelves gently and the swimming is safe, so is particularly suitable for families.

Ao Khlong Nin

Ao Khlong Nin is a bit of a mixed bag in terms of accommodation, ranging from basic backpacker places through to the top-of-the-range resorts. There is, as they say, just about something for everyone. The beach itself is picturesque with rocks dotted about and not just a single sweep of sand; the sand is white and fine. The downside is that this means that swimming, in places, can be tricky. Usually, though, it is possible to find a safe place to swim.

Ao Kantiang

Ao Kantiang was once the cheap and secluded hideaway for many Europeans and Scandinavians who spent months resting in bungalows overlooking the bay. With golden sand, steeply sloping hillsides and only a small village, the only accommodation was locally owned and operated and set well back from the local community. All that has changed with the arrival of the **Pimalai Resort**. This luxury resort has completely altered the feel of this bay. Speedboats send guests off to a floating jetty (thus avoiding putting any money into local coffers through the ferry and avoiding the road which was substantially torn up by the construction vehicles building the resort). The Scandinavians still frequent this beach, as do wealthy European retirees.

Ao Khlong Jaak
Ao Khlong Jaak used to be one of the most peaceful bays on Koh Lanta, a relatively small bay with sloping hills to the north and south and coconut plantations and grassland in the middle. However, there is rampant land speculation in this area now, as with all the beaches. In the bay area there is an elephant trekking station (up to the waterfall), and the barbed wire marking off land plots that was washed away by the waves will no doubt return. It is important to remember that during the dry season the waterfall turns to a trickle, as this is one of the main selling points of Klong Jark. However, it is still possible to find cheap accommodation and more independently minded tourists here.

Ao Mai Phai
Ao Mai Phai is the last bay before the national park and one of the few on the west coast of Lanta with good snorkelling opportunities. Again, it is a relatively small bay with steeply sloping hills leading down to the bay on the north and south and with a more extensive area of flatter land in the middle.

Moo Koh Lanta Marine National Park
① ฿400.
The park covers much of the southern part of the island and extends over numerous islands in the area including Koh Rok, Hin Muang and Hin Daeng. The national park headquarters is at Laem Tanod and involves either a boat trip or a long and painful drive. The road to the park is in very bad condition and practically impassable during the rainy season. The peninsula is named after the tanod trees (a type of sugar palm) that grow throughout the area and give it an almost prehistoric atmosphere. There are two bays and in the middle is the lighthouse (navy controlled but the peninsula is accessible to the public). One bay has fine soft sand and is great for swimming. The other, which faces west, bears the full brunt of the monsoons and is rocky and a good place to explore if you like rock pools. Beyond the visitor centre and the toilet and shower block, is a lily pond and the park headquarters. Just beyond this, is a nature trail which takes you up a fairly precipitous path into the forest and then along a contour around the back of the offices in a half loop ending at the road entering the park. It's a well-designed trail though not suitable for children or the elderly because the path is very steep in the early parts and can be slippery. Take plenty of water and some snacks with you. The bay is surrounded by forested hills and filled with forest sounds and the gentle or not so gentle sound of waves crashing on to the rocks or beach (depending on the season). It is a beautiful spot to spend a day swimming and walking, and then watching the sunset from the viewpoint on Laem Tanod.

Koh Lanta Noi
If you take the car ferry route to Lanta Yai, Lanta Noi is the island you cross between the two ferry crossings. Undeveloped for tourism, this island is dominated by mangrove forest and paperbark forest. Few tourists visit the island, but it is worth making a quick visit from Sala Dan using the small long-tailed boats. This will take you to the pier used for

the district office (now located on Lanta Noi but once based in Ban Koh Lanta Yai). From here you can walk for at least a couple of hours along a stretch of beach complete with casuarina trees and paperbark forest. With good views to the coast and across to islands, this is a pleasant place from which to escape the noise and dust of the main island. Also on Lanta Noi, but on the main road and in the only village passed en route to Koh Lanta, is a women's group shop that sells the woven matting bags, mats, etc that you may see in souvenir shops on Lanta Yai. Prices here are not much lower than what you'd pay in the shops, but at least all of the money goes to the makers. The quality of the weaving here is very high.

Had Thung Thale Non-Hunting Area, Koh Klang

① There are few organized tours to this area, but you can self-drive. Signs are reasonably well marked – it's about 17 km off the main road down a couple of turn-offs and through some small villages and plantations.

Had Thung Thale Non-Hunting Area is on Koh Klang, but you'll have a hard time spotting that fact even if you do drive over to Lanta Yai and take the car ferries. Koh Klang is joined to the mainland by a bridge. The non-hunting area comprises several hundred hectares of beautiful paperbark forest (*pa samet*), coastal grasslands and casuarina forest, and is bordered with some beautiful long stretches of grey/white beaches. Rarely visited, occasionally it is taken over completely with local school trips for their scouting activities and government groups on corporate bonding sessions – the same sort that go to Tarutao. There are several conservation projects sponsored by the king. The paperbark forests have a bleak but beautiful aspect, are fragrant and present relatively easy walking opportunities.

◉ Koh Lanta listings

For Sleeping and Eating price codes and other relevant information, see pages 44-49.

● Sleeping

Most bungalow operations are scattered down the west coast of Koh Lanta Yai and usually offer free pick-ups from the pier at Sala Dan. Even if you do not have a place sorted out, you will be inundated with reps on the boats traversing between the various islands, most with photo albums showing pics – though not very reliable ones – of their resorts and promising discounts because they like you. You might find the hail-fellow-well-met routine unravels once they hand over the key to your room but it is still best to stay on good terms, as there is considerable communication between the various touts. Travel agents and tour companies in Krabi and Ao Nang advertise accommodation on Koh Lanta so it is possible to get a pretty good idea of the various places before arriving. The choice is basically between simple concrete bungalows (some with a/c), bamboo or wood bungalows (usually fan), luxury resorts one step away from a theme song, and chic spa boutique resorts that offer total comfort and brand T-shirts. Some resorts have been nicknamed 'chicken farms' for their unimaginative and overcrowded lay-out and there are more and more of these turning up, erected in cleared land that has been scraped clean of trees and foliage. Further south along the coast, there are some new and more interesting resorts and the whole area is much less crowded and has a peaceful atmosphere (although there are regular parties during the high season). There is considerable variation between high season (Nov-May) and low season (Jun-Oct) rates, with a lowseason rate being roughly half that of the high season rate.

Ban Koh Lanta Yai *p546, map p544*
The tiny old town of Lanta keenly displays the charm of a non-segregated version of tourism as opposed to the Thai-corp style where tourists stay in one place and residents stay in another. It must be said that there are very few places to stay here – a good sign as the village is reliant on other forms of income and hasn't succumbed to the draw of the tourist dollar.

A-B Mango House, middle of the main street, T075-697181, www.kolanta.net/south ern lantaresort.htm. Very nicely restored old wooden house overlooking the sea. Rooms are nicely decorated and some have views over to Bubu island. No a/c and shared facilities throughout. Was once, allegedly, a government-run opium den. The owners also have a number of villas and houses for rent (**A-C**). Certainly one of the most original places to stay on the island and a massive departure from the clichéd resorts aimed at package tourists or dull-as-dishwater bamboo huts that are the preserve of the unadventurous backpacker. Highly recommended.

Koh Bubu *p546*
C-D Boo Boo Island Resort, T075-612536. Restaurant and little else except sea and solitude. The electricity goes off after 2200 and you are left to the sound of the waves and the moonlight. That said, the beds are rather uncomfortable and the beach is difficult to swim off during low tide because of the sea urchins.

Ao Khlong Dao *p546, map p544*
LL Costa Lanta, Moo 3, T02-6623550, www.costalanta.com. Tranquillity and privacy are the order of the day at this exclusive resort. Whilst modernism may not be to everybody's taste, this resort has succeeded in creating a very different ambiance, somewhere between modern urban living and beach hide-away. Standard rooms have huge, floor to ceiling teak doors that concertina back to completely open 2 sides to the elements, flooding the rooms

with natural light. As you would expect there is a swimming pool and restaurant. Recommended for its serenity.

LL-AL Lanta Sand Resort and Spa, Ao Khlong Dao edging to Ao Phra-Ae, T075-684633, www.lantasand.com. Excellent reports from this luxury resort next to **Sayang Resort**. Spacious rooms plus amazing bathroom with glass wall so that the monkeys can peer in while you are taking a bath. The tubs are also a good size. Good service, fine food. Prices double during high season. Recommended.

LL-AL Royal Lanta, 222 Moo 3, Khlong Dao Beach, Sala Dan, T075-684361, www.royal lanta.com. Aiming for the family market with children's pool and playground. Also offers spa, minimart, internet and good coffee shop selling tasty cakes. Impersonal large restaurant, rather bare rooms. Over 50 cottages with red steeply pitched roofs.

L-A DR Lanta Bay Resort, 206 Moo 3, T075-684383, www.drlantaresort.com. Typical resort-style accommodation ranging from rooms to bungalows. All rooms come with TV, fridge, a/c, safety deposit box and hot water. The management try to be as accommodating as possible. Possibly overpriced.

L-C Holiday Villa, 220 Moo 3, Sala Dan, T075-684370, www.holidayvillalanta.com. This is a large 42-room hotel at the southern end of Ao Khlong Dao. Big concrete suite bungalows and a pool. Rooms are spacious but rather dark, and the furniture and decorations look somewhat out of place in this seaside setting. Tiled floors make for a clean, cool surface.

AL-A Lanta Sea House, 15 Moo 3, Sala Dan, T075-684073-4, www.lantaseahouse resort.com. Bungalows near beach, and pool. Consistently well-kept establishment. 2 grades of room, both are clean and well supplied, the more expensive have spacious balconies and their own bathroom. Very good value in the low season.

AL-B Andaman Lanta Resort, 142 Moo 3, Khlong Dao Beach, T075-684200-2, www.andamanlantaresort.com. Towards the south, this was the first real hotel on Koh Lanta, which is used as a selling point. The 2-storey building of 69 rooms is not very pretty, and although there is a pool, these rooms are overpriced for what they are. The blue-roofed bungalow rooms are better value and nicer. Not the friendliest place.

AL-B Golden Bay, 22 Moo 3, T075-684161, www.goldenbaylanta.com. There are 3 styles of room, all with TV, fridge, a/c and hot water. Hotel room ambience. Friendly, helpful owners and an easy place to get to. Awesome restaurant serving some of the best Thai and Isaan food on the beach.

AL-B Southern Lanta Resort, 105 Moo 3, T075-684175, www.southernlanta.com. Concrete bungalows, clean if a tad boring. Price varies with location. All rooms have a/c, TV, fridge. There is a restaurant, swimming pool, shop and internet. Staff are friendly, helpful and speak very good English. Renovations planned for next season.

A Lanta Mermaid Boutique House, 333 Moo 3 Khlong Dao Beach, T075-684364, www.lantamermaid.com. Well-designed and contemporary small hotel set on the main road 200 m from the beach. Rooms are all a/c and en suite with balconies and cable TV – the ones at the back are both quieter and cheaper.

A-B Lanta Bee Garden, 199 Moo 3, T075-684227, www.lantabeegarden.com. Clean but unimaginative chalet-style bungalows. Both fan and a/c are available, some rooms have a bathtub.

A-D Lanta Garden Home Resort, 18 Moo 3, T075-684084, www.krabidir.com/lanta gardenhome. This resort offers a variety of accommodation. The cheapest have fan and shared facilities; the most expensive, have hot water, a/c and beachside location.

A-D Sayang Beach, situated just south of the Lanta Villa between Khlong Dao and Ao Phra-Ae, T08-1476 6357 (mob), www.say angbeachlanta.com. This operation is run by a local family that took care to protect the environment while constructing their

bungalows (unlike many), leaving trees to provide necessary shade and ambience. Excellent food cooked by one of the daughters, with fresh fish nightly. The bungalows are large; the ones towards the beachfront are better quality, while the others at the back are rather too close together.

A-E Chaba Bungalows & Art Gallery, 20 Moo 3, Khlong Dao beach, T075-684 118, www.krabidir.com/chababungalows. Walk along Khlong Dao beach and you'll eventually come across a series of strange, brightly coloured, amorphous shapes. This is the original frontage for this tiny self-made resort. The rooms and bungalows, while offering some attempt to get away from the usual resort offerings, are not that inspired. Having said that, Chaba is very friendly with an un-corporate feel and the rooms/bungalows are good value. The art gallery holds various exhibitions differing in quality. Good food. Recommended.

B-C Sun, Fun & Sea Resort, 240 Moo 3, T075-684025. Both fan and a/c rooms have hot water but both are dated and the beds uncomfortably old. Good location but still overpriced.

B-D Lanta Island Resort, 10 Moo 3, T075-684124, www.lantaislandresort.com. These concrete fan and a/c bungalows, in a jungle setting, are clean enough but a little tired looking. The cheaper huts are further back from the beach. Staff are helpful and there is a swimming pool.

E Hans Restaurant & Bungalows, next to Fun, Sun & Sea, T075-684152. Basic, clean wooden bugalows with cold water bathrooms. Fresh coffee available. Nothing special, but the location is great.

Ao Phra-Ae (Long Beach) p546, map p544

AL-A Chaw Ka Cher Lanta Tropicana Resort, 352 Moo 2, T08-1895 9718 (mob), www.lantatropicanaresort.com. Set on a hill just off the main road at the far southern end of Ao Phra-Ae, this is a very friendly and beautifully set out resort. The gorgeous bungalows have open-air bathrooms and are much bigger than anything in a similar price-range on the beach. Pool, excellent restaurant, free internet, huge library. 500 m from the beach; owners supply bicycles to get you there. Recommended.

AL-B Relax Bay, 111 Moo 2, T075-684194, www.relaxbay.com. 48 large wooden bungalows, some basic some VIP, raised high off the ground and scattered through a beachside grove, unusual angles to the roofs and comfortable verandas. Very quiet, all rooms have glass and/or mosquito panels in the windows, fans and shower rooms in the open air adjoining. Spartan decor – airy. 2 beach bars and café, French owned and managed. Excellent service and lay-out. Recommended.

AL-C Palm Beach Resort, 47 Moo 3, T075-684603, www.lantapalmbeach resort.com. Although the concrete a/c and fan bungalows are the same old same old, they are clean and the staff are helpful. Next to a hippy-like village, situated on the beach, which is full of bars and restaurants.

AL-E Mook Lanta, 343 Moo 2, T075-684638, www.mooklanta.com. Both the bungalows and rooms have been built with considerable attention to detail. All rooms, even fan, come with hot water and Wi-Fi access. Beautifully designed with nice finishes such as silk throws, mood lighting and curtains. The management go out of their way to be helpful. Also offers massage and spa services. Highly recommended.

A-B Lanta Long Beach, 172 Moo 3, T075-684198, www.lantalongbeach.com. A/c or fan thatched bamboo huts with mosquito nets provided. Also family bungalows with Bali-style bathrooms. Nice feature of sliding doors. Verandas too and a new bar.

A-D Thai House Beach Resort, 38/2 Moo 2, T075-684289, www.thaihousebeachresort. net. This resort is on the beach and offers a range of rooms, including some spacious bungalows, a/c and fan. Friendly management offers discounts for long-term stays.

B Freedom Estate, 157 Moo 2, www.free domestate.com. At the back of Ao Phra-Ae and up Lanta hill, overlooking the beach. 6 self-contained and serviced fan units with gas-oven kitchens, good for families who tire of eating out all the time, but you would need access to transport into the markets in Sala Dan or the old town. You could also try buying fish directly from the Chao Le fishermen in the Old Town. Balcony. Excellent value in the low season. Recommended.

B Last Horizon Resort, 175 Moo 2, Baan Phu Klom Beach, www.lantalanta.com/last_ horizon_resort/index.html. last_horizon@ hotmail.com. 25 nicely designed stone bungalows in a coconut grove with attached showers, 24-hr electricity, restaurant and beach bar. Friendly management, motor-bikes for hire, tours arranged. The beach here is only suitable for swimming at high tide. Recommended.

C-E Lanta Sunny House, 42 Moo 2, Ao Phra-Ae, T075-684347. Fan or a/c rooms. Tired looking guesthouse which has seen better days. The beach is a short walk down an alleyway. Restaurant and internet.

C-E Somewhere Else, next to Lanta Sand Resort, T09-7311312. The bamboo huts with decorative woven walls are rather dark inside. Fan and mosquito net. Pretty bathrooms with cold water. Size of room dictates the price. Great cabanas right on the beach.

D Blue Marlin Resort, next to Lanta Marina. Simple bamboo huts. Friendly staff, nice rustic feel to this whole area, given the absence of concrete bungalows, and the simple design of bungalows and restaurants.

D-E Blue Sky Resort & Restaurant, 238 Moo 3, T075-684871, www.krabidir.com/ blueskylanta. Bamboo huts, very clean and surprisingly spacious. Good mix of nationalities stay here. Check for discounts if you are staying for a while. Super friendly staff. Recommended for its beachfront location.

E-F Lanta Marina Resort, 147 Moo 2, www.kolanta.net/LANTAMARINA.htm. Bamboo bungalows on stilts which look a bit like haystacks but are comfortably, if basically, furnished with mattresses on the floor and mosquito nets, some with bathrooms attached. Good access to beach with swimming.

F Sea Culture House, 317 Moo 3, T075-684 541. Next to Relax Bay on a very quiet stretch of beach with soft sand – the sea here is good for swimming. Basic wooden bungalows which are sturdier than they look. Bathroom inside. Owner also rents out tents for ฿100. For this price and location, recommended.

Hat Khlong Khoang *p547, map p544*

A-E Lanta Emerald Resort, 154 Moo 2, T075-667037. Bamboo fan bungalows at the back and concrete a/c rooms nearer the beach. Family atmosphere and a laid-back vibe with many people returning year after year. Swimming pool, internet and restaurant.

B Nice and Easy, 315 Moo 2, T075-667105. It's easy to spot this resort as the owner's art deco house-cum-spaceship, fronts onto the beach. The a/c bungalows resemble Swiss cottages inside, very quaint with frilly curtains. There is a small pool and the staff are friendly.

B-D Lanta Riviera Bungalow, 121 Moo 1, Sala Dan, T075-667044, www.lanta riviera.com. Bungalows with fan or a/c and attached shower, quiet and relaxed atmosphere. Bar, restaurant, internet and swimming pool. Recently renovated.

B-E Where Else Resort, next to Bee Bee, T075-667173. This place has bags of character and a lot of thought has gone into the design of the bamboo bungalows. These rustic huts are half hidden in the jungle garden, just back from the beach. All have bathrooms, mosquito screens and hammocks on the balcony. The ones at the back are a little cramped together. Recommended.

C-E Lanta Thip House, 361 Khlong Khoang Beach, T075-684-888, www.lantathip house.com. Small hotel set on the main road about 200 m from the northern end of the beach. Rooms are all a/c, en suite and have a contemporary, modern feel. Friendly owners and excellent food and coffee.

D Fisherman's Cottage, 190 Moo 2, Klong Khong Beach, T08-1476 1529 (mob), www.krabidir.com/fishermanscottage. Collection of 11 moody, atmospheric bungalows, all with sea views, on a steep bend of the main island road before the turn-off to the national park. Decorated with style, most of the many owners and staff appear to be artists. Trendy, though there is a family cottage, and the staff are very family friendly – so is the beach area which is gently shelving and a safe place to swim. Good ambient music at the bar – also deep house and hip hop. Recommended.

E-F Lanta Coconut Green Field, 78 Moo 2, Tambon Sala Dan, T075-684284, www.kolanta.net/coconutgreenfield.htm. Pleasant bamboo bungalows in a coconut plantation by a rocky shore. Friendly staff and peaceful setting. Restaurant and bar (**Robinhood Bar**) with movie showings.

Khlong Toab *p547, map p544*

LL-AL Rawi Warin Resort and Spa, 139 Moo 8, T075-607400, www.rawi warin.com. The most luxurious and most expensive resort on the island. This is a massive development of stunning pool villas (US$2000 a night), incredible facilities including a floating swimming pool and a private cinema. There's even a music room featuring a US$150,000 stereo system built by the hi-fi-obsessed Chinese owner. Awesome service, food and everything – it remains to be seen if it can fill its very expensive rooms.

A-B Lanta Palace, 29 Moo 8, T075-662571, www.lantapalace.com. Looks like something straight out of a European seaside resort, with white concrete cottages in a small garden. The bungalows are a bit too close together, but this is a quiet part of the coastline, comfortable and popular with families.

C-D Lanta River Sand T075-662660, www.lantariversand.com. This is actually between Khlong Toab and Klong Nin beaches. Touted as being made from 'ecological materials grown locally' (or trees), these

15 simple bamboo bungalows are set around a brackish water lagoon and in amongst trees with lots of mosquitos. It is also the sister resort of **Lanta Marina**. Interesting and in a more secluded location, even if a little dark. Also a reasonable-ish price for these parts.

Ao Khlong Nin *p547, map p544*

AL Sri Lanta, Moo 6, T075-662688, www.srilanta.com. Spacious, well-designed bamboo and wood bungalows with a/c (but sadly no mosquito screening or ceiling fans) and hot showers. The bathrooms are semi-outdoors. Beautiful black-tiled pool right on the beach. Fan-cooled restaurant in similar style and a spa in garden area adjacent to the pool and other facilities. Beautiful spot on the bay with rocks adding character to the area, but still with access to a sandy beach for swimming. Attracts prosperous Scandinavians. Recommended.

AL-B Narima Bungalow Resort, 98 Moo 5, Klong Nin, T075-662668, www.narima-lanta.com. Large bungalows with wooden floors overlooking a quiet part of beach. Wall of sliding glass doors. Doctors own this place. The restaurant here also serves a greater variety of Thai dishes than most places. Pool, exercise bicycle, DVDs, CDs and a mini-library. Good reductions if you stay for 7 or 14 nights. Recommended.

AL-C Dream Team, 38 Moo 5, www.dream-team-beach-resort.th66.com. Good restaurant using their own home-grown produce. Wooden houses with fans and a/c and night time electricity, steps leading up, gardens but facing a rocky beach.

A-B Lanta Paradise, 67 Moo 6, www.lantalanta.com/lanta_paradise_bungalows/index.html. Doesn't have such a pleasant beach, all beds have mosquito nets and fans. Some bungalows are behind the road away from the beach. But atmosphere more hippy-trippy here even if it does have a pool. Tour desk. Motorbike rental available.

A-D Lanta Miami, 13 Moo 6, T075-697081, www.lantamiami.com. A/c and fan available. Family-run, all rooms come with attached

bathrooms. Rooms are quite closely packed with vertigo-inducing pseudo-marquetry stripes across floor and ceiling and shiny walls. Looks far more peaceful from outside with wide verandas and rustic wooden clapboard fronts. Snorkelling organized from here. Wide range of room rates.

A-F Lanta Nature Beach Resort, 54 Moo 6, www.krabidir.com/lantanaturebeach. Good bungalows, friendly and helpful owners. Again more of a traveller feel to this place. Good discounts in the off season, reflected in the price range quoted.

E Atcha Hut, 70 Moo 6, T094-704607, www.atchahut.com. This area has a bohemian arty feel to it. The concrete bungalows have been finished to resemble an adobe finish and for this price, right on the beach, they are a steal. The owner has tried to create an artistic vibe rather than just a business, although the party atmosphere might be a little too much for those seeking tranquillity and solitude. Beachfront bar and yoga classes. There are more good value bungalows further down.

Ao Kantiang *p547, map p544*

LL Pimalai Resort, 99 Moo 5, Ba Kan Tiang Beach, T075-607999, www.pimalai.com. Yet another resort to make big claims about the pristine nature of its setting with the implication that staying here will not be causing damage to the environment or local culture. Huge resort, beautifully designed rooms, although parts of the garden look very sparse and there's an awful lot of concrete used in creating terraces, steps and roads. The resort also encroaches onto the beach – something which undoes its avowed eco-aims in one fell swoop. All facilities are on offer as one would expect for a resort of this type. More of the same to come.

A-B Lanta Marine Park Resort, 58 Moo 5, www.krabidir.com/lantampv/index.htm. Set up high on the hill overlooking Ao Kantiang with great views of the bay from the bungalows in the front. Several styles of bungalows: the small bamboo ones set back from the view are the cheapest; the larger concrete ones with views from the balconies are the most expensive. Rooms are spacious and comfortable. The walk up to the bungalows will keep you fit. Free pick-up from Sala Dan.

Ao Khlong Jaak *p548, map p544*
AL-A Andalanta Resort, T075-612084, www.discoverythailand.net/kohlanta/water fall_bay.html. Well-run resort set amid trees and by the beach. Variety of wood bungalows, good facilities. Boat trips are organized to nearby islands and other places of interest.
F-G Khlong Jark Bungalows. Simple bamboo bungalows. Frogs in the room can be very pleasant to hear late at night. Good slap-dash atmosphere. Closed in low season.

Ao Mai Phai *p548, map p544*
There are several bungalow resorts in this bay from **Bamboo Bay Resort** to **Last Resort**. All offer roughly the same style accommodation in **D-G** range with simple bamboo bungalows and varying degrees of access to the sea/ views, etc. All seem friendly. It's difficult to get to in the rainy season given the bad state of the road, but a good escape from the more built-up resort areas on Koh Lanta and within easy reach of the national park.

❶ Eating

All the guesthouses and hotels provide restaurants with similar menus.

Sala Dan *p545, map p544*
In Sala Dan there are some small cafés, **Swiss Bakery** and **Santos**, good pastries and coffee. 3 restaurants overlook the bay between Lanta Yai and Lanta Noi (rather windy):
❡ **Seaview 1** (aka **Monkey in the Back**). Slow service, good seafood, no electricity, cheap.
❡ **Seaview 2** Larger menu, Thai and seafood, friendly, cheap. The enormous scones are tasty and filling.

Ban Koh Lanta Yai *p546, map p544*
❡❡❡-❡❡ **Mango Bar & Bistro**, below Mango House guesthouse. Decent Thai and Western food in this great little hangout. Bar serves cocktails and various whiskies.
❡❡ **Krue Lanta Yai Restaurant**, at the end of 'town', T075-697062. Hours variable. A restaurant on the pier along a walkway filled with plants. Good selection of fresh seafood nicely prepared. Recommended.
❡ **Rom Thai**, on the pier. Downmarket; also sells seafood but not as sophisticated a menu as **Krue Lanta Yai**.

Ao Khlong Dao *p546, map p544*
❡❡❡ **Sayang Beach Resort Restaurant**, Khlong Dao Beach by **Lanta Sand Resort and Spa**. Excellent Malay-Thai fusion cuisine here – among the best along the west coast cooked with real flair and precision. Recommended.
❡❡❡-❡❡ **Chaba Bungalows & Art Gallery**, 20 Moo 3, Khlong Dao beach, T075-684 118. Eclectic array of good Mexican-, Thai- and Mediterranean-inspired food in this funky restaurant.
❡❡❡-❡❡ **Costa Lanta Restaurant**, northern stretch of the beach. Lunch and dinner, served in exquisite surroundings. This spacious building mixes concrete, wood and fabrics to create a very special ambience. Delicious Thai food and a decent wine list. The bar is perfect to relax with a drink, after a hard day on the beach; this isn't the place to lounge about in a bikini or Speedos. Recommended.
❡❡❡-❡❡ **Golden Bay**, see Sleeping, above. Beachside restaurant in the bungalow operation of the same name. Excellent Thai and Isaan food on sale here. They also BBQ a fresh catch of seafood daily and offer discounts in low season. Reasonably priced in comparison to other places.
❡❡ **Danny's**, southern end of Khlong Dao beach. Huge menu of seafood, Thai and international, Sun evening Thai buffets are very popular.

Ao Phra-Ae (Long Beach) *p546,*
map p544

Retro Restaurant & Bar, on the main road, located behind **Red Snapper**. Rustic restaurant made from natural local materials, touches most bases on the culinary spectrum: Thai, pizza, pasta and the usual, other European fare.

Mr Wee Pizzeria, near the **Ozone Bar**. Rather good oven pizza in an open-air beachfront restaurant. Fire shows and cheap drinks too. Hip hop and soul – thumpy and predictable but the pizza hits the spot.

Hat Khlong Khoang *p547, map p544*

Bulan Lanta, opposite **Sonya Homestay**. Impressive range of Thai food to satisfy your taste buds. Some Western food, such as chips and burgers. Also open for breakfast. Check out the specials board.

Ao Khlong Nin *p547, map p544*

Cook Kai, just across the road from the beach, opposite the **Apichayavee Residence**. This family run restaurant serves a great range of Thai dishes including a comprehensive selection of vegetarian food. Food is served in a traditional Thai building with ornamental seashell chandeliers that tinkle in the sea breeze, making it a beautiful setting to enjoy lunch or dinner Recommended.

Green Leaf Café, on the main road, opposite the entrance to the **Where Else Resort**. A warm welcome awaits at this comfy café, which has a rather homely feel. The English and Thai owners offer up real coffees, generous baguettes, served on fresh multi grain bread and healthy salads. For a *farang* food fix, highly recommended.

O Shopping

Koh Lanta *p543, map p544*
Basic supplies are available in Sala Dan and Ban Koh Lanta Yai. Numerous mini-marts are springing up along the main road.

Hammocks
Hammock House, main street, Ban Koh Lanta Yai. A great little shop in an old wooden house. The owner is very friendly and provides visitors with a 'Lanta Biker Map' as well as trying to sell well-made hammocks and art.

Handicrafts.
Huan Mae Khum Pan, on the main road near Lanta residence, www.huanmaek hampan-handdicraft.com. Lanna style clothing, furniture and decorative pieces. The owner Pom, is extremely friendly, helpful and speaks excellent English.

▲ Activities and tours

Koh Lanta *p543, map p544*
Cookery classes
Time for Lime, 72/2 Mo 3, T075-684590, T08-9474 5171 (mob), www.timeforlime.net. Contact Junie Kovacs. Learn Thai cookery on the beach.

Diving and snorkelling
There are several schools in Sala Dan (some with German spoken); check equipment before signing on. Snorkelling is known locally as 'snorking'. Most guesthouses hire out equipment for about ฿100 per day, although the quality varies.

    Blue Planet Divers, 3 Moo 1, T075-684 165; **Lanta Discovery Divers**, Long Beach Resort, T075-684035/08-1797 2703 (mob); **Scool Divers**, T075-684654. See also Tour operators, below.

Horse riding
Mr Yat Riding School, Ao Phra-Ae. Riding along the beach and in the forest.

Tour operators
The following are well run and friendly, and can offer motorcycle rental, boat and bus tickets: **Amour Travel and Tour**, Khlong Dao beachfront, T075-684897; **IC Travel**, Sala Dan; **Makaira Tour Centre**, 18 Moo 1 Sala Dan;

O & M Travel, Sala Dan; **Sala Dan Travel Centre**, Sala Dan.

Most bungalows can make travel arrangements and offer day trips to Trang's Andaman Islands (see page 561), ฿950-1400 per person (depending on the type of boat), including lunch and snorkelling gear. (Note that it is a long trip – 3 hrs each way – and some people find the noise unbearable for just 1 or 2 hrs' snorkelling.) You can also organize trips from Ban Koh Lanta Yai. For long-tailed boat trips, including fishing and camping tours, contact **Sun Fishing and Island Tours**, main waterfront Rd, Lanta Old town, T08-7891 6619 (mob), www.lantalongtail.com. Boats leaving from this side of the island can save a couple of hours from the return trip to Koh Ngai and will take you to explore some of the islands on the east side. There are a couple of small tour shops running these businesses in the old town, and **Khrua Lanta Yai** also runs boat trips. **Freedom Adventures**, T08-4910 9132 (mob), www.freedom-adventures.com, organize various day trips (from ฿1300) and camping adventures (from ฿2800). Encourage your boatman to buoy, rather than use an anchor which damages the coral. Comprehensive island tours are offered by a number of tour agencies based in Sala Dan. **Opal** has reasonably priced tours and excellent service. **South Nature Travel** offers a full tour of the island including sea canoes.

Transport

Koh Lanta *p543, map p544*
Bicycles
The laterite roads are rough. Mountain bikes can be hired from bungalows for ฿150 per

day, motorbikes for ฿250 per day. Alternatively, go to Sala Dan.

Boat
Boats leave from Sala Dan on the northern tip of the island and from Lanta Pier on the southeast coast. To **Phi Phi**, there are 2 departures a day, 0800 and 1300, ฿350. Includes transfer from resort to the pier. To **Phuket** boats leave daily, 0800 and 1300, ฿750, and connect with a minivan, ฿196. To **Krabi**, there's 1 ferry daily at 0800, 2 hrs, ฿350. There is no ferry to Krabi from Lanta (and vice versa) in the wet season. During the high season there are daily boats between Lanta and **Phi Phi**.

Hire long-tailed boats from bungalows for ฿1200 per person, based on 4 people per trip, per day. This price includes all snorkelling gear and food

Minivan
Minivans to **Trang** leave on the hour 0700-1500, ฿250; To **Krabi**, every hour from 0600-1500, ฿200, or ฿300 to the airport.

Pick-up trucks
Some ply the island, but can be horrendously expensive, others serve individual bungalows.

Directory

Koh Lanta *p543, map p544*
Banks Siam City Bank Exchange, Sala Dan. ATMs are now common place. **Medical services** Health centre, Sala Dan. Hospital, Lanta Pier. **Police** Sala Dan. **Post office** Lanta Pier.

Trang and its islands

→ *Colour map 4, C2-3.*

On first sight, Trang looks like a somewhat drab but industrious Chinese-Thai town, filled with temples and decent schools – in other words – a good place to raise your children. Everything shuts down at around 2230 in the evening and even the traffic signals seem to go to sleep while early morning is filled with bustling tradespeople, eager to make their fortunes and provide for their families. But there is an underlying cranky charm and no-nonsense energy to this town which is famous for its char-grilled pork, sweet cakes and as the birthplace of former Prime Minister Chuan Leekpai. Its unique entertainments include bullfights (bull to bull) and bird-singing competitions (bird to bird) while the people are hugely friendly and exceptionally helpful the minute they realize that you like Trang too.

Finally, Trang has a nine-day Vegetarian Festival in October, similar to that celebrated in Phuket. Vegetarian patriots, dressed all in white, parade the street, dancing through clouds of exploding fireworks, with the revered few shoving various objects through their cheeks. Trang is also an excellent jumping-off point for Koh Lanta, Krabi and the exotic coral islands just off the coast.
▶▶ *For listings see pages 563-570.*

Ins and outs

Getting there and around

Trang has an airport, 20 minutes from town, and an air-conditioned minibus costs ฿100 and drops you outside the train station. It is possible to charter a tuk-tuk for ฿150, but this depends very much on your bartering skills. Buses arrive at the Thanon Huay Yod terminal, including buses from Satun, which used to arrive at Thanon Ratsada. To visit the islands you need to arrange minibuses to Pak Bara in the high season (May to November). There are also two overnight trains from Bangkok which stop at the station on the western end of Thanon Rama VI. ▶▶ *See Transport, page 569, for further information.*

Best time to visit

The best time to visit is between January and April, out of the monsoon season. In the low season, some of the islands close down except for one or two bungalow set-ups so you do need to check availability. If you have found a place during the low season then you need a bus to Langu and from there a tuk-tuk, *songthaew* or cab (if you can find one).

Background

The town was established as a trading centre in the first century AD and flourished between the seventh and 12th centuries. Its importance rested on its role as a relay point for communications between the east coast of Thailand and Palembang (Srivijaya) in Sumatra. It was then known as Krung Thani and later as Trangkhapura, the 'City of Waves'. The name was shortened in the 19th century to Trang. During the Ayutthaya period, the town was located at the mouth of the river and was a popular port of entry for Western visitors continuing north to Ayutthaya. Later, during King Mongkut's reign, the town was moved inland because of frequent flooding.

The arrival of the Teochew (Chinese) community in the latter half of the 19th century was a boon to the local economy which, until the introduction of rubber from Malaysia, was reliant on tin mining. Trang's rubber plantations were the first in Thailand (the first tree was planted just south of the city) and its former ruler, Phraya Rasdanupradit Mahitsara Phakdi, is credited with encouraging the spread of its cultivation. He also built the twisting road from Trang across the Banthat Range to Phattalung. There is a statue of him 1 km out of town on the Phattalung road.

Trang ◉🏨❀◔▲◉◑ ➤ pp563-570. Colour map 4, C3.

Trang has retained the atmosphere of a Chinese immigrant community, many of whom would be descendents of those who fled the corrupt and oppressive Manchu government. The airport is 7 km from town and a minivan to the town centre is ฿100 per person. There are good Chinese restaurants and several Chinese shrines dotted throughout the town

Trang

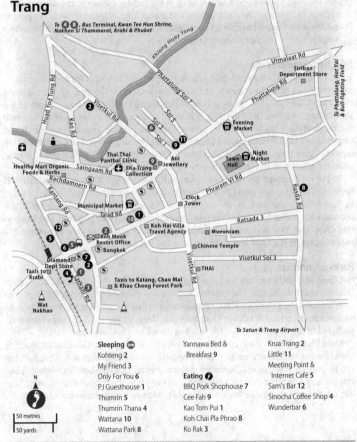

Sleeping 🛏
Kohteng **2**
My Friend **3**
Only For You **6**
PJ Guesthouse **1**
Thumrin **5**
Thumrin Thana **4**
Wattana **10**
Wattana Park **8**

Yannawa Bed &
Breakfast **9**

Eating 🍴
BBQ Pork Shophouse **7**
Cee Fah **9**
Kao Tom Pui **1**
Koh Chai Pla Phrao **8**
Ko Rak **3**

Krua Trang **2**
Little **11**
Meeting Point &
Internet Café **5**
Sam's Bar **12**
Sinocha Coffee Shop **4**
Wunderbar **6**

Sungei Golok–Rantau Panjang

There are buses from most southern towns to **Kuala Lumpur** via this border crossing. The border at 1700 and not all buses make it there before then, so be prepared to spend a night here.

that hold individual festivals. The **Kwan Tee Hun shrine**, dedicated to a bearded war god, is in Ban Bang Rok, 3 km north of Trang on Route 4. The Vegetarian Festival centres around the **Kiw Ong Eia Chinese Temple** and **Muean Ram**. There is also the **Rajamangkala Aquarium** ① *T075-248201-5, open daily during 'official hours'*, which lies 30 km from the city on the road to Pakmeng and is housed in the Fishery Faculty of the Rajamangkala Institute of Technology. The aquarium has 61 tanks of freshwater and marine life. Former **Prime Minister Chuan Leekpai's house** (ask locally for directions) has also become a pilgrimage spot of sorts and is open to visitors.

Beaches around Trang

Trang's embryonic tourism industry has so far escaped the hard sell of Phuket and Pattaya – excellent news for nature lovers, reef divers and explorers. The strip of coast running south from Pakmeng (38 km west from Trang) round to Kantang, boasts some of the south's best beaches. Unfortunately, it is also a relatively expensive place to stay with frankly exorbitant rates charged at some of the more popular beaches and islands and very ordinary food. **Pakmeng and Chang Lang** beaches are the most accessible – 40 km west of Trang town. The sea is poor here for swimming but it's a nice place to walk, although scarcely as scenic as the beaches of Koh Lanta or Krabi.

To the north, down the road from Sikao, is **Hua Hin** which has a good beach and is famed for its *hoi tapao* – sweet-fleshed oysters. Unfortunately the oyster season climaxes in November – the peak of the wet season. Hua Hin Bay is dotted with limestone outcrop islets. Other beaches to the south include **Hat San**, **Hat Yong Ling**, **Hat Yao** and **Hat Chao Mai**; private ventures are not permitted at any of the beaches within the national park (ie Hat Chao Mai, Hat Yong Ling and Hat San).

Parks around Trang

Hat Chao Mai National Park has some impressive caves near the village, known for their layered curtain stalactites. The beaches and many of the offshore islands fall under the jurisdiction of the 230-sq-km Hat Chao Mai National Park. Accommodation is available at park headquarters (6 km outside Chao Mai). See Sleeping, page 565. To get to the park, you need to take a minibus from the minibus station on Thaklang Road (฿100).

Khao Chong Forest Park, 20 km from town, off the Trang–Phattalung road, supports one of the few remaining areas of tropical forest in the area and has two waterfalls, Nam Tok Ton Yai and Nam Tok Ton Noi. Government resthouses are available here. To reach the park, you can take a local bus (from the bus station on Huay Yod Road), bound for Phattalung or Hat Yai, ฿15 or a *songthaew* from near the old market on Ratchadumnuen Road, ฿25.

Trang's Andaman Islands number 47 in total and spread out to the south of Koh Lanta. More tourists are visiting the islands, and the beauty, rich birdlife and the clear waters that surround them make upmarket future development highly likely. The islands can be reached from several small ports and fishing villages along the Trang coast, the main ones being Pakmeng (take a minibus from Thaklang Road, ฿60) and Kantang, 24 km from Trang. It is also possible to charter boats with the Muslim fishermen who live on the islands. The best time to visit the area is between January and April. The weather is unsuitable for island-hopping from May to December and although it is sometimes still possible to charter boats out of season, it can be expensive and risky: the seas are rough, the water is cloudy and you may be stranded by a squall or equally by the boatmen's incompetency and a vessel which was never seaworthy in the first place. There is a also a tendency to overbook these boats and consequent delays as the operators wait for further customers. ➻ *See Sleeping, page 565, for accommodation on the islands.*

Koh Ngai (Hai)
This 5-sq-km island is cloaked in jungle and fringed with glorious beaches. It also enjoys fabulous views of the limestone stacks that pepper the sea around it. A coral reef sweeps down the eastern side, ending in two big rocks, between which rips a strong current – but the coral around these rocks is magnificent. Koh Ngai is the clichéd resort island retreat where you wake up, eat and sleep at the same place. There are only three resorts on this island and no local community. If you like this sort of intense group intimacy, Koh Ngai is perfect but guests have complained of cabin fever setting in after a week. It is more suited to honeymooners or those who will stay here as a base and do day trips to other islands. Although Koh Ngai forms the southernmost part of Krabi province and is most easily reached from Pakmeng in Trang province, 16 km away, it is also possible to get there from Koh Phi Phi and Koh Lanta. Tourists also stop here on island-hopping day trips to eat at one of the three resorts and to snorkel in the magnificently clear waters which are rich with marine life.

Koh Chuak and **Koh Waen** (between Koh Hai and Koh Muk) are also snorkellers' havens – the latter is the best reef for seafan corals.

Koh Muk (Mook)
On the western side of Koh Muk is the **Emerald Cave** (Tham Morakot) – known locally as Tham Nam – which can only be entered by boat (or fearless swimmers) at low tide, through a narrow opening. After the blackness of the 80-m-long passage it opens into daylight again at an inland beach straight out of Jurassic Park – emerald water ringed with powdery white sand and a backdrop of precipitous cliffs that look as if they are made of black lava frozen over the centuries. The cave was only discovered during a helicopter survey not very long ago and is thought to have been a pirates' lair. **Be warned**, you can only leave the pool at low tide. Unfortunately this is being oversold and there have been groups of Southeast Asian tourists who combine the swimming into the cave with positive reinforcement songs that can be heard up to a mile away as everyone shouts in unison – 'we can do this' and 'we will succeed, onward, onward'. Unless you are in with the crowd, this is unfailingly depressing and destroys the mystique of this one-off place. The only way around the group scene is to hire a long-tailed boat privately and try to go at an early hour although the tide does dictate when it is safe to swim in. The death of some

tourists in the Emerald Cave at the peak of the tsunami may have dampened people's urge to visit, particularly as it is a daunting swim. If you hire a private boatmen, he can swim in with you and hold your hand which helps immensely. A torch is also a good idea as is snorkelling gear, which you may just be brave enough to try on the way out. If you do snorkel, you will be rewarded with schools of hundreds of brightly-coloured tropical fish swimming around you. The trick in getting through the cave psychologically intact is to look backwards as you swim so that you can always see a little light reflected on the cave walls. However, unless you are with a boatman who knows the way, this is impossible as you do need to turn left at some point. The entire swim only takes about 15-20 minutes. The island's west coast has white beaches backed by high cliffs where swallows nest. There are also beautiful beaches on the east coast facing the craggy mainland.

Trang's Andaman Islands

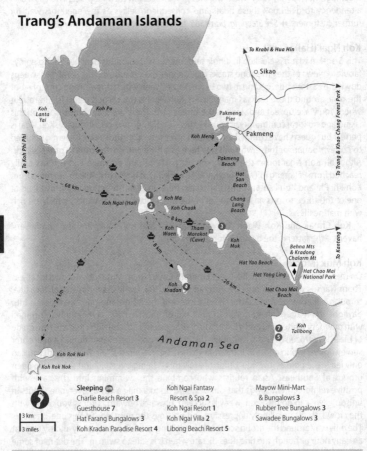

Sleeping 🛏️
Charlie Beach Resort **3**
Guesthouse **7**
Hat Farang Bungalows **3**
Koh Kradan Paradise Resort **4**

Koh Ngai Fantasy
Resort & Spa **2**
Koh Ngai Resort **1**
Koh Ngai Villa **2**
Libong Beach Resort **5**

Mayow Mini-Mart
& Bungalows **3**
Rubber Tree Bungalows **3**
Sawadee Bungalows **3**

Koh Kradan

Koh Kradan, most of which falls within the bounds of the Chao Mai National Park, is regarded as the most beautiful of Trang's islands, with splendid beaches and fine coral, on the east side. Two Japanese warships sunk during the Second World War lie off the shore and are popular dive spots. The area not encompassed by the national park is a mixture of rubber smallholdings and coconut groves. The island – bar the park area – is privately owned, having been bought by tycoon Mon Sakunmethanon in 1985 for ฿5 million. It only has two places to stay, see Sleeping, page 566. There has been talk of a day centre set up by one of the major resort groups which would have a restaurant, bar and boutique but nothing has been finalized yet.

Koh Talibong (Libong)

Koh Talibong (Libong), which is part of the Petra Islands group to the south, is renowned for its oysters and birdlife. The Juhoi Cape and the eastern third of the island is a major stopping-off point for migratory birds, and in March and April the island is an ornithologist's El Dorado. Typical visitors, on their way back to northern latitudes, include brown-headed gulls, crab plovers, four species of terns, waders, curlews, godwits, redshanks, greenshanks, reef egrets and black-necked storks. From October to March the island is famed for its unique Hoi Chakteen oysters. The rare manatee (*Manatus senegalensis*) and the green turtle also inhabit the waters off the island. The best coral reef is off the southwest coast, directly opposite the **Libong Beach Resort**. Snorkelling equipment is available from the resort which also provides fishing gear. Libong's main town is Ban Hin Kao, where the daily ferry from Kantang docks. Motorcycle taxis take visitors along rough trails to the island's beaches and villages. There is one hotel on the island and no nightlife. The population is almost exclusively Muslim, and alcohol is not widely available so you would need to stock up in Trang.

Koh Sukorn (Muu), Koh Petra, Koh Lao Lieng (Nua and Tai)

Koh Sukorn, Koh Petra, Koh Lao Lieng (Nua and Tai) are also part of the Petra Islands group, off Palien, 47 km south of Trang, and can be reached from there or Kantang. Koh Sukorn (locally known as Koh Muu – or Pig Island) is inhabited by Muslims, who do not seem to mind the name. Apart from its golden powdery beaches, its main claim to fame are the mouth-watering watermelons that are grown here (March/April).

Koh Petra and **Koh Lao Lieng** have sheer cliffs which are the domain of the birds' nest collectors who risk life and limb for swiftlet saliva (see box, page 535). The islands have excellent sandy beaches on their east coasts and impressive reefs which are exposed at low tide. Dolphins can often be seen offshore.

◉ Trang and its islands listings

For Sleeping and Eating price codes and other relevant information, see pages 44-49.

● Sleeping

Trang *p559, map p559*
Trang makes a good base if you want to explore the south; most places are handily

situated between the clock tower and the railway station.
A-C Thumrin Thana, 69/8 Huay Yod Rd, T075-223223. Considered to be the No 1 hotel in town with 285 rooms. It's a couple of kilometres from the town centre so not an ideal choice if you arrive on the sleeper train from Bangkok. All rooms are en suite,

a/c and with colour TVs. They have a pool.

A-D Wattana Park, 315/7 Huay Yod Rd, T075-216216. A little way out from the town centre on the road in from Krabi. A modern hotel with good rooms and friendly service – probably the best value business-class hotel in Trang. Does not have a pool. Recommended.

C-E Thumrin, Phraram VI Rd, T075-211011. Downmarket sister hotel to the **Thumrin Thana**, though the a/c en suite rooms are decent enough, service is fine and location good. Often used as a stopover point for long-distance buses from Malaysia and can be booked out.

E My Friend, 25/17 Sathani Rd, T075-255 447, www.myfriend-trang.com. All rooms in this clean, well-run guesthouse are en suite with TV and a/c. Convenient location near the station – they'll let you check in early, if they have availability; good news for those arriving on the sleeper train from Bangkok. Internet, lots of local information, staff are helpful and friendly though don't speak much English. Free tea and filter coffee.

E-G Yannawa Bed and Breakfast, 94 Visetkul Rd, T075-216617. Clean, comfortable rooms in a shophouse. Good price and helpful staff. The rooms at the top are not as dark but avoid the noisy street at the front. The single rooms are the best value. Recommended at this price.

F Only For You, Patalung Soi 1, T08-13974574 (mob). Breezy, cool house, 5 mins' walk from the centre of town, with 2 bedrooms, bathroom and a kitchen. Ideal for those wanting to stay in Trang for at least a week (minimum). Rate includes utilities. Very good value.

F Wattana, 127 Phraram VI Rd, T075-218 184. Good value, basic rooms, all en suite with fan or a/c, in this Chinese-style hotel.

F-G Kohteng, 77-79 Phraram VI Rd, T075-218622. Very basic rooms – the a/c options represent best value. Staff can be rude and unfriendly.

G PJ Guesthouse, 25/12 Sathani Rd, T075-217500. Home-like set-up with traveller ambience and attention to detail. Rooms are small but not too dark and very clean. Shared shower and toilet per floor. Tour service downstairs. Motorbike rental. Joy and Pong are helpful owners and both speak good English. Good location about 100 m from the station. Recommended for those on a tight budget.

Beaches around Trang p560

AL-L Amari Trang Beach Resort, 199 Moo 5, Had Pak Meng, Changlang Beach, T075-205 888, www.amari.com. Newly opened spa and 138 seafront rooms in a contemporary, minimalist low-rise. The **Amari** also has a speedboat shuttle to the exclusive private day resort of Koh Kradan which you may need as the beach here is poor and not particularly clean. For entertainment in this isolated spot the **Amari** offers 5 restaurants and a pool.

L-C Lay Trang Resort, Pakmeng, T075-274 228. A bungalow resort just up from the pier. Good seafood restaurant, well-built and well-equipped resort. Sea canoes and guides for hire. The resort will also arrange camping on the nearby islands, complete with picnic and mobile phone.

D-C Pakmeng Resort, Pakmeng, T075-274 112, www.pakmengresort.com. Turn left after reaching the main seafront and continue on towards the national park. The resort is on the left and is well marked. Wooden bungalows with attached bathroom and fan and some a/c. The resort backs onto the main khlong leading to the river. Good restaurant. Motorbikes (₿350 per day) and bicycles (₿100 per day) for rent.

D-G Barn Chom Talay – Seaview Guest House, Hat Yao. Dormitory room and bungalows all clean and well-furnished. The daughter of the owners speaks excellent English. Also offers every type of tour, including kayak rental, trips to the nearby caves and boat tours to the islands. A pleasant out-of-the-way place to stay. Recommended.

Parks around Trang *p560*
**E-F Hat Chao Mai National Park
Bungalows**. There's no restaurant here –
you can buy food from a very small shop
in Chao Mai village.

Koh Ngai (Hai) *p561*
LL-A Koh Ngai Fantasy Resort and Spa,
next door to **Koh Ngai Villa**, T075-206923,
www.kohhai.com. A/c bungalows and
family suites. Obscured in the foliage of
this idyllic island. Pool. Stately rooms. Has
been upgraded since its early days and
now has decent food.
LL-B Koh Ngai Resort, 142/1 Moo 4,
T075-590035, www.kohngairesort.com. In
the southeastern corner of the island, with
its own magnificent private beach, this is
a massive development, with around
60 suites, cottages, villas and bungalows
all a/c with private balconies. Overpriced,
but the service is friendly and the food has
improved. Dominates the beachfront.
B-E Koh Ngai Villa, halfway up the eastern
side of the island, facing the reef, T075-210
496, www.krabidir.com/kohngaivilla/
index/html. A range of new and old chalets,
some with a/c, others with mosquito nets,
restaurant, tents also available (฿150). The
food is awful, service unfriendly, and the
rooms overpriced but the beach is gorgeous.

Koh Muk (Mook) *p561*
The majority of the accommodation here
shuts 6 months of the year due to navigational difficulties and drought. Koh Muk has
seen a bit of a boom accommodation-wise
for an island with this size of a beach – less
than 1 km with rocks both ends – there are
now around 20 resorts. The other side of
the island also has accommodation, none
are recommended as the village is fairly
unsightly, the beach filthy and the still
pools of stagnant water likely to encourage
dengue fever.
AL-C Charlie Beach Resort, T075-2032813,
www.kohmook.com. Smack bang in the
centre of the beach. The bungalows are

faultlessly clean and the restaurant and bar
serve reasonable food. Staff can be surly and
unfriendly. Very conscious of its monopoly
and is overpriced.
B-E Rubber Tree Bungalows, T075-215972,
www.mookrubbertree.com. Across from
Mayow, up a long wooden staircase cut
into the hill are these marvellous family-run
bungalows. Attached toilet and bathroom.
These are set in a working rubber tree
plantation so that you may be woken early in
the morning by the lanterns of the rubber
tree tappers. You are welcome to observe
them at work. The attached restaurant has
easily the best food on the island – cooked
by a northern Thai native. Let her choose
what to cook if you can't decide. This is a
magical place to have an evening drink
with dozens of twinkling lights providing a
dreamy backdrop. Recommended.
C-E Hat Farang Bunglaows, near Mayow
on the hilly part. 13 bamboo bungalows with
attached bathroom and toilet. It doesn't get
much light as it's in the foliage but it is close
to the beach.
D Sawadee Bungalows, next to Charlie's,
T075-2079645, sawadeeresort64@
yahoo.com. Basic wooden bungalows on
stilts set into hill. Own bathroom. Romantic
spot as it is at the end of the beach where it
is rather rocky and private. Good view of
sunset. Attached restaurant serves bland
portions of Thai food but is OK for morning
coffee and fruit salad. Attracts divers, surfers,
travellers. Electricity only 4 hrs a day.
E-F Mayow Mini-Mart and Bungalows,
over a little wooden walkway to the right
of **Sawadee**. 5 bungalows with showers
and toilet outside. Mayow is the name of
the female owner and she also has a café/
kitchen which does good fried fish and
banana fritters along with Thai curries.
It also operates **Dugong Dugong Travel**,
which arranges snorkelling and diving.
F-G Mookies, down the lane/dirt path
towards the sea gypsy village (there is only
one path on from Rubber Tree), T08-7275
6533 (mob), mookiebrian@yahoo.com.

Open all year. Cross over a wooden bridge and follow the disco music to **Mookie's Bar**, where you are likely to find Aussie Mookie reading pulp fiction and drinking in the mid-afternoon. This is a completely eccentric set-up. Rooms are large with spring mattresses and 24-hr electricity with light and fan inside. While the toilet and shower is shared, they are kept clean to military standards. The shower outside also has hot water. Highly recommended. See also Eating, below.

Koh Kradan *p563*
C-B Koh Kradan Paradise Resort, book through Trang office, 25/36 Sathani Rd, T075-211391. The Trang office also runs a daily boat service to the island. Expensive, concrete bungalows that have been painted to look like wooden bungalows,and are failing miserably. Recent visitors have been disappointed as the resort is run-down with poor rooms at this price. Visitors regularly complain that the restaurant is one of the poorest in Thailand. However, the staff are friendly and the island is wonderful. Tents are available.

Koh Talibong (Libong) *p563*
A-D Libong Beach Resort, Ban Lan Khao, T075-225205, www.libongbeachresort.com. Large open-fronted restaurant with about 15 basic bungalows set in a coconut grove facing onto a sandy beach. Overpriced, as is most of Trang's island accommodation.
B-D Guesthouse, 5 km from the main town Ban Hin Khao, run by the **Conservation of Wildlife Committee** at Laem Juhol on the east coast. The guesthouse must be booked in advance, and food is not available; contact the secretary at the Libong Regional Department, PO Box 5, Kantang, Trang 92110, T075-251932.

Koh Sukhorn (Muu), Koh Petra, Koh Lao Lieng (Nua and Tai) *p563*
Koh Sukhorn (Muu)
B-C Sukorn Cabana Resort, T075-225894, www.sukorncabana.com. Bungalows and

tents, so suitable for families and backpackers. Bungalows are set in coconut trees with attached bathrooms.
B-D Sukhorn Beach Bungalows, T075-211 457, www.sukorn-island-trang.com. Owned by a Dutchman, some individual bungalows, some attached. Excellent restaurant, private beach frontage, bikes for rent, tours arranged.

● Eating

Trang *p559, map p559*
Trang's BBQ pork is delicious and one of the town's few claims to national fame. It is made from a traditional recipe brought here by the town's immigrant Chinese community and is usually served with rice or dim sum. It's the speciality of several Chinese restaurants and can also be bought from street vendors and is usually only available from 0900-1500ish. Opposite the **Meeting Point** are stalls and a **Roti Bread Place** as well as **M & P Bakery**. There is an excellent, small night market, selling everything from seasonal fruit through to Isaan food, just off of Phraram VI Rd past the town hall. Open every night 1800-2100. You can also find a few night stalls in the square in front of the railway station. During the day, the municipal market near Rachdamnern Rd is great for fresh fruit and a huge assortment of other munchies. There is a local evening market on the corner of Ruenrom Rd and Pattalung Rd, perfect if you fancy experimenting with local delicacies.

There are several restaurants on Visetkul Rd offering excellent Thai food, and a couple of coffee shops catering to more Western tastes. This area appears to be a hub for tourism development with souvenir shops on the corner opposite the clock tower and on the road itself.
¶¶ Koh Chai Pla Phrao, Rusda Rd. Look for a bright yellow sign (Thai only) and a big open-plan eatery for one of the most popular places in Trang. Don't be fooled by the cheap plastic furniture, the Thai food here is awesome. House speciality is grilled fish –

so fresh it will be staring back at you – or steamed fish with a mood altering chilli and lime sauce. Highly recommended.

Krua Trang, Visetkul Rd. Excellent Thai food and draft Carlsberg beer. The stuffed steamed seabass is a specialty and is delicious, filleted, stuffed with shrimp and vegetables and then steamed. The entire range of food is impressive. Staff are friendly and helpful at recommending dishes.

BBQ Pork Shophouse, corner of a small *soi* on Kantang Rd. This tiny Chinese place is often packed to the rafters with families queuing for either takeaway or a table. Only really sells one dish – BBQ pork smothered in a sweet gravy with leafy green vegetables on rice. You can also get chicken satay if you ask nicely. Highly recommended.

Cee Fah, Pattalung Rd Soi 5. Deliciously cheap and healthy vegetarian Thai food.

Kao Tom Pui Restaurant, 111 Phraram IV Rd, T075-210127. Since 1967. Family restaurant, very popular with the locals, an unpretentious café setting with Sino-Portugese feel. Does cauldrons of seafood soup, excellent seafood dishes, including steamed bass. Good vegetables – morning glory with garlic especially nice. Regulars include local gangsters and their girls and large families. Recommended.

Ko Rak (also called **Somrak**), 158-160 Kantang Rd. Friendly shophouse-style eatery surrounded by a throng of stalls which sell tender duck and pork rice and noodles. The family who runs this packed place is originally from the Chinese island of Hainan and first came to Trang over 70 years ago. Full of bustle and good grub. Recommended.

Little Restaurant, a stones throw further up Pattalung Rd from from the **Cee Fah** restaurant. Serves both Western and local food, popular with the small expat community.

Meeting Point Restaurant and Internet Café, right along from the railway station. This does a good breakfast, decent coffees in an airy café with tiled ceramic floor and wooden benches. For some reason there

are pictures of Native Americans on the wall. Also has a little bar. Recommended.

Pong O Cha, where Wisekul Rd meets Huai Yod Rd. Popular with locals for tasty traditional Thai breakfasts, cakes and coffee. Opens very early.

Sam's Bar, opposite the railway station. Happy hour 1600-1800. Also does fantastic salads and sandwiches. The baguettes are loaded with fresh salad from the deli and are recommended if you are craving some *farang* food.

Sinocha Coffee Shop, next to train station. Does a good selection of coffees and decent pastries, tasty Thai food and ice cream. Popular hang-out with tuk-tuk drivers and locals.

Wunderbar, 24 Sathani Rd. Western cuisine in small dark wooden café. Good selection of magazines and papers. Decent breakfast and excellent place to pick up information. Also does cheeses if you have a hankering for dairy products. Comforting drinking hole in the evening.

Beaches around Trang *p560*
Hat Yao Seafood, Hat Yao. A very good restaurant which is open-fronted and looks out onto the beach.

Koh Muk (Mook) *p561*
Mookies Bar. Does spare ribs, hamburgers, grilled chicken, but you need to order ahead of time so he can get the supplies from the mainland. The entertainment here is provided through the colourful tales of Russell who first came to Thailand in 1969.

⊛ Festivals and events

Trang *p559*
Oct Vegetarian Festival (movable). 9-day festival in which a strict vegetarian diet is observed to purify the body. Mediums pierce their cheeks and tongues with spears and walk on hot coals. On the 6th day a procession makes its way around town, in which everyone dresses in traditional

costumes. The same event occurs in Phuket, see page 464.

O Shopping

Trang p559, map p559
Best buys in Trang include locally woven cotton and wickerwork and sponge cake. Thaklang and Municipal markets are next door to each other in the centre of town, off Rachdamnern Rd.
Ani, Pattalung Rd, T08-1397 4574 (mob). Huge range of jewellery, much of it made on the premises.
Charonemwit Bookstore, 88-88/1 Phraram VI Rd and Kantang Rd. For English-language magazines and books. Family-run and very helpful staff.
Fha Trang Collection, 283 Radchadam-neon Rd, T075-217004. Posh and pretty souvenirs reasonably priced. Embroidered shoes, scarves, artistic mobiles and folk craft. There is also a second-hand book-shop next door.
Trang Sura Thip Whiskey Shop, 69/1 Phraram VI, near the clocktower. This tobacco and whiskey shop looks like a log cabin on the inside. Good selection of whiskies and liquors.

▲ Activities and tours

Trang p559, map p559
Bull fighting
Fights between bulls take place at random, depending on whether the farmers have a suitable bull. The only way to find out about whether they are taking place is to ask around. But be warned – this is a very much a local entertainment and you might get some curious looks when you ask, particularly if you are a woman. Scarcely any women attend these events. The fights are usually held during the week and only in the daytime. They occur in a field off Trang-Pattalung Rd near the Praya Ratsadanupradit Monument.

The best way to get there is by tuk-tuk, which takes about 20 mins from the railway station. They are always packed by an excitable betting crowd screaming with dismay or joy and there are plenty of stalls about selling drinks and foods, including noodles and fruit. Dusty and hot but exciting.

Snorkelling
Trang Travel, Thumrin Sq. Equipment for hire.

Therapies
Ministry of Health Spa, Panthai Clinic, 32-34-36 Saingam Rd. This superb spa does everything from ear candles to moxibusiton (Gwyneth Paltrow is a great fan of this detoxification process which involves hot suction caps). You can get acupuncture here and Chinese remedies, as well as Thai massage. Reasonable prices in beautiful surroundings. Highly professional.
Yannawa Bed and Breakfast, see Sleeping, above. There is a well-run small spa in the guesthouse, offering footmassage and Thai massage at reasonable rates. A cut above the usual offerings with this walk-in shophouse.

Tour operators
Choa Mai Tour Ltd, 15 Satanee Rd, contact Jongkoolnee Usaha, T075-216380, www.chaomai-tour-trang.com. Reliable and trustworthy, they go out of their way to help, can make hotel reservations, offer tourist information, airport reservations and a/c bus or van, and tours. A 1 day Andaman Sea tour, ฿850, plus National Park fee of ฿200. Good level of English spoken. Recommended.
PJ Guesthouse, 25/12 Sathani Rd. Run an excellent and well-informed travel service that is as much about you getting to experience local life as making money. They can set you up with private cars and also English-speaking tuk-tuk drivers who organize Trang tours (from ฿200/hour) showing you all the nooks and crannies of this vibrant town. Recommended.

Underwater weddings
Trang Underwater Weddings. These occur in Feb. For information contact the Trang Chamber of Commerce, T075-5225353.

Koh Ngai (Hai) *p561*
Diving
Rainbow Divers, Koh Ngai Resort, T075-206962, www.rainbow-diver.com. Open mid-Nov until the end of Apr. Run by a German couple, they offer PADI courses and excursions.

❍ Transport

Trang *p559, map p559*
Air
Daily connections on THAI to **Bangkok**, 1020 and 1145, 2 hrs 10 mins. Daily flights at 1020 and 1145 with **Nok air**, fares start at ฿1800, www.nokair.com.

Airline offices **Nok Air**, Trang Airport, T075-212229, **Thai**, 199 Visetkul Rd (not in the centre of town), T075-218066.

Boat
For information on reaching Malaysia from Trang, see border box, page 577.

Boats leave from **Pakmeng**, about 25 km west of Trang. Boats from Pakmeng to **Koh Hai**, 45 mins, **Koh Muk**, 1 hr, **Koh Kradan**, 1½ hrs, same price ฿1000 one way, for all destinations. To Ko Muk and Koh Kradan, take a boat from Kuantungku pier, minibuses leave every 30 mins from the minibus station, ฿100. To **Koh Libong**, take a minibus to Hat Yao pier, ฿80, then a long-tailed boat, 0700-1600, ฿80 per person.

To **Koh Tarutao**, (Nov-May), take a ferry from Ban Pak Bara pier, 0900, 1100, 1330 and an irregular service at 1630, 1½ hrs. You must buy a National Park ticket, ฿400

To **Langkawi**, a minivan from your hotel to Tammalang Pier in **Satun**, 2hrs, ฿300, then a ferry boat, ฿400.

Kradan Island Resort operates a boat, minimum 4 people, ฿400 oneway, including minivan from Trang. For **Koh Talibong** (Libong)take a taxi from Trang to **Kantang**, ฿350, for the taxi. From there a ferry leaves daily at 1200 for Koh Talibong's (Libong's) 'capital' of Ban Hin Khao and motorcycles take visitors the 5 km to the only hotel, the Libong Beach Resort. **Trang Travel**, opposite the Thumrin Hotel in Trang, also operates a boat which can be chartered to any of the islands. For those with less time on their hands, they offer day excursions.

To reach **Singapore**, book through an agency, 16 hrs, ฿750.

Bus
Buses to **Bangkok** leave from the bus station on Ploenpitak Rd. Normal a/c at 1630 and 1730, ฿671. VIP at 1730, ฿781. Super VIP at 1700 and 1730, ฿1040. To **Phuket**, regular services from Ploenpitak Rd, from 0600-1800, normal a/c ฿290, VIP ฿340. These buses also stop at **Krabi**. To **Saturn**, non a/c A150, from the bus terminal on Huai Yod Rd. To **Phattalung**, a non a/c bus runs from Ploenpitak Rd, 1½ hrs, A50.

Minibuses to **Koh Lanta** leave from outside KK Travel, opposite the train station, every hour from 0930-1630, ฿250, 2½ hrs. This is by far the easiest way to get to the island, the minivan drops you off at your resort so you avoid the touts at Sala Dan. Minivan to **Hat Yai** from Huai Yod Rd, every hour 0600-1700, 2 hrs, ฿100. To **Phattalung**, 1 hr, A100; to **Nakhon Si Thammarat**, from Wisekul Rd, every hour from 0600-1700, 2½ hrs, ฿200. To **Ban Pak Bura**, organize a minivan from your hotel, or book through agency, 2 hrs, ฿300. To **Surat Thani**, minivan from Thaklang Rd, near the fruit market, 3 hrs, ฿170.

Motorbike
PJ Guesthouse can arrange hire from ฿250 per day.

Train

Train to **Bangkok** leave twice daily at 1320 sleeper and 1720 (sleeper). For the sleeper, an upper bed is ฿821, a lower bed is ฿871.

Songthaew

Shared taxi to **Satun**, 6 people, ฿200 each, from Ratsada Rd. To **Ban Pak Bura**, take a *songthaew* from Satun, ฿20. To **Hat Yai**, 6 people, from 0600-1700, leaves when full, ฿120 each.

❶ Directory

Trang *p559, map p559*
Banks Banks are clustered along Phraram VI Rd. **Internet** Plenty of internet locations along Phraram VI Rd; also one at **My Friend Guesthouse**. **Post office** Jermpanya Rd.

Tarutao National Park and the far south

→ Colour map 5, C4.

While some say that Tarutao is merely a mispronunciation of the Malay words ta lo trao, meaning 'plenty of bay', when first spying this ominous humped island rising out of the sea, it is far easier to believe a second interpretation. That is, that Tarutao comes from the Malay word for old, mysterious and primitive. Resonating with a murky history of pirates, prisoners and ancient curses, it is no wonder the island was picked for the flop reality television series Survivor in 2002. Despite dynamite-fishing in some areas, the island waters still have reasonable coral, and provide some of the best dive sites in Thailand – particularly around the stone arch on Koh Khai. Adang Island has magnificent coral reefs. These are part of Thailand's best-preserved marine park, where turtles, leopard sharks, whales and dolphins can be spotted.

Inland, however, is a different story. Over half of Koh Tarutao is dense dark rainforest with only a single 12-km road cutting through the length of the island and scant paths leading into a potentially lethal jungle filled with poisonous snakes and volatile beasts like the wild boar. Created in 1974, the marine national park comprises 51 islands – the main ones being Tarutao, Adang, Rawi, Lipe, Klang, Dong and Lek. Tarutao Park itself is divided into two main sections – the Tarutao archipelago and the Adang-Rawi archipelago.

In the far south, there is the Muslim town of Satun with its preserved shophouses and the Thale Ban National Park. ▶▶ *For listings, see pages 578-584.*

Tarutao National Park

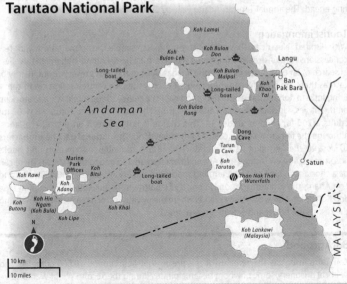

Ins and outs

Getting there

Koh Tarutao lies off the coast 30 km south of Pak Bara; Koh Adang, Rawi and Lipe are another 40 km out into the Andaman Sea, while Koh Bulon-Leh is 20 km due west of Pak Bara. Beware of travelling to any of these islands during bad weather; it is dangerous and a number of boats have foundered.

Getting to Tarutao National Park requires some planning. For much of the year, it is not advisable to take a boat to these beautiful islands. Ferries run from October to June, but speedboats or privately hired long-tailed boats can be chartered at other times of year. If you are based on Koh Lipe or Koh Bulon-Leh then hiring private long-tails to other islands is advised as you will otherwise be facing a roundabout route from Satun or **Ban Pak Bara**, thus adding hours to your journey. Ferries depart from Ban Pak Bara and also from Satun's Thammalang pier. ▶▶ *See Transport, page 583, for further information.*

Getting around

Rented bicycles provide an adequate means of traversing Tarutao's main road which is a gruelling route of steep curves occupied at times by cobras and pythons sunning themselves. The only other road on the island is around 6 km long and was built by the prisoners to link the two jails.

Best time to visit

November to April are the best months; the coolest are November and December. The park is officially closed from the end of May to 15 October, but it is still possible to get there. Services run providing the weather is alright. Koh Bulon-Leh is accessible year round, although most resorts are closed for six months of the year so it is wise to ring ahead. The annual Tarutao-Adang Fishing Cup Festival takes place in March.

Tourist information

With limited electricity, basic beach restaurants, simple accommodation and few concessions to mainstream tourism, the islands attract hardier, more bohemian travellers in search of an unspoilt paradise. Koh Lipe has most of the area's resorts. Bring plenty of cash as there are no banks on the islands, and only the dive centres accept credit cards. Bring food to Koh Tarutao as the park shop has little choice so you might want to stock up on the basics – including alcohol and even fruit. The entrance fee to Tarutao is ฿400 for adults, ฿200 for children under 14. This charge is not enforced on the other islands, although the ferry to Koh Lipe costs a fairly steep ฿550. The **national park headquarters** ① *close to the ferry port at Pak Bara, T074-781285,* provides information and books accommodation on Tarutao and Adang (messages are radioed to the islands). There can be a shortage in high season. Camping spaces are usually available. On Koh Tarutao and Koh Adang the accommodation is Forestry Department (ie government) run; Koh Lipe and Koh Bulon-Leh are the only islands where the private sector has a presence, meaning the resorts are better and activities more varied.

Background

Koh Tarutao boasts the remains of the prison that held around 10,000 criminals and political prisoners, some of whom became pirates during the Second World War to stave off starvation. Island rumour also has it that somewhere on Koh Tarutao a tonne of gold dust looted from a French ship still remains buried along with the murdered pirates that attacked the unfortunate vessel. Not all of the prisoners on this island were pirates. Indeed the translator of the English/Thai dictionary – Sor Settabut – completed the T section of the book at Tarutao. Another scholar – Prince Sithiporn Kridaka – continued his study of crop diversification that helped modernize Thailand's agriculture. The prince, who was educated largely in England and was a lifelong Anglophile, had been interned for his involvement in attempts to send railway cars to jam tracks on which tanks were being brought to defend Bangkok during widespread insurrections in 1932. The prince was also known for having invented Thailand's first shorthand – still used today – and for forming a boy scout troop among the youths at a government opium factory that he was sent to manage. Imprisoned for 11 years, the prince fell prey to life-threatening dysentery. Yet, it is now believed that the political prisoners received the best of the treatment on Koh Tarutao, where the general criminals may even have served them. Certainly the two groups did not mix, with the criminals held in the eastern part at the present-day Taloh Wow Cove and the political prisoners detained at Udang Cove in the southern tip. But all suffered during the Second World War when the island was completely cut off – along with essential food supplies. In cahoots with the guards, prisoners took to ambushing passing ships, originally for food and then for anything of value. This only came to an end in 1947 when the British, who had retaken Malaya, sent in the Royal Navy to quell the pirates. Afterwards, the island was left in total isolation with the prison gradually reduced to the remains of the prison director's house on top of a dune along with a sawmill below and a mysterious hole indicating a torture cellar. Legend has it that, centuries ago, a princess of Langkawi who had been accused of misdeeds declared that the island would never be discovered. Certainly much of Koh Tarutao holds on to its mystery with its brooding interior and inaccessibility throughout the rainy season.

Tarutao archipelago ●❼▲⊜ » pp578-584.

Koh Tarutao

The mountainous island of Tarutao is the largest of the islands, 26 km long and 11 km wide and covering 151 sq km. A mountainous spine runs north–south down the centre of the island, with its highest point reaching 708 m. The interior remains largely forested, cloaked in dense semi-evergreen rainforest. The main beaches are **Ao Moh Lai**, **Hin Ngam**, **Ao Phante**, **Ao Chak** and **Ao Sone**, mostly on the west of the island which has long sweeps of sand punctuated by headlands and mangrove. Ao Sone, for example, is a 3 km-long stretch of sand fringed with casuarina trees. (Much of the mangrove was cut for charcoal during the early 1960s before the national park was finally gazetted in 1974.) Notorious as the beach where a lone pirate killed a camping tourist in the 1980s, this eerie strip has quite a physical presence, unlike any of the other beaches along the west coast. The water is aggressive and choppy while Tarutao looms out from the water. This haunting beach, while it does have refreshments at one end, is not as busy as the others. Well worth the visit to Tarutao for the feeling that not everything has been tamed. You can also spot the delightfully electric kingfisher here.

    Tae Bu cliff, just behind the park headquarters on Ao Phante, has good sunset views. You climb up an imaginative route which includes a path cut into the hill, rickety wooden plank steps and extraordinary rock formations, all the while hearing the sound of monkeys, mouse deer, hornbills and perhaps wild boar. Finally you reach the top and a lookout point over the beach and surrounding forest, which is not as satisfying as the walk itself. You may also find it taken over by groups of young park staff – especially in the early morning.

The prison at Ao Talo U-Dang, in the south, was established in 1939 and was once used as a concentration camp for Thailand's political prisoners; the graveyard, charcoal furnaces and a fish fermentation plant are still there. The other main camp, at Ao Talo Wao on the east side of the island, was used for high-security criminals. During the Second World War, when communications were slow and difficult, the remoteness of the island meant it was cut off from supplies of food. After 700 out of the 3000 prisoners died, the desperate inmates and some of the guards became pirates to stay alive. The prisons have been partially restored as historical monuments. Today the only people living on the island are the park wardens and other staff.

Coconut plantations still exist on Tarutao but the forests have barely been touched, providing a habitat for flying lizards, wild cats, lemur, wild boar, macaques, mouse deer and feral cows, believed to have bred when the prisoners were taken from the island. Crocodiles once inhabited Khlong Phante and there is a large cave on the Choraka (crocodile) water system known as **Crocodile Cave** (bring a torch). The best way to see wildlife on Koh Tarutao is to walk down the 12-km road during the dry season when animals come out in search of water. There are also many species of bird on the islands including colonies of swiftlets found in the numerous limestone caves – mainly on **Koh Lo Tong** (to the south of Tarutao) and **Koh Ta Kieng** (to the northeast). Large tracts of mangrove forest are found here, especially along Khlong Phante Malacca, on Tarutao. The islands are also known for their trilobite fossils, 400 to 500 million years old, found not just on Tarutao but all over the national park.

While the waters around Tarutao are home to four species of turtle (the Pacific Ridleys, green, hawksbill and leatherback), whales and dolphins are also occasionally seen; the sea is clearer further west in the waters of the Adang-Rawi archipelago (see below).

Koh Bulon-Leh

① *Numerous resorts and fishermen operate boat tours around the area, costing about ฿800 for a ½-day of swimming, snorkelling and sometimes fishing. Whales, dolphins and turtles are common.*

These two islands have both developed into beach resorts fairly recently. But while Koh Lipe has had Chao Le for perhaps centuries, only in the past 50 years or so has Koh Bulon-Leh had year-round residents: a Muslim population of around 50. The reason for this is down to the superstition of the Moken fisherpeople who believed the island was cursed and that everyone who lived there met an untimely died. This kept the island uninhabited until after the Second World War; since then it was discovered that the high mortality rate was due to tuberculosis.

The lifestyle here is exceedingly laid-back and in the more expensive resorts – boho-chic. One of the perks to having had few tourists and a rather isolated position, is that visitors will often join simple pleasures like the evening rugby games by the school or fishing trips with the locals. The island has attracted many returnees – many from Italy and France – and of a wide age range. More upmarket than Koh Lipe, it does offer greater comfort to the well-heeled who sometimes stay for months at a time.

Development is still relatively low-key but land speculation has been going on since the 1990s and investors are no doubt hoping that Koh Bulon-Leh will develop, especially as it is relatively near the pier at Pak Bara. Koh Bulon-Leh is less than 20 km north of

Koh Tarutao and about the same distance west of Ban Pak Bara. While it is part of the same archipelago as Tarutao, the island is outside the boundaries of the national park. Furthermore, it has two caves of interest: **Bat Cave**, which houses a small colony of fruit bats, and **Nose Cave**, where it's possible to dive in from one side, swim under the rocks and among thousands of little fish (but beware the moray eel) and come up on the other side.

Adang-Rawi archipelago ⊜⊕⊕⊿⊜ ➼ pp578-584.

Koh Adang and Koh Rawi

Adang and Rawi lie 43 km west of Tarutao and are the main islands in the archipelago of the same name. They offer a stark contrast to Tarutao. While Tarutao is composed of limestone and sandstone, the rugged hills of Adang and Rawi are granite. Adang's highest mountain rises to 703 m while Rawi's is 463 m in height. Koh Adang is almost entirely forested and there is a trail that leads up to the summit, Chado Cliff, for good views over Koh Lipe and the Andaman Sea. There are also a handful of trails through the dense vegetation; to spot the shy inhabitants – including a variety of squirrels, mouse deer and wild pigs – it is best to wait half an hour or so in silence. The main beaches on Adang are Khai, Laem Son, Ao Lo Lae Lae and Lo Lipa, and Sai Khao on Rawi.

Koh Lipe

Still a tropical idyll occupied by Chao Le fisherpeople although the main beach – Pattaya – is now fairly densely populated by tourist bungalows and resorts, though thankfully all are rather low-key and there are no multi-story complexes yet.

Koh Lipe is a beautiful island that attracts many returnees, mainly because of the laid-back and gentle populace, excellent snorkelling in some of the clearest waters in the Andaman Sea, blindingly white sand beaches and terrific seafood. The island is also extremely popular with young families. While much of the accommodation is poorly thought out, the island is still a delightful getaway with an unspoilt charm and snorkelling that is highly rewarding. Among the marine life that can be spotted in coral reefs only 60 m out are trumpet fish, sergeant majors, blue-spotted ribbontail rays, angel fish and anemones. There are also fishing and diving expeditions and an excellent massage operation on Pattaya Beach, set up by staff trained by Wat Po – especially Mr Chai (nickname) Bovornpar and Mrs Thanaporn Chimmalee, who also offers reflexology and other body treatments. The Chao Le have also managed to keep their culture and language and hold a traditional ceremony called *pla juk* twice a year. For this, a miniature boat is built out of *rakam* and *teenped* wood by the villagers. Once the boat is completed, offerings are placed in it, and the Chao Le dance until dawn and then launch the boat out to sea, loaded with the village's communal bad luck. One hopes that Bangkok interests which are casting their eye Lipe-way will not take away what little control the Chao Le still have and bring them bad luck in the long run.

There is a proposal to lay the island's first paved road behind the beach resorts for the island's small fleet of motorbikes, the engines of which soon fill with sand from too much use on the beach. Now only paths criss-cross the island. The combination of a tiny island and rampant tourist bungalow expansion creates a dilemma as the accommodation along both sides hems in the resident Chao Le and intrudes on their privacy. Some resorts even back directly onto villages with the unfortunate effect that tourists in bikinis can too easily stroll into a communal shower occupied by the modest Chao Le, as few of their homes have running water and bathrooms. It is also true that while certain resorts have a surface aura of cleanliness and order, this is quickly dispelled by the smell of burning plastic as rubbish disposal here is largely accomplished on a chaotic and sporadic basis.

The Chao Le areas are clearly at shanty town level which makes one wonder what benefits they are receiving from unchecked tourism. Indeed, it was only in 1940 that Koh Lipe officially became Thai territory – up to then it was unclear whether the Chao Le here were Malay or Thai. Locals maintain that the Thai authorities encouraged them to plant coconut trees to show that they had settled, presumably on the basis that occupation is as good as ownership.

Other islands

Koh Hin Ngam (**Koh Bula**) is southwest of Adang. The name means 'beautiful rocks' and this striking beach is covered in smooth oval stones that appear to have been polished by hand and that twinkle as the waves wash over them. According to legend, these stones should never be removed or the ghost of Hin Ngami will curse you with bad luck. There is excellent snorkelling. **Koh Khai** has the famous stone arch depicted on many postcards, white powdery sand beaches and some excellent diving. *Khai* means 'egg' in Thai, as this island was a popular turtle nesting site in the past. **Chabang**'s sunken reef is home to hundreds of soft corals of many different colours that make for wonderfully rewarding snorkelling.

The far south ●●▲●● ‣ *pp578-584.*

Approached through towering karst peaks and bordered by limestone hills, Satun is a pleasant town with friendly, mostly Muslim inhabitants. Its only real tourist attraction is old town and the Kuden Mansion – a good example of British colonial architecture built by Penang artisans – which can be seen in a day. Most people use the town as a stopover en route to boats for Koh Tarutao, Koh Lipe and Malaysia. Thale Ban National Park, filled with birds and animals and forest trails is 37 km from Satun.

Satun province, which borders Malaysia on the west coast near the Straits of Malacca in the Indian Ocean, now falls within the danger zones for terrorist activity, particularly following the bombing at Hat Yai airport in 2005 (see box, page 672).

Satun → *Colour map 5, C4.*

Surrounded by mountains, Satun is cut off from the Malaysian Peninsula and the eastern side of the Kra Isthmus. Few towns in Thailand, particularly provincial capitals, have escaped thoughtless redevelopment. Satun, though, has done better than most. It has an attractive, low-key centre with preserved shophouses and is Malay in feel; 85% of the population are thought to be Muslim. Few tourists include Satun on their itinerary. Instead, they make a beeline for Ban Pak Bara, 60 km or so north of town and catch a boat to the Tarutao islands (see page 572). But perhaps Satun deserves a few more visitors.

The province seems to have spent the last century searching for an identity separate from that of its neighbours. In the early years of the last century it was administered as part of Kedah, in Malaysia. In 1909, following a treaty between Thailand and Britain, it came under the authority of Phuket. Fifteen years later it found itself being administered from Nakhon Si Thammarat, and it was not until 1932 that it managed to carve out an independent niche for itself when it was awarded provincial status by Bangkok.

The town's main mosque, the **Mesjid Bombang**, was built in 1979 after the previous mosque – also in the shape of a pyramid – fell prey to rot and was torn down. The mosque

Border essentials: Thailand–Malaysia

Satun–Kuala Perlis

Ferries leave from Satun for Malaysia and dock at one of two places, depending on the tide. If the tide is sufficiently high, boats leave from the jetty at the end of Samanta Prasit Road. At low water boats dock at Tammalang Pier, south of Satun. *Songthaews* run to the pier from Buriwanit Road.

There are four ferries daily from Satun and Langkawi Island (at 0845, 1200, 1530 and 1700). Tickets can be purchased in advance from Charan Tour, see page 583.

From **Trang**, get a shared taxi to Satun from Ratsada Road. (one hour 10 minutes, ฿200 per person, six people needed).

is on Satunthani Road. More interesting perhaps are the preserved **Chinese shophouses** on Buriwanit Road. They are thought to be around 150 years old; fortunately the town's authorities issued a preservation order on the buildings before they could be torn down and replaced by something hideous. **Ku Den's Mansion**, on Satunthani Road, dates from the 1870s. It was originally the governor's residence. The windows and doors share a Roman motif while the two-storey roof is in Thai Panyi style.

Thale Ban National Park

ⓘ *Thale Ban National Park Office, Amphoe Khuan Don, Satun Province, T074-797073. Open daily during daylight hours. Take Highway 4, 406 and 4184 to the park. By public transport catch a songthaew from Samantha Prasit Rd (by the pier) to Wang Prajan. From here there are occasional songthaews the last few kilometres, or take a motorcycle taxi.*

Bordering Malaysia, the Thale Ban National Park was gazetted in 1980 after four years of wrangling and threats from local so-called *ithiphon muut*, or 'dark influences'. It is a small park, covering just over 100 sq km, 37 km from Satun and 90 km from Hat Yai. How it got its name is the source of some dispute. Some people believe it is derived from the Malay words *loet roe ban*, meaning sinking ground; others that it comes from the Thai word *thale*, meaning sea.

The best time to visit Thale Ban is between December and April, when rainfall in this wet area (2662 mm per year) is at its minimum.

At the core of the park is a lake that covers some 30 ha, between the mountains Khao Chin to the east at 720 m and Khao Wangpra to the west. The park has a large bird population: hawks, hornbills, falcons and many migratory birds. Animals include dusky-leaf monkeys, white-handed gibbon, lesser mousedeer, wild boar and, it is said, the Sumatran rhinoceros. Forest trails lead from the headquarters and it is not unusual to see hornbills, langurs, macaques or even wild pigs. The round trip takes about four hours.

A hiking trail leads from the park headquarters to the summit of **Khao Chin** where it is possible to camp. There are also waterfalls and caves; the most frequently visited waterfall is **Ya Roi**, 5 km north of the park headquarters and accessible by vehicles. The falls plunge through nine levels; at the fifth is a good pool for swimming. En route to Ya Roi is a modest cave: **Ton Din**.

For Sleeping and Eating price codes and other relevant information, see pages 44-49.

◉ Sleeping

Tarutao National Park *p571, map p571*
Ban Pak Bara
D-E Pak Nam Resort, Koh Kebang, 15-min long-tailed taxi trip from Pak Bara pier, T074-781129. A more salubrious alternative to the country club. 17 bungalows and A-frame huts, all with fan and attached bathroom. Excellent restaurant but the water is dirty.
E Bara Resort, on the beach. A/c bungalows with hot water. Nice view but noisy and dusty from traffic.
E Best House Resort, close to the pier, T074-783058/783568. Offers 10 a/c and clean bungalows with comfortable beds, friendly owners and a good restaurant. Recommended.
E-F Panyong Country Club Resort, 20-30 mins' drive from Pak Bara pier, near Langu town (free transport is provided), T074-781230. A grand name for a simple set-up with basic a/c and fan wooden bungalows and a restaurant in a garden overlooking nipa palms, mangroves and some marshland. It's about a 200-m walk to a beach on a shallow bay. The beach is nothing special although the views are nice, and the resort is quiet.
F Diamond Beach, T074-783138. Bungalows with sea views.

Koh Tarutao *p573*
Book through the National Park office in Bangkok, T02-579052, or the Pak Bara office, T074-783485. Accommodation is in the north and west of Tarutao. There are 3 choices: multi-occupancy bungalows which can accommodate families or groups, longhouses and tents. The 3 main beaches – **Ao Pante**, **Ao Molae** and **Ao Sone** all offer some or all of these types, with Ao Pante, the one closest

to the pier and where the park warden offices are, offering the most selection. The rooms may also have shared outside toilets. The bungalows are sparsely furnished wooden structures, set along the side of the road against the cliffs. In the morning, the monkeys raiding the bins can be terrifically noisy but there are marvellous hornbills to offset that. Tents are on the beach with a public shower and toilet. Check your tent for size and condition. If you intend to stay for more than 2 nights it's best to buy a tent from the mainland; it will pay for itself and be clean, in good condition and odour-free. The treatment given to tent visitors varies. Hired tent cost ฿100-200; own tent ฿60. Best spots for camping are on Ao Jak and Ao Sone. You can also camp on the beach close to the national park bungalows (฿30 per night per person, as in other Thai national parks).
Ban Molae, Ao Molae. ฿1000. 4-person bungalows that are more upmarket and look rather like wendy houses. 2 rooms and 2 toilets.
Ban Nangnoi, Ao Pante. ฿650. 6-person bungalow. 2 rooms and 2 toilets.
Ban Tabang, Ao Pante. ฿1200. 4-person bungalow with 2 rooms and 2 toilets.
Ban Taboon, Ao Pante. ฿1000. 4-person bungalow. 2 rooms and 1 toilet.
Samed Dang Long House, Ao Pante. ฿500. 4 people per room. Toilet outside.
Samed Kaw Long House, Ao Pante. ฿500. 4 people per room. Toilet outside.

Koh Bulon-Leh *p574*
If you want to camp, **Charan Tour** can rent tents (see Satun tour operators, page 583.
C-D Ban Sulaida Bungalows, near Panka Noi Bay. Pleasant, clean rooms set in carefully tended gardens, with friendly owner who gives discounts for longer stays. 5 mins from the beach, but this is not the white-sand idyll of the eastern coast, although it's good for snorkelling. Small, airy restaurant

is decorated with shells, hanging bird nests and plants, serving good seafood.

C-D Pansand Resort, T08-1397 0802 (mob), or **First Andaman Travel** (Trang), T075-218 035. Open Oct-Jun. Well-maintained and welcoming bungalows with attached bathrooms and dormitories. The views are good, and the garden pleasant – it even has British-style park benches. Good watersports. It also organizes camping, snorkelling and boat trips and an evening internet service. Set in from main beach but this is a plus as it makes it feel more exclusive. Recommended.

C-E Bulon Viewpoint Resort and Tours. Some bungalows get little light and have poor views, others have great views, spotless bathrooms and plenty of sunshine. These are some of the most secure bungalows in Bulon-Leh. Good landscaping; the manager loves birds and insects. From the drop-off point on the beach you have a 15 to 20-min walk up a dirt path that becomes paved. Offers internet and has a good bar on the beach.

D Chaolae Food and Bungalows, up hill further on from **Bulon Viewpoint Resort**. Run by a Chao Le family. 8 raised brick and bamboo bungalows – all adorable. It has sunken bathrooms with squat toilet and shower but no fans. However, the trees provide respite from the heat. Tucked away so you might miss it but it is well worth the hunt. Plenty of personal touches. Sweet restaurant with shell mobiles and lined with cacti and brightly hued flowers in pots. You can choose your fish from the daily catch for beautiful cooking with herbs and spices. Recommended.

E Bulon Le Resort, T08-1897 9084 (mob). Well positioned where the boats dock over-looking a beautiful beach. A wide range of bungalows from nice, spacious, almost colonial options to the more basic, single rooms with spotless shared bathrooms. All in good shape and run by friendly and helpful management. Electricity 1800-0200. Good restaurant and the island's best breakfast. Recommended.

E Marina Bungalows, T074-728032, www.marina-kobulon.com. These wooden-log, fan bungalows set into the hill going up towards Panka Bay are charming and romantic but overpriced. They are more treehouse than bungalow – you can see the ground through the spaces in the log floor and there is no glass in the windows. But, even if snakes and palm rats can clamber through the logs at night there are perks like comfortable double beds, clean linen and large verandas big enough for hammocks. For those who don't mind roughing it.

E Panka Bay Resort, up the hill and down on the Panka Bay side of the island, T074-711 982, T074-783097. The only resort here. There are 21 bungalows at this Muslim Malay/Thai family-run establishment, all with varying advantages. Some have better views and bigger porches or are sheltered by trees. They are arranged along the beach and in tiers up a hill with handmade stone and sand steps built by the family. The beach is not great as it has a rocky shore but you can walk to the other beach in 20 mins and see some amazing bird and lizard life on the way. Excellent service – they offer a free pick up from the **Bulon-Le Resort**. Another perk is electricity until 0500. Huge restaurant with superb Thai-Malay fusion food. Recommended.

Koh Adang and Koh Rawi p575

Accommodation is all on the southern swathe of Adang island, with longhouses offering **B-D** rates, where some rooms accommodate sometimes up to 10 people.

Tents are available on Adang: big ฿200, small ฿100, own tent ฿60 at Laem Son. There is a simple restaurant. The island essentially closes down during the rainy season.

The bungalows here differ in terms of the perks offered, ie hot showers.
Laem Son, ฿400. 4 people per bungalow. Big tents (8-10 people), ฿300, medium/middle tents (3-5 people), ฿300, small tents (2 people), ฿150.

Rawi Long House, ฿400. 4 people per room. Toilet outside.

Koh Lipe p575

In recent years, accommodation on Lipe has expanded rapidly. A few years ago the Chao Le mainly operated the guesthouses, but more commercially astute outsiders have muscled in on the tourism industry. Electricity is usually only available from dusk onwards, mosquito nets are provided but not all places have fans or a/c that work. Where there is hot water it is more like warm water with poor pressure. The bungalows are either concrete or bamboo and fall within the **D-F** price range although most are within the **E-F** range and fairly basic. Most of the action is on **Pattaya Beach**, which has powder-soft white sand and crystal-blue water ideal for swimming. On the opposite side of the island is the smaller, slightly less dazzling **Sunset Beach**. **Sunlight Beach** is in from the dusty path that leads to the village – the beach here is beautiful and peaceful with water clear and blue enough to hurt your eyes and the water is shallow for some distance making it better for paddling than swimming.

A-E Varin Resort, Pattaya Beach, T074-728 080/081-5982225. The most upmarket spot on the beach, these 109 exceptionally clean bungalows, suites and villas are set in an attractive, if fairly cramped and regimental layout facing each other. Still, it offers the highest standard of accommodation on Lipe. There are nice personal touches such as the giant ceramic pots by the porches that are filled with water so you can wash your feet. The operation is run by a Muslim Thai/Malay family. The restaurant is a little characterless but service is excellent and attentive. Recommended.

C Asia Resort, Sunlight Beach, T074-728117. A divers' resort lacking in character. About 20 thatched bungalows on stilts set along a dusty path.

C-E Lipe Resort, Pattaya Beach, T074-724 336, www.liperesort.com. A mix of around 70 fan and a/c bungalows of varying sizes, set in part among the pine trees and all fairly clean with lino/tile floors and attached toilets. The more expensive white wooden bungalows at the front are better value and have large verandas while others sit over an unattractive crowded waterlogged inlet. There are also cheaper longhouses at the back. Electricity is available from 1800-0600, and when the internet works, it costs ฿5 per min. While some of the bungalows are attractive, the owner is a major detraction with guests complaining of intimidation. However, the ground-level staff go out of their way even if there is high staff turnover. The large, airy restaurant faces onto the beach.

C-E Mountain Resort, bay to west of Sunlight Beach, T074-728131, www.mt-resort.com. One of Lipe's best resorts with spacious grounds and corrugated-roofed bamboo bungalows. The rooms have 24-hr electricity, large verandas and basic tiled bathrooms. The large romantic wooden restaurant is set on a shaded cliff high above idyllic views over the sandbanks with great sea breeze. Steep steps down the cliff lead to a gorgeous shallow beach and the **Karma** beach bar. Fan and a/c rooms. Recommended.

D-F Andaman Resort, Sunlight Beach, T074-728017. A mix of 40 concrete, log and bamboo bungalows generously spaced along a pristine quiet beach and well-shaded by trees. The best rooms are the white and blue concrete row on the beach near the restaurant, although they lack some of the other huts' character. Clean, quiet, bright rooms popular with families. Owned a Chao Le-Chinese-Thai family. Recommended.

E Pooh's, Sunlight Beach, T074-722220. 6 clean fan bungalows set in Pooh's excellent, friendly, family-run complex of bar, internet, restaurant, travel agency and dive shop. Nice enough bungalows but they are not on the beach. Breakfast and 10 mins on the internet are included. Convenient for early morning coffee and everything else at this

one-stop operation run by the affable Mr Pooh ('crab' in English). Guests get a discount at the dive shop. Recommended.
E-F Daya Resort, Pattaya Beach, T074-728 030. Offers 48 bungalows with attached Western toilets and some rooms set in gardens and boasting the island's most popular seafood restaurant. However, bungalows are rather dirty and run-down in concrete and bamboo – also far too cramped.
E-F Pattaya Song (Two), Pattaya Beach, T074-728034. These 39 fan bungalows are set in the hillside overlooking the water with an ideal view. Unfortunately, you have to navigate a rickety wooden staircase just above the rocks. The rooms are only partly clean and the whole set-up feels a bit like a squat. Too bad because the restaurant does good Italian meals and the views are marvellous. Aim for the more sturdy concrete bungalows at the front rather than the bamboo shacks out back. Run by Stefano from Bologna, a larger-than-life character and avid fisherman who set up in Koh Lipe years ago.
E-F Porn Bungalows, Sunset Beach, T08-9464 5765 (mob). A Chao-Le run operation headed by Mr Gradtai. Fairly self-contained resort with simple woven bamboo huts on a beautiful beach; incredibly popular with return visitors – especially families with small children. The staff can take time to warm to newcomers but it's worth the work. The restaurant is a bit overpriced but the menu of the nearby **Flour Power** bakery is an excellent alternative (see Eating, below).
F Fishery Bay, Sunset Beach, T08-9739 4647 (mob). 7 municipal concrete bungalows with wide verandas set amid trees. Some have bathrooms shared between adjacent rooms. There are also 6 basic wooden huts on stilts with bathrooms on a small beach over the headland.
F Pink Resort, Pattaya Beach, T08-1598 3519 (mob). A cute name for a rather cute set-up next to **Lipe Resort**. The 12 bungalows are still nice, clean and new. Fishing trips can also be organized from here. Recommended.

F Viewpoint Resort, east end of Sunlight Beach, T08-6961 5967 (mob). 15 basic and rickety bungalows on a pretty but small beach, studded with boulders and overlooking the nearby islands. Built on a hill so plenty of step climbing is needed to get to each bungalow. Quiet and secluded. Restaurant attached.

Satun *p576*
E Wangmai, 43 Satunthani Rd, T074-711 607. A/c, restaurant, white 5-storey dated, slightly musty place with good facilities and clean rooms. Decent level of comfort and well priced.
E-F Sinkiat Thani, 50 Buri Wanit Rd, T074-721055. A hotel with a modicum of style. 108 large, well-kept rooms. Great views from the upper floors; guesthouse annex across the road with cheaper but spotless fan rooms. Satun's best hotel with low-season discounts. Claims to have the first disco in Satun.
G Rain Tong, Samantha Prasit Rd, at the western end, by the river. Cheap, dank flophouse with attached dirty bathrooms and cold-water showers.

Thale Ban National Park *p577*
There are 10 bungalows for rent around the lake, sleeping between 8 and 15. There is also a restaurant and an information centre at the park headquarters. Tents are available for hire from the park headquarters.

🍴 Eating

Koh Tarutao *p573*
Just one Thai restaurant with coupon system for paying for food: purchase your coupons at the table next to the restaurant, and return any not used for a cash refund.

Koh Bulon-Leh *p574*
⸙ Orchid, near Ban Sulaida Bungalows, see Sleeping, above. A good, cheap restaurant.

Koh Lipe p575

Excellent simple seafood served along the main Pattaya Beach when tables and chairs are laid out at night. You can choose the cut and fish. **Varin Resort** also does marvellous salads and baked potatoes with the fish.

¶¶¶ **Pooh's**, on the path between **Chao Le Resort** and Pattaya Beach, T074-722220. Usually the busiest place, offering music, a good bar and tasty meals in a well-decorated, relaxed airy setting. The bakery also serves up typically delicious goods.

¶¶ **Daya**, west end of Pattaya Beach. One of the best places for barbecued fish thanks to an exquisite marinade.

¶¶ **Pattaya Song restaurant**, west end of Pattaya Beach, next to **Daya**. Italian pasta dishes and pizza as well as Thai food.

¶ **Banana Tree Restaurant**, in the village (take a left at **Forra Dive Centre**). An off-beach setting with shady floor seating under the trees. A popular spot with an extensive Thai menu, it shows movies in the evenings.

¶ **Flour Power Bakery**, Sunset Beach, behind **Sabye Sports**. It has expanded its seating area along with its repertoire to include a mouthwatering selection of Thai and Western dishes, such as lemon chicken, as well as its staple fruit pies, brownies, fresh bread and cinnamon rolls. The vegetarian selection is good and all meals are served with fresh bread or baked potatoes and salad.

¶ **Thai Pancake Shop**, opposite the massage centre. A popular spot serving pancakes, sandwiches, burgers, breakfasts, simple Thai dishes, lassis, shakes and excellent cocktails.

Satun p576

Pretty much opposite the **Sinkiat Thani** are several small restaurants serving Malay food and a *roti* shop selling banana, egg and plain *rotis* in the mornings.

¶¶-¶ **Banburee**, Buriwanit Rd. 1 of 2 places with English signs. Modern establishment behind the **Sinkiat Thani**.

¶¶-¶ **Kualuang**, Satuntanee Phiman. Best in a group of small restaurants.

¶ **The Baker's**, Satuntanee Phiman, main street into town. Pastries, ice cream and soft drinks.

¶ **Smile**, round the corner from **Wangmai Hotel** on Satuntanee Phiman Rd. Fast food, budget prices.

¶ **Suhana**, 16/7 Buriniwet Rd. The other English-signed place on this road behind the mosque. Muslim food.

Foodstalls

Night market with stalls serving Thai and Malay dishes on Satun Thani Soi 3. There are plenty of roadside food vendors – particularly on Samantha Prasit Rd. All serve cheap rice and noodles.

⚙ Bars and clubs

Koh Lipe p575

As the volume of tourist trade picks up, more of these are springing up. On Pattaya Beach there's **Time to Chill** probably the pick of the bunch due to the super-friendly dreadlocked owner Mut and a lovely laid-back atmosphere; **Monkey Bar**, **Moon Light Bar**, and **Peace and Love Bar**, all of which are relaxed with mats and candles on the beach. **Jack's Jungle Bar**, up in the hills (follow the signs from the village). Has a more upbeat feel and is popular with the diving crowd. Make sure you bring a torch for the trek home.

Karma beach bar, on the charming bay below the **Mountain Resort**. A popular bar. The owners are friendly and it normally has a great island-idyll atmosphere.

Pooh's remains a favourite watering hole and is rather more upmarket than the beach bars with a stage for live bands.

▲ Activities and tours

Tarutao National Park p571, map p571
Diving and snorkelling

Some of the best areas for coral are in the

waters northwest of Koh Rang Nok, north-west of Tarutao, southeast of Koh Rawi, around Koh Klang between Tarutao and Adang, and off Koh Kra off Koh Lipe's east coast. Equipment is for hire on Adang and Lipe.

Kayaking
Paddle Asia, 19/3 Rasdanusorn Rd, Phuket, T/F076-240893, www.paddleasia.com. Offers kayaking/snorkelling tours to Tarutao.

Tours and tour operators
For tours to Tarutao, see also Satun, below.
Khun Udom, T08-1897 4765 (mob). A licensed tour guide with a good knowledge of the islands.
Tarutao Travel, in La-Ngu town (on the way to Pak Bara Pier), Ban Pak Bara, T074-781284/781360.
Udom Tour, Ban Pak Bara, just before the port, T08-1897 4765 (mob).

Koh Lipe p575
Tours and tour operators
Heading further west from Lipe, there are countless islands and coral reefs teeming with a staggering variety of fish – the locals know all the good spots. The best locations, only 1 or 2 hrs away, include Koh Dong, Koh Pung and Koh Tong, Koh Hin Son, Koh Hin Ngam and Koh Chabang.

Outfits include **Dang's Tours**, a stone's throw from Pooh's on the way to Chao Ley Resort, just one of the outfits that arranges all day snorkelling tours for around ฿1000 per boat for 6 people; **Forra Dive Centre**, near Chao Ley Resort; **Jack's Tours**, on the beach at Koh Lipe; **Lotus Dive** (Pooh's), **Ocean Pro Divers** near Leepay Resort. **Sabye Sports**, next to **Porn Bungalows**, T/F074-734104, T08-9464 5884 (mob), info@sabye-divers.com. The island's first scuba-diving and sports centre, offers diving and rents canoes (฿500 per day) and snorkelling equipment (฿200 per day). **Starfish Scuba**, next to the **Leepay Resort**, Pattaya Beach, T074-728089, www.starfish scuba.com. Also offers diving courses.

Satun p576
Tour operators
Charan Tour, 19/6 Satunthani Rd, T074-711 453/01-9573908. Runs boat tours every day to the islands between Oct-May. Lunch and snorkelling equipment are provided. Has a good reputation.

⊖ Transport

Tarutao National Park p571, map p571
Boat
To **Koh Lipe**, 2½-3½ hrs. Transfer from ferry to long-tailed boat to Koh Lipe and Koh Adang, ฿30. Boats can also be chartered from Tarutao. To **Satun** from Tarutao at 1700.

Ferries leave from Pak Bara, T074-783010. Call for departure times and prices. To see all the islands, the ฿900 return ticket allows stops at **Tarutao**, **Lipe**, **Adang** and **Bulon**. Boats to **Koh Tarutao** (docking at Ao Phante Malaka on the island's west coast) at 1030 and 1330 from Nov-May (1½ hrs, ฿300 return) and then on to Koh Lipe and Koh Adang (3 hrs, ฿900 return).

Speedboats also leave for Tarutao, Lipe and Adang during the season at 0900 and 1300. The ferry stops at Tarutao (฿400 one way) and then continues for ฿1300 return.

The daily boat to **Koh Bulon-Leh** leaves at 1400 (1½ hrs, ฿500 return).

It is often too rough between May and Oct for ferries to operate, and the park is officially closed in any case. However, boats can be chartered throughout the year (฿1500 plus). Long-tailed boat charters from Pak Bara to **Koh Bulon-Leh** cost ฿700-1000 per boat.

Bus
There are regular buses from **Ban Pak Bara** to **Trang** and **Satun**, 60 km south. Connections to **Hat Yai**, 1½ hrs. Hat Yai is 158 km east of Pak Bara (1½hrs).

Koh Bulon-Leh *p574*
Boat
From Bulon-Leh to **Koh Tarutao** and
Ban Pak Bara, the boats leave at 0900
and 1200. Boats travel on from Koh Bulon-
Leh to **Koh Adang** and **Koh Lipe** at 1430.

Koh Lipe *p575*
Boat
There's a return ferry at 0900 from
Lipe to **Koh Tarutao**.

Satun *p576*
Air
Hay Yai airport offers several daily connecting
flights to Bangkok with **Air Asia**, **Nok Air** and
Orient Thai Airlines.

Boat
There is 1 boat a day from Tammalang Pier
(Satun) to the islands (**Tarutao** and **Lipe**) at
1100, ฿900 return. It is also possible to charter
a boat from Satun, but it is a lot cheaper catch
an early bus to **Pak Bara** and take 1 of the
regular boats from there (see above).

Bus
Overnight connections with **Bangkok**,
15 hrs. Buses for Bangkok leave from Sarit
Phuminaraot Rd. Regular connections with
Hat Yai and **Trang** from opposite the wat on
Buriwanit Rd. To **Pak Bara**, buses leave from
Plaza Market. The buses connect with ferries.

Taxi
To **Hat Yai** from Bureevanith Rd; to **Trang**,
from taxi rank next to Chinese temple.

❶ Directory

Satun *p576*
Banks On Buriwanit and Satunthani Rd.
Thai Military, Buriwanit Rd, across from Hat
Yai taxi rank on Buriwanit Rd; Thai Farmers,
opposite the market. **Immigration** Office
at the end of Buriwanit Rd. **Internet** Near
the Sinkiat Hotel, Satunthani Rd is an internet
café **Satun Cybernet** offers connections for
฿30 per hr. **Post office** Samantha Prasit Rd,
near Intersection with Satun Thani Rd.
Telephone Attached to the GPO.

Contents

Gulf of Thailand

At a glance

◉ **Getting around** The islands are served by boats and some planes. The railway line from Bangkok runs down the spine.

◉ **Time required** 1-2 weeks, some people stay permanently.

☼ **Weather** Dive conditions around Koh Tao are best from Feb-May.

✖ **When not to go** The Chinese monsoon hits a bit later than on the western half of the country. Expect rains in Nov and Dec.

N
20 km
20 miles

Phetburi
Phet Buri Reservoir
Tha Yang
Hat Chao Sumran
Nong
Bight of Bangkok
Kaeng Krachan National Park
Cha-am
Thongklua
Pak Ngam
1 Hua Hin
Rt 4
Pran Buri Reservoir
Pranburi
Rai Mai
Phu Noi
Khao Sam Roi Yod National Park
Bang Pu
Samrong
Khung Tanot

BURMA (MYANMAR)

Prachuap Khiri Khan

Rt 4

Thap Sakae

Ban Krut

Bang Saphan
Koh Talu

Mai Sombun
Koh Wiang

Rt 4
Ao Bang Saphan

Chumphon
Pak Nam Chumphon

Kra Buri
Ao Sawi
Ao Sawi

Khao Thaiu
Gulf of Thailand

Ranong
Lang Suan

Phato
Isthmus of Kra
Khuan
Rt 41

Nam Sai
Tha Chana
Koh Tao
4

Wat Suan Mok
Ban Mae Hat

Ang Thong Marine National Park
Thong Sala
3

Koh Ang Tong
Koh Phangan

Chaiya
Koh Phaluai
Nathon
Bophut

Koh Nok
Koh Samui
2

Ao Ban Don
Ta Phao
Tha Thong

Tha Chang
Don Sak

Kanchanadit
Khanom

Phun Phin
Krut

Surat Thani
Khao Nan National Park
Sichon
Tha Mak

Kwang
Rt 401
Rt 41

Khao Wong
Khao Luang National Park

Rt 415

Khao To
Than Phut
Laem Talumphet

Phraegaeng
Nakhon Si Thammarat
Ao Nakhon

Ao Luk Nua
Rt 4037

Rt 41
Chawang
5

★ **Don't miss ...**
1 **Hua Hin**, page 591.
2 **Massage on Koh Samui**, pages 637, 638 and 639.
3 **Full Moon Party, Koh Phangan**, page 645.
4 **Jamahkiri Spa and Resort, Koh Tao**, page 665.
5 **Nakhon Si Thammarat**, page 671.

Beaches, resorts, national parks and cultured towns garland the length of the Gulf Coast, with the islands offering unbridled hedonism. Phetburi, south of Bangkok, is peppered with wats and a hilltop royal palace affording sweeping views of the plains, while Khao Sam Roi Yod National Park provides a glimpse of the rare dusky langur. Cha-am, Hua Hin and Prachuap Khiri Khan provide old-world charm, excellent spas, some outstanding resorts and fewer tourists.

The appeal of the northern Gulf Coast towns is eclipsed by the delights of Koh Samui, Koh Phangan and Koh Tao. These islands have it all: there are the pampering palaces, appealing resorts, fine dining, streets of thumping bars, action-packed beaches and quiet bays on Koh Samui; meanwhile, once a month on the smaller Koh Phangan, the world's largest outdoor party spins on the sands at Hat Rin when 10,000 people flock to dance and drink in the glow of the full moon. Around the rest of the island, particularly the east coast, the perfect getaways are waiting in cove after cove with sapphire seas tainted only by a glint of granite.

Further north at Koh Tao, the underwater world is an attraction with so many shallow reefs offshore. Around the island remote bays are guarded by huge granite boulder formations and surrounded by perfect tropical seas. At night Hat Sai Ri is enlivened by funky bars and beachfront dining.

The thriving town of Nakhon Si Thammarat, unmuddied by full-scale tourism, offers an opportunity to see the unusual art of shadow puppetry and savour confectioners' delicate pastries.

Phetburi to Chumphon

The historic town of Phetburi (or Phetchaburi), with perhaps the best-preserved Ayutthayan wats in Thailand, is 160 km south of Bangkok and can be visited as a day trip from the capital. It is a historic provincial capital on the banks of the Phetburi River and is one of the oldest cities in Thailand and, because it was never sacked by the Burmese, is unusually intact.

Another 70 km south is Hua Hin, one of Thailand's premier beach resorts and the destination of choice for generations of Thai royalty. These days Hua Hin has been overshadowed – at least in terms of numbers – by Phuket and Pattaya. Yet this resort town manages to maintain a lot more character than its bigger rivals, with a virtually intact waterfront of old wooden fishing houses, most of which, admittedly, have been turned into restaurants.

Close by is Cha-am, a smaller seaside resort mostly frequented by blue-collar Thais looking for some good grilled pork, sun and sea. If you want to get into some wilder surroundings head for the Khao Sam Roi Yod National Park with its rare dusky langurs. Further south is the pleasant resort of Prachuap Khiri Khan, with the stunning beach of Ao Manao, and the long, less-developed coast down to Chumphon. Chumpon offers some local attractions such as trekking, kayaking, kitesurfing and diving but is mainly the launch pad to the island of Koh Tao. ▸▸ For listings, see pages 598-610.

Phetburi and around ⬤🚗❀🏨🍴 ▸▸ pp598-610.

Ins and outs → *Colour map 3, C3.*
Getting there and around Trains take 2½ hours from Bangkok and the station is about 1.5 km northwest of the town centre. The main bus terminal is about the same distance west of town, at the foot of Phra Nakhon Khiri (Khao Wang), but the air-conditioned bus terminal is more central, some 500 m north of the centre. Buses take about two hours from Bangkok. *Songthaews* meet the buses and take passengers into the town centre. There are connections south to Cha-am, Hua Hin and onward. Phetburi – or at least its centre – is small enough to explore on foot. ▸▸ *See also Transport, page 608.*

Background
Initially, Phetburi's wealth and influence was based upon the coastal salt pans found in the vicinity of the town, and which Thai chronicles record as being exploited as early as the 12th century. By the 16th century, Phetburi was supplying salt to most of Siam and the Malay Peninsula. It became particularly important during the Ayutthaya period (14th century) and because the town was not sacked by the Burmese (as Ayutthaya was in 1767) its fine examples of Ayutthayan art and architecture are in good condition. Later, during the 19th century, Phetburi became a popular retreat for the Thai royal family and they built a palace here. Today, Phetburi is famous for its paid assassins who usually carry out their work from the backs of motorcycles with large-calibre pistols. Each time there is a national election, 15 to 20 politicians and their canvassers (so-called *hua khanen*) are killed. As in Chonburi, Thailand's other capital of crime, the police seem strangely unable to charge anyone.

Phetburi
Phetburi has numerous wats. Those mentioned below are some of the more interesting examples. Although it is possible to walk around these wats in half a day, travelling by

saamlor is much less exhausting. Note that often the ordination halls (bots) are locked; if the abbot can be found, he may be persuaded to open them up.

Situated in the centre of town on Damnoenkasem Road, **Wat Phra Sri Ratana Mahathat** can be seen from a distance. It is dominated by five much-restored, Khmer-style white *prangs*, probably dating from the Ayutthaya period (14th century); the largest is 42 m high. Inside the bot, richly decorated with murals, are three highly regarded Buddha images, arranged one in front of the other: **Luangpor Mahathat**, **Luangpor Ban Laem** and **Luangpor Lhao Takrao**. The principal image depicts the crowned Buddha. The complex makes an attractive cluster of buildings. Musicians and dancers are paid by those who want to give thanks for wishes granted.

Across Chomrut Bridge and east along Pongsuriya Road is **Wat Yai Suwannaram**; it's on the right-hand side, within a spacious compound and a large pond. The wat was built during the Ayutthaya period and then extensively restored during the reign of Rama V. The bot contains some particularly fine Ayutthayan murals showing celestial beings and, facing the principal Buddha image, Mara tempting the Buddha. Note the six-toed bronze Buddha image on the rear wall which is thought to be pre-Ayutthayan in date. Behind the bot is a large teak pavilion (*sala kan parian*) with three doorways at the front and two at the back. The front door panels have fine coloured-glass insets, while the mark on the right-hand panel is said to have been made by a Burmese warrior en route to attack Ayutthaya.

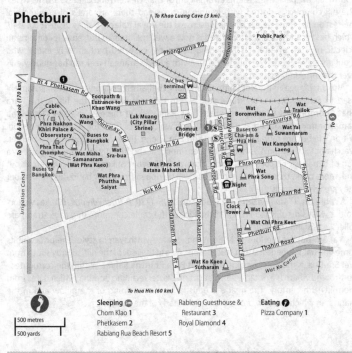

Phetburi

Sleeping
Chom Klao 1
Phetkasem 2
Rabiang Rua Beach Resort 5

Rabieng Guesthouse & Restaurant 3
Royal Diamond 4

Eating
Pizza Company 1

The wat also houses an elegant, old wooden library. **Wat Boromvihan** and **Wat Trailok** are next to one another on the opposite side of the road and are being restored. They are distinctive only for their wooden dormitories (*kuti*) on stilts.

South down Phokarong Road and west a short distance along Phrasong Road, is **Wat Kamphaeng Laeng**. The five Khmer laterite *prangs* (one in very poor condition) have been dated to the 12th century and are reminiscent of those in the northeast of the country. Little of the original stucco work remains, but they are nonetheless rather pleasing. Surrounded by thick laterite walls, the wat may have originally been a Hindu temple – a statue of a Hindu goddess was found here in 1956.

West back towards the centre of town and south down Matayawong Road, are, in turn, **Wat Phra Song**, **Wat Laat** and **Wat Chi Phra Keut**, all on the left-hand side of the road. Just before reaching a bridge over Wat Ko Canal, is **Wat Ko Kaeo Sutharam**. The bot contains early 18th-century murals showing scenes from the Buddha's life and from Buddhist cosmology. The fact that the mural of the Buddha subduing Mara is on the rear wall, behind the principal Buddha image, has led to speculation that the entrance to the building was relocated at some time, possibly to gain access to a newly constructed road. The wat also houses interesting quarters for monks – long wooden buildings on stilts, similar to those at Wat Boromvihan.

At the western edge of the city is **Phra Nakhon Khiri**, popularly known as **Khao Wang** (Palace on the Mountain), built in 1858 during the reign of Rama IV. Perched on the top of a 95-m hill, the palace represents an amalgam of Thai, Western and Chinese artistic styles. The hill complex is dotted with frangipani trees and there are areas of architectural interest on the three peaks. On the west rise is the **Royal Palace** ① *daily 0900-1600, ฿40*, which has recently been restored and is now a well-maintained museum. It contains an eclectic mixture of artefacts (including bed pans) collected by Ramas IV and V who regularly stayed here. The building is airy with a Mediterranean feel and has good views over the surrounding plain.

Also on this peak is the **Hor Chatchavan Viangchai**, an observatory tower which Rama IV used to further his astronomical studies. On the central rise of the hill is the **Phra That Chomphet**, a white stupa erected by Rama IV. On the east rise sits **Wat Maha Samanaram** (also known as Wat Phra Kaeo), which dates from the Ayutthayan period. Within the bot are mural paintings by Khrua In Khong, quite a well-known Thai painter. Watch out for the monkeys here; they seem innocent and friendly enough until you buy a bag of bananas or a corn on the cob. Sprawls between monkeys are quick to break out and, more often than not, the whole bag will be ripped from your hand. Just remember they are wild animals!

A **cable car** ① *Mon-Fri 0815-1700, Sat-Sun, 0815-1730, ฿30, children ฿10*, takes visitors up the west side of Khao Wang. At the foot of the cable car (more of a cable-tram) are toilets, cafés and souvenir stalls.

Wat Sra-bua, at the foot of Khao Wang, is late Ayutthayan in style. The bot exhibits some fine gables, pedestal and stucco work. Also at the foot of the hill, slightly south from Wat Sra-bua, is the poorly maintained **Wat Phra Phuttha Saiyat**. Within the corrugated-iron-roofed viharn is a notable 43-m brick and plaster reclining Buddha, which dates from the mid-18th century. The image is unusual in the moulding of the pillow and in the manner in which the arm protrudes into the body of the building.

Around Phetburi

Khao Luang Cave, 3 km north of Phetburi on Route 3173 (take a *saamlor*), contains stalactites, stupas and multitudes of second-rate Buddha images in various poses. This cave was frequently visited by Europeans who came to Phetburi in the 19th century. Mary Lovina Court (1886), an early example of the inquisitive but destructive Western tourist, wrote: "At the mouth of the cave we found some curious rocks, and succeeded in breaking off several good specimens." There is a large reclining Buddha inside the cave. Mary Court ended her sojourn telling some Buddhist visitors about "the better God than the idols by which they had knelt". On the right-hand side, at the entrance to the cave, is a monastery called **Wat Bun Thawi** with attractive carved-wooden door panels.

South from Phetburi ⊖✪☻⊕❶ ➤ *pp598-610.*

Cha-am

Cha-am is reputed to have been a stopping place for King Naresuan's troops when they were travelling south. The name Cha-am may have derived from the Thai word *cha-an*, meaning to clean the saddle. Cha-am is a beach resort with some excellent hotels and a sizeable building programme of new hotels and condominiums for wealthy Bangkokians. The beach is a classic stretch of golden sand, filled with beach umbrellas and inner-tube renters. The northern end of the beach is much quieter, with a line of trees providing cooling shade. The town also has a good reputation for the quality of its seafood and grilled pork. It has become a popular weekend spot, so sizeable discounts are available during the week when most hotels are close to empty. At the weekend something of a transformation occurs and it buzzes with life for 48 hours before returning to its comatose state. The **tourist office** ① *Phetkasem Rd, close to the post office, T032-471005, www.tat. or.th/central2, daily 0830-1630*, is responsible for the areas of Cha-am and Prachuap Khiri Khan, Phetburi and Hua Hin. Air-conditioned buses from Bangkok drop you right on the beach but other buses from Phetburi or Hua Hin stop on the Phetkasem Highway at its junction with Narathip Road. Motorbike taxis from here to the beach cost ฿20.

Between Cha-am and Hua Hin, **Maruekkhathayawan Palace** ① *daily 0800-1600, entry by donation*, was designed by an Italian and built by Rama VI in 1924; the king is reputed to have had a major influence in its design. The palace is made of teak and the name means 'place of love and hope', which is rather charming. It consists of 16 pavilions in a very peaceful setting. To get there, take a *saamlor* or catch a bus heading for Hua Hin and walk 2 km from the turn-off.

Hua Hin and around ⊖✪☻❀⊙▲⊖❶ ➤ *pp598-610.*

Thailand's first beach resort, Hua Hin, has had an almost continuous royal connection since the late 19th century. In 1868, King Mongkut journeyed to Hua Hin to observe a total eclipse of the sun. In 1910, Prince Chakrabongse, brother of Rama VI, visited Hua Hin on a hunting trip and was so enchanted by the area that he built himself a villa. These days Hua Hin is a thriving resort town that, in places, has managed to retain some of its charm – particularly the waterfront. The suburbs are filled with holiday villas, while most of the high-end hotels are several kilometres to the north of the town. These luxury places are some of the best in Thailand, if not the world, and are a big draw for many visitors.

Ins and outs

Getting there There are daily flights with SGA who run a 12-seat Cessna from Bangkok to Hua Hin's Bofai Airport, T032-520343. A taxi from the airport costs ฿40-50, a local bus costs ฿10. The **train station** ① *Damnoenkasem Rd, T032-511073, T032-5111690*, is on the western edge of town, within walking distance of the centre. The journey from Bangkok takes three hours and there are onward connections to all points south. The bus terminal is quite central and provides regular connections with Bangkok and many southern towns.

Getting around Hua Hin is an increasingly compact beach resort and many of the hotels and restaurants are within walking distance of one another. There is also a good network of public transport: *songthaews* run along fixed routes, there are taxis and *saamlors*, and bicycles, motorbikes and cars are all available for hire. *Saamlors* can be hired for ฿50 around town, ฿150 for a sightseeing tour. *Songthaew* rout to Khao Takiab, ฿15.

Tourist information **Tourist office** ① *114 Phetkasem Rd, T032-532433, Mon-Fri 0830-1200, 1300-2000.* Also useful is www.huahin.go.th.

Background

The first of the royal palaces, **Saen Samran House**, was built by Prince Naris, son of Rama V. In the early 1920s, King Vajiravudh (Rama VI) – no doubt influenced by his brother Chakrabongse – began work on a teakwood palace, '**Deer Park**'. The final stamp of royal approval came in the late 1920s, when King Phrajadipok (Rama VII) built another palace, which he named **Klai Kangwon**, literally 'Far From Worries'. It was designed by one of Prince Naris' sons. The name could not have been more inappropriate: the king was staying at Klai Kangwon in 1932 when he was dislodged from the throne by a coup d'état.

Early guidebooks, nostalgic for English seaside towns, named the resort Hua Hin-on-Sea. *Hua* (head) *Hin* (rock) refers to a stone outcrop at the end of the fine white-sand beach. The resort used to promote itself as the 'Queen of Tranquillity'; until the 1980s, it was a forgotten backwater of an earlier, and less frenetic, tourist era. However, in the last few years the constant influx of tourists has livened up the atmosphere considerably; with massage parlours, tourist shops and numerous Western restaurants and bars lining the streets, it's hard to get a moment's peace. And just when you think the town is as chock-a-block as possible, the sound of drills and construction work reminds you otherwise. Condominiums are springing up all along the coast to cater for wealthy holidaymakers from Bangkok; high-rise buildings scar the horizon and vehicles clog the streets. New golf courses are being constructed to serve Thailand's growing army of golfers – as well as avid Japanese players – and the olde-worlde charm that was once Hua Hin's great selling point has been lost.

Sights

As Hua Hin is billed as a beach resort people come here expecting a beautiful tropical beach but that isn't quite the case. Many of the nicest stretches of sand are in front of hotels – the **Hilton**, **Marriott** and **Sofitel** in particular.

The famous **Railway Hotel** was built in 1923 by a Thai prince, Purachatra, who headed the State Railways of Thailand. It became Thailand's premier seaside hotel, but by the 1960s had fallen into rather glorious disrepair. It experienced a short burst of stardom when the building played the role of the **Phnom Penh Hotel** in the film the *Killing Fields*, but it still seemed destined to rot into oblivion. Saved by privatization, it was renovated

Hua Hin

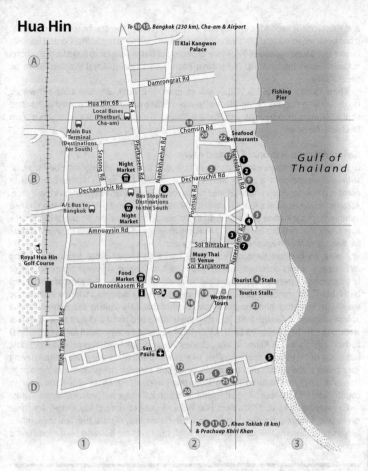

To ⑩⑮, Bangkok (230 km), Cha-am & Airport

□ Klai Kangwon Palace

Gulf of Thailand

Fishing Pier

Damrongrat Rd

Hua Hin 68
Local Buses (Phetburi, Cha-am)

Main Bus Terminal (Destinations for South)

Srasong Rd

Phetkasem Rd

Neebkhachat Rd

Chomsin Rd

⑱

⑳ ㉒ Seafood Restaurants

Night Market

⑰ ❶
❷ ❾
❻

Dechanuchit Rd

A/c Bus to Bangkok

Dechanuchit Rd

Poonsuk Rd

Naresdamri Rd

❽ Bus Stop for Destinations to the South

Night Market

❹ ❸

Amnuaysin Rd

❸
❼

Royal Hua Hin Golf Course

Food Market

Soi Bintabat

Muay Thai Venue

Soi Kanjanoma

❻

Damnoenkasem Rd

Tourist ❹ Stalls

Tourist Stalls

Riab Tang Rot Fai Rd

i ✉ ☎ ❽ ⑯ ⑲ Western Tours ㉓

San Paulo ✚

⑫

㉑ ❶ @
㉕ ⑭

⑤

⑤⑪⑬

⑤

To ⑤⑪⑬, Khao Takiab (8 km) & Prachuap Khiri Khan

Gulf of Thailand

N

|—| 100 metres
|—| 100 yards

Sleeping 🛏
A&B **1** *D2*
All Nations Guesthouse **2** *B2*
All Seasons Guest House **8** *C2*
Anantara Resort & Spa **10** *A2*

Araya **20** *B2*
Bird Guesthouse **3** *B3*
Central Hua Hin Village **4** *C3*
Chiva Som International Health Resort **5** *D2*
Chomsin Hua Hin **18** *B2*
City Beach Resort **6** *C2*
Evason Hua Hin Resort & Spa **13** *D2*
Fulay Guesthouse **9** *B3*
Hilton Hua Hin Resort & Spa **7** *C3*
Hua Hin Marriott Resort & Spa **12** *D2*

Hyatt Regency Hua Hin **11** *D2*
Jinning Beach **14** *D2*
Patchara House **16** *C2*
Pattana Guesthouse **17** *B2*
PP Villa & Puang Pen **19** *C2*
Royal Beach **21** *D2*
Sheraton Hua Hin Resort & Spa **15** *A2*
Sofitel Central Hua Hin Resort **23** *C3*
Sunshine Guesthouse **25** *D2*

Supasuda/Ananthara Guesthouse **22** *B2*
White Villa **26** *D2*

Eating 🍴
Brasserie de Paris **1** *B3*
Chao Lay **2** *B3*
Hua Hin Brewing Co **7** *C3*
Jeak Peak **8** *B2*
Lo Stivale **3** *C2*
Maharaja **6** *B3*
Veranda Grill **5** *D3*
World News Coffee **4** *B3*

and substantially expanded in 1986 and is now an excellent five-star hotel. Unfortunately, it has been renamed, and goes under the unromantic name of the Sofitel Central Hua Hin Resort (see Sleeping, page 601). At the other end of Damnoenkasem Road from the hotel is the railway station itself. The station has a rather quaint Royal Waiting Room on the platform.

Khao Takiab (Chopstick Hill), south of town, is a dirty, unremarkable hill with a large standing Buddha facing the sea. Nearby is **Khao Krilat**, a rock covered in assorted shrines, stupas, ponds, salas and Buddha images. To get there, take a local bus from Dechanuchit Road.

Kaeng Krachan National Park and caves

ⓘ *Until recently, entrance to the park was only ฿20, but was suddenly increased to ฿200 with another charge of ฿200 for the Pa La-U waterfalls. Due to this dramatic increase, a number of tour operators have decided to boycott the park, in the hope the price will drop. Accommodation is available at the park HQ, see Sleeping, page 602. To get to the park, take a minibus from the station on Srasong Rd to the village of Fa Prathan, 53 km (฿15). For the caves, take the same bus but get off at Nongphlab village (฿10) and ask at the police station for directions. The caves are a 45-min to 1-hr walk.*

The park, 63 km northwest of Hua Hin, is Thailand's largest protected area covering 2915 sq km. It was gazetted in 1981 and is said to support significant populations of large mammal species (elephant, tiger, leopard, gibbon, the Malayan pangolin) and birds (hornbills, minivets, pheasants and bee-eaters). Endangered species include the woolly-necked stork and the plain-pouched hornbill. Few visitors see many of these animals though. Extensive trails lead through undisturbed forest and past a succession of waterfalls (the best being **Pa La-U**, which has 11 tiers and is renowned for its butterflies) to hot springs and a Karen village. Guides are advisable and charge ฿500 per day, but many of them don't speak English, so make sure you meet the guide before paying your money. The Tenasserim mountain range cuts through the park; the highest peak stands at 1207 m. **Phanoen Thung Mountain** offers superb views of the surrounding countryside. It's a six-hour hike to the summit; warm clothes are needed for chilly mornings.

En route to Pa La-U, 27 km from Hua Hin and close to Nongphlab village, are three caves: **Dao**, **Lablae** and **Kailon**, which contain the usual array of stalactites and stalagmites. Guides with lanterns will take visitors through the caves for ฿30 and boat trips can be made on the reservoir.

South of Hua Hin ⬤❼❷❶ ›› *pp598-610.*

Khao Sam Roi Yod National Park

ⓘ *Park HQ, T032-619078, ฿200, children ฿100. Take a bus from Hua Hin to Pranburi (there are also trains to Pranburi, as well as trains and buses from Bangkok). From Pranburi it is necessary to charter a songthaew (฿250) or take a motorcycle taxi (฿150) to the park HQ. Be sure you are taken to Khao Sam Roi Yod National Park, and not Khao Sam Roi Yod village. For Laem Sala Beach (located within the park), there are regular songthaews from Pranburi market to Bang Pu village from 0800-1600, ฿20. Or take a tour with one of the many tour operators in town, ฿900.*

Khao Sam Roi Yod National Park ('Mountain of Three Hundred Peaks') occupies an area of limestone hills surrounded by saltwater flats and borders the Gulf of Thailand. It lies about 45 km south of Hua Hin, east off Route 4. Its freshwater marshes provide 11 different categories of wetland habitat – as much as the Red River Delta in Vietnam which covers an area nearly 200 times greater. The area is a haven for waterbirds and has been extensively developed (and exploited) as a centre for prawn and fish farming, limiting the marshland available to the waterbirds who breed here. The park has the advantage of being relatively small (98 sq km) with readily accessible sights: wildlife (including the rare and shy serow), forest walks and quiet beaches. The main beach is Laem Sala where a campsite, bungalows and a restaurant are located. Search the beach here for sand dollars and mother of pearl.

There are also some caves. **Phraya Nakhon**, close to Ban Bang Pu beach, has two large sinkholes where the roof collapsed a century ago, and a pavilion which was built in 1896 for the visit of King Rama V and is currently being restored. The climb to the cave takes one hour and can be slippery. If you are lucky you may spot some rare dusky langurs with their babies. **Sai Cave** contains impressive stalactites and stalagmites and a 'petrified waterfall' created from dripping water. At least 237 species of land and waterbirds have been recorded including painted storks, herons, egrets and many different waders. To visit the caves and beaches, boats can be hired from local fishermen at the park HQ (฿200-700). Schools of dolphins are often sighted on the way.

The biggest challenge facing the park – which supports a remarkable range of habitats for such a small area – is encroachment by private shrimp ponds. More than a third of the park area was cleared for fish and shrimp farming in 1992. Ironically, most of the prawn farms are now deserted, due to prawn disease. Available at the park HQ is a very useful guide with comprehensive details on fauna, flora and other natural sights in the park.

Prachuap Khiri Khan

Prachuap Khiri Khan is a small and peaceful resort with a long, crescent-shaped beach. At either end of the crescent, vegetation-draped limestone towers rear up from the sea creating beautiful symmetry and stunning views. The town is more popular with Thais than with *farangs* and has a reputation for good seafood. Bob, who runs the internet office and tourist information in the **Hadthong Hotel**, speaks good English and is helpful. Buses no longer come into town, they pull over on the highway where you will need to catch a motorbike or a tuk-tuk into town. The **railway station** ① *T032-611175*, is on the west side of town.

At the northern end of town, at the end of Salashiep/Sarathip Road, is **Khao Chong Krachok**. An exhausting 15- to 20-minute climb up the 'Mountain with the Mirror' – past armies of aggressive, preening monkeys – is rewarded with fine views of the surrounding countryside and bay. At the summit there is an unremarkable shrine built in 1922 containing a footprint of the Buddha.

There is a good **night market** at the corner of Phitakchat and Kong Kiat roads and a daily market with stacks of fruit along Maitri Ngam (the road south of the post office, opposite the **Hadthong Hotel**). The daily market which runs along Salashiep/Sarathip Road has stalls of orchids, fruit and metal sculptures. South of the **Hadthong Hotel** on Susuek Road are a couple of Chinese shophouses.

Ao Manao, a gorgeous bay 5 km south of town, is one of best beaches on this stretch of coast. A gently sloping slice of sand is fringed by refreshing woodlands and framed by distant islands. At some points of the year the place can get infested with jellyfish, so bring a rash guard. Ao Manao was also the site of the Japanese invasion of the Second World War and is sited slap bang in the middle of a military base. This is no bad thing as development is strictly controlled – you'll find none of the usual trappings expected at other Thai resort towns. There is also one military-run hotel, good, cheap Thai food, toilets, deckchairs and umbrellas to hire. To get there, take a motorbike taxi or tuk-tuk (฿30).

Bang Saphan to Chumphon

South of Prachuap Khiri Khan, the coastline to Chumphon is dotted with hotels and resorts; all are signposted in English off the main Route 4. At **Bang Saphan**, 60 km south of Prachuap Khiri Khan, several small beach resorts are developing, geared as much to Thais as to foreigners. **Hat Somboon** is the nearest beach to Bang Saphan, just 1 km away. The position is attractive enough although the sand soon degenerates into mud below the low-water mark. Continuing south from Bang Saphan are a series of other small groups of resorts and guesthouses – all still very low key.

Around 5 km further south is a ferry link to the offshore island of **Koh Talu** (15 minutes from the mainland by boat from Bang Saphan Noi). It is an excellent dive site with particularly good deep water diving and turtles. The name of the island is derived from its extraordinary 45-m hill which is shot through with a 30-m hole (*talu* means to pass through). For land lubbers there are rare bats and an abundance of swiftlets. The nests of the latter are harvested for bird's nest soup (see page 535).

North of Bang Saphan is the village of **Ban Krut**. The village and beach area are particularly appealing. There's a **tourist information office** ① *T032-695337*. The drive from the main road through to the beach passes a charming town with mostly wooden buildings, and then winds past a lovely rural scene of large raintrees and lily ponds. The beach area is lined with casuarina trees and coconut palms. The northern end leads past the usual line of small beachside restaurants, through a fishing community and then up to a large Buddha image on the northern hillside overlooking the bay. It is at the southern end of the bay where most of the accommodation is concentrated. Ban Krut is on the north-south railway line and can be reached by slow train.

Chumphon ☺️🔟🔺🔟🔟 ›› pp598-610.

Chumphon is considered the 'gateway to the south' and is where the southern highway divides, one route running west and then south on Route 4 to Ranong, Phuket and the Andaman Sea; the other, south on Route 41 to Surat Thani, Koh Samui, Nakhon Si Thammarat and the waters of the Gulf of Thailand.

There isn't much to see in the town itself, although there are some good beaches and islands nearby; the town is an access point for Koh Tao (see page 659). The station is at the west end of Krom Luang Chumphon Road, where the trains from Bangkok arrive.

The waters off the coast provide excellent diving opportunities. There are dive sites around the islands of **Koh Ngam Noi** (parcelled out to bird's nest concessionaires) and **Koh Ngam Yai**. Rock outcrops like **Hin Lak Ngam** and **Hin Pae**, are also becoming increasingly popular with dive companies for their coral gardens, caves and rock piles. Of particular note are the 500 varieties of rare black corals found in the vicinity of Hin Lak Ngam. The sea here is plankton-rich, which means an abundance of sea life including whaleshark, other species of shark, and sea turtles, as well as coral gardens. Visibility, though, is variable and certainly not as crystalline as on the Andaman Sea side of the isthmus. On a good day it may be more than 20 m, but at low tide less than half of this.

In his book *Surveying and exploring in Siam* (1900), James McCarthy writes of 'Champawn' marking the beginning of the Malay Peninsula. A group of French engineers had already visited the area with a view to digging a canal through the Kra Isthmus and it was clearly a little place at that time: the "harbour was full of rocks covered with oysters. The usual cocoa-nut palms and grass shanties marked the position of the village".

Around Chumphon

Pak Nam Chumphon, 11 km southeast of Chumphon on Route 4901 (take a *songthaew* from opposite the morning market on the southern side of town), lies on the coast at the mouth of the Chumphon River. It's a big fishing village with boats for hire to the nearby islands where swiftlets build their nests. The swiftlets are used to make the Chinese speciality of bird's nest soup – *yanwo*, in Chinese (see box, page 535). Many concessionaires are accompanied by bodyguards; visitors should seek permission before venturing to the nest sites. Islands include **Koh Phrao**, **Koh Lanka Chiu** and **Koh Rang Nok**. Other activities such as diving, jungle treks and boat trips to the caves can be organized through a guesthouse or travel agent (see Tour operators, page 608).

Chumphon

Sleeping		Eating	Transport
Chumphon Gardens **6**	New Infinity & Tour	Lanna Han Isaan **3**	A/c Bus Station **1**
Easy Divers **7**	Operator **2**	Puean Djai **1**	Local Buses **3**
Farang Bar & Travel	Paradorn Inn **5**	Spaghetti House **2**	Minibus to Surat Thani **4**
Agency **8**	Suriwong Chumphon **4**		Minivans to Ranong **6**
Jansom Chumphon **3**			Songthaews to Tayang Pier
New Chumphon			& Thuang Wua Laeu **5**
Guesthouse **1**			

Much of the coastline and islands off Chumphon form part of the **Chumphon Marine National Park** (Mu Ko Chumphon). The park headquarters ① *T077-558144*, is 8 km from Hat Si Ree and can provide details of bungalows and campsites. The park contains mangrove forest, limestone mountain forest as well as marine life offshore.

Hat Thung Wua Laen, 18 km north of Chumphon, is a beautiful beach – a broad curving bay and a long stretch of white sand, which slopes gently towards the sea, though this also means it's a long walk out to the water at low tide. From November to January, when the winds are high and sea unsuitable for bathing, this beach turns into something of a mecca for kitesurfers – some claim that here you can find the best kitesurfing conditions in Southeast Asia. There are also a number of hotels and bungalows operating here but the beach is still mercifully free of tourist paraphernalia and even when most accommodation is fully occupied the area is large enough to maintain a sense of peace and seclusion. In March the waters become inundated with plankton, which locals harvest using nets. It is considered a delicacy and is known as *kuey*. To get to the beach, take a *songthaew* (฿20) from the market in Chumphon; you can also charter a tuk-tuk (฿250).

Another beach, **Hat Sai Ri**, is 3 km south of Hat Pharadon and close to Koh Thong Luang. There is good snorkelling in the area. There is also a shrine to His Royal Highness Prince Chumphon, the self-styled father of the Royal Thai Navy. To get to Hat Sai Ri take a *songthaew* (฿20) from opposite the New Infinity Travel Agency in Chumpon, or from the post office.

At **Amphoe Lang Suan**, 62 km south of Chumphon, there are two beautiful caves – **Tham Khao Ngoen** and **Tham Khao Kriep**. There are 370 steps leading to the latter which is studded with stalagmites and stalactites. The district is also locally renowned for the quality of its fruit. You can take a bus there from the bus station in Chumphon.

⊚ Phetburi to Chumpon listings

For Sleeping and Eating price codes and other relevant information, see pages 44-49.

● Sleeping

Phetburi and around *p588, map p589*
Phetburi has limited accommodation with most visitors passing through as daytrippers.
A Rabiang Rua Beach Resort, 80/1-5 Moo 1 Anamai Rd, Chao Samran Beach, T032-44136, www.rabiangrua.com. On the beach, with great views and within easy reach of Phetburi, this is the first really comfortable, intimate and de luxe place to stay. Rooms are in 'boats' (rice-barge style) set around a small pool. Popular with Thai families. Bedrooms are strong on wood features, but light and airy nonetheless. Furnishings are refreshingly simple and although it's an odd-looking place to stay, it is fun and the staff are friendly. Bungalows also available. Recommended.

B-D Royal Diamond Hotel, 555 Phetka-sem Rd, T032-411061, www.royaldiamond hotel.com. Luxurious hotel compared to most others in Phetburi. The 58 rooms have a/c and are adequately furnished. The restaurant does a range of international food. There's a beer garden and pleasant, peaceful atmosphere. Internet access.
D-F Phetkasem, 86/1 Phetkasem Rd, T032-425581. Best-value place to stay in this category. 30 clean rooms, some with a/c. Friendly management. There is no restaurant but it is located very close to some of the best eats in Phetburi (see Eating, below). Motorcycle rent ฿250 and Thai massage ฿350.
F-G Chom Klao, 1 Tewet Rd, on the east bank of the river diagonally opposite the **Rabieng Guesthouse**, with duck-blue shutters, T032-425398. Clean, quiet and fair-sized rooms, though they are bare

and unattractive. The rooms with views over the river are by far the best and have balcony areas. More expensive rooms have shower rooms attached, ones without have basins. Friendly, helpful and informative management.
F-G Rabieng Guesthouse, Damnoen-kasem Rd, T032-425707. Wood-panelled rooms with tiled floors on the ground floor. Pokier rooms upstairs but all are clean. A good night's sleep is impossible, though, if your room faces the noisy bridge. Open-air seating area upstairs and cleanish communal facilities. Appealing restaurant overlooking the river serving a very wide range of dishes (see Eating, below). Motorbikes can be rented out for ฿250 per day, bicycles for ฿120. Laundry service. Trekking and rafting tours in the national parks are available. Good English is spoken.

Cha-am p591
A number of hotels on the seafront offer more bungalows and simple rooms in the **B-C** price range, with a few in the **D** range. Unless you speak Thai, it will be difficult to make a phone booking, but it is highly likely that you'll find available rooms on arrival. Mid-week tends to be quieter and cheaper.
LL-A Bann Pantai, Ruamchit Rd, T032-433 111, www.bannpantai.com. New in 2008, an upmarket mini-resort complex, complete with nice pool, contemporary-Thai styled bungalows and some cheaper rooms. Everything (a/c, en suite, cable TV) you'd expect from a place in this price range. Low-season, mid-week prices can be negotiated down.
LL-A Long Beach Cha-am Hotel, 225/75 Ruamchit Rd, T032-472444, www.longbeach-chaam.com. Huge concrete multi-story pile set back from the main beach road. The views are fantastic and most rooms have sea-facing balconies, with the fresh breezes negating the need for a/c, which they all have as well. Friendly place though ultimately a little dull.
L-A Dusit Resort, 1349 Phetkasem Rd, T032-520008, www.dusit.com. Large, stylish hotel block (300 rooms), with polo 'motifs'

throughout. Superb facilities including range of watersports, fitness centre, spa, tennis courts, horse riding and a huge swimming pool, Thai arts and crafts demonstrations.
L-A Regent, 849/21 Phetkasem Rd, south of the main beach area, T032-451240, www.regent-chaam.com. A/c, restaurants, pools, hotel and cottage accommodation on a 120-ha site, and every conceivable facility including squash and tennis courts, and a fitness centre.
L-C Methavalai, 220 Ruamchit Rd, T032-433250, www.methavalai.com. A/c bunga-lows, some with several bedrooms – ideal for families – and a small area of private beach, pool, good seafood and Thai restaurant.
A-E Santisuk, 263/3 Ruamchit Rd, south of the main stretch, T032-471212. Range of accommodation – some with a/c – including wooden cottages or a hotel block. Both are good.
C-E Dee-Lek, 225/30-33, Ruamchit Road, T032-470548. Friendly little guesthouse on the main beach road. The pricier rooms have nice balconies overlooking the beach and everything is clean, tidy – maybe a little dull – and comes with hotwater, tv and a/c. Also serve decent food (see Eating, below). Recommended.
C-E Viwathana, 263/21 Ruamchit Rd, T032-471289. One of the longer-established, with some simple, fan-cooled wooden bungalows as well as a new brick-built block. All are set in a garden of sorts. The more expensive bungalows have 2 or 3 rooms and a/c. Good value for families.
D-E Jitravee, 241/20 Ruamchit Rd, T032-471382. Clean rooms, friendly. More expensive rooms have a/c, TV, fridge, room service, bathroom. Cheaper rooms have clean, shared bathroom, some English spoken.
E-F Pratarnchoke House, 240/3 Ruam-chit Rd, T032-471215. Range of rooms available here from simple fan-cooled, through to more luxurious a/c rooms with bathrooms. Some English spoken.

Hua Hin and around *p591, map p593*
Many hotels reduce prices in the low season.
Rack rates are extortionate. For better deals
check the internet or tour operators. Prices
quoted here are for high season.

Slightly more expensive guesthouses
are to be found just south of the town in
an area called Soi Thipurai.
LL-AL Anantara Resort and Spa,
43/1 Phetkasem Rd, T032-520250,
www.anantara.com. 187 rooms in teak
pavilions set around a gorgeous pool.
There's an Italian, Thai and international
restaurant and good sports facilities but
no beach to speak of. The spa is run by
Mandara Spa, www.mandaraspa-asia.com.
Recommended.
**LL-AL Chiva Som International Health
Resort**, 73/4 Phetkasem Rd, T032-536536,
www.chivasom.com. This is a luxury health
resort (*Chiva-Som* means Haven of Life) set
in 3 ha of luxury grounds which ooze calm
and peace. It has a large spa building housing
a spacious gym, Roman bath, enormous
jacuzzi, circular steam room and dance
studio. There is also an outdoor freshwater
pool close to the sea. With health consultants,
hydrotherapy and lots of herbal tea and
healthy food, this is the place to come to lose
weight or firm up those buttocks without
feeling that life is too miserable. There are
numerous treatment and accommodation
packages on offer.
LL-AL Evason Hua Hin Resort and Spa,
9 Paknampran Beach, Prachuap Khiri Khan,
T032-618200, www.six-senses.com. About
20 km south of Hua Hin (not far from Pranburi)
is this stylish resort, set in spacious grounds
with a beautiful pool. It is hard to beat for
anyone wanting to 'get away from it all'.
The owners have created a unique
environment, with light and airy rooms,
furnished with contemporary, locally
produced furniture. Some of the more
expensive villas have private plunge pools.
The groundbreaking **Earth Spa** – conical
naturally cooled mud huts – provides the
last word in pampering as well as health

programmes for the more committed. There
are plenty of other (complimentary) facilities
including watersports (sailing, kayaking),
tennis courts, a gym, archery. The kids' club
has a separate pool and playground plus daily
activities. Low-season prices are good value.
Recommended.
LL-AL Hilton Hua Hin Resort and Spa,
33 Naresdamri Rd, T032-512879,
www.hilton.com. This rather unappealing
white tower block dominates the town
centre. However, it is a very pleasant and
comfortable hotel offering a luscious spa,
lovely pool, restaurants and a nice stretch
of beach. The 296 rooms are attractively
decorated although the bathrooms are
lacking in grandeur in comparison. Views
from the rooms are superb. Staff are
helpful and friendly.
**LL-AL Hua Hin Marriott Resort and
Spa**, 107/1 Phetkasem Rd, T032-511881,
www.marriotthotels.com. A large resort
with a very attractive lobby. The **Mandara
Spa** architecture and ambience is beautiful,
with a blend of Thai and Balinese style and
large stepping stones to cross ponds. The
216 rooms enjoy top facilities. The beach in
front of the hotel is white, clean and pleasant.
The pool gets extremely busy and there are
4 restaurants and 2 bars. Good sports
facilities, including tennis, fitness centre,
watersports and a kids' club. Recommended.
LL-AL Hyatt Regency Hua Hin, 99 Hua
Hin-Khao Takiap Rd, T032-521234,
www.huahin.regency.hyatt.com. All the
facilities you'd expect from a top-class
hotel, including an extensive range of watersports and cyber-games centre. It is a lovely
low-rise luxurious resort of 204 rooms set in
an expanse of well-maintained gardens.
**LL-AL Sheraton Hua Hin Resort and
Spa**, 1573 Petchkasem Rd, T032-708000,
www.sheraton.com/huahin. With its
entrance set on the main road between
Hua Hin and Cha-am, this is the kind of
resort you're not really meant to leave.
The best and most unique feature is the
giant, snaking swimming pool which can

be reached straight off the balconies of most groundfloor rooms. Otherwise it's a bog-standard 5-star place with all the usual trimmings – the beachside bar is a nice spot for a drink.

LL-AL Sofitel Central Hua Hin Resort, 1 Damnoenkasem Rd, T032-512021, www.sofitel.com. Hua Hin's original premier hotel, formerly the **Railway Hotel**. A beautiful place set in luscious gardens with some very creative topiary. It maintains excellent levels of service and enjoys a very good position on the beach, and while the new rooms are small they are well appointed. Rooms are beautifully decorated and bathrooms are finished with marble. Lovely grounds with pools right near the beach and frangipani trees, and an interesting small museum. In addition the seafood restaurant here – with a French chef – is truly worth seeking out. Colonial tea on the steps of the tea room and museum should not be missed. The hotel also boasts the **Centara Spa**. Recommended.

L-AL Central Hua Hin Village, 1 Damnoenkasem Rd, T032-512021, www.centralhotel resorts.com. 41 Thai village bungalows in a garden setting with direct access to the beach. Has all facilities: sauna, pool, spa, tennis courts, etc. The bungalows' design is totally in keeping with the traditional local style and are really charming. The whole resort is attractively petite compared to the towering **Hilton** which dwarfs it. Surprisingly spacious on the inside and again decorated in keeping with Hua Hin's tradition (albeit one which is being lost in most parts) of an elegant beach resort of a bygone era. The **Centara Spa**, 0900-2100, offers massage pavillions in the hotel grounds as well as massage rooms and sauna in the main spa buildings.

A-C Araya, 15/1 Chomsin Rd, T032-531130, www.araya-residence.com. Officially this is a small apartment block that offers monthly and annual rates on the rooms. They also offer rooms by the night and while it's not the cheapest Araya does represent excellent value. With enough contemporary design

and art to add to the 'cool' factor, the rooms are comfy and spacious. The best (and most expensive) are the two rooftop 'villas', which come complete with huge, private roof terrace, flatscreen TV, DVD players, fridge and free Wi-Fi. All this and it's in a great location and friendly to boot. Highly recommended.

A-C City Beach Resort, 16 Damnoen-kasem Rd, T032-512870. 162 very outdated and overpriced rooms. Restaurant, strange pool, pub with live music and karaoke. A good central location, though. Staff are helpful and there is an excellent breakfast included in the price.

A-D Supasuda/Ananthara Guesthouse, 1/8 Chomsin Rd, T032-516650, www.spg house.com. Sweet, stylish and friendly guesthouse opposite the pier in the heart of old Hua Hin. Rooms are all a/c, with TV and en suite – some have balconies/sea-views and there's even a private terrace on the roof. There's also a relaxing lounge bar on the ground floor. At present seems to be trading under 2 names. Recommended.

A-E Fulay Guesthouse, 110/1 Naresdamri Rd, T032-513145, www.fulay-huahin.com. A delightful little place with old world look, with teak frontage and white carved wooden railings and splashes of pastel green. Only a/c rooms have hot water. Fan rooms have shared bathrooms. Good restaurant. The Thai house is a cute little getaway on the top deck with ocean views.

B-E Jinning Beach, 113/25-26 Phetkasem Rd, T032-532597, www.jinningbeachguest house.com. 15 a/c rooms with minibar and TV. Not as friendly as the others in this street.

B-E Sunshine Guesthouse, 113/30 Soi Hua Hin, Phetkasem Rd, T032-515309, sunshine guesthouse@yahoo.com. Super-friendly management at this guesthouse, which is slightly cheaper than the others. Rooms have minibars, a/c and TVs. Internet café in the lobby.

C-D Chomsin Hua Hin Hotel, 130/4 Chom-sin Rd, T032-515348, www.chomsinhua hin.com. Smart, well-tended boutique joint on a nice quiet street in central Hua Hin.

All rooms come with a/c, en suite and TV – some have balconies. Rooms are excellent value, plus there's a small café downstairs. Good value and recommended.

C-D PP Villa and Puang Pen Hotel, 11 Damnoenkasem Rd, T032-533785, ppvillahotel@hotmail.com. 40 plainly decorated a/c rooms, pool. Recommended for excellent value and its central location, but some reception staff can be very rude.

C-E All Seasons Guest House, Naresdamri Rd. English guesthouse in nice back street location. All rooms are en suite and a/c – the best ones have huge balconies.

C-E White Villa, 125/1 Phetkasem Rd, T032-532971, wwwhuahinwhitevilla.com. Sleek, modern small hotel, in a busy location. Has pool and each en suite room comes with its own balcony, a/c and cable TV.

D A&B, 113/16-17 Phetkasem Rd, T032-532340, www.abguesthouse.com. Friendly Swedish management at this guesthouse with 12 ultra-clean rooms and bathrooms. TV, a/c and fridge.

D-E Patchara House, Naresdamri Rd, T032-511787. Some rooms with a/c, clean, friendly, room service, hot water, TV, pleasant restaurant. Recommended.

D-E Royal Beach, 113/13 Phetkasem Rd, T032-532210, royalbeach@hotmail.com. 12 rooms with minibar and TV available.

E-F Bird Guesthouse, 31/2 Naret Damri Rd, T032-511630, birdguesthousehuahin@hotmail.com. 10 rooms on a wooden platform on stilts above the beach. Atmospheric place with friendly management. There is no restaurant but you can get breakfast here, sitting area with views over the sea, more ambience and character than most. Rooms with a/c cost more.

E-G All Nations Guesthouse, 10 Dechanuchit Rd, T032-512747, cybercafehuahin@hotmail.com. Rooms with fan or a/c with your own balcony, clean. One of the cheapest in Hua Hin. English owner serves up English breakfasts. Free pool table.

F Pattana Guesthouse, 52 Naresdamri Rd, T032-513393, huahinpattana@hotmail.com.

Attractive location down a small alley. 13 twin-bedded rooms with fans in 2 original Thai teakwood buildings set around a flower-filled compound, some rooms with own bathrooms. 50 m from the beach, breakfast available.

Kaeng Krachan National Park and caves *p594*

C-D Bungalows sleeping 5-6 are available at the park HQ but you must bring all necessities with you (eg blankets, food and water) as nothing is provided.

Khao Sam Roi Yod National Park *p594*

C-D Bungalows either for hire in their entirety or per couple. Camping ground, with tents for hire, ฿100. You can also pitch your own tent here for around ฿20. Bungalows are available at both the park HQ and at Laem Sala Beach. Remember to take mosquito repellent.

Prachuap Khiri Khan *p595*

With the influx of Thais at weekends, accommodation is hard to find. During the week, room rates can be negotiated down.

C-D Prachuap Beach Hotel, 123 Susuek Rd, T032-601288, www.prachuapbeach.com. Decent enough hotel beside the sea – everything is en suite, with a/c, TV, balconies, etc. Should be pointed out, despite this optimistically named hotel, there is no 'beach' in Prachuap town centre.

D Fah Chom Klun, Ao Manao beachfront, T032-661088. This military-run establishment is the only accommodation next to the Ao Manao beach and is often booked out. Rooms are basic and spotlessly clean – all en suite, some have sea views. Recommended though reservations are essential.

D Sun Beach Guesthouse, 60 Chaitalae Rd, T032-604770, www.sunbeach-guesthouse.com. Brand new property on the seafront. Has a pool and each en suite room is comfortably fitted complete with a/c and balcony, though the 'sea view' claim is a bit tenuous. Friendly atmosphere.

D-E Golden Beach Hotel, 113-115 Suan-son Rd, north of town past Khao Chong Krachock, 600 m north of the river, south of **Happy Inn**, T032-601622, goldenbeach hostel@ hotmail.com. Basic clean rooms with a/c but rooms are smaller than at **Happy Inn**.

D-E Hadthong, 21 Susuek Rd, T032-601050, www.hadthong.com. Comfortable rooms (but small bathrooms in the standard rooms) overlooking the sea with great views. The pool also enjoys views of the bay. It is good value and the best hotel in town. The restaurant serves good Thai food and a reasonable breakfast.

E Happy Inn, 600 m north of Khao Chong Krachok, T032-601840. Quite, nice a/c bungalows with TV and bathroom attached. Just across the road from the beach, beside the river.

E-F Yuttichai, 115 Kong Kiat Rd, T032-611 055. This is a large, characterful family-run place. The vast front living area is like a little museum. Clean rooms with own bathroom and fans have Oriental toilets and shared bathrooms have Western toilets.

Bang Saphan to Chumphon *p596*

The southern end of the bay near Ban Krut village has a variety of accommodation from large wood and bamboo bungalows to colourful concrete houses reminiscent of some European seaside resorts. Many of the latter are let in a timeshare style or are owned by Bangkokians looking for a quieter (and cheaper) place to stay than Hua Hin or Cha-am. The area tends to attract families rather than individuals or couples and consequently has excellent accommodation for larger groups, such as 2- or 3-bedroom bungalow houses which can be good value. Most resorts have ample and landscaped grounds. Accommodation tends to be quite simple but is clean and comfortable. There are very few restaurants at the resorts and it's quite a walk to the main restaurant area.

D-E Nipa Beach Bungalows, Hat Somboon. A/c, hot water, telephone and TV. Good value and comfortable.

Chumphon *p596, map p597*

B-E Chumphon Gardens, 66/1 Tha Tapao Rrd, T077-506888. New hotel in central location, though set back a little from the road, so quiet. The cheaper rooms are excellent value – clean, with TV, en suite. Recommended.

C-D Jansom Chumphon, 188/138 Saladaeng Rd, T077-502504, jansombeach@ yahoo.com. Clean rooms with a/c and spacious bathrooms, but the place is quite run-down and the curtains need replacing. Restaurant serves a wide range of Thai food. The breakfast is measly. Disco attached.

C-E Paradorn Inn, 180/12 Soi Paradorn, Saladaeng Rd, T077-511500, www.chum phon-paradorn.com. A/c rooms with TV that are brighter, whiter and nicer than anything the competition offers. The restaurant has bamboo furniture and offers a wide range of reasonably priced food (0800-2200).

E Suriwong Chumphon Hotel, 125/30 Saladaeng Rd, T077-511203. Basically furnished rooms which are a little dark. Some bathrooms have damp ceilings but are OK. Reception is not too friendly. Better value can be found elsewhere.

G Easy Divers, Tha Tapao Rd, T077-570085. 6 twin or triple rooms that are a decent size and clean but windowless. Clean and pleasant shared bathrooms.

G Farang Bar and Travel Agency, Tha Tapao Rd, T077-501003. 9 dark, airless rooms with fan next to the restaurant with very clean toilets and showers out the back.

G New Chumphon Guesthouse 27 Soi 1 Krom Luang Rd, T032-502900. Clean, cosy rooms with wood-panelled floors upstairs and darker, cheaper rooms downstairs. Shared bathrooms. Homely atmosphere, friendly and helpful with management who speak good English. Tours to caves and waterfalls also arranged. Motorbike rental ฿200.

G New Infinity, 68/2 Tha Taphao Rd, T077-570176. Offers 6 rooms, 1 is larger with balcony, some smaller ones have no windows – all have fans, very basic but clean, shared bathrooms. Friendly and helpful management. Good travel service offered here, see Tour operators, below.

Beaches

There are a number of hotels and bungalow operations at Hat Thung Wua Lean. In terms of accommodation, the **Chumpon Cabana** is the most upmarket and right on the beach. Bungalow resorts are mostly separated from the beach by the road (but this is narrow and not busy), and usually set in smallish gardens.
B-D Chumphon Cabana Resort, 69 Moo 8, T077-560245-7, www.cabana.co.th. Some nicely decorated a/c bungalows set in attractive gardens and 2 hotel blocks all with a/c and hot water. The newer buildings have all been designed on energy-saving principles in keeping with the owner's environmental concerns. The resort has all the usual facilities including a pool, good watersports (including a PADI dive centre), a very peaceful location and a great view of the beach from the restaurant and some of the bungalows.
B-E Chuan Phun Lodge, 54/3 Moo 8, Thungwualaen Beach, T077-560120/230. Attractive en suite rooms in this new lodge/ hotel – the ones at the front have sea-facing balconies. Good value.
B-F Clean Wave, 54 Moo 8, Thungwualaen Beach, T077-560151. Some rooms with a/c. Cheaper fan-cooled bungalows.
E Thungwualaen Resort, 61/3 Moo 8, Thungwualaen Beach, T08-1970 1387 (mob). Nice bungalows set just back from the beach. Very friendly owner who speaks some English.
E-F Sea Beach Resort and Bungalow, 4/2 Moo 8, Thungwualaen Beach, T077-560115. Clean, cheap bungalows, some a/c, some fan, at this friendly resort, a favourite of the kitesurfing community.
F Seaside Guesthouse, 14/9 Moo 8, Saplee, T077-560178. Decent enough little guesthouse a little way from the beach on the road in from Chumphon town. Every room is en suite but there is no hot water. Some rooms are a/c.

F Thawat Hotel, 135 Khao Ngern Rd, Amphoe Lang Suan, T077-541046. Offers 100 rooms, some with fan and some a/c.

❶ Eating

Phetburi and around *p588, map p589*
Phetburi is well known for its desserts including *khanom mo kaeng* (a hard custard made of mung bean, egg, coconut and sugar, baked over an open fire), *khao kriap* (a pastry with sesame, coconut and sugar) and excellent *kluai khai* (sweet bananas). There are several restaurants along Phetkasem Rd selling Phetburi desserts.
⑪ The Pizza Company, Phetkasem Rd. Will satisfy pizza cravings. Free delivery available.
⑨ Rabieng Restaurant Guesthouse, Damnoenkasem Rd. Open 0830-0100. Attractively furnished riverside restaurant, serving a good range of Thai and Western food. The spicy squid salad is particularly good. Breakfasts are small and overpriced. Recommended.

Foodstalls

There is a small but excellent **night market** at the southern end of Surinreuchai Rd underneath the clock tower – you can get a range of delicious snacks here and may want to try the local *patai* (omelette/pan-cake fried with mussels and served with bamboo shoots).

Cha-am *p591*
There are plenty of seafood restaurants along Ruamchit Rd, mostly serving the same dishes, including chilli crab and barbecued snapper with garlic. On the road into town from the highway you'll find dozens of places selling excellent grilled pork and Isaan-style food.
⑪ Dee Lek, see Sleeping, above. This is a friendly-beachside café/restaurant selling decent Thai and European food. Friendly as well.
⑨ Moo Hang Nai Wang, almost opposite the KS golf sign on the road in from the highway.

This small shack, with Thai signage only, is arguably the best purveyor of authentic Isaan food on this stretch. Succulent grilled pork and chicken come with superlative, spicy papaya salad and filling sticky rice. It might require a bit of asking but this place is highly recommended for those wishing to be more adventurous in their culinary choices.

¶ **Neesky Cafe**, almost on the corner of the beach road and the road linking to the highway. This small, thatched place serves Thai food, steaks and supposedly the best burger in Thailand.

Hua Hin and around p591, map p593
Try the central market for breakfast. Good seafood is widely available particularly at the northern end of Naresdamri Rd. Most of the fish comes straight from the boats which land their catch at the pier at the northern end of the bay. There is also a concentration of restaurants and bars geared to *farang* visitors along Naresdamri Rd and surrounding lanes.

¶¶¶ **Brasserie de Paris**, 3 Naresdamri Rd, T032-530637. A French restaurant with a great position on the seafront sandwiched between the squid piers. Attentive and prompt service. The speciality of Hua Hin crab is absolutely delicious.

¶¶¶ **Palm Pavillion**, Sofitel Central, 1 Damnoenkasem Rd, 1900-2300. This seafood restaurant is probably the best in Hua Hin. Don't expect the usual range of Thai dishes; the chef is French.

¶¶¶-¶¶ **Hua Hin Brewing Co**, 33 Naresdamri Rd, T032-512888. 0900-0200. A partly open-air chaotic seafood restaurant serving good barbecued food. Also serves 3 home brews. Under-staffed during busy periods.

¶¶¶-¶¶ **Lo Stivale**, 132 Naresdamri Rd, T032-513800. Open 1030-2230. The best Italian restaurant in town although the pizzas are pretty standard. The house speciality of short pasta with crab meat and tomato sauce is recommended. Terrace and indoor seating available. Good and prompt service. Popular with foreign families. Recommended.

¶¶¶ **Chao Lay**, 15 Naresdamri Rd, T032-513436. Daily 1000-2200. This place with its blue and white checked cloths on a stilted building jutting out into the sea is hugely popular with Thais. It has 2 decks and is a great place from where to watch the sunset. Fruits of the sea including steamed squid, huge seabass, rock lobster and prawns, are served up with military precision.

¶¶-¶ **Maharaja**, 25 Naresdamri Rd, T032-530 347. Reasonable prices at this highly a/c Indian which is all peach decor, flower fabrics and fake chandeliers. Great naan bread and curries. Attentive service.

¶¶-¶ **Veranda Grill**, Veranda Lodge, 113 Hua Hin 67, Phetkasem Rd, T032-533 678, www.verandalodge.com. 0700-2300. Enjoy terraced dining on lapis lazuli blue tiles overlooking the beach. The basil air-dried squid is worth savouring.

¶ **Jeak Peak**, on the corner of Naebkhaehat and Dechanuchit roads. This small shop house is one of Hua Hin's most famous and longest standing noodle shops. Renowned for it's seafood noodles and pork satay, this shop has been in the same location for 63 years and has lots of olde worlde charm. It's often packed but the sometime queues are worth it. Recommended.

Cafés and bakeries
Museum and tea shop, Sofitel Central, see Sleeping, above. Take colonial tea here for a taste of old-world charm. Earl Grey followed by ham buns, scones, jam and cream, biscuits and peach tarts is a treat for ฿315.

World News Coffee, Naresdamri Rd, next to the **Hilton**. Daily 800-2230. Bagels, cakes, coffee and newspapers – at a price. Internet access too.

Foodstalls
There is an excellent **food market** opposite the Town Hall on Damnoenkasem Rd. The night market just off Phetkasem Rd does the usual selection of cheap Thai food as well as seafood that is so fresh that they have to tie the crabs' and lobsters' pincers shut.

Prachuap Khiri Khan p595

Prachuap is famous for its seafood and there are a number of excellent restaurants (as well as some more average ones) in the centre of town and along the seafront. If you venture to Ao Manao there are plenty of small places selling very good Thai food.

₦₦-₦ Laplom Seafood, north of the river. Offers an extensive range of seafood, probably the best selection in town (with a few meat dishes too), reasonably priced and friendly.

₦₦-₦ Shiew Ocha II, on the seafront towards the north of the town. Good range of seafood and meat dishes.

₦₦-₦ Mong Lai, 2.5 km north of Laplom on the north end of the bay below the mountain. Country-style restaurant that is well known for its spicy dishes.

₦₦-₦ Panphochana, in the centre of town, 2 doors down from the Hadthong Hotel, T032-611195. Open 1000-2200. Welcoming, English-speaking owner, offers a vast range of seafood, pork and chicken. Breakfasts also served. Interior and outdoor dining possible with great views of the bay.

₦₦-₦ Plern Smud, on the seafront next to the Hadthong Hotel, T03-611115. Serves a large range of seafood and other meat dishes. As well as a full English breakfast you can try fried pig's stomach here. Super-friendly service.

Chumphon p596, map p597

₦₦-₦ Farang Bar and Travel Agency, Tha Tapao Rd, T077-501003. 0430-0100. Thai-style soups and salads, noodles, spaghetti dishes and baguettes. Porridge for breakfast too. Cocktails are served at ฿100. Drink and eat while watching a movie. The night staff here are a lot friendlier than the day staff.

₦₦-₦ Puean Djai Restaurant, opposite the railway station. Open 1000-0200. This restaurant is in an attractive garden setting. Very tasty pizzas using cheese from an Italian cheese factory in Prachuap Khiri Khan. Pasta, crêpes and Thai cuisine also concocted.

₦ Lanna Han Isaan, set near the railway tracks in a cute garden. Delicious, cheap

Isaan food that is very popular with locals. The food here is very spicy so ask for *pet nit noi* (a little spicy).

₦ Spaghetti House, 188/132 Saladaeng Rd, T077-507320, 0900-2200. A comfortable a/c restaurant serving tasty and filling spaghetti at reasonable prices. Also delicious smoothies and ice creams with some unusual offerings: Japanese cucumber and the famous durian ice creams. There's also a coffee house inside. Staff are really friendly. Recommended.

Foodstalls

There are 2 night markets on Krom Luang Chumphon Rd and on Tha Taphao Rd.

☺ Entertainment

Hua Hin and around p591, map p593
The sois between Poonsuk and Naresdamri roads are stuffed, cheek by jowl, with bars catering to most tastes. The **Hua Hin Brewing Co** (see Eating, above), has a vast cavern-like pub with a giant screen for sports, open until 0200.

☺ Festivals and events

Phetburi and around p588, map p589
Feb Phra Nakhon Khiri Fair (movable) *son et lumière* show.

Hua Hin and around p591, map p593
Jun Hua Hin Jazz Festival, www.huahin jazzfestival.com. Organized by the Hilton. Stages are set up in front of the Sofitel Central and railway station.
Sep The King's Cup Elephant Polo tournament, www.thaielepolo.com. Takes place at the Som Dej Phra Suriyothai military ground, south of Hua Hin. It is organized by the Anantara Hotel and has become quite an attraction in recent years.

O Shopping

Hua Hin and around *p591, map p593*
The most distinctive buy is a locally produced printed cotton called *pha khommaphat*. The usual tourist shops and stalls can be found lining most streets in the town.

Night market, Dechanuchit Rd, close to the bus station. Dusk-2200. Sells a range of goods including Tibetan jewellery, paper dragons, T-shirts, cassettes, watches and silk scarves.

Books
Bookazine, 116 Naresdamri Rd, T032-532 071. Open 0900-2200. English-language books, magazines and stationery.

Silk
Jim Thompson shop in the Sofitel Central or the Hilton.
Rashnee Thai Silk Village, 18/1 Naeb-khehehars Rd, T032-531155. Open 0900-2100. Allows visitors to see the full silk-making process from worm to finished product.

▲ Activities and tours

Hua Hin and around *p591, map p593*
There are watersports and horse riding along the beach.

Golf
There are 5 championship golf courses close to Hua Hin including the **Royal Hua Hin**, the **Springfield Royal Country Club**, the **Palm Hills Golf Resort and Country Club**, **Lake View** and **Majestic Creek Country Club**.
Royal Hua Hin Golf Course, behind the railway station, T032-512475, royal_golf@hotmail.com. Designed in 1924 by a Scottish engineer working on the Royal Siamese Railway. It is the oldest in Thailand. Open to the public daily 0530-1930. Green fees ฿1500 at the weekend and ฿1200 during the week.

Muay Thai (Thai boxing)
Muay Thai Boxing Garden, 8/1 Th Phunsuk, T032-515269. Every Tue and Sat, 2100, ฿300 plus free drink.

Therapies
Anantara Spa, attached to the resort of the same name. Set in a quiet area with 6 suites in individual courtyards with baths filled with frangipani. Offers spa indulgence packages, which are reduced during the low season of Apr-Oct. These include accommodation and meals. The signature treatment is a 3-hr warm sesame compress.
Mandara Spa, at the **Marriott**, see Sleeping, above, T032-511881, ext 1810, www.mandara spa.com. Open 0800-2000. A heavenly experience. Its signature treatment is a red mud body detox (฿3100). Aroma-stone therapy (฿5520). Thai massage (฿2400) and body scrubs (exotic lime and ginger salt glow, ฿3300) are also offered.
Six Senses Earth Spa, at the Evason, see Sleeping, above. Awesome treatments, everything from reiki to basic Swedish massage, are available at this award-winning spa. The Earth Spa is sited in environmentally friendly mud huts which are designed to stay cool without a/c. Prices are high (฿2500-6000) but this is one of the most approachable and luxurious spas in Hua Hin. Recommended.
The Spa, at the Hilton, see Sleeping, above. Open 1000-2100. Has a large menu of different massages, facials using Guinot products, Thai fruit wrap (฿1850) and ancient Thai massage (฿1090). Twin share packages enjoy a 20% discount.

Tour operators
Tour operators are concentrated on Damnoenkasem and Phetkasem roads.
Western Tours, 1 Damnoenkasem Rd, T032-533303, www.westerntours huahin.com. Daily tours, THAI agent, transport tickets. Its trip to Khao Sam Roi Yod (฿900) is recommended. Kayaking, elephant riding and golf tours organized.

Chumphon *p596, map p597*

Diving

Easy Divers, Ta Taphao Rd, T077-570085, www.chumphoneasydivers.net. Takes divers to sites around the 41 islands off Chumphon. Also has bungalows and a restaurant at Thung Makham Noi and a guesthouse in Chumphon, see Sleeping, page 603.

Kitesurfing

The beach at Chumphon is fast becoming one of the premium kitesurfing locations in the country. At the moment there is only one operator offering classes.

Kite Thailand, in Chumphon in a small office next to **Seabeach Bungalows**, T08-1090 3730 (mob), T08-9970 1797 (mob), www.kite thailand.com. The friendly Dutch owner also runs sessions for all levels – a taster day, including all equipment costs ฿4000 per person, a full 3-day course about ฿12,000.

Tour operators

Fame Tour and Service, 118/20-21 Salad-aeng Rd, T077-571077, www.chumphon-kohtao.com. Open 0430-2400. Tours, boat tickets (taxi to pier included), visa extension, internet, motorbike and car rental, restaurant, taxi, shower service (free, but ฿20 if towel required) and guesthouse. Internet ฿1 per min. Sells various tours including trekking to Pak Lake (wild buffaloes, elephants and monkeys), long-tailed boat cruises on the Lang Suan River, and whitewater rafting on the Luang Suan River and Bout Fai River. Prices vary according to season and number of guests, but except to pay roughly ฿1000.

Farang Bar and Travel Agency, Tha Taphao Rd, T077-501003, farangbar@yahoo.com. Friendly staff offering lots of information and selling all tickets. Free taxi to train station offered. Also restaurant and rooms to rent.

Kiat travel, 115 Tha Taphao Rd, T077-502127, www.chumphonguide.com.

New Infinity Travel Agency, 68/2 Tha Taphao Rd, T077-570176, T08-1687 1825 (mob), new_infinity@hotmail.com.

Open 0600-2400. Offers all tourist services, including a guesthouse, run by the very helpful manager. Internet ฿1 per min. Free transfer to the Lomprayah and Songserm boats, ฿50 for transfer to night boat. Free transfers for guests to train or bus station. Motorbike rental ฿200 per day. Whitewater rafting, ฿550 per person. 1-day snorkelling trip to a choice of 3 islands, ฿700. Agent for **Chumphon Cabana**. It also does a visa run from Chumpon to Ranong and the border. Leave at 0545 return 1145. Burmese immigration, ฿300. Motorbike hire ฿200 per day, 4WD ฿1500 per day.

Songserm, Tha Tapao Rd, next to **New Infinity Travel**, T077-506205.

☉ Transport

Phetburi and around *p588, map p589*

Bus

Regular a/c connections with **Bangkok**'s Southern bus terminal near the Thonburi train station (2 hrs); non-a/c buses from the terminal near Khao Wang (2 hrs). Also connections with **Cha-am** (1½ hrs), **Hua Hin** (2¼ hrs, ฿35) and other southern destinations, between 0600-1800. These buses leave from the centre of town. Buses from Phetburi run past the turn-off for Kaeng Krachan Dam (Route 3175). From here, there are occasional minibuses which take visitors to the dam and the national park head-quarters (another 8 km), or hitch a lift.

Motorbike

These can be rented from **Rabieng Guesthouse** for ฿250 per day.

Saamlor

These can be hired for about ฿100 per hr.

Train

Regular connections with **Bangkok**'s Hualamphong station (2½ hrs), trains mostly leave in the morning. There are trains to **Hua Hin**, **Surat Thani** and southern destinations.

Cha-am *p591*
Bus
Cha-am is 25 km north of Hua Hin. There are regular connections with **Bangkok**'s Southern bus terminal (2½ hrs), **Phetburi**, **Hua Hin** and south destinations. To get to other southern destinations catch a bus to Hua Hin and change there.

Hua Hin and around *p591, map p593*
Air
SGA operates the Hua Hin Air Shuttle 3 times a day to **Bangkok**, 45 mins, ฿3100 one way, ฿5200 return. If you can afford it this is an great way to return to Bangkok. SGA only operate a 12-seat Cessna and this small aircraft flies low straight over the centre of Bangkok giving incredible views of the entire city.

Airline offices SGA, T032-522300, www.sga.aero.

Bicycle
Can be hired for ฿100 per day, on Damnoenkasem and Phetkasem roads.

Bus
There are 3 bus stations. The a/c bus station to BKK is on Srasong Rd, next to the Chatchai market, T032-511654. Regular a/c connections with **Bangkok**'s Southern bus terminal near the Thonburi train station, 3½ hrs, ฿128, every 40 mins from 0300-2100. A/c buses to the south leave from the main terminal and from opposite the Bangkok bus terminal on Srasong Rd, T08-1108 5319 (mob). Departures between 2100-2300. To **Prachuap Khiri Khan**, ฿40-50, **Chumphon**, ฿80-120, **Surat Thani**, ฿180-200. Local buses to **Phetburi**, ฿30, and **Cha-am**, ฿20, leave from Srasong Rd between streets 70 and 72 off Phetkasem Rd.

Car
It is presently a 3-hr drive to **Bangkok**, along a hazardous 2-lane highway (particularly bad over the first 80 km to Phetburi), jammed with *siplors* (10-wheel trucks).

Car hire Jeeps can be hired for ฿1000-1500 per day on Damnoenkasem and Phetkasem roads. **Avis**, www.avisthailand.com, has offices at the Hyatt, Sofitel Central and Hilton. Prices from ฿1350 per day. One-way rentals are possible.

Motorbike
Can be hired for ฿200 per day upwards, on Damnoenkasem and Phetkasem roads.

Taxis
Taxis run along prescribed routes for set fares. There's a taxi stand on Phetkasem Rd, opposite **Chatchai Hotel**. Taxis can be hired for the day for ฿1500 plus petrol.
Baipoo Service, Baipoo shop, Dechanuchit Rd, T08-1307 2352 (mob), baipoo_shop4@hotmail.com. A reliable taxi service which charges about ฿1000 per 100 km. Also rents motorbikes and cars.
Motorcycle taxis (identified by 'taxi' sign) will take you wherever you want to go. A taxi to **Bangkok** is 3 hrs (฿1600-1800).

Train
Regular connections with **Bangkok**'s Hualamphong station, same train as to Phetburi (3½-4 hrs). Regular connections with **Phetburi** (1 hr).
Lomprayah, Soi Kanjanomai, T032-533 738, runs bus and boat transport to Koh Tao, ฿850, Phangan, ฿1200 and Samui, ฿1400, with its own bus and catamaran.

Prachuap Khiri Khan *p595*
Bus
To **Bangkok**'s Southern bus terminal, 5 hrs; also destinations south including **Chumphon**.

Saamlor
Prachuap has its own distinctive form of tuk-tuk – motorcycles with sidecars and bench seats.

Train
Regular connections with **Bangkok**, 5 hrs, **Hua Hin** and destinations south.

Chumphon *p596, map p597*

Boat

Koh Tao (see page 659) can be reached by boat from 2 piers, one 10 km southeast of the town, the other 30 km away at Thung Makham Noi. Tickets for these boats can be bought at all the travel agents in town.

Lomprayah speed ferry uses the Thung Makham Noi Pier. Leaving at 0700 and 1300, 1½ hrs, ฿550. **Songserm** leaves Chumphon at 0700, ฿400. Arrives **Koh Tao** 0945, leaves at 1030 arriving at **Koh Phangan** at 1200, leaving at 1230 arriving **Koh Samui** at 1330. The return boat leaves Koh Samui at 1100, arriving Koh Phangan at 1200, leaving at 1230 arriving Koh Tao at 1430, leaving at 1500 arriving in Chumphon at 1730.

The night boat, ฿300 leaves at 2300 (you get a blanket and pillow on this one), 6 hrs on Mon, Wed and Fri returning Tue, Thu and Sat and daily at 2400, 6 hrs, ฿250.

Bus

The terminal is 15 km outside of town, ฿200 per person in taxi to get there. There are regular a/c connections with **Chokeanan Tour** off Pracha Uthid Rd, T077-511480, office hours 0430-2130. To **Bangkok**, 1030, 1400, 2130, 7 hrs, ฿322; to **Phuket** ฿300, and **Ranong** at 0800, 1000 and 1200. To **Hat Yai**, 0830, 0930, 1130, 2130, ฿320. Minivans to **Surat Thani** leave from Krom Louang Rd, next to the 7-11 shop; depart when full (2½ hrs, ฿150). Minivans to **Ranong** depart every 40 mins from 0600-1700, ฿90, from in front of the closed Tha Taphao hotel.

Taxi

To **Hat Thung Wua Laen**, ฿250, one way; **Hat Sai Ree** ฿200, one way; **Thung Makam** (for the **Lomprayah** catamaran) ฿250; **Tha Yang** pier ฿50; to **Muang Mai**, the new out of town bus station, 15 km away, ฿200.

Train

Regular connections with **Bangkok**'s Hualamphong station, (7½-9 hrs) and all stops south.

---

❶ Directory

Phetburi and around *p588, map p589*
Banks Siam Commercial Bank, on Damnoenkasem Rd, changes cash and TCs, and has an ATM. There are also several banks on Pongsuriya Rd. **Telephone** Overseas calls can be made from the post office on Ratwithi Rd.

Cha-am *p591*
Banks There are several banks on either side of Phetkasem Rd where the buses pull up. **Post office** The main post office is on the Narathip Rd, close to the bus station and Phetkasem Highway. Overseas calls can be made from here. There is also a small post office on Ruamchit Rd.

Hua Hin and around *p591, map p593*
Banks There are dozens of banks, ATMs and currency exchange booths all over town. **Internet** A number of small internet cafés have opened up around town. Also at **CAT** office, see Telephone, below, ฿100 for 3hrs. **Medical services** Medihouse Pharmacy, Naresdamri Rd, daily 0930-2300; San Paulo Hospital, Phetkasem Rd, opposite the Marriott, T032-532581. **Police** Damnoen-kasem Rd, T032-515995. **Post office** 21 Damnoenkasem Rd. **Telephone** CAT, Damnoenkasem Rd, www.cattelecom.co.th. Next to the post office, 0830-2300.

Prachuap Khiri Khan *p595*
Banks Bangkok Bank, corner of Sarathip/Salashiep and Maitri Ngam rosds, 1 block west of the **Hadthong Hotel**, has an ATM. **Internet** In the CAT phone office attached to the post office; in Hadthong Hotel, ฿30/hr. **Post office** Opposite the Hadthong Hotel.

Chumphon *p596, map p597*
Banks Thai Farmers' Bank, Saladaeng Rd. **Post office** Paramin Manda Rd, 1 km out of town on the left-hand side. **Telephone** Paramin Manda Rd. For overseas calls, slightly further than the post office, on the right.

Surat Thani and around

The riverside town of Surat Thani is the main launch pad for transport to the gulf islands of Samui, Phangan and Tao. North of the town is the ancient settlement of Chaiya, once an important outpost of the Srivijayan Empire that was based in Sumatra. Also north is Wat Suan Mok, a Buddhist retreat, known for its meditation courses which are open to foreigners. The pig-tailed macaque has been trained to collect the millions of coconuts that grow in the region and on the islands. There's a macaque training centre outside Surat Thani that can be visited. ▸▸ *For listings, see pages 614-616.*

Surat Thani ▤🚲❄🛺🚌🄲 ▸▸ *pp614-616. Colour map 4, B2.*

Surat Thani or 'City of the Good People' is a provincial capital and although the town has an interesting riverfront worth a visit and some fabulously stocked markets, its main purpose is as a transportation hub to the gulf islands or south to Krabi. About 50 km north of Surat Thani is the important historic town of Chaiya.

Getting there

The airport is 28 km south of town on Phetkasem Road, T077-253500. The station is at Phun Phin, T077-311213, 14 km west of Surat Thani. From Bangkok's Hualamphong station there are about five trains a night, with the 1820 departure being the most highly sought after, arriving at a convenient time to catch an early morning ferry to Koh Samui. Local buses travel to town regularly, stopping at the Talat Kaset Nung (1) terminal, ฿12, from 0500-1900 (40 minutes). Buses also meet the train to transfer passengers to the ferry terminals for Koh Samui, Koh Phangan and Koh Tao.

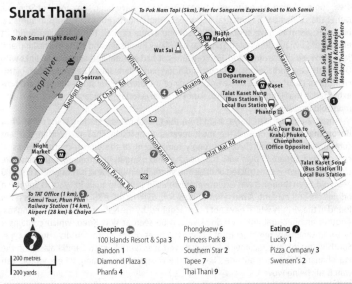

Surat Thani

To Pok Nam Tapi (5km), Pier for Songserm Express Boat to Koh Samui

To Koh Samui (Night Boat)

Tapi River

Ton Pho Rd

Night Market

Wat Sai

Wiset ad Rd

Bandon Rd

Si Chaiya Rd

Na Muang Rd

Mitkasem Rd

Department Store

Kaset

Talat Kaset Nung (Bus Station I) Local Bus Station

Phantip

To Don Sak, Nakhon Si Thammarat, Thaksin Hospital & Kradejae Monkey Training Centre

Seatran

Chonkasem Rd

Talat Mai Rd

A/c Tour Bus to Krabi, Phuket, Chumphon (Office Opposite)

Talat Mai 3

Talat Kaset Song (Bus Station II) Local Bus Station

Night Market

Permlit Pracha Rd

To TAT Office (1 km), Samui Tour, Phun Phin Railway Station (14 km), Airport (28 km) & Chaiya

N

200 metres
200 yards

Sleeping 🛏
100 Islands Resort & Spa 3
Bandon 1
Diamond Plaza 5
Phanfa 4

Phongkaew 6
Princess Park 8
Southern Star 2
Tapee 7
Thai Thani 9

Eating 🍴
Lucky 1
Pizza Company 3
Swensen's 2

The two central bus stations in Surat Thani are within easy walking distance of one another. Talat Kaset Nung (I) is for local buses and buses to Phun Phin, and Talat Kaset Song (II) is for longer-distance journeys. From Bangkok's Southern bus terminal, air-conditioned buses leave between 2000-2200 (12 hours). A popular option is to catch the 1800 bus from Khaosan Road (Bangkok). Passengers can then make their way to Koh Samui (see page 617).

Tourist information

The tourist office, **TAT** ① *5 Talat Mai Rd, T077-288817, tatsurat@tat.or.th, daily 0830-1200, 1300-1630,* is near **Wang Tai Hotel**, southwest of the town, is a good source of information for less-frequented sights in the province.

Sights

Boats can be hired for trips on the river (฿200 for up to six people). The better journey is upstream. There is a big **Chinese temple** and an attractive old viharn in the compound of **Wat Sai**, both on Thi Lek Road. The town brightens up considerably during the **Chak Phra Festival** in September or October (see Festivals, page 615).

Chaiya and around → *Colour map 4, B2.*

① *Northbound trains from Surat Thani's Phun Phin station stop at Chaiya (40 mins). There are regular buses from Surat Thani to Chaiya from Talat Kaset Nung (I). Regular songthaews from close to Talat Kaset Song (II) (฿30).*

This city, lying 50 km north of Surat Thani on Route 41, was an important outpost of the Sumatra-based Srivijayan Empire and dates from the late seventh century making it one of the most ancient settlements in Thailand. Given the quantity of antiquities found in the area, some scholars have suggested that Chaiya may have been the capital of Srivijaya, rather than Palembang (Sumatra) as is usually thought. Recent excavations in Sumatra, however, seem to have confirmed Palembang as the capital. The Mahayana Buddhist empire of Srivijaya dominated Sumatra, the Malay Peninsula, and parts of Thailand and Java between the seventh and 13th centuries. It had cultural and commercial links with Dvaravati, Cambodia, north and south India and particularly Java. The syncretic art of this civilization clearly reveals these links. Many of the artefacts found in the area are now exhibited in the National Museum in Bangkok. Chaiya today is a pleasant, clean town with many old wooden houses.

About 2 km outside Chaiya, 1 km from the Chaiya railway station, stands **Wat Phra Boromthat Chaiya**, one of the most revered temples in Thailand. Within the wat compound, the central *chedi* is strongly reminiscent of the eighth-century *candis* of central Java, square in plan with four porches and rising in tiers topped with miniature *chedis*. The *chedi* is constructed of brick and vegetable mortar and is thought to be 1200 years old. Even though it was extensively restored in 1901 and again in 1930, its Srivijayan origins are still evident. A **museum** ① *Wed-Sun, 0900-1600, ฿30,* nearby, exhibits relics found in the vicinity which have not been 'acquired' by the National Museum in Bangkok. Another architectural link with Srivijaya can be seen at **Wat Kaeo**, which contains a restored sanctuary reminiscent of Cham structures of the ninth century (Hoa-lai type, South Vietnam), but again with Javanese overtones (with links to Candi Kalasan on the Prambanan Plain). Just outside Chaiya is the village of Poomriang, where visitors can watch silk being woven.

Wat Suan Mok

ⓘ *50 km north of Surat Thani on Route 41, T077-431597, www.suanmokkh.org. Take a bus from Talat Kaset Nung (I); the road passes the wat (1 hr). The town of Chaiya is closer to the monastery, so if arriving by train direct from Bangkok alight here and catch a songthaew to Wat Suan Mok.*

Wat Suan Mok, or Wat Suan Mokkhabalarama, is a popular forest wat (*wat pa*), which has become an international Buddhist retreat. Courses for Westerners are run with the aid of a number of foreign monks and novices. The monastery was founded by one of Thailand's most revered monks, the late Buddhadasa Bhikkhu, on a peaceful plot of land covering around 50 ha of fields and forest. Since he died in 1993, the monastery has been run by monks who have continued to teach his reformist philosophy of eschewing consumerism and promoting simplicity and purity. (Buddhadasa Bhikku developed and refined the study of Buddhist economics and he follows a long tradition in Thailand of scholar-monks.)

Ten-day *anapanasati* meditation courses are held here, beginning on the first day of each month. Enrolment onto the course takes place on the last day of the previous month, on a first-come first-served basis. Courses are ฿1500, which covers the cost of the meals (rice and vegetable dishes at 0800 and 1300). For those considering taking the course, bear in mind that students sleep on straw mats, are woken by animal noises at 0400, bathe in a communal pool, and are expected to help with chores around the monastery. No alcohol, drugs or tobacco are permitted and the sexes tend to be segregated. If intending to visit the monastery or enrol on a course, it is worth bringing a torch and mosquito repellent (or buy these at the shop by the entrance).

Kradaejae Monkey Training Centre

ⓘ *T08-9871 8017 (mob), call to make a reservation. The centre is south of Surat Thani on Route 401, towards Nakhon Si Thammarat, 2 km off the main road. Take a songthaew or bus from Surat Thani heading towards Nakhon Si Thammarat, on Talat Mai Rd, which becomes Route 401. The turning to the centre is on the right-hand side, just over the Thathong Bridge, past a wat and a school.*

The only monkey capable of being trained to pick coconuts is the pig-tailed macaque (*ling kung* in Thai). The female is not usually trained as it is smaller and not as strong as the male; strength is needed to break off the stem of the coconut. The training can start when the animals are eight months old. The course lasts three to five months, and when fully trained, the monkeys can pick as many as 800 coconuts in a day and will work for 12 to 15 years. "Working monkeys are very cheap – they cost no more than ฿10 a day but make millions of baht a year", according to Somphon Saekhow, founder of a coconut-collecting school.

Surat Thani and around listings

For Sleeping and Eating price codes and other relevant information, see pages 44-49.

Sleeping

Surat Thani and around *p611, map p*

A-D Diamond Plaza, 83/27 Srivichai Rd, T077-205333, www.diamondplaza hotels.com. Just by the highway as you approach from Phun Phin, near the 100 Islands Resort. A ropey hotel that has seen far better days. Facilities include a fitness centre, swimming pool and a brothel.

A-D Southern Star, 253 Chonkasem Rd, T077-216414. The most luxurious hotel in the centre of town. The 150 rooms are tastefully decorated and are well equipped with satellite TV and minibar. There are 2 restaurants, one on the 16th floor which, in spite of great views over the city, is not recommended. For those looking for nightlife, the Southern Star is also home to the largest disco in the south.

D-E 100 Islands Resort and Spa, 19/6 Moo 3, T077-201150-8, www.roikoh.com. An attractive hotel on the highway, diagonally opposite the Tesco Lotus and Boots, right out of town. Some of the pleasantly decorated rooms open out directly onto the pool. There's a restaurant, jacuzzi, sauna and karaoke. Good value and recommended despite location.

E Phongkaew Hotel, 126/3 Talat Mai Rd, T077-223410. Small, tidy rooms, complete a/c, hot water, free Wi-Fi and cable TV, make this one of the best deals in town. Friendly and in a good location near the TAT office. Recommended.

E Princess Park Hotel, 19/19 Bypass Rd, T077-405989. Small hotel next door to the 100 Islands Resort. Rooms are clean and well appointed, with TV, fridge, hot water and a/c. Good value.

F-G Bandon, 268/2 Na Muang Rd, T077-272 167. The entrance is through a busy Chinese restaurant. Clean, tiled rooms, some a/c,

all with private shower rooms. Rooms get quite stuffy though even with the fan at full throttle. Good value and quiet.

F-G Tapee, 100 Chonkasem Rd, T077-272 575. Large, nice, clean rooms, some a/c, with large shower rooms and TV.

F-G Thai Thani, 442/306-8 Talat Mai Rd, T077-272977. Large, cleanish rooms with attached shower rooms. More expensive rooms have a/c and TV. Bleak corridors and a bit rough around the edges but conveniently positioned for an early bus.

G Phanfa, 247/2-5 Namuang Rd, T077-272288. These large, cleanish rooms with attached shower rooms are the cheapest in town but the place is dour and the corridors bleak.

Eating

Surat Thani and around *p611, map p*

♥♥ Lucky, 452/84-85 Talat Mai Rd, T077-270 3267. Open 0900-2200. Lots of fried fish – snapper, mullet and butterfish – served up in the airy dining room with its faux-ranch ambience. Friendly, English-speaking staff.

♥♥-♥ The Pizza Company, Na Muang Rd, T1112, is close to Swensen's in a large building. It serves what you expect but is recommended for being able to get a stab at a decent salad.

♥ Swensen's, Na Muang Rd, next to the Sahathai Department Store. Open 1000-2200. Sells dozens of ice creams in a/c coolness.

Foodstalls

Foodstalls on Ton Pho Rd, near to the intersection with Na Muang Rd, sell delicious mussel omelettes. There's a good **night market** on Na Muang Rd, and on Ton Pho Rd and vicinity. There's a plentiful supply of fruit and *khanom* stalls along the waterfront. Market next to the local bus terminal (Talat Kaset I).

⊛ Festivals and events

Surat Thani and around *p611, map p*
Aug Rambutan Fair (movable).
Oct-Nov Chak Phra Festival (movable)
marks the end of the 3-month Buddhist
Rains Retreat and the return to earth of the
Buddha. Processions of Buddha images and
boat races on the Tapi River, in longboats
manned by up to 50 oarsmen. Gifts are
offered to monks as this is also *krathin*,
celebrated across Buddhist Thailand,
see also Essentials, page 51.

▲ Activities and tours

Surat Thani and around *p611, map p*
Swimming
Non-residents can use the pools at the
Diamond Plaza Hotel for ฿50.

Tour operators
See also Transport, below.
Phangan Tour, 2000, 402/2 Talat Mai Rd,
T077-205799. Office hours 0530-2200.
Buses for the ferries leave Surat Thani at
0530, 0830, 1230, 1600 arriving at **Koh
Phangan** 4 hrs later, ฿270. The return
ferries depart Koh Phangan at 0700,
1000, 1300, 1700, 4 hrs.
Phantip Travel, 293/6-8 Talat Mai Rd,
T077-272230. A well-regarded and helpful
agency dealing with boats, buses, trains
and planes. Recommended.
Samui Tour, 346/36 Talat Mai Rd,
T077-282352. Office hours 0600-1700. Deals
with **Raja** ferries to **Koh Samui** and **Phangan**
and provides the bus transfer to Don Sak.
Raja ferries depart Don Sak for **Koh Samui**
hourly 0800-1800 returning 0730-1900,
1½ hrs on the boat. Bus transfers to the
ferry arranged from 0650-1630. Pick-ups
from the station at 0600 and 0800.
Songserm Travel Centre Co Ltd, 29/47 M
Mitkasem Rd, 077-205418-9, Surat Thani
pier, T077-289894, advtour_bangkok@
yahoo.com. Also at the port, although very

unhelpful here. May be best to deal with them
through other agents. With **Songserm**, you
can arrange trips to **Koh Samui**, 0800, 2 hrs,
฿150; to **Koh Phangan**, 0800, 3 hrs 40 mins,
฿250; through to **Koh Tao**, ฿500. The bus
from Surat Thani is included in the price.

⊖ Transport

Surat Thani and around *p611, map p*
Air
One-two-go has daily flights to **Bangkok**.
THAI has twice daily connections with
Bangkok as does **Air Asia**.
  Airline offices Air Asia, www.aira
sia.com; **One-two-go**, T1126, www.fly12
go.com; THAI, 3/27-28 Karunrat Rd,
T075-273710.

Boat
See also Tour operators, above.
  Seatran Ferry, Bandon Rd, T077-275060/
251555, www.seatranferry.com, office hours
0500-1800, there's a coffee bar, toilets and
bag-guarding service at the office. Buses
leave Surat Thani for Don Sak every hour
0530-1730. Boats leave Don Sak hourly
0600-1900 for **Koh Samui**. The return
times are the same from Nathon but the first
return ferry is at 0500 and the last at 1800,
฿180, children ฿130, including bus transfer
from Surat Thani with **Phantip Travel**, see
Tour operators, above. Just ferry ticket, ฿110
(2½ hrs). Combination tickets with trains
and buses are available. The train from
Bangkok that arrives at Phun Phin is met
by **Phantip Travel** for the 0900 ferry. The
return through journey to Bangkok leaves
Nathon at 1430 for the 1300 ferry back to
Surat Thani. Airport transfer with Samui
boat ticket, ฿280. Just downtown transfer,
฿70. Seatran ferries go to **Koh Phangan**
3 times daily, ฿280, children ฿180, for the
bus and boat. The 0730, 1230, 1530 (direct),
3½ hrs from Surat Thani, returning 0600
(direct), 0700, 1300. **Seatran** also plans to
start direct services to **Koh Tao**.

Night boats leave from the pier behind the Seatran office. To **Koh Tao**, 2300, 8 hrs, ฿500. To **Koh Samui**, 2300, 6 hrs, ฿150. To **Koh Phangan**, ฿250. See also Transport for Koh Samui, page 639.

Bus

Some private companies run bus services to **Bangkok** (10 hrs, ฿285-440) and **Krabi** (3-4 hrs, ฿80), see Tour operators above for listings. The advantage of taking a tour bus from here to Krabi is that they go all the way into Krabi town, to the Chao Fah Pier, rather than stopping at the bus station, out of town.

To **Trang**, (minibus) 3 hrs, 0700-1730, ฿130; **Phuket**, 4-6 hrs, 0640-1800, ฿113-203. The Phuket buses stop at **Khao Sok National Park**, 2½ hrs, ฿80-100; **Nakhon Si Thammarat**, 2½ hrs, 0630-1800, ฿60; **Krabi**, 3-4 hrs, 0630-1710, ฿80-130 (bus and minibus) and **Hat Yai** 5 hrs, 0600-1730, ฿126-227 (minibus and bus); to **Ranong**, 3½-5 hrs, 0600-1630, ฿80-130 (bus and minibus); to **Chumphon**, 2½-3½ hrs, 030-1730, ฿80-130 bus and minibus); to **Khanom**, 19 hrs, 0700-1800, ฿70. Regular a/c connections with **Bangkok**'s southern bus terminal in Thonburi (10 hrs), 0730-2100, from the out of town terminal, T077-200031.

A/c minibus For some destinations there are few buses but minibuses leave for most places regularly from the bus terminal, Talat Kaset 2, and cost 50% more than the a/c bus. To **Nakhon Si Thammarat**, from 442/347 Talat Mai 33, every 30 mins, 0600-1800, 2 hrs, ฿110.

International connections There are a/c buses from Surat Thani to **Kuala Lumpur** (Malaysia) and **Singapore**.

Songthaew
Known as 'taxis'. These are ubiquitous and cost from ฿5-20 a ride.

Train
Trains out of Phun Phin are often full; advance booking can be made at **Phantip Travel**, see tour operators, above. **Songserm Travel Service** also arranges reservations. There are connections with **Hua Hin**, **Trang**, **Yala**, **Hat Yai** and **Sungei Golok**.

There are 11 trains a day from Phun Phin to Hualamphong station, **Bangkok**, 11-13 hrs. The most comfortable times for overnight journeys are the 1950, 2108, 2123, 2246 and 2306, although these book up early. They take around 11-12 hrs.

International connections An international express train leaves Surat Thani for **Butterworth** (Malaysia) at 0131 (11 hrs) where it continues on to **Kuala Lumpur** and **Singapore**.

● Directory

Surat Thani and around p611, map p
Banks Several banks with ATMs on Na Muang and Chonkasem roads. **Internet** There are about 4 internet shops on Chonkasem Rd between Talat Mai Rd and the **Southern Star**, all charging ฿20 per hr. There is also internet in a café at the front of the Thai Thani hotel. **Medical services** Taksin Hospital, Talat Mai Rd, heading south towards Nakhon, T077-273239.
Post office Near the corner of Talat Mai and Chonkasem roads and on the corner of Na Muang and Chonkasem roads.

Koh Samui

Koh Samui is the third largest of Thailand's islands, after Phuket and Koh Chang. Over the last decade tourism has exploded and now that it is accessible by air, the palm-studded tropical island is making the transition from a backpackers' haven into a sophisticated beach resort. The most recent development has also seen an identity shift from a simple party and pampering paradise to upmarket spa destination. Unlike Phuket, it still caters for the budget traveller with a variety of bungalows scattered around its shores. Its popularity is deserved as it boasts some beautiful bays with sandy beaches hemmed by coconut palms seducing many a traveller in search of a paradise beach. But the only area of the island left relatively undeveloped is the southern tip, where the ring-road snakes inland from the coast, leaving a quiet corner away from the thud of dance music. However, Koh Samui is slowly disappearing under concrete and billboards as the tourism bandwagon continues to gather speed. The two most popular beaches are still Lamai and Chaweng, both on the east side of the island. They are the longest uninterrupted beaches on the island, with good swimming and watersports and busy nightlife. Mae Nam and Bophut, on the north shore, are a little more laid-back and a number of good quality, low-cost accommodations can still be found there, although expensive resorts rather than backpacker options are rapidly taking over.

There are still isolated spots, mainly in the south and west. For a much quieter scene, head for the remote bungalows down the west shore, although it is best to hire a vehicle as many of them are off the main road. An advantage of staying on this side of the island is the sunsets.

Close to Koh Samui are the beautiful islands of the Ang Thong Marine National Park, see page 620. ➤➤ *For listings, see pages 623-641.*

Ins and outs

Getting there

Flying is the easiest and quickest option. It is relatively expensive but hassle free. The **airport** ① *T077-428500*, in the northeast, is privately owned by **Bangkok Airways**. There are multiple daily connections with Bangkok, as well as flights from Phuket and Pattaya, and international connections with Singapore and Hong Kong. The airport has an information desk which deals with hotel reservations (note that this is owned by Bangkok Airways and attempts are made to divert clients to Samui Palm Beach – owned by the airline) and reconfirmation of flights. There is also a restaurant, free left luggage and through check-in for international flights for a large number of airlines, Hertz and Budget car rental, currency exchange and an ATM. Transport to town or the beach is by air-conditioned minibus to Bophut, Mae Nam, Chaweng (฿150), Choeng Mon, Lamai (฿300) and Big Buddha. Prices are inflated. There's a **limousine service** ① *T077-245598, samuiaccom@hotmail.com*, at domestic arrivals. The alternative is to walk out onto the road but it is a 1-km walk and tricky with luggage.

Take a ferry from one of Surat Thani's piers, which takes about two hours. The slow overnight boat to Samui leaves from Surat Thani (Don Sak) at 2300, arriving in Nathon at around 0500, ideal for those who arrive late in town and don't want to stay in Surat Thani. Expect to pay around ฿250. Or catch a boat from Chumphon to Koh Tao and from there to Koh Samui via Koh Phangan. But this is a much longer sea journey and only really makes sense if intending to stop off on Koh Tao. The State Railway runs a rail/bus/ferry service from Bangkok to Koh Samui (18 hours), this needs to be booked two-three days in advance.

It is not necessary to buy a 'combination' ticket (available from any travel agent in Bangkok); buses from all the ferry companies meet the trains at Phun Phin (see page 616) to transfer passengers to the ferry terminals. ▸▸ See Transport, page 639, for further information.

Getting around

Koh Samui is a large island – well over 20 km both long and wide. Beaches, hotels and guesthouses can be found on most of the coastline, although the two most popular and developed beaches are both on the east coast, Chaweng and Lamai. The main town of Nathon, where most of the ferries dock, is on the west side of the island. A ring road follows the coast along the north and east sides of the island, but runs inland cutting off the southwestern corner. Many resorts are on small tracks off this main circuit road running down to the beach. The most common form of transport, *songthaews* circulate between the island's northern and eastern beaches during daylight hours. Their final destination is usually written on the front of the vehicle and they stop anywhere when flagged down (prices start at ฿50 per person but are often inflated and some haggling

Koh Samui

	Bill Resort **2**	Lucky Mother **5**	Simple Life Bungalow **16**
	Chalee Villa **3**	New Lapaz Villa **7**	Spa Resort **13**
	Emerald Cove **8**	Phalarn Inn 33 **4**	Sunbeam **14**
	Imperial **10**	Pinnacle Samui Resort	Wiesenthal Resort **11**
	Lipa Lodge **12**	& Spa **1**	
Sleeping	Lipa Lovely Resort **15**	Seafan Beach Resort **6**	
Amari Palm Reef **9**			

may be required). Occasional nighttime *songthaews* run from 1830 and charge double. From Nathon, *songthaews* travel in a clockwise direction to Chaweng and anti-clockwise to Lamai. There are scores of places renting out motorbikes and jeeps but note that the accident rate on Koh Samui is horrendously high (see box, page 640).

Best time to visit

March to June is hot and fine with a good breeze and only the occasional thunderstorm. At this time of year good discounts are available on accommodation. June to October is also sunny and hot, with short showers. The 'worst' time of year is October to February, when the monsoon breaks and rain is more frequent. However, even during this period daily hours of sunshine average five to seven hours.

Tourist information

The **TAT office** ① *370 Moo 3, T077-420720, daily 0830-1630*, is helpful. Several tourist magazines and maps are distributed free of charge. Be aware that there are agencies advertising themselves as TAT booking offices in Bangkok. Customers book accommodation through them and then on arrival, if they don't like the sleeping choice they have no means to redress it. The official TAT is not a booking office. Companies using its acronym write it as follows: t.a.t. The official **Tourism Authority of Thailand** is just TAT.

Background

Koh Samui is the largest in an archipelago of 80 islands, only six of which are inhabited. Many of Koh Samui's inhabitants were not Thai, but Chinese from Hainan who settled on the island between 150 and 200 years ago. Although the Chinese across Thailand have assimilated to such a degree that they are almost invisible, a number of traditional homes can still be seen.

About 60,000 people live on Koh Samui, many of whom are fishermen-turned-hoteliers. As one of Thailand's most popular tourist destinations, the number of annual visitors is many times this figure. The first foreign tourists began stepping ashore on Samui in the mid-1960s. At that time there were no hotels, electricity (except generator-supplied), telephones or surfaced roads, just an over-abundance of coconuts. This is still evident because, apart from tourism, the mainstay of the economy is coconuts; two million are exported to Bangkok each month. Monkeys are taught to scale the trees and pluck down the ripe nuts; even this traditional industry has cashed in on tourism – visitors can watch the monkeys at work. A monkey training centre has been established outside Surat Thani, see page 613.

For the moment at least, Koh Samui – *in toto* – has managed to absorb a massive increase in tourist numbers without eroding the qualities that brought people to the island in the first place (although some long-term visitors would dispute that). Currently much of the island looks like a construction site as every available piece of land is built on.

Around the island ⊕❷❸❹⦿▲❺ ➤➤ *pp623-641. Colour map 4, B2.*

The island's main attractions are its wonderful beaches; most people head straight to one, where they remain until they leave. However, there are motorbikes or jeeps for hire to explore inland and there are a multitude of activities on offer, see Activities and tours, page 636. Evidence of the immigration of Hainanese can be seen reflected in the traditional architecture of the island. Houses, though they may also incorporate Indian, Thai and Khmer elements, are based on the Hainanese style. The use of fretwork to decorate balconies and windows, the tiled, pitched roofs and the decoration of the eaves make the older houses of Samui distinctive in Thai terms. Sadly, it is unlikely that many will survive the next decade or two. They are being torn down to make way for more modern structures, or renovated and extended in such a way that their origins are obscured.

Two-thirds of the island is forested and hilly with some impressive waterfalls (in the wet season). Hin Lad Waterfall and Wat are 3 km south of Nathon and can be reached from the town on foot, or by road 1 km off Route 4169. It's a 45-minute walk from the car park. Na Muang Waterfall, in the centre of the island, has a 30-m drop and a good pool for swimming. As the only waterfall on the island which is accessible by paved road it is busy at weekends and on holidays.

Nathon → *Colour map 4, B3.*
Nathon is Koh Samui's capital and is where the ferry docks. It is a town geared to tourists, with travel agents, exchange booths, clothes stalls, bars and restaurants. Nathon consists of three roads running parallel to the seafront, with two main roads at either end linking them. Although it is used mainly as a transit point, it still has a friendly feel. *Songthaews* travel from Nathon to all the beaches. Motorbikes wait at the end of the pier, *songthaews* wait next to the second southernmost pier.

Ang Thong ('Golden Basin') Marine National Park
① *Daily tours leave from piers around the island. There are no public boats but you can leave the tour, stay on Koh Wua Talap and rejoin it several days later at no extra charge (make sure you tell the ferry driver which day you want to be picked up).*
The park is made up of 40 islands lying northwest of Koh Samui, featuring limestone massifs, tropical rainforests and beaches. Particular features are **Mae Koh** (a beautiful beach) and **Thale Nai** (an emerald saltwater lake), both on **Koh Mae Koh** and **Koh Sam Sao**; the latter has a coral reef and a huge rock arch as well as a hill providing good views of the surrounding islands. The area is the major spawning ground of the short-bodied mackerel, a popular edible fish in Thailand. There is also good snorkelling (the main attraction), swimming and walking. The park's headquarters are on **Koh Wua Talap**. Visibility is at its best between late March and October.

North coast
Bang Po (Ban Poh) A quiet, secluded and clean beach which is good for swimming. One of the better options for those wanting to escape the buzz of Chaweng and Lamai.

Mae Nam A clean, serene beach with lots of coconut palms and fringed with coral reefs to tempt swimmers and snorkellers. It is a popular spot and a number of new, beautifully designed resorts have opened here.

Bophut Bophut is one of the few places on the island where there are still traditional wooden Samui houses with Chinese lettering above the doors. It has grown increasingly popular in the last few years and there are now currency exchanges, bookshops, yoga schools, bars, restaurants and good watersports facilities, yet these haven't really spoilt the ambience. The beach is straight and narrow and lacks the sweeping expanse of Chaweng, or the quiet intimacy of Laem Set, yet the place maintains a refined and friendly village

Sea and weather conditions on Koh Samui

March-October Light winds averaging 5 knots, calm seas, the driest period but downpours can still occur. Water visibility is good. This is the period of the south-west monsoon and though generally calm, Bophut and Mae Nam can be windy, with choppy conditions offshore. Chaweng is normally calm.

October-February The northeast monsoon brings rain and stronger winds, averaging 10-15 knots but with gusts of 30 knots on some days. Sea conditions are sometimes rough and water visibility is generally poor although Koh Tao, see page 659, offers good year-round diving.

---

atmosphere with the string of restaurants making the beachfront a popular evening location. Most hotels offer fishing, snorkelling and sightseeing charters, although there are also plenty of independent outfits. As with most of the more remote beaches on Samui, the *songthaews* that are allotted for the beach run rather infrequently. It is possible to charter them and there are always motorcycle taxis around.

Big Buddha (Bang Ruk) This small bay has typically been a favourite stomping ground with expats although in recent years it has become increasingly popular with travellers. Accommodation is rather cramped and it also tends to be noisy as the bungalows are squashed between the beach and the road. However, the beach is quiet and palm-fringed and the water is always good. During the choppier weather from October to February, this sheltered cove is a popular haven with fishing boats.

The **Temple of the Big Buddha** sits on an island linked to the mainland by a short causeway, near Bophut beach. This unremarkable, rather featureless, modern seated image is 12 m high. In recent years the site has been smartened up and made into a 'proper' tourist attraction; there are now 50 or so trinket stalls at the entrance and several foodstalls. It has become a popular spot on the motorbike touring trail.

Samrong Bay Set at the far northeastern corner of the island, this spot is also known as 'Secret Beach'. But it is not a secret any longer as there are two major resorts here. The scenery is more wild and raw.

Choeng Mon At the northeast of the island is arguably the prettiest bay. The crescent of extremely fine white sand has an island at its eastern end, attached to the mainland by a sandbar, traversable at low tide. While in places it is rocky underfoot in the centre of the bay, the sand continues well out to sea. The restaurant scene is pretty lively, particularly in the centre of the beach where bamboo tables with oil lamps reach right down to the water's edge and there are a couple of beach bars at the eastern end. The beach is most popular with couples and families. There is a *songthaew* station at the far eastern side of the area, behind the beach.

South of Choeng Mon, there's good snorkelling at **Yai Noi**, north of Chaweng.

East coast
Chaweng This is the biggest beach on the island, split into three areas – north, central and Chaweng Noi. **Chaweng Noi** is to the south, round a headland, and has three of

the most expensive hotels on the island. **Central Chaweng** is an attractive sweep of sand with lovely water for swimming and is lined with resorts, bungalows, restaurants and bars. The town that has grown up here is entirely geared towards tourists and in recent years it has become swamped. Along the road behind the beach there is a further proliferation of bars, clubs, tourist agencies, restaurants, fast-food chains, stalls and watersports facilities. However, the infrastructure has not kept pace with the concrete expansion and the drains stink in the searing heat. In comparison to the other beaches on the island it is crowded and getting more resort-ridden by the year, but it's still Samui's most popular and by far the busiest beach. Despite the facilities and energetic activities on offer, most visitors prefer to sunbathe.

Chaweng to Lamai There is not much beach along this stretch of coast but there is some snorkelling off the rocky shore. Snorkelling is best at **Coral Cove**, between Chaweng and Lamai.

Lamai Koh Samui's 'second' beach is 5 km long and has a large assortment of accommodation. The beach is nice but rugged and not as attractive as Chaweng and the sea is rocky underfoot in many places. Cheaper accommodation can be found more readily here than on Chaweng. Just south of Lamai, there is a cultural hall and a group of phallic rock formations known as **Grandmother** and **Grandfather rocks** (*Hinyai* and *Hinta*). There's an array of tourist shops leading up to it. Companies along the main road parallel to the beach offer fishing and snorkelling trips around the islands.

Depending on who you talk to, or who you are, this is either a rather tawdry, down-market Pattaya, or an idiosyncratic, slightly hip and colourful Hua Hin. It is not particularly peaceful or picturesque. It can be fun and some people love it. The original town of Ban Lamai is quiet and separate from the tourist part, which is usually quiet during the day as most of the tourists are on the beach. The sea at Lamai can be wild and challenging during the early months of the year, and suitable only for the most competent of swimmers. Due to the tide there are not as many watersports here and the sea can appear murky, particularly at the northern end. Many hotels and restaurants are geared to the German market.

South coast
The small, often stony, beaches that line the south coast from Ban Hua Thanon west to Thong Krut are quieter and less developed with only a handful of hotels and bungalows, although construction continues at a breathless pace and the area is littered with endless 'land for sale' boards. While most tourists head for the white sands and sweeping shores elsewhere, there are some beautiful little coves peppered along this southerly stretch.

Ban Hua Thanon Ban Hua Thanon is an attractive rambling village with wooden shophouses and *kwaytio* stalls – and the only Muslim community on Koh Samui. The forebears of the inhabitants come from Pattani in Thailand's far south. With its stony beach being the biggest anchorage for fishing boats on the island, this village is quiet and rarely visited by tourists. North of the village are a couple of restaurants, well situated with cooling sea breezes, see Eating, page 635.

Na Khai Na Khai is a small beach with just a handful of resorts. The swimming can be rocky, but if you are looking for a quiet place to stay and don't require a classic sweep of golden sand, then this is an option.

Laem Set This is not really much of a beach compared with Chaweng and Lamai. However, it is quiet, clean and palm fringed and there is some reasonable snorkelling.

Samui Butterfly Garden ① *T077-424020, 0830-1730, ฿170*, is set on the side of the hill behind **Laem Set Inn** opposite **Central Samui Village**. It features a screened butterfly garden with a limited collection of butterflies, a display of (dead) insects, moths and butterflies, a few beehives, a hillside observatory, observation platforms for views of the coast, a glass-bottomed boat for viewing a coral reef and a restaurant.

Thong Krut Thong Krut Bay and the hamlet of Ban Thong Krut are at the southern extremity of the island. The stony beach is around a kilometre long and the swimming is average but there are excellent views from here and it is peaceful and undeveloped with just a handful of shops including a little supermarket and **The Beach**, **Java** and **Green Ta'Lay** restaurants. Boat trips to Koh Tan and Koh Matsum or to fish and snorkel can be arranged through various companies in the village.

Nearby, is the **Samui Snake Farm** ① *88/2 Moo 4, T077-423247*. Shows are held at 1100 and 1400. The commentary is hilarious. Not for the squeamish.

Koh Tan and Koh Matsum **Koh Tan** lies due south of Thong Krut and is about 3 km long and 2 km wide. It was first colonized by Hainanese; there is a Chinese cemetery with those first colonizers' graves on the island. There are three small villages and a few bungalow developments on the island which, although undeveloped, are not blessed with spotless beaches and crystal-clear waters. Still, it is quiet and just about away from it all.

Koh Matsum is a sorry sight – all the coconut trees have been stripped by beetles, leaving a desolate landscape.

West coast
Like the south coast, the western coastline south of Nathon is undeveloped with secluded coves and beautiful sunsets. Phangka, near the southwest tip of the island, has good snorkelling in the quiet waters of a small bay; Thong Yang, further north, is an isolated beach, relatively untouched by frantic development. The vehicle ferry from Don Sak, on the mainland, docks here.

◉ Koh Samui listings

For Sleeping and Eating price codes and other relevant information, see pages 44-49.

● Sleeping

Accommodation prices tend to soar during the peak months but are a bargain off season. Prices on Koh Samui have doubled in the past few years and it's rare to find fan bungalows under ฿400-500 in the high season. Backpacker havens are being forced out to make way for high-end establishments. High season roughly runs from Jul-Aug, Dec-Apr.

Nathon *p620, map p618*
C-E Jinta Hotel, 310 Moo 3, T077-420630, www.tapee.com. Modern, attractive hotel on the seafront with 37 a/c and fan rooms with fridges and TVs. The more expensive modern rooms are a considerable improvement.
D-E Palace Hotel, on the seafront road, T077-421079. Offers 33 a/c, clean, adequate and well-maintained rooms with hot water.

Ang Thong Marine National Park
p620, map p618
Koh Wua Talap, National Park office, T077-2806025, T077-280222. Bungalows,

long-houses, camping, showers and a restaurant are available along with a small visitors' centre. Accommodation sleeps up to 8 people. See the national park website, www.dnp.go.th, for details and online booking.

North coast p620, map p618
Bang Po (Ban Poh)
C-E Phalarn Inn 33, T077-247111, phalarn_inn@hotmail.com. Set back some way from the beach. Concrete bungalows with big balconies, TV and a/c have a garish colour scheme. Cheaper fan rooms are available. Not the best deal considering the location but pleasant grounds, friendly staff and a good restaurant, motorbike rental, package tours and ticket reservations.
D-E Sunbeam, T077-420600. Secluded bungalows, quiet location, clean, friendly, private beach.

Mae Nam
LL Santiburi, 12/12 Moo 1, T077-425031, www.santiburi.com. A superb and incredibly large resort of 91 beautifully furnished Thai-style villas and suites with a massive pool, watersports, sauna, tennis and squash courts, on a quiet beach. The spa (1100-2300) offers a full range of massage, reflexology and facials. There's also a **Hertz** desk. For the golf course, see Activities and tours, page 637.
LL-C Pinnacle Samui Resort & Spa, 26/4 Moo 4, T077-425321, www.pinnacle hotels.com. The well established garden hides the 80 bungalows, creating a more intimate feel. All rooms have a good range of facilities but the interiors are a tad dated. There is a swimming pool, but pool villas are available for those who don't like to share. Suitable for families.
AL-E New Lapaz Villa, Next to Paradise Resort, T077-425402, www.newlapaz.com. Wide range of accommodation available from basic wooden bungalows, which are typical of the budget options, except that they have hot showers. The new midrange concrete bungalows are modern with built-in wardrobes, and include nice touches such as

dressing gowns and umbrellas in the rooms. The most expensive option has a separate lounge area, a bathtub and overlooks the beach. Swimming pool and restaurant.
AL-E Palm Point Village, 15 mins' walk from Mae Nam village, T077-425095, www.palmpointsamui.com. This place has good-value wooden and concrete bungalows on a lovely steep-sloping beach. The more expensive rooms have a/c and balcony. Cheaper fan rooms available. Good food and motorbikes for hire.
A-B Seafan Beach Resort, 11/1 Moo 4, T077-425204, www.seafanresort.com. Charming a/c luxury wooden bungalows on stilts, with whirlpools, attractive gardens, a pool and a restaurant.
A-C Maenam Resort, 1/3 Moo 4, T077-247 287, www.maenamresort.com. Alpinesque bungalows with little balconies, wicker furniture, wardrobes, desk and a/c in luscious gardens. Some have wonderful positions set on the gently sloping beach with shallow waters. Popular with young families. Friendly management. Recommended.
B-C Harry's Bungalows, 26/9 Wat Napralan, T077-425447, www.harrys-samui.com. 50m from the beach, reached by climbing wooden steps over a wall that encloses the resort. 19 bungalows spread out amongst a huge garden. Plenty of areas to relax, including a swimming pool. Rooms are spacious, complete with a/c, cable TV, safety deposit box, however the furniture is of disappointingly low quality. Free transfers from piers (airport ฿400) and Wi-Fi are a bonus.
B-E Home Bay Resort, 26/11 Moo 4, T077-247214. Old wooden bungalows with fan have been well maintained. The a/c rooms are cavernous and are decorated with bamboo matting. Modern bathrooms with hot water showers. Located on a tranquil stretch of beach.
B-E Moonhut Bungalows, 67/2 Moo 1, T077-425247, www.kohsamui.com/moonhut. Various types of room, from fan huts, in a luscious garden, at the rear, to more expensive

a/c which have a sea view. All have been finished to a high standard and are spotlessly clean. Popular with families.

B-E Shady Resort, 1/7 Moo 4, T077-425392, www.shady-resort.com. Offers 20 bungalows on a yellow-sand beach bordered by bowing coconut palms. Rooms are nice, white and bright with desks and fridges. A/c bungalows with gardens are the most expensive. Friendly and good value.

D-E See Daeng, 190 Moo 1, T08-9588 8859 (mob), www.seedaengsamui.com. Comfortable rooms in a wooden building perpendicular to the beach. They all have a small balcony and the room at the front has a sea view. Swiss and Thai owned. Discount for long-term stays.

D-E Wandee Bungalow, 151/1 Moo 1, T077-425609, wandeebungalow@ hotmail.com. 3 rows of spacious, if a little Spartan, concrete bungalows parallel to the beach. Windows on 3 sides flood the rooms with natural light. Restaurant on the beach. Very peaceful.

D-F Seashore 1, next to Seashore 2, T077-425280. Offers 2 options: small, cheap, cheerful and very basic wooden bungalows with fan or spacious, newer log cabin-style rooms with a/c, some of which are right on the beach. Pool table and beachfront bar.

E Poo Bungalows, 190 Moo 1, T077-247252. Row of wooden bungalows wedged down a narrow alley behind the owner's hairdressing shop. Fan rooms are a little dark and bathrooms tired looking, but for this price are actually very good, they even come with a TV. Discounts given for long-term stays.

E-F Sea Shore 2, next to Moonhut Bungalows, T077-425192. Concrete bungalows all with fan and bathroom inside. The rooms are rather bizarrely arranged just off the beach. Friendly Thai owner. Excellent value for the location.

Bophut Village

LL-A The Waterfront, 71/2 Moo 1, T077-427165, www.thewaterfrontbophut.com. Modern and attractive bungalows set around a small pool close to the beach but still in the village itself. Renovated and expanded by its British owners in 2003, it has a cosy atmosphere and is popular with families. Rooms have kettles and DVD player. Free childminding and Wi-Fi. The low-season prices are a bargain.

LL-B Eden Bungalows, 91 Moo1, T077-427645, www.edenbungalows.com. This French-owned oasis is delightful. 15 tiled double and family fan or a/c rooms with large bathrooms and romantically dim lighting. They are cleverly arranged around a small pool, and plenty of vegetation, giving an impression of space. Fairly pricey but the ambience is worth it.

LL-B Smile House Resort, 93 Moo 1, T077-425361, www.smilehouse-samui net.com. Choice of either a/c or fan bungalows in a pleasant layout. Both are kept meticulously clean and have unusual Chinese lampstands but small bathrooms. There is a large pool on the roadside, so it is a little public. The fan rooms are good value considering the access to the pool. There's a beachside restaurant over the road.

A-B The Red House, 51/8 Moo 1, T077-425686, www.design-visio.com. This delightful place has 4 boudoirs with balconies which are elegantly furnished with Chinese textiles in deep reds, and attractive furniture. The 4-poster beds look over the sea. The downstairs is a shoe emporium. Friendly and recommended.

A-C Shades, 99/1 Moo 1. Large attractive traditional Thai-style wooden bungalows with large verandas overlooking a pretty, secluded garden. All rooms have a/c and are minimally furnished but immaculate with large comfortable bed, TV, fridge, bath and kettle. There is a beachside restaurant across the road. The resort also offers 5 self-contained luxury apartments nearby.

B The Lodge, 91/1 Moo 1, T077-425337, www.apartmentsamui.com. This small, appealing hotel has 10 well-decorated a/c rooms, all of which have satellite TV, a minibar, and en suite bathroom. While there is no restaurant, there is a bar that serves basic Western food.

B-E Khun Thai Guesthouse, 88/6 Moo 6, T077-245118. Set back from the road, down a very quiet cul-de-sac, but still only a minute walk from the beach, this bright orange family home has numerous rooms on offer. A few don't have external windows, but most are bright and airy. All have hot water and TV. The ฿500 rooms are the best value.

C-E Oasis Bungalows, opposite **Starfish & Coffee**, see Eating, below, T077-425143. The alleyway beside the restaurant opens onto a beautiful garden with 6 bungalows ranging from concrete fan huts to larger, newer wooden bungalows. All have TV and hot water showers. Good value.

Bophut Beach

LL Anantara, 101/3 Bophut, T077-428300, www.anantara.com. With resorts and spas throughout Thailand, Anantara's well-designed Samui resort is chic and comfortable with a luxurious yet traditional feel. The striking lobby is dominated by a cluster of lanterns and doors imprinted with golden stencilling. This opens out onto a stunning, rectangular lotus pond. The infinity pool overlooks a well-kept section of the beach. The spa (1000-2200) is a cool oasis in the grounds. The Italian full-moon restaurant occupies a stylish raised platform with superb views.

LL-L Paradise Beach Resort, 18/8 Moo 1, T077-247227, www.samuiparadise beach.com. Now a **Best Western** with 95 bungalows on the beach and in a main building. Attractive touches in rooms include brightly coloured silk cushions and drapes on the beds. Each room has a double and single bed. There's a large secluded and nicely shaded pool, a kids' paddling pool, slides, dive shop, canoeing, windsurfing, massage and a growing number of fabulous restaurants – Thai and seafood. There's only a small beach but sunbeds are perched on a sandy terrace with great views of Koh Phangan. Popular with families.

LL-L Zazen, west side of Bophut beach, T077-425085, www.samuizazen.com. This is a compact resort full of surprising design details like the distinctly exotic interiors and North African style beachfront façade. The small beach is framed by a headland to the west, although the sea is not at its best here. Bungalows and spa massage cabins nestle amid the vegetation. There is a beach bar and the fashionable fusion restaurant, see Eating, below.

AL-B World Resort, 175/Moo 1, T077-425355, www.samuiworldresort.com. Fan and a/c, spacious wood-panelled bungalows. There is a large pool and a beach restaurant that serves Thai and Western food.

A-D Sandy Resort and Spa, 177/1 Bophut Beach, T077-425353, www.sandysamui.com Fan-cooled bungalows and a/c rooms in a somewhat ugly 2-storey building. There are 2 restaurants, one on the beach.

B-D Free House, at the western end of the beach, T077-427516. Freehousesamui.com. 14 smart, good-value modern bungalows. Like most places on the island they are rather squashed into limited space but the beachfront restaurant is popular.

C-D Cocunut Calm Beach, 180 Moo1, T077-427558, thamrug@hotmail.com. Mixture of concrete and bamboo bungalows reasonably spaced amongst coconut palms. Some effort has gone into making them presentable. Both fan and a/c are available.

D-E Chalee Villa, right at the western tip of the beach, T078-857884. This is a blast from the past with simple Thai-style beach bungalows spread leisurely along the shore a few metres from the waves. Basic, but clean and comfortable with friendly staff and a relaxed ambience – the best of the strip's budget accommodation.

Big Buddha (Bang Ruk)

AL-B Como Resort, western end of the beach, T077-425210, www.kohsamuibeach resort.com. With a little pool and relaxed atmosphere, **Como** has 11 smart little bungalows with hot water and TVs.

The friendly restaurant and quiet setting make it ideal for families.

A-C Secret Garden, 22/1 Moo 4, T077-245255, www.secretgarden.co.th. The cheaper rooms are in a converted building, the others are concrete bungalows. All rooms in this small resort have a/c, TV, fridge and hot water. Clean and comfortable, friendly British owner.

B-C Elemental, T08-1370 3980 (mob), areyouelemental.blogspot.com. Boutique-style beach bar and super-chic bungalows established by a British-Canadian couple in 2006. 4 stylish modern bungalows sleep up to 3, with the more expensive options offering living rooms overlooking the beach.

B-E Oriental Resort, 30/5 Moo 4, T077-427 192, www.kohsamui.net/orientalsamui. The fan rooms are at the back, stuck down the side of the resort and are dark, small and very basic – therefore overpriced. The a/c rooms have sea views and are lighter, airier and in much better condition. The pool is more for dipping than swimming.

D-E Chez Ban Ban, T077-245135, www.samui-info.com/ban-ban. Quaint brick bungalows in a well-kept garden overlooking the centre of the beach. The Swiss owner's influence is clear in the design and on the menu, which offers escargots and fondue. VIP bungalows are split-level while more basic, excellent value rooms are simple and clean with TV and fridge. Pretty restaurant with pool table and petanque.

D-E Shambala, 23/2 Moo 4, T077-425330, www.samui-shambala.com. A well-kept bohemian beach resort with 14 cute, bright, blue, fan bungalows amid a sweet garden with flourishing bougainvillea. A good choice for those looking for a serene, budget option and relaxed atmosphere. There's a great chill-out area with books and games and a detailed information board. Run by friendly and helpful Brits Julz and Jessica. Recommended.

E-F Sunset Song Bungalow, 33/4 Moo 4, T077-425155. Log cabin-style bungalows with fan or a/c in a small garden fronting

onto the beach. For this price you have to overlook the fact that the rooms are in need of some repair, however the beds are comfy.

Samrong Bay

LL Sila Evason Hideaway, T077-245678, www.sixsenses.com. Infamous ultra-chic and exclusive resort and spa with cool, calm and minimalist lines. 66 hidden villas with rectangular private pools and luxury sundecks. There are 2 restaurants (see Eating, below), a gym, shop and Six Senses Spa (1000-2200). The massage rooms overlook the sea. The Drinks on the Hill bar has cracking cocktails – especially the bellinis. Recommended.

AL-A Arayaburi, formerly Bay View Village, 6/14 Moo 5, T077-427500, www.samui-hotels.com/arayaburi/. Offers 65 villas, with small private terraces that are fairly closely packed. Superior rooms are nice and light and there are flowers on all beds. Garden view bungalows do not get much of a view. Beachside pool, bike, motorbike and canoe hire available. It shares a private beach with the Sila Evason Hideaway.

Choeng Mon

LL Sala Samui, www.salasamui.com. Stunning luxury hotel with award winning design. The beachside pool surrounded by decking and hidden private villas with pools, raised relaxing platforms and outdoor bathtubs. There's a Mediterranean feel. The Mandara spa is open 1000-2200.

LL Tongsai Bay, T077-245480, www.tongsai bay.co.th. Luxury resort with bungalows scattered across a hillside coconut planta-tion, overlooking a private bay. Watersports, tennis courts, gym and 2 pools (1 sea water) close to the sea. 3 restaurants, including beachside bar and café. Buggies are used to get around the resort but there are several flights of stairs to access some rooms.

L-A The White House, centre of the beach, 59/3 Moo 5, T077-245315, www.hotelthe whitehouse.com. Set in a delightful shady tropical garden, this is a small collection of large white houses with Thai details. The hotel also has a medium-sized pool in a cosy position just behind the beach and restaurants. A refined place. Recommended.

AL Imperial Boat House, 83 Moo 5, T077-425041, www.imperialhotels.com. 34 converted teak rice barges make for unusual suites, 182 other rooms in 3-storey ranch-style blocks, with limited views and rather disappointing compared to the boats. Watersports are available and a boat-shaped pool adds to the theme-park feel. The garden pool is more secluded. The buffet breakfast is extensive. But it is outdated compared to its elegant neighbours.

C Choeng Mon Guesthouse, centre of the beach, www.choeng monburi.com. 20 rooms right on the beach which offer a cheap alternative on this attractive bay. No pool.

East coast *p621, map p618*
Chaweng

Although Chaweng is more upmarket than Lamai, it contains a rather jarring combination of international hotels and basic bungalows. Visitors can stay in US$150 hotels then cross the road and have a full American breakfast for under US$2.

LL Blue Lagoon, northern end, T077-422037, www.bluelagoonhotel.com. Well designed with 60 rooms in 2-storey Thai-style blocks. The resort also features an international restaurant and a large pool.

LL Poppies, T077-422419, www.poppies samui.com. Beautifully designed to maximize space, these a/c Thai-style houses have open-air bathrooms and are set in a tropical garden with water running through it. There is an excellent, popular open-air restaurant (see Eating, below) and a small pool. The Swiss management offers outstanding service and one of its marketing gimmicks has been to set up a live video cam overlooking Chaweng beach 24 hrs a day.

LL-AL Centara Samui Beach Resort, T077-230500, www.centarahotels resorts.com. An elegant, if expensive, low-rise Greek temple comes to the Orient-style resort. Wood-panelled blocks with good facilities set in a palm grove. There's a large pool, health centre and 4 good restaurants. Popular.

LL-AL First Bungalow Beach Resort, T077-422327, www.firstbungalowsamui.com. As implied by its name, this was the first resort to appear on Chaweng beach and the a/c bungalows are spacious and nicely laid out.

LL-AL Imperial, southern end, T02-261 9000, www.imperialsamui.com. The first 5-star hotel on the island has rooms in a large 5-storey Tuscan-style block. The hotel also has salt and freshwater pools.

L-AL Impiana, T077-422011, www.impiana. com. A new modernized block with pool and 2 good restaurants. The downstairs Thai operation boasts a nice beach, while upstairs is **Tamarind's Restaurant** (1800-2230), which offers well-received Pacific-rim cuisine.

L-A Al's Resort, 200 Moo 2, T077-422154, www.alsresort.com. The rooms are reasonable enough but this resort operates an unfair cancellation policy; the staff can also be extremely rude and unhelpful. If you do stay here you are advised to only pay on a day-to-day basis.

AL Tradewinds, 17/14 Moo 3, T077-230602, www.tradewinds-samui.com. An appealing resort as the excellent bungalows are set out in an attractive part of the beach. As a result of its size, it is an intimate place and is peaceful at night. There is a beachside bar and restaurant.

AL-A Amari Palm Reef, northern end, T077-422015, www.amari.com. The hotel is built on both sides of the main road. The original part is on the seaward side of the road. Rooms here are in blocks in a garden compound. There is also a rather public swimming pool next to the beach and it is all slightly cramped. On the other side of the road are the newer Thai-style bungalows and duplexes. There is a quieter, more secluded pool, a tennis court, dive centre, the **Sivara spa** and an average restaurant.

AL-A Corto Maltese, 119/3 Moo 2, T077-230041, www.corto-samui.com.

Interestingly designed small resort, next to the beach, far removed from the generic hotel room design. The bright blue huts have colourfully and playfully sculptured interiors, which are very comfortable, with a/c, fridge and TV as standard. Spilt level flooring separates the lounge from the sleeping area and bathroom. Swimming pool, jacuzzi and beachfront restaurant. Recommended.

AL-B Samui Resotel (previously **Munchies**), T077-422374, www.samuiresotel.com. A range of well-decorated fan rooms and luxurious suites. They are, predictably, too close to one another, but emerge as being better than most because of the pleasant beachside restaurant and live music.

AL-C Long Beach Lodge, 14 Chaweng Beach, Moo 2, T077-422372, longbeach_samui@ hotmail.com. A large coconut-studded plot for so few bungalows. Laid back and peaceful. Bungalows are a reasonable size and a/c rooms are good value.

A-B The Island, northern end, T077-424202. Huts on the beach with an attractive garden and run by foreigners. There's a pool and the bar is open after 2200.

B Beach Love, next to Impiana, T077-422531, beachlovesamui@hotmail.com. Modern building built on stilts so that all 4 rooms have sea views. The rear backs on to the road. Cool urban interiors with concrete screed flooring, pale blue colour scheme and sleek white sanitary ware. TV, a/c, fridge, bay window and balcony. Very chic.

B-C Chaweng Centre Hotel, 14/41 Chaweng Beach Rd, T077-413747, chaweng center@hotmail.com. Modern hotel in the village a short walk from the beach. The rooms overlooking the road are the cheapest and have been recently refurbished with mattresses on a raised platform, modern Japanese style. All rooms have a/c, TV, fridge and hot water.

B-C Samui Coral Resort, opposite the Green Mango, T077-231005, www.samui coralresort.com. 2 rows of 2 storey concrete buildings perpendicular to the beach. All have a/c, TV, fridge and low quality furniture.

There are also cheaper wooden fan bungalows, which are, surprisingly, closer to the beach. Swimming pool and restaurant. Unfortunately rude staff.

B-E Lucky Mother, northern end, T077-230 931. Friendly, clean, excellent food, some private bathrooms. Several different types of accommodation on offer.

C-E Somwang House, 159/6 Moo 2, T077-422269, somwanghouse_hotel@ hotmail.com. A good budget option. Wooden bungalows with a/c and hot shower – proximity to the beach bars may be too noisy for some. More expensive rooms are in a bright green building further back from the beach.

Chaweng to Lamai

L-A Coral Cove Chalet, T077-422260, www.coralcovechalet.com. Charming chalets on a hillside linked by decking walkways with steps down to small private beach which has little sand but some good snorkelling off-shore. It is a well run with a tropical ambience. There's a small pool. Reception staff could be friendlier.

Lamai

LL-B Spa Resort, T077-230855, www.spas amui.com. As far as holistic health resorts go, this is excellent: the services provided are good value, the staff welcoming and restaurant award winning. Run by an American and his Thai wife, it has a sauna, steam room and a small pool and offers daily yoga, t'ai chi and meditation. The cheaper bungalows with attached bathrooms are excellent value. The rocky, shallow beach here is busy with boats. There is a sister resort in Lamai valley with a free shuttle running between the 2. Book ahead. See also Therapies, page 636.

L-C Bill Resort, T077-424403, www.bill resort.com. A fabulously quirky and stylish retreat with excellent standards of service and accommodation on an attractive and fairly secluded beach. The resort, with its range of well spaced, elegantly designed and well-furnished rooms, climbs a hillside giving it a slightly magical village feel. Pool, jacuzzi, restaurant and travel services. Recommended.

AL-A Aloha, T077-424418, www.aloha samui.com. Well-designed a/c rooms in this relaxing resort. There is a good pool and the restaurant offers a range of great seafood. Tours can be booked here.

AL-C Long Island Resort,146/24 Moo 4, T077-418456. Under new management but still offers a variety of quality accommodation including cheaper rooms. All are charming and artistically decorated with bamboo furniture and balconies, but bungalows are dark and bathrooms are small. The most expensive bungalows have multiple windows and are on the beach with decking onto the sand.

AL-C Sand Sea Resort & Spa, northern e nd of Lamai beach, T077-424026, www.samuisandsea.com. A mixture of concrete and wooden bungalows. All have tiled bathrooms and are mosquito proof. The gardens are nice and there are good views of the sea. It has a restaurant and 20-m swimming pool. During the low season room rates are cut by up to a third.

A-E Sea Breeze, 124/3 Moo 3, T077-960 601. One of the oldest places on the island offering basic fan rooms and comfortable a/c bungalows with hot water. The restaurant serves Thai and Western food at reasonable prices and the staff are friendly.

C-D Lamai Coconut Resort, 124/4 Moo 3, T077-232169. With 33 immaculate bungalows close to the beach, this resort has some of Lamai's best-value rooms. With shiny wooden floors, linen, fridges, elegant furniture and large windows, the bungalows feel rather luxurious despite the modest fan room rate. Recommended.

C-D Suan Thale, T077-424230. A/c and fan rooms in bungalow 'blocks' on a large plot. The rooms are reasonable with a bit more character than most.

C-E Lamai Resort, next to **Sandsea Resort**, T077-424124, lamairesort@hotmail.com. Simple, spacious log-style cabins with

balcony affording a slither of a sea view and concrete a/c bungalows on the beach with TV and fridge.

C-F Amadeus Bungalows, 129 Moo 3 Maret, T077-424568. Run by a sweet old Thai family, there are a/c rooms available in a new building or cheap wooden huts on stilts up on the hill side, the sea can be seen from the balconies. The beach is a 5-min walk.

D-F Beer's House, 161/4 Moo 4, T077-231 088, www.beerhousebungalow.com. Small wooden bungalows, some are right on the beach, others are in a garden. The cheapest option have a shared bathroom. Good value.

E Coconut Beach Resort, 124/22 Moo 3, T077-424209. Clean, simple wooden bungalows hidden amongst coconut palms. Bathrooms have squat toilets. A new hotel is under construction at the rear of the resort, but this shouldn't change the laid back vibe.

E-F New Hut, next to **Beer's House**, T077-230437. Simple, but good quality, 'A' frame bamboo huts, slap bang on the beach, with mattress on the floor, mosquito net, fan and shared bathroom. There are also bungalows with bathroom inside available. Funky restaurant. Recommended.

South coast p622, map 618
Na Khai

L-B Samui Orchid Resort, 33/2 Moo 2, T077-424017, www.samuiorchid.com. Rooms are cheap looking with old carpets, old-fashioned accessories and clashing colours. Beds are small. The 2 pools and beach are decent but the on-site zoo with tigers and birds is a sorry sight. Sealion training is available, T077-418 987, www.sealionsearch-rescue.com.

Laem Set

LL Kamalaya, 102/9 Moo 3, Laem Set Rd, T077-429800, www.kamalaya.com. This 'wellness sanctuary and holistic spa' is the latest, distinctly upmarket place to cater for Samui's spiritual tourists. Oriental and Western healing practices influence treat-ments. The excellent hillside spa is centred around a monk's cave and commands spectacular views. A range of exceptionally stylish rooms are available overlooking the small sandy bay. The service is unbeatable and both restaurant and poolside shalas offer detox specialities as well as indulgent delights at reasonable prices. Non-residents are welcomed. Recommended.

LL-A Centara Villas Samui (formerly Central Samui Village), opposite the butterfly garden (see page 623), T077-424 020, www.centarahotelsresorts.com. An unfortunate addition to this once-peaceful beach. The emphasis is on 'rustic' living, with 100 villas, set rather too close together in a tropical garden. 3 pools, spa, bikes for hire and beachside sports on offer. Well equipped.

LL-C Laem Set Inn, 110 Moo 2, Hua Thanon, T077-424393, www.laemset.com. Formerly an exclusive, secluded resort in an attractive compound, many of the 50 rooms are now shabby and overpriced. Several private a/c suites with small pools attached and views of the private beach. A number of the buildings are reconstructed traditional wooden Samui houses but much of the decoration is deeply eccentric with a homestay feel. There is a restaurant (0600-2200), pool, children's playground and spa (1000-1900). The room rate includes use of mountain bikes, kayaks, pedal boats, masks and snorkels. Suitable for families with a day nursery, babysitting and playground. They hold cookery courses.

Thong Krut

C-E Thong Krut Bungalow, 30/5 Moo 5, T077-334052, tktour@thaimail.com. Close to the road but quiet, friendly and unspoilt. Fan rooms are scruffy and stuffy with 2 beds. The beach in front of these huts needs a good tidy. A/c rooms are a better option. Also runs **TK Tour** – snorkelling, kayaking and fishing trips.

E-F Emerald Cove, 62 Moo 4 Taling Ngam, Phanga Beach, T077-334100. Although isolated and poorly signposted, this attractive spot on the southwest corner of the island is worth seeking out. 10 en suite bungalows, with the more expensive rooms featuring a

rock-lined bathroom, TV, fridge, kitchen sink and oddly dated decor. Recommended.

Koh Tan and Koh Matsum

You cannot stay on Koh Matsum. Charter a boat for ฿400.

D-E Coral Beach Bungalow, Koh Tan, T077-274100. Several attractive well-spaced wooden bungalows on a secluded beach varying in quality with some more substantial brick huts. There is an pretty garden and a restaurant serving Thai and Western dishes.

West coast *p623, map p618*

AL-A Lipa Lodge, T077-423028, lipalodge@hotmail.com. These attractive white, thatched bungalows with modern fittings are scattered around a lawn on a gorgeous beach. The restaurant (0800-2200) serves international cuisine.

AL-B Lipa Lovely Resort, (formerly Big John Resort & Seafood) 912 Moo 2, Lipanoi, T077-415537, www.bigjohnsamui.com. Around 30 bungalows spread across 2 adjacent resorts, the garden rooms are a little over-priced and cramped. Most bungalows have a TV, DVD player, kitchen sink and fridge. They are set around a pool. The beach is not as attractive as that at **Lipa Lodge** up the coast. Part of this set up is **Big John Seafood**, near the old car ferry, see Eating, below.

AL-B Wiesenthal Resort, 227 Moo 3 Taling Ngam, T077-235165, www.sawadee.com/ hotel/samui/wiesenthal/. Standing out among its competitors on the west of the island, this German-owned business is clean, excellent value and sits directly on an attractive beach with great views out to sea. The spotless octagonal a/c rooms have TVs and fridges. Recommended.

C-D Simple Life Bungalow, Tong Ta Node Beach, T077-334191. Offers 10 basic bungalows packed together but commanding a view of the small sweeping beach and Koh Matsum and Koh Tan can be seen from the shore. Rustic beach restaurant with bamboo furniture and simple fare. A one-day snorkel-ling and fishing trip to Koh Tan is ฿850.

🍴 Eating

Nathon *p620, map p618*
There are plenty of places to eat here, particularly good are the 'coffee shop' patisseries – there are a couple off the main road and some on the seafront. Seafood restaurants are also found on the seafront.

🍴 Mai-Tai, 259/8 Moo 3, T077-236488. Open 0900-2100. German restaurant serving fantastic meats, sausages and cheeses, can also be bought by weight. The Hungarian goulash is admired by locals.

🍴 Sunset, 175/3 Moo 3, T077-421244. Open 1000-2200. South end of town overlooking the sea. Great Thai food, especially the fish dishes.

🍴-🍴 Coffee Island, opposite the pier, T077-423153. Open 0600-2400. Open-fronted café with good Colombian, Brazilian and Ethiopian coffee and a full range of cakes as well as steaks, shakes, curry and seafood.

🍴 About Art and Craft, 90/3 Moo 3, T08-1499 9354 (mob). Mon-Sat 0900-1700. Lovely veggie dishes, sandwiches, breakfasts, fresh juices and shakes plus great hot muffins and sauce. Sit amid the pottery and artwork created by the owners. The Thai salad with glass noodles makes a great lunch.

🍴 RT Bakery. Wide range of international dishes. Excellent breakfasts, rolls and croissants.

🍴 Tang, near the market at the south end of main road. Serves up pizza, pasta, sandwiches and pastries.

North coast *p620, map p618*
Mae Nam
Angela's Bakery, 64/29 Moo 1, opposite the police station on the main road, T077-427396. Open 0800-1800. Sells sandwiches, bagels, cakes and pretzels, and also has a deli offering cheeses and cold meat. Popular with foreigners.

Bophut
There are a number of restaurants that set up elaborate displays of local seafood. Naturally, the choice on offer varies from day to day.

The choice has expanded astronomically over recent years, with a string of new eateries popping up, so below is just a selection.

🍴🍴-🍴🍴 Happy Elephant, 79/1 Moo 1, on the beachfront, T077-245347. Open 1230-2200. A popular stop with travellers serving good seafood. The fish with ginger and mushroom sauce are delicious. Shark steaks and fondues also available. Staff cook on the street. Its speciality is hot stone steaks. There's a decent wine cellar.

🍴🍴-🍴🍴 La Sirene, 65/1 Moo 1, T077-425 301. Open 1000-2300. A delightful little restaurant run by a friendly Frenchman. The seafood is fresh and locally caught and displayed outside the restaurant, the coffee is excellent too. French and Thai food offered. Recommended.

🍴🍴🍴-🍴🍴 Villa Bianca, 79/3 Moo 1, T077-245 041. Open 1200-1500, 1800-2400. A good Italian-run restaurant in a romantic Bophut setting. Everything, even the ice cream, is made on the premises.

🍴🍴🍴-🍴🍴 Zazen Restaurant, Zazen Resort, T077-425085. A gourmet hot spot in Bophut with a Belgian chef serving up his signature 'organic and orgasmic' fusion cuisine. Candle-lit beachfront dining, excellent wine cellar.

🍴🍴 Alla Baia, 49/1 Moo 1, T077-245566. Open 1100-2300. Right on the seafront, this affordable Italian boasts impressive views of Koh Phangan in a delightful Mediterranean-style setting. Veteran chef Mario prepares his pasta and pizzas, and pulls in a good proportion of Bophut's hungry population.

🍴🍴 Starfish & Coffee, 51/7 Moo 1, T077-427201. Open 1100-0100. Another lovely setting for a meal or a quick drink on the outside terrace in this big airy building. Plenty of seafood and international cuisine in the maroon-themed restaurant with wrought-iron and leopard-print decor.

🍴🍴-🍴 Chandra, east of the pier. A tiny tea-shop overlooking the sea along with a shop selling clothes, jewellery and little decorated paperweights.

🍴🍴-🍴 The Love Kitchen, T077-430290, www.absoluteyogasamui.com. The latest addition to the healthy food scene. Delicious organic café, excellent juice bar, bakery and lounge.

¥¥-¥ Yoga Café, to the right of the pier, T077-245046, www.healthyandfun.net. Wholefood café with movie screenings, naturopathy, astrology, reiki, palmistry, tarot, numerology consultations, dance classes and a kids' zone.

¥ Coffee Junction, 37 Moo 1, T08-9866 1085 (mob). Open 0800-2200. A good spot to watch the comings and goings from the pier or to wait for your boat. Good coffee but tasteless brownies.

Big Buddha (Bang Ruk)
¥¥¥-¥¥ Oceans 11, Bang Rak, next to Shambala, T077-245134. International, Thai and seafood. Great views of the sea and nearby islands from the balcony bar. Lunch, dinner and cocktails.

¥¥¥-¥ BBC (Big Buddha Café), 202 Moo 5, right next to the wat, T08-1788 9051 (mob). Open 0900-2300. High-quality Thai and international food, reasonably priced in this island-style open-plan layout; an enjoyable place to sit and watch the sunset. BBC offers all-you-can eat BBQs, a full English Sun lunch, lobster thermidor as a special and live. There's an ATM.

¥¥ Antica Locanda, opposite Shambala. Italian and Thai owners. Good-quality Italian food, including delicious pasta dishes. Popular with the local expat community.

¥ Elephant & Castle. Open 0900-0200. Upholds the English tradition. Excellent choice of food.

Samrong Bay
¥¥¥ Dining on the Rocks, Sila Evason Hideaway. Eating here on a large wood platform is a fine dining experience with some of the most tantalizingly meals on the island. The 'Experiences' menu offers reduction of coconut and truffle with rosemary-roasted chicken. From the à la carte menu start with oysters in gazpacho followed by roasted duck with citrus and

lavender and finish with jasmine tea chocolate pots. This is a wonderful gourmet experience with great wines on offer.

Choeng Mon
Choeng Mon is blessed with a number of excellent eateries. This is a selection of the best.

¥¥¥ Royal Siam Restaurant, Samui Peninsula Spa & Resort, T077-428100. Open 1100-2300. Dine in style at this superb location overlooking the infinity pool and the sea. The *gaeng poo*, blue crab curry with vermicelli, is absolutely delicious. Service is attentive but not intrusive.

¥¥¥ Tongsai Bay, see Sleeping, above. This luxury hotel offers 3 restaurants, all of which are top notch. The decking – or 'Plaza' as they call it – of Chef Chom's restaurant has a marvellous view of the bay with space for 130 guests. There's a wide range of Thai dishes, all of which are outstanding. It's less expensive than it has been, but it's still top end.

¥¥ Honey Seafood Restaurant and Bar, at the most easterly tip of the beach. Great seafood. Recommended.

¥¥-¥ Otto's Pub and Restaurant, centre of the beach. Thai food and a Thai interpretation of pizza and pasta dishes.

¥ O Soleil, towards the western end. Best value for local specialities.

East coast *p621, map p618*
Chaweng
Chaweng offers a range of international restaurants as well as plenty of seafood. It also features many international food chains.

¥¥¥ Betelnut Restaurant, 43/04 Moo 3, just over the road from Central Samui Beach Resort, T077-413370. Open 1800-2300. This small, exclusive restaurant serves fashionable Californian/Thai fusion cuisine that has locals and guests returning. Excellent food and service. Booking recommended.

¥¥¥ Chez Andy, 164/2 Chaweng Beach Rd, T077-422593. Open 1600-2300. A popular Swiss grill house with roof-garden dining.

It also provides Thai food and the garden serves beer from a microbrewery and BBQ meals.

¶¶¶ Hagi, Central Samui Beach Resort. Open 1800-2230. Japanese restaurant in sophisticated surroundings.

¶¶¶ La Brasserie, Beachcomber Hotel, 3/5 Moo 2, T077-422041. Open 0700-2230. Italian and Thai food. A pleasant beachfront experience, white-clothed tables are softened by night lanterns. The Sat night European set menu at ฿495 is a giveaway with 3 courses and a glass of red wine.

¶¶¶ Poppies, see Sleeping, above. An excellent Thai and international restaurant, one of the best on the beach. Live classical guitar accompaniment on Tue, Thu and Fri and a Thai night on Sat. Booking recommended.

¶¶¶ Spice Island, part of the Central Samui Beach Resort. 1800-2230. Sit either in the a/c or the relaxing beachside part of the restaurant and try a wide range of excellent, sophisticated Thai dishes.

¶¶¶ Vecchia Napoli, on the *soi* behind Starbucks, T077-231229. Beautifully decorated with a few tables spilling out from the airy inside onto the street. Friendly Italian owner who ensures his guests are happy. Always buzzing with Italians.

¶¶¶ Zico's, 38/2 Moo 3, opposite Central Samui Beach Resort, T077-231560. Open 1800-2230. This 150-seater, predominantly BBQ, Brazilian restaurant is one of a wave of upmarket eateries. Contemporary Brazilian decor, roving musicians and waiters bring the action to the tables. Recommended but be prepared to spend.

¶¶¶-¶¶ Sandies, Silver Sand Resort, T077-422777. Open 0630-2400. Dine at candlelit tables on the beach accompanied by live music at this lovely spot. The shark steak in garlic butter is particularly recommended. The service is excellent but check your bill.

¶¶¶-¶¶ The Three Monkeys, 13/11 Moo 2, Chaweng Beach Rd. 1030-0200. Great grub including chicken, salmon and beef dishes. The 'mango monkey' – marinated king prawns with a mango sauce – is filling and delicious. Canned Guinness, TV and a pool table available. Happy hour is 1430-1630 and there's free internet access.

¶¶ Caffé e Cucina, North Chaweng, T08-1894 2576 (mob). A pizzeria run by Angelo from Rome. Good Italian food, friendly and excellent value. Recommended.

¶¶ The Deck, Beach Rd. 0800-0200. Great location in the centre of the action and noise. Enjoy or tolerate the Fri night Elvis impersonator strutting his stuff in the **Quarterdeck** pub, opposite. Upstairs there's a great chilled-out drinking deck overlooking the main road with floor cushions to relax on. It serves Thai, Western and fusion dishes. Avoid the Thai fishcake starter.

¶¶ Gringos Cantina, behind The Islander Restaurant, T077-413267. Authentic Tex Mex.

¶¶ The Islander, near SoiGreen Mango, T077-230836. For anyone missing English dishes, this place provides 'full-monty' breakfasts, Sun roast with all the trimmings as well as pizzas, curry and lasagne.

¶¶ Mamma Roma, 155/30 Moo 2, T077-230649. Open 1100-2300. Notable for its signature pizza of tomato, cheese, ham, salami, olives and capers, which is tasty. There's also home-made pasta here and seafood dishes, but these are expensive.

¶¶ Osteria, along from the Chaweng Resort, T077-422530. Open 0900-0100. Good pizza and pasta.

¶¶ Will Wait Bakery, T077-230093. Open 0700-0100. For excellent pastries and breakfast or late night snacks.

¶ Sojeng Kitchen, 155/9 Chaweng Beach, T08-1892 2841 (mob). Open 1000-2200. Opposite My Friend Travel Agency, offers tasty food at excellent prices.

Lamai

There are several seafood restaurants along the Lamai beach road offering a wide choice, although nowhere is particularly good and cheap. International cuisine is widely available along the road parallel to the beach in restaurants such as Il Tempio.

ŤŤŤ Sala Thai, T077-233180. Serves good Thai food, seafood, steaks and Italian. It is, however, overpriced.

ŤŤ Will Wait Bakery, T077-0424263. Delicious pastries, croissants and pizzas. A popular breakfast joint.

ŤŤ-Ť The Spa, Spa Resort. An award-winning restaurant that serves a range of attractively presented vegetarian and Thai food, as well as detoxing/healthy specialities and great seafood. Well-priced menu, friendly service and a relaxed ambience. Recommended.

West coast *p622, map p618*
There are 2 restaurants in Ban Hua Thanon. Try **Hua Thanan** for seafood or **Aow Thai**, T077-418348, for northeastern Thai food.

Ť Big John Seafood Restaurant, Lipa Lovely Resort, near the old car ferry, see Sleeping, above. Away from the frenetic buzzing of Chaweng and Lamai, this is a great place for food and ambience. The sunsets are arguably the best on the island and you can dine inside listening to live music and the lobsters are enormous. There's a free pick-up service to and from your hotel within a 10-km range.

❶ Bars and clubs

North coast *p620, map p618*
Bophut

Billabong Surf Club, 79/2 Moo 1, T077-430 144. A full-on sports bar with TVs and sports pictures plastering the wall and a small balcony for drinking.

Frog and Gecko, 91/2 Moo 1, T077-425248. Open 1200-0200. The first of several English pubs/sports bars on the beachfront run by Graham and Raphaela. The music and Thai food is good. They show all major sporting events on a big screen, as well as recent movies. The pool table is ฿20 a game. Pub quiz Wed nights at 2000. Popular.

The Tropicana, T077-425304. With large fish tanks built into the walls, The Tropicanaca makes a refreshing change from the popular sports bars. It's run by friendly Paul and Lek.

East coast *p621, map p618*
Chaweng

Most of the bars are at the northern end of the strip, which is also home to a variety of go-go bars mixed in with the occasional European-style pubs. The girls who work at the bars outnumber patrons by about 4 to 1.

Dew Drop Huts. Tends to draw a young crowd and puts on beach parties during high season.

Green Mango, on the main road. A rather jaunty venue with Western DJs playing garage and house music. Also host to live Thai bands performing Western pop and rock.

The Reggae Pub, Chaweng lagoon, T077-422331. This huge bar, club and live music destination a little out of town is popular as a party destination, but pick your night as sometimes it's more techno than reggae.

Sound Pub, close to **Green Mango**. Classier than the rest of the bars on this street, which are mainly girly joints. There's a DJ and tables.

Tropical Murphys, 14/40 Chaweng Rd, T077-413614. Open 0900-0200. Opposite McDonald's in Central Chaweng. An Irish pub and the only place on the island serving draught Guinness and Kilkenny. Live music most nights and Tue night pub quizzes.

Lamai

Most are located down the *sois* which link the main road and the beach.

Bauhaus is a large, popular venue consisting of a pub, restaurant and discotheque. Shows mainstream Western movies during the day and early evening and hosts live bands.

❷ Entertainment

East coast *p621, map p618*
Chaweng

Cabaret Christy's. If you fancy sampling some of Thailand's drag cabaret acts then is the place to go. Performances start around 2300 and last about 1 hr.

Star Club, 200/11 Chaweng Rd, T077-414218. A rival to **Christy's**. Puts on a pretty hilarious

show with audience participation, a lot of feathers and make-up at 2230 nightly. Beers are ฿100. No admission charge, customers must buy drinks. Recommended.
Muay Thai (Thai boxing) Chaweng Stadium, T077-413504, free transfers. 8 fights from 2100.

Lamai
Buffalo fighting In the stadium at the north end (and several others around the island). Far tamer than it sounds, animals are rarely injured in the 'fights' and it's more a show of tradition than a fierce face-off. Ask at your hotel for date of the next event.
Muay Thai (Thai boxing) At Lamai's new stadium. Fights 2-3 times weekly during high season, ฿500.

O Shopping

Nathon *p620, map p618*
Nathon is a good centre for shopping on the island. It is worth a visit to browse through the stalls and take a walk down the main road, past the fresh market on the left and on down to the 'hardware' market on the right. The stalls provide the usual T-shirts, CDs/DVDs, watches and handicrafts. The inner road – Angthong Rd – is worth walking down too.

North coast *p620, map p618*
Bophut
There are a number of shops along the main road of Bophut. There is a good German, English and French bookshop, and shops selling art, gifts, clothes and produce from around Thailand, Laos and Cambodia.

East coast *p621, map p618*
Chaweng
The main shopping centre on the island, Chaweng caters for the visiting crowds, providing necessities in the supermarkets, pharmacies and opticians, along with plenty of tourist tat and upmarket designer clothes/swimwear stores. A plethora of tailors pepper

Chaweng, including **Armani International Suits**, **Joop!** and **Baron Fashion**.

There is a wide range of shops along the beach road, where most things can be bought. Many places remain open until late. There is the usual array of tourist shops selling beachwear, T-shirts, jewellery and handicrafts. A number of minimarts are scattered along the main road and the British-owned pharmacy chain, **Boots**. **Bookazine**, which sells newspapers, magazines and books, is next to Tropical Murphy's. For genuine branded surfwear, including Quiksilver and Roxy, try the shops next to McDonald's in the centre of town.

Lamai
Jewellery, beachwear and clothing boutiques are along the main road.

▲ Activities and tours

There are now numerous activities, including horse riding, elephant trekking, jungle canopy rides, training to be a sealion trainer, sail boat tours, snorkelling, kayaking, cooking classes, even football golf. See flyers, tour agents and adverts in the free visitors' guides.

The best time for **diving** is Apr and the best water is to be found around Koh Tao, Tan, Matsum and the Marine Park. Visibility is obviously variable, depending on the weather. Most of the schools dotted around the island organize all dive courses. PADI Open Water courses cost around ฿15,500. There is a hyperbaric chamber at Big Buddha.

Spas and **massage** places have mushroomed in the last few years. There are some gorgeous spas attached to hotels as well as day spas. Treatments vary in prices and scope. See under each area for details.

Nathon *p620, map p618*
Spas and therapies
Samui Dharma Healing Centre, 63 Moo Tee 1, Ao Santi Beach, near Nathon, T077-234170, www.dharmahealingintl.com. Alternative

health programmes to inspire and rejuvenate. 7- to 21-day fasting courses are directed according to Dharma Buddhist principles in alternative health: fasting, colonic irrigation, yoga, reflexology, iridology and many other therapies. Accommodation is available.

Tour operators
There are many travel agents cluttered along the seafront (particularly around the pier) and main roads, providing ticketing and tours.

Ang Thong Marine National Park
p620, map p618
Tour operators
National park tax (฿200) is included in all tour prices. Operators include **Big John**, T077-421 744; **Caveman**, T08-62822983, www.samui reef.com; and **Seatran**, T077-426000.

North coast *p620, map p618*
Cookery courses
Blue Banana, 2 Moo 4, Big Buddha Beach, T077-245080. Classes with 'Toy'.

Diving
Aquademia, Bophut, T077-427203, www.aquademiadive.com.
Bo Phut Diving School, next to Eden Bungalows, Bophut, T077-425496, www.bophut diving.com. Also offers snorkelling trips.
Captain Caveman, at the **Shambala Resort**, Big Buddha, and on Chaweng Beach Rd, T08-6282 2983 (mob), www.samuireef.com. Office hours 1000-2100, closed Sun am. A 5-star PADI dive centre. Prides itself on small classes. Snorkelling trips to Ang Thong Marine National Park, ฿3750, to Koh Tao and Nangyuan and Mango Bay, ฿2500.
Easy Divers, Big Buddha, T077-448129, www.easydivers-thailand.com.
Easy Divers, Bophut, T077-245026, www.easydivers-thailand.com.
Paradise Beach Resort, Mae Nam. One of many resorts offering diving.
Samui International Diving School, Big Buddha, 30/1 Moo 4, T08-9772 4002 (mob), www.dial-samui.com.

Fishing and watersports
Fishing and snorkelling are organized by most accommodation providers as well as individual tour operators scattered throughout the village of Bophut.
Pra-Yai Fishing and Tours, Big Buddha T077-427155. Open 0800-2200. Offering both day- and night-fishing tours, as well as private speed-boat chartering.

Golf
Minigolf International, Choeng Mon, T08-1787 9148 (mob), yogibearhaha@ hotmail.com. 0900-1830. 18 tracks near Choeng Mon.
Santiburi Golf, Mae Nam, T077-425031, www.santiburi.com. An 18-hole course that opened in 2003. Designed by Pirapon Namatra and Edward Thiele. Green fees, ฿3350. Hotel guests enjoy a 20% discount.

Spas and therapies
Thalasso Spa, Samui Peninsula Spa & Resort, T077-428100, www.samuipeninsula.com. Professional treatments in attractive rooms; mud treatments are the speciality.

Tour operators
One Hundred Degrees East, 23/2 Moo 4, Big Buddha, T08-6282 2983 (mob), www.100degreeseast.com. Charter trips run by Ivan Douglas who runs **Captain Caveman**. Private charters. A direct charter from Samui to Tao is ฿18,000.

East coast *p621, map p618*
Bowling
Living Bowl, 2nd floor, Living Square Shopping Centre, above McDonald's, Chaweng, T077-413258.

Bungee jumping
Sami Bungy Jump and Entertainment Complex, Reggae Pub Rd, Chaweng, T08-1891 3314 (mob). Daily from 1000. Offers hourly jumps (50 m), huge pool and sun lounge area.

Cookery courses
Samui Institute of Thai Culinary Arts, Chaweng, T077-413172, www.sitca.net. Thai cooking and fruit- and vegetable-carving courses. All equipment is provided, and you can keep the recipes. The lunchtime cooking class costs ฿1850 per person, the evening class ฿1850 per person. Carving courses (6 hrs of lessons over 3 days) are ฿4950 per person. To get there, get dropped off at (or walk to) the **Central Samui Beach Resort** on Chaweng Beach. Walk up the side street for about 150 m across from the **Central** with **Classic Gems** jewellery store at the corner. The Institute is on the right side.

Diving
Big Blue Diving, South Chaweng Beach Rd, Chaweng, T077-422617, www.bigbluediving samui.com. Popular Swedish dive centre.
Calypso Diving, southern end of Chaweng beach, T077-422437, www.calypso-diving.com.
Discovery Dive Centre, Amari Palm Reef Resort, T077-413196, www.discoverydivers.com.
The Dive Shop, central Chaweng Beach Rd, Chaweng, T077-230232, www.thediveshop.net.
Easy Divers, head office, Chaweng, T077-413373, www.easydivers-thailand.com.
Easy Divers, near **Lamai Resort** (north end of Lamai beach), T077-231990, www.easy divers-thailand.com. German, English and Swedish spoken.
Pro Divers, Lamai, T077-233399, www.prodivers.nu.
Samui International Diving School, Chaweng Beach Rd, Chaweng, T077-422386, www.planet-scuba.net.

Mountain biking
Red Bicycle, T077-232136, www.red bicycle.org. Hires bikes and offers guided trips.

Watersports
Masks and fins can be hired from most bungalows in Chaweng. For diving, see above.

Blue Stars Sea Kayaking, Chaweng Beach Rd, T077-413231, www.bluestars.info.
Samui Ocean Sports, on the beach at **Chaweng Regent Hotel**, Chaweng, T08-1940 1999 (mob), www.samui.sawadee.com/oceansports. Offers a wide range of activities and lessons: kayaking, snorkelling, windsurfing, catsailing and yachting.
Tan Speed Project, in front of Banana fan. Offer banana boats, ฿400 per person per 15 mins.
Treasure Island, behind the **Islander Restaurant**, Chaweng, T077-413267. Open 1100-2400. Kayaking.

Spas and therapies
It's boom time for any kind of healing centre and Chaweng has not missed a trick here. As well as several spas within hotels, there are some independent establishments in town.
Four Seasons Tropical Spa, next to the **Baan Samui Resort**, close to McDonald's, T077-414141, www.spafourseasons.com. A recommended relaxing experience.
Spa Resort, Lamai, T077-230855, www.spasamui.com, at the north end of the beach with a sister resort in the hills. See Sleeping, above. Offers 'exotic rejuvenation', anything from a herbal steam room to a 'liver flush fast' as well as yoga, t'ai chi and meditation. Day visitors are welcomed. A 3½-day fast costs ฿12,000.
Tamarind Springs, 205/7 Thong Takian, Lamai, T077-230571, www.tamarind retreat.com. 1000-2000. Just up the hill from Spa Samui is possibly the island's most relaxing and authentic spa in a spectacular natural setting. Treatment packages include body scrubs and a variety of massages, which include the divine combination of herbal spa and waterfall dip pool. It has a strong complementary health philosophy and makes much of its environmental consciousness. There is an excellent, peaceful restaurant but sadly the accommodation here has closed.

Tour operators

There are dozens along Chaweng Beach Rd. **My Friend Travel Agency**, 14/62-64 Mo 2, Chaweng Beach Rd, Chaweng, T077-413364. Open 1000-2300. Run by a friendly and helpful woman called Amporn who speaks English.
Travel Solutions, Chaweng, T077-230203, www.travelsoultions.co.th. Down the side of **The Pizza Company** opposite the **Baan Samui Resort**. Highly recommended, Western-Thai run business with over 13 years' of experience in the industry. Trustworthy information and travel advice/bookings.

South coast *p622, map 618*
Tour operators

GUP Travel, 109 Moo 2, Laem Set, T077-232021, www.guptravel.com. This is a particularly good company, whose English-, Swedish- and Thai-speaking staff offer a professional service.

Therapies

Kamalaya, 102/9 Moo 3, Laem Set Rd, Laem Set, T077-429800, www.kamalaya.com. The latest addition to Samui's sophisticated holistic spa scene, **Kamalaya** offers non-residents access to its healing events as well as yoga, t'ai chi, cleanses, massage and oriental and Western healing practices at its stunning hillside spa. See also Sleeping, page 630.

Watersports

Jetskis, windsurfing and snorkelling equipment is available for hire at the southern end of the beach.

● Transport

Koh Samui *p617, maps p618*
Air

Bangkok Airways is a private airline, which accounts for the inflated airport international departure tax (฿700 from Koh Samui, ฿300 for domestic departure tax, although this

should now be included in the ticket price). There are multiple daily connections with **Bangkok** and regular flights to **Phuket**, **U-Tapao** (Pattaya), **Krabi**, **Chiang Mai**, **Hong Kong** and **Singapore**. Berjaya Air, T077-414302, flies twice a week to **Kuala Lumpur**; Thai Airways fly to Bangkok.

   Airline offices Bangkok Airways, at southern end of Chaweng, T077-422513.

Boat

There are numerous daily boat options. Schedules, journey times and prices change according to the season. Tickets from travel agents will cost more but include scheduling advice and transfers. See transport sections for **Surat Thani**, **Koh Phangan** and **Koh Tao** for boat services to Samui. See also Bophut and Big Buddha, below, for services from the north coast to Koh Phangan and Koh Tao.

   Songserm Travel, seafront road, Nathon, T077-420157, office hours 0800-1800, runs express passenger boats daily. These boats leave from the southern pier in Nathon. To **Surat Thani**, 1330, 2½ hrs, ฿180; to **Koh Phangan** and on to **Koh Tao**, 1100, 40 mins and 2½ hrs, ฿200 and 350 respectively.

   Seatran, office on pier, daily 0500-1700, T077-4260012, operates boats to **Surat Thani** from the main northerly pier in Nathon hourly from 0500-1800 with the bus arriving in Surat Thani 2½ hrs later, ฿180, including bus. Also has 2 daily departures, 0800 and 1330 to **Koh Phangan** (฿250), **Koh Tao** (฿550), **Chumphon** (฿900), **Hua Hin** (฿900) and **Bangkok** (฿1000). Price includes transfer from hotel to Bang Ruk pier.

   Boats leave Nathon at 2100, arriving in **Don Sak** at around 0300/0400, ฿250.

   The **Raja** ferry leaves from the Tong Yang pier, south of Nathon, to **Don Sak**. To get to Tong Yang, take a *songthaew* from Nathon or the beaches.

   Cattcorp, from Coral Grand Pier to **Koh Phangan**, 0750, 30 mins, ฿250; to **Koh Tao**, 0750, 1½ hrs, ฿550.

Road madness on Samui, Phagnan and Tao

By some measures, Thailand has the world's highest death rate on the roads. Koh Samui has the highest rate in Thailand and accidents, fatal and otherwise, are certainly horrifyingly common. (The islands are full of walking wounded wearing bandages on their arms legs and faces). There are several reasons for this state of affairs:

→ narrow and impossibly steep roads
→ poorly maintained vehicles/machines
→ visitors unused to driving on the left
→ visitors unused to driving in Thailand.

First-time riders can be absolutely fine when bowling along most of the time, however, should something happen ahead that makes an emergency stop necessary, they simply don't have the natural reflexes to handle their bikes appropriately

→ locals driving without lights
→ visitors drink-driving or on drugs

This means that visitors should be careful when driving on the islands and make sure that they test their motorbike or car before completing a rental agreement. It is also advised that people do not leave their passports as collateral. Should there be an accident, it leaves the renter of the vehicle at the mercy of its owner.

For more details on driving in Thailand see Essentials, page 40.

Haad Rin Queen, T077-375113, from Big Buddha Pier to Hat Rin on **Koh Phangan**, 1030, 1300, 1600, 1830, 50 mins, ฿150.

Speed Boat Line from Bophut to Thong Sala on **Koh Phangan**, 0430, 0900, 1200, 1430, 20 mins, ฿400.

Bus

There are several buses that leave Surat Thani for the overnight trip to **Bangkok**. Ask the tour operators or an agency on the island.

Car and motorbike hire

This is cheaper from the town of Nathon than on the beaches. Motorbikes cost ฿150-200 per day, and around ฿250 for an automatic, not including insurance although the price is negotiable if you rent for several days. Helmets must be provided. The fine for not wearing one is ฿200-500.

Jeep/car hire is ฿800-1000 per day, including insurance or ฿1000-1800 if you hire from an international company such as **Budget** (see box, above, for cautions about driving).

Motorbike taxi

Available all over the island. They wait in clusters wearing coloured cloth jackets. **Nathon–Chaweng**, ฿150-180. **Bophut–Chaweng**, ฿100. **Nathon–Maenam**, ฿100.

Taxi

Expensive yellow meter taxis cruise the island all day. They are scarce after 0100 but any bar or hotel owner will know one. The taxis do not use their meters and even if requested they may be fixed. The minimum fare is ฿50. Fares do vary according to the time of day. On average a fare from **Nathon–Chaweng** and from **Bophut–Chaweng** is ฿500. The majority of taxis are to be found in Chaweng. A taxi can be chartered for ฿400 per hr.

Train

Travel agencies in town can provide details and tickets that combine the boat from Samui, bus from Don Sak to the railway station and then the train ticket, or some of these combinations.

Footprint Mini Atlas
Thailand

VIETNAM

LAOS

❶

Pai
Chiang Rai
Mae Hong Son
Chiang Mai
Nan
Lampang
Phrae

❷

BURMA (MYANMAR)

Uttaradit
Sukhothai
Phitsanulok

Nong Khai
Udon Thani
That Phanom

Tak
Mae Sot

Khon Kaen

Nakhon Sawan

Nakhon Ratchasima (Korat)

Ubon Ratchathani

Ayutthaya
Kanchanaburi
Nonthaburi
BANGKOK
Ratchaburi
Chonburi
Phetburi
Pattaya
Hua Hin
Chantaburi

Andaman Sea

CAMBODIA

Gulf of Thailand

❸

Chumphon

Koh Samui
Surat Thani
Nakhon Si Thammarat

Krabi
Phuket
Phuket City
Koh Lanta
Trang

South China Sea

❹

Hat Yai
Songkhla

❺

MALAYSIA

Altitude in metres
3000
1000
200
100
0
Neighbouring country
Expressway
Main road (National highway)
Other road
Railway

N

100 km
100 miles

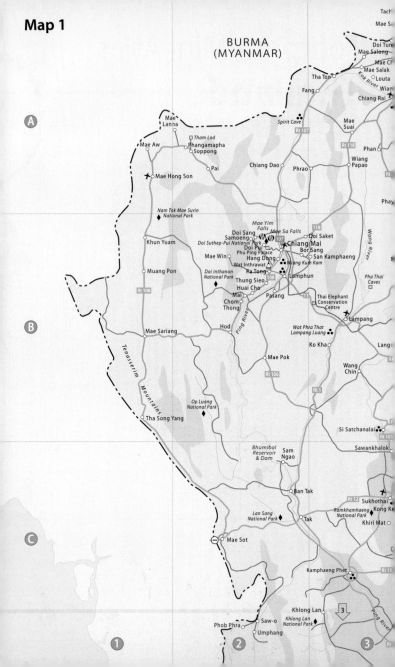

Map 1

BURMA (MYANMAR)

Tach
Mae S

Doi Tun
Mae Salong
Mae Ci
Mae Salak
Louta
Wian
Tha Ton
Fang
Chiang Rai

Mae Lanna
Tham Lod
Phangamapha
Soppong
Pai
Chiang Dao
Phrao
Spirit Cave
Rt 107
Mae Suai
Rt 118
Phan
Wiang Papao

Mae Aw
Mae Hong Son
Rt

Nam Tok Mae Surin
National Park

Mae Yim Falls
Mae Sa Falls
Doi Saket
Doi Sang
Samoeng
Doi Suthep-Pui National Park
Doi Pui
Phu Ping Palace
Hang Dong
Wat Inthrawat
Pa Tong
Rt 107
118
Chiang Mai
Bor Sang
San Kamphaeng
Wiang Kum Kam
Pha Thai Caves
Phay

Khun Yuam
Mae Win
Doi Inthanon National Park
Thung Sieo
Huai Cho
Mai
Chom Thong
Pasang
Lamphun
Rt 108
Rt 108
Rt 11
Thai Elephant Conservation Centre
Lampang
Wang River
Muang Pon

Mae Sariang
Hod
Ping River
Wat Phra That Lampang Luang
Ko Kha
Lang

Mae Pok
Wang Chin
Rt 106

Tenasserim Mountains
Op Luang National Park
Si Satchanalai
Rt 101

Tha Song Yang
Sawankhalok

Bhumibol Reservoir & Dam
Sam Ngao

Ban Tak
Rt 12
Sukhothai
Ramkhamhaeng National Park
Kong K
Khiri Mat

Lan Sang National Park
Tak

Mae Sot
Kamphaeng Phet
Rt 11

Phob Phra
Saw-o
Umphang
Khlong Lan
Khlong Lan National Park
3
Ping River
Rt

A
B
C
1
2
3

Map 2

LAOS

Mekong River

Amphoe Na Noi

Sao Din

Rt 101

Phrae

Sung Men

Den Chai

Sirikit
Reservoir

Uttaradit

Sangkhom

VIENTIANE
Friendship
Bridge

Pak
Chom

Si Chiangmai

Tha Bo

Non Kha

Chiang Khan

Ban Paak
Huay

Tha Li

Phu Phra Bat
Historical Park

Ban Bang
Phuan

Phu Phra Bat

Ban Phu

Rt 211

Rt 2

Ngoi

Phu Rua
National Park

Loei

Udon Thani

Phu Luang

Rt 2020

Rt 210

Nong Bua Lamphu

Erawan Cave

Non Cham

Kong
Krailat

Rt 11

Phitsanulok

Yaeng

Phu Hin
Rongkla
National Park

Thung Salaeng
National Park

Rt 203

Rt 12

Lom Sak

Phu Kradung
National Park

Rt 201

Phu Phan Kham
National Park

Phu Wiang
National Park

Ubon Rat
Reservoir

Phu Wiang

Phu Kradung
(1571m)

Phetchabun Hills

Phra Cave

Rt 115

Phichit

Taphan
Hin

Bang Mun Nak

Rt 113

Phetchabun

Chumphae

Khon Kaen

Rt 2057

Mancha Kiri

Rt 201

Pa Sak River

Yom River

Ping River

Rt 21

Chumsaeng

Nong Bua

Nakhon
Sawan

Rt 11

Phaisali

Ban Nok
Charoen

Si Thep

Chaiyaphum

Samran

Chonnabot
Ban Phai

Phon

Rt 202

Bua Yai

Rt 2

Pratha

Prase
Puayr

Ban Prasat

Phimai

Prasat Phranomwan

Uthai Thani

Chai Nat

Don Chedi

Suphanburi

hong

Chao Phraya River

Khok Samrong

Rt 205

Chai Badan

Rt 201

Rt 205

Nakhon
Ratchasima
(Korat)

Singburi

Rt 32

Lopburi

Wat Phra
Buddhabat

Ang Thong

Tha Rua

Pa Mok

Rt 21

Pak Chong

Rt 2

Kaeng Khoi

Saraburi

Khao Yai
National Park

Ban Dan Kwian

Pak Thong Chai

Chokchai

Nong Ki

Nang Rong

Ba
Tak

Phnom Rung

Muang

Rt 304

ong Phi Nong

Don Tum

Pathum
Thani

Sam Khok

Bang Sai

Ayutthaya

Bang Pain

Nong Khae

Nakhon
Nayok

Thanya Buri

Rt 305

Prachin Buri

Kok Ph

To Phaya

1

2

3

Map 3

Khlong Lan
Saw-o
Phob Phra   Umphang
Khlong Lan
National Park

Pling River

Rt 1

Nakhon Saw

A

Khao Yai
(1554m)

Uthai Thani

Chai

Thung Yai
Wildlife Sanctuary

Saam Ong
(Three Pagodas Pass)
Huai Kha Khaeng
Wildlife Sanctuary

Sangkhlaburi   Khao Laem
National Park

Khao Laem
Reservoir

Srinakharin
Reservoir

Dan Chang

Don Che

Khao Daen
(1249m)   Thong Pha Phum

Si Sawat   Nong Pru

Rt 323

Tham Than Lot
National Park

Nong
Pradu   Suphant

Erawan
National Park

Ban Sai Yok
Sai Yok
National Park
Sai Yok Noi
Lawa
Caves

Park Entrance

Bo Phloi
(Gem Mines)

Kwai Yai River

Uthong

Tha Kham   Song Phi No

Rt 32

Nam
Tok

Sai Tok

Nong Pradok
Railway Station

Kanchanaburi

Don Tun

B

BURMA
(MYANMAR)

▲ (1558m)

Muang Singh
Historical Park

Kwai Noi River

Tha Muang   Rt 323

Nakhon Pathom

Ban Pong   Rose Gar

▲ (1565m)

Thung Ri

Clom Bung

Tenasserim
Mountains

Photharam

Ratchaburi   Rt 325

Damnoen Saduak

Myinmoletkat
Taung
(2072m)

Tha Yung   Pak Tho

Samu
Songkhr

Phetburi   Hat Chao Sumran
Tha Yang

Phet Buri
Reservoir

Kaeng Krachan
National Park

Nong Pradu

Cha-am

Thongkhlua
Pak Ngam

Hua Hin

C

Pran Buri
Reservoir

Pranburi

Phu N
Bang

Andaman Sea

Rai Mai
Sam Roi Yod
Khao Sam Roi Yod NP

Samrong

Khu
Tan

Don Yai

Rt 4

Prachuap
Khiri Khan

N

20 km
20 miles

↑ 1   ↓ 4

1   **2**   **3**

Map 4

BURMA (MYANMAR)

Prachuap Khiri Khan
Thap Sakae
Ban Krut
Bang Saphan
Koh Talu
Mai Sombun
Ao Bang Saphan
Chumphon
Pak Nam Chumphon
Kra Buri
Ao Sawi
Khao Thaiu
Ao Sawi
Rt 4

Gulf of Thailand

Koh Tao
Ban Mae Hat

Similan Islands

Koh Bon
Koh Ba Ngu (9)
Koh Similan (8)
Hin Luk Chang (7)
Koh Pa Yu (7)
Koh Miang (4)
Koh Pa Yan (3)
Koh Pa Yang (2)
Koh Hu Yong (1)

To Phuket (5hrs) ▼ *To Takua Pa (3hrs)*

Similan Islands
Boat to Koh Similan, 110km from Patong, Koh Phuket

Phuket

Kawthoung
Ranong
Lang Suan
Phato
Khuan
Nam Sai
Isthmus of Kra
Koh Chang
Koh Phayam
Hat Bang Baen

Ang Thong Marine National Park
Koh Ang Tong
Kah Ang Tong
Koh Phaluai
Koh Nok
Ta Phao
Thong Sala
Nathon
Bophut
Tong Yang
Koh Phangan
Koh Samui
Chong Samui

Tha Chana
Wat Suan Mok
Chaiya
Ao Ban Don
Tha Thong
Don Sak
Kanchanadit
Khanom

Andaman Sea

Koh Surin Nua
Koh Surin Tai
Koh Ra
Koh Prathong
Laem Son National Park
Koh Kam Yai
Koh Kam Noi

Kuraburi
Chieo Lan Reservoir

Tha Chang
Phun Phin
Surat Thani
Krut
Khao Nan National Park
Sichon
Tha Mak

Takua Pa
Laem Pakarang
Bang Sak
Khao Lak
Khao Sok National Park
Kwang
Khao Wong
Khao Luang National Park
Rt 401

To Koh Similan
Khao Lak
Lam Ru National Park
Thap Lamu
Thai Muang National Park
Phangnga
Thai Muang
Kapong
Khao To
Than Phut
Phraegaeng
Chawang
Khiriwong
Lan Saka
Nakhon Si Thammarat
Ron Phibun
Laem Talumphet
Ao Nakhon
Rt 403

Wat Suwan Kuha
Thai Muang
Khok Kloi
Sarasin Bridge
Khao Lampee-Had Thai Muang National Park
Rt 4152
Ao Luk Nua
Ao Luk
Dong Tau
Chong Lom
Chai Mai
Bo Lo
Rt 408

Nai Yang National Park
Thalang
Phuket
Cherng Talay
Kamala
Patong Beach
Karon Beach
Kata Beach
Nai Harn
Promthep Cape

Khao Phrao Thaeo Wildlife Park
Ko Wa Yai
Koh Yao Noi
Koh Yao Yai
Wat Tham Sua
Wat Tham Khao Thao
Chong Phli
Ao Nang
Krabi
Talat Kao
Hua Sai

Phuket City
Koh Siray
Makham Bay National Park
Koh Maiton
Koh Hii (Coral Island)
Koh Naka Yai
Tha Rua
Koh Boda
Koh Siboya
Laem Kruat
Tha Pradu
Huai Yot
Chai Khlong
Rt 404
Phattalung
Ranat
Di Luang

Phi Phi
Koh Phi Phi Le
Koh Jum
Koh Klang
Khlong Phon
Hat Nopparat Thara
Bo Muang
Na Wong
Thale Noi Bird Sanctuary
Thale Noi
Thale Luang

Koh Lanta Noi
Ban Sala Dan
Koh Lanta Yai
Ban Koh Lanta Yai
Ko Po
Ton Chot
Pakmeng
Trang
Kantang
Rt 403
Sating Phra

Koh Ngai (Hai)
Koh Meng
Koh Ma
Koh Chuak
Koh Muk
Koh Kradan
Hat Chao Mai National Park
Bo Pradu

N

20 km
20 miles

Map 5

Boat to Chumphon,
85km from Ban
Mae Hat, Koh Tao

Ban Mae
Hat
Koh Tao

Ang Thong
Marine
National Park
Koh Ang Tong
Koh Phaluai
Koh Nok
~Ta Phao
Don Sak
Kanchanadit
Krut

Thong
Sala
Koh Phangan
Nathon
Bophut
Koh Samui
Tong Yang
Chong Samui

Khanom

Sichon
Tha Mak

Gulf of Thailand

N

20 km
20 miles

A

Khao Luang
National Park

Nakhon Si
Thammarat
Chawang
Lan Saka

Laem
Talumphet
Ao
Nakhon

Rt 41
Chong
Lom
Chai Mai

Ron
Phibun
Rt 403
Rt 408
Bo Lo

Hua Sai

B

Tha Pradu
Huai Yot
Chai Khlong
Rt 41
Rt 4
Thale Noi Bird
Sanctuary
Thale
Noi
Ranot
Rt 408

Ton Chot
Trang
Na Wong
Phattalung
Thale
Luang

Rt 404
Rt 403
Kantang
at Chao Mai
ational Park

Di Luang
Sating Phra

Bo Pradu

'oh
bong
Palian
Koh Sukorn

Thung Wa

Rattaphum
Thale Sap
Songkhla
Koh Yo
Koh No &
Koh Maew
Songkhla

Rt 406
Hat Yai
Rt 407
Chum Pho

Koh Lamai
Koh Bulon Don
Koh Bulon-Leh
Koh Bulon
Rang
Koh
Khai Yai
Langu
Ban Pak Bara

Chalung

Rt 416

Khlong Ngae
Thale Ban
National Park
Rt 4
Na Thawi
Chana
Thepha
Rachadapisek
Pattani
Talo Kapo
Panare

Laem Pho

Khae Khae

Tarutao
ational
Park
Koh Le La
Koh Klang
Koh Lo
Koh Singha
Koh Palitong
Koh
Tanga
Koh Tarutao

Satun
Sadao

Yarang
Wasukri
Saiburi

Yala

Langkawi
Island

Kuala Perlis

MALAYSIA

Narathiwat

Koh Rawi
Koh
Butong
Koh
Adang
Koh Lipe
Koh
Tanga
Koh
Tarang

Boat from
Koh Tarutao

Ban Nang Sata

Rangae
Tak Bai

C

Bang Lang
Reservoir
Than To

Sungei Golok

Andaman Sea

4

Betong

5

6

Bangkok Skytrain & Metro

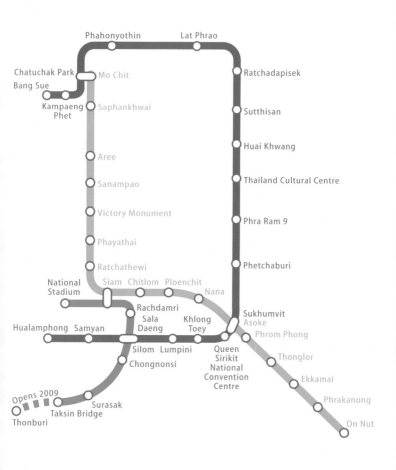

Phahonyothin
Lat Phrao
Chatuchak Park
Mo Chit
Bang Sue
Ratchadapisek
Kampaeng Phet
Saphankhwai
Sutthisan
Aree
Huai Khwang
Sanampao
Thailand Cultural Centre
Victory Monument
Phra Ram 9
Phayathai
Phetchaburi
Ratchathewi
National Stadium
Siam Chitlom Ploenchit
Nana
Rachdamri
Sukhumvit
Sala Daeng
Khlong Toey
Asoke
Hualamphong Samyan
Phrom Phong
Silom Lumpini
Thonglor
Chongnonsi
Queen Sirikit National Convention Centre
Ekkamai
Opens 2009
Phrakanong
Surasak
Taksin Bridge
On Nut
Thonburi

N

Not to scale

Skytrain Sukhumvit Line

Skytrain Silom Line

Metro

Interchange

Distance chart

Bangkok
245	Chantaburi

```
Bangkok
245  Chantaburi
696  1106 Chiang Mai
785  1200 182  Chiang Rai
463  708  1159 1248 Chumphon
128  373  765  844  478  Kanchanaburi
947  520  1629 732  912  535  Khon Kaen
814  1059 1510 1599 363  828  1263 Krabi
924  1169 579  672  1387 983  956  1738 Mae Hong Son
259  332  777  870  922  345  190  1382 1012 Nakhon Ratchasima
780  1025 1476 1565 330  795  1329 233  1704 1039 Nakhon Si Thammarat
615  687  818  899  1078 701  166  1429 1122 356  1395 Nong Khai
147  110  843  932  610  275  494  961  1071 335  597  691  Pattaya
123  368  819  908  340  144  572  691  1047 382  658  738  270  Phetburi
862  1107 1558 1627 412  877  1311 176  1786 862  336  1477 1009 740  Phuket
427  672  298  400  891  370  378  1241 578  514  1207 544  575  550  1289 Sukhothai
828  1073 1524 1617 378  842  1277 131  1752 1087 123  1443 975  705  312  1255 Trang
629  700  937  1014 1092 712  282  1441 1238 282  1365 448  705  765  1493 660  1457 Ubon Ratchathani
564  635  767  847  1027 650  115  1378 1071 152  1344 51   640  687  1426 493  1392 401  Udon Thani
```

Distances in kilometres   1 kilometre = 0.62 miles

Map symbols

- □ Capital city
- ○ Other city, town
- International border
- Regional border
- ⊖ Customs
- Contours (approx)
- ▲ Mountain, volcano
- ⤵ Mountain pass
- Escarpment
- Glacier
- Salt flat
- Rocks
- Seasonal marshland
- Beach, sandbank
- Waterfall
- Reef
- ═══ Motorway
- ─── Main road
- ─── Minor road
- Track
- Footpath
- ─── Railway
- Railway with station
- ✈ Airport
- Bus station
- Ⓜ Metro station

- ---- Cable car
- +++++ Funicular
- Ferry
- Pedestrianized street
- Tunnel
- One way-street
- Steps
- Bridge
- Fortified wall
- Park, garden, stadium
- Sleeping
- Eating
- Bars & clubs
- Building
- Sight
- Cathedral, church
- Chinese temple
- Hindu temple
- Meru
- Mosque
- Stupa
- Synagogue
- Tourist office
- Museum
- Post office
- Police

- Ⓢ Bank
- @ Internet
- Telephone
- Market
- Medical services
- Parking
- Petrol
- Golf
- Archaeological site
- ♦ National park, wildlife reserve
- Viewing point
- Campsite
- Refuge, lodge
- Castle, fort
- Diving
- Deciduous, coniferous, palm trees
- Hide
- Vineyard, winery
- Distillery
- Shipwreck
- Historic battlefield
- Related map

Index

Nathon *p620, map p618*
Car and motorbike hire
Motorbikes and jeeps can be hired
in Nathon.

North coast *p620, map p618*
Boat
Lomprayah, main road, Mae Nam, on the
corner of the road to the Baan Fah Resort,
office Mon-Sat 0800-1700, telephone lines
open daily 077-427765, www.lomprayah.com.
Daily service departing from Wat Na Phra
Lam pier 0800 and 1230 to **Koh Phangan**,
฿250, additional service at 1700; to **Koh
Tao**, ฿550; to **Chumporn**, ฿900; to **Hua Hin**
฿1000; and **Bangkok**, ฿1000. Price includes
transfer to pier. Service to Full Moon Party,
฿850, one way.
  From **Big Buddha Pier**, next to 7/11.
To Hat Rin on **Koh Phangan**, 1030, 1300,
1600, 1830, 50 mins, ฿150. Petcherat
Marina, 82/1 Moo 4, Bophut, T077-425262,
www.samuispeed boat.com. Boats go to
Hat Rin on **Koh Phangan**, every full moon,
from Petcherat Marina, Big Buddha,
1700-2400 hourly, 30 mins, ฿700 return.
Return 0100-0800. Boats leave when full.
Make sure the boat you board does not
exceed capacity and has lifejackets (in
Jan 2005 an overloaded boat capsized
with the loss of more than a dozen lives).

Car and motorbike hire
In Mae Nam hire is available on the beach
or at resorts.
  In Choeng Mon there's **Avis**, T077-425454;
and **TA Car Rental**, T077-245129, opposite
The White House and The Boathouse.

East coast *p621, map p618*
Car and motorbike hire
In Lamai jeeps and motorbikes are widely
available for hire.

● Directory

Koh Samui *p617, map p618*
Banks Until recently Nathon was the only
place with a bank, now there are countless
exchanges and ATMs scattered all over the
island. In **Nathon**, exchange booths and
banks along the seafront and main roads.
Bophut has several bank booths as well as
tour agencies change money. In **Chaweng**,
money changing and ATMs are along
Chaweng Beach Rd. In **Lamai**, currency
exchanges are along the main parallel to
the beach and there are ATMs in town.
Immigration on main road next to the
police station, Nathon, T077-421069, Mon-Fri
0830-1200 and 1300-1630. Visas can be
extended here. **Internet** There are internet
cafés in all the beach resorts, ฿1 per min, and
most travel agencies. **Medical services**
24-hr emergency clinic and the **Samui
International Hospital**, Chaweng, T077-
422272, www.sih.co.th (also has a dental
clinic). It is best to take injured people to
the hospital; the ambulance service can be
slow. A reasonable level of English is spoken.
In **Bophut**, there is **Bandon International
Hospital**, T077-245236, www.bandon
hospital.com. In **Big Buddha**, Hyperbaric
Services, 34/8 Moo 4, at Big Buddha,
T077-427427, T08-1084 8485 (mob),
www.ssnsnetwork.com. **Police** Tourist
police, 3 km south of Nathon, T077-4212815,
open 24 hrs, past turning to Hin Lad Waterfall.
T1169 emergency, T191 police. **Post office**
Nathon Post Office, to the north of the pier,
international telephone and poste restante
service and CAT internet, Mon-Fri 0830-1630,
Sat-Sun 0830-1200. Lamai Post Office, south
end of the main road. **Telephone** Calls are
much cheaper if made at the post office. High
street 'booths' are 3-4 times more expensive.
International calls can also be made from
many hotels and travel agents.

Koh Phangan

→ *Colour map 4, B3.*

Koh Phangan is the gulf's party island. World renowned for the Full Moon Party, it attracts thousands of young people looking for the night of their life on the sands at Hat Rin, the most developed part of the island. The pace of development on the island has been rapid. Although still unspoilt in part, in the main it is not as beautiful as parts of Koh Samui and Koh Tao although the beaches at Hat Rin and some along the east coast are attractive and – except for Hat Rin – uncrowded. The water is good for snorkelling, particularly during the dry season when clarity is at its best. Boats leave from Thong Sala, the island's main town, for nearby Ang Thong Marine National Park (see page 620). Between May and September the tide is out all day between Mae Hat and Hat Rin. Fishing and coconut production remain mainstays of the economy, and villages still have a traditional air – although tourism is now by far the largest single industry. ▸▸ *For listings, see pages 647-658.*

Ins and outs

Getting there
There is no airport on the island so everyone arrives by boat. There are daily ferries from Don Sak Pier and Bandon near Surat Thani on the mainland and also from the larger, neighbouring island of Koh Samui and its northerly neighbour, Koh Tao. Minibus taxis meet the boats and take people from Thong Sala pier to Hat Rin for ฿100 and to Thong Nai Pan for ฿150. The quickest way to Koh Phangan is to fly from Bangkok to Koh Samui (see page 639) and then to catch an express boat from Samui to Koh Phangan. Alternatively, it is possible to fly to Surat Thani and take a boat from there. ▸▸ *See Transport, page 657, for further information.*

Getting around
Koh Phangan stretches 15 km north to south and 10 km east to west. The main settlement is Thong Sala. Thong Sala and Hat Rin are connected by a paved road. Two roads run between Thong Sala and Ao Chao Lok Lum: the west coast route and the one through the centre of the island. Around the remainder of the island there is a limited network of poor roads and tracks, and the stretch from Ban Khai to Hat Rin is steep and treacherous and inadvisable for anything but a 4WD during the rainy season. The number of accidents is huge. For off-the-road beaches it is often easiest to travel by long-tailed boat. Motorbikes and mountain bikes are available for hire, and the most appealing areas to ride are in the north and west of the island, which are flat. *Songthaews* run from the pier to any of the bays served by road. A trip to Hat Rin from Thong Sala is ฿80-100. The cost to the other bays depends on how many people are going with you. At Hat Rin *songthaews* wait close to the **Drop in Club Resort** between Hat Rin East and West. For a few beaches walking is the best option. See also box on road madness, page 640.

Tourist information
There is no official tourist information on the island. The TAT on Koh Samui, see page 619, is responsible for the island. See www.kohphangan.com and www.phangan.info, for information.

Koh Phangan offers natural sights such as waterfalls, forests, coral and viewpoints but little of historical or cultural interest. Sometimes the best way to explore the island is on foot, following tracks that link the villages and beaches, which cannot be negotiated by *songthaew* or motorbike. It is possible to walk on a trail from Hat Rin up the east coast to Hat Thien, although other paths are swiftly swallowed up by the forest.

Although it's possible to navigate the roads by motorbike, first-timers should think seriously before heading southeast to Hat Rin, as the roads are often at a 40° gradient which makes them treacherous at best and a death trap when wet. The high number of walking wounded is testimony to the danger of these hilly roads.

Thong Sala and around

The main town of Koh Phangan is the port of Thong Sala (pronounced Tong-sala) where most boats from Koh Samui, Surat Thani and Koh Tao dock. Thong Sala has banks, ATMs,

Koh Phangan

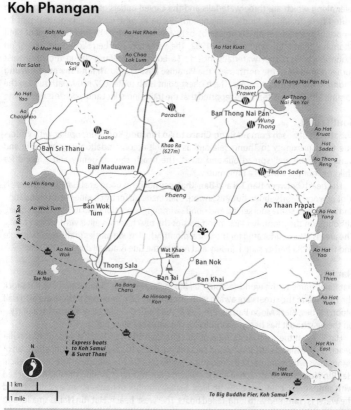

telephone, internet access, travel agents, a small supermarket, dive shops, motorbike hire and a second-hand bookstore. Humming during the day with all the departures and arrivals, this can be a bit of a ghost town during the evenings, although it's a pleasant place to spend the night, with some good restaurants.

On the coast to the east of Thong Sala, outside Ban Tai, is **Wat Khao Tum** and the **Vipassana Meditation Centre** ① *all-inclusive fees are ฿4500 for 10 days, contact Wat Khao Tum, Koh Phangan, Surat Thani, for more information, or www.watkowtahm.org, where they provide a contact and booking facility*. There are views from the hilltop wat to Samui and the Ang Thong Islands. Ten-day meditation courses are held every month with 20-day courses and three-month retreats also available. All the courses are conducted in English and taught by Australian-US couple Rosemary and Steve Weissman who have been here since 1988.

The interior

Phaeng Waterfall is to be found in the interior of the island, about 4.5 km from Thong Sala and 2 km from the village of Maduawan. The walk east to Hat Sadet runs parallel to a river along which are three waterfalls and the carved initials of several Thai kings who visited here, including King Chulalongkorn (Rama V), who was so enamoured that he reportedly came here on 10 occasions between 1888 and 1909, and the present King Bhumibol (Rama IX), who came in 1962. The waterfalls can be reached on foot or on mountain bikes. Other waterfalls include **Ta Luang** and **Wang Sai** in the northwest corner, **Paradise** in the north (near the Paradise Resort), and **Thaan Prawet** and **Wung Thong** in the northeast corner. The highest point is **Khao Ra** (627 m). A path runs to the summit although visitors have reported that the trail is indistinct and a guide is necessary.

South coast

The stretch of beach from **Ao Bang Charu** to **Ao Hinsong Kon** is unpopular with visitors due to its proximity to Thong Sala and as a result accommodation is good value and bungalows are well spread out and quiet. The beach shelves gently and is good for children, but the water is a little murky.

The beach between **Ban Tai** and **Ban Khai** may not be as good as at Hat Rin and there is a lot of wood debris about, but this is more than made up for by cheaper accommodation and less noise. Some snorkelling and good swimming is possible and it is generally quiet, although on the monthly black moon parties the beach comes alive with techno beats. The area is also well-located for the twice-monthly half moon parties in the nearby jungle and the Wat Po herbal sauna. In July and August the tide is out all day.

Hat Rin

Hat Rin is home to the world-famous Full Moon Parties when thundering bass-lines rock the beach and the streets are awash with alcohol (see box, page 645). There are also Half Moon Parties, Black Moon Parties, Pre-Full Moon Parties – in fact any excuse for a party – on the beach so it has become famous for the almighty blow outs.

Hat Rin is at the southeastern tip of Koh Phangan and has the best and most popular beach on the island with some good snorkelling. It also has the greatest concentration of bungalows which are packed close together (except on the hillsides). The 'east' beach, **Hat Rin Nok**, is more attractive and is cleaned every morning. During the day it is packed with sunbathers, coloured blow-up lilos, a small number of hawkers, volleyball nets and the water is crammed with long-tailed boats. The 'west' beach, **Hat Rin Nai**, is smaller and

Full Moon Parties

The Full Moon Parties, which have been going since 1989, are now accompanied by Half and Black Moon Parties, Saturday Night Parties and Pre-Full Moon Parties. Unfortunately, over the past few years rape and violent robbery have badly tarnished the friendly party atmosphere. Of course, many people do attend without any problems but caution is highly recommended as Thai criminal gangs now seem to be targeting party goers. There have also been several stories of post-party boats to Koh Samui being dangerously overloaded, and it is recommended that you avoid these boats completely.

On full moon night, if you are not planning to party till dawn, it is advisable to stay on Hat Rin West or elsewhere on the island, unless you feel you can sleep to the boom of the bass from the beach. Up to 10,000 people turn up on Hat Rin East every month to dance to the excellent music, watch the jugglers, fire eaters and fireworks displays and drink themselves into oblivion. Even the dogs take part as partygoers paint their pooches in psychedelic paint!

Tips for the party

→ Don't bring valuables with you; if a safety deposit box is an option at your bungalow, leave everything there. Don't leave anything of value in bungalows that are easily broken into. Reportedly it's a big night for burglars.

→ Do not eat or drink anything that is offered by strangers.

→ Wear shoes. The beach gets littered with broken glass and some people suffer serious injury from this.

→ If you lose your brain and your way (and a lot of people do) carry the business (name) card of your bungalow to show sober folk once you've left the party.

→ Don't take drugs. It's not worth the risk. At almost every party plainclothes policemen take a number of Westerners down to the jail from where they will only be released on bail if they can pay the fine. Otherwise they will be held for five to six weeks prior to trial.

Further information can be found on the following websites: www.fullmoon.phangan.info; www.halfmoonfestival.com; and www.kohphangan.com.

almost non-existent at high tide; accommodation is slightly cheaper here. The two beaches, less than 10 minutes' walk apart, are both wonderfully quiet until about 1300, as most people are sleeping off the night's excesses. At night the noise from generators and the bars can be overpowering on Hat Rin Nok but a few minutes' walk away from the action towards Hat Rin Nai, the music, incredibly, is inaudible – this applies on full moon nights too. Theft has become a real problem in the area, use safety deposit boxes for valuables and secure bungalows with extra locks wherever possible – especially when sleeping.

East coast

These beaches and coves form **Hat Thien to Hat Sadet** are only accessible by boat. The stretch of stony coastline at Hat Thien doesn't afford much for those hoping to lie and fry, but its rocky, tree-lined character makes it an attractive and rugged area. It's not a bad option at all: there are cheap guesthouses and it's possible to walk over the headland to Hat Yuan where the beautiful and popular white-sand beach is much more palatable to sun worshippers.

Ao Thong Nai Pan Noi and **Ao Thong Nai Pan Yai** is a double bay boasting some of the most beautiful, quiet, white-sand beaches on the island, romantically hemmed in by the mountains and with among the highest recurring visitor rates. The attractive beach is topped by boulders at its northern end, hiding the enormous Santhiya resort spread up the hill beyond. Yai has more palms leaning over the beach and so is slightly more picturesque than Noi, but Noi has a wider beach and is a bit more bustling. There are several shops, ATMs and bars behind Noi beach and bikes can be rented. There's also internet, snorkel gear and kayaks for hire on the beach. It is said to have been Rama V's favourite beach on the island, and it's not hard to see why – plenty of people come here for a short holiday and end up staying for months. It remains fairly off the beaten tourist track and is more a place to relax for those whose main aim is not to party. The journey by truck from Thong Sala takes almost an hour and the road is muddy in the rainy season, but it does take you through untouched jungle and so is quite an experience. It is also possible to get a boat from Hat Rin which is much more comfortable.

North coast
About 5 km northwest of Thong Nai Pan, **Ao Hat Kuat**, more commonly known by its English translation 'Bottle Beach', is even more isolated, with a beautiful beach. Staff at the bungalows here are not as friendly as they could be. Despite developing a reputation as a bit of a British ghetto and a huge new development here, it retains its escapist appeal.

Along a rutted track, **Ao Hat Khom** is another relaxed place and many stay for weeks. The bay is fringed by a reef offering some of the best snorkelling on Phangan, however, because the seabed shelves gently, swimming is sometimes only really possible at high tide and getting out to the reef can be tricky.

Ao Chao Lok Lum is a deep, sheltered bay on Koh Phangan's north coast. There is now an excellent road from Thong Sala to here and this fishing village is gradually developing into a quiet, comparatively refined resort, with the best part of the beach being to the east. In the village of Ban Chao Lok Lum there are bikes and diving equipment for rent. There's also a 7-11 shop and an ATM.

Hat Salat is one of the most peaceful parts of the island, though due to its picturesque bay it is also one of the fastest-developing spots. **Ao Mae Hat** has a super beach with a sandy bank extending outwards and along which it is possible to walk to Koh Ma when it hasn't rained for some time. There are palm trees, a few bungalows and good snorkelling.

West coast
Ao Hat Yao is an attractive curved, clean beach on the west coast with good swimming and snorkelling, 20 minutes by *songthaew* from Thong Sala. Bungalows are spread out and quiet.

To the south of Ao Hat Yao, **Ao Chaophao** is a relatively quiet and undeveloped bay with just a handful of places to stay. The perfect crescent of sand and sunsets make the bay particularly attractive. There is also good swimming because the seabed shelves steeply before reaching the reef around 100 m offshore where there is good snorkelling. At the southern end is an attractive lagoon and the coast here also has some remnant mangroves.

Ao Sri Thanu is a long but rather narrow beach, 15 minutes by *songthaew* from Thong Sala. It is a peaceful spot to spend a few days and is sparsely settled but is not very attractive. Behind the beach is a freshwater lake fringed by pine trees which is ideal for swimming.

North of Thong Sala and south of Ban Sri Thanu, the beaches at **Ao Wok Tum** are average and the swimming is poor. Accommodation is good value though.

North of Thong Sala and south of Ban Sri Thanu, the beaches between **Ao Hin Kong** and **Ao Nai Wok** aren't particularly striking and swimming is difficult as the seabed shelves so gently. However, it is quite attractive with shallow boulders near Cookies and it is not rocky underfoot for the first 10 m or so. Accommodation is good value.

⦿ Koh Phangan listings

For Sleeping and Eating price codes and other relevant information, see pages 44-49.

⦿ Sleeping

There is just one big hotel in Thong Sala, **Phangan Centrepoint**. Hat Rin is more expensive than other beaches and some accommodation is outrageously overpriced. During the high season (Dec-Feb and Jul-Sep), prices are 50% higher than in the low season: bargain if bungalows seem empty. Over full moon most places insist on a 7-night stay at inflated prices. Don't turn up expecting to find a room in Hat Rin. At peak times around the full moon accommodation runs out and you may have to stay further afield; Thong Sala is a good option.

Thong Sala and around *p643, map p643*
C-D Phangan Centrepoint, 26/6 Moo 1, T077-377232. Right in the centre of town, upmarket spacious hotel-style a/c rooms with cable TV based around a dazzlingly modern shopping plaza.
D Phangan Chai Hotel, 45/65 Moo 1, T077-377068. All rooms are a/c, with garden or sea views, fridge, shower and Western toilet. Decor leaves something to be desired.
D-E Buakao Inn Guest House, 146 Thong-sala, T077-377226. Comfortably furnished rooms with TV, all en suite, the cheapest is fan only, the rest are a/c. During full moon Parties price rises to ฿1500 per night and must be booked for a minimum of 3 nights.

South coast *p644, map p643*
Bang Charu and Ao Hinsong Kon
AL-A First Villa, T077-377225. Impeccably clean a/c and fan rooms along a private

beachfront and in a pleasant tropical garden. Rooms are upmarket if slightly garish, some with private jacuzzi.
B-C Charm Beach Resort, T077-377165, www.charmbeachresort.com. The bungalows are well laid out and the most expensive are a/c. The cheap rooms, which are bamboo and thatch huts, are particularly good value but often full. The restaurant serves Thai and European food. Swimming pool.
B-D Phangan Beach Resort, 112/1 Moo 1, T077-238809, phanganbeachresort@hot mail.com. Very cosy a/c and fan bungalows. Spacious and clean with a sliding door leading to an open-air bathroom. Comfortable with nice finishes. Set in a garden that leads straight to the beach.
F Liberty Bungalows, T077-238171, libertybantai@hotmail.com. This is a nice compound of 10 bungalows with bamboo furnishings and hammocks set amid bougainvillea and cactus. Rooms are clean and comfortable with attached shower rooms. The more expensive ones are on the beach. There's music and movies in the restaurant and volleyball on the beach.

Ban Tai and Ban Khai
AL-C Milky Bay Resort, Ban Tai, T077-238 566, www.milkybay.com. Stylishly designed resort with plush a/c rooms and bungalows on the beach and excellent facilities. Pool, bar, gym with Thai boxing, pool tables, massage shalas, herbal steam room and Thai and Italian restaurant as well as beachfront barbecues.
A-B Hansa Resort, Ban Tai, T077-377494, www.hansaresort.com. Popular picturesque resort with traditional beach bungalows complete with a/c, TV and minibar.

B-E Mac's Bay Resort, T077-238443, www.macbayresort.com. Popular with Israelis, there are basic huts and smart white concrete bungalows, lined up attractively on the beach. Slightly better than most, well run and clean. The more expensive rooms are large and have attached shower rooms and a/c. There is a restaurant with a wide menu with nightly videos plus table tennis. Money exchange and an international collect-call service.

B-F Phangnan Rainbow, 25/3 Moo 4, T077-238236. Very comfortable fan rooms with high-quality furnishings. The cheapest bungalows have a shared bathroom. Location and size determines the price, some have a sea view. Very friendly family fun resort. Restaurant. Make sure the taxi driver takes you to Bankai Beach and not Hat Hin, where there is another resort of the same name. Recommended.

C-F Triangle Lodge, Ban Tai, T077-377 432, www.phangan.info/trianglelodge. The more expensive bungalows on the beach sport nicely carved wooden balcony decoration. The restaurant is appealing as it has a wide and imaginative menu with tasty interpretations of Western dishes and the staff are friendly. Bikes for rent.

E-F Lee Garden Resort Ban Khai, T077-238 150, lees_garden@yahoo.com. A scattering of bungalows set in a garden next to the beach with balconies and hammocks in a quiet location. There are funky tunes, a giant tree swing, good food and great views. Well run.

Hat Rin p644, map p643
Hat Rin Nok
Bear in mind that accommodation gets booked up around the full moon so it's worth arriving a week in advance or booking.

L-A Phangan Bay Shore Resort, T077-375 224, T077-375227, www.phanganbayshore. com. Nice bungalows set in rows leading down to the beach. The most expensive are well kept with a/c, fridge, TV and hot water but little furniture and cheap fluorescent lights. There are hammocks on the verandas.

L-B Palita Lodge, T801-375170, www.koh phanganlodge.com. The management have moved upmarket with the construction of 10 immaculate suites with rock bath tubs that fill from a fountain and rain showers, 2 seating areas and smart venetian blinds. Breakfast is included.

L-B Sunrise Resort, 136 Moo 6, T077-375 145. Clean hotel rooms with small balcony, a/c, fridge and hot water. Popular with the Israeli crowd and is usually full over the full moon period. Swimming pool.

A-B Delight Resort, 140 Hat Rin, T077-375 527, www.delightresort.com. A street back from the beach, this new place offers comfortable a/c rooms. There's a restaurant and a large clothes store next to it. ฿500-700.

AL-B Tommy Resort, T077-375215, F077-375253. Tommy's moving rapidly upmarket with 22 pleasant traditional-style bungalows near the beach that have TV, fridges and hot water. The dingy restaurant reflects its backpacker past.

A-D Haadrin Resort, 128/9 Moo 6, T077-375258. Ranges from fan huts to a/c rooms, basic but clean. Price includes breakfast. Stones throw from the Full Moon Beach.

B-D Sea Garden Resort & Spa, 137 Moo 6, T077-375281, www.seagarden_resort.com. Bungalows and a/c rooms in a 2 storey building, peaceful garden setting across the road from the beach. Cheapest rooms are fan only, whilst the de luxe rooms have bathtub and stereo. Good value for the area.

C-F Paradise, T077-375244. The originators of the Full Moon Party, the management of this set-up run around 50 bungalows, most of which are tatty, some significantly bigger and better than others, with hot water and a/c; all have attached showers. Pleasant garden although it might be too close to the nightclubs for many. Some bungalows can accommodate 4 people in 2 double beds, which makes it the best-value option. There were reports of rooms being systematically burgled at night in 2006. The owners also run a restaurant, **The Rock** (see Eating, below).

D-E Baan Talay, 74/1 Moo 6, T077-375083, www.phangan.info/baantalay. In the village between the sunrise and sunset beaches. Comfortable. Well-furnished rooms, either fan or a/c. Hot water showers. Good value.

D-E Bongo Bunglows, 94/9 Moo 6, T077-375268. Offers 2 rows of huge concrete and brick huts spread down a long narrow garden. Both fan and a/c are available. Bathrooms could be cleaner.

D-E Same Same, T077-375200, www.same-same.com. A popular bar and basic guesthouse which receives good reports among the backpacker scene.

Hat Rin Nai

The advantage of staying on Hat Rin Nai is that it is quieter and on full moon nights the party cannot be heard. It's a short stroll to the centre of Hat Rin and Hat Rin Nok beach.

L-A Phangan Buri Resort & Spa, T077-375 481, www.phanganburiresort.net. A more expensive resort away from the crowds with a lovely beachfront pool and another further back. Bungalows are attractively furnished and are nicely spaced in rows leading down to the beach. Non-guests can use the pool for ฿100.

B-C Neptune's Villa, T077-375251, neptune1@thaimail.com. There are a/c concrete bungalows and 2nd-floor rooms with great views of the sea and a fairly pleasant beach. Overpriced in peak season.

B-D Hillside Bungalows, a few metres along the road to Thong Sala, T077-375102. This friendly spot is run by relaxed Nepali Tacco. Almost doubles its prices at full moon. Smart rooms with fridge and hot water.

B-E Blue Marine, 110/6 Haad Rin, T077-375079. Even the fan rooms, the cheapest option, have TV, minibar and hot water. A/c available. Spacious and clean, right next to the beach. Good value.

B-E Friendly Guesthouse, next to Black & White, T077-375167. Some rooms in a 2 storey Chinese looking building. Bungalows are also available. Fan and a/c, all rooms have hot water showers. The decor is a bit garish. If you check in 3 days before the full moon the price remains the same.

C-F Black & White, 110/2 Moo 6, T077-375187. There are over 60 rooms at this resort ranging from fan bungalows to a/c rooms in a modern building. Very close to sunset beach.

D-F Charung Bungalow, T077-375168, charungbungalows@hotmail.com. Simple bungalows with attached shower room and fan. Hammocks in front of every room. The restaurant's snooker table needs serious attention.

Leela Beach

A little further out of town, on the western side of the Had Rin's peninsular, Leela beach is worth the effort to reach for its beauty and complete sense of removal from the hedonism of the party scene.

AL-E Sarikantang, Hat Sikantang, towards the headland, T077-375055, www.sarikantang.com. Gorgeous rooms with large windows at this luscious resort with a beachfront pool. The cheaper, wooden rooms are good value. It's a 10-min walk to the centre of Hat Rin.

D-F Lighthouse Bungalows, T077-375075, www.lighthousebungalows.com. This great place is a 20-min walk from Hat Rin on the western side of the headland. It is reached by a long romantic wooden causeway around the rocks to the bungalows of various sizes and prices. The staff are friendly and helpful and there's a sociable restaurant, which is an excellent place to make friends before the full moon madness. The sunsets are fantastic. Recommended.

East coast *p645, map p643*
Hat Thien to Hat Sadet

AL-F The Sanctuary, Hat Yuan, T08-1271 3614 (mob), www.the sanctuary-kpg.com. Renowned for its post and pre-party 'detox and retox' programmes and unbeatably bohemian beach atmosphere. Managed by Westerners it offers everything from fasts and colonic-cleansing courses to a treat-heavy menu, cocktails and wine in the boulder-strewn café. Accommodation ranges from dorms for under ฿250 to palatial open-plan hilltop houses. The vegetarian and seafood restaurant with its home-grown produce and bakery is pricey but top quality. Self-development courses in yoga, meditation and massage run year round. Only accessible by boat or a long walk through jungle.

D-E Haad Tien Resort, T08-1229 3919 (mob). There is no road access to this peaceful resort which is 15 mins from Hat Rin by boat. 22 a/c bungalows and rooms either on the beach or overlooking the sea. Swimming pool. Some rooms possibly overpriced.

D-E Mai Pen Rai, Hat Sadet, T077-445090, www.thansadet.com. Basic fan bungalows with attached bathrooms on the beach with newer ones on the hillside. Near the biggest waterfall and although on a less than impressive beach it has a sleepy charm. Many Thai kings have visited and the present king owns the land.

E-F Horizon Boxing Camp, between Ao Hat Yuan and Ao Hat Thien, T072-778570, www.horizonmuaythai.com. Basic thatched huts with outside toilets and some more expensive en suite options, overlooking the beach. The impressive boxing gym and ring sets it apart from competitors.

Ao Thong Nai Pan Yai
B-E Nice Beach Resort, T077-238547. The 27 unimaginative bungalows have seen better days and the staff could be friendlier.

C-E Dreamland, T077-238539, www.dream landresort.net. Attempting to make the leap to a more luxurious resort, with a recently built swimming pool. New concrete villas were being built at the time of writing; time will tell whether or not the transition is successful.

C-G Su's Bakery & Bungalows, 11/2 Baan Thong Nai Pan, T077-238924, subakery-2004 @hotmail.com. A range of accommodation, a minutes walk from the beach, ranging from a wooden hut to a fully kitted out house

with kitchen, a/c, hot water, TV and even a washing machine, making it an excellent option for families.

F Dolphin Bungalows, Bar & Restaurant, southern end of the beach, kimgiet@ hotmail.com. Enjoys almost legendary status amongst guests that keep returning year after year. Spectacularly and lovingly landscaped jungle-garden houses the beachfront bar and restaurant (see Eating, below) and further back, hides the wooden fan bungalows, which are all en suite with hammocks on the balcony. Everything here has been designed with genuine care for the environment. Highly recommended.

F Pingjun, T077-445062. A friendly resort with large bungalows all of which have verandas, hammocks, fans and en suite bathrooms. Popular restaurant.

F White Sand, at the southern end of the beach, T077-445123. This is one of the beach's best budget options. Serves some of the best Thai food on the beach, reasonably priced and the staff are friendly. Recommended.

Ao Thong Nai Pan Noi
LL-L Panviman Resort, T077-445101, www.panviman.com. A large upmarket resort with peculiar grotto-style concrete villas and exclusive suites in the hotel set high on the cliffs commanding impressive views. Its circular formal restaurant over-looks the sea.

A-E Baan Panburi Village, T077-238599, www.baanpanburivillage.com. 2 huge red and green lanterns mark the entrance of this traditional, picturesque resort. A range of simple a/c or fan bungalows with wooden shutters, balconies and hammocks and more basic thatched beach huts amid frangipani trees in a spacious, well-tended garden. At the time of writing large scale construction was underway transforming the area into a high-end luxury resort.

A-E Tong Ta Pan, T077-238538, www.thong tapan.com. Large white villas set either on a picturesque rocky hillside or on the beach. The upmarket interiors are pleasantly furnished and have large tiled bathrooms with hot water. Excursions and water sports club.

B-E Star Hut, T077-445006, star_hut@ hotmail.com. The largest and most popular place on the beach. The wood and bamboo huts with thatched roofs are attractive although too close together. Some are fan only and others have a/c. The good restaurant serves cheap Thai and Western food. It is well managed. A bus runs 3 times daily to Thong Sala.

North coast *p646, map p643*
Ao Hat Kuat
Construction of a large hotel on Bottle Beach is underway.

D-E Bottle Beach Bungalow No 1, T077-445152, bottlebeach@hotmail.com. The first and most upmarket of 3 resorts run by the same family, this is the smartest of the **Bottle Beaches** and features polished wood bungalows under coconut palms. The bungalows are set in a nice garden with little platform verandas right on the beach. The wooden ones have a Swiss feel. All have shower and fan. More expensive rooms have 4 beds.

D-F Bottle Beach Bungalow No 3, T077-445127. The smallest of the 3 with fan bungalows, some right on beach. The concrete bungalows come with pleasant roof annexes. It also has an attractive beachfront restaurant.

E Smile, T077-445155. Blue-roofed bungalows set up amongst the boulders reached by little stone paths and rooms with jungle views are particularly peaceful. It has an attractive restaurant with hanging shell mobiles and newspapers. There's a tree swing and sofa swings on the beach. Recommended.

F Bottle Beach Bungalow No 2, T077-445156. Fairly rustic and slightly cheaper blue bungalows with a little less character right on the beach at the southern end of the bay which vary in price according to size. All have fan and bathroom. There's a nice restaurant on the beach too.

Ao Hat Khom
D-F Coconut Beach, furthest end of the beach, T077-374298, www.coconutbeach-bungalows.com. At the end of a steep and treacherous dirt track. Concrete bungalows on the cliff side which leads down to the beachfront restaurant and the soft, white-sandy beach.

D-F Ocean View Resort, T077-377231. Up on the headland with a great view and a range of bungalow options – the creatively designed more expensive ones with views are a particular bargain. The restaurant also has lovely sea views and serves good vegetarian food.

E-F Coral Bay, T077-374245. Bungalows from the more basic with shared bathrooms, to posh ones with interesting bathrooms built into the rock. All have mosquito nets. The resort also rents snorkelling equipment.

Ao Chao Lok Lum
AL-A Chaloklum Bay T077-374147-8, www.chaloklumbay.com. Attractive beachfront bungalows on stilts with a/c and hot water or fan. There are also a couple of large, attractive beach houses for groups or families. Shop on site.

B-E Malibu Beach Resort, after Wantana Resort, T077-374057. Simple, well-maintained and clean bamboo huts with attached bath-rooms. Further back are a/c bungalows which are large but rather dark inside. The bathrooms are also spacious with bathtub. Plenty of hammocks hanging from the trees. Beach BBQ.

B-E Niramon Villas, next to **Fanta Bungalows**, T077-374115. Large concrete bungalows on stilts, some with sea views. Comfortably furnished with a/c, minibar, cable TV and hot water. The beach is a short walk away over a rather precarious wooden suspension bridge. Friendly management. Plans for a swimming pool.

B-F Fanta Bungalows, 113/1 Moo 7, T077-374132. Clean, well-kept wooden bungalows, some are right on the beach. All have bathroom inside and mosquito

net. There's a large a/c bungalow on the beach too. Good deal for the location.
D-F Wattana Resort, T077-374022. The larger rooms have balconies on 2 sides with hammocks and mosquito screens. The cheaper rooms are large, but basic, with mosquito nets.

Hat Salat and Ao Mae Hat
LL-AL Green Papaya Resort, T077-349280, www.greenpapayaresort.com. 18 luxury wooden cottages and rooms with stylish interiors set in a lush garden around a beachfront pool.
AL-B Salad Beach Resort, T077-349149, www.saladbeachphangan.com. Bungalows and 2-storey rooms with fan or a/c, TV and hot water set around a lovely pool. There's a pool table and jacuzzi too.
A-B Salad Hut, T077-349246, salad_hut@ hotmail.com. A smaller cluster of attractive bungalows including 4 family rooms. The bungalows facing the beach have nice big rooms with carved balconies complete with a day-bed and 2 hammocks. There's a restaurant, snorkelling and boat trips. Friendly management.
B-F Wang Sai Resort, Ao Mae Hat, T077-374238. In a beautiful setting behind a stream close to the sandbar, the attractive bungalows, some perched on boulders, are clean and well maintained, although few have sea views. It is quiet and secluded but the sea is not so clear here. Snorkelling equipment for hire, book exchange and volleyball net. Restaurant serves cheap Thai and Western food.
E My Way Bungalows, T077-349267. Bamboo fan bungalows with thatched roofs and hammocks. Electricity stops at 2300. Clean, with bathroom attached. The restaurant serves good, cheap Thai cuisine.
E-F Island View Cabana, Ao Mae Hat, T077-374172. One of the oldest places on the island, set in a wide part of the beach where a sandbar stretches out to Koh Ma which provides good snorkelling. Simple huts, some have attached shower rooms

with Western toilets. The restaurant serves good, cheap food, pool table. This is a popular, well-organized place.

West coast p646, map p643
Ao Hat Yao
AL-C Long Bay, T077-349057, www.long-bay.com. A classy option with swish, modern a/c rooms and some cheaper fan options all with relative luxuries such as dressing tables and wardrobes, set around a large swimming pool by the sea.
A-E High Life Resort, Moo 8, T077-349114, www.highlifebungalow.com. Various rooms from fan to a/c with jacuzzi and TV. There's a swimming pool and the beach is a 5 min walk away. Attracts a young crowd, possibly overpriced.
B-E Sandy Bay, T077-349119. A good selection of smart spacious a/c and traditional fan bungalows on the beach. All are kept clean and have large verandas with hammocks or varnished wood furniture. This is a popular place with tables and chairs on the sand and the best restaurant on the beach which mainly serves cheap Thai food. Kayaking and island trips offered. Movies shown. Haad Yao Divers attached. Recommended.

Ao Chaophao
AL-B Sunset Cove, Sea & Forest Boutique Resort, 78/11 Moo 8, T077-349211, www.thaisunsetcove.com. All rooms have a/c and are furnished to a very high standard, with comfy duvets on the beds and open bathrooms. The cottages have a separate lounge area and wooden bathtubs. Infinity edge swimming pool and jacuzzi.
B-D Seaflower, T077-349090. Prices vary with distance from the beach. Run by a Canadian-Thai couple, well-laid out wooden bungalows, with high peaked thatched roofs set in a mature, shady garden. Camping expeditions, snorkelling (equipment is free for guests), fishing, cliff diving and caving trips. Restaurant has an interesting menu. Recommended.

C-F Jungle Huts, T077-349088. Offers
2 rows of large and airy huts made of board,
timber and thatch with attached shower
rooms ranging from the cheapest with just
fans to those with a/c. Hammocks on the
large verandas. Restaurant specializes in
cocktails, plus Thai and Western dishes.
Motorbike rental available.

D-E West Coast Bungalow, Moo 8 Had
Chaophao, T08-7898 4220 (mob). Breezy,
light and spacious bungalows on a steep
rise above the sea. Coffee- and tea-making
facilities in the rooms. Both a/c and
fan available.

E-F Haad Chaophao Resort. Bungalows
set in pleasant garden. All have verandas,
attached shower rooms and mosquito nets.
Restaurant with backpacker staples.

Ao Sri Thanu

A-C Chills Bay Resort, T08-9036 7128 (mob),
www.chillresort.com. 9 stylish bungalows
with fan or a/c on the beach facing the
sunset. The more expensive have high-
raftered ceilings with living rooms and loft
bedrooms. Unusual rock swimming pool.

B-F Nice Sea Resort, Sritanu Village,
T077-349177. From the road cross a rickety
wooden bridge. Bamboo fan bungalows,
some with hot water. Basic but clean. There
is also a large brick bungalow with a/c and
TV. Large sandy beach.

C-F Laem Son, T077-349032. Family-run
pretty blue bungalows close to a pine
plantation and set back a bit off the beach.
There's a volleyball net and beach bar. There
are no rocks and the sea is sandy underfoot.
It's one of the nicest places on this stretch
and is popular.

E-F Seaview Rainbow, Moo 8, T077-349
084. Little log cabins next to the beach
with bathrooms inside, mosquito screen
and balcony. Restaurant.

Ao Hin Kong and Ao Nai Wok

B Moo 6, Moo 6 Hinkong Beach, T077-238
520. Absolutely stunning villas with kitchen,
lounge area and bathroom. Finished to an

extremely high standard with a/c, cable TV
and hot water showers. Across the road
from the beach. Restaurant coming soon.
Discount for stays longer than a week.
Highly recommended.

B-E Bounty Bungalows, Ao Plaay Laem,
T077-349105. Offers 15 clean and attractive
board huts with tiled shower rooms and
fans run by friendly staff. Snorkelling gear
available. There's also a restaurant. There
are lovely granite boulders in front.

C-F Phangan Bungalows, Aow Nai Wog,
T077-377191. Different size wood and
bamboo huts at various prices. Raised on
stilts with generous balconies these
bungalows are popular with people
staying long term. Very peaceful.

D-F Cookies, Ao Plaay Laem, T077-377
499, cookies_bungalow@hotmail.com.
30 attractive bamboo bungalows, set in a
green garden with a small splash pool.
Some have shared bathroom, some have
a/c and DVD players. The restaurant has a
raised platform and the beach is secluded
and attractive. Run by the friendly Aom and
An. The watersports club offers windsurfing,
kayaking and laser boats. Recommended.

E Blue Sea Bungalows, 69/4 Moo 4 Ao
Plaay Laem, T08-1844 7736 (mob). This resort
has just 5 sturdy and spacious bungalows
at an angle facing the sea. This is a very quiet
spot attracting a more mature crowd not
interested in partying. All have bathrooms
inside. Restaurant.

E-F Mellow, 69/1 Nai Wok Beach, T077-
238601, www.phanganmellow.com.
Old school wooden bungalows bang
smack on the beach. All have bathrooms
inside, are clean and well maintained.
Super-friendly owner shows movies in
the restaurant. Excellent value.

🍴 Eating

Many visitors eat at their bungalows and
some serve excellent, cheap seafood.
Prices are fairly standard though it's worth

checking to avoid a shock at the end of your stay. There are also increasing numbers of restaurants in virtually every village. Word-of-mouth recommendations are the best guide; new ones open all the time. See each area for details.

Thong Sala and around p643, map p643

Absolute Island, T077-349109. A cliff-top restaurant with gorgeous views and a romantic ambience which serves up great Thai food and seafood.

Big Mango, T077-377300. Thai fusion and barbecue in attractive, plant-strewn indoor and outdoor dining areas. Specialities include alligator and ostrich.

Pizza Chiara, on the town's main road. Authentic pasta and pizza (it is run by an Italian). Spaghetti carbonara is delicious.

Yellow Café, T077-238615. A popular stop, painted yellow and looking out onto the pier. Menu includes full English breakfasts and baked potatoes.

Phantip Food Market, just before the 7/11 on the main road to the pier. Reasonable examples of Thai street food.

Hat Rin p644, map p643

Bamboozle, Hat Rin West, T07-8964941. Open until late. This is run by an Englishman and his Thai wife. Serves Mexican food. There's covered seating or a little garden with tables and umbrellas and a row of terracotta lamps marking the boundaries of the restaurant.

Lazy House, on the road to Hat Rin West. Run by an Englishman and offering full English breakfast and movies all day. Wooden and cosy, it's popular with expats.

Lucky Crab, T077-375124. The original seafood place in Hat Rin, on the main road between east and west. Full of 'unlucky' crabs, since its popularity and extensive menu means they're eaten at a rate of knots. It is usually packed every night but often under-staffed, leading to excruciatingly inefficient service. Punters eat at long tables in a party atmosphere. The soups and salads are also excellent.

Nic's Restaurant & Bar, Moo 5, T08-7007 3769, www.nics-restaurant.com. 1700-late. A welcome stylish addition to the area, serving delicious, but very reasonably priced, tapas, pasta, pizza and Thai food. After beach specials 1800-2000, 50% off listed drinks. DJs from KL play funky house around the time of the Full Moon Parties. Chill out areas and big screen showing major sporting events. Highly recommended.

Outback Bar and Restaurant, T077-375 126. Big TV screens make this a popular place with the sporting crowd. Big cushions and comfy seating add to its pull. Its full-monty breakfast is mighty fine.

The Rock, run by Paradise Bungalows. The Rock has unbeatable views of the beach, and dishes out exquisite seafood, an unusual range of bar snacks including the ever-popular garlic bread and salads, imported organic coffee, super cocktails and higher quality wine than you'll find anywhere else. Relaxing music makes for a welcome break from the booming tunes elsewhere. Recommended.

Nira's Bakery, T077-375109. Open 24 hrs. A bakery selling a gorgeous range of cakes, pastries, brownies and bread. The spinach and feta pastries and spinach muffins are recommended. The nextdoor café (0800-2400) does great coffee, spirulina shakes and breakfasts. Watch *BBC World* out the back or sit roadside on wooden picnic tables and chairs.

Om Ganesh, at Hat Rin pier, T077-375123. An old favourite for Indian food, offers delicious traditional tandoori, curries and thalis. Also the Himalayan Art Gallery next door with art for sale.

East coast p645, map p643

Dolphin Bar & Restaurant, see Sleeping, above. Breakfast and lunch, tapas served in the evenings. Excellent range of international food served at various seating areas from raised platforms to cabanas hidden in the jungle. The ingredients are of the highest quality and the food here is amongst the best on the island. The cocktails are worth a try too. Highly Recomended.

Su's Bakery, Thong Nai Pan Yai, first shop on the left as you enter the village. Fantastic thin-base pizzas are definitely worth the walk from the beach to the village. Very popular with regulars. Fresh coffees, brownies and banana cake are also a big hit. Recommended.

Memory, Thong Nai Pan Yai, opposite Nu Bar. Serves some of the best Thai food on the beach. Very friendly owner, Nat.

North coast p646, map p643

Sheesha, Chao Lok Lum, T077-374161. A funky addition to the north coast catering for this craze that has seized Phangan and Koh Tao. International food, cocktails, dancefloor, sundeck and private outdoor booths for sucking on a variety of fruity tobacco flavours.

West coast p646, map p643

Garden Bistro, Ao Hin Kong. Range of healthy cereals and shakes, as well as fried breakfasts. Intimate garden setting next to the beach. Run by an affable Brit.

Bars and clubs

Hat Rin p644, map p643

At full moon, every shop, bar and restaurant turns itself into a bar selling plastic buckets stuffed with spirits and mixers. The 3 best and loudest clubs on Hat Rin Beach East are **Vinyl Club**, **Zoom Bar** and the **Drop in Club**, www.dropinclub.com, which play upbeat dance music and not just on full moon nights.
Backyard Club, on Hat Rin West. Infamous for its Full Moon after-parties which start at 1100 with the best of the DJs.
Cactus Club, a little further down the beach with a great bar right on the beach, plays a more melodic set than most with hip hop, R'n'B and a bit of rock.
Esco Bar, fabulous position on some rocks overlooking the sea at Hat Rin West between

the **Siam Healing Centre** and the **Phangan Buri Resort**. Open 1200-2400. Reggae seems the order of the day at this great little wooden bar.
Nargile House, close to the **Drop in Bar** on Hat Rin East. Open until late. Smoking the sheesha at tables costs ฿300 at this roadside bar. Alcohol also available.

East coast p645, map p643

In Thong Nai Pan Noi there's the notoriously hip **Flip Flop Pharmacy**, on the beach, then along the road there's the low-level wooden **Jungle Bar**, the more rocking **Rasta Baby**, the Mexican bar and restaurant **Que Pasa** and the **Hideaway Bar**, decorated in bunting.

West coast p646, map p643

The Eagle, Ao Hat Yao, T04-8397143. A good option for a bit of house.
The Pirate's Bar, Ao Chaophao, accessed through the **Seatanu Bungalows**. Hosts the moon set party, 3 days before full moon. The bar in the shape of a ship is set in the tiniest of coves accessed by a wooden bridge that winds around boulders.

Entertainment

Hat Rin p644, map p643
Cabaret
Cabaret is sometimes held at **Coral Bungalows** on Hat Rin West. See flyers for details.

Muay Thai (Thai boxing)
3 stadiums in Thong Sala, 1 in Had Rin and 1 on Tong Nai Pan Noi. Look out for flyers for fight days. Expect to pay around ฿500.

Shopping

Hat Rin p644, map p643
Fashion
Shops selling leather goods, funky fashions and books abound in Hat Rin. **JD Exotic** sells

swish shirts for men and **Napo-po** sells stylish boho fashions, accessories and photographs. **Fusion** offers funkier, contemporary fashions.

Furniture

Beautiful World, T077-238935, www.beauti fulworldthailand.com, on the road to Thong Sala, sells stylish contemporary and antique furniture and interior accessories.

▲ Activities and tours

Koh Phangan *p642, map p643*
Diving

For the trained diver, the west coast offers the best diving with hard coral reefs at depths up to about 20 m. There are also some islets which offer small walls, soft coral and filter corals. Dive trips are also available to further sites such as **Koh Wao Yai** in the north of the Ang Thong Marine National Park or **Hin Bai** (Sail Rock). Here the dives are deeper.
Chaloklum Diving, Chao Lok Lum Village, T077-374025, www.chaloklum-diving.com. One of the longest-standing operations on the island with an excellent reputation. Small group policy guarantees personal attention.
Crystal Dive, Hat Rin T077-375535, www.crystaldive.com. This booking branch of the respected dive resort in Koh Tao is run by **Backpackers Information Centre**.
Lotus Diving, Ao Chao Lok Lum, T077-374097, www.lotusdiving.com. Offers PADI courses and dive trips.
Phangan Divers, based in Hat Rin, near the pier on the west side, Ao Hat Yao, Ao Thong Nai Pan and Koh Ma, T077-375 117, www.phangandivers.com.
Tropical Dive Club, Thong Nai Pan Noi, T077-445081, www.tropicaldiveclub.com.

Fishing and sailing

Castaway Cats, T08-9289 3355 (mob), www.cast awaycats.net. Private charters on the catamaran *Nok Talay*.
Rin Beach Tours, T08-1979 5939 (mob). Day or night fishing on Thai boats.

Gym and Muay Thai (Thai boxing)

Jungle Gym, Hat Rin, T077-375115, www.jungle gym.co.th. Thai boxing courses as well as aerobics, yoga and other training and courses.
Muay Thai Boxing Training, Tong Sala, T08-6953 8253 (mob). Run by a Thai boxing champion there are 2-hr introductory classes or 1-month courses available.

Snorkelling

Coral is to be found off most beaches, except for those on the east coast. Particularly good are those in **Mae Hat** where corals are just a few metres below the surface.

Tour operators and travel agents

Numerous operators run trips around the island to several beaches and waterfalls and the price includes food and drink on the tour.
Backpackers, Hat Rin, T077-375535, www.backpackersthailand.com. An invaluable source of information and the only TAT-registered independent travel agent on the island. Run by Thai-British couple Rashi and Bambi who are experts on accommodation, tickets, health and safety. The agency also organizes lifeguard and full moon volunteer services on Hat Rin beach. Their website contains plenty of reliable advice, articles and updates.
Phangan Adventure, Ao Chao Lok Lum, T077-374142, www.phanganadventure.com. Boat trips, snorkelling, fishing trips, wake-boarding, kayaking trips and rental, and mountain-bike tours and rental.
Reggae Magic Boat Trip, Reggae Magic Bar, Hat Rin East, T08-1606 8159 (mob). Long-tailed boat trips to the highlights of the island with post-trip party and dinner.
Thong Sala Centre, 44/13 Thong Sala Pier, T077-238984, jamareei@hotmail.com. Run by twin sisters for the last 25 years. Can organize boat, train, plane tickets and offer sound travel advice. Trustworthy.

Paintball

Paintball Warfare T077-377300, paintball
warfare@hotmail.com. A huge paintball
battlefield in Thong Sala, open daily
1000-1800, ฿300 for a full day.

Therapies

Chakra, Hat Rin, off the main drag leading
up from the pier, T077-375401, www.chakra
yoga.com. Open until 2400. Run by a real
master, Yan, and his English wife Ella.
Whether you're looking for simple relaxation,
or you've a specific complaint that needs
working on, the staff here dish out any
number of good traditional body, face and
foot Thai massages, reiki, reflexology and
acupressure treatments. For those looking
to learn the art themselves, they also run
certificated courses: traditional Thai massage
(30 hrs), reiki, levels 1-4; oil massage
(30 hrs), foot and head massage (15 hrs),
and massage therapy course – similar to
acupuncture, but with thumbs instead
of needles (30 hrs).

Monte Vista Retreat Centre, Thong Sala
T077-238951, www.montevistathailand.com.
The latest addition to the island's holistic
health scene and already winning rave reviews.
Daily yoga and meditation, cleansing and
fasting courses, in-house training for reiki,
palm and psychic readings, herbal facials
and several types of massage. Basic
accommodation also available.

The Sanctuary, Hat Yuan, T08-1271 3614
(mob), www.thesanctuary-kpg.com. See
Hat Thien, Sleeping, page 649.

Wat Pho Herbal Sauna, close to Ban
Tai beach on the southwest coast. This
traditional herbal sauna is run on donations
and uses traditional methods and ingredients.

The Yoga Retreat, Hat Salad, T077-374
310, www.yogaretreat-kohphangan.com.
A family business run by qualified instructors
offering courses in yoga, pilates, Alexander
technique and chakra healing in the peaceful jungle.

☉ Transport

Koh Phangan *p642, map p643*
Boat
Boats to Hat Rin run from both Thong Sala
and Ban Khai.

Long-tailed boats take passengers from
Hat Rin, Ao Thong Nai Pan, Ao Hat Yao and
Ao Hat Kuat to Thong Sala and Ban Khai
piers for somewhat inflated prices. Most
boats dock at the pier at Thong Sala,
although there's a ferry, the *Haad Rin
Queen*, T077-375113, from **Big Buddha
pier** on **Samui**, 50 mins, 1030, 1300, 1600
and 1830 going straight to Hat Rin (฿150).
It returns at 0930, 1140, 1430, 1730.

From **Thong Sala** to Koh Samui, with
Songsern, T077-377704, to Nathon pier,
0700, 1230, ฿200. **Mae Nam beach** with
Lomprayah, T077-238411, 1100, 1600,
฿250. **Big Buddha pier** with Seatran,
T077-238679, 1100, 1630, ฿250.

Speed Boat Line to **Bophut**, **Koh Samui**,
0600, 0930, 1300, 1530, 20 mins. To **Koh
Tao** from Thong Sala with Seatran, 0830,
1400, 1½ hrs, ฿350; Lomprayah, 0830, 1300,
1 hr 20 mins, ฿350; Songsern, 1230, ฿250.

To Surat Thani from Thong Sala with
Songsern, 1230, ฿300; Raja Ferry, 0700,
1100, 1300, 1700, 2½ hrs, ฿310. Prices
include bus ticket to bus and train stations.
The night boat leaves Koh Phangan for
Surat Thani at 2200 (although times can
vary, so it's worth checking in good time),
6 hrs, ฿300.

To **Chumphon** with Lomprayah at 0830,
3 hrs 15 mins, and 1230, 3 hrs 40 mins, ฿900.

Motorcycle hire

Available in Thong Sala and from the more
popular beaches. Some guesthouses also
hire out motorbikes, from ฿200 per day.

Train

The **State Railways of Thailand** runs a train/
bus/ferry service between Koh Phangan and
Bangkok's Hualamphong Station.

❶ Directory

Koh Phangan *p642, map p643*

Banks There are banks with ATMs on the main road in Thong Sala. International money transfer, **Moneygram** is available at the **Siam Bank**. There are many ATMs in Hat Rin and plenty of foreign exchange outlets. **Medical Services** Koh Phangan Hospital, about 2.5 km north of Thong Sala, offers 24-hr emergency services. Facilities are better in Samui or Bangkok.

Bandon International Hospital, in Hat Rin, T077-375471, is a 24-hr private clinic with English-speaking staff. **Internet** There are now plenty of internet cafés, all vying for business and charging ฿2 per min. **Police** about 2 km north of Thong Sala, T077-377114; **Tourist Police**, T077-421281. **Post office** Hat Rin, close to pier, Mon-Fri 0830-1640, Sat 0900-1200. **Telephone** Virtually every agency and internet café offer IDD telephones, around ฿25 per min for international calls.

Koh Tao

→ Colour map 4, B3.
Koh Tao, the smallest of the three famous islands in the Gulf of Thailand, is a big dive and snorkelling centre with plenty of shallow coral beds and tropical fish. The waters – especially in the south and east – are stunning, a marbling of turquoise blue, sapphire, emerald and seaweed green. For non-divers this small island offers a surprisingly high number of exceptionally well-designed, independent upmarket resorts, with the added bonus of quiet beach life by day and fairly sophisticated nightlife due to the underwater preferences of the majority of visitors. The name Koh Tao, translated as 'turtle island', relates to the shape of the island. ▶ For listings, see pages 662-670.

Ins and outs

Getting there
Several companies operate regular express boats from Chumphon, Surat Thani, Koh Samui and Koh Phangan as well as a slow, night ferry direct from Surat Thani. Songserm, www.songserm-expressboat.com, sells a combination ticket to and from Bangkok to Koh Tao, ฿550. Leave Bangkok at 1800 and arrive in Chumphon at 0200. Passengers then sleep on the office floor before getting the 0700 boat to Koh Tao. The return journey leaves Chumphon at 2030 to Bangkok. The rail connection from Bangkok to Koh Tao leaves Bangkok at 2250 and arrives in Chumphon at 0552. Ticket price depends on class.

Getting around
There is just one surfaced road on Koh Tao, which runs from the north end of Sai Ri to Chalok Ban Kao, passing through Ban Mae Hat. Motorbike taxis and pick-ups are the main form of local transport. These can be found just north of the dock next to the exchange booth. They operate from dawn to 2300; rates tend to double after dark. Motorbikes, jeeps and bicycles are available for hire. Long-tailed boats can be chartered to reach more remote beaches and coves, either by the trip, hour or day. ▶ *See Transport, page 669, for further information.*

Tourist information
The **TAT** office on Koh Samui, see page 619, is responsible for Koh Tao but there is no official office on the island. The website www.kohtao.com, provides lots of information or see the free quarterly *Koh Tao Info* magazine, www.kohtaoinfo.tv.

Avoid bringing any plastic bottles or tin cans to the island as these are difficult to dispose of. Some environmentalists advise people to drink cans rather than bottles of beer as few businesses find it economically viable to recycle bottles and simply dump them. In addition, due to reduced rainfall in recent years, water is now a great problem on the island, and much of it is imported from the mainland. Visitors should use it sparingly.

Background

The accessibility of interesting marine life at depths available to beginners, the fairly gentle currents and the relatively low costs all contribute to making Koh Tao a particularly good place to learn to dive. The presence of giant manta rays and whalesharks (plankton feeders which can reach 6 m) means that more experienced divers will also find something of interest here. With these attractions in its favour, Koh Tao's reputation as a good, low-cost dive centre has grown rapidly, and in the space of just 10 years the island has made the transition from backwater to mainstream destination. See Diving, page 668. Improved transport links with the mainland have also made the island more accessible to the short-stay tourist, and so it is no surprise that the former economic mainstay of coconuts has now been eclipsed by the still-expanding tourist trade. Already, the number of rooms for tourists outnumbers the Thai residents on the island. Sensibly, though, as on Koh Samui, there are height restrictions on new buildings and this, in conjunction with the poor infrastructure, means the 'palm tree horizon' has not yet been blotted by multi-storey monstrosities. However, there do seem to be a worrying number of tall hotels being built. While most people come here for the swimming, snorkelling and diving – as well as beach life – the fact that most paths are not vehicle-friendly makes the island walker-friendly and there are some good trails to explore. Land-based wildlife includes monitor lizards, fruit bats and various non-venomous snakes. If planning to go on walks it is worth purchasing V Honsombud's *Guide Map of Koh Phangan & Koh Tao*.

Around the island ⬤🄋🄊 » pp662-670.

Ban Mae Hat and the west coast
The harbour is at the island's main village of Ban Mae Hat. On both sides of the harbour there are small beaches with a few resorts. These areas have easy access to the town. There are numerous shops from fashion boutiques to bookstores and supermarkets and some of the best restaurants as well as a burgeoning nightlife, post office, money exchanges, dive shops, tour operators, transport and foodstalls.

To the north of Ban Mae Hat on the west coast, is the white-sand curved beach of **Hat Sai Ri**. Stretching to around 2 km, it is the longest beach on the island, the sweep of sand is only interrupted by the occasional large boulder. It has the widest range of accommodation, and many restaurants, shops, dive centres and bars. Although it is a bustling beach with some great bars, the debris – plastic bottles, rotting wood and the like – left by the retreating tide is really unsightly.

North coast
The little cove of **Ao Mamuang** is only accessible by boat so it remains quiet and unfrequented. It is a great place for solitude and there is some good snorkelling.

Koh Tao

Koh Nang Yuan

Ao Mamuang (Mango Bay)

Ao Kluai Tuen

Khao Hat Sai Re

To Chumphon

Ao Hin Wong

Hat Sai Ri

Ao Mao

Laem Thian

Ban Mae Hat

Jansom Bay

Hat Sai Nuan

Ao Ta Not

To Thong Sala (Koh Phangan) & Koh Samui

Lang Khaai Bay

Ao Chun Chua

Ao Leuk

Ao Chalok Ban Kao

Ao Thian Ok

Hat Sai Daeng

Hat Taa Toh Yai

Laem Tato

N

| 1 km |
| 1 mile |

Sleeping
Beach Side Resort **1**
Charm Churee Villa & Spa **2**
Diamond Resort **5**
New Heaven **7**

OK II Bungalows **8**
Pahnun View Bungalows **6**
Sai Thong Resort & Spa **3**
Siam Cookies **3**
Snorkelling Point Resort **6**
View Rock Resort **4**

Off the northwest coast of Koh Tao is **Koh Nang Yuan**. Once a detention centre for political prisoners, this privately owned island consists of three peaks and three connecting sandbars, making it a mini-archipelago. It's surrounded by crystal-clear water and some wonderful coral. **Lomprayah** runs boats to the island at 1030, 1500 and 1800, returning at 0830, 1330 and 1630.

East coast

Ao Hin Wong is a peaceful bay with fantastic views but no beach. However, you can swim off the rocks and boulders and there is some great snorkelling – turtles have been spotted here. The accommodation consists of simple huts tumbling down the steep hillsides.

South of Ao Hin Wong, the bay of **Ao Mao** has just one resort and some great snorkelling, particularly at the **Laem Thian** pinnacle. It is among the more remote and secluded places to stay on Koh Tao.

Continuing south, the bay of **Ao Ta Not** is served by a poor road but vehicles brave the conditions to ferry guests. This is one of the more remote bays and it has a good beach. Although it is not as pretty as Hin Wong, it is wider, has boulders, and more facilities, more expensive accommodation, restaurants, watersports and scuba-diving (see page 668).

Lang Khaai Bay is littered with dozens of boulders which are reached from a steep slope. The bay is good for snorkelling but there is only a tiny slither of beach.

The beach at **Ao Leuk** shelves more steeply than most of the others around Koh Tao and so is good for swimming and has some of the best snorkelling on the island. This is a quiet beach in spite of visiting groups.

South coast

Next to Ao Chalok Ban Kao, **Ao Thian Ok**, also known as Shark Bay, is a beautiful, privately owned bay with the **Jamahkiri Spa and Resort** set on one hillside. The sea is a stunning mix of blues and greens while the attractive beach is lined with a strip of coconut palms. The bay is known for the black-tip reef sharks that congregate here.

The area of **Taa Toh** 'lagoon' is on the south coast and consists of three beaches, the largest of which is **Hat Taa Toh Yai**. There is good snorkelling on the far side of the lagoon from Hat Taa Toh Yai with reef sharks and more. There is easy access from here to Chalok Ban Kao.

Ao Chalok Ban Kao is a gently shelving beach, enclosed within a horseshoe bay on the south coast capped with weirdly shaped giant boulders. It has a good range of accommodation, restaurants and nightlife. This large bay also has the highest concentration of diving resorts.

Hat Sai Nuan is a quiet, isolated bay, only accessible by long-tailed boat or by a pleasant 30-minute walk around the hilly headland. There are just a handful of places to stay and a relaxed atmosphere. It is arguably the best spot on the island.

For Sleeping and Eating price codes and other relevant information, see pages 44-49.

◉ Sleeping

The densest areas of accommodation are **Hat Sai Ri** and **Ao Chalok Ban Kao**. These offer restaurants, bars and easy access to the dive schools. If you are looking for a greater sense of remoteness, the other bays are more secluded. This has largely been due to the poor roads which makes them difficult to reach without a trek or taxi boat.

Despite the rapid rate of bungalow construction it remains difficult for non-divers to find empty, cheap accommodation unassisted during the high season. If you don't want to risk having to hike around in search of free rooms, the simplest option is to follow a tout from the pier. You can always move out the following day, but book the next place in advance.

Alternatively, make your way straight to one of the more remote bays where places are often less booked out. If diving, you should head straight for the dive shops where they will find you a place to stay in affiliated accommodation – often at a subsidized rate on the days when you are diving.

The other unusual point about accommodation in Koh Tao is the early checkout times. These reflect the need to free up rooms for those arriving on the early boats from the mainland. Most guesthouses have restaurants attached but guests have sometimes been evicted from their bungalows if they have not been spending enough in the restaurant so it is worth enquiring if there is a minimum expenditure before checking in.

Ban Mae Hat and the west
coast *p660, map p660*
Ban Mae Hat
LL-AL Sensi Paradise, T077-456244, www.sensiparadise.com. A great range of rooms. At the top of the price range the buildings are sensitively designed wooden affairs with traditional Thai architectural features and are incredibly romantic. The garden is also richly planted and the small bay behind the resort is truly idyllic. The pretty beach in front is tiny with several boulders.
LL-A Charm Churee Villa and Spa, Jansom Bay, T077-456393, www.charm chureevilla.com. The island's most stylishly upmarket resort, in an exquisite cove, just south of Mae Hat. Bungalows on stilts are perched on the hillside, amongst coconut trees, with wonderful sea views from the balconies. Seafood restaurant, beach bar and spa. Tranquillity guaranteed. Recommended.
AL-C Koh Tao Royal Resort, T077-456156. Smart, well-maintained wood and bamboo bungalows. Cheaper rooms climb the hill behind the beach. Lively restaurant in a great location. It has a reasonable secluded beach.
A-B Beach Club, T077-456222, www.kohtao beachclub.com. Attractive, airy rooms with high bamboo-lined ceilings, some with a/c. Discounts for divers available.
A-B Beach Side Resort, 24/5 Baan Mae Haad, T077-456565. Immaculate, newly built, large concrete and teak bungalows with hot water showers can either be a/c or fan. There are 2 rooms right on the beach, for the others it's a 30-sec walk past the restaurant. Friendly owners. Discount for stays of 3 days or more.
A-D Crystal Dive Resort, just left of the pier on the beach, T077-456106, www.crystal dive.com. One of the longest-standing dive centres on the island and awarded the prestigious PADI Gold Palm 5 star IDC Resort qualification for its excellent facilities. A range of rooms and bungalows are available with good rates for divers. Pool, restaurant, bar with large screen movies shown, yoga school attached.

Hat Sai Ri
L-AL Koh Tao Cabana, T077-456505, www.kohtaocabana.com. 33 villas built into

the headland at the northern end of the beach including 10 attractively designed white circular villas – which have a Mediterranean feel – climbing up the hillside. Bathrooms are open-air and built into rock faces. There are pleasant gardens with attractive wooden sun loungers.

L-A Koh Tao Coral Grand Resort, T077-456 431, www.kohtaocoral.com. Large, dusty pink cabins with wooden floors, TVs, fridges, coffee-making facilities and shower rooms dot the landscape of this quiet resort popular with couples and families. The pool is close to the beach with sun loungers and the restaurant is on the beach. The sea is beautiful at this northern end of the beach. Dive centre attached, www.coralgrand divers.com. Recommended.

L-A Thipwimarn Resort, T077-456409, www.thipwimarnresort.com. Beyond the northern end of the beach on the northwest headland, this beautiful, relatively new place has 11 bungalows perched on the rocks. Its infinity pool enjoys spectacular views. The deservedly popular restaurant overlooks Sai Ri Bay and the sea.

AL-D Seashell Resort, T077-456299, www.kohtaoseashell.com. Attractive wood and bamboo huts with spacious verandas in well-manicured grounds. Some a/c rooms and family bungalows available. Divers get cheaper rates. Roasted rice with shrimp and pineapple is among the best dishes at the restaurant. Movies shown. Massage available and courses in massage too. PADI dive centre attached, T077-456300, seashell divers@hotmail.com.

AL-E Ban's Diving Resort, T077-456466, www.amazingkohtao.com. This resort offers everything from gorgeous a/c luxury rooms with silk furnishings and large balconies to plain fan rooms around the pool for divers. Partial views of the sea. As well as diving, wake-boarding, waterskiing and kayaking is offered, ฿200 per hr. Recommended.

AL-E Bow Thong Beach, T077-456351. Offers 30 well-spaced white-board bungalows with an attractive restaurant

(0500-1900), private and quieter than most. Pleasant and good value.

A-D Tommy's Dive Resort, T077-456039. Attractive large a/c rooms with spacious bathrooms in well-furnished concrete bungalows close to the beach, or smaller rooms above the office with or without a/c. All rooms are clean and roomy, homely family bungalows are also available.

A-E Sai Ree Huts, T077-456000, saireeh hutresort@hotmail.com. Bamboo weave and timber bungalows with hammocks and a swing on the beach. A/c and fan rooms available.

B-E AC Resort, T077-456197, www.ac resort.com. Well-maintained bungalows in a pleasing resort on the 'wrong' side of the road with mosquito screens on the windows and nets over the beds. Tiled shower rooms, fan and verandas. The resort has a nice pool. **Phoenix Divers**, www.phoenix-divers.com, is attached. Divers using the school get cheaper accommodation.

B-E AC Two Resort, T077-456195. On the landward side of the road, this small, older resort has large rooms with small bath rooms, fan and veranda. They are a little dark but set in an appealing ramshackle garden. The excellent Thai food restaurant overlooks the sea and holds popular parties. There is also a supermarket.

B-E SB Cabana, opposite Scuba Junction, T077-456005. Typical wooden bungalows in an excellent location very near to the beach. Some fan, some a/c, all with bathroom. Managed by a cantankerous old woman.

B-F DD Hut Bungalows, Moo 2, T077-456 077, deedee_hut@hotmail.com. All the bungalows have bathrooms, which makes the cheapest ones a good deal. A/c rooms are also available. Relaxed atmosphere. Property leads down to the sea, but there isn't a beach here. Restaurant.

B-F Here & Now, Sai Ri Beach, T077-456730, www.hereandnow.be. 12 simple rooms with a spiritual bent, blocked off from the main route to the water by ropes strung across the path. Fairly wild surrounds. Shared and private showers. This is the last establishment on the northwest headland of the island, north of Sai Ri beach. You can swim off the rocks into the sea. The restaurant has a great view of Nang Yuan Island, which apparently inspired the novel *The Beach*.

B-F Sairee Cottage, T077-456374, nitsairee@hotmail.com. A well-established resort with the more expensive rooms on the beach in a grassy compound with the remainder across the road. Relaxed and friendly. The restaurant serves reasonably priced food and cocktails.

C-E In Touch Resort, T077-456514. Very funky resort with an equally cool beachfront restaurant. Brightly coloured individual huts have lots of character. Arranged in a garden opposite the beach, the fan option are the best designed. The cheapest huts are wooden bungalows with open-air bathrooms. Recommended.

C-E View Cliff, T077-456353, viewclifftao@hotmail.com. A mixture of concrete, wood and bamboo huts mostly with twin beds, some a/c, all clean.

C-F Blue Wind Bakery and Resort, T077-456116, bluewind_wa@yahoo.com. A small, friendly and attractive place with excellent value fan and a/c rooms and a charming beach restaurant. Pretty wood bungalows nestled in a beautiful mature garden. Their bakery serves pastries, pasta and ice cream. Daily yoga classes. Recommended.

C-F Queen Resort, T077-456002, moo_mmm@hotmail.com. Rooms with fan, a/c and rooms with shared bathroom available. Some blocks look right out over the sea. ฿20 to use the shower for non-guests. Friendly management.

C-F Sun Sea, on the northwest headland, north of Sai Ri Beach. T08-9037 4195 (mob). 10 bungalows with fans and shower rooms amid boulder-strewn land that attracts dozens of butterflies. Rooms are also available to rent by the month. Most rooms have great views out to sea. The place needs a tidy up. There is no restaurant or access to the beach.

E-F Sun Lord, T077-456139. Only accessible along an unconvincing track through the jungle on the northwest headland of the island, north of Sai Ri Beach with fantastic views. The cheapest rooms, made of bamboo and without showers, are perched precariously on huge granite boulders. Beneath them there is good coral, perfect for snorkelling.

North coast *p660, map p660*
LL-B Nangyuan Island Dive Resort, Koh Nang Yuan, T077-456088, www.nangyuan.com. The only bungalow complex on this beautiful trio of islands has a/c rooms. PADI dive courses and diving trips arranged. Facilities and atmosphere are excellent but it's a little overpriced. Environmental awareness is encouraged. Guests receive a free transfer to Koh Samui.

A-C Mango Bay Grand Resort, Ao Mamuang, T077-456097, www.kohtaomangobay.com. 15 bungalows, various prices, on stilts overlooking the bay in this secluded spot. This bay is popular for snorkelling.

East coast *p661, map p660*
Ao Hin Wong
B-F View Rock Resort, T077-456548. Popular with Germans, this isolated resort clings to a steep hill as it tumbles to the rocky shore. The more expensive of the 14 rooms have a/c and 2 beds, while the cheapest have shared toilets. Taxi boats from Ban Mae Hat cost ฿50, one way.

D-F Hin Wong Bungalows, T077-456006. The newer wooden huts with verandas overlooking the sea are pretty. Plenty of windows to let in the sea breeze, reasonably priced restaurant, snorkelling equipment and canoes for hire. Discounts available after 3 nights. Electricity available 1800-0600. Mol, the friendly owner, used to have a gallery in town and can paint to order.

E Green Tree Resort, T077-456742. White bungalows at a budget price and a decent restaurant set in jungle. Snorkelling equipment available for free. Welcoming owners.

Laem Thian

C-E Laem Thian, T077-456477, ping pong_laemthian@hotmail.com. Range of budget rooms and bungalows from rustic to modern hotel all with attached showers and fans and set in an attractive secluded bay. Free pick-up service from ferry. Electricity 1800-0700.

Ao Ta Not

A-E Tanote Family Bay Dive Resort, T077-456757. At the northern end of the bay, spread out amid the rocks, this resort offers cheap, dark fan rooms or more expensive brighter rooms with balconies. All have tables and chairs. No special rates for divers, www.calypso-diving-kohtao.de. Taxi to main island pier twice a day. Restaurant open 0700-2200.

C-E Diamond Resort, 40/7 Aow Tanote, T077-456591. The cheaper rooms are excellent value; they have cold water showers but are very comfortable and spacious with plenty of windows. Homely feel. Only fan available. Next to a very quiet beach. Restaurant, with others within walking distance. Recommended.

C-F Poseidon, T077-456735, poseidon kohtao@hotmail.com. Cheaper rooms are small, stuffy and dark but with balconies and some are set right back from the beach. It's a small set up with only 14 bungalows and a restaurant, see Eating, below. A taxi leaves the resort daily at 1300 for the island pier.

E-F Mountain Reef Resort, T077-456697/9. At the southern end of the bay. A family-run resort which will take guests out fishing for their dinner. Larger rooms are more expensive – go for the ones overlooking the beach which get great sunrise views. There's a daily taxi to the island pier. Friendly and welcoming staff.

Lang Khaai Bay

E Snorkelling Point Resort, next to Pahnun View, T077-456264. Brand new wooden bungalows with impressive views of the bay. Super comfy beds and a hammock on the balcony. 24-hr electricity. Restaurant. Owner speaks a very good level of English.

F Pahnun View Bungalows, Aow Lang Khaay, T077-456541, pahnun_kohtao@ hotmail.com. Bamboo huts on the cliff-side with fan, mosquito net and bathroom. Painted light blue inside, making them bright and cool. Sweeping views from the balcony and restaurant. There's no beach.

Ao Leuk

The only 2 establishments on this beach are small and simple and neither have fans in the rooms.

B-E Aow Leuk Bungalows, T077-456 692. Offers 13 bungalows, with the more expensive ones being closer to the beach. Restaurant, snorkel hire and taxi service available.

D-F Nice Moon Bungalows, T077-456737, nicemoon43@hotmail.com. About 200 m south of the beach on cliffs overlooking the bay. Free snorkelling equipment, friendly and informative. Restaurant serves delicious Thai food. Recommended.

South coast p661, map p660
Ao Thian Ok

LL-L Jamahkiri Spa & Resort, T077-456 400, www.jamahkiri.com. A well-designed and exceptionally private resort which incorporates large boulders into the fabric of the buildings. The handful of boutique rooms with their exquisite interiors, floor to ceiling windows and wide balconies all sit on concrete stilts looking out to sea. Private sun decks lead straight into Shark Bay. The restaurant enjoys an incredible view over the bay. The spa's fresh aloe vera wraps are recommended for sunburn. Free pick-up for the resort, restaurant and spa. There's car, kayak and snorkel hire. See also Therapies, page 669.

AL-C New Heaven, next to OK II, T077-456462, www.newheavenkohtao.com. Very nicely furnished dark teak bungalows with tropical-looking bathrooms. Restaurant has sweeping views of the bay. The newer, more expensive bungalows have a/c. From this cliff-side setting, the sea, which is good for snorkelling, is a short walk away.

D OK II Bungalows, 44/1 Aow Taa Choa, T077-456506. Wooden fan bungalows nestled on the cliff leading down to the water's edge. The ones at the front command an interrupted view of the sea.

D-E Rocky Resort, T077-456035. It's all about the stunning location in this beautiful bay. Bungalows, though a little weathered, are built around the boulders and many have balconies over the sea with tables and chairs. Basic, but well spaced out and friendly with reasonably priced food.

Ao Chalok Ban Kao

B-E- Bhora Bhora, T077-456044, www.bhorabhora.com. 21 spacious rooms in wood or concrete with nice bamboo beds and mosquito screens on the windows. The resort takes pride in its relaxed, traveller-style atmosphere and unique rooms, some including sections of massive granite boulders as part of the walls and the wooden rooms having bathroom walls made of glass bottles set in concrete. Restaurant 1800-2400. Rates include breakfast. Recommended.

C-D View Point Resort, T077-456444, www.viewpoint.com. The large bamboo and thatch rooms in Balinese-style are clean, attractive and quiet, with gorgeous views. The cheapest have shared showers. Good bargains for divers. Fairly secluded. Recommended.

E Sunshine 2, T077-456154. Offers 62 attractive blue-roofed wooden bungalows lined with bamboo weave with tiled bathrooms. Set a little back from the beach in nicely manicured gardens. The more expensive ones have a/c. Friendly restaurant.

Hat Sai Nuan

A-G Sai Thong Resort and Spa, T077-456476. A rather special and secluded spot, well worth taking the trip off the beaten track for. Accommodation ranges from

cheap hillside huts with shared bathrooms to slightly overpriced but romantic beach-front bungalows. The simple outdoor spa has a distinctly bohemian appeal, set among jungle and offering relaxation treatments in a small saltwater pool. Relaxed restaurant with cushions, hammocks, a garden and small private beach. Recommended.

B-E Siam Cookies, T077-456301. Attractive bamboo huts. The cheaper rooms share clean and well-maintained shower rooms.

C-F Tao Thong Villa, T077-456078. On the headland so seaviews on both sides. Simple wood and bamboo huts with large verandas, well placed to make the most of sea breezes. Excellent location. Cheapest rooms have shared bathroom.

🍴 Eating

Ban Mae Hat and the west coast *p660, map p660*
Ban Mae Hat

🍴🍴 **Café del Sol**, Mae Hat Sq, T077-456578. Open 0800-2300. Great place for breakfast. It also serves sandwiches, bruschetta and coffee, and for dinner the French/Italian chef prepares salmon or steak and other international cuisine.

🍴🍴 **El Gringo**, Pier Rd, T077-456323. Open 0800-2300. The full Mexican works with fajitas, nachos, steaks and burgers served on tables overlooking the main road. Takeaways and deliveries possible.

🍴🍴 **Farango Pizzeria**, Pier Rd, T077-456205. Open 1200-1500, 1800-2200. Italian restaurant which serves excellent pizzas and salads and has a delivery and takeaway service.

🍴 **Puk's Thai Kitchen**, Mae Hat Sq, T077-456685. Open 0800-late. Serves Thai but also does a full English breakfast.

Hat Sai Ri

🍴🍴🍴 **Papa's Tapas**, opposite Siam Scuba Dive Center, Sai Ri village, T077-456298. Open 1900-late. A sophisticated addition to the island and Thailand's only absinthe bar.

Sample wonderfully concocted Asian fusion tapas with attention to detail – the tandoori prawn and the panacotta are delicious. Indulge in the alcoholic creations of Jesper, the mixologist, who was once asked to shake up Absolut Vodka's cocktail list. For a bittersweet killer try the chilli-lemongrass (lemongrass, chilli, coconut liqueur, vodka and gin). Retire to the sheesha lounge or smoke one at your table. A great gourmet extravaganza. Recommended.

Thipwimarn Restaurant, on the north-west headland, T077-456409. Open 0700-2200. This has become one of the more popular spots for fashionable dining due to the stunning views over Sai Ri bay and excellent Thai food and seafood. Free pick-up.

Noori India, on the hill between Mae Had and Sai Ri, T08-7892 9970 (mob). Taking over Shalimar restaurant's crown as the Indian restaurant of choice in Sai Ri, this thatched restaurant serves up a magnificent array of delicious dishes including vegetarian specials and great lunch deals. Delivery available.

White Elephant, main road, Sai Ri Village, T08-9292 8249 (mob). A sweet restaurant in a little garden with a pond serving up delicious seafood and succulent duck dishes.

Blue Wind Bakery, towards the northern end of the beach, T077-456116. Specializes in breads and desserts and serves reasonable sandwiches. Also offers fresh pasta including speciality fillings.

Intouch Restaurant and Bar, T077-456 514. Breakfasts (including porridge), burgers, sandwiches, soups, salads and noodles form part of a vast menu at this place which has decking on the beach. Relax in a hammock, play pool or eat looking over the sea.

Suthep Restaurant, centre of the beach. Thai food, lasagne, fish cakes, fish pie, burgers, great mashed potato, toad in the hole and Marmite sandwiches. The Bailey's cheesecake is an indulgence. Cushion seating. Popular with long-term residents. Good value. Stops serving at 2200.

Coffee Boat, on the main road just before the main drag down to the beach in Sai Ri

village, T077-456178. A cheap and cheerful authentic Thai diner and bakery. Ample proportions of tasty, hot Thai food. Cakes made to order.

Pon Bakery, close to Sai Ree Cottage, T077-456655. Rye, granary and sour-dough bread sold.

East coast *p661, map p660*
Ao Ta Not
Poseidon, T077-456735. Open 0730-2200. A popular restaurant serving fried fish, a good range of vegetarian dishes and unusual milk-shakes – including cookie vanilla flavour and prune lassies.

Mountain Reef, T077-456697/9. Breakfasts of hash browns and peanut butter bagels.

South coast *p661, map p660*
Ao Chalok Ban Kao
New Heaven, rather a climb, at the top of the hill, T077-456462. Evenings only. A bit pricey but good food and fantastic views over the gorgeous Thian Og Bay.

Sunshine Dive School. Has a BBQ evening buffet every night with baked potatoes, garlic bread, calamari, kebabs, salad and some rice dishes.

Taraporn Bar & Restaurant, across the slatted walkway at the west of the beach. Seating on hammocks, cushions and mats on the floor. The restaurant itself is on stilts above the sea. A great venue.

Viewpoint Restaurant, beyond the Bubble Dive Resort at the eastern end of the beach, T077-456777. Open 0700-2200. Wide menu of Thai and some Western food that is filling and tasty served in this laid-back restaurant. Also perched above the sea it enjoys great views of the horseshoe-shaped Chalok Ban Kao Bay.

Bars and clubs

Koh Tao, once a quiet neighbour of Koh Phangan, is now well provided with night spots. The best way to discover what is happening is to look out for flyers and advertisements in shop windows.

Ban Mae Hat and the west
coast *p660, map p660*
Ban Mae Hat
Dragon Bar, Pier Rd. Wooden tables spill onto the street from this relatively new bar playing different music every night: indie, 1980s, hip hop, jazz and alternative rock. Look out for flyers.

Safety Stop Pub, Mae Hat Sq, close to the pier. Popular with tourists and locals, with a late night disco on Sat nights and sports coverage throughout the week.

Whitening, on the road to the Sensi Paradise Resort. The staple diver's after-hours spot with a pleasant bar on the beach and decent menu. Fri night parties.

Hat Sai Ri
Choppers, Sai Ri Village, T077-456641. Open 0800-late. A popular large, Western-style pub which shows sport. It pastes timetables for all events outside the pub. Friendly staff.

Dry Bar. A popular place amongst the trees on the beach decked out with Chinese lanterns, fairy lights and candles in the sand.

Lotus Beach Bar, close to Papa's Tapas. This is where it's at on Mon nights. Fancy dress parties are popular. Free drinks and buckets for punters. Loud tunes until the early hours and flame throwers until the fires completely die.

Pure, south Sai Ri beach. The hippest place in town stylishly scattered with big red bean bags. Open every night until 0200 but watch out for the popular party nights.

South coast *p661, map p660*
Ao Chalok Ban Kao
Babaloo Excellent bar set in the rocks and decorated with sculptures, open from 2100. Party night is Mon.

▲ Activities and tours

Koh Tao *p661, map p660*
Diving
Diving is popular year round here. It is said to be the cheapest place in Thailand to learn to dive, and the shallow waters and plenty of underwater life, make it an easy and interesting place to do so. There's a **recompression chamber** in Ban Mae Hat (Badalveda, opposite the main petrol station on the island, north up the main road and turn right, T077-456664, vedainfo@badalveda.com).

Dive schools have an arrangement where they charge roughly the same for an **Open Water** course (฿9000). Fixed prices also apply to other courses: ฿8500 for **Advanced**, and ฿9500 for rescue. What varies are the sizes of the groups and the additional perks such as a free dive or free/subsidized accommodation. A discover scuba dive is around ฿3000, and a fun-dive for qualified divers is around ฿1800, although the more dives you do the cheaper each dive becomes. All schools accept credit cards. If you are considering diving but want to watch the divers in action before making the investment, many of the dive schools are prepared to take you out to dive sites with their groups. You only pay for the snorkelling equipment.

Asia Divers, Ban Mae Hat, T077-456054, www.asia-divers.com.

Ban's, Hat Sai Ri, T077-456466, www.amazingkohtao.com.

Big Blue, Ban Mae Hat, T077-456050, or Hat Sai Ri, T077-456179, www.bigbluediving.com.

Big Bubble, Chalok Ban Kao, T077-456669, www.tauchen-diving.de.

Black Tip Diving and Watersports, at Ban Mae Hat, T077-456204, and at Ao Ta Not, T077-456488, blacktipdiving@yahoo.com.

Buddha View Dive Resort, Chalok Ban Kao, T077-456074, www.buddhaview-diving.com.

Calypso Diving, Ao Ta Not, T077-456745, eugentao@yahoo.de.

Crystal Dive Resort, Ban Mae Hat and Sai Ri, T077-456107, www.crystaldive.com.

Easy Divers, Ban Mae Hat, T077-456010, www.thaidive.com.

Kho Tao Divers, Hat Sai Ri, T08-6069 9244 (mob), kohtaodivers@hotmail.com.

Planet Scuba, Ban Mae Hat, T077-456110, www.planet-scuba.net.

Scuba Junction, Sai Ri Beach, T077-456164, www.scuba-junction.com.

Siam Scuba Dive Center, Sai Ri village, T077-456628, www.scubadive.com.

Muay Thai (Thai boxing)
Sai Ri Stadium, near Asia Divers. ฿500. Look out for flyers for dates.

Snorkelling kayaking and surfing
Many of the guesthouses hire out their own equipment, but this can be of low quality and dirty. The most reliable gear is that hired from the dive shops. You generally pay ฿50 for the mask and snorkel and a further ฿50 for fins. Boats around the island cost around ฿500 per person for a day trip with stops for snorkelling.

Kayak hire is available from hotels and guesthouses, including **Ban's Diving Resort**, page 663.

Zunami, Mae Hat Sq, Ban Mae Hat, has the latest surf fashions.

Therapies
Jamahkiri Spa & Resort, Ao Thian Ok, T077-456400. 1000-2200. Free pick-ups available. Indulge in one of the reasonably priced packages available at this spa in grounds overlooking the sea. The aloe vera body wrap is the signature experience and produces quite a strange sensation. There's a steam sauna and facials and a variety of massages are available. After your massage have a drink overlooking the sea. Recommended.

Tour operators
A long-tailed boat trip around the island starts from about ฿1500 for up to 4 people.

🚌 Transport

Koh Tao *p661, map p660*
Bicycle hire
Mountain bikes are available for hire from guesthouses and travel agencies.

Boat
There are boats of various speeds and sizes going to and from Koh Tao. Connections are with **Chumphon** (see page 610), and **Koh Samui**, via Koh Phangan.

To **Chumphon** with Lomprayah, T077-456176, office hours 0830-1900, 1015 and 1425, 2hrs, ฿550; with **Songserm**, T077-456274, 1430, 3 hrs, ฿400; with **Seatran**, T077-456907, 1000, 1600, 2hrs, ฿550; with Ko Jaroen, T08-1797 0276 (mob), the nightboat at 2200, 5 hrs.

To **Koh Samui**, Lomprayah is the most comfortable, with a/c and TV and shortest journey time, 0930, 1½ hrs, ฿300, and 1500, 1½ hrs, ฿450; with **Songserm**, T077-456274, 1000, 2 hrs 45 mins, ฿250; with **Seatran**, T077-456907, 0930 and 1500, 1½ hrs, ฿550.

To **Koh Phangan** with Lomprayah, 0930 and 1500, 1 hr, ฿200; with **Songserm**, T077-456274, 1000, 1½ hrs, ฿170; with **Seatran**, 0930 and 1500, 1 hr, ฿350.

To **Surat Thani** with Songserm, 1000, 6½ hrs, ฿550; with the nightboat, 2100, 8½ hrs, ฿550; with **Seatran**, 0930 and 1500, ฿550, free transfer from Bang Ruk pier to Nathorn on Samui for boats to Surat Thani

To **Hua Hin** with Lomprayah, 1015 and 1425, ฿850.

To **Bangkok** with Lomprayah, with boat and VIP bus, 1015 and 1445, ฿850.

Motorbike hire
Unless you are an experienced dirt bike rider this is not really an advisable form of transport as reaching any of the isolated bays involves going along narrow, twisting, bumpy, severely potholed tracks.

Lederhosenbikes, Ban Mae Hat, T08-1752 8994 (mob), www.cycling-koh-tao.com. Rents bikes from ฿200 per day.

Travel warning: the Malaysian border

This guide does not cover the provinces of Narathiwat, Songkhla, Pattani and Yala, which extend to the Malaysian border. At the beginning of 2007, due to the ongoing political situation in Southern Thailand the UK Foreign and Commonwealth Office (www.fco.gov.uk) and the US State Department (www.state.gov) both issued travel warnings advising visitors NOT to travel to, or through, these provinces. These warnings are still in place as this book goes to press in 2009.

Travellers should also be reminded that when such warnings are issued, if you chose to ignore them, insurance companies may withdraw their cover. This situation and warnings are also subject to change and visitors should check the present situation before they make plans to travel. See pages 64 and 674.

Taxi

Taxis and motorbike taxis wait at the end of Mae Hat pier. Sharing taxis makes sense as the cost is per journey, not per person. From Mae Hat to Ao Ta Not costs ฿200-300 with a minimum of 4 in the car. To Sai Ri or Chalok, ฿150-200.

❶ Directory

Koh Tao p661, map p660
Banks There is an exchange office just east of the pier in Ban Mae Hat, run by the **Krung Thai Bank**, 0900-1600. **Siam City Bank**, Pier Rd, Ban Mae Hat, east of the pier on the left with ATM, exchange and TCs changed, Mon-Fri 0830-1630. There are also a couple of ATMs between Ban Mae Hat and Sai Ri and in Chalok. **Internet** There are numerous internet cafés in Ban Mae Hat and Sai Ri and Chalok, ฿2 per min everywhere.
Medical services Badalaveda Diving Medicine Centre, Sai Ri, T077-456664; Koh Tao Physician Clinic, Sai Ri T077-456037, T081-7375444, 0800-1900; Koh Tao Health Centre, Mae Hat, T077-456007. **Post office** Thongnual Rd, Mae Hat, straight up from the pier and turn left, Mon-Fri 0830-1630.
Telephone Facilities are easily available on Sai Ri Beach, Ao Chalok Ban Kao and Ban Mae Hat.

Nakhon Si Thammarat and around

→ Colour map 4, C3.

Nakhon Si Thammarat ('the Glorious city of the Dead') or Nagara Sri Dhammaraja ('the city of the Sacred Dharma Kings') has masqueraded under many different aliases: Marco Polo referred to it as Lo-Kag, the Portuguese called it Ligor – thought to have been its original name – while to the Chinese it was Tung Ma-ling. Today, it is the second biggest city in the south and most people know it simply as Nakhon or Nakhon Si.

It is not a very popular tourist destination and it has a rather unsavoury reputation as one of the centres of mafia activity in Thailand, but otherwise it is friendly and manageable with a wide range of hotels, some excellent restaurants, a good museum and a fine monastery in Wat Phra Mahathat. It is also famed for its shadow puppetry.

Around Nakhon are the quiet beaches of Khanom and Nai Phlao. The Khao Luang and Khao Nan national parks offer waterfalls, caves, whitewater rafting and homestays. ▸▸ *For listings, see pages 679-682.*

Nakhon ⊜❼❻❸❶❻❻ ▸▸ *pp679-682.*

Ins and outs

Getting there Nakhon is a provincial capital and therefore well connected. There is an airport north of town with daily flights to Bangkok. Nakhon lies on the main north–south railway line linking Bangkok with points south and the station is within easy walking distance of the town centre. The station is on Yommarat Road, but most southbound trains stop at the junction of Khao Chum Thong, 30 km west of Nakhon, from where you must take a bus or taxi. Only two trains go into Nakhon itself. The main bus station (for non-air-conditioned connections) is 1 km out of town over the bridge on Karom Rd, west of the mosque. It has connections with Bangkok and most destinations in the south. There are also minibus and shared taxi services to many destinations in the south. ▸▸ *See Transport, page 681, for further information.*

Getting around The centre is comparatively compact and navigable on foot. But for sights on the edge of town – like Wat Phra Mahathat – it is necessary to catch a public *songthaew*, *saamlor* or motorcycle taxi. The *songthaew* is the cheapest option, a trip across town costs ฿10. The old pedal *saamlor* is still in evidence though it is gradually being pushed out by the noisier and more frightening motorcycle taxi, of which there seem to be hundreds.

Tourist information TAT ① *Sanam Na Muang, Rachdamnern Rd, T075-346515-6, www.tat. or.th/south2 (Thai only), daily 0830-1630*, is situated in an old, attractive club building. The staff here produce a helpful pamphlet and hand-out sheets of information on latest bus and taxi prices. It is a useful first stop.

Background

Nakhon is surrounded by rich agricultural land and has been a rice exporter for centuries. The city has links with both the Dvaravati and Srivijayan empires. Buddhist monks from Nakhon are thought to have propagated religion throughout the country perhaps even influencing the development of Buddhism in Sukhothai, Thailand's former great kingdom.

Red Zone, Yellow Zone, Green Zone

For the first time since the violent Communist insurgency of the 1970s, the infamous red zone coding has been brought back, this time in the deep south against villages believed to be sympathetic to Islamic militants.

Critics of the contentious coding tactic say that the zoning, which is directly linked to funding for villages, will exacerbate tensions and help breed future militants.

Red zones, which are to have all funds cut, are villages with active militants. Yellow zones, which will have their funding slashed, are villages where locals offer aid and shelter to militants. Green zones, which will receive the most funds, are villages that do not engage in terrorist activity and which could provide moles for information about militant activities.

The draconian measures came in the wake of more than 2000 fatalities which were blamed on Islamic militants. While the majority of victims at first were police and soldiers, Buddhist monks and teachers fast became victims. Tourists are seldom targeted, though many foreign governments recommend that their nationals completely avoid the area (see box, page 674). Over the years several incidents have intensified both insurgency and government efforts, not least the notorious death in detention of over 80 Muslim men at Tak Bai in 2004, and the murders of dozens of Thai military personnel. This conflict was also used as excuse by the Thai military after it began pushing back male Muslim refugees from Burma (the Rohingya) in December 2008 (see box, page 222).

Nakhon was at its most powerful and important during King Thammasokarat's reign in the 13th century, when it was busily trading with south India and Ceylon. But as Sukhothai and then Ayutthaya grew in influence, the city went into a gradual decline. During the 17th century, King Narai's principal concubine banished the bright young poet Si Phrat to Nakhon. Here he continued to compose risqué rhymes about the women of the governor's court. His youthful impertinence lost him his head.

Nakhon used to have the dubious honour of being regarded as one of the crime capitals of Thailand – a position it had held, apparently, since the 13th century. Locals maintain that the city has now cleaned up its act and Nakhon is probably best known today for its prawn farms (see box, page 676) and nielloware industry (see page 74?). The shop where the industry started some 50 years ago still stands on Sitama Road and production techniques are demonstrated on Si Thammasok I Road. Elsewhere, other than in a few handicraft shops on Tha Chang Road, nielloware is an elusive commodity, although the National Museum has some examples on display. The art and craft and performance of shadow puppetry is also being kept alive in Nakhon, see page 681 and Background, page 745.

Wat Phra Mahathat

ⓘ T075-345172, cloisters open daily 0800-1630.

A 2-km-long wall formerly enclosed the old city and its wats – only a couple of fragments of this remain (the most impressive section is opposite the town jail on Rachdamnern Road). Wat Phra Mahathat, 2 km south of town on Rachdamnern Road, is the oldest temple in town and the biggest in South Thailand – as well as being one of the region's

Nakhon Si Thammarat

most important. The wat dates from AD 757 and was originally a Srivijayan Mahayana Buddhist shrine. The 77-m high stupa, *Phra Boromathat* – a copy of the Mahathupa in Ceylon – was built early in the 13th century to hold relics of the Buddha from Ceylon. The wat underwent extensive restoration in the Ayutthayan period and endured further alterations in 1990. The *chedi's* square base, its voluptuous body and towering spire are all Ceylonese-inspired. Below the spire is a small square platform decorated with bas-reliefs in gold of monks circumambulating (*pradaksina*) the monument. The spire itself is said to be topped with 962 kg of gold, while the base is surrounded by small stupas. The covered cloisters at its base contain many beautiful, recently restored Buddha images all in the image of subduing Mara. The base is dotted with attractive elephant heads. Also here is **Vihara Bodhi Langka** ⓘ *0800-1600, entry by donation*, a jumbled treasure trove of a museum. It contains a large collection of archaeological artefacts, donated jewellery, bodhi trees, Buddhas and a collection of sixth- to 13th-century Dvaravati sculpture – some of the latter are particularly fine. The mural at the bottom of the stairs tells the story of the early life of the Buddha, while the doorway at the top is decorated with figures of Vishnu and Phrom dating from the Sukhothai period.

Phra Viharn Luang

The nearby Phra Viharn Luang (to the left of the main entrance to the stupa) is an impressive building, with an intricately painted and decorated ceiling, dating from the 18th century. The best time to visit the

Sleeping		Hao Coffee Shop **3**
Grand Park **1**		Krour Nakorn **3**
Nakhon Garden Inn **3**		
Thai **4**		**Minibuses**
Thai Lee **5**		Minivan to Hat Yai **5**
Thaksin **6**		Minivan to Surat Thani
Twin Lotus **2**		& Khanom **4**
		Share taxi terminal to
Eating		Airport, Trang & Songkhla **2**
A&A **1**		To Phuket **3**

Terrorism in the deep south

Along with Narathiwat, Songkhla, Pattani and Yala, Satun province was a hotbed for Islamic insurgents during the 1970s and 1980s until a government amnesty saw 20,000 fighters handing in their arms in 1987. Then, in December 2001, it all began again with hit-and-run attacks on police, military outposts, schools and commercial sites.

The Australian government, following the Bali bombings, warned its citizens to exercise particular vigilance in Satun province and overland travel to the Malaysian border. The UK Foreign Office advises against all but essential travel to the four southern provinces. Among the risks are kidnapping from resorts and piracy in the Straits of Malacca.

Much of the violence has been blamed on Thaksin Shinawatra's hair-brained attempts to stamp out the separatist movement by rounding up suspected militants (but on the basis of unsound intelligence), thus creating a wave of resentment in the region. The military leaders who deposed the oligarch-turned-politician in late 2006 made overtures to the separatists, apologising for Thaksin's policies, with mixed success.

Much of the tension in Satun province and throughout the deep south can be traced back to the late 1890s when these provinces – once part of Muslim and animist Malaysia – were Siamised, their names translated to Thai and the people reclassified as Malay-Thais. Satun was formerly called Setol. But the south also claims that, because it is not fully Thai, it is punished with low funding and poor schools and has become a dumping ground for corrupt and inept military and government officials. Certainly, banditry is rife throughout the southern provinces.

The Bahasa-speaking inhabitants certainly see themselves as more Malaysian than Thai and this is evident in the excellent cuisine, which is not as hot as Thai food but is spicier with quieter, more layered curries and a subtler sweetness. And the restaurant owners may often tell you that the ingredients are all Malaysian.

The far south also has spectacular national parks, including Tarutao with its marine life and awe-inspiring scenery.

---

monastery is in October during the Tenth Lunar Month Festival when Wat Mahathat becomes a hive of activity. Foodstalls, travelling cinemas, shadow-puppet masters, the local mafia, businessmen in their Mercedes, monks and handicraft sellers all set up shop, making the wat endlessly interesting.

Puppet workshop and museum
ⓘ *110/18 Si Thammasok, Soi 3, T075-346394, daily 0830-1700, 20-min performance, ฿100 for 2; 3 or more ฿50 each.*
Not far from Wat Mahathat is the puppet workshop of Nakhon's most famous *nang thalung* master – Khun Suchart Subsin. His workshop is signposted off the main road near the Chinese temple (hard to miss). As well as giving shows (see Entertainment, page 681) and selling examples of his work starting at ฿200 or so for a simple elephant, the compound itself is interesting and peaceful with craftsmen hammering out puppets under thatched awnings and dozens of buffalo skulls hung everywhere. There is also a small museum exhibiting puppet characters from as far back as the 18th century.

Saan Chao Mae Thap Thim Chinese Pagoda

ⓘ *It's a 2-km hike out to the monastery; blue songthaews constantly ply the road to the monastery and back (฿6).*

Returning to the main road, this Chinese pagoda offers a respite from Theravada Buddhist Thailand. Magnificent dragons claw their way up the pillars and inside, wafted by incense, are various Chinese gods, Bodhisattvas and demons.

Nakhon Si Thammarat National Museum

ⓘ *Rachdamnern Rd, about 700 m beyond Wat Mahathat, Wed-Sun 0830-1630, ฿30. The museum is a 2-km walk from most of the hotels; catch one of the numerous blue songthaews running along Rachdamnern Rd and ask for 'Pipitipan Nakhon Si Thammarat' (฿6).*

The Nakhon branch of the National Museum is one of the town's most worthwhile sights. The impressive collection includes many interesting Indian-influenced pieces as well as rare pieces from the Dvaravati and later Ayutthaya periods. Some exhibits are labelled in English. The section on art in South Thailand explains and charts the development of the unusual local Phra Phutthasihing (or Buddha Sihing) style of Buddha image, which was popular locally in the 16th century. Also in this section is the oldest Vishnu statue in Southeast Asian art (holding a conch shell on his hip), which dates from the fifth century. The museum has sections on folk arts and crafts and local everyday implements. To the right of the entrance hall, in the prehistory section, stand two large Dongson bronze kettle drums – two of only 12 found in the country. The one decorated with four ornamental frogs is the biggest ever found in Thailand.

Chapel of Phra Buddha Sihing

The Chapel of Phra Buddha Sihing, sandwiched between two large provincial office buildings just before Rachdamnern Road splits in two, may contain one of Thailand's most important Buddha images. During the 13th century an image, magically created, was shipped to Thailand from Ceylon (hence the name – Sihing for the Sinhalese people). The Nakhon statue, like the other two images that claim to be the Phra Buddha Sihing (one in Bangkok, see page 85, and one in Chiang Mai, northern Thailand, see page 239), is not Ceylonese in style at all; it conforms with the Thai style of the peninsula.

Wat Wang Tawan Tok

Back in the centre of town is Wat Wang Tawan Tok, across Rachdamnern Road from the bookshop. It has, at the far side of its sprawling compound, a southern Thai-style wooden house built between 1888 and 1901. Originally the house (which is really three houses in one) was constructed without nails – it has since been poorly repaired using them. The door panels, window frames and gables, all rather weather-beaten now, were once intricately carved but it is still infinitely more appealing than the concrete shophouses going up all over Thailand.

Hindu temples

There are two 13th- to 14th-century Hindu temples in the city, along Rachdamnern Road. **Hor Phra Isuan**, next to the Semamuang Temple, houses an image of Siva, the destroyer. Opposite is **Hor Phra Narai** which once contained images of Vishnu, now in the city museum.

Making a killing from the tiger prawn

The coastline north from Sating Phra and Ranot is one of Thailand's major prawn-farming areas. The paddy fields have been dug out, aerators have been installed and since the early 1980s the farmers of the area have taken out large loans to get into the lucrative business of farming tiger prawns. Environmentally the effects have sometimes been disastrous. The protective mangroves and nipa palms were uprooted to make more space for prawns and in so doing destroyed the breeding grounds for many fish and crustacea as well as promoting erosion along the exposed shoreline. The water from the ponds polluted nearby ricelands and viral infections often killed the prawns that farmers had invested so much money in raising. In recent years the government has been researching and promoting more sustainable prawn aquaculture.

Morning market

A worthwhile early-morning walk is west across the bridge along Karom Road to the morning market (about 1 km), which sells fresh food. This gets going early and is feverish with activity from around 0630.

Thai Traditional Medicine Centre

① *Take a local bus, ฿8.*
On the outskirts of the city, after Wat Mahathat is the small **Wat Sa-la Mechai**. While the temple is fairly ordinary, at one end of the temple grounds is a recently established centre for traditional medicine, including massage. If you want a traditional massage, it costs about ฿100 per hour – you pay before you begin. You can also take a course in massage, paying by the hour, and learn more about traditional herbal medicine (there is a small garden of medicinal plants at the front).

Around Nakhon ⊕❼▲⊖ » *pp679-682.*

Khanom and Nai Phlao beaches

① *Regular buses from Nakhon (฿20), a/c micro buses (฿60) leave from Wat Kit Rd and also from Surat Thani. The beaches are about 8 km off the main road; turn at the Km 80 marker.*
Eighty kilometres north of Nakhon, near Khanom district, there are some secluded stretches of shoreline: Khanom beach (2 km from town), Nai Phlao beach to the south, and a couple of other bays are opening up to development. This area is predominantly visited by Thai tourists. Newer operations seem to be targeting Western tourists who are beginning to look towards the mainland in this area for reasonably priced peace and quiet, and convenience they have failed to find on Samui. There are better beaches in Thailand but you're likely to have most of what you find to yourself – particularly if you come mid-week. Khanom beach is a long run of coconut-grove fringed sand that slopes steeply into the sea. Development is picking up here but it still has a remote feeling. Khanom town is a very lively rough and ready fishing port. There are few facilities aimed at *farang* in this town meaning that it offers a genuine slice of Thai rural life to the more adventurous traveller. Nai Phlao beach offers a much shorter run of beach and has a greater concentration of resorts. That's not saying much though as it still feels like a

relatively untouched spot, despite the best efforts of the new development at the **Chada Racha Resort** to introduce an unhealthy dose of concrete to the coastline.

Khao Luang National Park

ⓘ *To get to Karom Waterfall take a bus to Lan Saka (then walk 3 km to falls) or charter a minibus direct. To get to Phrom Lok Waterfall take a minibus from Nakhon then hire a motorbike taxi for the last very pleasant 8 km. The villagers at Khiriwong village can organize trips up Khao Luang mountain but do not speak English. See Activities and tours for further options, homestays and guides. Songthaews leave Nakhon for Khiriwong every 15 mins or so (β15).*

The Khao Luang National Park is named after Khao Luang, a peak of 1835 m – the highest in the south – which lies less than 10 km west of Nakhon. Within the boundaries of the

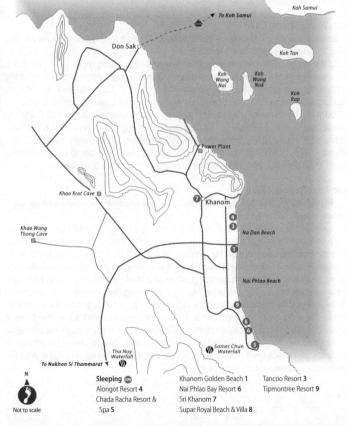

Beaches north of Nakhon Si Thammarat

Sleeping 🛏
Alongot Resort **4**
Chada Racha Resort & Spa **5**
Khanom Golden Beach **1**
Nai Phlao Bay Resort **6**
Sri Khanom **7**
Supar Royal Beach & Villa **8**
Tancoo Resort **3**
Tipmontree Resort **9**

mountainous, 570-sq-km national park are three waterfalls. **Karom Waterfall** lies 30 km from Nakhon, off Route 4015, and has a great location with views over the lowlands. Also here are cool forest trails and fast-flowing streams. The park is said to support small populations of tiger, leopard and elephant, although many naturalists believe they are on the verge of extinction here. **Phrom Lok Waterfall** is about 25 km from Nakhon, off Route 4132. However, the most spectacular of the waterfalls is **Krung Ching** – 'waterfall of a hundred thousand raindrops' – 70 km out of town, and a 4-km walk from the park's accommodation. The 1835-m climb up **Khao Luang** starts from Khiriwong village, 23 km from Nakhon, off Route 4015. The mountain is part of the Nakhon Si Thammarat range, running from Koh Samui south through Surat Thani to Satun. The scenic village, surrounded by forest, was partially destroyed by mudslides in 1988 – an event which led to the introduction of a nationwide logging ban at the beginning of 1989. The climb takes three days and is very steep in parts, with over 60° slopes. If you plan to do this walk on your own, there is no accommodation so it is necessary to carry your own equipment and food. See also Sleeping, below.

Khao Wang Thong Cave
ⓘ *Charter a songthaew for around ฿800 per day. The entrance is past the cave keeper's house, 15 mins' walk uphill from the village.*
One of the less-publicized sights in the Nakhon area is Khao Wang Thong Cave. The cave is on the south side of the middle peak of three limestone mountains near Ban Khao Wang Thong in Khanom district. It lies 100 km north of Nakhon, 11 km off Route 4142. Villagers and a group of Nakhon conservationists saved the cave from a dolomite mining company in 1990. A few tight squeezes and a short ladder climb are rewarded by some of Thailand's most spectacular cave formations. Its four spacious chambers – one of which has been dubbed 'the throne hall' – are decorated with gleaming white curtain stalactites. It is presently maintained by groups of local villagers and plans are afoot to install a lighting system. Until then, it is advisable that you bring your own torch (flashlight).

Khao Nan National Park
ⓘ *Take the main route up to Khanom beyond Ta Sala and turn left down the road from where there are signposts to the park.*
Just north of Khao Luang National Park is the new Khao Nan National Park. At 1430 m, Khao Nan Yai is not as high as Khao Luang, but is still tall enough to support cloud forest on its summit. The national park has a beautiful waterfall near its entrance, lush forests, waterfalls and caves. One cave, **Tham Hong**, has a waterfall inside it and is well worth visiting, and fairly easily accessible but you'll need a torch. Treks to the top of Khao Nan Yai taking three to four days are organized by the Forestry Department staff. You should call the Forestry Department in Bangkok at least a couple of days in advance to arrange a guide. The treks go to the top of Khao Nan where you can camp out in cloud forest. Temperatures at the top are always cool and there is a wide variety of ferns and mosses in the understorey of the forest. Khao Nan and Khao Luang are also known for *pa pra* – a deciduous tree which loses its leaves during the dry season (February to April) with the leaves first changing colour to a brilliant red.

For Sleeping and Eating price codes and other relevant information, see pages 44-49.

⊙ Sleeping

Nakhon *p671, map p673*
At the top level of accommodation, Nakhon has a 5-star hotel, and the middle range now has a couple of hotels worthy of a mention, but as for the rest, there is little to choose between them.

A-D Twin Lotus Hotel, 97/8 Hatankarn-khukwag Rd, outskirts of the town centre, T075-323777. Nearly 400 a/c rooms with TV and minibars, and a good-sized swimming pool and fitness centre. The usual services expected for a top-end hotel. The reasonable tariff includes a good buffet-style breakfast. A well-run and well-maintained hotel.

D-E Grand Park Hotel, 1204/79 Pak Nakhon Rd, T075-317666-73. Opposite the Nakhon Garden Inn, this is a bit of a block architecturally and doesn't really live up to its grand name, but it has adequate rooms and is centrally located with lots of parking. A/c, hot water, bathtubs, TV, minibar. One of the better hotels in this category.

D-E Thaksin Hotel, 1584/23 Si Prat Rd. T075-342790, www.thaksinhotel.com. Comfortable, good-value rooms, with cable TV, en suite and a/c. Decent location, friendly and some English spoken. Recommended.

E Nakhon Garden Inn, 1/4 Pak Nakhon Rd, T075-344831. One of the nicest mid-range places to stay – a rustic feel for Nakhon, with 2 brick buildings on either side of a large garden compound with clean a/c rooms and hot water. The rooms have been nicely decorated – rather dark, but good value and a bit different from most of the places in the city centre. Recommended.

E-F Thai Hotel, 1375 Rachdamnern Rd, T075-341509. Some a/c in newer rooms away from the noise of the street with beds large enough to sleep 4. Restaurant and internet access too. Over the Twin

Lotus Hotel, it has the advantage of a central location.

F-G Thai Lee, 1130 Rachdamnern Rd, T075-356948. Large, bright, clean rooms with fan and attached bathroom (Western toilet), best-value accommodation in the lower end of the market.

Khanom and Nai Phlao beaches *p676, map p677*

L-A Chada Racha Resort and Spa, Nai Phlao beach 99, T075-527833, www.chadaracha.com. An attempt to create a luxury resort on a rocky outcrop at the far end of Nai Phlao beach, this place comes across as overpriced and pretentious. There are some decent views from the villas and rooms. All the usual amenities – pool, a/c, cable TV, en suite rooms, spa and restaurant.

A-C Khanom Golden Beach Hotel, 59/3 Moo 4, Ban Na Dan, T075-326690, khanom@nksrat.ksc.co.th. Hotel block with pool, snooker room, children's room, tour desk, restaurant and rental of windsurf boards, sailing dinghies and bicycles. Friendly and professional staff. Rooms are rather characterless but clean and comfortable. The larger more expensive suites are very spacious and well equipped.

B-D Supar Royal Beach Hotel, 51/4 Moo 8, Hat Nai Phlao, T075-528417. Hotel block under same management as the Supar Villa. Clean rooms, tiled floors, generally very characterless but every room has a sea view.

D Alongot Resort, Khanom beach, T075-529119. The promising exterior of these bungalows is ruined by very drab interiors. The location is great – right in the middle of Khanom beaches' long sweep. They sell a decent array of food as well. Friendly.

D-E Nai Phlao Bay Resort, 51/3 Ban Nai Phlao, T075-529039. Large resort with a/c rooms, restaurant and impersonal service. Average bungalows set back from the beach – nice tree-lined lawn. Quite pricey for what it is.

E Tipmontree Resort, 12 Moo 7, Hat Nai Phret, T075-528147. Large comfortable bungalows with basic amenities on pretty beachfront. Laid-back, friendly staff.
F Sri Khanom Hotel, 77 Tambon Rd, T075-529259. Only hotel in Khanom town. No English is spoken at this friendly, family-run hotel. Some rooms are worn and grim – go for the ones on the upper floors for more air and light. No hot water though all rooms are en suite. Aimed at Thai businessmen.
F Tancoo Resort, 23/9 Moo 2, Hat Na Dan, T075-529491. Fairly old and quite rough bungalow accommodation but well kept and clean. Fan only, nice location.

Khao Luang National Park *p677*
The **B** bungalows at the park office of the Karom Waterfall sleep up to 10 people. Camping is possible if you have your own gear. The 2nd park office at Krung Ching Waterfall, T075-309644-5, has 2 guest-houses **AL-C** and a campsite. For homestay, see Activities and tours, below.

Eating

Nakhon *p671, map p673*
Prawns are Nakhon's speciality and farms abound in the area. Good seafood (including saltwater prawns) is available at reasonable prices in most of the town's restaurants. Roadside stalls sometimes sell a Nakhon speciality: small prawns in their shells, deep fried in a spicy batter and served as a sort of prawn pattie. The Bovorn Bazaar, in the centre of town off Rachdamnern Rd, is a good place to start in any hunt for food. It has restaurants, a bakery, a bar and a coffee shop.
TT A & A Restaurant, T075-311047. Open 0700-2400. A/c restaurant just down the road from the Nakhorn Garden Inn and marked with flags boasting fresh coffee. Serves Thai-style toasted bread with jam, marmalade, condensed milk and sugar, excellent coffee, and very tasty Thai food. It also does Western breakfasts for a very reasonable price. Try the pork rib noodle soup and the fried minced chicken noodles. The brownies and sticky cakes, puddings and jellies are delicious. There's a menu in English.
TT-T 99 Rock Bar and Grill, Bovorn Bazaar, Rachdamnern Rd, T075-317999. Open 1100-1400, 1600-2300. A Western-style bar with cold beer and a menu including pasta, pizzas, baked potatoes and grilled chicken.
T Hao Coffee Shop, Bovorn Bazaar, off Rachdamnern Rd. It is charmingly decorated with antiques and assorted oddities and is like a museum piece with glass display cabinets everywhere. Recommended.
T Krour Nakorn, at the back of Bovorn Bazaar off Rachdamnern Rd next to the massive trunk of an Indian rubber tree. Pleasant eating spot, with open verandas, art work, wicker chairs and a reasonable line in seafood and other spicy dishes. You get given an entire tray of herbs and vegetables to go with your meal. Recommended.

Bakeries
Ligo, Rachdamnern Rd and Bovorn Bazaar. A good selection of pastries and doughnuts.
Sinocha (sign only in Thai), down the narrow alleyway by the Thai Hotel. Perhaps even better than Ligos, it sells Danish pastries, doughnuts, more sickly concoctions, as well as a good range of dim sum. Recommended.

Foodstalls
Nam Cha Rim Tang is a stall in the Bovorn Bazaar, which sets up early evening and produces exceedingly good banana rotis. Lining Rachdamnern Rd, along the wall of the playing fields, there are countless stalls selling *som tam*, a chilli-hot papaya salad from Thailand's northeastern region usually served with grilled chicken (*kai yaang*).

Khanom and Nai Phlao beaches *p676, map p677*
There are lots of foodstalls in Khanom town on Tambon Rd. On the beaches the only food is provided by the hotels, resorts and bungalows operators.

🎭 Entertainment

Nakhon *p671, map p673*
Shadow plays
Most of the plays relate tales from the **Ramakien** (see page 86) and the *Jataka* tales. Narrators sing in ear-piercing falsetto accompanied by a band comprising *tab* (drums), *pi* (flute), *mong* (bass gong), *saw* (fiddle) and *ching* (miniature cymbals). There are 2 sizes of puppets. *Nang yai* (large puppets) which may be 2 m tall, and *nang lek* (small puppets) (see page 745). Shows and demonstrations of how the puppets are made can be seen at the workshop of **Suchart Subsin**, 110/18 Si Thammasok Soi 3 (take the road opposite Wat Phra Mahathat, turn left – at the top of the *soi* Suchart Subsin's house is signposted – and walk 50 m). This group has undertaken several royal performances.

🎉 Festivals and events

Nakhon *p671, map p673*
Feb Hae Pha Khun That A 3-day event when homage is paid to locally enshrined relics of the Buddha.
Sep-Oct Tenth Lunar Month Festival (movable) A 10-day celebration, the climax of which is the colourful procession down Rachdamnern Rd to Wat Phra Mahathat.

🛍 Shopping

Nakhon *p671, map p673*
Nakhon is the centre of the south Thai handicrafts industry. Nielloware, *yan liphao* basketry (woven from strands of vine of the same name), shadow puppets, Thai silk brocades and *pak yok* weaving are local specialities.

Handicrafts
Shops on Tha Chang Rd, notably the **Thai Handicraft Centre** (in the lime green wooden house on the far side of the road

behind the tourist office), **Nabin House** and **Manat Shop**. With the exception of the **Thai Handicraft Centre**, silverware predominates.

Shadow puppets
From the craftsmen at **Suchart Subsin's House**, Si Thammasok Rd, Soi 3 (see Entertainment, above) and stalls around Wat Phra Mahathat.

🅰 Activities and tours

Khao Luang National Park *p677*
Tours in the province can be also organized through companies in Nakhon Sri Thammarat or at the park office.
Khiriwong Agro Tourism Promotion Center, Moo 5, Tambon Kam Lon, Amphoe Lan Saka (near the park office), T075-309010, T08-1229 0829 (mob). Offers tours to Krung Ching Waterfall, including whitewater rafting. Can organize homestays and guides.
TVS-REST, T02-6910437-9, www.ecotour. in.th/indexen.html. A Thai not-for-profit organization involved in community development, offers tours and visits to Khiriwong village, with activities and accommodation at the village and with treks into the forest. The tour leaves from Bangkok and costs ฿3600.

🚌 Transport

Nakhon *p671, map p673*
Air
There are 4 daily connections with **Bangkok** with **Nok Air**, www.nokair.com; and **PB Air**, www.pbair.com.

Bus
Most people pick up a bus as it works its way through town.
Overnight connections with **Bangkok**'s Southern bus terminal, 12 hrs, ฿350. Regular non a/c and a/c connections with **Krabi**, 3 hrs, ฿65; **Surat Thani**, 2½-3 hrs, ฿55;

Hat Yai, 3 hrs, ฿73; **Phuket**, 8 hrs, ฿125; **Trang**, 2 hrs, ฿65; **Songkhla**, 3 hrs, ฿70; and with other southern towns.

A number of minibus services also operate to destinations in the south including **Hat Yai**, ฿90; **Phuket**, ฿500; **Krabi**, ฿120; **Trang** ฿80; and **Surat Thani**, ฿110. They tend to be marginally quicker and slightly more expensive than a/c coaches. See map for locations but check beforehand as their 'patches' seem to change from time to time.

Shared taxi
For shared taxis, the terminal is on Yommarat Rd. Prices are fixed (they are listed on a board at the terminal) and most large centres in the south are served from here including **Hat Yai**, **Phuket**, **Krabi**, **Trang**, **Surat Thani**, **Phattalung** and **Songkhla**.

Train
Overnight connections with **Bangkok**.

⊕ Directory

Nakhon *p671, map p673*
Banks Bangkok, 1747 Rachdamnern Rd. There are numerous other banks in the centre. **Internet** Inside the Bovorn Bazaar. **Post office** Rachdamnern Rd (opposite the police station). There is also a small post office opposite the **Nakhon Garden Inn** on Pak Nakhon Rd. **Telephone** Attached to the post office on Rachdamnern Rd, overseas calls available.

Contents

Background

History

Prehistory

Research since the end of the Second World War has shown Thailand to be a 'hearth' – or core area – in Southeast Asian prehistory. Discoveries at archaeological sites such as Ban Chiang (see page 374) and Non Nok Tha in the northeast, Spirit Cave in the north, and Ban Kao in the west have revealed evidence of early agriculture (possibly, 7000 BC) – particularly rice cultivation – pottery (3500 BC) and metallurgy (2500 BC). Although heated arguments over the significance and the dating of the finds continue, there is no doubt that important technologies were being developed and disseminated from an early date. These finds have altered the view of this part of the world from being a 'receptacle' for outside influences to being an area of innovation in its own right.

Today, the population of Thailand is made up of Tai-speaking peoples. It has long been thought that the Tai migrated from southern China about 2000 years ago, filtering down the valleys and along the river courses that cut north–south down the country. These migrants settled in the valleys of north Thailand, on the Khorat Plateau, and in parts of the lower Chao Phraya Basin. Even at this early date there was a clear division between hill and lowland people. The lowland Tai mastered the art of wet rice cultivation (see page 760), supporting large populations and enabling powerful states and impressive civilizations to evolve. In the highlands, people worked with the forest, living in small itinerant groups, eking out a living through shifting cultivation or hunting and gathering. In exchange for metal implements, salt and pottery, the hill peoples would trade natural forest products: honey, resins such as lac, wild animal skins, ivory and herbs. Even today, lowland 'civilized' Thais view the *pa* (forest) as a *thuan* (wild place), inhabited by spirits and hill peoples. This is reflected in the words used to denote 'civilized' lowland Thais – *Khon Muang* (People of the Town), and 'barbaric' upland people – *Khon Pa* (People of the Forest).

Mon, Srivijayan and Khmer influences

Before the Tais emerged as the dominant force in the 13th century, Thailand was dominated by **Mon** and **Khmer peoples**. The Mon were a people and a civilization centred on the western edge of the central plains. They established the enigmatic kingdom of Dvaravati, see below, of which very little is known even to the extent that the location of its capital is far from certain. From the small collection of inscriptions and statues scholars do know, however, that the kingdom was Buddhist and extended eastwards towards Cambodia, northwards towards Chiang Mai, and westwards into Burma. The Khmer were the people, and (usually) a kingdom, centred on present-day Cambodia with their capital at Angkor. They controlled large areas of Thailand (particularly the northeast) and Laos (the south) as well as Cambodia.

Prior to the 13th century the people of the **Srivijayan Kingdom** also extended their influence across Thailand. This was a Hindu-Buddhist kingdom that had its capital near present-day Palembang (Sumatra) and which built its wealth on controlling the trade through the Straits of Melaka between China and India/Middle East. Because of the monsoon winds (northeast/southwest) boats powered by sail had to 'winter' in island Southeast Asia, waiting for the winds to change before they could continue their journeys. Srivijaya, for which we have little solid evidence, is thought to have been one of the most – if not the most – powerful maritime kingdom in the region.

The Dvaravati, Srivijaya and Khmer empires in Thailand (6th-14th centuries)

Dvaravati	**6th-11th centuries (west, central and northern Thailand)**
	AD 661 (19 February): Haripunchaya reputed to have been founded at Lamphun in northern Thailand by a group of Buddhist holy men.
	Late 7th century: Queen Chamadevi, a daughter of the ruler of Lopburi, becomes queen of the Mon (Dvaravati) Kingdom of Haripunchaya.
Srivijaya	**7th-13th centuries (southern Thailand)**
	7th century: evidence of a thriving Buddhist entrepôt based at Palembang in Sumatra, with a presence in southern Thailand.
	13th-14th centuries: Srivijaya loses its control of the Malay peninsula and southern Thailand to the young and vigorous Tai states of Sukhothai and, later, Ayutthaya.
Khmer	**9th-13th centuries (northeast and central Thailand)**
	AD 889-900: reign of Yasovarman I. He expands the Khmer Empire onto the Khorat Plateau of northeast Thailand.
	1001-1002: reign of Udayadityavarman, who mounts an invasion of Haripunjaya following an attack by Haripunjaya on the Khmer town of Lopburi.
	12th century: Lopburi is regarded by Angkor as Syam – ie Siam.
	1113-1150: reign of Suryavarman II.
	1181-c1219: reign of the great Jayavarman VII, who develops the Angkorian communications system, helping to hold together his vast empire. Lopburi is firmly incorporated into the Khmer Empire.
	1220-1243: reign of Indravarman II.

Dvaravati

The Mon Kingdom of Dvaravati was centred close to Bangkok, with cities at modern-day Uthong and Nakhon Pathom, and was an artistic and political outlier of the Mon Empire of Burma. Dvaravati relics have also been found in the north and northeast, along what are presumed to have been the trade routes between Burma east to Cambodia, north to Chiang Mai and northeast to the Khorat Plateau and Laos. The Dvaravati Kingdom lasted from the sixth to the 11th centuries; only the tiny Mon kingdom of Haripunjaya, with its capital at Lamphun in the north, managed to survive annexation by the powerful Khmer Empire and remained independent until the 13th century. Unfortunately, virtually nothing of the architecture of the Dvaravati period remains. Buildings were constructed of laterite blocks, faced with stucco (a mixture of sand and lime) and, apparently, bound together with vegetable glue. In Thailand, only the stupa of Wat Kukut outside Lamphun shows Dvaravati architecture (it was last rebuilt in 1218, see page 735). Dvaravati sculpture is much better represented and the National Gallery in Bangkok has some fine examples. The sculptors of the period drew their inspiration from India's late-Gupta cave temples, rendering human form almost supernaturally.

Srivijaya

The powerful Srivijayan Empire, with its capital at Palembang in Sumatra, extended its control over south Thailand from the seventh to the 13th centuries. Inscriptions and sculptures dating from the Srivijayan period have been found near the modern Thai towns of Chaiya and Sating Phra in Surat Thani, and Songkhla provinces. They reveal an eclectic mixture of Indian, Javanese, Mon and Khmer artistic influences, and incorporate both Hindu and Mahayana Buddhist iconography. Probably the best examples of what little remains of Srivijayan architecture in Thailand are Phra Boromthat and a sanctuary at Wat Kaeo, both in Chaiya (see page 612).

The Khmer

Of all the external empires to impinge on Thailand before the rise of the Tai, the most influential was the Khmer. Thailand lay on the fringes of the Angkorian Kingdom, but nonetheless many Thai towns are Khmer in origin: That Phanom, Sakhon Nakhon and Phimai in the northeast; Lopburi, Suphanburi and Ratburi in the lower central plain; and Phitsanulok, Sawankhalok and Sukhothai in the upper central plain.

The peak of the Khmer period in Thailand lasted from the 11th to the 13th centuries, corresponding with the flowering of the Angkorian period in Cambodia. However, antiquities have been found that date back as far as the seventh and eighth century AD. The period of Khmer inspiration is referred to as 'Lopburi', after the Central Thai town of the same name which was a Khmer stronghold. The most impressive architectural remains are to be found in the northeastern region: Phimai, not far from Nakhon Ratchasima (Korat) (see page 335), Muang Tham (see page 339) and Phnom Rung (see page 337), both south of Buriram. As Cambodia's treasures are still relatively expensive and hard to get to, these 'temple cities' are a substitute, giving some idea of the economic power and artistic brilliance of the Khmer period. There are also many lesser Khmer ruins scattered over the northeastern region, many barely researched, and these offer worthwhile forays for those with a real interest in Thailand's historical and archaeological past.

The Tai

The Tai did not begin to exert their dominance over modern Thailand until the 12th and 13th centuries when the Khmer Empire had begun to decline. By then they had taken control of Lamphun in the north, founded Chiang Mai, established the Sukhothai Kingdom in the Yom River valley, and gained control of the southern peninsula. From the 13th century onwards, the history of Thailand becomes a history of the Tai people.

An important unit of organization among the Tai was the *muang*. Today, *muang* is usually translated as 'town'. But it means much more than this, and to an extent defies translation. The *muang* was a unit of control, and denoted those people who came under the sway of a *chao* or lord. In a region where people were scarce but land was abundant, the key to power was to control manpower, and thereby to turn forest into rice land. At the beginning of the 13th century, some Tai lords began to extend their control over neighbouring *muang*, forging kingdoms of considerable power. In this way, the Tai began to make a history of their own, rather than merely to be a part of history.

Chiang Mai or Lanna Thai

In northern Thailand, various Tai chiefs began to expand at the expense of the Mon. The most powerful of these men was **King Mengrai**, born in October 1239 at Chiang Saen,

Lanna Thai (1239-1660)

1239	King Mengrai, the founder of the Lanna Kingdom, is born in Chiang Saen.
1259	Mengrai becomes the ruler of Chiang Saen, succeeding his father.
1262	Mengrai founds Chiang Rai.
1281	After years of preparation, Mengrai takes the Haripunchaya Kingdom based at Lamphun.
1289	Mengrai takes Pegu (Burma) and extends his empire into Burma.
1292	Mengrai establishes Chiang Mai as his new capital.
1317	Mengrai dies and the Lanna Kingdom enters a period of instability.
1355	King Ku Na of Lanna brings some stability and direction back to the kingdom; he is a fine scholar and a cultured man.
1369	King Ku Na invites a monk from Sukhothai to establish a monastery in Chiang Mai.
1404-1405	Lanna is invaded by a large Chinese army from Yunnan; they are repulsed after the king raises an army said to be 300,000-strong.
1442-1443	Ayutthaya sends an army against Lanna and the principality of Nan revolts against Lanna domination. In time, Lanna defeats both.
1456-1457	The beginning of a long period of conflict between Lanna and Ayutthaya over control of the upper central plains and lower north, which continues until about 1486.
1478-1479	A Vietnamese army from Luang Prabang (Laos) tries to take Nan, and is repulsed.
1526	The death of King Muang Kaeo marks the beginning of the decline of Lanna.
1546	Lanna comes under the suzerainty of Lane Xang (Laos).
1564-1660	Lanna is controlled over much of the period by Burma, whose king puts a series of puppet rulers on the throne of Lanna.
1595	Kings of Lane Xang and Nan try to oust the Burmese from Lanna, but fail.
1660	King Narai takes Chiang Mai and Lampang, but is eventually repulsed by a Burmese army.

a fortified town on the Mekong. It is said that Mengrai, concerned that the constant warring and squabbling between the lords of the north was harming the population, took it upon himself to unite the region under one king. That, inevitably, was himself. Entranced by the legendary wealth of Haripunjaya, Mengrai spent almost a decade hatching a plot to capture this powerful prize. He sent one of his scribes – Ai Fa – to ingratiate himself with the king of Haripunjaya, and having done this encouraged the scribe to sow seeds of discontent. By 1280, the king of Haripunjaya was alienated from his court and people, and in 1281, Mengrai attacked with a huge army and took the city without great trouble. Mengrai then set about uniting his expansive, new kingdom. This was helped to a significant degree by the propagation of Ceylonese Theravada Buddhism, which transcended tribal affiliations and helped to create a new identity of northern Thai. The Lanna (literally 'million rice fields') Thai Kingdom created by Mengrai was to remain the dominant power in the north until the mid-16th century, and was not truly incorporated into the Thai state until the 19th century.

In 1296, Mengrai built a new capital, which he named Chiang Mai – or 'New Town' (see page 233). The art of this era is called Chiang Saen and dates from the 11th century. It is still in evidence throughout the north – in Chiang Saen, Chiang Mai, Lamphun and Lampang – and shows strong stylistic links with Indian schools of art.

Sukhothai

South of Chiang Mai, at the point where the rivers of the north spill out onto the wide and fertile central plains, a second Thai Kingdom was evolving during the 13th century: the Sukhothai Kingdom. Sri Indraditya was the first known king of Sukhothai, in the 1240s when it was a small kingdom, and it remained a weak local power until the reign of its most famous king, **Ramkhamhaeng** (c1279-1298) or 'Rama the Brave', who gained his name – so it is said – after defeating an enemy general in single-handed elephant combat at the age of 19. When Ramkhamhaeng ascended to the throne in 1275, Sukhothai was a relatively small kingdom occupying part of the upper central plain. When he died in 1298, extensive swathes of land came under the king of Sukhothai's control, and only King Mengrai of Lanna and King Ngam Muang of Phayao could be regarded as his equals. In his first few years as king, Ramkhamhaeng had incorporated the area around Sukhothai into his mandala alongside Sawankhalok, Uttaradit, Kamphaeng Phet and Tak. But King Ramkhamhaeng is remembered as much for his artistic achievements as for his raw power. Under Khmer tutelage, he is said to have devised the Thai writing system and also made a number of administrative reforms. The inscription No 1 from his reign, composed in 1292, is regarded as the first work of Thai literature, and contains the famous lines:

"In the time of King Ramkhamhaeng, this land of Sukhothai is thriving. In the water there are fish, in the fields there is rice. The lord of the realm does not levy toll on his subjects for travelling the roads; they lead their cattle to trade or ride their horses to sell; whoever wants to trade in elephants does so; whoever wants to trade in horses, does so; whoever wants to trade in silver and gold, does so. When any commoner or man of rank dies, his estate – his elephants, wives, children, granaries, rice, retainers and groves of areca and betel – is left in its entirety to his son ... When [the king] sees someone's rice he does not covet it, when he sees someone's wealth he does not get angry ... He has hung a bell in the opening of the gate over there: if any commoner in the land has a grievance which sickens his belly and gripes his heart, and which he wants to make known to his ruler and lord, it is easy; he goes and strikes the bell which the king has hung there; King Ramkhamhaeng, the ruler of the kingdom, hears the call; he goes and questions the man, examines the case, and decides it justly for him. So the people of this *muang* [city/state] of Sukhotai praise him."

Every Thai schoolchild is taught to memorize the opening lines of the inscription, ones which seemingly just about every book on Thailand also repeats: *Nai naam mii plaa, nai naa mii khao*: "in the water there are fish, in the fields there is rice".

Although the kingdom of Sukhothai owed a significant cultural and artistic debt to the Khmers, by the 13th century the Tais of Sukhothai were beginning to explore and develop their own interpretations of politics, art and life. The kingdom promoted Theravada Buddhism (see page 750), sponsoring missionary monks to spread the word. In 1298, Ramkhamhaeng died and was succeeded by his son Lo Thai. His father's empire began to wane and by 1321 Sukhothai had declined in influence and become a small principality among many competing states. For many Thais today, the Sukhothai period – which lasted a mere 200 years – represents the apogee, the finest flowering of Thai brilliance. A visit to the ruins of Sukhothai or its sister city of Si Satchanalai reinforces this (see pages 196-207).

Ayutthaya (1314-1767)

1314	Birth of Uthong, reputed to have been the founder of Ayutthaya
1351	Ayutthaya is established and Uthong – renamed King Ramathibodi – ascends to the throne.
1390	King Ramesuan captures Chiang Mai.
1409-1424	Reign of King Intharacha.
1424	Following King Intharacha's death, his two elder sons contest a duel on elephant back for the throne – both die from their injuries, allowing a third son to accede.
1431-1432	King Borommaracha II takes and then sacks Angkor in Cambodia.
1448-88	Reign of King Boromtrailokant, best known for his administrative and legal reforms.
1507-1515	Drawn-out war between Ayutthaya and Lanna.
1549	Burmese invade and are repulsed.
1555	Naresuan, later to free Ayutthaya from the yoke of the Burmese, is born.
1558	Burmese take Chiang Mai.
1564	Burmese invade Ayutthaya.
1569	Burmese take the city of Ayutthaya and put their own puppet ruler, Maha Thammaracha, on the throne. The Burmese period lasts until 1593.
1570-1587	Cambodians forces invade Ayutthaya on six occasions in 18 years.
1585-1587	Naresuan defies and defeats the Burmese occupiers on two occasions.
1593	The Burmese send a massive army to defeat Naresuan, and are vanquished at Nong Sarai. Ayutthaya is restored as an independent kingdom.
1608	Siam sends its first diplomatic mission to Europe and trade relations, especially with the Dutch, grow.
1662	King Narai mounts an invasion of Burma.
1664	Trading treaty concluded with the Dutch.
1687	A large French diplomatic mission arrives in Ayutthaya.
1688	Narai's death leads to the Ayutthaya 'Revolution' and the execution of Constantine Phaulcon. Links with Europe and Western traders and emissaries are cut.
1733-1758	Reign of King Boromtrailokant, marking the apogee of Ayutthaya's power.
1760	Burmese forces beseige Ayutthaya, but retreat.
1766-1767	Burmese forces, after defeating Chiang Mai and other northern towns, beseige, capture and sack Ayutthaya, marking the end of the Ayutthaya period.

Ayutthaya

From the mid-14th century

In the middle of the 14th century, Sukhothai's influence began to be challenged by another Thai kingdom, Ayutthaya. Located over 300 km south on the Chao Phraya River, Ayutthaya was the successor to the Mon Kingdom of Lavo (Lopburi). It seems that from the 11th century, Tais began to settle in the area and were peacefully incorporated into the Mon state, where they gradually gained influence. Finally, in 1351, a Tai lord took control of the area and founded a new capital at the confluence of the Pa Sak, Lopburi and Chao Phraya rivers. He called the city Ayutthaya – after the sacred town of Ayodhya in the Hindu epic, the Ramayana (see page 86). This kingdom would subsequently be known as Siam. From 1351, Ayutthaya began to extend its power south as far as Nakhon Si Thammarat, and east to Cambodia, raiding Angkor in the late 14th century and taking the city in 1432. The palace at Angkor was looted by the Thai forces and the Khmers abandoned their capital, fleeing eastwards towards present-day Phnom Penh. Although Sukhothai and Ayutthaya initially vied with one another for supremacy, Ayutthaya proved the more powerful. In 1438, King Boromraja II placed his seven-year-old son, Ramesuan (later to become King Boromtrailokant), on the throne, signalling the end of Sukhothai as an independent power.

During the Ayutthayan period, the basis of Thai common law was introduced by King Ramathibodi (1351-1369), who drew upon the Indian legal code of Manu, while the powerful King Boromtrailokant (1448-1488) centralized the administration of his huge kingdom and introduced various other civil, economic and military reforms. Perhaps the most important was the *sakdi naa* system, in which an individual's social position was related to the size of his landholdings. The heir apparent controlled 16,000 ha, the highest official 1600 ha, and the lowest commoner 4 ha. A code of conduct for royalty was also introduced, with punishments again linked to position: princes of high rank who had violated the law were to be bound by gold fetters, those of lower rank by silver. The execution of a member of the royal family was, it has been said, carried out by placing them in a sack and either beating them to death with scented sandalwood clubs or having them trampled by white elephants. Even kicking a palace door would, in theory, lead to the amputation of the offending foot.

By King Boromtrailokant's reign, Ayutthaya had extended its control over 500,000 sq km, and the capital had a population of 150,000. Although the art of Ayutthaya is not as 'pure' as that of Sukhothai, the city impressed 16th- and 17th-century European visitors. The German surgeon Christopher Fryke remarked that "there is not a finer city in all India". Perhaps it was the tiger and elephant fights that excited the Europeans so much. The elephants (regarded as noble and representing the state) were expected to win by tossing the tiger (regarded as wild and representing disorder) repeatedly into the air. The fact that the tigers were often tied to a stake or attacked by several elephants at once must have lengthened the odds against them. (In Vietnam it was reported that tigers sometimes had their claws removed and jaws sewn together.) Despite the undoubted might of Ayutthaya and the absolute power that lay within each monarch's grasp, kings were not, in the main, able to name their successors. Blood was not an effective guarantee to kingship and a strong competitor could easily usurp a rival, even though he might – on paper – have a better claim to the throne. As a result, the history of Ayutthaya is peppered with court intrigues, bloody succession struggles and rival claims.

16th-18th centuries (Burmese invasion)

During this period, the fortunes of the Ayutthayan Kingdom were bound up with those of Burma. Over a 220-year period, the Burmese invaded on no less than six occasions. The first time was in 1548 when the Burmese king of Pegu, Tabengshweti, encircled the capital. King Mahachakrapat only survived the ensuing battle when one of his wives drove her elephant in front of an approaching warrior. Elephants figured heavily in war and diplomacy during the Ayutthayan period: Tabengshweti justified his invasion by

The early Chakri period (1767-1855)

1767	Ayutthaya sacked and capital moves to Thonburi.
1769-1770	Taksin begins to piece Siam back together when he takes control of Cambodia, Phitsanulok, Nakhon Si Thammarat and Fang.
1782	Rama I relocates capital from Thonburi to Bangkok.
1785	Burmese mount a huge invasion force, which is eventually repulsed.
1787	Burmese invade Lanna; also repulsed.
1788-1789	The Pali-language Buddhist Tripitaka is re-written in definitive style.
1800	Threat from Burma is ended and Siam becomes the leading power in the area.
1805	As part of his modernization programme, Rama I gives a committee of judges the job of reforming the Siamese legal code. They produce the Three Seals Laws.
1812	Growing friction between Siam and Vietnam.
1813	Siamese suzerainty of Cambodia ends, with Vietnam filling the void.
1821	John Crawfurd visits Siam on behalf of the governor-general of British India.
1825	John Burney is sent as British emissary to Siam.
1826	The commercial and diplomatic Burney Treaty is signed.
1827	King Anou of Laos invades northeastern Siam; his forces are eventually decimated and Vientiane is sacked by the Siamese army.
1829	Anou is captured and dies in captivity in Bangkok.
1833-1834	A Siamese and Lao army invades Cambodia; it is defeated by Vietnamese forces and Cambodia falls within the Vietnamese sphere of influence.
1855	Signing of the Bowring Treaty.

pointing out that he had no white elephants, the holiest of beasts (the Buddha's last reincarnation before his enlightenment was as a white elephant). The Ayutthayan king meanwhile had a whole stable of them, and was not willing to part with even one. Although this attack failed, in 1569, King Bayinnaung mounted another invasion and plundered the city, making Ayutthaya a vassal state. When the Burmese withdrew to Pegu, they left a ravaged countryside devoid of people, and large areas of rice land returned to scrub and forest. But a mere 15 years later, Prince Naresuan re-established Thai sovereignty, and began to lay the foundations for a new golden age in which Ayutthaya would be more powerful and prosperous than ever before (see page 167).

17th century (commercial and diplomatic expansion)

The 17th century saw a period of intense commercial contact with the Dutch, English and French. In 1608, Ayutthaya sent a diplomatic mission to the Netherlands and in 1664 a trading treaty was concluded with the Dutch. Even as early as the 17th century, Thailand had a flourishing prostitution industry. In the 1680s an official was given a monopoly of prostitution in the capital; he used 600 women to generate considerable state revenues. The kings of Ayutthaya also made considerable use of foreigners as advisers and ministers at the court. The most influential foreign family was founded by two Persian brothers, who arrived at the beginning of the 17th century. However, the best known was the

Penis balls and sexual roles in historical southeast Asia

One notable feature of Thai – and more widely, Southeast Asian – society is the relative autonomy of women. This is most clearly illustrated in sexual relations. As the historian Anthony Reid wrote in his book *Southeast Asia in the Age of Commerce 1450-1680*: "Southeast Asian literature of the period leaves us in little doubt that women took a very active part in courtship and lovemaking, and demanded as much as they gave by way of sexual and emotional gratification". He then went on to describe the various ways – often involving painful surgery – that men would try to satisfy their partners. Metal pins, for example, were inserted into the penis, and wheels, studs and spurs attached as accessories to increase the female's pleasure. Alternatively, metal balls or bells, sometimes made of gold or ivory, would be inserted beneath the skin of the penis. Numerous early European visitors expressed their astonishment at the practice. Tome Pires, the 16th-century Portuguese apothecary, observed that Pegu lords in Burma "wear as many as nine gold ones [penis bells], with beautiful treble, contralto and tenor tones, the size of the Alvares plums in our country; and those who are too poor … have them in lead … Malay women rejoice greatly when the Pegu men come to their country … [because of] their sweet harmony". Whereas, in Africa, genital surgery was, and is, often intended to suppress pleasure for women or increase it for men, in Southeast Asia the reverse was the case. The surgery described above was also widely practised in Burma, Siam, Makassar, among the Torajans of Sulawesi, and Java.

Greek adventurer Constantine Phaulcon, who began his life in the East as a mere cabin boy with the East India Company and rose to become one of King Narai's (1656-1688) closest advisers and one of the kingdom's most influential officials before being executed in 1688. He was implicated in a plot with the French against King Narai and his execution heralded 100 years of relative isolation as the Thais became wary of, and avoided close relations with, the West.

18th century (Ayutthaya's zenith)

The height of Ayutthaya's power and glory is often associated with the reign of King Boromkot (literally, 'the King in the urn [awaiting cremation]', as he was the last sovereign to be honoured in this way). Boromkot ruled from 1733 to 1758 and he fulfilled many of the imagined pre-requisites of a great king: he promoted Buddhism and ruled effectively over a vast territory. But, in retrospect, signs of imperial senility were beginning to materialize even as Ayutthaya's glory was approaching its zenith. In particular, King Boromkot's sons began to exert their ambitions. Prince Senaphithak, the eldest, went so far as to have some of the king's officials flogged; in retaliation, one of the officials revealed that the prince had been having an affair with one of Boromkot's three queens. He admitted to the liaison and was flogged to death, along with his lover.

The feud with Burma was renewed in 1760 when the Burmese King Alaungpaya invaded Thailand. His attack was repulsed after one of the siege guns exploded, seriously injuring the Burmese king. He died soon afterwards during the arduous march back to Pegu. Three years later his successor, King Hsinbyushin, raised a vast army and took Chiang Mai, Lamphun and Luang Prabang (Laos). By 1765, the Burmese were ready to mount a second assault on Ayutthaya. Armies approached from the north and west and at the beginning of 1766 met up outside the city, from where they laid siege to the capital. King Suriyamarin offered to surrender, but King Hsinbyushin would hear nothing of it. The city fell after a year, in 1767. David Wyatt, in *Thailand: A short history*, wrote: "The Burmese wrought awful desolation. They raped, pillaged and plundered and led tens of thousands of captives away to Burma. They put the torch to everything flammable and even hacked at images of the Buddha for the gold with which they were coated. King Suriyamarin is said to have fled the city in a small boat and starved to death 10 days later."

The city was too damaged to be renovated for a second time, and the focus of the Thai state moved southwards once again – to Thonburi, and from there to Bangkok.

Bangkok and the Rattanakosin period

After the sacking of Ayutthaya in 1766-1767, **General Taksin** moved the capital 74 km south to Thonburi, on the other bank of the Chao Pharaya River from modern day Bangkok. Taksin's original name was Sin. Proving himself an adept administrator, he was appointed Lord of Tak (a city in the upper central plain), or Phraya Tak. Hence his name Tak-sin. From Thonburi, Taksin successfully fought Burmese invasions, until the stress caused his mental health to deteriorate to the extent that he was forced to abdicate in 1782. A European visitor wrote in a letter that "He [Taksin] passed all his time in prayer, fasting, and meditation, in order by these means to be able to fly through the air". He became madder by the month and on 6 April 1782 a group of rebels marched on Thonburi, captured the king and asked one of Taksin's generals, Chao Phya Chakri, to assume the throne. The day that Chao Phya Chakri became King Ramathobodi, 6 April, remains a public holiday in Thailand – Chakri Day – and marks the beginning of the current Chakri Dynasty. Worried about the continuing Burmese threat, Rama I (as Chao Phya Chakri is known) moved his capital to the opposite, and safer, bank of the Chao Phraya River, founded Bangkok and began the process of consolidating his kingdom. By the end of the century, the Burmese threat had dissipated, and the Siamese were once again in a position to lead the Tai world.

19th century (Rama II's reign)

During Rama II's reign (1809-1824), a new threat emerged to replace the Burmese: that of the Europeans. In 1821, the English *East India Company* sent John Crawfurd as an envoy to Siam to open up trading relations. Although the king and his court remained unreservedly opposed to unfettered trade, Crawfurd's visit served to impress upon those more prescient Siamese where the challenges of the 19th century would lie.

Rama II's death and succession illustrates the dangers inherent in having a claim to the throne of Siam, even in the 19th century. The court chronicles record that in 1824 Prince Mongkut (the second son of Rama II) was ordained as a monk because the death of a royal elephant indicated it was an 'ill-omened time'. Historians believe that Rama II, realizing his death was imminent, wished to protect the young prince by bundling him off to a monastery, where the robes of a monk might protect him from court intrigues.

Rama III was the son of Rama II by a junior wife. When King Rama II died he was chosen by the accession council over Mongkut because the latter was in the monkhood. Rama III's reign (1824-1851) saw an invasion by an army led by the Lao King Anou. In 1827, Anou took Nakhon Ratchasima on the edge of the central plain and was within striking distance of Bangkok before being defeated. After their victory, the Siamese marched on Vientiane, plundering the city and subjugating the surrounding countryside. In 1829, King Anou himself was captured and transported to Bangkok, where he was displayed to the public in a cage. Anou died shortly after this humiliation – some say of shame, others say of self-administered poison. Before he died he is said to have laid a curse on the Chakri dynasty, swearing that never again would a Chakri king set foot on Lao soil. None has, and when the present King Bhumibol attended the opening of the Thai–Lao Friendship bridge over the Mekong in 1994, he did so from a sand bar in the middle of the river.

There were also ructions at the court in Bangkok: in 1848 Prince Rakrannaret (a distant relative of Rama III's) was found guilty of bribery and corruption and, just for good measure, homosexuality and treason as well. Rama III had him beaten to death with sandalwood clubs, in time-honoured Thai fashion.

The 19th century was a dangerous time for Siam. Southeast Asia was being methodically divided between Britain, France and Holland as they scrambled for colonial territories. The same fate might have befallen Siam, had it not been blessed with two brilliant kings: **King Mongkut (Rama IV – 1851-1868)** and **King Chulalongkorn (Rama V – 1868-1910)**.

Mongkut (the second son of Rama II) was a gifted scholar. He learnt English and Latin and when he sat his oral Pali examination, performed brilliantly. Indeed, his 27 years in a monastery allowed him to study the religious texts to such depth that he concluded that all Siamese ordinations were invalid. He established a new sect based upon the stricter Mon teachings, an order which became known as the *Thammayutika* or 'Ordering Adhering to the Dharma'. To distinguish themselves from those 'fallen' monks who made up most of the Sangha, they wore their robes with both shoulders covered. Mongkut derisively called the main Thai order – the *Mahanikai* – the 'Order of Long-standing Habit'.

But Mongkut was not an other-wordly monk with scholarly inclinations. He was a rational, pragmatic man who well appreciated the economic and military might of the Europeans. He recognized that if his kingdom was to survive he would have to accept and acquiesce to the colonial powers, rather than try to resist them. He did not accede to the throne until he was 47, and it is said that during his monastic studies he came to realize that if China, the Middle Kingdom, had to bow to Western pressure, then he would have to do the same.

He set about modernizing his country, along with the support of other modern-thinking princes. He established a modern ship-building industry, trained his troops in European methods and studied Western medicine. Most importantly, in 1855, he signed the **Bowring Treaty** with Britain, giving British merchants access to the Siamese market, and setting in motion a process of agricultural commercialization and the clearing of the vast central plains for rice cultivation. As David Wyatt wrote: "At the stroke of a pen, old Siam faced the thrust of a surging economic and political power with which they were unprepared to contend or compete". Mongkut's meeting with Sir John Bowring illustrates the lengths to which he went to meet the West on its own terms: he received the British envoy and offered him port and cigars from his own hand, an unheard of action in Thai circles.

It would seem that King Mongkut and **Sir John Bowring** were like-minded men. Both were scholars who believed in the power of rational argument. Bowring was a close friend of the philosophers Jeremy Bentham and John Stuart Mill, and he wrote a number of articles for the *Westminster Review*. He was a radical reformer, in favour of free trade and prison reform and bitterly opposed to slavery. He was a member of the House of Commons for six years, governor of Hong Kong, and Her Majesty's Consul in Canton (China). He was a remarkable man, just as Mongkut was a remarkable man, and his achievements during his 80-year life were enough to satisfy the ambitions of a dozen men. It seems that

Bowring used a mixture of veiled military force and rational argument to encourage Mongkut to sign the Bowring Treaty, perhaps the single most important treaty in Thailand's history. Bowring's account of his visit, the two volume *The kingdom and people of Siam*, published in 1857, is a remarkably perceptive work, especially given the brevity of Bowring's visit to Siam. As David Wyatt wrote in a reprint of the work (Oxford University Press, 1977), the book is undoubtedly "the finest account of Thailand at the middle of the 19th century, when it stood on the threshold of revolutionary change".

Unfortunately, in the West, Mongkut is not known for the skilful diplomacy that kept at bay expansionist nations considerably more powerful than his own, but for his characterization in the film *The King and I* (in which he is played by Yul Brynner). Poorly adapted from Anna Leonowens' own distorted accounts of her period as governess in the Siamese court, both the book and the film offend the Thai people. According to contemporary accounts, Mrs Leonowens was a bad tempered lady obviously given to flights of fantasy. She never became a trusted confidant of King Mongkut, who scarcely needed her limited skills, and there is certainly no evidence to indicate that he was attracted to her sexually. It appears that she was plain in appearance.

King Mongkut died on 1 October 1868 and was succeeded by his 15-year-old son **Chulalongkorn**. However, for the next decade a regent controlled affairs of state, and it was not until 1873, when Chulalongkorn was crowned for a second time, that he could begin to mould the country according to his own vision. The young king quickly showed himself to be a reformer like his father – for in essence Mongkut had only just begun the process of modernization. Chulalongkorn set about updating the monarchy by establishing ministries and ending the practice of prostration. He also accelerated the process of economic development by constructing roads, railways, schools and hospitals. The opium trade was regulated, court procedures streamlined and slavery finally completely abolished in 1905. Although a number of princes were sent abroad to study – Prince Rajebuidirekrit went to Oxford – Chulalongkorn had to also rely on foreign advisors to help him undertake these reforms. In total he employed 549 foreigners – the largest number being British, but also Dutch, Germans, French and Belgians. Chulalongkorn even held fancy dress parties at New Year and visited Europe twice. These visits included trips to the poor East End of London and showed Chulalongkorn that for all the power of Britain and France, they were still unable to raise the living standards of a large part of the population much above subsistence levels.

These reforms were not introduced without difficulty. The *Hua Boran* ('The Ancients'), as the king derogatorily called them, strongly resisted the changes and in late December 1874 Prince Wichaichan attempted to take the royal palace and usurp the king. The plot was thwarted at the last possible moment, but it impressed upon Chulalongkorn that reform could only come slowly. Realizing he had run ahead of many of his subjects in his zeal for change, he reversed some of his earlier reforms and toned down others. Nevertheless, Siam remained on the path of modernization – albeit progressing at a rather slower pace. As during Mongkut's reign, Chulalongkorn also managed to keep the colonial powers at bay. Although the king himself played a large part in placating the Europeans by skilful diplomacy and by presenting an image of urbane sophistication, he was helped in this respect by a brilliant minister of foreign affairs, his son, Prince Devawongse (1858-1923), who controlled Siam's foreign relations for 38 years. Devawongse looked into European systems of government with the aim of reforming Siam's administration and even attended the celebrations marking Queen Victoria's 50 years on the throne of Great Britain in 1887. During his time controlling Siam's foreign affairs, a new administrative system and a new system of ministries was introduced to extend Bangkok's power to the outer provinces.

The fundamental weakness of the Siamese state, in the face of the European powers, was illustrated in the dispute with France over Laos. Despite attempts by Prince Devawongse to manufacture a compromise, the French forced Siam to cede Laos to France in 1893 and to pay compensation – even though they had little claim to the territory. (The land on the far banks of the Mekong came under Thai suzerainty. The French annexed Laos on some rather dubious evidence that Vietnam – which they controlled – claimed suzerainty over Laos.) As it is said, power grows out of the barrel of a gun, and Chulalongkorn could not compete with France in terms of military might. After this humiliating climbdown, the king essentially retired from public life, broken in spirit and health. In 1909, the British chipped away at more of Siam's territory, gaining rights of suzerainty over the Malay states of Kelantan, Terengganu, Kedah and Perlis. In total, Siam relinquished nearly 500,000 sq km of territory to maintain the integrity of the core of the kingdom. King Chulalongkorn died on 24 October 1910, sending the whole nation into deep and genuine mourning.

20th century

The kings that were to follow Mongkut and Chulalongkorn could not have been expected to have had such illustrious, brilliant reigns. Absolute kingship was becoming increasingly incompatible with the demands of the modern world, and the kings of Thailand were resisting the inevitable. Rama VI, **King Vajiravudh** (1910-1925), second son of Chulalongkorn, was educated at Oxford and Sandhurst Military Academy and seemed well prepared for kingship. However, he squandered much of the wealth built up by Chulalongkorn and ruled in a rather heavy-handed uncoordinated style. He did try to inculcate a sense of 'nation' with his slogan 'king, nation, religion', but seemed more interested in Western theatre and literature than in guiding Siam through a difficult period in its history. He died at the age of only 44, leaving an empty treasury.

Like his older brother, **King Prajadhipok** (Rama VII – 1925-1935), was educated in Europe: at Eton, the Woolwich Military Academy and at the École Supérieure de Guerre in France. But he never expected to become king and was thrust onto the throne at a time of great strain. Certainly, he was more careful with the resources that his treasury had to offer, but could do little to prevent the country being seriously affected by the Great Depression of the 1930s. The price of rice, the country's principal export, declined by two-thirds and over the same two-year period (1930-1932) land values in Bangkok fell by 80%. The economy was in crisis and the government appeared to have no idea how to cope. In February 1932, King Prajadhipok told a group of military officers:

"The financial war is a very hard one indeed. Even experts contradict one another until they become hoarse. Each offers a different suggestion. I myself know nothing at all about finances, and all I can do is listen to the opinions of others and choose the best. I have never experienced such a hardship; therefore if I have made a mistake I really deserve to be excused by the officials and people of Siam".

The people, both the peasantry and the middle class, were dissatisfied by the course of events and with their declining economic position. But neither group was sufficiently united to mount a threat to the king and his government. Nevertheless, Prajadhipok was worried: there was a prophesy linked to Rama I's younger sister Princess Narinthewi, which predicted that the Chakri Dynasty would survive for 150 years and end on 6 April 1932.

Thailand enters the modern period (1911-1946)

1910	King Chulalongkorn dies, his second son Vajiravudh accedes to the throne.
1911	Wild Tiger Corp established – an adult unit and a youth unit, is formed which became Thailand's scout movement. They also became ultra-nationalist and ultra-monarchist and were implicated, for example, in the massacre of students outside Thammasat University in 1976.
1912	Attempted coup against the king is thwarted.
1917	A small force of Siamese soldiers is sent to Europe to fight with the Allies in the First World War.
1919-1920	Appalling rice harvest and other economic problems lead to severe economic difficulties.
1925	King Vajiravudh dies at the age of only 44 on 26 November.
1927	King Prajadhipok (educated at Eton and the Woolwich Military Academy) writes a paper on 'Democracy in Siam', and also appoints an advisory council to deliberate on government reform.
1930-1932	Great Depression hits Siam.
1932	The Revolution of 24 June, and Siam becomes a constitutional monarchy. Phraya Mano becomes the first prime minister.
1935	King Prajadiphok abdicates on 2 March. King Ananda Mahidol comes to the throne aged just 10. Two princes rule while he is finishing his schooling in Switzerland.
1938	Phibun Songkram becomes prime minister introduces nationalistic and anti-Chinese policies.
1939	Phibun changes the country's name from Siam to Thailand.
1940	Thai forces invade Laos and Cambodia following the German defeat of France.
1941	Japanese forces invade Thailand, and Bangkok is forced to agree a military alliance with Japan in December.
1944	Phibun is forced to resign with the Japanese on the verge of defeat.
1945	King Ananda Mahidol returns to Thailand to take his throne.
1946	King Ananda Mahidol is killed in mysterious circumstances. His brother King Bhumibol Adulyadej comes to the throne.

The Revolution of 1932

The date itself passed without incident, but just 12 weeks later on 24 June a clique of soldiers and civilians staged a **coup d'état**, while the king was holidaying at the seaside resort of Hua Hin. This episode is often called the Revolution of 1932, but it was not in any sense a revolution involving a large rump of the people. It was orchestrated by a small elite, essentially for the elite. The king accepted the terms offered to him, and wrote:

"I have received the letter in which you invite me to return to Bangkok as a constitutional monarch. For the sake of peace; and in order to save useless bloodshed; to avoid confusion and loss to the country; and, more, because I have already considered making this change myself, I am willing to co-operate in the establishment of a constitution under which I am willing to serve."

Reign of Prince Ananda Mahidol

However, King Prajadhipok had great difficulty adapting to his lesser role and, falling out with the military, he abdicated in favour of his young nephew, Prince Ananda Mahidol, in 1935. The prince at the time was only 10 years old, and at school in Switzerland, so the newly created National Assembly appointed two princes to act as regents. From this point, until after the Second World War, the monarchy was only partially operative. Ananda was out of the country for most of the time, and the civilian government took centre stage. Ananda was not to physically reoccupy the throne until December 1945 and just six months later he was found dead in bed, a bullet through his head. The circumstances behind his death have never been satisfactorily explained and it remains a subject on which Thais are not openly permitted to speculate. Books investigating the death are still banned in Thailand.

Phibun Songkhram and Pridi Panomyong

While the monarchy receded from view, the civilian government was going through the intrigues and power struggles that were to become such a feature of the future politics of the country. The two key men at this time were the army officer Phibun Songkhram and the left-wing idealist lawyer Pridi Panomyong. Between them they managed to dominate Thai politics until 1957.

When **Prime Minister Pridi Panomyong** tried to introduce a socialist economic programme in 1933, pushing for the state control of the means of production, he was forced into exile in Europe. This is often seen as the beginning of the tradition of authoritarian, right-wing rule in Thailand (although to be fair, Pridi's vision of economic and political reform was poorly thought through and rather romantic). Nonetheless, with Pridi in Paris – at least for a while – it gave the more conservative elements in the government the chance to promulgate an anti-communist law, and thereby to usher in a period of ultra-nationalism. Anti-Chinese propaganda became more shrill, with some government positions being reserved for ethnic Tais. In 1938 the populist writer Luang Wichit compared the Chinese in Siam with the Jews in Germany, and thought that Hitler's policies might be worth considering for his own country.

This shift in policy can be linked to the influence of one man: Luang Phibun Songkhram. Born of humble parents in 1897, he worked his way up through the army ranks and then into politics. He became prime minister in 1938 and his enduring influence makes him the most significant figure in 20th-century Thai politics. Under his direction, Siam became more militaristic, xenophobic, as well as 'religiously' nationalistic, avidly pursuing the reconversion of Siamese Christians back to Buddhism. As if to underline these developments, in 1939 Siam adopted a new name: Thailand. Phibun justified this change on the grounds that it would indicate that the country was controlled by Thais and not by the Chinese or any other group.

Second World War

During the Second World War, Phibun Songkhram sided with the Japanese who he felt sure would win. He saw the war as an opportunity to take back some of the territories lost to the French (particularly) and the British. In 1940, Thai forces invaded Laos and Western Cambodia. A year later, the Japanese used the kingdom as a launching pad for their assaults on the British in Malaya and Burma. Thailand had little choice but to declare war on the Allies and to agree a military alliance with Japan in December 1941. As allies of the Japanese, Phibun's ambassadors were instructed to declare war on Britain and the

Thai, Siamese or Tai?

Is a Thai a Tai? And is this the same as a Siamese? Sometimes. Thai here is used to mean a national of Thailand. Prior to the Second World War, Thailand was known as Siam, a name by which Europeans had referred to the kingdom from the 16th century. However, in 1939 Prime Minister Phibun Songkhram decided a change was in order, largely because he wished to disassociate his country from the past, but also because of his xenophobia towards the Chinese. The name he chose is a more direct translation of the Thai term *prathet Thai*, and firmly established Thailand as the 'country of the Tais'. Nonetheless, because the change is associated with the right-wing Phibun government, some academics still refuse to use the name and talk, rather pointlessly, of Siam.

Tai here is used to refer to the Tai-speaking peoples who are found not just in Thailand, but also in Burma, Laos and southern China. Some Thais are not Tai (for example, the Malay-speaking Thais of the south), while many Tais are not Thais. As David Wyatt wrote in his *Thailand: A Short History*: "The modern Thai may or may not be descended by blood from the late-arriving Tai. He or she may instead be the descendant of still earlier Mon or Khmer inhabitants of the region, or of much later Chinese or Indian immigrants. Only over many centuries has a 'Thai' culture, a civilization and identity emerged as the product of interaction between Tai and indigenous and immigrant cultures."

A slightly different issue is the question of what makes a Thai a Thai. In other words, what are the defining characteristics of Thai-ness. This is shaky ground, dotted with metaphorical minefields. Ethnicity is noted on every Thai's identity card, but there is no system governing the categories applied. A person with 'Chinese' parents is counted a 'Thai', yet a Muslim Thai from the south is counted a 'Muslim', not a Thai. Some would say that there is method in this muddle, and that being a Theravada Buddhist is a critical component of being counted a true 'Thai'. Rather less contentious is an uncritical love of the king. All schoolchildren are taught that Thai-ness is encapsulated in three symbols, 'King, Nation, Religion', and this goes much of the way to explaining what the average Thai views as representative of being a Thai.

United States. However, the ambassador in Washington, Seni Pramoj, refused to deliver the declaration (he considered it illegal) and Thailand never formally declared war on the USA. In Thailand itself, Pridi, who had returned as regent to the young monarch King Ananda, helped to organize the Thai resistance – the Free Thai Movement. They received help from the US Office of Strategic Services (OSS) and the British Force 136, and also from many Thais. As the tide of the war turned in favour of the Allies, so Prime Minister Phibun was forced to resign. He spent a short time in gaol in Japan, but was allowed to return to Thailand in 1947.

Post-war Thailand

After the war, Seni Pramoj, Thailand's ambassador in the USA, became prime minister. He was soon succeeded by Pridi Panomyong, who had gathered a good deal of support due to the role he played during the conflict. However, in 1946 King Ananda was mysteriously found shot dead in his royal apartments and Pridi was implicated in a plot. He was forced to resign, so enabling Phibun to become prime minister once again – a post he kept until 1957. Phibun's fervent anti-communist stance quickly gained support in the USA, which contributed generous amounts of aid as the country became a front-line state in the battle against the 'red tide' that seemed to be engulfing Asia. Phibun's closest brush with death occurred in June 1951. He was leading a ceremony on board a dredge, the *Manhattan*, when he was taken prisoner during a military coup and transferred to the Thai navy flagship *Sri Ayutthaya*. The air force and army stayed loyal to Phibun, and planes bombed the ship. As it sank, the prime minister was able to swim to safety. The attempted coup resulted in 1200 deaths – mostly civilians. For the navy, it has meant that ever since it has been treated as the junior member of the armed forces, receiving far less resources than the army and air force.

Prime Minister Phibun Songkhram was deposed following a coup d'état in 1957, and was replaced by **General Sarit Thanarat**. General Sarit established the National Economic Development Board (now the National Economic and Social Development Board) and introduced Thailand's first five-year national development plan in 1961. He was a tough, uncompromising leader, and following his death in 1963 was replaced by another General – **Thanom Kitticachorn**. With the war in Indochina escalating, Thanom allowed US planes to be based in Thailand, from where they flew bombing sorties over the Lao panhandle and Vietnam. In 1969 a general election was held, which Thanom won, but as the political situation in Thailand deteriorated, so Prime Minister Thanom declared martial law. However, unlike his predecessors Sarit and Phibun, Thanom could not count on the loyalty of all elements within the armed forces, and although he tried to take the *nak laeng* (strongman) approach, his administration always had a frailty about it. In addition, historian David Wyatt argues that developments in Thai society, particularly an emergent middle-class and an increasingly combative body of students, made controlling the country from the centre rather harder than it had been over the previous decades.

October Revolution

It was Thailand's students who precipitated probably the single most tumultuous event since the Revolution of 1932. The student body felt that Thanom had back-tracked and restricted the evolution of a more open political system in the country. In June 1973 they began to demonstrate against the government, printing highly critical pamphlets and calling for the resignation of Thanom. A series of demonstrations, often centred on Sanaam Luang near the radical Thammasat University and the Grand Palace, brought crowds of up to 500,000 onto the streets. During the demonstrations, Thanom lost the support of the army: the Commander-in-Chief, General Krit Sivara, was unwilling to send his troops out to quell the disturbances, while Thanom, apparently, was quite willing to kill thousands if necessary. With the army unwilling to confront the students, and with the king – crucially – also apparently siding with Thanom's army opponents, he was forced to resign from the premiership and fled the country.

David Wyatt wrote of the October Revolution: "In many important respects, the events of October 1973 deserved far more the name 'revolution' than either the events of 1932 or the authoritarian program of Sarit. They brought about an end to one-man, authoritarian rule; and if they did not bring an end to the military role in politics, then they at least signalled a new consciousness of the necessity of sharing political power more widely than had ever been the case in the past."

The October Revolution ushered in a period of turbulent democratic government in Thailand, the first such period in the country's history. It was an exciting time: radical scholars could openly speak and publish, students could challenge the establishment, labour unions could organize and demonstrate, and leftist politicians could make their views known. But it was also a period of political instability. While there had been just five prime ministers between 1948 and 1973, the three years following 1973 saw the rapid coming and going of another four: Sanya Dharmasakti (October 1973-February 1975), Seni Pramoj (February-March 1975), Kukrit Pramoj (March 1975-January 1976) and Seni Pramoj (April-October 1976). This instability was reinforced by the feeling among the middle classes that the students were pushing things too far. The fall of Vietnam, Cambodia and Laos to communism left many Thais wondering whether they would be the next 'domino' to topple. This gave an opening for rightist groups to garner support, and anti-communist organizations like the Red Gaurs and the Village Scouts gained in influence and began, with the support and connivance of the police, to harrass and sometimes murder left-wingers. "Violence, vituperation, and incivility" as Wyatt wrote "were now a part of public life as they never had been before in Thailand."

Thammasat University Massacre

This was the background that led the army to feel impelled to step in once again. However, the trigger for the appalling events of October 1976 was the return of former Prime Minister Thanom from exile, who joined the *sangha* and became a monk. Installed in a Bangkok monastery, Thanom was visited by members of the royal family. The students took this as royal recognition of a man who had led the country into violence and to the edge of civil war. Demonstrations broke out in Bangkok, again centred on Sanaam Luang and the nearby Democracy Monument. This time, though, the students were not able to face down the forces of the Right. Newspapers printed pictures apparently showing the crown prince being burnt in effigy by students at Thammasat, and right wing groups, along with the police and the army, advanced on the university on 6 October. Details of the hours that followed are hazy. However, it seems clear that an orgy of killing ensued. With the situation rapidly deteriorating, the army stepped in and imposed martial law. Tanin Kraivixien was installed as prime minister, to be replaced the following year by Kriangsak Chomanan.

In 1996, on the 20th anniversary of the massacre, newspapers in Thailand were filled with the reminiscences of those from both sides who were involved. The bones of the tragic episode were picked over exhaustively and the still grieving parents of some of those who were murdered or 'disappeared' were interviewed. Such was the coverage of the event – far more detailed and honest than anything at the time – that it was almost as if the Thai nation were engaged in a collective catharsis, cauterizing the wounds of 20 years earlier. Yet in a way the debate over the massacre said as much about the present as the past. Kasian Tejapira, one of the student leaders involved, and by 1996 a university lecturer, suggested that the anniversary was an opportunity "to redefine the meaning of Thai identity – one that is anti-elitist and not conservative; one that was put down at Thammasat 20 years ago". The former student activists are now in positions of power and influence. Some are wealthy businessmen, others university lecturers, while more still are involved in politics. Most seem to have retained their commitment to building a just society.

The 1976 massacre was a shot in the arm for the **Communist Party of Thailand (CPT)**. Left-wing intellectuals and many students, feeling that they could no longer influence events through the political system, fled to the jungle and joined the CPT. The victories of the communists in neighbouring Indochina also reinforced the sense that ultimately the CPT would emerge victorious. By the late 1970s the ranks of the party had swelled to

Jit Poumisak's radical history

Most histories of Thailand tell a conservative tale: of peasants working in the fields, protected by the merit of a benevolent king. Indeed, many Thai historians seem to go out of their way to paint a picture of Thailand's history, which is notable for its conservativism. It is no accident that perhaps the greatest early Thai historian, Damrong Rajanubhab, was himself a Chakri prince. Throughout the 19th century and the first half of the 20th century, Thai scholars eschewed radicalism and perpetuated a conservative view of Thai history.

In 1957 this cosy world was disrupted by the publication (in Thai) of Jit Poumisak's *The real face of Thai feudalism today*. The book turned Thai history on its head. For the first time, it presented a picture of Thailand where feudalism, and not just benevolent monarchs, reigned; where the masses were engaged in a struggle against oppressive rulers; where history

was interpreted through economics; and where the social system governed relations between classes. It was Thailand's history with a Marxist visage.

Jit's reinterpretation of Thai history was, at least in the Thai context, astounding for its daring. Religion and culture were recast as the agents through which kings maintained their positions of power. Peasants – the great mass of the population – became pawns manipulated in the interests of the ruling classes, their impoverished position both maintained and justified in terms of religion and culture.

Unsurprisingly, Jit's work was not received warmly by Thailand's elite. In 1958 the book was banned and Jit was imprisoned for sedition. In 1973 it was republished during Thailand's experiment in democracy, only to be banned again in 1977, as the forces of dictatorship gained the upper hand. In 1979 it was reprinted for a third time as the threat of communism

around 14,000 armed guerrillas, who controlled large areas of the northeast, north and south. However, with the ascendancy of Prem Tinsulanond to the premiership in 1980 and a rapidly changing global political environment, the CPT fragmented and quickly lost support. Its leaders were divided between support for China and the Cambodian Khmer Rouge on the one hand, and the Soviet Union and Vietnam on the other. When the government announced an amnesty in 1980, many of the students who had fled into the forests and hills following the riots of 1973 returned to mainstream politics, exhausted and disenchanted with revolutionary life. In true Thai style, they were largely forgiven and re-integrated into society. Those who died on Sanaam Luang and in the streets leading off it have never been acknowledged, and in many cases their parents were never informed that they had been killed – nor were they allowed to collect their children's bodies. As the Thai historian Thongchai Winichakul lamented on the 20th anniversary of the massacre in 1996, this showed the extent to which Thai society still valued national stability over individual rights: "Life is more significant than the nation."

Prem Tinsulanond presided over the most stable period in Thai politics since the end of the Second World War. He finally resigned in 1988, and by then Thailand – or so most people thought – was beginning to outgrow the habit of military intervention in civilian politics. Chatichai Choonhaven replaced Prem after general elections in 1988, by which time the country was felt to be more stable and economically prosperous than at any time in recent memory. During his reign, the present King Bhumibol has played a crucial role in

receded and remains in print, required reading by every student of Thai history.

During the brief phase of democratic politics between 1973 and 1976, Jit became a central figure in the Left's struggle against the Right. Students read his works and seminars were arranged to discuss his life and thoughts. Jit became an emblem of – and an emblem for – the Left. By all accounts he was a brilliant scholar with a highly original mind.

His radical inclinations first became evident in 1953 when he was appointed editor of the Chulalongkorn University Yearbook. But just before the book went to press, the university authorities tried to halt its publication, claiming it was seditious. A university assembly was called to discuss the affair and some 3000 students attended. Jit made an impassioned and eloquent speech defending his editorial role, but just as the audience seemed to be swinging in his favour a group of engineering students rushed the stage and knocked Jit unconscious.

From that moment on, Jit was on the outside. He continued to enrage the authorities with his radical writings. He was arrested and interrogated by the police. He moved closer to the Communist Party of Thailand – although he was not made a member until after his death. The final break with the establishment came in 1965, when he left Bangkok and fled to the jungle to join in the Communist Party of Thailand's struggle against the government. Less than a year later, in May 1966, he was shot and killed in Sakhon Nakhon province in the northeastern region. Accounts differ on who shot him. However, it seems that a local headman killed him, possibly as he and a fellow insurgent stopped to barter for supplies. According to one source, a hand was cut from the corpse and sent to Bangkok for identification.

maintaining social stability, while the political system has been in turmoil. He is highly revered by his subjects, and has considerable power to change the course of events.

There are essentially two views on the role of the king in contemporary Thailand. The general view is that he has influence far beyond that which his constitutional position strictly permits, but that he is careful not to over-exercise that power and only intervenes at times of crisis. The king, in short, is his own man and acts in the best interests of the Thai people. The alternative view is that after his coronation, influential courtiers and generals tried to diminish the power of the king by making him a semi-divine figurehead and surrounding him in protocol. The king became a tool used by right-wing dictators and the army to justify their authoritarian ways. (For further background on the king, see box page 710.)

From massacre to crisis: 1991-1997

The widely held belief that the Thai political system had come of age proved ill-founded. In February 1991, with the prime minister daring to challenge the armed forces, **General Suchinda Kraprayoon** staged a bloodless coup d'état and ousted the democratically elected government of Chatichai Choonhavan. The last decade of the 20th century was a pretty eventful one for Thailand. At the end of the year, egged on by two generals-turned-politicians – Chamlong Srimuang and Chaovalit Yongchaiyut – 100,000 people gathered in Bangkok to protest against a Suchinda and military-imposed constitution.

Elections in March 1992 produced no clear winner and General Suchinda tearfully agreed to become premier – something he had previously promised he would not do. Chamlong Srimuang took this as his cue to call his supporters onto the streets and announced he was going on hunger strike. Tens of thousands of people gathered around the parliament buildings and Sanaam Luang, near the Grand Palace. Suchinda buckled under this weight of public outrage and appeared to agree to their demands. But Suchinda went back on his word, and in response tens of thousands of demonstrators returned to the streets. Suchinda called in the army and scores of people were killed.

Three days after the confrontation between the army and the demonstrators, **King Bhumibol** ordered both Suchinda and opposition leader Chamlong – who had to be released from gaol for the meeting – to his palace. There, television cameras were waiting to witness Suchinda's global, public humiliation. He and Chamlong prostrated themselves on the floor while the king lectured them, asking rhetorically: "What is the use of victory when the winner stands on wreckage?" Immediately afterwards, the army and the demonstrators withdrew from the streets. On Friday, Suchinda offered his resignation to the king, and on Saturday, less than one week after the killing began, Suchinda Kraprayoon fled the country. In a televised address, Suchinda accepted responsibility for the deaths.

After the riots of May 1992, and General Suchinda's humiliating climbdown, Anand Panyarachun was appointed interim prime minister. New elections were set for September, which the Democrat Party won. **Chuan Leekpai** was appointed 1992's fourth prime minister. Chuan, a mild-mannered southerner from a poor background (his father was a fish vendor in Trang) gained his law degree while living as a novice monk in a monastery. Never one for flashiness and quick fixes, Chuan became known as Chuan Chuengcha – or Chuan the slowmover. He may have been slow but his government lasted more than 2½ years, making it the longest serving elected government in Thai history, before he was forced to resign over a land scandal.

The Chart Thai Party, led by 62-year-old **Banharn Silpa-Archa**, won the election – or at least the largest number of seats – and formed a coalition government of seven parties. Bangkok's intelligentsia were horrified. Like Chuan, Banharn came from a poor background and was very much a self-made man. But in almost all other respects, Banharn and Chuan could not have been more different. Banharn's Chart Thai was closely associated with the military junta and was viewed as incorrigibly corrupt. As British political scientist Duncan McCargo explained: "there's no movement for [true] democracy. There's nothing but the money, and the results [of the election] bear that out". Two Chart Thai candidates in the elections were even accused of involvement in the narcotics trade. Thanong Wongwan was indicted in California with drug trafficking, where he was reportedly known as 'Thai Tony', and the party's deputy leader Vatana Asavahame had a visa request turned down by the US authorities on similar grounds. Banharn was even accused of plagiarism in his Masters thesis, which is said to bear a striking similarity to a paper by his academic advisor – who Banharn appointed to his cabinet.

While the press may have hated Banharn (*The Nation* stated that "the only way for 1996 to be a good year is for the Banharn government to go"), he survived because he was an arch populist politician. He used to step from his limousine and order local officials to mend roads, provide electricity, or improve health services. Here was a man getting things done, sweeping away red tape, and putting the interests of ordinary people first. But while Banharn might have been able to ignore the press, he couldn't ignore the king. In late summer 1995, Banharn's government found itself explicitly criticized by the palace when the king highlighted government failures to address Bangkok's infrastructural mess and its shortcomings in dealing with serious flooding. Ministers, the king said, only "talk, talk, talk and argue, argue, argue". Taking the king's cue, the great and the good including businessmen, influential civil servants, four former Bank of Thailand governors, opposition politicians (of course), even his own daughter, demanded that he step down. On 21 September 1996 Banharn announced his resignation. The king dissolved parliament.

The elections of 17 November 1996 were close, with **Chaovalit Yongchaiyudh's** New Aspirations Party (NAP) just managing to win the largest number of seats, and after the usual bickering and horse-trading he managed to stitch together a six-party coalition controlling 221 seats in the 393-seat House of Representatives. Chaovalit, a canny 64-year-old former army commander-in-chief, never completely managed to hide his ambition to become premier. He was an old-style patronage politician who depended on his links with the army and on handing out lucrative concessions to his supporters. "Transparency", as Democrat MP Surin Pitsuwan was quoted as saying in August 1996, "is not in his dictionary".

In retrospect, the mid-1990s were a watershed in contemporary Thailand's history. On 18 July 1995 the Princess Mother (the king's mother) died. After the king she was probably the most revered person in the country. Born a commoner and trained as a nurse, she married a prince. Their two sons, Mahidol and Bhumipol, unexpectedly became kings (Mahidol for only a short time before his tragic death). Her funeral in 1996 was a grandiose affair and her death has been likened to that of Britain's Princess Diana. Even Bangkok's massage parlours closed as a mark of respect. 1996 also saw the 50th anniversary of King Bhumibol's accession to the throne and the country threw a massive party to celebrate the event. The celebrations were as much a mark of Thailand's coming of age as of the king's golden jubilee. No expense was spared by the newly self-confident Tiger Thailand. Both events – the Princess Mother's funeral and the king's jubilee – were, for those so inclined, omens. The night before the funeral there was an unseasonable rainstorm; and during the procession of royal boats on the Chao Phraya it also poured. The king's boat was washed off course and had to be rescued by the navy. As it turned out, 1996 was the last year when money was no object.

Modern Thailand

Bust, boom and bust

As Thailand entered the 21st century and the third millennium, the country was also, rather shakily, recovering from the deepest contraction of the economy since the 1930s. Until July 1997, everything was hunky dory in Thailand. Or that, at least, is what the World Bank and most business people and pundits thought. The kingdom's economy was expanding at close to double-digit rates and the country was being showered with strings of congratulatory epithets. It was a 'miracle' economy, an Asian 'tiger' or 'dragon' ready to pounce on an unsuspecting world. Thailand has become the 'Cinderella' of Southeast Asia – a beautiful woman long disguised beneath shabby clothes – and academics and journalists were turning out books with glowing titles like *Thailand's Boom* (1996), *Thailand's Turn: Profile of a New Dragon* (1992) and *Thailand's Macro-economic Miracle* (1996). Wealth was growing, poverty falling and Bangkok was chock-full of designer shops, meeting the consumer needs of a growing, and increasingly hedonistic, middle-class.

Post-war Thailand

1946	King Bhumibol accedes to the throne.
1951	Attempted coup by the Navy against Prime Minister Phibun Songkhram is thwarted by the army and air force.
1957	Sarit Thanarat becomes prime minister; he ushers in the era of modern development, known as *samai pattana*.
1961	Publication of Thailand's first 'Five Year Development Plan'.
1963	Thanom Kitticachorn replaces Sarit as PM following Sarit's death.
1964	US military aircraft are based on Thai soil. Operations increase as the Vietnam War escalates.
1967	Thailand becomes a founder member of the Association of Southeast Asian Nations (ASEAN).
1967	Bangkok agrees to send troops to support the USA in South Vietnam.
1968	45,000 US personnel in Thailand and more than 600 aircraft.
1973	Massive demonstrations at Thammasat University in support of democracy leads to the resignation of Thanom.
1973-1976	Period of turbulent democratic government.
1976	Massacre of students at Thammasat University in Bangkok as the military steps in again. A shot in the arm for the CPT.
Late 1970s	CPT has 14,000 men and women under arms.
1980	Prem Tinsulanond becomes prime minister.
Mid-1980s	CPT a spent force. Thailand enters its period of rapid economic growth.
1988	Democratic elections, Chatichai Choonhaven becomes prime minister.
1991	Suchinda Kraprayoon leads successful coup against Chatichai.
1992	Massacre of anti-dictatorship demonstrators in Sanaam Luang. Democratic elections.
1995	The king of Thailand celebrates 50 years on the throne.
1997	Baht is devalued and Thailand's economic crisis begins.
2001	Thaksin Shinawatra becomes prime minister after landslide election victory.
2004	The separatist struggle in southern Thailand intensifies. Tak Bai incident in which 85 detained Muslim demonstrators from southern Thailand are suffocated. Asian Tsunami hits southern Thailand – huge casualties, including thousands of tourists and illegal foreign labourers.
2005	Thaksin re-elected in massive landslide.
2006	Huge demonstrations in Bangkok against Thaksin's rule after allegations of corruption and lese-majesty. Thaksin calls election – opposition refuse to stand and results are annulled. 19 September, Thaksin deposed in a military coup.
2007	New military junta-inspired Consitution and Thaksin's supporters in People's Power Party (PPP) come to power after landslide victory
2008	People's Alliance for Democracy (PAD) occupy government house. In November, they occupy Bangkok's airports stranding 300,000 tourists. PPP government dissolved by the courts. Abhisit is named Prime Minister.
2009	Democrat government cracks down on burgeoning anti-royalist movement. Pro-democracy, anti-military movement (Red Shirts) holds demontrations.

Of course even in the heady days of double-digit economic growth there were those who questioned the direction and rapidity of the country's development, and the social, economic and environmental tensions and conflicts that arose. By the mid-1990s Bangkok was overstretched, its transport system on the verge of collapse and the air barely fit to breath. While the elite few breezed from boutique to club in their air-conditioned Mercedes, around one million people were living in slum settlements in the capital. Deforestation had become so rampant, and so uncontrolled, that the government felt impelled to impose a nationwide logging ban in 1989. Even the kingdom's national parks were being systematically poached and encroached. In the poor northeastern region, incomes had stagnated, causing social tensions to become more acute and millions to migrate to the capital each dry season in a desperate search for work. In some villages in the north, meanwhile, AIDS had already spread to the extent that scarcely a household was not touched by the epidemic.

Most of these problems, though, were viewed by many analysts as side effects of healthy economic growth – problems to be managed through prudent planning and not reasons to doubt the wisdom of the country's broader development strategy.

Economic crisis

Then everything went horribly wrong. The local currency, the baht, went into freefall, the stockmarket crashed, unemployment more than doubled, and the economy contracted. Bankrupt business people, the *nouveau pauvre*, cashed in their Mercedes, and wives were put on strict spending diets. Almost overnight, apparently prescient commentators, who had remained strangely silent during the years of growth, were offering their own interpretations of Thailand's fall from economic grace. A distinct whiff of schadenfreude filled the air. Epithet writers went back to their computers and came up with titles like the 'Asian contagion', the 'Asian mirage', 'Frozen miracles' and 'Tigers lose their grip'. In Thailand itself, locals began to talk of the *Thaitanic* as it sank faster than the doomed liner.

The financial crisis of July 1997 quickly became a much wider economic crisis. The failure of the economy was, in turn, interpreted as a failure of government. Prime Minister Chaovalit Yongchaiyut tried to sound convincing in the face of a collapsing currency and a contracting economy, but he resigned before the year was out. Chuan Leekpai, his successor, manfully struggled to put things to rights but after little more than two years at the helm was trounced in a general election in early 2001 by telecoms billionaire Thaksin Shinawatra. Perhaps most importantly in the long term, while Thailand was on the economic ropes, Parliament approved a radically new constitution aimed at cleaning up Thailand's notoriously corrupt political system.

Politics

Politics during an economic crisis: 1997-2000

Chaovalit was, in a sense, unlucky to take over the reins of government when he did. Economic conditions were a cause for concern in the country in late 1996, but no one – scholar or pundit – predicted the economic meltdown that was just a few months away. He appointed the well-respected Amnuay Virawan as finance minister. But the collapse of the baht, the Bangkok stock market, the property and finance sectors, and a haemorrhaging loss of domestic and international confidence created conditions that were impossible to manage. Even so, his performance was hardly memorable. As *The Economist* tartly put it, "he dithered when decisions were needed, bumbled when clear words might have helped, and smiled benignly while the economy got worse". The central bank spent a staggering US$10 billion trying to defend the baht's peg to the US dollar, and interest rates were raised to 1300% for offshore borrowers in an ultimately futile attempt to keep the speculators at bay. The baht was allowed to float on 2 July, ending 13 years of being pegged to the US dollar. Two cabinet reshuffles during August did little to stem the criticism of Chaovalit and his administration, and there was talk of military intervention – though the army commander-in-chief quickly distanced himself from any such suggestion. In September, Chaovalit used his promised support for a vote on a new constitution (see below) to defeat a no-confidence motion. Even so, the end of Chaovalit's administration was in sight. On 7 November, Chaovalit resigned as prime minister after less than a year in power.

Following Chaovalit's resignation, **Chuan Leekpai**, leader of the Democrat Party, stitched together a new seven-party, 208-person coalition and became prime minister for the second time. Given talk of military intervention a few months earlier, it was a relief to many that Thailand had achieved a peaceful change of government. The key question, however, was whether Chuan could do any better than Chaovalit, particularly given the mixed make-up of his coalition government. Chuan and his finance minister, Tarrin Nimmanahaeminda (the fourth finance minister of the year) vigorously implemented the International Monetary Fund's rescue package and even managed to negotiate a slight loosening of the terms of the package.

The economic crisis enabled a coterie of young, reform-minded politicians to gain high office – like urbane, US-educated foreign minister Surin Pitsuwan. Fed up with coups and corruption, and backed by an increasingly assertive middle-class, these politicians were committed to change. As Chuan's special assistant, Bunaraj Smutharaks, explained to journalist Michael Vatikiotis, "If we don't seize this opportunity to instigate change, the future generations will see this [economic] crisis as a lost opportunity". (Far Eastern Economic Review, 30.06.98)

Under Chuan's leadership, Thailand became a role model for the IMF and foreign investors applauded the government's attempts to put things in order. The difficulty that Chuan faced throughout his second stint as premier was that the economy didn't bounce back after Thailand Inc had taken the IMF's unpalatable medicine. Many foreign commentators praised Chuan's efforts seeing him as honest and pragmatic. But domestic commentators tended to depict him as bumbling and ineffectual, toadying to the IMF while Thailand's poor were squeezed by multilateral organizations and Thai companies were sold to foreign interests at 'fire sale' prices

Thaksin Shinawatra takes over

The beginning of January 2001 saw the election of **Thaksin Shinawatra** and the Thai Rak Thai party, in a landslide victory over Chuan Leekpai and the Democrats. Thaksin won for two reasons: first, he made grand promises and second, his opponent, Chuan, was stuck with the charge that he had sold the country out to the IMF and foreign business interests. A good dose of populism won the day. But his victory was remarkable in one telling respect: for the first time in Thai political history a party won (almost) a majority of seats in the lower House of Representatives. While Thaksin decided to form a coalition he had no need to do this. And a few months after the election a minor party, Seritham, with 14 MPs, merged with Thai Rak Thai to give Thaksin an absolute majority. Here was a man with an unprecedented mandate to rule.

Getting to grips with corruption

Why is Thailand so corrupt? Some people point to the fact that Thailand is a 'soft' state without the rigid rules of countries like Singapore. Being soft means that people can argue that corruption is really not that bad – just part of the cultural landscape. Polls reveal that most Thais do not regard giving a few hundred baht to a public servant to ensure speedy service as wrong. The low salaries paid to civil servants and others in public service is often cited as an explanation, yet the logic becomes circular: civil servants are paid little because they are corrupt and they are corrupt because their salaries are so low. Suthichai Yoon, a commentator for *The Nation*, described in 1998 how senior officers in the Police Department set targets for the number of motorists who have to be fined. For each fine, the policeman on the beat receives 20%, the rest being passed up the ladder to line the pockets of more senior officers.

There is now a more concerted effort to educate people regarding the corrosive effects of corruption: the mis-allocation of resources, the lower economic growth rate, the loss of competitiveness – and the fact that it is the poor who are hurt most by corruption. All-in-all, corruption is far from being just a harmless part of the cultural landscape. In April 2002 police spokesman Major-General Pongsapat Pongcharoen told journalist Shawn Crispin, "Many Thai people are sick and tired of police corruption. Thai society is changing – the police must change too."

Yet by early 2009, nothing seems to have changed – the Thai police still take bribes and even senior government figures appear to be on the take. It is quite clear that for Thailand to fully root out corruption, a wholesale cultural sea-change needs to take place.

Thaksin won the election by promising the world – or at least rather more than the dour Chuan could manage. Fed up with 3½ years of belt tightening, the electorate grabbed at Thaksin's pledge to grant one million baht (US$23,200) to each of Thailand's 70,000 villages, a debt moratorium for poorer farmers, cheap medical care, and more. But Thaksin was more than just a populist prime minister; he brought to Thai politics a business sense honed whilst managing one of the country's most successful companies. Rather than handing out bottles of fish sauce and ฿100 notes to poor farmers in a crass attempt to buy their support he employed pollsters and consultants to judge the mood of the electorate. Moreover, he delivered on his promises: the debt moratorium was introduced in July 2001 and in October 2001 health care became available to all Thais at a standard rate of ฿30 per visit.

There are those, however, who feared that Thaksin was too powerful. Like Italian Prime Minister Silvio Berlusconi, he not only headed the country, but also the country's largest and most influential media group. He had little time for the checks and balances of the new constitution (designed to prevent Thailand reverting to its old political ways) and when his family's company purchased the only remaining private television station, iTV, journalists and commentators critical of his ways were promptly sacked.

King Bhumibol and the monarchy

Although Thailand has been a constitutional monarchy since the revolution of 1932, King Bhumibol Adulyadej and the royal family have an influence that far exceeds their formal constitutional powers. It seems that the leaders of the revolution shied away from emasculating the monarchy, and decided to keep the king at the centre of the Thai social and political universe. Nonetheless, the only truly active king since 1932 has been the present one, King Bhumibol, who acceded to the throne in 1945 and in 1995 celebrated 50 years as sovereign.

King Bhumibol Adulyadej – the name means Strength of the Land, Incomparable Power – has virtually single-handedly resurrected the Thai monarchy. The king was born in the USA, where his father was a doctor in Boston. He graduated in engineering from Lausanne, Switzerland and speaks English and French. He is a skilled jazz saxophonist (he has played with Benny Goodman) and an accomplished yachtsman (he won a gold medal at the Asian Games).

After returning from his studies abroad to become king he entered the monkhood, and since then has continuously demonstrated his concern for the welfare of his people. The king and his queen, Sirikit, travel the country overseeing development projects which they finance, visiting remote villages and taking a keen interest in the poor. The king has largely managed to maintain his independence from the hurly-burly of Thai politics. When he has intervened, he has done so with great effect. In October 1973, after the riots at Thammasat University, he requested that Prime Minister Thanom, along with his henchmen Praphat and Narong, leave the country to stem the tide of civil disorder. They obeyed. In a repeat of the events of 1973, in May 1992 the king called Prime Minister General Suchinda Kraprayoon to his palace where, recorded on television, he was publicly – though not overtly – humiliated for ordering the army to quell demonstrations against his premiership. Three days later, Suchinda had resigned and left the country. Most recently, at the end of January 2003, he requested that Thais rallying outside the Cambodian embassy in Bangkok intent on responding to the torching of Thailand's embassy

Liberal authoritarian

As his first term progressed Thaksin revealed an authoritarian side that was increasingly alarming. With an economic boom slowly re-establishing itself, a whole set of social problems had to be evaporated. To this end, in 2003, a war against drugs was declared. This wasn't a poster campaign nor an attempt to stop smuggling. It involved the whole-sale extra-judicial murder of thousands of suspected drug dealers, drug addicts and anyone else the police didn't really like that much. Some commentators felt that the notoriously corrupt Thai police were just getting rid of their competition, others agreed that this form of social cleansing was the only way to control the nefarious criminals who ran the illegal drug trade. Organizations such as Amnesty condemned the deaths – many victims were shot in the back or executed with a single head shot while restrained – although the international community, to its shame, was largely silent.

The year 2003 also marked the invasion of Iraq with Thailand taking its place as the 10th largest member in the coalition of the willing. This was a bold step for a country not

in Phnom Penh calm down and go home. So they did.

The undoubted love and respect that virtually all Thais hold for their king raises the question of the future and whether the monarchy can remain a stabilizing force. The suitability of his eldest son Crown Prince Vajiralongkorn has been questioned, while his eldest daughter Crown Princess Sirindhorn is respected and loved almost as much as the king himself. In January 1993, Vajiralongkorn – in an unprecedented move – lashed out at his critics. He was quoted in the *Bangkok Post* as saying: "[They say] I act as a powerful chao poh [Godfather] providing protection for sleazy business… Do I look like a chao poh type? The money I spend is earned honestly. I do not want to touch money earned illegally or through the suffering of others."Thais worried about the succession are comforted by a legend that the Chakri Dynasty would only have nine monarchs: King Bhumibol is the ninth.

Visitors should avoid any open criticism of the royal family: lese-majesty is still an offence in Thailand, punishable by up to 15 years in prison. In early 1995 Frenchman Lech Tomacz Kisielwicz uttered an expletive on a THAI flight, apparently directed at fellow passenger Thai Princess Soamswali and her daughter. On arrival at Don Muang Airport he found himself arrested and then incarcerated, before being released on bail. When the Far Eastern Economic Review commented on the king's allegedly less than positive views of Prime Minister Thaksin and the latter's business links with the Crown Prince in a short piece in January 2002, the prime minister became so worried that the two journalists involved had their visas revoked, only to be reinstated after they had apologised. In cinemas, the national anthem is played before the film and the audience – including foreigners – are expected to stand. In towns in the countryside, at 0800 every morning, the national anthem is relayed over PA systems, and pedestrians are again expected to stop what they are doing and stand to attention. It is in ways like this that the continuing influential role of the monarchy becomes clear.

known for foreign adventure. The troops, all of whom were used in civil activities, left in 2004, just in time for the beginning of an insurgency in the south of Thailand.

Southern insurgency

The Muslim south has long felt separate from the mainstream of Thai society. And with another period of economic prosperity in place – something which hardly touched the Muslims of the south – a series of demonstrations, killings and bombings occurred. However, it wasn't until October 2004 that an event took place that gave this insurrection a sense of legitimacy and urgency.

After a violent demonstration outside a government building in the small town of Tak Bai, hundreds of Muslim demonstrators were arrested. Beaten and shackled, they were then loaded into army trucks like human logs, stacked one on top of another, four or five deep. More than 80 people died of suffocation. A wave of violence followed with Buddhist monks and teachers becoming targets and explosions a regular occurrence.

Thaksin's response to the situation was surreal. He ordered school children around Thailand to make origami cranes – the bird is a symbol of peace and goodwill in Asian cultures. Millions were loaded onto planes and dropped onto the Islamic communities of the south. The bizarre rationale was that the tiny paper birds would show the Muslims that the rest of the country cared about them. The insurgency gathered pace, draconian emergency rule was declared – suspending many judicial and constitutional rights – and by September 2005 the death toll had reached 1000.

Second term

The December 2004 tsunami came to overshadow many of the events in the south. Thaksin's handling of this disaster was seen by most – at least initially – to be efficient and statesman-like. An election was called soon after in February 2005 and with the economy in a full-scale boom and free face whitening cream for female voters, Thaksin's TRT won a landslide.

Yet, Thaksin's style of rule, popular with the impoverished masses but not with the middle classes and Bangkok elite, soon began to divide Thailand. Early in 2006, and fuelled by an alleged tax-avoidance scam by the Shinawatra family who'd just sold their large telecoms company into foreign hands, a series of demonstrations aimed at Thaksin's ruling party began to turn into a serious movement, the **Peoples' Alliance for Democracy (PAD)**. Alongside this, Thaksin was accused by certain parts of the media of not showing sufficient respect to the king and even of lese-majesty – a serious offence in Thailand.

With demonstrations now becoming massive affairs of up to 200,000 people, and with deadlock on the streets, Thaksin was desperate to re-assert his authority and called a snap election pencilled in for April 2006. His opponents, led by the Democrat Party, realizing they could never beat Thaksin at the ballot box, decided to withdraw all their candidates, effectively boycotting the election. This led to a constitutional crisis that eventually caused the annulment of the ensuing Thaksin landslide. A period of stalemate ensued, only resolved after a series of negotiations when Thaksin agreed to take on the role of caretaker prime minister and stand down by October 2006 when new elections would be called.

Military coup

September 2006 changed everything. On the morning of the 19 September (UK time) the BBC's news website began reporting that Prime Minister Thaksin – then in New York at a UN conference – had declared a state of emergency. By the afternoon the BBC were reporting that tanks were on the streets and Thaksin's government had been replaced by an army council – a full scale military coup had taken place.

If you walked around the streets of the capital a few days later you'd be forgiven for wondering whether anything had happened at all. In a move designed to win over the masses a national holiday was declared and by the end of the first week locals were delivering flowers and food to the army. A typically Thai sense of surreal fun descended on the capital and tourists posed with the tanks for photo-ops. The coup had seemed to unite the nation: peace prevailed.

Within a few weeks a new prime minister, **General Surayud Chulanont**, was installed and the hard-fought-for, though ultimately flawed, 1997 constitution was shredded. New elections and a new constitution were mooted for later in 2007 and a civilian cabinet was put in place. With Thaksin skulking in China and the country seemingly united behind the king, a feeling of optimism grew.

It didn't last long. After the civilian unity cabinet made a series of poor judgements regarding foreign investment leading to a mini stock market crash, several bombs exploded in Bangkok on New Year's Eve, killing nine people, authority seemed to be draining from the new regime.

By the middle of 2007 a great deal of uncertainty had crept back into Thai society. Efforts were being made to root out the supposed corruption of the Thaksin years and to create a more enduring constitution. Yet the process of redrafting the constitution was decidedly problematic. Key voices, such as social and trade union activists, were left off the body responsible for drafting the new document. When it did finally arrive it contained the seeds for less democracy rather than more – the upper chamber was to be largely appointed and the military were to be given broad and sweeping new powers during times of 'national emergency'.

In late 2007 the country took part in a referendum on the draft document, supervised by the military, and the constitution was passed with 57.8% of the total vote. However, this figure does not reflect the fact that criticism of the draft and opposition to the constitutional referendum was made a criminal act by the military. No real public debate was allowed to take place yet 42.2% still voted no – hardly a resounding victory given the circumstances.

On 23 December 2007 a general election was called, and with Thaksin's TRT party officially dissolved the new Thaksin-inspired **People's Power Party** (**PPP**) promptly took power. The new prime minister, **Samak Sundaravej** (a former right-wing firebrand who was implicated in stirring up the Thammasat massacre in 1976), promptly declared by the press as a 'Thaksin nominee' yet he had 233 MPs to draw from in the new 480 seat parliament. The opposition, the Democrat Party led by British-born ex-Etonian Abhisit Vejjajiva, managed to secure only a third of seats – a huge failure for the favoured party – and so Prime Minister Samak created a coalition containing several other smaller parties that brought his MP count up to 315. In effect, Thailand was exactly back were it started before the 2006 coup – with Thaksin's people firmly back in control. The only relief for the establishment that had overthrown Thaksin in 2006 was that the Election Commission had called into question the activities that occurred prior to the 23 December general election by certain PPP and coalition members (they also were set to investigate Democrat Party activity – something that strangely never took place – this investigation into the PPP was to have a huge impact in late 2008).

Crisis year: 2008

Thaksin returned to Thailand in February 2008 to a mixture of jubilation and outright hostility. By May 2008 the PAD were back out on the streets, fearful that Thaksin was once again pulling the strings and that the 2006 coup they'd helped precipitate had been rendered meaningless by the PPP's general election victory. This time, though, things were different. Previously, the PAD had a broad base that had supported the pre-2006 coup, but as a result of their increasingly excessive actions, the PAD became alienated. In short, the PAD had transformed from a popular movement into an extremist vanguard.

In August the yellow-shirted PAD (yellow is the king's colour) seized Government House, the home of the Thai cabinet, facilitated strikes with its allies in the public service trade unions and, in actions that would foretell of things to come, briefly occupied Krabi and Phuket airports. Thaksin, who was awaiting trial on a number of corruption charges presciently took flight to the opening of the Beijing Olympics with a diplomatic passport (by February 2009 he had not returned to Thailand and is yet to serve the resulting prison sentence).

PAD demagogue and media tycoon Sondhi Limthongkul kept up a steady flow of pro-PAD/anti-Thaksin propaganda on his ASTV television station, while the demonstrators entrenched themselves in Government House. Armed PAD goons (many of them allegedly street criminals or ex-army colleagues of another senior figure in the PAD, ex-Thai army Major General Chamlong Srimuang) placed razor wire around the encamped demonstrators and dragged anyone who they suspected of opposing them off the street to be beaten or humiliated. The PAD needed some form of defence as regular attacks, some involving RPGs and explosives, occurred.

As the rhetoric and ranting became increasingly hysterical, Prime Minister Samak, who was also moonlighting as a TV chef, vowed to hold onto power. But in another bizarre twist, his culinary endeavours ended him up in hot water – Thai prime ministers are forbidden from earning money from other sources (he was paid peanuts for his chef appearances) and Samak was removed from his position by a military appointed court.

Samak's replacement, the mild-mannered **Somchai Wongsawat** (Thaksin's brother-in-law), was initially accepted by Sondhi as a compromise prime minister. Nonetheless Somchai's appointment did nothing to placate the PAD and a new list of demands was produced, including the establishment of something called 'New Politics'. The PAD's (now firmly backed by middle-class Bangkokians and sectors of the elite) belief was that the wrong thinking of the uneducated, poor masses of Isaan and the north had led to Thaksin's rise to power. In order to get around the 'failings' of 'democracy' the PAD now wanted a 70% unelected parliament filled with army officers and bureaucrats appointed by the king and his advisors. Any notion of the PAD being agents for democracy was now melting away and with them regularly engaging in nationalistic tub thumping (see Phra Viharn box, page 350) the highly respected Asian Human Rights Commission declared of the PAD "although they may not describe themselves as fascist, they have fascist qualities."

With the beginning of October things took another dramatic turn. Due to the PAD blockade, the Somchai government was unable to announce or implement the policies they had been democratically elected to carry out (Thailand's constitution states that a government cannot implement all but the most very basic policies if they cannot be announced) and so they sent in the riot police to throw out the increasingly fanatical PAD from Government House. The result was hundreds injured and at least one dead PAD demonstrator. The PAD fully renounced non-violence and stated that their new aim was to provoke a coup and get their supporters in the Democrat Party installed as the party of government. As all this was being played out, on 21 October the absent and still massively popular Thaksin was sentenced to two years' imprisonment for his role in a crooked land deal. Tensions continued to rise.

With the Thai queen attending the funeral of the dead PAD activist and Thaksin speaking via telephone to mass rallies of Red Shirts (a popular anti-PAD and anti-coup movement) Thailand seemed to be splitting apart.

Then in late November, the PAD, with their popular support draining away, took their most dramatic action to date and while clutching portraits of the king occupied both of Bangkok's main airports in what they termed 'Operation Hiroshima'.

The most obvious impact on the international community was that Thailand's tourism industry ground to a complete halt. Hotels and resorts stood empty as no flights could take off or land through the nation's main entry points. Images of hundreds of thousands of stranded tourists flashed around the world – the 'Land of Smiles' was transforming into angry frowns. More importantly, but less high profile, Suvarnambhumi airport was also one of busiest cargo airports in the world, largely being built to export the goods made in the vast factories of Thailand's eastern seaboard. With the world in economic meltdown the last thing Thailand needed was a seriously damaging incident like this. But still the PAD held sway, refusing to budge until the PPP government resigned.

What was incomprehensible for outsiders was the way in which the PAD had so easily taken over important facilities such as Bangkok's main airports. The entire internal mechanics of Thai politics was momentarily laid bare. The PAD had been able to take control of the airports because their backers in the elite were linked to both the military and other shadowy power structures. No police officer or soldier would stand against the PAD as it would mean standing against a group whose actions were perceived to have the backing of Thailand's highest institutions. The result was that democracy in Thailand was unofficially suspended – the will of the people had been circumnavigated by 3000 violent demonstrators and their secretive backers.

Thailand seemed to be heading towards another coup, but the military was rumoured to be split. If the army did take to the streets on this occasion it was unlikely they would receive the same passive response they did in 2006 and civil war was a likely outcome.

In the end a military coup wasn't necessary. On 2 December the constitutional court dissolved the PPP (and coalition members Chart Thai and Matchima) banning many of its key people, including Prime Minister Somchai, from politics for five years. While none of the PPP's MPs and cabinet members had any allegations of any wrongdoing against them the Election Commission had brought charges against a single PPP official for misconduct during the December 2007 general election (similar charges against the Democrat Party were conveniently forgotten). The military-sponsored Thai constitution of 2007 was explicit that any political party official found guilty of one of a number of offences meant that that entire party could be dissolved and its executive banned. And so, with all hint of Thaksin's influence now absent from government and any semblance of democracy finally demolished the PAD departed the airports and claimed outright victory. Many commentators quite fittingly called this a 'judicial coup.'

But things weren't quite over. The PPP had anticipated such a move by the courts and had founded a new political party, the **Puea Thai Party** (**PTP**), which wouldn't fall under the constitutional court's verdict. Yet the PTP's numbers were immediately reduced due not only to the banning of up to 37 PPP and coalition MPs but also intervention by the Abhisit led Democrat Party and the head of the Thai military, General Anupong.

In the first few days after the dissolution and with MPs still figuring out where their 'loyalties' might lie, the Democrats were the de-facto largest party in the Thai government giving them the right to try and form a government. With reports of MP's being bought for millions of baht and General Anupong meeting with potential Democrat-coalition partners to 'advise' them what to do, **Prime Minister Abhisit** was voted in with a majority of standing MPs on 15 December. What was most remarkable about this coalition was that key Thaksin allies, most notably the Newin Faction (led by a banned politician Newin Chidchob), were now sided with the Democrats – Newin was previously a bogeyman for both the PAD and Abhisit's democrats.

With the shiny, handsome, alternative rock-loving PM Abhisit installed, a new era of accountability and democracy was promised. Abhisit himself had personally vowed to root out corruption and restore the rule of law, yet things started to go wrong almost immediately. The new foreign minister, Kasit, told the press how much he enjoyed attending the PAD occupations at the airports and several other key PAD supporters were installed in government positions. The obvious implication was that the highly illegal and murderously violent activities of the PAD wouldn't only be tolerated but even validated by the new administration. A huge clampdown on lese majeste was implemented by the Democrats (see pp for more details) with over 4000 perceived anti-royal websites closed and several anti-PAD/anti-2006 coup activists arrested. Organizations such as Amnesty

International, whose local chairperson was linked to the PAD, refused to take up lese-majesty cases and the elite seemed to have a free hand in rolling back 20 years of democratic advances.

At this point the Harry Nicolaides case came to court (see box, page 54) and the international media began to openly question the role of the Thai elite in recent events – even if leading NGOs such as Amnesty refused. The *Economist* was in the vanguard of the international press and published a series of damning articles aimed at the most senior elements in the Thai elite – the result was that several editions of the magazine were effectively banned in Thailand.

As if to show how widespread the rot had advanced in Thai society, on New Years' Eve 2008 a huge fire engulfed one of Bangkok's most popular nightclubs, Santika. Once again unsavoury images of Thailand flooded the international media – over 60 horribly burned bodies, most young party goers and several tourists, were pulled from Santika's ruins.

It didn't end there. A story concerning the treatment of several hundred Burmese refugees – from an ethnic Muslim group known as the Rohingya – at the hands of the Thai military began to circulate in the international press. Apparently the Rohingya were attempting to reach Malaysia by sea but had drifted off-course and ended up in Thai waters instead. Caught by the Thai navy the Rohingya were allegedly beaten, starved and then towed out to sea and set adrift on unseaworthy boats with little or no food and water. Those that refused to board the boats were murdered. Up to 500 Rohingya were thought to have perished, with similar independent allegations of maltreatment at the hands of the Thai military surfacing in both India and Indonesia. The Democrat Party-led government's reaction was to blame the media – some even called it a BBC hoax. Abhisit, his much vaunted humanist credentials on the line, refused to take a hardline against the military who'd seemingly carried out the Rohingya murders – after all this was the same military who'd helped both him and the Democrats gain power.

And it wasn't all quiet on the home front either. The red-shirted **National United Front of Democracy Against Dictatorship (UDD)**, who'd formed out of a broad coalition of pro-Thaksin, anti-2006 coup and anti-PAD activists, took to the streets. Tens of thousands of people took part in almost completely peaceful demonstrations with their key demand being a general election (The Democrat Party haven't won an election since 1976) and the prosecution of PAD activists. All the UDD's demands were rejected by the government who now seemingly lurched from crisis to crisis – several members of the Democrats were then involved in corruption scandals surrounding the sale of tinned milk.

As 2009 entered March and with Thailand now caught between years of Thaksin-inspired cronyism/corruption and the current flagrant disregard for both the rule of law and democracy by the elite, more bitter divisions certainly await the kingdom. It is almost impossible to predict any outcome at this point but with an ageing king on the throne and demonstrators back on the streets, Thailand's democratic future, as it enters a period of massive economic downturn, is looking decidedly bleak.

Culture

Lao

The largest, and least visible, 'minority' group in Thailand are the Lao of the northeastern region, who constitute nearly a third of the total population of the country. The region and its people are also referred to as 'Isan' (meaning northeastern) and they are often regarded by central Thais as being the equivalent of country bumpkins. Their linguistic and cultural distinctiveness, and the patronizing attitude of the central authorities, led considerable numbers of the population in the northeast, as in the south, to support the CPT during the 1960s and 1970s. The murder, by the police, of prominent northeastern politicians during this period also did little to help integrate northeasterners into the fabric of Thailand. Although the situation has since stabilized, and separatist sentiments are much reduced, the northeast is still the poorest and least developed part of the country, with the highest incidence of poverty, malnutrition and child mortality. As a result, the government invests considerable resources trying to develop the area.

Sino-Thais (Chinese)

Anything between 9% and 15% of the population of Thailand is thought to be Sino-Thai (depending on how 'Chinese' is defined). Hundreds of thousands emigrated from China during the 19th and early 20th centuries, escaping the poverty and lack of opportunity in their homeland. In Thailand they found a society and a religion that was inclusive rather than exclusive. Forced to learn Thai to communicate with the ruling classes (rather than English, French or Dutch, as in neighbouring colonial countries), they were relatively quickly and easily assimilated into Thai society. They took Thai names, inter-married with Thais and converted to Buddhism (although they were not required to renounce ancestor worship): in short, they became Thai. As elsewhere in the region, these Chinese immigrants proved to be remarkably adept at money-making and today control a disproportionate slice of businesses.

While the Chinese are well integrated into Thai society compared with other countries in the region like Malaysia and Indonesia, there have been times when the Chinese have felt the hot breath of Tai nationalism. In 1914 King Rama VI wrote an essay under the *nom de plume* Atsawaphaahu, entitled *The Jews of the East*, blaming many of his country's problems on the Chinese. During Phibun Songkram's premiership between 1938 and 1944, anti-Chinese xenophobia was also pronounced and was a major reason why, in 1939, the country's name was changed from Siam to Thailand. This was to be a country of the Tais, and not any other ethnic group. Even today, it is common for government documents to maintain that the plight of the farmer is due to the unscrupulous practices of Chinese traders and moneylenders.

Although the Chinese have been well assimilated into the fabric of the nation, Bangkok still supports a large Chinatown. Here, Mandarin is spoken, shop signs are in Chinese, and Chinese cultural and religious traits are clearly in evidence.

Some commentators report a resurgence of pride in being Chinese. From the 1930s through to the 1980s the Chinese wished to blend in, but wealth has brought confidence and Sino-Thais are once more learning the 'mother' tongue (Mandarin), praying to Mahayanist and Taoist deities like Kuan Im (Kuan Yin), and travelling to China to discover their roots. Partly, this makes good economic sense. Trade with China is booming and China is the great emerging economic (and military) powerhouse in the Asia-Pacific. To be able to converse in Mandarin and draw on family links with the homeland is perceived to be good for business. There are dangers in this rediscovered love of China, however: Thailand's past shows periods of xenophobia when Sino-Thais have been persecuted and their businesses burnt, and most are quick to assert that their allegiances are with Thailand.

Thai Malays

Of the various minority ethnic and religious groups in Thailand, the Thai Malays and Thai Muslims have often felt most alienated from the Thai nation. Not only do many in the southern four provinces of the country (Yala, Narathiwat, Pattani and Satun) speak Malay rather than Thai, but the great majority (about 80%) are also Muslim rather than Buddhist. The fact that the government has sometimes been rather heavy handed in its approach to their welfare and citizenship gave great impetus to the growth of the Communist Party of Thailand (CPT) in the south, during the 1960s and 1970s. Pattani was only incorporated into the Thai state at the beginning of the 20th century, and even then just loosely. It was not until the 1930s that the government in Bangkok began to try and assimilate the far south, and many of the problems that remain evident today in relations between Tai-Thais and Thai-Malays can be dated from that period.

Relations are far better today, but it is still true that few Thai Muslims have been recruited into the civil service or army, and schools in the south still give lessons in Thai and present an essentially 'Tai' view of the country. (It is for this reason that the majority of Muslim parents still choose to send their children to private Islamic *pondok* schools, even though it means paying fees.) The Islamic revival in Southeast Asia has brought the issue of Muslim disaffection in the south to the fore once again.

King Bhumibol has done more than most to incorporate the Thai Malays into the fabric of the nation. He presents awards for Koranic study and regularly visits the region, staying in his palace at Narathiwat. Today most Thai Muslims, rather than calling for a separate state, use the political system to raise their profile and make their voices heard. The difficulty is that the acceptance that they should work within the system to achieve change has been accompanied by the spread of orthodox, conservative Islam. Unlike the Chinese, Thai Muslims are unwilling to compromise over matters of faith and simply blend in with the masses.

In April 1997 the Thai army clashed with armed separatists linked with the Barisan Revolusi Nasional (BRN), in Narathiwat province. While few people believe that the BRN, or other similar groups, represent a threat to the integrity of the Thai state, clashes like this demonstrate that the task of integrating the far south into the mainstream of Thai political life is still to be completed.

Hilltribes

Thailand's assorted hilltribes, concentrated in the north and west, number over 800,000 people. For more information, see Chiang Mai, page 232.

Hilltribe economy and culture

Traditionally, most of the hilltribes in Thailand practised slash and burn agriculture, also known as swiddening or shifting cultivation. They would burn a small area of forest, cultivate it for a few years by planting rice, corn and other crops, and then, when the soil was exhausted, abandon the land until the vegetation had regenerated to replenish the soil. Some groups shifted fields in a 10- to 15-year rotation; others moved the entire village, relocating in a fresh area of forest when the land had become depleted of nutrients. To obtain salt, metal implements and other goods that could not be made or found in the hills, the tribal peoples would trade forest products such as resins and animal skins with the settled lowland Thais. This simplified picture of the hilltribe economy is being gradually eroded for a variety of reasons, the most significant being that today there is simply not enough land available in most areas to practise such an extensive system of agriculture.

The Karen (Kariang, Yang)

Origins

The Karen, also known as the Kariang or Yang, are found along the Thai-Burmese border, concentrated in the Mae Hong Son region. They are the largest tribal group in Thailand, numbering about 270,000. Their origins are in Burma, where today many more are fighting a long-term and low-intensity war against the Burmese authorities for greater autonomy. The Karen started to infiltrate into Thailand in the 18th century and moved into areas occupied by the Lawa, possibly the oldest established tribe in Thailand. The evidence of this contact between the two groups can still be seen in the dress, ornamentation and implements of the Karen.

Economy and society

The Karen are divided into two main sub-groups, the Sgaw and the Pwo and these are divided into two sub-groups, the Pa-O and Bwe. The Sgaw and the Pwo are also known as the White Karen. The differences between the two principal groups are in language and dress. The Pwo make up about 20% of the total population and the Sgaw the remaining 80%. Most Karen live in mountain villages and practise shifting cultivation of the rotating field type (that is they move their fields, but not their villages). They prevent soil erosion on the steep slopes by taking care to maintain belts of forest growth between 'swiddens' or fields, by leaving saplings and tree roots to help bind the soil, and by not turning the soil before planting. When a community grows so large that the distance to the outer fields becomes excessive, a group of villagers establish a satellite village beyond the boundaries of the mother village. However, with the pressure on land and the incentive to commercialize production, this traditional pioneering strategy is often no longer possible. Karen are being forced to try and increase yields by developing irrigation, and some Karen have moved down into the valleys and taken up settled agriculture, imitating the methods of the lowland Thais.

Karen houses are built on stilts out of bamboo, with thatched roofs. Animals are kept under the house at night for protection against wild animals and rustlers. Most houses have only one room and a spacious veranda. A household usually consists of a husband and wife plus their unmarried children. Should a man's wife die, he is not permitted to remarry until his children have left the home, as this would cause conflict with the spirits. Indeed, much of Karen life is dictated by the spirits. The most important is the 'Lord of Land and Water', who controls the productivity of the land and calls upon the rice spirit to grow. Also important is the matrilineal ancestor guardian spirit, *bga*.

The priest is the most revered individual in the village: he is the ritual leader and it is he who sets dates for the annual ceremonies. The post is an ancestral one and only changes when the priest dies – at which time the village must change location as well (although the distance may only be nominal). As the Karen have been incorporated into the Thai state, so increasing numbers have turned to Buddhism. The role of European missionaries in the highland areas also means that there are significant numbers of Christian Karen. A central Karen myth tells of a younger 'white brother' from across the water, who would arrive with the skills of writing given to him by God. This no doubt helped the missionaries enormously when they arrived, pasty faced and clutching bibles. In most cases, however, while converting to Buddhism or Christianity, the Karen have at the same time maintained a healthy belief in their traditional spirits.

Women in Thai society

Although the logic of Buddhism relegates women to a subordinate position, women in Thailand have considerable influence. In the rural north and northeast, land was traditionally inherited by the female members of a household (usually the youngest daughter), and husbands reside with their wives. It is common to find the wife controlling the finances in a family, determining where and how much fertilizer to buy, and even giving her husband an 'allowance'. This has been noted for centuries: in 1433 the Chinese Muslim traveller Ma Huan recorded: "It is their [Siamese] custom that all affairs are managed by their wives... all trading transactions great and small". Although in public the role of the man is accentuated, in private, equality of the sexes or the reverse is more usually the case. In the fields, ploughing is usually done by men, but other tasks are equally shared – and often women do more than their fair share.

The relative strength of the woman's role even extends to sexual relations. Ma Huan's 15th-century account of Siam noted how men would have penis balls inserted under their foreskin to increase their partner's pleasure: "If it is the king... or a great chief or a wealthy man, they use gold to make hollow beads, inside which a grain of sand is placed... They make a tinkling sound, and this is regarded as beautiful".

The contrast between the subordinate position of women in Thai society and their much more influential underlying role is a recurring theme. This would seem to lend credence to the old Thai adage that the two front legs of an elephant are male and the two rear legs,

female – the implication being that men lead the way and women follow. Female traders and businesswomen, for instance, are well represented – indeed, there are thought to be more female than male traders. But at the same time, their influential role in private enterprise arises partly because they are largely excluded from high office in the public sector. As a result, ambitious women are forced to enter the private sector. Politics is an almost exclusively male domain. It took 17 years from when women were granted equal political rights to men in 1932 for the first female MP to enter parliament. But even today women are grossly under-represented. In the elections of 2000 just 21 of the 200 seats in the senate were filled by women.

The few women who do become MPs, Juree Vichit-Vadakan wrote, "are perceived to be mere decorative flowers to brighten and lighten the atmosphere" (*Bangkok Post*, 25.3.97). They are not expected to contribute much to the political process and are not taken seriously by their male counterparts. Thai law also reveals a streak of discrimination: Thai men are permitted to demand a divorce if their wives have just one affair; Thai women can only request a divorce if their husband honours another woman as his wife – he can have as many affairs as he likes.

In previously booming Thailand, taking a *mia noi* (minor wife) became de rigeur, and having a mistress was rather like having a limited edition Mercedes with a badge showing membership of the Royal Bangkok Sports Club. When it comes to *mia noi*, there is an unwritten set of rules over how they are to be treated, rules that are accepted by both errant husbands and their (first) wives. It is only when these rules are transgressed that all hell breaks loose. *Mia noi* get BMWs; first wives get rather staider Mercedes, probably with a chauffeur thrown in for good measure. The *mia noi* will drive herself, wearing Armani sunglasses and perhaps a Versace suit. *Mia noi* are to be enjoyed in (semi) private. They can be taken for discreet weekends, or out to dinner, but they must not attend official functions and should not grace society pages arm-in-arm with their men. As long as the men and their *mia noi* stick to the rules, things seem to work just fine.

The collapse in the Thai economy changed things. For most men, there was simply not as much money to throw around on luxuries like minor wives. However, the *mia noi* of senior politicians may have benefited from the rules introduced in late 1997 that require cabinet ministers to declare their assets. Apparently, some politicians, rather than have their improbably extensive holdings exposed to the glare of publicity, transferred cars, houses and other baubles to their minor wives. Even first wives have got something out of the new asset-revealing measures. Former Prime Minister Chaovalit Yongchaiyut, who resigned in 1997, valued his own assets at ฿17m; his wife's amounted to ฿124m.

Not every woman in Thailand becomes a *mia noi*, of course. In fact it has been argued that education and a career have put many middle-class Thai women off marriage of any sort, whether as first or second wives. They are reluctant to 'marry down' to secure a partner and instead develop their careers and gain social status in that way. While women do face discrimination, Thai society does give them the social space to acquire status on their own, independent of a husband. Some Thai women sense a change in the role and position of women in Thailand, especially in politics. In the 1998 local government elections, nearly 1500 women were voted in as village heads. This may be just 2.5% of the total, but to have a women as a village head was hitherto almost unheard of. Moreover, in the municipal and provincial council elections of early 2000, the proportion of women winning seats reached 10% of the total, double the figure for the previous elections. Perhaps things are changing; but there's still some way to go before Thailand metamorphoses into a tropical Sweden. Maybe it will only be when Buddhism becomes more amenable to the idea that men and women are equal that really profound change will occur.

The Buddha, so far as we know, did not make the road to enlightenment gender specific. Yet women cannot be ordained in Thailand, and religious schools are male-only establishments. There are nuns – *mae chi* – but they are not generally held in high regard. Thai feminists are trying to break down these religious barriers. In 2001, the (female) Buddhist scholar Chatsumarn Kabilsingh went to Sri Lanka (where these things are possible) to be ordained. She returned to Bangkok to try and establish a 'monastery' for women. The conservative clergy reacted with anger and incomprehension. How could a woman possibly imagine that she was equal to a man in these matters?

Hilltribe calendar

	Karen	Hmong	Mien (Yao)
January	village ceremony	New Year festival	embroidering
February	site selection	scoring poppies	scoring poppies
March	clearing field	clearing field	clearing field
April	burning field	burning field	burning field
May	rice planting	rice planting	rice/maize planting
June	field spirit offering	weeding	weeding
July	field spirit offering	weeding	weeding
August	weeding	weeding	harvesting
September	rat trapping	poppy seeding	poppy seeding
October	rice harvest	thinning poppy field	rice harvest
November	rice harvest	rice harvest	rice harvest
December	rice threshing	New Year festival	rice threshing

Source: Tribal Research Institute, Chiang Mai University.

Material culture

The Karen are prolific weavers. Weaving is done on simple backstrap looms and many Karen still spin their own thread. The upper garments worn by men, women and children are all made in the same way: two strips of material are folded in half, the fold running along the shoulder. They are then sewn together along the centre of the garment and down the sides, leaving holes for the head and arms. The stitching is not merely functional, it is an integral part of the design. Until girls marry, they wear only this garment, full length to just below their knees and made of white cotton. The Sgaw embroider a band of red or pink around their waists, the Pwo embroider red diamond patterns along the lower edge. Married women wear this garment as an over-blouse and they also wear a sarong. The over-blouse is considerably more elaborate than that of the girls: Job's-tear seeds (seeds from a grass) are woven into the design, or a pattern is woven around the border. Pwo women tend to embroider all over the blouse.

The sarong is made up of two strips of material, sewn horizontally and stitched to make a tubular skirt. They are held up with a cord or metal belt and are worn knee or ankle-length, longer for formal occasions. The colour is predominantly red. Men's shirts are usually hip length, with elaborate embroidery. They wear sarongs or Thai peasant-style pants.

The Sgaw women and girls wear strands of small beads, which hang from mid-chest to waist length, normally red, white or yellow. The Pwo wear them around their neck and to mid-chest length and they are mostly black. Their necklaces are made from old 'bullet coins', strung on braided red thread. Pwo women wear lots of bracelets of silver, copper, brass or aluminium. Sgaw are more moderate in their use of jewellery. All Karen wear silver cup-shaped earrings, which often have coloured tufts of wool attached.

Akha	Lisu	Lahu
weaving	New Year Festival	scoring poppies
clearing fields	Second New Year festival	New Year Festival
burning field	clearing field	burning field
rice spirit ceremony	burning field	field spirit house
rice planting	rice dibbling	rice planting
weeding	weeding	weeding
weeding	weeding	weeding
swinging ceremony	soul calling ceremony	weeding
poppy seeding	maize harvest	maize harvest
rice harvest	poppy seeding	field spirit offering
rice harvest	rice harvest	rice harvest
New Year festival	rice threshing	field spirit offering

The Hmong (or Meo)

Origins

The Hmong, also known as the Meo, are the second largest tribal group in Thailand, numbering about 82,000. Although their origins are rather hazy, the Hmong themselves claim that they have their roots in the icy north. They had arrived in Laos by 1850 and by the end of the 19th century had migrated into the provinces of Chiang Rai and Nan. Today they are scattered right across the northern region and have spread over a larger area than any other tribe, apart from the Karen.

Economy and society

There are two sub-groups of the Hmong, the Blue and the White Hmong. Blue Hmong (aka Black Meo, Flowery Meo or Striped Meo) women wear the distinctive indigo-dyed pleated skirt with a batik design which you often see in northern Thailand. During ceremonial occasions White Hmong women wear white pleated skirts. Day-to-day they wear indigo-dyed trousers (see below). The Hmong value their independence, and tend to live at high altitudes, away from other tribes. This independence, and their association with poppy cultivation, has meant that of all the hilltribes it is the Hmong who have been most severely persecuted by the Thai authorities. They are persecuted by the Thai government for three main reasons: because they were (much less so now) to be a security risk, prone to banditry and so on; because they cultivate the higher lands and clear primary forest on watersheds, and are therefore seen as environmentally destructive; and because they were the main cultivators of opium in the north (again, less so now). Finally, and in general, they are seen as the 'hardest' of the hill peoples and commercially savvy. Like most hilltribes, they practise shifting cultivation, moving their villages when the surrounding land has been exhausted. The process of moving is stretched out over two seasons: an advance party finds a suitable site, builds tWemporary shelters, clears the land and plants rice, and only after the harvest do the rest of the inhabitants follow on.

Hmong villages tend not to be fenced, while their houses are built of wood or bamboo at ground level. Each house has a main living area and two or three sleeping rooms. The extended family is headed by the oldest male: he settles family disputes and has supreme authority over family affairs. Like the Karen, the Hmong too are spirit worshippers and believe in household spirits. Every house has an altar, where protection for the household is sought. Despite 21st-century pressures (particularly scarcity of land), they maintain a strong sense of identity. The children may be educated in Thai schools, but they invariably return to farming alongside their parents.

Material culture

The Hmong are the only tribe in Thailand who make batik. Indigo-dyed batik makes up the main panel of their skirts, with appliqué and embroidery added to it. The women wear black leggings from their knees to their ankles, black jackets (with embroidery), and a black panel or 'apron', held in place with a cummerbund. Even the smallest children wear clothes of intricate design with exquisite needlework. Today much of the cloth is purchased from the market or from traders; traditionally it would have been woven by hand on a foot-treddle/back-strap loom.

The White Hmong tend to wear less elaborate clothing from day to day, saving it for special occasions only. Hmong men wear loose-fitting black trousers, black jackets (sometimes embroidered) and coloured or embroidered sashes.

The Hmong particularly value silver jewellery: it signifies wealth and a good life. Men, women and children wear silver: tiers of neck rings, heavy silver chains with lock-shaped pendants, earrings and pointed rings on every finger. All the family jewellery is brought out at New Year and is an impressive sight, symbolizing the wealth of the family.

Even though the Hmong are perhaps the most independent of all the hilltribes, they too are being drawn into the 'modern' world. Some still grow the poppy at higher elevations, but the general shortage of land is forcing them to descend to lower altitudes, to take up irrigated rice farming, to grow cash crops, and to mix with the lowland Thais. This has led to conflicts between the Hmong and the lowlanders as they compete for the same resources – previously they would have been occupying quite different ecological niches.

The Lahu (or Mussur)

Origins

The Lahu in Thailand are found along the Burmese border and number about 60,000. They originated in Yunnan (South China) and migrated from Burma into Thailand at the end of the 19th century. Today, the majority of Thai Lahu are found in the provinces of Chiang Mai and Chiang Rai. There are a number of Lahu sub-groups, each with slightly different traditions and clothing. The two dominant groups are the Black Lahu and the Yellow Lahu, which themselves are subdivided.

Economy and society

Traditionally, the Lahu lived at relatively high elevations, 1200 m or higher. Pressure on land and commercialization has encouraged most of these groups to move down the slopes, and most of these have now taken up irrigated rice farming in the small, high valleys that dissect the northern region of Thailand.

Villages are about 30 houses strong, with about six people in each house. Their houses are built on stilts and consist of the main living area, a bedroom, a spirit altar and a fireplace. Houses are usually built of wood or bamboo, and thatch. The men are less dominant in the family hierarchy than in other tribes: they help around the home and share in the care of their children and livestock, as well as gathering water and firewood. A typical household is nuclear rather than extended, consisting of a man, his wife and their unmarried children. It is also not unusual for a married daughter and her husband and children to live in the household.

The Lahu believe in spirits, in the soul and in a God. Missionary work by Christians, and also by Buddhists, means that many Lahu villages are now ostensibly Christian or Buddhist. It is estimated that one-third of all Lahu live within Christian communities. But this does not mean that they have rejected their traditional beliefs: they have adopted new religions, while at the same time maintaining their animistic ones.

Material culture

Because each Lahu group has distinct clothing and ornamentation, it is difficult to characterize a 'general' dress for the tribe as a whole. To simplify, Lahu dress is predominantly black or blue, with border designs of embroidery or appliqué. Some wear short jackets and sarongs, others wear longer jackets and leggings. Most of their cloth is now bought and machine-made; traditionally it would have been handwoven. The jackets are held together with large, often elaborate, silver buckles. All Lahu make caps for their children and the cloth shoulder bag is also a characteristic Lahu accessory.

Ornamentation is similarly varied. The Lahu Nyi women wear wide silver bracelets, neck rings and earrings. The Lahu Sheh Leh wear large numbers of small white beads around their necks and silver bracelets. The Lahu Na wear engraved and moulded silver bracelets, and on special occasions heavy silver chains, bells and pendants. The Lahu Shi wear red and white beads around their necks and heavy silver earrings.

The Akha (or Kaw)

Origins

The Akha, or Kaw, number about 33,000 in Thailand and are found in a relatively small area of the north, near Chiang Rai. They have their origins in Yunnan, southern China, and from there spread into Burma (where there are nearly 200,000) and rather later into Thailand. The first Akha village was not established in Thailand until the very beginning of the 20th century. They prefer to live along ridges, at about 1000 m.

Economy and society

The Akha are shifting cultivators, growing primarily dry rice on mountainsides but also a wide variety of vegetables. The cultivation of rice is bound up with myths and rituals: the rice plant is regarded as a sentient being, and the selection of the swidden, its clearance, the planting of the rice seed, the care of the growing plants, and finally the harvest of the rice, must all be done according to the Akha Way. Any offence to the rice soul must be rectified by ceremonies.

Akha villages are identified by their gates, a village swing and high-roofed houses on posts. They have no word for religion, but believe in the 'Akha Way'. They are able to recite the names of all their male ancestors (60 names or more) and they keep an ancestral altar in their homes, at which food is offered up at important times in the year such as New Year, during the village swing ceremony, and after the rice harvest.

At the upper and lower ends of the village are gates which are renewed every year. Visitors should walk through them in order to rid themselves of the spirit of the jungle. The gates are sacred and must not be defiled. Visitors must not touch the gates and should avoid going through them if they do not intend to enter a house in the village. A pair of wooden male and female carved figures are placed inside the entrance to signify that this is the realm of human beings. The two most important Akha festivals are the four-day Swinging Ceremony celebrated during August, and New Year when festivities also extend over four days.

Material culture

Akha clothing is made of homespun blue-black cloth, which is appliquéd for decoration. Particularly characteristic of the Akha is their headdress, which is adorned with jewellery. The basic clothing of an Akha woman is a headdress, a jacket, a short skirt worn on her hips, with a sash and leggings worn from the ankle to below the knee. They wear their jewellery as an integral part of their clothing, mostly sewn to their headdresses. Girls wear similar clothing to the women, except that they sport caps rather than the elaborate headdress of the mature women. The change from girl's clothes to women's clothes occurs through four stages during adolescence. Unmarried girls can be identified by the small gourds tied to their waist and headdress.

Men's clothing is much less elaborate. They wear loose-fitting Chinese-style black pants, and a black jacket which may be embroidered. Both men and women use cloth shoulder bags.

Today, the Akha are finding it increasingly difficult to follow the 'Akha Way'. Their complex rituals set them apart from both the lowland Thais and from the other hilltribes. There is no land, no game, and the modern world has little use or time for their ways. The conflicts and pressures that the Akha currently face, and their inability to reconcile the old with the new, is claimed by some to explain why the incidence of opium addiction among the Akha is so high.

The Mien (or Yao)

Origins

The Mien, or Yao, are unique among the hilltribes in that they have a tradition of writing based on Chinese characters. Mien legend has it that they came from 'across the sea' during the 14th century, although it is generally thought that their roots are in southern China. They first migrated into Thailand from Laos in the mid-19th century and they currently number about 36,000, mostly in the provinces of Chiang Rai and Nan, close to the Laotian border.

Economy and society

The Mien village is not enclosed and is usually found on sloping ground. The houses are large, wooden affairs, as they need to accommodate an extended family of sometimes 20 or more members. They are built on the ground, not on stilts, and have one large living area and four or more bedrooms. As with other tribes, the construction of the house must be undertaken carefully. The house needs to be orientated appropriately, so that the spirits are not disturbed, and the ancestral altar installed on an auspicious day.

The Mien combine two religious beliefs: on the one hand they recognize and pay their dues to spirits and ancestors (informing them of family developments); on the other, they follow Taoism as it was practised in China in the 13th and 14th centuries. The Taoist rituals are expensive, and the Mien appear to spend a great deal of their lives struggling to save enough money to afford the various ceremonies, such as weddings, merit-making and death ceremonies. The Mien economy is based upon the shifting cultivation of dry rice, corn and small quantities of opium poppy.

Material culture

The Mien women dress distinctively, with black turbans and red-ruffed tunics, making them easy to distinguish from the other hilltribes. All their clothes are made of black or indigo-dyed homespun cotton, which is then embroidered using distinctive cross-stitching. Their trousers are the most elaborate garments. Unusually, they sew from the back of the cloth and cannot see the pattern they are making. The children wear embroidered caps, with red pompoms on the top and by the ears. The men's dress is a simple indigo-dyed jacket and trousers, with little embroidery.

The Htin

Origins

The Htin go by a number of other names: Tin, Thin or Kha T'in in Thailand, and Phai or Kha Phai in Laos. They are said to prefer Mal or Prai. The Htin have probably been living in Thailand for a considerable time, although their arrival in the country and their origins are not well documented. In total there were 32,755 Htin living in Thailand in 1995.

Economy and society

The Htin are concentrated in Nan province along the border with Laos and, traditionally, were migratory shifting cultivators growing glutinous (sticky) dry rice and a range of other dryland crops. Some continue to cultivate opium, although these are very small in number. Today, because of land shortages, few can continue to cultivate land in their traditional, extensive manner. The emphasis of the Htin economy may remain on farming but few are food secure and they need to engage in other activities to meet their needs. The general view, however, is that the Htin have found it difficult to adapt to modern, commercial life and have been marginalized by the process of modernization, unable to compete effectively with other groups.

The Htin are monogamous and matrilocal (ie the husband lives with his wife), like many other people in northern and northeastern Thailand. There has been some conversion of Htin to Buddhism, mostly among those living on lower slopes where they have come into contact with lowland Tai settlements. The majority, though, are still animist. While their religious beliefs may have shown some resilience, the same is not true

A Thai hilltribe clothing primer

These days many hilltribe people wear jeans and t-shirts; they mostly dress up for tourists.

Karen are among the best and most prolific of hilltribe weavers. Their traditional striped warp *ikat*, dyed in soft hues, is characteristically inter-sewn with job's seeds. Girls wear creamy white smocks with red stitching, whilst women wear coloured smocks and strings of beads. Their tunics are made up of two lengths of cloth, worn vertically, sewn together down the centre and sides, leaving a hole for the neck and the arms.

Hmong (Meo) produce exquisite embroidery made up of appliquéd layers of fabric of geometric shapes, worn by men, women and children. Some of the patternwork on their pleated skirts is achieved by batik (the only hilltribe to do this). Jackets are of black velvet or satinized cotton, with embroidered lapels. They wear black or white leggings and sashes to hold up their skirts. Hand weaving is a dying art among the Hmong.

Lahu (Mussur) groups traditionally wore a diverse array of clothing. All embroider, but many have now abandoned the use of traditional dress. Another common feature is the shoulder bag – primarily red in the case of the Lahu Nyi (the 'Red' Lahu), black among the Lahu Sheh Leh (and often tasselled), black with patchwork for the Lahu Na, and often striped in the case of the Lahu Shi.

Mien (Yao) embroidery is distinguished by cross-stitching on indigo fabric, worn as baggy trousers and turbans. They are one of the easiest of the hilltribes to identify because of their distinctive red-collared jackets. Virtually none of the cloth is hand woven – it is bought and then sometimes re-dyed before being decorated.

Akha are most easily distinguished by their elaborate head-dresses, made up of silver beads, coins and buttons. Akha cloth is limited to plain weave, dyed with indigo (after weaving) – and still often made from home-grown cotton. This is then decorated with embroidery, shells, buttons, silver and seeds. Akha patch-work is highly intricate work, involving the assembly of tiny pieces of cloth.

Lisu wear very brightly coloured clothing and (at festivals) lots of jewellery. Particularly notable are the green and blue kaftans with red sleeves, worn with baggy Chinese trousers and black turbans. Lisu weaving has virtually died out.

of their material culture. Very few Htin wear their traditional clothes, except for a handful of older women.

The Kha Haw

The Kha Haw are one of the smallest (in number) groups of hill people living in Thailand. When they were last surveyed in the mid-1990s there was just a single Kha Haw village of 28 houses and 196 individuals. This village is situated in Nan province's district of Rae. They are also one of the most recent to have settled in the country, arriving not more than 50 years ago. Like the Htin, the Kah Haw were traditionally migratory shifting cultivators growing glutinous dry rice.

The Lisu (or Lisaw)

Origins
The Lisu number some 25,000 in Thailand, and live in the mountainous region northwest of Chiang Mai. They probably originated in China, at the headwaters of the Salween River, and did not begin to settle in Thailand until the early 20th century.

Economy and society
The Lisu grow rice and vegetables for subsistence and opium for sale. Rice is grown at lower altitudes and the opium poppy at over 1500 m. Villages are located so that the inhabitants can maintain some independence from the Thai authorities. At the same time they need to be relatively close to a market so that they can trade.

Lisu houses may be built either on the ground or raised above it: the former are more popular at higher altitudes as they are said to be warmer. The floors and walls are made from wood and bamboo, and the roof is thatched. The house is divided into a bedroom, a large living area, and contains a guest platform. Within each house there will also be a fireplace and an ancestral altar.

Each village has a 'village guardian spirit shrine' which is located above the village, in a roofed pavilion that women are forbidden to enter. Local disputes are settled by a headman, and kinship is based upon patrilineal clans. As well as the village guardian, the Lisu worship Wu Sa (the creator) and a multitude of spirits of the forest, ancestors, trees, the sun, moon and everyday objects. Coupled with this, the Lisu fear possession by *phi pheu* (weretigers) and *phu seu* (vampires).

Material culture
Lisu clothing is some of the most brightly coloured, and most distinctive, of all the hilltribes. They make up their clothes from machine-made cloth. The women wear long tunics – often bright blue, with red sleeves and pattern-work around the yoke – black knee-length pants and red leggings. A wide black sash is wound tightly round the waist. Looped around this at the back is a pair of tassels consisting of many tightly woven threads, with pompoms attached to the ends (sometimes as many as 500 strands in a pair of tassels). Turbans, again with coloured tassels attached, are worn for special occasions. The man's attire is simpler: a black jacket, blue or green trousers and black leggings.

The most important ceremony is New Year (celebrated on the same day as the Chinese), when the villagers dress up in all their finery and partake in a series of rituals. At this time, the women wear copious amounts of silver jewellery: tunics with rows of silver buttons sewn onto them, and abundant heavy necklaces.

The Lawa (or Lua)

Origins
The Lawa, known as the Lua by the Thai, are only to be found in northern Thailand. They are thought to have migrated into the valley of the Mae Ping in the seventh century and were among the very first hilltribe settlers in present-day Thailand. In the 1995 census they numbered 15,711 individuals, mostly concentrated to the southeast of Mae Hong Son, to the southwest of Chiang Mai and in the upland areas around Umpai. However a significant number have probably assimilated into mainstream Thai society and, as a tribal minority, have effectively disappeared from view.

Economy and society

Those who maintain their traditional ways practice rotational shifting cultivation. They are regarded as among the most environmentally aware of swidden cultivators. A fair number have embraced wet rice culture, although whether they are hill or padi farmers they tend to be subsistence oriented in terms of production. In addition to farming, the Lawa have a long tradition of working as iron smiths and most have also taken on supplementary non-farm income earning activities. Due to limited land and environmental degradation few can survive adequately from agriculture alone.

In terms of social structure, the Lawa are monogamous and patrilineal. While many have converted to Buddhism, this is creatively combined with ancestor worship and their former animist belief system. The Lawa have wavy hair and the men, often, quite thick beards. Unfortunately very few wear their traditional clothes, most having adopted Thai/Western dress. But among those who do, the women wear plain cotton clothes: off-white (girls) or blue blouses (married women), which are sometimes embroidered on the sleeves. Leggings are also worn by women, although jewellery and silver bracelets are rarely displayed. Men have given up their traditional dress almost entirely.

The Khamu

The Khamu are mainly concentrated in neighbouring Laos and there are few living in Thailand – in 1995, just 10,153 concentrated in Nan province close to the border with Laos. There are also, however, settlements in Lampang, Chiang Rai and as far away as Kanchanaburi in the west of Thailand. They are thought to have settled here from Luang Prabang, Xieng Khouang and Vientiane in Laos, arriving first of all as labourers. Most have assimilated to varying degrees into mainstream Thai society although some have established themselves as swidden farmers and maintained their ethnic distinctiveness.

Their dress is similar to that of the Lawa but, for the women, with more embroidery, jewellery and beads. During festivals men wear distinctive embroidered long-sleeved jackets fastened at the side at the neck. Day-to-day however the men wear lowland Thai clothes. There are also strong linguistic similarities between the Khamu and Lawa.

The Khamu are patrilineal and patrilocal and many continue with their animist beliefs. They construct spirit gates on the approach to the village and make offerings of food and sacrifice chickens to the spirits. To varying degrees elements of Buddhism have been incorporated into their traditional belief system and some have also converted to Christianity. The Khamu practise shifting cultivation in addition to hunting, fishing and the collection of non-timber forest products. Like other groups, because of the falling productivity of agriculture they also engage in various non-farm occupations, working as labourers on construction sites, for example.

Other ethnic groups

Phu Thai

The Phu Thai are a sub-group of the Thai. There are over 150,000 Phu Thai speakers in Thailand, and close to this number also in Laos and Vietnam. They wear distinctive *pha sin* tube skirts and also have their own dances and ceremonies similar to those of the Lao of northeastern Thailand and Laos. Perhaps the most familiar custom is the *ba sii* ceremony when sacred thread, *sai sin*, is tied around a person's wrists.

Mlabri

The elusive Mlabri 'tribe' of eastern Thailand represent one of the few remaining groups of hunter-gatherers in Southeast Asia. They are also known as the Phi Tong Luang or 'Spirits of the Yellow Leaves', because when their shelters of rattan and banana leaves turn yellow, they take this as a sign from the spirits that it is time to move on.

Padaung

The Padaung are a Burmese people from the state of Kayah who were forced out of Burma during their long struggle for autonomy. They have become refugees in northern Thailand and objects of tourist fascination, also known as the 'long-necked Karen' or, derogatorily, as the 'giraffe people' because of the wearing of neck coils. See box, page 280.

Suay

The Suay are a 'tribe' of elephant catchers speaking their own dialect of Thai and with their own customs. They are thought to have come from Cambodia and settled in Thailand where they honed their skills of catching, taming and training elephants. Unfortunately, with the end of logging in Thailand the work of elephants – and therefore of the Suay – has dried up. They have become a people without a purpose.

Refugees

Thailand's relative economic prosperity, coupled with the wars that have afflicted neighbouring countries, have brought in waves of refugees to the kingdom in recent years. Following the victory of communist forces in Cambodia and Laos in the mid-1970s, many thousands fled to the safety of Thailand. Those escaping the atrocities of the Khmer Rouge (more than 300,000 people) settled in refugee camps along the southern rim of the northeastern region and have since been repatriated. The several hundred thousand Lao who crossed the Mekong River as the Pathet Lao took control of Laos took shelter in refugee camps along the northern sweep of the northeast. These camps too have been closed and their inmates largely resettled in the USA, Australia, France and Canada.

More recently, the crushing of the democracy movement in Burma in 1988 caused several tens of thousands of Burmese to flee to Thailand. More than 100,000 continue to live in camps along the Thai-Burmese border, from Prachuap Khiri Khan in the south to Mae Hong Son in the north. Guesthouses in Mae Sot, and also in Sangkhlaburi, often collect clothes and medicines for distribution to the refugee camps. These political refugees, fleeing persecution – or the fear of persecution – in their own countries, have been joined since the late 1980s by a new army of economic refugees. In 1997 there were an estimated one million illegal migrant workers in Thailand, most of them (around 75%) from Burma, but with large numbers also from China, Laos, Cambodia and Vietnam, and smaller populations from India, Bangladesh and Pakistan. There are probably more illegal labour migrants and refugees in Thailand than there are hill peoples, making them the largest 'minority' group in the country.

In mid-1996 the government announced it would permit illegal migrants already in the country (but not new arrivals) to work for two years before their repatriation. At the end of the three-month amnesty that was granted to allow illegal immigrants to register, the Immigration Department had compiled a list of 342,000 names. The reason for this strange policy decision was that Thailand, at that time, was woefully short of cheap labour: rapid economic growth had priced many Thai workers out of the lower paid, unskilled manual jobs, and illegal labour migrants from neighbouring Burma, Cambodia and Laos were seen as a neat (and cheap) way to fill the gap. Jobs in road maintenance, sugar cane cutting, construction, food packing and freezing, for example, were characteristically filled by immigrants willing to take so-called '3-D jobs' (dangerous, dirty and demeaning – sometimes, for good measure, difficult, too).

With the economic crisis, the logic of the government's decision was, seemingly, undermined. In 1997 and 1998, Thais were being laid off as factories shut down. Immigrant workers, in their turn, were displaced as the sensibilities of Thais over what they did eased in the face of economic necessity. The result was that tens of thousands of Burmese found themselves living in camps on the Thai-Burmese border, waiting for repatriation. But while the crisis certainly made life hard for Thailand's economic migrants, many continued to fill the least attractive jobs. There is little doubt that many thousands of Burmese, Cambodian and Lao workers remain in Thailand, many illegally, often taking on the jobs which are too dirty, dangerous and poorly paid to attract the average Thai.

Language

According to the Thai census, 97% of the population of Thailand speak Thai, the national language. However, it would be more accurate to say that 97% of the population speak one of several related 'Tai' dialects.

The Thai language is an amalgam of Mon and Khmer, and the ancient Indian languages, Pali and Sanskrit. It has also been influenced by Chinese dialects and by Malay. There remains strong academic disagreement as to whether it should be seen as primarily a language of the Sino-Tibetan group, or more closely linked to Austronesian languages. It is usually accepted that the Thai writing system was devised by King Ramkhamhaeng in 1283, who modelled it on an Indian system using Khmer characters (although see page 198). The modern Thai alphabet contains 44 consonants, 24 vowels and four diacritical tone marks. Words often link with other languages, particularly technical words. For example, *praisani*/post office (Sanskrit), *khipanawut*/guided missile (Pali) and *supermarket*/supermarket (English). There is a royal court language (*rachasap*) with a specialized vocabulary, as well as a vocabulary to be used when talking to monks. ▶▶ *See Useful words and phrases, page 774.*

The usual view of Thailand is one of homogeneity in language terms. Even long-term residents and those who speak Thai will observe that the kingdom is almost monolingual. But, as William Smalley, a linguistics professor at Bethel College and a former missionary linguist in Vietnam, Laos and Thailand, explained in his book *Linguistic Diversity and National Unity: Language Ecology in Thailand* (University of Chicago Press: Chicago, 1994), there are over 80 languages spoken in Thailand and great diversity in linguistic terms. What is interesting is that despite this great diversity, language has not become a divisive and politicized issue. There are those in the northeast and the south who argue the case for a greater recognition of regional languages – Lao (or Isan) and Pak Tai respectively – but so-called Standard Thai is still perceived to be the language of *all* Thais. Thus, the view of Thailand being a country of 'one' language, though it may in academic terms be incorrect, in functional and political terms is broadly accurate.

Thailand is a country with a united sense of itself, yet with a fragmented linguistic pattern. Successive governments have contributed to this by portraying the country as culturally homogenous and assuming that everyone who speaks one of a number of Tai dialects speaks Thai. William Smalley illustrates this diversity by giving the example of a teacher from the northeast: "A high school teacher in the provincial capital of Surin in northeast Thailand speaks the northern Khmer language of the area to her neighbours and in many other informal situations around town. She learned it by living and working in the city for several years. On the other hand, she speaks Lao with her husband, a government official, because that is his mother tongue. She learned it (and met him) when she was in training as a teacher in the Lao-speaking area of the northeast. She teaches in Standard Thai, which she herself learned in school. She talks to her children in Lao or northern Khmer or Standard Thai, as seems appropriate at the time. When she returns to her home village, an hour's ride by bus to the east of Surin, she speaks Kuy, her own native language, the language of her parents, the language in which she grew up." (Smalley 1994:1)

Thailand's four main regional languages are Lao (spoken in the northeast), Kham Muang ('language of the principalities', spoken in the north), Thai Klang (spoken in the central region) and Pak Tai ('southern tongue', spoken in the south). These four languages, and Standard Thai, are spoken by the following proportions of the total population: Thai Klang (27%), Lao (23%), Standard Thai (20%), Kam Muang (9%), Pak Tai (8%). **Note** Thai Klang (Central Thai) is not the same as Standard Thai.

Thai, like many languages, has borrowed extensively from the English language. However, Thai has always pillaged other languages – particularly Chinese, Khmer, Pali and Sanskrit. Sometimes there are different words for pieces of modern technology that span this divide. For example, anyone being taught formal Thai will learn that the word for television is *thoorathat*. This is constructed from two classical words meaning 'far away' and 'view'. However, saying *thoorathat* is a little like saying gramophone in English, and may elicit a giggle. Most Thais now talk about the *thii wii*, clearly borrowed from the English. There are many other Thai words with English borrowings: *thek* from discotheque, *piknik* from picnic, *chut* from suit (for a set of something), and so on.

Literature

The first piece of Thai literature is recognized as being King Ramkhamhaeng's inscription No 1 of 1292 (see page 688). The *Suphasit Phra Ruang* (The maxims of King Ruang), perhaps written by King Ramkhamhaeng himself, is regarded as the first piece of Thai poetry of the genre, known as *suphasit*. It shows clear links with earlier Pali works and with Indian-Buddhist religious texts, and an adaptation of the original can be seen carved in marble at Wat Pho in Bangkok (see page 82).

Another important early piece of prose is the *Traiphum Phra Ruang* (Three worlds of Phra Ruang), probably written by King Lithai in the mid-14th century. The work investigates the Three Buddhist realms – earth, heaven and hell – and also offers advice on how a *cakravartin* (universal monarch) should govern. According to Phra Ruang, or the *Traibhumikata*, it is regarded as the masterpiece of Tai Buddhist cosmology. Authorship is usually attributed to King Lithai of Sukhothai, although this is far from conclusively settled. He is thought to have written the book while heir apparent, in 1345. The book sets out the desired relationship of a ruler to his subjects and the characteristics of a righteous monarch. The merit of the ruler spreads out like an umbrella to touch and shield all those who come within its protecting and civilizing powers. In this way the *Three Worlds* is seen to describe the form and function of the Tai city state or *müang*, most clearly reflected in Sukhothai and Si Satchanalai.

The literary arts flourished during the Ayutthayan period, particular poetry. Five forms of verse evolved during this period, and they are still in use today – *chan, kap, khlong, klon* and *rai*. The first two are Indian in origin, the last three are Thai. Each has strict rules of rhyme and structure.

The genre of poetry known as *nirat* reached its height during the reign of King Narai (1656-1688). These are long narrative poems, written in *khlong* form, usually describing a journey. They have proved useful to historians and other scholars in their attempts to reconstruct Thai life. The poem *Khlong Kamsuan Siprat* is regarded as the masterpiece of this genre. Unfortunately, many of the manuscripts of these Ayutthayan works were lost when the Burmese sacked the city in 1767.

During the Rattanakosin period, focused on Bangkok/Thonburi, the first piece of Thai prose fiction was written – a historical romance written by Chao Phraya Phra Khlang. The first full version of the Ramakien was also produced in *klon* verse form (see page 86). The acknowledged poetic genius of the period was Sunthorn Phu (1786-1855), who the Thais think of as their Shakespeare, whose masterpiece is the 30,000 line romance *Phra Aphaimani* (see page 415).

The revolution of 1932 led to a transformation in Thai literature. The first novel to be received with acclaim was Prince Arkartdamkeung Rapheephat's *Lakhon haeng chiwit* (The Circus of Life), published in 1929. Sadly, this gifted novelist died at the age of 27. Two other talented novelists were the commoner Si Burapha, whose masterpiece is *Songkhram chiwit* (War of Life, 1932), and the female writer Dokmai Sot, whose publications include *Phu dii* (The Good Person, 1937). The works of Dokmai Sot, like those of Prince Akat, deal with the theme of the clash of Thai and Western cultures. Their works are particularly pertinent today, when many educated Thais are re-examining their cultural roots.

Since the Second World War, second rate love/romance writing has flourished. The plots vary only marginally from book to book: love triangles, jealousy, macho men, faithful women … This dismal outpouring is partly balanced by a handful of quality works. Notable are those of Kukrit Pramoj, a journalist and former prime minister, whose most famous and best work is *Si phaen din* (The Four Reigns, 1953). This traces the history of a noble family from the late-19th century to the end of the Second World War – a sort of Barbara Cartland à la Thailand.

From the political turmoil of the 1950s through to the present day, but particularly from 1973 to 1976, literature began to be used more explicitly as a tool of political commentary and criticism. *Phai daeng* (Red Bamboo, 1954) is a carefully constructed anti-communist novel by Kukrit Pramoj, while the poems of Angkhan Kanlayanaphong became favourites of the radical student movement of the 1970s. Many of the more radical novelists were gaoled during the 1950s, of whom the most talented was probably Si Burapha. He, and the other radical novelists' and poets' work, represent a genre of socialist realism in which the country's afflictions are put down to capitalism and right-wing politics. But perhaps the most successful of Thai novels are those that deal with the trials and tribulations of rural life: Kamphoon Boontawee's *Luuk Isan* (Child of the Northeast, 1976) and Khammaan Khonkai's *Khru ban nok* (The Rural Teacher), later made into the film *The Teacher of Mad Dog Swamp*. ➤➤ *See Books, page 771.*

Art and architecture

The various periods of Thai art and architecture were characterized by their own distinctive styles. For illustrations, see the Buddha images on page 743.

One of the problems with reconstructing the artistic heritage of any Southeast Asian civilization is that most buildings were built of wood. Wood was abundant, but it also rotted quickly in the warm and humid climate. Although there can be no doubt that fine buildings made of wood were constructed by the various kingdoms of Thailand, much of the art that remains, and on which our appreciation is built, is made of stone, brick or bronze. There are few wooden buildings more than a century or so old.

Dvaravati style (sixth-11th centuries)

The Dvaravati Kingdom is rather an enigma to art historians. Theravada Buddhist objects have been unearthed in various parts of the central plains which date from the sixth century onwards, among them coins with the inscription "the merit of the king of Dvaravati". The capital of this kingdom was probably Nakhon Pathom, west of Bangkok, and it is thought that the inhabitants were Mon in origin. The kingdom covered much of Lower Burma and Central Thailand, and may have been influential from as early as the third century to as late as the 13th.

Dvaravati Buddha images show stylistic similarities with Indian Gupta and post-Gupta images (fourth to eighth centuries), and with pre-Pala (also Indian) images (eighth-11th centuries). Most are carved in stone, with only small images cast in bronze. Standing images tend to be presented in the attitude of Vitarkamudra (see page 743), and later carvings show more strongly indigenous facial features: a flatter face, prominent eyes, and thick nose and lips. Fragments of red paint have been discovered on some images, leading art historians to believe that the carvings would originally have been painted.

Also characteristic of Dvaravati art are terracotta sculptures – some intricately carved, such as those found at Nakhon Pathom and exhibited in the museum there – carved bas-reliefs and stone Wheels of Law. As well as Nakhon Pathom, Dvaravati art has also been discovered at Uthong in Suphanburi province, and Muang Fa Daed in Kalasin (northeastern region). But perhaps the finest and most complete remnants of the Dvaravati tradition are in the town of Lamphun, formerly Haripunjaya (see below).

Haripunjaya style (seventh-13th centuries)

It seems that during the seventh century the Dvaravati-influenced inhabitants of Lopburi (Lavo) migrated north to found a new city: Haripunjaya, now called Lamphun (see page 248). Although the art of this Mon outlier was influenced by the Indian Pala tradition, as well as by Khmer styles, it maintained its independence long after the rest of the Dvaravati Kingdom had been subsumed by the stronger Tai kingdoms. It was not until the late-13th century that Haripunjaya was conquered by the Tais, and as a result is probably the oldest preserved city in Thailand.

Srivijaya (eighth-13th centuries)

The Srivijayan Empire was a powerful maritime empire that extended from Java northwards into Thailand, and had its capital at Palembang in Sumatra. Like Dvaravati art, Srivijaya art was also heavily influenced by Indian traditions. It seems likely that this part of Thailand was on the trade route between India and China, and as a result local artists were well aware of Indian styles. A problem with characterizing the art of this period, which spanned five centuries, is that it is very varied.

Srivijaya was a Mahayana Buddhist Empire, and numerous Avalokitesvara Bodhisattvas have been found, in both stone and bronze, at Chaiya (see page 612). Some of these are wonderfully carved, and particularly notable is the supremely modelled bronze Avalokitesvara (eighth century, 63 cm high), unearthed at Chaiya and now housed in the National Museum in Bangkok. In fact, so much Srivijayan art has been discovered around this town that some experts went so far as to argue that Chaiya, and not Palembang, was the capital of Srivijaya. Unfortunately, however, there are few architectural remnants from the period. Two exceptions are Wat Phra Boromthat and Wat Kaeo, both at Chaiya (see page 612).

Khmer or Lopburi style (seventh-14th centuries)

Khmer art has been found in the eastern, central and northeastern regions of the country, and is closely linked to the art and architecture of Cambodia. It is usually referred to as Lopburi style, because the town of Lopburi in the central plains is assumed to have been a centre of the Khmer Empire in Thailand (see page 174). The art is Mahayana Buddhist in inspiration and stylistic changes mirror those in Cambodia. In Thailand, the period of Khmer artistic influence begins with the reign of Suryavarman I (1002-1050) and includes Muang Tham, Prasat Phranomwan and the beginnings of Phanom Rung; Phimai, the most visited of the Khmer Shrines, was built during the reign of the great King Jayavarman VII (1181-1217).

Lopburi Buddhas are authoritative, with flat, square faces and a protuberance on the crown of the head signifying enlightenment. They are the first Buddhas to be portrayed in regal attire, as the Khmers believed that the king, as a *deva raja* (god king), was himself divine. They were carved in stone or cast in bronze. Sadly, many of the finer Khmer pieces have been smuggled abroad. Khmer temples in Thailand are among the most magnificent structures in Southeast Asia. The biggest are those of the north-eastern region, including Phimai, Muang Tham and Phanom Rung, although Khmer architecture is also found as far afield as Lopburi and at Muang Kao outside Kanchanaburi.

Chiang Saen or Chiang Mai style (11th-18th centuries)

This period marks the beginning of Tai art. Earlier works were derivative, being essentially the art of empires and kingdoms whose centres of power lay beyond the country – like Cambodia (Khmer), Sumatra (Srivijaya) and Burma (Mon/Dvaravati). There are two styles within this northern tradition: the Chiang Saen and Chiang Mai (or Later Chiang Saen) schools. The Chiang Saen style, in which the Buddha is portrayed with a round face, arched eyebrows and prominent chin, is stylistically linked to Pala art of India. Nevertheless, local artists incorporated their own vision and produced unique and beautiful images. The earliest

Khmer-style Prang

date from around the 11th century and their classification refers to the ancient town of Chiang Saen, situated on the Mekong in northern Thailand, where many of the finest pieces have been found. The second style is known as Later Chiang Saen or, less confusingly, Chiang Mai. The influence of Sukhothai can be seen in the works from this period: oval face, more slender body and with the robe over the left shoulder. Images date from the mid-14th century.

Buddha images from both of the northern periods were carved in stone or semi-precious stone, and cast in bronze. The most famous Buddha of all, the Emerald Buddha housed in Wat Phra Kaeo in Bangkok, may have been carved in northern Thailand during the Late Chiang Saen/Chiang Mai period, although this is not certain.

Architecturally, the 'northern school' began to make a pronounced contribution from the time of the founding of the city of Chiang Mai in 1296. Perhaps the finest example from this period – indeed, some people regard the buildings that make up the complex as the finest in all Thailand – is the incomparable Wat Lampang Luang, outside the town of Lampang in the north.

Sukhothai style (late 13th to early 15th centuries)

The Sukhothai Buddha is one of the first representations of the Ceylonese Buddha in Siam, the prototypes being from Anuradhapura, Sri Lanka (Ceylon). The Buddha is usually represented in the round, either seated cross-legged in the attitude of subduing Mara; or the languid, one-foot forward standing position, with one hand raised, in the attitude of giving protection as the enlightened one descends from the Tavatimsa Heaven. Most were cast in bronze, as Thailand is noticeably lacking in good stone. Some art historians have also argued that Sukhothai artists disliked the violence of chiselling stone, maintaining that

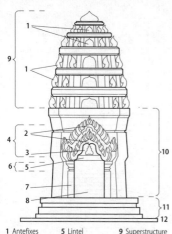

as peaceful Thais and good Buddhists they would have preferred the art of modelling bronze. This is fanciful in the extreme.

For the seated Buddha, the surfaces are smooth and curved, with an oval head and elongated features, small hair curls, arched eyebrows and a hooked nose. The classic, enigmatic Sukhothai smile is often said to convey inner contentment. The head is topped by a tall flame-like motif or *ketumula*. The shoulders are broad and the waist is narrow. The length of cloth hanging over the left shoulder drops quite a long way down to the navel, and terminates in a notched design.

The graceful walking Buddha (perhaps the greatest single artistic innovation of the Sukhothai period) features rather strange projecting heels (which follows the ancient writings describing the Buddha's physical appearance). The figure is almost androgynous – this was Buddha depicted having achieved enlightenment, which meant that

1 Antefixes	5 Lintel	9 Superstructure
2 Arches	6 Capital	10 Cell
3 Tympanum	7 Pilaster	11 Base
4 Pediment	8 Niche or door	12 Platform

13th-century Khmer Sanctuary Tower after Stratton and Scott, 1981

sexual characteristics no longer existed. The finest examples were produced in the decades immediately prior to Ayutthaya conquering the city in 1438.

Steve van Beek and Luca Tettoni wrote in *The Arts of Thailand*: "Sukhothai sculpture suggests a figure in the process of dematerializing, halfway between solid and vapour. He doesn't walk so much as float. He doesn't sit, he levitates, and belies his masculine nature which should be inflexible. Even his diaphanous robes portray a Buddha which has already shed the trappings of this world."

The initial influence upon Sukhothai art and architecture was from Cambodia. Khmer influence can be seen reflected, for example, in the distinctive 'prang' towers of the period (see illustration). Subsequent stupas can be classified into three styles. First, there is the Ceylonese bell-shaped stupa (see illustration, below). This is characterized by a square base surrounded by caryatids, above which is another base with niches containing Buddha images. Wat Chang Lom, in Si Satchanalai, is a good example. The second style of stupa is the lotus bud *chedi*, examples of which can be found at Wat Mahathat and Wat Trapang Ngoen in Sukhothai, Wat Chedi Jet Thaew in Si Satchanalai, and also in Kamphaeng Phet, Tak, Phitsanulok and Chiang Mai. The third style of stupa constructed during this period is believed to be derived from Srivijayan prototypes, although the links are not well established. It is, however, very distinctive, consisting of a square base, above which is a square main body, superimposed with pedestals, containing niches within which are standing Buddha images. Above the main body are bell-shaped *andas* of reducing size.

Examples of this style can be found on the corner stupas at Wat Mahathat and some subsidiary stupas at Wat Chedi Jet Thaew (Si Satchanalai). Mention should be made of the mondop, built in place of the stupa on a square plan and always containing a large Buddha image. A good example is Wat Sri Chum (Sukhothai). It is said that the stupa 'evolved' as the Buddha lay dying. One of the disciples, Ananda, asked how they might remember the Enlightened One after his death, to which the Buddha replied it was the doctrine, not himself, that should be remembered. As this reply was clearly unsatisfactory to his distraught followers, the Buddha added that after cremation a relic of his body might be placed within a mound of earth – which, over time, became the stupa.

Ayutthayan style (mid-14th to mid-18th centuries)

Both the art and architecture of this period can be split into four sub-periods spanning the years from 1351 to 1767, when Ayutthaya was sacked by the Burmese.

As far as Ayutthayan Buddha images are concerned, for much of the time the artists of the city drew upon the works of other kingdoms for inspiration. To begin with, Uthong Buddhas were popular (themselves drawing upon Khmer prototypes).

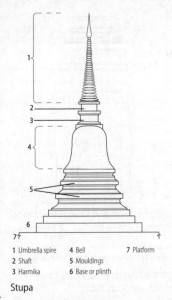

1 Umbrella spire	4 Bell	7 Platform
2 Shaft	5 Mouldings	
3 Harmika	6 Base or plinth	

Stupa

Then, from the mid-15th century, Sukhothai styles became highly influential – although the images produced looked rather lifeless and are hardly comparable with the originals. In the mid-16th century, when Cambodia came under Thai control, Ayutthayan artists looked to, and imitated, Khmer sculpture (identifiable by the double lips and indistinct moustache). Finally, in the Late Ayutthayan period, a home-grown but rather fussy style arose, with the Buddha often portrayed crowned.

The first of the four sub-periods of Ayutthayan architecture commenced in 1351 and may have been influenced by the *prang* of Wat Phra Sri Ratana Mahathat in Lopburi, though *prangs* at Ayutthaya are slightly taller. The second period (1488-1629) is dominated by the round Ceylonese-style stupa, the major example of this being Wat Phra Sri Samphet. During the third period (the first half of the 17th century), the king sent architects to Cambodia to study the architectural characteristics of the Khmer monuments. As a result, the *prang* became fashionable again – Wat Watthanaram and Wat Chumphon (Bang Pa-In) were built at this time. The final period was from 1732 until the sacking of Ayutthaya by the Burmese in 1767. The many-rabbeted *chedis* were popular during this period, although fewer new buildings were constructed as King Boromkot was more interested in restoring existing buildings. Most of the *viharns* and *ubosoths* have long since perished. What remains dates mainly from the Late Ayutthayan period.

Bangkok style (late 18th to 20th centuries)

The Bangkok or Rattanakosin period dates from the founding of the Chakri Dynasty in 1782. But, initially at least, the need for Buddha images was met not by making new ones, but by recovering old ones. King Rama I ordered that images be collected from around his devastated kingdom and brought to Bangkok. About 1200 were recovered in this way,

Wat Suwannaram (Bangkok)

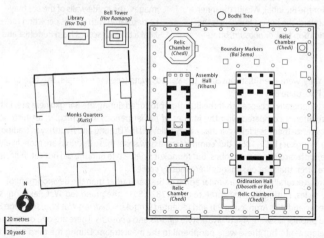

The Thai wat

Wats are usually separated from the secular world by **two walls**. Between these outer and inner walls are found the **monks quarters** or dormitories (*kutis*), perhaps a **bell tower** *(hor rakang)* that is used to toll the hours and to warn of danger and, in larger complexes, schools and other administrative buildings. Traditionally, the *kutis* were placed on the south side of the wat. It was believed that if the monks slept directly in front of the principal Buddha image, they would die young; if they slept to the left, they would become ill; and if they slept behind it, there would be discord in the community of monks. This section of the compound is known as the *sanghavasa*, or *sanghawat* (ie for the Sangha – the monkhood).

The inner wall, which in bigger wats often takes the form of a **gallery** or cloister (*phra rabieng*) lined with Buddha images, represents the division between the worldly and the holy, the sacred and the profane. It is used as a quiet place for meditation. This part of the wat compound is known as the *buddhavasa*, or *phutthawat* (ie for the Buddha). Within the inner courtyard, the holiest building is the **ordination hall**, or *ubosoth*, often

shortened to just **bot**. This building is reserved for monks only. It is built on consecrated ground, and has a ring of eight stone tablets or boundary markers (*bai sema*), sometimes contained in mini-pavilions, arranged around it at the cardinal and subcardinal points. These *bai sema* are shaped like stylized leaves of the bodhi tree, and often carved with representations of Vishnu, Siva, Brahma or Indra, or of *nagas*. Buried in the ground beneath the *bai sema* are *luuk nimit* – stone spheres – and sometimes gold and jewellery. The *bai sema* mark the limit of earthly power – within the stones, not even a king can issue orders.

The *bot* is characteristically a large, rectangular building with high walls and multiple sloping roofs, covered in glazed clay tiles (or wood tiles, in the north). At each end of the roof are *chofaa*, or 'bunches of sky', which represent garuda grasping two *nagas* in its talons. Inside, often through elaborately carved and inlaid doors, is a Buddha image. There may also be numerous subsidiary images. The inside walls of the *bot* may be decorated with murals depicting the Jataka tales, or scenes from Buddhist and

and they were then distributed to the various wats (see for example, the fine array at Wat Pho, page 82).

It is generally accepted that the Buddhas produced during the Bangkok era are, in the main, inferior compared with the images of earlier periods. In particular, art historians characterize them as 'lifeless'. Initially, they followed the Uthong and Ayutthayan traditions. King Mongkut (1851-1868) did 'commission' a new style: these Buddhas are more lively in style, with carefully carved robes. But Mongkut's new-style Buddha did not catch on, and more often than not old images were merely copied.

Architecturally, there is a similar aping of the past rather than the development of any new styles. During the first three reigns (1782-1851), the *prang* (eg Wat Rakhang, see page 96; and Wat Arun, page 93) and redented (angular) *chedi* (eg Wat Pho, see page 82) were popular, as were Ayutthayan-style *viharns* and *ubosoths*. There are one or two new developments, but these were peripheral to the mainstream. During the third reign, for example, the influence of Chinese art becomes quite pronounced. Other 'oddities' include

Hindu cosmology. Like the Buddha image, these murals are meant to serve as meditation aids. It is customary for pilgrims to remove their shoes on entering any Buddhist building (or private house for that matter), although in state ceremonies, officials in uniform are not required to do so.

The other main building within the inner courtyard is the **assembly hall**, or **viharn**, but not all wats have one, and some may have more than one. Architecturally, this is often indistinguishable from the *bot*. It contains the wat's principal Buddha images. The main difference between the *bot* and *viharn* is that the latter does not stand on consecrated ground, and can be identified by the absence of any *bai sema* – stone tablets – set around it. The *viharn* is for general use and, unlike the *bot*, is rarely locked. Both *bot* and *viharn* are supposed to face water, because the Buddha himself was facing a river when he achieved enlightenment under the bodhi tree. If there is no natural body of water, the monks may dig a pond. In the late Ayutthayan period, the curved lines of

the *bot* and *viharn* were designed to symbolize a boat.

Also found in the inner courtyard may be a number of other structures. Among the more common are **chedis**, bell-shaped **relic chambers** with tapering spires. In larger wats these can be built on a massive scale (such as the one at Nakhon Pathom), and contain holy relics of the Buddha himself. More often, *chedis* are smaller affairs containing the ashes of royalty, monks or pious lay people. A rarer Khmer architectural feature sometimes found in Thai wats is the **prang**, also a relic chamber. The best known of these angular corn-cob-shaped towers is the one at Wat Arun in Bangkok (see page 95).

Another rarer feature is the **library** or scripture repository (*hor trai*), usually a small, tall-sided building where the Buddhist scriptures can be stored safely, high off the ground.

Salas are open-sided **rest pavilions**, which can be found anywhere in the wat compound; the *sala kan parian* or **study hall** is the largest and most impressive of these and is almost like a *bot* or *viharn* without walls. Here the monks say their prayers at noon.

the early 20th-century Wat Nivet Thamaprawat at Bang Pa-in, which is Gothic in inspiration (see page 112), and Wat Benchamabophit in Bangkok, which is a fusion of Eastern and Western styles (see page 100). In general, Rattanakosin wat buildings are airier and less ornate than those of Ayutthaya.

Thai murals

Like sculptural art in Thailand, paintings – usually murals – were devotional works. They were meant to serve as meditation aids, and therefore tended to follow established 'scripts' that any pilgrim could 'read' with ease. These scripts were primarily based on the *Ramakien* (see page 86), the *Jataka* tales and the *Traiphum* (The Three Worlds), see also page 733. Most such murals are found, appropriately, on the interior walls of *bots* and *viharns*. Unfortunately, there are no murals to compete in antiquity with carvings in stone, although they were certainly produced during the Sukhothai period and probably much earlier. The use of paint on dry walls (frescoes are painted onto wet plaster and survive

Mudras and the Buddha image

An artist producing an image of the Buddha does not try to create an original piece of art: he or she is trying to be faithful to a tradition which can be traced back over centuries. It is important to appreciate that the Buddha image is not merely a work of art, but an object of – and for – worship. Sanskrit poetry even sets down the characteristics of the Buddha – albeit in rather unlikely terms: legs like a deer, arms like an elephant's trunk, a chin like a mango stone and hair like the stings of scorpions. The Pali texts of Theravada Buddhism add the 108 auspicious signs, long toes and fingers of equal length, body like a banyan tree and eyelashes like a cow's. The Buddha can be represented either sitting, lying (indicating paranirvana) or standing, and (in Thailand) occasionally walking. He is often represented standing on an open lotus flower: the Buddha was born into an impure world, and likewise the lotus germinates in mud, but rises above the filth to flower. Each image will be represented in a particular mudra or 'attitude', of which there are 40. The most common are:

Abhayamudra
Dispelling fear or giving protection; right hand (sometimes both hands) raised, palm outwards, usually with the Buddha in a standing position.

Varamudra
Giving blessing or charity; the right hand pointing downwards, the palm facing outwards, with the Buddha either seated or standing.

Vitarkamudra
Preaching mudra; the ends of the thumb and index finger of the right hand touch to form a circle, symbolizing the Wheel of Law. The Buddha can be seated or standing.

Dharmacakramudra
'Spinning the Wheel of Law'; a preaching mudra symbolizing the teaching of the first sermon. Hands are held in front of the chest, thumbs and index fingers of both joined, one facing inwards, one outwards.

Bhumisparcamudra
'Calling the earth goddess to witness' or 'touching the earth'; the right hand rests on the right knee, with the tips of the fingers 'touching ground', thus calling the earth goddess Thoranee to witness his enlightenment and victory over Mara, the king of demons. The Buddha is always seated.

Dhyanamudra
Meditation; both hands open, palms upwards, in the lap, right over left.

Vajrasana
Yogic posture of meditation; cross-legged, both soles of the feet visible.

Virasana (paryankasana)
Yogic posture of meditation; cross-legged, but with the right leg on top of the left, covering the left foot.

Buddha under Naga
A common image in Khmer art; the Buddha is shown seated in an attitude of meditation, with a cobra rearing up over his head. This refers to an episode in the Buddha's life when he was meditating: a rain storm broke and Nagaraja, the king of the nagas (snakes), curled up under the Buddha (seven coils) and then used his seven-headed hood to protect the Holy One from the falling rain.

Buddha calling for rain
The Buddha is standing, arms held at the side of the body, fingers pointing down.

Bhumisparcamudra – calling the earth goddess to witness. Sukhothai period, 13th-14th century.

Dhyanamudra – meditation. Sukhothai period, 13th-14th century.

Abhayamudra – dispelling fear or giving protection. Lopburi Buddha, Khmer style, 12th century.

Vitarkamudra – preaching, 'spinning the Wheel of Law'. Dvaravati Buddha, 7th-8th century seated in the 'European' manner.

Abhayamudra – dispelling fear or giving protection; subduing Mara position. Lopburi Buddha, Khmer style, 13th century.

The Buddha – 'Calling for rain'.

much better) made the works susceptible to damp and heat. None has survived that pre-dates the Ayutthaya period and only a handful are more than 150 years old.

The sequence of the murals tend to follow a particular pattern: beneath the windows on the long walls are episodes from the Buddha's life; behind the principal Buddha image, the Three Worlds – heaven, earth and hell (see illustration page 743); and on the end wall facing the Buddha, the contest with Mara. But, in amongst these established themes, the artist was free to incorporate scenes from everyday life and local tales and myths. These are often the most entertaining sections. All were portrayed without perspective using simple lines and blocks of uniform colour, with no use of shadow and shading.

Modern Thai architecture

Few visitors – or residents for that matter – see much but crudity in modern Thai buildings: elegant wooden shophouses are torn down to make way for the worst in concrete crassness; office buildings are erected with apparently not a shred of thought as to their effects on the surrounding environment; multi-storeyed condominiums are built with abandon and bad taste. This is tragic, given the beauty and environmental common sense that informed traditional designs. Much like Singapore, in a few years' time the Thais may be frantically putting back what they have so recently pulled down. But there are Thai architects who are attempting to develop a modern Thai architecture that does not merely ape the worst in Western designs, and there are some notable new buildings.

In wat architecture, there is a move away from the gaudy, rather over-worked (to Western eyes) traditions of the Bangkok period, towards a sparer, almost ascetic vision. Bright colours have been replaced by expanses of white and subdued hues; the hectic angles of tradition, with simpler geometric shapes. Monasteries like Wat Sala Loi, in Nakhon Ratchasima (Korat) in the northeast, and Wat Dhammakaya in Pathum Thani province, keep decoration to a minimum. Wirot Srisuro, of Khon Kaen University and the architect of Wat Sala Loi, explained to the *Bangkok Post*: "Buddhism teaches us to follow the middle path, to avoid extravagance. Our buildings should reflect this thinking by staying simple." Although Ajaan Wirot's work and that of other modernists has attracted great attention – much of it negative – far more monasteries are being built in traditional style, but with cement and concrete blocks replacing brick and stucco.

Cinema

Thailand has a suddenly resurgent domestic film industry, so much so that some critics are writing of a 'New Thai Cinema'. Certainly something new is stirring, but it must be remembered that this comes after years of dross when Thai cinema was notable only for poor quality and crass story lines. In 1997, the year of the economic crisis in Thailand, it seemed that Thai cinema was in terminal decline. Just 17 films were made that year, compared to an average of 100 per year throughout the 1970s. But 1997 was also the year when a generation of new directors began to make a difference. Penek Rattanaruang made *Fun Bar Karaoke*, which was screened to some critical acclaim at the Berlin International Film Festival. A year later, Nonzee Nimibutr made *Dang Bireley's and Young Gangster* a film which, importantly, was not only critically acclaimed but also commercially successful. Other notable directors include Oxide Pang who made *Who is running?* and Wisit Sasanatieng who directed *Tear of the Black Tiger*. But the biggest film of many years – indeed of all time – is the historical epic *Suriyothai* released in 2002. This was not only hugely expensive for a Thai film but has also proved to be well received by the public and pundits alike. The Bangkok International Art Film Festival was inaugurated in 1997.

It is not just Thai cinema that has seen a resurgence over the last few years. So too has Thailand as a production centre for overseas films. Excellent locations, value for money, and an increasingly professional support network have all raised the profile of the country.

Dance, drama and music

The great Indian epic, the Ramayana (in Thai known as the Ramakien, see page 86), has been an important influence on all Thai arts, but most clearly in dance and drama such as *nang* and *nang thalung* (shadow plays, see below), *khon* (masked dramas) and *lakhon* (classical dance dramas). Also important is the likay (folk drama).

Dance
Lakhon are dance dramas known to have been performed in the 17th century, and probably evolved from Javanese prototypes. They became very popular not just in the court, but also in the countryside and among the common people. Consisting of three main forms, they draw upon the Jatakas (tales of the former lives of the historic Buddha), the Ramakien, and upon local fables, legends and myths, for their subject matter. Performers wear intricate costumes based on ancient dress, and character parts (such as demons and yogis) wear masks. In genuine *lakhon*, all performers – bar clowns – are played by women. A chorus sing the parts, not the actors.

Drama
Khon masked drama evolved in the royal court of Siam, although its roots lie in folk dances of the countryside. Performers don elaborate jewelled costumes, men wearing masks and women crowns or gilded headdresses. Music accompanies the dance, and words and songs are performed by an off-stage chorus. Many dances are interpretations of traditional myths, and performers begin their training at an early age.

The **ramwong** is a dance often performed at ceremonies and originates from the central region. The **fawn** is a similar northern dance. Slow, graceful, synchronized dancing, accompanied by drums and symbols – in which hand movements are used to evoke meaning – characterize the dance. Ungainly Westerners are often encouraged to perform these dances, to the obvious amusement of Thais.

It is thought that **likay** evolved from Muslim Malay religious performances. It was adopted by the Thais and in time became primarily a comedy folk art enjoyed by common people, with singing and dancing. In recent years, *likay* artists have begun to incorporate political jibes into their repertoires. Cultured people in Bangkok used to consider *likay* rough and unsophisticated, but in recent years it has gained greater recognition as an art form.

Nang shadow plays, with characters beautifully engraved on leather, are frequently performed at cremation ceremonies, particularly in the south (see page 681). There are usually 10 puppeteers in a *nang* troupe, who wear traditional costume and are often made-up. The narrator (usually the oldest member of the troupe) offers some help with the story line, while a traditional *phipat* band provides musical accompaniment. The classical *phipat* orchestra consists of gongs and cymbals (*ching*), a xylophone (*ranat ek*), drums and a traditional wind instrument, rather like an oboe, called a *phi nai*.

Muay Thai (Thai boxing)

Along with Siamese cats and inaccurate films, Thailand is known in the West for Muay Thai – literally Thai boxing – or 'kick boxing'. This art of self-defence is first mentioned in the Burmese chronicles of 1411. King Naresuan (1590-1605), one of Thailand's greatest monarchs, made Muay Thai a compulsory element of military training and gradually it developed into a sport. Today it is Thailand's most popular sport and is one of the few ways that a poor country boy can turn his rags into riches. It is no coincidence that most of Thailand's best boxers have come from the harsh and impoverished northeastern region, which seems to turn out a never-ending stream of tough, determined young men.

A boy will begin training at the age of six or seven; he will be fighting by the age of 10, and competing in professional bouts at 16. Few boxers continue beyond the age of 25. In the countryside, boys herding buffalo will kick trees to hone their skills and learn to transcend pain, all with the intention of using their strength and agility to fight their way out of poverty. Trainers from Bangkok send scouts up-country to tour the provinces, in search of boys with potential.

In Muay Thai, any part of the body can be used to strike an opponent, except the head. Gloves were only introduced in the 1930s; before then, fists were wrapped in horse hide and studded with shell or glass fragments set in glue. Fatalities were common, and for a time in the 1920s Muay Thai was officially banned. Today, fights are staged much like boxing in the West: they are held in a ring, with gloves, and consist of five three-minute rounds, with two-minute rest periods between each round. Before beginning, the boxers prostrate themselves on the canvas while an orchestra of drums and symbols raises the tension. The opponents *wai* to each corner before the music stops, and the fight begins. Punching is rare – far more effective are the kicks and vicious elbow stabs. The intensity of many contests make Western heavyweight boxing seem slow and ponderous. As Doug Lansky, who sent us an amusing email, commented:

"These kickboxers may have been small, but I wouldn't want to step into a ring with any of them. They are kicking machines. Apparently, defence has not been introduced in this sport. It was like watching a battery commercial where two robots go at it until the cheaper battery runs out of power, or in this case, one of the fighters runs out of blood."

Nang was probably introduced into Thailand from Java during the early Ayutthaya period. *Nang thalung* puppets are smaller, more finely carved, and usually have articulated arms (see page 750). In both cases, the figures 'perform' in front of, or behind, a screen, usually enacting stories from the Ramakien. Like *likay*, *nang* and *nang thalung* have, in the past, been looked down upon as rather crude, unsophisticated arts.

Unfortunately for those who are trying to preserve traditional Thai arts, they are gradually, but steadily, losing their popular appeal. Although tourists may expect and hope to see a performance, most Thais would rather watch the TV or go to the movies.

Music

Thai traditional music is a blending of musical elements from a number of cultures, namely Chinese, Indian and Khmer. This applies not just to the instruments, but also to the melodies. Although Thai music can therefore be seen to be derivative, it nonetheless developed into a distinctive form that is regarded as belonging to the 'high' musical cultures of Southeast Asia. In the past, talented young musicians would become attached to the king's court or that of a nobleman, and would there receive training from established musicians. Musicians and composers independent of such patronage were rare, and public guilds seldom lasted very long.

With the ending of the absolute monarchy in 1932, the role of the nobility in supporting musicians began to die. Traditional music became viewed as 'un-modern' and performances were actively discouraged by the authorities. It has only been in about the last 25 years that an interest in traditional Thai music has re-emerged. But because of the years of neglect, the pool of talented musicians is very small.

Although court music may have withered, folk music remained popular and vibrant throughout this period – and perhaps nowhere more so than in the northeastern region of the country. Here *mor lam* singers are renowned, and in some cases they have become national celebrities. Accompanied by the haunting sound of the *khaen* (bamboo pipes) and singing 'songs from the rice fields' about rural poverty and unrequited love, they are among the most traditional of performers.

While non-Thai music (both Western and Eastern) is popular in Thailand there is also a booming local **popular music** industry. Some of this draws on local musical traditions. For example, a band called Fong Nam plays traditional *phipat* music using modern instruments such as electric keyboards. More popular still are re-workings of traditional folk music traditions to serve a population – particularly in rural areas – who are struggling with the pressures of modernization. So *luk thung* and the accompanying *likay* theatre are played and sung using electric guitars and keyboards. The themes, though, generally remain the same: lost love and the hard life of the farmer. That said, in the 1960s and particularly during the 1970s a new genre of *luk thung* appeared in Thailand: the protest song. Foremost among the bands to politicize music in this manner was the band Caravan, one of Thailand's most successful groups. Songwriters began to struggle with issues of poverty, democracy and the environment. Caravan split up in the 1980s and perhaps Thailand's biggest rock band now (although they play only very occasionally) is Carabao. Like Caravan, Carabao is a band with a social conscience writing and playing songs that dwell on the destructiveness of consumerism and the tragedy of AIDS in Thailand. More popular among younger Thais is the more sugary band Bird who have embraced rap and disco and given them a Thai flavour.

Textiles

Thai traditional textiles have experienced something of a rebirth since the end of the Second World War, with the support of the royal family, NGOs and the Jim Thompson Thai Silk Company. In 1947, Jim Thompson – an American resident in Bangkok – sent a sample of Thai silk to the editor of *Vogue* in New York. Then a near moribund industry, today it produces over 10,000,000 m of silk a year. In the past, cloth was made from silk, cotton or hemp. Because of a shortage of such natural yarns, it is common today to find cloth being woven from synthetic yarn. Likewise, chemical aniline dyes are used in place of natural animal and vegetable dyes although there has been a revival of interest in vegetable dyes, (particularly on cotton) in recent years. Among the most distinctive of Thai textiles is *matmii* cloth, produced using the *ikat* dyeing technique (see below). The dyed yarn is then woven into cloth using plain weave, float weave, supplementary weft and tapestry weave techniques. In the north, hill peoples also produce appliqué cloth.

Silk weaving appears to be of considerable antiquity in Thailand. Excavations at Ban Chiang in the northeast (see page 374) have revealed silk threads, in association with artifacts dated to 1000-2000 BC. If this is corroborated by other evidence (it remains contested), then the accepted view that the technology of sericulture filtered south from China will have to be revised. According to legend, the origins of sericulture date back to 4000 BC, when China's first emperor noticed that the leaves of the mulberry trees in his garden were being eaten at a prodigious rate by a small grub. Having eaten their fill, the voracious grubs spun cocoons of fine thread. Lei Zu, a concubine, collected the cocoons and dropped some into boiling water, whereupon they unravelled into long lengths of fine, but strong, thread.

The silk 'worm' lives for just 20 days, and 35,000 hatch from 30 g of eggs. In their short lives, this number of worms consume mulberry leaves (fresh, preferably young) three times a day, or 680 kg in under three weeks. Laid out on circular bamboo trays, the noise of 35,000 tiny jaws chomping their way through barrow-loads of leaves is like a gentle rustling sound. Susceptible to cold, disease, pest attack and all manner of other threats, the worms must be lovingly cultivated if they are to live long enough to weave their cocoons of silk. After they have formed cocoons – a process which takes around 36 hours – the worm metamorphoses into the silk moth. This gives the silk reelers just 10 days before the moth chews its way out of the cocoon, destroying the silk thread in the process. The cocoons are dropped into boiling water, killing the forming moth, and then unreeled, often by hand. A single cocoon can yield a thread between 200 m and 1500 m long, and about 12,500 cocoons are needed to produce 1 kg of silk yarn.

Clothing

The *pha sin* is an ankle length tubular piece of cloth, made up of three pieces and worn by women. The *hua sin* (waistband) is usually plain, the *pha sin* (main body of the skirt) is plain or decorated, while the *dtin sin* (lower hem) may be intricately woven. Traditionally, the pha sin was worn with a *pha sabai* (blouse or shawl), although it is common today to see women wearing T-shirts with the *pha sin*.

The *pha sarong* is the male equivalent of the *pha sin* and is now a rare sight. As the name suggests, it is a tubular piece of cloth which is folded at the front and secured with a belt. It is worn with either a Western-style shirt or a *prarachatan* (a tight-collared long-sleeved shirt).

Cloth

Matmii ikat – woven cotton cloth – is characteristic of the northeastern region. Designs are invariably geometric and it is very unusual to find a piece which has not been dyed using chemicals. Designs are handed down by mothers to their daughters and encompass a broad range from simple *sai fon* ('falling rain') designs, where random sections of weft are tied, to the more complex *mee gung* and *poom som*. The less common *pha kit* is a supplementary weft ikat, although the designs are similar to those found in matmii. The characteristic 'axe cushions' – or *mawn kwan* – of the northeast are usually made from this cloth, which is thick and loosely woven. These cushions are traditionally given to monks (usually at the end of the Buddhist Rains Retreat) to rest upon. *Pha fai* is a simple cotton cloth, in blue or white and sometimes simply decorated, made for everyday use and also as part of the burial ceremony, when a white length of *pha fai* is draped over the coffin. Centres of weaving in the northeast include: Khon Kaen, Udon Thani, Renu Nakhon (outside That Phanom), Surin, and Pak Thong Chai (outside Korat).

Except for the hilltribe textiles (see page 728), weaving in the north and central regions is far less diverse than that of the northeast. Indeed, most of the cloth that is handwoven is produced in Lao (ie northeastern) villages that have been relocated to this part of the country. Distinctive *pha sin* are woven by the Thai Lu of Phrae and Nan, featuring brightly coloured horizontal stripes interspersed with triangular designs. Centres of weaving in the north include: Pasang and San Kamphaeng (both outside Chiang Mai), and Nan and Phrae.

The textiles of southern Thailand exhibit links with those of Malaysia and Sumatra. In general, the handwoven textile tradition is weak in this part of the country. *Pha yok* is similar to *songket* (a Malay cloth), consisting of cotton or silk interwoven with gold or silver yarns. *Han karok* is a technique in which two-coloured twisted thread is woven. Centres of production in the south include villages around Trang and in the Songkhla Lake area.

Crafts

Mother-of-pearl

The method used to produce mother-of-pearl in Thailand differs from that in China and Vietnam. The 'pearl' is from the turban shell, from which pieces are cut and sanded to a thickness of 1 mm. These are then glued to a wooden panel and the gaps between the design filled with layers of lac (a resin), before being highly polished. This art form reached its peak during the 17th and 18th centuries. Masterpieces include the doors at Wat Pho, Wat Phra Kaeo and Wat Benchamabophit (all in Bangkok), and the footprint of the Buddha at Wat Phra Singh in Chiang Mai. In Vietnam and China, the wood is chiselled-out and the mother-of-pearl cut to fit the incisions.

Nielloware

To produce nielloware, a dark amalgam of lead, copper and silver metals is rubbed into etched silver. The craft was introduced to Nakhon Si Thammarat (see page 671) from India and then spread north. It is used to decorate trays, betel boxes, vases and other small objects.

Khon masks

Khon masks depict characters from the Ramakien (the Thai Ramayana) and are made from plaster moulds. Layers of paper are pasted over the mould, glued, and then coated in lac. The masks are then painted and decorated.

Lacquerware

In the production of lacquerware, three layers of lacquer from the sumac tree (*Gluta usitata*) are brushed onto a wood or wicker base, and each layer polished with charcoal. Then a fourth layer of lac is added, and once more highly polished with charcoal. After drying, the piece is inscribed with a sharp instrument and then soaked in a red dye for two to three days. The polished black part of the surface resists the dye, while the inscribed areas take it. Because this traditional method is so time-consuming, artists today tend to paint the design on to the lacquer. The art dates from the mid-Ayutthaya period and was possibly introduced by visiting Japanese artists. Some of the finest examples of lacquerware are to be found at Bangkok's Suan Pakkard Palace (see page 100).

Kites

Kite-flying has been a popular pastime in Thailand, certainly from the Sukhothai period (where it is described in the chronicles). During the Ayutthaya period, an imperial edict forbade kite-flying over the Royal Palace, while La Loubère's journal (1688) records that it was a favourite sport of noblemen. Today it is most common to see competitions between *chula* (formerly 'kula') and *pukpao*, at Sanaam Luang in Bangkok. The *chula* kite is over 2 m in length, while the diamond-shaped *pukpao* is far smaller and more agile. The frame is made from bamboo, cut before the onset of the rains and, preferably, left to mature. The bamboo is then split and the paper skin attached, according to a long-established system.

Puppets

Nang yai puppets, literally 'large skin', are carved from buffalo or cow hide and may be over 2 m in height. Though they can be skilfully decorated, *nang yai* are mechanically simple: there are no moving parts. Interestingly, some characters require particular types of hide. For example, a Rishi must be cut from the skin of a cow or bull that has been struck by lightning or died after a snakebite, or from a cow that has died calving. After curing and stretching the hide on a frame, the figure is carved out and then painted (if it is to be used for night performances, it is painted black).

Nang thalung are smaller than *nang yai* and are related to Javanese prototypes. They are more complex and have even stranger hide requirements than the *nang yai*: traditionally, key characters such as Rishi and Isavara need to be made from the soles of a dead (luckily) *nang thalung* puppet master. If master puppeteers are thin on the ground, then an animal that has died a violent death is acceptable. For the clown character, a small piece of skin from the sexual organ of a master puppeteer (again dead) should be attached to the lower lip of the puppet. One arm of the figure is usually articulated by a rod, enabling the puppet master to provide some additional expression to the character.

Religion

The Thai census records that 94% of the population is Buddhist. In Thailand's case, this means Theravada Buddhism, also known as Hinayana Buddhism. Of the other 6% of the population, 3.9% are Muslim (living predominantly in the south of the country), 1.7% Confucianist (mostly Sino-Thais living in Bangkok) and 0.6% Christian (mostly hilltribe people living in the north). Though the king is designated the protector of all religions, the constitution stipulates that he must be a Buddhist.

Theravada Buddhism

Theravada Buddhism was introduced into Southeast Asia in the 13th century, when monks trained in Ceylon (Sri Lanka) returned actively to spread the word. As a universal and a popular religion, it quickly gained converts and spread rapidly amongst the Tai. Theravada Buddhism, from the Pali word *thera* (elders), means the 'way of the elders' and is distinct from the dominant Buddhism practised in India, Mahayana Buddhism or the 'Greater Vehicle'. The sacred language of Theravada Buddhism is Pali rather than Sanskrit, Bodhisattvas (future Buddhas) are not given much attention, and emphasis is placed upon a precise and 'fundamental' interpretation of the Buddha's teachings, as they were originally recorded.

Buddhism, as it is practised in Thailand, is not the 'other-worldly' religion of Western conception. Ultimate salvation – enlightenment, or *nirvana* – is a distant goal for most people. Thai Buddhists pursue the Law of Karma, the reduction of suffering. Meritorious acts are undertaken and demeritorious ones avoided so that life, and more particularly future life, might be improved. Outside many wats it is common to see caged birds or turtles being sold: these are purchased and set free, and in this way the liberator gains merit. 'Karma' (act or deed, from Pali – *kamma*) is often thought in the West to mean 'fate'. It does not. It is true that previous karma determines a person's position in society, but there is still room for individual action, and a person is ultimately responsible for that action. It is the law of cause and effect.

It is important to draw a distinction between 'academic' Buddhism, as it tends to be understood in the West, and 'popular' Buddhism, as it is practised in Thailand. In Thailand, Buddhism is a syncretic religion: it incorporates elements of Brahmanism, animism and ancestor worship. Amulets are worn to protect against harm and are often sold in temple compounds (see page 94). Brahmanistic 'spirit' houses can be found outside most buildings (see box, above). In the countryside, farmers have what they consider to be a healthy regard for the *phi* (spirits) and demons that inhabit the rivers, trees and forests. Astrologers are widely consulted by urban and rural dwellers alike. It is these aspects of Thai Buddhism which help to provide worldly assurance, and they are perceived to be complementary, not in contradiction, with Buddhist teachings. But Thai Buddhism is not homogeneous. There are deep scriptural and practical divisions between 'progressive' monks and the *sangha* (the monkhood) hierarchy, for example.

The wat and the life of a monk

Virtually every village in Thailand has its wat. There is no English equivalent of the Thai word. It is usually translated as either monastery or temple, although neither is correct. It is easiest to get around this problem by simply calling them wats.

While secularization has undoubtedly undermined the role of Buddhism, and therefore the place of the wat, they still remain the focus of any community. The wat serves as a place of worship, education, meeting and healing. Without a wat, a village cannot be viewed as a 'complete' community, there are some 30,000 scattered across the country, supporting a population of around 300,000 monks and novices. During Lent the population of monks and novices swells by some 100,000 as people are ordained for the Buddhist Rains Retreat that runs from July to October. Large wats may have up to 600 monks and novices, but most in the countryside will have less than 10, many only one or two.

The wat represents the mental heart of each community, and most young men at some point in their lives will become ordained as monks, usually during the Buddhist Rains Retreat. Previously, this period represented the only opportunity for a young man to gain an education and to learn how to read. The surprisingly high literacy rate in Thailand before universal education was introduced (although some would maintain that this was hardly *functional* literacy) is explained by the presence of temple education.

The wat does not date as far back as one might imagine. Originally, there were no wats, as monks were wandering ascetics. It seems that although the word 'wat' was in use in the 14th century, these were probably just shrines, and were not monasteries. By the late 18th century, the wat had certainly metamorphosed into a monastery, so sometime in the intervening four centuries, shrine and monastery had united into a whole.

Royal wats, or *wat luang* – of which there are only 186 in the country – can usually be identified by the use of the prefixes *Rat*, *Raja* or *Racha* in their names. (Different ways of

House of spirits

It does not take long for a first-time visitor to Thailand to notice the miniature houses, often elaborately decorated, that sit in the corner of most house compounds. Private homes, luxury hotels and international banks do not seem to be without them; the more grandiose the building, the more luxurious their miniature alter ego. The house outside the World Trade Centre is one of the most ostentatious. Some look like gaudy miniature Thai wats made from cement and gilded; other, more traditional examples are attractively weathered wooden houses. *Phi* (spirits) are apparently not adverse to living in Corbusier-eque modern affairs, like the angular house outside the Pan Pacific Hotel at the end of Silom and Surawong roads.

These *san phra phum* or 'spirit houses' are home to the resident spirit or *phra phum* of the compound, who has the power to help in emergencies but also to wreak havoc should the spirit not be contented. Small models of the guardian spirit and his retainers, moulded from plaster, usually occupy the building. The spirit occupies the inner room of the abode, and is usually represented as a figure holding a sword or fly whisk in the right hand and a book in the left. The book is a death register. Around the house on the raised platform (the spirit house should be at or above eye level) are arranged the retainers: servants, animals and entertainers. Sunday is traditionally designated house cleaning day.

Usually the spirit house will occupy one corner of the house compound – the shadow of the main house should never fall on the spirit house. This would court disaster and entice the spirit to move from its residence into the main house. But the art of placing the spirit house goes much further than just keeping it out of the shadow of the main house and is akin to the Chinese art of geomancy or feng shui. Often, when misfortune strikes a family, one of their first actions is to refurbish and move the spirit house. In the normal run of events though, the spirit merely needs placating with food, incense, flowers, candles and other offerings. Each has its own character and tastes: one family, facing serious difficulties, employed a *mor du* ('seeing doctor', a medium) to be told that, as their spirit was a Muslim, he had been offended by being offered pork. The family changed the spirit's diet and the difficulties melted away. Guests who stay the night should ideally ask the spirit for permission and then visit the shrine again before leaving.

transliterating Thai into English arrive at slightly different spellings of the prefix.) This indicates royal patronage. Wats that contain important relics also have the prefix *Maha* or Great – as in Wat Mahathat. Community wats make up the rest and number about 30,000. Although wats vary a great deal in size and complexity, there is a traditional layout to which most conform (see box, page 740).

It seems that wats are often short-lived. Even great wats, if they lose their patronage, are deserted by their monks and fall into ruin. Unlike Christian churches, they depend on constant support from the laity; the wat owns no land or wealth, and must depend on gifts of food to feed the monks and money to repair and expand the fabric of its buildings.

Ordination

Today, ordination into the monkhood is seen as an opportunity to study the Buddhist scriptures, to prepare for a responsible moral life – to become 'ripe'. Farmers sometimes still say that just as a girl who cannot weave is *dip* ('raw') and *suk* (not yet 'ripe') for marriage, so the same is true of a man who has not entered the monkhood. An equally important reason for a man to become ordained is so that he can accumulate merit for his family, particularly for his mother, who as a woman cannot become ordained. The government still allows civil servants to take leave, on full pay, to enter the monkhood for three months. Women gain merit by making offerings of food each morning to the monks and by performing other meritorious deeds. They can also become nuns. In 1399, the Queen of Sukhothai prayed that through such actions she might be fortunate enough to be 'reborn as a male'. Lectures on Buddhism and meditation classes are held at the World Fellowship of Buddhists in Bangkok.

For male Thais from poor backgrounds the monkhood may be the only way that they can continue their education beyond primary level. In 1995 there were almost 87,000 novice monks in monasteries in Thailand; many come from poor, rural families. In light of this, there is clearly an incentive for youngsters to join the monkhood not for spiritual reasons, but for pecuniary and educational ones. This is beginning to worry some in the Buddhist hierarchy who would like to think that novices join primarily to become monks, not to become educated. It is a drain on their resources – the government only pays 20% of the costs of educating these novices – and in some instances may pollute the atmosphere of the *wat*. In addition, it means that the quality of monks is probably lower than many in the Buddhist hierarchy would wish. The Venerable Phra Dhammakittiwong, the abbot of Wat Rachaorot and a member of the Supreme Sangha Council, was quoted in 1997 saying, quite plainly, that the problem with Thai Buddhism is that "people who are considered bright and smart do not want to become monks" (*The Nation*, 20.7.97). Nonetheless, there have been some notable successes of this form of education: former Prime Minister Chuan Leekpai, who comes from a poor southern family, studied law for six years while a novice.

Another problem which has emerged in recent years is that of empty wats. Of the country's 30,000 wats, around 5000 are thought to stand empty. Often people give alms to build new monasteries, as this is the main means of gaining merit. But Thailand is not producing enough monks to man these new monasteries. There is, simply, over-building and under-manning. This has led some Buddhist scholars to question the assumption that building more wats is good for Thai society. In mid-1998 the Sangha Supreme Council took the unprecedented step of ordering monasteries to stop all new, non-essential construction work. The overt reason was to pare down costs in the face of the economic crisis; an additional reason was probably the belief that construction had got out of hand as monasteries vied with each other in the size and opulence of their buildings.

The Thammakai movement and Santi Asoke

As Thailand has modernized, so there have appeared new Buddhist 'sects' designed to appeal to the middle class, sophisticated, urban Thai. The Thammakai movement, for example, counts among its supporters large numbers of students, businessmen, politicians and members of the military. Juliane Schober maintains that the movement has garnered support from these groups because it has managed to appeal to those people who are experiencing "disenchantment with modern Thai society, but [are] reluctant to forego the benefits of modernization". "Through effective use of modern media,

In Siddhartha's footsteps: a short history of Buddhism

Buddhism was founded by Siddhartha Gautama, a prince of the Sakya tribe of Nepal, who probably lived between 563 and 483 BC. He achieved enlightenment and buddha means 'fully enlightened one', or 'one who has woken up'. He is known by a number of titles. In the West, he is usually referred to as The Buddha, ie the historic Buddha (but not just Buddha); more common in Southeast Asia is the title Sakyamuni, or Sage of the Sakyas (referring to his tribal origins).

Over the centuries, the life of the Buddha has become part legend, and the Jataka tales are colourful and convoluted. (These are tales of the former lives of the historic Buddha as he passed through a series of births and re-births on the way to nirvana. There are 547 in total. Some of the tales are more popular than others although this varies between countries and cultures.) But central to any Buddhist's belief is that he was born under a sal tree, he achieved enlightenment under a bodhi tree in the Bodh Gaya Gardens (India), he preached the First Sermon at Sarnath and that he died at Kusinagara (all in India or Nepal).

The Buddha was born at Lumbini (in present-day Nepal), as Queen Maya was on her way to her parents' home. She had had a very auspicious dream before the child's birth of being impregnated by an elephant, whereupon a sage prophesied Siddhartha would become either a great king or a great spiritual leader. His father, being keen that the first option of the prophesy be fulfilled, brought him up in all the princely skills – at which Siddhartha excelled – and ensured that he only saw beautiful things, not the harsher elements of life.

Despite his father's efforts, Siddhartha saw four things while travelling between palaces: a helpless old man, a very sick man, a corpse being carried by relatives, and an ascetic, calm and serene man as he begged for food. The young prince renounced his princely origins and left home to study under a series of spiritual teachers. He finally discovered the path to enlightenment at the Bodh Gaya Gardens. He then proclaimed his thoughts to a

marketing, fund raising strategies, and mass appeal of religious consumerism", the author suggests, "it offers its followers concrete methods for attaining spiritual enlightenment in this life and membership in a pristine Buddhist community that promises to restore the nation's moral life, individual peace, and material success." During 1998 the Thammakai movement was criticized for its unorthodox money-raising activities – getting supporters to solicit door-to-door – and in November the Education Ministry ordered an investigation of its activities by the Supreme Sangha Council. The movement is trying to raise US$360 m to build a massive *chedi*, but claims of miracles are raising suspicions that the hard sell has gone too far. The movement has even won a business management prize. But as defenders point out, miracles and claims that generous donors will be rewarded in heaven is common to many Thai monasteries. What really bugs the opposition is that the Thammakai movement is so successful.

Another movement with a rather different philosophy is Santi Asoke. This movement rejects consumerism and materialism in all its guises, and enjoins its members to "eat less, use little, work a lot, and save the rest for society". Both Santi Asoke and Thammakai have come in for a great deal of scrutiny and have been criticized for their recruiting methods

small group of disciples at Sarnath, near Benares, and continued to preach and attract followers until he died at the age of 81 at Kusinagara.

In the First Sermon at the deer park in Sarnath, the Buddha preached the Four Truths – still considered the root of Buddhist belief and practical experience: suffering exists; there is a cause of suffering; suffering can be ended; and to end suffering it is necessary to follow the 'Noble Eightfold Path' – namely, right speech, livelihood, action, effort, mindfulness, concentration, opinion and intention.

Soon after the Buddha began preaching, a monastic order – the Sangha – was established. As the monkhood evolved in India, it also began to fragment into different sects. An important change was the belief the Buddha was transcendent: he had never been born, nor had he died; he had always existed and his life on earth had been mere illusion. The emergence of these new concepts helped to turn what up until then was an ethical code of conduct

into a religion. It eventually led to the appearance of Mahayana Buddhism, which split from the more traditional Theravada 'sect'.

Despite the division of Buddhism into two sects, the central tenets of the religion are common to both. Specifically, the principles pertaining to the Four Noble Truths, the Noble Eightfold Path, the Dependent Origination, the Law of Karma, and nirvana. In addition, the principles of non-violence and tolerance are also embraced by both. In essence, the differences between the two are of emphasis and interpretation. Theravada Buddhism is strictly based on the original Pali Canon, while the Mahayana tradition stems from later Sanskrit texts. Mahayana Buddhism also allows a broader and more varied interpretation of the doctrine. Other important differences are that while the Theravada tradition is more 'intellectual' and self-obsessed, with an emphasis upon the attaining of wisdom and insight for oneself, Mahayana Buddhism stresses devotion and compassion towards others.

and their fundamentalist positions. They are indicative, in the eyes of some Thais, of a crisis in Thai Buddhism.

A crisis in Thai Buddhism?

The intrusion of modern life and mores into the wat has created considerable tensions for the *sangha* in Thailand, reflected in a growing number of scandals. At the beginning of 1995 a monk, Phra Sayan, took the law into his own hands when he beheaded his abbot, Chamnong, for having sexual relations with a woman. He explained his actions in the context of a very popular Chinese television series about the legendary Song Dynasty magistrate Judge Pao, who rights wrongs and fights for the little person, by explaining: "Judge Pao used to say, 'Even if the emperor commits crimes, he should be punished just like ordinary people.' So there was no excuse for the abbot."

More recently, in late December 2000, Abbot Wanchai Oonsap was captured on camera dressed as an army colonel, disguised behind dark glasses and underneath a wig, with a bevy of girls in tow and an assortment of pornographic videos and empty bottles of spirits in the house where he was living it up. Earlier, Phra Pativetviset was found at a

The practice of Islam: living by the Prophet

Islam is an Arabic word meaning 'submission to God'. As Muslims often point out, it is not just a religion but a total way of life. The main Islamic scripture is the Koran or Quran, the name being taken from the Arabic al-qur'an or 'the recitation'. The Koran is divided into 114 sura, or 'units'. Most scholars are agreed that the Koran was partially written by the Prophet Mohammad. In addition to the Koran there are the hadiths, from the Arabic word *hadith* meaning 'story', which tell of the Prophet's life and works. These represent the second most important body of scriptures.

The practice of Islam is based upon five central tenets, known as the Pillars of Islam: *Shahada* (profession of faith), *Salat* (worship), *Zakat* (charity), *Saum* (fasting) and *Haj* (pilgrimage). The mosque is the centre of religious activity. The two most important mosque officials are the *imam* – (leader) – and the *khatib* (preacher) – who delivers the Friday sermon.

The **Shahada** is the confession, and lies at the core of any Muslim's faith. It involves reciting, sincerely, two statements: 'There is no god, but God', and 'Mohammad is the Messenger [Prophet] of God'. A Muslim will do this at every **Salat**. This is the daily prayer ritual which is performed five times a day, at sunrise, midday, mid-afternoon, sunset and at night. There is also the important Friday noon worship. The Salat is performed by a Muslim bowing and then prostrating himself in the direction of Mecca (in Malaysian *kiblat*, in Arabic *qibla*). In hotel rooms throughout there is nearly always a little arrow, painted on the ceiling – or sometimes inside a wardrobe – indicating the direction of Mecca and labelled *kiblat*. The faithful are called to worship by a mosque official. Beforehand, a worshipper must wash to ensure ritual purity. The Friday midday service is performed in the mosque and includes a sermon given by the khatib.

A third essential element of Islam is **Zakat** – charity or alms-giving. A Muslim

karaoke bar where the girls pronounced him a real 'party animal'. Of the last few years numerous other monks have been implicated in drug dealing, rape and murder– one was even caught having sex under a crematorium.

The wider problem concerns how monk superstars deal with their fame and fortune. While monks are technically prohibited from handling money, the exigencies of modern life mean that most cannot avoid it. This, in turn, opens monks up to a whole series of temptations that their predecessors, living in rural monasteries never faced.

In short, keeping the Buddhist precepts is far harder in modern than in traditional Thailand. Many Thais lament the visible signs of worldly wealth that monks display. It is this gradual erosion of the ideals that monks should embrace, rather than the odd lurid scandal, which is the more important. Many monks come from poor backgrounds and few are well educated. The temptations are all too clear in a society where a newly wealthy laity see the lavish support of individual monks and their monasteries as a means to accumulate merit. Thais talk with distaste of *Buddhapanich* (commercialized Buddhism) where amulets are sold for US$20,000 and monks attain the status and trappings of rock stars. It was reported in 1995 that one wat had earned a business school marketing award. The abbot of Wat Bon Rai in northern Thailand, Luang Poh Koon, gave away nearly

is supposed to give up his 'surplus' (according to the Koran); through time this took on the form of a tax levied according to the wealth of the family. In Malaysia there is no official Zakat as there is in Saudi Arabia, but good Muslims are expected to contribute a tithe (one-tenth) to the Muslim community.

The fourth pillar of Islam is **Saum** or fasting. The daytime month-long fast of Ramadan is a time of contemplation, worship and piety – the Islamic equivalent of Lent. Muslims are expected to read one-thirtieth of the Koran each night. Muslims who are ill or on a journey have dispensation from fasting, but otherwise they are only permitted to eat during the night until "so much of the dawn appears that a white thread can be distinguished from a black one".

The **Haj** or Pilgrimage to the holy city of Mecca in Saudi Arabia is required of all Muslims once in their lifetime if they can afford to make the journey and are physically able to. It is restricted to a certain time of the year, beginning on the eighth day of the Muslim month of Dhu-l-Hijja. Men who have been on the Haj are given the title Haji, and women *hajjah*.

The Koran also advises on a number of other practices and customs, in particular the prohibitions on usury, the eating of pork, the taking of alcohol, and gambling.

While the provinces of the far south of Thailand support a majority Muslim population, Islam has not – in general – been radicalized to the extent it has in some other countries and regions. The veil, for example, is not widely worn while the consumption of alcohol is fairly widespread. There has been an Islamic revival of sorts, and an increased interest in Islamic scholarship, but this has been restricted to a small segment of the population. There may have been considerable disquiet at the US-led invasion of Iraq and calls for boycotts of US products and companies but this should not been interpreted as a sea-change in attitudes. Indeed, many Thai Buddhists share these concerns.

฿64 million in 1994. The reason why he managed to generate such staggering sums is because people believe he can bring wealth and health. Each morning his monastery throngs with people, itching to hand over cash in the hope that it will be a wise investment. It is thought that he takes US$1000 a day in this manner. Taken together, Thailand's monasteries have a turnover of billions of baht; individual monks have personal bank accounts running into millions. It is this concern for money, in a religion where monks take a vow of poverty, which critics find particularly worrying.

Most of these stories of greed, commercialism and sexual peccadillos rarely make the leap from the Thai to the international media. However, the murder in January 1996 of Johanne Masheder, a British tourist, by a monk at Wat Tham Kao Poon (a cave wat), outside the town of Kanchanaburi in western Thailand, led Western journalists to look more closely at Buddhism in Thailand. In court it was revealed that the monk, Yodchart Suaphoo, was a former member of the Thai underworld and had already served time for rape. How could he have possibly been allowed to join the monkhood, many foreigners wondered. Yet taking the saffron robes of the monk has been a traditional way for men to make up for past crimes. Dictators, hit-and-run drivers, drug addicts hoping to dry out, even murderers, have all found sanctuary in Thailand's monasteries. As Police

Colonel Vorathep Mathwaj, head of the Investigation Division of the Immigration police, put it: "This does not look good for Thailand and our monkhood". A month after his arrest, Yodchart was sentenced to death by firing squad after a one-day trial. He pleaded to be taken to the mouth of the cave and shot right away, but his wish was not granted. His death sentence was later commuted to life – as is usual in Thailand.

The Sangha Council, which is supposed to police the monkhood, has, at times, seemed perplexed as to what to do. In July 1998, for example, they found Phra Khru Sopitsutkhun, the abbot of Wat Sanam Chang in Chachoengsao, not guilty of bringing Buddhism into bad repute with his murals of naked men and women, his image of the Buddha in the so-called Superman mudra – arms outstretched and foot planted firmly on a globe – and his sale of lustral water. The *Bangkok Post* deplored the Council's unwillingness to confront unsavoury commercialism within the *sangha*, and viewed the case of as an example of "Buddhism gone horribly wrong" (*Bangkok Post*, 22.07.98).

Sulak Sivaraksa, one of Thailand's most respected scholars and critics, has suggested that there is a "crisis at the core of organized Thai Buddhism". In his view, Buddhism has simply failed to adapt in line with wider changes in economy and society. It evolved as a religion suited to a country where there was a feudal court system and where most people were subsistence farmers. Now most people live in the cash economy and work in modern sectors of the economy. These views are not restricted to those outside the monkhood. Prayudh Payutto, perhaps Thailand's greatest living monk-scholar, was quoted in 1996 as saying "More and more monks are living luxurious lives", adding that they "are no longer keeping to the letter or to the spirit of the rules [the 227 precepts]". Even more dramatically, Sompong Rachano, the director of the Religious Affairs' Buddhist Monastery Division, stated in 1997 that "Not many Buddhist monks can adhere to the 227 Buddhist precepts, few can discuss the teachings of the Buddha with lay people and fewer still – perhaps one in a thousand – have the ability to deliver a sermon before a congregation" (*The Nation*, 20.7.97).

Islam
While Thailand is often portrayed as a 'Buddhist Kingdom', the provinces of the far south are majority Muslim. This is because these provinces have, historically, come under the cultural influence of the former sultanates of the Malay peninsula. See box, page 756.

Christianity
When Europeans first made trading contact with the Kingdom of Ayutthaya some of these early visitors also aimed to convert Siam to Christianity. This reached a peak when the Greek adventurer Constantine Phaulcon inveigled his way to becoming Mahatthai or chief minister to King Narai and, it is said, held the ambition of converting the king to Roman Catholicism. This came to nothing, and Phaulcon lost his life. Since then missionaries have had the odd success in the Buddhist heartland of Thailand but it still remains a solidly Buddhist nation. Missionaries, though, have had far more success among the formerly largely animist hill peoples. Here significant numbers of Karen and Lahu, and other minority groups, have converted to Christianity.

Land and environment

Geography

Thailand covers an area of 500,000 sq km (about the size of France) and had a population in 2001 of 62.3 million, which is growing at 1.5% per year. It shares its borders with Burma, Laos, Cambodia and Malaysia. Administratively, the country is divided into five main regions: the North, Northeast, Central Plains, South and the Bangkok Metropolitan Region. Two smaller, additional regions are also sometimes identified: the East and West. Each of these seven regions has its own distinctive geographical character.

The **Central region** is Thailand's 'rice bowl', encompassing the wide and fertile central plains: this is the economic and cultural heartland of the Thai (or Tai) nation. The construction of dams, and the spread of irrigation in the region, has enabled Thailand to become, and remain, the world's largest rice exporter. Yet most farms remain small, family-owned affairs. Towards the southern extremity of the central plains lies the **Bangkok Metropolitan Region**. With an official population of 8.16 million (2007), it is many times larger than Thailand's second city and is the country's economic and political hub. Indeed, it has outgrown its administrative borders and the population of the entire urban agglomeration is nearer to 10 million. Bangkok supports both the greatest density of businesses, as well as the key institutions of government.

The **North** is Thailand's largest region, and includes the kingdom's second city of Chiang Mai. It is a mountainous region with narrow river valleys, and supports most of the minority hilltribes. The area was not incorporated fully into the Thai state until the 19th century. Doi Pha Hom Pok, the country's highest peak at 2300 m, is located in Chiang Mai Province.

The **Northeast** or '**Isan**' is the second largest, and poorest, region of Thailand. It is also known as the Khorat Plateau and is environmentally harsh. The people of the Northeast speak a dialect of Thai – Lao – and they are culturally distinct in terms of food, dress and ritual. Most are rice farmers living in approaching 29,000 villages.

Just south of the Northeast, sandwiched between the sea and the Damrek hills, is the **Eastern region**. This has become an overspill area for Bangkok, with businesses moving to take advantage of cheaper land and less congested infrastructure. The Eastern region also contains the renowned seaside resort of Pattaya.

To the west of the central plains and Bangkok is the **Western region**. Until recently this was a relatively undeveloped, mountainous and largely forested area. But over the past 10-20 years, pioneer agriculturalists and logging companies have moved into the West, clearing large tracts of forest, and planting the land with cash crops such as sugar-cane and cassava. Despite these developments, the beautiful mountains which rise up towards the border with Burma remain relatively unspoilt. Towns here have a 'frontier' atmosphere.

Thailand's seventh region is the **South**, which stretches 1150 km south to the border with Malaysia. The far south has more in common with island Southeast Asia than mainland Southeast Asia; the climate is tropical, many of the inhabitants are Malay, Islam is the main religion and rubber is the dominant crop. Most visitors visit the beach resorts of Koh Samui, Phuket, Koh Phi Phi, Hua Hin and Koh Phangan.

Below the region, there are a series of further administrative subdivisions. First, the *changwat*, or province, of which there are 75 (Bangkok is a separate administrative division), each with a governor at its head. Below the province is the *amphoe*, or district, numbering 811 in all, each headed by a *nai amphoe*, or district officer. Then comes the *tambon*, a 'commune' of villages, of which there are 7409, each with a *kamnan* in charge. And finally, the lowest level of administration is the *mubaan* (the village) of which there are 67,581, each headed by a democratically elected *phuuyaibaan*, or village head.

Climate

Thailand lies within the humid tropics and remains hot throughout the year. Mean temperatures vary between 24°C in the far North to 29°C in the Central region, while rainfall ranges from 1200 mm in parts of the Northeast to over 4000 mm in some parts of the South (eg Ranong) and East (eg Khlong Yai, Chantaburi). Far more important than these mean annual figures are seasonal fluctuations in rainfall and, to a lesser extent, temperature. With the exception of the southern isthmus, which receives rainfall throughout the year, Thailand has a dry season which stretches from November to April, corresponding with the period of the northeast monsoon, and a wet season from May to October, corresponding with the southwest monsoon.

The distinction between the dry and the rainy seasons is most pronounced in the northeast, where as much as 98% of rain falls between April and October. Nonetheless, like the English, Thai's talk endlessly about the weather. The seasons (ie the rains) determine the very pattern of life in the region. Rice cultivation, and its associated festivals, is dependent in most areas on the arrival of the rains, and religious ceremonies are timed to coincide with the seasons.

The dry season can be divided into two: cool and hot. During the cool season in the north, (December to February), it can become distinctly chilly, with temperatures falling to as low as 7°C at night. The hot season runs between March and May and temperatures may exceed 40°C, before the cooling rains arrive towards the end of the period. But for much of the time, and in most places, it is hot whatever the month.

Seasons → *For further information on when to go, see page 20.*
Hot season March-May, dry with temperatures 27-35°C, but sometimes in the 40s for extended periods.

Wet or rainy season June-October, wet with lower temperatures (due to the cooling effect of the rain and increased cloud cover) 24-32°C, but higher humidity.

Cool season December-February, when conditions are at their most pleasant, with little rain and temperatures ranging from 18-32°C.

Seasons in the South Similar weather to that of the Malay peninsula, with hot, humid and sunny weather most of the year. Chance of rain at any time, although more likely during the period of the two monsoons, May-October (particularly on west side of the peninsula) and November-April (particularly on east coast).

Wet rice cultivation

Rice probably spread into Southeast Asia from a core area, which spanned the highlands from Assam (India) to north Vietnam. Some of the earliest evidence of agriculture in the world has been uncovered in and around the village of Ban Chiang in northeastern Thailand, and also from Bac-son in north Vietnam. However, archaeologists are far from agreed about the dating and significance of the evidence. Some believe that rice may have been cultivated as early as 7000 BC; others say it dates back no further than 3000-2000 BC.

By the time the first Europeans arrived in the 15th century, the crop was well established as the staple for the region. Today, other staples are frowned upon, being widely regarded as 'poor man's food'. The importance of rice can be seen reflected in the degree to which culture and crop have become intermeshed, and in the mythology and ceremony associated with its cultivation. The American anthropologist DeYoung, who worked in a village in central Thailand in the late 1950s, wrote that the farmer: "reverences the crop he grows as a sentient being; he marks its stages of growth by ceremonies; and he propitiates the spirit of the soil in which it grows and the good or evil spirits that may help or harm it. He considers rice to possess a life spirit (kwan) and to grow much as a human being grows; when it bears grain, it has become 'pregnant' like a mother, and the rice is the seed or child of the Rice Goddess."

Wet rice, more than any other staple crop, is dependent on an ample and constant supply of water. The links between rice and water, wealth and poverty, and abundance and famine are clear. Throughout the region, there are numerous rituals and songs which honour the 'gift of water' and dwell upon the vagaries of the monsoon. Water-throwing festivals, designed to induce abundant rainfall, are widespread, and if they do not have the desired effect villagers will often resort to magic. The struggle to ensure a constant supply of water can also be seen reflected in the sophisticated *müang fai*, traditional irrigation systems of northern Thailand. Less obvious, but no less ingenious and complex, is that farmers without the benefits of irrigation have also developed sophisticated cultivation strategies designed to maintain production through flood and drought.

While rice remains Thailand's key crop and a marker of Thai-ness, it does not occupy the central position in life and livelihood that it once did. Young people, increasingly, wish to avoid the drudgery of farming which has become, through the twin effects of education and the media, a low status occupation. Anyone spending time in the northern region or the central plains may notice uncultivated land, effectively abandoned because there is no one to farm it. (An alternative explanation is that it has been purchased for speculative reasons.) Many farmers have sold their buffalo and bought rotavators (known as *kwai lek* or iron buffalo) because they plough the land more quickly and don't have to be fed, grazed and bedded. Broadcasting has replaced transplanting in some areas because it saves time. There are even cases of weekend farmers who travel up from Bangkok on Saturdays to keep their farms ticking over. Today, it is not uncommon for rural households to earn 50% or more of their income from non-farm sources. In the countryside, older Thais sometimes lament this loss of subsistence innocence, but the young, of course, will have nothing of it. The future, so far as they are concerned, does not lie in farming.

Flora and fauna

It has been estimated that Thailand supports 18,000 species of plant, 6000 insect species, 1000 kinds of bird, and 300 species of mammal. Even so, it is difficult not to escape the conclusion that the kingdom's flora and fauna are woefully depleted. As recently as 1950, over half the country's land area was forested. Today, barely a day goes by before yet another scandal with an environmental tinge is revealed in the newspapers. This concern for the environment, though, is comparatively recent, dating only from 1973. In that year, an army helicopter crashed, and as investigators picked over the wreckage they discovered not just the bodies of the crew and passengers, but also the corpses of several protected wild animals. It became clear that the human victims – prominent army officers – had been illegally hunting in the Thung Yai Naresuan Wildlife Sanctuary. A public scandal ensued and the environmental movement in Thailand was born.

From the mid-1980s, the environment became an issue of considerable political importance and public concern in Thailand. In no small way this was linked to the environmental destruction that had accompanied the country's rush to development: the stripping of much of the forest resource, the devastation of coastal mangroves, the decimation of many large mammals, the pollution of rivers, the denudation of watersheds, widespread soil erosion, rampant over-fishing, and more. Newspapers increasingly began to highlight abuses of power and environmental pressure groups such as the Project for Ecological Recovery (PER) enjoyed growing public support. To begin with the government and business saw such environmental movements as 'the enemy', to be vanquished. Today, however grudgingly, the government and most major players have come to realize that the environment cannot be ignored, and nor can public concerns. Agencies and research outfits such as the Thailand Environment Institute (TEI) work with the mainstream and plans formulated by the National Economic and Social Development Board are thoroughly 'green'. Of course cynics and critics see this as largely window dressing and that beneath the sheen of greenery are groups and individuals who have changed barely at all.

Flora

Thailand's dominant natural vegetation is **tropical forest**. In the south, parts of the west, and in pockets such as Chanthaburi province in the east, this means 'jungle' or tropical rain forest. Tigers, elephants, banteng (wild ox), sambar (deer) and tapirs still roam the lowland forests, although not in great numbers. Thailand's forests have been depleted to a greater extent than in any other country in Southeast Asia (with the one exception of Singapore, which doesn't really count). In 1938, 70% of Thailand's land area was forested; by 1961 this had been reduced to just over 50%. Today, natural forest cover accounts for only a little more than 15% of the land area and projections indicate that by 2010 this will have declined to less than 10%. The Royal Forestry Department still insists on a figure of over 20% and puts the area of National Reserve Forest at 40%, despite the fact that over large areas not a single tree remains standing, a glance at satellite images will show both figures to be palpably fraudulent.

The causes of this spectacular, and depressing, destruction of Thailand's forests are numerous: simple population growth, commercial logging, commercialization and the spread of cash cropping, and dam construction. Cronyism and corruption, which is part and parcel of logging across the region, has also marred the management of Thailand's forests. In late 1988, such was the public outcry after floods in the south killed 300 people – and whose severity was linked in the public imagination to deforestation – that a nationwide logging ban was introduced in January 1989. Few doubt, though, that deforestation continues. 'The Forestry Department', as Nok Nguak (a pseudonym) argued, "can be described at best as ineffective and at worst as one the main culprits in the destruction of our forests" (*Bangkok Post*, 24.03.98). In February 1998 it was revealed that a logging mafia, in league with the Royal Forestry Department (RFD), had been instrumental in the logging of protected forest in the Salween area near Mae Hong Son, in Northern Thailand. After the revelation of a ฿5 million bribe, *The Nation* opined that the RFD was 'hopelessly corrupt'.

The tropical rainforests of Thailand, although not comparable with those of Malaysia and Indonesia, have a high diversity of species, exceeding 100 per hectare in some areas. In total, it is estimated that Thailand supports 20,000-25,000 species of plant.

In the north and the northeast the vegetation adapts to a climate, with a dry season that stretch over months. For this reason, the forests here support fewer species than in the south. In many cases they are also highly degraded due to logging and farming. Other sub-types of tropical forest in Thailand include semi-evergreen forest (in the peninsula and north along the border with Burma), dry evergreen forest (in the wetter parts of the northeast and the north), *ixed deciduous* and dry dipterocarp savannah forest (mostly in the northeast and parts of the northern central plains).

Fauna

Thailand's fauna is even more threatened than its forests. Of the kingdom's 282 species of mammal, 40 are endangered and 14 are critically endangered. For its birds, the picture is equally gloomy: 190 endangered species out of 928, with 38 critically endangered. While for the country's reptiles and amphibians, there are 37 endangered species out of 405, of which seven are on the critical list. A century ago, wild elephants and tigers roamed the Bang Kapi area east of Bangkok – now it is overrun with shopping malls. It was only in 1960 that a law was enacted protecting wild animals, and even today it doesn't take an investigative journalist to find endangered – and protected – animals for sale, whether whole (and alive) or in bits.

Thailand supports a rich and varied fauna, partly because it lies on the boundary between several zoogeographic regions: the Indochinese, Indian and Sundaic. It also lies on a crossroads between north and south, acting as a waystation for animals dispersing north from the Sundaic islands, and south from the Asian mainland. The problem in trying to maintain the biodiversity is that most of the national parks and wildlife sanctuaries are thought to be too small to be sustainable. A single male tiger, for example, needs about 50 sq km of forest to survive; some of Thailand's parks cover less than 100 sq km.

Mammals During the 1980s, some of Thailand's endangered species of mammal disappeared entirely. The Javan and Sumatran rhinoceros, the kouprey (*Bos sauveli*), the wild water buffalo and Eld's deer (*Cervus eldi*) are probably all extinct in Thailand, or on the verge of extinction. The world's last Schomburgk's deer (*Cervus schomburgki*) was kept as a pet in the grounds of a Buddhist monastery in Samut Sakhon province before, reputedly, being clubbed to death by a drunk in 1938.

The reasons for this pattern of extermination are not difficult to fathom: destruction of habitat and over-hunting (see below). Thailand does have national legislation protecting rare species from hunting, capturing and trade, but too often the legislation is ignored and even officials have actively flouted the law, sometimes hunting in national parks. Of Thailand's 282 species of mammal, 40 are listed in the International Union for the Conservation of Nature and Natural Resources' (IUCNs) Red List of Endangered Species. These include the pileated gibbon (*Hylobates pileatus*), the clouded leopard (*Neofelis nebulosa*), the Malayan tapir (*Tapirus indicus*) and the tiger (*Panthera tigris*). Indeed, almost all Thailand's large mammals are in danger of extinction in the country.

Birds Birdlife in Thailand is also under pressure. Birds' habitats are being destroyed, pollution is increasing, and hunting is barely controlled. Even in Thailand's national parks, a lack of resources and widespread corruption mean that bird populations are under threat.

Elephants have nowhere to go

According to the World Wide Fund for Nature, there are 2705 domesticated elephants in Thailand and 1975 wild animals. In 1782 there were around 200,000; by 1900 this had declined to less than 100,000. But the trained elephants and their mahouts are out of a job and out of luck. With the imposition of a logging ban in 1989, their traditional work in the forests of the country all but dried up. Some took the rather degrading alternative option of working in tourist-oriented elephant 'camps', where the stately pachyderms are forced to play football and harmonicas. But there is a limit to the tourist potential of the elephant, and many of these down-on-their-luck animals and mahouts took to begging for food. As it is Bangkok where most of the money is to be found, it was Bangkok where elephants gravitated. Because the elephant is the holiest of beasts, Buddhists can make merit by buying sugar cane and bananas for the animals. It was in this way that the mahouts managed to feed their mounts – at an estimated cost of ฿2000-3000 a month.

But in 2000 the governor of Bangkok banned elephants from the city. The mahouts saw the hands of environmentalists in this ban – and in particular, foreign environmentalists. It was suggested that Roger Lohanan, of the Thai Society for the Prevention of Cruelty to Animals, and Solaida Salwala, of the Asian Elephant Lovers Foundation, had been instrumental in convincing the governor that elephants are not designed for city life. There were reports of elephants being hit by cars, having their feet lacerated by nails and broken glass, and going berserk in the heat and fumes. Mahouts were accused of cruelty, and of furthering their own interests at the expense of the elephants. The mahouts reacted furiously, accusing the elephant

Over the last three decades or so, 80% of Thailand's forests have disappeared, and with them, many bird habitats. Birds are also hunted by farmers for food and virtually any size and shape of bird is considered fair game. The rarer and more colourful species are hunted by collectors for the bird trade – for which Thailand is a centre. It is not unusual to walk in the countryside and neither see nor hear a bird of any type. Three of Thailand's birds are listed by the IUCN as threatened with extinction: the giant ibis (*Pseudibis gigantea*), the Chinese egret (*Egretta eulophotes*), and the white-winged wood duck (*Cairina scutulata*).

In total, Thailand has 928 species of bird – more than double the number found in Europe – which account for a 10th of the world's species. This richness of birdlife is due to the varied nature of Thailand's habitats and the country's position at the junction of three zoological realms. The country is also an important wintering area for migrant birds from the northern latitudes.

Reptiles and amphibians Thailand supports an impressive and varied population of snakes, lizards and other assorted cold-blooded creatures. In total there are 298 reptile and 107 amphibian species, of which 37 are regarded as endangered. The closest most people come to a snake (at least knowingly) is at Bangkok's Red Cross Snake Farm, or at the snake farm near the Floating Market in Thonburi.

The large **non-venomous** pythons are active around dusk and kill their prey by constriction. The reticulated python (*Python reticulatus*) can grow to a length of 15 m and,

lovers of ignorance. One mahout, 60-year-old Ta Jongjaingam, even asked "Why do they let the Burmese and Khmers stay [in Bangkok]– but not our elephants?". As is usual with these things in Thailand, lots of slightly crazed people (and some sensible ones) wrote letters to the newspapers, arguing one way or the other.

In 2002 the US-based People for the Ethical Treatment of Animals (PETA) publicized a film showing young elephants being tortured in northern Thailand. Again Thailand found itself in the dock. Thai officials and experts claimed that the film has been doctored and was not representative of the animals' treatment in the kingdom; PETA, meanwhile, called for a tourist ban of Thailand and proposed a law for elephant welfare. This, for most Thais, was going too far: foreigners interfering in the sovereign affairs of a country and suggesting to Thais how they should look after their national symbol. It does seem a rather heavy-handed way of dealing with the issue and while publicity might have been gained rather more would have been achieved with a subtler approach.

Some people have pointed out that even before the logging ban, life was not always a bed of bananas for the elephants. There have been reports that they were fed on amphetamines to keep them working, and when they became too ill or exhausted they were simply sold – often to be slaughtered. An elephant trunk is said to be worth ฿40,000 and the genitals ฿15,000- 20,000; a good pair of tusks considerably more than this.

Unfortunately, Thailand is really not in a position to support a large number of elephants any longer. There is neither the work, the space, nor the interest. Even wild elephants are becoming a pest in some areas, as they venture out of national park areas and destroy crops.

although non-venomous, has a powerful bite. Other smaller pythons include the blood python (*Python curtus*) and rock python (*Python molurus bivittatus*).

Some of the most beautiful non-venomous snakes in Thailand are the racers (genus Elaphe and Gonyosoma). They live in a variety of habitats, and because they are diurnal are often seen. The visually striking, gold-coloured copperhead racer (*Elephe radiata*) can grow to a length of 2 m and lives in open grasslands. The bright green, red-tailed racer (*Gonyosoma oxycephalum*) lives in trees; it can also grow to 2 m and is easily identified by its brown tail. Other snakes found in Thailand include the rat snakes (genus Zaocys and Ptyas), the beautiful whip-like bronzebacks (genus Dendrelaphis), and the keelbacks (sub-family Natricinae).

It is partly the dread – often misplaced – of **venomous** snakes that make them so fascinating. There are two types: the front-fanged (more venomous) and back-fanged (mildly venomous) snakes. The latter include whip snakes (genus Ahaetulla and Dryophiops), water snakes (sub-family Homalopsinae) and cat snakes (genus Boiga). The former include cobras, the best known of which is the king cobra (*Ophiophagus hannah*), common Chinese cobra (*Naja naja atra*) and the monocled cobra (*Naja naja kaouthia*). The king cobra is said to be the longest venomous snake in the world; it has been known to reach lengths of up to 6 m. It is also among the most dangerous due to its aggressive nature. One specimen shot in the mountains of Nakhon Si Thammarat in 1924 measured 5.6 m. Their venom is a very powerful neurotoxin, and victims can be dead within half an hour.

It has even been claimed that elephants have died after being bitten, the snake puncturing the soft skin at the tip of the trunk. King cobras are found throughout the country, in most habitats. It should be emphasized that despite their aggressiveness, few people die from cobra bites in Thailand.

The venom of **sea snakes** (family *Hydrophiidae*) is even more powerful than that of cobras, and the common sea snake's (*Enhydrina schistosa*) is said to be the most toxic of any snake. Fortunately, sea snakes are not particularly aggressive, and it is rare for swimmers to be bitten. Twenty-two species have been found in the waters of Southeast Asia, and all bar one (*Laticauda colubrina*, which lays its eggs in rock crevices) produce their young live. They grow to a length of 2 m and feed on fish.

Snakes of the viper family (*Viperidae*) grow to a length of 1 m, and the kraits (genus Bungarus) to 2 m. Vipers are easily identifiable by their arrow-shaped heads. The vipers' long fangs, their position at the front of the mouth, and their aggressiveness, makes them more dangerous than other more poisonous species. The Malayan pit viper (*Agkistrodon rhodostoma*) and Pope's pit viper (*Trimeresurus popeiorum*) are both highly irritable. Kraits, though possessing a toxic venom which has been known to kill, are of sleepy temperament and rarely attack unless provoked. The banded krait (*Bungarus fasciatus*), with its black and yellow striped body, is very distinctive.

A rather different, and less dangerous – at least in its current form – reptile is *Siamotyrannus isanensis*, a tyrannosaur beloved of school children around the world. On 19 June 1996, Thai and French palaeontologists announced the discovery of a 7-m-long tyrannosaur. This may not be the largest member of the family ('rex' is twice the size) but it is the oldest, predating the next most senior by 20 million years. It is also Thailand's very own dinosaur (see page 364).

Insects Insects are not usually at the top of a visitor's agenda to Thailand. But, as with the kingdom's birds and flora, the country also has a particularly rich insect population due to its position at a crossroads between different, and varied, zoogeographic zones. There are over 1400 species of butterfly and moth (*Lepidoptera*), including one of the world's largest moths, the giant atlas (*Attacus atlas*) which has a wing span of up to 28 cm. Beetles are even more numerous, although how numerous is not known: one single square kilometre of the Thung Yai-Huai Kha Khaeng area was found to support 10,000 species alone.

Marine life Thailand's coastline abuts onto both the Indian Ocean (Andaman Sea) and the South China Sea (Gulf of Thailand), and therefore has marine flora and fauna characteristic of both regions. In the Gulf, 850 species of open-water fish have been identified including tuna, of which Thailand is the world's largest exporter (although most are now caught outside Thailand's waters). In the Andaman Sea, game fish such as blue and black marlin, barracuda, sailfish and various sharks are all present.

Among sea mammals, Thailand's shores provide nesting sites for four species of **sea turtle**: the leatherback, green, Ridley's and the hawksbill turtle. The latter is now very rare, while a fifth species, the loggerhead turtle, has disappeared from Thailand's shores and waters. Other marine mammals include several species of sea snake (see above), the saltwater crocodile (which may now be extinct), three species of dolphin, and the dugong or sea cow.

Coral reefs probably contain a richer profusion of life than any other ecosystem – even exceeding the tropical rainforest in terms of species diversity. Those in Thailand's Andaman Sea are among the finest in the region – and maritime parks like the Surin and Similan islands have been gazetted to help protect these delicate habitats. Although the country's

The 'Siamese' cat

There were, originally, 23 breeds of cat that came from Thailand. Of these, only one is regarded by cat fanciers as the Siamese Cat – the Korat or Si Sawat. The original 23 breeds are described in the *Cat Book Poems*, a 14th-century manuscript including paintings and verse now housed in Bangkok's National Library. Of the 23, 17 were regarded as good luck cats, and the remaining six as cats of ill fortune. Today, however, only six of the original 23 breeds remain and, fortunately, all are good luck cats.

Korat (officially, Nakhon Ratchasima) is a large town in Thailand's northeastern region, and the original name of the Siamese cat is said to have arisen when King Rama V (1868-1910) asked a court official where a particularly beautiful cat came from, to be told 'Korat'. Certainly, Western visitors to this part of the north-east remarked on the breed's existence at the beginning of the 20th century.

It was not, however, until 1959 that the first confirmed pair of Korats were imported into the US. Today the Korat is more usually called Si Sawat, a reference to the cat's colour (silver-blue). The sawat is a grey-green non-edible fruit; sawat also happens to mean good fortune. Why the Si Sawat is associated with good luck is not clear. It has been said that its colour is symbolic of silver, signifying good fortune. Others have argued that the colour is akin to rain clouds, indicating a bountiful rice crop. Even the colour of the cat's eyes have been likened to the colour of ripening rice. A pair of Si Sawats given to a bride before marriage is said to bring good fortune to the partnership. Other than the Korat's distinctive colour, it is also unique in that its hair does not float off when it is stroked, making the animal particularly suitable for those with a cat allergy.

For further information, contact: Rose Meldrum, President, Korat Cat Fanciers' Association Inc, 6408 Shinnwood Road, Wilmington, NC 28409, USA; or The Cat Fanciers' Association Inc, PO Box 1005, Manasquan NJ 08736-1005, USA.

---

reefs remain under-researched, 210 species of hard coral and 108 coral reef fish have so far been identified in the Andaman Sea. Literally tens of thousands of other marine organisms, including soft corals, crustacea, echinoderms and worms, would have to be added to this list to build up a true picture of the ecosystem's diversity.

But like the rest of Thailand's natural heritage, life under the sea is also threatened. Collin Piprell and Ashley J Boyd vividly recount this story in their book *Thailand's Coral Reefs: Nature under Threat* (see Books, page 772). Some reefs have been virtually wiped out by human depredations (for example, that off Koh Larn near Pattaya). Fish stocks in the Gulf of Thailand are seriously depleted and the destruction of mangroves along both the eastern and western seaboards has seriously eroded the main breeding grounds for many fish. Untreated effluent and raw sewage are dumped into the Gulf and, because it is an almost enclosed body of water, this tends to become concentrated. Marine biologists have identified some instances of sex-changes in shellfish communities – apparently because of the build-up of toxic compounds.

It has to be acknowledged that although tourism in some areas of Thailand has an interest in maintaining the sanctity of the marine environment, it has also been a major cause of destruction. Anchors, rubbish and sewerage, the thrashing fins of novice divers, and the selfish grabbing hands of collectors of shells, all contribute to the gradual erosion

Thailand's blooming business

Thailand's forests, wetlands and grasslands support over 1000 varieties of orchid and the country has become Southeast Asia's largest exporter of the blooms. In 1991, flower exports – mostly orchids – earned US$80 million. The industry began in the 1950s, but only really expanded in the mid-1980s as orchid farms were established around Bangkok. Of the various genuses, the most popular is Dendrobium, which is particularly suited to Thailand's seasonal climate and has the added attraction of blooming throughout the year.

Over half of Thailand's orchid exports go to Japan – where customers have a particular predilection for pink and purple blooms. Despite such healthy growth, there are fears that a change of fashion in Japan might undermine the market. The price of the pink Sonia dendrobium has declined from ฿5-6 to ฿2-3 per bloom. An area of the economy which has bloomed even faster than orchids is that of artificial flower production. In 1996, exports of plastic and silk flowers and foliage totalled nearly US$70 million.

of the habitat that tourists come to experience. Other sources of destruction have less or nothing to do with tourism: the accumulation of toxic chemicals, Thailand's voracious fishermen, cyanide and dynamite fishing, the trade in aquarium fish, and collection and sale of certain species for their use in traditional Chinese medicines. The kingdom is, for example, the world's largest exporter of seahorses. Around 15 tonnes of the dried creatures are exported each year, mostly to Taiwan and Hong Kong, where their crushed bodies are believed to be an aphrodisiac and a cure for certain respiratory ailments. Like the kingdom's forests, there are fears that within a decade there might be little left for the discerning diver to enjoy.

National parks

In 1961 Khao Yai became Thailand's first national park – although King Ramkhamhaeng of Sukhothai created a royal reserve in the 13th century, and the grounds of Buddhist wats have always provided havens for wildlife. By late 1995 there were 81 parks covering over 41,000 sq km spread throughout the kingdom, encompassing all the principal ecological zones – and more have been gazetted since. Including Thailand's 35 wildlife sanctuaries (which cover another 29,000 sq km), and 48 non-hunting areas, nearly 15% of Thailand's land area is protected in some way. Though impressive on paper, this does not mean that there are some 70,000 sq km of protected forest, grassland, swamp and sea. Settled and shifting agriculturalists live in many parks, illegal logging is widespread (though better controlled today than in the 1980s), and poaching continues to be a problem. Poor pay, lack of manpower and corruption all contribute to the difficulties of maintaining the integrity of these 'protected' areas. Some 40 park wardens have been murdered doing their job.

There has been an increase of late in public awareness towards wildlife and the environment. Certainly, there have been some notable successes: the logging ban of 1989, the shelving of the plan to build the Nam Choan dam in the contiguous Huai Kha Khaeng and Tha Thungna Wildlife Sanctuaries (see page 186), and – without being patronizing – a far wider concern for the environment amongst average Thais. But the battle is far from won. Loggers, poachers and tree plantation companies wield enormous financial and political power. In 1990, such was the exasperation of Sueb Makasathien, the highly regarded director of the incomparable Huai Kha Khaeng Wildlife Sanctuary, that he committed suicide. It is generally agreed that Sueb killed himself because he was unable to prevent corrupt officials, loggers and poachers from degrading his park – 2400 sq km of the finest forest in all Southeast Asia. (Sueb was hoping to get the sanctuary accepted as a World Heritage area by UNESCO.) Tourism has also left its mark on the parks. Khao Yai is now so popular as a weekend trip from Bangkok that its capacity has been exceeded, while coastal and island marine parks suffer from refuse-littered beaches and campsites. The National Parks Division's management of the country's protected areas has been woefully inadequate. Koh Samet and Koh Phi Phi, both national parks, are – illegally – covered with accommodation developments. Khao Yai, Thailand's first park, has hotels and golf courses within its area. The Thaplan National Park in the northeast is extensively logged by army-backed interests. The national parks, as they stand, are being ruined by poor management.

Central region **Phu Hin Rongkla National Park**: As much of historical as natural interest, this park was a centre for Communist Party activities during the 1970s. The park rises to nearly 2000 m and has a good range of wildlife including small populations of bear and tiger. **Thung Salaeng National Park**: best known for its birdlife which is easy to view in the park's open meadows. Species include hornbills, pheasants and eagles. **Khlong Lan National Park**: one of Thailand's most pristine, and rugged, protected areas; good for trekking.

Northern region **Doi Inthanon National Park**: a very popular national park within easy reach of Chiang Mai. Named after Thailand's highest peak, which climbs to more than 2500 m. Wide range of flora, waterfalls, hiking trails and good facilities.

Northeastern region **Khao Yai National Park**: Thailand's first park and one of the most popular. Gets particularly crowded at weekends; good facilities, trails, waterfalls, but wildlife tends to keep well out of the way of people. **Kaeng Tana National Park**: on the Mun River; it is possible to swim here in the dry season. **Phu Wiang National Park**: best known as the site of numerous dinosaur bone 'quarries', which it is possible to explore. **Phu Kradung National Park**: a popular place for student groups who climb the 1500-m-high mountain after which this park is named. Particularly known for its wild flowers, range of vegetation types, and 130 species of bird. Good trekking.

Eastern region **Khao Laem Ya National Park**: the island resort of Koh Samet comes within the boundaries of this marine park; very popular but not the best protected marine area. **Koh Chang National Park**: this is focused on the large island of Koh Chang. Good diving and snorkelling as well as waterfalls and trekking trails on the island.

Western region **Erawan National Park**: a very popular park with waterfalls, some stunning landscapes, caves, trails and good facilities. **Tham Than Lot National Park**: this small park has a rich diversity of fauna and the cave of Than Lot, after which it is named.

Southern region **Kaeng Krachan National Park**: a large park covering almost 2000 sq km. Extensive trails, mountain hikes and waterfalls. **Khao Sam Roi Yod National Park**: the best place in Thailand to see water birds; good facilities. **Khao Sok National Park**: one of

Thailand's finest protected areas with a wide range of forest types and good trails. **Similan Islands National Park**: arguably Thailand's best marine park; excellent diving. **Koh Surin National Park**: another fine marine park in the Andaman Sea; the reefs here are said to be the most diverse in Thailand. **Tarutao National Park**: Thailand's first protected marine area and one of the best; closed between May and October. **Ang Thong National Park**: a protected marine area close to the resort island of Koh Samui, so the dive sites are much frequented. **Khao Luang National Park**: this encompasses the southern region's highest peak, Khao Luang (1835 m). Mountain trails and waterfalls.

Books

Hilltribes

Boyes, Jon and **Piraban S**, *A life apart: viewed from the hills* (1992) Silkworm Books: Bangkok. This has been written with the trekker in mind. It is a series of hilltribe vignettes, written from the tribal people's perspective. In this respect the book is fine; where it fails is in providing a context for these vignettes. Here the authors over-generalize and sometimes provide misleading information. Take the book for the thumbnail sketches of life, not for accuracy.

Guntamala, Ada and **Kornvika, Puapratum**, *Trekking through Northern Thailand* (1992) Silkworm Books: Chiang Mai.

Lewis, Paul and **Lewis, Elaine**, *Peoples of the Golden Triangle: six tribes in Thailand* (1984) Thames and Hudson: London. Glossy coffee-table book with a good supporting text. Too heavy to take on the road, but a good book for before or after.

McKinnon, John and **Vienne, Bernard**, *Hill tribes today: problems in change* (1989) White-Lotus/Orstom: Bangkok. This volume, though beginning to become rather dated in some respects, is accurate and informative. It also suffers from being a fairly hefty tome to lug around the hills.

Tapp, Nicholas, *The Hmong of Thailand: opium people of the Golden Triangle* (1986) report No 4, Anti-slavery Society: London. *Sovereignty and rebellion: the White Hmong of Northern Thailand* (1989) Oxford University Press: Singapore. Nick Tapp is an anthropologist at the Australian National University. This book is intended mostly for an academic audience; it is interesting because it tries to challenge the

established wisdom that the Hmong are a 'bad' tribe.

Living in Thailand

Cornwel-Smith, Phil, *Very Thai* (2004), River Books. An essential guide to all those indecipherable elements of Thai popular culture that bewitch and bewilder. Everything from hairdos to tattoos are dealt with here. The book is also filled with some great photography.

A useful book delving deeper into the do's and don'ts of living in Thailand is Robert and Nanthapa Cooper's *Culture shock: Thailand*, Time Books International: Singapore (1990). It is available from most bookshops.

Textiles

Conway, Susan, *Thai Textiles* (1992) British Museum Press: London. A richly illustrated book with informative text, placing Thai textiles in the context of Thai society and history.

Thai literature available in English

Increasing numbers of Thai novels and short stories are being translated into English. In particular, TMC (Thai Modern Classics) are publishing a number of what their editorial team regard as the best works of Thai literature. By mid-1995 3 volumes had come out: Arkartdamkeung Rapheephat's *The Circus of Life*, Sila Khoamchai's *The Path of the Tiger*, and an anthology of pieces from 20 Thai novels. All are very competitively priced and more have been published since then.

Boontawee, Kampoon, *A Child of the Northeast [Luuk Isan]* (1988) Duang Kamol: Bangkok. This novel covers a year in the life of a village in the northeast in the 1930s. It centres on the experiences of an 8-year-old boy, Koon, and concentrates on the struggle to make ends meet in a capricious land. The image here of traditional life could be usefully set against Pira Sudham's more golden view of the past. The original Thai version of the book won the 1976 Best Novel of the Year award and is highly recommended.

Botan, *Letters from Thailand* (1991) Duang Kamol Books: Bangkok. Award-winning novel by Thai-Chinese author, set up as a series of letters from a young immigrant in 1950s and 1960s Bangkok to his mother back in China. Was used in Thai schools to give pupils an insight into how foreigners see Thailand.

Ekachai, Sanitsuda, *Behind the Smile: Voices of Thailand* (1990) Thai Development Support Committee: Bangkok. This is not a novel, but a series of vignettes of contemporary Thai life, written in English by a Bangkok Post reporter. They are well written, perceptive and stimulating, providing a realistic view of the pressures, aspirations and opportunities facing ordinary people in Thailand. A more recent, more expensive and considerably glossier book, by the same author, is *Seeds of Hope: Local Initiatives in Thailand* (1994) which also focuses on the theme of development, but with an emphasis on self-help and the work of NGOs.

Khonkhai, Khammaan, *The Teacher of Mad Dog Swamp* (1992) Silkworm Books: Bangkok. A book about life in the northeast, this centres upon the experiences of a diligent young teacher who, on graduation, is sent to an up-country primary school. Almost inevitably, his concern for the people of the area results in him being labelled a communist. The book provides an excellent insight into the concerns of villagers and also incorporates a political plot. It was originally published in Thai as *Khru Ban Nok (Rural Teacher)* in 1978; the author was brought up in the northeast

and trained as a teacher, the book is semi-autobiographical.

Pramoj, Kukrit, *The Four Reigns [Si phaen din]* (1953) DK Books: Bangkok. This novel, one of the most famous written in Thai, is a historical saga recounting the experiences of a noble Thai family through the reign of 4 kings from the late-19th century. Written by a former Thai prime minister, some view it as a masterpiece of Thai literature; others simply see it as a historical novel in the Cartland/Cookson mould. Entertaining, but hardly high art.

Rayawa, Nikorn, *High Banks, Heavy Logs* (1992) Penguin. The story of a woodcarver in northern Thailand and his struggle against change, and the declining moral and artistic standards that are seen to accompany change.

Siburapha, *Behind the painting and other stories* (1990) OUP: Singapore. These short stories, only recently translated into English by David Smyth – who teaches Thai at the School of Oriental and African Studies in London – are written by an author who is regarded as one of the 'greats' of modern Thai literature. He was at the forefront of the transformation of Thai literature into a modern genre, and was also an influential social and political activist.

Srinawk, Khamsing, *The Politician and Other Stories* (1991) OUP: Singapore. This volume consists of 12 short stories. The author comes from a farming background and the stories describe the difficulties that rural households face in coming to terms with modernization.

Sudham, Pira, *Monsoon Country* (1988), *People of Esarn* (1987), *Siamese Drama* (1983), *Pira Sudham's Best* (1993). All 4 of these books are published by Shire Books; Bankok and are widely available in Bangkok and essentially have the same tale to tell: country life in the poor northeastern region. Pira comes from a rural background and won a scholarship to study English in New Zealand; he has since become a bit of a gadfly in *farang* circles. However, it is intriguing that his books have not been translated into Thai and his main admirers remain *farangs*; indeed, many Thais find his rather romantic view of rural life somewhat unconvincing. His books are rather similar in style and content; there is little to identify Pira as one of the greats of Thai literature, but they are worth reading nonetheless – although some of his views should be viewed with scepticism.

Wildlife

Lekagul, Boonsong and **McNeely, JA**, *Mammals of Thailand* (1988) Association for the Conservation of Wildlife.

Lekagul, Boonsong and **Cronin, Edward**, *Bird guide of Thailand* (1974) Association for the Conservation of Wildlife: Bangkok. For keen ornithologists.

Lekagul, Boonsong and **Round, Philip**, *The Birds of Thailand* (1991) Sahakarn Bhaet: Bangkok.

Lekagul, Boonsong, et al, *Fieldguide to the Butterflies of Thailand* (1977) Association for the Conservation of Wildlife: Bangkok. Available from most large bookshops in Bangkok.

Piprell, Collin and **Boyd, Ashley J**, *Thailand's Coral Reefs: Nature under Threat* (1995) Bangkok: White Lotus. A well-illustrated plea for the conservation of the kingdom's reefs.

Contents

Footprint features

Footnotes

Useful words and phrases

Thai is a tonal language with five tones: mid tone (no mark), high tone (´), low tone (`), falling tone (^), and rising tone (ˇ). Tones are used to distinguish between words which are otherwise the same. For example, 'see' pronounced with a low tone means 'four'; with a rising tone, it means 'colour'. Thai is not written in Roman script but using an alphabet derived from Khmer. The Romanization given below is only intended to help in pronouncing Thai words. There is no accepted method of Romanization and some of the sounds in Thai cannot be accurately reproduced using Roman script.

Polite particles
At the end of sentences males use the polite particle *krúp*, and females, *kâ* or *ká*.

Learning Thai
The list of words and phrases below is only very rudimentary. For anyone serious about learning Thai it is best to buy a dedicated Thai language text book or to enrol on a Thai course. Recommended among the various 'teach yourself Thai' books is Somsong Buasai and David Smyth's *Thai in a Week*, Hodder & Stoughton: London (1990). A useful mini-dictionary is the Hugo *Thai phrase book* (1990). For those interested in learning to read and write Thai, the best 'teach yourself' course is the *Linguaphone* course.

General words and phrases

Yes/no	*chái/mâi chái, or krúp (kâ)/mâi krúp (kâ)*
Thank you/no thank you	*kòrp-kOOn/mâi ao kòrp-kOOn*
Hello, good morning, goodbye	*sa-wùt dee krúp(kâ)*
What is your name? My name is …	*Koon chêu a-rai krúp (kâ)? Pom chêu …*
Excuse me, sorry!	*kor-tôht krúp(kâ)*
Can/do you speak English?	*KOON pôot pah-sah ung-grìt*
a little, a bit	*nít-nòy*
Where's the …?	*yòo têe-nai …?*
How much is …?	*tâo-rài …?*
Pardon?	*a-rai ná?*
I don't understand	*pom (chún) mâi kao jái*
How are you?	*Mâi sa-bai*
Not very well	*sa-bai dee mái?*

At hotels

What is the charge each night?	*kâh hôrng wun la tâo-rài?*
Is the room air conditioned?	*hôrng dtìt air reu bplào?*
Can I see the room first please?	*kor doo hôrng gòrn dâi mái?*
Does the room have hot water?	*hôrng mii náhm rórn mái?*
Does the room have a bathroom?	*hôrng mii hôrng náhm mái?*
Can I have the bill please?	*kor bin nòy dâi mái?*

Travelling

Where is the train station?	*sa-tahn-nee rót fai yòo têe-nai?*
Where is the bus station?	*sa-tahn-nee rót may yòo têe-nai?*
How much to go to ...?	*bpai ... tâo-rài?*
That's expensive	*pairng bpai nòy*
What time does the bus/	
train leave for ...?	*rót may/rót fai bpai ...òrk gèe mohng?*
Is it far?	*glai mái?*
Turn left/turn right	*lée-o sái / lée-o kwah*
Go straight on	*ler-ee bpai èek*
It's straight ahead	*yòo dtrong nâh*

At restaurants

Can I see a menu?	*kor doo may-noo nòy?*
Can I have ...?/ I would like ...?	*Kor ...*
Is it very (hot) spicy?	*pèt mâhk mái?*
I am hungry	*pom (chún) hew*
Breakfast	*ah-hahn cháo*
Lunch	*ah-hahn glanhg wun*

Time and days

in the morning	*dtorn cháo*	Monday	*wun jun*
in the afternoon	*dtorn bài*	Tuesday	*wun ung-kahn*
in the evening	*dtorn yen*	Wednesday	*wun pÓOt*
today	*wun née*	Thursday	*wun pá-réu-hùt*
tomorrow	*prÔOng née*	Friday	*wun sÒOk*
yesterday	*mêu-a wahn née*	Saturday	*wun sao*
		Sunday	*wun ah-tít*

Numbers

1	*nèung*	20	*yêe-sìp*
2	*sorng*	21	*yêe-sìp-et*
3	*sahm*	22	*yêe-sìp-sorng... etc*
4	*sèe*	30	*sahm-sìp*
5	*hâa*	100	*(nèung) róy*
6	*hòk*	101	*(nèung) róy-nèung*
7	*jèt*	150	*(nèung) róy-hâh-sìp*
8	*bpàirt*	200	*sorng róy ... etc*
9	*gâo*	1000	*(nèung) pun*
10	*sìp*	10,000	*mèun*
11	*sìp-et*	100,000	*sairn*
12	*sìp-sorng ... etc*	1,000,000	*láhn*

Basic vocabulary

airport	*a-nahm bin*	beautiful	*oo-ay*
bank	*ta-nah-kahn*	big	*yài*
bathroom	*hôrng náhm*	boat	*reu-a*
beach	*hàht*	bus	*ót may*

bus station	*sa-tah-nee rót may*	open	*bpèrt*
buy	*séu*	police	*dtum-ròo-ut*
chemist	*ráhn kai yah*	police station	*sa-tah-nee,*
clean	*sa-àht*		*dtum-ròo-ut*
closed	*bpìt*	post office	*bprai-sa-nee*
cold	*yen*	restaurant	*ráhn ah-hahn*
day	*wun*	road	*thanon*
delicious	*a-ròy*	room	*hôrng*
dirty	*sòk-ga-bpròk*	shop	*ráhn*
doctor	*mor*	sick (ill)	*mâi sa-bai*
eat	*gin (kâo)*	silk	*mai*
embassy	*sa-tahn tôot*	small	*lék*
excellent	*yêe-um*	stop	*yÒOt*
expensive	*pairng*	taxi	*táirk-sêe*
food	*ah-hahn*	that	*nún*
fruit	*pon-la-mái*	this	*née*
hospital	*rohng pa-yah-bahn*	ticket	*dtoo-a*
hot (temp)	*rórn*	toilet	*hôrng náhm*
hot (spicy)	*pèt*	town	*meu-ung*
hotel	*rôhng rairm*	train station	*sa-tah-nee rót fai*
island	*gòr*	very	*mâhk*
market	*dta-làht*	water	*náhm*
medicine	*yah*	what	*a-rai*

Glossary

A

Amitabha the Buddha of the Past (see Avalokitsvara)

Amphoe district; administrative division below the province

Amulet protective medallion

Ao bay

Arhat a person who has perfected himself; images of former monks are sometimes carved into arhat

Avadana Buddhist narrative, telling of the deeds of saintly souls

Avalokitsvara also known as Amitabha and Lokeshvara, the name literally means 'World Lord'; he is the compassionate male Bodhisattva, the saviour of Mahayana Buddhism, and represents the central force of creation in the universe; usually portrayed with a lotus and water flask

B

Bai sema boundary stones marking consecrated ground around a Buddhist bot

Ban village; shortened from muban

Baray man-made lake or reservoir

Batik a form of resist dyeing

Bhikku Buddhist monk

Bodhi the tree under which the Buddha achieved enlightenment (*Ficus religiosa*)

Bodhisattva a future Buddha. In Mahayana Buddhism, someone who has attained enlightenment, but who postpones nirvana to help others reach it.

Bor Kor Sor (BKS) Government bus terminal

Bot Buddhist ordination hall, of rectangular plan, identifiable by the boundary stones placed around it; an abbreviation of ubosoth

Brahma the Creator, one of the gods of the Hindu trinity, usually represented with four faces, and often mounted on a hamsa

Brahmin a Hindu priest

Bun to make merit

C

Caryatid elephants, often used as buttressing decorations

Celadon pottery ware with blue/green to grey glaze

Chakri the current royal dynasty in Thailand. They have reigned since 1782

Champa rival empire of the Khmers, of Hindu culture, based in present-day Vietnam

Changwat province

Chao title for Lao and Thai kings

Chat honorific umbrella or royal multi-tiered parasol

Chedi from the Sanskrit *cetiya* (Pali, *caitya*), meaning memorial. Usually a religious monument (often bell-shaped), containing relics of the Buddha or other holy remains. Used interchangeably with stupa

Chofa 'sky tassel' on the roof of wat buildings

CPT Communist Party of Thailand

D

Deva a Hindu-derived male god

Devata a Hindu-derived goddess

Dharma the Buddhist law

Dipterocarp family of trees (*Dipterocarpaceae*), characteristic of Southeast Asia's forests

Dvarapala guardian figure, usually placed at the entrance to a temple

F

Farang Westerner

G

Ganesh elephant-headed son of Siva

Garuda mythical divine bird, with predatory beak and claws, and human body; the king of birds, enemy of naga and mount of Vishnu

Gautama the historic Buddha

Geomancy the art of divination by lines and figures

Gopura crowned or covered gate, entrance to a religious area

H

Hamsa sacred goose, Brahma's mount; in Buddhism represents the flight of the doctrine

Hang yaaw long-tailed boat, used on canals

Harmika box-like part of a Burmese stupa that often acts as a reliquary casket

Hat beach

Hinayana 'Lesser Vehicle', major Buddhist sect in Southeast Asia, usually termed Theravada Buddhism

Hong swan

Hor kong a pavilion built on stilts, where the monastery drum is kept

Hor takang bell tower

Hor tray/trai library where manuscripts are stored in a Thai monastery

Hti 'umbrella' surmounting Burmese temples, often encrusted with jewels

I

Ikat tie-dyeing method of patterning cloth

Indra the Vedic god of the heavens, weather and war

J

Jataka(s) the birth stories of the Buddha; they normally number 547, although an additional three were added in Burma for reasons of symmetry in mural painting and sculpture. The last 10 are the most important

K

Kala (makara) literally 'death' or 'black'; a demon ordered to consume itself, often sculpted with grinning face and bulging eyes over entranceway to act as a door guardian; also known as kirtamukha

Kathin/krathin a one-month period during the eighth lunar month, when lay people present new robes and other gifts to monks

Ketumula flame-like motif above the Buddha head

Khao mountain

Khlong canal

Khruang amulet

Kinaree half-human, half-bird, usually depicted as a heavenly musician

Kirtamukha see kala

Koh island

Koutdi see kuti

Krating wild bull, most commonly seen on bottles of *Red Bull* (Krating Daeng) drink

Krishna incarnation of Vishnu

Kuti living quarters of Buddhist monks in a monastery complex

L

Laem cape (as in bay)

Lakhon traditional Thai classical music

Lak muang city pillar

Laterite bright red tropical soil/stone, commonly used in Khmer monuments

Linga phallic symbol and one of the forms of Siva. Embedded in a pedestal, shaped to allow drainage of lustral water poured over it; the linga typically has a succession of cross sections: from square at the base, through octagonal, to round. These symbolize, in order, the trinity of Brahma, Vishnu and Siva

Lintel a load-bearing stone spanning a doorway; often heavily carved

Lokeshvara see Avalokitsvara

M

Mahabharata a Hindu epic text, written about 2000 years ago

Mahayana 'Greater Vehicle', Buddhist sect

Maitreya the future Buddha

Makara a mythological aquatic reptile, somewhat like a crocodile and sometimes with an elephant's trunk; often found along with the *kala* framing doorways

Mandala a focus for meditation; a representation of the cosmos

Mara personification of evil and tempter of the Buddha

Matmii Northeastern Thai cotton ikat

Meru sacred or cosmic mountain at the centre of the world in Hindu-Buddhist cosmology; home of the gods.

Mon race and kingdom of southern Burma and central Thailand, from 7th-11th century

Mondop from the sanskrit, *mandapa*. A cube-shaped building, often topped with a cone-like structure, used to contain an object of worship like a footprint of the Buddha

Muang 'town' in Thai, but also sometimes 'municipality' or 'district'

Muban village, usually shortened to ban

Mudra symbolic gesture of the hands of the Buddha

N

Naga benevolent mythical water serpent, enemy of Garuda

Naga makara fusion of naga and makara

Nalagiri the elephant let loose to attack the Buddha, who calmed him

Namtok waterfall

Nandi/nandin bull, mount of Siva

Nang thalung shadow play/puppets

Nikhom resettlement village

Nirvana release from the cycle of suffering in Buddhist belief; 'enlightenment'

P

Pa kama Lao men's all-purpose cloth, usually woven with checked pattern

paddy/padi unhulled rice

Pali sacred language of Theravada Buddhism

Parvati consort of Siva

Pha sin tubular bit of cloth, similar to sarong

Phi spirit

Phnom/phanom Khmer for hill/mountain

Phra sinh see pha sin

Pradaksina pilgrims' clockwise circumambulation of holy structure

Prah sacred

Prang form of stupa built in Khmer style, shaped like a corncob

Prasada stepped pyramid (see prasat)

Prasat residence of a king or of the gods (sanctuary tower), from the Indian prasada

Q

Quan Am Chinese goddess of mercy

R

Rai unit of measurement, 1 ha = 6.25 rai

Rama incarnation of Vishnu, hero of the Indian epic, the *Ramayana*

Ramakien Thai version of the *Ramayana*

Ramayana Hindu romantic epic, known as *Ramakien* in Thailand

S

Saamlor three-wheeled bicycle taxi

Sakyamuni the historic Buddha

Sal the Indian sal tree (*Shorea robusta*), under which the historic Buddha was born

Sala open pavilion

Sangha the Buddhist order of monks

Sawankhalok type of ceramic

Singha mythical guardian lion

Siva the Destroyer, one of the three gods of the Hindu trinity

Sofa see dok sofa

Songthaew 'two rows': pick-up truck with benches along either side

Sravasti the miracle at Sravasti, the Buddha subdues the heretics in front of a mango tree

Stele inscribed stone panel

Stucco plaster, often heavily moulded

Stupa chedi

T

Talaat market
Tambon a commune of villages
Tam bun see bun
Tavatimsa heaven of the 33 gods, at the summit of Mount Meru
Tazaungs small pavilions, found within Burmese temple complexes
Tham cave
Thanon street in Thai
That shrine housing Buddhist relics, an edifice commemorating the Buddha's life or the funerary temple for royalty
Thein Burmese ordination hall
Theravada 'Way of the Elders'; major Buddhist sect, also known as Hinayana Buddhism ('Lesser Vehicle')
Traiphum the three worlds of Buddhist cosmology – heaven, hell and earth
Trimurti Hindu trinity of gods: Brahma, the Creator, Vishnu the Preserver, Siva the Destroyer
Tripitaka Theravada Buddhism's Pali canon

U

Ubosoth see bot

Urna the dot or curl on the Buddha's forehead
Usnisa the Buddha's top knot or 'wisdom bump',

V

Vahana a mythical beast, upon which a deva or god rides
Viharn an assembly hall in a Buddhist monastery; may hold Buddha images
Vishnu the Protector, one of the gods of the Hindu trinity

W

Wai Thai greeting, with hands held together at chin height as if in prayer
Wat Buddhist 'monastery'

Z

Zayat prayer pavilion found in Burmese temple complexes
Zedi Burmese term for a stupa

Food glossary → See also Thai dishes, page 783.

a-haan food
ba-mii egg noodles
bia beer
chaa tea
check bin/bill cheque
chorn spoon
gaeng curry
gaeng chud soup
jaan plate
kaafae (ron) coffee (hot)
kaew glass
kai chicken
kap klaem snacks to be eaten when drinking
khaaw/khao rice
khaaw niaw sticky rice
khaaw tom rice gruel
khai egg
khai dao fried egg
khanom sweet, dessert or cake
khanom cake cake
khanom pang bread
khanom pang ping toast
khing ginger
khuan scramble
khuat bottle
kin to eat
kleua salt
krueng kieng side dishes
kung crab
kwaytio noodle soup, white noodles
laap pa raw fish crushed into a paste, marinated in lemon juice and mixed with chopped mint, chilli and rice grains
laap sin raw meat dish, see above
lao liquor
man root vegetable

man farang potatoes
manaaw lemon
mekong a Thai whisky
mit knife
muu pork
nam chaa tea
nam kheng ice
nam kuat bottled water
nam manaaw soda lime soda
nam plaa fish sauce
nam plaa prik fish sauce with chilli
nam plaaw plain water
nam som orange juice
nam taan sugar
nam tom boiled water
nom milk
nua meat (usually beef)
phak vegetables
phat to stir fry
phet hot (chilli)
phon lamai fruit
pla fish
priaw sour
priaw waan sweet and sour
prik hot chilli
raan a-haan restaurant
ratnaa in gravy
rawn hot (temperature)
sa-te satay
sorm fork
talaat market
thao mai luai morning glory
thua nut/bean
tom to boil
tort to deep fry
waan sweet
yam salad
yen cold

Distinctive fruits

Custard apple (*Annona cherimola Mill*) Scaly green skin, squeeze the skin to open the fruit and scoop out the flesh with a spoon. June-September.

Durian (*Durio zibethinus*) A large prickly fruit, with yellow flesh, about the size of a football. Infamous for its pungent smell. While it is today regarded by many visitors as simply revolting, early Europeans (16th-18th centuries) raved about it. Borri (1744) thought it was "God himself, who had produc'd that fruit". But by 1880 Burbridge was writing: "Its odour – one scarcely feels justified in using the word 'perfume' – is so potent, so vague, but withal so insinuating, that it can scarcely be tolerated inside the house". Banned from hotel rooms throughout the region, and beloved by most Southeast Asians, it has an alluring taste. Durian-flavoured chewing gum, ice cream and jams are all available. May-August.

Jackfruit (*Artocarpus heteropyllus*) Similar in appearance to durian but not as spiky. Yellow flesh, tasting slightly like custard. January-June.

Mango (*Mangifera indica*) A rainforest fruit which is now cultivated. Widely available in the West; there are hundreds of different varieties with subtle variations in flavour. Delicious eaten with sticky rice and a sweet sauce. The best mangoes in the region are considered to be those from South Thailand. March-June.

Mangosteen (*Garcinia mangostana*) An aubergine-coloured hard shell covers this small fruit which is about the size of a tennis ball. Cut or squeeze the purple shell to reach its sweet white flesh which is prized by many visitors above all others. In 1898, an American resident of Java wrote, erotically and in obvious ecstasy: "The five white segments separate easily, and they melt on the tongue with a touch of tart and a touch of sweet; one moment a memory of the juiciest, most fragrant apple, at another a remembrance of the smoothest cream ice, the most exquisite and delicately flavoured fruit-acid known – all of the delights of nature's laboratory condensed in that ball of neige parfumée". Southeast Asians believe it should be eaten as a chaser to durian. April-September.

Papaya (*Carica papaya*) A New-World fruit introduced into Southeast Asia in the 16th century. Large, round or oval in shape, yellow or green-skinned with bright orange flesh and a mass of round, black seeds in the middle. The flesh, in texture and taste, is somewhere between a mango and a melon. Some maintain it tastes 'soapy'. Year round.

Pomelo (*Citrus Grande*) A large round fruit the size of anything from an ostrich egg to a football, with thick, green skin and pith, and flesh similar to a grapefruit's, but less acidic. August-November.

Rambutan (*Nephelium lappaceum*) The bright red and hairy rambutan – rambut is the Malay word for 'hair' – with its slightly rubbery but sweet flesh is a close relative of the lychee of southern China. The Thai word for rambutan is *ngoh*. May-September.

Salak (*Salacca edulis*) A small pear-shaped fruit about the size of a large plum with a rough, brown, scaly skin (somewhat like a miniature pangolin) and yellow-white, crisp flesh. It is related to the sago and rattan trees.

Tamarind (*Tamarindus indicus*) Brown seedpods with dry brittle skins and a brown tart-sweet fruit which grow on a tree introduced into India. The flesh has a high tartaric acid content and is used to flavour curries, jams, jellies and chutneys as well as for cleaning brass and copper. December-February.

Thai dishes

It is impossible to provide a comprehensive list of Thai dishes. However (and at the risk of offending connoisseurs by omitting their favourites), popular dishes include:

Soups (*gaeng chud*)
Kaeng juut bean curd and vegetable soup, non-spicy
Khaaw tom rice soup with egg and pork (a breakfast dish) or chicken, fish or prawn. It is said that it can cure fevers and other illnesses. Probably best for a hangover.
Kwaytio Chinese noodle soup served with a variety of additional ingredients, often available from roadside stalls and from smaller restaurants – mostly served up until lunchtime.
Tom ka kai chicken in coconut milk with laos (loas, or ka, is an exotic spice)
Tom yam kung hot and sour prawn soup spiced with lemon grass, coriander and chillies

Rice-based dishes
Single-dish meals served at roadside stalls and in many restaurants (especially cheaper ones).
Khaaw gaeng curry and rice
Khaaw man kai rice with chicken
Khaaw mu daeng rice with red pork
Khaaw naa pet rice with duck
Khaaw phat kai/mu/kung fried rice with chicken/pork/prawn

Noodle-based dishes
Ba-mii haeng wheat noodles served with pork and vegetables
Khaaw soi a form of *Kwaytio* with egg noodles in a curry broth
Kwaytio haeng wide noodles served with pork and vegetables
Mee krop Thai crisp-fried noodles
Phak sii-u noodles fried with egg, vegetables and meat/prawns
Phat thai Thai fried noodles

Curries (*gaeng*)
Gaeng khiaw waan kai/nua/phet/pla green chicken/beef/duck/fish curry (the colour is due to the large number of whole green chillies pounded to make the paste that forms the base of this very hot curry)
Gaeng mussaman Muslim beef curry served with potatoes
Gaeng phanaeng chicken/beef curry
Gaeng phet kai/nua hot chicken/beef curry
Gaeng plaa duk catfish curry

Meat dishes
Kai/mu/nua phat kapow fried meat with basil and chillies
Kai/nua phat prik fried chicken/beef with chillies
Kai tort Thai fried chicken
Kai tua chicken in peanut sauce
Kai yang garlic chicken
Laap chopped (once raw, now frequently cooked) meat with herbs and spices
Mu waan sweet pork
Nua priaw waan sweet and sour beef
Priao wan sweet and sour pork with vegetables

Seafood
Haw mok steamed fish curry
Luuk ciin fishballs
Plaa nerng steamed fish
Plaa pao grilled fish
Plaa priaw waan whole fried fish with ginger sauce
Plaa too tort Thai fried fish
Thotman plaa fried curried fish cakes

Salads (*yam*)
Som tam green papaya salad with tomatoes, chillies, garlic, chopped dried shrimps and lemon (can be extremely hot)
Yam nua Thai beef salad

Vegetables
Phak phat ruam mit mixed fried vegetables

Sweets (*kanom*)
Kanom mo kaeng baked custard squares
Khaaw niaw mamuang sticky rice and mango (a seasonal favourite)
Khaaw niaw sankhayaa sticky rice and custard
Kluay buat chee bananas in coconut milk
Kluay tort Thai fried bananas
Leenchee loi mek chilled lychees in custard

Fruits → *(see also box, page 782)*
Chomphu rose apple
Khanun jackfruit. Jan-Jun
Kluay banana. Year round

Lamyai longan; thin brown shell with translucent fruit similar to lychee. Jun-Aug
Lamut sapodilla
Linchi lychee. Apr-Jun
Majeung star apple
Makham wan tamarind. Dec-Feb
Malakho papaya. Year round
Mamuang mango. Mar-Jun
Manaaw lime. Year round
Mang khud mangosteen. Apr-Sep
Maprao coconut. Year round
Ngo rambutan. May-Sep
Noi na custard (or sugar) apple. Jun-Sep
Sapparot pineapple. Apr-Jun, Dec-Jan
Som orange. Year round
Som o pomelo. Aug-Nov
Taeng mo watermelon. Oct-Mar
Thurian durian. May-Aug

Index → *Entries in bold refer to maps.*

Advertisers' index

Acknowledgements

Andrew Spooner would like to thank Travelmood, Roger Moore, Nanthida Rakwong, Craig Douglas, Paolo Bigolli, Ben Sudhikam, Dave Unkovich, Ruengsang Sripaoraya, TAT, Pop Ruttanaporn, Felicity Laughton, Sara Chare, Elizabeth Taylor, Alan Murphy, Sarah Sorenson, Kassia Gawronski and all at Footprint. I would also like to thank Jenny Hedstrom, Matt Crook and Stratford Blyth for their research contributions. This book wouldn't have possible without the staff at Greenery House nor Khun A's patience and driving skills.

The health section was written by Professor Larry Goodyer, Head of the Leicester School of Pharmacy and director of Nomad Medical.

The diving section was written by Master Scuba Diver, Beth Tierney who contributes to several international magazines. Her editorial work covers both land and dive travel, marine biology and conservation. Beth and her husband Shaun, an underwater photographer, are co-authors for Footprint's *Diving the World*. Thanks also to William Gray and Caroline Sygle, authors of Footprint's *Travel with Kids* and *Body & Soul escapes*, for contributing to the colour section of this guide.

Credits

Footprint credits

Editor: Sara Chare
Map editor: Sarah Sorensen
Colour section: Kassia Gawronski
Managing Director: Andy Riddle
Commercial Director: Patrick Dawson
Publisher: Alan Murphy
Editorial: Felicity Laughton, Nicola Gibbs,
Ria Gane, Jen Haddington, Alice Jell
Cartography: Robert Lunn, Kevin Feeney,
Emma Bryers
Cover design: Robert Lunn
Design: Mytton Williams
Sales and marketing: Liz Harper,
Zoë Jackson, Hannah Bonnell
Advertising sales manager: Renu Sibal
Finance and administration:
Elizabeth Taylor

Photography credits

Front cover: Traditional boat_Alamy_
ANH5G7_Jon Arnold Images Ltd
Back cover: Chillies on sale in a market in
North Thailand_SuperStock_1566-456100_
age fotostock.jpg

Print

Manufactured in India by Nutech
Photolithographers, Delhi
Pulp from sustainable forests

Footprint feedback

We try as hard as we can to make each
Footprint guide as up to date as possible
but, of course, things always change. If you
want to let us know about your experiences –
good, bad or ugly – then don't delay, go to
www.footprintbooks.com and send in
your comments.

Publishing information

Footprint Thailand
7th edition
© Footprint Handbooks Ltd
May 2009

ISBN: 978 1 906098 667
CIP DATA: A catalogue record for this book
is available from the British Library

® Footprint Handbooks and the Footprint
mark are a registered trademark of Footprint
Handbooks Ltd

Published by Footprint
6 Riverside Court
Lower Bristol Road
Bath BA2 3DZ, UK
T +44 (0)1225 469141
F +44 (0)1225 469461
www.footprintbooks.com

Distributed in the USA by Globe Pequot Press,
Guilford, Connecticut

Trails of Asia

Journey through lost kingdoms and
discover the hidden history of Asia
letting Asian Trails be your guide!

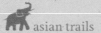
asian·trails